MW00617989

THE SPANISH VERB FINDER

REVISED

Approximately 2,243 irregular Spanish verbs, 34,550 irregular verb forms, 40,500 definitions including 4,850 Spanish verbs arranged alphabetically with definitions and infinitives identified. This revised version also includes the identification of each irregular verb form by mode, person and number.

by

KENNETH P. THEDA

B.A., Howard Payne University
M.A., California State University, Long Beach
Ed.D., Texas Tech University

ISBN 0-9617570-0-0

PRINTED IN THE UNITED STATES OF AMERICA

To my wife, Betty, for her patience, and to my son, Gary, who wrote the fabulous computer programs which made the compilation of this books possible.

SAMPLE OF ENGLISH VERB CONJUGATION

Infinitive	to help
Present Participle	helping
Past Participle	helped
Present Indicative	I help, you help. he (she/it) helps; we help, you all help, they help
Imperfect Indicative	I was helping, you were helping, he (she/it) was helping; we were helping, you all were helping, they were helping
Preterit or Past	I helped, you helped, he (she/it) helped; we helped, you all helped, they helped
Future	I shall help, you will help, he (she/it) will help; we shall help, you all will help, they will help
Conditional	I should help. you would help, he (she/it) would help; we should help, you all would help, they would help
Present Subjunctive	that I may help, that you may help, the he (she/it) may help; that we may help, that you all may help, that they may help
Imperfect Suabjunctive	that I might help, that you might help, that he(she/it) might help; that we might help, that you all might help, that they might help

ABBREVIATIONS USED

cond. - conditional	ind. - indicative	pl. - plural
fut. - future	irr. - irregular	pres. - present
imp. - imperfect	part. - participle	reg. - regular
impve. - imperative	pers. - person	sing. - singular
		subj. - subjunctive

SAMPLE OF REGULAR SIMPLE TENSE - AR CONJUGATION

AYUDAR - to help

Pres. Part.	ayud	ando					
Past Part.	ayud	ado					
		Singular			**Plural**		
Present	ayud	o	as	a	amos	áis	an
Imperfect	ayud	aba	abas	aba	ábamos	abais	aban
Preterit	ayud	é	aste	ó	amos	asteis	aron
Future	ayudar	é	ás	á	emos	éis	án
Conditional	ayudar	ía	ías	ía	íamos	íais	ían
Pres. Subj.	ayud	e	es	e	emos	éis	en
Imp. Subj.	ayud	ara	aras	ara	áramos	arais	aran
Imp. Subj.	ayud	ase	ases	ase	ásemos	aseis	asen
Imperative	ayud		a	e	emos	ad	en

SAMPLE OF REGULAR SIMPLE TENSE -ER CONJUGATION

CORRER - to run

Pres. Part.	corr	iendo					
Past Part.	corr	ido					
		Singular			**Plural**		
Present	corr	o	es	e	emos	éis	en
Imperfect	corr	ía	ías	ía	íamos	íais	ían
Preterit	corr	í	iste	ió	imos	isteis	ieron
Future	correr	é	ás	á	emos	éis	án
Conditional	correr	ía	ías	ía	íamos	íais	ían
Pres. Subj.	corr	a	as	a	amos	áis	an
Imp. Subj.	corr	iera	ieras	iera	iéramos	ierais	ieran
Imp. Subj.	corr	iese	ieses	iese	iésemos	ieseis	iesen
Imperative	corr		e	a	amos	ed	an

SAMPLE OF REGULAR SIMPLE TENSE -IR CONJUGATION

CUBRIR - to cover

Pres. Part.	cubr	iendo					
Past Part.	cubr	ido					
		Singular			**Plural**		
Present	cubr	o	es	e	imos	ís	en
Imperfect	cubr	ía	ías	ía	íamos	íais	ían
Preterit	cubr	í	iste	ió	imos	isteis	ieron
Future	cubrir	é	ás	á	emos	éis	án
Conditional	cubrir	ía	ías	ía	íamos	íais	ían
Pres. Subj.	cubr	a	as	a	amos	áis	an
Imp. Subj.	cubr	iera	ieras	iera	iéramos	ierais	ieran
Imp. Subj.	cubr	iese	ieses	iese	iésemos	ieseis	iesen
Imperative	cubr		e	a	amos	id	an

A

abajándose lowering oneself; pres. part. / *abajarse*.

abajaos (you all) lower yourselves; impve. 2nd pers. pl. / *abajarse*.

abajarse to lower oneself or humilitate oneself. reg.

abájate (you) lower yourself; impve. 2nd pers. sing. / *abajarse*.

abajémonos let us lower ourselves; impve. 1st pers. pl. / *abajarse*.

abájense let them lower themselves; impve. 3rd pers. pl. / *abajarse*.

abájese let him (her/it) lower himself (herself/itself); impve. 3rd pers. sing. / *abajarse*.

abalance 1. that I may balance; pres. subj. 1st pers. sing. / *abalanzar* 2. that he (she/it) may balance; pres. subj. 3rd pers. sing. 3. let him (her/it) balance; impve. 3rd pers. sing.

abalancé I balanced; past 1st pers. sing. / *abalanzar*.

abalancéis that you (all) may balance; pres. subj. 2nd pers. pl. / *abalanzar*.

abalancémonos let us rush headlong; impve. 1st pers. pl. / *abalanzarse*.

abalancemos 1. that we may balance; pres. subj. 1st pers. pl. / *abalanzar*. 2. let us balance.; impve. 1st pers. pl.

abalancen 1. that they may balance; pres. subj. 3rd pers. pl. / *abalanzar*. 2. let them balance.; impve. 3rd pers. pl.

abaláncense let them rush headlong; impve. 3rd pers. pl. / *abalanzarse*.

abalances that you may balance; pres. subj. 2nd pers. sing. / *abalanzar*.

abaláncese let him (her/it) rush headlong; impve. 3rd pers. sing. / *abalanzarse*.

abalanzándose rushing headlong; pres. part. / *abalanzarse*.

abalanzaos (you all) rush headlong; impve. 2nd pers. pl. / *abalanzarse*.

abalanzar to balance or to hurl. irr.

abalanzarse to rush headlong. irr.

abalánzate (you) rush headlong; impve. 2nd pers. sing. / *abalanzarse*.

abalear to riddle with bullets. reg.

abanderar to register. reg.

abanderice 1. that I may cause to take sides; pres. subj. 1st pers. sing. / *abanderizar*. 2. that he (she/it) may cause to take sides; pres. subj. 3rd pers. sing. 3. let him (her/it) cause to take sides; impve. 3rd pers. sing.

abandericé I caused to take sides; past 1st pers. sing. / *abanderizar*.

abandericéis that you (all) may cause to take sides; pres. subj. 2nd pers. pl. / *abanderizar*

abandericémonos let us take sides; impve. 1st pers. pl. / *abanderizarse*.

abandericemos 1. that we may cause to take sides; pres. subj. 1st pers. pl. / *abanderizar*. 2. let us cause to take sides.; impve. 1st pers. pl.

abandericen 1. that they may cause to take sides; pres. subj. 3rd pers. pl. / *abanderizar*. 2. let them cause to take sides.; impve. 3rd pers. pl.

abanderícense let them take sides; impve. 3rd pers. pl. / *abanderizarse*.

abanderices that you may cause to take sides; pres. subj. 2nd pers. sing. / *abanderizar*.

abanderícese let him (her/it) take sides; impve. 3rd pers. sing. / *abanderizarse*.

abanderizándose taking sides; pres. part. / *abanderizarse*.

abanderizaos (you all) take sides; impve. 2nd pers. pl. / *abanderizarse*.

abanderizar to cause to take sides or to split into factions. irr.

abanderizarse to take sides. irr.

abanderízate (you) take sides; impve. 2nd pers. sing. / *abanderizarse*.

abandonándose despairing; pres. part. / *abandonarse*.

abandonaos (you all) despair; impve. 2nd pers. pl. / *abandonarse*.

abandonar to abandon. reg.

abandonarse to despair. reg.

abandónate (you) despair; impve. 2nd pers. sing. / *abandonarse*.

abandonémonos let us despair; impve. 1st pers. pl. / *abandonarse*.

abandónense let them despair; impve. 3rd pers. pl. / *abandonarse*.

abandónese let him (her/it) despair; impve. 3rd pers. sing. / *abandonarse*.

abanicar to fan. irr.

abanique 1. that I may fan; pres. subj. 1st pers. sing. / *abanicar*. 2. that he (she/it) may fan; pres. subj. 3rd pers. sing. 3. let him (her/it) fan; impve. 3rd pers. sing.

abaniqué I fanned; past 1st pers. sing. / *abanicar*.

abaniquéis that you (all) may fan; pres. subj. 2nd pers. pl. / *abanicar*.

abaniquemos 1. that we may fan; pres. subj. 1st pers. pl. / *abanicar*. 2. let us fan; impve. 1st pers. pl.

abaniquen 1. that they may fan; pres. subj. 3rd pers. pl. / *abanicar*. 2. let them fan; impve. 3rd pers. pl.

abaniques that you may fan; pres. subj. 2nd pers. sing. / *abanicar*.

abaratándose falling in price; pres. part. / *abaratarse*.

abaratar to cheapen or lower the price of. reg.

abaratarse to fall in price. reg.

abarátense let them fall in price; impve. 3rd pers. pl. / *abaratarse*.

abarátese let it fall in price; impve. 3rd pers. sing. / *abaratarse*.

abarcar to embrace or to contain. irr.

abarloar to dock. reg.

abarque 1. that I may embrace; pres. subj. 1st pers. sing. / *abarcar*. 2. that he (she/it) may embrace; pres. subj. 3rd pers. sing. 3. let him (her/it) embrace; impve. 3rd pers. sing.

abarqué I embraced; past 1st pers. sing. / *abarcar*.

abarquéis that you (all) may embrace; pres. subj. 2nd pers. pl. / *abarcar.*

abarquemos 1. that we may embrace; pres. subj. 1st pers. pl. / *abarcar.* 2. let us embrace; impve. 1st pers. pl.

abarquen 1. that they may embrace; pres. subj. 3rd pers. pl. / *abarcar.* 2. let them embrace; impve. 3rd pers. pl.

abarques that you may embrace; pres. subj. 2nd pers. sing. / *abarcar.*

abarquillándose warping; pres. part. / *abarquillarse.*

abarquillaos (you all) warp; impve. 2nd pers. pl. / *abarquillarse.*

abarquillar to curl up. reg.

abarquillarse to warp. reg.

abarquíllate (you) warp; impve. 2nd pers. sing. / *abarquillarse.*

abarquillémonos let us warp; impve. 1st pers. pl. / *abarquillarse.*

abarquíllense let them warp; impve. 3rd pers. pl. / *abarquillarse.*

abarquíllese let him (her/it) warp; impve. 3rd pers. sing. / *abarquillarse.*

abarrancándose getting into a predicament; pres. part. / *abarrancarse.*

abarrancaos (you all) get into a predicament; impve. 2nd pers. pl. / *abarrancarse.*

abarrancar to erode. irr.

abarrancarse to get into a predicament. irr.

abarráncate (you) get into a predicament; impve. 2nd pers. sing. / *abarrancarse.*

abarranque 1. that I may erode; pres. subj. 1st pers. sing. / *abarrancar.* 2. that he (she/it) may erode; pres. subj. 3rd pers. sing. 3. let him (her/it) erode; impve. 3rd pers. sing.

abarranqué I eroded; past 1st pers. sing. / *abarrancar.*

abarranquéis that you (all) may erode; pres. subj. 2nd pers. pl. / *abarrancar.*

abarranquémonos let us get into a predicament; impve. 1st pers. pl. / *abarrancarse.*

abarranquemos 1. that we may erode; pres. subj. 1st pers. pl. / *abarrancar.* 2. let us erode; impve. 1st pers. pl.

abarranquen 1. that they may erode; pres. subj. 3rd pers. pl. / *abarrancar.* 2. let them erode; impve. 3rd pers. pl.

abarránquense let them get into a predicament; impve. 3rd pers. pl. / *abarrancarse.*

abarranques that you may erode; pres. subj. 2nd pers. sing. / *abarrancar.*

abarránquese let him (her/it) get into a predicament; impve. 3rd pers. sing. / *abarrancarse.*

abarrotar to stuff or cram. reg.

abastar to supply. reg.

abasteceos (you all) obtain supplies; impve. 2nd pers. pl. / *abastecerse.*

abastecer to supply. irr.

abastecerse to obtain supplies. irr.

abastécete (you) obtain supplies; impve. 2nd pers. sing. / *abastecerse.*

abasteciéndose obtaining supplies; pres. part. / *abastecerse.*

abastezca 1. that I may supply; pres. subj. 1st pers. sing. / *abastecer.* 2. that he (she/it) may supply; pres. subj. 3rd pers. sing. 3. let him (her/it) supply; impve. 3rd pers. sing.

abastezcáis that you (all) may supply; pres. subj. 2nd pers. pl. / *abastecer.*

abastezcámonos let us obtain supplies; impve. 1st pers. pl. / *abastecerse.*

abastezcamos 1. that we may supply; pres. subj. 1st pers. pl. / *abastecer.* 2. let us supply; impve. 1st pers. pl.

abastezcan 1. that they may supply; pres. subj. 3rd pers. pl. / *abastecer.* 2. let them supply; impve. 3rd pers. pl.

abastézcanse let them obtain supplies; impve. 3rd pers. pl. / *abastecerse.*

abastezcas that you may supply; pres. subj. 2nd pers. sing. / *abastecer.*

abastézcase let him (her/it) obtain supplies; impve. 3rd pers. sing. / *abastecerse.*

abastezco I supply; pres. ind. 1st pers. sing. / *abastecer.*

abatámonos let us become discouraged; impve. 1st pers. pl. / *abatirse.*

abátanse let them become discouraged; impve. 3rd pers. pl. / *abatirse.*

abátase let him (her/it) become discouraged; impve. 3rd pers. sing. / *abatirse.*

abátete (you) become discouraged; impve. 2nd pers. sing. / *abatirse.*

abatiéndose becoming discouraged; pres. part. / *abatirse.*

abatíos (you all) become discouraged; impve. 2nd pers. pl. / *abatirse.*

abatir to bring down. reg.

abatirse to become discouraged. reg.

abdicar to abdicate. irr.

abdique 1. that I may abdicate; pres. subj. 1st pers. sing. / *abdicar.* 2. that he (she/it) may abdicate; pres. subj. 3rd pers. sing. 3. let him (her/it) abdicate; impve. 3rd pers. sing.

abdiqué I abdicated; past 1st pers. sing. / *abdicar.*

abdiquéis that you (all) may abdicate; pres. subj. 2nd pers. pl. / *abdicar.*

abdiquemos 1. that we may abdicate; pres. subj. 1st pers. pl. / *abdicar.* 2. let us abdicate; impve. 1st pers. pl.

abdiquen 1. that they may abdicate; pres. subj. 3rd pers. pl. / *abdicar.* 2. let them abdicate; impve. 3rd pers. pl.

abdiques that you may abdicate; pres. subj. 2nd pers. sing. / *abdicar.*

abierto opened; past part. / *abrir.*

abigarrar to variegate or to dapple. reg.

abismándose grieving deeply; pres. part. / *abismarse.*

abismaos (you all) grieve deeply; impve. 2nd pers. pl. / *abismarse.*

abismar to overwhelm or to depress. reg.

abismarse to grieve deeply or to be absorbed or engrossed. reg.

abísmate (you) grieve deeply; impve. 2nd pers. sing. / *abismarse.*

abismémonos let us grieve deeply; impve. 1st pers. pl. / *abismarse.*

abísmense let them grieve deeply; impve. 3rd pers. pl. / *abismarse.*

abísmese let him (her/it) grieve deeply; impve. 3rd pers. sing. / *abismarse.*

abjurar to abjure or to renounce. reg.

ablandándose relenting; pres. part. / *ablandarse.*

ablandaos (you all) relent; impve. 2nd pers. pl. / *ablandarse.*

ablandar to soften. reg.

ablandarse to relent. reg.

ablándate (you) relent; impve. 2nd pers. sing. / *ablandarse.*

ablandecer to mollify. irr.

ablandémonos let us relent; impve. 1st pers. pl. / *ablandarse.*

ablándense let them relent; impve. 3rd pers. pl. / *ablandarse.*

ablándese let him (her/it) relent; impve. 3rd pers. sing. / *ablandarse.*

ablandezca 1. that I may mollify; pres. subj. 1st pers. sing. / *ablandecer.* 2. that he (she/it) may mollify; pres. subj. 3rd pers. sing. 3. let him (her/it) mollify; impve. 3rd pers. sing.

ablandezcáis that you (all) may mollify; pres. subj. 2nd pers. pl. / *ablandecer.*

ablandezcamos 1. that we may mollify; pres. subj. 1st pers. pl. / *ablandecer.* 2. let us mollify; impve. 1st pers. pl.

ablandezcan 1. that they may mollify; pres. subj. 3rd pers. pl. / *ablandecer.* 2. let them mollify; impve. 3rd pers. pl.

ablandezcas that you may mollify; pres. subj. 2nd pers. sing. / *ablandecer.*

ablandezco I mollify; pres. ind. 1st pers. sing. / *ablandecer.*

abnegándose denying oneself; pres. part. / *abnegarse.*

abnegaos (you all) deny yourselves; impve. 2nd pers. pl. / *abnegarse.*

abnegar to renounce. irr.

abnegarse to deny oneself. irr.

abnegué I renounced; past 1st pers. sing. / *abnegar.*

abneguéis that you (all) may renounce; pres. subj. 2nd pers. pl. / *abnegar.*

abneguémonos let us deny ourselves; impve. 1st pers. pl. / *abnegarse.*

abneguemos 1. that we may renounce; pres. subj. 1st pers. pl. / *abnegar.* 2. let us renounce; impve. 1st pers. pl.

abniega 1. he (she/it) renounces; pres. ind. 3rd pers. sing. / *abnegar.* 2. (you) renounce; impve. 2nd pers. sing.

abniegan they renounce; pres. ind. 3rd pers. pl. / *abnegar.*

abniegas you renounce; pres.ind. 2nd pers. sing. / *abnegar.*

abniégate (you) deny yourself; impve. 2nd pers. sing. / *abnegarse.*

abniego I renounce; pres. ind. 1st pers. sing. / *abnegar.*

abniegue 1. that I may renounce; pres. subj. 1st pers. sing. / *abnegar.* 2. that he (she/it) may renounce; pres. subj. 3rd pers. sing. 3. let him (her/it) renounce; impve. 3rd pers. sing.

abnieguen 1. that they may renounce; pres. subj. 3rd pers. pl. / *abnegar.* 2. let them renounce; impve. 3rd pers. pl.

abniéguense let them deny themselves; impve. 3rd pers. pl. / *abnegarse.*

abniegues that you may renounce; pres. subj. 2nd pers. sing. / *abnegar.*

abniéguese let him (her/it) deny himself (herself/itself); impve. 3rd pers. sing. / *abnegarse.*

abobándose becoming silly; pres. part. / *abobarse.*

abobaos (you all) become silly; impve. 2nd pers. pl. / *abobarse.*

abobar to stupefy. reg.

abobarse to become silly. reg.

abóbate (you) become silly; impve. 2nd pers. sing. / *abobarse.*

abobémonos let us become silly; impve. 1st pers. pl. / *abobarse.*

abóbense let them become silly; impve. 3rd pers. pl. / *abobarse.*

abóbese let him (her/it) become silly; impve. 3rd pers. sing. / *abobarse.*

abocándose meeting together; pres. part. / *abocarse.*

abocaos (you all) meet together; impve. 2nd pers. pl. / *abocarse.*

abocar to face or come to grips with. irr.

abocardar to ream or countersink. reg.

abocarse to meet or come together. irr.

abócate (you) meet together; impve. 2nd pers. sing. / *abocarse.*

abocetar to sketch roughly. reg.

abochornándose becoming embarrassed; pres. part. / *abochornarse.*

abochornaos (you all) be embarrassed; impve. 2nd pers. pl. / *abochornarse.*

abochornar to swelter or to overheat. reg.

abochornarse to be embarrassed or to blush. reg.

abochórnate (you) be embarrassed; impve. 2nd pers. sing. / *abochornarse.*

abochornémonos let us be embarrassed; impve. 1st pers. pl. / *abochornarse.*

abochórnense let them be embarrassed; impve. 3rd pers. pl. / *abochornarse.*

abochórnese let him (her/it) be embarrassed; impve. 3rd pers. sing. / *abochornarse.*

abofetear to slap. reg.

abogar to plead or intercede. irr.

abogue 1. that I may plead; pres. subj. 1st pers. sing. / *abogar*. 2. that he (she/it) may plead; pres. subj. 3rd pers. sing. 3. let him (her/it) plead; impve. 3rd pers. sing.

abogué I pleaded; past 1st pers. sing. / *abogar*.

aboguéis that you (all) may plead; pres. subj. 2nd pers. pl. / *abogar*.

aboguemos 1. that we may plead; pres. subj. 1st pers. pl. / *abogar*. 2. let us plead; impve. 1st pers. pl.

aboguen 1. that they may plead; pres. subj. 3rd pers. pl. / *abogar*. 2. let them plead; impve. 3rd pers. pl.

abogues that you may plead; pres. subj. 2nd pers. sing. / *abogar*.

abolir to abolish. irr. used only in forms that have an i in the ending.

abolsándose becoming baggy; pres. part. / *abolsarse*.

abolsarse to become baggy. reg.

abólsense let them become baggy; impve. 3rd pers. pl. / *abolsarse*.

abólsese let it become baggy; impve. 3rd pers. sing. / *abolsarse*.

abollar to dent or bump. reg.

abollonar to emboss. reg.

abombándose smelling bad; pres. part. / *abombarse*.

abombaos (you all) smell bad; impve. 2nd pers. pl. / *abombarse*.

abombar to cause to bulge or swell. reg.

abombarse to smell bad. reg.

abómbense let them smell bad; impve. 3rd pers. pl. / *abombarse*.

abómbese let it smell bad; impve. 3rd pers. sing. / *abombarse*.

abominar to abominate or to detest. reg.

abonándose subscribing to; pres. part. / *abonarse*.

abonaos (you all) subscribe to; impve. 2nd pers. pl. / *abonarse*.

abonar to credit or to fertilize. reg.

abonarse to subscribe to. reg.

abónate (you) subscribe to; impve. 2nd pers. sing. / *abonarse*.

abonémonos let us subscribe to; impve. 1st pers. pl. / *abonarse*.

abónense let them subscribe to; impve. 3rd pers. pl. / *abonarse*.

abónese let him (her/it) subscribe to; impve. 3rd pers. sing. / *abonarse*.

aboque 1. that I may face; pres. subj. 1st pers. sing. / *abocar*. 2. that he (she/it) may face; pres. subj. 3rd pers. sing. 3. let him (her/it) face; impve. 3rd pers. sing.

aboqué I faced; past 1st pers. sing. / *abocar*.

aboquéis that you (all) may face; pres. subj. 2nd pers. pl. / *abocar*.

aboquémonos let us meet together; impve. 1st pers. pl. / *abocar*.

aboquemos 1. that we may face; pres. subj. 1st pers. pl. / *abocar*. 2. let us face; impve. 1st pers. pl.

aboquen 1. that they may face; pres. subj. 3rd pers. pl. / *abocar*. 2. let them face; impve. 3rd pers. pl.

abóquense let them meet together; impve. 3rd pers. pl. / *abocarse*.

aboques that you may face; pres. subj. 2nd pers. sing. / *abocar*.

abóquese let him (her/it) meet together; impve. 3rd pers. sing. / *abocarse*.

abordar to board (a ship) or to approach. reg.

aborrascándose becoming stormy; pres. part. / *aborrascarse*.

aborrascaos (you all) become stormy; impve. 2nd pers. pl. / *aborrascarse*.

aborrascarse to become stormy. irr.

aborráscate (you) become stormy; impve. 2nd pers. sing. / *aborrascarse*.

aborrasque 1. that I may become stormy; pres. subj. 1st pers. sing. / *aborrascarse*. 2. that he (she/it) may become stormy; pres. subj. 3rd pers. sing.

aborrasqué I became stormy; past 1st pers. sing. / *aborrascarse*.

aborrasquéis that you (all) may become stormy; pres. subj. 2nd pers. pl. / *aborrascarse*.

aborrasquémonos let us become stormy; impve. 1st pers. pl. / *aborrascarse*.

aborrasquemos that we may become stormy; pres. subj. 1st pers. pl. / *aborrascarse*.

aborrasquen that they may become stormy; pres. subj. 3rd pers. pl. / *aborrascarse*.

aborrásquense let them become stormy; impve. 3rd pers. pl. / *aborrascarse*.

aborrasques that you may become stormy; pres. subj. 2nd pers. sing. / *aborrascarse*.

aborrásquese let him (her/it) become stormy; impve. 3rd pers. sing. / *aborrascarse*.

aborrecer to hate or abhor. irr.

aborrezca 1. that I may hate; pres. subj. 1st pers. sing. / *aborrecer*. 2. that he (she/it) may hate; pres. subj. 3rd pers. sing. 3. let him (her/it) hate; impve. 3rd pers. sing.

aborrezcáis that you (all) may hate; pres. subj. 2nd pers. pl. / *aborrecer*.

aborrezcamos 1. that we may hate; pres. subj. 1st pers. pl. / *aborrecer*. 2. let us hate; impve. 1st pers. pl.

aborrezcan 1. that they may hate; pres. subj. 3rd pers. pl. / *aborrecer*. 2. let them hate; impve. 3rd pers. pl.

aborrezcas that you may hate; pres. subj. 2nd pers. sing. / *aborrecer*.

aborrezco I hate; pres. ind. 1st pers. sing. / *aborrecer*.

abortar to abort or miscarry. reg.

abotagándose feeling bloated; pres. part. / *abotagarse*.

abotagaos (you all) feel bloated; impve. 2nd pers. pl. / *abotagarse*.

abotagar to bloat. irr.

abotagarse to be or feel bloated. irr.

abotágate (you) feel bloated; impve. 2nd pers. sing. / *abotagarse*.

abotague 1. that I may bloat; pres. subj. 1st pers. sing. / *abotagar*. 2. that he (she/it) may bloat; pres. subj. 3rd pers. sing. 3. let him (her/it) bloat; impve. 3rd pers. sing.

abotagué I bloated; past 1st pers. sing. / *abotagar.*

abotaguéis that you (all) may bloat; pres. subj. 2nd pers. pl. / *abotagar.*

abotaguémonos let us feel bloated; impve. 1st pers. pl. / *abotagarse.*

abotaguemos 1. that we may bloat; pres. subj. 1st pers. pl. / *abotagar.* 2. let us bloat; impve. 1st pers. pl.

abotaguen 1. that they may bloat; pres. subj. 3rd pers. pl. / *abotagar.* 2. let them bloat; impve. 3rd pers. pl.

abotáguense let them feel bloated; impve. 3rd pers. pl. / *abotagarse.*

abotagues that you may bloat; pres. subj. 2nd pers. sing. / *abotagar.*

abotáguese let him (her/it) feel bloated; impve. 3rd pers. sing. / *abotagarse.*

abotonándose buttoning up; pres. part. / *abotonarse.*

abotonaos (you all) button up; impve. 2nd pers. pl. / *abotonarse.*

abotonar to button or bud. reg.

abotonarse to button up. reg.

abotónate (you) button up; impve. 2nd pers. sing. / *abotonarse.*

abotonémonos let us button up; impve. 1st pers. pl. / *abotonarse.*

abotónense let them button up; impve. 3rd pers. pl. / *abotonarse.*

abotónese let him (her/it) button up; impve. 3rd pers. sing. / *abotonarse.*

abovedar to vault or arch. reg.

abozalar to muzzle. reg.

abrace 1. that I may hug; pres. subj. 1st pers. sing. / *abrazar.* 2. that he (she/it) may hug; pres. subj. 3rd pers. sing. 3. let him (her/it) hug; impve. 3rd pers. sing.

abracé I hugged; past 1st pers. sing. / *abrazar.*

abracéis that you (all) may hug; pres. subj. 2nd pers. pl. / *abrazar.*

abracémonos let us embrace; impve. 1st pers. pl. / *abrazarse.*

abracemos 1. that we may hug; pres. subj. 1st pers. pl. / *abrazar.* 2. let us hug; impve. 1st pers. pl.

abracen 1. that they may hug; pres. subj. 3rd pers. pl. / *abrazar.* 2. let them hug; impve. 3rd pers. pl.

abrácense let them embrace; impve. 3rd pers. pl. / *abrazarse.*

abraces that you may hug; pres. subj. 2nd pers. sing. / *abrazar.*

abrácese let him (her/it) embrace; impve. 3rd pers. sing. / *abrazarse.*

abrámonos let us open up; impve. 1st pers. pl. / *abrirse.*

abramos 1. that we may open; pres. subj. 1st pers. pl. / *abrir.* 2. let us open; impve. 1st pers. pl.

abran 1. that they may open; pres. subj. 3rd pers. pl. / *abrir.* 2. let them open; impve. 3rd pers. pl.

ábranse let them open up; impve. 3rd pers. pl. / *abrirse.*

abras that you may open; pres. subj. 2nd pers. sing. / *abrir.*

abrasándose burning up; pres. part. / *abrasarse.*

abrasar to burn. reg.

abrasarse to burn up or to be consumed. reg.

ábrase let him (her/it) open up; impve. 3rd pers. sing. / *abrirse.*

abrásense let them burn up; impve. 3rd pers. pl. / *abrasarse.*

abrásese let it burn up; impve. 3rd pers. sing. / *abrasarse.*

abrazándose embracing; pres. part. / *abrazarse.*

abrazaos (you all) embrace; impve. 2nd pers. pl. / *abrazarse.*

abrazar to embrace or hug. irr.

abrazarse to embrace. irr.

abrázate (you) embrace; impve. 2nd pers. sing. / *abrazarse.*

abre 1. he (she/it) opens; pres. ind. 3rd pers. sing. / *abrir.* 2. (you) open; impve. 2nd pers. sing.

abren they open; pres. ind. 3rd pers. pl. / *abrir.*

abres you open; pres.ind. 2nd pers. sing. / *abrir.*

ábrete (you) open up; impve. 2nd pers. sing. / *abrirse.*

abrevar to water (cattle) or to soak. reg.

abreviar to abbreviate or shorten. reg.

abrí I opened; past 1st pers. sing. / *abrir.*

abrid (you all) open; impve. 2nd pers. pl. / *abrir.*

abriendo opening; pres. part. / *abrir.*

abriéndose opening up; pres. part. / *abrirse.*

abrieron they opened; past 3rd pers. pl. / *abrir.*

abrigándose finding shelter; pres. part. / *abrigarse.*

abrigaos (you all) find shelter; impve. 2nd pers. pl. / *abrigarse.*

abrigar to shelter or protect. irr.

abrigarse to find shelter or to wrap oneself up. irr.

abrígate (you) find shelter; impve. 2nd pers. sing. / *abrigarse.*

abrigue 1. that I may shelter; pres. subj. 1st pers. sing. / *abrigar.* 2. that he (she/it) may shelter; pres. subj. 3rd pers. sing. 3. let him (her/it) shelter; impve. 3rd pers. sing.

abrigué I sheltered; past 1st pers. sing. / *abrigar.*

abriguéis that you (all) may shelter; pres. subj. 2nd pers. pl. / *abrigar.*

abriguémonos let us find shelter; impve. 1st pers. pl. / *abrigarse.*

abriguemos 1. that we may shelter; pres. subj. 1st pers. pl. / *abrigar.* 2. let us shelter; impve. 1st pers. pl.

abriguen 1. that they may shelter; pres. subj. 3rd pers. pl. / *abrigar.* 2. let them shelter; impve. 3rd pers. pl.

abríguense let them find shelter; impve. 3rd pers. pl. / *abrigarse.*

abrigues that you may shelter; pres. subj. 2nd pers. sing. / *abrigar.*

abríguese let him (her/it) find shelter; impve. 3rd pers. sing. / *abrigarse.*

abrillantar to brighten or polish. reg.

abrió he (she/it) opened; past 3rd pers. sing. / *abrir*.

abríos (you all) open up; impve. 2nd pers. pl. / *abrirse*.

abrir to open or to unlock. irr.

abrirse to open up. irr.

abro I open; pres. ind. 1st pers. sing. / *abrir*.

abrochar to hook or fasten or button. reg.

abrogar to abrogate or repeal or annul. irr.

abrogue 1. that I may abrogate; pres. subj. 1st pers. sing. / *abrogar*. 2. that he (she/it) may abrogate; pres. subj. 3rd pers. sing. 3. let him (her/it) abrogate; impve. 3rd pers. sing.

abrogué I abrogated; past 1st pers. sing. / *abrogar*.

abroguéis that you (all) may abrogate; pres. subj. 2nd pers. pl. / *abrogar*.

abroguemos 1. that we may abrogate; pres. subj. 1st pers. pl. / *abrogar*. 2. let us abrogate; impve. 1st pers. pl.

abroguen 1. that they may abrogate; pres. subj. 3rd pers. pl. / *abrogar*. 2. let them abrogate; impve. 3rd pers. pl.

abrogues that you may abrogate; pres. subj. 2nd pers. sing. / *abrogar*.

abrumándose becoming hazy; pres. part. / *abrumarse*.

abrumar to overwhelm or to trouble. reg.

abrumarse to become hazy or foggy. reg.

abrúmense let them become hazy; impve. 3rd pers. pl. / *abrumarse*.

abrúmese let it become hazy; impve. 3rd pers. sing. / *abrumarse*.

absolver to absolve or aquit. irr.

absorber to absorb. reg. except pp.

absorto absorbed; past part. / *absorber*.

absten (you) abstain; impve. 2nd pers. sing. / *abstenerse*.

abstendrá he (she/it) will abstain; fut. 3rd pers. sing. / *abstenerse*.

abstendrán they will abstain; fut. 3rd pers. pl. / *abstenerse*.

abstendrás you will abstain; fut. 2nd pers. sing. / *abstenerse*.

abstendré I shall abstain; fut. 1st pers. sing. / *abstenerse*.

abstendréis you (all) will abstain; fut. 2nd pers. pl. / *abstenerse*.

abstendremos we shall abstain; fut. 1st pers. pl. / *abstenerse*.

abstendría 1. I should abstain; cond. 1st pers. sing. / *abstenerse*. 2. he (she/it) would abstain; cond. 3rd pers. sing.

abstendríais you (all) would abstain; cond. 2nd pers. pl. / *abstenerse*.

abstendríamos we should abstain; cond. 1st pers. pl. / *abstenerse*.

abstendrían they would abstain; cond. 3rd pers. pl. / *abstenerse*.

abstendrías you would abstain; cond. 2nd pers. sing. / *abstenerse*.

absteneos (you all) abstain; impve. 2nd pers. pl. / *abstenerse*.

abstenerse to abstain. irr.

absténete (you) abstain; impve. 2nd pers. sing. / *abstenerse*.

abstenga 1. that I may abstain; pres. subj. 1st pers. sing. / *abstenerse*. 2. that he (she/it) may abstain; pres. subj. 3rd pers. sing.

abstengáis that you (all) may abstain; pres. subj. 2nd pers. pl. / *abstenerse*.

abstengámonos let us abstain; impve. 1st pers. pl. / *abstenerse*.

abstengamos that we may abstain; pres. subj. 1st pers. pl. / *abstenerse*.

abstengan that they may abstain; pres. subj. 3rd pers. pl. / *abstenerse*.

absténganse let them abstain; impve. 3rd pers. pl. / *abstenerse*.

abstengas that you may abstain; pres. subj. 2nd pers. sing. / *abstenerse*.

absténgase let him (her/it) abstain; impve. 3rd pers. sing. / *abstenerse*.

abstengo I abstain; pres. ind. 1st pers. sing. / *abstenerse*.

abstenido abstained; past part. / *abstenerse*.

absteniéndose abstaining; pres. part. / *abstenerse*.

abstiene he (she/it) abstains; pres. ind. 3rd pers. sing. / *abstenerse*.

abstienen they abstain; pres. ind. 3rd pers. pl. / *abstenerse*.

abstienes you abstain; pres.ind. 2nd pers. sing. / *abstenerse*.

abstraed (you all) abstract; impve. 2nd pers. pl. / *abstraer*.

abstraeos (you all) become absorbed; impve. 2nd pers. pl. / *abstraerse*.

abstraer to abstract. irr.

abstraerse to become absorbed or abstracted. irr.

abstráete (you) become absorbed; impve. 2nd pers. sing. / *abstraerse*.

abstraído abstracted; past part. / *abstraer*.

abstraiga 1. that I may abstract; pres. subj. 1st pers. sing. / *abstraer*. 2. that he (she/it) may abstract; pres. subj. 3rd pers. sing. 3. let him (her/it) abstract; impve. 3rd pers. sing.

abstraigáis that you (all) may abstract; pres. subj. 2nd pers. pl. / *abstraer*.

abstraigámonos let us become absorbed; impve. 1st pers. pl. / *abstraerse*.

abstraigamos 1. that we may abstract; pres. subj. 1st pers. pl. / *abstraer*. 2. let us abstract; impve. 1st pers. pl.

abstraigan 1. that they may abstract; pres. subj. 3rd pers. pl. / *abstraer*. 2. let them abstract; impve. 3rd pers. pl.

abstraíganse let them become absorbed; impve. 3rd pers. pl. / *abstraerse*.

abstraigas that you may abstract; pres. subj. 2nd pers. sing. / *abstraer*.

abstraígase let him (her/it) become absorbed; impve. 3rd pers. sing. / *abstraerse*.

abstraigo I abstract; pres. ind. 1st pers. sing. / *abstraer*.

abstraje I abstracted; past 1st pers. sing. / *abstraer.*

abstrajera 1. that I might abstract; imp. subj. 1st pers. sing. / *abstraer.* 2. that he (she/it) might abstract; imp. subj. 3rd pers. sing.

abstrajerais that you (all) might abstract; imp. subj. 2nd pers pl. / *abstraer.*

abstrajéramos that we might abstract; imp. subj. 1st pers. pl. / *abstraerse.*

abstrajeran that they might abstract; imp. subj. 3rd pers. pl. / *abstraer.*

abstrajeras that you might abstract; imp. subj. 2nd pers. sing. / *abstraer.*

abstrajeron they abstracted; past 3rd pers. pl. / *abstraer.*

abstrajese 1. that I might abstract; imp. subj. 1st pers. sing. / *abstraer.* 2. that he (she/it) might abstract; imp. subj. 3rd pers. sing.

abstrajeseis that you (all) might abstract; imp. subj. 2nd pers pl. / *abstraer.*

abstrajésemos that we might abstract; imp. subj. 1st pers. pl. / *abstraer.*

abstrajesen that they might abstract; imp. subj. 3rd pers. pl. / *abstraer.*

abstrajeses that you might abstract; imp. subj. 2nd pers. sing. / *abstraer.*

abstrajimos we abstracted; past 1st pers. pl. / *abstraer.*

abstrajiste you abstracted; past 2nd pers. sing. / *abstraer.*

abstrajisteis you (all) abstracted; past 2nd pers. pl. / *abstraer.*

abstrajo he (she/it) abstracted; past 3rd pers. sing. / *abstraer.*

abstrayendo abstracting; pres. part. / *abstraer.*

abstrayéndose becoming absorbed; pres. part. / *abstraerse*

abstuve I abstained; past 1st pers. sing. / *abstenerse.*

abstuviera 1. that I might abstain; imp. subj. 1st pers. sing. / *abstenerse.* 2. that he (she/it) might abstain; imp. subj. 3rd pers. sing.

abstuvierais that (you) all might abstain; imp. subj. 2nd pers pl. / *abstenerse.*

abstuviéramos that we might abstain; imp. subj. 1st pers. pl. / *abstenerse.*

abstuvieran that they might abstain; imp. subj. 3rd pers. pl. / *abstenerse.*

abstuvieras that you might abstain; imp. subj. 2nd pers. sing. / *abstenerse.*

abstuvieron they abstained; past 3rd pers. pl. / *abstenerse.*

abstuviese 1. that I might abstain; imp. subj. 1st pers. sing. / *abstenerse.* 2. that he (she/it) might abstain; imp. subj. 3rd pers. sing.

abstuvieseis that you (all) might abstain; imp. subj. 2nd pers pl. / *abstenerse.*

abstuviésemos that we might abstain; imp. subj. 1st pers. pl. / *abstenerse.*

abstuviesen that they might abstain; imp. subj. 3rd pers. pl. / *abstenerse.*

abstuvieses that you might abstain; imp. subj. 2nd pers. sing. / *abstenerse.*

abstuvimos we abstained; past 1st pers. pl. / *abstenerse.*

abstuviste you abstained; past 2nd pers. sing. / *abstenerse.*

abstuvisteis you (all) abstained; past 2nd pers. pl. / *abstenerse.*

abstuvo he (she/it) abstained; past 3rd pers. sing. / *abstenerse.*

absuelto absolved; past part. / *absolver.*

absuelva 1. that I may absolve; pres. subj. 1st pers. sing. / *absolver.* 2. that he (she/it) may absolve; pres. subj. 3rd pers. sing. 3. let him (her/it) absolve; impve. 3rd pers. sing.

absuelvan 1. that they may absolve; pres. subj. 3rd pers. pl. / *absolver.* 2. let them absolve; impve. 3rd pers. pl.

absuelvas that you may absolve; pres. subj. 2nd pers. sing. / *absolver.*

absuelve 1. he (she/it) absolves; pres. ind. 3rd pers. sing. / *absolver.* 2. (you) absolve; impve. 2nd pers. sing.

absuelven they absolve; pres. ind. 3rd pers. pl. / *absolver.*

absuelves you absolve; pres.ind. 2nd pers. sing. / *absolver.*

absuelvo I absolve; pres. ind. 1st pers. sing. / *absolver.*

abultar to bulge or enlarge. reg.

abundar to abound. reg.

aburguesándose acquiring bourgeois attitudes; pres. part. / *aburguesarse.*

aburguesaos (you all) acquire bourgeois attitudes; impve. 2nd pers. pl. / *aburguesarse.*

aburguesarse to acquire bourgeois attitudes. reg.

aburguésate (you) acquire bourgeois attitudes; impve. 2nd pers. sing. / *aburguesarse.*

aburguesémonos let us acquire bourgeois attitudes; impve. 1st pers. pl. / *aburguesarse.*

aburguésense let them acquire bourgeois attitudes; impve. 3rd pers. pl. / *aburguesarse.*

aburguésese let him (her/it) acquire bourgeois attitudes; impve. 3rd pers. sing. / *aburguesarse.*

aburilar to engrave. reg.

aburrámonos let us become bored; impve. 1st pers. pl. / *aburrirse.*

aburrándose becoming brutish; pres. part. / *aburrarse.*

abúrranse let them become bored; impve. 3rd pers. pl. / *aburrirse.*

aburraos (you all) become brutish; impve. 2nd pers. pl. / *aburrarse.*

aburrarse to become brutish. reg.

abúrrase let him (her/it) become bored; impve. 3rd pers. sing. / *aburrirse.*

abúrrate (you) become brutish; impve. 2nd pers. sing. / *aburrarse.*

aburrémonos let us become brutish; impve. 1st pers. pl. / *aburrarse.*

abúrrense let them become brutish; impve. 3rd pers. pl. / *aburrarse.*

abúrrese let him (her/it) become brutish; impve. 3rd pers. sing. / *aburrarse.*

abúrrete (you) become bored; impve. 2nd pers. sing. / *aburrirse.*

aburriéndose becoming bored; pres. part. / *aburrirse.*

aburríos (you all) become bored; impve. 2nd pers. pl. / *aburrirse.*

aburrir to bore or vex. reg.

aburrirse to become bored. reg.

abusar to abuse or misuse. reg.

acabad (you all) finish; impve. 2nd pers. pl. / *acabar.*

acabado finished; past part. / *acabar.*

acabando finishing; pres. part. / *acabar.*

acabándose growing feeble; pres. part. / *acabarse.*

acabaos (you all) grow feeble; impve. 2nd pers. pl. / *acabarse.*

acabar to finish or end. reg.

acabarse to grow feeble. reg.

acábate (you) grow feeble; impve. 2nd pers. sing. / *acabarse.*

acabémonos let us grow feeble; impve. 1st pers. pl. / *acabarse.*

acábense let them grow feeble; impve. 3rd pers. pl. / *acabarse.*

acábese let him (her/it) grow feeble; impve. 3rd pers. sing. / *acabarse.*

acaecer to happen or occur. irr

acaeza 1. that I may happen; pres. subj. 1st pers. sing. / *acaecer.* 2. that he (she/it) may happen; pres. subj. 3rd pers. sing. 3. let him (her/it) happen; impve. 3rd pers. sing.

acaezáis that you (all) may happen; pres. subj. 2nd pers. pl. / *acaecer.*

acaezamos 1. that we may happen; pres. subj. 1st pers. pl. / *acaecer.* 2. let us happen; impve. 1st pers. pl.

acaezan 1. that they may happen; pres. subj. 3rd pers. pl. / *acaecer.* 2. let them happen; impve. 3rd pers. pl.

acaezas that you may happen; pres. subj. 2nd pers. sing. / *acaecer.*

acaezo I happen; pres. ind. 1st pers. sing. / *acaecer.*

acalambrándose having cramps; pres. part. / *acalambrarse.*

acalambraos (you all) have cramps; impve. 2nd pers. pl. / *acalambrarse.*

acalambrarse to have cramps. reg.

acalámbrate (you) have cramps; impve. 2nd pers. sing. / *acalambrarse.*

acalambrémonos let us have cramps; impve. 1st pers. pl. / *acalambrarse.*

acalámbrense let them have cramps; impve. 3rd pers. pl. / *acalambrarse.*

acalámbrese let him (her/it) have cramps; impve. 3rd pers. sing. / *acalambrarse.*

acalenturándose becoming feverish; pres. part. / *acalenturarse.*

acalenturaos (you all) become feverish; impve. 2nd pers. pl. / *acalenturarse.*

acalenturar to be feverish. reg.

acalenturarse to become feverish. reg.

acalentúrate (you) become feverish; impve. 2nd pers. sing. / *acalenturarse.*

acalenturémonos let us become feverish; impve. 1st pers. pl. / *acalenturarse.*

acalentúrense let them become feverish; impve. 3rd pers. pl. / *acalenturarse.*

acalentúrese let him (her/it) become feverish; impve. 3rd pers. sing. / *acalenturarse.*

acalorándose getting excited; pres. part. / *acalorarse.*

acaloraos (you all) get excited; impve. 2nd pers. pl. / *acalorarse.*

acalorar to heat or excite. reg.

acalorarse to get excited. reg.

acalórate (you) get excited; impve. 2nd pers. sing. / *acalorarse.*

acalorémonos let us get excited; impve. 1st pers. pl. / *acalorarse.*

acalórense let them get excited; impve. 3rd pers. pl. / *acalorarse.*

acalórese let him (her/it) get excited; impve. 3rd pers. sing. / *acalorarse.*

acallar to quiet or silence. reg.

acampándose camping; pres. part. / *acamparse.*

acampaos (you all) camp; impve. 2nd pers. pl. / *acamparse.*

acampar to camp. reg.

acamparse to camp. reg.

acámpate (you) camp; impve. 2nd pers. sing. / *acamparse.*

acampémonos let us camp; impve. 1st pers. pl. / *acamparse.*

acámpense let them camp; impve. 3rd pers. pl. / *acamparse.*

acámpese let him (her/it) camp; impve. 3rd pers. sing. / *acamparse.*

acanalar to groove or flute. reg.

acantonar to quarter (troops). reg.

acaparar to monopolize. reg.

acaramelándose cloying; pres. part. / *acaramelarse.*

acaramelaos (you all) be cloying; impve. 2nd pers. pl. / *acaramelarse.*

acaramelar to ice or candy. reg.

acaramelarse to be cloying. reg.

acaramélate (you) be cloying; impve. 2nd pers. sing. / *acaramelarse.*

acaramelémonos let us be cloying; impve. 1st pers. pl. / *acaramelarse.*

acaramélense let them be cloying; impve. 3rd pers. pl. / *acaramelarse.*

acaramélese let him (her/it) be cloying; impve. 3rd pers. sing. / *acaramelarse.*

acarar to confront. reg.

acardenalándose being covered with bruises; pres. part. / *acardenalarse.*

acardenalaos (you all) be covered with bruises; impve. 2nd pers. pl. / *acardenalarse.*

acardenalar to beat black and blue. reg.

acardenalarse to be covered with bruises. reg.

acardenálate (you) be covered with bruises; impve. 2nd pers. sing. / *acardenalarse.*

acardenalémonos let us be covered with bruises; impve. 1st pers. pl. / *acardenalarse.*

acardenálense let them be covered with bruises; impve. 3rd pers. pl. / *acardenalarse.*

acardenálese let him (her/it) be covered with bruises; impve. 3rd pers. sing. / *acardenalarse.*

acarear to confront. reg.

acariciar to caress or cherish. reg.

acarrear to cart or carry. reg.

acatar to respect or revere. reg.

acatarrándose getting chilled; pres. part. / *acatarrarse.*

acatarraos (you all) get chilled; impve. 2nd pers. pl. / *acatarrarse.*

acatarrar to catch cold. reg.

acatarrarse to get chilled. reg.

acatárrate (you) get chilled; impve. 2nd pers. sing. / *acatarrarse.*

acatarrémonos let us get chilled; impve. 1st pers. pl. / *acatarrarse.*

acatárrense let them get chilled; impve. 3rd pers. pl. / *acatarrarse.*

acatárrese let him (her/it) get chilled; impve. 3rd pers. sing. / *acatarrarse.*

acaudalar to hoard. reg.

acaudillar to lead or command. reg.

acceder to accede or agree. reg.

accidentándose fainting; pres. part. / *accidentarse.*

accidentaos (you all) faint; impve. 2nd pers. pl. / *accidentarse.*

accidentarse to faint or have a seizure. reg.

accidéntate (you) faint; impve. 2nd pers. sing. / *accidentarse.*

accidentémonos let us faint; impve. 1st pers. pl. / *accidentarse.*

accidéntense let them faint; impve. 3rd pers. pl. / *accidentarse.*

accidéntese let him (her/it) faint; impve. 3rd pers. sing. / *accidentarse.*

accionar to make gestures or operate. reg.

acece 1. that I may pant; pres. subj. 1st pers. sing. / *acezar.* 2. that he (she/it) may pant; pres. subj. 3rd pers. sing. 3. let him (her/it) pant; impve. 3rd pers. sing.

acecé I panted; past 1st pers. sing. / *acezar.*

acecéis that you (all) may pant; pres. subj. 2nd pers. pl. / *acezar.*

acecemos 1. that we may pant; pres. subj. 1st pers. pl. / *acezar.* 2. let us pant; impve. 1st pers. pl.

acecen 1. that they may pant; pres. subj. 3rd pers. pl. / *acezar.* 2. let them pant; impve. 3rd pers. pl.

aceces that you may pant; pres. subj. 2nd pers. sing. / *acezar.*

acecinar to salt and smoke or dry (meat). reg.

acechar to watch or to spy. reg.

acedándose souring; pres. part. / *acedarse.*

acedaos (you all) sour; impve. 2nd pers. pl. / *acedarse.*

acedar to sour. reg.

acedarse to sour. reg.

acédate (you) sour; impve. 2nd pers. sing. / *acedarse.*

acedémonos let us sour; impve. 1st pers. pl. / *acedarse.*

acédense let them sour; impve. 3rd pers. pl. / *acedarse.*

acédese let him (her/it) sour; impve. 3rd pers. sing. / *acedarse.*

aceitar to oil or lubricate. reg.

acelerar to accelerate or hasten. reg.

acendrar to refine (metals) or purify. reg.

acentúa 1. he (she/it) accents; pres. ind. 3rd pers. sing. / *acentuar.* 2. (you) accent; impve. 2nd pers. sing.

acentúan they accent; pres. ind. 3rd pers. pl. / *acentuar.*

acentuándose becoming worse; pres. part. / *acentuarse.*

acentúaos (you all) become worse; impve. 2nd pers. pl. / *acentuarse.*

acentuar to accent or emphasize. irr.

acentuarse to become worse (as an illness). irr.

acentúas you accent; pres. ind. 2nd pers. sing. / *acentuar.*

acentúate (you) become worse; impve. 2nd pers. sing. / *acentuarse.*

acentúe 1. that I may accent; pres. subj. 1st pers. sing. / *acentuar.* 2. that he (she/it) may accent; pres. subj. 3rd pers. sing. 3. let him (her/it) accent; impve. 3rd pers. sing.

acentuémonos let us become worse; impve. 1st pers. pl. / *acentuarse.*

acentúen 1. that they may accent; pres. subj. 3rd pers. pl. / *acentuar.* 2. let them accent; impve. 3rd pers. pl.

acentúense let them become worse; impve. 3rd pers. pl. / *acentuarse.*

acentúes that you may accent; pres. subj. 2nd pers. sing. / *acentuar.*

acentúese let him (her/it) become worse; impve. 3rd pers. sing. / *acentuarse.*

acentúo I accent; pres. ind. 1st pers. sing. / *acentuar.*

acepillar to brush or to plane. reg.

aceptar to accept or to honor. reg.

acerándose taking courage; pres. part. / *acerarse.*

aceraos (you all) take courage; impve. 2nd pers. pl. / *acerarse.*

acerar to edge with steel or to pave. reg.

acerarse to take courage. reg.

acérate (you) take courage; impve. 2nd pers. sing. / *acerarse.*

acercándose approaching; pres. part. / *acercarse.*

acercaos (you all) approach; impve. 2nd pers. pl. / *acercarse.*

acercar to bring near or draw up. irr.

acercarse to come near or approach. irr.

acércate (you) approach; impve. 2nd pers. sing. / *acercarse.*

acerémonos let us take courage; impve. 1st pers. pl. / *acerarse.*

acérense let them take courage; impve. 3rd pers. pl. / *acerarse.*

acérese let him (her/it) take courage; impve. 3rd pers. sing. / *acerarse.*

acerque 1. that I may bring near; pres. subj. 1st pers. sing. / *acercar.* 2. that he (she/it) may bring near; pres. subj. 3rd pers. sing. 3. let him (her/it) bring near; impve. 3rd pers. sing.

acerqué I brought near; past 1st pers. sing. / *acercar.*

acerquéis that you (all) may bring near; pres. subj. 2nd pers. pl. / *acercar.*

acerquémonos let us approach; impve. 1st pers. pl. / *acercarse.*

acerquemos 1. that we may bring near; pres. subj. 1st pers. pl. / *acercar.* 2. let us bring near; impve. 1st pers. pl.

acerquen 1. that they may bring near; pres. subj. 3rd pers. pl. / *acercar.* 2. let them bring near; impve. 3rd pers. pl.

acérquense let them approach; impve. 3rd pers. pl. / *acercarse.*

acerques that you may bring near; pres. subj. 2nd pers. sing. / *acercar.*

acérquese let him (her/it) approach; impve. 3rd pers. sing. / *acercarse.*

acerrojar to bolt or lock. reg.

acertar to hit (the mark) or guess correctly. irr.

acezar to pant or gasp. irr.

acicalándose dressing up; pres. part. / *acicalarse.*

acicalaos (you all) dress up; impve. 2nd pers. pl. / *acicalarse.*

acicalar to polish or adorn. reg.

acicalarse to dress up. reg.

acicálate (you) dress up; impve. 2nd pers. sing. / *acicalarse.*

acicalémonos let us dress up; impve. 1st pers. pl. / *acicalarse.*

acicálense let them dress up; impve. 3rd pers. pl. / *acicalarse.*

acicálese let him (her/it) dress up; impve. 3rd pers. sing. / *acicalarse.*

acicatear to spur or prod. reg.

acidificar to acidify. reg.

acierta 1. he (she/it) hits; pres. ind. 3rd pers. sing. / *acertar.* 2. (you) hit; impve. 2nd pers. sing.

aciertan they hit; pres. ind. 3rd pers. pl. / *acertar.*

aciertas you hit; pres. ind. 2nd pers. sing. / *acertar.*

acierte 1. that I may hit; pres. subj. 1st pers. sing. / *acertar.* 2. that he (she/it) may hit; pres. subj. 3rd pers. sing. 3. let him)her/it) hit; impve. 3rd pers. sing.

acierten 1. that they may hit; pres. subj. 3rd pers. pl. / *acertar.* 2. let them hit; impve. 3rd pers. pl.

aciertes that you may hit; pres. subj. 2nd pers. sing. / *acertar.*

acierto I hit; pres. ind. 1st pers. sing. / *acertar.*

aclamar to acclaim. reg.

aclarándose becoming clear; pres. part. / *aclararse.*

aclarar to clarify or rinse. reg.

aclararse to become clear. reg.

aclárense let them become clear; impve. 3rd pers. pl. / *aclararse.*

aclárese let it become clear; impve. 3rd pers. sing. / *aclararse.*

aclimatar to acclimatize. reg.

aclocándose hatching; pres. part. / *aclocarse.*

aclocaos (you all) hatch; impve. 2nd pers. pl. / *aclocarse.*

aclocarse to brood or hatch. reg.

acloqué I hatched; past 1st pers. sing. / *aclocarse.*

acloquéis that you (all) may hatch; pres. subj. 2nd pers. pl. / *aclocarse.*

acloquémonos let us hatch; impve. 1st pers. pl. / *aclocarse.*

acloquemos that we may hatch; pres. subj. 1st pers. pl. / *aclocarse.*

aclueca he (she/it) hatches; pres. ind. 3rd pers. sing. / *aclocarse.*

acluecan they hatch; pres. ind. 3rd pers. pl. / *aclocarse.*

acluecas you hatch; pres. ind. 2nd pers. sing. / *aclocarse.*

acluécate (you) hatch; impve. 2nd pers. sing. / *aclocarse.*

aclueco I hatch; pres. ind. 1st pers. sing. / *aclocarse.*

aclueque 1. that I may hatch; pres. subj. 1st pers. sing. / *aclocarse.* 2. that he (she/it) may hatch; pres. subj. 3rd pers. sing.

acluequen that they may hatch; pres. subj. 3rd pers. pl. / *aclocarse.*

acluéquense let them hatch; impve. 3rd pers. pl. / *aclocarse.*

aclueques that you may hatch; pres. subj. 2nd pers. sing. / *aclocarse.*

acluéquese let him (her/it) hatch; impve. 3rd pers. sing. / *aclocarse.*

acobardándose becoming frightened; pres. part. / *acobardarse.*

acobardaos (you all) become frightened; impve. 2nd pers. pl. / *acobardarse.*

acobardar to frighten or intimidate. reg.

acobardarse to become frightened. reg.

acobárdate (you) become frightened; impve. 2nd pers. sing. / *acobardarse.*

acobardémonos let us become frightened; impve. 1st pers. pl. / *acobardarse.*

acobárdense let them become frightened; impve. 3rd pers. pl. / *acobardarse.*

acobárdese let him (her/it) become frightened; impve. 3rd pers. sing. / *acobardarse.*

acodándose leaning; pres. part. / *acodarse.*

acodaos (you all) lean; impve. 2nd pers. pl. / *acodarse.*

acodarse to rest the elbow or to lean. reg.

acódate (you) lean; impve. 2nd pers. sing. / *acodarse.*

acodémonos let us lean; impve. 1st pers. pl. / *acodarse.*

acódense let them lean; impve. 3rd pers. pl. / *acodarse.*

acódese let him (her/it) lean; impve. 3rd pers. sing. / *acodarse.*

acodillar to bend in the form of an elbow. reg.

acogeos (you all) take refuge; impve. 2nd pers. pl. / *acogerse.*

acoger to receive or give shelter. irr.

acogerse to take refuge. irr.

acógete (you) take refuge; impve. 2nd pers. sing. / *acogerse.*

acogiéndose taking refuge; pres. part. / *acogerse.*

acogotar to kill with a blow in the nape of the neck. reg.

acoja 1. that I may receive; pres. subj. 1st pers. sing. / *acoger.* 2. that he (she/it) may receive; pres. subj. 3rd pers. sing. 3. let him (her/it) receive; impve. 3rd pers. sing.

acojáis that you (all) may receive; pres. subj. 2nd pers. pl. / *acoger.*

acojámonos let us take refuge; impve. 1st pers. pl. / *acogerse.*

acojamos 1. that we may receive; pres. subj. 1st pers. pl. / *acoger.* 2. let us receive; impve. 1st pers. pl.

acojan 1. that they may receive; pres. subj. 3rd pers. pl. / *acoger.* 2. let them receive; impve. 3rd pers. pl.

acójanse let them take refuge; impve. 3rd pers. pl. / *acogerse.*

acojas that you may receive; pres. subj. 2nd pers. sing. / *acoger.*

acójase let him (her/it) take refuge; impve. 3rd pers. sing. / *acogerse.*

acojinar to cushion or quilt. reg.

acojo I receive; pres. ind. 1st pers. sing. / *acoger.*

acolchar to quilt or pad. reg.

acombar to bend or warp. reg.

acomedíos (you all) volunteer; impve. 2nd pers. pl. / *acomedirse.*

acomedirse to volunteer. irr.

acometer to attack or undertake. reg.

acomida 1. that I may volunteer; pres. subj. 1st pers. sing. / *acomedirse.* 2. that he (she/it) may volunteer; pres. subj. 3rd pers. sing.

acomidáis that you (all) may volunteer; pres. subj. 2nd pers. pl. / *acomedirse.*

acomidámonos let us volunteer; impve. 1st pers. pl. / *acomedirse.*

acomidamos that we may volunteer; pres. subj. 1st pers. pl. / *acomedirse.*

acomidan that they may volunteer; pres. subj. 3rd pers. pl. / *acomedirse.*

acomídanse let them volunteer; impve. 3rd pers. pl. / *acomedirse.*

acomidas that you may volunteer; pres. subj. 2nd pers. sing. / *acomedirse.*

acomídase let him (her/it) volunteer; impve. 3rd pers. sing. / *acomedirse.*

acomide he (she/it) volunteers; pres. ind. 3rd pers. sing. / *acomedirse.*

acomiden they volunteer; pres. ind. 3rd pers. pl. / *acomedirse.*

acomides you volunteer; pres. ind. 2nd pers. sing. / *acomedirse.*

acomídete (you) volunteer; impve. 2nd pers. sing. / *acomedirse.*

acomidiéndose volunteering; pres. part. / *acomedirse.*

acomidiera 1. that I might volunteer; imp. subj. 1st pers. sing. / *acomedirse.* 2. that he (she/it) might volunteer; imp. subj. 3rd pers. sing.

acomidierais that you (all) might volunteer; imp. subj. 2nd pers pl. / *acomedirse.*

acomidiéramos that we might volunteer; imp. subj. 1st pers. pl. / *acomedirse.*

acomidieran that they might volunteer; imp. subj. 3rd pers. pl. / *acomedirse.*

acomidieras that you might volunteer; imp. subj. 2nd pers. sing. / *acomedirse.*

acomidieron they volunteered; past 3rd pers. pl. / *acomedirse.*

acomidiese 1. that I might volunteer; imp. subj. 1st pers. sing. / *acomedirse.* 2. that he (she/it) might volunteer; imp. subj. 3rd pers. sing.

acomidieseis that you (all) might volunteer; imp. subj. 2nd pers pl. / *acomedirse.*

acomidiésemos that we might volunteer; imp. subj. 1st pers. pl. / *acomedirse.*

acomidiesen that they might volunteer; imp. subj. 3rd pers. pl. / *acomedirse.*

acomidieses that you might volunteer; imp. subj. 2nd pers. sing. / *acomedirse.*

acomidió he (she/it) volunteered; past 3rd pers. sing. / *acomedirse.*

acomido I volunteer; pres. ind. 1st pers. sing. / *acomedirse.*

acomodándose making oneself comfortable; pres. part. / *acomodarse.*

acomodaos (you all) make yourselves comfortable; impve. 2nd pers. pl. / *acomodarse.*

acomodar to accommodate or to arrange. reg.

acomodarse to make oneself comfortable. reg.

acomódate (you) make yourself comfortable; impve. 2nd pers. sing. / *acomodarse.*

acomodémonos let us make ourselves comfortable; impve. 1st pers. pl. / *acomodarse.*

acomódense let them make themselves comfortable; impve. 3rd pers. pl. / *acomodarse.*

acomódese let him (her/it) make himself (herself/itself) comfortable; impve. 3rd pers. sing. / *acomodarse.*

acompañar to accompany or enclose (in a letter). reg.

acompasar to measure with dividers. reg.

aconchándose forming a deposit; pres. part. / *aconcharse.*

aconchar to cup -as the hands. reg.

aconcharse to form a deposit or settle. reg.

acónchense let them form a deposit; impve. 3rd pers. pl. / *aconcharse.*

acónchese let it form a deposit; impve. 3rd pers. sing. / *aconcharse.*

acondicionándose becoming conditioned; pres. part. / *acondicionarse.*

acondicionaos (you all) become conditioned; impve. 2nd pers. pl. / *acondicionarse.*

acondicionar to condition or prepare. reg.

acondicionarse to become conditioned. reg.

acondiciónate (you) become conditioned; impve. 2nd pers. sing. / *acondicionarse.*

acondicionémonos let us become conditioned; impve. 1st pers. pl. / *acondicionarse.*

acondiciónense let them become conditioned; impve. 3rd pers. pl. / *acondicionarse.*

acondiciónese let him (her/it) become conditioned; impve. 3rd pers. sing. / *acondicionarse.*

acongojándose being distressed; pres. part. / *acongojarse.*

acongojaos (you all) be distressed; impve. 2nd pers. pl. / *acongojarse.*

acongojar to grieve or afflict. reg.

acongojarse to be distressed. reg.

acongójate (you) be distressed; impve. 2nd pers. sing. / *acongojarse.*

acongojémonos let us be distressed; impve. 1st pers. pl. / *acongojarse.*

acongójense let them be distressed; impve. 3rd pers. pl. / *acongojarse.*

acongójese let him (her/it) be distressed; impve. 3rd pers. sing. / *acongojarse.*

aconsejándose taking advice; pres. part. / *aconsejarse.*

aconsejaos (you all) take advice; impve. 2nd pers. pl. / *aconsejarse.*

aconsejar to advise or counsel. reg.

aconsejarse to take advice. reg.

aconséjate (you) take advice; impve. 2nd pers. sing. / *aconsejarse.*

aconsejémonos let us take advice; impve. 1st pers. pl. / *aconsejarse.*

aconséjense let them take advice; impve. 3rd pers. pl. / *aconsejarse.*

aconséjese let him (her/it) take advice; impve. 3rd pers. sing. / *aconsejarse.*

aconsonantar to rhyme. reg.

acontecer to happen. irr. used only in inf. and 3rd pers.

acontezca 1. that it may happen; pres. subj. 3rd pers. sing. / *acontecer.* 2. let it happen; impve. 3rd pers. sing.

acontezcan 1. that those may happen; pres. subj. 3rd pers. pl. / *acontecer.* 2. let them happen; impve. 3rd pers. pl.

acopiar to gather or store up. reg.

acoplándose joining; pres. part. / *acoplarse.*

acoplaos (you all) join; impve. 2nd pers. pl. / *acoplarse.*

acoplar to couple or adjust. reg.

acoplarse to join. reg.

acóplate (you) join; impve. 2nd pers. sing. / *acoplarse.*

acoplémonos let us join; impve. 1st pers. pl. / *acoplarse.*

acóplense let them join; impve. 3rd pers. pl. / *acoplarse.*

acóplese let him (her/it) join; impve. 3rd pers. sing. / *acoplarse.*

acoquinar to intimidate or scare. reg.

acorace 1. that I may armor; pres. subj. 1st pers. sing. / *acorazar.* 2. that he (she/it) may armor; pres. subj. 3rd pers. sing. 3. let him (her/it) armor; impve. 3rd pers. sing.

acoracé I armored; past 1st pers. sing. / *acorazar.*

acoracéis that you (all) may armor; pres. subj. 2nd pers. pl. / *acorazar.*

acoracemos 1. that we may armor; pres. subj. 1st pers. pl. / *acorazar.* 2. let us armor; impve. 1st pers. pl.

acoracen 1. that they may armor; pres. subj. 3rd pers. pl. / *acorazar.* 2. let them armor; impve. 3rd pers. pl.

acoraces that you may armor; pres. subj. 2nd pers. sing. / *acorazar.*

acorazar to armor. irr.

acorchándose shriveling; pres. part. / *acorcharse.*

acorchaos (you all) shrivel; impve. 2nd pers. pl. / *acorcharse.*

acorcharse to shrivel. reg.

acórchate (you) shrivel; impve. 2nd pers. sing. / *acorcharse.*

acorchémonos let us shrivel; impve. 1st pers. pl. / *acorcharse.*

acórchense let them shrivel; impve. 3rd pers. pl. / *acorcharse.*

acórchese let him (her/it) shrivel; impve. 3rd pers. sing. / *acorcharse.*

acordándose remembering; pres. part. / *acordarse.*

acordaos (you all) remember; impve. 2nd pers. pl. / *acordarse.*

acordar to agree upon or to decide. irr.

acordarse to remember. irr.

acordelar to measure with a cord. reg.

acordémonos let us remember; impve. 1st pers. pl. / *acordarse.*

acordonar to tie with a cord. reg.

acornear to gore or butt. reg.

acorralar to corral. reg.

acorrer to avail. reg.

acorrucándose huddling ; pres. part. / *acorrucarse.*

acorrucaos (you all) huddle; impve. 2nd pers. pl. / *acorrucarse.*

acorrucarse to huddle or crouch. irr.

acorrúcate (you) huddle; impve. 2nd pers. sing. / *acorrucarse.*

acorruqué I huddled; past 1st pers. sing. / *acorrucarse.*

acorruque 1. that I may huddle; pres. subj. 1st pers. sing. / *acorrucarse.* 2. that he (she/it) may huddle; pres. subj. 3rd pers. sing.

acorruquéis that you (all) may huddle; pres. subj. 2nd pers. pl. / *acorrucarse.*

acorruquémonos let us huddle; impve. 1st pers. pl. / *acorrucarse.*

acorruquemos that we may huddle; pres. subj. 1st per pl. / *acorrucarse.*

acóplese let him (her/it) join; impve. 3rd pers. sing. / *acoplarse.*

acorruquen that they may huddle; pres. subj. 3rd pers. pl. / *acorrucarse.*

acorrúquense let them huddle; impve. 3rd pers. pl. / *acorrucarse.*

acorruques that you may huddle; pres. subj. 2nd pers. sing. / *acorrucarse.*

acorrúquese let him (her/it) huddle; impve. 3rd pers. sing. / *acorrucarse.*

acortándose shrinking; pres. part. / *acortarse.*

acortaos (you all) shrink; impve. 2nd pers. pl. / *acortarse.*

acortar to shorten. reg.

acortarse to shrink or be shy. reg.

acórtate (you) shrink; impve. 2nd pers. sing. / *acortarse.*

acortémonos let us shrink; impve. 1st pers. pl. / *acortarse.*

acórtense let them shrink; impve. 3rd pers. pl. / *acortarse.*

acórtese let him (her/it) shrink; impve. 3rd pers. sing. / *acortarse.*

acosar to pursue or harass. reg.

acostándose going to bed; pres. part. / *acostarse.*

acostaos (you all) go to bed; impve. 2nd pers. pl. / *acostarse.*

acostar to put to bed or lay flat. irr.

acostarse to go to bed or lie down. irr.

acostémonos let us go to bed; impve. 1st pers. pl. / *acostarse.*

acostumbrándose getting accustomed; pres. part. / *acostumbrarse.*

acostumbraos (you all) get accustomed; impve. 2nd pers. pl. / *acostumbrarse.*

acostumbrar to accustom or train. reg.

acostumbrarse to get accustomed. reg.

acostúmbrate (you) get accustomed; impve. 2nd pers. sing. / *acostumbrarse.*

acostumbrémonos let us get accustomed; impve. 1st pers. pl. / *acostumbrarse.*

acostúmbrense let them get accustomed; impve. 3rd pers. pl. / *acostumbrarse.*

acostúmbrese let him (her/it) get accustomed; impve. 3rd pers. sing. / *acostumbrarse.*

acotar to mark off or annotate. reg.

acrecentándose advancing; pres. part. / *acrecentarse.*

acrecentaos (you all) advance; impve. 2nd pers. pl. / *acrecentarse.*

acrecentar to increase. irr.

acrecentarse to advance. irr.

acrecentémonos let us advance; impve. 1st pers. pl. / *acrecentarse.*

acreceos (you all) advance; impve. 2nd pers. pl. / *acrecerse.*

acrecer to increase or advance. irr.

acrecerse to advance. irr.

acrécete (you) advance; impve. 2nd pers. sing. / *acrecerse.*

acreciéndose advancing; pres. part. / *acrecerse.*

acrecienta 1. he (she/it) increases; pres. ind. 3rd pers. sing. / *acrecentar.* 2. (you) increase; impve. 2nd pers. sing.

acrecientan they increase; pres. ind. 3rd pers. pl. / *acrecentar.*

acrecientas you increase; pres.ind. 2nd pers. sing. / *acrecentar.*

acreciéntate (you) advance; impve. 2nd pers. sing. / *acrecentarse.*

acreciente 1. that I may increase; pres. subj. 1st pers. sing. / *acrecentar.* 2. that he (she/it) may increase; pres. subj. 3rd pers. sing. 3. let him (her/it) increase; impve. 3rd pers. sing.

acrecienten 1. that they may increase; pres. subj. 3rd pers. pl. / *acrecentar.* 2. let them increase; impve. 3rd pers. pl.

acreciéntense let them advance; impve. 3rd pers. pl. / *acrecentarse.*

acrecientes that you may increase; pres. subj. 2nd pers. sing. / *acrecentar.*

acreciéntese let him (her/it) advance; impve. 3rd pers. sing. / *acrecentarse.*

acreciento I increase; pres. ind. 1st pers. sing. / *acrecentar.*

acreditándose gaining a reputation; pres. part. / *acreditarse.*

acreditaos (you all) gain a reputation; impve. 2nd pers. pl. / *acreditarse.*

acreditar to accredit or to assure. reg.

acreditarse to gain a reputation. reg.

acredítate (you) gain a reputation; impve. 2nd pers. sing. / *acreditarse.*

acreditémonos let us gain a reputation; impve. 1st pers. pl. / *acreditarse.*

acredítense let them gain a reputation; impve. 3rd pers. pl. / *acreditarse.*

acredítese let him (her/it) gain a reputation; impve. 3rd pers. sing. / *acreditarse.*

acrezca 1. that I may increase; pres. subj. 1st pers. sing. / *acrecer.* 2. that he (she/it) may increase; pres. subj. 3rd pers. sing. 3. let him (her/it) increase; impve. 3rd pers. sing.

acrezcáis that you (all) may increase; pres. subj. 2nd pers. pl. / *acrecer.*

acrezcámonos let us advance; impve. 1st pers. pl. / *acrecerse.*

acrezcamos 1. that we may increase; pres. subj. 1st pers. pl. / *acrecer.* 2. let us increase; impve. 1st pers. pl.

acrezcan 1. that they may increase; pres. subj. 3rd pers. pl. / *acrecer.* 2. let them increase; impve. 3rd pers. pl.

acrézcanse let them advance; impve. 3rd pers. pl. / *acrecerse.*

acrezcas that you may increase; pres. subj. 2nd pers. sing. / *acrecer.*

acrézcase let him (her/it) advance; impve. 3rd pers. sing. / *acrecerse.*

acrezco I increase; pres. ind. 1st pers. sing. / *acrecer.*

acribar to sift. reg.

acribillar to riddle or perforate. reg.

acriminar to accuse or incriminate. reg.

acriollándose adopting latin american customs; pres. part. / *acriollarse.*

acriollaos (you all) adopt latin american customs; impve. 2nd pers. pl. / *acriollarse.*

acriollarse to adopt latin american customs. reg.

acrióllate (you) adopt latin american customs; impve. 2nd pers. sing. / *acriollarse.*

acriollémonos let us adopt latin american customs; impve. 1st pers. pl. / *acriollarse.*

acrióllense let them adopt latin american customs; impve. 3rd pers. pl. / *acriollarse.*

acrióllese let him (her/it) adopt latin american customs; impve. 3rd pers. sing. / *acriollarse.*

acrisolar to refine or purify. reg.

activar to activate or expedite. reg.

actúa 1. he (she/it) acts; pres. ind. 3rd pers. sing. / *actuar* 2. (you) act; impve. 2nd pers. sing.

actualice 1. that I may bring up to date; pres. subj. 1st pers. sing. / *actualizar.* 2. that he (she/it) may bring up to date; pres. subj. 3rd pers. sing. 3. let him (her/it) bring up to date; impve. 3rd pers. sing.

actualicé I brought up to date; past 1st pers. sing. / *actualizar.*

actualicéis that you (all) may bring up to date; pres. subj. 2nd pers. pl. / *actualizar.*

actualicemos 1. that we may bring up to date; pres. subj. 1st pers. pl. / *actualizar.* 2. let us bring up to date; impve. 1st pers. pl.

actualicen 1. that they may bring up to date; pres. subj. 3rd pers. pl. / *actualizar.* 2. let them bring up to date; impve. 3rd pers. pl.

actualices that you may bring up to date; pres. subj. 2nd pers. sing. / *actualizar.*

actualizar to bring up to date. irr.

actúan they act; pres. ind. 3rd pers. pl. / *actuar.*

actuar to act or perform. irr.

actúas you act; pres. ind. 2nd pers. sing. / *actuar.*

actúe 1. that I may act; pres. subj. 1st pers. sing. / *actuar.* 2. that he (she/it) may act; pres. subj. 3rd pers. sing. 3. let him (her/it) act; impve. 3rd pers. sing.

actúen 1. that they may act; pres. subj. 3rd pers. pl. / *actuar.* 2. let them act; impve. 3rd pers. pl.

actúes that you may act; pres. subj. 2nd pers. sing. / *actuar.*

actúo I act; pres. ind. 1st pers. sing. / *actuar.*

acuartelar to quarter (troops). reg.

acuatice 1. that I may alight on the water; pres. subj. 1st pers. sing. / *acuatizar.* 2. that he (she/it) may alight on the water; pres. subj. 3rd pers. sing. 3. let him (her/it) alight on the water; impve. 3rd pers. sing.

acuaticé I alighted on the water; past 1st pers. sing. / *acuatizar.*

acuaticéis that you (all) may alight on the water; pres. subj. 2nd pers. pl. / *acuatizar.*

acuaticemos 1. that we may alight on the water; pres. subj. 1st pers. pl. / *acuatizar.* 2. let us alight on the water; impve. 1st pers. pl.

acuaticen 1. that they alight on the water; pres. subj. 3rd pers. pl. / *acuatizar.* 2. let them alight on the water; impve. 3rd pers. pl.

acuatices that you may alight on the water; pres. subj. 2nd pers. sing. / *acuatizar.*

acuatizar to alight on the water. irr.

acuciar to urge or to stimulate. reg.

acuclillándose squatting; pres. part. / *acuclillarse.*

acuclillaos (you all) squat; impve. 2nd pers. pl. / *acuclillarse.*

acuclillarse to squat or to crouch. reg.

acuclíllate (you) squat; impve. 2nd pers. sing. / *acuclillarse.*

acuclillémonos let us squat; impve. 1st pers. pl. / *acuclillarse.*

acuclíllense let them squat; impve. 3rd pers. pl. / *acuclillarse.*

acuclíllese let him (her/it) squat; impve. 3rd pers. sing. / *acuclillarse.*

acuchillándose fighting with knives; pres. part. / *acuchillarse.*

acuchillaos (you all) fight with knives; impve. 2nd pers. pl. / *acuchillarse.*

acuchillar to stab. reg.

acuchillarse to fight with knives. reg.

acuchíllate (you) fight with knives; impve. 2nd pers. sing. / *acuchillarse.*

acuchillémonos let us fight with knives; impve. 1st pers. pl. / *acuchillarse.*

acuchíllense let them fight with knives; impve. 3rd pers. pl. / *acuchillarse.*

acuchíllese let him (her/it) fight with knives; impve. 3rd pers. sing. / *acuchillarse.*

acudir to betake oneself or to assist. reg.

acuerda 1. he (she/it) agrees upon; pres. ind. 3rd pers. sing. / *acordar.* 2. (you) agree upon; impve. 2nd pers. sing.

acuerdan they agree upon; pres. ind. 3rd pers. pl. / *acordar.*

acuerdas you agree upon; pres.ind. 2nd pers. sing. / *acordar.*

acuérdate (you) remember; impve. 2nd pers. sing. / *acordarse.*

acuerde 1. that I may agree upon; pres. subj. 1st pers. sing. / *acordar.* 2. that he (she/it) may agree upon; pres. subj. 3rd pers. sing. 3. let him (her/it) agree upon; impve. 3rd pers. sing.

acuerden 1. that they may agree upon; pres. subj. 3rd pers. pl. / *acordar.* 2. let them agree upon; impve. 3rd pers. pl.

acuérdense let them remember; impve. 3rd pers. pl. / *acordarse.*

acuerdes that you may agree upon; pres. subj. 2nd pers. sing. / *acordar.*

acuérdese let him (her/it) remember; impve. 3rd pers. sing. / *acordarse.*

acuerdo I agree upon; pres. ind. 1st pers. sing. / *acordar.*

acuesta 1. he (she/it) puts to bed; pres. ind. 3rd pers. sing. / *acostar.* 2. (you) put to bed; impve. 2nd pers. sing.

acuestan they put to bed; pres. ind. 3rd pers. pl. / *acostar.*

acuestas you put to bed; pres. ind. 2nd pers. sing. / *acostar.*

acuéstate (you) go to bed; impve. 2nd pers. sing. / *acostarse.*

acueste 1. that I may put to bed; pres. subj. 1st pers. sing. / *acostar.* 2. that he (she/it) may put to bed; pres. subj. 3rd pers. sing. 3. let him (her/it) put to bed; impve. 3rd pers. sing.

acuesten 1. that they may put to bed; pres. subj. 3rd pers. pl. / *acostar.* 2. let them put to bed; impve. 3rd pers. pl.

acuéstense let them go to bed; impve. 3rd pers. pl. / *acostarse.*

acuestes that you may put to bed; pres. subj. 2nd pers. sing. / *acostar.*

acuéstese let him (her/it) go to bed; impve. 3rd pers. sing. / *acostarse.*

acuesto I put to bed; pres. ind. 1st pers. sing. / *acostar.*

acuitándose grieving; pres. part. / *acuitarse.*

acuitaos (you all) grieve; impve. 2nd pers. pl. / *acuitarse.*

acuitar to afflict or oppress. reg.

acuitarse to grieve. reg.

acuítate (you) grieve; impve. 2nd pers. sing. / *acuitarse.*

acuitémonos let us grieve; impve. 1st pers. pl. / *acuitarse.*

acuítense let them grieve; impve. 3rd pers. pl. / *acuitarse.*

acuítese let him (her/it) grieve; impve. 3rd pers. sing. / *acuitarse.*

acumular to accumulate or amass. reg.

acunar to cradle. reg.

acuñar to coin or to wedge. reg.

acurrucándose cuddling; pres. part. / *acurrucarse.*

acurrucaos (you all) cuddle; impve. 2nd pers. pl. / *acurrucarse.*

acurrucarse to cuddle. irr.

acurrúcate (you) cuddle; impve. 2nd pers. sing. / *acurrucarse.*

acurruqué I cuddled; past 1st pers. sing. / *acurrucarse.*

acurruque 1. that I may cuddle; pres. subj. 1st pers. sing. / *acurrucarse.* 2. that he (she/it) may cuddle; pres. subj. 3rd pers. sing.

acurruquéis that you (all) may cuddle; pres. subj. 2nd pers. pl. / *acurrucarse.*

acurruquémonos let us cuddle; impve. 1st pers. pl. / *acurrucarse.*

acurruquemos that we may cuddle; pres. subj. 1st pers. pl. / *acurrucarse.*

acurruquen that they may cuddle; pres. subj. 3rd pers. pl. / *acurrucarse.*

acurrúquense let them cuddle; impve. 3rd pers. pl. / *acurrucarse.*

acurruques that you may cuddle; pres. subj. 2nd pers. sing. / *acurrucarse.*

acurrúquese let him (her/it) cuddle; impve. 3rd pers. sing. / *acurrucarse.*

acusándose confessing; pres. part. / *acusarse.*

acusaos (you all) confess; impve. 2nd pers. pl. / *acusarse.*

acusar to accuse. reg.

acusarse to confess. reg.

acúsate (you) confess; impve. 2nd pers. sing. / *acusarse.*

acusémonos let us confess; impve. 1st pers. pl. / *acusarse.*

acúsense let them confess; impve. 3rd pers. pl. / *acusarse.*

acúsese let him (her/it) confess; impve. 3rd pers. sing. / *acusarse.*

achacar to impute or to blame. irr.

achaflanar to bevel. reg.

achantándose cringing; pres. part. / *achantarse.*

achantaos (you all) cringe; impve. 2nd pers. pl. / *achantarse.*

achantarse to cringe or cower. reg.

achántate (you) cringe; impve. 2nd pers. sing. / *achantarse.*

achantémonos let us cringe; impve. 1st pers. pl. / *achantarse.*

achántense let them cringe; impve. 3rd pers. pl. / *achantarse.*

achántese let him (her/it) cringe; impve. 3rd pers. sing. / *achantarse.*

achaque 1. that I may impute; pres. subj. 1st pers. sing. / *achacar.* 2. that he (she/it) may impute; pres. subj. 3rd pers. sing. 3. let him (her/it) impute; impve. 3rd pers. sing.

achaqué I imputed; past 1st pers. sing. / *achacar.*

achaquéis that you (all) may impute; pres. subj. 2nd pers. pl. / *achacar.*

achaquemos 1. that we may impute; pres. subj. 1st pers. pl. / *achacar.* 2. let us impute; impve. 1st pers. pl.

achaquen 1. that they may impute; pres. subj. 3rd pers. pl. / *achacar.* 2. let them impute; impve. 3rd pers. pl.

achaques that you may impute; pres. subj. 2nd pers. sing. / *achacar.*

achatar to flatten. reg.

achicándose humbling oneself; pres. part. / *achicarse.*

achicaos (you all) humble yourselves; impve. 2nd pers. pl. / *achicarse.*

achicar to reduce or diminish. irr.

achicarse to humble oneself. irr.

achícate (you) humble yourself; impve. 2nd pers. sing. / *achicarse.*

achicharrar to scorch or overcook. reg.

achique 1. that I may reduce; pres. subj. 1st pers. sing. / *achicar.* 2. that he (she/it) may reduce; pres. subj. 3rd pers. sing. 3. let him (her/it) reduce; impve. 3rd pers. sing.

achiqué I reduced; past 1st pers. sing. / *achicar.*

achiquéis that you (all) may reduce; pres. subj. 2nd pers. pl. / *achicar.*

achiquémonos let us humble ourselves; impve. 1st pers. pl. / *achicarse.*

achiquemos 1. that we may reduce; pres. subj. 1st pers. pl. / *achicar.* 2. let us reduce; impve. 1st pers. pl.

achiquen 1. that they may reduce; pres. subj. 3rd pers. pl. / *achicar.* 2. let them reduce; impve. 3rd pers. pl.

achiquense let them humble themselves; impve. 3rd pers. pl. / *achicarse.*

achiques that you may reduce; pres. subj. 2nd pers. sing. / *achicar.*

achíquese let him (her/it) humble himself (herself/itself); impve. 3rd pers. sing. / *achicarse.*

achispar to make tipsy. reg.

achochar to become senile. reg.

adaptar to adapt or fit. reg.

adecentar to make decent (in appearance). reg.

adecuar to fit or accommodate. reg.

adelantándose getting ahead; pres. part. / *adelantarse.*

adelantaos (you all) get ahead; impve. 2nd pers. pl. / *adelantarse.*

adelantar to advance or promote. reg.

adelantarse to get ahead. reg.

adelántate (you) get ahead; impve. 2nd pers. sing. / *adelantarse.*

adelantémonos let us get ahead; impve. 1st pers. pl. / *adelantarse.*

adelántense let them get ahead; impve. 3rd pers. pl. / *adelantarse.*

adelántese let him (her/it) get ahead; impve. 3rd pers. sing. / *adelantarse.*

adelgace 1. that I may thin out; pres. subj. 1st pers. sing. / *adelgazar.* 2. that he (she/it) may thin out; pres. subj. 3rd pers. sing. 3. let him (her/it) thin out; impve. 3rd pers. sing.

adelgacé I thinned out; past 1st pers. sing. / *adelgazar.*

adelgacéis that you (all) may thin out; pres. subj. 2nd pers. pl. / *adelgazar.*

adelgacémonos let us grow slender; impve. 1st pers. pl. / *adelgazarse.*

adelgacemos 1. that we may thin out; pres. subj. 1st pers. pl. / *adelgazar.* 2. let us thin out; impve. 1st pers. pl.

adelgacen 1. that they may thin out; pres. subj. 3rd pers. pl. / *adelgazar.* 2. let them thin out; impve. 3rd pers. pl.

adelgácense let them grow slender; impve. 3rd pers. pl. / *adelgazarse.*

adelgaces that you may thin out; pres. subj. 2nd pers. sing. / *adelgazar.*

adelgácese let him (her/it) grow slender; impve. 3rd pers. sing. / *adelgazarse.*

adelgazándose growing slender; pres. part. / *adelgazarse.*

adelgazaos (you all) grow slender; impve. 2nd pers. pl. / *adelgazarse.*

adelgazar to thin out or to taper. irr.

adelgazarse to grow slender. irr.

adelgázate (you) grow slender; impve. 2nd pers. sing. / *adelgazarse.*

adentrándose entering; pres. part. / *adentrarse.*

adentraos (you all) enter; impve. 2nd pers. pl. / *adentrarse.*

adentrarse to enter or to penetrate. reg.

adéntrate (you) enter; impve. 2nd pers. sing. / *adentrarse.*

adentrémonos let us enter; impve. 1st pers. pl. / *adentrarse.*

adéntrense let them enter; impve. 3rd pers. pl. / *adentrarse.*

adéntrese let him (her/it) enter; impve. 3rd pers. sing. / *adentrarse.*

aderece 1. that I may adorn; pres. subj. 1st pers. sing. / *aderezar.* 2. that he (she/it) may adorn; pres. subj. 3rd pers. sing. 3. let him (her/it) adorn; impve. 3rd pers. sing.

aderecé I adorned; past 1st pers. sing. / *aderezar.*

aderecéis that you (all) may adorn; pres. subj. 2nd pers. pl. / *aderezar.*

aderecemos 1. that we may adorn; pres. subj. 1st pers. pl. / *aderezar.* 2. let us adorn; impve. 1st pers. pl.

aderecen 1. that they may adorn; pres. subj. 3rd pers. pl. / *aderezar.* 2. let them adorn; impve. 3rd pers. pl.

adereces that you may adorn; pres. subj. 2nd pers. sing. / *aderezar.*

aderezar to adorn. irr.

adestrándose practicing; pres. part. / *adestrarse.*

adestraos (you all) practice; impve. 2nd pers. pl. / *adestrarse.*

adestrar to train or guide. irr.

adestrarse to practice. irr.

adestrémonos let us practice; impve. 1st pers. pl. / *adestrarse.*

adeudándose running into debt; pres. part. / *adeudarse.*

adeudaos (you all) run into debt; impve. 2nd pers. pl. / *adeudarse.*

adeudar to owe. reg.

adeudarse to run into debt. reg.

adeúdate (you) run into debt; impve. 2nd pers. sing. / *adeudarse.*

adeudémonos let us run into debt; impve. 1st pers. pl. / *adeudarse.*

adeúdense let them run into debt; impve. 3rd pers. pl. / *adeudarse.*

adeúdese let him (her/it) run into debt; impve. 3rd pers. sing. / *adeudarse.*

adheríos (you all) adhere; impve. 2nd pers. pl. / *adherirse.*

adherir to stick or adhere. irr.

adherirse to adhere. irr.

adhiera 1. that I may stick; pres. subj. 1st pers. sing. / *adherir.* 2. that he (she/it) may stick; pres. subj. 3rd pers. sing. 3. let him (her/it) stick; impve. 3rd pers. sing.

adhieran 1. that they may stick; pres. subj. 3rd pers. pl. / *adherir.* 2. let them stick; impve. 3rd pers. pl.

adhiéranse let them adhere; impve. 3rd pers. pl. / *adherirse*.

adhieras that you may stick; pres. subj. 2nd pers. sing. / *adherir*.

adhiérase let him (her/it) adhere; impve. 3rd pers. sing. / *adherirse*.

adhiere 1. he (she/it) sticks; pres. ind. 3rd pers. sing. / *adherir*. 2. (you) stick; impve. 2nd pers. sing.

adhieren they stick; pres. ind. 3rd pers. pl. / *adherir*.

adhieres you stick; pres. ind. 2nd pers. sing. / *adherir*.

adhiérete (you) adhere; impve. 2nd pers. sing. / *adherirse*.

adhiero I stick; pres. ind. 1st pers. sing. / *adherir*.

adhiráis that you (all) may stick; pres. subj. 2nd pers. pl. / *adherir*.

adhirámonos let us adhere; impve. 1st pers. pl. / *adherirse*.

adhiramos 1. that we may stick; pres. subj. 1st pers. pl. / *adherir*. 2. let us stick; impve. 1st pers. pl.

adhiriendo sticking; pres. part. / *adherir*.

adhiriéndose adhering; pres. part. / *adherirse*.

adhiriera 1. that I might stick; imp. subj. 1st pers. sing. / *adherir*. 2. that he (she/it) might stick; imp. subj. 3rd pers. sing.

adhirierais that you (all) might stick; imp. subj. 2nd pers pl. / *adherir*.

adhiriéramos that we might stick; imp. subj. 1st pers. pl. / *adherir*.

adhirieran that they might stick; imp. subj. 3rd pers. pl. / *adherir*.

adhirieras that you might stick; imp. subj. 2nd pers. sing. / *adherir*.

adhirieron they stuck; past 3rd pers. pl. / *adherir*.

adhiriese 1. that I might stick; imp. subj. 1st pers. sing. / *adherir*. 2. that he (she/it) might stick; imp. subj. 3rd pers. sing.

adhirieseis that you (all) might stick; imp. subj. 2nd pers pl. / *adherir*.

adhiriésemos that we might stick; imp. subj. 1st pers. pl. / *adherir*.

adhiriesen that they might stick; imp. subj. 3rd pers. pl. / *adherir*.

adhirieses that you might stick; imp. subj. 2nd pers. sing. / *adherir*.

adhirió he (she/it) stuck; past 3rd pers. sing. / *adherir*.

adicionar to add or to augment. reg.

adiestra 1. he (she/it) trains; pres. ind. 3rd pers. sing. / *adestrar*. 2. (you) train; impve. 2nd pers. sing.

adiestran they train; pres. ind. 3rd pers. pl. / *adestrar*.

adiestrándose practicing; pres. part. / *adiestrarse*.

adiestraos (you all) practice; impve. 2nd pers. pl. / *adiestrarse*.

adiestrar to train or to instruct. reg.

adiestrarse to practice. reg.

adiestras you train; pres. ind. 2nd pers. sing. / *adestrar*.

adiéstrate (you) practice; impve. 2nd pers. sing. / *adiestrarse*.

adiestre 1. that I may train; pres. subj. 1st pers. sing. / *adestrar*. 2. that he (she/it) may train; pres. subj. 3rd pers. sing. 3. let him (her/it) train; impve. 3rd pers. sing.

adiestrémonos let us practice; impve. 1st pers. pl. / *adiestrarse*.

adiestren 1. that they may train; pres. subj. 3rd pers. pl. / *adestrar*. 2. let them train; impve. 3rd pers. pl.

adiéstrense let them practice; impve. 3rd pers. pl. / *adiestrarse*.

adiestres that you may train; pres. subj. 2nd pers. sing. / *adestrar*.

adiéstrese let him (her/it) practice; impve. 3rd pers. sing. / *adiestrarse*.

adiestro I train; pres. ind. 1st pers. sing. / *adestrar*.

adivinar to predict or guess. reg.

adjudicándose appropriating; pres. part. / *adjudicarse*.

adjudicaos (you all) appropriate; impve. 2nd pers. pl. / *adjudicarse*.

adjudicar to award or adjudge. irr.

adjudicarse to appropriate to oneself. irr.

adjudícate (you) appropriate; impve. 2nd pers. sing. / *adjudicarse*.

adjudique 1. that I may award; pres. subj. 1st pers. sing. / *adjudicar*. 2. that he (she/it) may award; pres. subj. 3rd pers. sing. 3. let him (her/it) award; impve. 3rd pers. sing.

adjudiqué I awarded; past 1st pers. sing. / *adjudicar*.

adjudiquéis that you (all) may award; pres. subj. 2nd pers. pl. / *adjudicar*.

adjudiquémonos let us appropriate; impve. 1st pers. pl. / *adjudicarse*.

adjudiquemos 1. that we may award; pres. subj. 1st pers. pl. / *adjudicar*. 2. let us award; impve. 1st pers. pl.

adjudiquen 1. that they may award; pres. subj. 3rd pers. pl. / *adjudicar*. 2. let them award; impve. 3rd pers. pl.

adjudíquense let them appropriate; impve. 3rd pers. pl. / *adjudicarse*.

adjudiques that you may award; pres. subj. 2nd pers. sing. / *adjudicar*.

adjudíquese let him (her/it) appropriate; impve. 3rd pers. sing. / *adjudicarse*.

adjuntar to enclose or to attach. reg.

administrándose receiving the last sacrament; pres. part. / *administrarse*.

administraos (you all) receive the last sacrament; impve. 2nd pers. pl. / *administrarse*.

administrar to administer or manage. reg.

administrarse to receive the last sacrament. reg.

adminístrate (you) receive the last sacrament; impve. 2nd pers. sing. / *administrarse*.

administrémonos let us receive the last sacrament; impve. 1st pers. pl. / *administrarse*.

adminístrense let them receive the last sacrament; impve. 3rd pers. pl. / *administrarse*.

adminístrese let him (her/it) receive the last sacrament; impve. 3rd pers. sing. / *administrarse*.

admirándose being astonished; pres. part. / *admirarse.*

admiraos (you all) be astonished; impve. 2nd pers. pl. / *admirarse.*

admirar to admire. reg.

admirarse to be astonished or amazed. reg.

admírate (you) be astonished; impve. 2nd pers. sing. / *admirarse.*

admirémonos let us be astonished; impve. 1st pers. pl. / *admirarse.*

admírense let them be astonished; impve. 3rd pers. pl. / *admirarse.*

admírese let him (her/it) be astonished; impve. 3rd pers. sing. / *admirarse.*

admitir to admit or accept. reg.

adobar to prepare (food). reg.

adoctrinar to indoctrinate. reg.

adoleceos (you all) condole; impve. 2nd pers. pl. / *adolecerse.*

adolecer to be ill. irr.

adolecerse to condole. irr.

adolécete (you) condole; impve. 2nd pers. sing. / *adolecerse.*

adoleciéndose condoling; pres. part. / *adolecerse.*

adolezca 1. that I may be ill; pres. subj. 1st pers. sing. / *adolecer.* 2. that he (she/it) may be ill; pres. subj. 3rd pers. sing. 3. let him (her/it) be ill; impve. 3rd pers. sing.

adolezcáis that you (all) may be ill; pres. subj. 2nd pers. pl. / *adolecer.*

adolezcámonos let us condole; impve. 1st pers. pl. / *adolecerse.*

adolezcamos 1. that we may be ill; pres. subj. 1st pers. pl. / *adolecer.* 2. let us be ill; impve. 1st pers. pl.

adolezcan 1. that they may be ill; pres. subj. 3rd pers. pl. / *adolecer.* 2. let them be ill; impve. 3rd pers. pl.

adolézcanse let them condole; impve. 3rd pers. pl. / *adolecerse.*

adolezcas that you may be ill; pres. subj. 2nd pers. sing. / *adolecer.*

adolézcase let him (her/it) condole; impve. 3rd pers. sing. / *adolecerse.*

adolezco I am ill; pres. ind. 1st pers. sing. / *adolecer.*

adoptar to adopt. reg.

adoquinar to pave. reg.

adorar to adore or worship. reg.

adormeceos (you all) become sleepy; impve. 2nd pers. pl. / *adormecerse.*

adormecer to lull to sleep. irr.

adormecerse to become sleepy. irr.

adormécete (you) become sleepy; impve. 2nd pers. sing. / *adormecerse.*

adormeciéndose becoming sleepy; pres. part. / *adormecerse.*

adormezca 1. that I may lull to sleep; pres. subj. 1st pers. sing. / *adormecer.* 2. that he (she/it) may lull to sleep; pres. subj. 3rd pers. sing. 3. let him (her/it) lull to sleep; impve. 3rd pers. sing.

adormezcáis that you (all) may lull to sleep; pres. subj. 2nd pers. pl. / *adormecer.*

adormezcámonos let us become sleepy; impve. 1st pers. pl. / *adormecerse.*

adormezcamos 1. that we may lull to sleep; pres. subj. 1st pers. pl. / *adormecer.* 2. let us lull to sleep; impve. 1st pers. pl.

adormezcan 1. that they may lull to sleep; pres. subj. 3rd pers. pl. / *adormecer.* 2. let them lull to sleep; impve. 3rd pers. pl.

adormézcanse let them become sleepy; impve. 3rd pers. pl. / *adormecerse.*

adormezcas that you may lull to sleep; pres. subj. 2nd pers. sing. / *adormecer.*

adormézcase let him (her/it) become sleepy; impve. 3rd pers. sing. / *adormecerse.*

adormezco I lull to sleep; pres. ind. 1st pers. sing. / *adormecer.*

adormilándose dozing; pres. part. / *adormilarse.*

adormilaos (you all) doze; impve. 2nd pers. pl. / *adormilarse.*

adormilarse to doze or drowse. reg.

adormílate (you) doze; impve. 2nd pers. sing. / *adormilarse.*

adormilémonos let us doze; impve. 1st pers. pl. / *adormilarse.*

adormílense let them doze; impve. 3rd pers. pl. / *adormilarse.*

adormílese let him (her/it) doze; impve. 3rd pers. sing. / *adormilarse.*

adormitándose becoming drowsy; pres. part. / *adormitarse.*

adormitaos (you all) become drowsy; impve. 2nd pers. pl. / *adormitarse.*

adormitarse to become drowsy. reg.

adormítate (you) become drowsy; impve. 2nd pers. sing. / *adormitarse.*

adormitémonos let us become drowsy; impve. 1st pers. pl. / *adormitarse.*

adormítense let them become drowsy; impve. 3rd pers. pl. / *adormitarse.*

adormítese let him (her/it) become drowsy; impve. 3rd pers. sing. / *adormitarse.*

adornar to adorn or decorate. reg.

adosar to lean something against another. reg.

adquiera 1. that I may acquire; pres. subj. 1st pers. sing. / *adquirir.* 2. that he (she/it) may acquire; pres. subj. 3rd pers. sing. 3. let him (her/it) acquire; impve. 3rd pers. sing.

adquieran 1. that they may acquire; pres. subj. 3rd pers. pl. / *adquirir.* 2. let them acquire; impve. 3rd pers. pl.

adquieras that you may acquire; pres. subj. 2nd pers. sing. / *adquirir.*

adquiere 1. he (she/it) acquires; pres. ind. 3rd pers. sing. / *adquirir.* 2. (you) acquire; impve. 2nd pers. sing.

adquieren they acquire; pres. ind. 3rd pers. pl. / *adquirir.*

adquieres you acquire; pres.ind. 2nd pers. sing. / *adquirir.*

adquiero I acquire; pres. ind. 1st pers. sing. / *adquirir.*

adquirir to acquire or obtain. irr.

adscribir to ascribe or to attribute. reg. except for past part.
adscripto ascribed; past part. / *adscribir.*
adscrito ascribed; past part. / *adscribir.*
aducir to cite or allege. irr.
adueñándose taking possession; pres. part. / *adueñarse.*
adueñaos (you all) take possession; impve. 2nd pers. pl. / *adueñarse.*
adueñarse to take possession. reg.
aduéñate (you) take possession; impve. 2nd pers. sing. / *adueñarse.*
adueñémonos let us take possession; impve. 1st pers. pl. / *adueñarse.*
aduéñense let them take possession; impve. 3rd pers. pl. / *adueñarse.*
aduéñese let him (her/it) take possession; impve. 3rd pers. sing. / *adueñarse.*
aduje I cited; past 1st pers. sing. / *aducir.*
adujera 1. that I might cite; imp. subj. 1st pers. sing. / *aducir.* 2. that he (she/it) might cite; imp. subj. 3rd pers. sing.
adujerais that you (all) might cite; imp. subj. 2nd pers pl. / *aducir.*
adujéramos that we might cite; imp. subj. 1st pers. pl. / *aducir.*
adujeran that they might cite; imp. subj. 3rd pers. pl. / *aducir.*
adujeras that you might cite; imp. subj. 2nd pers. sing. / *aducir.*
adujeron they cited; past 3rd pers. pl. / *aducir.*
adujese 1. that I might cite; imp. subj. 1st pers. sing. / *aducir.* 2. that he (she/it) might cite; imp. subj. 3rd pers. sing.
adujeseis that you (all) might cite; imp. subj. 2nd pers pl. / *aducir.*
adujésemos that we might cite; imp. subj. 1st pers. pl. / *aducir.*
adujesen that they might cite; imp. subj. 3rd pers. pl. / *aducir.*
adujeses that you might cite; imp. subj. 2nd pers. sing. / *aducir.*
adujimos we cited; past 1st pers. pl. / *aducir.*
adujiste you cited; past 2nd pers. sing. / *aducir.*
adujisteis you (all) cited; past 2nd pers. pl. / *aducir.*
adujo he (she/it) cited; past 3rd per. sing. / *aducir.*
adular to flatter. reg.
adulterar to adulterate or make impure. reg.
aduzca 1. that I may cite; pres. subj. 1st pers. sing. / *aducir.* 2. that he (she/it) may cite; pres. subj. 3rd pers. sing. 3. let him (her/it) cite; impve. 3rd pers. sing.
aduzcáis that you (all) may cite; pres. subj. 2nd pers. pl. / *aducir.*
aduzcamos 1. that we may cite; pres. subj. 1st pers. pl. / *aducir.* 2. let us cite; impve. 1st pers. pl.
aduzcan 1. that they may cite; pres. subj. 3rd pers. pl. / *aducir.* 2. let them cite; impve. 3rd pers. pl.
aduzcas that you may cite; pres. subj. 2nd pers. sing. / *aducir.*

aduzco I cite; pres. ind. 1st pers. sing. / *aducir.*
advertir to notice or to warn. irr.
advierta 1. that I may notice; pres. subj. 1st pers. sing. / *advertir.* 2. that he (she/it) may notice; pres. subj. 3rd pers. sing. 3. let him (her/it) notice; impve. 3rd pers. sing.
adviertan 1. that they may notice; pres. subj. 3rd pers. pl. / *advertir.* 2. let them notice; impve. 3rd pers. pl.
adviertas that you may notice; pres. subj. 2nd pers. sing. / *advertir.*
advierte 1. he (she/it) notices; pres. ind. 3rd pers. sing. / *advertir.* 2. (you) notice; impve. 2nd pers. sing.
advierten they notice; pres. ind. 3rd pers. pl. / *advertir.*
adviertes you notice; pres.ind. 2nd pers. sing. / *advertir.*
advierto I notice; pres. ind. 1st pers. sing. / *advertir.*
advirtáis that you (all) may notice; pres. subj. 2nd pers. pl. / *advertir.*
advirtamos 1. that we may notice; pres. subj. 1st pers. pl. / *advertir.* 2. let us notice; impve. 1st pers. pl.
advirtiendo noticing; pres. part. / *advertir.*
advirtiera 1. that I might notice; imp. subj. 1st pers. sing. / *advertir.* 2. that he (she/it) might notice; imp. subj. 3rd pers. sing.
advirtierais that you (all) might notice; imp. subj. 2nd pers pl. / *advertir.*
advirtiéramos that we might notice; imp. subj. 1st pers. pl. / *advertir.*
advirtieran that they might notice; imp. subj. 3rd pers. pl. / *advertir.*
advirtieras that you might notice; imp. subj. 2nd pers. sing. / *advertir.*
advirtieron they noticed; past 3rd pers. pl. / *advertir.*
advirtiese 1. that I might notice; imp. subj. 1st pers. sing. / *advertir.* 2. that he (she/it) might notice; imp. subj. 3rd pers. sing.
advirtieseis that you (all) might notice; imp. subj. 2nd pers pl. / *advertir.*
advirtiésemos that we might notice; imp. subj. 1st pers. pl. / *advertir.*
advirtiesen that they might notice; imp. subj. 3rd pers. pl. / *advertir.*
advirtieses that you might notice; imp. subj. 2nd pers. sing. / *advertir.*
advirtió he (she/it) noticed; past 3rd pers. sing. / *advertir.*
afamar to make famous. reg.
afanándose toiling; pres. part. / *afanarse.*
afanaos (you all) toil; impve. 2nd pers. pl. / *afanarse.*
afanar to urge or hurry. reg.
afanarse to toil. reg.
afánate (you) toil; impve. 2nd pers. sing. / *afanarse.*
afanémonos let us toil; impve. 1st pers. pl. / *afanarse.*
afánense let them toil; impve. 3rd pers. pl. / *afanarse.*
afánese let him (her/it) toil; impve. 3rd pers. sing. / *afanarse.*
afear to make ugly or to deform. reg.

afectándose feeling; pres. part. / *afectarse.*
afectaos (you all) feel; impve. 2nd pers. pl. / *afectarse.*
afectar to affect or to feign. reg.
afectarse to feel or to be moved. reg.
aféctate (you) feel; impve. 2nd pers. sing. / *afectarse.*
afectémonos let us feel; impve. 1st pers. pl. / *afectarse.*
aféctense let them feel; impve. 3rd pers. pl. / *afectarse.*
aféctese let him (her/it) feel; impve. 3rd pers. sing. / *afectarse.*
afeitándose shaving oneself; pres. part. / *afeitarse.*
afeitaos (you all) shave yourselves; impve. 2nd pers. pl. / *afeitarse.*
afeitar to shave. reg.
afeitarse to shave oneself or to put on make-up. reg.
afeítate (you) shave yourself; impve. 2nd pers. sing. / *afeitarse.*
afeitémonos let us shave ourselves; impve. 1st pers. pl. / *afeitarse.*
afeítense let them shave themselves; impve. 3rd pers. pl. / *afeitarse.*
afeítese let him (her) shave himself (herself); impve. 3rd pers. sing. / *afeitarse.*
afeminar to make effeminate. reg.
aferrándose clinging; pres. part. / *aferrarse.*
aferraos (you all) cling; impve. 2nd pers. pl. / *aferrarse.*
aferrar to grasp or seize. reg.
aferrarse to cling. reg.
aférrate (you) cling; impve. 2nd pers. sing. / *aferrarse.*
aferrémonos let us cling; impve. 1st pers. pl. / *aferrarse.*
aférrense let them cling; impve. 3rd pers. pl. / *aferrarse.*
aférrese let him (her/it) cling; impve. 3rd pers. sing. / *aferrarse.*
afiance 1. that I may fasten; pres. subj. 1st pers. sing. / *afianzar.* 2. that he (she/it) may fasten; pres. subj. 3rd pers. sing. 3. let him (her/it) fasten; impve. 3rd pers. sing.
afiancé I fastened; past 1st pers. sing. / *afianzar.*
afiancéis that you (all) may fasten; pres. subj. 2nd pers. pl. / *afianzar.*
afiancemos 1. that we may fasten; pres. subj. 1st pers. pl. / *afianzar.* 2. let us fasten; impve. 1st pers. pl.
afiancen 1. that they may fasten; pres. subj. 3rd pers. pl. / *afianzar.* 2. let them fasten; impve. 3rd pers. pl.
afiances that you may fasten; pres. subj. 2nd pers. sing. / *afianzar.*
afianzar to fasten or to give bond. irr.
aficionándose taking an interest in; pres. part. / *aficionarse.*
aficionaos (you all) take an interest in; impve. 2nd pers. pl. / *aficionarse.*
aficionar to inspire affection. reg.
aficionarse to take an interest in. reg.
aficiónate (you) take an interest in; impve. 2nd pers. sing. / *aficionarse.*
aficionémonos let us take an interest in; impve. 1st pers. pl. / *aficionarse.*

aficiónense let them take an interest in; impve. 3rd pers. pl. / *aficionarse.*
aficiónese let him (her/it) take an interest in; impve. 3rd pers. sing. / *aficionarse.*
afiebrándose becoming feverish; pres. part. / *afiebrarse.*
afiebraos (you all) become feverish; impve. 2nd pers. pl. / *afiebrarse.*
afiebrarse to become feverish. reg.
afiébrate (you) become feverish; impve. 2nd pers. sing. / *afiebrarse.*
afiebrémonos let us become feverish; impve. 1st pers. pl. / *afiebrarse.*
afiébrense let them become feverish; impve. 3rd pers. pl. / *afiebrarse.*
afiébrese let him (her/it) become feverish; impve. 3rd pers. sing. / *afiebrarse.*
afilar to sharpen. reg.
afiliándose affiliating with; pres. part. / *afiliarse.*
afiliaos (you all) affiliate with; impve. 2nd pers. pl. / *afiliarse.*
afiliar to affiliate or adopt. reg.
afiliarse to affiliate with. reg.
afilíate (you) affiliate with; impve. 2nd pers. sing. / *afiliarse.*
afiliémonos let us affiliate with; impve. 1st pers. pl. / *afiliarse.*
afilíense let them affiliate with; impve. 3rd pers. pl. / *afiliarse.*
afilíese let him (her/it) affiliate with; impve. 3rd pers. sing. / *afiliarse.*
afinar to complete or to tune. reg.
afincándose getting a foothold; pres. part. / *afincarse.*
afincaos (you all) get a foothold; impve. 2nd pers. pl. / *afincarse.*
afincar to acquire real estate. irr.
afincarse to get a foothold or to acquire real estate. irr.
afíncate (you) get a foothold; impve. 2nd pers. sing. / *afincarse.*
afinque 1. that I may get a foothold; pres. subj. 1st pers. sing. / *afincarse.* 2. that he (she/it) may get a foothold; pres. subj. 3rd pers. sing. 3. let him (her/it) acquire real estate; impve. 3rd pers. sing.
afinqué I got a foothold; past 1st pers. sing. / *afincarse.*
afinquéis that you (all) may get a foothold; pres. subj. 2nd pers. pl. / *afincarse.*
afinquémonos let us get a foothold; impve. 1st pers. pl. / *afincarse.*
afinquemos 1. that we may get a foothold; pres. subj. 1st pers. pl. / *afincarse.* 2. let us acquire real estate; impve. 1st pers. pl.
afinquen 1. that they may get a foothold; pres. subj. 3rd pers. pl. / *afincarse.* 2. let them acquire real estate; impve. 3rd pers. pl.
afínquense let them get a foothold; impve. 3rd pers. pl. / *afincarse.*
afinques that you may get a foothold; pres. subj. 2nd pers. sing. / *afincarse.*

afínquese let him (her/it) get a foothold; impve. 3rd pers. sing. / *afincarse*.

afirmándose steadying oneself; pres. part. / *afirmarse*.

afirmaos (you all) steady yourselves; impve. 2nd pers. pl. / *afirmarse*.

afirmar to affirm or assert. reg.

afirmarse to steady oneself. reg.

afírmate (you) steady yourself; impve. 2nd pers. sing. / *afirmarse*.

afirmémonos let us steady ourselves; impve. 1st pers. pl. / *afirmarse*.

afírmense let them steady themselves; impve. 3rd pers. pl. / *afirmarse*.

afírmese let him (her/it) steady himself (herself); impve. 3rd pers. sing. / *afirmarse*.

aflicto afflicted; past part. / *afligir*.

aflígete (you) grieve; impve. 2nd pers. sing. / *afligirse*.

afligiéndose grieving; pres. part. / *afligirse*.

afligíos (you all) grieve; impve. 2nd pers. pl. / *afligirse*.

afligir to afflict or grieve. irr.

afligirse to grieve. irr.

aflija 1. that I may afflict; pres. subj. 1st pers. sing. / *afligir*. 2. that he (she/it) may afflict; pres. subj. 3rd pers. sing. 3. let him (her/it) afflict; impve. 3rd pers. sing.

aflijáis that you (all) may afflict; pres. subj. 2nd pers. pl. / *afligir*.

aflijámonos let us grieve; impve. 1st pers. pl. / *afligirse*.

aflijamos 1. that we may afflict; pres. subj. 1st pers. pl. / *afligir*. 2. let us afflict; impve. 1st pers. pl.

aflijan 1. that they may afflict; pres. subj. 3rd pers. pl. / *afligir*. 2. let them afflict; impve. 3rd pers. pl.

aflíjanse let them grieve; impve. 3rd pers. pl. / *afligirse*.

aflijas that you may afflict; pres. subj. 2nd pers. sing. / *afligir*.

aflíjase let him (her/it) grieve; impve. 3rd pers. sing. / *afligirse*.

aflijo I afflict; pres. ind. 1st pers. sing. / *afligir*.

aflojándose growing weak; pres. part. / *aflojarse*.

aflojaos (you all) grow weak; impve. 2nd pers. pl. / *aflojarse*.

aflojar to loosen or relax. reg.

aflojarse to grow weak. reg.

aflójate (you) grow weak; impve. 2nd pers. sing. / *aflojarse*.

aflojémonos let us grow weak; impve. 1st pers. pl. / *aflojarse*.

aflójense let them grow weak; impve. 3rd pers. pl. / *aflojarse*.

aflójese let him (her/it) grow weak; impve. 3rd pers. sing. / *aflojarse*.

aflorar to come to the surface or to sift (flour). reg.

afluir to come together or to flow (into). irr.

afluya 1. that I may come together; pres. subj. 1st pers. sing. / *afluir*. 2. that he (she/it) may come together; pres. subj. 3rd pers. sing. 3. let him (her/it) come together; impve. 3rd pers. sing.

afluyáis that you (all) may come together; pres. subj. 2nd pers. pl. / *afluir*.

afluyamos 1. that we may come together; pres. subj. 1st pers. pl. / *afluir*. 2. let us come together; impve. 1st pers. pl.

afluyan 1. that they may come together; pres. subj. 3rd pers. pl. / *afluir*. 2. let them come together; impve. 3rd pers. pl.

afluyas that you may come together; pres. subj. 2nd pers. sing. / *afluir*.

afluye 1. he (she/it) comes together; pres. ind. 3rd pers. sing. / *afluir*. 2. (you) come together; impve. 2nd pers. sing.

afluyen they come together; pres. ind. 3rd pers. pl. / *afluir*.

afluyendo coming together; pres. part. / *afluir*.

afluyera 1. that I might come together; imp. subj. 1st pers. sing. / *afluir*. 2. that he (she/it) might come together; imp. subj. 3rd pers. sing.

afluyerais that you (all) might come together; imp. subj. 2nd pers pl. / *afluir*.

afluyéramos that we might come together; imp. subj. 1st pers. pl. / *afluir*.

afluyeran that they might come together; imp. subj. 3rd pers. pl. / *afluir*.

afluyeras that you might come together; imp. subj. 2nd pers. sing. / *afluir*.

afluyeron they came together; past 3rd pers. pl. / *afluir*.

afluyes you come together; pres.ind. 2nd pers. sing. / *afluir*.

afluyese 1. that I might come together; imp. subj. 1st pers. sing. / *afluir*. 2. that he (she/it) might come together; imp. subj. 3rd pers. sing.

afluyeseis that you (all) might come together; imp. subj. 2nd pers pl. / *afluir*.

afluyésemos that we might come together; imp. subj. 1st pers. pl. / *afluir*.

afluyesen that they might come together; imp. subj. 3rd pers. pl. / *afluir*.

afluyeses that you might come together; imp. subj. 2nd pers. sing. / *afluir*.

afluyo I come together; pres. ind. 1st pers. sing. / *afluir*.

afluyó he (she/it) came together; past 3rd pers. sing. / *afluir*.

afofándose fluffing up; pres. part. / *afofarse*.

afofaos (you all) fluff up; impve. 2nd pers. pl. / *afofarse*.

afofarse to fluff up. reg.

afófate (you) fluff up; impve. 2nd pers. sing. / *afofarse*.

afofémonos let us fluff up; impve. 1st pers. pl. / *afofarse*.

afófense let them fluff up; impve. 3rd pers. pl. / *afofarse*.

afófese let him (her/it) fluff up; impve. 3rd pers. sing. / *afofarse*.

afondándose sinking; pres. part. / *afondarse*.

afondaos (you all) sink; impve. 2nd pers. pl. / *afondarse*.

afondar to sink. reg.

afondarse to sink. reg.

afóndate (you) sink; impve. 2nd pers. sing. / *afondarse.*

afondémonos let us sink; impve. 1st pers. pl. / *afondarse.*

afóndense let them sink; impve. 3rd pers. pl. / *afondarse.*

afóndese let him (her/it) sink; impve. 3rd pers. sing. / *afondarse.*

aforar to appraise or to measure. reg.

afrancesar to frenchify. reg.

afrentar to affront or to offend. reg.

afrontar to confront or to face. reg.

agachándose crouching; pres. part. / *agacharse.*

agachaos (you all) crouch; impve. 2nd pers. pl. / *agacharse.*

agachar to bow down or to lower. reg.

agacharse to crouch. reg.

agáchate (you) crouch; impve. 2nd pers. sing. / *agacharse.*

agachémonos let us crouch; impve. 1st pers. pl. / *agacharse.*

agáchense let them crouch; impve. 3rd pers. pl. / *agacharse.*

agáchese let him (her/it) crouch; impve. 3rd pers. sing. / *agacharse.*

agangrenándose becoming gangrenous; pres. part. / *agangrenarse.*

agangrenaos (you all) become gangrenous; impve. 2nd pers. pl. / *agangrenarse.*

agangrenarse to become gangrenous. reg.

agangrénate (you) become gangrenous; impve. 2nd pers. sing. / *agangrenarse.*

agangrenémonos let us become gangrenous; impve. 1st pers. pl. / *agangrenarse.*

agangrénense let them become gangrenous; impve. 3rd pers. pl. / *agangrenarse.*

agangrénese let him (her/it) become gangrenous; impve. 3rd pers. sing. / *agangrenarse.*

agarrándose holding on; pres. part. / *agarrarse.*

agarraos (you all) hold on; impve. 2nd pers. pl. / *agarrarse.*

agarrar to grasp or to take root. reg.

agarrarse to hold on. reg.

agárrate (you) hold on; impve. 2nd pers. sing. / *agarrarse.*

agarrémonos let us hold on; impve. 1st pers. pl. / *agarrarse.*

agárrense let them hold on; impve. 3rd pers. pl. / *agarrarse.*

agárrese let him (her/it) hold on; impve. 3rd pers. sing. / *agarrarse.*

agarrotándose seizing as a bearing; pres. part. / *agarrotarse.*

agarrotar to strangle or to fasten tightly with ropes. reg.

agarrotarse to seize as a bearing or to stiffen as a muscle. reg.

agarrótense let them seize as a bearing; impve. 3rd pers. pl. / *agarrotarse.*

agarrótese let it seize as a bearing; impve. 3rd pers. sing. / *agarrotarse.*

agasajar to entertain. reg.

agazapándose crouching; pres. part. / *agazaparse.*

agazapaos (you all) crouch; impve. 2nd pers. pl. / *agazaparse.*

agazapar to catch or to grab. reg.

agazaparse to crouch. reg.

agazápate (you) crouch; impve. 2nd pers. sing. / *agazaparse.*

agazapémonos let us crouch; impve. 1st pers. pl. / *agazaparse.*

agazápense let them crouch; impve. 3rd pers. pl. / *agazaparse.*

agazápese let him (her/it) crouch; impve. 3rd pers. sing. / *agazaparse.*

agenciándose managing / *agenciarse.*

agenciaos (you all) manage; impve. 2nd pers. pl. / *agenciarse.*

agenciar to negotiate or promote. reg.

agenciarse to manage or to get along. reg.

agencíate (you) manage; impve. 2nd pers. sing. / *agenciarse.*

agenciémonos let us manage; impve. 1st pers. pl. / *agenciarse.*

agencíense let them manage; impve. 3rd pers. pl. / *agenciarse.*

agencíese let him (her/it) manage; impve. 3rd pers. sing. / *agenciarse.*

agigantar to exaggerate. reg.

agitándose becoming excited; pres. part. / *agitarse.*

agitaos (you all) become excited; impve. 2nd pers. pl. / *agitarse.*

agitar agitate or excite. reg.

agitarse to become excited. reg.

agítate (you) become excited; impve. 2nd pers. sing. / *agitarse.*

agitémonos let us become excited; impve. 1st pers. pl. / *agitarse.*

agítense let them become excited; impve. 3rd pers. pl. / *agitarse.*

agítese let him (her/it) become excited; impve. 3rd pers. sing. / *agitarse.*

aglomerándose crowding together; pres. part. / *aglomerarse.*

aglomeraos (you all) crowd together; impve. 2nd pers. pl. / *aglomerarse.*

aglomerar to agglomerate or mass together. reg.

aglomerarse to crowd together. reg.

aglomérate (you) crowd together; impve. 2nd pers. sing. / *aglomerarse.*

aglomerémonos let us crowd together; impve. 1st pers. pl. / *aglomerarse.*

aglomérense let them crowd together; impve. 3rd pers. pl. / *aglomerarse.*

aglomérese let him (her/it) crowd together; impve. 3rd pers. sing. / *aglomerarse.*

aglutinar to bind together. reg.

agobiar to oppress or weigh down. reg.

agolpándose rushing together; pres. part. / *agolparse*.

agolpaos (you all) rush together; impve. 2nd pers. pl. / *agolparse*.

agolpar to crowd. reg.

agolparse to rush together. reg.

agólpate (you) rush together; impve. 2nd pers. sing. / *agolparse*.

agolpémonos let us rush together; impve. 1st pers. pl. / *agolparse*.

agólpense let them rush together; impve. 3rd pers. pl. / *agolparse*.

agólpese let him (her/it) rush together; impve. 3rd pers. sing. / *agolparse*.

agonice 1. that I may agonize; pres. subj. 1st pers. sing. / *agonizar*. 2. that he (she/it) may agonize; pres. subj. 3rd pers. sing. 3. let him (her/it) agonize; impve. 3rd pers. sing.

agonicé I agonized; past 1st pers. sing. / *agonizar*.

agonicéis that you (all) may agonize; pres. subj. 2nd pers. pl. / *agonizar*.

agonicemos 1. that we may agonize; pres. subj. 1st pers. pl. / *agonizar*. 2. let us agonize; impve. 1st pers. pl.

agonicen 1. that they may agonize; pres. subj. 3rd pers. pl. / *agonizar*. 2. let them agonize; impve. 3rd pers. pl.

agonices that you may agonize; pres. subj. 2nd pers. sing. / *agonizar*.

agonizar to agonize or to be dying. irr.

agorar to foretell or divine. irr.

agostándose fading away; pres. part. / *agostarse*.

agostaos (you all) fade away; impve. 2nd pers. pl. / *agostarse*.

agostar to parch or dry up. reg.

agostarse to fade away. reg.

agóstate (you) fade away; impve. 2nd pers. sing. / *agostarse*.

agostémonos let us fade away; impve. 1st pers. pl. / *agostarse*.

agóstense let them fade away; impve. 3rd pers. pl. / *agostarse*.

agóstese let him (her/it) fade away; impve. 3rd pers. sing. / *agostarse*.

agotándose becoming run-down; pres. part. / *agotarse*.

agotaos (you all) become run-down; impve. 2nd pers. pl. / *agotarse*.

agotar to exhaust or to misspend. reg.

agotarse to become run-down or to become exhausted. reg.

agótate (you) become run-down; impve. 2nd pers. sing. / *agotarse*.

agotémonos let us become run-down; impve. 1st pers. pl. / *agotarse*.

agótense let them become run-down; impve. 3rd pers. pl. / *agotarse*.

agótese let him (her/it) become run-down; impve. 3rd pers. sing. / *agotarse*.

agraciar to embellish or adorn. reg.

agradándose being pleased at; pres. part. / *agradarse*.

agradaos (you all) be pleased at; impve. 2nd pers. pl. / *agradarse*.

agradar to please. reg.

agradarse to be pleased at. reg.

agrádate (you) be pleased at; impve. 2nd pers. sing. / *agradarse*.

agradecer to thank for or be grateful for. irr.

agradémonos let us be pleased at; impve. 1st pers. pl. / *agradarse*.

agrádense let them be pleased at; impve. 3rd pers. pl. / *agradarse*.

agrádese let him (her/it) be pleased at; impve. 3rd pers. sing. / *agradarse*.

agradezca 1. that I may thank for; pres. subj. 1st pers. sing. / *agradecer*. 2. that he (she/it) may thank for; pres. subj. 3rd pers. sing. 3. let him (her/it) thank for; impve. 3rd pers. sing.

agradezcáis that you (all) may thank for; pres. subj. 2nd pers. pl. / *agradecer*.

agradezcamos 1. that we may thank for; pres. subj. 1st pers. pl. / *agradecer*. 2. let us thank for; impve. 1st pers. pl.

agradezcan 1. that they may thank for; pres. subj. 3rd pers. pl. / *agradecer*. 2. let them thank for; impve. 3rd pers. pl.

agradezcas that you may thank for; pres. subj. 2nd pers. sing. / *agradecer*.

agradezco I thank for; pres. ind. 1st pers. sing. / *agradecer*.

agrandar to enlarge or to extend. reg.

agravándose getting worse; pres. part. / *agravarse*.

agravaos (you all) get worse; impve. 2nd pers. pl. / *agravarse*.

agravar to aggravate or make worse. reg.

agravarse to get worse. reg.

agrávate (you) get worse; impve. 2nd pers. sing. / *agravarse*.

agravémonos let us get worse; impve. 1st pers. pl. / *agravarse*.

agrávense let them get worse; impve. 3rd pers. pl. / *agravarse*.

agrávese let him (her/it) get worse; impve. 3rd pers. sing. / *agravarse*.

agraviándose taking offense; pres. part. / *agraviarse*.

agraviaos (you all) take offense; impve. 2nd pers. pl. / *agraviarse*.

agraviar to offend or insult. reg.

agraviarse to take offense. reg.

agraviate (you) take offense; impve. 2nd pers. sing. / *agraviarse*.

agraviémonos let us take offense; impve. 1st pers. pl. / *agraviarse*.

agravíense let them take offense; impve. 3rd pers. pl. / *agraviarse*.

agravíese let him (her/it) take offense; impve. 3rd pers. sing. / *agraviarse*.

agredir to attack or assault. used only in tenses with endings beginning with i.

agregándose joining; pres. part. / *agregarse*.

agregaos (you all) join; impve. 2nd pers. pl. / *agregarse*.

agregar to add. irr.

agregarse to join. irr.

agrégate (you) join; impve. 2nd pers. sing. / *agregarse*.

agregue 1. that I may add; pres. subj. 1st pers. sing. / *agregar*. 2. that he (she/it) may add; pres. subj. 3rd pers. sing. 3. let him (her/it) add; impve. 3rd pers. sing.

agregué I added; past 1st pers. sing. / *agregar*.

agreguéis that you (all) may add; pres. subj. 2nd pers. pl. / *agregar*.

agreguémonos let us join; impve. 1st pers. pl. / *agregarse*.

agreguemos 1. that we may add; pres. subj. 1st pers. pl. / *agregar*. 2. let us add; impve. 1st pers. pl.

agreguen 1. that they may add; pres. subj. 3rd pers. pl. / *agregar*. 2. let them add; impve. 3rd pers. pl.

agréguense let them join; impve. 3rd pers. pl. / *agregarse*.

agregues that you may add; pres. subj. 2nd pers. sing. / *agregar*.

agréguese let him (her/it) join; impve. 3rd pers. sing. / *agregarse*.

agremiándose joining a union; pres. part. / *agremiarse*.

agremiaos (you all) join a union; impve. 2nd pers. pl. / *agremiarse*.

agremiar to unionize. reg.

agremiarse to join a union. reg.

agremíate (you) join a union; impve. 2nd pers. sing. / *agremiarse*.

agremiémonos let us join a union; impve. 1st pers. pl. / *agremiarse*.

agremíense let them join a union; impve. 3rd pers. pl. / *agremiarse*.

agremíese let him (her/it) join a union; impve. 3rd pers. sing. / *agremiarse*.

agría it sours; pres. ind. 3rd pers. sing. / *agriar*.

agrían they sour; pres. ind. 3rd pers. pl. / *agriar*.

agriándose turning sour; pres. part. / *agriarse*.

agriar to sour. irr.

agriarse to turn sour. irr.

agríe 1. that it may sour; pres. subj. 3rd pers. sing. / *agriar*. 2. let it sour; impve. 3rd pers. sing.

agríen 1. that they may sour; pres. subj. 3rd pers. pl. / *agriar*. 2. let them sour; impve. 3rd pers. pl.

agríense let them turn sour; impve. 3rd pers. pl. / *agriarse*.

agríese let him (her/it) turn sour; impve. 3rd pers. sing. / *agriarse*.

agrietándose cracking; pres. part. / *agrietarse*.

agrietaos (you all) crack; impve. 2nd pers. pl. / *agrietarse*.

agrietarse to crack or to chap. reg.

agriétate (you)crack; impve. 2nd pers. sing. / *agrietarse*.

agrietémonos let us crack; impve. 1st pers. pl. / *agrietarse*.

agriétense let them crack; impve. 3rd pers. pl. / *agrietarse*.

agriétese let him (her/it) crack; impve. 3rd pers. sing. / *agrietarse*.

agrumar to curdle or clot. reg.

agrupándose clustering; pres. part. / *agruparse*.

agrupaos (you all) cluster; impve. 2nd pers. pl. / *agruparse*.

agrupar to group. reg.

agruparse to cluster. reg.

agrúpate (you) cluster; impve. 2nd pers. sing. / *agruparse*.

agrupémonos let us cluster; impve. 1st pers. pl. / *agruparse*.

agrúpense let them cluster; impve. 3rd pers. pl. / *agruparse*.

agrúpese let him (her/it) cluster; impve. 3rd pers. sing. / *agruparse*.

aguándose becoming diluted; pres. part. / *aguarse*.

aguantándose being silent; pres. part. / *aguantarse*.

aguantaos (you all) be silent; impve. 2nd pers. pl. / *aguantarse*.

aguantar to endure or tolerate. reg.

aguantarse to be silent or to restrain oneself. reg.

aguántate (you) be silent; impve. 2nd pers. sing. / *aguantarse*.

aguantémonos let us be silent; impve. 1st pers. pl. / *aguantarse*.

aguántense let them be silent; impve. 3rd pers. pl. / *aguantarse*.

aguántese let him (her/it) be silent; impve. 3rd pers. sing. / *aguantarse*.

aguar to dilute with water. irr.

aguardar to wait for or to expect. reg.

aguarse to become diluted. irr.

aguce 1. that I may sharpen; pres. subj. 1st pers. sing. / *aguzar*. 2. that he (she/it) may sharpen; pres. subj. 3rd pers. sing. 3. let him (her/it) sharpen; impve. 3rd pers. sing.

agucé I sharpened; past 1st pers. sing. / *aguzar*.

agucéis that you (all) may sharpen; pres. subj. 2nd pers. pl. / *aguzar*.

agucemos 1. that we may sharpen; pres. subj. 1st pers. pl. / *aguzar*. 2. let us sharpen; impve. 1st pers. pl.

agucen 1. that they may sharpen; pres. subj. 3rd pers. pl. / *aguzar*. 2. let them sharpen; impve. 3rd pers. pl.

aguces that you may sharpen; pres. subj. 2nd pers. sing. / *aguzar*.

agüe 1. that I may dilute with water; pres. subj. 1st pers. sing. / *aguar*. 2. that he (she/it) may dilute with water; pres. subj. 3rd pers. sing. 3. let him (her/ it) dilute with water; impve. 3rd pers. sing.

agüé I diluted with water; past 1st pers. sing. / *aguar*.

agüéis that you (all) may dilute with water; pres. subj. 2nd pers. pl. / *aguar*.

agüemos 1. that we may dilute with water; pres. subj. 1st pers. pl. / *aguar*. 2. let us dilute with water; impve. 1st pers. pl.

agüen 1. that they may dilute with water; pres. subj. 3rd pers. pl. / *aguar*. 2. let them dilute with water; impve. 3rd pers. pl.

agüense let them become diluted; impve. 3rd pers. pl. / *aguarse*.

agüera 1. he (she/it) foretells; pres. ind. 3rd pers. sing. / *agorar* 2. (you) foretell; impve. 2nd pers. sing.

agüeran they foretell; pres. ind. 3rd pers. pl. / *agorar*.

agüeras you foretell; pres.ind. 2nd pers. sing. / *agorar*.

agüere 1. that I may foretell; pres. subj. 1st pers. sing. / *agorar*. 2. that he (she/it) may foretell; pres. subj. 3rd pers. sing. 3. let him (her/it) foretell; impve. 3rd pers. sing.

agüeren 1. that they may foretell; pres. subj. 3rd pers. pl. / *agorar*. 2. let them foretell; impve. 3rd pers. pl.

agüeres that you may foretell; pres. subj. 2nd pers. sing. / *agorar*.

agüero I foretell; pres. ind. 1st pers. sing. / *agorar*.

agües that you may dilute with water; pres. subj. 2nd pers. sing. / *aguar*.

agüese let it become diluted; impve. 3rd pers. sing. / *aguarse*.

aguijar to spur or goad. reg.

aguijonear to prick or goad. reg.

agujerear to pierce or perforate. reg.

agusanándose becoming worm-eaten; pres. part. / *agusanarse*.

agusanarse to become worm-eaten. reg.

agusanense let them become worm-eaten; impve. 3rd pers. pl. / *agusanarse*.

agusánese let it become worm-eaten; impve. 3rd pers. sing. / *agusanarse*.

aguzar to sharpen or whet. irr.

ahechar to winnow. reg.

aherrojar to put in chains or irons. reg.

ahijar to adopt or to breed. reg.

ahilándose becoming faint; pres. part. / *ahilarse*.

ahilaos (you all) become faint; impve. 2nd pers. pl. / *ahilarse*.

ahilarse to become faint or to turn sour. reg.

ahílate (you) become faint; impve. 2nd pers. sing. / *ahilarse*.

ahilémonos let us become faint; impve. 1st pers. pl. / *ahilarse*.

ahílense let them become faint; impve. 3rd pers. pl. / *ahilarse*.

ahílese let him (her/it) become faint; impve. 3rd pers. sing. / *ahilarse*.

ahitándose gorging; pres. part. / *ahitarse*.

ahitaos (you all) gorge; impve. 2nd pers. pl. / *ahitarse*.

ahitar to satiate. reg.

ahitarse to gorge. reg.

ahítate (you) gorge; impve. 2nd pers. sing. / *ahitarse*.

ahitémonos let us gorge; impve. 1st pers. pl. / *ahitarse*.

ahítense let them gorge; impve. 3rd pers. pl. / *ahitarse*.

ahítese let him (her/it) gorge; impve. 3rd pers. sing. / *ahitarse*.

ahogándose feeling suffocated; pres. part. / *ahogarse*.

ahogar to drown or smother. irr.

ahogarse to feel suffocated. irr.

ahogue 1. that I may drown; pres. subj. 1st pers. sing. / *ahogar*. 2. that he (she/it) may drown; pres. subj. 3rd pers. sing. 3. let him (her/it) drown; impve. 3rd pers. sing.

ahogué I drowned; past 1st pers. sing. / *ahogar*.

ahoguéis that you (all) may drown; pres. subj. 2nd pers. pl. / *ahogar*.

ahoguemos 1. that we may drown; pres. subj. 1st pers. pl. / *ahogar*. 2. let us drown; impve. 1st pers. pl.

ahoguen 1. that they may drown; pres. subj. 3rd pers. pl. / *ahogar*. 2. let them drown; impve. 3rd pers. pl.

ahóguense let them feel suffocated; impve. 3rd pers. pl. / *ahogarse*.

ahogues that you may drown; pres. subj. 2nd pers. sing. / *ahogar*.

ahóguese let him (her/it) feel suffocated; impve. 3rd pers. sing. / *ahogarse*.

ahondar to go deep into or to investigate. reg.

ahorcajándose sitting astride; pres. part. / *ahorcajarse*.

ahorcajaos (you all) sit astride; impve. 2nd pers. pl. / *ahorcajarse*.

ahorcajarse to sit astride. reg.

ahorcájate (you) sit astride; impve. 2nd pers. sing. / *ahorcajarse*.

ahorcajémonos let us sit astride; impve. 1st pers. pl. / *ahorcajarse*.

ahorcájense let them sit astride; impve. 3rd pers. pl. / *ahorcajarse*.

ahorcájese let him (her/it) sit astride; impve. 3rd pers. sing. / *ahorcajarse*.

ahorcándose committing suicide by hanging; pres. part. / *ahorcarse*.

ahorcaos (you all) commit suicide by hanging; impve. 2nd pers. pl. / *ahorcarse*.

ahorcar to hang. irr.

ahorcarse to commit suicide by hanging. irr.

ahórcate (you) commit suicide by hanging; impve. 2nd pers. sing. / *ahorcarse*.

ahormar to fit or shape. reg.

ahorque 1. that I may hang; pres. subj. 1st pers. sing. / *ahorcar*. 2. that he (she/it) may hang; pres. subj. 3rd pers. sing. 3. let him (her/it) hang; impve. 3rd pers. sing.

ahorqué I hung; past 1st pers. sing. / *ahorcar*.

ahorquéis that you (all) may hang; pres. subj. 2nd pers. pl. / *ahorcar*.

ahorquémonos let us commit suicide by hanging; impve. 1st pers. pl. / *ahorcarse*.

ahorquemos 1. that we may hang; pres. subj. 1st pers. pl. / *ahorcar*. 2. let us hang; impve. 1st pers. pl.

ahorquen 1. that they may hang; pres. subj. 3rd pers. pl. / *ahorcar*. 2. let them hang; impve. 3rd pers. pl.

ahórquense let them commit suicide by hanging; impve. 3rd pers. pl. / *ahorcarse*.

ahorques that you may hang; pres. subj. 2nd pers. sing. / *ahorcar*.

ahórquese let him (her) commit suicide by hanging; impve. 3rd pers. sing. / *ahorcarse.*

ahorquillándose being forked; pres. part. / *ahorquillarse.*

ahorquillar to fork. reg.

ahorquillarse to be or become forked. reg.

ahorquíllense let them be forked; impve. 3rd pers. pl. / *ahorquillarse.*

ahorquíllese let it be forked; impve. 3rd pers. sing. / *ahorquillarse.*

ahorrar to save or to spare. reg.

ahuecándose getting conceited; pres. part. / *ahuecarse.*

ahuecar to hollow or scoop out. irr.

ahuecarse to get conceited. irr.

ahueque 1. that I may scoop out; pres. subj. 1st pers. sing. / *ahuecar.* 2. that he (she/it) may scoop out; pres. subj. 3rd pers. sing. 3. let him (her/it) scoop out; impve. 3rd pers. sing.

ahuequé I scooped out; past 1st pers. sing. / *ahuecar.*

ahuequéis that you (all) may scoop out; pres. subj. 2nd pers. pl. / *ahuecar.*

ahuequemos 1. that we may scoop out; pres. subj. 1st pers. pl. / *ahuecar.* 2. let us scoop out; impve. 1st pers. pl.

ahuequen 1. that they may scoop out; pres. subj. 3rd pers. pl. / *ahuecar.* 2. let them scoop out; impve. 3rd pers. pl.

ahuéquense let them get conceited; impve. 3rd pers. pl. / *ahuecarse.*

ahueques that you may scoop out; pres. subj. 2nd pers. sing. / *ahuecar.*

ahuéquese let him (her/it) get conceited; impve. 3rd pers. sing. / *ahuecarse.*

ahumándose getting smoky; pres. part. / *ahumarse.*

ahumar to smoke or fumigate. reg.

ahumarse to get smoky or to become tipsy. reg.

ahúmense let them get smoky; impve. 3rd pers. pl. / *ahumarse.*

ahúmese let it get smoky; impve. 3rd pers. sing. / *ahumarse.*

ahusándose tapering; pres. part. / *ahusarse.*

ahusaos (you all) taper; impve. 2nd pers. pl. / *ahusarse.*

ahusar to taper. reg.

ahusarse to taper. reg.

ahúsate (you) taper; impve. 2nd pers. sing. / *ahusarse.*

ahusémonos let us taper; impve. 1st pers. pl. / *ahusarse.*

ahúsense let them taper; impve. 3rd pers. pl. / *ahusarse.*

ahúsese let him (her/it) taper; impve. 3rd pers. sing. / *ahusarse.*

ahuyentándose fleeing; pres. part. / *ahuyentarse.*

ahuyentaos (you all) flee; impve. 2nd pers. pl. / *ahuyentarse.*

ahuyentar to frighten away or to banish. reg.

ahuyentarse to flee. reg.

ahuyéntate (you) flee; impve. 2nd pers. sing. / *ahuyentarse.*

ahuyentémonos let us flee; impve. 1st pers. pl. / *ahuyentarse.*

ahuyéntense let them flee; impve. 3rd pers. pl. / *ahuyentarse.*

ahuyéntese let him (her/it) flee; impve. 3rd pers. sing. / *ahuyentarse.*

airándose becoming angry; pres. part. / *airarse.*

airaos (you all) become angry; impve. 2nd pers. pl. / *airarse.*

airar to annoy or irritate. reg.

airarse to become angry. reg.

aírate (you) become angry; impve. 2nd pers. sing. / *airarse.*

aireándose catching cold; pres. part. / *airearse.*

aireaos (you all) catch cold; impve. 2nd pers. pl. / *airearse.*

airear to air or to ventilate. reg.

airearse to catch cold. reg.

airéate (you) catch cold; impve. 2nd pers. sing. / *airearse.*

aireémonos let us catch cold; impve. 1st pers. pl. / *airearse.*

airéense let them catch cold; impve. 3rd pers. pl. / *airearse.*

airéese let him (her/it) catch cold; impve. 3rd pers. sing. / *airearse.*

airémonos let us become angry; impve. 1st pers. pl. / *airarse.*

aírense let them become angry; impve. 3rd pers. pl. / *airarse.*

aírese let him (her/it) become angry; impve. 3rd pers. sing. / *airarse.*

aislándose secluding oneself; pres. part. / *aislarse.*

aislaos (you all) seclude yourselves; impve. 2nd pers. pl. / *aislarse.*

aislar to isolate or to insulate. reg.

aislarse to seclude oneself. reg.

aíslate (you) seclude yourself; impve. 2nd pers. sing. / *aislarse.*

aislémonos let us seclude ourselves; impve. 1st pers. pl. / *aislarse.*

aíslense let them seclude themselves; impve. 3rd pers. pl. / *aislarse.*

aíslese let him (her/it) seclude himself (herself/itself); impve. 3rd pers. sing. / *aislarse.*

ajar to rumple or spoil. reg.

ajetreándose hustling; pres. part. / *ajetrearse.*

ajetreaos (you all) hustle; impve. 2nd pers. pl. / *ajetrearse.*

ajetrearse to hustle or busy oneself. reg.

ajetréate (you) hustle; impve. 2nd pers. sing. / *ajetrearse.*

ajetreémonos let us hustle; impve. 1st pers. pl. / *ajetrearse.*

ajetréense let them hustle; impve. 3rd pers. pl. / *ajetrearse.*

ajetréese let him (her/it) hustle; impve. 3rd pers. sing. / *ajetrearse.*

ajustándose conforming; pres. part. / *ajustarse.*

ajustaos (you all) conform; impve. 2nd pers. pl. / *ajustarse*.

ajustar to adjust or to fit. reg.

ajustarse to conform or come to an agreement. reg.

ajústate (you) conform; impve. 2nd pers. sing. / *ajustarse*.

ajustémonos let us conform; impve. 1st pers. pl. / *ajustarse*.

ajústense let them conform; impve. 3rd pers. pl. / *ajustarse*.

ajústese let him (her/it) conform; impve. 3rd pers. sing. / *ajustarse*.

ajusticiar to execute or put to death. reg.

alabándose bragging; pres. part. / *alabarse*.

alabaos (you all) brag; impve. 2nd pers. pl. / *alabarse*.

alabar to praise or extol. reg.

alabarse to praise oneself or to brag. reg.

alábate (you) brag; impve. 2nd pers. sing. / *alabarse*.

alabeándose warping; pres. part. / *alabearse*.

alabeaos (you all) warp; impve. 2nd pers. pl. / *alabearse*.

alabear to warp. reg.

alabearse to warp. reg.

alabéate (you) warp; impve. 2nd pers. sing. / *alabearse*.

alabeémonos let us warp; impve. 1st pers. pl. / *alabearse*.

alabéense let them warp; impve. 3rd pers. pl. / *alabearse*.

alabéese let him (her/it) warp; impve. 3rd pers. sing. / *alabearse*.

alabémonos let us brag; impve. 1st pers. pl. / *alabarse*.

alábense let them brag; impve. 3rd pers. pl. / *alabarse*.

alábese let him (her/it) brag; impve. 3rd pers. sing. / *alabarse*.

alambicar to distil or to scrutinize. irr.

alambique 1. that I may distil; pres. subj. 1st pers. sing. / *alambicar*. 2. that he (she/it) may distil; pres. subj. 3rd pers. sing. 3. let him (her/it) distil; impve. 3rd pers. sing.

alambiqué I distilled; past 1st pers. sing. / *alambicar*.

alambiquéis that you (all) may distil; pres. subj. 2nd pers. pl. / *alambicar*.

alambiquemos 1. that we may distil; pres. subj. 1st pers. pl. / *alambicar*. 2. let us distil; impve. 1st pers. pl.

alambiquen 1. that they may distil; pres. subj. 3rd pers. pl. / *alambicar*. 2. let them distil; impve. 3rd pers. pl.

alambiques that you may distil; pres. subj. 2nd pers. sing. / *alambicar*.

alambrar to wire. reg.

alancear to lance or to spear. reg.

alardear to brag or to boast. reg.

alargándose becoming longer; pres. part. / *alargarse*.

alargar to lengthen or to prolong. irr.

alargarse to become longer. irr.

alargue 1. that I may lengthen; pres. subj. 1st pers. sing. / *alargar*. 2. that he (she/it) may lengthen; pres. subj. 3rd pers. sing. 3. let him (her/it) lengthen; impve. 3rd pers. sing.

alargué I lengthened; past 1st pers. sing. / *alargar*.

alarguéis that you (all) may lengthen; pres. subj. 2nd pers. pl. / *alargar*.

alarguemos 1. that we may lengthen; pres. subj. 1st pers. pl. / *alargar*. 2. let us lengthen; impve. 1st pers. pl.

alarguen 1. that they may lengthen; pres. subj. 3rd pers. pl. / *alargar*. 2. let them lengthen; impve. 3rd pers. pl.

alárguense let them become longer; impve. 3rd pers. pl. / *alargarse*.

alargues that you may lengthen; pres. subj. 2nd pers. sing. / *alargar*.

alárguese let it become longer; impve. 3rd pers. sing. / *alargarse*.

alarmándose being alarmed; pres. part. / *alarmarse*.

alarmaos (you all) be alarmed; impve. 2nd pers. pl. / *alarmarse*.

alarmar to alarm. reg.

alarmarse to be alarmed. reg.

alármate (you) be alarmed; impve. 2nd pers. sing. / *alarmarse*.

alarmémonos let us be alarmed; impve. 1st pers. pl. / *alarmarse*.

alármense let them be alarmed; impve. 3rd pers. pl. / *alarmarse*.

alármese let him (her/it) be alarmed; impve. 3rd pers. sing. / *alarmarse*.

albear to glow white or to rise at dawn. reg.

albergándose taking shelter; pres. part. / *albergarse*.

albergaos (you all) take shelter; impve. 2nd pers. pl. / *albergarse*.

albergar to house or shelter. irr.

albergarse to take shelter. irr.

albérgate (you) take shelter; impve. 2nd pers. sing. / *albergarse*.

albergue 1. that I may house; pres. subj. 1st pers. sing. / *albergar*. 2. that he (she/it) may house; pres. subj. 3rd pers. sing. 3. let him (she/it) house; impve. 3rd pers. sing.

albergué I housed; past 1st pers. sing. / *albergar*.

alberguéis that you (all) may house; pres. subj. 2nd pers. pl. / *albergar*.

alberguémonos let us take shelter; impve. 1st pers. pl. / *albergarse*.

alberguemos 1. that we may house; pres. subj. 1st pers. pl. / *albergar*. 2. let us house; impve. 1st pers. pl.

alberguen 1. that they may house; pres. subj. 3rd pers. pl. / *albergar*. 2. let them house; impve. 3rd pers. pl.

albérguense let them take shelter; impve. 3rd pers. pl. / *albergarse*.

albergues that you may house; pres. subj. 2nd pers. sing. / *albergar*.

albérguese let him (her/it) take shelter; impve. 3rd pers. sing. / *albergarse*.

alborear to dawn. reg.

alboroce 1. that I may gladden; pres. subj. 1st pers. sing. / *alborozar*. 2. that he (she/it) may gladden; pres. subj. 3rd pers. sing. 3. let him (her/it) gladden; impve. 3rd pers. sing.

alborocé I gladdened; past 1st pers. sing. / *alborozar*.

alborocéis that you (all) may gladden; pres. subj. 2nd pers. pl. / *alborozar*.

alborocémonos let us rejoice; impve. 1st pers. pl. / *alborozarse*.

alborocemos 1. that we may gladden; pres. subj. 1st pers. pl. / *alborozar*. 2. let us gladden; impve. 1st pers. pl.

alborocen 1. that they may gladden; pres. subj. 3rd pers. pl. / *alborozar*. 2. let him (her/it) gladden; impve. 3rd pers. pl.

alborócense let them rejoice; impve. 3rd pers. pl. / *alborozarse*.

alboroces that you may gladden; pres. subj. 2nd pers. sing. / *alborozar*.

alborócese let him (her/it) rejoice; impve. 3rd pers. sing. / *alborozarse*.

alborotándose getting excited; pres. part. / *alborotarse*.

alborotaos (you all) get excited; impve. 2nd pers. pl. / *alborotarse*.

alborotar to disturb or upset. reg.

alborotarse to get excited. reg.

alborótate (you) get excited; impve. 2nd pers. sing. / *alborotarse*.

alborotémonos let us get excited; impve. 1st pers. pl. / *alborotarse*.

alborótense let them get excited; impve. 3rd pers. pl. / *alborotarse*.

alborótese let him (her/it) get excited; impve. 3rd pers. sing. / *alborotarse*.

alborozándose rejoicing; pres. part. / *alborozarse*.

alborozaos (you all) rejoice; impve. 2nd pers. pl. / *alborozarse*.

alborozar to gladden or exhilarate. irr.

alborozarse to rejoice. irr.

alborózate (you) rejoice; impve. 2nd pers. sing. / *alborozarse*.

alcahuetear to procure or pander. reg.

alcalice 1. that I may alkalize; pres. subj. 1st pers. sing. / *alcalizar*. 2. that he (she/it) may alkalize; pres. subj. 3rd pers. sing. 3. let him (her/it) alkalize; impve. 3rd pers. sing.

alcalicé I alkalized; past 1st pers. sing. / *alcalizar*.

alcalicéis that you (all) may alkalize; pres. subj. 2nd pers. pl. / *alcalizar*.

alcalicemos 1. that we may alkalize; pres. subj. 1st pers. pl. / *alcalizar*. 2. let us alkalize; impve. 1st pers. pl.

alcalicen 1. that they may alkalize; pres. subj. 3rd pers. pl. / *alcalizar*. 2. let them alkalize; impve. 3rd pers. pl.

alcalices that you may alkalize; pres. subj. 2nd pers. sing. / *alcalizar*.

alcalizar to alkalize. irr.

alcance 1. that I may overtake; pres. subj. 1st pers. sing. / *alcanzar*. 2. that he (she/it) may overtake; pres. subj. 3rd pers. sing. 3. let him (her/it) overtake; impve. 3rd pers. sing.

alcancé I overtook; past 1st pers. sing. / *alcanzar*.

alcancéis that you (all) may overtake; pres. subj. 2nd pers. pl. / *alcanzar*.

alcancemos 1. that we may overtake; pres. subj. 1st pers. pl. / *alcanzar*. 2. let us overtake; impve. 1st pers. pl.

alcancen 1. that they may overtake; pres. subj. 3rd pers. pl. / *alcanzar*. 2. let them overtake; impve. 3rd pers. pl.

alcances that you (all) may overtake; pres. subj. 2nd pers. sing. / *alcanzar*.

alcanzar to overtake or to reach. irr.

alce 1. that I may raise; pres. subj. 1st pers. sing. / *alzar*. 2. that he (she/it) may raise; pres. subj. 3rd pers. sing. 3. let him (her/it) raise; impve. 3rd pers. sing.

alcé I raised; past 1st pers. sing. / *alzar*.

alcéis that you (all) may raise; pres. subj. 2nd pers. pl. / *alzar*.

alcémonos let us rebel; impve. 1st pers. pl. / *alzarse*.

alcemos 1. that we may raise; pres. subj. 1st pers. pl. / *alzar*. 2. let us raise; impve. 1st pers. pl.

alcen 1. that they may raise; pres. subj. 3rd pers. pl. / *alzar*. 2. let them raise; impve. 3rd pers. pl.

álcense let them rebel; impve. 3rd pers. pl. / *alzarse*.

alces that you may raise; pres. subj. 2nd pers. sing. / *alzar*.

álcese let him (her/it) rebel; impve. 3rd pers. sing. / *alzarse*.

alear to alloy or to flutter. reg.

aleccionar to coach or train. reg.

alegar to allege or to argue. irr.

alegorice 1. that I may allegorize; pres. subj. 1st pers. sing. / *alegorizar*. 2. that he (she/it) may allegorize; pres. subj. 3rd pers. sing. 3. let him (her/it) allegorize; impve. 3rd pers. sing.

alegoricé I allegorized; past 1st pers. sing. / *alegorizar*.

alegoricéis that you (all) may allegorize; pres. subj. 2nd pers. pl. / *alegorizar*.

alegoricemos 1. that we may allegorize; pres. subj. 1st pers. pl. / *alegorizar*. 2. let us allegorize; impve. 1st pers. pl.

alegoricen 1. that they may allegorize; pres. subj. 3rd pers. pl. / *alegorizar*. 2. let them allegorize; impve. 3rd pers. pl.

alegorices that you may allegorize; pres. subj. 2nd pers. pl. / *alegorizar*.

alegorizar to allegorize. irr.

alegrándose rejoicing; pres. part. / *alegrarse*.

alegraos (you all) rejoice; impve. 2nd pers. pl. / *alegrarse*.

alegrar to gladden or cheer up. reg.

alegrarse to rejoice or to be glad. reg.

alégrate (you) rejoice; impve. 2nd pers. sing. / *alegrarse*.

alegrémonos let us rejoice; impve. 1st pers. pl. / *alegrarse.*

alégrense let them rejoice; impve. 3rd pers. pl. / *alegrarse.*

alégrese let him (her/it) rejoice; impve. 3rd pers. sing. / *alegrarse.*

alegue 1. that I may allege; pres. subj. 1st pers. sing. / *alegar.* 2. that he (she/it) may allege; pres. subj. 3rd pers. sing. 3. let him (her/it) allege; impve. 3rd pers. sing.

alegué I alleged; past 1st pers. sing. / *alegar.*

aleguéis that you (all) may allege; pres. subj. 2nd pers. pl. / *alegar.*

aleguemos 1. that we may allege; pres. subj. 1st pers. pl. / *alegar.* 2. let us allege; impve. 1st pers. pl.

aleguen 1. that they may allege; pres. subj. 3rd pers. pl. / *alegar.* 2. let them allege; impve. 3rd pers. pl.

alegues that you may allege; pres. subj. 2nd pers. sing. / *alegar.*

alejándose withdawing; pres. part. / *alejarse.*

alejaos (you all) withdraw; impve. 2nd pers. pl. / *alejarse.*

alejar to remove or to separate. reg.

alejarse to withdraw or to recede. reg.

aléjate (you) withdraw; impve. 2nd pers. sing. / *alejarse.*

alejémonos let us withdraw; impve. 1st pers. pl. / *alejarse.*

aléjense let them withdraw; impve. 3rd pers. pl. / *alejarse.*

aléjese let him (her/it) withdraw; impve. 3rd pers. sing. / *alejarse.*

alelándose becoming stupid; pres. part. / *alelarse.*

alelaos (you all) become stupid; impve. 2nd pers. pl. / *alelarse.*

alelar to daze. reg.

alelarse to become stupid. reg.

alélate (you) become stupid; impve. 2nd pers. sing. / *alelarse.*

alelémonos let us become stupid; impve. 1st pers. pl. / *alelarse.*

alélense let them become stupid; impve. 3rd pers. pl. / *alelarse.*

alélese let him (her/it) become stupid; impve. 3rd pers. sing. / *alelarse.*

alentándose recovering; pres. part. / *alentarse.*

alentaos (you all) recover; impve. 2nd pers. pl. / *alentarse.*

alentar to inspire or to breathe. irr.

alentarse to recover. irr.

alentémonos let us recover; impve. 1st pers. pl. / *alentarse.*

alertándose being on one's guard; pres. part. / *alertarse.*

alertaos (you all) be on your guard; impve. 2nd pers. pl. / *alertarse.*

alertar to alert. reg.

alertargándose becoming lethargic; pres. part. / *alertargarse.*

alertargaos (you all) become lethargic; impve. 2nd pers. pl. / *alertargarse.*

alertargarse to become lethargic. irr.

alertárgate (you) become lethargic; impve. 2nd pers. sing. / *alertargarse.*

alertargue 1. that I may be lethargic; pres. subj. 1st pers. sing. / *alertargarse.* 2. that he (she/it) may be lethargic; pres. subj. 3rd pers. sing.

alertargué I became lethargic; past 1st pers. sing. / *alertargarse.*

alertarguéis that you (all) may be lethargic; pres. subj. 2nd pers. pl. / *alertagarse.*

alertarguémonos let us become lethargic; impve. 1st pers. pl. / *alertargarse.*

alertarguemos that we may be lethargic; pres. subj. 1st pers. pl. / *alertargarse.*

alertarguen that they may be lethargic; pres. subj. 3rd pers. pl. / *alertargarse.*

alertárguense let them become lethargic; impve. 3rd pers. pl. / *alertargarse.*

alertargues that you may be lethargic; pres. subj. 2nd pers. sing. / *alertargarse.*

alertárguese let him (her/it) become lethargic; impve. 3rd pers. sing. / *alertargarse.*

alertarse to be on one's guard. reg.

alértate (you) be on your guard; impve. 2nd pers. sing. / *alertarse.*

alertémonos let us be on our guard; impve. 1st pers. pl. / *alertarse.*

alértense let them be on their guard; impve. 3rd pers. pl. / *alertarse.*

alértese let him (her/it) be on his (her/it's) guard; impve. 3rd pers. sing. / *alertarse.*

aletear to flutter or flap. reg.

alfabetice 1. that I may alphabetize; pres. subj. 1st pers. sing. / *alfabetizar.* 2. that he (she/it) may alphabetize; pres. subj. 3rd pers. sing. 3. let him (her/it) alphabetize; impve. 3rd pers. sing.

alfabeticé I alphabetized; past 1st pers. sing. / *alfabetizar.*

alfabeticéis that you (all) may alphabetize; pres. subj. 2nd pers. pl. / *alfabetizar.*

alfabeticemos 1. that we may alphabetize; pres. subj. 1st pers. pl. / *alfabetizar.* 2. let us alphabetize; impve. 1st pers. pl.

alfabeticen 1. that they may alphabetize; pres. subj. 3rd pers. pl. / *alfabetizar.* 2. let them alphabetize; impve. 3rd pers. pl.

alfabetices that you may alphabetize; pres. subj. 2nd pers. sing. / *alfabetizar.*

alfabetizar to alphabetize. irr.

alfeñicándose becoming thin; pres. part. / *alfeñicarse.*

alfeñicaos (you all) become thin; impve. 2nd pers. pl. / *alfeñicarse.*

alfeñicar to frost with sugar. irr.

alfeñicarse to become thin. irr.

alfeñícate (you) become thin; impve. 2nd pers. sing. / *alfeñicarse.*

alfeñique 1. that I may frost with sugar; pres. subj. 1st pers. sing. / *alfeñicar*. 2. that he (she/it) may frost with suga; pres. subj. 3rd pers. sing. 3. let him (her/it) frost with sugar; impve. 3rd pers. sing.

alfeñiqué I frosted with sugar; past 1st pers. sing. / *alfeñicar*.

alfeñiquéis that you (all) may frost with sugar; pres. subj. 2nd pers. pl. / *alfeñicar*.

alfeñiquémonos let us become thin; impve. 1st pers. pl. / *alfeñicarse*.

alfeñiquemos 1. that we may frost with sugar; pres. subj. 1st pers. pl. / *alfeñicar*. 2. let us frost with sugar; impve. 1st pers. pl.

alfeñiquen 1. that they may frost with sugar; pres. subj. 3rd pers. pl. / *alfeñicar*. 2. let them frost with sugar; impve. 3rd pers. pl.

alfeñíquense let them become thin; impve. 3rd pers. pl. / *alfeñicarse*.

alfeñiques that you may frost with sugar; pres. subj. 2nd pers. sing. / *alfeñicar*.

alfeñíquese let him (her/it) become thin; impve. 3rd pers. sing. / *alfeñicarse*.

alfombrar to carpet. reg.

alforce 1. that I may tuck; pres. subj. 1st pers. sing. / *alforzar*. 2. that he (she/it) may tuck; pres. subj. 3rd pers. sing. 3. let him (her/it) tuck; impve. 3rd pers. sing.

alforcé I tucked; past 1st pers. sing. / *alforzar*.

alforcéis that you (all) may tuck; pres. subj. 2nd pers. pl. / *alforzar*.

alforcemos 1. that we may tuck; pres. subj. 1st pers. pl. / *alforzar*. 2. let us tuck; impve. 1st pers. pl.

alforcen 1. that they may tuck; pres. subj. 3rd pers. pl. / *alforzar*. 2. let them tuck; impve. 3rd pers. pl.

alforces that you may tuck; pres. subj. 2nd pers. sing. / *alforzar*.

alforzar to tuck. irr.

algodonar to stuff with cotton. reg.

alheñar to henna. reg.

alía 1. he (she/it) unites; pres. ind. 3rd pers. sing. / *aliar*. 2. (you) unite; impve. 2nd pers. sing.

alían they unite; pres. ind. 3rd pers. pl. / *aliar*.

aliándose becoming allied ; pres. part. / *aliarse*.

aliaos (you all) become allied; impve. 2nd pers. pl. / *aliarse*.

aliar to unite or ally. irr.

aliarse to become allied. irr.

alías you unite; pres. ind. 2nd pers. sing. / *aliar*.

alíate (you) become allied; impve. 2nd pers. sing. / *aliarse*.

alíe 1. that I may unite; pres. subj. 1st pers. sing. / *aliar*. 2. that he (she/it) may unite; pres. subj. 3rd pers. sing. 3. let him (her/it) unite; impve. 3rd pers. sing.

aliémonos let us become allied; impve. 1st pers. pl. / *aliarse*.

alíen 1. that they may unite; pres. subj. 3rd pers. pl. / *aliar*. 2. let them unite; impve. 3rd pers. pl.

alienar to alienate. reg.

alíense let them become allied; impve. 3rd pers. pl. / *aliarse*.

alienta 1. he (she/it) inspires; pres. ind. 3rd pers. sing. / *alentar*. 2. (you) inspire; impve. 2nd pers. sing.

alientan they inspire; pres. ind. 3rd pers. pl. / *alentar*.

alientas you inspire; pres. ind. 2nd pers. sing. / *alentar*.

aliéntate (you) recover; impve. 2nd pers. sing. / *alentarse*.

aliente 1. that I may inspire; pres. subj. 1st pers. sing. / *alentar*. 2. that he (she/it) may inspire; pres. subj. 3rd pers. sing. 3. let him (her/it) inspire; impve. 3rd pers. sing.

alienten 1. that they may inspire; pres. subj. 3rd pers. pl. / *alentar*. 2. let them inspire; impve. 3rd pers. pl.

aliéntense let them recover; impve. 3rd pers. pl. / *alentarse*.

alientes that you may inspire; pres. subj. 2nd pers. sing. / *alentar*.

aliéntese let him (her/it) recover; impve. 3rd pers. sing. / *alentarse*.

aliento I inspire; pres. ind. 1st pers. sing. / *alentar*.

alíes that you may unite; pres. subj. 2nd pers. sing. / *aliar*.

alíese let him (her/it) become allied; impve. 3rd pers. sing. / *aliarse*.

aligar to tie or to unite. reg.

aligerar to lighten or to ease. reg.

alijar to unload or to gin (cotton). reg.

alimentándose feeding oneself; pres. part. / *alimentarse*.

alimentaos (you all) feed yourselves; impve. 2nd pers. pl. / *alimentarse*.

alimentar to feed or to nourish. reg.

alimentarse to feed oneself. reg.

aliméntate (you) feed yourself; impve. 2nd pers. sing. / *alimentarse*.

alimentémonos let us feed ourselves; impve. 1st pers. pl. / *alimentarse*.

aliméntense let them feed themselves; impve. 3rd pers. pl. / *alimentarse*.

aliméntese let him (her/it) feed himself (herself/itself); impve. 3rd pers. sing. / *alimentarse*.

alindar to fix limits or to adorn. reg.

alineándose falling in line; pres. part. / *alinearse*.

alineaos (you all) fall in line; impve. 2nd pers. pl. / *alinearse*.

alinear to align. reg.

alinearse to fall in line. reg.

alinéate (you) fall in line; impve. 2nd pers. sing. / *alinearse*.

alineémonos let us fall in line; impve. 1st pers. pl. / *alinearse*.

alinéense let them fall in line; impve. 3rd pers. pl. / *alinearse*.

alinéese let him (her/it) fall in line; impve. 3rd pers. sing. / *alinearse*.

aliñar to dress or to season (food) or to adorn. reg.

alío I unite; pres. ind. 1st pers. sing. / *aliar*.

alisar to smooth or to polish. reg.

alistándose getting ready; pres. part. / *alistarse.*
alistaos (you all) get ready; impve. 2nd pers. pl. / *alistarse.*
alistar to enlist or to enroll. reg.
alistarse to get ready. reg.
alístate (you) get ready; impve. 2nd pers. sing. / *alistarse.*
alistémonos let us get ready; impve. 1st pers. pl. / *alistarse.*
alístense let them get ready; impve. 3rd pers. pl. / *alistarse.*
alístese let him (her/it) get ready; impve. 3rd pers. sing. / *alistarse.*
aliviándose getting better; pres. part. / *aliviarse.*
aliviaos (you all) get better; impve. 2nd pers. pl. / *aliviarse.*
aliviar to lighten or to ease. reg.
aliviarse to get better. reg.
alivíate (you) get better; impve. 2nd pers. sing. / *aliviarse.*
aliviémonos let us get better; impve. 1st pers. pl. / *aliviarse.*
alivíense let them get better; impve. 3rd pers. pl. / *aliviarse.*
alivíese let him (her/it) get better; impve. 3rd pers. sing. / *aliviarse.*
almacenar to store. reg.
almibrar to preserve in sugar or syrup. reg.
almidonar to starch. reg.
almohazar to curry. reg.
almonedear to auction. reg.
almorcé I ate lunch; past 1st pers. sing. / *almorzar.*
almorcéis that you (all) may eat lunch; pres. subj. 2nd pers. pl. / *almorzar.*
almorcemos 1. that we may eat lunch; pres. subj. 1st pers. pl. / *almorzar.* 2. let us eat lunch; impve. 1st pers. pl.
almorzar to eat lunch. irr.
almuerce 1. that I may eat lunch; pres. subj. 1st pers. sing. / *almorzar.* 2. that he (she/it) may eat lunch; pres. subj. 3rd pers. sing. 3. let him (her/it) eat lunch; impve. 3rd pers. sing.
almuercen 1. that they may eat lunch; pres. subj. 3rd pers. pl. / *almorzar.* 2. let them eat lunch; impve. 3rd pers. pl.
almuerces that you may eat lunch; pres. subj. 2nd pers. sing. / *almorzar.*
almuerza 1. he (she/it) eats lunch; pres. ind. 3rd pers. sing. / *almorzar.* 2. (you) eat lunch; impve. 2nd pers. sing.
almuerzan they eat lunch; pres. ind. 3rd pers. pl. / *almorzar.*
almuerzas you eat lunch; pres. ind. 2nd pers. sing. / *almorzar.*
almuerzo I eat lunch; pres. ind. 1st pers. sing. / *almorzar.*
alocar to drive mad. irr.
alojándose taking lodgings; pres. part. / *alojarse.*
alojaos (you all) take lodging; impve. 2nd pers. pl. / *alojarse.*

alojar to lodge. reg.
alojarse to take lodgings. reg.
alójate (you) take lodging; impve. 2nd pers. sing. / *alojarse.*
alojémonos let us take lodgings; impve. 1st pers. pl. / *alojarse.*
alójense let them take lodging; impve. 3rd pers. pl. / *alojarse.*
alójese let him (her/it) take lodging; impve. 3rd pers. sing. / *alojarse.*
alongar to enlarge or separate. irr.
alongué I enlarged; past 1st pers. sing. / *alongar.*
alonguéis that you (all) may enlarge; pres. subj. 2nd pers. pl. / *alongar.*
alonguemos 1. that we may enlarge; pres. subj. 1st pers. pl. / *alongar.* 2. let us enlarge; impve. 1st pers. pl.
aloque 1. that I may drive mad; pres. subj. 1st pers. sing. / *alocar.* 2. that he (she/it) may drive may; pres. subj. 3rd pers. sing. 3. let him (her/it) drive may; impve. 3rd pers. sing.
aloqué I drove mad; past 1st pers. sing. / *alocar.*
aloquéis that you (all) may drive mad; pres. subj. 2nd pers. pl. / *alocar.*
aloquemos 1. that we may drive mad; pres. subj. 1st pers. pl. / *alocar.* 2. let us drive mad; impve. 1st pers. pl.
aloquen 1. that they may drive mad; pres. subj. 3rd pers. pl. / *alocar.* 2. let them drive mad; impve. 3rd pers. pl.
aloques that you may drive mad; pres. subj. 2nd pers. sing. / *alocar.*
alquilándose hiring out; pres. part. / *alquilarse.*
alquilaos (you all) hire out; impve. 2nd pers. pl. / *alquilarse.*
alquilar to rent or to hire. reg.
alquilarse to hire out. reg.
alquílate (you) hire out; impve. 2nd pers. sing. / *alquilarse.*
alquilémonos let us hire out; impve. 1st pers. pl. / *alquilarse.*
alquílense let them hire out; impve. 3rd pers. pl. / *alquilarse.*
alquílese let him (her/it) hire out; impve. 3rd pers. sing. / *alquilarse.*
alquitranar to tar. reg.
alterándose becoming angry; pres. part. / *alterarse.*
alteraos (you all) become angry; impve. 2nd pers. pl. / *alterarse.*
alterar to alter or change. reg.
alterarse to become angry. reg.
altérate (you) become angry; impve. 2nd pers. sing. / *alterarse.*
altercar to argue or quarrel. irr.
alterémonos let us become angry; impve. 1st pers. pl. / *alterarse.*
altérense let them become angry; impve. 3rd pers. pl. / *alterarse.*
altérese let him (her/it) become angry; impve. 3rd pers. sing. / *alterarse.*

alternándose taking turns; pres. part. / *alternarse.*
alternaos (you all) take turns; impve. 2nd pers. pl. / *alternarse.*
alternar to alternate. reg.
alternarse to take turns. reg.
altérnate (you) take turns; impve. 2nd pers. sing. / *alternarse.*
alternémonos let us take turns; impve. 1st pers. pl. / *alternarse.*
altérnense let them take turns; impve. 3rd pers. pl. / *alternarse.*
altérnese let him (her/it) take turns; impve. 3rd pers. sing. / *alternarse.*
alterque 1. that I may argue; pres. subj. 1st pers. sing. / *altercar.* 2. that he (she/it) may argue; pres. subj. 3rd pers. sing. 3. let him (her/it) argue; impve. 3rd pers. sing.
alterqué I argued; past 1st pers. sing. / *altercar.*
alterquéis that you (all) may argue; pres. subj. 2nd pers. pl. / *altercar.*
alterquemos 1. that we may argue; pres. subj. 1st pers. pl. / *altercar.* 2. let us argue; impve. 1st pers. pl.
alterquen 1. that they may argue; pres. subj. 3rd pers. pl. / *altercar.* 2. let them argue; impve. 3rd pers. pl.
alterques that you may argue; pres. subj. 2nd pers. sing. / *altercar.*
alucinándose being deceived; pres. part. / *alucinarse.*
alucinaos (you all) be deceived; impve. 2nd pers. pl. / *alucinarse.*
alucinar to delude or to fascinate. reg.
alucinarse to be deceived. reg.
alucínate (you) be deceived; impve. 2nd pers. sing. / *alucinarse.*
alucinémonos let us be deceived; impve. 1st pers. pl. / *alucinarse.*
alucínense let them be deceived; impve. 3rd pers. pl. / *alucinarse.*
alucínese let him (her/it) be deceived; impve. 3rd pers. sing. / *alucinarse.*
aludir to allude or to refer indirectly. reg.
aluenga 1. he (she/it) enlarges; pres. ind. 3rd pers. sing. / *alongar.* 2. (you) enlarge; impve. 2nd pers. sing.
aluengan they enlarge; pres. ind. 3rd pers. pl. / *alongar.*
aluengas you enlarge; pres. ind. 2nd pers. sing. / *alongar.*
aluengo I enlarge; pres. ind. 1st pers. sing. / *alongar.*
aluengue 1. that I may enlarge; pres. subj. 1st pers. sing. / *alongar.* 2. that he (she/it) may enlarge; pres. subj. 3rd pers. sing. 3. let him (her/it) enlarge; impve. 3rd pers. sing.
aluenguen 1. that they may enlarge; pres. subj. 3rd pers. pl. / *alongar.* 2. let him (her/it) enlarge; impve. 3rd pers. pl.
aluengues that you (all) may enlarge; pres. subj. 2nd pers. pl. / *alongar.*
alumbrándose lighting one's way; pres. part. / *alumbrarse.*

alumbraos (you all) light your way; impve. 2nd pers. pl. / *alumbrarse.*
alumbrar to illuminate or to give birth. reg.
alumbrarse to light one's way or to get tipsy. reg.
alúmbrate (you) light your way; impve. 2nd pers. sing. / *alumbrarse.*
alumbrémonos let us light our way; impve. 1st pers. pl. / *alumbrarse.*
alúmbrense let them light their way; impve. 3rd pers. pl. / *alumbrarse.*
alúmbrese let him (her/it) light his (her/it's) way; impve. 3rd pers. sing. / *alumbrarse.*
alzándose rebelling; pres. part. / *alzarse.*
alzaos (you all) rebel; impve. 2nd pers. pl. / *alzarse.*
alzar to raise or cut (cords). irr.
alzarse to rebel. irr.
álzate (you) rebel; impve. 2nd pers. sing. / *alzarse.*
allanándose submitting; pres. part. / *allanarse.*
allanaos (you all) submit; impve. 2nd pers. pl. / *allanarse.*
allanar to level or flatten. reg.
allanarse to submit. reg.
allánate (you) submit; impve. 2nd pers. sing. / *allanarse.*
allanémonos let us submit; impve. 1st pers. pl. / *allanarse.*
allánense let them submit; impve. 3rd pers. pl. / *allanarse.*
allánese let him (her/it) submit; impve. 3rd pers. sing. / *allanarse.*
allegándose approaching; pres. part. / *allegarse.*
allegaos (you all) approach; impve. 2nd pers. pl. / *allegarse.*
allegar to collect or gather. irr.
allegarse to approach. irr.
allégate (you) approach; impve. 2nd pers. sing. / *allegarse.*
allegue 1. that I may collect; pres. subj. 1st pers. sing. / *allegar.* 2. that he (she/it) may collect; pres. subj. 3rd pers. sing. 3. let him (her/it) collect; impve. 3rd pers. sing.
allegué I collected; past 1st pers. sing. / *allegar.*
alleguéis that you (all) may collect; pres. subj. 2nd pers. pl. / *allegar.*
alleguémonos let us approach; impve. 1st pers. pl. / *allegarse.*
alleguemos 1. that we may collect; pres. subj. 1st pers. pl. / *allegar.* 2. let us collect; impve. 1st pers. pl.
alleguen 1. that they may collect; pres. subj. 3rd pers. pl. / *allegar.* 2. let them collect; impve. 3rd pers. pl.
alléguense let them approach; impve. 3rd pers. pl. / *allegarse.*
allegues that you may collect; pres. subj. 2nd pers. sing. / *allegar.*
alléguese let him (her/it) approach; impve. 3rd pers. sing. / *allegarse.*
amachetear to strike or cut with a machete. reg.
amaestrar to teach or to train. reg.
amagar to threaten or to strike at. irr.

amague 1. that I may threaten; pres. subj. 1st pers. sing. / *amagar*. 2. that he (she/it) may threaten; pres. subj. 3rd pers. sing. 3. let him (her/it) threaten; impve. 3rd pers. sing.

amagué I threatened; past 1st pers. sing. / *amagar*.

amaguéis that you (all) may threaten; pres. subj. 2nd pers. pl. / *amagar*.

amaguemos 1. that we may threaten; pres. subj. 1st pers. pl. / *amagar*. 2. let us threaten; impve. 1st pers. pl.

amaguen 1. that they may threaten; pres. subj. 3rd pers. pl. / *amagar*. 2. let them threaten; impve. 3rd pers. pl.

amagues that you may threaten; pres. subj. 2nd pers. sing. / *amagar*.

amainándose giving up; pres. part. / *amainarse*.

amainaos (you all) give up; impve. 2nd pers. pl. / *amainarse*.

amainar to relax or to die down. reg.

amainarse to give up. reg.

amaínate (you) give up; impve. 2nd pers. sing. / *amainarse*.

amainémonos let us give up; impve. 1st pers. pl. / *amainarse*.

amaínense let them give up; impve. 3rd pers. pl. / *amainarse*.

amaínese let him (her/it) give up; impve. 3rd pers. sing. / *amainarse*.

amalgamar to amalgamate or combine. reg.

amamantar to nurse or suckle. reg.

amancebándose living in concubinage; pres. part. / *amancebarse*.

amancebaos (you all) live in concubinage; impve. 2nd pers. pl. / *amancebarse*.

amancebarse to live in concubinage. reg.

amancébate (you) live in concubinage; impve. 2nd pers. sing. / *amancebarse*.

amancebémonos let us live in concubinage; impve. 1st pers. pl. / *amancebarse*.

amancébense let them live in concubinage; impve. 3rd pers. pl. / *amancebarse*.

amancébese let him (her/it) live in concubinage; impve. 3rd pers. sing. / *amancebarse*.

amancillar to stain or to defile. reg.

amándose loving one another; pres. part. / *amarse*.

amanecer to dawn. irr.

amanerándose becoming affected; pres. part. / *amanerarse*.

amaneraos (you all) become affected; impve. 2nd pers. pl. / *amanerarse*.

amanerarse to become affected. reg.

amanérate (you) become affected; impve. 2nd pers. sing. / *amanerarse*.

amanerémonos let us become affected; impve. 1st pers. pl. / *amanerarse*.

amanérense let them become affected; impve. 3rd pers. pl. / *amanerarse*.

amanérese let him (her/it) become affected; impve. 3rd pers. sing. / *amanerarse*.

amanezca 1. that it may dawn; pres. subj. 3rd pers. sing. / *amanecer*. 2. let it dawn; impve. 3rd pers. sing.

amansar to tame. reg.

amañándose adapting oneself; pres. part. / *amañarse*.

amañaos (you all) adapt yourselves; impve. 2nd pers. pl. / *amañarse*.

amañar to do cleverly. reg.

amañarse to adapt oneself or to be handy. reg.

amáñate (you) adapt yourself; impve. 2nd pers. sing. / *amañarse*.

amañémonos let us adapt ourselves; impve. 1st pers. pl. / *amañarse*.

amáñense let them adapt themselves; impve. 3rd pers. pl. / *amañarse*.

amáñese let him (her/it) adapt himself (herself/itself); impve. 3rd pers. sing. / *amañarse*.

amaos (you all) love one another; impve. 2nd pers. pl. / *amarse*.

amar to love. reg.

amargándose becoming bitter; pres. part. / *amargarse*.

amargaos (you all) become bitter; impve. 2nd pers. pl. / *amargarse*.

amargar to make bitter. irr.

amargarse to become bitter. irr.

amárgate (you) become bitter; impve. 2nd pers. sing. / *amargarse*.

amargue 1. that I may make bitter; pres. subj. 1st pers. sing. / *amargar*. 2. that he (she/it) may make bitter; pres. subj. 3rd pers. sing. 3. let him (her/it) make bitter; impve. 3rd pers. sing.

amargué I made bitter; past 1st pers. sing. / *amargar*.

amarguéis that you (all) may make bitter; pres. subj. 2nd pers. pl. / *amargar*.

amarguémonos let us become bitter; impve. 1st pers. pl. / *amargarse*.

amarguemos 1. that we may make bitter; pres. subj. 1st pers. pl. / *amargar*. 2. let us make bitter; impve. 1st pers. pl.

amarguen 1. that they may make bitter; pres. subj. 3rd pers. pl. / *amargar*. 2. let them make bitter; impve. 3rd pers. pl.

amárguense let them become bitter; impve. 3rd pers. pl. / *amargarse*.

amargues that you may make bitter; pres. subj. 2nd pers. sing. / *amargar*.

amárguese let him (her/it) become bitter; impve. 3rd pers. sing. / *amargarse*.

amarillear to color yellow. reg.

amarrar to tie or fasten. reg.

amarse to love one another. reg.

amartelándose falling in love; pres. part. / *amartelarse*.

amartelaos (you all) fall in love; impve. 2nd pers. pl. / *amartelarse*.

amartelar to court. reg.

amartelarse to fall in love. reg.

amartélate (you) fall in love; impve. 2nd pers. sing. / *amartelarse*.

amartelémonos let us fall in love; impve. 1st pers. pl. / *amartelarse.*

amartélense let them fall in love; impve. 3rd pers. pl. / *amartelarse.*

amartélese let him (her/it) fall in love; impve. 3rd pers. sing. / *amartelarse.*

amartillar to hammer or to cock (a gun). reg.

amasar to knead or to amass. reg.

ámate (you) love one another; impve. 2nd pers. sing. / *amarse.*

amayorazgar to entail. irr.

amayorazgue 1. that it may entail; pres. subj. 3rd pers. sing. / *amayorazgar.* 2. let it entail; impve. 3rd pers. sing.

ambicionar to seek or to covet. reg.

amblar to pace or to amble (as a horse). reg.

ambular to wander. reg.

amedrantar to frighten. reg.

amedrentándose becoming frightened; pres. part. / *amedrentarse.*

amedrentaos (you all) become frightened; impve. 2nd pers. pl. / *amedrentarse.*

amedrentar to frighten or intimidate. reg.

amedrentarse to become frightened. reg.

amedréntate (you) become frightened; impve. 2nd pers. sing. / *amedrentarse.*

amedrentémonos let us become frightened; impve. 1st pers. pl. / *amedrentarse.*

amedréntense let them become frightened; impve. 3rd pers. pl. / *amedrentarse.*

amedréntese let him (her/it) become frightened; impve. 3rd pers. sing. / *amedrentarse.*

ameliorar to better or improve. reg.

amémonos let us love one another; impve. 1st pers. pl. / *amarse.*

amenace 1. that I may menace; pres. subj. 1st pers. sing. / *amenazar.* 2. that he (she/it) may menace; pres. subj. 3rd pers. sing. 3. let him (her/it) menace; impve. 3rd pers. sing.

amenacé I menaced; past 1st pers. sing. / *amenazar.*

amenacéis that you (all) may menace; pres. subj. 2nd pers. pl. / *amenazar.*

amenacemos 1. that we may menace; pres. subj. 1st pers. pl. / *amenazar.* 2. let us menace; impve. 1st pers. pl.

amenacen 1. that they may menace; pres. subj. 3rd pers. pl. / *amenazar.* 2. let them menace; impve. 3rd pers. pl.

amenaces that you may menace; pres. subj. 2nd pers. sing. / *amenazar;*

amenazar to menace or threaten. irr.

amenguar to lessen or to dishonor. irr.

amengüe 1. that I may lessen; pres. subj. 1st pers. sing. / *amenguar.* 2. that he (she/it) may lessen; pres. subj. 3rd pers. sing. 3. let him (her/it) lessen; impve. 3rd pers. sing.

amengüé I lessened; past 1st pers. sing. / *amenguar.*

amengüéis that you (all) may lessen; pres. subj. 2nd pers. pl. / *amenguar.*

amengüemos 1. that we may lessen; pres. subj. 1st pers. pl. / *amenguar.* 2. let us lessen; impve. 1st pers. pl.

amengüen 1. that they may lessen; pres. subj. 3rd pers. pl. / *amenguar.* 2. let them lessen; impve. 3rd pers. pl.

amengües that you may lessen; pres. subj. 2nd pers. sing. / *amenguar.*

amenice 1. that I may make pleasant; pres. subj. 1st pers. sing. / *amenizar.* 2. that he (she/it) may make pleasant; pres. subj. 3rd pers. sing. 3. let him (her/it) make pleasant; impve. 3rd pers. sing.

amenicé I made pleasant; past 1st pers. sing. / *amenizar.*

amenicéis that you (all) may make pleasant; pres. subj. 2nd pers. pl. / *amenizar.*

amenicemos 1. that we may make pleasant; pres. subj. 1st pers. pl. / *amenizar.* 2. let us make pleasant; impve. 1st pers. pl.

amenicen 1. that they may make pleasant; pres. subj. 3rd pers. pl. / *amenizar.* 2. let them make pleasant; impve. 3rd pers. pl.

amenices that you may make pleasant; pres. subj. 2nd pers. sing. / *amenizar.*

amenizar to make pleasant. irr.

ámense let them love one another; impve. 3rd pers. pl. / *amarse.*

americanice 1. that I may americanize; pres. subj. 1st pers. sing. / *americanizar.* 2. that he (she/it) may americanize; pres. subj. 3rd pers. sing. 3. let him (her/it) americanize; impve. 3rd pers. sing.

americanicé I americanized; past 1st pers. sing. / *americanizar*

americanicéis that you (all) may americanize; pres. subj. 2nd pers. pl. / *americanizar.*

americanicemos 1. that we may americanize; pres. subj. 1st pers. pl. / *americanizar.* 2. let us americanize; impve. 1st pers. pl.

americanicen 1. that they may americanize; pres. subj. 3rd pers. pl. / *americanizar.* 2. let them americanize; impve. 3rd pers. pl.

americanices that you may americanize; pres. subj. 2nd pers. sing. / *americanizar.*

americanizar to americanize. irr.

americe 1. that I may land on the water; pres. subj. 1st pers. sing. / *amerizar.* 2. that he (she/it) may land on the water; pres. subj. 3rd pers. sing. 3. let him (her/it) land on the water; impve. 3rd pers. sing.

americé I landed on the water; past 1st pers. sing. / *amerizar.*

americéis that you (all) may land on water; pres. subj. 2nd pers. pl. / *amerizar.*

americemos 1. that we may land on water; pres. subj. 1st pers. pl. / *amerizar.* 2. let us land on water; impve. 1st pers. pl.

americen 1. that they may land on water; pres. subj. 3rd pers. pl. / *amerizar.* 2. let them land on water; impve. 3rd pers. pl.

americes that you may land on water; pres. subj. 2nd pers. sing. / *amerizar.*

amerizar to land on the water (in an aircraft). irr.

ámese let him (her/it) love others; impve. 3rd pers. sing. / *amarse.*

ametrallar to machine-gun or strafe. reg.

amilanándose becoming terrified; pres. part. / *amilanarse.*

amilanaos (you all) become terrified; impve. 2nd pers. pl. / *amilanarse.*

amilanar to frighten. reg.

amilanarse to become terrified. reg.

amilánate (you) become terrified; impve. 2nd pers. sing. / *amilanarse.*

amilanémonos let us become terrified; impve. 1st pers. pl. / *amilanarse.*

amilánense let them become terrified; impve. 3rd pers. pl. / *amilanarse.*

amilánese let him (her/it) become terrified; impve. 3rd pers. sing. / *amilanarse.*

amillarar to assess. reg.

aminorar to reduce or lessen. reg.

amistándose making friends; pres. part. / *amistarse.*

amistaos (you all) make friends; impve. 2nd pers. pl. / *amistarse.*

amistar to reconcile. reg.

amistarse to make friends. reg.

amístate (you) make friends; impve. 2nd pers. sing. / *amistarse.*

amistémonos let us make friends; impve. 1st pers. pl. / *amistarse.*

amístense let them make friends; impve. 3rd pers. pl. / *amistarse.*

amístese let him (her/it) make friends; impve. 3rd pers. sing. / *amistarse.*

amnistía 1. he (she/it) gives amnesty; pres. ind. 3rd pers. sing. / *amnistiar.* 2. (you) give amnesty; impve. 2nd pers. sing.

amnistían they give amnesty; pres. ind. 3rd pers. pl. / *amnistiar.*

amnistiar to give amnesty. irr.

amnistías you give amnesty; pres. ind. 2nd pers. sing. / *amnistiar.*

amnistíe 1. that I may give amnesty; pres. subj. 1st pers. sing. / *amnistiar.* 2. that he (she/it) may give amnesty; pres. subj. 3rd pers. sing. 3. let him (her/it) give amnesty; impve. 3rd pers. sing.

amnistíen 1. that they may give amnesty; pres. subj. 3rd pers. pl. / *amnistiar.* 2. let them give amnesty; impve. 3rd pers. pl.

amnistíes that you may give amnesty; pres. subj. 2nd pers. sing. / *amnistiar.*

amnistío I give amnesty; pres. ind. 1st pers. sing. / *amnistiar.*

amoblar to furnish. irr. same as amueblar.

amodorrándose becoming sleepy; pres. part. / *amodorrarse.*

amodorraos (you all) become sleepy; impve. 2nd pers. pl. / *amodorrarse.*

amodorrar to make drowsy. reg.

amodorrarse to become sleepy. reg.

amodórrate (you) become sleepy; impve. 2nd pers. sing. / *amodorrarse.*

amodorrémonos let us become sleepy; impve. 1st pers. pl. / *amodorrarse.*

amodórrense let them become sleepy; impve. 3rd pers. pl. / *amodorrarse.*

amodórrese let him (her/it) become sleepy; impve. 3rd pers. sing. / *amodorrarse.*

amohinar to annoy. reg.

amolándose going to rack and ruin; pres. part. / *amolarse.*

amolaos (you all) go to rack and ruin; impve. 2nd pers. pl. / *amolarse.*

amolar to sharpen or to grind or to annoy. irr.

amolarse to go to rack and ruin. irr.

amoldándose adapting oneself; pres. part. / *amoldarse.*

amoldaos (you all) adapt yourselves; impve. 2nd pers. pl. / *amoldarse.*

amoldar to mold. reg.

amoldarse to adapt oneself. reg.

amóldate (you) adapt yourself; impve. 2nd pers. sing. / *amoldarse.*

amoldémonos let us adapt ourselves; impve. 1st pers. pl. / *amoldarse.*

amóldense let them adapt themselves; impve. 3rd pers. pl. / *amoldarse.*

amóldese let him (her/it) adapt himself (herself/itself); impve. 3rd pers. sing. / *amoldarse.*

amolémonos let us go to rack and ruin; impve. 1st pers. pl. / *amolarse.*

amonestar to admonish or to warn. reg.

amontonándose crowding together; pres. part. / *amontonarse.*

amontonaos (you all) crowd together; impve. 2nd pers. pl. / *amontonarse.*

amontonar to heap up. reg.

amontonarse to crowd together or to fly into a rage. reg.

amontónate (you) crowd together; impve. 2nd pers. sing. / *amontonarse.*

amontonémonos let us crowd together; impve. 1st pers. pl. / *amontonarse.*

amontónense let them crowd together; impve. 3rd pers. pl. / *amontonarse.*

amontónese let him (her/it) crowd together; impve. 3rd pers. sing. / *amontonarse.*

amoratándose turning blue as with cold; pres. part. / *amoratarse.*

amorataos (you all) turn blue as with cold; impve. 2nd pers. pl. / *amoratarse.*

amoratarse to turn blue as with cold. reg.

amorátate (you) turn blue as with cold; impve. 2nd pers. sing. / *amoratarse.*

amoratémonos let us turn blue as with cold; impve. 1st pers. pl. / *amoratarse.*

amorátense let them turn blue as with cold; impve. 3rd pers. pl. / *amoratarse.*

amorátese let him (her/it) turn blue as with cold; impve. 3rd pers. sing. / *amoratarse.*

amordace 1. that I may gag; pres. subj. 1st pers. sing. / *amordazar*. 2. that he (she/it) may gag; pres. subj. 3rd pers. sing. 3. let him (her/it) gag; impve. 3rd pers. sing.

amordacé I gagged; past 1st pers. sing. / *amordazar*.

amordacéis that you (all) may gag; pres. subj. 2nd pers. pl. / *amordazar*.

amordacemos 1. that we may gag; pres. subj. 1st pers. pl. / *amordazar* 2. let us gag; impve. 1st pers. pl.

amordacen 1. that they may gag; pres. subj. 3rd pers. pl. / *amordazar*. 2. let them gag; impve. 3rd pers. pl.

amordaces that you may gag; pres. subj. 2nd pers. sing. / *amordazar*.

amordazar to gag or to muzzle. irr.

amorrándose sulking; pres. part. / *amorrarse*.

amorraos (you all) sulk ; impve. 2nd pers. pl. / *amorrarse*.

amorrar to sulk. reg.

amorrarse to sulk. reg.

amórrate (you) sulk; impve. 2nd pers. sing. / *amorrarse*.

amorrémonos let us sulk; impve. 1st pers. pl. / *amorrarse*.

amórrense let them sulk; impve. 3rd pers. pl. / *amorrarse*.

amórrese let him (her/it) sulk; impve. 3rd pers. sing. / *amorrarse*.

amortajar to shroud. reg.

amortice 1. that I may amortize; pres. subj. 1st pers. sing. / *amortizar*. 2. that he (she/it) may amortize; pres. subj. 3rd pers. sing. 3. let him (her/it) amortize; impve. 3rd pers. sing.

amorticé I amortized; past 1st pers. sing. / *amortizar*.

amorticéis that you (all) may amortize; pres. subj. 2nd pers. pl. / *amortizar*.

amorticemos 1. that we may amortize; pres. subj. 1st pers. pl. / *amortizar*. 2. let us amortize; impve. 1st pers. pl.

amorticen 1. that they may amortize; pres. subj. 3rd pers. pl. / *amortizar*. 2. let them amortize; impve. 3rd pers. pl.

amortices that you may amortize; pres. subj. 2nd pers. sing. / *amortizar*.

amortiguar to muffle or to deaden. irr.

amortigüe 1. that I may muffle; pres. subj. 1st pers. sing. / *amortiguar*. 2. that he (she/it) may muffle; pres. subj. 3rd pers. sing. 3. let him (her/it) muffle; impve. 3rd pers. sing.

amortigüé I muffled; past 1st pers. sing. / *amortiguar*.

amortigüéis that you (all) may muffle; pres. subj. 2nd pers. pl. / *amortiguar*.

amortigüemos 1. that we may muffle; pres. subj. 1st pers. pl. / *amortiguar* 2. let us muffle; impve. 1st pers. pl.

amortigüen 1. that they muffle; pres. subj. 3rd pers. pl. / *amortiguar*. 2. let them muffle; impve. 3rd pers. pl.

amortigües that you may muffle; pres. subj. 2nd pers. sing. / *amortiguar*.

amortizar to amortize or write off. irr.

amoscándose getting annoyed; pres. part. / *amoscarse*.

amoscaos (you all) get annoyed; impve. 2nd pers. pl. / *amoscarse*.

amoscarse to get annoyed. irr.

amóscate (you) get annoyed; impve. 2nd pers. sing. / *amoscarse*.

amosqué I got annoyed; past 1st pers. sing. / *amoscarse*.

amosque 1. that I may get annoyed; pres. subj. 1st pers. sing. / *amoscarse*. 2. that he (she/it) may get annoyed; pres. subj. 3rd pers. sing.

amosquéis that you (all) may get annoyed; pres. subj. 2nd pers. pl. / *amoscarse*.

amosquémonos let us get annoyed; impve. 1st pers. pl. / *amoscarse*.

amosquemos that we may get annoyed; pres. subj. 1st pers. pl. / *amoscarse*.

amosquen that they may get annoyed; pres. subj. 3rd pers. pl. / *amoscarse*.

amósquense let them get annoyed; impve. 3rd pers. pl. / *amoscarse*.

amosques that you may get annoyed; pres. subj. 2nd pers. sing. / *amoscarse*.

amósquese let him (her/it) get annoyed; impve. 3rd pers. sing. / *amoscarse*.

amostace 1. that I may irritate; pres. subj. 1st pers. sing. / *amostazar*. 2. that he (she/it) may irritate; pres. subj. 3rd pers. sing. 3. let him (her/it) irritate; impve. 3rd pers. sing.

amostacé I irritated; past 1st pers. sing. / *amostazar*.

amostacéis that you (all) may irritate; pres. subj. 2nd pers. pl. / *amostazar*.

amostacémonos let us get angry; impve. 1st pers. pl. / *amostazarse*.

amostacemos 1. that we may irritate; pres. subj. 1st pers. pl. / *amostazar* 2. let us irritate; impve. 1st pers. pl.

amostacen 1. that they may irritate; pres. subj. 3rd pers. pl. / *amostazar*. 2. let them irritate; impve. 3rd pers. pl.

amostácense let them get angry; impve. 3rd pers. pl. / *amostazarse*.

amostaces that you may irritate; pres. subj. 2nd pers. sing. / *amostazar*.

amostácese let him (her/it) get angry; impve. 3rd pers. sing. / *amostazarse*.

amostazándose getting angry; pres. part. / *amostazarse*.

amostazaos (you all) get angry; impve. 2nd pers. pl. / *amostazarse*.

amostazar to irritate or anger. irr.

amostazarse to get angry. irr.

amostázate (you) get angry; impve. 2nd pers. sing. / *amostazarse*.

amotinándose mutinying; pres. part. / *amotinarse*.

amotinaos (you all) mutiny; impve. 2nd pers. pl. / *amotinarse*.

amotinar to excite rebellion. reg.

amotinarse to mutiny. reg.

amotínate (you) mutiny; impve. 2nd pers. sing. / *amotinarse.*

amotinémonos let us mutiny; impve. 1st pers. pl. / *amotinarse.*

amotínense let them mutiny; impve. 3rd pers. pl. / *amotinarse.*

amotínese let him (her/it) mutiny; impve. 3rd pers. sing. / *amotinarse.*

amparándose claiming protection; pres. part. / *ampararse.*

amparaos (you all) claim protection; impve. 2nd pers. pl. / *ampararse.*

amparar to protect or to shelter. reg.

ampararse to claim protection. reg.

ampárate (you) claim protection; impve. 2nd pers. sing. / *ampararse.*

amparémonos let us claim protection; impve. 1st pers. pl. / *ampararse.*

ampárense let them claim protection; impve. 3rd pers. pl. / *ampararse.*

ampárese let him (her/it) claim protection; impve. 3rd pers. sing. / *ampararse.*

amplía 1. he (she/it) amplifies; pres. ind. 3rd pers. sing. / *ampliar.* 2. (you) amplify; impve. 2nd pers. sing.

amplían they amplify; pres. ind. 3rd pers. pl. / *ampliar.*

ampliar to enlarge or amplify. irr.

amplías you amplify; pres. ind. 2nd pers. sing. / *ampliar.*

amplíe 1. that I may amplify; pres. subj. 1st pers. sing. / *ampliar.* 2. that he (she/it) may amplify; pres. subj. 3rd pers. sing. 3. let him (her/it) amplify; impve. 3rd pers. sing.

amplíen 1. that they may amplify; pres. subj. 3rd pers. pl. / *ampliar.* 2. let them amplify; impve. 3rd pers. pl.

amplíes that you may amplify; pres. subj. 2nd pers. sing. / *ampliar.*

amplificar to amplify or magnify. irr.

amplifique 1. that I may amplify; pres. subj. 1st pers. sing. / *amplificar.* 2. that he (she/it) may amplify; pres. subj. 3rd pers. sing. 3. let him (her/it) amplify; impve. 3rd pers. sing.

amplifiqué I amplified; past 1st pers. sing. / *amplificar.*

amplifiquéis that you (all) may amplify; pres. subj. 2nd pers. pl. / *amplificar.*

amplifiquemos 1. that we may amplify; pres. subj. 1st pers. pl. / *amplificar.* 2. let us amplify; impve. 1st pers. pl.

amplifiquen 1. that they may amplify; pres. subj. 3rd pers. pl. / *amplificar.* 2. let them amplify; impve. 3rd pers. pl.

amplifiques that you may amplify; pres. subj. 2nd pers. sing. / *amplificar.*

amplío I amplify; pres. ind. 1st pers. sing. / *ampliar.*

ampollándose rising in bubbles; pres. part. / *ampollarse.*

ampollar to blister. reg.

ampollarse to rise in bubbles. reg.

ampóllense let them rise in bubbles; impve. 3rd pers. pl. / *ampollarse.*

ampóllese let it rise in bubbles; impve. 3rd pers. sing. / *ampollarse.*

amputar to amputate. reg.

amueblar to furnish. reg.

amuela 1. he (she/it) sharpens; pres. ind. 3rd pers. sing. / *amolar.* 2. (you) sharpen; impve. 2nd pers. sing.

amuelan they sharpen; pres. ind. 3rd pers. pl. / *amolar.*

amuelas you sharpen; pres. ind. 2nd pers. sing. / *amolar.*

amuélate (you) go to rack and ruin; impve. 2nd pers. sing. / *amolarse.*

amuele 1. that I may sharpen; pres. subj. 1st pers. sing. / *amolar.* 2. that he (she/it) may sharpen; pres. subj. 3rd pers. sing. 3. let him (her/it) sharpen; impve. 3rd pers. sing.

amuelen 1. that they may sharpen; pres. subj. 3rd pers. pl. / *amolar.* 2. let them sharpen; impve. 3rd pers. pl.

amuélense let them go to rack and ruin; impve. 3rd pers. pl. / *amolarse.*

amueles that you may sharpen; pres. subj. 2nd pers. sing. / *amolar.*

amuélese let him (her/it) go to rack and ruin; impve. 3rd pers. sing. / *amolarse.*

amuelo I sharpen; pres. ind. 1st pers. sing. / *amolar.*

amurallar to wall up. reg.

amurrándose becoming glum; pres. part. / *amurrarse.*

amurraos (you all) become glum; impve. 2nd pers. pl. / *amurrarse.*

amurrarse to become glum or discouraged. reg.

amúrrate (you) become glum; impve. 2nd pers. sing. / *amurrarse.*

amurrémonos let us become glum; impve. 1st pers. pl. / *amurrarse.*

amúrrense let them become glum; impve. 3rd pers. pl. / *amurrarse.*

amúrrese let him (her/it) become glum; impve. 3rd pers. sing. / *amurrarse.*

anadear to waddle. reg.

analice 1. that I may analyze; pres. subj. 1st pers. sing. / *analizar.* 2. that he (she/it) may analyze; pres. subj. 3rd pers. sing. 3. let him (her/it) analyze; impve. 3rd pers. sing.

analicé I analyzed; past 1st pers. sing. / *analizar.*

analicéis that you (all) may analyze; pres. subj. 2nd pers. pl. / *analizar.*

analicemos 1. that we may analyze; pres. subj. 1st pers. pl. / *analizar* 2. let us analyze; impve. 1st pers. pl.

analicen 1. that they may analyze; pres. subj. 3rd pers. pl. / *analizar.* 2. let them analyze; impve. 3rd pers. pl.

analices that you may analyze; pres. subj. 2nd pers. sing. / *analizar.*

analizar to analyze. irr.

anatematice 1. that I may anathematize; pres. subj. 1st pers. sing. / *anatematizar*. 2. that he (she/it) may anathematize; pres. subj. 3rd pers. sing. 3. let him (her/it) anathematize; impve. 3rd pers. sing.

anatematicé I anathematized; past 1st pers. sing. / *anatematizar*.

anatematicéis that you (all) may anathematize; pres. subj. 2nd pers. pl. / *anatematizar*.

anatematicemos 1. that we may anathematize; pres. subj. 1st pers. pl. / *anatematizar*. 2. let us anathematize; impve. 1st pers. pl.

anatematicen 1. that they may anathematize; pres. subj. 3rd pers. pl. / *anatematizar*. 2. let them anathematize; impve. 3rd pers. pl.

anatematices that you may anathematize; pres. subj. 2nd pers. sing. / *anatematizar*.

anatematizar to anathematize. irr.

anatomice 1. that I may anatomize; pres. subj. 1st pers. sing. / *anatomizar*. 2. that he (she/it) may anatomize; pres. subj. 3rd pers. sing. 3. let him (her/it) anatomize; impve. 3rd pers. sing.

anatomicé I anatomized; past 1st pers. sing. / *anatomizar*.

anatomicéis that you (all) may anatomize; pres. subj. 2nd pers. pl. / *anatomizar*.

anatomicemos 1. that we may anatomize; pres. subj. 1st pers. pl. / *anatomizar*. 2. let us anatomize; impve. 1st pers. pl.

anatomicen 1. that they may anatomize; pres. subj. 3rd pers. pl. / *anatomizar*. 2. let them anatomize; impve. 3rd pers. pl.

anatomices that you may anatomize; pres. subj. 2nd pers. sing. / *anatomizar*.

anatomizar to anatomize or dissect. irr.

anclar to anchor. reg.

ancorar to cast anchor. reg.

andándose passing; pres. part. / *andarse*.

andaos (you all) pass; impve. 2nd pers. pl. / *andarse*.

andar to walk or to go. irr.

andarse to pass. irr.

ándate (you) pass; impve. 2nd pers. sing. / *andarse*.

andémonos let us pass; impve. 1st pers. pl. / *andarse*.

ándense let them pass; impve. 3rd pers. pl. / *andarse*.

ándese let him (her/it) pass; impve. 3rd pers. sing. / *andarse*.

anduve I walked; past 1st pers. sing. / *andar*.

anduviera 1. that I might walk; imp. subj. 1st pers. sing. / *andar*. 2. that he (she/it) might walk; imp. subj. 3rd pers. sing.

anduvierais that you (all) might walk; imp. subj. 2nd pers pl. / *andar*.

anduviéramos that we might walk; imp. subj. 1st pers. pl. / *andar*.

anduvieran that they might walk; imp. subj. 3rd pers. pl. / *andar*.

anduvieras that you might walk; imp. subj. 2nd pers. sing. / *andar*.

anduvieron they walked; past 3rd pers. pl. / *andar*.

anduviese 1. that I might walk; imp. subj. 1st pers. sing. / *andar*. 2. that he (she/it) might walk; imp. subj. 3rd pers. sing.

anduvieseis that you (all) might walk; imp. subj. 2nd pers pl. / *andar*.

anduviésemos that we might walk; imp. subj. 1st pers. pl. / *andar*.

anduviesen that they might walk; imp. subj. 3rd pers. pl. / *andar*.

anduvieses that you might walk; imp. subj. 2nd pers. sing. / *andar*.

anduvimos we walked; past 1st pers. pl. / *andar*.

anduviste you walked; past 2nd pers. sing. / *andar*.

anduvisteis you (all) walked; past 2nd pers. pl. / *andar*.

anduvo he (she/it) walked; past 3rd pers. sing. / *andar*.

aneblándose clouding over; pres. part. / *aneblarse*.

aneblar to cloud or to darken. irr.

aneblarse to cloud over. irr.

anegándose becoming flooded; pres. part. / *anegarse*.

anegaos (you all) become flooded; impve. 2nd pers. pl. / *anegarse*.

anegar to drown or to flood. irr.

anegarse to become flooded or soaked. irr.

anégate (you) become flooded; impve. 2nd pers. sing. / *anegarse*.

anegue 1. that I may drown; pres. subj. 1st pers. sing. / *anegar*. 2. that he (she/it) may drown; pres. subj. 3rd pers. sing. 3. let him (her/it) drown; impve. 3rd pers. sing.

anegué I drowned; past 1st pers. sing. / *anegar*.

aneguéis that you (all) may drown; pres. subj. 2nd pers. pl. / *anegar*.

aneguémonos let us become flooded; impve. 1st pers. pl. / *anegarse*.

aneguemos 1. that we may drown; pres. subj. 1st pers. pl. / *anegar* 2. let us drown; impve. 1st pers. pl.

aneguen 1. that they may drown; pres. subj. 3rd pers. pl. / *anegar*. 2. let them drown; impve. 3rd pers. pl.

anéguense let them become flooded; impve. 3rd pers. pl. / *anegarse*.

anegues that you may drown; pres. subj. 2nd pers. sing. / *anegar*.

anéguese let him (her/it) become flooded; impve. 3rd pers. sing. / *anegarse*.

anestesiar to anesthetize. reg.

anexar to annex or to join. reg.

angostándose becoming narrow; pres. part. / *angostarse*.

angostaos (you all) become narrow; impve. 2nd pers. pl. / *angostarse*.

angostar to narrow or to contract. reg.

angostarse to become narrow. reg.

angóstate (you) become narrow; impve. 2nd pers. sing. / *angostarse*.

angostémonos let us become narrow; impve. 1st pers. pl. / *angostarse*.

angóstense let them become narrow; impve. 3rd pers. pl. / *angostarse*.

angóstese let him (her/it) become narrow; impve. 3rd pers. sing. / *angostarse.*

angustiándose feeling anguish; pres. part. / *angustiarse.*

angustiaos (you all) feel anguish; impve. 2nd pers. pl. / *angustiarse.*

angustiar to anguish or distress. reg.

angustiarse to feel anguish or to grieve. reg.

angustíate (you) feel anguish; impve. 2nd pers. sing. / *angustiarse.*

angustiémonos let us feel anguish; impve. 1st pers. pl. / *angustiarse.*

angustíense let them feel anguish; impve. 3rd pers. pl. / *angustiarse.*

angustíese let him (her/it) feel anguish; impve. 3rd pers. sing. / *angustiarse.*

anhelar to covet or long for. reg.

anidar to nest or inhabit. reg.

aniebla it clouds; pres. ind. 3rd pers. sing. / *aneblar.*

anieble 1. that it may cloud; pres. subj. 3rd pers. sing. / *aneblar.* 2. let it cloud; impve. 3rd pers. sing.

aniéblese let it cloud over; impve. 3rd pers. sing. / *aneblarse.*

animándose cheering up; pres. part. / *animarse.*

animaos (you all) cheer up; impve. 2nd pers. pl. / *animarse.*

animar to animate or to encourage. reg.

animarse to cheer up. reg.

anímate (you) cheer up; impve. 2nd pers. sing. / *animarse.*

animémonos let us cheer up; impve. 1st pers. pl. / *animarse.*

anímense let them cheer up; impve. 3rd pers. pl. / *animarse.*

anímese let him (her/it) cheer up; impve. 3rd pers. sing. / *animarse.*

aniñándose acting in a childish manner; pres. part. / *aniñarse.*

aniñaos (you all) act in a childish manner; impve. 2nd pers. pl. / *aniñarse.*

aniñarse to act in a childish manner. reg.

aníñate (you) act in a childish manner; impve. 2nd pers. sing. / *aniñarse.*

aniñémonos let us act in a childish manner; impve. 1st pers. pl. / *aniñarse.*

aníñense let them act in a childish manner; impve. 3rd pers. pl. / *aniñarse.*

aníñese let him (her/it) act in a childish manner; impve. 3rd pers. sing. / *aniñarse.*

aniquilándose being destroyed; pres. part. / *aniquilarse.*

aniquilaos (you all) be destroyed; impve. 2nd pers. pl. / *aniquilarse.*

aniquilar to annihilate or to destroy. reg.

aniquilarse to be destroyed. reg.

aniquílate (you) be destroyed; impve. 2nd pers. sing. / *aniquilarse.*

aniquilémonos let us be destroyed; impve. 1st pers. pl. / *aniquilarse.*

aniquílense let them be destroyed; impve. 3rd pers. pl. / *aniquilarse.*

aniquílese let him (her/it) be destroyed; impve. 3rd pers. sing. / *aniquilarse.*

anisar to flavor with aniseed. reg.

anochecer to grow dark. irr.

anochecerse to grow dark. irr.

anocheciéndose growing dark; pres. part. / *anochecerse.*

anochezca 1. that it may grow dark; pres. subj. 3rd pers. sing. / *anochecer.* 2. let it grow dark; impve. 3rd pers. sing.

anochézcanse let them grow dark; impve. 3rd pers. pl. / *anochecerse.*

anochézcase let it grow dark; impve. 3rd pers. sing. / *anochecerse.*

anodizar to anodize. reg.

anonadándose feeling crushed; pres. part. / *anonadarse.*

anonadaos (you all) feel crushed; impve. 2nd pers. pl. / *anonadarse.*

anonadar to annihilate or to humiliate. reg.

anonadarse to feel crushed. reg.

anonádate (you) feel crushed; impve. 2nd pers. sing. / *anonadarse.*

anonadémonos let us feel crushed; impve. 1st pers. pl. / *anonadarse.*

anonádense let them feel crushed; impve. 3rd pers. pl. / *anonadarse.*

anonádese let him (her/it) feel crushed; impve. 3rd pers. sing. / *anonadarse.*

anotar to annotate or note. reg.

anquilosándose becoming stiff in the joints; pres. part. / *anquilosarse.*

anquilosaos (you all) become stiff in the joints; impve. 2nd pers. pl. / *anquilosarse.*

anquilosarse to become stiff in the joints or to become mentally stagnant. reg.

anquilósate (you) become stiff in the joints; impve. 2nd pers. sing. / *anquilosarse.*

anquilosémonos let us become stiff in the joints; impve. 1st pers. pl. / *anquilosarse.*

anquilósense let them become stiff in the joints; impve. 3rd pers. pl. / *anquilosarse.*

anquilósese let him (her/it) become stiff in the joints; impve. 3rd pers. sing. / *anquilosarse.*

ansía 1. he (she/it) longs for; pres. ind. 3rd pers. sing. / *ansiar.* 2. (you) long for; impve. 2nd pers. sing. / *ansiar.*

ansían they long for; pres. ind. 3rd pers. pl. / *ansiar.*

ansiar to long for or desire earnestly. irr.

ansías you long for; pres. ind. 2nd pers. sing. / *ansiar.*

ansíe 1. that I may long for; pres. subj. 1st pers. sing. / *ansiar.* 2. that he (she/it) may long for; pres. subj. 3rd pers. sing. 3. let him (her/it) long for; impve. 3rd pers. sing.

ansíen 1. that they may long for; pres. subj. 3rd pers. pl. / *ansiar.* 2. let them long for; impve. 3rd pers. pl.

ansíes that you may long for; pres. subj. 2nd pers. sing. / *ansiar.*

ansío I long for; pres. ind. 1st pers. sing. / *ansiar.*

antagonice 1. that I may antagonize; pres. subj. 1st pers. sing. / *antagonizar*. 2. that he (she/it) may antagonize; pres. subj. 3rd pers. sing. 3. let him (her/it) antagonize; impve. 3rd pers. sing.

antagonicé I antagonized; past 1st pers. sing. / *antagonizar*.

antagonicéis that you (all) may antagonize; pres. subj. 2nd pers. pl. / *antagonizar*.

antagonicemos 1. that we may antagonize; pres. subj. 1st pers. pl. / *antagonizar*. 2. let us antagonize; impve. 1st pers. pl.

antagonicen 1. that they may antagonize; pres. subj. 3rd pers. pl. / *antagonizar*. 2. let them antagonize; impve. 3rd pers. pl.

antagonices that you may antagonize; pres. subj. 2nd pers. sing. / *antagonizar*.

antagonizar to antagonize. irr.

anteceder to precede. reg.

antedatar to antedate. reg.

antepagar to pay in advance. reg.

antepon (you) prefer; impve. 2nd pers. sing. / *anteponer*.

antepondrá he (she/it) will prefer; fut. 3rd pers. sing. / *anteponer*.

antepondrán they will prefer; fut. 3rd pers. pl. / *anteponer*.

antepondrás you will prefer; fut. 2nd pers. sing. / *anteponer*.

antepondré I shall prefer; fut. 1st pers. sing. / *anteponer*.

antepondréis you (all) will prefer; fut. 2nd pers. pl. / *anteponer*.

antepondremos we shall prefer; fut. 1st pers. pl. / *anteponer*.

antepondría 1. I should prefer; cond. 1st pers. sing. / *anteponer*. 2. he (she/it) would prefer; cond. 3rd pers. sing.

antepondríais you (all) would prefer; cond. 2nd pers. pl. / *anteponer*.

antepondríamos we should prefer; cond. 1st pers. pl. / *anteponer*.

antepondrían they would prefer; cond. 3rd pers. pl. / *anteponer*.

antepondrías you would prefer; cond. 2nd pers. sing. / *anteponer*.

anteponeos (you all) push yourselves forward; impve. 2nd pers. pl. / *anteponerse*.

anteponer to prefer or to place before. irr.

anteponerse to push oneself forward. irr.

anteponga 1. that I may prefer; pres. subj. 1st pers. sing. / *anteponer*. 2. that he (she/it) may prefer; pres. subj. 3rd pers. sing. 3. let him (her/it) prefer; impve. 3rd pers. sing.

antepongáis that you (all) may prefer; pres. subj. 2nd pers. pl. / *anteponer*.

antepongámonos let us push ourselves forward; impve. 1st pers. pl. / *anteponerse*.

antepongamos 1. that we may prefer; pres. subj. 1st pers. pl. / *anteponer* 2. let us prefer; impve. 1st pers. pl.

antepongan 1. that they may prefer; pres. subj. 3rd pers. pl. / *anteponer*. 2. let him (her/it) prefer; impve. 3rd pers. pl.

antepónganse let them push themselves forward; impve. 3rd pers. pl. / *anteponerse*.

antepongas that you may prefer; pres. subj. 2nd pers. sing. / *anteponer*.

antepóngase let him (her/it) push himself (herself/itself) forward; impve. 3rd pers. sing. / *anteponerse*.

antepongo I prefer; pres. ind. 1st pers. sing. / *anteponer*

anteponiéndose pushing oneself forward; pres. part. / *anteponerse*.

anteponte (you) push yourself forward; impve. 2nd pers. sing. / *anteponerse*.

antepuesto preferred; past part. / *anteponer*.

antepuse I preferred; past 1st pers. sing. / *anteponer*.

antepusiera 1. that I might prefer; imp. subj. 1st pers. sing. / *anteponer*. 2. that he (she/it) might prefer; imp. subj. 3rd pers. sing.

antepusierais that you (all) might prefer; imp. subj. 2nd pers pl. / *anteponer*.

antepusiéramos that we might prefer; imp. subj. 1st pers. pl. / *anteponer*.

antepusieran that they might prefer; imp. subj. 3rd pers. pl. / *anteponer*.

antepusieras that you might prefer; imp. subj. 2nd pers. sing. / *anteponer*.

antepusieron they preferred; past 3rd pers. pl. / *anteponer*.

antepusiese 1. that I might prefer; imp. subj. 1st pers. sing. / *anteponer*. 2. that he (she/it) might prefer; imp. subj. 3rd pers. sing.

antepusieseis that you (all) might prefer; imp. subj. 2nd pers pl. / *anteponer*.

antepusiésemos that we might prefer; imp. subj. 1st pers. pl. / *anteponer*.

antepusiesen that they might prefer; imp. subj. 3rd pers. pl. / *anteponer*.

antepusieses that you might prefer; imp. subj. 2nd pers. sing. / *anteponer*.

antepusimos we preferred; past 1st pers. pl. / *anteponer*

antepusiste you preferred; past 2nd pers. sing. / *anteponer*.

antepusisteis you (all) preferred; past 2nd pers. pl. / *anteponer*.

antepuso he (she/it) preferred; past 3rd pers. sing. / *anteponer*.

anticipándose getting ahead (of); pres. part. / *anticiparse*.

anticipaos (you all) get ahead (of); impve. 2nd pers. pl. / *anticiparse*.

anticipar to anticipate or to advance. reg.

anticiparse to get ahead (of). reg.

anticípate (you) get ahead (of); impve. 2nd pers. sing. / *anticiparse*.

anticipémonos let us get ahead (of); impve. 1st pers. pl. / *anticiparse*.

anticípense let them get ahead (of); impve. 3rd pers. pl. / *anticiparse.*

anticípese let him (her/it) get ahead (of); impve. 3rd pers. sing. / *anticiparse.*

anticuándose becoming outdated; pres. part. / *anticuarse.*

anticuaos (you all) become outdated; impve. 2nd pers. pl. / *anticuarse.*

anticuar to outdate. reg.

anticuarse to become outdated. reg.

anticúate (you) become outdated; impve. 2nd pers. sing. / *anticuarse.*

anticuémonos let us become outdated; impve. 1st pers. pl. / *anticuarse.*

anticúense let them become outdated; impve. 3rd pers. pl. / *anticuarse.*

anticúese let him (her/it) become outdated; impve. 3rd pers. sing. / *anticuarse.*

antojándose longing for; pres. part. / *antojarse.*

antojaos (you all) long for; impve. 2nd pers. pl. / *antojarse.*

antojarse to long for or to surmise. reg.

antójate (you) long for; impve. 2nd pers. sing. / *antojarse.*

antojémonos let us long for; impve. 1st pers. pl. / *antojarse.*

antójense let them long for; impve. 3rd pers. pl. / *antojarse.*

antójese let him (her/it) long for; impve. 3rd pers. sing. / *antojarse.*

anublándose becoming cloudy; pres. part. / *anublarse.*

anublar to cloud or to darken. reg.

anublarse to become cloudy. reg.

anúblese let it become cloudy; impve. 3rd pers. sing. / *anublarse.*

anudándose becoming knotted; pres. part. / *anudarse.*

anudaos (you all) become knotted; impve. 2nd pers. pl. / *anudarse.*

anudar to knot or to untie. reg.

anudarse to become knotted. reg.

anúdate (you) become knotted; impve. 2nd pers. sing. / *anudarse.*

anúdense let them become knotted; impve. 3rd pers. pl. / *anudarse.*

anúdese let him (her/it) become knotted; impve. 3rd pers. sing. / *anudarse.*

anulándose vanishing; pres. part. / *anularse.*

anulaos (you all) vanish; impve. 2nd pers. pl. / *anularse.*

anular to annul or to abolish. reg.

anularse to vanish. reg.

anúlate (you) vanish; impve. 2nd pers. sing. / *anularse.*

anulémonos let us vanish; impve. 1st pers. pl. / *anularse.*

anúlense let them vanish; impve. 3rd pers. pl. / *anularse.*

anúlese let him (her/it) vanish; impve. 3rd pers. sing. / *anularse.*

anunciar to announce or to advertise. reg.

añadir to add or to increase. reg.

añejándose becoming old; pres. part. / *añejarse.*

añejaos (you all) become old; impve. 2nd pers. pl. / *añejarse.*

añejar to make old. reg.

añejarse to become old or to age. reg.

añéjate (you) become old; impve. 2nd pers. sing. / *añejarse.*

añejémonos let us become old; impve. 1st pers. pl. / *añejarse.*

añéjense let them become old; impve. 3rd pers. pl. / *añejarse.*

añéjese let him (her/it) become old; impve. 3rd pers. sing. / *añejarse.*

añorar to yearn for or to regret. reg.

aojar to bewitch or give the evil eye. reg.

aovillándose rolling oneself into a ball; pres. part. / *aovillarse.*

aovillaos (you all) roll yourselves into a ball; impve. 2nd pers. pl. / *aovillarse.*

aovillar to wind (into balls). reg.

aovillarse to roll oneself into a ball. reg.

aovíllate (you) roll yourself into a ball; impve. 2nd pers. sing. / *aovillarse.*

aovillémonos let us roll ourselves into a ball; impve. 1st pers. pl. / *aovillarse.*

aovíllense let them roll themselves into a ball; impve. 3rd pers. pl. / *aovillarse.*

aovíllese let him (her/it) roll himself (herself/itself) into a ball; impve. 3rd pers. sing. / *aovillarse.*

apabilándose losing courage; pres. part. / *apabilarse.*

apabilaos (you all) lose courage; impve. 2nd pers. pl. / *apabilarse.*

apabilar to trim (wick). reg.

apabilarse to lose courage. reg.

apabílate (you) lose courage; impve. 2nd pers. sing. / *apabilarse.*

apabilémonos let us lose courage; impve. 1st pers. pl. / *apabilarse.*

apabílense let them lose courage; impve. 3rd pers. pl. / *apabilarse.*

apabílese let him (her/it) lose courage; impve. 3rd pers. sing. / *apabilarse.*

apabullar to crush or crumple. reg.

apacentándose pasturing; pres. part. / *apacentarse.*

apacentaos (you all) pasture; impve. 2nd pers. pl. / *apacentarse.*

apacentar to graze. irr.

apacentarse to pasture. irr.

apacentémonos let us pasture; impve. 1st pers. pl. / *apacentarse.*

apacienta 1. he (she/it) grazes; pres. ind. 3rd pers. sing. / *apacentar.* 2. (you) graze; impve. 2nd pers. sing.

apacientan they graze; pres. ind. 3rd pers. pl. / *apacentarse.*

apacientas you graze; pres. ind. 2nd pers. sing. / *apacentar*

apaciéntate (you) pasture; impve. 2nd pers. sing. / *apacentarse*.

apaciente 1. that I may graze; pres. subj. 1st pers. sing. / *apacentar*. 2. that he (she/it) may graze; pres. subj. 3rd pers. sing. 3. let him (her/it) graze; impve. 3rd pers. sing.

apacienten 1. that they may graze; pres. subj. 3rd pers. pl. / *apacentar*. 2. let them graze; impve. 3rd pers. pl.

apaciéntense let them pasture; impve. 3rd pers. pl. / *apacentarse*.

apacientes that you may graze; pres. subj. 2nd pers. sing. / *apacentar*.

apaciéntese let him (her/it) pasture; impve. 3rd pers. sing. / *apacentarse*.

apaciento I graze; pres. ind. 1st pers. sing. / *apacentar*.

apacigüándose calming down; pres. part. / *apaciguarse*.

apacigüaos (you all) calm down; impve. 2nd pers. pl. / *apaciguarse*.

apaciguar to appease or to pacify. irr.

apaciguarse to calm down. irr.

apacígüate (you) calm down; impve. 2nd pers. sing. / *apaciguarse*.

apacigüe 1. that I may appease; pres. subj. 1st pers. sing. / *apaciguar*. 2. that he (she/it) may appease; pres. subj. 3rd pers. sing. 3. let him (her/it) appease; impve. 3rd pers. sing.

apacigüé I appeased; past 1st pers. sing. / *apaciguar*.

apacigüéis that you (all) may appease; pres. subj. 2nd pers. pl. / *apaciguar*.

apacigüémonos let us calm down; impve. 1st pers. pl. / *apaciguarse*.

apacigüemos 1. that we may appease; pres. subj. 1st pers. pl. / *apaciguar* 2. let us appease; impve. 1st pers. pl.

apacigüen 1. that they may appease; pres. subj. 3rd pers. pl. / *apaciguar*. 2. let them appease; impve. 3rd pers. pl.

apacígüense let them calm down; impve. 3rd pers. pl. / *apaciguarse*.

apacigües that you may appease; pres. subj. 2nd pers. sing. / *apaciguar*.

apacígüese let him (her/it) calm down; impve. 3rd pers. sing. / *apaciguarse*.

apachurrar to crush or to flatten. reg.

apadrinar to sponsor or to act as a godfather. reg.

apagándose quenching; pres. part. / *apagarse*.

apagaos (you all) quench; impve. 2nd pers. pl. / *apagarse*.

apagar to extinguish or put out. irr.

apagarse to quench. irr.

apágate (you) quench; impve. 2nd pers. sing. / *apagarse*.

apague 1. that I may extinguish; pres. subj. 1st pers. sing. / *apagar*. 2. that he (she/it) may extinguish; pres. subj. 3rd pers. sing. 3. let him (her/it) extinguish; impve. 3rd pers. sing.

apagué I extinguished; past 1st pers. sing. / *apagar*.

apaguéis that you (all) may extinguish; pres. subj. 2nd pers. pl. / *apagar*.

apaguémonos let us quench; impve. 1st pers. pl. / *apagarse*.

apaguemos 1. that we may extinguish; pres. subj. 1st pers. pl. / *apagar* 2. let us extinguish; impve. 1st pers. pl.

apaguen 1. that they may extinguish; pres. subj. 3rd pers. pl. / *apagar*. 2. let them extinguish; impve. 3rd pers. pl.

apáguense let them quench; impve. 3rd pers. pl. / *apagarse*.

apagues that you may extinguish; pres. subj. 2nd pers. sing. / *apagar*.

apáguese let him (her/it) quench; impve. 3rd pers. sing. / *apagarse*.

apalabrándose agreeing; pres. part. / *apalabrarse*.

apalabraos (you all) agree; impve. 2nd pers. pl. / *apalabrarse*.

apalabrar to speak for or to discuss. reg.

apalabrarse to agree. reg.

apalábrate (you) agree; impve. 2nd pers. sing. / *apalabrarse*.

apalabrémonos let us agree; impve. 1st pers. pl. / *apalabrarse*.

apalábrense let them agree; impve. 3rd pers. pl. / *apalabrarse*.

apalábrese let him (her/it) agree; impve. 3rd pers. sing. / *apalabrarse*.

apalear to beat up or whip. reg.

apandillándose banding together; pres. part. / *apandillarse*.

apandillaos (you all) band together; impve. 2nd pers. pl. / *apandillarse*.

apandillarse to band together. reg.

apandíllate (you) band together; impve. 2nd pers. sing. / *apandillarse*.

apandillémonos let us band together; impve. 1st pers. pl. / *apandillarse*.

apandíllense let them band together; impve. 3rd pers. pl. / *apandillarse*.

apandíllese let him (her/it) band together; impve. 3rd pers. sing. / *apandillarse*.

apantanar to flood. reg.

apañándose scheming; pres. part. / *apañarse*.

apañaos (you all) scheme; impve. 2nd pers. pl. / *apañarse*.

apañar to seize or catch. reg.

apañarse to contrive or scheme. reg.

apáñate (you) scheme; impve. 2nd pers. sing. / *apañarse*.

apañémonos let us scheme; impve. 1st pers. pl. / *apañarse*.

apáñense let them scheme; impve. 3rd pers. pl. / *apañarse*.

apáñese let him (her/it) scheme; impve. 3rd pers. sing. / *apañarse*.

aparar to prepare. reg.

aparcar to park (car). irr.

apareándose being paired; pres. part. / *aparearse*.

apareaos (you all) be paired; impve. 2nd pers. pl. / *aparearse*.

aparear to mate or to couple. reg.
aparearse to be paired. reg.
aparéate (you) be paired; impve. 2nd pers. sing. /
aparearse.
apareceos (you all) show up; impve. 2nd pers. pl. /
aparecerse.
aparecer to appear. irr.
aparecerse to show up. irr.
aparécete (you) show up; impve. 2nd pers. sing. /
aparecerse.
apareciéndose showing up; pres. part. / *aparecerse.*
apareémonos let us be paired; impve. 1st pers. pl. /
aparearse.
aparéense let them be paired; impve. 3rd pers. pl. /
aparearse.
aparéese let him (her/it) be paired; impve. 3rd pers.
sing. / *aparearse.*
aparejándose equipping oneself; pres. part. /
aparejarse.
aparejaos (you all) equip yourselves; impve. 2nd
pers. pl. / *aparejarse.*
aparejar to prepare or to harness. reg.
aparejarse to equip oneself. reg.
aparéjate (you) equip yourself; impve. 2nd pers. sing.
/ *aparejarse.*
aparejémonos let us equip ourselves; impve. 1st pers.
pl. / *aparejarse.*
aparéjense let them equip themselves; impve. 3rd
pers. pl. / *aparejarse.*
aparéjese let him (her/it) equip himself
(herself/itself); impve. 3rd pers. sing. / *aparejarse.*
aparentar to seem or to pretend. reg.
aparezca 1. that I may appear; pres. subj. 1st pers.
sing. / *aparecer.* 2. that he (she/it) may appear; pres.
subj. 3rd pers. sing. 3. let him (her/it) appear;
impve. 3rd pers. sing.
aparezcáis that you (all) may appear; pres. subj. 2nd
pers. pl. / *aparecer.*
aparezcámonos let us show up; impve. 1st pers. pl. /
aparecerse.
aparezcamos 1. that we may appear; pres. subj. 1st
pers. pl. / *aparecer* 2. let us appear; impve. 1st pers.
pl.
aparezcan 1. that they may appear; pres. subj. 3rd
pers. pl. / *aparecer.* 2. let them appear; impve. 3rd
pers. pl.
aparézcanse let them show up; impve. 3rd pers. pl. /
aparecerse.
aparezcas that you may appear; pres. subj. 2nd pers.
sing. / *aparecer.*
aparézcase let him (her/it) show up; impve. 3rd pers.
sing. / *aparecerse.*
aparezco I appear; pres. ind. 1st pers. sing. / *aparecer.*
aparque 1. that I may park (a car); pres. subj. 1st
pers. sing. / *aparcar.* 2. that he (she/it) may park (a
car); pres. subj. 3rd pers. sing. 3. let him (her/it)
park (a car); impve. 3rd pers. sing.
aparqué I parked (a car); past 1st pers. sing. /
aparcar.

aparquéis that you (all) may park (a car); pres. subj.
2nd pers. pl. / *aparcar.*
aparquemos 1. that we may park (a car); pres. subj.
1st pers. pl. / *aparcar.* 2. let us park (a car); impve.
1st pers. pl.
aparquen 1. that they may park (a car); pres. subj.
3rd pers. pl. / *aparcar.* 2. let them park (a car);
impve. 3rd pers. pl.
aparques that you may park (a car); pres. subj. 2nd
pers. sing. / *aparcar.*
aparragándose nestling; pres. part. / *aparragarse.*
aparragaos (you all) nestle; impve. 2nd pers. pl. /
aparragarse.
aparragarse to nestle or crouch. reg.
aparrágate (you) nestle; impve. 2nd pers. sing. /
aparragarse.
aparragémonos let us nestle; impve. 1st pers. pl. /
aparragarse.
aparrágense let them nestle; impve. 3rd pers. pl. /
aparragarse.
aparrágese let him (her/it) nestle; impve. 3rd pers.
sing. / *aparragarse.*
apartándose withdrawing; pres. part. / *apartarse.*
apartaos (you all) withdraw; impve. 2nd pers. pl. /
apartarse.
apartar to separate. reg.
apartarse to withdraw. reg.
apártate (you) withdraw; impve. 2nd pers. sing. /
apartarse.
apartémonos let us withdraw; impve. 1st pers. pl. /
apartarse.
apártense let them withdraw; impve. 3rd pers. pl. /
apartarse.
apártese let him (her/it) withdraw; impve. 3rd pers.
sing. / *apartarse.*
apartidándose taking sides; pres. part. / *apartidarse.*
apartidaos (you all) take sides; impve. 2nd pers. pl. /
apartidarse.
apartidar to back or support. reg.
apartidarse to take sides. reg.
apartídate (you) take sides; impve. 2nd pers. sing. /
apartidarse.
apartidémonos let us take sides; impve. 1st pers. pl. /
apartidarse.
apartídense let them take sides; impve. 3rd pers. pl. /
apartidarse.
apartídese let him (her/it) take sides; impve. 3rd
pers. sing. / *apartidarse.*
apasionándose becoming fond (of); pres. part. /
apasionarse.
apasionaos (you all) become fond (of); impve. 2nd
pers. pl. / *apankonarse.*
apasionar to arouse passion. reg.
apasionarse to become fond (of). reg.
apasiónate (you) become fond (of); impve. 2nd pers.
sing. / *apasionarse.*
apasionémonos let us become fond (of); impve. 1st
pers. pl. / *apasionarse.*
apasiónense let them become fond (of); impve. 3rd
pers. pl. / *apasionarse.*

apasiónese let him (her/it) become fond (of); impve. 3rd pers. sing. / *apasionarse*.

apeándose alighting; pres. part. / *apearse*.

apeaos (you all) alight; impve. 2nd pers. pl. / *apearse*.

apear to dismount or to lower. reg.

apearse to alight. reg.

apéate (you) alight; impve. 2nd pers. sing. / *apearse*.

apechugar to push with the chest. irr.

apechugue 1. that I may push with my chest; pres. subj. 1st pers. sing. / *apechugar*. 2. that he (she/it) may push with his (her/it's) chest; pres. subj. 3rd pers. sing. 3. let him (her/it) push with his (her/it's) chest;

apechugué I pushed with my chest; past 1st pers. sing. / *apechugar*.

apechuguéis that you (all) may push with your chest; pres. subj. 2nd pers. pl. / *apechugar*.

apechuguemos 1. that we may push with our chest; pres. subj. 1st pers. pl. / *apechugar*. 2. let us push with our chest; impve. 1st pers. pl.

apechuguen 1. that they may push with their chest; pres. subj. 3rd pers. pl. / *apechugar*. 2. let them push with their chest; impve. 3rd pers. pl.

apechugues that you may push with your chest; pres. subj. 2nd pers. sing. / *apechugar*.

apedreándose being injured by hail; pres. part. / *apedrearse*.

apedreaos (you all) be injured by hail; impve. 2nd pers. pl. / *apedrearse*.

apedrear to stone. reg.

apedrearse to be injured by hail. reg.

apedréate (you) be injured by hail; impve. 2nd pers. sing. / *apedrearse*.

apedreémonos let us be injured by hail; impve. 1st pers. pl. / *apedrearse*.

apedréense let them be injured by hail; impve. 3rd pers. pl. / *apedrearse*.

apedréese let him (her/it) be injured by hail; impve. 3rd pers. sing. / *apedrearse*.

apeémonos let us alight; impve. 1st pers. pl. / *apearse*.

apéense let them alight; impve. 3rd pers. pl. / *apearse*.

apéese let him (her/it) alight; impve. 3rd pers. sing. / *apearse*.

apegándose becoming attached to; pres. part. / *apegarse*.

apegaos (you all) become attached to; impve. 2nd pers. pl. / *apegarse*.

apegarse to become attached to or to become fond of. irr.

apégate (you) become attached to; impve. 2nd pers. sing. / *apegarse*.

apegué I became attached to; past 1st pers. sing. / *apegarse*.

apegue 1. that I may become attached to; pres. subj. 1st pers. sing. / *apegarse*. 2. that he (she/it) may become attached to; pres. subj. 3rd pers. sing.

apeguéis that you (all) may become attached to; pres. subj. 2nd pers. pl. / *apegarse*.

apeguémonos let us become attached to; impve. 1st pers. pl. / *apegarse*.

apeguemos that we may become attached to; pres. subj. 1st pers. pl. / *apegarse*.

apeguen that they may become attached to; pres. subj. 3rd pers. pl. / *apegarse*.

apéguense let them become attached to; impve. 3rd pers. pl. / *apegarse*.

apegues that you may become attached to; pres. subj. 2nd pers. sing. / *apegarse*.

apéguese let him (her/it) become attached to; impve. 3rd pers. sing. / *apegarse*.

apelar to appeal or to refer. reg.

apelmace 1. that I may compress; pres. subj. 1st pers. sing. / *apelmazar*. 2. that he (she/it) may compress; pres. subj. 3rd pers. sing. 3. let him (her/it) compress; impve. 3rd pers. sing.

apelmacé I compressed; past 1st pers. sing. / *apelmazar*.

apelmacéis that you (all) may compress; pres. subj. 2nd pers. pl. / *apelmazar*.

apelmacemos 1. that we may compress; pres. subj. 1st pers. pl. / *apelmazar*. 2. let us compress; impve. 1st pers. pl.

apelmacen 1. that they may compress; pres. subj. 3rd pers. pl. / *apelmazar*. 2. let them compress; impve. 3rd pers. pl.

apelmaces that you may compress; pres. subj. 2nd pers. sing. / *apelmazar*.

apelmazar to compress or to make lumpy. irr.

apelotonándose clustering; pres. part. / *apelotonarse*.

apelotonaos (you all) cluster; impve. 2nd pers. pl. / *apelotonarse*.

apelotonar to roll into a ball. reg.

apelotonarse to cluster. reg.

apelotónate (you) cluster; impve. 2nd pers. sing. / *apelotonarse*.

apelotonémonos let us cluster; impve. 1st pers. pl. / *apelotonarse*.

apelotónense let them cluster; impve. 3rd pers. pl. / *apelotonarse*.

apelotónese let him (her/it) cluster; impve. 3rd pers. sing. / *apelotonarse*.

apellidándose being named; pres. part. / *apellidarse*.

apellidaos (you all) be named; impve. 2nd pers. pl. / *apellidarse*.

apellidar to name. reg.

apellidarse to be named. reg.

apellídate (you) be named; impve. 2nd pers. sing. / *apellidarse*.

apellidémonos let us be named; impve. 1st pers. pl. / *apellidarse*.

apellídense let them be named; impve. 3rd pers. pl. / *apellidarse*.

apellídese let him (her/it) be named; impve. 3rd pers. sing. / *apellidarse*.

apenándose being grieved; pres. part. / *apenarse*.

apenaos (you all) be grieved; impve. 2nd pers. pl. / *apenarse*.

apenar to cause pain. reg.

apenarse to be grieved. reg.

apénate (you) be grieved; impve. 2nd pers. sing. / *apenarse.*

apenémonos let us be grieved; impve. 1st pers. pl. / *apenarse.*

apénense let them be grieved; impve. 3rd pers. pl. / *apenarse.*

apénese let him (her/it) be grieved; impve. 3rd pers. sing. / *apenarse*531Y.

aperar to repair or equip (farm machinery). reg.

apercibámonos let us get ready; impve. 1st pers. pl. / *apercibirse.*

apercíbanse let them get ready; impve. 3rd pers. pl. / *apercibirse.*

apercíbase let him (her/it) get ready; impve. 3rd pers. sing. / *apercibirse.*

apercíbete (you) get ready; impve. 2nd pers. sing. / *apercibirse.*

apercibiéndose getting ready; pres. part. / *apercibirse.*

apercibíos (you all) get ready; impve. 2nd pers. pl. / *apercibirse.*

apercibir to prepare. reg.

apercibirse to get ready. reg.

apesadumbrándose being grieved; pres. part. / *apesadumbrarse.*

apesadumbraos (you all) be grieved; impve. 2nd pers. pl. / *apesadumbrarse.*

apesadumbrar to cause trouble. reg.

apesadumbrarse to be grieved. reg.

apesadúmbrate (you) be grieved; impve. 2nd pers. sing. / *apesadumbrarse.*

apesadumbrémonos let us be grieved; impve. 1st pers. pl. / *apesadumbrarse.*

apesadúmbrense let them be grieved; impve. 3rd pers. pl. / *apesadumbrarse.*

apesadúmbrese let him (her/it) be grieved; impve. 3rd pers. sing. / *apesadumbrarse.*

apesgándose becoming aggrieved; pres. part. / *apesgarse.*

apesgaos (you all) become aggrieved; impve. 2nd pers. pl. / *apesgarse.*

apesgar to overburden. irr.

apesgarse to become aggrieved. irr.

apésgate (you) become aggrieved; impve. 2nd pers. sing. / *apesgarse.*

apesgue 1. that I may overburden; pres. subj. 1st pers. sing. / *apesgar.* 2. that he (she/it) may overburden; pres. subj. 3rd pers. sing. 3. let him (her/it) overburden; impve. 3rd pers. sing.

apesgué I overburdened; past 1st pers. sing. / *apesgar.*

apesguéis that you (all) may overburden; pres. subj. 2nd pers. pl. / *apesgar.*

apesguémonos let us become aggrieved; impve. 1st pers. pl. / *apesgarse.*

apesguemos 1. that we may overburden; pres. subj. 1st pers. pl. / *apesgar.* 2. let us overburden; impve. 1st pers. pl.

apesguen 1. that they may overburden; pres. subj. 3rd pers. pl. / *apesgar.* 2. let them overburden; impve. 3rd pers. pl.

apésguense let them become aggrieved; impve. 3rd pers. pl. / *apesgarse.*

apesgues that you may overburden; pres. subj. 2nd pers. sing. / *apesgar.*

apésguese let him (her/it) become aggrieved; impve. 3rd pers. sing. / *apesgarse.*

apestándose turning putrid; pres. part. / *apestarse.*

apestar to infect. reg.

apestarse to turn putrid. reg.

apéstense let them turn putrid; impve. 3rd pers. pl. / *apestarse.*

apéstese let it turn putrid; impve. 3rd pers. sing. / *apestarse.*

apetecer to long for or to crave. irr.

apetezca 1. that I may long for; pres. subj. 1st pers. sing. / *apetecer.* 2. that he (she/it) may long for; pres. subj. 3rd pers. sing. 3. let him (her/it) long for; impve. 3rd pers. sing.

apetezcáis that you (all) may long for; pres. subj. 2nd pers. pl. / *apetecer.*

apetezcamos 1. that we may long for; pres. subj. 1st pers. pl. / *apetecer* 2. let us long for; impve. 1st pers. pl.

apetezcan 1. that they may long for; pres. subj. 3rd pers. pl. / *apetecer.* 2. let them long for; impve. 3rd pers. pl.

apetezcas that you may long for; pres. subj. 2nd pers. sing. / *apetecer.*

apetezco I long for; pres. ind. 1st pers. sing. / *apetecer.*

apiadándose pitying; pres. part. / *apiadarse.*

apiadaos (you all) pity; impve. 2nd pers. pl. / *apiadarse.*

apiadar to inspire pity. reg.

apiadarse to pity. reg.

apiádate (you) pity; impve. 2nd pers. sing. / *apiadarse.*

apiadémonos let us pity; impve. 1st pers. pl. / *apiadarse.*

apiádense let them pity; impve. 3rd pers. pl. / *apiadarse.*

apiádese let him (her/it) pity; impve. 3rd pers. sing. / *apiadarse.*

apicarándose becoming depraved; pres. part. / *apicararse.*

apicaraos (you all) become depraved; impve. 2nd pers. pl. / *apicararse.*

apicararse to become depraved. reg.

apicárate (you) become depraved; impve. 2nd pers. sing. / *apicararse.*

apicarémonos let us become depraved; impve. 1st pers. pl. / *apicararse.*

apicárense let them become depraved; impve. 3rd pers. pl. / *apicararse.*

apicárese let him (her/it) become depraved; impve. 3rd pers. sing. / *apicararse.*

apilándose piling up; pres. part. / *apilarse.*

apilaos (you all) pile up; impve. 2nd pers. pl. / *apilarse.*

apilar to pile up. reg.

apilarse to pile up. reg.

apílate (you) pile up; impve. 2nd pers. sing. / *apilarse.*

apilémonos let us pile up; impve. 1st pers. pl. / *apilarse.*

apílense let them pile up; impve. 3rd pers. pl. / *apilarse.*

apílese let him (her/it) pile up; impve. 3rd pers. sing. / *apilarse.*

apimpollándose sprouting; pres. part. / *apimpollarse.*

apimpollaos (you all) sprout; impve. 2nd pers. pl. / *apimpollarse.*

apimpollarse to sprout. reg.

apimpóllate (you) sprout; impve. 2nd pers. sing. / *apimpollarse.*

apimpollémonos let us sprout; impve. 1st pers. pl. / *apimpollarse.*

apimpóllense let them sprout; impve. 3rd pers. pl. / *apimpollarse.*

apimpóllese let him (her/it) sprout; impve. 3rd pers. sing. / *apimpollarse.*

apiñándose piling up ; pres. part. / *apiñarse.*

apiñaos (you all) pile up; impve. 2nd pers. pl. / *apiñarse.*

apiñar to crowd or to squeeze. reg.

apiñarse to pile up. reg.

apíñate (you) pile up; impve. 2nd pers. sing. / *apiñarse.*

apiñémonos let us pile up; impve. 1st pers. pl. / *apiñarse.*

apíñense let them pile up; impve. 3rd pers. pl. / *apiñarse.*

apíñese let him (her/it) pile up; impve. 3rd pers. sing. / *apiñarse.*

apisonar to tamp or pack down. reg.

aplacándose calming down; pres. part. / *aplacarse.*

aplacaos (you all) calm down; impve. 2nd pers. pl. / *aplacarse.*

aplacar to appease or pacify. irr.

aplacarse to calm down or to subside. irr.

aplácate (you) calm down; impve. 2nd pers. sing. / *aplacarse.*

aplace 1. that I may postpone; pres. subj. 1st pers. sing. / *aplazar.* 2. that he (she/it) may postpone; pres. subj. 3rd pers. sing. 3. let him (her/it) postpone; impve. 3rd pers. sing.

aplacé I postponed; past 1st pers. sing. / *aplazar.*

aplacéis that you (all) may postpone; pres. subj. 2nd pers. pl. / *aplazar.*

aplacemos 1. that we may postpone; pres. subj. 1st pers. pl. / *aplazar* 2. let us postpone; impve. 1st pers. pl.

aplacen 1. that they may postpone; pres. subj. 3rd pers. pl. / *aplazar.* 2. let them postpone; impve. 3rd pers. pl.

aplaces that you may postpone; pres. subj. 2nd pers. sing. / *aplazar.*

aplanándose being flattened; pres. part. / *aplanarse.*

aplanar to level or to flatten. reg.

aplanarse to be flattened or to become discouraged. reg.

aplanchar to iron or press linen. reg.

aplánense let them be flattened; impve. 3rd pers. pl. / *aplanarse.*

aplanese let it be flattened; impve. 3rd pers. sing. / *aplanarse.*

aplaque 1. that I may appease; pres. subj. 1st pers. sing. / *aplacar.* 2. that he (she/it) may appease; pres. subj. 3rd pers. sing. 3. let him (her/it) appease; impve. 3rd pers. sing.

aplaqué I appeased; past 1st pers. sing. / *aplacar.*

aplaquéis that you (all) may appease; pres. subj. 2nd pers. pl. / *aplacar.*

aplaquémonos let us calm down; impve. 1st pers. pl. / *aplacarse.*

aplaquemos 1. that we may appease; pres. subj. 1st pers. pl. / *aplacar* 2. let us appease; impve. 1st pers. pl.

aplaquen 1. that they may appease; pres. subj. 3rd pers. pl. / *aplacar.* 2. let them appease; impve. 3rd pers. pl.

apláquense let them calm down; impve. 3rd pers. pl. / *aplacarse.*

aplaques that you may appease; pres. subj. 2nd pers. sing. / *aplacar.*

apláquese let him (her/it) calm down; impve. 3rd pers. sing. / *aplacarse.*

aplastándose collapsing; pres. part. / *aplastarse.*

aplastaos (you all) collapse; impve. 2nd pers. pl. / *aplastarse.*

aplastar to crush or squash. reg.

aplastarse to collapse. reg.

aplástate (you) collapse; impve. 2nd pers. sing. / *aplastarse.*

aplastémonos let us collapse; impve. 1st pers. pl. / *aplastarse.*

aplástense let them collapse; impve. 3rd pers. pl. / *aplastarse.*

aplástese let him (her/it) collapse; impve. 3rd pers. sing. / *aplastarse.*

aplaudir to applaud. reg.

aplazar to postpone or to call together. irr.

aplicándose applying oneself; pres. part. / *aplicarse.*

aplicaos (you all) apply yourselves; impve. 2nd pers. pl. / *aplicarse.*

aplicar to apply. irr.

aplicarse to apply oneself. irr.

aplícate (you) apply yourself; impve. 2nd pers. sing. / *aplicarse.*

aplique 1. that I may apply; pres. subj. 1st pers. sing. / *aplicar.* 2. that he (she/it) may apply; pres. subj. 3rd pers. sing. 3. let him (her/it) apply; impve. 3rd pers. sing.

apliqué I applied; past 1st pers. sing. / *aplicar.*

apliquéis that you (all) may apply; pres. subj. 2nd pers. pl. / *aplicar.*

apliquémonos let us apply ourselves; impve. 1st pers. pl. / *aplicarse.*

apliquemos 1. that we may apply; pres. subj. 1st pers. pl. / *aplicar* 2. let us apply; impve. 1st pers. pl.

apliquen 1. that they may apply; pres. subj. 3rd pers. pl. / *aplicar.* 2. let them apply; impve. 3rd pers. pl.

aplíquense let them apply themselves; impve. 3rd pers. pl. / *aplicarse.*

apliques that you may apply; pres. subj. 2nd pers. sing. / *aplicar.*

aplíquese let him (her/it) apply himself (herself/itself); impve. 3rd pers. sing. / *aplicarse.*

aplomándose collapsing; pres. part. / *aplomarse.*

aplomaos (you all) collapse; impve. 2nd pers. pl. / *aplomarse.*

aplomar to make plumb. reg.

aplomarse to collapse or to become ashamed. reg.

aplómate (you) collapse; impve. 2nd pers. sing. / *aplomarse.*

aplomémonos let us collapse; impve. 1st pers. pl. / *aplomarse.*

aplómense let them collapse; impve. 3rd pers. pl. / *aplomarse.*

aplómese let him (her/it) collapse; impve. 3rd pers. sing. / *aplomarse.*

apocándose humbling oneself; pres. part. / *apocarse.*

apocaos (you all) humble yourselves; impve. 2nd pers. pl. / *apocarse.*

apocar to lessen. irr.

apocarse to humble oneself. irr.

apócate (you) humble yourself; impve. 2nd pers. sing. / *apocarse.*

apodar to nickname or to ridicule. reg.

apoderándose taking possession; pres. part. / *apoderarse.*

apoderaos (you all) take possession; impve. 2nd pers. pl. / *apoderarse.*

apoderar to empower. reg.

apoderarse to take possession. reg.

apodérate (you) take possession; impve. 2nd pers. sing. / *apoderarse.*

apoderémonos let us take possession; impve. 1st pers. pl. / *apoderarse.*

apodérense let them take possession; impve. 3rd pers. pl. / *apoderarse.*

apodérese let him (her/it) take possession; impve. 3rd pers. sing. / *apoderarse.*

apolillándose becoming moth-eaten; pres. part. / *apolillarse.*

apolillar to eat holes (moths). reg.

apolillarse to become moth-eaten. reg.

apolíllense let them become moth-eaten; impve. 3rd pers. pl. / *apolillarse.*

apolíllese let it become moth-eaten; impve. 3rd pers. sing. / *apolillarse.*

apologice 1. that I may apologize; pres. subj. 1st pers. sing. / *apologizar.* 2. that he (she/it) may apologize; pres. subj. 3rd pers. sing. 3. let him (her/it) apologize; impve. 3rd pers. sing.

apologicé I apologized; past 1st pers. sing. / *apologizar.*

apologicéis that you (all) may apologize; pres. subj. 2nd pers. pl. / *apologizar.*

apologicemos 1. that we may apologize; pres. subj. 1st pers. pl. / *apologizar.* 2. let us apologize; impve. 1st pers. pl.

apologicen 1. that they may apologize; pres. subj. 3rd pers. pl. / *apologizar.* 2. let them apologize; impve. 3rd pers. pl.

apologices that you may apologize; pres. subj. 2nd pers. sing. / *apologizar.*

apologizar to apologize or to defend. irr.

apoltronándose growing lazy; pres. part. / *apoltronarse.*

apoltronaos (you all) grow lazy; impve. 2nd pers. pl. / *apoltronarse.*

apoltronarse to grow lazy or cowardly. reg.

apoltrónate (you) grow lazy; impve. 2nd pers. sing. / *apoltronarse.*

apoltronémonos let us grow lazy; impve. 1st pers. pl. / *apoltronarse.*

apoltrónense let them grow lazy; impve. 3rd pers. pl. / *apoltronarse.*

apoltrónese let him (her/it) grow lazy; impve. 3rd pers. sing. / *apoltronarse.*

apoque 1. that I may lessen; pres. subj. 1st pers. sing. / *apocar.* 2. that he (she/it) may lessen; pres. subj. 3rd pers. sing. 3. let him (her/it) lessen; impve. 3rd pers. sing.

apoqué I lessened; past 1st pers. sing. / *apocar.*

apoquéis that you (all) may lessen; pres. subj. 2nd pers. pl. / *apocar.*

apoquémonos let us humble ourselves; impve. 1st pers. pl. / *apocarse.*

apoquemos 1. that we may lessen; pres. subj. 1st pers. pl. / *apocar* 2. let us lessen; impve. 1st pers. pl.

apoquen 1. that they may lessen; pres. subj. 3rd pers. pl. / *apocar.* 2. let them lessen; impve. 3rd pers. pl.

apóquense let them humble themselves; impve. 3rd pers. pl. / *apocarse.*

apoques that you may lessen; pres. subj. 2nd pers. sing. / *apocar.*

apóquese let him (her/it) humble himself (herself/itself); impve. 3rd pers. sing. / *apocarse.*

aporrándose becoming urgent; pres. part. / *aporrarse.*

aporraos (you all) become urgent; impve. 2nd pers. pl. / *aporrarse.*

aporrar to stand tongue-tied. reg.

aporrarse to become urgent. reg.

apórrate (you) become urgent; impve. 2nd pers. sing. / *aporrarse.*

aporreándose studying hard; pres. part. / *aporrearse.*

aporreaos (you all) study hard; impve. 2nd pers. pl. / *aporrearse.*

aporrear to beat. reg.

aporrearse to study hard. reg.

aporréate (you) study hard; impve. 2nd pers. sing. / *aporrearse.*

aporreémonos let us study hard; impve. 1st pers. pl. / *aporrearse.*

aporréense let them study hard; impve. 3rd pers. pl. / *aporrearse.*

aporréese let him (her/it) study hard; impve. 3rd pers. sing. / *aporrearse.*

aporrémonos let us become urgent; impve. 1st pers. pl. / *aporrarse.*

apórrense let them become urgent; impve. 3rd pers. pl. / *aporrarse.*

apórrese let him (her/it) become urgent; impve. 3rd pers. sing. / *aporrarse.*

aportándose appearing; pres. part. / *aportarse.*

aportaos (you all) appear; impve. 2nd pers. pl. / *aportarse.*

aportar to bring or to arrive in port. reg.

aportarse to appear or to approach. reg.

apórtate (you) appear; impve. 2nd pers. sing. / *aportarse.*

aportémonos let us appear; impve. 1st pers. pl. / *aportarse.*

apórtense let them appear; impve. 3rd pers. pl. / *aportarse.*

apórtese let him (her/it) appear; impve. 3rd pers. sing. / *aportarse.*

aportillar to open a hole in or to break up. reg.

aposentándose lodging; pres. part. / *aposentarse.*

aposentaos (you all) lodge; impve. 2nd pers. pl. / *aposentarse.*

aposentar to lodge. reg.

aposentarse to lodge. reg.

aposéntate (you) lodge; impve. 2nd pers. sing. / *aposentarse.*

aposentémonos let us lodge; impve. 1st pers. pl. / *aposentarse.*

aposéntense let them lodge; impve. 3rd pers. pl. / *aposentarse.*

aposéntese let him (her/it) lodge; impve. 3rd pers. sing. / *aposentarse.*

apostándose stationing oneself; pres. part. / *apostarse.*

apostaos (you all) station yourselves; impve. 2nd pers. pl. / *apostarse.*

apostar to bet. irr.

apostarse to station oneself. irr.

apostatar to apostatize. reg.

apostémonos let us station; impve. 1st pers. pl. / *apostarse.*

apostillar to make notes in the margin. reg.

apostrofar to apostrophize or to insult. reg.

apoyándose leaning upon; pres. part. / *apoyarse.*

apoyaos (you all) lean upon; impve. 2nd pers. pl. / *apoyarse.*

apoyar to lean or to rest. reg.

apoyarse to lean upon. reg.

apóyate (you) lean upon; impve. 2nd pers. sing. / *apoyarse.*

apoyémonos let us lean upon; impve. 1st pers. pl. / *apoyarse.*

apóyense let them lean upon; impve. 3rd pers. pl. / *apoyarse.*

apóyese let him (her/it) lean upon; impve. 3rd pers. sing. / *apoyarse.*

apreciar to appreciate or to value. reg.

aprehender to apprehend. reg.

apremiar to press or to compel. reg.

aprender to learn. reg.

aprensar to press or to calendar. reg.

apresar to seize or to grab. reg.

aprestándose getting ready; pres. part. / *aprestarse.*

aprestaos (you all) get ready; impve. 2nd pers. pl. / *aprestarse.*

aprestar to prepare. reg.

aprestarse to get ready. reg.

apréstate (you) get ready; impve. 2nd pers. sing. / *aprestarse.*

aprestémonos let us get ready; impve. 1st pers. pl. / *aprestarse.*

apréstense let them get ready; impve. 3rd pers. pl. / *aprestarse.*

apréstese let him (her/it) get ready; impve. 3rd pers. sing. / *aprestarse.*

apresurándose making haste; pres. part. / *apresurarse.*

apresuraos (you all) make haste; impve. 2nd pers. pl. / *apresurarse.*

apresurar to hurry. reg.

apresurarse to make haste. reg.

apresúrate (you) make haste; impve. 2nd pers. sing. / *apresurarse.*

apresurémonos let us make haste; impve. 1st pers. pl. / *apresurarse.*

apresúrense let them make haste; impve. 3rd pers. pl. / *apresurarse.*

apresúrese let him (her/it) make haste; impve. 3rd pers. sing. / *apresurarse.*

apretándose overeating; pres. part. / *apretarse.*

apretaos (you all) overeat; impve. 2nd pers. pl. / *apretarse.*

apretar to tighten or to pinch. irr.

apretarse to overeat. irr.

apretémonos let us overeat; impve. 1st pers. pl. / *apretarse.*

apretujar to squeeze or to press tight. reg.

aprieta 1. he (she/it) tightens; pres. ind. 3rd pers. sing. / *apretar.* 2. (you) tighten; impve. 2nd pers. sing.

aprietan they tighten; pres. ind. 3rd pers. pl. / *apretar.*

aprietas you tighten; pres. ind. 2nd pers. sing. / *apretar.*

apriétate (you) overeat; impve. 2nd pers. sing. / *apretarse.*

apriete 1. that I may tighten; pres. subj. 1st pers. sing. / *apretar.* 2. that he (she/it) may tighten; pres. subj. 3rd pers. sing. 3. let him (her/it) tighten; impve. 3rd pers. sing.

aprieten 1. that they may tighten; pres. subj. 3rd pers. pl. / *apretar.* 2. let them tighten; impve. 3rd pers. pl.

apriétense let them overeat; impve. 3rd pers. pl. / *apretarse.*

aprietes that you may tighten; pres. subj. 2nd pers. sing. / *apretar.*

apriétese let him (her/it) overeat; impve. 3rd pers. sing. / *apretarse.*

aprieto I tighten; pres. ind. 1st pers. sing. / *apretar.*

aprisionar to imprison or to tie. reg.

aprobar to approve or to pass an examination. irr.

aprontar to get ready or to expedite. reg.

apropiándose taking possession of; pres. part. / *apropiarse.*

apropiaos (you all) take possession of; impve. 2nd pers. pl. / *apropiarse.*

apropiar to adapt or to fit. reg.

apropiarse to take possession of. reg.

apropíate (you) take possession of; impve. 2nd pers. sing. / *apropiarse.*

apropiémonos let us take possession of; impve. 1st pers. pl. / *apropiarse.*

apropíense let them take possession of; impve. 3rd pers. pl. / *apropiarse.*

apropíese let him (her/it) take possession of; impve. 3rd pers. sing. / *apropiarse.*

apropincuándose approaching; pres. part. / *apropincuarse.*

apropincuaos (you all) approach; impve. 2nd pers. pl. / *apropincuarse.*

apropincuarse to approach. reg.

apropincúate (you) approach; impve. 2nd pers. sing. / *apropincuarse.*

apropincuémonos let us approach; impve. 1st pers. pl. / *apropincuarse.*

apropincúense let them approach; impve. 3rd pers. pl. / *apropincuarse.*

apropincúese let him (her/it) approach; impve. 3rd pers. sing. / *apropincuarse.*

aprovechándose taking advantage; pres. part. / *aprovecharse.*

aprovechaos (you all) take advantage; impve. 2nd pers. pl. / *aprovecharse.*

aprovechar to profit or to make good use of. reg.

aprovecharse to take advantage. reg.

aprovéchate (you) take advantage; impve. 2nd pers. sing. / *aprovecharse.*

aprovechémonos let us take advantage; impve. 1st pers. pl. / *aprovecharse.*

aprovéchense let them take advantage; impve. 3rd pers. pl. / *aprovecharse.*

aprovéchese let him (her/it) take advantage; impve. 3rd pers. sing. / *aprovecharse.*

aprovisionar to supply or provide. reg.

aproximándose approaching; pres. part. / *aproximarse.*

aproximaos (you all) approach; impve. 2nd pers. pl. / *aproximarse.*

aproximar to approximate or to move near. reg.

aproximarse to approach or to get near. reg.

aproxímate (you) approach; impve. 2nd pers. sing. / *aproximarse.*

aproximémonos let us approach; impve. 1st pers. pl. / *aproximarse.*

aproxímense let them approach; impve. 3rd pers. pl. / *aproximarse.*

aproxímese let him (her/it) approach; impve. 3rd pers. sing. / *aproximarse.*

aprueba 1. he (she/it) approves; pres. ind. 3rd pers. sing. / *aprobar.* 2. (you) approve; impve. 2nd pers. sing.

aprueban they approve; pres. ind. 3rd pers. pl. / *aprobar.*

apruebas you approve; pres. ind. 2nd pers. sing. / *aprobar.*

apruebe 1. that I may approve; pres. subj. 1st pers. sing. / *aprobar.* 2. that he (she/it) may approve; pres. subj. 3rd pers. sing. 3. let him (her/it) approve; impve. 3rd pers. sing.

aprueben 1. that they may approve; pres. subj. 3rd pers. pl. / *aprobar.* 2. let them approve; impve. 3rd pers. pl.

apruebes that you may approve; pres. subj. 2nd pers. sing. / *aprobar.*

apruebo I approve; pres. ind. 1st pers. sing. / *aprobar.*

apuesta 1. he (she/it) bets; pres. ind. 3rd pers. sing. / *apostar.* 2. (you) bet; impve. 2nd pers. sing.

apuestan they bet; pres. ind. 3rd pers. pl. / *apostar.*

apuestas you bet; pres. ind. 2nd pers. sing. / *apostar.*

apuéstate (you) station yourself; impve. 2nd pers. sing. / *apostarse.*

apueste 1. that I may bet; pres. subj. 1st pers. sing. / *apostar.* 2. that he (she/it) may bet; pres. subj. 3rd pers. sing. 3. let him (her/it) bet; impve. 3rd pers. sing.

apuesten 1. that they may bet; pres. subj. 3rd pers. pl. / *apostar.* 2. let them bet; impve. 3rd pers. pl.

apuéstense let them station themselves; impve. 3rd pers. pl. / *apostarse.*

apuestes that you may bet; pres. subj. 2nd pers. sing. / *apostar.*

apuéstese let him (her/it) station himself (herself/itself); impve. 3rd pers. sing. / *apostarse.*

apuesto I bet; pres. ind. 1st pers. sing. / *apostar.*

apuntalar to prop or give support. reg.

apuntándose beginning to turn sour; pres. part. / *apuntarse.*

apuntar to aim or to point. reg.

apuntarse to begin to turn sour or to enroll. reg.

apúntense let them begin to turn sour; impve. 3rd pers. pl. / *apuntarse.*

apúntese let it begin to turn sour; impve. 3rd pers. sing. / *apuntarse.*

apuñalar to stab. reg.

apuñear to punch. reg.

apuñetear to punch. reg.

apurándose hurrying up; pres. part. / *apurarse.*

apuraos (you all) hurry up; impve. 2nd pers. pl. / *apurarse.*

apurar to hurry or to annoy. reg.

apurarse to hurry up or to get worried. reg.

apúrate (you) hurry up; impve. 2nd pers. sing. / *apurarse.*

apurémonos let us hurry up; impve. 1st pers. pl. / *apurarse.*

apúrense let them hurry up; impve. 3rd pers. pl. / *apurarse.*

apúrese let him (her/it) hurry up; impve. 3rd pers. sing. / *apurarse.*

aquejar to grieve or to ail. reg.

aquerenciándose becoming fond; pres. part. / *aquerenciarse.*

aquerenciaos (you all) become fond; impve. 2nd pers. pl. / *aquerenciarse.*

aquerenciarse to become fond. reg.

aquerencíate (you) become fond ; impve. 2nd pers. sing. / *aquerenciarse.*

aquerenciémonos let us become fond ; impve. 1st pers. pl. / *aquerenciarse.*

aquerencíense let them become fond; impve. 3rd pers. pl. / *aquerenciarse.*

aquerencíese let him (her/it) become fond ; impve. 3rd pers. sing. / *aquerenciarse.*

aquietándose calming down; pres. part. / *aquietarse.*

aquietaos (you all) calm down; impve. 2nd pers. pl. / *aquietarse.*

aquietar to quiet or to hush. reg.

aquietarse to calm down. reg.

aquiétate (you) calm down; impve. 2nd pers. sing. / *aquietarse.*

aquietémonos let us calm down; impve. 1st pers. pl. / *aquietarse.*

aquiétense let them calm down; impve. 3rd pers. pl. / *aquietarse.*

aquiétese let him (her/it) calm down; impve. 3rd pers. sing. / *aquietarse.*

aquilatar to assay or to appraise. reg.

aquistar to acquire. reg.

arabice 1. that I may arabize; pres. subj. 1st pers. sing. / *arabizar.* 2. that he (she/it) may arabize; pres. subj. 3rd pers. sing. 3. let him (her/it) arabize; impve. 3rd pers. sing.

arabicé I arabized; past 1st pers. sing. / *arabizar.*

arabicéis that you (all) may arabize; pres. subj. 2nd pers. pl. / *arabizar.*

arabicémonos let us go arab; impve. 1st pers. pl. / *arabizarse.*

arabicemos 1. that we may arabize; pres. subj. 1st pers. pl. / *arabizar.* 2. let us arabize; impve. 1st pers. pl.

arabicen 1. that they may arabize; pres. subj. 3rd pers. pl. / *arabizar.* 2. let them arabize; impve. 3rd pers. pl.

arabícense let them go arab; impve. 3rd pers. pl. / *arabizarse.*

arabices that you may arabize; pres. subj. 2nd pers. sing. / *arabizar.*

arabícese let him (her/it) go arab; impve. 3rd pers. sing. / *arabizarse.*

arabizándose going arab; pres. part. / *arabizarse.*

arabizaos (you all) go arab; impve. 2nd pers. pl. / *arabizarse.*

arabizar to arabize. irr.

arabizarse to go arab. irr.

arabízate (you) go arab; impve. 2nd pers. sing. / *arabizarse.*

arañar to scratch. reg.

arar to plow or to till. reg.

arbitrándose managing well; pres. part. / *arbitrarse.*

arbitraos (you all) manage well; impve. 2nd pers. pl. / *arbitrarse.*

arbitrar to arbitrate. reg.

arbitrarse to manage well. reg.

arbítrate (you) manage well; impve. 2nd pers. sing. / *arbitrarse.*

arbitrémonos let us manage well; impve. 1st pers. pl. / *arbitrarse.*

arbítrense let them manage well; impve. 3rd pers. pl. / *arbitrarse.*

arbítrese let him (her/it) manage well; impve. 3rd pers. sing. / *arbitrarse.*

arbolar to hoist. reg.

archivar to file. reg.

arder to burn or to rage. reg.

arengar to harangue. irr.

arengue 1. that I may harangue; pres. subj. 1st pers. sing. / *arengar.* 2. that he (she/it) may harangue; pres. subj. 3rd pers. sing. 3. let him (her/it) harangue; impve. 3rd pers. sing.

arengué I harangued; past 1st pers. sing. / *arengar.*

arenguéis that you (all) may harangue; pres. subj. 2nd pers. pl. / *arengar.*

arenguemos 1. that we may harangue; pres. subj. 1st pers. pl. / *arengar.* 2. let us harangue; impve. 1st pers. pl.

arenguen 1. that they may harangue; pres. subj. 3rd pers. pl. / *arengar.* 2. let them harangue; impve. 3rd pers. pl.

arengues that you may harangue; pres. subj. 2nd pers. sing. / *arengar.*

argamasar to cement or plaster. reg.

argentar to silver plate or to polish. reg.

argüir to argue or to infer. irr.

argumentar to argue or to deduce. reg.

arguya 1. that I may argue; pres. subj. 1st pers. sing. / *argüir.* 2. that he (she/it) may argue; pres. subj. 3rd pers. sing. 3. let him (her/it) argue; impve. 3rd pers. sing.

arguyáis that you (all) may argue; pres. subj. 2nd pers. pl. / *argüir.*

arguyamos 1. that we may argue; pres. subj. 1st pers. pl. / *argüir.* 2. let us argue; impve. 1st pers. pl.

arguyan 1. that they may argue; pres. subj. 3rd pers. pl. / *argüir.* 2. let them argue; impve. 3rd pers. pl.

arguyas that you may argue; pres. subj. 2nd pers. sing. / *argüir.*

arguye 1. he (she/it) argues; pres. ind. 3rd pers. sing. / *argüir.* 2. (you) argue; impve. 2nd pers. sing.

arguyen they argue; pres. ind. 3rd pers. pl. / *argüir.*

arguyendo arguing; pres. part. / *argüir.*

arguyera 1. that I might argue; imp. subj. 1st pers. sing. / *argüir.* 2. that he (she/it) might argue; imp. subj. 3rd pers. sing.

arguyerais that you (all) might argue; imp. subj. 2nd pers pl. / *argüir.*

arguyéramos that we might argue; imp. subj. 1st pers. pl. / *argüir.*

arguyeran that they might argue; imp. subj. 3rd pers. pl. / *argüir.*

arguyeras that you might argue; imp. subj. 2nd pers. sing. / *argüir*.

arguyeron they argued; past 3rd pers. pl. / *argüir*.

arguyes you argue; pres. ind. 2nd pers. sing. / *argüir*.

arguyese 1. that I might argue; imp. subj. 1st pers. sing. / *argüir*. 2. that he (she/it) might argue; imp. subj. 3rd pers. sing.

arguyeseis that you (all) might argue; imp. subj. 2nd pers pl. / *argüir*.

arguyésemos that we might argue; imp. subj. 1st pers. pl. / *argüir*.

arguyesen that they might argue; imp. subj. 3rd pers. pl. / *argüir*.

arguyeses that you might argue; imp. subj. 2nd pers. sing. / *argüir*.

arguyo I argue; pres. ind. 1st pers. sing. / *argüir*.

arguyó he (she/it) argued; past 3rd pers. sing. / *argüir*.

armándose arming oneself; pres. part. / *armarse*.

armaos (you all) arm yourselves; impve. 2nd pers. pl. / *armarse*.

armar to arm or to assemble. reg.

armarse to arm oneself or to be stubborn. reg.

ármate (you) arm yourself; impve. 2nd pers. sing. / *armarse*.

armémonos let us arm ourselves; impve. 1st pers. pl. / *armarse*.

ármense let them arm themselves; impve. 3rd pers. pl. / *armarse*.

ármese let him (her/it) arm himself (herself/itself); impve. 3rd pers. sing. / *armarse*.

armonice 1. that I may harmonize; pres. subj. 1st pers. sing. / *armonizar*. 2. that he (she/it) may harmonize; pres. subj. 3rd pers. sing. 3. let him (her/it) harmonize; impve. 3rd pers. sing.

armonicé I harmonized; past 1st pers. sing. / *armonizar*.

armonicéis that you (all) may harmonize; pres. subj. 2nd pers. pl. / *armonizar*.

armonicemos 1. that we may harmonize; pres. subj. 1st pers. pl. / *armonizar*. 2. let us harmonize; impve. 1st pers. pl.

armonicen 1. that they may harmonize; pres. subj. 3rd pers. pl. / *armonizar*. 2. let them harmonize; impve. 3rd pers. pl.

armonices that you may harmonize; pres. subj. 2nd pers. sing. / *armonizar*.

armonizar to harmonize. irr.

aromatice 1. that I may perfume; pres. subj. 1st pers. sing. / *aromatizar*. 2. that he (she/it) may perfume; pres. subj. 3rd pers. sing. 3. let him (her/it) perfume; impve. 3rd pers. sing.

aromaticé I perfumed; past 1st pers. sing. / *aromatizar*.

aromaticéis that you (all) may perfume; pres. subj. 2nd pers. pl. / *aromatizar*.

aromaticemos 1. that we may perfume; pres. subj. 1st pers. pl. / *aromatizar*. 2. let us perfume; impve. 1st pers. pl.

aromaticen 1. that they may perfume; pres. subj. 3rd pers. pl. / *aromatizar*. 2. let them perfume; impve. 3rd pers. pl.

aromatices that you may perfume; pres. subj. 2nd pers. sing. / *aromatizar*.

aromatizar to perfume. irr.

arpar to rend or to claw. reg.

arponar to harpoon. reg.

arponear to harpoon. reg.

arquear to arch or to bow or to retch. reg.

arracimándose forming in a cluster; pres. part. / *arracimarse*.

arracimaos (you all) form in a cluster; impve. 2nd pers. pl. / *arracimarse*.

arracimar to cluster. reg.

arracimarse to form in a cluster. reg.

arracímate (you) form in a cluster; impve. 2nd pers. sing. / *arracimarse*.

arracimémonos let us form in a cluster; impve. 1st pers. pl. / *arracimarse*.

arracímense let them form in a cluster; impve. 3rd pers. pl. / *arracimarse*.

arracímese let him (her/it) form in a cluster; impve. 3rd pers. sing. / *arracimarse*.

arraigándose becoming establshed; pres. part. / *arraigarse*.

arraigaos (you all) become established; impve. 2nd pers. pl. / *arraigarse*.

arraigar to take root. irr.

arraigarse to become established. irr.

arraígate (you) become established; impve. 2nd pers. sing. / *arraigarse*.

arraigue 1. that I may take root; pres. subj. 1st pers. sing. / *arraigar*. 2. that he (she/it) may take root; pres. subj. 3rd pers. sing. 3. let him (her/it) take root; impve. 3rd pers. sing.

arraigué I took root; past 1st pers. sing. / *arraigar*.

arraiguéis that you (all) may take root; pres. subj. 2nd pers. pl. / *arraigar*.

arraiguémonos let us become established; impve. 1st pers. pl. / *arraigarse*.

arraiguemos 1. that we may take root; pres. subj. 1st pers. pl. / *arraigar*. 2. let us take root; impve. 1st pers. pl.

arraiguen 1. that they may take root; pres. subj. 3rd pers. pl. / *arraigar*. 2. let them take root; impve. 3rd pers. pl.

arraíguense let them become established; impve. 3rd pers. pl. / *arraigarse*.

arraigues that you may take root; pres. subj. 2nd pers. sing. / *arraigar*.

arraíguese let him (her/it) become established; impve. 3rd pers. sing. / *arraigarse*.

arrancar to uproot or to start out. irr.

arranchar to snatch or to cohabit. reg.

arranque 1. that I may uproot; pres. subj. 1st pers. sing. / *arrancar*. 2. that he (she/it) may uproot; pres. subj. 3rd pers. sing. 3. let him (her/it) uproot; impve. 3rd pers. sing.

arranqué I uprooted; past 1st pers. sing. / *arrancar*.

arranquéis that you (all) may uproot; pres. subj. 2nd pers. pl. / *arrancar*.

arranquemos 1. that we may uproot; pres. subj. 1st pers. pl. / *arrancar* 2. let us uproot; impve. 1st pers. pl.

arranquen 1. that they may uproot; pres. subj. 3rd pers. pl. / *arrancar*. 2. let them uproot; impve. 3rd pers. pl.

arranques that you may uproot; pres. subj. 2nd pers. sing. / *arrancar*.

arrasándose clearing up (of the sky); pres. part. / *arrasarse*.

arrasar to demolish or to fill to the brim. reg.

arrasarse to clear up (of the sky). reg.

arrásese let it clear up (of the sky); impve. 3rd pers. sing. / *arrasarse*.

arrastrándose crawling; pres. part. / *arrastrarse*.

arrastraos (you all) crawl; impve. 2nd pers. pl. / *arrastrarse*.

arrastrar to drag or to haul. reg.

arrastrarse to creep or crawl. reg.

arraátrate (you) crawl; impve. 2nd pers. sing. / *arrastrarse*.

arrastrémonos let us crawl; impve. 1st pers. pl. / *arrastrarse*.

arraétrense let them crawl; impve. 3rd pers. pl. / *arrastrarse*.

arraétrese let him (her/it) crawl; impve. 3rd pers. sing. / *arrastrarse*.

arrear to drive (animals) or to steal livestock. reg.

arrebatándose being carried away emotionally; pres. part. / *arrebatarse*.

arrebataos (you all) be carried away emotionally; impve. 2nd pers. pl. / *arrebatarse*.

arrebatar to carry off. reg.

arrebatarse to be carried away emotionally. reg.

arrebátate (you) be carried away emotionally; impve. 2nd pers. sing. / *arrebatarse*.

arrebatémonos let us be carried away emotionally; impve. 1st pers. pl. / *arrebatarse*.

arrebátense let them be carried away emotionally; impve. 3rd pers. pl. / *arrebatarse*.

arrebátese let him (her/it) be carried away emotionally; impve. 3rd pers. sing. / *arrebatarse*.

arrebolándose turning red; pres. part. / *arrebolarse*.

arrebolaos (you all) turn red; impve. 2nd pers. pl. / *arrebolarse*.

arrebolar to redden. reg.

arrebolarse to turn red. reg.

arrebólate (you) turn red; impve. 2nd pers. sing. / *arrebolarse*.

arrebolémonos let us turn red; impve. 1st pers. pl. / *arrebolarse*.

arrebólense let them turn red; impve. 3rd pers. pl. / *arrebolarse*.

arrebólese let him (her/it) turn red; impve. 3rd pers. sing. / *arrebolarse*.

arrebujándose covering up oneself well; pres. part. / *arrebujarse*.

arrebujaos (you all) cover up yourselves well; impve. 2nd pers. pl. / *arrebujarse*.

arrebujar to huddle or bundle up. reg.

arrebujarse to cover oneself up well. reg.

arrebújate (you) cover up yourself well; impve. 2nd pers. sing. / *arrebujarse*.

arrebujémonos let us cover up ourselves well; impve. 1st pers. pl. / *arrebujarse*.

arrebújense let them cover up themselves well; impve. 3rd pers. pl. / *arrebujarse*.

arrebújese let him (her/it) cover up himself (herself/itself) well; impve. 3rd pers. sing. / *arrebujarse*.

arreciándose growing stronger; pres. part. / *arreciarse*.

arreciaos (you all) grow stronger; impve. 2nd pers. pl. / *arreciarse*.

arreciar to increase in intensity. reg.

arreciarse to grow stronger. reg.

arrecíate (you) grow stronger; impve. 2nd pers. sing. / *arreciarse*.

arreciémonos let us grow stronger; impve. 1st pers. pl. / *arreciarse*.

arreciéndose becoming numb; pres. part. / *arrecirse*.

arrecíense let them grow stronger; impve. 3rd pers. pl. / *arreciarse*.

arrecíese let him (her/it) grow stronger; impve. 3rd pers. sing. / *arreciarse*.

arrecíos (you all) become numb; impve. 2nd pers. pl. / *arrecirse*.

arrecirse to become numb. irr. verb occurs only in those forms where the i is present in the verb ending.

arredrándose being scared; pres. part. / *arredrarse*.

arredraos (you all) be scared; impve. 2nd pers. pl. / *arredrarse*.

arredrar to drive back or to frighten. reg.

arredrarse to be or to get scared. reg.

arrédrate (you) be scared; impve. 2nd pers. sing. / *arredrarse*.

arredrémonos let us be scared; impve. 1st pers. pl. / *arredrarse*.

arrédrense let them be scared; impve. 3rd pers. pl. / *arredrarse*.

arrédrese let him (her/it) be scared; impve. 3rd pers. sing. / *arredrarse*.

arregace 1. that I may tuck up; pres. subj. 1st pers. sing. / *arregazar*. 2. that he (she/it) may tuck up; pres. subj. 3rd pers. sing. 3. let him (her/it) tuck up; impve. 3rd pers. sing.

arregacé I tucked up; past 1st pers. sing. / *arregazar*.

arregacéis that you (all) may tuck up; pres. subj. 2nd pers. pl. / *arregazar*.

arregacemos 1. that we may tuck up; pres. subj. 1st pers. pl. / *arregazar* 2. let us tuck up; impve. 1st pers. pl.

arregacen 1. that they may tuck up; pres. subj. 3rd pers. pl. / *arregazar*. 2. let them tuck up; impve. 3rd pers. pl.

arregaces that you may tuck up; pres. subj. 2nd pers. sing. / *arregazar*.

arregazar to tuck up. irr.

arreglándose settling differences; pres. part. / *arreglarse.*

arreglaos let us settle differences; impve. 1st pers. pl. / *arreglarse.*

arreglar to regulate or to adjust. reg.

arreglarse to settle differences. reg.

arréglate (you) settle differences; impve. 2nd pers. sing. / *arreglarse.*

arreglémonos let us settle differences; impve. 1st pers. pl. / *arreglarse.*

arréglense let them settle differences; impve. 3rd pers. pl. / *arreglarse.*

arréglese let him (her/it) settle differences; impve. 3rd pers. sing. / *arreglarse.*

arrellanándose lounging; pres. part. / *arrellanarse.*

arrellanaos (you all) lounge; impve. 2nd pers. pl. / *arrellanarse.*

arrellanarse to lounge or stretch out. reg.

arrellánate (you) lounge; impve. 2nd pers. sing. / *arrellanarse.*

arrellanémonos let us lounge; impve. 1st pers. pl. / *arrellanarse.*

arrellánense let them lounge; impve. 3rd pers. pl. / *arrellanarse.*

arrellánese let him (her/it) lounge; impve. 3rd pers. sing. / *arrellanarse.*

arremangándose resolving firmly; pres. part. / *arremangarse.*

arremangaos (you all) resolve firmly; impve. 2nd pers. pl. / *arremangarse.*

arremangar to tuck up or turn up. irr.

arremangarse to resolve firmly. irr.

arremángate (you) resolve firmly; impve. 2nd pers. sing. / *arremangarse.*

arremangue 1. that I may tuck up; pres. subj. 1st pers. sing. / *arremangar.* 2. that he (she/it) may tuck up; pres. subj. 3rd pers. sing. 3. let him (her/it) tuck up; impve. 3rd pers. sing.

arremangué I tucked up; past 1st pers. sing. / *arremangar.*

arremanguéis that you (all) may tuck up; pres. subj. 2nd pers. pl. / *arremangar.*

arremanguémonos let us resolve firmly; impve. 1st pers. pl. / *arremangarse.*

arremanguemos 1. that we may tuck up; pres. subj. 1st pers. pl. / *arremangar.* 2. let us tuck up; impve. 1st pers. pl.

arremanguen 1. that they may tuck up; pres. subj. 3rd pers. pl. / *arremangar.* 2. let them tuck up; impve. 3rd pers. pl.

arremánguense let them resolve firmly; impve. 3rd pers. pl. / *arremangarse.*

arremangues that you may tuck up; pres. subj. 2nd pers. sing. / *arremangar.*

arremánguese let him (her/it) resolve firmly; impve. 3rd pers. sing. / *arremangarse.*

arremeter to attack. reg.

arremolinándose whirling; pres. part. / *arremolinarse.*

arremolinaos (you all) whirl; impve. 2nd pers. pl. / *arremolinarse.*

arremolinarse to whirl. reg.

arremolínate (you) whirl; impve. 2nd pers. sing. / *arremolinarse.*

arremolinémonos let us whirl; impve. 1st pers. pl. / *arremolinarse.*

arremolínense let them whirl; impve. 3rd pers. pl. / *arremolinarse.*

arremolínese let him (her/it) whirl; impve. 3rd pers. sing. / *arremolinarse.*

arrendar to rent or to bridle or to mimic. irr.

arrepentí I repented; past 1st pers. sing. / *arrepentirse.*

arrepentíos (you all) repent; impve. 2nd pers. pl. / *arrepentirse.*

arrepentirse to repent. irr.

arrepentiste you repented; past 2nd pers. sing. / *arrepentirse.*

arrepienta 1. that I may repent; pres. subj. 1st pers. sing. / *arrepentirse.* 2. that he (she/it) may repent; pres. subj. 3rd pers. sing.

arrepientan that they may repent; pres. subj. 3rd pers. pl. / *arrepentirse.*

arrepiéntanse let them repent; impve. 3rd pers. pl. / *arrepentirse.*

arrepientas that you may repent; pres. subj. 2nd pers. sing. / *arrepentirse.*

arrepiéntase let him (her/it) repent; impve. 3rd pers. sing. / *arrepentirse.*

arrepiente he (she/it) repents; pres. ind. 3rd pers. sing. / *arrepentirse.*

arrepienten they repent; pres. ind. 3rd pers. pl. / *arrepentirse.*

arrepientes you repent; pres.ind. 2nd pers. sing. / *arrepentirse.*

arrepiéntete (you) repent; impve. 2nd pers. sing. / *arrepentirse.*

arrepiento I repent; pres. ind. 1st pers. sing. / *arrepentirse.*

arrepintáis that you (all) may repent; pres. subj. 2nd pers. pl. / *arrepentirse.*

arrepintámonos let us repent; impve. 1st pers. pl. / *arrepentirse.*

arrepintamos that we may repent; pres. subj. 1st pers. pl. / *arrepentirse.*

arrepintiéndose repenting; pres. part. / *arrepentirse*

arrepintiera 1. that I might repent; imp. subj. 1st pers. sing. / *arrepentirse.* 2. that he (she/it) might repent; imp. subj. 3rd pers. sing.

arrepintierais that you (all) might repent; imp. subj. 2nd pers pl. / *arrepentirse.*

arrepintiéramos that we might repent; imp. subj. 1st pers. pl. / *arrepentirse.*

arrepintieran that they might repent; imp. subj. 3rd pers. pl. / *arrepentirse.*

arrepintieras that you might repent; imp. subj. 2nd pers. sing. / *arrpentirse.*

arrepintieron they repented; past 3rd pers. pl. / *arrepentirse.*

arrepintiese 1. that I might repent; imp. subj. 1st pers. sing. / *arrepentirse.* 2. that he (she/it) might repent; imp. subj. 3rd pers. sing.

arrepintieseis that you (all) might repent; imp. subj. 2nd pers pl. / *arrepentirse.*

arrepintiésemos that we might repent; imp. subj. 1st pers. pl. / *arrepentirse.*

arrepintiesen that they might repent; imp. subj. 3rd pers. pl. / *arrepentirse.*

arrepintieses that you might repent; imp. subj. 2nd pers. sing. / *arrepentirse.*

arrepintió he (she/it) repented / past 3rd pers. sing. / *arrepentirse.*

arrestándose daring; pres. part. / *arrestarse.*

arrestaos (you all) dare; impve. 2nd pers. pl. / *arrestarse.*

arrestar to arrest or to imprison. reg.

arrestarse to dare or venture. reg.

arréstate (you) dare; impve. 2nd pers. sing. / *arrestarse.*

arrestémonos let us dare; impve. 1st pers. pl. / *arrestarse.*

arréstense let them dare; impve. 3rd pers. pl. / *arrestarse.*

arréstese let him (her/it) dare; impve. 3rd pers. sing. / *arrestarse.*

arría 1. he (she/it) lowers; pres. ind. 3rd pers. sing. / *arriar.* 2. (you) lower; impve. 2nd pers. sing.

arrían they lower; pres. ind. 3rd pers. pl. / *arriar.*

arriándose waning; pres. part. / *arriarse.*

arriar to lower. irr.

arriarse to wane. irr.

arrías you lower; pres. ind. 2nd pers. sing. / *arriar.*

arribar to arrive. reg.

arríe 1. that I may lower; pres. subj. 1st pers. sing. / *arriar.* 2. that he (she/it) may lower; pres. subj. 3rd pers. sing. 3. let him (her/it) lower; impve. 3rd pers. sing.

arríen 1. that they may lower; pres. subj. 3rd pers. pl. / arriar. 2. *let them lower; impve. 3rd pers. pl.*

arrienda 1. he (she/it) rents; pres. ind. 3rd pers. sing. / *arrendar.* 2. (you) rent; impve. 2nd pers. sing.

arriendan they rent; pres. ind. 3rd pers. pl. / *arrendar.*

arriendas you rent; pres. ind. 2nd pers. sing. / *arrendar.*

arriende 1. that I may rent; pres. subj. 1st pers. sing. / *arrendar.* 2. that he (she/it) may rent; pres. subj. 3rd pers. sing. 3. let him (her/it) rent; impve. 3rd pers. sing.

arrienden 1. that they may rent; pres. subj. 3rd pers. pl. / *arrendar.* 2. let them rent; impve. 3rd pers. pl.

arriendes that you may rent; pres. subj. 2nd pers. sing. / *arrendar.*

arriendo I rent; pres. ind. 1st pers. sing. / *arrendar.*

arríense let them wane; impve. 3rd pers. pl. / *arriarse.*

arríes that you may lower; pres. subj. 2nd pers. sing. / *arriar.*

arríese let it wane; impve. 3rd pers. sing. / *arriarse.*

arriesgándose daring; pres. part. / *arriesgarse.*

arriesgaos (you all) dare; impve. 2nd pers. pl. / *arriesgarse.*

arriesgar to risk. irr.

arriesgarse to dare. irr.

arriésgate (you) dare; impve. 2nd pers. sing. / *arriesgarse.*

arriesgue 1. that I may risk; pres. subj. 1st pers. sing. / *arriesgar.* 2. that he (she/it) may risk; pres. subj. 3rd pers. sing. 3. let him (her/it) risk; impve. 3rd pers. sing.

arriesgué I risked; past 1st pers. sing. / *arriesgar.*

arriesguéis that you (all) may risk; pres. subj. 2nd pers. pl. / *arriesgar.*

arriesguémonos let us dare; impve. 1st pers. pl. / *arriesgarse.*

arriesguemos 1. that we may risk; pres. subj. 1st pers. pl. / *arriesgar* 2. let us risk; impve. 1st pers. pl.

arriesguen 1. that they may risk; pres. subj. 3rd pers. pl. / *arriesgar.* 2. let them risk; impve. 3rd pers. pl.

arriesguense let them dare; impve. 3rd pers. pl. / *arriesgarse.*

arriesgues that you may risk; pres. subj. 2nd pers. sing. / *arriesgar.*

arriésguese let him (her/it) dare; impve. 3rd pers. sing. / *arriesgarse.*

arrimándose leaning on; pres. part. / *arrimarse.*

arrimaos (you all) lean on; impve. 2nd pers. pl. / *arrimarse.*

arrimar to bring close. reg.

arrimarse to lean on. reg.

arrímate (you) lean on; impve. 2nd pers. sing. / *arrimarse.*

arrimémonos let us lean on; impve. 1st pers. pl. / *arrimarse.*

arrímense let them lean on; impve. 3rd pers. pl. / *arrimarse.*

arrímese let him (her/it) lean on; impve. 3rd pers. sing. / *arrimarse.*

arrinconándose retiring; pres. part. / *arrinconarse.*

arrinconaos (you all) retire; impve. 2nd pers. pl. / *arrinconarse.*

arrinconar to corner. reg.

arrinconarse to retire. reg.

arrincónate (you) retire; impve. 2nd pers. sing. / *arrinconarse.*

arrinconémonos let us retire; impve. 1st pers. pl. / *arrinconarse.*

arrincónense let them retire; impve. 3rd pers. pl. / *arrinconarse.*

arrincónese let him (her/it) retire; impve. 3rd pers. sing. / *arrinconarse.*

arrío I lower; pres. ind. 1st pers. sing. / *arriar.*

arriscándose becoming angry; pres. part. / *arriscarse.*

arriscaos (you all) become angry; impve. 2nd pers. pl. / *arriscarse.*

arriscar to risk or to venture. irr.

arriscarse to become angry or to flare up. irr.

arríscate (you) become angry; impve. 2nd pers. sing. / *arriscarse.*

arrisque 1. that I may risk; pres. subj. 1st pers. sing. / *arriscar.* 2. that he (she/it) may risk; pres. subj. 3rd pers. sing. 3. let him (her/it) risk; impve. 3rd pers. sing.

arrisqué I risked; past 1st pers. sing. / *arriscar.*

arrisquéis that you (all) may risk; pres. subj. 2nd pers. pl. / *arriscar.*

arrisquémonos let us become angry; impve. 1st pers. pl. / *arriscarse.*

arrisquemos 1. that we may risk; pres. subj. 1st pers. pl. / *arriscar* 2. let us risk; impve. 1st pers. pl.

arrisquen 1. that they may risk; pres. subj. 3rd pers. pl. / *arriscar.* 2. let them risk; impve. 3rd pers. pl.

arrísquense let them become angry; impve. 3rd pers. pl. / *arriscarse.*

arrisques that you may risk; pres. subj. 2nd pers. sing. / *arriscar.*

arrísquese let him (her/it) become angry; impve. 3rd pers. sing. / *arriscarse.*

arrizar to reef or to tie. reg.

arrobándose being enraptured; pres. part. / *arrobarse.*

arrobaos (you all) be enraptured; impve. 2nd pers. pl. / *arrobarse.*

arrobar to charm. reg.

arrobarse to be enraptured. reg.

arróbate (you) be enraptured; impve. 2nd pers. sing. / *arrobarse.*

arrobémonos let us be enraptured; impve. 1st pers. pl. / *arrobarse.*

arróbense let them be enraptured; impve. 3rd pers. pl. / *arrobarse.*

arróbese let him (her/it) be enraptured; impve. 3rd pers. sing. / *arrobarse.*

arrodillándose kneeling; pres. part. / *arrodillarse.*

arrodillaos (you all) kneel; impve. 2nd pers. pl. / *arrodillarse.*

arrodillar to kneel. reg.

arrodillarse to kneel. reg.

arrodíllate (you) kneel; impve. 2nd pers. sing. / *arrodillarse.*

arrodillémonos let us kneel; impve. 1st pers. pl. / *arrodillarse.*

arrodíllense let them kneel; impve. 3rd pers. pl. / *arrodillarse.*

arrodíllese let him (her/it) kneel; impve. 3rd pers. sing. / *arrodillarse.*

arrogándose appropriating; pres. part. / *arrogarse.*

arrogaos (you all) appropriate; impve. 2nd pers. pl. / *arrogarse.*

arrogar to adopt. irr.

arrogarse to appropriate. irr.

arrógate (you) appropriate; impve. 2nd pers. sing. / *arrogarse.*

arrogue 1. that I may adopt; pres. subj. 1st pers. sing. / *arrogar.* 2. that he (she/it) may adopt; pres. subj. 3rd pers. sing. 3. let him (her/it) adopt; impve. 3rd pers. sing.

arrogué I adopted; past 1st pers. sing. / *arrogar.*

arroguéis that you (all) may adopt; pres. subj. 2nd pers. pl. / *arrogar.*

arroguémonos let us appropriate; impve. 1st pers. pl. / *arrogarse.*

arroguemos 1. that we may adopt; pres. subj. 1st pers. pl. / *arrogar* 2. let us adopt; impve. 1st pers. pl.

arroguen 1. that they may adopt; pres. subj. 3rd pers. pl. / *arrogar.* 2. let them adopt; impve. 3rd pers. pl.

arróguense let them appropriate; impve. 3rd pers. pl. / *arrogarse.*

arrogues that you may adopt; pres. subj. 2nd pers. sing. / *arrogar.*

arróguese let him (her/it) appropriate; impve. 3rd pers. sing. / *arrogarse.*

arrojándose rushing; pres. part. / *arrojarse.*

arrojaos (you all) rush; impve. 2nd pers. pl. / *arrojarse.*

arrojar to fling or to expel. reg.

arrojarse to rush or to vomit. reg.

arrójate (you) rush; impve. 2nd pers. sing. / *arrojarse.*

arrojémonos let us rush; impve. 1st pers. pl. / *arrojarse.*

arrójense let them rush; impve. 3rd pers. pl. / *arrojarse.*

arrójese let him (her/it) rush; impve. 3rd pers. sing. / *arrojarse.*

arrollar to roll up or to defeat. reg.

arropándose clothing; pres. part. / *arroparse.*

arropaos (you all) clothe; impve. 2nd pers. pl. / *arroparse.*

arropar to cover or to wrap. reg.

arroparse to clothe. reg.

arrópate (you) clothe; impve. 2nd pers. sing. / *arroparse.*

arropémonos let us clothe; impve. 1st pers. pl. / *arroparse.*

arrópense let them clothe; impve. 3rd pers. pl. / *arroparse.*

arrópese let him (her/it) clothe; impve. 3rd pers. sing. / *arroparse.*

arrostrándose fighting face to face; pres. part. / *arrostrarse.*

arrostraos (you all) fight face to face; impve. 2nd pers. pl. / *arrostrarse.*

arrostrar to face or to defy. reg.

arrostrarse to fight face to face. reg.

arróstrate (you) fight face to face; impve. 2nd pers. sing. / *arrostrarse.*

arrostrémonos let us fight face to face; impve. 1st pers. pl. / *arrostrarse.*

arróstrense let them fight face to face; impve. 3rd pers. pl. / *arrostrarse.*

arróstrese let him (her/it) fight face to face; impve. 3rd pers. sing. / *arrostrarse.*

arrugándose shriveling; pres. part. / *arrugarse.*

arrugaos (you all) shrivel; impve. 2nd pers. pl. / *arrugarse.*

arrugar to wrinkle. irr.

arrugarse to shrivel. irr.

arrúgate (you) shrivel; impve. 2nd pers. sing. / *arrugarse.*

arrugue 1. that I may wrinkle; pres. subj. 1st pers. sing. / *arrugar.* 2. that he (she/it) may wrinkle; pres. subj. 3rd pers. sing. 3. let him (her/it) wrinkle; impve. 3rd pers. sing.

arrugué I wrinkled; past 1st pers. sing. / *arrugar.*

arruguéis that you (all) may wrinkle; pres. subj. 2nd pers. pl. / *arrugar*.

arruguémonos let us shrivel; impve. 1st pers. pl. / *arrugarse*.

arruguemos 1. that we may wrinkle; pres. subj. 1st pers. pl. / *arrugar* 2. let us wrinkle; impve. 1st pers. pl.

arruguen 1. that they may wrinkle; pres. subj. 3rd pers. pl. / *arrugar*. 2. let them wrinkle; impve. 3rd pers. pl.

arrúguense let them shrivel; impve. 3rd pers. pl. / *arrugarse*.

arrugues that you may wrinkle; pres. subj. 2nd pers. sing. / *arrugar*.

arrúguese let him (her/it) shrivel; impve. 3rd pers. sing. / *arrugarse*.

arruinándose going bankrupt; pres. part. / *arruinarse*.

arruinaos (you all) go bankrupt; impve. 2nd pers. pl. / *arruinarse*.

arruinar to ruin. reg.

arruinarse to go bankrupt. reg.

arruínate (you) go bankrupt; impve. 2nd pers. sing. / *arruinarse*.

arruinémonos let us go bankrupt; impve. 1st pers. pl. / *arruinarse*.

arruínense let them go bankrupt; impve. 3rd pers. pl. / *arruinarse*.

arruínese let him (her/it) go bankrupt; impve. 3rd pers. sing. / *arruinarse*.

arrullar to lull or to coo. reg.

arrumándose becoming overcast; pres. part. / *arrumarse*.

arrumar to stow (cargo). reg.

arrumarse to become overcast. reg.

arrumbándose getting seasick; pres. part. / *arrumbrarse*.

arrumbaos (you all) get seasick; impve. 2nd pers. pl. / *arrumbrarse*.

arrumbar to cast aside or to take bearings. reg.

arrumbarse to get seasick. reg.

arrúmbate (you) get seasick; impve. 2nd pers. sing. / *arrumbrarse*.

arrumbémonos let us get seasick; impve. 1st pers. pl. / *arrumbrarse*.

arrúmbense let them get seasick; impve. 3rd pers. pl. / *arrumbrarse*.

arrúmbese let him (her/it) get seasick; impve. 3rd pers. sing. / *arrumbrarse*.

arrúmense let them become overcast; impve. 3rd pers. pl. / *arrumarse*.

arrúmese let it become overcast; impve. 3rd pers. sing. / *arrumarse*.

articular to articulate. reg.

artillar to arm with guns. reg.

asaetear to shoot with an arrow or to harness. reg.

asaltar to assault. reg.

asándose feeling very hot; pres. part. / *asarse*.

asaos (you all) feel very hot; impve. 2nd pers. pl. / *asarse*.

asar to roast. reg.

asarse to feel very hot. reg.

ásate (you) feel very hot; impve. 2nd pers. sing. / *asarse*.

ascender to ascend or to promote. irr.

ascienda 1. that I may ascend; pres. subj. 1st pers. sing. / *ascender*. 2. that he (she/it) may ascend; pres. subj. 3rd pers. sing. 3. let him (her/it) ascend; impve. 3rd pers. sing.

asciendan 1. that they may ascend; pres. subj. 3rd pers. pl. / *ascender*. 2. let them ascend; impve. 3rd pers. pl.

asciendas that you may ascend; pres. subj. 2nd pers. sing. / *ascender*.

asciende 1. he (she/it) ascends; pres. ind. 3rd pers. sing. / *ascender*. 2. (you) ascend; impve. 2nd pers. sing.

ascienden they ascend; pres. ind. 3rd pers. pl. / *ascender*.

asciendes you ascend; pres. ind. 2nd pers. sing. / *ascender*.

asciendo I ascend; pres. ind. 1st pers. sing. / *ascender*.

aseándose cleaning oneself up; pres. part. / *asearse*.

aseaos (you all) clean yourselves up; impve. 2nd pers. pl. / *asearse*.

asear to clean or to make neat. reg.

asearse to clean oneself up. reg.

aséate (you) clean yourself up; impve. 2nd pers. sing. / *asearse*.

asechar to ambush. reg.

asediar to besiege or to nag. reg.

aseémonos let us clean ourselves up; impve. 1st pers. pl. / *asearse*.

aséense let them clean themselves up; impve. 3rd pers. pl. / *asearse*.

aséese let him (her/it) clean himself (herself/itself) up; impve. 3rd pers. sing. / *asearse*.

asegurándose making sure; pres. part. / *asegurarse*.

aseguraos (you all) make sure; impve. 2nd pers. pl. / *asegurarse*.

asegurar to make safe or to assure. reg.

asegurarse to make sure. reg.

asegúrate (you) make sure; impve. 2nd pers. sing. / *asegurarse*.

aseguremos let us make sure; impve. 1st pers. pl. / *asegurarse*.

asegúrense let them make sure; impve. 3rd pers. pl. / *asegurarse*.

asegúrese let him (her/it) make sure; impve. 3rd pers. sing. / *asegurarse*.

asemejándose resembling; pres. part. / *asemejarse*.

asemejaos (you all) resemble; impve. 2nd pers. pl. / *asemejarse*.

asemejar to make similar or to compare. reg.

asemejarse to resemble. reg.

aseméjate (you) resemble; impve. 2nd pers. sing. / *asemejarse*.

asemejémonos let us resemble; impve. 1st pers. pl. / *asemejarse*.

aseméjense let them resemble; impve. 3rd pers. pl. / *asemejarse*.

aseméjese let him (her/it) resemble; impve. 3rd pers. sing. / *asemejarse.*

asémonos let us feel very hot; impve. 1st pers. pl. / *asarse.*

ásense let them feel very hot; impve. 3rd pers. pl. / *asarse.*

asentándose settling; pres. part. / *asentarse.*

asentaos (you all) settle; impve. 2nd pers. pl. / *asentarse.*

asentar to seat or to hone. irr.

asentarse to settle. irr.

asentémonos let us settle; impve. 1st pers. pl. / *asentarse.*

asentí I assented; pres. ind. 1st pers. sing. / *asentir.*

asentir to assent or to concede. irr.

asentiste you assented; past 2nd pers. sing. / *asentir.*

aserrar to saw. irr.

aserruchar to saw (by hand). reg.

ásese let him (her/it) feel very hot; impve. 3rd pers. sing. / *asarse.*

asesinar to assassinate or murder. reg.

asesorándose taking advice; pres. part. / *asesorarse.*

asesoraos (you all) take advice; impve. 2nd pers. pl. / *asesorarse.*

asesorar to give advice. reg.

asesorarse to take advice. reg.

asesórate (you) take advice; impve. 2nd pers. sing. / *asesorarse.*

asesorémonos let us take advice; impve. 1st pers. pl. / *asesorarse.*

asesórense let them take advice; impve. 3rd pers. pl. / *asesorarse.*

asesórese let him (her/it) take advice; impve. 3rd pers. sing. / *asesorarse.*

asestar to aim. reg.

ásete (you) take hold; impve. 2nd pers. sing. / *asirse.*

aseverar to assert. reg.

asfaltar to pave with asphalt. reg.

asfixiar to suffocate or to smother. reg.

asga 1. that I may seize; pres. subj. 1st pers. sing. / *asir.* 2. that he(she/it) may seize; pres. subj. 3rd pers. sing. 3. let him (her/it) seize; impve. 3rd pers. sing.

asgáis that you (all) may seize; pres. subj. 2nd pers. pl. / *asir.*

asgámonos let us take hold; impve. 1st pers. pl. / *asirse.*

asgamos 1. that we may seize; pres. subj. 1st pers. pl. / *asir* 2. let us seize; impve. 1st pers. pl.

asgan 1. that they may seize; pres. subj. 3rd pers. pl. / *asir.* 2. let them seize; impve. 3rd pers. pl.

ásganse let them take hold; impve. 3rd pers. pl. / *asirse.*

asgas that you may seize; pres. subj. 2nd pers. sing. / *asir.*

ásgase let him (her/it) take hold; impve. 3rd pers. sing. / *asirse.*

asgo I seize; pres. ind. 1st pers. sing. / *asir.*

asiéndose taking hold; pres. part. / *asirse.*

asienta 1. he (she/it) seats; pres. ind. 3rd pers. sing. / *asentar.* 2. (you) seat; impve. 2nd pers. sing.

asienta 1. that I may assent; pres. subj. 1st pers. sing. / *asentir.* 2. that he (she/it) may assent; pres. subj. 3rd pers. sing. 3. let him (her/it) assent; impve. 3rd pers. sing.

asientan they seat; pres. ind. 3rd pers. pl. / *asentar.*

asientan 1. that they may assent; pres. subj. 3rd pers. pl. / *asentir.* 2. let them assent; impve. 3rd pers. pl.

asientas you seat; pres. ind. 2nd pers. sing. / *asentar.*

asientas that you may assent; pres. subj. 2nd pers. sing. / *asentir.*

asiéntate (you) settle; impve. 2nd pers. sing. / *asentarse.*

asiente 1. that I may seat; pres. subj. 1st pers. sing. / *asentar.* 2. that he (she/it) may seat; pres. subj. 3rd pers. sing. 3. let him (her/it) seat; impve. 3rd pers. sing.

asiente 1. he (she/it) assents; pres. ind. 3rd pers. sing. / *asentir.* 2. (you) assent; impve. 2nd pers. sing.

asienten 1. that they may seat; pres. subj. 3rd pers. pl. / *asentar.* 2. let them seat; impve. 3rd pers. pl.

asienten they assent; pres. ind. 3rd pers. pl. / *asentir.*

asiéntense let them settle; impve. 3rd pers. pl. / *asentarse.*

asientes that you may seat; pres. subj. 2nd pers. sing. / *asentar.*

asientes you assent; pres. ind. 2nd pers. sing. / *asentir.*

asiéntese let him (her/it) settle; impve. 3rd pers. sing. / *asentarse.*

asiento I seat; pres. ind. 1st pers. sing. / *asentar.*

asiento I assent; pres. ind. 1st pers. sing. / *asentir.*

asierra 1. he (she/it) saws; pres. ind. 3rd pers. sing. / *aserrar.* 2. (you) saw; impve. 2nd pers. sing.

asierran they saw; pres. ind. 3rd pers. pl. / *aserrar.*

asierras you saw; pres. ind. 2nd pers. sing. / *aserrar.*

asierre 1. that I may saw; pres. subj. 1st pers. sing. / *aserrar.* 2. that he (she/it) may saw; pres. subj. 3rd pers. sing. 3. let him (her/it) saw; impve. 3rd pers. sing.

asierren 1. that they may saw; pres. subj. 3rd pers. pl. / *aserrar.* 2. let them saw; impve. 3rd pers. pl.

asierres that you may saw; pres. subj. 2nd pers. sing. / *aserrar.*

asierro I saw; pres. ind. 1st pers. sing. / *aserrar.*

asignar to assign. reg.

asilar to shelter or to put in an asylum. reg.

asimilándose being alike; pres. part. / *asimilarse.*

asimilaos (you all) be alike; impve. 2nd pers. pl. / *asimilarse.*

asimilar to assimilate or to resemble. reg.

asimilarse to be alike. reg.

asimílate (you) be alike; impve. 2nd pers. sing. / *asimilarse.*

asimilémonos let us be alike; impve. 1st pers. pl. / *asimilarse.*

asimílense let them be alike; impve. 3rd pers. pl. / *asimilarse.*

asimílese let him (her/it) be alike; impve. 3rd pers. sing. / *asimilarse.*

asintáis that you (all) may assent; pres. subj. 2nd pers. pl. / *asentir.*

asintamos 1. that we may assent; pres. subj. 1st pers. pl. / *asentir* 2. let us assent; impve. 1st pers. pl.

asintiendo assenting; pres. part. / *asentir.*

asintiera 1. that I might assent; imp. subj. 1st pers. sing. / *asentir.* 2. that he (she/it) might assent; imp. subj. 3rd pers. sing.

asintierais that you (all) might assent; imp. subj. 2nd pers pl. / *asentir.*

asintiéramos that we might assent; imp. subj. 1st pers. pl. / *asentir.*

asintieran that they might assent; imp. subj. 3rd pers. pl. / *asentir.*

asintieras that you might assent; imp. subj. 2nd pers. sing. / *asentir.*

asintieron they assented; past 3rd pers. pl. / *asentir.*

asintiese 1. that I might assent; imp. subj. 1st pers. sing. / *asentir.* 2. that he (she/it) might assent; imp. subj. 3rd pers. sing.

asintieseis that you (all) might assent; imp. subj. 2nd pers pl. / *asentir.*

asintiésemos that we might assent; imp. subj. 1st pers. pl. / *asentir.*

asintiesen that they might assent; imp. subj. 3rd pers. pl. / *asentir.*

asintieses that you might assent; imp. subj. 2nd pers. sing. / *asentir.*

asintió he (she/it) assented; past 3rd pers. sing. / *asentir.*

asíos (you all) take hold; impve. 2nd pers. pl. / *asirse.*

asir to seize. irr.

asirse to take hold. irr.

asistir to assist or to be present. reg.

asociándose joining; pres. part. / *asociarse.*

asociaos (you all) join; impve. 2nd pers. pl. / *asociarse.*

asociar to associate. reg.

asociarse to join or to become a partner. reg.

asocíate (you) join; impve. 2nd pers. sing. / *asociarse.*

asociémonos let us join; impve. 1st pers. pl. / *asociarse.*

asocíense let them join; impve. 3rd pers. pl. / *asociarse.*

asocíese let him (her/it) join; impve. 3rd pers. sing. / *asociarse.*

asolándose drying up; pres. part. / *asolarse.*

asolaos (you all) dry up; impve. 2nd pers. pl. / *asolarse.*

asolar to destroy or to parch. irr.

asolarse to dry up. irr.

asoleándose getting sunburned; pres. part. / *asolearse.*

asoleaos (you all) get sunburned; impve. 2nd pers. pl. / *asolearse.*

asolear to sun. reg.

asolearse to get sunburned. reg.

asoléate (you) get sunburned; impve. 2nd pers. sing. / *asolearse.*

asoleémonos let us get sunburned; impve. 1st pers. pl. / *asolearse.*

asoléense let them get sunburned; impve. 3rd pers. pl. / *asolearse.*

asoléese let him (her/it) get sunburned; impve. 3rd pers. sing. / *asolearse.*

asolémonos let us dry up; impve. 1st pers. pl. / *asolarse.*

asomándose lookng out; pres. part. / *asomarse.*

asomaos (you all) look out; impve. 2nd pers. pl. / *asomarse.*

asomar to show. reg.

asomarse to look out or to lean out. reg.

asómate (you) look out; impve. 2nd pers. sing. / *asomarse.*

asombrándose being astonished; pres. part. / *asombrarse.*

asombraos (you all) be astonished; impve. 2nd pers. pl. / *asombrarse.*

asombrar to amaze or to darken. reg.

asombrarse to be astonished or to be frightened. reg.

asómbrate (you) be astonished; impve. 2nd pers. sing. / *asombrarse.*

asombrémonos let us be astonished; impve. 1st pers. pl. / *asombrarse.*

asómbrense let them be astonished; impve. 3rd pers. pl. / *asombrarse.*

asómbrese let him (her/it) be astonished; impve. 3rd pers. sing. / *asombrarse.*

asomémonos let us look out; impve. 1st pers. pl. / *asomarse.*

asómense let them look out; impve. 3rd pers. pl. / *asomarse.*

asómese let him (her/it) look out; impve. 3rd pers. sing. / *asomarse.*

asosegándose calming down; pres. part. / *asosegarse.*

asosegaos (you all) calm down; impve. 2nd pers. pl. / *asosegarse.*

asosegar to calm. irr.

asosegarse to calm down. irr.

asosegué I calmed; past 1st pers. sing. / *asosegar.*

asoseguéis that you (all) may calm; pres. subj. 2nd pers. pl. / *asosegar.*

asoseguémonos let us calm down; impve. 1st pers. pl. / *asosegarse.*

asoseguemos 1. that we may calm; pres. subj. 1st pers. pl. / *asosegar* 2. let us calm; impve. 1st pers. pl.

asosiega 1. he (she/it) calms; pres. ind. 3rd pers. sing. / *asosegar.* 2. (you) calm; impve. 2nd pers. sing.

asosiegan they calm; pres. ind. 3rd pers. pl. / *asosegar.*

asosiegas you calm; pres. ind. 2nd pers. sing. / *asosegar.*

asosiégate (you) calm down; impve. 2nd pers. sing. / *asosegarse.*

asosiego I calm; pres. ind. 1st pers. sing. / *asosegar*

asosiegue 1. that I may calm; pres. subj. 1st pers. sing. / *asosegar.* 2. that he (she/it) may calm; pres. subj. 3rd pers. sing. 3. let him (her/it) calm; impve. 3rd pers. sing.

asosieguen 1. that they may calm; pres. subj. 3rd pers. pl. / *asosegar*. 2. let them calm; impve. 3rd pers. pl.

asosiéguense let them calm down; impve. 3rd pers. pl. / *asosegarse*.

asosiegues that you may calm; pres. subj. 2nd pers. sing. / *asosegar*.

asosiéguese let him (her/it) calm down; impve. 3rd pers. sing. / *asosegarse*.

aspándose taking great pains; pres. part. / *asparse*.

aspaos (you all) take great pains; impve. 2nd pers. pl. / *asparse*.

aspar to reel or to crucify. reg.

asparse to take great pains. reg.

áspate (you) take great pains; impve. 2nd pers. sing. / *asparse*.

aspémonos let us take great pains; impve. 1st pers. pl. / *asparse*.

áspense let them take great pains; impve. 3rd pers. pl. / *asparse*.

áspese let him (her/it) take great pains; impve. 3rd pers. sing. / *asparse*.

aspirar to aspire or to suck in. reg.

asquear to disgust or to sicken. reg.

astillándose splintering; pres. part. / *astillarse*.

astillaos (you all) splinter; impve. 2nd pers. pl. / *astillarse*.

astillar to chip or to splinter. reg.

astillarse to splinter. reg.

astíllate (you) splinter; impve. 2nd pers. sing. / *astillarse*.

astillémonos let us splinter; impve. 1st pers. pl. / *astillarse*.

astíllense let them splinter; impve. 3rd pers. pl. / *astillarse*.

astíllese let him (her/it) splinter; impve. 3rd pers. sing. / *astillarse*.

astringir to astringe. irr.

astrinja 1. that I may astringe; pres. subj. 1st pers. sing. / *astringir*. 2. that he (she/it) may astringe; pres. subj. 3rd pers. sing. 3. let him (her/it) astringe; impve. 3rd pers. sing.

astrinjáis that you (all) may astringe; pres. subj. 2nd pers. pl. / *astringir*.

astrinjamos 1. that we may astringe; pres. subj. 1st pers. pl. / *astringir*. 2. let us astringe; impve. 1st pers. pl.

astrinjan 1. that they may astringe; pres. subj. 3rd pers. pl. / *astringir*. 2. let them astringe; impve. 3rd pers. pl.

astrinjas that you may astringe; pres. subj. 2nd pers. sing. / *astringir*.

astrinjo I astringe; pres. ind. 1st pers. sing. / *astringir*.

asuela 1. he (she/it) destroys; pres. ind. 3rd pers. sing. / *asolar*. 2. (you) destroy; impve. 2nd pers. sing.

asuelan they destroy; pres. ind. 3rd pers. pl. / *asolar*.

asuelas you destroy; pres. ind. 2nd pers. sing. / *asolar*.

asuélate (you) dry up; impve. 2nd pers. sing. / *asolarse*.

asuele 1. that I may destroy; pres. subj. 1st pers. sing. / *asloar*. 2. that he (she/it) may destroy; pres. subj. 3rd pers. sing. 3. let him (her/it) destroy; impve. 3rd pers. sing.

asuelen 1. that they may destroy; pres. subj. 3rd pers. pl. / *asolar*. 2. let them destroy; impve. 3rd pers. pl.

asuélense let them dry up; impve. 3rd pers. pl. / *asolarse*.

asueles that you may destroy; pres. subj. 2nd pers. sing. / *asolar*.

asuélese let him (her/it) dry up; impve. 3rd pers. sing. / *asolarse*.

asuelo I destroy; pres. ind. 1st pers. sing. / *asolar*.

asumir to assume. reg.

asustándose being frightened; pres. part. / *asustarse*.

asustaos (you all) be frightened; impve. 2nd pers. pl. / *asustarse*.

asustar to frighten. reg.

asustarse to be frightened. reg.

asústate (you) be frightened; impve. 2nd pers. sing. / *asustarse*.

asustémonos let us be frightened; impve. 1st pers. pl. / *asustarse*.

asústense let them be frightened; impve. 3rd pers. pl. / *asustarse*.

asústese let him (her/it) be frightened; impve. 3rd pers. sing. / *asustarse*.

atacar to attack. irr.

atajándose being abashed; pres. part. / *atajarse*.

atajaos (you all) be abashed; impve. 2nd pers. pl. / *atajarse*.

atajar to cut off or to intercept. reg.

atajarse to be abashed. reg.

atájate (you) be abashed; impve. 2nd pers. sing. / *atajarse*.

atajémonos let us be abashed; impve. 1st pers. pl. / *atajarse*.

atájense let them be abashed; impve. 3rd pers. pl. / *atajarse*.

atájese let him (her/it) be abashed; impve. 3rd pers. sing. / *atajarse*.

atándose getting tied up; pres. part. / *atarse*.

atañer to concern. irr. this verb is used primarily only in the 3rd person present indicative.

ataos (you all) get tied up; impve. 2nd pers. pl. / *atarse*.

ataque 1. that I may attack; pres. subj. 1st pers. sing. / *atacar*. 2. that he (she/it) may attack; pres. subj. 3rd pers. sing. 3. let him (her/it) attack; impve. 3rd pers. sing.

ataqué I attacked; past 1st pers. sing. / *atacar*.

ataquéis that you (all) may attack; pres. subj. 2nd pers. pl. / *atacar*.

ataquemos 1. that we may attack; pres. subj. 1st pers. pl. / *atacar* 2. let us attack; impve. 1st pers. pl.

ataquen 1. that they may attack; pres. subj. 3rd pers. pl. / *atacar*. 2. let them attack; impve. 3rd pers. pl.

ataques that you may attack; pres. subj. 2nd pers. sing. / *atacar*.

atar to tie. reg.

atarantar to stun or to confuse. reg.

atareándose working hard; pres. part. / *atarearse*.

atareaos (you all) work hard; impve. 2nd pers. pl. / *atarearse*.

atarear to load with work. reg.

atarearse to work hard. reg.

ataréate (you) work hard; impve. 2nd pers. sing. / *atarearse*.

atareémonos let us work hard; impve. 1st pers. pl. / *atarearse*.

atareénse let them work hard; impve. 3rd pers. pl. / *atarearse*.

atareése let him (her/it) work hard; impve. 3rd pers. sing. / *atarearse*.

atarse to get tied up or to be confused. reg.

atarugándose choking; pres. part. / *atarugarse*.

atarugaos (you all) choke; impve. 2nd pers. pl. / *atarugarse*.

atarugar to wedge or to plug. irr.

atarugarse to choke. irr.

atarúgate (you) choke; impve. 2nd pers. sing. / *atarugarse*.

atarugue 1. that I may wedge; pres. subj. 1st pers. sing. / *atarugar*. 2. that he (she/it) may wedge; pres. subj. 3rd pers. sing. 3. let him (her/it) wedge; impve. 3rd pers. sing.

atarugué I wedged; past 1st pers. sing. / *atarugar*.

ataruguéis that you (all) may wedge; pres. subj. 2nd pers. pl. / *atarugar*.

ataruguémonos let us choke; impve. 1st pers. pl. / *atarugarse*.

ataruguemos 1. that we may wedge; pres. subj. 1st pers. pl. / *atarugar* 2. let us wedge; impve. 1st pers. pl.

ataruguen 1. that they may wedge; pres. subj. 3rd pers. pl. / *atarugar*. 2. let them wedge; impve. 3rd pers. pl.

atarúguense let them choke; impve. 3rd pers. pl. / *atarugarse*.

atarugues that you may wedge; pres. subj. 2nd pers. sing. / *atarugar*.

atarúguese let him (her/it) choke; impve. 3rd pers. sing. / *atarugarse*.

atasajar to jerk (meat). reg.

atascándose becoming clogged; pres. part. / *atascarse*.

atascaos (you all) become clogged; impve. 2nd pers. pl. / *atascarse*.

atascar to stop up. irr.

atascarse to become clogged. irr.

atáscate (you) become clogged; impve. 2nd pers. sing. / *atascarse*.

atasque 1. that I may stop up; pres. subj. 1st pers. sing. / *atascar*. 2. that he (she/it) may stop up; pres. subj. 3rd pers. sing. 3. let him (her/it) stop up; impve. 3rd pers. sing.

atasqué I stopped up; past 1st pers. sing. / *atascar*.

atasquéis that you (all) may stop up; pres. subj. 2nd pers. pl. / *atascar*.

atasquémonos let us become clogged; impve. 1st pers. pl. / *atascarse*.

atasquemos 1. that we may stop up; pres. subj. 1st pers. pl. / *atascar* 2. let us stop up; impve. 1st pers. pl.

atasquen 1. that they may stop up; pres. subj. 3rd pers. pl. / *atascar*. 2. let them stop up; impve. 3rd pers. pl.

atásquense let them become clogged; impve. 3rd pers. pl. / *atascarse*.

atasques that you may stop up; pres. subj. 2nd pers. sing. / *atascar*.

atásquese let him (her/it) become clogged; impve. 3rd pers. sing. / *atascarse*.

átate (you) get tied up; impve. 2nd pers. sing. / *atarse*.

atavía 1. he (she/it) adorns; pres. ind. 3rd pers. sing. / *ataviar*. 2. (you) adorn; impve. 2nd pers. sing.

atavían they adorn; pres. ind. 3rd pers. pl. / *ataviar*.

ataviándose dressing up; pres. part. / *ataviarse*.

ataviaos (you all) dress up; impve. 2nd pers. pl. / *ataviarse*.

ataviar to adorn. irr.

ataviarse to dress up. irr.

atavías you adorn; pres. ind. 2nd pers. sing. / *ataviar*.

atavíate (you) dress up; impve. 2nd pers. sing. / *ataviarse*.

atavíe 1. that I may adorn; pres. subj. 1st pers. sing. / *ataviar*. 2. that he (she/it) may adorn; pres. subj. 3rd pers. sing. 3. let him (her/it) adorn; impve. 3rd pers. sing.

ataviémonos let us dress up; impve. 1st pers. pl. / *ataviarse*.

atavíen 1. that they may adorn; pres. subj. 3rd pers. pl. / *ataviar*. 2. let them adorn; impve. 3rd pers. pl.

atavíense let them dress up; impve. 3rd pers. pl. / *ataviarse*.

atavíes that you may adorn; pres. subj. 2nd pers. sing. / *ataviar*.

atavíese let him (her/it) dress up; impve. 3rd pers. sing. / *ataviarse*.

atavío I adorn; pres. ind. 1st pers. sing. / *ataviar*.

atece 1. that I may tan; pres. subj. 1st pers. sing. / *atezar*. 2. that he (she/it) may tan; pres. subj. 3rd pers. sing. 3. let him (her/it) tan; impve. 3rd pers. sing.

atecé I tanned; past 1st pers. sing. / *atezar*.

atecéis that you (all) may tan; pres. subj. 2nd pers. pl. / *atezar*.

atecemos 1. that we may tan; pres. subj. 1st pers. pl. / *atezar* 2. let us tan; impve. 1st pers. pl.

atecen 1. that they may tan; pres. subj. 3rd pers. pl. / *atezar*. 2. let them tan; impve. 3rd pers. pl.

ateces that you may tan; pres. subj. 2nd pers. sing. / *atezar*.

atediándose being bored; pres. part. / *atediarse*.

atediaos (you all) be bored; impve. 2nd pers. pl. / *atediarse*.

atediar to disgust. reg.

atediarse to be bored. reg.

atedíate (you) be bored; impve. 2nd pers. sing. / *atediarse.*

atediémonos let us be bored; impve. 1st pers. pl. / *atediarse.*

atedíense let them be bored; impve. 3rd pers. pl. / *atediarse.*

atediese let him (her/it) be bored; impve. 3rd pers. sing. / *atediarse.*

atémonos let us get tied up; impve. 1st pers. pl. / *atarse.*

atemorice 1. that I may frighten; pres. subj. 1st pers. sing. / *atemorizar.* 2. that he (she/it) may frighten; pres. subj. 3rd pers. sing. 3. let him (her/it) frighten; impve. 3rd pers. sing.

atemoricé I frightened; past 1st pers. sing. / *atemorizar.*

atemoricéis that you (all) may frighten; pres. subj. 2nd pers. pl. / *atemorizar.*

atemoricémonos let us become frightened; impve. 1st pers. pl. / *atemorizar.*

atemoricemos 1. that we may frighten; pres. subj. 1st pers. pl. / *atemorizar* 2. let us frighten; impve. 1st pers. pl.

atemoricen 1. that they may frighten; pres. subj. 3rd pers. pl. / *atemorizar.* 2. let them frighten; impve. 3rd pers. pl.

atemorícense let them become frightened; impve. 3rd pers. pl. / *atemorizarse.*

atemorices that you may frighten; pres. subj. 2nd pers. sing. / *atemorizar.*

atemorícese let him (her/it) become frightened; impve. 3rd pers. sing. / *atemorizarse.*

atemorizándose becoming frightened; pres. part. / *atemorizarse.*

atemorizaos (you all) become frightened; impve. 2nd pers. pl. / *atemorizarse.*

atemorizar to frighten or to intimidate. irr.

atemorizarse to become frightened. irr.

atemorízate (you) become frightened; impve. 2nd pers. sing. / *atemorizarse.*

aten (you) depend; impve. 2nd pers. sing. / *atenerse.*

atender to heed or to assist. irr.

atendrá he (she/it) will depend; fut. 3rd pers. sing. / *atenerse.*

atendrán they will depend; fut. 3rd pers. pl. / *atenerse.*

atendrás you will depend; fut. 2nd pers. sing. / *atenerse.*

atendré I shall depend; fut. 1st pers. sing. / *atenerse.*

atendréis you (all) will depend; fut. 2nd pers. pl. / *atenerse.*

atendremos we shall depend; fut. 1st pers. pl. / *atenerse.*

atendría 1. I should depend; cond. 1st pers. sing. / *atenerse.* 2. he (she/it) would depend; cond. 3rd pers. sing.

atendríais you (all) would depend; cond. 2nd pers. pl. / *atenerse.*

atendríamos we should depend; cond. 1st pers. pl. / *atenerse.*

atendrían they would depend; cond. 3rd pers. pl. / *atenerse.*

atendrías you would depend; cond. 2nd pers. sing. / *atenerse.*

ateneos (you all) depend; impve. 2nd pers. pl. / *atenerse.*

atenerse to depend or to rely. irr.

aténete (you) depend; impve. 2nd pers. sing. / *atenerse.*

atenga 1. that I may depend; pres. subj. 1st pers. sing. / *atenerse.* 2. that he (she/it) may depend; pres. subj. 3rd pers. sing.

atengáis that you (all) may depend; pres. subj. 2nd pers. pl. / *atenerse.*

atengámonos let us depend; impve. 1st pers. pl. / *atenerse.*

atengamos that we may depend; pres. subj. 1st pers. pl. / *atenerse.*

atengan that they may depend; pres. subj. 3rd pers. pl. / *atenerse.*

aténganse let them depend; impve. 3rd pers. pl. / *atenerse.*

atengas that you may depend; pres. subj. 2nd pers. sing. / *atenerse.*

aténgase let him (her/it) depend; impve. 3rd pers. sing. / *atenerse.*

atengo I depend; pres. ind. 1st pers. sing. / *atenerse.*

ateniéndose depending; pres. part. / *atenerse.*

átense let them get tied up; impve. 3rd pers. pl. / *atarse.*

atentar to attempt a crime. irr.

atenúa 1. he (she/it) attenuates; pres. ind. 3rd pers. sing. / *atenuar.* 2. (you) attenuate; impve. 2nd pers. sing.

atenúan they attenuate; pres. ind. 3rd pers. pl. / *atenuar.*

atenuar to attenuate. irr.

atenúas you attenuate; pres. ind. 2nd pers. sing. / *atenuar.*

atenúe 1. that I may attenuate; pres. subj. 1st pers. sing. / *atenuar.* 2. that he (she/it) may attenuate; pres. subj. 3rd pers. sing. 3. let him (her/it) attenuate; impve. 3rd pers. sing.

atenúen 1. that they may attenuate; pres. subj. 3rd pers. pl. / *atenuar.* 2. let them attenuate; impve. 3rd pers. pl.

atenúes that you may attenuate; pres. subj. 2nd pers. sing. / *atenuar.*

atenúo I attenuate; pres. ind. 1st pers. sing. / *atenuar.*

aterecer to become numb with cold. irr.

aterezca 1. that I may become numb with cold; pres. subj. 1st pers. sing. / *aterecer.* 2. that he (she/it) may become numb with cold; pres. subj. 3rd pers. sing. 3. let him (her/it) become numb with cold; impve. 3rd pers. sing.

aterezcáis that you (all) may become numb with cold; pres. subj. 2nd pers. pl. / *aterecer.*

aterezcamos 1. that we may become numb with cold; pres. subj. 1st pers. pl. / *aterecer.* 2. let us become numb with cold; impve. 1st pers. pl.

aterezcan 1. that they may become numb with cold; pres. subj. 3rd pers. pl. / *aterecer.* 2. let them become numb with cold; impve. 3rd pers. pl.

aterezcas that you may become numb with cold; pres. subj. 2nd pers. sing. / *aterecer.*

aterezco I become numb with cold; pres. ind. 1st pers. sing. / *aterecer.*

ateriéndose becoming numb with cold; pres. part. / *aterirse.*

ateríos (you all) become numb with cold; impve. 2nd pers. pl. / *aterirse.*

aterirse to become numb with cold. irr. this verb is used only in the forms that have an I in the ending.

aterrajar to thread or tap. reg.

aterrándose being appalled; pres. part. / *aterrarse.*

aterrándose standing inshore; pres. part. / *aterrarse.*

aterraos (you all) be appalled; impve. 2nd pers. pl. / *aterrarse.*

aterraos (you all) stand inshore; impve. 2nd pers. pl. / *aterrarse.*

aterrar to terrify. reg.

aterrar to demolish. irr.

aterrarse to be appalled. reg.

aterrarse to stand inshore. irr.

atérrate (you) be appalled; impve. 2nd pers. sing. / *aterrarse.*

aterrémonos let us be appalled; impve. 1st pers. pl. / *aterrarse.*

aterrémonos let us stand inshore; impve. 1st pers. pl. / *aterrarse.*

atérrense let them be appalled; impve. 3rd pers. pl. / *aterrarse.*

atérrese let him (her/it) be appalled; impve. 3rd pers. sing. / *aterrarse.*

aterrice 1. that I may land; pres. subj. 1st pers. sing. / *aterrizar.* 2. that he (she/it) may land; pres. subj. 3rd pers. sing. 3. let him (her/it) land; impve. 3rd pers. sing.

aterricé I landed; past 1st pers. sing. / *aterrizar.*

aterricéis that you (all) may land; pres. subj. 2nd pers. pl. / *aterrizar.*

aterricemos 1. that we may land; pres. subj. 1st pers. pl. / *aterrizar* 2. let us land; impve. 1st pers. pl.

aterricen 1. that they may land; pres. subj. 3rd pers. pl. / *aterrizar.* 2. let them land; impve. 3rd pers. pl.

aterrices that you may land; pres. subj. 2nd pers. sing. / *aterrizar.*

aterrizar to land. irr.

aterronándose lumping; pres. part. / *aterronarse.*

aterronaos (you all) lump; impve. 2nd pers. pl. / *aterronarse.*

aterronar to make lumpy. reg.

aterronarse to lump. reg.

aterrónate (you) lump; impve. 2nd pers. sing. / *aterronarse.*

aterronémonos let us lump; impve. 1st pers. pl. / *aterronarse.*

aterrónense let them lump; impve. 3rd pers. pl. / *aterronarse.*

aterrónese let him (her/it) lump; impve. 3rd pers. sing. / *aterronarse.*

aterrorice 1. that I may terrify; pres. subj. 1st pers. sing. / *aterrorizar.* 2. that he (she/it) may terrify; pres. subj. 3rd pers. sing. 3. let him (her/it) terrify; impve. 3rd pers. sing.

aterroricé I terrified; past 1st pers. sing. / *aterrorizar.*

aterroricéis that you (all) may terrify; pres. subj. 2nd pers. pl. / *aterrorizar.*

aterroricémonos let us become terrified; impve. 1st pers. pl. / *aterrorizarse.*

aterroricemos 1. that we may terrify; pres. subj. 1st pers. pl. / *aterrorizar.* 2. let us terrify; impve. 1st pers. pl.

aterroricen 1. that they may terrify; pres. subj. 3rd pers. pl. / *aterrorizar.* 2. let them terrify; impve. 3rd pers. pl.

aterrorícense let them become terrified; impve. 3rd pers. pl. / *aterrorizarse.*

aterrorices that you may terrify; pres. subj. 2nd pers. sing. / *aterrorizar.*

aterrorícese let him (her/it) become terrified; impve. 3rd pers. sing. / *aterrorizarse.*

aterrorizándose becoming terrified; pres. part. / *aterrorizarse.*

aterrorizaos (you all) become terrified; impve. 2nd pers. pl. / *aterrorizarse.*

aterrorizar to terrify. irr.

aterrorizarse to become terrified. irr.

aterrorízate (you) become terrified; impve. 2nd pers. sing. / *aterrorizarse.*

atesar to stiffen or to tense. irr.

átese let him (her/it) get tied up; impve. 3rd pers. sing. / *atarse.*

atesorar to save up or to hoard. reg.

atestándose overeating; pres. part. / *atestarse.*

atestaos (you all) overeat; impve. 2nd pers. pl. / *atestarse.*

atestar to attest. reg.

atestar to cram. irr.

atestarse to overeat. irr.

atestémonos let us overeat; impve. 1st pers. pl. / *atestarse.*

atestiguar to testify or to witness. irr.

atestigüe 1. that I may testify; pres. subj. 1st pers. sing. / *atestiguar.* 2. that he (she/it) may testify; pres. subj. 3rd pers. sing. 3. let him (her/it) testify; impve. 3rd pers. sing.

atestigüé I testified; past 1st pers. sing. / *atestiguar.*

atestigüéis that you (all) may testify; pres. subj. 2nd pers. pl. / *atestiguar.*

atestigüemos 1. that we may testify; pres. subj. 1st pers. pl. / *atestiguar.* 2. let us testify; impve. 1st pers. pl.

atestigüen 1. that they may testify; pres. subj. 3rd pers. pl. / *atestiguar.* 2. let them testify; impve. 3rd pers. pl.

atestigües that you may testify; pres. subj. 2nd pers. sing. / *atestiguar.*

atezar to tan or to make smooth. irr.

atiborrar to stuff. reg.

atice 1. that I may stir (the fire); pres. subj. 1st pers. sing. / *atizar*. 2. that he (she/it) may stir (the fire); pres. subj. 3rd pers. sing. 3. let him (her/it) stir the fire; impve. 3rd pers. sing.

aticé I stirred (the fire); past 1st pers. sing. / *atizar*.

aticéis that you (all) may stir (the fire); pres. subj. 2nd pers. pl. / *atizar*.

aticemos 1. that we may stir (the fire); pres. subj. 1st pers. pl. / *atizar*. 2. let us stir (the fire); impve. 1st pers. pl.

aticen 1. that they may stir (the fire); pres. subj. 3rd pers. pl. / *atizar*. 2. let them stir (the fire); impve. 3rd pers. pl.

atices that you may stir (the fire); pres. subj. 2nd pers. sing. / *atizar*

atienda 1. that I may heed; pres. subj. 1st pers. sing. / *atender*. 2. that he (she/it) may heed; pres. subj. 3rd pers. sing. 3. let him (her/it) heed; impve. 3rd pers. sing.

atiendan 1. that they may heed; pres. subj. 3rd pers. pl. / *atender*. 2. let them heed; impve. 3rd pers. pl.

atiendas that you may heed; pres. subj. 2nd pers. sing. / *atender*.

atiende 1. he (she/it) heeds; pres. ind. 3rd pers. sing. / *atender*. 2. (you) heed; impve. 2nd pers. sing.

atienden they heed; pres. ind. 3rd pers. pl. / *atender*.

atiendes you heed; pres. ind. 2nd pers. sing. / *atender*.

atiendo I heed; pres. ind. 1st pers. sing. / *atender*.

atiene he (she/it) depends; pres. ind. 3rd pers. sing. / *atenerse*.

atienen they depend; pres. ind. 3rd pers. pl. / *atenerse*.

atienes you depend; pres. ind. 2nd pers. sing. / *atenerse*.

atienta 1. he (she/it) attempts a crime; pres. ind. 3rd pers. sing. / *atentar*. 2. (you) attempt a crime; impve. 2nd pers. sing.

atientan they attempt a crime; pres. ind. 3rd pers. pl. / *atentar*.

atientas you attempt a crime; pres. ind. 2nd pers. sing. / *atentar*.

atiente 1. that I may attempt a crime; pres. subj. 1st pers. sing. / *atentar*. 2. that he (she/it) may attempt a crime; pres. subj. 3rd pers. sing. 3. let him (her/it) attempt a crime; impve. 3rd pers. sing.

atienten 1. that they may attempt a crime; pres. subj. 3rd pers. pl. / *atentar*. 2. let them attempt a crime; impve. 3rd pers. pl.

atientes that you may attempt a crime; pres. subj. 2nd pers. sing. / *atentar*.

atiento I attempt a crime; pres. ind. 1st pers. sing. / *atentar*.

atierra 1. he (she/it) demolishes; pres. ind. 3rd pers. sing. / *aterrar*. 2. (you) demolish; impve. 2nd pers. sing.

atierran they demolish; pres. ind. 3rd pers. pl. / *aterrar*.

atierras you demolish; pres. ind. 2nd pers. sing. / *aterrar*.

atiérrate (you) stand inshore; impve. 2nd pers. sing. / *aterrarse*.

atierre 1. that I may demolish; pres. subj. 1st pers. sing. / *aterrar*. 2. that he (she/it) may demolish; pres. subj. 3rd pers. sing. 3. let him (her/it) demolish; impve. 3rd pers. sing.

atierren 1. that they may demolish; pres. subj. 3rd pers. pl. / *aterrar*. 2. let them demolish; impve. 3rd pers. pl.

atiérrense let them stand inshore; impve. 3rd pers. pl. / *aterrarse*.

atierres that you may demolish; pres. subj. 2nd pers. sing. / *aterrar*.

atiérrese let him (her/it) stand inshore; impve. 3rd pers. sing. / *aterrarse*.

atierro I demolish; pres. ind. 1st pers. sing. / *aterrar*.

atiesar to stiffen. reg.

atiesta 1. he (she/it) crams; pres. ind. 3rd pers. sing. / *atestar*. 2. (you) cram; impve. 2nd pers. sing.

atiestan they cram; pres. ind. 3rd pers. pl. / *atestar*.

atiestas you cram; pres. ind. 2nd pers. sing. / *atestar*.

atiéstate (you) overeat; impve. 2nd pers. sing. / *atestarse*.

atieste 1. that I may cram; pres. subj. 1st pers. sing. / *atestar*. 2. that he (she/it) may cram; pres. subj. 3rd pers. sing. 3. let him (her/it) cram; impve. 3rd pers. sing.

atiesten 1. that they may cram; pres. subj. 3rd pers. pl. / *atestar*. 2. let them cram; impve. 3rd pers. pl.

atiéstense let them overeat; impve. 3rd pers. pl. / *atestarse*.

atiestes that you may cram; pres. subj. 2nd pers. sing. / *atestar*.

atiéstese let him (her/it) overeat; impve. 3rd pers. sing. / *atestarse*.

atiesto I cram; pres. ind. 1st pers. sing. / *atestar*.

atildar to punctuate or to adorn or to find fault with. reg.

atinar to guess right. reg.

atiriéndose becoming numb with cold; pres. part. / *aterirse*.

atiriera 1. that I might become numb with cold; imp. subj. 1st pers. sing. / *aterirse*. 2. that he (she/it) might become numb with cold; imp. subj. 3rd pers. sing.

atirierais that you (all) might become numb with cold; imp. subj. 2nd pers pl. / *aterirse*.

atiriéramos that we might become numb with cold; imp. subj. 1st pers. pl. / *aterirse*.

atirieran that they might become numb with cold; imp. subj. 3rd pers. pl. / *aterirse*.

atirieras that you might become numb with cold; imp. subj. 2nd pers. sing. / *aterirse*.

atirieron they became numb with cold; past 3rd pers. pl. / *aterirse*.

atiriese 1. that I might become numb with cold; imp. subj. 1st pers. sing. / *aterirse*. 2. that he (she/it) might become numb with cold; imp. subj. 3rd pers. sing.

atirieseis that you (all) might become numb with cold; imp. subj. 2nd pers pl. / *aterirse*.

atiriésemos that we might become numb with cold; imp. subj. 1st pers. pl. / *aterirse*.

atiriesen that they might become numb with cold; imp. subj. 3rd pers. pl. / *aterirse.*

atirieses that you might become numb with cold; imp. subj. 2nd pers. sing. / *aterirse.*

atirió he (she/it) became numb with cold; past 3rd pers. sing. / *aterirse.*

atisbar to spy or to examine closely. reg.

atizar to stir (the fire) or to rouse. irr.

atolondrándose getting muddled; pres. part. / *atolondrarse.*

atolondraos (you all) get muddled; impve. 2nd pers. pl. / *atolondrarse.*

atolondrar to confuse. reg.

atolondrarse to get muddled. reg.

atolóndrate (you) get muddled; impve. 2nd pers. sing. / *atolondrarse.*

atolondrémonos let us get muddled; impve. 1st pers. pl. / *atolondrarse.*

atolóndrense let them get muddled; impve. 3rd pers. pl. / *atolondrarse.*

atolóndrese let him (her/it) get muddled; impve. 3rd pers. sing. / *atolondrarse.*

atollándose bogging down; pres. part. / *atollarse.*

atollaos (you all) bog down; impve. 2nd pers. pl. / *atollarse.*

atollar to get stuck in the mud. reg..

atollarse to bog down. reg.

atóllate (you) bog down; impve. 2nd pers. sing. / *atollarse.*

atollémonos let us bog down; impve. 1st pers. pl. / *atollarse.*

atóllense let them bog down; impve. 3rd pers. pl. / *atollarse.*

atóllese let him (her/it) bog down; impve. 3rd pers. sing. / *atollarse.*

atomice 1. that I may spray; pres. subj. 1st pers. sing. / *atomizar.* 2. that he (she/it) may spray; pres. subj. 3rd pers. sing. 3. let him (her/it) spray; impve. 3rd pers. sing.

atomicé I sprayed; past 1st pers. sing. / *atomizar.*

atomicéis that you (all) may spray; pres. subj. 2nd pers. pl. / *atomizar.*

atomicemos 1. that we may spray; pres. subj. 1st pers. pl. / *atomizar.* 2. let us spray; impve. 1st pers. pl.

atomicen 1. that they may spray; pres. subj. 3rd pers. pl. / *atomizar.* 2. let them spray; impve. 3rd pers. pl.

atomices that you may spray; pres. subj. 2nd pers. sing. / *atomizar.*

atomizar to spray. irr.

atontándose becoming stupid; pres. part. / *atontarse.*

atontaos (you all) become stupid; impve. 2nd pers. pl. / *atontarse.*

atontar to stun or to stupefy. reg.

atontarse to become stupid. reg.

atóntate (you) become stupid; impve. 2nd pers. sing. / *atontarse.*

atontémonos let us become stupid; impve. 1st pers. pl. / *atontarse.*

atóntense let them become stupid; impve. 3rd pers. pl. / *atontarse.*

atóntese let him (her/it) become stupid; impve. 3rd pers. sing. / *atontarse.*

atorándose getting stuck in the mud; pres. part. / *atorarse.*

atoraos (you all) get stuck in the mud; impve. 2nd pers. pl. / *atorarse.*

atorar to choke. reg.

atorarse to get stuck in the mud. reg..

atórate (you) get stuck in the mud; impve. 2nd pers. sing. / *atorarse.*

atorémonos let us get stuck in the mud; impve. 1st pers. pl. / *atorarse.*

atórense let them get stuck in the mud; impve. 3rd pers. pl. / *atorarse.*

atórese let him (her/it) get stuck in the mud; impve. 3rd pers. sing. / *atorarse.*

atormentándose distressing oneself; pres. part. / *atormentarse.*

atormentaos (you all) distress yourselves; impve. 2nd pers. pl. / *atormentarse.*

atormentar to torment or to tease. reg.

atormentarse to distress oneself. reg.

atorméntate (you) distress yourself; impve. 2nd pers. sing. / *atormentarse.*

atormentémonos let us distress ourselves; impve. 1st pers. pl. / *atormentarse.*

atorméntense let them distress themselves; impve. 3rd pers. pl. / *atormentarse.*

atorméntese let him (her/it) distress himself (herself/itself); impve. 3rd pers. sing. / *atormentarse.*

atornillar to screw. reg.

atosigándose being hurried; pres. part. / *atosigarse.*

atosigaos (you all) be hurried; impve. 2nd pers. pl. / *atosigarse.*

atosigar to poison or to harass. irr.

atosigarse to be hurried. irr.

atosígate (you) be hurried; impve. 2nd pers. sing. / *atosigarse.*

atosigue 1. that I may poison; pres. subj. 1st pers. sing. / *atosigar.* 2. that he (she/it) may poison; pres. subj. 3rd pers. sing. 3. let him (her/it) poison; impve. 3rd pers. sing.

atosigué I poisoned; past 1st pers. sing. / *atosigar.*

atosiguéis that you (all) may poison; pres. subj. 2nd pers. pl. / *atosigar.*

atosiguémonos let us be hurried; impve. 1st pers. pl. / *atosigarse.*

atosiguemos 1. that we may poison; pres. subj. 1st pers. pl. / *atosigar.* 2. let us poison; impve. 1st pers. pl.

atosiguen 1. that they may poison; pres. subj. 3rd pers. pl. / *atosigar.* 2. let them poison; impve. 3rd pers. pl.

atosíguense let them be hurried; impve. 3rd pers. pl. / *atosigarse.*

atosigues that you may poison; pres. subj. 2nd pers. sing. / *atosigar.*

atosíguese let him (her/it) be hurried; impve. 3rd pers. sing. / *atosigarse.*

atrabancándose rushing into things; pres. part. / *atrabancarse.*

atrabancaos (you all) rush into things; impve. 2nd pers. pl. / *atrabancarse.*

atrabancar to rush awkwardly or to run over. irr.

atrabancarse to rush into things. irr.

atrabáncate (you) rush into things; impve. 2nd pers. sing. / *atrabancarse.*

atrabanque 1. that I may rush awkwardly; pres. subj. 1st pers. sing. / *atrabancar.* 2. that he (she/it) may rush awkwardly; pres. subj. 3rd pers. sing. 3. let him (her/it) rush awkwardly; impve. 3rd pers. sing.

atrabanqué I rushed awkwardly; past 1st pers. sing. / *atrabancar.*

atrabanquéis that you (all) may rush awkwardly; pres. subj. 2nd pers. pl. / *atrabancar.*

atrabanquémonos let us rush into things; impve. 1st pers. pl. / *atrabancarse.*

atrabanquemos 1. that we may rush awkwardly; pres. subj. 1st pers. pl. / *atrabancar.* 2. let us rush awkwardly; impve. 1st pers. pl.

atrabanquen 1. that they may rush awkwardly; pres. subj. 3rd pers. pl. / *atrabancar.* 2. let them rush awkwardly; impve. 3rd pers. pl.

atrabánquense let them rush into things; impve. 3rd pers. pl. / *atrabancarse.*

atrabanques that you may rush awkwardly; pres. subj. 2nd pers. sing. / *atrabancar.*

atrabánquese let him (her/it) rush into things; impve. 3rd pers. sing. / *atrabancarse.*

atracándose overeating; pres. part. / *atracarse.*

atracaos (you all) overeat; impve. 2nd pers. pl. / *atracarse.*

atracar to cram or to rob or to dock. irr.

atracarse to overeat. irr.

atrácate (you) overeat; impve. 2nd pers. sing. / *atracarse.*

atraer to attract or to allure. irr.

atrafagar to toil. irr.

atrafague 1. that I may toil; pres. subj. 1st pers. sing. / *atrafagar.* 2. that he (she/it) may toil; pres. subj. 3rd pers. sing. 3. let him (her/it) toil; impve. 3rd pers. sing.

atrafagué I toiled; past 1st pers. sing. / *atrafagar.*

atrafaguéis that you (all) may toil; pres. subj. 2nd pers. pl. / *atrafagar.*

atrafaguemos 1. that we may toil; pres. subj. 1st pers. pl. / *atrafagar.* 2. let us toil; impve. 1st pers. pl.

atrafaguen 1. that they may toil; pres. subj. 3rd pers. pl. / *atrafagar.* 2. let them toil; impve. 3rd pers. pl.

atrafagues that you may toil; pres. subj. 2nd pers. sing. / *atrafagar.*

atragantándose choking; pres. part. / *atragantarse.*

atragantaos (you all) choke; impve. 2nd pers. pl. / *atragantarse.*

atragantarse to choke or to gag. reg.

atragántate (you) choke; impve. 2nd pers. sing. / *atragantarse.*

atragantémonos let us choke; impve. 1st pers. pl. / *atragantarse.*

atragántense let them choke; impve. 3rd pers. pl. / *atragantarse.*

atragántese let him (her/it) choke; impve. 3rd pers. sing. / *atragantarse.*

atraiga 1. that I may attract; pres. subj. 1st pers. sing. / *atraer.* 2. that he (she/it) may attract; pres. subj. 3rd pers. sing. 3. let him (her/it) attract; impve. 3rd pers. sing.

atraigáis that you (all) may attract; pres. subj. 2nd pers. pl. / *atraer.*

atraigamos 1. that we may attract; pres. subj. 1st pers. pl. / *atraer.* 2. let us attract; impve. 1st pers. pl.

atraigan 1. that they may attract; pres. subj. 3rd pers. pl. / *atraer.* 2. let them attract; impve. 3rd pers. pl.

atraigas that you may attract; pres. subj. 2nd pers. sing. / *atraer.*

atraigo I attract; pres. ind. 1st pers. sing. / *atraer.*

atraje I attracted; past 1st pers. sing. / *atraer.*

atrajera 1. that I might attract; imp. subj. 1st pers. sing. / *atraer.* 2. that he (she/it) might attract; imp. subj. 3rd pers. sing.

atrajerais that you (all) might attract; imp. subj. 2nd pers pl. / *atraer.*

atrajéramos that we might attract; imp. subj. 1st pers. pl. / *atraer.*

atrajeran that they might attract; imp. subj. 3rd pers. pl. / *atraer.*

atrajeras that you might attract; imp. subj. 2nd pers. sing. / *atraer.*

atrajeron they attracted; past 3rd pers. pl. / *atraer.*

atrajese 1. that I might attract; imp. subj. 1st pers. sing. / *atraer.* 2. that he (she/it) might attract; imp. subj. 3rd pers. sing.

atrajeseis that you (all) might attract; imp. subj. 2nd pers pl. / *atraer.*

atrajésemos that we might attract; imp. subj. 1st pers. pl. / *atraer.*

atrajesen that they might attract; imp. subj. 3rd pers. pl. / *atraer.*

atrajeses that you might attract; imp. subj. 2nd pers. sing. / *atraer.*

atrajimos we attracted; past 1st pers. pl. / *atraer.*

atrajiste you attracted; past 2nd pers. sing. / *atraer.*

atrajisteis you (all) attracted; past 2nd pers. pl. / *atraer.*

atrajo he (she/it) attracted; past 3rd pers. sing / *atraer.*

atrampándose being trapped; pres. part. / *atramparse.*

atrampaos (you all) be trapped; impve. 2nd pers. pl. / *atramparse.*

atramparse to be trapped. reg.

atrámpate (you) be trapped; impve. 2nd pers. sing. / *atramparse.*

atrampémonos let us be trapped; impve. 1st pers. pl. / *atramparse.*

atrámpense let them be trapped; impve. 3rd pers. pl. / *atramparse.*

atrámpese let him (her/it) be trapped; impve. 3rd pers. sing. / *atramparse.*

atrancándose getting crammed; pres. part. / *atrancarse*.

atrancaos (you all) get crammed; impve. 2nd pers. pl. / *atrancarse*.

atrancar to bolt or to be stubborn. irr.

atrancarse to get crammed. irr.

atráncate (you) get crammed; impve. 2nd pers. sing. / *atrancarse*.

atranque 1. that I may bolt; pres. subj. 1st pers. sing. / *atrancar*. 2. that he (she/it) may bolt; pres. subj. 3rd pers. sing. 3. let him (her/it) bolt; impve. 3rd pers. sing.

atranqué I bolted; past 1st pers. sing. / *atrancar*.

atranquéis that you (all) may bolt; pres. subj. 2nd pers. pl. / *atrancar*.

atranquémonos let us get crammed; impve. 1st pers. pl. / *atrancarse*.

atranquemos 1. that we may bolt; pres. subj. 1st pers. pl. / *atrancar*. 2. let us bolt; impve. 1st pers. pl.

atranquen 1. that they may bolt; pres. subj. 3rd pers. pl. / *atrancar*. 2. let them bolt; impve. 3rd pers. pl.

atránquense let them get crammed; impve. 3rd pers. pl. / *atrancarse*.

atranques that you may bolt; pres. subj. 2nd pers. sing. / *atrancar*.

atránquese let him (her/it) get crammed; impve. 3rd pers. sing. / *atrancarse*.

atrapar to trap or to catch. reg.

atraque 1. that I may cram; pres. subj. 1st pers. sing. / *atracar*. 2. that he (she/it) may cram; pres. subj. 3rd pers. sing. 3. let him (her/it) cram; impve. 3rd pers. sing.

atraqué I crammed; past 1st pers. sing. / *atracar*.

atraquéis that you (all) may cram; pres. subj. 2nd pers. pl. / *atracar*.

atraquémonos let us overeat; impve. 1st pers. pl. / *atracarse*.

atraquemos 1. that we may cram; pres. subj. 1st pers. pl. / *atracar*. 2. let us cram; impve. 1st pers. pl.

atraquen 1. that they may cram; pres. subj. 3rd pers. pl. / *atracar*. 2. let them cram; impve. 3rd pers. pl.

atráquense let them overeat; impve. 3rd pers. pl. / *atracarse*.

atraques that you may cram; pres. subj. 2nd pers. sing. / *atracar*.

atráquese let him (her/it) overeat; impve. 3rd pers. sing. / *atracarse*.

atrasándose being late; pres. part. / *atrasarse*.

atrasaos (you all) be late; impve. 2nd pers. pl. / *atrasarse*.

atrasar to delay. reg.

atrasarse to be late or to fall behind. reg.

atrásate (you) be late; impve. 2nd pers. sing. / *atrasarse*.

atrasémonos let us be late; impve. 1st pers. pl. / *atrasarse*.

atrásense let them be late; impve. 3rd pers. pl. / *atrasarse*.

atrásese let him (her/it) be late; impve. 3rd pers. sing. / *atrasarse*.

atravesándose getting in the way; pres. part. / *atravesarse*.

atravesaos (you all) get in the way; impve. 2nd pers. pl. / *atravesarse*.

atravesar to cross or to pierce. irr.

atravesarse to get in the way. irr.

atravesémonos let us get in the way; impve. 1st pers. pl. / *atravesarse*.

atraviesa 1. he (she/it) crosses; pres. ind. 3rd pers. sing. / *atravesar*. 2. (you) cross; impve. 2nd pers. sing.

atraviesan they cross; pres. ind. 3rd pers. pl. / *atravesar*.

atraviesas you cross; pres. ind. 2nd pers. sing. / *atravesar*.

atraviésate (you) get in the way; impve. 2nd pers. sing. / *atravesarse*.

atraviese 1. that I may cross; pres. subj. 1st pers. sing. / *atravesar*. 2. that he (she/it) may cross; pres. subj. 3rd pers. sing. 3. let him (her/it) cross; impve. 3rd pers. sing.

atraviesen 1. that they may cross; pres. subj. 3rd pers. pl. / *atravesar*. 2. let them cross; impve. 3rd pers. pl.

atraviésense let them get in the way; impve. 3rd pers. pl. / *atravesarse*.

atravieses that you may cross; pres. subj. 2nd pers. sing. / *atravesar*.

atraviésese let him (her/it) get in the way; impve. 3rd pers. sing. / *atravesarse*.

atravieso I cross; pres. ind. 1st pers. sing. / *atravesar*.

atrayendo attracting; pres. part. / *atraer*.

atreguar to grant a truce or an extension to. irr.

atregüe 1. that I may grant a truce; pres. subj. 1st pers. sing. / *atreguar* 2. that he (she/it) may grant a truce; pres. subj. 3rd pers. sing. 3. let him (her/it) grant a truce; impve. 3rd pers. sing.

atregüé I granted a truce; past 1st pers. sing. / *atreguar*.

atregüéis that you (all) may grant a truce; pres. subj. 2nd pers. pl. / *atreguar*.

atregüemos 1. that we may grant a truce; pres. subj. 1st pers. pl. / *atreguar*. 2. let us grant a truce; impve. 1st pers. pl.

atregüen 1. that they may grant a truce; pres. subj. 3rd pers. pl. / *atreguar*. 2. let them grant a truce; impve. 3rd pers. pl.

atregües that you may grant a truce; pres. subj. 2nd pers. sing. / *atreguar*.

atrevámonos let us dare; impve. 1st pers. pl. / *atreverse*.

atrévanse let them dare; impve. 3rd pers. pl. / *atreverse*.

atrévase let him (her/it) dare; impve. 3rd pers. sing. / *atreverse*.

atreveos (you all) dare; impve. 2nd pers. pl. / *atreverse*.

atreverse to dare or to be insolent. reg.

atrévete (you) dare; impve. 2nd pers. sing. / *atreverse*.

atreviéndose daring; pres. part. / *atreverse*.

atribuíos (you all) assume; impve. 2nd pers. pl. / *atribuirse*.

atribuir to attribute. irr.

atribuirse to assume. irr.

atribulándose being distressed; pres. part. / *atribularse*.

atribulaos (you all) be distressed; impve. 2nd pers. pl. / *atribularse*.

atribular to grieve or to vex. reg.

atribularse to be distressed. reg.

atribúlate (you) be distressed; impve. 2nd pers. sing. / *atribularse*.

atribulémonos let us be distressed; impve. 1st pers. pl. / *atribularse*.

atribúlense let them be distressed; impve. 3rd pers. pl. / *atribularse*.

atribúlese let him (her/it) be distressed; impve. 3rd pers. sing. / *atribularse*.

atribuya 1. that I may attribute; pres. subj. 1st pers. sing. / *atribuir*. 2. that he (she/it) may attribute; pres. subj. 3rd pers. sing. 3. let him (her/it) attribute; impve. 3rd pers. sing.

atribuyáis that you (all) may attribute; pres. subj. 2nd pers. pl. / *atribuir*.

atribuyámonos let us assume; impve. 1st pers. pl. / *atribuirse*.

atribuyamos 1. that we may attribute; pres. subj. 1st pers. pl. / *atribuir*. 2. let us attribute; impve. 1st pers. pl.

atribuyan 1. that they may attribute; pres. subj. 3rd pers. pl. / *atribuir*. 2. let them attribute; impve. 3rd pers. pl.

atribúyanse let them assume; impve. 3rd pers. pl. / *atribuirse*.

atribuyas that you may attribute; pres. subj. 2nd pers. sing. / *atribuir*.

atribúyase let him (her/it) assume; impve. 3rd pers. sing. / *atribuirse*.

atribuye 1. he (she/it) attributes; pres. ind. 3rd pers. sing. / *atribuir*. 2. (you) attribute; impve. 2nd pers. sing.

atribuyen they attribute; pres. ind. 3rd pers. pl. / *atribuir*.

atribuyendo attributing; pres. part. / *atribuir*.

atribuyéndose assuming; pres. part. / *atribuirse*.

atribuyera 1. that I might attribute; imp. subj. 1st pers. sing. / *atribuir*. 2. that he (she/it) might attribute; imp. subj. 3rd pers. sing.

atribuyerais that you (all) might attribute; imp. subj. 2nd pers pl. / *atribuir*.

atribuyéramos that we might attribute; imp. subj. 1st pers. pl. / *atribuir*.

atribuyeran that they might attribute; imp. subj. 3rd pers. pl. / *atribuir*.

atribuyeras that you might attribute; imp. subj. 2nd pers. sing. / *atribuir*.

atribuyeron they attributed; past 3rd pers. pl. / *atribuir*.

atribuyes you attribute; pres. ind. 2nd pers. sing. / *atribuir*.

atribuyese 1. that I might attribute; imp. subj. 1st pers. sing. / *atribuir*. 2. that he (she/it) might attribute; imp. subj. 3rd pers. sing.

atribuyeseis that you (all) might attribute; imp. subj. 2nd pers pl. / *atribuir*.

atribuyésemos that we might attribute; imp. subj. 1st pers. pl. / *atribuir*.

atribuyesen that they might attribute; imp. subj. 3rd pers. pl. / *atribuir*.

atribuyeses that you might attribute; imp. subj. 2nd pers. sing. / *atribuir*.

atribúyete (you) assume; impve. 2nd pers. sing. / *atribuirse*.

atribuyo I attribute; pres. ind. 1st pers. sing. / *atribuir*.

atribuyó he (she/it) attributed; past 3rd pers. sing. / *atribuir*.

atrincherándose taking cover; pres. part. / *atrincherarse*.

atrincheraos (you all) take cover; impve. 2nd pers. pl. / *atrincherarse*.

atrincherar to entrench. reg.

atrincherarse to take cover. reg.

atrinchérate (you) take cover; impve. 2nd pers. sing. / *atrincherarse*.

atrincherémonos let us take cover; impve. 1st pers. pl. / *atrincherarse*.

atrinchérense let them take cover; impve. 3rd pers. pl. / *atrincherarse*.

atrinchérese let him (her/it) take cover; impve. 3rd pers. sing. / *atrincherarse*.

atrofiándose atrophying; pres. part. / *atrofiarse*.

atrofiarse to atrophy. reg.

atrofíense let them atrophy; impve. 3rd pers. pl. / *atrofiarse*.

atrofíese let him (her/it) atrophy; impve. 3rd pers. sing. / *atrofiarse*.

atronándose being thunderstruck; pres. part. / *atronarse*.

atronar to deafen or to stun. irr.

atronarse to be thunderstruck. irr.

atropellándose rushing; pres. part. / *atropellarse*.

atropellaos (you all) rush; impve. 2nd pers. pl. / *atropellarse*.

atropellar to trample down. reg.

atropellarse to fall all over oneself or to rush. reg.

atropéllate (you) rush; impve. 2nd pers. sing. / *atropellarse*.

atropellémonos let us rush; impve. 1st pers. pl. / *atropellarse*.

atropéllense let them rush; impve. 3rd pers. pl. / *atropellarse*.

atropéllese let him (her/it) rush; impve. 3rd pers. sing. / *atropellarse*.

atruena 1. he (she/it) deafens; pres. ind. 3rd pers. sing. / *atronar*. 2. (you) deafen; impve. 2nd pers. sing.

atruenan they deafen; pres. ind. 3rd pers. pl. / *atronar*.

atruenas you deafen; pres. ind. 2nd pers. sing. / *atronar.*

atruene 1. that I may deafen; pres. subj. 1st pers. sing. / *atronar.* 2. that he (she/it) may deafen; pres. subj. 3rd pers. sing. 3. let him (her/it) deafen; impve. 3rd pers. sing.

atruenen 1. that they may deafen; pres. subj. 3rd pers. pl. / *atronar.* 2. let them deafen; impve. 3rd pers. pl.

atruénense let them be thunderstruck; impve. 3rd pers. pl. / *atronarse.*

atruenes that you may deafen; pres. subj. 2nd pers. sing. / *atronar.*

atruénese let it be thunderstruck; impve. 3rd pers. sing. / *atronarse.*

atrueno I deafen; pres. ind. 1st pers. sing. / *atronar.*

aturdámonos let us be stunned; impve. 1st pers. pl. / *aturdirse.*

atúrdanse let them be stunned; impve. 3rd pers. pl. / *aturdirse.*

atúrdase let him (her/it) be stunned; impve. 3rd pers. sing. / *aturdirse.*

atúrdete (you) be stunned; impve. 2nd pers. sing. / *aturdirse.*

aturdiéndose being stunned; pres. part. / *aturdirse.*

aturdíos (you all) be stunned; impve. 2nd pers. pl. / *aturdirse.*

aturdir to stun or bewilder. reg.

aturdirse to be stunned. reg.

aturrullar to confuse. reg.

aturullar to confuse. reg.

atusar to trim. reg.

atuve I depended; past 1st pers. sing. / *atenerse.*

atuviera 1. that I might depend; imp. subj. 1st pers. sing. / *atenerse.* 2. that he (she/it) might depend; imp. subj. 3rd pers. sing.

atuvierais that you (all) might depend; imp. subj. 2nd pers pl. / *atenerse.*

atuviéramos that we might depend; imp. subj. 1st pers. pl. / *atenerse.*

atuvieran that they might depend; imp. subj. 3rd pers. pl. / *atenerse*

atuvieras that you might depend; imp. subj. 2nd pers. sing. / *atenerse.*

atuvieron they depended; past 3rd pers. pl. / *atenerse.*

atuviese 1. that I might depend; imp. subj. 1st pers. sing. / *atenerse.* 2. that he (she/it) might depend; imp. subj. 3rd pers. sing.

atuvieseis that you (all) might depend; imp. subj. 2nd pers pl. / *atenerse.*

atuviésemos that we might depend; imp. subj. 1st pers. pl. / *atenerse.*

atuviesen that they might depend; imp. subj. 3rd pers. pl. / *atenerse.*

atuvieses that you might depend; imp. subj. 2nd pers. sing. / *atenerse.*

atuvimos we depended; past 1st pers. pl. / *atenerse.*

atuviste you depended; past 2nd pers. sing. / *atenerse.*

atuvisteis you (all) depended; past 2nd pers. pl. / *atenerse.*

atuvo he (she/it) depended; past 3rd pers. sing. / *atenerse.*

augurar to foretell or to predict. reg.

aúlla 1. he (she/it) howls; pres. ind. 3rd pers. sing. / *aullar.* 2. (you) howl; impve. 2nd pers. sing.

aúllan they howl; pres. ind. 3rd pers. pl. / *aullar.*

aullar to howl. irr.

aúllas you howl; pres. ind. 2nd pers. sing. / *aullar.*

aúlle 1. that I may howl; pres. subj. 1st pers. sing. / *aullar.* 2. that he (she/it) may howl; pres. subj. 3rd pers. sing. 3. let him (her/it) howl; impve. 3rd pers. sing.

aúllen 1. that they may howl; pres. subj. 3rd pers. pl. / *aullar.* 2. let them howl; impve. 3rd pers. pl.

aúlles that you may howl; pres. subj. 2nd pers. sing. / *aullar.*

aúllo I howl; pres. ind. 1st pers. sing. / *aullar.*

aumentándose increasing; pres. part. / *aumentarse.*

aumentaos (you all) increase; impve. 2nd pers. pl. / *aumentarse.*

aumentar to augment. reg.

aumentarse to increase. reg.

auméntate (you) increase; impve. 2nd pers. sing. / *aumentarse.*

aumentémonos let us increase; impve. 1st pers. pl. / *aumentarse.*

auméntense let them increase; impve. 3rd pers. pl. / *aumentarse.*

auméntese let him (her/it) increase; impve. 3rd pers. sing. / *aumentarse.*

aunar to unite or to assemble. reg.

aúpa 1. he (she/it) gives a hoist up; pres. ind. 3rd pers. sing. / *aupar.* 2. (you) give a hoist up; impve. 2nd pers. sing.

aúpan they give a hoist up; pres. ind. 3rd pers. pl. / *aupar.*

aupar to give a hoist up or to hitch up. irr.

aúpas you give a hoist up; pres. ind. 2nd pers. sing. / *aupar.*

aúpe 1. that I may give a hoist up; pres. subj. 1st pers. sing. / *aupar.* 2. that he (she/it) may give a hoist up; pres. subj. 3rd pers. sing. 3. let him (her/it) give a hoist up; impve. 3rd pers. sing.

aúpen 1. that they may give a hoist up; pres. subj. 3rd pers. pl. / *aupar.* 2. let them give a hoist up; impve. 3rd pers. pl.

aúpes that you may give a hoist up; pres. subj. 2nd pers. sing. / *aupar.*

aúpo I give a hoist up; pres. ind. 1st pers. sing. / *aupar.*

auscultar to sound or examine by listening to (the heart). reg.

ausentándose leaving; pres. part. / *ausentarse.*

ausentaos (you all) leave; impve. 2nd pers. pl. / *ausentarse.*

ausentar to send away. reg.

ausentarse to leave. reg.

auséntate (you) leave; impve. 2nd pers. sing. / *ausentarse*.

ausentémonos let us leave; impve. 1st pers. pl. / *ausentarse*.

auséntense let them leave; impve. 3rd pers. pl. / *ausentarse*.

auséntese let him (her/it) leave; impve. 3rd pers. sing. / *ausentarse*.

auspiciar to sponsor. reg.

autenticar to authenticate. irr.

autentique 1. that I may authenticate; pres. subj. 1st pers. sing. / *autenticar*. 2. that he (she/it) may authenticate; pres. subj. 3rd pers. sing. 3. let him (her/it) authenticate; impve. 3rd pers. sing.

autentiqué I authenticated; past 1st pers. sing. / *autenticar*.

autentiquéis that you (all) may authenticate; pres. subj. 2nd pers. pl. / *autenticar*.

autentiquemos 1. that we may authenticate; pres. subj. 1st pers. pl. / *autenticar*. 2. let us authenticate; impve. 1st pers. pl.

autentiquen 1. that they may authenticate; pres. subj. 3rd pers. pl. / *autenticar*. 2. let them authenticate; impve. 3rd pers. pl.

autentiques that you may authenticate; pres. subj. 2nd pers. sing. / *autenticar*.

automatice 1. that I may automate; pres. subj. 1st pers. sing. / *automatizar*. 2. that he (she/it) may automate; pres. subj. 3rd pers. sing. 3. let him (her/it) automate; impve. 3rd pers. sing.

automaticé I automated; past 1st pers. sing. / *automatizar*.

automaticéis that you (all) may automate; pres. subj. 2nd pers. pl. / *automatizar*.

automaticemos 1. that we may automate; pres. subj. 1st pers. pl. / *automatizar*. 2. let us automate; impve. 1st pers. pl.

automaticen 1. that they may automate; pres. subj. 3rd pers. pl. / *automatizar*. 2. let them automate; impve. 3rd pers. pl.

automatices that you may automate; pres. subj. 2nd pers. sing. / *automatizar*.

automatizar to automate. irr.

autorice 1. that I may authorize; pres. subj. 1st pers. sing. / *autorizar*. 2. that he (she/it) may authorize; pres. subj. 3rd pers. sing. 3. let him (her/it) authorize; impve. 3rd pers. sing.

autoricé I authorized; past 1st pers. sing. / *autorizar*.

autoricéis that you (all) may authorize; pres. subj. 2nd pers. pl. / *autorizar*.

autoricemos 1. that we may authorize; pres. subj. 1st pers. pl. / *autorizar*. 2. let us authorize; impve. 1st pers. pl.

autoricen 1. that they may authorize; pres. subj. 3rd pers. pl. / *autorizar*. 2. let them authorize; impve. 3rd pers. pl.

autorices that you may authorize; pres. subj. 2nd pers. sing. / *autorizar*.

autorizar to authorize. irr.

auxilía 1. he (she/it) aids; pres. ind. 3rd pers. sing. / *auxiliar*. 2. (you) aid; impve. 2nd pers. sing.

auxilían they aid; pres. ind. 3rd pers. pl. / *auxiliar*.

auxiliar to aid or assist. irr.

auxilías you aid; pres. ind. 2nd pers. sing. / *auxiliar*.

auxilíe 1. that I may aid; pres. subj. 1st pers. sing. / *auxiliar*. 2. that he (she/it) may aid; pres. subj. 3rd pers. sing. 3. let him (her/it) aid; impve. 3rd pers. sing.

auxilíen 1. that they may aid; pres. subj. 3rd pers. pl. / *auxiliar*. 2. let them aid; impve. 3rd pers. pl.

auxilíes that you may aid; pres. subj. 2nd pers. sing. / *auxiliar*.

auxilío I aid; pres. ind. 1st pers. sing. / *auxiliar*.

avalar to stand security for. reg.

avalorar to enhance the value of or to evaluate. reg.

avalúa 1. he (she/it) estimates; pres. ind. 3rd pers. sing. / *avaluar*. 2.(you) estimate; impve. 2nd pers. sing.

avalúan they estimate; pres. ind. 3rd pers. pl. / *avaluar*.

avaluar to estimate or to value. irr.

avalúas you estimate; pres. ind. 2nd pers. sing. / *avaluar*.

avalúe 1. that I may estimate; pres. subj. 1st pers. sing. / *avaluar*. 2. that he (she/it) may estimate; pres. subj. 3rd pers. sing. 3. let him (her/it) estimate; impve. 3rd pers. sing.

avalúen 1. that they may estimate; pres. subj. 3rd pers. pl. / *avaluar*. 2. let them estimate; impve. 3rd pers. pl.

avalúes that you may estimate; pres. subj. 2nd pers. sing. / *avaluar*.

avalúo I estimate; pres. ind. 1st pers. sing. / *avaluar*.

avance 1. that I may advance; pres. subj. 1st pers. sing. / *avanzar*. 2. that he (she/it) may advance; pres. subj. 3rd pers. sing. 3. let him (her/it) advance; impve. 3rd pers. sing.

avancé I advanced; past 1st pers. sing. / *avanzar*.

avancéis that you (all) may advance; pres. subj. 2nd pers. pl. / *avanzar*.

avancemos 1. that we may advance; pres. subj. 1st pers. pl. / *avanzar*. 2. let us advance; impve. 1st pers. pl.

avancen 1. that they may advance; pres. subj. 3rd pers. pl. / *avanzar*. 2. let them advance; impve. 3rd pers. pl.

avances that you may advance; pres. subj. 2nd pers. sing. / *avanzar*.

avanzar to advance. irr.

avasallándose submitting; pres. part. / *avasallarse*.

avasallaos (you all) submit; impve. 2nd pers. pl. / *avasallarse*.

avasallar to subject. reg.

avasallarse to submit. reg.

avasállate (you) submit; impve. 2nd pers. sing. / *avasallarse*.

avasallémonos let us submit; impve. 1st pers. pl. / *avasallarse*.

avasállense let them submit; impve. 3rd pers. pl. / *avasallarse*.

avasállese let him (her/it) submit; impve. 3rd pers. sing. / *avasallarse*.

avece 1. that I may accustom; pres. subj. 1st pers. sing. / *avezar*. 2. that he (she/it) may accustom; pres. subj. 3rd pers. sing. 3. let him (her/it) accustom; impve. 3rd pers. sing.

avecé I accustomed; past 1st pers. sing. / *avezar*.

avecéis that you (all) may accustom; pres. subj. 2nd pers. pl. / *avezar*

avecémonos let us become accustomed; impve. 1st pers. pl. / *avezarse*.

avecemos 1. that we may accustom; pres. subj. 1st pers. pl. / *avezar*. 2. let us accustom; impve. 1st pers. pl.

avecen 1. that they may accustom; pres. subj. 3rd pers. pl. / *avezar*. 2. let them accustom; impve. 3rd pers. pl.

avécense let them become accustomed; impve. 3rd pers. pl. / *avezarse*.

aveces that you may accustom; pres. subj. 2nd pers. sing. / *avezar*.

avécese let him (her/it) become accustomed; impve. 3rd pers. sing. / *avezarse*.

avecinándose approaching; pres. part. / *avecinarse*.

avecinaos (you all) approach; impve. 2nd pers. pl. / *avecinarse*.

avecinarse to approach. reg.

avecínate (you) approach; impve. 2nd pers. sing. / *avecinarse*.

avecindándose settling; pres. part. / *avecindarse*.

avecindaos (you all) settle; impve. 2nd pers. pl. / *avecindarse*.

avecindar to domicile. reg.

avecindarse to settle or to take up residence. reg.

avecíndate (you) settle; impve. 2nd pers. sing. / *avecindarse*.

avecindémonos let us settle; impve. 1st pers. pl. / *avecindarse*.

avecíndense let them settle; impve. 3rd pers. pl. / *avecindarse*.

avecíndese let him (her/it) settle; impve. 3rd pers. sing. / *avecindarse*.

avecinémonos let us approach; impve. 1st pers. pl. / *avecinarse*.

avecínense let them approach; impve. 3rd pers. pl. / *avecinarse*.

avecínese let him (her/it) approach; impve. 3rd pers. sing. / *avecinarse*.

avejentándose aging prematurely; pres. part. / *avejentarse*.

avejentaos (you all) age prematurely; impve. 2nd pers. pl. / *avejentarse*.

avejentarse to age prematurely. reg.

avejéntate (you) age prematurely; impve. 2nd pers. sing. / *avejentarse*.

avejentémonos let us age prematurely; impve. 1st pers. pl. / *avejentarse*.

avejéntense let them age prematurely; impve. 3rd pers. pl. / *avejentarse*.

avejéntese let him (her/it) age prematurely; impve. 3rd pers. sing. / *avejentarse*.

avejigar to blister. reg.

avellanándose shriveling; pres. part. / *avellanarse*.

avellanaos (you all) shrivel; impve. 2nd pers. pl. / *avellanarse*.

avellanar to countersink. reg.

avellanarse to shrivel. reg.

avellánate (you) shrivel; impve. 2nd pers. sing. / *avellanarse*.

avellanémonos let us shrivel; impve. 1st pers. pl. / *avellanarse*.

avellánense let them shrivel; impve. 3rd pers. pl. / *avellanarse*.

avellánese let him (her/it) shrivel; impve. 3rd pers. sing. / *avellanarse*.

aven (you) reconcile; impve. 2nd pers. sing. / *avenir*.

avendrá he (she/it) will reconcile; fut. 3rd pers. sing. / *avenir*.

avendrán they will reconcile; fut. 3rd pers. pl. / *avenir*.

avendrás you will reconcile; fut. 2nd pers. sing. / *avenir*.

avendré I shall reconcile; fut. 1st pers. sing. / *avenir*.

avendréis you (all) will reconcile; fut. 2nd pers. pl. / *avenir*.

avendremos we shall reconcile; fut. 1st pers. pl. / *avenir*.

avendría 1. I should reconcile; cond. 1st pers. sing. / *avenir*. 2. he (she/it) would reconcile; cond. 3rd pers. sing.

avendríais you (all) would reconcile; cond. 2nd pers. pl. / *avenir*.

avendríamos we should reconcile; cond. 1st pers. pl. / *avenir*.

avendrían they would reconcile; cond. 3rd pers. pl. / *avenir*.

avendrías you would reconcile; cond. 2nd pers. sing. / *avenir*.

avénete (you) agree; impve. 2nd pers. sing. / *avenirse*.

avenga 1. that I may reconcile; pres. subj. 1st pers. sing. / *avenir*. 2. that he (she/it) may reconcile; pres. subj. 3rd pers. sing. 3. let him (her/it) reconcile; impve. 3rd pers. sing.

avengáis that you (all) may reconcile; pres. subj. 2nd pers. pl. / *avenir*.

avengámonos let us agree; impve. 1st pers. pl. / *avenirse*.

avengamos 1. that we may reconcile; pres. subj. 1st pers. pl. / *avenir*. 2. let us reconcile; impve. 1st pers. pl.

avengan 1. that they may reconcile; pres. subj. 3rd pers. pl. / *avenir*. 2. let them reconcile; impve. 3rd pers. pl.

avénganse let them agree; impve. 3rd pers. pl. / *avenirse*.

avengas that you may reconcile; pres. subj. 2nd pers. sing. / *avenir*.

avéngase let him (her/it) agree; impve. 3rd pers. sing. / *avenirse*.

avengo I reconcile; pres. ind. 1st pers. sing. / *avenir*.
aveníos (you all) agree; impve. 2nd pers. pl. / *avenirse*.
avenir to reconcile. irr.
avenirse to agree or to compromise. irr.
aventajándose getting ahead of; pres. part. / *aventajarse*.
aventajaos (you all) get ahead of; impve. 2nd pers. pl. / *aventajarse*.
aventajar to excel. reg.
aventajarse to get ahead of. reg.
aventájate (you) get ahead of; impve. 2nd pers. sing. / *aventajarse*.
aventajémonos let us get ahead of; impve. 1st pers. pl. / *aventajarse*.
aventájense let them get ahead of; impve. 3rd pers. pl. / *aventajarse*.
aventájese let him (her/it) get ahead of; impve. 3rd pers. sing. / *aventajarse*.
aventándose puffing up; pres. part. / *aventarse*.
aventaos (you all) puff up; impve. 2nd pers. pl. / *aventarse*.
aventar to fan or to winnow. irr.
aventarse to puff up. irr.
aventémonos let us puff up; impve. 1st pers. pl. / *aventarse*.
aventurándose taking a chance; pres. part. / *aventurarse*.
aventuraos (you all) take a chance; impve. 2nd pers. pl. / *aventurarse*.
aventurar to venture or hazard. reg.
aventurarse to take a chance. reg.
aventúrate (you) take a chance; impve. 2nd pers. sing. / *aventurarse*.
aventurémonos let us take a chance; impve. 1st pers. pl. / *aventurarse*.
aventúrense let them take a chance; impve. 3rd pers. pl. / *aventurarse*.
aventúrese let him (her/it) take a chance; impve. 3rd pers. sing. / *aventurarse*.
avergoncé I shamed; past 1st pers. sing. / *avergonzar*.
avergoncéis that you (all) may shame; pres. subj. 2nd pers. pl. / *avergonzar*.
avergoncémonos let us be ashamed; impve. 1st pers. pl. / *avergonzarse*.
avergoncemos 1. that we may shame; pres. subj. 1st pers. pl. / *avergonzar*. 2. let us shame; impve. 1st pers. pl.
avergonzándose being ashamed; pres. part. / *avergonzarse*.
avergonzaos (you all) be ashamed; impve. 2nd pers. pl. / *avergonzarse*.
avergonzar to shame. irr.
avergonzarse to be ashamed. irr.
avergüence 1. that I may shame; pres. subj. 1st pers. sing. / *avergonzar*. 2. that he (she/it) may shame; pres. subj. 3rd pers. sing. 3. let him (her/it) shame; impve. 3rd pers. sing.

avergüencen 1. that they may shame; pres. subj. 3rd pers. pl. / *avergonzar*. 2. let them shame; impve. 3rd pers. pl.
avergüéncense let them be ashamed; impve. 3rd pers. pl. / *avergonzarse*.
avergüences that you may shame; pres. subj. 2nd pers. sing. / *avergonzar*.
avergüéncese let him (her/it) be ashamed; impve. 3rd pers. sing. / *avergonzarse*.
avergüenza 1. he (she/it) shames; pres. ind. 3rd pers. sing. / *avergonzar*. 2. (you) shame; impve. 2nd pers. sing.
avergüenzan they shame; pres. ind. 3rd pers. pl. / *avergonzar*.
avergüenzas you shame; pres. ind. 2nd pers. sing. / *avergonzar*.
avergüénzate (you) be ashamed; impve. 2nd pers. sing. / *avergonzarse*.
avergüenzo I shame; pres. ind. 1st pers. sing. / *avergonzar*.
avería 1. he (she/it) damages; pres. ind. 3rd pers. sing. / *averiar*. 2. (you) damage; impve. 2nd pers. sing.
averían they damage; pres. ind. 3rd pers. pl. / *averiar*.
averiándose breaking down; pres. part. / *averiarse*.
averiaos (you all) break down; impve. 2nd pers. pl. / *averiarse*.
averiar to damage. irr.
averiarse to break down. irr.
averías you damage; pres. ind. 2nd pers. sing. / *averiar*.
averíate (you) break down; impve. 2nd pers. sing. / *averiarse*.
averíe 1. that I may damage; pres. subj. 1st pers. sing. / *averiar*. 2. that he (she/it) may damage; pres. subj. 3rd pers. sing. 3. let him (her/it) damage; impve. 3rd pers. sing.
averiémonos let us break down; impve. 1st pers. pl. / *averiarse*.
averíen 1. that they may damage; pres. subj. 3rd pers. pl. / *averiar*. 2. let them damage; impve. 3rd pers. pl.
averíense let them break down; impve. 3rd pers. pl. / *averiarse*.
averíes that you may damage; pres. subj. 2nd pers. sing. / *averiar*.
averíese let him (her/it) break down; impve. 3rd pers. sing. / *averiarse*.
averiguar to find out. irr.
averigüe 1. that I may find out; pres. subj. 1st pers. sing. / *averiguar*. 2. that he (she/it) may find out; pres. subj. 3rd pers. sing. 3. let him (her/it) find out; impve. 3rd pers. sing.
averigüé I found out; past 1st pers. sing. / *averiguar*.
averigüéis that you (all) may find out; pres. subj. 2nd pers. pl. / *averiguar*.
averigüemos 1. that we may find out; pres. subj. 1st pers. pl. / *averiguar*. 2. let us find out; impve. 1st pers. pl.
averigüen 1. that they may find out; pres. subj. 3rd pers. pl. / *averiguar*. 2. let them find out; impve. 3rd pers. pl.

averigües ·that you may find out; pres. subj. 2nd pers. sing. / *averiguar.*

averío I damage; pres. ind. 1st pers. sing. / *averiar.*

averruega he (she/it) becomes warty; pres. ind. 3rd pers. sing. / *averrugarse.*

averruegan they become warty; pres. ind. 3rd pers. pl. / *averrugarse.*

averruegas you become warty; pres. ind. 2nd pers. sing. / *averrugarse.*

averruégate (you) become warty; impve. 2nd pers. sing. / *averrugarse.*

averruego I become warty; pres. ind. 1st pers. sing. / *averrugarse.*

averrueguen that they may become warty; pres. subj. 3rd pers. pl. / *averrugarse.*

averruéguense let them become warty; impve. 3rd pers. pl. / *averrugarse.*

averruegues that you may become warty; pres. subj. 2nd pers. sing. / *averrugarse.*

averruéguese let him (her/it) become warty; impve. 3rd pers. sing. / *averrugarse.*

averrugándose becoming warty; pres. part. / *averrugarse.*

averrugaos (you all) become warty; impve. 2nd pers. pl. / *averrugarse.*

averrugarse to become warty. irr.

averrugue 1. that I may become warty; pres. subj. 1st pers. sing. / *averrugarse.* 2. that he (she/it) may become warty; pres. subj. 3rd pers. sing.

averrugué I became warty; past 1st pers. sing. / *averrugarse.*

averruguéis that you (all) may become warty; pres. subj. 2nd pers. pl. / *averrugarse.*

averruguémonos let us become warty; impve. 1st pers. pl. / *averrugarse.*

averruguemos that we may become warty; pres. subj. 1st pers. pl. / *averrugarse.*

avezándose becoming accustomed; pres. part. / *avezarse.*

avezaos (you all) become accustomed; impve. 2nd pers. pl. / *avezarse.*

avezar to accustom or to habituate. irr.

avezarse to become accustomed. irr.

avézate (you) become accustomed; impve. 2nd pers. sing. / *avezarse.*

avía 1. he (she/it) gets ready; pres. ind. 3rd pers. sing. / *aviar.* 2. (you) get ready; impve. 2nd pers. sing.

avían they get ready; pres. ind. 3rd pers. pl. / *aviar.*

aviándose fitting oneself out; pres. part. / *aviarse.*

aviaos (you all) fit yourselves out; impve. 2nd pers. pl. / *aviarse.*

aviar to get ready or to equip. irr.

aviarse to fit oneself out. irr.

avías you get ready; pres. ind. 2nd pers. sing. / *aviar.*

avíate (you) fit yourself out; impve. 2nd pers. sing. / *aviarse.*

avíe 1. that I may get ready; pres. subj. 1st pers. sing. / *aviar.* 2. that he (she/it) may get ready; pres. subj. 3rd pers. sing. 3. let him (her/it) get ready; impve. 3rd pers. sing.

aviémonos let us fit ourselves out; impve. 1st pers. pl. / *aviarse.*

avíen 1. that they may get ready; pres. subj. 3rd pers. pl. / *aviar.* 2. let them get ready; impve. 3rd pers. pl.

aviene he (she/it) reconciles; pres. ind. 3rd pers. sing. / *avenir.*

avienen they reconcile; pres. ind. 3rd pers. pl. / *avenir.*

avienes you reconcile; pres. ind. 2nd pers. sing. / *avenir.*

avíense let them fit themselves out; impve. 3rd pers. pl. / *aviarse.*

avienta 1. he (she/it) fans; pres. ind. 3rd pers. sing. / *aventar.* 2. (you) fan; impve. 2nd pers. sing.

avientan they fan; pres. ind. 3rd pers. pl. / *aventar.*

avientas you fan; pres. ind. 2nd pers. sing. / *aventar.*

aviéntate (you) puff up; impve. 2nd pers. sing. / *aventarse.*

aviente 1. that I may fan; pres. subj. 1st pers. sing. / *aventar.* 2. that he (she/it) may fan; pres. subj. 3rd pers. sing. 3. let him (her/it) fan; impve. 3rd pers. sing.

avienten 1. that they may fan; pres. subj. 3rd pers. pl. / *aventar.* 2. let them fan; impve. 3rd pers. pl.

aviéntense let them puff up; impve. 3rd pers. pl. / *aventarse.*

avientes that you may fan; pres. subj. 2nd pers. sing. / *aventar.*

aviéntese let him (her/it) puff up; impve. 3rd pers. sing. / *aventarse.*

aviento I fan; pres. ind. 1st pers. sing. / *aventar.*

avíeis that you may get ready; pres. subj. 2nd pers. sing. / *aviar.*

avíese let him (her/it) fit himself (herself/itself) out; impve. 3rd pers. sing. / *aviarse.*

avillanándose degenerating; pres. part. / *avillanarse.*

avillanaos (you all) degenerate; impve. 2nd pers. pl. / *avillanarse.*

avillanar to debase. reg.

avillanarse to degenerate. reg.

avillánate (you) degenerate; impve. 2nd pers. sing. / *avillanarse.*

avillanémonos let us degenerate; impve. 1st pers. pl. / *avillanarse.*

avillánense let them degenerate; impve. 3rd pers. pl. / *avillanarse.*

avillánese let him (her/it) degenerate; impve. 3rd pers. sing. / *avillanarse.*

avinagrándose becoming sour; pres. part. / *avinagrarse.*

avinagraos (you all) become sour; impve. 2nd pers. pl. / *avinagrarse.*

avinagrar to make sour. reg.

avinagrarse to become sour. reg.

avinágrate (you) become sour; impve. 2nd pers. sing. / *avinagrarse.*

avinagrémonos let us become sour; impve. 1st pers. pl. / *avinagrarse.*

avinágrense let them become sour; impve. 3rd pers. pl. / *avinagrarse.*

avinágrese let him (her/it) become sour; impve. 3rd pers. sing. / *avinagrarse*.

avine I reconciled; past 1st pers. sing. / *avenir*.

aviniendo reconciling; pres. part. / *avenir*.

aviniéndose agreeing; pres. part. / *avenirse*.

aviniera 1. that I might reconcile; imp. subj. 1st pers. sing. / *avenir*. 2. that he (she/it) might reconcile; imp. subj. 3rd pers. sing.

avinierais that you (all) might reconcile; imp. subj. 2nd pers pl. / *avenir*.

aviniéramos that we might reconcile; imp. subj. 1st pers. pl. / *avenir*.

avinieran that they might reconcile; imp. subj. 3rd pers. pl. / *avenir*.

avinieras that you might reconcile; imp. subj. 2nd pers. sing. / *avenir*.

avinieron they reconciled; past 3rd pers. pl. / *avenir*.

aviniese 1. that I might reconcile; imp. subj. 1st pers. sing. / *avenir*. 2. that he (she/it) might reconcile; imp. subj. 3rd pers. sing.

avinieseis that you (all) might reconcile; imp. subj. 2nd pers pl. / *avenir*.

aviniésemos that we might reconcile; imp. subj. 1st pers. pl. / *avenir*.

aviniesen that they might reconcile; imp. subj. 3rd pers. pl. / *avenir*.

avinieses that you might reconcile; imp. subj. 2nd pers. sing. / *avenir*.

avinimos we reconciled; past 1st pers. pl. / *avenir*.

aviniste you reconciled; past 2nd pers. sing. / *avenir*.

avinisteis you (all) reconciled; past 2nd pers. pl. / *avenir*.

avino he (she/it) reconciled; past 3rd pers. sing. / *avenir*.

avío I get ready; pres. ind. 1st pers. sing. / *aviar*.

avisar to inform or to advise. reg.

avispándose becoming restless; pres. part. / *avisparse*.

avispaos (you all) become restless; impve. 2nd pers. pl. / *avisparse*.

avispar to spur or to incite. reg.

avisparse to become restless. reg.

avíspate (you) become restless; impve. 2nd pers. sing. / *avisparse*.

avispémonos let us become restless; impve. 1st pers. pl. / *avisparse*.

avíspense (you all) become restless; impve. 2nd pers. pl. / *avisparse*.

avíspese let him (her/it) become restless; impve. 3rd pers. sing. / *avisparse*.

avistándose having a meeting; pres. part. / *avistarse*.

avistaos (you all) have a meeting; impve. 2nd pers. pl. / *avistarse*.

avistar to glimpse. reg.

avistarse to have a meeting. reg.

avístate (you) have a meeting; impve. 2nd pers. sing. / *avistarse*.

avistémonos let us have a meeting; impve. 1st pers. pl. / *avistarse*.

avístense let them have a meeting; impve. 3rd pers. pl. / *avistarse*.

avístese let him (her/it) have a meeting; impve. 3rd pers. sing. / *avistarse*.

avivar to revive or to encourage. reg.

avizorar to watch. reg.

ayudar to help. reg.

ayunar to fast. reg.

azadonar to hoe. reg.

azafranar to flavor or color with saffron. reg.

azogándose being in a state of agitation; pres. part. / *azogarse*.

azogaos (you all) be in a state of agitation; impve. 2nd pers. pl. / *azogarse*.

azogar to coat with mercury. irr.

azogarse to be in a state of agitation. irr.

azógate (you) be in a state of agitation; impve. 2nd pers. sing. / *azogarse*.

azogue 1. that I may coat with mercury; pres. subj. 1st pers. sing. / *azogar*. 2. that he (she/it) may coat with mercury; pres. subj. 3rd pers. sing. 3. let him (her/it) coat with mercury; impve. 3rd pers. sing.

azogué I coated with mercury; past 1st pers. sing. / *azogar*.

azoguéis that you (all) may coat with mercury; pres. subj. 2nd pers. pl. / *azogar*.

azoguémonos let us be in a state of agitation; impve. 1st pers. pl. / *azogarse*.

azoguemos 1. that we may coat with mercury; pres. subj. 1st pers. pl. / *azogar*. 2. let us coat with mercury; impve. 1st pers. pl.

azoguen 1. that they may coat with mercury; pres. subj. 3rd pers. pl. / *azogar*. 2. let them coat with mercury; impve. 3rd pers. pl.

azóguense let them be in a state of agitation; impve. 3rd pers. pl. / *azogarse*.

azogues that you may coat with mercury; pres. subj. 2nd pers. sing. / *azogar*.

azóguese let him (her/it) be in a state of agitation; impve. 3rd pers. sing. / *azogarse*.

azolvándose getting clogged; pres. part. / *azolvarse*.

azolvaos (you all) get clogged; impve. 2nd pers. pl. / *azolvarse*.

azolvar to clog or obstruct. reg.

azolvarse to get clogged. reg.

azólvate (you) get clogged; impve. 2nd pers. sing. / *azolvarse*.

azolvémonos let us get clogged; impve. 1st pers. pl. / *azolvarse*.

azólvense let them get clogged; impve. 3rd pers. pl. / *azolvarse*.

azólvese let him (her/it) get clogged; impve. 3rd pers. sing. / *azolvarse*.

azorándose being startled; pres. part. / *azorarse*.

azoraos (you all) be startled; impve. 2nd pers. pl. / *azorarse*.

azorar to disturb or to abash or to excite. reg.

azorarse to be startled. reg.

azórate (you) be startled; impve. 2nd pers. sing. / *azorarse*.

azorémonos let us be startled; impve. 1st pers. pl. / *azorarse*.

azórense let them be startled; impve. 3rd pers. pl. / *azorarse*.

azórese let him (her/it) be startled; impve. 3rd pers. sing. / *azorarse*.

azotar to whip. reg.

azucarándose becoming sweet; pres. part. / *azucararse*.

azucaraos (you all) become sweet; impve. 2nd pers. pl. / *azucararse*.

azucarar to sugar. reg.

azucararse to become sweet or to turn to sugar. reg.

azucárate (you) become sweet; impve. 2nd pers. sing. / *azucararse*.

azucarémonos let us become sweet; impve. 1st pers. pl. / *azucararse*.

azucárense let them become sweet; impve. 3rd pers. pl. / *azucararse*.

azucárese let him (her/it) become sweet; impve. 3rd pers. sing. / *azucararse*.

azuce 1. that I may urge; pres. subj. 1st pers. sing. / *azuzar*. 2. that he (she/it) may urge; pres. subj. 3rd pers. sing. 3. let him (her/it) urge; impve. 3rd pers. sing.

azucé I urged; past 1st pers. sing. / *azuzar*.

azucéis that you (all) may urge; pres. subj. 2nd pers. pl. / *azuzar*.

azucemos 1. that we may urge; pres. subj. 1st pers. pl. / *azuzar*. 2. let us urge; impve. 1st pers. pl.

azucen 1. that they may urge; pres. subj. 3rd pers. pl. / *azuzar*. 2. let them urge; impve. 3rd pers. pl.

azuces that you may urge; pres. subj. 2nd pers. sing. / *azuzar*.

azulándose turning blue; pres. part. / *azularse*.

azulaos (you all) turn blue; impve. 2nd pers. pl. / *azularse*.

azular to color blue. reg.

azularse to turn blue. reg.

azúlate (you) turn blue; impve. 2nd pers. sing. / *azularse*.

azulejar to tile. reg.

azulémonos let us turn blue; impve. 1st pers. pl. / *azularse*.

azúlense let them turn blue; impve. 3rd pers. pl. / *azularse*.

azúlese let him (her/it) turn blue; impve. 3rd pers. sing. / *azularse*.

azuzar to urge or to set on. irr.

B

babear to drivel or slobber. reg.

babosear to drool or to act like a fool. reg.

bailar to dance or to spin around. reg.

bailotear to jig or to dance badly. reg.

bajándose alighting; pres. part. / *bajarse*.

bajaos (you all) alight; impve. 2nd pers. pl. / *bajarse*.

bajar to lower or to descend. reg.

bajarse to alight or to grovel. reg.

bájate (you) alight; impve. 2nd pers. sing. / *bajarse*.

bajémonos let us alight; impve. 1st pers. pl. / *bajarse*.

bájense let them alight; impve. 3rd pers. pl. / *bajarse*.

bájese let him (her/it) alight; impve. 3rd pers. sing. / *bajarse*.

baladrar to shout or screech. reg.

baladronear to boast. reg.

balanceándose swaying; pres. part. / *balancearse*.

balanceaos (you all) sway; impve. 2nd pers. pl. / *balancearse*.

balancear to balance. reg.

balancearse to rock or sway. reg.

balancéate (you) sway; impve. 2nd pers. sing. / *balancearse*.

balanceémonos let us sway; impve. 1st pers. pl. / *balancearse*.

balancéense let them sway; impve. 3rd pers. pl. / *balancearse*.

balancéese let him (her/it) sway; impve. 3rd pers. sing. / *balancearse*.

balar to bleat. reg.

balbucear to stammer or to babble. reg.

balbucir to stammer. irr. used only in those forms where the i is present in the verb endings.

baldar to cripple or to trump (a card). reg.

baldear to flush with water. reg.

baldonar to insult. reg.

baldosar to tile. reg.

balear to shoot at. reg.

balotar to ballot. reg.

balsear to cross by ferry. reg.

ballestear to shoot with a crossbow. reg.

bamboleándose staggering; pres. part. / *bambolearse*.

bamboleaos (you all) stagger; impve. 2nd pers. pl. / *bambolearse*.

bambolear to sway or to swing. reg.

bambolearse to stagger. reg.

bamboléate (you) stagger; impve. 2nd pers. sing. / *bambolearse*.

bamboleémonos let us stagger; impve. 1st pers. pl. / *bambolearse*.

bamboléense let them stagger; impve. 3rd pers. pl. / *bambolearse*.

bamboléese let him (her/it) stagger; impve. 3rd pers. sing. / *bambolearse*.

bandeándose shifting for oneself; pres. part. / *bandearse*.

bandeaos (you all) shift for yourselves; impve. 2nd pers. pl. / *bandearse*.

bandearse to shift for oneself. reg.

bandéate (you) shift for yourself; impve. 2nd pers. sing. / *bandearse*.

bandeémonos let us shift for ourselves; impve. 1st pers. pl. / *bandearse*.

bandéense let them shift for themselves; impve. 3rd pers. pl. / *bandearse*.

bandéese let him (her/it) shift for himself (herself/itself); impve. 3rd pers. sing. / *bandearse*.

banquetear to banquet. reg.
bañándose taking a bath; pres. part. / *bañarse*.
bañaos (you all) take a bath; impve. 2nd pers. pl. / *bañarse*.
bañar to bathe or to dip. reg.
bañarse to take a bath. reg.
báñate (you) take a bath; impve. 2nd pers. sing. / *bañarse*.
bañémonos let us take a bath; impve. 1st pers. pl. / *bañarse*.
báñense let them take a bath; impve. 3rd pers. pl. / *bañarse*.
báñese let him (her/it) take a bath; impve. 3rd pers. sing. / *bañarse*.
baquetear to beat or to annoy. reg.
barajándose getting mixed up; pres. part. / *barajarse*.
barajaos (you all) get mixed up; impve. 2nd pers. pl. / *barajarse*.
barajar to mix or to squabble. reg.
barajarse to get mixed up. reg.
barájate (you) get mixed up; impve. 2nd pers. sing. / *barajarse*.
barajémonos let us get mixed up; impve. 1st pers. pl. / *barajarse*.
barájense let them get mixed up; impve. 3rd pers. pl. / *barajarse*.
barájese let him (her/it) get mixed up; impve. 3rd pers. sing. / *barajarse*.
baratear to sell cheap. reg.
baraústa 1. he (she/it) aims; pres. ind. 3rd pers. sing. / *baraustar*. 2. (you) aim; impve. 2nd pers. sing.
baraústan they aim; pres. ind. 3rd pers. pl. / *baraustar*.
baraustar to aim or to ward off. irr.
baraústas you aim; pres. ind. 2nd pers. sing. / *baraustar*.
baraúste 1. that I may aim; pres. subj. 1st pers. sing. / *baraustar*. 2. that he (she/it) may aim; pres. subj. 3rd pers. sing. 3. let him (her/it) aim; impve. 3rd pers. sing.
baraústen 1. that they may aim; pres. subj. 3rd pers. pl. / *baraustar*. 2. let him (her/it) aim; impve. 3rd pers. pl.
baraústes that you may aim; pres. subj. 2nd pers. sing. / *baraustar*.
baraústo I aim; pres. ind. 1st pers. sing. / *baraustar*.
barbarice 1. that I may barbarize; pres. subj. 1st pers. sing. / *barbarizar* 2. that he (she/it) may barbarize; pres. subj. 3rd pers. sing. 3. let him (her/it) barbarize; impve. 3rd pers. sing.
barbaricé I barbarized; past 1st pers. sing. / *barbarizar*.
barbaricéis that you (all) may barbarize; pres. subj. 2nd pers. pl. / *barbarizar*.
barbaricemos 1. that we may barbarize; pres. subj. 1st pers. pl. / *barbarizar*. 2. let us barbarize; impve. 1st pers. pl.
barbaricen 1. that they may barbarize; pres. subj. 3rd pers. pl. / *barbarizar*. 2. let them barbarize; impve. 3rd pers. pl.

barbarices that you may barbarize; pres. subj. 2nd pers. sing. / *barbarizar*.
barbarizar to barbarize or to say outrageous things. irr.
barbear to reach with the chin. reg.
barbechar to plow. reg.
barbotar to mumble or to mutter. reg.
barbotear to mumble or to mutter. reg.
barbullar to chatter noisely. reg.
barloar to bring alongside. reg.
barloventear to ply windward. reg.
barnice 1. that I may varnish; pres. subj. 1st pers. sing. / *barnizar*. 2. that he (she/it) may varnish; pres. subj. 3rd pers. sing. 3. let him (her/it) varnish; impve. 3rd pers. sing.
barnicé I varnished; past 1st pers. sing. / *barnizar*.
barnicéis that you (all) may varnish; pres. subj. 2nd pers. pl. / *barnizar*.
barnicemos 1. that we may varnish; pres. subj. 1st pers. pl. / *barnizar*. 2. let us varnish; impve. 1st pers. pl.
barnicen 1. that they may varnish; pres. subj. 3rd pers. pl. / *barnizar*. 2. let them varnish; impve. 3rd pers. pl.
barnices that you may varnish; pres. subj. 2nd pers. sing. / *barnizar*.
barnizar to varnish or to polish. reg.
barrar to daub or to mire. reg.
barrenar to drill or to scuttle (a ship). reg.
barrer to sweep or brush against. reg.
barruntar to foresee or to suspect. reg.
basándose en relying on; pres. part. / *basarse en*.
basaos en (you all) rely on; impve. 2nd pers. pl. / *basarse en*.
basar to base or to support. reg.
basarse en to rely on. reg.
básate en (you) rely on; impve. 2nd pers. sing. / *basarse en*.
basémonos en let us rely on; impve. 1st pers. pl. / *basarse en*.
básense en let them rely on; impve. 3rd pers. pl. / *basarse en*.
básese en let him (her/it) rely on; impve. 3rd pers. sing. / *basarse en*.
basquear to be nauseated. reg.
bastándose being self-sufficient; pres. part. / *bastarse*.
bastaos (you all) be self-sufficient; impve. 2nd pers. pl. / *bastarse*.
bastar to suffice. reg.
bastardear to degenerate. reg.
bastarse to be self-sufficient. reg.
bástate (you) be self-sufficient; impve. 2nd pers. sing. / *bastarse*.
bastear to stitch loosely. reg.
bastémonos let us be self-sufficient; impve. 1st pers. pl. / *bastarse*.
bástense let them be self-sufficient; impve. 3rd pers. pl. / *bastarse*.

bástese let him (her/it) be self-sufficient; impve. 3rd pers. sing. / *bastarse.*

bastillar to hem. reg.

batallar to battle or to struggle. reg.

batámonos let us fight; impve. 1st pers. pl. / *batirse.*

batanear to beat or to thrash. reg.

bátanse let them fight; impve. 3rd pers. pl. / *batirse.*

bátase let him (her/it) fight; impve. 3rd pers. sing. / *batirse.*

batear to bat (baseball). reg.

bátete (you) fight; impve. 2nd pers. sing. / *batirse.*

batiéndose fighting; pres. part. / *batirse.*

batíos (you all) fight; impve. 2nd pers. pl. / *batirse.*

batir to beat or to ruin. reg.

batirse to fight. reg.

bautice 1. that I may baptize; pres. subj. 1st pers. sing. / *bautizar.* 2. that he (she/it) may baptize; pres. subj. 3rd pers. sing. 3. let him (her/it) baptize; impve. 3rd pers. sing.

bauticé I baptized; past 1st pers. sing. / *bautizar.*

bauticéis that you (all) may baptize; pres. subj. 2nd pers. pl. / *bautizar.*

bauticemos 1. that we may baptize; pres. subj. 1st pers. pl. / *bautizar.* 2. let us baptize; impve. 1st pers. pl.

bauticen 1. that they may baptize; pres. subj. 3rd pers. pl. / *bautizar.* 2. let them baptize; impve. 3rd pers. pl.

bautices that you may baptize; pres. subj. 2nd pers. sing. / *bautizar.*

bautizar to baptize or to christen. irr.

bazucar to stir or to meddle with. irr.

bazuque 1. that I may stir; pres. subj. 1st pers. sing. / *bazucar.* 2. that he (she/it) may stir; pres. subj. 3rd pers. sing. 3. let him (her/it) stir; impve. 3rd pers. sing.

bazuqué I stirred; past 1st pers. sing. / *bazucar.*

bazuquear to stir or to meddle with. reg.

bazuquéis that you (all) may stir; pres. subj. 2nd pers. pl. / *bazucar.*

bazuquemos 1. that we may stir; pres. subj. 1st pers. pl. / *bazucar.* 2. let us stir; impve. 1st pers. pl.

bazuquen 1. that they may stir; pres. subj. 3rd pers. pl. / *bazucar.* 2. let them stir; impve. 3rd pers. pl.

bazuques that you may stir; pres. subj. 2nd pers. sing. / *bazucar.*

beatificar to beautify or to sanctify. irr.

beatifique 1. that I may beautify; pres. subj. 1st pers. sing. / *beatificar.* 2. that he (she/it) may beautify; pres. subj. 3rd pers. sing. 3. let him (her/it) beautify; impve. 3rd pers. sing.

beatifiqué I beautified; past 1st pers. sing. / *beatificar.*

beatifiquéis that you (all) may beautify; pres. subj. 2nd pers. pl. / *beatificar.*

beatifiquemos 1. that we may beautify; pres. subj. 1st pers. pl. / *beatificar.* 2. let us beautify; impve. 1st pers. pl.

beatifiquen 1. that they may beautify; pres. subj. 3rd pers. pl. / *beatificar.* 2. let them beautify; impve. 3rd pers. pl.

beatifiques that you may beautify; pres. subj. 2nd pers. sing. / *beatificar.*

bebámonos let us swallow; impve. 1st pers. pl. / *beberse.*

bébanse let them swallow; impve. 3rd pers. pl. / *beberse.*

bébase let him (her/it) swallow; impve. 3rd pers. sing. / *beberse.*

bebeos (you all) swallow; impve. 2nd pers. pl. / *beberse.*

beber to drink or to absorb. reg.

beberse to swallow. reg.

bébete (you) swallow; impve. 2nd pers. sing. / *beberse.*

bebiéndose swallowing; pres. part. / *beberse.*

befar to scoff or to jeer at. reg.

beldar to winnow. irr.

bellaquear to cheat or to play tricks. reg.

bendecir to bless. irr.

bendi (you) bless; impve. 2nd pers. sing. / *bendecir.*

bendice he (she/it) blesses; pres. ind. 3rd pers. sing. / *bendecir.*

bendicen they bless; pres. ind. 3rd pers. pl. / *bendecir.*

bendices you bless; pres. ind. 2nd pers. sing. / *bendecir.*

bendiciendo blessing; pres. part. / *bendecir.*

bendiga 1. that I may bless; pres. subj. 1st pers. sing. / *bendecir.* 2. that he (she/it) may bless; pres. subj. 3rd pers. sing. 3. let him (her/it) bless; impve. 3rd pers. sing.

bendigáis that you (all) may bless; pres. subj. 2nd pers. pl. / *bendecir.*

bendigamos 1. that we may bless; pres. subj. 1st pers. pl. / *bendecir.* 2. let us bless; impve. 1st pers. pl.

bendigan 1. that they may bless; pres. subj. 3rd pers. pl. / *bendecir.* 2. let them bless; impve. 3rd pers. pl.

bendigas that you may bless; pres. subj. 2nd pers. sing. / *bendecir.*

bendigo I bless; pres. ind. 1st pers. sing. / *bendecir.*

bendije I blessed; past 1st pers. sing. / *bendecir.*

bendijera 1. that I might bless; imp. subj. 1st pers. sing. / *bendecir.* 2. that he (she/it) might bless; imp. subj. 3rd pers. sing.

bendijerais that you (all) might bless; imp. subj. 2nd pers pl. / *bendecir.*

bendijéramos that we might bless; imp. subj. 1st pers. pl. / *bendecir.*

bendijeran that they might bless; imp. subj. 3rd pers. pl. / *bendecir.*

bendijeras that you might bless; imp. subj. 2nd pers. sing. / *bendecir.*

bendijeron they blessed; past 3rd pers. pl. / *bendecir.*

bendijese 1. that I might bless; imp. subj. 1st pers. sing. / *bendecir.* 2. that he (she/it) might bless; imp. subj. 3rd pers. sing.

bendijeseis that you (all) might bless; imp. subj. 2nd pers pl. / *bendecir.*

bendijésemos that we might bless; imp. subj. 1st pers. pl. / *bendecir.*

bendijesen that they might bless; imp. subj. 3rd pers. pl. / *bendecir.*

bendijeses that you might bless; imp. subj. 2nd pers. sing. / *bendecir.*

bendijimos we blessed; past 1st pers. pl. / *bendecir.*

bendijiste you blessed; past 2nd pers. sing. / *bendecir.*

bendijisteis you (all) blessed; past 2nd pers. pl. / *bendecir.*

bendijo he (she/it) blessed; past 3rd pers. sing. / *bendecir.*

bendirá he (she/it) will bless; fut. 3rd pers. sing. / *bendecir.*

bendirán they will bless; fut. 3rd pers. pl. / *bendecir*

bendirás you will bless; fut. 2nd pers. sing. / *bendecir.*

bendiré I shall bless; fut. 1st pers. sing. / *bendecir.*

bendiréis you (all) will bless; fut. 2nd pers. pl. / *bendecir*

bendiremos we shall bless; fut. 1st pers. pl. / *bendecir.*

bendiría 1. I should bless; cond. 1st pers. sing. / *bendecir.* 2. he (she/it) would bless; cond. 3rd pers. sing.

bendiríais you (all) would bless; cond. 2nd pers. pl. / *bendecir.*

bendiríamos we should bless; cond. 1st pers. pl. / *bendecir.*

bendirían they would bless; cond. 3rd pers. pl. / *bendecir.*

bendirías you would bless; cond. 2nd pers. sing. / *bendecir.*

bendito blessed; past part. / *bendecir*

beneficiándose profiting; pres. part. / *beneficiarse*

beneficiaos (you all) profit; impve. 2nd pers. pl. / *beneficiarse.*

beneficiar to benefit or to cultivate or to exploit. reg.

beneficiarse to profit. reg.

beneficíate (you) profit; impve 2nd pers. sing. / *beneficiarse.*

beneficiémonos let us profit; impve. 1st pers pl. / *beneficiarse.*

beneficíense let them profit; impve. 3rd pers. pl. / *beneficiarse.*

beneficíese let him (her/it) profit; impve. 3rd pers. sing. / *beneficiarse.*

bermejear to look or become bright red. reg.

berrear to bellow or to scream. reg.

besándose bumping heads; pres. part. / *besarse.*

besaos (you all) bump heads; impve. 2nd pers. pl. / *besarse.*

besar to kiss. reg.

besarse to bump heads. reg.

bésate (you) bump heads; impve. 2nd pers. sing. / *besarse.*

besémonos let us bump heads; impve. 1st pers. pl. / *besarse.*

bésense let them bump heads; impve. 3rd pers. pl. / *besarse.*

bésese let him (her/it) bump heads; impve. 3rd pers. sing. / *besarse.*

besucar to kiss repeatedly. irr.

besuque 1. that I may kiss repeatedly; pres. subj. 1st pers. sing. / *besucar.* 2. that he (she/it) may kiss repeatedly; pres. subj. 3rd pers. sing. 3. let him (her/it) kiss repeatedly; impve. 3rd pers. sing.

besuqué I kissed repeatedly; past 1st pers. sing. / *besucar.*

besuquear to kiss excessively or to smooch. reg.

besuquéis that you (all) may kiss repeatedly; pres. subj. 2nd pers. pl. / *besucar.*

besuquemos 1. that we may kiss repeatedly; pres. subj. 1st pers pl. / *besucar.* 2. let us kiss repeatedly; impve. 1st pers. pl.

besuquen 1. that they may kiss repeatedly; pres. subj. 3rd pers. pl. / *besucar.* 2. let them kiss repeatedly; impve. 3rd pers. pl.

besuques that you may kiss repeatedly; pres. subj. 2nd pers. sing. / *besucar.*

betunar to tar or to polish (shoes). reg.

bichar to spy on or to pry. reg.

bielda 1. he (she/it) winnows; pres. 3rd pers. sing./ *beldar.* 2. (you) winnow; impve 2nd pers. sing.

bieldan they winnow; pres. 3rd pers. sing. / *beldar.*

bieldas you winnow; pres. ind. 2nd pers. sing. / *beldar.*

bielde 1. that I may winnow; pres. subj. 1st pxers. sing. / *beldar.* 2. that he (she/it) may winnow; pres. subj. 3rd pers. sing. 3. let him (her/it) winnow; impve. 3rd pers. sing.

bielden 1. that they may winnow; pres. subj. 3rd pers. pl. / *beldar.* 2. let them winnow; impve. 3rd pers. pl.

bieldes that you may winnow; pres. subj. 2nd pers. sing. / *beldar.*

bieldo I winnow; pres. ind. 1st pers. sing. / *beldar.*

bienquerer to be fond of. irr.

bienquerrá he (she/it) will be fond of; fut. 3rd pers. sing. / *bienquerer.*

bienquerrán they will be fond of; fut. 3rd pers. pl. / *bienquerer.*

bienquerrás you will be fond of; fut. 2nd pers. sing. / *bienquerer.*

bienquerré I shall be fond of; fut. 1st pers. sing. / *bienquerer.*

bienquerréis you (all) will be fond of; fut. 2nd pers. pl. / *bienquerer.*

bienquerremos we shall be fond of; fut. 1st pers. pl. / *bienquerer.*

bienquerría 1. I should be fond of; cond. 1st pers. sing. / *bienquerer.* 2. he (she/it) would be fond of; cond. 3rd pers. sing.

bienquerríais you (all) would be fond of; cond. 2nd pers. pl. / *bienquerer.*

bienquerríamos we should be fond of; cond. 1st pers. pl. / *bienquerer.*

bienquerrían they would be fond of; cond. 3rd pers. pl. / *bienquerer.*

bienquerrías you would be fond of; cond. 2nd pers. sing. / *bienquerer.*

bienquiera 1. that I may be fond of; pres. subj. 1st pers. sing. / *bienquerer.* 2. that he (she/it) may be fond of; pres. subj. 3rd pers. sing. 3. let him (her/it) be fond of; impve. 3rd pers. sing.

bienquieran 1. that they may be fond of; pres. subj. 3rd pers. pl. / *bienquerer.* 2. let them be fond of; impve. 3rd pers. pl.

bienquieras that you may be fond of; pres. subj. 2nd pers. sing. / *bienquerer.*

bienquiere 1. he (she/it) is fond of; pres. ind. 3rd pers. sing. / *bienquerer.* 2. (you) be fond of; impve. 2nd pers. sing.

bienquieren they are fond of; pres. ind. 3rd pers. pl. / *bienquerer.*

bienquieres you are fond of; pres. ind. 2nd pers. sing. / *bienquerer.*

bienquiero I am fond of; pres. ind. 1st pers. sing. / *bienquerer.*

bienquise I was fond of; past 1st pers. sing. / *bienquerer.*

bienquisiera 1. that I might be fond of; imp. subj. 1st pers. sing. / *bienquerer.* 2. that he (she/it) might be fond of; imp. subj. 3rd pers. sing.

bienquisierais that you (all) might be fond of; imp. subj. 2nd pers pl. / *bienquerer.*

bienquisiéramos that we might be fond of; imp. subj. 1st pers. pl. / *bienquerer.*

bienquisieran that they might be fond of; imp. subj. 3rd pers. pl. / *bienquerer.*

bienquisieras that you might be fond of; imp. subj. 2nd pers. sing. / *bienquerer.*

bienquisieron they were fond of; past 3rd pers. pl. / *bienquerer.*

bienquisiese 1. that I might be fond of; imp. subj. 1st pers. sing. / *bienquerer* 2. that he (she/it) might be fond of; imp. subj. 3rd pers. sing.

bienquisieseis that you (all) might be fond of; imp. subj. 2nd pers pl. / *bienquerer.*

bienquisiésemos that we might be fond of; imp. subj. 1st pers. pl. / *bienquerer.*

bienquisiesen that they might be fond of; imp. subj. 3rd pers. pl. / *bienquerer.*

bienquisieses that you might be fond of; imp. subj. 2nd pers. sing. / *bienquerer.*

bienquisimos we were fond of; past 1st pers. pl. / *bienquerer.*

bienquisiste you were fond of; past 2nd pers. sing. / *bienquerer.*

bienquisisteis you (all) were fond of; past 2nd pers. pl. / *bienquerer.*

bienquiso he (she/it) was fond of; past 3rd pers. sing. / *bienquerer.*

bienquistándose settling their differences; pres. part. / *bienquistarse.*

bienquistaos (you all) settle their differences; impve. 2nd pers. pl. / *bienquistarse.*

bienquistar to reconcile. reg.

bienquistarse to settle their differences. reg.

bienquístate (you) settle their differences; impve. 2nd pers. sing. / *bienquistarse.*

bienquistémonos let us settle their differences; impve. 1st pers. pl. / *bienquistarse.*

bienquístense let them settle their differences; impve. 3rd pers. pl. / *bienquistarse.*

bienquístese let him (her/it) settle their differences; impve. 3rd pers. sing. / *bienquistarse.*

bienvivir to live in comfort or to live right. reg.

bifurcándose forking; pres. part. / *bifurcarse.*

bifurcaos (you all) fork; impve. 2nd pers. pl. / *bifurcarse.*

bifurcarse to fork or to branch off. irr.

bifúrcate (you) fork; impve. 2nd pers. sing. / *bifurcarse.*

bifurque 1. that I may fork; pres. subj. 1st pers. sing. / *bifurcarse.* 2. that he (she/it) may fork; pres. subj. 3rd pers. sing.

bifurqué I forked; past 1st pers. sing. / *bifurcarse.*

bifurquéis that you (all) may fork; pres. subj. 2nd pers. pl. / *bifurcarse.*

bifurquémonos let us fork; impve. 1st pers. pl. / *bifurcarse.*

bifurquemos that we may fork; pres. subj. 1st pers. pl. / *bifurcarse.*

bifurquen that they may fork; pres. subj. 3rd pers. pl. / *bifurcarse.*

bifúrquense let them fork; impve. 3rd pers. pl. / *bifurcarse.*

bifurques that you may fork; pres. subj. 2nd pers. sing. / *bifurcarse.*

bifúrquese let him (her/it) fork; impve. 3rd pers. sing. / *bifurcarse.*

binar to plow the ground for the second time. reg.

birlar to snatch away or to bring down with one blow. reg.

bisar to repeat. reg.

bisbisar to mutter. reg.

bisecar bisect. irr.

biselar to bevel. reg.

biseque 1. that I may bisect; pres. subj. 1st pers. sing. / *bisecar.* 2. that he (she/it) may bisect; pres. subj. 3rd pers. sing. 3. let him (her/it) bisect; impve. 3rd pers. sing.

bisequé I bisected; past 1st pers. sing. / *bisecar.*

bisequéis that you (all) may bisect; pres. subj. 2nd pers. pl. / *bisecar.*

bisequemos 1. that we may bisect; pres. subj. 1st pers. pl. / *bisecar.* 2. let us bisect; impve. 1st pers. pl.

bisequen 1. that they may bisect; pres. subj. 3rd pers. pl. / *bisecar.* 2. let them bisect; impve. 3rd pers. pl.

biseques that you may bisect; pres. subj. 2nd pers. sing. / *bisecar.*

bizcar to wink or to squint. irr.

bizmar to poultice. reg.

bizque 1. that I may wink; pres. subj. 1st pers. sing. / *bizcar.* 2. that he (she/it) may wink; pres. subj. 3rd pers. sing. 3. let him (her/it) wink; impve. 3rd pers. sing.

bizqué I winked; past 1st pers. sing. / *bizcar.*

bizquéis that you (all) may wink; pres. subj. 2nd pers. pl. / *bizcar.*

bizquemos 1. that we may wink; pres. subj. 1st pers. pl. / *bizcar.* 2. let us wink; impve. 1st pers. pl.

bizquen 1. that they may wink; pres. subj. 3rd pers. pl. / *bizcar.* 2. let them wink; impve. 3rd pers. pl.

bizques that you may wink; pres. subj. 2nd pers. sing. / *bizcar.*

blandeándose softening; pres. part. / *blandearse.*

blandeaos (you all) soften; impve. 2nd pers. pl. / *blandearse.*

blandear to mollify. reg.

blandearse to soften or to give in. reg.

blandéate (you) soften; impve. 2nd pers. sing. / *blandearse.*

blandeémonos let us soften; impve. 1st pers. pl. / *blandearse.*

blandéense let them soften; impve. 3rd pers. pl. / *blandearse.*

blandéese let him (her/it) soften; impve. 3rd pers. sing. / *blandearse.*

blandiéndose waving about; pres. part. / *blandirse.*

blandíos (you all) wave about; impve. 2nd pers. pl. / *blandirse.*

blandir to brandish. irr. occurring only in those forms where the i is present in verb ending.

blandirse to wave about or to shake. irr.

blanqueándose blanching; pres. part. / *blanquearse.*

blanqueaos (you all) blanch; impve. 2nd pers. pl. / *blanquearse.*

blanquear to whiten or to bleach. reg.

blanquearse to blanch. reg.

blanquéate (you) blanch; impve. 2nd pers. sing. / *blanquearse.*

blanquecer to whiten or to blanch. irr.

blanqueémonos let us blanch; impve. 1st pers. pl. / *blanquearse.*

blanquéense let them blanch; impve. 3rd pers. pl. / *blanquearse.*

blanquéese let him (her/it) blanch; impve. 3rd pers. sing. / *blanquearse.*

blanquezca 1. that I may whiten; pres. subj. 1st pers. sing. / *blanquecer.* 2. that he (she/it) may whiten; pres. subj. 3rd pers. sing. 3. let him (her/it) whiten; impve. 3rd pers. sing.

blanquezcáis that you (all) may whiten; pres. subj. 2nd pers. pl. / *blanquecer.*

blanquezcamos 1. that we may whiten; pres. subj. 1st pers. pl. / *blanquecer.* 2. let us whiten; impve. 1st pers. pl.

blanquezcan 1. that they may whiten; pres. subj. 3rd pers. pl. / *blanquecer.* 2. let them whiten; impve. 3rd pers. pl.

blanquezcas that you may whiten; pres. subj. 2nd pers. sing. / *blanquecer.*

blanquezco I whiten; pres. ind. 1st pers. sing. / *blanquecer.*

blasfemar to blaspheme or to curse. reg.

blasonar to boast. reg.

blindar to armor or to shield. reg.

blofear to bluff. reg.

bloquear to blockade. reg.

bobear to act or to talk like a fool. reg.

bocinar to blow a horn. reg.

bochar to hit the jack (in bowls) or to snub. reg.

bogar to row or to sail. irr.

bogue 1. that I may row; pres. subj. 1st pers. sing. / *bogar.* 2. that he (she/it) may row; pres. subj. 3rd pers. sing. 3. let him (her/it) row; impve. 3rd pers. sing.

bogué I rowed; past 1st pers. sing. / *bogar.*

boguéis that you (all) may row; pres. subj. 2nd pers. pl. / *bogar.*

boguemos 1. that we may row; pres. subj. 1st pers. pl. / *bogar.* 2. let us row; impve. 1st pers. pl.

boguen 1. that they may row; pres. subj. 3rd pers. pl. / *bogar.* 2. let them row; impve. 3rd pers. pl.

bogues that you may row; pres. subj. 2nd pers. sing. / *bogar.*

boicotear to boycott or to picket. reg..

boleándose balking; pres. part. / *bolearse.*

boleaos (you all) balk; impve. 2nd pers. pl. / *bolearse.*

bolear to play billiards or to bowl or to fib. reg.

bolearse to balk or to blush. reg. ar conju.

boléate (you) balk; impve. 2nd pers. sing. / *bolearse.*

boleémonos let us balk; impve. 1st pers. pl. / *bolearse.*

boléense let them balk; impve. 3rd pers. pl. / *bolearse.*

boléese let him (her/it) balk; impve. 3rd pers. sing. / *bolearse.*

bolsear to pick the pocket. reg.

bombar to pump. reg.

bombardear to bombard or to bomb. reg.

bombear to pump or to bomb or to praise. reg.

boquear to gape or to be dying. reg.

borbollar to bubble out or to boil up. reg.

borbollear to bubble out or to gush out. reg.

borbotar to bubble up or to spurt. reg.

bordar to embroider. reg.

bordeándose approaching; pres. part. / *bordearse.*

bordeaos (you all) approach; impve. 2nd pers. pl. / *bordearse.*

bordear to border or to skirt. reg.

bordearse to approach. reg.

bordéate (you) approach; impve. 2nd pers. sing / *bordearse.*

bordeémonos let us approach; impve. 1st pers. pl. / *bordearse.*

bordéense let them approach; impve. 3rd pers. pl. / *bordearse.*

bordéese let him (her/it) approach; impve. 3rd pers. sing. / *bordearse.*

bordonear to roam or to buzz (by airplane). reg.

borlándose getting a doctor's degree; pres. part. / *borlarse.*

borlaos (you all) get a doctor's degree; impve. 2nd pers. pl. / *borlarse.*

borlarse to get a doctor's degree. reg.

bórlate (you) get a doctor's degree; impve. 2nd pers. sing. / *borlarse.*

borlémonos let us get a doctor's degree; impve. 1st pers. pl. / *borlarse.*

bórlense let them get a doctor's degree; impve. 3rd pers. pl. / *borlarse.*

bórlese let him (her) get a doctor's degree / *borlarse.*

borneándose warping; pres. part. / *bornearse.*

bornear to twist or to set. reg.
bornearse to warp or to bulge. reg.
bornéense let them warp; impve. 3rd pers. pl. / *bornearse*.
bornéese let it warp; impve. 3rd pers. sing. / *bornearse*.
borrajear to doodle or scribble. reg.
borrar to erase or to blur. reg.
borronear to blotch or to sketch roughly. reg.
bosquejar to sketch or to outline. reg.
bostece 1. that I may yawn; pres. subj. 1st pers. sing. / *bostezar* 2. that he (she/it) may yawn; pres. subj. 3rd pers. sing. 3. let him (her/it) yawn; impve. 3rd pers. sing.
bostecé I yawned; past 1st pers. sing. / *bostezar*.
bostecéis that you (all) may yawn; pres. subj. 2nd pers. pl. / *bostezar*.
bostecemos 1. that we may yawn; pres. subj. 1st pers. pl. / *bostezar*. 2. let us yawn; impve. 1st pers. pl.
bostecen 1. that they may yawn; pres. subj. 3rd pers. pl. / *bostezar*. 2. let them yawn; impve. 3rd pers. pl.
bosteces that you may yawn; pres. subj. 2nd pers. sing. / *bostezar*.
bostezar to yawn. irr.
botándose lying down; pres. part. / *botarse*.
botaos (you all) lie down; impve. 2nd pers. pl. / *botarse*.
botar to hurl or to launch or to bounce. reg.
botarse to lie down. reg.
bótate (you) lie down; impve. 2nd pers. sing. / *botarse*.
botémonos let us lie down; impve. 1st pers. pl. / *botarse*.
bótense let them lie down; impve. 3rd pers. pl. / *botarse*.
bótese let him (her/it) lie down; impve. 3rd pers. sing. / *botarse*.
boxear to box. reg.
boyar to float. reg.
bracear to swing the arms or to brew. reg.
bramar to roar or to rage. reg.
bravear to bluster or to bully. reg.
brear to annoy or to molest. reg.
bregar to struggle or to work hard. irr.
bregue 1. that I may struggle; pres. subj. 1st pers. sing. / *bregar*. 2. that he (she/it) may struggle; pres. subj. 3rd pers. sing. 3. let him (her/it) struggle; impve. 3rd pers. sing.
bregué I struggled; past 1st pers. sing. / *bregar*.
breguéis that you (all) may struggle; pres. subj. 2nd pers. pl. / *bregar*.
breguemos 1. that we may struggle; pres. subj. 1st pers. pl. / *bregar*. 2. let us struggle; impve. 1st pers. pl.
breguen 1. that they may struggle; pres. subj. 3rd pers. pl. / *bregar*. 2. let them struggle; impve. 3rd pers. pl.
bregues that you may struggle; pres. subj. 2nd pers. sing. / *bregar*.
brescar to take out the honeycombs. reg.

brillar to shine. reg.
brincar to jump or to bounce. irr.
brindándose offering one's help; pres. part. / *brindarse*.
brindaos (you all) offer your help; impve. 2nd pers. pl. / *brindarse*.
brindar to offer or to drink to the health of. reg.
brindarse to offer one's help. reg.
bríndate (you) offer your help; impve. 2nd pers. sing. / *brindarse*.
brindémonos let us offer our help; impve. 1st pers. pl. / *brindarse*.
bríndense let them offer their help; impve. 3rd pers. pl. / *brindarse*.
bríndese let him (her/it) offer his (her/its) help; impve. 3rd pers. sing. / *brindarse*.
brinque 1. that I may jump; pres. subj. 1st pers. sing. / *brincar*. 2. that he (she/it) may jump; pres. subj. 3rd pers. sing. 3. let him (her/it) jump; impve. 3rd pers. sing.
brinqué I jumped; past 1st pers. sing. / *brincar*.
brinquéis that you (all) may jump; pres. subj. 2nd pers. pl. / *brincar*.
brinquemos 1. that we may jump; pres. subj. 1st pers. pl. / *brincar*. 2. let us jump; impve. 1st pers. pl.
brinquen 1. that they may jump; pres. subj. 3rd pers. pl. / *brincar*. 2. let them jump; impve. 3rd pers. pl.
brinques that you may jump; pres. subj. 2nd pers. sing. / *brincar*.
bromeándose jesting; pres. part. / *bromearse*.
bromeaos (you all) jest; impve. 2nd pers. pl. / *bromearse*.
bromear to joke or to have fun. reg.
bromearse to jest. reg.
broméate (you) jest; impve. 2nd pers. sing. / *bromearse*.
bromeémonos let us jest; impve. 1st pers. pl. / *bromearse*.
broméense let them jest; impve. 3rd pers. pl. / *bromearse*.
broméese let him (her/it) jest; impve. 3rd pers. sing. / *bromearse*.
bronceándose becoming tanned; pres. part. / *broncearse*.
bronceaos (you all) become tanned; impve. 2nd pers. pl. / *broncearse*.
broncear to bronze. reg.
broncearse to become tanned. reg.
broncéate (you) become tanned; impve. 2nd pers. sing. / *broncearse*.
bronceémonos let us become tanned; impve. 1st pers. pl. / *broncearse*.
broncéense let them become tanned; impve. 3rd pers. pl. / *broncearse*.
broncéese let him (her/it) become tanned; impve. 3rd pers. sing. / *broncearse*.
brotar to bud or sprout. reg.
brozar to brush (type). reg.
brujear to practice witchcraft. reg.
brujulear to scrutinize. reg.

bruñendo burnishing; pres. part. / *bruñir.*
bruñera 1. that I might burnish; imp. subj. 1st pers. sing. / *bruñir.* 2. that he (she/it) might brunish; imp. subj. 3rd pers. sing.
bruñerais that you (all) might burnish; imp. subj. 2nd pers pl. / *bruñir.*
bruñéramos that we might burnish; imp. subj. 1st pers. pl. / *bruñir.*
bruñeran that they might burnish; imp. subj. 3rd pers. pl. / *bruñir.*
bruñeras that you might burnish; imp. subj. 2nd pers. sing. / *bruñir.*
bruñeron they burnished; past 3rd pers. pl. / *bruñir.*
bruñese 1. that I might burnish; imp. subj. 1st pers. sing. / *bruñir.* 2. that he (she/it) might burnish; imp. subj. 3rd pers. sing.
bruñeseis that you (all) might burnish; imp. subj. 2nd pers pl. / *bruñir.*
bruñésemos that we might burnish; imp. subj. 1st pers. pl. / *bruñir.*
bruñesen that they might burnish; imp. subj. 3rd pers. pl. / *bruñir.*
bruñeses that you might burnish; imp. subj. 2nd pers. sing. / *bruñir.*
bruñir to burnish. irr.
bruñó he (she/it) burnished; past 3rd pers. sing. / *bruñir.*
brutalice 1. that I may brutalize; pres. subj. 1st pers. sing. / *brutalizar.* 2. that he (she/it) may brutalize; pres. subj. 3rd pers. sing. 3. let him (her/it) brutilize; impve. 3rd pers. sing.
brutalicé I brutalized; past 1st pers. sing. / *brutalizar.*
brutalicéis that you (all) may brutalize; pres. subj. 2nd pers. pl. / *brutalizar.*
brutalicemos 1. that we may brutalize; pres. subj. 1st pers. pl. / *brutalizar.* 2. let us brutalize; impve. 1st pers. pl.
brutalicen 1. that they may brutalize; pres. subj. 3rd pers. pl. / *brutalizar.* 2. let them brutalize; impve. 3rd pers. pl.
brutalices that you may brutalize; pres. subj. 2nd pers. sing. / *brutalizar.*
brutalizar to brutalize. irr.
buce 1. that I may dip; pres. subj. 1st pers. sing. / *buzar.* 2. that he (she/it) may dip; pres. subj. 3rd pers. sing. 3. let him (her/it) dip; impve. 3rd pers. sing.
bucé I dipped; past 1st pers. sing. / *buzar.*
bucear to dive or to explore thoroughly a subject. reg.
bucéis that you (all) may dip; pres. subj. 2nd pers. pl. / *buzar.*
bucemos 1. that we may dip; pres. subj. 1st pers. pl. / *buzar.* 2. let us dip; impve. 1st pers. pl.
bucen 1. that they may dip; pres. subj. 3rd pers. pl. / *buzar.* 2. let them dip; impve. 3rd pers. pl.
buces that you may dip; pres. subj. 2nd pers. sing. / *buzar.*
bufándose swelling; pres. part. / *bufarse.*
bufaos (you all) swell; impve. 2nd pers. pl. / *bufarse.*
bufar to snort or to puff angrily. reg.

bufarse to swell or budge. reg.
búfate (you) swell ; impve. 2nd pers. sing. / *bufarse.*
bufémonos let us swell; impve. 1st pers. pl. / *bufarse.*
búfense let them swell; impve. 3rd pers. pl. / *bufarse.*
búfese let him (her/it) swell; impve. 3rd pers. sing. / *bufarse.*
bufoneándose jesting; pres. part. / *bufonearse.*
bufoneaos (you all) jest; impve. 2nd pers. pl. / *bufonearse.*
bufonear to clown or to jest. reg.
bufonearse to jest. reg.
bufonéate (you) jest; impve. 2nd pers. sing. / *bufonearse.*
bufoneémonos let us jest; impve. 1st pers. pl. / *bufonearse.*
bufonéense let them jest; impve. 3rd pers. pl. / *bufonearse.*
bufonéese let him (her/it) jest; impve. 3rd pers. sing. / *bufonearse.*
bullámonos let us budge; impve. 1st pers. pl. / *bullirse.*
búllanse let them budge; impve. 3rd pers. pl. / *bullirse.*
búllase let him (her/it) budge; impve. 3rd pers. sing. / *bullirse.*
bullendo boiling; pres. part. / *bullir.*
bulléndose budging; pres. part. / *bullirse.*
bullera 1. that I might boil; imp. subj. 1st pers. sing. / *bullir.* 2. that he (she/it) might boil; imp. subj. 3rd pers. sing.
bullerais that you (all) might boil; imp. subj. 2nd pers pl. / *bullir.*
bulléramos that we might boil; imp. subj. 1st pers. pl. / *bullir.*
bulleran that they might boil; imp. subj. 3rd pers. pl. / *bullir.*
bulleras that you might boil; imp. subj. 2nd pers. sing. / *bullir.*
bulleron they boiled; past 3rd pers. pl. / *bullir*
bullese 1. that I might boil; imp. subj. 1st pers. sing. / *bullir.* 2. that he (she/it) might boil; imp. subj. 3rd pers. sing.
bulleseis that you (all) might boil; imp. subj. 2nd pers pl. / *bullir.*
bullésemos that we might boil; imp. subj. 1st pers. pl. / *bullir.*
bullesen that they might boil; imp. subj. 3rd pers. pl. / *bullir.*
bulleses that you might boil; imp. subj. 2nd pers. sing. / *bullir.*
búllete (you) budge; impve. 2nd pers. sing. / *bullirse.*
bullir to boil or to stir. irr.
bullirse to budge. irr.
bulló he (she/it) boiled; past 3rd pers. sing. / *bullir.*
bullos (you all) budge; impve. 2nd pers. pl. / *bullirse.*
burbujear to bubble or to burble. reg.
burilar to engrave. reg.
burlándose de making fun of; pres. part. / *burlarse de.*

burlaos de (you all) make fun of; impve. 2nd pers. pl. / *burlarse de.*

burlar to mock or to deceive. reg.

burlarse de to make fun of. reg.

búrlate de (you) make fun of; impve. 2nd pers. sing. / *burlarse de.*

burlémonos de let us make fun of; impve. 1st pers. pl. / *burlarse de.*

búrlense de let them make fun of; impve. 3rd pers. pl. / *burlarse de.*

búrlese de let him (her/it) make fun of; impve. 3rd pers. sing. / *burlarse de.*

buscar to seek or to look for. irr.

busque 1. that I may seek; pres. subj. 1st pers. sing. / *buscar.* 2. that he (she/it) may seek; pres. subj. 3rd pers. sing. 3. let him (her/it) seek; impve. 3rd pers. sing.

busqué I sought; past 1st pers. sing. / *buscar.*

busquéis that you (all) may seek; pres. subj. 2nd pers. pl. / *buscar.*

busquemos 1. that we may seek; pres. subj. 1st pers. pl. / *buscar.* 2. let us seek; impve. 1st pers. pl.

busquen 1. that they may seek; pres. subj. 3rd pers. pl. / *buscar.* 2. let them seek; impve. 3rd pers. pl.

busques that you may seek; pres. subj. 2nd pers. sing. / *buscar.*

buzar to dip. irr.

C

cabalgar to ride horseback. irr.

cabalgue 1. that I may ride horseback; pres. subj. 1st pers. sing. / *cabalgar.* 2. that he (she/it) may ride horseback; pres. subj. 3rd pers. sing. 3. let him (her/it) ride horseback; impve. 3rd pers. sing.

cabalgué I rode horseback; past 1st pers. sing. / *cabalgar.*

cabalguéis that you (all) may ride horseback; pres. subj. 2nd pers. pl. / *cabalgar.*

cabalguemos 1. that we may ride horseback; pres. subj. 1st pers. pl. / *cabalgar.* 2. let us ride horseback; impve. 1st pers. pl.

cabalguen 1. that they may ride horseback; pres. subj. 3rd pers. pl. / *cabalgar.* 2. let them ride horseback; impve. 3rd pers. pl.

cabalgues that you may ride horseback; pres. subj. 2nd pers. sing. / *cabalgar.*

caballear to like riding horseback. reg.

caballerear to simulate gentility. reg.

cabecear to nod or to pitch (as a boat). reg.

caber to fit or to contain or to be admissible. irr.

cabestrar to halter. reg.

cabestrear to be led easily by the halter. reg.

cabildear to lobby. reg.

cablegrafía 1. he (she/it) cables; pres. ind. 3rd pers. sing. / *cablegrafiar.* 2. (you) cable; impve. 2nd pers. sing.

cablegrafían they cable; pres. ind. 3rd pers. pl. / *cablegrafiar.*

cablegrafiar to cable. irr.

cablegrafías you cable; pres.ind. 2nd pers. sing. / *cablegrafiar.*

cablegrafíe 1. that I may cable; pres. subj. 1st pers. sing. / *cablegrafiar.* 2. that he (she/it) may cable; pres. subj. 3rd pers. sing. 3. let him (her/it) cable; impve. 3rd pers. sing.

cablegrafíen 1. that they may cable; pres. subj. 3rd pers. pl. / *cablegrafiar.* 2. let them cable; impve. 3rd pers. pl.

cablegrafíes that you may cable; pres. subj. 2nd pers. sing. / *cablegrafiar.*

cablegrafío I cable; pres. ind. 1st pers. sing. / *cablegrafiar.*

cabrá he (she/it) will fit; fut. 3rd pers. sing. / *caber.*

cabrán they will fit; fut. 3rd pers. pl. / *caber.*

cabrás you will fit; fut. 2nd pers. sing. / *caber.*

cabré I shall fit; fut. 1st pers. sing. / *caber.*

cabréis you (all) will fit; fut. 2nd pers. pl. / *caber.*

cabremos we shall fit; fut. 1st pers. pl. / *caber.*

cabría 1. I should fit; cond. 1st pers. sing. / *caber.* 2. he (she/it) would fit; cond. 3rd pers. sing.

cabríais you (all) would fit ; cond. 2nd pers. pl. / *caber.*

cabríamos we should fit; cond. 1st pers. pl. / *caber.*

cabrían they would fit; cond. 3rd pers. pl. / *caber.*

cabrías you would fit; cond. 2nd pers. sing. / *caber.*

cabriolar to caper or to prance. reg.

cabriolear to caper or to prance. reg.

cacarear to cackle or to boast. reg.

cace 1. that I may chase; pres. subj. 1st pers. sing. / *cazar.* 2. that he (she/it) may chase; pres. subj. 3rd pers. sing. 3. let him (her/it) chase; impve. 3rd pers. sing.

cacé I chased; past 1st pers. sing. / *cazar.*

cacéis that you (all) may chase; pres. subj. 2nd pers. pl. / *cazar.*

cacemos 1. that we may chase; pres. subj. 1st pers. pl. / *cazar.* 2. let us chase; impve. 1st pers. pl.

cacen 1. that they may chase; pres. subj. 3rd pers. pl. / *cazar.* 2. let them chase; impve. 3rd pers. pl.

caces that you may chase; pres. subj. 2nd pers. sing. / *cazar.*

cachar to shatter or to split lengthwise. reg.

cachear to frisk (a suspect). reg.

cachifollar to snub or to cheat. reg.

caducar to be senile or to be out of date. irr.

caduque 1. that I may be senile; pres. subj. 1st pers. sing. / *caducar.* 2. that he (she/it) may be senile; pres. subj. 3rd pers. sing. 3. let him (her/it) be senile; impve. 3rd pers. sing.

caduqué I was senile; past 1st pers. sing. / *caducar.*

caduquéis that you (all) may be senile; pres. subj. 2nd pers. pl. / *caducar.*

caduquemos 1. that we may be senile; pres. subj. 1st pers. pl. / *caducar.* 2. let us be senile; impve. 1st pers. pl.

caduquen 1. that they may be senile; pres. subj. 3rd pers. pl. / *caducar.* 2. let them be senile; impve. 3rd pers. pl.

caduques that you may be senile; pres. subj. 2nd pers. sing. / *caducar*.

caeos (you all) fall down; impve. 2nd pers. pl. / *caerse*.

caer to fall or to suit. irr.

caerse to fall down. irr.

cáete (you) fall down; impve. 2nd pers. sing. / *caerse*.

cagar to soil or to defecate. irr.

cague 1. that I may soil; pres. subj. 1st pers. sing. / *cagar*. 2. that he (she/it) may soil; pres. subj. 3rd pers. sing. 3. let him (her/it) soil; impve. 3rd pers. sing.

cagué I soiled; past 1st pers. sing. / *cagar*.

caguéis that you (all) may soil; pres. subj. 2nd pers. pl. / *cagar*.

caguemos 1. that we may soil; pres. subj. 1st pers. pl. / *cagar*. 2. let us soil; impve. 1st pers. pl.

caguen 1. that they may soil; pres. subj. 3rd pers. pl. / *cagar*. 2. let them soil; impve. 3rd pers. pl.

cagues that you may soil; pres. subj. 2nd pers. sing. / *cagar*.

caído fell or fallen ; past part. / *caer*.

caiga 1. that I may fall; pres. subj. 1st pers. sing. / *caer*. 2. that he (she/it) may fall; pres. subj. 3rd pers. sing. 3. let him (her/it) fall; impve. 3rd pers. sing.

caigáis that you (all) may fall; pres. subj. 2nd pers. pl. / *caer*.

caigámonos let us fall down; impve. 1st pers. pl. / *caerse*.

caigamos 1. that we may fall; pres. subj. 1st pers. pl. / *caer*. 2. let us fall; impve. 1st pers. pl.

caigan 1. that they may fall; pres. subj. 3rd pers. pl. / *caer*. 2. let them fall; impve. 3rd pers. pl.

caíganse let them fall down; impve. 3rd pers. pl. / *caerse*.

caigas that you may fall; pres. subj. 2nd pers. sing. / *caer*.

caígase let him (her/it) fall down; impve. 3rd pers. sing. / *caerse*.

caigo I fall; pres. ind. 1st pers. sing. / *caer*.

calabacear to flunk or to fail. reg.

calafatear to calk. reg.

calándose getting soaked; pres. part. / *calarse*.

calaos (you all) get soaked; impve. 2nd pers. pl. / *calarse*.

calar to pierce or to soak. reg.

calarse to get soaked. reg.

cálate (you) get soaked; impve. 2nd pers. sing. / *calarse*.

calaverear to act foolishly. reg.

calcar to trace or to copy. irr.

calce 1. that I may put on (shoes/etc.); pres. subj. 1st pers. sing. / *calzar*. 2. that he (she/it) may put on (shoes/etc.); pres. subj. 3rd pers. sing. 3. let him (her/it) put on (shoes/etc.); impve. 3rd pers. sing.

calcé I put on (shoes/etc.); past 1st pers. sing. / *calzar*.

calcéis that you (all) may put on (shoes/etc.); pres. subj. 2nd pers. pl. / *calzar*.

calcemos 1. that we may put on (shoes/etc.); pres. subj. 1st pers. pl. / *calzar*. 2. let us put on (shoes/etc.); impve. 1st pers. pl.

calcen 1. that they may put on (shoes/etc.); pres. subj. 3rd pers. pl. / *calzar*. 2. let them put on (shoes/etc.); impve. 3rd pers. pl.

calces that you may put on (shoes/etc.); pres. subj. 2nd pers. sing. / *calzar*.

calcificar to calcify. irr.

calcifique 1. that it may calcify; pres. subj. 3rd pers. sing. / *calcificar*. 2. let it calcify; impve. 3rd pers. sing.

calcifiquen 1. that they may calcify; pres. subj. 3rd pers. pl. / *calcificar*. 2. let them calcify; impve. 3rd pers. pl.

calcinar to calcine or to burn. reg.

calcular to calculate. reg.

caldeándose getting hot; pres. part. / *caldearse*.

caldeaos (you all) get hot; impve. 2nd pers. pl. / *caldearse*.

caldear to heat. reg.

caldearse to get hot. reg.

caldéate (you) get hot; impve. 2nd pers. sing. / *caldearse*.

caldeémonos let us get hot; impve. 1st pers. pl. / *caldearse*.

caldéense let them get hot; impve. 3rd pers. pl. / *caldearse*.

caldéese let him (her/it) get hot; impve. 3rd pers. sing. / *caldearse*.

calémonos let us get soaked; impve. 1st pers. pl. / *calarse*.

cálense let them get soaked; impve. 3rd pers. pl. / *calarse*.

calentándose warming oneself; pres. part. / *calentarse*.

calentaos (you all) warm yourselves; impve. 2nd pers. pl. / *calentarse*.

calentar to warm or to spank. irr.

calentarse to warm oneself. irr.

calentémonos let us warm ourselves; impve. 1st pers. pl. / *calentarse*.

cálese let him (her/it) get soaked; impve. 3rd pers. sing. / *calarse*.

calibrar to calibrate. reg.

calienta 1. he (she/it) warms; pres. ind. 3rd pers. sing. / *calentar*. 2. (you) warm; impve. 2nd pers. sing.

calientan they warm; pres. ind. 3rd pers. pl. / *calentar*.

calientas you warm; pres. ind. 2nd pers. sing. / *calentar*.

caliéntate (you) warm yourself; impve. 2nd pers. sing. / *calentarse*.

caliente 1. that I may warm; pres. subj. 1st pers. sing. / *calentar*. 2. that he (she/it) may warm; pres. subj. 3rd pers. sing. 3. let him (her/it) warm; impve. 3rd pers. sing.

calienten 1. that they may warm; pres. subj. 3rd pers. pl. / *calentar*. 2. let them warm; impve. 3rd pers. pl.

caliéntense let them warm themselves; impve. 3rd pers. pl. / *calentarse.*

calientes that you may warm; pres. subj. 2nd pers. sing. / *calentar.*

caliéntese let him (her/it) warm himself (herself/itself); impve. 3rd pers. sing. / *calentarse.*

caliento I warm; pres. ind. 1st pers. sing. / *calentar.*

calificándose registering as a voter; pres. part. / *calificarse.*

calificaos (you all) register as a voter; impve. 2nd pers. pl. / *calificarse.*

calificar to qualify. irr.

calificarse to register as a voter or to prove one's noble birth. irr.

califícate (you) register as a voter; impve. 2nd pers. sing. / *calificarse.*

califique 1. that I may qualify; pres. subj. 1st pers. sing. / *calificar.* 2. that he (she/it) may qualify; pres. subj. 3rd pers. sing. 3. let him (her/it) qualify; impve. 3rd pers. sing.

califiqué I qualified; past 1st pers. sing. / *calificar.*

califiquéis that you (all) may qualify; pres. subj. 2nd pers. pl. / *calificar.*

califiquémonos let us register as a voter; impve. 1st pers. pl. / *calificarse.*

califiquemos 1. that we may qualify; pres. subj. 1st pers. pl. / *calificar.* 2. let us qualify; impve. 1st pers. pl.

califiquen 1. that they may qualify; pres. subj. 3rd pers. pl. / *calificar.* 2. let them qualify; impve. 3rd pers. pl.

califíquense let them register as a voter; impve. 3rd pers. pl. / *calificarse.*

califiques that you may qualify; pres. subj. 2nd pers. sing. / *calificar.*

califíquese let him (her/it) register as a voter; impve. 3rd pers. sing. / *calificarse.*

calmándose quieting down; pres. part. / *calmarse.*

calmaos (you all) quiet down; impve. 2nd pers. pl. / *calmarse.*

calmar to calm. reg.

calmarse to quiet down. reg.

cálmate (you) quiet down; impve. 2nd pers. sing. / *calmarse.*

calmémonos let us quiet down; impve. 1st pers. pl. / *calmarse.*

cálmense let them quiet down; impve. 3rd pers. pl. / *calmarse.*

cálmese let him (her/it) quiet down; impve. 3rd pers. sing. / *calmarse.*

calofriándose shivering because of cold; pres. part. / *calofriarse.*

calofriaos (you all) shiver because of cold; impve. 2nd pers. pl. / *calofriarse.*

calofriarse to shiver because of cold. reg.

calofríate (you) shiver because of cold; impve. 2nd pers. sing. / *calofriarse.*

calofriémonos let us shiver because of cold; impve. 1st pers. pl. / *calofriarse.*

calofríense let them shiver because of cold; impve. 3rd pers. pl. / *calofriarse.*

calofríese let him (her/it) shiver because of cold; impve. 3rd pers. sing. / *calofriarse.*

calosfriándose shivering; pres. part. / *calosfriarse.*

calosfriaos (you all) shiver; impve. 2nd pers. pl. / *calosfriarse.*

calosfriarse to shiver. reg.

calosfríate (you) shiver; impve. 2nd pers. sing. / *calosfriarse.*

calosfriémonos let us shiver; impve. 1st pers. pl. / *calosfriarse.*

calosfríense let them shiver; impve. 3rd pers. pl. / *calosfriarse.*

calosfríese let him (her/it) shiver; impve. 3rd pers. sing. / *calosfriarse.*

calque 1. that I may trace; pres. subj. 1st pers. sing. / *calcar.* 2. that he (she/it) may trace; pres. subj. 3rd pers. sing. 3. let him (her/it) trace; impve. 3rd pers. sing.

calqué I traced; past 1st pers. sing. / *calcar.*

calquéis that you (all) may trace; pres. subj. 2nd pers. pl. / *calcar.*

calquemos 1. that we may trace; pres. subj. 1st pers. pl. / *calcar.* 2. let us trace; impve. 1st pers. pl.

calquen 1. that they may trace; pres. subj. 3rd pers. pl. / *calcar.* 2. let them trace; impve. 3rd pers. pl.

calques that you may trace; pres. subj. 2nd pers. sing. / *calcar.*

calumniar to slander. reg.

calzar to put on (shoes/etc.). irr.

callándose keeping silent; pres. part. / *callarse.*

callaos (you all) keep silent; impve. 2nd pers. pl. / *callarse.*

callar to be silent. reg.

callarse to keep silent. reg.

cállate (you) keep silent; impve. 2nd pers. sing. / *callarse.*

callejear to wander the streets. reg.

callémonos let us keep silent; impve. 1st pers. pl. / *callarse.*

cállense let them keep silent; impve. 3rd pers. pl. / *callarse.*

cállese let him (her/it) keep silent; impve. 3rd pers. sing. / *callarse.*

cambalachear to swap. reg.

cambiar to change or exchange. reg.

camelar to flirt or seduce. reg.

caminar to travel or to walk. reg.

campanear to ring or to chime. reg.

campanillear to tinkle or to ring. reg.

campar to camp or to stand out. reg.

campear to pasture or to excel. reg.

camuflar to camouflage. reg.

canalice 1. that I may channel; pres. subj. 1st pers. sing. / *canalizar.* 2. that he (she/it) may channel; pres. subj. 3rd pers. sing. 3. let him (her/it) channel; impve. 3rd pers. sing.

canalicé I channeled; past 1st pers. sing. / *canalizar.*

canalicéis that you (all) may channel; pres. subj. 2nd pers. pl. / *canalizar*.

canalicemos 1. that we may channel; pres. subj. 1st pers. pl. / *canalizar*. 2. let us channel; impve. 1st pers. pl.

canalicen 1. that they may channel; pres. subj. 3rd pers. pl. / *canalizar*. 2. let them channel; impve. 3rd pers. pl.

canalices that you may channel; pres. subj. 2nd pers. sing. / *canalizar*.

canalizar to channel. irr.

cancelar to cancel. reg.

cancerándose becoming cancerous; pres. part. / *cancerarse*.

cancerar to canker. reg.

cancerarse to become cancerous. reg.

cancérense let them become cancerous; impve. 3rd pers. pl. / *cancerarse*.

cancérese let him (her/it) become cancerous; impve. 3rd pers. sing. / *cancerarse*.

candar to lock or to shut. reg.

cangrenándose becoming gangrenous; pres. part. / *cangrenarse*.

cangrenarse to become gangrenous. reg.

cangrénense let them become gangrenous; impve. 3rd pers. pl. / *cangrenarse*.

cangrénese let it become gangrenous; impve. 3rd pers. sing. / *cangrenarse*.

canjear to exchange. reg.

canonice 1. that I may canonize; pres. subj. 1st pers. sing. / *canonizar*. 2. that he (she/it) may canonize; pres. subj. 3rd pers. sing. 3. let him (her/it) canonize; impve. 3rd pers. sing.

canonicé I canonized; past 1st pers. sing. / *canonizar*.

canonicéis that you (all) may canonize; pres. subj. 2nd pers. pl. / *canonizar*.

canonicemos 1. that we may canonize; pres. subj. 1st pers. pl. / *canonizar*. 2. let us canonize; impve. 1st pers. pl.

canonicen 1. that they may canonize; pres. subj. 3rd pers. pl. / *canonizar*. 2. let them canonize; impve. 3rd pers. pl.

canonices that you may canonize; pres. subj. 2nd pers. sing. / *canonizar*.

canonizar to canonize. irr.

cansándose getting tired; pres. part. / *cansarse*.

cansaos (you all) get tired; impve. 2nd pers. pl. / *cansarse*.

cansar to tire. reg.

cansarse to get tired. reg.

cánsate (you) get tired; impve. 2nd pers. sing. / *cansarse*.

cansémonos let us get tired; impve. 1st pers. pl. / *cansarse*.

canésense let them get tired; impve. 3rd pers. pl. / *cansarse*.

canésese let him (her/it) get tired; impve. 3rd pers. sing. / *cansarse*.

cantar to sing or to confess. reg.

cantonar to quarter (troops). reg.

cantonear to lounge on street corners. reg.

canturrear to hum or sing softly. reg.

canturriar to hum or sing softly. reg.

cañonear to bombard. reg.

capacitar to enable or to authorize. reg.

capar to castrate or to curtail. reg.

capear to wave the cape at a bull. reg.

capitalice 1. that I may capitalize; pres. subj. 1st pers. sing. / *capitalizar*. 2. that he (she/it) may captilize; pres. subj. 3rd pers. sing. 3. let him (her/it) capitalize; impve. 3rd pers. sing.

capitalicé I capitalized; past 1st pers. sing. / *capitalizar*.

capitalicéis that you (all) may capitalize; pres. subj. 2nd pers. pl. / *capitalizar*.

capitalicemos 1. that we may capitalize; pres. subj. 1st pers. pl. / *capitalizar*. 2. let us capitalize; impve. 1st pers. pl.

capitalicen 1. that they may capitalize; pres. subj. 3rd pers. pl. / *capitalizar*. 2. let them capitalize; impve. 3rd pers. pl.

capitalices that you may capitalize; pres. subj. 2nd pers. sing. / *capitalizar*.

capitalizar to capitalize. irr.

capitanear to captain or to command. reg.

capitular to capitulate or to accuse. reg.

capolar to chop or mince. reg.

capotar to turn over. reg.

capotear to wave (a cloak) or to evade. reg.

captándose winning; pres. part. / *captarse*.

captaos (you all) win; impve. 2nd pers. pl. / *captarse*.

captar to captivate or to attract. reg.

captarse to win. reg.

cáptate (you) win; impve. 2nd pers. sing. / *captarse*.

captémonos let us win; impve. 1st pers. pl. / *captarse*.

cáptense let them win; impve. 3rd pers. pl. / *captarse*.

cáptese let him (her/it) win; impve. 3rd pers. sing. / *captarse*.

capturar to capture. reg.

caracolear to caper. reg.

caracterice 1. that I may characterize; pres. subj. 1st pers. sing. / *caracterizar*. 2. that he (she/it) may characterize; pres. subj. 3rd pers. sing. 3. let him (her/it) characterize; impve. 3rd pers. sing.

caracXericé I characterized; past 1st pers. sing. / *caracterizar*.

caractericéis that you (all) may characterize; pres. subj. 2nd pers. pl. / *caracterizar*.

caractericemos 1. that we may characterize; pres. subj. 1st pers. pl. / *caracterizar*. 2. let us characterize; impve. 1st pers. pl.

caractericen 1. that they may characterize; pres. subj. 3rd pers. pl. / *caracterizar*. 2. let them characterize; impve. 3rd pers. pl.

caracterices that you may characterize; pres. subj. 2nd pers. sing. / *caracterizar*.

caracterizar to characterize. irr.

carambolear to carom. reg.

caramelice 1. that I may caramelize; pres. subj. 1st pers. sing. / *caramelizar*. 2. that he (she/it) may caramelize; pres. subj. 3rd pers. sing. 3. let him (her/it) caramelize; impve. 3rd pers. sing.

caramelicé I caramelized; past 1st pers. sing. / *caramelizar*.

caramelicéis that you (all) may caramelize; pres. subj. 2nd pers. pl. / *caramelizar*.

caramelicemos 1. that we may caramelize; pres. subj. 1st pers. pl. / *caramelizar*. 2. let us caramelize; impve. 1st pers. pl.

caramelicen 1. that they may caramelize; pres. subj. 3rd pers. pl. / *caramelizar*. 2. let them caramelize; impve. 3rd pers. pl.

caramelices that you may carmelize; pres. subj. 2nd pers. sing. / *caramelizar*.

caramelizar to carmelize or to sugar coat. irr.

carbonar to make charcoal. reg.

carbonatar to carbonate. reg.

carbonear to char. reg.

carbonice 1. that I may char; pres. subj. 1st pers. sing. / *carbonizar*. 2. that he (she/it) may char; pres. subj. 3rd pers. sing. 3. let him (her/it) char; impve. 3rd pers. sing.

carbonicé I charred; past 1st pers. sing. / *carbonizar*.

carbonicéis that you (all) may char; pres. subj. 2nd pers. pl. / *carbonizar*.

carbonicémonos let us carbonize; impve. 1st pers. pl. / *carbonizarse*.

carbonicemos 1. that we may char; pres. subj. 1st pers. pl. / *carbonizar*. 2. let us char; impve. 1st pers. pl.

carbonicen 1. that they may char; pres. subj. 3rd pers. pl. / *carbonizar*. 2. let them char; impve. 3rd pers. pl.

carbonícense let them carbonize; impve. 3rd pers. pl. / *carbonizarse*.

carbonices that you may char; pres. subj. 2nd pers. sing. / *carbonizar*.

carbonícese let him (her/it) carbonize; impve. 3rd pers. sing. / *carbonizarse*.

carbonizándose carbonizing; pres. part. / *carbonizarse*.

carbonizaos (you all) carbonize; impve. 2nd pers. pl. / *carbonizarse*.

carbonizar to carbonize or to char. irr.

carbonizarse to carbonize. irr.

carbonízate (you) carbonize; impve. 2nd pers. sing. / *carbonizarse*.

carcómanse let them become worm-eaten; impve. 3rd pers. pl. / *carcomerse*.

carcómase let it become worm-eaten; impve. 3rd pers. sing. / *carcomerse*.

carcomer to knaw away or to erode. reg.

carcomerse to become worm-eaten. reg.

carcomiéndose becoming worm-eaten; pres. part. / *carcomerse*.

cardar to card or comb (wool). reg.

careándose meeting face to face; pres. part. / *carearse*.

careaos (you all) meet face to face; impve. 2nd pers. pl. / *carearse*.

carear to confront or to compare. reg.

carearse to meet face to face. reg.

caréate (you) meet face to face; impve. 2nd pers. sing. / *carearse*.

carecer to lack or to want. irr.

careémonos let us meet face to face; impve. 1st pers. pl. / *carearse*.

caréense let them meet face to face; impve. 3rd pers. pl. / *carearse*.

caréese let him (her/it) meet face to face; impve. 3rd pers. sing. / *carearse*.

carezca 1. that I may lack; pres. subj. 1st pers. sing. / *carecer* 2. that he (she/it) may lack; pres. subj. 3rd pers. sing. 3. let him (her/it) lack; impve. 3rd pers. sing.

carezcáis that you (all) may lack; pres. subj. 2nd pers. pl. / *carecer*.

carezcamos 1. that we may lack; pres. subj. 1st pers. pl. / *carecer*. 2. let us lack; impve. 1st pers. pl.

carezcan 1. that they may lack; pres. subj. 3rd pers. pl. / *carecer*. 2. let them lack; impve. 3rd pers. pl.

carezcas that you may lack; pres. subj. 2nd pers. sing. / *carecer*.

carezco I lack; pres. ind. 1st pers. sing. / *carecer*.

cargándose getting rid of; pres. part. / *cargarse*.

cargaos (you all) get rid of; impve. 2nd pers. pl. / *cargarse*.

cargar to load or to charge or to bother. irr.

cargarse to get rid of or to lean or to sway. irr.

cárgate (you) get rid of; impve. 2nd pers. sing. / *cargarse*.

cargue 1. that I may load; pres. subj. 1st pers. sing. / *cargar*. 2. that he (she/it) may load; pres. subj. 3rd pers. sing. 3. let him (her/it) load; impve. 3rd pers. sing.

cargué I loaded; past 1st pers. sing. / *cargar*.

carguéis that you (all) may load; pres. subj. 2nd pers. pl. / *cargar*.

carguémonos let us get rid of; impve. 1st pers. pl. / *cargarse*.

carguemos 1. that we may load; pres. subj. 1st pers. pl. / *cargar*. 2. let us load; impve. 1st pers. pl.

carguen 1. that they may load; pres. subj. 3rd pers. pl. / *cargar*. 2. let them load; impve. 3rd pers. pl.

cárguense let them get rid of; impve. 3rd pers. pl. / *cargarse*.

cargues that you may load; pres. subj. 2nd pers. sing. / *cargar*.

cárguese let him (her/it) get rid of; impve. 3rd pers. sing. / *cargarse*.

cariándose becoming decayed; pres. part. / *cariarse*.

cariarse to become decayed. reg.

caricaturar to caricature. reg.

caricaturice 1. that I may caricature; pres. subj. 1st pers. sing. / *caricaturizar*. 2. that he (she/it) may caricature; pres. subj. 3rd pers. sing. 3. let him (her/it) caricature; impve. 3rd pers. sing.

caricaturicé I caricatured; past 1st pers. sing. / *caricaturizar.*
caricaturicéis that you (all) may caricature; pres. subj. 2nd pers. pl. / *caricaturizar.*
caricaturicemos 1. that we may caricature; pres. subj. 1st pers. pl. / *caricaturizar.* 2. let us caricature; impve. 1st pers. pl.
caricaturicen 1. that they may caricature; pres. subj. 3rd pers. pl. / *caricaturizar.* 2. let them caricature; impve. 3rd pers. pl.
caricaturices that you may caricature; pres. subj. 2nd pers. sing. / *caricaturizar.*
caricaturizar to caricature. irr.
caríense let them become decayed; impve. 3rd pers. pl. / *cariarse.*
caríese let it become decayed; impve. 3rd pers. sing. / *cariarse.*
carmenar to untangle or to cheat. reg.
carnear to butcher or to kill. reg.
carpintear to carpenter. reg.
carpir to weed. reg.
carraspear to clear one's throat or to be hoarse. reg.
carretear to cart or to haul. reg.
carteándose corresponding; pres. part. / *cartearse.*
carteaos (you all) correspond; impve. 2nd pers. pl. / *cartearse.*
cartear to correspond or to play low cards. reg.
cartearse to correspond. reg.
cartéate (you) correspond; impve. 2nd pers. sing. / *cartearse.*
carteémonos let us correspond; impve. 1st pers. pl. / *cartearse.*
cartéense let them correspond; impve. 3rd pers. pl. / *cartearse.*
cartéese let him (her/it) correspond; impve. 3rd pers. sing. / *cartearse.*
cartografía 1. he (she/it) charts; pres. ind. 3rd pers. sing. / *cartografiar.* 2. (you) chart; impve. 2nd pers. sing.
cartografían they chart; pres. ind. 3rd pers. pl. / *cartografiar.*
cartografiar to chart. irr.
cartografías you chart; pres. ind. 2nd pers. sing. / *cartografiar.*
cartografíe 1. that I may chart; pres. subj. 1st pers. sing. / *cartografiar.* 2. that he (she/it) may chart; pres. subj. 3rd pers. sing. 3. let him (her/it) chart; impve. 3rd pers. sing.
cartografíen 1. that they may chart; pres. subj. 3rd pers. pl. / *cartografiar.* 2. let them chart; impve. 3rd pers. pl.
cartografíes that you may chart; pres. subj. 2nd pers. sing. / *cartografiar.*
cartografío I chart; pres. ind. 1st pers. sing. / *cartografiar.*
casándose getting married; pres. part. / *casarse.*
casaos (you all) get married; impve. 2nd pers. pl. / *casarse.*
casar to marry or to wed. reg.
casarse to get married. reg.

cásate (you) get married; impve. 2nd pers. sing. / *casarse.*
cascabelear to lead on or to entice. reg.
cascándose breaking open; pres. part. / *cascarse.*
cascaos (you all) break open; impve. 2nd pers. pl. / *cascarse.*
cascar to crack or to break. irr.
cascarse to break open. irr.
cáscate (you) break open; impve. 2nd pers. sing. / *cascarse.*
casémonos let us get married; impve. 1st pers. pl. / *casarse.*
cásense let them get married; impve. 3rd pers. pl. / *casarse.*
cásese let him (her/it) get married; impve. 3rd pers. sing. / *casarse.*
casque 1. that I may crack; pres. subj. 1st pers. sing. / *cascar.* 2. that he (she/it) may crack; pres. subj. 3rd pers. sing. 3. let him (her/it) crack; impve. 3rd pers. sing.
casqué I cracked; past 1st pers. sing. / *cascar.*
casquéis that you (all) may crack; pres. subj. 2nd pers. pl. / *cascar.*
casquémonos let us break open; impve. 1st pers. pl. / *cascarse.*
casquemos 1. that we may crack; pres. subj. 1st pers. pl. / *cascar.* 2. let us crack; impve. 1st pers. pl.
casquen 1. that they may crack; pres. subj. 3rd pers. pl. / *cascar.* 2. let them crack; impve. 3rd pers. pl.
cásquense let them break open; impve. 3rd pers. pl. / *cascarse.*
casques that you may crack; pres. subj. 2nd pers. sing. / *cascar.*
cásquese let him (her/it) break open; impve. 3rd pers. sing. / *cascarse.*
castañetear to shake the castanets or to chatter (teeth) or to shiver. reg.
castellanice 1. that I may hispanicize; pres. subj. 1st pers. sing. / *castellanizar.* 2. that he (she/it) may hispanicize; pres. subj. 3rd pers. sing. 3. let him (her/it) hispanicize; impve. 3rd pers. sing.
castellanicé I hispanicized; past 1st pers. sing. / *castellanizar.*
castellanicéis that you (all) may hispanicize; pres. subj. 2nd pers. pl. / *castellanizar.*
castellanicemos 1. that we may hispanicize; pres. subj. 1st pers. pl. / *castellanizar.* 2. let us hispanicize; impve. 1st pers. pl.
castellanicen 1. that they may hispanicize; pres. subj. 3rd pers. pl. / *castellanizar.* 2. let them hispanicize; impve. 3rd pers. pl.
castellanices that you may hispanicize; pres. subj. 2nd pers. sing. / *castellanizar.*
castellanizar to castilianize or hispanicize. irr.
castigar to chastise or to punish. irr.
castigue 1. that I may chastise; pres. subj. 1st pers. sing. / *castigar.* 2. that (she/it) may chastise; pres. subj. 3rd pers. sing. 3. let him (her/it) chastise; impve. 3rd pers. sing.
castigué I chastised; past 1st pers. sing. / *castigar.*

castiguéis that you (all) may chastise; pres. subj. 2nd pers. pl. / *castigar*.

castiguemos 1. that we may chastise; pres. subj. 1st pers. pl. / *castigar*. 2. let us chastise; impve. 1st pers. pl.

castiguen 1. that they may chastise; pres. subj. 3rd pers. pl. / *castigar*. 2. let them chastise; impve. 3rd pers. pl.

castigues that you may chastise; pres. subj. 2nd pers. sing. / *castigar*.

castrar to castrate or to prune. reg.

catalogar to catalog or to test. irr.

catalogue 1. that I may catalog; pres. subj. 1st pers. sing. / *catalogar*. 2. that he (she/it) may catalog; pres. subj. 3rd pers. sing. 3. let him (her/it) catalog; impve. 3rd pers. sing.

catalogué I cataloged; past 1st pers. sing. / *catalogar*.

cataloguéis that you (all) may catalog; pres. subj. 2nd pers. pl. / *catalogar*.

cataloguemos 1. that we may catalog; pres. subj. 1st pers. pl. / *catalogar*. 2. let us catalog; impve. 1st pers. pl.

cataloguen 1. that they may catalog; pres. subj. 3rd pers. pl. / *catalogar*. 2. let them catalog; impve. 3rd pers. pl.

catalogues that you may catalog; pres. subj. 2nd pers. sing. / *catalogar*.

catar to taste or to inspect. reg.

catear to explore or to seek. reg.

catequice 1. that I may catechize; pres. subj. 1st pers. sing. / *catequizar*. 2. that he (she/it) may catechize; pres. subj. 3rd pers. sing. 3. let him (her/it) catechize; impve. 3rd pers. sing.

catequicé I catechetized; past 1st pers. sing. / *catequizar*.

catequicéis that you (all) may catechize; pres. subj. 2nd pers. pl. / *catequizar*.

catequicemos 1. that we may catechize; pres. subj. 1st pers. pl. / *catequizar*. 2. let us catechize; impve. 1st pers. pl.

catequicen 1. that they may catechize; pres. subj. 3rd pers. pl. / *catequizar*. 2. let them catechize; impve. 3rd pers. pl.

catequices that you may catechize; pres. subj. 2nd pers. sing. / *catequizar*.

catequizar to catechize or give religious instruction or to persuade. irr.

caucionar to caution or guard against or to guarantee. reg.

causar to cause or to produce. reg.

cautelándose preventing; pres. part. / *cautelarse*.

cautelaos (you all) prevent; impve. 2nd pers. pl. / *cautelarse*.

cautelar to guard against or to prevent. reg.

cautelarse to prevent. reg.

cautélate (you) prevent; impve. 2nd pers. sing. / *cautelarse*.

cautelémonos let us prevent; impve. 1st pers. pl. / *cautelarse*.

cautélense let them prevent; impve. 3rd pers. pl. / *cautelarse*.

cautélese let him (her/it) prevent; impve. 3rd pers. sing. / *cautelarse*.

cauterice 1. that I may cauterize; pres. subj. 1st pers. sing. / *cauterizar*. 2. that he (she/it) may cauterize; pres. subj. 3rd pers. sing. 3. let him (her/it) cauterize; impve. 3rd pers. sing.

caubericé I cauterized; past 1st pers. sing. / *cauterizar*.

cautericéis that you (all) may cauterize; pres. subj. 2nd pers. pl. / *cauterizar*.

cautericemos 1. that we may cauterize; pres. subj. 1st pers. pl. / *cauterizar*. 2. let us cauterize; impve. 1st pers. pl.

cautericen 1. that they may cauterize; pres. subj. 3rd pers. pl. / *cauterizar*. 2. let them cauterize; impve. 3rd pers. pl.

cauterices that you may cauterize; pres. subj. 2nd pers. sing. / *cauterizar*.

cauterizar to cauterize. irr.

cautivar to captivate or to capture. reg.

cavar to dig or to penetrate deeply. reg.

cavilar to muse or mull over. reg.

cayendo falling; pres. part. / *caer*.

cayéndose falling down; pres. part. / *caerse*.

cayera 1. that I might fall; imp. subj. 1st pers. sing. / *caer*. 2. that he (she/it) might fall; imp. subj. 3rd pers. sing.

cayerais that you (all) might fall; imp. subj. 2nd pers pl. / *caer*.

cayéramos that we might fall; imp. subj. 1st pers. pl. / *caer*.

cayeran that they might fall; imp. subj. 3rd pers. pl. / *caer*.

cayeras that you might fall; imp. subj. 2nd pers. sing. / *caer*.

cayeron they fell; past 3rd pers. pl. / *caer*.

cayese 1. that I might fall; imp. subj. 1st pers. sing. / *caer*. 2. that he (she/it) might fall; imp. subj. 3rd pers. sing.

cayeseis that you (all) might fall; imp. subj. 2nd pers pl. / *caer*.

cayésemos that we might fall; imp. subj. 1st pers. pl. / *caer*.

cayesen that they might fall; imp. subj. 3rd pers. pl. / *caer*.

cayeses that you might fall; imp. subj. 2nd pers. sing. / *caer*.

cayó he (she/it) fell; past 3rd pers. sing. / *caer*.

cazar to chase or to hunt. irr.

cazcalear to bumble about. reg.

cebándose raging; pres. part. / *cebarse*.

cebaos (you all) rage; impve. 2nd pers. pl. / *cebarse*.

cebar to feed or fatten (animals) or to encourage (a passion) or to start. reg.

cebarse to rage. reg.

cébate (you) rage; impve. 2nd pers. sing. / *cebarse*.

cebémonos let us rage; impve. 1st pers. pl. / *cebarse*.

cébense let them rage; impve. 3rd pers. pl. / *cebarse*.

cébese let him (her/it) rage; impve. 3rd pers. sing. / *cebarse*.

cecear to lisp. reg.

ceder to cede or to yield. reg.
cegar to go blind or to blind. irr.
cegué I went blind; past 1st pers. sing. / *cegar*.
ceguéis that you (all) may go blind; pres. subj. 2nd pers. pl. / *cegar*.
ceguemos 1. that we may go blind; pres. subj. 1st pers. pl. / *cegar*. 2. let us go blind; impve. 1st pers. pl.
cejar to go back or to give in. reg.
celar to watch carefully or to hide. reg.
celebrándose taking place; pres. part. / *celebrarse*.
celebrar to celebrate or to take place. reg.
celebrarse to take place. reg.
celébrense let them take place; impve. 3rd pers. pl. / *celebrarse*.
celébrese let it take place; impve. 3rd pers. sing. / *celebrarse*.
cellisquear to sleet. reg.
cementar to cement or to case harden. reg.
cenar to have supper. reg.
cencerrear to clatter or clang. reg.
censar to take a census. reg.
censurar to censure or criticize. reg.
centellar to sparkle or to flash. reg.
centellear to sparkle or to twinkle. reg.
centralice 1. that I may centralize; pres. subj. 1st pers. sing. / *centralizar*. 2. that he (she/it) may centralize; pres. subj. 3rd pers. sing. 3. let him (her/it) centralize; impve. 3rd pers. sing.
centralicé I centralized; past 1st pers. sing. / *centralizar*.
centralicéis that you (all) may centralize; pres. subj. 2nd pers. pl. / *centralizar*.
centralicémonos let us centralize; impve. 1st pers. pl. / *centralizarse*.
centralicemos 1. that we may centralize; pres. subj. 1st pers. pl. / *centralizar*. 2. let us centralize; impve. 1st pers. pl.
centralicen 1. that they may centralize; pres. subj. 3rd pers. pl. / *centralizar*. 2. let them centralize; impve. 3rd pers. pl.
centralícense let them centralize; impve. 3rd pers. pl. / *centralizarse*.
centralices that you may centralize; pres. subj. 2nd pers. sing. / *centralizar*.
centralícese let him (her/it) centralize; impve. 3rd pers. sing. / *centralizarse*.
centralizándose centralizing; pres. part. / *centralizarse*.
centralizaos (you all) centralize; impve. 2nd pers. pl. / *centralizarse*.
centralizar to centralize. irr.
centralizarse to centralize. irr.
centralízate (you) centralize; impve. 2nd pers. sing. / *centralizarse*.
centrándose being centered; pres. part. / *centrarse*.
centraos (you all) be centered; impve. 2nd pers. pl. / *centrarse*.
centrar to center. reg.
centrarse to be centered. reg.

céntrate (you) be centered; impve. 2nd pers. sing. / *centrarse*.
centrémonos let us be centered; impve. 1st pers. pl. / *centrarse*.
céntrense let them be centered; impve. 3rd pers. pl. / *centrarse*.
céntrese let him (her/it) be centered; impve. 3rd pers. sing. / *centrarse*.
centuplicar to centuple. irr.
centuplique 1. that I may centuple; pres. subj. 1st pers. sing. / *centuplicar*. 2. that he (she/it) may centuple; pres. subj. 3rd pers. sing. 3. let him (her/it) centuple; impve. 3rd pers. sing.
centupliqué I centupled; past 1st pers. sing. / *centuplicar*.
centupliquéis that you (all) may centuple; pres. subj. 2nd pers. pl. / *centuplicar*.
centupliquemos 1. that we may centuple; pres. subj. 1st pers. pl. / *centuplicar*. 2. let us centuple; impve. 1st pers. pl.
centupliquen 1. that they may centuple; pres. subj. 3rd pers. pl. / *centuplicar*. 2. let them centuple; impve. 3rd pers. pl.
centupliques that you may centuple; pres. subj. 2nd pers. sing. / *centuplicar*.
ceñí I girded; pres. ind. 1st pers. sing. / *ceñir*.
ceñíos (you all) limit yourselves; impve. 2nd pers. pl. / *ceñirse*.
ceñir to gird or encircle. irr.
ceñirse to limit oneself. irr.
cepillar to brush or to plane. reg.
cercar to fence in or to besiege. irr.
cercenar to pare or to reduce. reg.
cerciorándose finding out; pres. part. / *cerciorarse*.
cercioraos (you all) find out; impve. 2nd pers. pl. / *cerciorarse*.
cerciorar to assure. reg.
cerciorarse to find out. reg.
cerciórate (you) find out; impve. 2nd pers. sing. / *cerciorarse*.
cerciorémonos let us find out; impve. 1st pers. pl. / *cerciorarse*.
cerciórense let them find out; impve. 3rd pers. pl. / *cerciorarse*.
cerciórese let him (her/it) find out; impve. 3rd pers. sing. / *cerciorarse*.
cerdear to totter or to scrape roughly. reg.
cernámonos let us hover; impve. 1st pers. pl. / *cernerse*.
cerneos (you all) hover; impve. 2nd pers. pl. / *cernerse*.
cerner to sift or to blossom. irr.
cernerse to hover. irr.
cerniéndose hovering; pres. part. / *cernerse*.
cernir to strain or to sift. irr.
cerque 1. that I may fence in; pres. subj. 1st pers. sing. / *cercar*. 2. that he (she/it) may fence in; pres. subj. 3rd pers. sing. 3. let him (her/it) fence in; impve. 3rd pers. sing.
cerqué I fenced in; past 1st pers. sing. / *cercar*.

cerquéis that you (all) may fence in; pres. subj. 2nd pers. pl. / *cercar.*

cerquemos 1. that we may fence in; pres. subj. 1st pers. pl. / *cercar.* 2. let us fence in; impve. 1st pers. pl.

cerquen 1. that they may fence in; pres. subj. 3rd pers. pl. / *cercar.* 2. let them fence in; impve. 3rd pers. pl.

cerques that you may fence in; pres. subj. 2nd pers. sing. / *cercar.*

cerrándose becoming cloudy; pres. part. / *cerrarse.*

cerrar to close or to lock. irr.

cerrarse to become cloudy. irr.

cerrillar to knurl. reg.

certificar to certify. irr.

certifique 1. that I may certify; pres. subj. 1st pers. sing. / *certificar.* 2. that he (she/it) may certify; pres. subj. 3rd pers. sing. 3. let him (her/it) certify; impve. 3rd pers. sing.

certifiqué I certified; past 1st pers. sing. / *certificar.*

certifiquéis that you (all) may certify; pres. subj. 2nd pers. pl. / *certificar.*

certifiquemos 1. that we may certify; pres. subj. 1st pers. pl. / *certificar* 2. let us certify; impve. 1st pers. pl.

certifiquen 1. that they may certify; pres. subj. 3rd pers. pl. / *certificar.* 2. let them certify; impve. 3rd pers. pl.

certifiques that you may certify; pres. subj. 2nd pers. sing. / *certificar.*

cesar to cease. reg.

cicatrice 1. that I may heal; pres. subj. 1st pers. sing. / *cicatrizar.* 2. that he (she/it) may heal; pres. subj. 3rd pers. sing. 3. let him (her/it) heal; impve. 3rd pers. sing.

cicatricé I healed; past 1st pers. sing. / *cicatrizar.*

cicatricéis that you (all) may heal; pres. subj. 2nd pers. pl. / *cicatrizar.*

cicatricémonos let us heal; impve. 1st pers. pl. / *cicatrizarse.*

cicatricemos 1. that we may heal; pres. subj. 1st pers. pl. / *cicatrizar* 2. let us heal; impve. 1st pers. pl.

cicatricen 1. that they may heal; pres. subj. 3rd pers. pl. / *cicatrizar.* 2. let them heal; impve. 3rd pers. pl.

cicatrícense let them heal; impve. 3rd pers. pl. / *cicatrizarse.*

cicatrices that you may heal; pres. subj. 2nd pers. sing. / *cicatrizar.*

cicatrícese let him (her/it) heal; impve. 3rd pers. sing. / *cicatrizarse.*

cicatrizándose healing; pres. part. / *cicatrizarse.*

cicatrizaos (you all) heal; impve. 2nd pers. pl. / *cicatrizarse.*

cicatrizar to heal. irr.

cicatrizarse to heal. irr.

cicatrízate (you) heal; impve. 2nd pers. sing. / *cicatrizarse.*

ciega 1. he (she/it) goes blind; pres. ind. 3rd pers. sing. / *cegar.* 2. (you) go blind; impve. 2nd pers. sing.

ciegan they go blind; pres. ind. 3rd pers. pl. / *cegar.*

ciegas you go blind; pres. ind. 2nd pers. sing. / *cegar.*

ciego I go blind; pres. ind. 1st pers. sing. / *cegar.*

ciegue 1. that I may go blind; pres. subj. 1st pers. sing. / *cegar.* 2. that he (she/it) may go blind; pres. subj. 3rd pers. sing. 3. let him (her/it) go blind; impve. 3rd pers. sing.

cieguen 1. that they may go blind; pres. subj. 3rd pers. pl. / *cegar.* 2. let them go blind; impve. 3rd pers. pl.

ciegues that you may go blind; pres. subj. 2nd pers. sing. / *cegar.*

cierna 1. that I may sift; pres. subj. 1st pers. sing. / *cerner.* 2. that he (she/it) may sift; pres. subj. 3rd pers. sing. 3. let him (her/it) sift; impve. 3rd pers. sing.

ciernan 1. that they may sift; pres. subj. 3rd pers. pl. / *cerner.* 2. let them sift; impve. 3rd pers. pl.

ciérnanse let them hover; impve. 3rd pers. pl. / *cernerse.*

ciernas that you may sift; pres. subj. 2nd pers. sing. / *cerner.*

ciérnase let him (her/it) hover; impve. 3rd pers. sing. / *cernerse.*

cierne 1. he (she/it) sifts; pres. ind. 3rd pers. sing. / *cerner.* 2. (you) sift; impve. 2nd pers. sing.

ciernen they sift; pres. ind. 3rd pers. pl. / *cerner.*

ciernes you sift; pres. ind. 2nd pers. sing. / *cerner.*

ciérnete (you) hover; impve. 2nd pers. sing. / *cernerse.*

cierno I sift; pres. ind. 1st pers. sing. / *cerner.*

cierra 1. he (she/it) closes; pres. ind. 3rd pers. sing. / *cerrar.* 2. (you) close; impve. 2nd pers. sing.

cierran they close; pres. ind. 3rd pers. pl. / *cerrar.*

cierras you close; pres. ind. 2nd pers. sing. / *cerrar.*

cierre 1. that I may close; pres. subj. 1st pers. sing. / *cerrar.* 2. that he (she/it) may close; pres. subj. 3rd pers. sing. 3. let him (her/it) close; impve. 3rd pers. sing.

cierren 1. that they may close; pres. subj. 3rd pers. pl. / *cerrar.* 2. let them close; impve. 3rd pers. pl.

ciérrense let them become cloudy; impve. 3rd pers. pl. / *cerrarse.*

cierres that you may close; pres. subj. 2nd pers. sing. / *cerrar.*

ciérrese let it become cloudy; impve. 3rd pers. sing. / *cerrarse.*

cierro I close; pres. ind. 1st pers. sing. / *cerrar.*

cifrar to write in code. reg.

cilindrar to roll. reg.

cimarronear to drink mate without sugar. reg.

cimbrándose swinging; pres. part. / *cimbrarse.*

cimbraos (you all) swing; impve. 2nd pers. pl. / *cimbrarse.*

cimbrar to brandish. reg.

cimbrarse to swing or sway. reg.

címbrate (you) swing; impve. 2nd pers. sing. / *cimbrarse.*

cimbreándose vibrating; pres. part. / *cimbrearse.*

cimbreaos (you all) vibrate; impve. 2nd pers. pl. / *cimbrearse.*

cimbrear to brandish. reg.

cimbrearse to vibrate. reg.

cimbréate (you) vibrate; impve. 2nd pers. sing. / *cimbrearse*.

cimbreémonos let us vibrate; impve. 1st pers. pl. / *cimbrearse*.

cimbréense let them vibrate; impve. 3rd pers. pl. / *cimbrearse*.

cimbréese let him (her/it) vibrate; impve. 3rd pers. sing. / *cimbrearse*.

cimbrémonos let us swing; impve. 1st pers. pl. / *cimbrarse*.

címbrense let them swing; impve. 3rd pers. pl. / *cimbrarse*.

címbrese let him (her/it) swing; impve. 3rd pers. sing. / *cimbrarse*.

cimentar to lay the foundation for or to refine. irr.

cimienta 1. he (she/it) lays the foundation for; pres. ind. 3rd pers. sing. / *cimentar* 2. (you) lay the foundation for; impve. 2nd pers. sing.

cimientan they lay the foundation for; pres. ind. 3rd pers. pl. / *cimentar*.

cimientas you lay the foundation for; pres. ind. 2nd pers. sing. / *cimentar*.

cimiente 1. that I may lay the foundation for; pres. subj. 1st pers. sing. / *cimentar*. 2. that he (she/it) may lay the foundation for; pres. subj. 3rd pers. sing. 3. let him (her/it) lay the foundation for; impve. 3rd pers. sing.

cimienten 1. that they may lay the foundation for; pres. subj. 3rd pers. pl. / *cimentar*. 2. let them lay the foundation for; impve. 3rd pers. pl.

cimientes that you may lay the foundation for; pres. subj. 2nd pers. sing. / *cimentar*.

cimiento I lay the foundation for; pres. ind. 1st pers. sing. / *cimentar*.

cincelar to chisel or to engrave. reg.

cinchar to cinch. reg.

cinematografía 1. he (she/it) films; pres. ind. 3rd pers. sing. / *cinematografiar*. 2. (you) film; impve. 2nd pers. sing.

cinematografían they film; pres. ind. 3rd pers. pl. / *cinematografiar*.

cinematografiar to film. irr.

cinematografías you film; pres. ind. 2nd pers. sing. / *cinematografiar*.

cinematografíe 1. that I may film; pres. subj. 1st pers. sing. / *cinematografiar*. 2. that he (she/it) may film; pres. subj. 3rd pers. sing. 3. let him (her/it) film; impve. 3rd pers. sing.

cinematografíen 1. that they may film; pres. subj. 3rd pers. pl. / *cinematografiar*. 2. let them film; impve. 3rd pers. pl.

cinematografíes that you may film; pres. subj. 2nd pers. sing. / *cinematografiar*.

cinematografío I film; pres. ind. 1st pers. sing. / *cinematografiar*.

cinglar to forge (iron). reg.

cinglar to scull (a boat). reg.

cintilar to sparkle. reg.

ciña 1. that I may gird; pres. subj. 1st pers. sing. / *ceñir*. 2. that he (she/it) may gird; pres. subj. 3rd pers. sing. 3. let him (her/it) gird; impve. 3rd pers. sing.

ciñáis that you (all) may gird; pres. subj. 2nd pers. pl. / *ceñir*.

ciñámonos let us limit ourselves; impve. 1st pers. pl. / *ceñirse*.

ciñamos 1. that we may gird; pres. subj. 1st pers. pl. / *ceñir*. 2. let us gird; impve. 1st pers. pl.

ciñan 1. that they may gird; pres. subj. 3rd pers. pl. / *ceñir*. 2. let them gird; impve. 3rd pers. pl.

ciñanse let them limit themselves; impve. 3rd pers. pl. / *ceñirse*.

ciñas that you may gird; pres. subj. 2nd pers. sing. / *ceñir*.

ciñase let him (her/it) limit himself (herself/itself); impve. 3rd pers. sing. / *ceñirse*.

ciñe 1. he (she/it) girds; pres. ind. 3rd pers. sing. / *ceñir*. 2. (you) gird; impve. 2nd pers. sing.

ciñen they gird; pres. ind. 3rd pers. pl. / *ceñir*.

ciñendo girding; pres. part. / *ceñir*.

ciñéndose limiting oneself; pres. part. / *ceñirse*.

ciñera 1. that I might gird; imp. subj. 1st pers. sing. / *ceñir*. 2. that he (she/it) might gird; imp. subj. 3rd pers. sing.

ciñerais that you (all) might gird; imp. subj. 2nd pers pl. / *ceñir*.

ciñéramos that we might gird; imp. subj. 1st pers. pl. / *ceñir*.

ciñeran that they might gird; imp. subj. 3rd pers. pl. / *ceñir*.

ciñeras that you might gird; imp. subj. 2nd pers. sing. / *ceñir*.

ciñeron they girded; past 3rd pers. pl. / *ceñir*.

ciñes you gird; pres. ind. 2nd pers. sing. / *ceñir*.

ciñese 1. that I might gird; imp. subj. 1st pers. sing. / *ceñir*. 2. that he (she/it) might gird; imp. subj. 3rd pers. sing.

ciñeseis that you (all) might gird; imp. subj. 2nd pers pl. / *ceñir*.

ciñésemos that we might gird; imp. subj. 1st pers. pl. / *ceñir*.

ciñesen that they might gird; imp. subj. 3rd pers. pl. / *ceñir*.

ciñeses that you might gird; imp. subj. 2nd pers. sing. / *ceñir*.

cíñete (you) limit yourself; impve. 2nd pers. sing. / *ceñirse*.

ciño I gird; pres. ind. 1st pers. sing. / *ceñir*.

ciñó he (she/it) girded; past 3rd pers. sing. / *ceñir*.

circuir to encircle. irr.

circular to circulate. reg.

circuncidar to circumcise. reg.

circundar to surround. reg.

circunnavegar to circumnavigate. irr.

circunnavegue 1. that I may circumnavigate; pres. subj. 1st pers. sing. / *circunnavegar*. 2. that he (she/it) may circumnavigate; pres. subj. 3rd pers. sing. 3. let him (her/it) circumnavigate; impve. 3rd pers. sing.

circunnavegué I circumnavigated; past 1st pers. sing. / *circunnavegar*.

circunnavegéuis that you (all) may circumnavigate; pres. subj. 2nd pers. pl. / *circunnavegar*.

circunnaveguemos 1. that we may circumnavigate; pres. subj. 1st pers. pl. / *circunnavegar*. 2. let us circumnavigate; impve. 1st pers. pl.

circunnaveguen 1. that they may circumnavigate; pres. subj. 3rd pers. pl. / *circunnavegar*. 2. let them circumnavigate; impve. 3rd pers. pl.

circunnavegues that you may circumnavigate; pres. subj. 2nd pers. sing. / *circunnavegar*.

circunscribir to circumscribe or to limit. reg. except for pp.

circunscripto circumscribed; past part. / *circunscribir*.

circunscrito circumscribed; past part. / *circunscribir*.

circunvalar to surround. reg.

circunven (you) circumvent; impve. 2nd pers. sing. / *circunvenir*.

circunvendrá he (she/it) will circumvent; fut. 3rd pers. sing. / *circunvenir*.

circunvendrán they will circumvent; fut. 3rd pers. pl. / *circunvenir*.

circunvendrás you will circumvent; fut. 2nd pers. sing. / *circunvenir*.

circunvendré I shall circumvent; fut. 1st pers. sing. / *circunvenir*.

circunvendréis you (all) will circumvent; fut. 2nd pers. pl. / *circunvenir*.

circunvendremos we shall circumvent; fut. 1st pers. pl. / *circunvenir*.

circunvendría 1. I should circumvent; cond. 1st pers. sing. / *circunvenir*. 2. he (she/it) would circumvent; cond. 3rd pers. sing.

circunvendríais you (all) would circumvent; cond. 2nd pers. pl. / *circunvenir*.

circunvendríamos we should circumvent; cond. 1st pers. pl. / *circunvenir*.

circunvendrían they would circumvent; cond. 3rd pers. pl. / *circunvenir*.

circunvendrías you would circumvent; cond. 2nd pers. sing. / *circunvenir*.

circunvenga 1. that I may circumvent; pres. subj. 1st pers. sing. / *circunvenir*. 2. that he (she/it) may circumvent; pres. subj. 3rd pers. sing. 3. let him (her/it) circumvent; impve. 3rd pers. sing.

circunvengáis that you (all) may circumvent; pres. subj. 2nd pers. pl. / *circunvenir*.

circunvengamos 1. that we may circumvent; pres. subj. 1st pers. pl. / *circunvenir*. 2. let us circumvent; impve. 1st pers. pl.

circunvengan 1. that they may circumvent; pres. subj. 3rd pers. pl. / *circunvenir*. 2. let them circumvent; impve. 3rd pers. pl.

circunvengas that you may circumvent; pres. subj. 2nd pers. sing. / *circunvenir*.

circunvengo I circumvent; pres. ind. 1st pers. sing. / *circunvenir*.

circunvenir to circumvent. irr.

circunviene he (she/it) circumvents; pres. ind. 3rd pers. sing. / *circunvenir*.

circunvienen they circumvent; pres. ind. 3rd pers. pl. / *circunvenir*.

circunvienes you circumvent; pres. ind. 2nd pers. sing. / *circunvenir*.

circunvine I circumvented; pres. ind. 1st pers. sing. / *circunvenir*.

circunviniendo circumventing; pres. part. / *circunvenir*.

circunviniera 1. that I might circumvent; imp. subj. 1st pers. sing. / *circunvenir*. 2. that he (she/it) might circumvent; imp. subj. 3rd pers. sing.

circunvinierais that you (all) might circumvent; imp. subj. 2nd pers pl. / *circunvenir*.

circunviniéramos that we might circumvent; imp. subj. 1st pers. pl. / *circunvenir*.

circunvinieran that they might circumvent; imp. subj. 3rd pers. pl. / *circunvenir*.

circunvinieras that you might circumvent; imp. subj. 2nd pers. sing. / *circunvenir*.

circunvinieron they circumvented; past 3rd pers. pl. / *circunvenir*.

circunviniese 1. that I might circumvent; imp. subj. 1st pers. sing. / *circunvenir*. 2. that he (she/it) might circumvent; imp. subj. 3rd pers. sing.

circunvinieseis that you (all) might circumvent; imp. subj. 2nd pers pl. / *circunvenir*.

circunviniésemos that we might circumvent; imp. subj. 1st pers. pl. / *circunvenir*.

circunviniesen that they might circumvent; imp. subj. 3rd pers. pl. / *circunvenir*.

circunvinieses that you might circumvent; imp. subj. 2nd pers. sing. / *circunvenir*.

circunvinimos we circumvented; past 1st pers. pl. / *circunvenir*.

circunviniste you circumvented; past 2nd pers. sing. / *circunvenir*.

circunvinisteis you (all) circumvented; past 2nd pers. pl. / *circunvenir*.

circunvino he (she/it) circumvented; past 3rd pers. sing. / *circunvenir*.

circunvolar to fly around. irr.

circunvuela 1. he (she/it) flies around; pres. ind. 3rd pers. sing. / *circunvolar*. 2. (you) fly around; impve. 2nd pers. sing.

circunvuelan they fly around; pres. ind. 3rd pers. pl. / *circunvolar*.

circunvuelas you fly around; pres. ind. 2nd pers. sing. / *circunvolar*.

circunvuele 1. that I may fly around; pres. subj. 1st pers. sing. / *circunvolar*. 2. that he (she/it) may fly around; pres. subj. 3rd pers. sing. 3. let him (her/it) fly around; impve. 3rd pers. sing.

circunvuelen 1. that they may fly around; pres. subj. 3rd pers. pl. / *circunvolar*. 2. let them fly around; impve. 3rd pers. pl.

circunvueles that you may fly around; pres. subj. 2nd pers. sing. / *circunvolar*.

circunvuelo I fly around; pres. ind. 1st pers. sing. / *circunvolar*.

circuya 1. that I may encircle; pres. subj. 1st pers. sing. / *circuir* 2. that he (she/it) may encircle; pres. subj. 3rd pers. sing. 3. let him (her/it) encircle; impve. 3rd pers. sing.

circuyáis that you (all) may encircle; pres. subj. 2nd pers. pl. / *circuir*.

circuyamos 1. that we may encircle; pres. subj. 1st pers. pl. / *circuir*. 2. let us encircle; impve. 1st pers. pl.

circuyan 1. that they may encircle; pres. subj. 3rd pers. pl. / *circuir*. 2. let them encircle; impve. 3rd pers. pl.

circuyas that you may encircle; pres. subj. 2nd pers. sing. / *circuir*.

circuye 1. he (she/it) encircles; pres. ind. 3rd pers. sing. / *circuir*. 2. (you) encircle; impve. 2nd pers. sing.

circuyen they encircle; pres. ind. 3rd pers. pl. / *circuir*.

circuyendo encircling; pres. part. / *circuir*.

circuyera 1. that I might encircle; imp. subj. 1st pers. sing. / *circuir*. 2. that he (she/it) might encircle; imp. subj. 3rd pers. sing.

circuyerais that you (all) might encircle; imp. subj. 2nd pers pl. / *circuir*.

circuyéramos that we might encircle; imp. subj. 1st pers. pl. / *circuir*.

circuyeran that they might encircle; imp. subj. 3rd pers. pl. / *circuir*.

circuyeras that you might encircle; imp. subj. 2nd pers. sing. / *circuir*.

circuyeron they encircled; past 3rd pers. pl. / *circuir*.

circuyes you encircle; pres. ind. 2nd pers. sing. / *circuir*.

circuyese 1. that I might encircle; imp. subj. 1st pers. sing. / *circuir*. 2. that he (she/it) might encircle; imp. subj. 3rd pers. sing.

circuyeseis that you (all) might encircle; imp. subj. 2nd pers pl. / *circuir*.

circuyésemos that we might encircle; imp. subj. 1st pers. pl. / *circuir*.

circuyesen that they might encircle; imp. subj. 3rd pers. pl. / *circuir*.

circuyeses that you might encircle; imp. subj. 2nd pers. sing. / *circuir*.

circuyo I encircle; pres. ind. 1st pers. sing. / *circuir*.

circuyó he (she/it) encircled; past 3rd pers. sing. / *circuir*.

citar to make an appointment with or to quote. reg.

civilice 1. that I may civilize; pres. subj. 1st pers. sing. / *civilizar*. 2. that he (she/it) may civilize; pres. subj. 3rd pers. sing. 3. let him (her/it) civilize; impve. 3rd pers. sing.

civilicé I civilized; past 1st pers. sing. / *civilizar*.

civilicéis that you (all) may civilize; pres. subj. 2nd pers. pl. / *civilizar*.

civilicemos 1. that we may civilize; pres. subj. 1st pers. pl. / *civilizar*. 2. let us civilize; impve. 1st pers. pl.

civilicen 1. that they may civilize; pres. subj. 3rd pers. pl. / *civilizar*. 2. let them civilize; impve. 3rd pers. pl.

civilices that you may civilize; pres. subj. 2nd pers. sing. / *civilizar*.

civilizar to civilize. irr.

clamar to clamor or to whine. reg.

clamorear to clamor or to toll. reg.

clareándose becoming transparent; pres. part. / *clarearse*.

clareaos (you all) become transparent; impve. 2nd pers. pl. / *clarearse*.

clarear to grow light or to clear up. reg.

clarearse to become transparent. reg.

claréate (you) become transparent; impve. 2nd pers. sing. / *clarearse*.

clarecer to dawn. irr.

clareémonos let us become transparent; impve. 1st pers. pl. / *clarearse*.

claréense let them become transparent; impve. 3rd pers. pl. / *clarearse*.

claréese let him (her/it) become transparent; impve. 3rd pers. sing. / *clarearse*.

clarezca 1. that it may dawn; pres. subj. 3rd pers. sing. / *clarecer* 2. let it dawn; impve. 3rd pers. sing.

clarificar to clarify. irr.

clarifique 1. that I may clarify; pres. subj. 1st pers. sing. / *clarificar*. 2. that he (she/it) may clarify; pres. subj. 3rd pers. sing. 3. let him (her/it) clarify; impve. 3rd pers. sing.

clarifiqué I clarified; past 1st pers. sing. / *clarificar*.

clarifiquéis that you (all) may clarify; pres. subj. 2nd pers. pl. / *clarificar*.

clarifiquemos 1. that we may clarify; pres. subj. 1st pers. pl. / *clarificar*. 2. let us clarify; impve. 1st pers. pl.

clarifiquen 1. that they may clarify; pres. subj. 3rd pers. pl. / *clarificar*. 2. let them clarify; impve. 3rd pers. pl.

clarifiques that you may clarify; pres. subj. 2nd pers. sing. / *clarificar*.

clasificándose qualifying; pres. part. / *clasificarse*.

clasificaos (you all) qualify; impve. 2nd pers. pl. / *clasificarse*.

clasificar to classify. irr.

clasificarse to qualify. irr.

clasifícate (you) qualify; impve. 2nd pers. sing. / *clasificarse*.

clasifique 1. that I may classify; pres. subj. 1st pers. sing. / *clasificar*. 2. that he (she/it) may classify; pres. subj. 3rd pers. sing. 3. let him (her/it) classify; impve. 3rd pers. sing.

clasifiqué I classified; past 1st pers. sing. / *clasificar*.

clasifiquéis that you (all) may classify; pres. subj. 2nd pers. pl. / *clasificar*.

clasifiquémonos let us qualify; impve. 1st pers. pl. / *clasificarse*.

clasifiquemos 1. that we may classify; pres. subj. 1st pers. pl. / *clasificar*. 2. let us classify; impve. 1st pers. pl.

clasifiquen 1. that they may classify; pres. subj. 3rd pers. pl. / *clasificar*. 2. let them classify; impve. 3rd pers. pl.

clasifíquense let them qualify; impve. 3rd pers. pl. / *clasificarse*.

clasifiques that you may classify; pres. subj. 2nd pers. sing. / *clasificar*.

clasifíquese let him (her/it) qualify; impve. 3rd pers. sing. / *clasificarse*.

claudicar to limp or to bungle. irr.

claudique 1. that I may limp; pres. subj. 1st pers. sing. / *claudicar*. 2. that he (she/it) may limp; pres. subj. 3rd pers. sing. 3. let him (her/it) limp; impve. 3rd pers. sing.

claudiqué I limped; past 1st pers. sing. / *claudicar*.

claudiquéis that you (all) may limp; pres. subj. 2nd pers. pl. / *claudicar*.

claudiquemos 1. that we may limp; pres. subj. 1st pers. pl. / *claudicar*. 2. let us limp; impve. 1st pers. pl.

claudiquen 1. that they may limp; pres. subj. 3rd pers. pl. / *claudicar*. 2. let them limp; impve. 3rd pers. pl.

claudiques that you may limp; pres. subj. 2nd pers. sing. / *claudicar*.

clausurar to close or to stop the operation of. reg.

clavándose being deceived; pres. part. / *clavarse*.

clavaos (you all) be deceived; impve. 2nd pers. pl. / *clavarse*.

clavar to nail or to cleat. reg.

clavarse to be deceived. reg.

clávate (you) be deceived; impve. 2nd pers. sing. / *clavarse*.

clavémonos let us be deceived; impve. 1st pers. pl. / *clavarse*.

clávense let them be deceived; impve. 3rd pers. pl. / *clavarse*.

clávese let him (her/it) be deceived; impve. 3rd pers. sing. / *clavarse*.

clavetear to stud with nails or to tip with metal. reg.

clisar to stereotype. reg.

clocar to cluck. irr.

cloque 1. that I may cluck; pres. subj. 1st pers. sing. / *clocar*. 2. that he (she/it) may cluck; pres. subj. 3rd pers. sing. 3. let him (her/it) cluck; impve. 3rd pers. sing.

cloqué I clucked; past 1st pers. sing. / *clocar*.

cloquear to cluck or to cackle. reg.

cloquéis that you (all) may cluck; pres. subj. 2nd pers. pl. / *clocar*.

cloquemos 1. that we may cluck; pres. subj. 1st pers. pl. / *clocar*. 2. let us cluck; impve. 1st pers. pl.

cloquen 1. that they may cluck; pres. subj. 3rd pers. pl. / *clocar*. 2. let them cluck; impve. 3rd pers. pl.

cloques that you may cluck; pres. subj. 2nd pers. sing. / *clocar*.

cloroformice 1. that I may chloroform; pres. subj. 1st pers. sing. / *cloroformizar*. 2. that he (she/it) may chloroform; pres. subj. 3rd pers. sing. 3. let him (her/it) chloroform; impve. 3rd pers. sing.

cloroformicé I chloroformed; past 1st pers. sing. / *cloroformizar*.

cloroformicéis that you (all) may chloroform; pres. subj. 2nd pers. pl. / *cloroformizar*.

cloroformicemos 1. that we may chloroform; pres. subj. 1st pers. pl. / *cloroformizar*. 2. let us chloroform; impve. 1st pers. pl.

cloroformicen 1. that they may chloroform; pres. subj. 3rd pers. pl. / *cloroformizar*. 2. let them chloroform; impve. 3rd pers. pl.

cloroformices that you may chloroform; pres. subj. 2nd pers. sing. / *cloroformizar*.

cloroformizar to chloroform. irr.

clueca 1. he (she/it) clucks; pres. ind. 3rd pers. sing. / *clocar*. 2. (you) cluck; impve. 2nd pers. sing.

cluecan they cluck; pres. ind. 3rd pers. pl. / *clocar*.

cluecas you cluck; pres. ind. 2nd pers. sing. / *clocar*.

clueco I cluck; pres. ind. 1st pers. sing. / *clocar*.

clueque 1. that I may cluck; pres. subj. 1st pers. sing. / *clocar*. 2. that he (she/it) may cluck; pres. subj. 3rd pers. sing. 3. let him (her/it) cluck; impve. 3rd pers. sing.

cluequen 1. that they may cluck; pres. subj. 3rd pers. pl. / *clocar*. 2. let them cluck; impve. 3rd pers. pl.

clueques that you may cluck; pres. subj. 2nd pers. sing. / *clocar*.

coaccionar to compel. reg.

coadyuvar to contribute or to help. reg.

coagulándose clotting; pres. part. / *coagularse*.

coagular to coagulate or to curdle. reg.

coagularse to clot. reg.

coagúlense let them clot; impve. 3rd pers. pl. / *coagularse*.

coagúlese let it clot; impve. 3rd pers. sing. / *coagularse*.

coartar to limit or to restrict. reg.

cobijar to cover or to shelter. reg.

cobrándose recovering; pres. part. / *cobrarse*.

cobraos (you all) recover; impve. 2nd pers. pl. / *cobrarse*.

cobrar to collect or to cash. reg.

cobrarse to recover. reg.

cóbrate (you) recover; impve. 2nd pers. sing. / *cobrarse*.

cobrémonos let us recover; impve. 1st pers. pl. / *cobrarse*.

cóbrense let them recover; impve. 3rd pers. pl. / *cobrarse*.

cóbrese let him (her/it) recover; impve. 3rd pers. sing. / *cobrarse*.

cocear to kick. reg.

coceos (you all) suffer intensely; impve. 2nd pers. pl. / *cocerse*.

cocer to boil. irr.

cocerse to suffer intensely. irr.

cociéndose suffering intensely; pres. part. / *cocerse*.

cocinar to cook. reg. ar conju.
codeándose hobnobing; pres. part. / *codearse*.
codeaos (you all) hobnob; impve. 2nd pers. pl. / *codearse*.
codear to elbow or to nudge. reg. ar conju.
codearse to hobnob or to mingle. reg. ar conju.
codéate (you) hobnob; impve. 2nd pers. sing. / *codearse*.
codeémonos let us hobnob; impve. 1st pers. pl. / *codearse*.
codeense let them hobnob; impve. 3rd pers. pl. / *codearse*.
codéese let him (her/it) hobnob; impve. 3rd pers. sing. / *codearse*.
codiciar to covet. reg. ar conju.
codificar to codify. irr.
codifique 1. that I may codify; pres. subj. 1st pers. sing. / *cofificar*. 2. that he (she/it) may codify; pres. subj. 3rd pers. sing. 3. let him (her/it) codify; impve. 3rd pers. sing.
codifiqué I codified; past 1st pers. sing. / *codificar*.
codifiquéis that you (all) may codify; pres. subj. 2nd pers. pl. / *codificar*.
codifiquemos 1. that we may codify; pres. subj. 1st pers. pl. / *codificar*. 2. let us codify; impve. 1st pers. pl.
codifiquen 1. that they may codify; pres. subj. 3rd pers. pl. / *codificar*. 2. let them codify; impve. 3rd pers. pl.
codifiques that you may codify; pres. subj. 2nd pers. sing. / *codificar*.
coercer to coerce. irr.
coerza 1. that I may coerce; pres. subj. 1st pers. sing. / *coercer*. 2. that he (she/it) may coerce; pres. subj. 3rd pers. sing. 3. let him (her/it) coerce; impve. 3rd pers. sing.
coerzáis that you (all) may coerce; pres. subj. 2nd pers. pl. / *coercer*.
coerzamos 1. that we may coerce; pres. subj. 1st pers. pl. / *coercer*. 2. let us coerce; impve. 1st pers. pl.
coerzan 1. that they may coerce; pres. subj. 3rd pers. pl. / *coercer*. 2. let them coerce; impve. 3rd pers. pl.
coerzas that you may coerce; pres. subj. 2nd pers. sing. / *coercer*.
coerzo I coerce; pres. ind. 1st pers. sing. / *coercer*.
coexistir to coexist. reg.
coger to seize or to fit. irr.
cohabitar to cohabit. reg.
cohechar to bribe or to plough. reg.
cohibir to restrain or to inhibit. reg.
cohonestar to gloss over. reg.
coimear to graft. reg.
coincidir to coincide or to concur. reg.
coja 1. that I may seize; pres. subj. 1st pers. sing. / *coger*. 2. that he (she/it) may seize; pres. subj. 3rd pers. sing. 3. let him (her/it) seize; impve. 3rd pers. sing.
cojáis that you (all) may seize; pres. subj. 2nd pers. pl. / *coger*.

cojamos 1. that we may seize; pres. subj. 1st pers. pl. / *coger*. 2. let us seize; impve. 1st pers. pl.
cojan 1. that they may seize; pres. subj. 3rd pers. pl. / *coger*. 2. let them seize; impve. 3rd pers. pl.
cojas that you may seize; pres. subj. 2nd pers. sing. / *coger*
cojear to limp or to wobble. reg.
cojo I seize; pres. ind. 1st pers. sing. / *coger*.
colaborar to collaborate. reg. ar conju.
colándose slipping in; pres. part. / *colarse*.
colaos (you all) slip in; impve. 2nd pers. pl. / *colarse*.
colar to strain or filter or to sneak in. irr.
colarse to slip in or to seep. irr.
colchar to quilt. reg.
colear to wag the tail. reg.
coleccionar to collect. reg.
colectar to collect. reg.
colectivice 1. that I may collectivize; pres. subj. 1st pers. sing. / *colectivizar*. 2. that he (she/it) may collectivize; pres. subj. 3rd pers. sing. 3. let him (her/it) collectivize; impve. 3rd pers. sing.
colectivicé I collectivized; past 1st pers. sing. / *colectivizar*.
colectivicéis that you (all) may collectivize; pres. subj. 2nd pers. pl. / *colectivizar*.
colectivicemos 1. that we may collectivize; pres. subj. 1st pers. pl. / *colectivizar*. 2. let us collectivize; impve. 1st pers. pl.
colectivicen 1. that they may collectivize; pres. subj. 3rd pers. pl. / *colectivizar*. 2. let them collectivize; impve. 3rd pers. pl.
colectivices that you may collectivize; pres. subj. 2nd pers. sing. / *colectivizar*.
colectivizar to collectivize. irr.
colegir to gather or to infer. irr.
colémonos let us slip in; impve. 1st pers. pl. / *colarse*.
colgar to hang up or to attribute. irr.
colgué I hung up; past 1st pers. sing. / *colgar*.
colguéis that you (all) may hang up; pres. subj. 2nd pers. pl. / *colgar*.
colguemos 1. that we may hang up; pres. subj. 1st pers. pl. / *colgar*. 2. let us hang up; impve. 1st pers. pl.
coligándose banding together; pres. part. / *coligarse*.
coligaos (you all) band together; impve. 2nd pers. pl. / *coligarse*.
coligarse to band together. irr.
colígate (you) band together; impve. 2nd pers. sing. / *coligarse*.
colige 1. he (she/it) gathers; pres. ind. 3rd pers. sing. / *colegir*. 2. (you) gather; impve. 2nd pers. sing.
coligen they gather; pres. ind. 3rd pers. pl. / *colegir*.
coliges you gather; pres. ind. 2nd pers. sing. / *colegir*.
coligiendo gathering; pres. part. / *colegir*.
coligiera 1. that I might gather; imp. subj. 1st pers. sing. / *colegir*. 2. that he (she/it) might gather; imp. subj. 3rd pers. sing.
coligierais that you (all) might gather; imp. subj. 2nd pers pl. / *colegir*.

coligiéramos that we might gather; imp. subj. 1st pers. pl. / *colegir*.

coligieran that they might gather; imp. subj. 3rd pers. pl. / *colegir*.

coligieras that you might gather; imp. subj. 2nd pers. sing. / *colegir*.

coligieron they gathered; past 3rd pers. pl. / *colegir*.

coligiese 1. that I might gather; imp. subj. 1st pers. sing. / *colegir*. 2. that he (she/it) might gather; imp. subj. 3rd pers. sing.

coligieseis that you (all) might gather; imp. subj. 2nd pers pl. / *colegir*.

coligiésemos that we might gather; imp. subj. 1st pers. pl. / *colegir*.

coligiesen that they might gather; imp. subj. 3rd pers. pl. / *colegir*.

coligieses that you might gather; imp. subj. 2nd pers. sing. / *colegir*.

coligió he (she/it) gathered; past 3rd pers. sing. / *colegir*.

coligue 1. that I may band togther; pres. subj. 1st pers. sing. / *coligarse*. 2. that he (she/it) may band together; pres. subj. 3rd pers. sing.

coligué I banded together; past 1st pers. sing. / *coligarse*.

coliguéis that you (all) may band together; pres. subj. 2nd pers. pl. / *coligarse*.

coliguémonos let us band together; impve. 1st pers. pl. / *coligarse*.

coliguemos that we may band together; pres. subj. 1st pers. pl. / *coligarse*.

coliguen that they may band together; pres. subj. 3rd pers. pl. / *coligarse*.

colíguense let them band together; impve. 3rd pers. pl. / *coligarse*.

coligues that you may band together; pres. subj. 2nd pers. sing. / *coligarse*.

colíguese let him (her/it) band together; impve. 3rd pers. sing. / *coligarse*.

colija 1. that I may gather; pres. subj. 1st pers. sing. / *colegir*. 2. that he (she/it) may gather; pres. subj. 3rd pers. sing. 3. let him (her/it) gather; impve. 3rd pers. sing.

colijáis that you (all) may gather; pres. subj. 2nd pers. pl. / *colegir*.

colijamos 1. that we may gather; pres. subj. 1st pers. pl. / *colegir*. 2. let us gather; impve. 1st pers. pl.

colijan 1. that they may gather; pres. subj. 3rd pers. pl. / *colegir*. 2. let them gather; impve. 3rd pers. pl.

colijas that you may gather; pres. subj. 2nd pers. sing. / *colegir*.

colijo I gather; pres. ind. 1st pers. sing. / *colegir*.

colindar to border (on). reg.

colmar to fill to the brim. reg.

colocar to place or to get employment. irr.

colonice 1. that I may colonize; pres. subj. 1st pers. sing. / *colonizar*. 2. that he (she/it) may colonize; pres. subj. 3rd pers. sing. 3. let him (her/it) colonize; impve. 3rd pers. sing.

colonicé I colonized; past 1st pers. sing. / *colonizar*.

colonicéis that you (all) may colonize; pres. subj. 2nd pers. pl. / *colonzar*.

colonicemos 1. that we may colonize; pres. subj. 1st pers. pl. / *clonizar*. 2. let us colonize; impve. 1st pers. pl.

colonicen 1. that they may colonize; pres. subj. 3rd pers. pl. / *colonizar*. 2. let them colonize; impve. 3rd pers. pl.

colonices that you may colonize; pres. subj. 2nd pers. sing. / *colonizar*.

colonizar to colonize. irr.

coloque 1. that I may place; pres. subj. 1st pers. sing. / *colocar*. 2. that he (she/it) may place; pres. subj. 3rd pers. sing. 3. let him (her/it) place; impve. 3rd pers. sing.

coloqué I placed; past 1st pers. sing. / *colocar*.

coloquéis that you (all) may place; pres. subj. 2nd pers. pl. / *colocar*.

coloquemos 1. that we may place; pres. subj. 1st pers. pl. / *colocar*. 2. let us place; impve. 1st pers. pl.

coloquen 1. that they may place; pres. subj. 3rd pers. pl. / *colocar*. 2. let them place; impve. 3rd pers. pl.

coloques that you may place; pres. subj. 2nd pers. sing. / *colocar*.

colorar to color or to dye. reg.

colorear to color or to make plausible. reg.

colorir to color or to turn red. irr. occurs only in those forms where the i is present in the verb ending.

coludámonos let us act in collusion; impve. 1st pers. pl. / *coludirse*.

colúdanse let them act in collusion; impve. 3rd pers. pl. / *coludirse*.

colúdase let him (her/it) act in collusion; impve. 3rd pers. sing. / *coludirse*.

colúdete (you) act in collusion; impve. 2nd pers. sing. / *coludirse*.

coludiéndose acting in collusion; pres. part. / *coludirse*.

coludíos (you all) act in collusion; impve. 2nd pers. pl. / *coludirse*.

coludir to act in collusion. reg.

coludirse to act in collusion. reg.

columbrar to glimpse or to infer. reg.

columpiándose swaying; pres. part. / *columpiarse*.

columpiaos (you all) sway; impve. 2nd pers. pl. / *columpiarse*.

columpiar to swing or sway. reg.

columpiarse to sway or to rock. reg.

columpíate (you) sway; impve. 2nd pers. sing. / *columpiarse*.

columpiémonos let us sway; impve. 1st pers. pl. / *columpiarse*.

columpíense let them sway; impve. 3rd pers. pl. / *columpiarse*.

columpíese let him (her/it) sway; impve. 3rd pers. sing. / *columpiarse*.

comadrear to gossip or to tattle. reg.

comámonos let us eat up; impve. 1st pers. pl. / *comerse*.

comandar to command. reg.

comanditar to invest (in a business). reg.

cómanse let them eat up; impve. 3rd pers. pl. / *comerse*.

comarcar to border. irr.

comarque 1. that I may border; pres. subj. 1st pers. sing. / *comarcar*. 2. that he (she/it) may border; pres. subj. 3rd pers. sing. 3. let him (her/it) border; impve. 3rd pers. sing.

comarqué I bordered; past 1st pers. sing. / *comarcar*.

comarquéis that you (all) may border; pres. subj. 2nd pers. pl. / *comarcar*.

comarquemos 1. that we may border; pres. subj. 1st pers. pl. / *comarcar*. 2. let us border; impve. 1st pers. pl.

comarquen 1. that they may border; pres. subj. 3rd pers. pl. / *comarcar*. 2. let them border; impve. 3rd pers. pl.

comarques that you may border; pres. subj. 2nd pers. sing. / *comarcar*.

cómase let him (her/it) eat up; impve. 3rd pers. sing. / *comerse*.

combándose sagging; pres. part. / *combarse*.

combaos (you all) sag; impve. 2nd pers. pl. / *combarse*.

combar to bend or warp. reg.

combarse to sag or to bulge. reg.

combatámonos let us struggle; impve. 1st pers. pl. / *combatirse*.

combátanse let them struggle; impve. 3rd pers. pl. / *combatirse*.

combátase let him (her/it) struggle; impve. 3rd pers. sing. / *combatirse*.

cómbate (you) sag; impve. 2nd pers. sing. / *combarse*.

combátete (you) struggle; impve. 2nd pers. sing. / *combatirse*.

combatiéndose struggling; pres. part. / *combatirse*.

combatíos (you all) struggle; impve. 2nd pers. pl. / *combatirse*.

combatir to combat or to attack. reg.

combatirse to struggle. reg.

combémonos let us sag; impve. 1st pers. pl. / *combarse*.

cómbense let them sag; impve. 3rd pers. pl. / *combarse*.

cómbese let him (her/it) sag; impve. 3rd pers. sing. / *combarse*.

combinar to combine or to work out. reg.

comediar to halve. reg.

comedíos (you all) be polite; impve. 2nd pers. pl. / *comedirse*.

comedirse to be polite or to control oneself. irr.

comencé I began; past 1st pers. sing. / *comenzar*.

comencéis that you (all) may begin; pres. subj. 2nd pers. pl. / *comenzar*.

comencemos 1. that we may begin; pres. subj. 1st pers. pl. / *comenzar*. 2. let us begin; impve. 1st pers. pl.

comentar to comment on. reg.

comenzar to begin or to commence. irr.

comeos (you all) eat up; impve. 2nd pers. pl. / *comerse*.

comer to eat. reg.

comercialice 1. that I may commercialize; pres. subj. 1st pers. sing. / *comercializar*. 2. that he (she/it) may commercialize; pres. subj. 3rd pers. sing. 3. let him (her/it) commercialize; impve. 3rd pers. sing.

comercialicé I commercialized; past 1st pers. sing. / *comercializar*.

comercialicéis that you (all) may commercialize; pres. subj. 2nd pers. pl. / *comercializar*.

comercialicemos 1. that we may commercialize; pres. subj. 1st pers. pl. / *comercializar*. 2. let us commercialize; impve. 1st pers. pl.

comercialicen 1. that they may commercialize; pres. subj. 3rd pers. pl. / *comercializar*. 2. let them commercialize; impve. 3rd pers. pl.

comercialices that you may commercialize; pres. subj. 2nd pers. sing. / *comercializar*.

comercializar to commercialize. irr.

comerciar to trade or to deal. reg.

comerse to eat up. reg.

cómete (you) eat up; impve. 2nd pers. sing. / *comerse*.

cometer to commit or to entrust. reg.

comida 1. that I may be polite; pres. subj. 1st pers. sing. / *comedirse*. 2. that he (she/it) may be polite; pres. subj. 3rd pers. sing.

comidáis that you (all) may be polite; pres. subj. 2nd pers. pl. / *comedirse*.

comidámonos let us be polite; impve. 1st pers. pl. / *comedirse*.

comidamos that we may be polite; pres. subj. 1st pers. pl. / *comedirse*.

comidan that they may be polite; pres. subj. 3rd pers. pl. / *comedirse*.

comídanse let them be polite; impve. 3rd pers. pl. / *comedirse*.

comidas that you may be polite; pres. subj. 2nd pers. sing. / *comedirse*.

comídase let him (her/it) be polite; impve. 3rd pers. sing. / *comedirse*.

comide he (she/it) is polite; pres. ind. 3rd pers. sing. / *comedirse*.

comiden they are polite; pres. ind. 3rd pers. pl. / *comedirse*.

comides you are polite; pres. ind. 2nd pers. sing. / *comedirse*.

comídete (you) be polite; impve. 2nd pers. sing. / *comedirse*.

comidiéndose being polite; pres. part. / *comedirse*.

comidiera 1. that I might be polite; imp. subj. 1st pers. sing. / *comedirse*. 2. that he (she/it) might be polite; imp. subj. 3rd pers. sing.

comidierais that you (all) might be polite; imp. subj. 2nd pers pl. / *comedirse*.

comidiéramos that we might be polite; imp. subj. 1st pers. pl. / *comedirse*.

comidieran that they might be polite; imp. subj. 3rd pers. pl. / *comedirse*.

comidieras that you might be polite; imp. subj. 2nd pers. sing. / *comedirse*.

comidieron they were polite; past 3rd pers. pl. / *comedirse*.

comidiese 1. that I might be polite; imp. subj. 1st pers. sing. / *comedirse* 2. that he (she/it) might be polite; imp. subj. 3rd pers. sing.

comidieseis that you (all) might be polite; imp. subj. 2nd pers pl. / *comedirse*.

comidiésemos that we might be polite; imp. subj. 1st pers. pl. / *comedirse*.

comidiesen that they might be polite; imp. subj. 3rd pers. pl. / *comedirse*.

comidieses that you might be polite; imp. subj. 2nd pers. sing. / *comedirse*.

comidió he (she/it) was polite; past 3rd pers. sing. / *comedirse*.

comido I am polite; pres. ind. 1st pers. sing. / *comedirse*.

comience 1. that I may begin; pres. subj. 1st pers. sing. / *comenzar*. 2. that he (she/it) may begin; pres. subj. 3rd pers. sing. 3. let him (her/it) begin; impve. 3rd pers. sing.

comiencen 1. that they may begin; pres. subj. 3rd pers. pl. / *comenzar*. 2. let them begin; impve. 3rd pers. pl.

comiences that you may begin; pres. subj. 2nd pers. sing. / *comenzar*.

comiéndose eating up; pres. part. / *comerse*.

comienza 1. he (she/it) begins; pres. ind. 3rd pers. sing. / *comenzar*. 2. (you) begin; impve. 2nd pers. sing.

comienzan they begin; pres. ind. 3rd pers. pl. / *comenzar*.

comienzas you begin; pres. ind. 2nd pers. sing. / *comenzar*.

comienzo I begin; pres. ind. 1st pers. sing. / *comenzar*.

comiquear to put on amateur plays. reg.

comisar to impound. reg.

comisionar to commission. reg.

comisquear to nibble. reg.

compactar to make compact. reg.

compadeceos (you all) concur; impve. 2nd pers. pl. / *compadecerse*.

compadecer to pity or sympathize with. irr.

compadecerse to concur. irr.

compadécete (you) concur; impve. 2nd pers. sing. / *compadecerse*.

compadeciéndose concurring; pres. part. / *compadecerse*.

compadezca 1. that I may pity; pres. subj. 1st pers. sing. / *compadecer*. 2. that he (she/it) may pity; pres. subj. 3rd pers. sing. 3. let him (her/it) pity; impve. 3rd pers. sing.

compadezcáis that you (all) may pity; pres. subj. 2nd pers. pl. / *compadecer*.

compadezcámonos let us concur; impve. 1st pers. pl. / *compadecerse*.

compadezcamos 1. that we may pity; pres. subj. 1st pers. pl. / *compadecer*. 2. let us pity; impve. 1st pers. pl.

compadezcan 1. that they may pity; pres. subj. 3rd pers. pl. / *compadecer*. 2. let them pity; impve. 3rd pers. pl.

compadézcanse let them concur; impve. 3rd pers. pl. / *compadecerse*.

compadezcas that you may pity; pres. subj. 2nd pers. sing. / *compadecer*.

compadézcase let him (her/it) concur; impve. 3rd pers. sing. / *compadecerse*.

compadezco I pity; pres. ind. 1st pers. sing. / *compadecer*.

compadrar to become friends with. reg.

compadrear to be chummy. reg.

compaginándose fitting; pres. part. / *compaginarse*.

compaginaos (you all) fit; impve. 2nd pers. pl. / *compaginarse*

compaginar to arrange or to page. reg.

compaginarse to fit or to agree. reg.

compagínate (you) fit; impve. 2nd pers. sing. / *compaginarse*

compaginémonos let us fit; impve. 1st pers. pl. / *compaginarse*

compagínense let them fit; impve. 3rd pers. pl. / *compaginarse*

compagínese let him (her/it) fit; impve. 3rd pers. sing. / *compaginarse*

comparar to compare. reg.

comparecer to appear. irr.

comparezca 1. that I may appear; pres. subj. 1st pers. sing. / *comparecer*. 2. that he (she/it) may appear; pres. subj. 3rd pers. sing. 3. let him (her/it) appear; impve. 3rd pers. sing.

comparezcáis that you (all) may appear; pres. subj. 2nd pers. pl. / *comparecer*.

comparezcamos 1. that we may appear; pres. subj. 1st pers. pl. / *comparecer*. 2. let us appear; impve. 1st pers. pl.

comparezcan 1. that they may appear; pres. subj. 3rd pers. pl. / *comparecer*. 2. let them appear; impve. 3rd pers. pl.

comparezcas that you may appear; pres. subj. 2nd pers. sing. / *comaprecer*.

comparezco I appear; pres. ind. 1st pers. sing. / *comparecer*.

compartir to share or to divide. reg.

compasar to measure or to cut to size. reg.

compeler to compel. reg. except for pp.

compendiar to summarize or to condense. reg.

compenetrándose immersing oneself; pres. part. / *compenetrarse*.

compenetraos (you all) immerse yourselves; impve. 2nd pers. pl. / *compenetrarse*.

compenetrarse to immerse oneself. reg.

compenétrate (you) immerse yourself; impve. 2nd pers. sing. / *compenetrarse*.

compenetrémonos let us immerse ourselves; impve. 1st pers. pl. / *compenetrarse*.

compenétrense let them immerse themselves; impve. 3rd pers. pl. / *compenetrarse*.

compenétrese let him (her/it) immerse himself (herself/itself); impve. 3rd pers. sing. / *compenetrarse*.

compensar to compensate or to make equal. reg.

competer to be one's concern. reg.

competir to compete. irr.

compilar to compile. reg.

compita 1. that I may compete; pres. subj. 1st pers. sing. / *competir*. 2. that he (she/it) may compete; pres. subj. 3rd pers. sing. 3. let him (her/it) compete; impve. 3rd pers. sing.

compitáis that you (all) may compete; pres. subj. 2nd pers. pl. / *competir*.

compitamos 1. that we may compete; pres. subj. 1st pers. pl. / *competir*. 2. let us compete; impve. 1st pers. pl.

compitan 1. that they may compete; pres. subj. 3rd pers. pl. / *competir*. 2. let them compete; impve. 3rd pers. pl.

compitas that you may compete; pres. subj. 2nd pers. sing. / *competir*.

compite 1. he (she/it) competes; pres. ind. 3rd pers. sing. / *competir*. 2. (you) compete; impve. 2nd pers. sing.

compiten they compete; pres. ind. 3rd pers. pl. / *competir*.

compites you compete; pres. ind. 2nd pers. sing. / *competir*.

compitiendo competing; pres. part. / *competir*.

compitiera 1. that I might compete; imp. subj. 1st pers. sing. / *competir*. 2. that he (she/it) might compete; imp. subj. 3rd pers. sing.

compitierais that you (all) might compete; imp. subj. 2nd pers pl. / *competir*.

compitiéramos that we might compete; imp. subj. 1st pers. pl. / *competir*.

compitieran that they might compete; imp. subj. 3rd pers. pl. / *competir*.

compitieras that you might compete; imp. subj. 2nd pers. sing. / *competir*.

compitieron they competed; past 3rd pers. pl. / *competir*.

compitiese 1. that I might compete; imp. subj. 1st pers. sing. / *competir*. 2. that he (she/it) might compete; imp. subj. 3rd pers. sing.

compitieseis that you (all) might compete; imp. subj. 2nd pers pl. / *competir*.

compitiésemos that we might compete; imp. subj. 1st pers. pl. / *competir*.

compitiesen that they might compete; imp. subj. 3rd pers. pl. / *competir*.

compitieses that you might compete; imp. subj. 2nd pers. sing. / *competir*.

compitió he (she/it) competed; past 3rd pers. sing. / *competir*.

compito I compete; pres. ind. 1st pers. sing. / *competir*.

complaceos (you all) be pleased; impve. 2nd pers. pl. / *complacerse*.

complacer to please. irr.

complacerse to be pleased or to take pleasure (in). irr.

complácete (you) be pleased; impve. 2nd pers. sing. / *complacerse*.

complaciéndose being pleased; pres. part. / *complacerse*.

complazca 1. that I may please; pres. subj. 1st pers. sing. / *complacer*. 2. that he (she/it) may please; pres. subj. 3rd pers. sing. 3. let him (her/it) please; impve. 3rd pers. sing.

complazcáis that you (all) may please; pres. subj. 2nd pers. pl. / *complacer*.

complazcámonos let us be pleased; impve. 1st pers. pl. / *complacerse*.

complazcamos 1. that we may please; pres. subj. 1st pers. pl. / *complacer*. 2. let us please; impve. 1st pers. pl.

complazcan 1. that they may please; pres. subj. 3rd pers. pl. / *complacer*. 2. let them please; impve. 3rd pers. pl.

complázcanse let them be pleased; impve. 3rd pers. pl. / *complacerse*.

complazcas that you may please; pres. subj. 2nd pers. sing. / *complacer*.

complázcase let him (her/it) be pleased; impve. 3rd pers. sing. / *complacerse*.

complazco I please; pres. ind. 1st pers. sing. / *complacer*.

complega that he (she/it) may please; pres. subj. 3rd pers. sing. / *complacer*.

complegue that he (she/it) may please; pres. subj. 3rd pers. sing. / *complacer*.

complementar to complement. reg.

completar to complete. reg.

complicar to complicate. irr.

complique 1. that I may complicate; pres. subj. 1st pers. sing. / *complicar*. 2. that he (she/it) may complicate; pres. subj. 3rd pers. sing. 3. let him (her/it) complicate; impve. 3rd pers. sing.

compliqué I complicated; past 1st pers. sing. / *complicar*.

compliquéis that you (all) may complicate; pres. subj. 2nd pers. pl. / *complicar*.

compliquemos 1. that we may complicate; pres. subj. 1st pers. pl. / *complicar* 2. let us complicate; impve. 1st pers. pl.

compliquen 1. that they may complicate; pres. subj. 3rd pers. pl. / *complicar*. 2. let them complicate; impve. 3rd pers. pl.

compliques that you may complicate; pres. subj. 2nd pers. sing. / *complicar*.

complugo he (she/it) pleased; past 3rd pers. sing. / *complacer*.

compluguiera that he (she/it) might please; imp. subj. 3rd pers. sing. / *complacer*.

compluguieron they pleased; past 3rd pers. pl. / *complacer*.

compluguiese that he (she/it) might please; imp. subj. 3rd pers. sing. / *complacer*.

compon (you) fix; impve. 2nd pers. sing. / *componer*.

compondrá he (she/it) will fix; fut. 3rd pers. sing. /
componer.
compondrán they will fix; fut. 3rd pers. pl. /
componer.
compondrás you will fix; fut. 2nd pers. sing. /
componer.
compondré I shall fix; fut. 1st pers. sing. / *componer.*
compondréis you (all) will fix; fut. 2nd pers. pl. /
componer.
compondremos we shall fix; fut. 1st pers. pl. /
componer.
compondría 1. I should fix; cond. 1st pers. sing. /
componer. 2. he (she/it) would fix; cond. 3rd pers.
sing.
compondríais you (all) would fix; cond. 2nd pers. pl.
/ *componer.*
compondríamos we should fix; cond. 1st pers. pl. /
componer.
compondrían they would fix; cond. 3rd pers. pl. /
componer.
compondrías you would fix; cond. 2nd pers. sing. /
componer.
componeos (you all) come to terms; impve. 2nd pers.
pl. / *componerse.*
componer to fix or to compose. irr.
componerse to come to terms or to put on makeup.
irr.
componga 1. that I may fix; pres. subj. 1st pers. sing. /
componer. 2. that he (she/it) may fix; pres. subj. 3rd
pers. sing. 3. let him (her/it) fix; impve. 3rd pers.
sing.
compongáis that you (all) may fix; pres. subj. 2nd
pers. pl. / *componer.*
compongámonos let us come to terms; impve. 1st
pers. pl. / *componerse.*
compongamos 1. that we may fix; pres. subj. 1st pers.
pl. / *componer.* 2. let us fix; impve. 1st pers. pl.
compongan 1. that they may fix; pres. subj. 3rd pers.
pl. / *componer.* 2. let them fix; impve. 3rd pers. pl.
compónganse let them come to terms; impve. 3rd
pers. pl. / *componerse.*
compongas that you may fix; pres. subj. 2nd pers.
sing. / *componer.*
compóngase let him (her/it) come to terms; impve.
3rd pers. sing. / *componerse.*
compongo I fix; pres. ind. 1st pers. sing. / *componer.*
componiendo fixing; pres. part. / *componer.*
componiéndose coming to terms; pres. part. /
componerse.
componte (you) come to terms; impve. 2nd pers.
sing. / *componerse.*
comportándose behaving; pres. part. / *comportarse.*
comportaos (you all) behave; impve. 2nd pers. pl. /
comportarse.
comportar to endure or to tolerate. reg.
comportarse to behave. reg.
compórtate (you) behave; impve. 2nd pers. sing. /
comportarse.
comportémonos let us behave; impve. 1st pers. pl. /
comportarse.

compórtense let them behave; impve. 3rd pers. pl. /
comportarse.
compórtese let him (her/it) behave; impve. 3rd pers.
sing. / *comportarse*
comprar to buy or to shop. reg.
comprender to comprehend or to include. reg.
comprimámonos let us restrain ourselves; impve. 1st
pers. pl. / *comprimirse.*
comprímanse let them restrain themselves; impve.
3rd pers. pl. / *comprimirse.*
comprímase let him (her/it) restrain himself
(herself/itself); impve. 3rd pers. sing. / *comprimirse.*
comprímete (you) restrain yourself; impve. 2nd pers.
sing. / *comprimirse.*
comprimiéndose restraining oneself; pres. part. /
comprometerse.
comprimíos (you all) restrain yourself; impve. 2nd
pers. pl. / *comprimirse.*
comprimir to compress or to repress. reg.
comprimirse to restrain oneself. reg.
comprobar to verify or to prove. irr.
comprometámonos let us promise; impve. 1st pers.
pl. / *comprometerse.*
comprométanse let them promise; impve. 3rd pers.
pl. / *comprometerse.*
comprométase let him (her/it) promise; impve. 3rd
pers. sing. / *comprometerse*
comprometeos (you all) promise; impve. 2nd pers.
pl. / *comprometerse.*
comprometer to compromise. reg.
comprometerse to promise. reg.
comprométete (you) promise; impve. 2nd pers. sing. /
comprometerse.
comprometiéndose promising; pres. part. /
comprometerse.
comprueba 1. he (she/it) verifies; pres. ind. 3rd pers.
sing. / *comprobar.* 2. (you) verify; impve. 2nd pers.
sing.
comprueban they verify; pres. ind. 3rd pers. pl. /
comprobar.
compruebas you verify; pres. ind. 2nd pers. sing. /
comprobar.
compruebe 1. that I may verify; pres. subj. 1st pers.
sing. / *comprobar.* 2. that he (she/it) may veify; pres.
subj. 3rd pers. sing. 3. let him (her/it) verify; impve.
3rd pers. sing.
comprueben 1. that they may verify; pres. subj. 3rd
pers. pl. / *comprobar.* 2. let them verify; impve. 3rd
pers. pl.
compruebes that you may verify; pres. subj. 2nd pers.
sing. / *comprobar.*
compruebo I verify; pres. ind. 1st pers. sing. /
comprobar.
compuesto fixed; past part. / *componer.*
compulsar to collate or to check. reg.
compulso compelled; past part. / *compeler.*
compúngete (you) feel regret; impve. 2nd pers. sing. /
compungirse.
compungiéndose feeling regret; pres. part. /
compungirse.

compungíos (you all) feel regret; impve. 2nd pers. pl. / *compungirse.*

compungir to move to remorse. irr.

compungirse to feel regret or remorse. irr.

compunja 1. that I may move to remorse; pres. subj. 1st pers. sing. / *compungir.* 2. that he (she/it) may move to remorse; pres. subj. 3rd pers. sing. 3. let him (her/it) move to remorse; impve. 3rd pers. sing.

compunjáis that you (all) may move to remorse; pres. subj. 2nd pers. pl. / *compungir.*

compunjámonos let us feel regret; impve. 1st pers. pl. / *compungirse.*

compunjamos 1. that we may move to remorse; pres. subj. 1st pers. pl. / *compungir.* 2. let us move to remorse; impve. 1st pers. pl.

compunjan 1. that they may move to remorse; pres. subj. 3rd pers. pl. / *compungir.* 2. let them move to remorse; impve. 3rd pers. pl.

compúnjanse let them feel regret; impve. 3rd pers. pl. / *compungirse.*

compunjas that you may move to remorse; pres. subj. 2nd pers. sing. / *compungir.*

compúnjase let him (her/it) feel regret; impve. 3rd pers. sing. / *compungirse*

compunjo I move to remorse; pres. ind. 1st pers. sing. / *compungir.*

compuse I fixed; past 1st pers. sing. / *componer.*

compusiera 1. that I might fix; imp. subj. 1st pers. sing. / *componer.* 2. that he (she/it) might fix; imp. subj. 3rd pers. sing.

compusierais that you (all) might fix; imp. subj. 2nd pers pl. / *componer.*

compusiéramos that we might fix; imp. subj. 1st pers. pl. / *componer.*

compusieran that they might fix; imp. subj. 3rd pers. pl. / *componer.*

compusieras that you might fix; imp. subj. 2nd pers. sing. / *componer.*

compusieron they fixed; past 3rd pers. pl. / *componer.*

compusiese 1. that I might fix; imp. subj. 1st pers. sing. / *componer.* 2. that he (she/it) might fix; imp. subj. 3rd pers. sing.

compusieseis that you (all) might fix; imp. subj. 2nd pers pl. / *componer.*

compusiésemos that we might fix; imp. subj. 1st pers. pl. / *componer.*

compusiesen that they might fix; imp. subj. 3rd pers. pl. / *componer.*

compusieses that you might fix; imp. subj. 2nd pers. sing. / *componer.*

compusimos we fixed; past 1st pers. pl. / *componer.*

compusiste you fixed; past 2nd pers. sing. / *componer.*

compusisteis you (all) fixed; past 2nd pers. pl. / *componer.*

compuso he (she/it) fixed; past 3rd pers. sing. / *componer.*

computar to compute. reg.

comulgar to commune or to take communion. irr.

comulgue 1. that I may commune; pres. subj. 1st pers. sing. / *comulgar.* 2. that he (she/it) may commune; pres. subj. 3rd pers. sing. 3. let him (her/it) commune; impve. 3rd pers. sing.

comulgué I communed; past 1st pers. sing. / *comulgar.*

comulguéis that you (all) may commune; pres. subj. 2nd pers. pl. / *comulgar.*

comulguemos 1. that we may commune; pres. subj. 1st pers. pl. / *comulgar.* 2. let us commune; impve. 1st pers. pl.

comulguen 1. that they may commune; pres. subj. 3rd pers. pl. / *comulgar.* 2. let them commune; impve. 3rd pers. pl.

comulgues that you may commune; pres. subj. 2nd pers. sing. / *comulgar.*

comunicándose being in touch with; pres. part. / *comunicarse.*

comunicaos (you all) be in touch with; impve. 2nd pers. pl. / *comunicarse.*

comunicar to communicate. irr.

comunicarse to be in touch with or to connect. irr.

comunícate (you) be in touch with; impve. 2nd pers. sing. / *comunicarse.*

comunice 1. that I may communize; pres. subj. 1st pers. sing. / *comunizar.* 2. that he (she/it) may communize; pres. subj. 3rd pers. sing. 3. let him (her/it) communize; impve. 3rd pers. sing.

comunicé I communized; past 1st pers. sing. / *comunizar.*

comunicéis that you (all) may communize; pres. subj. 2nd pers. pl. / *comunizar.*

comunicemos 1. that we may communize; pres. subj. 1st pers. pl. / *comunizar.* 2. let us communize; impve. 1st pers. pl.

comunicen 1. that they may communize; pres. subj. 3rd pers. pl. / *comunizar.* 2. let them communize; impve. 3rd pers. pl.

comunices that you may communize; pres. subj. 2nd pers. sing. / *comunicar.*

comunique 1. that I may communicate; pres. subj. 1st pers. sing. / *comunicar* 2. that he (she/it) may communicate; pres. subj. 3rd pers. sing. 3. let him (her/it) communicate; impve. 3rd pers. sing.

comuniqué I communicated; past 1st pers. sing. / *comunicar.*

comuniquéis that you (all) may communicate; pres. subj. 2nd pers. pl. / *comunicar.*

comuniquémonos let us be in touch with; impve. 1st pers. pl. / *comunicarse.*

comuniquemos 1. that we may communicate; pres. subj. 1st pers. pl. / *comunicar.* 2. let us communicate; impve. 1st pers. pl.

comuniquen 1. that they may communicate; pres. subj. 3rd pers. pl. / *comunicar.* 2. let them communicate; impve. 3rd pers. pl.

comuníquense let them be in touch with; impve. 3rd pers. pl. / *comunicarse.*

comuniques that you may communicate; pres. subj. 2nd pers. sing. / *comunicar.*

comuníquese let him (her/it) be in touch with; impve. 3rd pers. sing. / *comunicarse*

comunizar to communize. irr.

concadenar to concatenate. reg.

concatenar to concatenate. reg.

concebir to conceive or to imagine. irr.

conceder to concede or to grant. reg.

concentrándose concentrating; pres. part. / *concentrarse.*

concentraos (you all) concentrate; impve. 2nd pers. pl. / *concentrarse.*

concentrar to concentrate. reg.

concentrarse to concentrate. reg.

concéntrate (you) concentrate; impve. 2nd pers. sing. / *concentrarse.*

concentrémonos let us concentrate; impve. 1st pers. pl. / *concentrarse.*

concéntrense let them concentrate; impve. 3rd pers. pl. / *concentrarse.*

concéntrese let him (her/it) concentrate; impve. 3rd pers. sing. / *concentrarse*

conceptúa 1. he (she/it) reputes; pres. ind. 3rd pers. sing. / *conceptuar.* 2. (you) repute; impve. 2nd pers. sing.

conceptúan they repute; pres. ind. 3rd pers. pl. / *conceptuar.*

conceptuar to repute or to deem. irr.

conceptúas you repute; pres. ind. 2nd pers. sing. / *conceptuar.*

conceptúe 1. that I may repute; pres. subj. 1st pers. sing. / *conceptuar.* 2. that he (she/it)may repute; pres. subj. 3rd pers. sing. 3. let him (her/it) repute; impve. 3rd pers. sing.

conceptúen 1. that they may repute; pres. subj. 3rd pers. pl. / *conceptuar.* 2. let them repute; impve. 3rd pers. pl.

conceptúes that you may repute; pres. subj. 2nd pers. sing. / *conceptuar.*

conceptúo I repute; pres. ind. 1st pers. sing. / *conceptuar.*

concerniendo concerning; pres. part. / *concernir.*

concerniéndose concerning oneself; pres. part. / *concernirse.*

concerníos (you all) concern yourselves; impve. 2nd pers. pl. / *concernirse.*

concernir to concern. irr.

concernirse to concern oneself. irr.

concertándose agreeing; pres. part. / *concertarse.*

concertaos (you all) agree; impve. 2nd pers. pl. / *concertarse.*

concertar to arrange or to concert. irr.

concertarse to agree or come to terms. irr.

concertémonos let us agree; impve. 1st pers. pl. / *concertarse.*

conciba 1. that I may concieve; pres. subj. 1st pers. sing. / *concebir.* 2. that he (she/it) may concieve; pres. subj. 3rd pers. sing. 3. let him (her/it) concieve; impve. 3rd pers. sing.

concibáis that you (all) may conceive; pres. subj. 2nd pers. pl. / *concebir.*

concibamos 1. that we may conceive; pres. subj. 1st pers. pl. / *concebir.* 2. let us conceive; impve. 1st pers. pl.

conciban 1. that they may conceive; pres. subj. 3rd pers. pl. / *concebir.* 2. let them conceive; impve. 3rd pers. pl.

concibas that you may conceive; pres. subj. 2nd pers. sing. / *concebir.*

concibe 1. he (she/it) conceives; pres. ind. 3rd pers. sing. / *concebir.* 2. (you) conceive; impve. 2nd pers. sing.

conciben they conceive; pres. ind. 3rd pers. pl. / *concebir.*

concibes you conceive; pres. ind. 2nd pers. sing. / *concebir.*

concibiendo conceiving; pres. part. / *concebir.*

concibiera 1. that I might conceive; imp. subj. 1st pers. sing. / *concebir.* 2. that he (she/it) might conceive; imp. subj. 3rd pers. sing.

concibierais that you (all) might conceive; imp. subj. 2nd pers pl. / *concebir.*

concibiéramos that we might conceive; imp. subj. 1st pers. pl. / *concebir.*

concibieran that they might conceive; imp. subj. 3rd pers. pl. / *concebir.*

concibieras that you might conceive; imp. subj. 2nd pers. sing. / *concebir.*

concibieron they conceived; past 3rd pers. pl. / *concebir.*

concibiese 1. that I might conceive; imp. subj. 1st pers. sing. / *concebir.* 2. that he (she/it) might conceive; imp. subj. 3rd pers. sing.

concibieseis that you (all) might conceive; imp. subj. 2nd pers pl. / *concebir.*

concibiésemos that we might conceive; imp. subj. 1st pers. pl. / *concebir.*

concibiesen that they might conceive; imp. subj. 3rd pers. pl. / *concebir.*

concibieses that you might conceive; imp. subj. 2nd pers. sing. / *concebir.*

concibió he (she/it) conceived; past 3rd pers. sing. / *concebir.*

concibo I conceive; pres. ind. 1st pers. sing. / *concebir.*

concierna that it may concern ; pres. subj. 3rd pers. sing. / *concernirse.*

conciernan that they may concern; pres. subj. 3rd pers. pl. / *concernirse.*

conciérnanse let them concern themselves; impve. 3rd pers. pl. / *concernirse.*

conciérnase let him (her/it) concern himself (herself/itself); impve. 3rd pers. sing. / *concernirse.*

concierne it concerns; pres. ind. 3rd pers. sing. / *concernir.*

conciernen they concern; pres. ind. 3rd pers. pl. / *concernir.*

concierta 1. he (she/it) arranges; pres. ind. 3rd pers. sing. / *concertar.* 2. (you) arrange; impve. 2nd pers. sing.

conciertan they arrange; pres. ind. 3rd pers. pl. / *concertar*

conciertas you arrange; pres. ind. 2nd pers. sing. / *concertar*.

conciértate (you) agree; impve. 2nd pers. sing. / *concertarse*.

concierte 1. that I may arrange; pres. subj. 1st pers. sing. / *concertar*. 2. that he (she/it) may arrange; pres. subj. 3rd pers. sing. 3. let him (her/it) arrange; impve. 3rd pers. sing.

concierten 1. that they may arrange; pres. subj. 3rd pers. pl. / *concertar*. 2. let them arrange; impve. 3rd pers. pl.

conciértense let them agree; impve. 3rd pers. pl. / *concertarse*.

conciertes that you may arrange; pres. subj. 2nd pers. sing. / *concertar*.

conciértese let him (her/it) agree; impve. 3rd pers. sing. / *concertarse*.

concierto I arrange; pres. ind. 1st pers. sing. / *concertar*.

conciliándose winning; pres. part. / *conciliarse*.

conciliaos (you all) win; impve. 2nd pers. pl. / *conciliarse*.

conciliar to conciliate or to reconcile. reg.

conciliarse to win or to gain (esteem). reg.

concíliate (you) win; impve. 2nd pers. sing. / *conciliarse*.

conciliémonos let us win; impve. 1st pers. pl. / *conciliarse*.

concilíense let them win; impve. 3rd pers. pl. / *conciliarse*.

concilíese let him (her/it) win; impve. 3rd pers. sing. / *conciliarse*.

concitar to incite. reg.

concluíos (you all) end; impve. 2nd pers. pl. / *concluirse*.

concluir to conclude or to convince. irr.

concluirse to end. irr.

concluya 1. that I may conclude; pres. subj. 1st pers. sing. / *concluir*. 2. that he (she/it) may conclude; pres. subj. 3rd pers. sing. 3. let him (her/it) conclude; impve. 3rd pers. sing.

concluyáis that you (all) may conclude; pres. subj. 2nd pers. pl. / *concluir*.

concluyámonos let us end; impve. 1st pers. pl. / *concluirse*.

concluyamos 1. that we may conclude; pres. subj. 1st pers. pl. / *concluir*. 2. let us conclude; impve. 1st pers. pl.

concluyan 1. that they may conclude; pres. subj. 3rd pers. pl. / *concluir*. 2. let them conclude; impve. 3rd pers. pl.

conclúyanse let them end; impve. 3rd pers. pl. / *concluirse*.

concluyas that you may conclude; pres. subj. 2nd pers. sing. / *concluir*.

conclúyase let him (her/it) end; impve. 3rd pers. sing. / *concluirse*.

concluye 1. he (she/it) concludes; pres. ind. 3rd pers. sing. / *concluir*. 2. (you) conclude; impve. 2nd pers. sing.

concluyen they conclude; pres. ind. 3rd pers. pl. / *concluir*.

concluyendo concluding; pres. part. / *concluir*.

concluyéndose ending; pres. part. / *concluirse*.

concluyera 1. that I might conclude; imp. subj. 1st pers. sing. / *concluir*. 2. that he (she/it) might conclude; imp. subj. 3rd pers. sing.

concluyerais that you (all) might conclude; imp. subj. 2nd pers pl. / *concluir*.

concluyéramos that we might conclude; imp. subj. 1st pers. pl. / *concluir*.

concluyeran that they might conclude; imp. subj. 3rd pers. pl. / *concluir*.

concluyeras that you might conclude; imp. subj. 2nd pers. sing. / *concluir*.

concluyeron they concluded; past 3rd pers. pl. / *concluir*.

concluyes you conclude; pres. ind. 2nd pers. sing. / *concluir*.

concluyese 1. that I might conclude; imp. subj. 1st pers. sing. / *concluir*. 2. that he (she/it) might conclude; imp. subj. 3rd pers. sing.

concluyeseis that you (all) might conclude; imp. subj. 2nd pers pl. / *concluir*.

concluyésemos that we might conclude; imp. subj. 1st pers. pl. / *concluir*.

concluyesen that they might conclude; imp. subj. 3rd pers. pl. / *concluir*.

concluyeses that you might conclude; imp. subj. 2nd pers. sing. / *concluir*.

conclúyete (you) end; impve. 2nd pers. sing. / *concluirse*.

concluyo I conclude; pres. ind. 1st pers. sing. / *concluir*.

concluyó he (she/it) concluded; past 3rd pers. sing. / *concluir*.

concomámonos let us shrug; impve. 1st pers. pl. / *concomerse*.

concómanse let them shrug; impve. 3rd pers. pl. / *concomerse*.

concómase let him (her/it) shrug; impve. 3rd pers. sing. / *concomerse*.

concomeos (you all) shrug; impve. 2nd pers. pl. / *concomerse*.

concomerse to shrug or to twitch with an itch. reg.

concómete (you) shrug; impve. 2nd pers. sing. / *concomerse*.

concomiéndose shrugging; pres. part. / *concomerse*.

concordar to agree to or to accord or to harmonize. irr.

concretándose limiting oneself; pres. part. / *concretarse*.

concretaos (you all) limit yourselves; impve. 2nd pers. pl. / *concretarse*.

concretar to limit or to make concrete. reg.

concretarse to limit oneself. reg.

concrétate (you) limit yourself; impve. 2nd pers. sing. / *concretarse*.

concretémonos let us limit ourselves; impve. 1st pers. pl. / *concretarse*.

concrétense let them limit themselves; impve. 3rd pers. pl. / *concretarse.*

concrétese let him (her/it) limit himself (herself/itself); impve. 3rd pers. sing. / *concretarse.*

concuerda 1. he (she/it) agrees; pres. ind. 3rd pers. sing. / *concordar.* 2. (you) agree; impve. 2nd pers. sing.

concuerdan they agree; pres. ind. 3rd pers. pl. / *concordar.*

concuerdas you agree; pres. ind. 2nd pers. sing. / *concordar.*

concuerde 1. that I may agree; pres. subj. 1st pers. sing. / *concordar.* 2. that he (she/it) may agree; pres. subj. 3rd pers. sing. 3. let him (her/it) agree; impve. 3rd pers. sing.

concuerden 1. that they may agree; pres. subj. 3rd pers. pl. / *concordar.* 2. let them agree; impve. 3rd pers. pl.

concuerdes that you may agree; pres. subj. 2nd pers. sing. / *concordar.*

concuerdo I agree; pres. ind. 1st pers. sing. / *concordar.*

conculcar to trample on or to violate. irr.

conculque 1. that I may trample on; pres. subj. 1st pers. sing. / *conculcar.* 2. that he (she/it) may trample on; pres. subj. 3rd pers. sing. 3. let him (her/it) trample on; impve. 3rd pers. sing.

conculqué I trampled on; past 1st pers. sing. / *conculcar.*

conculquéis that you (all) may trample on; pres. subj. 2nd pers. pl. / *conculcar.*

conculquemos 1. that we may trample on; pres. subj. 1st pers. pl. / *conculcar.* 2. let us trample on; impve. 1st pers. pl.

conculquen 1. that they may trample on; pres. subj. 3rd pers. pl. / *conculcar.* 2. let them trample on; impve. 3rd pers. pl.

conculques that you may trample on; pres. subj. 2nd pers. sing. / *conculcar.*

concurrir to concur or to assemble or to compete. reg.

conchabándose conspiring; pres. part. / *conchabarse.*

conchabaos (you all) conspire; impve. 2nd pers. pl. / *conchabarse.*

conchabar to join. reg.

conchabarse to conspire. reg.

conchábate (you) conspire; impve. 2nd pers. sing. / *conchabarse.*

conchabémonos let us conspire; impve. 1st pers. pl. / *conchabarse.*

conchábense let them conspire; impve. 3rd pers. pl. / *conchabarse.*

conchábese let him (her/it) conspire; impve. 3rd pers. sing. / *conchabarse.*

condecorar to decorate or to honor. reg.

condenándose being damned; pres. part. / *condenarse.*

condenaos (you all) be damned; impve. 2nd pers. pl. / *condenarse.*

condenar to condemn. reg.

condenarse to be damned. reg.

condénate (you) be damned; impve. 2nd pers. sing. / *condenarse.*

condenémonos let us be damned; impve. 1st pers. pl. / *condenarse.*

condénense let them be damned; impve. 3rd pers. pl. / *condenarse.*

condénese let him (her/it) be damned; impve. 3rd pers. sing. / *condenarse.*

condensándose condensing; pres. part. / *condensarse.*

condensaos (you all) condense; impve. 2nd pers. pl. / *condensarse.*

condensar to condense. reg.

condensarse to condense. reg.

condénsate (you) condense; impve. 2nd pers. sing. / *condensarse.*

condensémonos let us condense; impve. 1st pers. pl. / *condensarse.*

condénsense let them condense; impve. 3rd pers. pl. / *condensarse.*

condénsese let him (her/it) condense; impve. 3rd pers. sing. / *condensarse.*

condescender to condescend or to comply. irr.

condescienda 1. that I may condescend; pres. subj. 1st pers. sing. / *condescender.* 2. that he (she/it) may condescend; pres. subj. 3rd pers. sing. 3. let him (her/it) condescend; impve. 3rd pers. sing.

condesciendan 1. that they may condescend; pres. subj. 3rd pers. pl. / *condescender.* 2. let them condescend; impve. 3rd pers. pl.

condesciendas that you may condescend; pres. subj. 2nd pers. sing. / *condescender.*

condesciende 1. he (she/it) condescends; pres. ind. 3rd pers. sing. / *condescender.* 2. (you) condescend; impve. 2nd pers. sing.

condescienden they condescend; pres. ind. 3rd pers. pl. / *condescender.*

condesciendes you condescend; pres. ind. 2nd pers. sing. / *condescender.*

condesciendo I condescend; pres. ind. 1st pers. sing. / *condescender.*

condicionar to condition or to agree. reg.

condimentar to season. reg.

condolámonos let us condole; impve. 1st pers. pl. / *condolerse.*

condoleos (you all) condole; impve. 2nd pers. pl. / *condolerse.*

condolerse to condole or to sympathize (with). irr.

condoliéndose condoling; pres. part. / *condolerse.*

condonar to condone or to pardon. reg.

condúcete (you) behave; impve. 2nd pers. sing. / *conducirse.*

conduciéndose behaving; pres. part. / *conducirse.*

conducíos (you all) behave; impve. 2nd pers. pl. / *conducirse.*

conducir to conduct or to lead. irr.

conducirse to behave or act. irr.

conduela 1. that I may condole; pres. subj. 1st pers. sing. / *condolerse.* 2. that he (she/it) may condole; pres. subj. 3rd pers. sing.

conduelan that they may condole; pres. subj. 3rd pers. pl. / *condolerse.*

conduélanse let them condole; impve. 3rd pers. pl. / *condolerse.*

conduelas that you may condole; pres. subj. 2nd pers. sing. / *condolerse.*

conduélase let him (her/it) condole; impve. 3rd pers. sing. / *condolerse.*

conduele he (she/it) condoles; pres. ind. 3rd pers. sing. / *condolerse.*

conduelen they condole; pres. ind. 3rd pers. pl. / *condolerse.*

condueles you condole; pres. ind. 2nd pers. sing. / *condolerse.*

conduélete (you) condole; impve. 2nd pers. sing. / *condolerse.*

conduelo I condole; pres. ind. 1st pers. sing. / *condolerse.*

conduje I conducted; past 1st pers. sing. / *conducir.*

condujera 1. that I might conduct; imp. subj. 1st pers. sing. / *conducir.* 2. that he (she/it) might conduct; imp. subj. 3rd pers. sing.

condujerais that you (all) might conduct; imp. subj. 2nd pers pl. / *conducir.*

condujéramos that we might conduct; imp. subj. 1st pers. pl. / *conducir.*

condujeran that they might conduct; imp. subj. 3rd pers. pl. / *conducir.*

condujeras that you might conduct; imp. subj. 2nd pers. sing. / *conducir.*

condujeron they conducted; past 3rd pers. pl. / *conducir.*

condujese 1. that I might conduct; imp. subj. 1st pers. sing. / *conducir.* 2. that he (she/it) might conduct; imp. subj. 3rd pers. sing.

condujeseis that you (all) might conduct; imp. subj. 2nd pers pl. / *conducir.*

condujésemos that we might conduct; imp. subj. 1st pers. pl. / *conducir.*

condujesen that they might conduct; imp. subj. 3rd pers. pl. / *conducir.*

condujeses that you might conduct; imp. subj. 2nd pers. sing. / *conducir.*

condujimos we conducted; past 1st pers. pl. / *conducir.*

condujiste you conducted; past 2nd pers. sing. / *conducir.*

condujisteis you (all) conducted; past 2nd pers. pl. / *conducir.*

condujo he (she/it) conducted; past 3rd pers. sing. / *conducir.*

conduzca 1. that I may conduct; pres. subj. 1st pers. sing. / *conducir.* 2. that he (she/it) may conduct; pres. subj. 3rd pers. sing. 3. let him (her/it) conduct; impve. 3rd pers. sing.

conduzcáis that you (all) may conduct; pres. subj. 2nd pers. pl. / *conducir.*

conduzcámonos let us behave; impve. 1st pers. pl. / *conducirse.*

conduzcamos 1. that we may conduct; pres. subj. 1st pers. pl. / *conducir.* 2. let us conduct; impve. 1st pers. pl.

conduzcan 1. that they may conduct; pres. subj. 3rd pers. pl. / *conducir.* 2. let them conduct; impve. 3rd pers. pl.

condúzcanse let them behave; impve. 3rd pers. pl. / *conducirse.*

conduzcas that you may conduct; pres. subj. 2nd pers. sing. / *conducir.*

condúzcase let him (her/it) behave; impve. 3rd pers. sing. / *conducirse.*

conduzco I conduct; pres. ind. 1st pers. sing. / *conducir.*

conectar to connect. reg.

conexionar to connect. reg.

confabulándose confabulating; pres. part. / *confabularse.*

confabulaos (you all) confabulate; impve. 2nd pers. pl. / *confabularse.*

confabular to confabulate. reg.

confabularse to confabulate. reg.

confabúlate (you) confabulate; impve. 2nd pers. sing. / *confabularse.*

confabulémonos let us confabulate; impve. 1st pers. pl. / *confabularse.*

confabúlense let them confabulate; impve. 3rd pers. pl. / *confabularse.*

confabúlese let him (her/it) confabulate; impve. 3rd pers. sing. / *confabularse.*

confeccionar to make or to prepare. reg.

confederándose confederating; pres. part. / *confederarse.*

confederaos (you all) confederate; impve. 2nd pers. pl. / *confederarse.*

confederar to confederate. reg.

confederarse to confederate. reg.

confedérate (you) confederate; impve. 2nd pers. sing. / *confederarse.*

confederémonos let us confederate; impve. 1st pers. pl. / *confederarse.*

confedérense let them confederate; impve. 3rd pers. pl. / *confederarse.*

confedérese let him (her/it) confederate; impve. 3rd pers. sing. / *confederarse.*

conferenciar to confer or to hold a conference. reg.

conferir to confer or to bestow. irr.

confesándose making confession; pres. part. / *confesarse.*

confesaos (you all) make confession; impve. 2nd pers. pl. / *confesarse.*

confesar to confess. irr.

confesarse to make confession. irr.

confesémonos let us make confession; impve. 1st pers. pl. / *confesarse.*

confía 1. he (she/it) confides; pres. ind. 3rd pers. sing. / *confiar.* 2. (you) confide; impve. 2nd pers. sing.

confían they confide; pres. ind. 3rd pers. pl. / *confiar.*

confiándose relying; pres. part. / *confiarse.*

confiaos (you all) rely; impve. 2nd pers. pl. / *confiarse.*

confiar to confide or to hope. irr.

confiarse to rely. irr.

confías you confide; pres. ind. 2nd pers. sing. / *confiar.*

confíate (you) rely; impve. 2nd pers. sing. / *confiarse.*

confíe 1. that I may confide; pres. subj. 1st pers. sing. / *confiar.* 2. that he (she/it) may confide; pres. subj. 3rd pers. sing. 3. let him (her/it) confide; impve. 3rd pers. sing.

confiémonos let us rely; impve. 1st pers. pl. / *confiarse.*

confíen 1. that they may confide; pres. subj. 3rd pers. pl. / *confiar.* 2. let them confide; impve. 3rd pers. pl.

confíense let them rely; impve. 3rd pers. pl. / *confiarse.*

confiera 1. that I may confer; pres. subj. 1st pers. sing. / *conferir.* 2. that he (she/it) may confer; pres. subj. 3rd pers. sing. 3. let him (her/it) confer; impve. 3rd pers. sing.

confieran 1. that they may confer; pres. subj. 3rd pers. pl. / *conferir.* 2. let them confer; impve. 3rd pers. pl.

confieras that you may confer; pres. subj. 2nd pers. sing. / *conferir.*

confiere 1. he (she/it) confers; pres. ind. 3rd pers. sing. / *conferir.* 2. (you) confer; impve. 2nd pers. sing.

confieren they confer; pres. ind. 3rd pers. pl. / *conferir.*

confieres you confer; pres. ind. 2nd pers. sing. / *conferir.*

confiero I confer; pres. ind. 1st pers. sing. / *conferir.*

confíes that you may confide; pres. subj. 2nd pers. sing. / *confiar.*

confiesa 1. he (she/it) confesses; pres. ind. 3rd pers. sing. / *confesar.* 2. (you) confess; impve. 2nd pers. sing.

confiesan they confess; pres. ind. 3rd pers. pl. / *confesar.*

confiesas you confess; pres. ind. 2nd pers. sing. / *confesar.*

confiésate (you) make confession; impve. 2nd pers. sing. / *confesarse.*

confiese 1. that I may confess; pres. subj. 1st pers. sing. / *confesar.* 2. that he (she/it) may confess; pres. subj. 3rd pers. sing. 3. let him (her/it) confess; impve. 3rd pers. sing.

confiese let him (her/it) rely; impve. 3rd pers. sing. / *confiarse.*

confiesen 1. that they may confess; pres. subj. 3rd pers. pl. / *confesar.* 2. let them confess; impve. 3rd pers. pl.

confiésense let them make confession; impve. 3rd pers. pl. / *confesarse.*

confieses that you may confess; pres. subj. 2nd pers. sing. / *confesar.*

confiésese let him (her/it) make confession; impve. 3rd pers. sing. / *confesarse.*

confieso I confess; pres. ind. 1st pers. sing. / *confesar.*

configurar to shape or give configuration to. reg.

confinar to confine or to border. reg.

confío I confide; pres. ind. 1st pers. sing. / *confiar.*

confiráis that you (all) may confer; pres. subj. 2nd pers. pl. / *conferir.*

confiramos 1. that we may confer; pres. subj. 1st pers. pl. / *conferir.* 2. let us confer; impve. 1st pers. pl.

confiriendo conferring; pres. part. / *conferir.*

confiriera 1. that I might confer; imp. subj. 1st pers. sing. / *conferir.* 2. that he (she/it) might confer; imp. subj. 3rd pers. sing.

confirierais that you (all) might confer; imp. subj. 2nd pers pl. / *conferir.*

confiriéramos that we might confer; imp. subj. 1st pers. pl. / *cOnferir.*

confirieran that they might confer; imp. subj. 3rd pers. pl. / *conferir.*

confirieras that you might confer; imp. subj. 2nd pers. sing. / *conferir.*

confirieron they conferred; past 3rd pers. pl. / *conferir.*

confiriese 1. that I might confer; imp. subj. 1st pers. sing. / *conferir.* 2. that he (she/it) might confer; imp. subj. 3rd pers. sing.

confirieseis that you (all) might confer; imp. subj. 2nd pers pl. / *conferir.*

confiriésemos that we might confer; imp. subj. 1st pers. pl. / *conferir.*

confiriesen that they might confer; imp. subj. 3rd pers. pl. / *conferir.*

confirieses that you might confer; imp. subj. 2nd pers. sing. / *conferir.*

confirió he (she/it) conferred; past 3rd pers. sing. / *conferir.*

confirmar to confirm. reg.

confiscar to confiscate. irr.

confisque 1. that I may confiscate; pres. subj. 1st pers. sing. / *confiscar.* 2. that he (she/it) may confiscate; pres. subj. 3rd pers. sing. 3. let him (her/it) confiscate; impve. 3rd pers. sing.

confisqué I confiscated; past 1st pers. sing. / *confiscar.*

confisquéis that you (all) may confiscate; pres. subj. 2nd pers. pl. / *confiscar.*

confisquemos 1. that we may confiscate; pres. subj. 1st pers. pl. / *confiscar* 2. let us confiscate; impve. 1st pers. pl.

confisquen 1. that they may confiscate; pres. subj. 3rd pers. pl. / *confiscar.* 2. let them confiscate; impve. 3rd pers. pl.

confisques that you may confiscate; pres. subj. 2nd pers. sing. / *confiscar.*

confitar to candy or glaze. reg.

conflagrar to set ablaze. reg.

confluir to join or to meet together. irr.

confluya 1. that I may join; pres. subj. 1st pers. sing. / *confluir.* 2. that he (she/it) may join; pres. subj. 3rd pers. sing. 3. let him (her/it) join; impve. 3rd pers. sing.

confluyáis that you (all) may join; pres. subj. 2nd pers. pl. / *confluir.*
confluyamos 1. that we may join; pres. subj. 1st pers. pl. / *confluir.* 2. let us join; impve. 1st pers. pl.
confluyan 1. that they may join; pres. subj. 3rd pers. pl. / *confluir.* 2. let them join; impve. 3rd pers. pl.
confluyas that you may join; pres. subj. 2nd pers. sing. / *confluir.*
confluye 1. he (she/it) joins; pres. ind. 3rd pers. sing. / *confluir.* 2. (you) join; impve. 2nd pers. sing.
confluyen they join; pres. ind. 3rd pers. pl. / *confluir.*
confluyendo joining; pres. part. / *confluir.*
confluyera 1. that I might join; imp. subj. 1st pers. sing. / *confluir.* 2. that he (she/it) might join; imp. subj. 3rd pers. sing.
confluyerais that you (all) might join; imp. subj. 2nd pers pl. / *confluir.*
confluyéramos that we might join; imp. subj. 1st pers. pl. / *confluir.*
confluyeran that they might join; imp. subj. 3rd pers. pl. / *confluir.*
confluyeras that you might join; imp. subj. 2nd pers. sing. / *confluir.*
confluyeron they joined; past 3rd pers. pl. / *confluir.*
confluyes you join; pres. ind. 2nd pers. sing. / *confluir.*
confluyese 1. that I might join; imp. subj. 1st pers. sing. / *confluir.* 2. that he (she/it) might join; imp. subj. 3rd pers. sing.
confluyeseis that you (all) might join; imp. subj. 2nd pers pl. / *confluir.*
confluyésemos that we might join; imp. subj. 1st pers. pl. / *confluir.*
confluyesen that they might join; imp. subj. 3rd pers. pl. / *confluir.*
confluyeses that you might join; imp. subj. 2nd pers. sing. / *confluir.*
confluyo I join; pres. ind. 1st pers. sing. / *confluir.*
confluyó he (she/it) joined; past 3rd pers. sing. / *confluir.*
conformándose submitting; pres. part. / *conformarse.*
conformaos (you all) submit; impve. 2nd pers. pl. / *conformarse.*
conformar to conform or to adapt. reg.
conformarse to submit or to resign oneself. reg.
confórmate (you) submit; impve. 2nd pers. sing. / *conformarse.*
conformémonos let us submit; impve. 1st pers. pl. / *conformarse.*
confórmense let them submit; impve. 3rd pers. pl. / *conformarse.*
confórmese let him (her/it) submit; impve. 3rd pers. sing. / *conformarse.*
confortar to comfort or to invigorate. reg.
confraternar to fraternize. reg.
confraternice 1. that I may fraternize; pres. subj. 1st pers. sing. / *confraternizar.* 2. that he (she/it) may fraternize; pres. subj. 3rd pers. sing. 3. let him (her/it) fraternize; impve. 3rd pers. sing.

confraternicé I fraternized; past 1st pers. sing. / *confraternizar.*
confraternicéis that you (all) may fraternize; pres. subj. 2nd pers. pl. / *confraternizar.*
confraternicemos 1. that we may fraternize; pres. subj. 1st pers. pl. / *confraternizar.* 2. let us fraternize; impve. 1st pers. pl.
confraternicen 1. that they may fraternize; pres. subj. 3rd pers. pl. / *confraternizar.* 2. let them fraternize; impve. 3rd pers. pl.
confraternices that you may fraternize; pres. subj. 2nd pers. sing. / *confraternizar.*
confraternizar to fraternize. irr.
confrontándose facing; pres. part. / *confrontarse.*
confrontaos (you all) face; impve. 2nd pers. pl. / *confrontarse.*
confrontar to confront or to compare. reg.
confrontarse to face. reg.
confróntate (you) face; impve. 2nd pers. sing. / *confrontarse.*
confrontémonos let us face; impve. 1st pers. pl. / *confrontarse.*
confróntense let them face; impve. 3rd pers. pl. / *confrontarse.*
confróntese let him (her/it) face; impve. 3rd pers. sing. / *confrontarse.*
confundámonos let us make a mistake; impve. 1st pers. pl. / *confundirse.*
confúndanse let them make a mistake; impve. 3rd pers. pl. / *confundirse.*
confúndase let him (her/it) make a mistake; impve. 3rd pers. sing. / *confundirse.*
confúndete (you) make a mistake; impve. 2nd pers. sing. / *confundirse.*
confundiéndose making a mistake; pres. part. / *confundirse.*
confundíos (you all) make a mistake; impve. 2nd pers. pl. / *confundirse.*
confundir to confuse. reg.
confundirse to make a mistake. reg.
confutar to confute. reg.
congelar to congeal or to freeze. reg.
congeniar to be congenial. reg.
congestionar to congest. reg.
conglomerar to conglomerate. reg.
congraciar to ingratiate or to win over. reg.
congratulándose rejoicing; pres. part. / *congratularse.*
congratulaos (you all) rejoice; impve. 2nd pers. pl. / *congratularse.*
congratular to congratulate. reg.
congratularse to rejoice. reg.
congratúlate (you) rejoice; impve. 2nd pers. sing. / *congratularse.*
congratulémonos let us rejoice; impve. 1st pers. pl. / *congratularse.*
congratúlense let them rejoice; impve. 3rd pers. pl. / *congratularse.*
congratúlese let him (her/it) rejoice; impve. 3rd pers. sing. / *congratularse.*
congregándose assembling; pres. part. / *congregarse.*

congregaos (you all) assemble; impve. 2nd pers. pl. / *congregarse*.

congregar to congregate. irr.

congregarse to assemble. irr.

congrégate (you) assemble; impve. 2nd pers. sing. / *congregarse*.

congregue 1. that I may congregate; pres. subj. 1st pers. sing. / *congregar*. 2. that he (she/it) may congregate; pres. subj. 3rd pers. sing. 3. let him (her/it) congregate; impve. 3rd pers. sing.

congregué I congregated; past 1st pers. sing. / *congregar*.

congreguéis that you (all) may congregate; pres. subj. 2nd pers. pl. / *congregar*.

congreguémonos let us assemble; impve. 1st pers. pl. / *congregarse*.

congreguemos 1. that we may congregate; pres. subj. 1st pers. pl. / *congregar* 2. let us congregate; impve. 1st pers. pl.

congreguen 1. that they may congregate; pres. subj. 3rd pers. pl. / *congregar*. 2. let them congregate; impve. 3rd pers. pl.

congréguense let them assemble; impve. 3rd pers. pl. / *congregarse*.

congregues that you may congregate; pres. subj. 2nd pers. sing. / *congregar*.

congréguese let him (her/it) assemble; impve. 3rd pers. sing. / *congregarse*.

conjecturar to conjecture. reg.

conjeturar to conjecture. reg.

conjugar to conjugate. irr.

conjugue 1. that I may conjugate; pres. subj. 1st pers. sing. / *conjugar*. 2. that he (she/it) may conjugate; pres. subj. 3rd pers. sing. 3. let him (her/it) conjugate; impve. 3rd pers. sing.

conjugué I conjugated; past 1st pers. sing. / *conjugar*.

conjuguéis that you (all) may conjugate; pres. subj. 2nd pers. pl. / *conjugar*.

conjuguemos 1. that we may conjugate; pres. subj. 1st pers. pl. / *conjugar*. 2. let us conjugate; impve. 1st pers. pl.

conjuguen 1. that they may conjugate; pres. subj. 3rd pers. pl. / *conjugar* 2. let them conjugate; impve. 3rd pers. pl.

conjugues that you may conjugate; pres. subj. 2nd pers. sing. / *conjugar*.

conjurándose conspiring; pres. part. / *conjurarse*.

conjuraos (you all) conspire; impve. 2nd pers. pl. / *conjurarse*.

conjurar to entreat or to conspire. reg.

conjurarse to conspire. reg.

conjúrate (you) conspire; impve. 2nd pers. sing. / *conjurarse*.

conjurémonos let us conspire; impve. 1st pers. pl. / *conjurarse*.

conjúrense let them conspire; impve. 3rd pers. pl. / *conjurarse*.

conjúrese let him (her/it) conspire; impve. 3rd pers. sing. / *conjurarse*.

conllevar to share (a burden). reg.

conmemorar to commemorate. reg.

conmemsurar to commensurate. reg.

conminar to threaten or to denounce. reg.

conmovámonos let us be moved; impve. 1st pers. pl. / *conmoverse*.

conmoveos (you all) be moved; impve. 2nd pers. pl. / *conmoverse*.

conmover to move or to disturb. irr.

conmoverse to be moved. irr.

conmoviéndose being moved; pres. part. / *conmoverse*.

conmueva 1. that I may move; pres. subj. 1st pers. sing. / *conmover*. 2. that he (she/it) may move; pres. subj. 3rd pers. sing. 3. let him (her/it) move; impve. 3rd pers. sing.

conmuevan 1. that they may move; pres. subj. 3rd pers. pl. / *conmover*. 2. let them move; impve. 3rd pers. pl.

conmuévanse let them be moved; impve. 3rd pers. pl. / *conmoverse*.

conmuevas that you may move; pres. subj. 2nd pers. sing. / *conmover*.

conmuévase let him (her/it) be moved; impve. 3rd pers. sing. / *conmoverse*.

conmueve 1. he (she/it) moves; pres. ind. 3rd pers. sing. / *conmover*. 2. (you) move; impve. 2nd pers. sing.

conmueven they move; pres. ind. 3rd pers. pl. / *conmover*.

conmueves you move; pres. ind. 2nd pers. sing. / *conmover*.

conmuévete (you) be moved; impve. 2nd pers. sing. / *conmoverse*.

conmuevo I move; pres. ind. 1st pers. sing. / *conmover*.

conmutar to commute or to exchange. reg.

connaturalice 1. that I may become acclimatized; pres. subj. 1st pers. sing. / *connaturalizarse*. 2. that he (she/it) may become acclimatized; pres. subj. 3rd pers. sing. 3. let him (her/it) become acclimatized; impve. 3rd pers. sing.

connaturalicé I became acclimatized; past 1st pers. sing. / *connaturalizarse*.

connaturalicéis that you (all) may become acclimatized; pres. subj. 2nd pers. pl. / *connaturalizarse*.

connaturalicémonos let us become acclimatized; impve. 1st pers. pl. / *connaturalizarse*.

connaturalicemos that we may become acclimatized; pres. subj. 1st pers. pl. / *connaturalizarse*.

connaturalicen that they may become acclimatized; pres. subj. 3rd pers. pl. / *connaturalizarse*.

connaturalícense let them become acclimatized; impve. 3rd pers. pl. / *connaturalizarse*.

connaturalices that you may become acclimatized; pres. subj. 2nd pers. sing. / *connaturalizarse*.

connaturalícese let him (her/it) become acclimatized; impve. 3rd pers. sing. / *connaturalizarse*.

connaturalizándose becoming acclimatized; pres. part. / *connaturalizarse*.

connaturalizaos (you all) become acclimatized; impve. 2nd pers. pl. / *connaturalizarse*.

connaturalizarse to become acclimatized. irr.

connaturalízate (you) become acclimatized; impve. 2nd pers. sing. / *connaturalizarse*.

connotar to connote or to imply. reg.

conocer to know or to become acquainted with. irr.

conozca 1. that I may know; pres. subj. 1st pers. sing. / *conocer*. 2. that he (she/it) may know; pres. subj. 3rd pers. sing. 3. let him (her/it) know; impve. 3rd pers. sing.

conozcáis that you (all) may know; pres. subj. 2nd pers. pl. / *conocer*.

conozcamos 1. that we may know; pres. subj. 1st pers. pl. / *conocer*. 2. let us know; impve. 1st pers. pl.

conozcan 1. that they may know; pres. subj. 3rd pers. pl. / *conocer*. 2. let them know; impve. 3rd pers. pl.

conozcas that you may know; pres. subj. 2nd pers. sing. / *conocer*.

conozco I know; pres. ind. 1st pers. sing. / *conocer*.

conquistar to conquer. reg.

consagrándose devoting oneself; pres. part. / *consagrarse*.

consagraos (you all) devote yourselves; impve. 2nd pers. pl. / *consagrarse*.

consagrar to consecrate. reg.

consagrarse to devote oneself. reg.

conságrate (you) devote yourself; impve. 2nd pers. sing. / *consagrarse*.

consagrémonos let us devote ourselves; impve. 1st pers. pl. / *consagrarse*.

conságrense let them devote themselves; impve. 3rd pers. pl. / *consagrarse*.

conságrese let him (her/it) devote himself (herself/itself); impve. 3rd pers. sing. / *consagrarse*.

conseguir to get or to manage. irr.

consentíos (you all) come apart; impve. 2nd pers. pl. / *consentirse*.

consentir to consent or to permit. irr.

consentirse to come apart. irr.

conservándose taking care of oneself; pres. part. / *conservarse*.

conservaos (you all) take care of yourselves; impve. 2nd pers. pl. / *conservarse*.

conservar to conserve or to keep. reg.

conservarse to take care of oneself. reg.

consérvate (you) take care of yourself; impve. 2nd pers. sing. / *conservarse*.

conservémonos let us take care of ourselves; impve. 1st pers. pl. / *conservarse*.

consérvense let them take care of themselves; impve. 3rd pers. pl. / *conservarse*.

consérvese let him (her/it) take care of himself (herself/itself); impve. 3rd pers. sing. / *conservarse*.

considerar to consider. reg.

consienta 1. that I may consent; pres. subj. 1st pers. sing. / *consentir*. 2. that he (she/it) may consent; pres. subj. 3rd pers. sing. 3. let him (her/it) consent; impve. 3rd pers. sing.

consientan 1. that they may consent; pres. subj. 3rd pers. pl. / *consentir*. 2. let them consent; impve. 3rd pers. pl.

consiéntanse let them come apart; impve. 3rd pers. pl. / *consentirse*.

consientas that you may consent; pres. subj. 2nd pers. sing. / *consentir*.

consiéntase let him (her/it) come apart; impve. 3rd pers. sing. / *consentirse*.

consiente 1. he (she/it) consents; pres. ind. 3rd pers. sing. / *consentir*. 2. (you) consent; impve. 2nd pers. sing.

consienten they consent; pres. ind. 3rd pers. pl. / *consentir*.

consientes you consent; pres. ind. 2nd pers. sing. / *consentir*.

consiéntete (you) come apart; impve. 2nd pers. sing. / *consentirse*.

consiento I consent; pres. ind. 1st pers. sing. / *consentir*.

consiga 1. that I may get; pres. subj. 1st pers. sing. / *conseguir*. 2. that he (she/it) may get; pres. subj. 3rd pers. sing. 3. let him (her/it) get; impve. 3rd pers. sing.

consigáis that you (all) may get; pres. subj. 2nd pers. pl. / *conseguir*.

consigamos 1. that we may get; pres. subj. 1st pers. pl. / *conseguir*. 2. let us get; impve. 1st pers. pl.

consigan 1. that they may get; pres. subj. 3rd pers. pl. / *conseguir*. 2. let them get; impve. 3rd pers. pl.

consigas that you may get; pres. subj. 2nd pers. sing. / *conseguir*.

consignar to consign or to assign. reg.

consigo I get; pres. ind. 1st pers. sing. / *conseguir*.

consigue 1. he (she/it) gets; pres. ind. 3rd pers. sing. / *conseguir*. 2. (you) get; impve. 2nd pers. sing.

consiguen they get; pres. ind. 3rd pers. pl. / *conseguir*.

consigues you get; pres. ind. 2nd pers. sing. / *conseguir*.

consiguiendo getting; pres. part. / *conseguir*.

consiguiera 1. that I might get; imp. subj. 1st pers. sing. / *conseguir*. 2. that he (she/it) may get; imp. subj. 3rd pers. sing.

consiguierais that you (all) might get; imp. subj. 2nd pers pl. / *conseguir*.

consiguiéramos that we might get; imp. subj. 1st pers. pl. / *conseguir*.

consiguieran that they might get; imp. subj. 3rd pers. pl. / *conseguir*.

consiguieras that you might get; imp. subj. 2nd pers. sing. / *conseguir*.

consiguieron they got; past 3rd pers. pl. / *conseguir*.

consiguiese 1. that I might get; imp. subj. 1st pers. sing. / *conseguir*. 2. that he (she/it) might get; imp. subj. 3rd pers. sing.

consiguieseis that you (all) might get; imp. subj. 2nd pers pl. / *conseguir*.

consiguiésemos that we might get; imp. subj. 1st pers. pl. / *conseguir*.

consiguiesen that they might get; imp. subj. 3rd pers. pl. / *conseguir*.

consiguieses that you might get; imp. subj. 2nd pers. sing. / *conseguir*.

consiguió he (she/it) got; past 3rd pers. sing. / *conseguir*.

consintáis that you (all) may consent; pres. subj. 2nd pers. pl. / *consentir*.

consintámonos let us come apart; impve. 1st pers. pl. / *consentirse*.

consintamos 1. that we may consent; pres. subj. 1st pers. pl. / *consentir* 2. let us consent; impve. 1st pers. pl.

consintiendo consenting; pres. part. / *consentir*.

consintiéndose coming apart; pres. part. / *consentirse*.

consintiera 1. that I might consent; imp. subj. 1st pers. sing. / *consentir*. 2. that he (she/it) might consent; imp. subj. 3rd pers. sing.

consintierais that you (all) might consent; imp. subj. 2nd pers pl. / *consentir*.

consintiéramos that we might consent; imp. subj. 1st pers. pl. / *consentir*.

consintieran that they might consent; imp. subj. 3rd pers. pl. / *consentir*.

consintieras that you might consent; imp. subj. 2nd pers. sing. / *consentir*.

consintieron they consented; past 3rd pers. pl. / *consentir*.

consintiese 1. that I might consent; imp. subj. 1st pers. sing. / *consentir*. 2. that he (she/it) might consent; imp. subj. 3rd pers. sing.

consintieseis that you (all) might consent; imp. subj. 2nd pers pl. / *consentir*.

consintiésemos that we might consent; imp. subj. 1st pers. pl. / *consentir*.

consintiesen that they might consent; imp. subj. 3rd pers. pl. / *consentir*.

consintieses that you might consent; imp. subj. 2nd pers. sing. / *consentir*.

consintió he (she/it) consented; past 3rd pers. sing. / *consentir*.

consistir to consist. reg.

consolar to console. irr.

consolidándose becoming consolidated; pres. part. / *consolidarse*.

consolidaos (you all) become consolidated; impve. 2nd pers. pl. / *consolidarse*.

consolidar to consolidate. reg.

consolidarse to become consolidated. reg.

consolídate (you) become consolidated; impve. 2nd pers. sing. / *consolidarse*.

consolidémonos let us become consolidated; impve. 1st pers. pl. / *consolidarse*.

consolídense let them become consolidated; impve. 3rd pers. pl. / *consolidarse*.

consolídese let him (her/it) become consolidated; impve. 3rd pers. sing. / *consolidarse*.

consonar to harmonize or to rhyme. irr.

conspirar to conspire. reg.

constar to be clear or to be composed of. reg.

constatar to prove or to establish. reg.

constelar to spangle. reg.

consternar to consternate or to dismay. reg.

constipándose catching cold; pres. part. / *constiparse*.

constipaos (you all) catch cold; impve. 2nd pers. pl. / *constiparse*.

constipar to stop up or to constipate. reg.

constiparse to catch cold. reg.

constípate (you) catch cold; impve. 2nd pers. sing. / *constiparse*.

constipémonos let us catch cold; impve. 1st pers. pl. / *constiparse*.

constípense let them catch cold; impve. 3rd pers. pl. / *constiparse*.

constípese let him (her/it) catch cold; impve. 3rd pers. sing. / *constiparse*.

constituíos (you all) set yourselves up; impve. 2nd pers. pl. / *constituirse*.

constituir to constitute or to establish. irr.

constituirse to set oneself up. irr.

constituya 1. that I may constitute; pres. subj. 1st pers. sing. / *constituir* 2. that he (she/it) may constitute; pres. subj. 3rd pers. sing. 3. let him (her/it) constitute; impve. 3rd pers. sing.

constituyáis that you (all) may constitute; pres. subj. 2nd pers. pl. / *constituir*.

constituyámonos let us set ourselves up; impve. 1st pers. pl. / *constituirse*.

constituyamos 1. that we may constitute; pres. subj. 1st pers. pl. / *constituir*. 2. let them constitute; impve. 1st pers. pl.

constituyan 1. that they may constitute; pres. subj. 3rd pers. pl. / *constituir*. 2. let them constitute; impve. 3rd pers. pl.

constitúyanse let them set themselves up; impve. 3rd pers. pl. / *constituirse*.

constituyas that you may constitute; pres. subj. 2nd pers. sing. / *constituir*.

constitúyase let him (her/it) set himself (herself/itself) up; impve. 3rd pers. sing. / *constituirse*.

constituye 1. he (she/it) constitutes; pres. ind. 3rd pers. sing. / *constituir*. 2. (you) constitute; impve. 2nd pers. sing.

constituyen they constitute; pres. ind. 3rd pers. pl. / *constituir*.

constituyendo constituting; pres. part. / *constituir*.

constituyéndose setting oneself up; pres. part. / *constituirse*.

constituyera 1. that I might constitute; imp. subj. 1st pers. sing. / *constituir*. 2. that he (she/it) might constitute; imp. subj. 3rd pers. sing.

constituyerais that you (all) might constitute; imp. subj. 2nd pers pl. / *constituir*.

constituyéramos that we might constitute; imp. subj. 1st pers. pl. / *constituir*.

constituyeran that they might constitute; imp. subj. 3rd pers. pl. / *constituir*.

constituyeras that you might constitute; imp. subj. 2nd pers. sing. / *constituir*.

constituyeron they constituted; past 3rd pers. pl. / *constituir*.

constituyes you constitute; pres. ind. 2nd pers. sing. / *constituir.*

constituyese 1. that I might constitute; imp. subj. 1st pers. sing. / *constituir.* 2. that he (she/it) might constitute; imp. subj. 3rd pers. sing.

constituyeseis that you (all) might constitute; imp. subj. 2nd pers pl. / *constituir.*

constituyésemos that we might constitute; imp. subj. 1st pers. pl. / *constituir.*

constituyesen that they might constitute; imp. subj. 3rd pers. pl. / *constituir.*

constituyeses that you might constitute; imp. subj. 2nd pers. sing. / *constituir.*

constituyo I constitute; pres. ind. 1st pers. sing. / *constituir.*

constituyó he (she/it) constituted; past 3rd pers. sing. / *constituir.*

constreñir to constrain or to compel. irr.

constriña 1. that I may constrain; pres. subj. 1st pers. sing. / *constreñir.* 2. that he (she/it) may constrain; pres. subj. 3rd pers. sing. 3. let him (her/it) constrain; impve. 3rd pers. sing.

constriñáis that you (all) may constrain; pres. subj. 2nd pers. pl. / *constreñir.*

constriñamos 1. that we may constrain; pres. subj. 1st pers. pl. / *constreñir.* 2. let us constrain; impve. 1st pers. pl.

constriñan 1. that they may constrain; pres. subj. 3rd pers. pl. / *constreñir.* 2. let them constrain; impve. 3rd pers. pl.

constriñas that you may constrain; pres. subj. 2nd pers. sing. / *constreñir.*

constriñe 1. he (she/it) constrains; pres. ind. 3rd pers. sing. / *constreñir.* 2. (you) constrain; impve. 2nd pers. sing.

constriñen they constrain; pres. ind. 3rd pers. pl. / *constreñir.*

constriñendo constraining; pres. part. / *constreñir.*

constriñera 1. that I might constrain; imp. subj. 1st pers. sing. / *constreñir.* 2. that he (she/it) might constrain; imp. subj. 3rd pers. sing.

constriñerais that you (all) might constrain; imp. subj. 2nd pers pl. / *constreñir.*

constriñéramos that we might constrain; imp. subj. 1st pers. pl. / *constreñir.*

constriñeran that they might constrain; imp. subj. 3rd pers. pl. / *constreñir.*

constriñeras that you might constrain; imp. subj. 2nd pers. sing. / *constreñir.*

constriñeron they constrained; past 3rd pers. pl. / *constreñir.*

constriñes you constrain; pres. ind. 2nd pers. sing. / *constreñir.*

constriñese 1. that I might constrain; imp. subj. 1st pers. sing. / *constreñir.* 2. that he (she/it) might constrain; imp. subj. 3rd pers. sing.

constriñeseis that you (all) might constrain; imp. subj. 2nd pers pl. / *constreñir.*

constriñésemos that we might constrain; imp. subj. 1st pers. pl. / *constreñir.*

constriñesen that they might constrain; imp. subj. 3rd pers. pl. / *constreñir.*

constriñeses that you might constrain; imp. subj. 2nd pers. sing. / *constreñir.*

constriño I constrain; pres. ind. 1st pers. sing. / *constreñir.*

constriñó he (she/it) constrained; past 3rd pers. sing. / *constreñir.*

construir to construct or to construe. irr.

construya 1. that I may construct; pres. subj. 1st pers. sing. / *construir.* 2. that he (she/it) may construct; pres. subj. 3rd pers. sing. 3. let him (her/it) construct; impve. 3rd pers. sing.

construyáis that you (all) may construct; pres. subj. 2nd pers. pl. / *construir.*

construyamos 1. that we may construct; pres. subj. 1st pers. pl. / *construir.* 2. let us construct; impve. 1st pers. pl.

construyan 1. that they may construct; pres. subj. 3rd pers. pl. / *construir.* 2. let them construct; impve. 3rd pers. pl.

construyas that you may construct; pres. subj. 2nd pers. sing. / *construir.*

construye 1. he (she/it) constructs; pres. ind. 3rd pers. sing. / *construir.* 2. (you) construct; impve. 2nd pers. sing.

construyen they construct; pres. ind. 3rd pers. pl. / *construir.*

construyendo constructing; pres. part. / *construir.*

construyera 1. that I might construct; imp. subj. 1st pers. sing. / *construir* 2. that he (she/it) might construct; imp. subj. 3rd pers. sing.

construyerais that you (all) might construct; imp. subj. 2nd pers pl. / *construir.*

construyéramos that we might construct; imp. subj. 1st pers. pl. / *construir.*

construyeran that they might construct; imp. subj. 3rd pers. pl. / *construir.*

construyeras that you might construct; imp. subj. 2nd pers. sing. / *construir.*

construyeron they constructed; past 3rd pers. pl. / *construir.*

construyes you construct; pres. ind. 2nd pers. sing. / *construir.*

construyese 1. that I might construct; imp. subj. 1st pers. sing. / *construir* 2. that he (she/it) might construct; imp. subj. 3rd pers. sing.

construyeseis that you (all) might construct; imp. subj. 2nd pers pl. / *construir.*

construyésemos that we might construct; imp. subj. 1st pers. pl. / *construir.*

construyesen that they might construct; imp. subj. 3rd pers. pl. / *construir.*

construyeses that you might construct; imp. subj. 2nd pers. sing. / *construir.*

construyo I construct; pres. ind. 1st pers. sing. / *construir.*

construyó he (she/it) constructed; past 3rd pers. sing. / *construir.*

consuela 1. he (she/it) consoles; pres. ind. 3rd pers. sing. / *consolar*. 2. (you) console; impve. 2nd pers. sing.

consuelan they console; pres. ind. 3rd pers. pl. / *consolar*.

consuelas you console; pres. ind. 2nd pers. sing. / *consolar*.

consuele 1. that I may console; pres. subj. 1st pers. sing. / *consolar*. 2. that he (she/it) may console; pres. subj. 3rd pers. sing. 3. let him (her/it) console; impve. 3rd pers. sing.

consuelen 1. that they may console; pres. subj. 3rd pers. pl. / *consolar*. 2. let them console; impve. 3rd pers. pl.

consueles that you may console; pres. subj. 2nd pers. sing. / *consolar*.

consuelo I console; pres. ind. 1st pers. sing. / *comsolar*.

consuena 1. he (she/it) harmonizes; pres. ind. 3rd pers. sing. / *consonar*. 2. (you) harmonize; impve. 2nd pers. sing.

consuenan they harmonize; pres. ind. 3rd pers. pl. / *consonar*.

consuenas you harmonize; pres. ind. 2nd pers. sing. / *consonar*.

consuene 1. that I may harmonize; pres. subj. 1st pers. sing. / *consonar*. 2. that he (she/it) may harmonize; pres. subj. 3rd pers. sing. 3. let him (her/it) harmonize; impve. 3rd pers. sing.

consuenen 1. that they may harmonize; pres. subj. 3rd pers. pl. / *consonar* 2. let them harmonize; impve. 3rd pers. pl.

consuenes that you may harmonize; pres. subj. 2nd pers. sing. / *consonar*.

consueno I harmonize; pres. ind. 1st pers. sing. / *consonar*.

consultar to consult. reg.

consumámonos let us waste away; impve. 1st pers. pl. / *consumirsse*.

consúmanse let them waste away; impve. 3rd pers. pl. / *consumirsse*.

consumar to consummate or to perfect. reg.

consúmase let him (her/it) waste away; impve. 3rd pers. sing. / *consumirsse*.

consúmete (you) waste away; impve. 2nd pers. sing. / *consumirsse*.

consumiéndose wasting away; pres. part. / *consumirsse*.

consumíos (you all) waste away; impve. 2nd pers. pl. / *consumirsse*.

consumir to consume. reg.

consumirse to waste away. reg.

consunto consumed / *consumir*. alternate pp.

contagiándose becoming infected; pres. part. / *contagiarse*.

contagiaos (you all) become infected; impve. 2nd pers. pl. / *contagiarse*.

contagiar to infect. reg.

contagiarse to become infected. reg.

contagíate (you) become infected; impve. 2nd pers. sing. / *contagiarse*.

contagiémonos let us become infected; impve. 1st pers. pl. / *contagiarse*.

contagíense let them become infected; impve. 3rd pers. pl. / *contagiarse*.

contagíese let him (her/it) become infected; impve. 3rd pers. sing. / *contagiarse*.

contaminar to contaminate. reg.

contar to count or to tell. irr.

contemplar to contemplate or to be lenient towards. reg.

contemporice 1. that I may temporize; pres. subj. 1st pers. sing. / *contemporizar*. 2. that he (she/it) may temporize; pres. subj. 3rd pers. sing. 3. let him (her/it) temporize; impve. 3rd pers. sing.

contemporicé I temporized; past 1st pers. sing. / *contemporizar*.

contemporicéis that you (all) may temporize; pres. subj. 2nd pers. pl. / *contemporizar*.

contemporicemos 1. that we may temporize; pres. subj. 1st pers. pl. / *constemporizar*. 2. let us temporize; impve. 1st pers. pl.

contemporicen 1. that they may temporize; pres. subj. 3rd pers. pl. / *contemporizar*. 2. let them temporize; impve. 3rd pers. pl.

contemporices that you may temporize; pres. subj. 2nd pers. sing. / *contemporizar*.

contemporizar to temporize. irr.

conten (you) contain; impve. 2nd pers. sing. / *contener*.

contender to contend or to struggle. irr.

contendrá he (she/it) will contain; fut. 3rd pers. sing. / *contener*.

contendrán they will contain; fut. 3rd pers. pl. / *contener*.

contendrás you will contain; fut. 2nd pers. sing. / *contener*.

contendré I shall contain; fut. 1st pers. sing. / *contener*.

contendréis you (all) will contain; fut. 2nd pers. pl. / *contener*.

contendremos we shall contain; fut. 1st pers. pl. / *contener*.

contendría 1. I should contain; cond. 1st pers. sing. / *contener*. 2. he (she/it) would contain; cond. 3rd pers. sing.

contendríais you (all) would contain; cond. 2nd pers. pl. / *contener*.

contendríamos we should contain; cond. 1st pers. pl. / *contener*.

contendrían they would contain; cond. 3rd pers. pl. / *contener*.

contendrías you would contain; cond. 2nd pers. sing. / *contener*.

conteneos (you all) refrain yourselves; impve. 2nd pers. pl. / *contenerse*.

contener to contain. irr.

contenerse to refrain oneself. irr.

conténete (you) refrain yourself; impve. 2nd pers. sing. / *contenerse*.

contenga 1. that I may contain; pres. subj. 1st pers. sing. / *contener*. 2. that he (she/it) may contain; pres. subj. 3rd pers. sing. 3. let him (her/it) contain; impve. 3rd pers. sing.

contengáis that you (all) may contain; pres. subj. 2nd pers. pl. / *contener*.

contengámonos let us refrain ourselves; impve. 1st pers. pl. / *contenerse*.

contengamos 1. that we may contain; pres. subj. 1st pers. pl. / *contener*. 2. let us contain; impve. 1st pers. pl.

contengan 1. that they may contain; pres. subj. 3rd pers. pl. / *contener*. 2. let them contain; impve. 3rd pers. pl.

conténganse let them refrain themselves; impve. 3rd pers. pl. / *contenerse*.

contengas that you may contain; pres. subj. 2nd pers. sing. / *contener*.

conténgase let him (her/it) refrain himself (herself/itself); impve. 3rd pers. sing. / *contenerse*.

contengo I contain; pres. ind. 1st pers. sing. / *contener*.

conteniéndose refraining oneself; pres. part. / *contenerse*.

contentándose being satisfied; pres. part. / *contentarse*.

contentaos (you all) be satisfied; impve. 2nd pers. pl. / *contentarse*.

contentar to content or to please. reg.

contentarse to be satisfied. reg.

conténtate (you) be satisfied; impve. 2nd pers. sing. / *contentarse*.

contentémonos let us be satisfied; impve. 1st pers. pl. / *contentarse*.

conténtense let them be satisfied; impve. 3rd pers. pl. / *contentarse*.

conténtese let him (her/it) be satisfied; impve. 3rd pers. sing. / *contentarse*.

contestar to answer or to agree. reg.

contienda 1. that I may contend; pres. subj. 1st pers. sing. / *contender*. 2. that he (she/it) may contend; pres. subj. 3rd pers. sing. 3. let him (her/it) contend; impve. 3rd pers. sing.

contiendan 1. that they may contend; pres. subj. 3rd pers. pl. / *contender*. 2. let them contend; impve. 3rd pers. pl.

contiendas that you may contend; pres. subj. 2nd pers. sing. / *contender*.

contiende 1. he (she/it) contends; pres. ind. 3rd pers. sing. / *contender*. 2. (you) contend; impve. 2nd pers. sing.

contienden they contend; pres. ind. 3rd pers. pl. / *contender*.

contiendes you contend; pres. ind. 2nd pers. sing. / *contender*.

contiendo I contend; pres. ind. 1st pers. sing. / *contender*.

contiene he (she/it) contains; pres. ind. 3rd pers. sing. / *contener*.

contienen they contain; pres. ind. 3rd pers. pl. / *contener*.

contienes you contain; pres. ind. 2nd pers. sing. / *contener*.

continúa 1. he (she/it) continues; pres. ind. 3rd pers. sing. / *continuar*. 2. (you) continue; impve. 2nd pers. sing.

continúan they continue; pres. ind. 3rd pers. pl. / *continuar*.

continuándose keeping on; pres. part. / *continuarse*.

continuaos (you all) keep on; impve. 2nd pers. pl. / *continuarse*.

continuar to continue or to stay. irr.

continuarse to keep on. irr.

continúas you continue; pres. ind. 2nd pers. sing. / *continuar*.

continúate (you) keep on; impve. 2nd pers. sing. / *continuarse*.

continúe 1. that I may continue; pres. subj. 1st pers. sing. / *continuar*. 2. that he (she/it) may continue; pres. subj. 3rd pers. sing. 3. let him (her/it) continue; impve. 3rd pers. sing.

continuémonos let us keep on; impve. 1st pers. pl. / *continuarse*.

continúen 1. that they may continue; pres. subj. 3rd pers. pl. / *continuar*. 2. let them continue; impve. 3rd pers. pl.

continúense let them keep on; impve. 3rd pers. pl. / *continuarse*.

continúes that you may continue; pres. subj. 2nd pers. sing. / *continuar*.

continúese let him (her/it) keep on; impve. 3rd pers. sing. / *continuarse*.

continúo I continue; pres. ind. 1st pers. sing. / *continuar*.

contoneándose strutting; pres. part. / *contonearse*.

contoneaos (you all) strut; impve. 2nd pers. pl. / *contonearse*.

contonearse to strut or to waddle. reg.

contonéate (you) strut; impve. 2nd pers. sing. / *contonearse*.

contoneémonos let us strut; impve. 1st pers. pl. / *contonearse*.

contonéense let them strut; impve. 3rd pers. pl. / *contonearse*.

contonéese let him (her/it) strut; impve. 3rd pers. sing. / *contonearse*.

contorceos (you all) writhe; impve. 2nd pers. pl. / *contorcerse*.

contorcerse to writhe. irr.

contorciéndose writhing; pres. part. / *contorcerse*.

contornar to outline or to go around. reg.

contornear to trace or to go around. reg.

contorzáis that you (all) may writhe; pres. subj. 2nd pers. pl. / *contorcerse*.

contorzamos that we may writhe; pres. subj. 1st pers. pl. / *contorcerse*.

contraatacar to counterattack. irr.

contraataque 1. that I may counterattack; pres. subj. 1st pers. sing. / *contraatacar*. 2. that he (she/it) may counterattack; pres. subj. 3rd pers. sing. 3. let him (her/it) counterattack; impve. 3rd pers. sing.

contraataqué I counterattacked; past 1st pers. sing. / *contraatacar.*

contraataquéis that you (all) may counterattack; pres. subj. 2nd pers. pl. / *contraatacar.*

contraataquemos 1. that we may counterattack; pres. subj. 1st pers. pl. / *contraatacar.* 2. let us counterattack; impve. 1st pers. pl.

contraataquen 1. that they may counterattack; pres. subj. 3rd pers. pl. / *contraatacar.* 2. let them counterattack; impve. 3rd pers. pl.

contraataques that you may counterattack; pres. subj. 2nd pers. sing. / *contraatacar.*

contrabalancear to counterbalance. reg.

contrabandear to smuggle. reg.

contradecir to contradict. irr.

contradi (you) contradict; impve. 2nd pers. sing. / *contradecir.*

contradice he (she/it) contradicts; pres. ind. 3rd pers. sing. / *contradecir.*

contradicen they contradict; pres. ind. 3rd pers. pl. / *contradecir.*

contradices you contradict; pres. ind. 2nd pers. sing. / *contradecir.*

contradiciendo contradicting; pres. part. / *contradecir.*

contradicho contradicted; past part. / *contradecir.*

contradiga 1. that I may contradict; pres. subj. 1st pers. sing. / *contradecir.* 2. that he (she/it) may contradict; pres. subj. 3rd pers. sing. 3. let him (her/it) contradict; impve. 3rd pers. sing.

contradigáis that you (all) may contradict; pres. subj. 2nd pers. pl. / *contradecir.*

contradigamos 1. that we may contradict; pres. subj. 1st pers. pl. / *contradecir.* 2. let us contradict; impve. 1st pers. pl.

contradigan 1. that they may contradict; pres. subj. 3rd pers. pl. / *contradecir.* 2. let them contradict; impve. 3rd pers. pl.

contradigas that you may contradict; pres. subj. 2nd pers. sing. / *contradecir.*

contradigo I contradict; pres. ind. 1st pers. sing. / *contradecir.*

contradije I contadicted; past 1st pers. sing. / *contradecir.*

contradijera 1. that I might contradict; imp. subj. 1st pers. sing. / *contradecir.* 2. that he (she/it) might contradict; imp. subj. 3rd pers. sing.

contradijerais that you (all) might contradict; imp. subj. 2nd pers pl. / *contradecir.*

contradijéramos that we might contradict; imp. subj. 1st pers. pl. / *contradecir.*

contradijeran that they might contradict; imp. subj. 3rd pers. pl. / *contradecir.*

contradijeras that you might contradict; imp. subj. 2nd pers. sing. / *contradecir.*

contradijeron they contradicted; past 3rd pers. pl. / *contradecir.*

contradijese 1. that I might contradict; imp. subj. 1st pers. sing. / *contradecir.* 2. that he (she/it) might contradict; imp. subj. 3rd pers. sing.

contradijeseis that you (all) might contradict; imp. subj. 2nd pers pl. / *contradecir.*

contradijésemos that we might contradict; imp. subj. 1st pers. pl. / *contradecir.*

contradijesen that they might contradict; imp. subj. 3rd pers. pl. / *contradecir.*

contradijeses that you might contradict; imp. subj. 2nd pers. sing. / *contradecir.*

contradijimos we contradicted; past 1st pers. pl. / *contradecir.*

contradijiste you contradicted; past 2nd pers. sing. / *contradecir.*

contradijisteis you (all) contradicted; past 2nd pers. pl. / *contradecir.*

contradijo he (she/it) contradicted; past 3rd pers. sing. / *contradecir.*

contradirá he (she/it) will contradict; fut. 3rd pers. sing. / *contradecir.*

contradirán they will contradict; fut. 3rd pers. pl. / *contradecir.*

contradirás you will contradict; fut. 2nd pers. sing. / *contradecir.*

contradiré I shall contradict; fut. 1st pers. sing. / *contradecir.*

contradiréis you (all) will contradict; fut. 2nd pers. pl. / *contradecir.*

contradiremos we shall contradict; fut. 1st pers. pl. / *contradecir.*

contradiría 1. I should contradict; cond. 1st pers. sing. / *contradecir.* 2. he (she/it) would contradict; cond. 3rd pers. sing.

contradiríais you (all) would contradict; cond. 2nd pers. pl. / *contradecir.*

contradiríamos we should contradict; cond. 1st pers. pl. / *contradecir.*

contradirían they would contradict; cond. 3rd pers. pl. / *contradecir.*

contradirías you would contradict; cond. 2nd pers. sing. / *contradecir.*

contraeos (you all) shrink; impve. 2nd pers. pl. / *contraerse.*

contraer to contract or to condense. irr.

contraerse to shrink. irr.

contráete (you) shrink; impve. 2nd pers. sing. / *contraerse.*

contrahacer to counterfeit or to copy. irr.

contrahaga 1. that I may counterfeit; pres. subj. 1st pers. sing. / *contrahacer.* 2. that he (she/it) may counterfeit; pres. subj. 3rd pers. sing. 3. let him (her/it) counterfeit; impve. 3rd pers. sing.

contrahagáis that you (all) may counterfeit; pres. subj. 2nd pers. pl. / *contrahacer.*

contrahagamos 1. that we may counterfeit; pres. subj. 1st pers. pl. / *contrahacer.* 2. let us counterfeit; impve. 1st pers. pl.

contrahagan 1. that they may counterfeit; pres. subj. 3rd pers. pl. / *contrahacer.* 2. let them counterfeit; impve. 3rd pers. pl.

contrahagas that you may counterfeit; pres. subj. 2nd pers. sing. / *contrahacer.*

contrahago I counterfeit; pres. ind. 1st pers. sing. / *contrahacer.*

contrahará he (she/it) will counterfeit; fut. 3rd pers. sing. / *contrahacer.*

contraharán they will counterfeit; fut. 3rd pers. pl. / *contrahacer.*

contraharás you will counterfeit; fut. 2nd pers. sing. / *contrahacer.*

contraharé I shall counterfeit; fut. 1st pers. sing. / *contrahacer.*

contraharéis you (all) will counterfeit; fut. 2nd pers. pl. / *contrahacer.*

contraharemos we shall counterfeit; fut. 1st pers. pl. / *contrahacer.*

contraharía 1. I should counterfeit; cond. 1st pers. sing. / *contrahacer* 2. he (she/it) would counterfeit; cond. 3rd pers. sing.

contraharíais you (all) would counterfeit; cond. 2nd pers. pl. / *contrahacer.*

contraharíamos we should counterfeit; cond. 1st pers. pl. / *contrahacer.*

contraharían they would counterfeit; cond. 3rd pers. pl. / *contrahacer.*

contraharías you would counterfeit; cond. 2nd pers. sing. / *contrahacer.*

contrahaz (you) counterfeit; impve. 2nd pers. sing. / *contrahacer.*

contrahecho counterfeited; past part. / *contrahacer.*

contrahice I counterfeited; past 1st pers. sing. / *contrahacer.*

contrahiciera 1. that I might counterfeit; imp. subj. 1st pers. sing. / *contrahacer.* 2. that he (she/it) might counterfeit; imp. subj. 3rd pers. sing.

contrahicierais that you (all) might counterfeit; imp. subj. 2nd pers pl. / *contrahacer.*

contrahiciéramos that we might counterfeit; imp. subj. 1st pers. pl. / *contrahacer.*

contrahicieran that they might counterfeit; imp. subj. 3rd pers. pl. / *contrahacer.*

contrahicieras that you might counterfeit; imp. subj. 2nd pers. sing. / *contrahacer.*

contrahicieron they counterfeited; past 3rd pers. pl. / *contrahacer.*

contrahiciese 1. that I might counterfeit; imp. subj. 1st pers. sing. / *contrahacer.* 2. that he (she/it) might counterfeit; imp. subj. 3rd pers. sing.

contrahicieseis that you (all) might counterfeit; imp. subj. 2nd pers pl. / *contrahacer.*

contrahiciésemos that we might counterfeit; imp. subj. 1st pers. pl. / *contrahacer.*

contrahiciesen that they might counterfeit; imp. subj. 3rd pers. pl. / *contrahacer.*

contrahicieses that you might counterfeit; imp. subj. 2nd pers. sing. / *contrahacer.*

contrahicimos we counterfeited; past 1st pers. pl. / *contrahacer.*

contrahiciste you counterfeited; past 2nd pers. sing. / *contrahacer.*

contrahicisteis you (all) counterfeited; past 2nd pers. pl. / *contrahacer.*

contrahizo he (she/it) counterfeited; past 3rd pers. sing. / *contrahacer.*

contraiga 1. that I may contract; pres. subj. 1st pers. sing. / *contraer.* 2. that he (she/it) may contract; pres. subj. 3rd pers. sing. 3. let him (her/it) contract; impve. 3rd pers. sing.

contraigáis that you (all) may contract; pres. subj. 2nd pers. pl. / *contraer.*

contraigámonos let us shrink; impve. 1st pers. pl. / *contraerse.*

contraigamos 1. that we may contract; pres. subj. 1st pers. pl. / *contraer.* 2. let us contract; impve. 1st pers. pl.

contraigan 1. that they may contract; pres. subj. 3rd pers. pl. / *contraer.* 2. let them contract; impve. 3rd pers. pl.

contraíganse let them shrink; impve. 3rd pers. pl. / *contraerse.*

contraigas that you may contact; pres. subj. 2nd pers. sing. / *contraer.*

contraígase let him (her/it) shrink; impve. 3rd pers. sing. / *contraerse.*

contraigo I contract; pres. ind. 1st pers. sing. / *contraer.*

contraje I contracted; pres. ind. 1st pers. sing. / *contraer.*

contrajera 1. that I might contract; imp. subj. 1st pers. sing. / *contraer.* 2. that he (she/it) might contract; imp. subj. 3rd pers. sing.

contrajerais that you (all) might contract; imp. subj. 2nd pers pl. / *contraer.*

contrajéramos that we might contract; imp. subj. 1st pers. pl. / *contraer.*

contrajeran that they might contract; imp. subj. 3rd pers. pl. / *contraer.*

contrajeras that you might contract; imp. subj. 2nd pers. sing. / *contraer.*

contrajeron they contracted; past 3rd pers. pl. / *contraer.*

contrajese 1. that I might contract; imp. subj. 1st pers. sing. / *contraer.* 2. that he (she/it) might contract; imp. subj. 3rd pers. sing.

contrajeseis that you (all) might contract; imp. subj. 2nd pers pl. / *contraer.*

contrajésemos that we might contract; imp. subj. 1st pers. pl. / *contraer.*

contrajeses that you might contract; imp. subj. 2nd pers. sing. / *contraer.*

contrajimos we contracted; past 1st pers. pl. / *contraer.*

contrajiste you contracted; past 2nd pers. sing. / *contraer.*

contrajisteis you (all) contracted; past 2nd pers. pl. / *contraer.*

contrajo he (she/it) contracted; past 3rd pers. sing. / *contraer.*

contramandar to countermand. reg.

contramarcar to countermark. irr.

contramarchar to countermarch or to reverse. reg.

contramarque 1. that I may countermark; pres. subj. 1st pers. sing. / *contramarcar.* 2. that he (she/it) may countermark; pres. subj. 3rd pers. sing. 3. let him (her/it) countermark; impve. 3rd pers. sing.

contramarqué I countermarked; past 1st pers. sing. / *contramarcar.*

contramarquéis that you (all) may countermark; pres. subj. 2nd pers. pl. / *contramarcar.*

contramarquemos 1. that we may countermark; pres. subj. 1st pers. pl. / *contramarcar.* 2. let us countermark; impve. 1st pers. pl.

contramarquen 1. that they may countermark; pres. subj. 3rd pers. pl. / *contramarcar.* 2. let them countermark; impve. 3rd pers. pl.

contramarques that you may countermark; pres. subj. 2nd pers. sing. / *contramarcar.*

contrapesar to counterbalance. reg.

contrapon (you) compare; impve. 2nd pers. sing. / *contraponer.*

contrapondrá he (she/it) will compare; fut. 3rd pers. sing. / *contraponer.*

contrapondrán they will compare; fut. 3rd pers. pl. / *contraponer.*

contrapondrás you will compare; fut. 2nd pers. sing. / *contraponer.*

contrapondré I shall compare; fut. 1st pers. sing. / *contraponer.*

contrapondréis you (all) will compare; fut. 2nd pers. pl. / *contraponer.*

contrapondremos we shall compare; fut. 1st pers. pl. / *contraponer.*

contrapondría 1. I should compare; cond. 1st pers. sing. / *contraponer.* 2. he (she/it) would compare; cond. 3rd pers. sing.

contrapondríais you (all) would compare; cond. 2nd pers. pl. / *contraponer.*

contrapondríamos we should compare; cond. 1st pers. pl. / *contraponer.*

contrapondrían they would compare; cond. 3rd pers. pl. / *contraponer.*

contrapondrías you would compare; cond. 2nd pers. sing. / *contraponer.*

contraponer to compare or to oppose. irr.

contraponga 1. that I may compare; pres. subj. 1st pers. sing. / *contraponer.* 2. that he (she/it) may compare; pres. subj. 3rd pers. sing. 3. let him (her/it) compare; impve. 3rd pers. sing.

contrapongáis that you (all) may compare; pres. subj. 2nd pers. pl. / *contraponer.*

contrapongamos 1. that we may compare; pres. subj. 1st pers. pl. / *contraponer.* 2. let us compare; impve. 1st pers. pl.

contrapongan 1. that they may compare; pres. subj. 3rd pers. pl. / *contraponer.* 2. let them compare; impve. 3rd pers. pl.

contrapongas that you may compare; pres. subj. 2nd pers. sing. / *contraponer.*

contrapongo I compare; pres. ind. 1st pers. sing. / *contraponer.*

contrapuesto compared; past part. / *contraponer.*

contrapuse I compared; past 1st pers. sing. / *contraponer.*

contrapusiera 1. that I might compare; imp. subj. 1st pers. sing. / *contraponer* 2. that he (she/it) might compare; imp. subj. 3rd pers. sing.

contrapusierais that you (all) might compare; imp. subj. 2nd pers pl. / *contraponer.*

contrapusiéramos that we might compare; imp. subj. 1st pers. pl. / *contraponer.*

contrapusieran that they might compare; imp. subj. 3rd pers. pl. / *contraponer.*

contrapusieras that you might compare; imp. subj. 2nd pers. sing. / *contraponer.*

contrapusieron they compared; past 3rd pers. pl. / *contraponer.*

contrapusiese 1. that I might compare; imp. subj. 1st pers. sing. / *contraponer* 2. that he (she/it) might compare; imp. subj. 3rd pers. sing.

contrapusieseis that you (all) might compare; imp. subj. 2nd pers pl. / *contaponer.*

contrapusiésemos that we might compare; imp. subj. 1st pers. pl. / *contraponer.*

contrapusiesen that they might compare; imp. subj. 3rd pers. pl. / *contraponer.*

contrapusieses that you might compare; imp. subj. 2nd pers. sing. / *contraponer.*

contrapusimos we compared; past 1st pers. pl. / *contraponer.*

contrapusiste you compared; past 2nd pers. sing. / *contraponer.*

contrapusisteis you (all) compared; past 2nd pers. pl. / *contraponer.*

contrapuso he (she/it) compared; past 3rd pers. sing. / *contraponer.*

contraría 1. he (she/it) contradicts; pres. ind. 3rd pers. sing. / *contrariar.* 2. (you) contradict; impve. 2nd pers. sing.

contrarían they contradict; pres. ind. 3rd pers. pl. / *contrariar.*

contrariar to contradict or to vex. irr.

contrarías you contradict; pres. ind. 2nd pers. sing. / *contrariar.*

contraríe 1. that I may contradict; pres. subj. 1st pers. sing. / *contrariar* 2. that he (she/it) may contradict; pres. subj. 3rd pers. sing. 3. let him (her/it) contradict; impve. 3rd pers. sing.

contraríen 1. that they may contradict; pres. subj. 3rd pers. pl. / *contrariar.* 2. let them contradict; impve. 3rd pers. pl.

contraríes that you may contradict; pres. subj. 2nd pers. sing. / *contrariar.*

contrarío I contradict; pres. ind. 1st pers. sing. / *contrariar.*

contrarrestar to counteract or to resist. reg.

contrastar to contrast. reg.

contratar to contract for or to hire. reg. ar conju.

contraven (you) contravene; impve. 2nd pers. sing. / *contravenir.*

contravendrá he (she/it) will contravene; fut. 3rd pers. sing. / *contravenir.*

contravendrán they will contravene; fut. 3rd pers. pl. / *contravenir.*

contravendrás you will contravene; fut. 2nd pers. sing. / *contravenir.*

contravendré I shall contravene; fut. 1st pers. sing. / *contravenir.*

contravendréis you (all) will contravene; fut. 2nd pers. pl. / *contravenir.*

contravendremos we shall contravene; fut. 1st pers. pl. / *contravenir.*

contravendría 1. I should contravene; cond. 1st pers. sing. / *contravenir.* 2. he (she/it) would contravene; cond. 3rd pers. sing.

contravendríais you (all) would contravene; cond. 2nd pers. pl. / *contravenir.*

contravendríamos we should contravene; cond. 1st pers. pl. / *contravenir.*

contravendrían they would contravene; cond. 3rd pers. pl. / *contravenir.*

contravendrías you would contravene; cond. 2nd pers. sing. / *contravenir.*

contravenga 1. that I may contravene; pres. subj. 1st pers. sing. / *contravenir.* 2. that he (she/it) may contravene; pres. subj. 3rd pers. sing. 3. let him (her/it) contravene; impve. 3rd pers. sing.

contravengáis that you (all) may contravene; pres. subj. 2nd pers. pl. / *contravenir.*

contravengamos 1. that we may contravene; pres. subj. 1st pers. pl. / *contravenir.* 2. let us contravene; impve. 1st pers. pl.

contravengan 1. that they may contravene; pres. subj. 3rd pers. pl. / *contravenir.* 2. let them contravene; impve. 3rd pers. pl.

contravengas that you may contravene; pres. subj. 2nd pers. sing. / *contravenir.*

contravengo I contravene; pres. ind. 1st pers. sing. / *contravenir.*

contravenir to contravene or to violate. irr.

contraviene he (she/it) contravenes; pres. ind. 3rd pers. sing. / *contravenir.*

contravienen they contravene; pres. ind. 3rd pers. pl. / *contravenir.*

contravienes you contravene; pres. ind. 2nd pers. sing. / *contravenir.*

contravine I contravened; pres. ind. 1st pers. sing. / *contravenir.*

contraviniendo contravening; pres. part. / *contravenir.*

contraviniera 1. that I might contravene; imp. subj. 1st pers. sing. / *contravenir.* 2. that he (she/it) might contravene; imp. subj. 3rd pers. sing.

contravinierais that you (all) might contravene; imp. subj. 2nd pers pl. / *contravenir.*

contraviniéramos that we might contravene; imp. subj. 1st pers. pl. / *contravenir.*

contravinieran that they might contravene; imp. subj. 3rd pers. pl. / *contravenir.*

contravinieras that you might contravene; imp. subj. 2nd pers. sing. / *contravenir.*

contravinieron they contravened; past 3rd pers. pl. / *contravenir.*

contraviniese 1. that I might contravene; imp. subj. 1st pers. sing. / *contravenir.* 2. that he (she/it) might contravene; imp. subj. 3rd pers. sing.

contravinieseis that you (all) might contravene; imp. subj. 2nd pers pl. / *contravenir.*

contraviniésemos that we might contravene; imp. subj. 1st pers. pl. / *contravenir.*

contraviniesen that they might contravene; imp. subj. 3rd pers. pl. / *contravenir.*

contravinieses that you might contravene; imp. subj. 2nd pers. sing. / *contravenir.*

contravinimos we contravened; past 1st pers. pl. / *contravenir.*

contraviniste you contravened; past 2nd pers. sing. / *contravened.*

contravinisteis you (all) contravened; past 2nd pers. pl. / *contravenir.*

contravino he (she/it) contravened; past 3rd pers. sing. / *contravenir.*

contrayendo contracting; pres. part. / *contraer.*

contrayéndose shrinking; pres. part. / *contraerse.*

contribuir to contribute. irr.

contribuya 1. that I may contribute; pres. subj. 1st pers. sing. / *contribuir* 2. that he (she/it) may contribute; pres. subj. 3rd pers. sing. 3. let them contribute; impve. 3rd pers. sing.

contribuyáis that you (all) may contribute; pres. subj. 2nd pers. pl. / *contribuir.*

contribuyamos 1. that we may contribute; pres. subj. 1st pers. pl. / *contribuir.* 2. let us contribute; impve. 1st pers. pl.

contribuyan 1. that they may contribute; pres. subj. 3rd pers. pl. / *contribuir.* 2. let them contribute; impve. 3rd pers. pl.

contribuyas that you may contribute; pres. subj. 2nd pers. sing. / *contribuir.*

contribuye 1. he (she/it) contributes; pres. ind. 3rd pers. sing. / *contribuir.* 2. (you) contribute; impve. 2nd pers. sing.

contribuyen they contribute; pres. ind. 3rd pers. pl. / *contribuir.*

contribuyendo contributing; pres. part. / *contribuir.*

contribuyera 1. that I might contribute; imp. subj. 1st pers. sing. / *contribuir.* 2. that he (she/it) might contribute; imp. subj. 3rd pers. sing.

contribuyerais that you (all) might contribute; imp. subj. 2nd pers pl. / *contribuir.*

contribuyéramos that we might contribute; imp. subj. 1st pers. pl. / *contribuir.*

contribuyeran that they might contribute; imp. subj. 3rd pers. pl. / *contribuir.*

contribuyeras that you might contribute; imp. subj. 2nd pers. sing. / *contribuir.*

contribuyeron they contributed; past 3rd pers. pl. / *contribuir.*

contribuyes you contribute; pres. ind. 2nd pers. sing. / *contribuir.*

contribuyese 1. that I might contribute; imp. subj. 1st pers. sing. / *contribuir.* 2. that he (she/it) might contribute; imp. subj. 3rd pers. sing.

contribuyeseis that you (all) might contribute; imp. subj. 2nd pers pl. / *contribuir.*

contribuyésemos that we might contribute; imp. subj. 1st pers. pl. / *contribuir.*

contribuyesen that they might contribute; imp. subj. 3rd pers. pl. / *contribuir.*

contribuyeses that you might contribute; imp. subj. 2nd pers. sing. / *contribuir.*

contribuyo I contribute; pres. ind. 1st pers. sing. / *contribuir.*

contribuyó he (she/it) contributed; past 3rd pers. sing. / *contribuir.*

contristar to sadden. reg.

controlar to control or to inspect. reg.

controvertir to controvert or to call in question. irr.

controvierta 1. that I may controvert; pres. subj. 1st pers. sing. / *controvertir.* 2. that he (she/it) may controvert; pres. subj. 3rd pers. sing. 3. let him (her/it) controvert; impve. 3rd pers. sing.

controviertan 1. that they may controvert; pres. subj. 3rd pers. pl. / *controvertir.* 2. let them controvert; impve. 3rd pers. pl.

controviertas that you may controvert; pres. subj. 2nd pers. sing. / *controvertir.*

controvierte 1. he (she/it) controverts; pres. ind. 3rd pers. sing. / *controvertir.* 2. (you) controvert; impve. 2nd pers. sing.

controvierten they controvert; pres. ind. 3rd pers. pl. / *controvertir.*

controviertes you controvert; pres. ind. 2nd pers. sing. / *controvertir.*

controvierto I controvert; pres. ind. 1st pers. sing. / *controvertir.*

controvirtáis that you (all) may controvert; pres. subj. 2nd pers. pl. / *controvertir.*

controvirtamos 1. that we may controvert; pres. subj. 1st pers. pl. / *controvertir.* 2. let us controvert; impve. 1st pers. pl.

controvirtiendo controverting; pres. part. / *controvertir.*

controvirtiera 1. that I might controvert; imp. subj. 1st pers. sing. / *controvertir.* 2. that he (she/it) might controvert; imp. subj. 3rd pers. sing.

controvirtierais that you (all) might controvert; imp. subj. 2nd pers pl. / *controvertir.*

controvirtiéramos that we might controvert; imp. subj. 1st pers. pl. / *controvertir.*

controvirtieran that they might controvert; imp. subj. 3rd pers. pl. / *controvertir.*

controvirtieras that you might controvert; imp. subj. 2nd pers. sing. / *controvertir.*

controvirtieron they controverted; past 3rd pers. pl. / *controvertir.*

controvirtiese 1. that I might controvert; imp. subj. 1st pers. sing. / *controvertir.* 2. that he (she/it) might controvert; imp. subj. 3rd pers. sing.

controvirtieseis that you (all) might controvert; imp. subj. 2nd pers pl. / *controvertir.*

controvirtiésemos that we might controvert; imp. subj. 1st pers. pl. / *controvertir.*

controvirtiesen that they might controvert; imp. subj. 3rd pers. pl. / *controvertir.*

controvirtieses that you might controvert; imp. subj. 2nd pers. sing. / *controvertir.*

controvirtió he (she/it) controverted; past 3rd pers. sing. / *controvertir.*

contuerce he (she/it) writhes; pres. ind. 3rd pers. sing. / *contorcerse.*

contuercen they writhe; pres. ind. 3rd pers. pl. / *contorcerse*

contuerces you writhe; pres. ind. 2nd pers. sing. / *contorcerse.*

contuércete (you) writhe; impve. 2nd pers. sing. / *contorcerse.*

contuerza 1. that I may writhe; pres. subj. 1st pers. sing. / *contorcerse.* 2. that he (she/it) may writhe; pres. subj. 3rd pers. sing.

contuerzan that they may writhe; pres. subj. 3rd pers. pl. / *contorcerse.*

contuérzanse let them writhe; impve. 3rd pers. pl. / *contorcerse.*

contuerzas that you may writhe; pres. subj. 2nd pers. sing. / *contorcerse.*

contuérzase let him (her/it) writhe; impve. 3rd pers. sing. / *contorcerse.*

contuerzo I writhe; pres. ind. 1st pers. sing. / *contorcerse.*

contundir to bruise. reg.

conturbar to perturb or to disquiet. reg.

contuve I contained; past 1st pers. sing. / *contener.*

contuviera 1. that I might contain; imp. subj. 1st pers. sing. / *contener.* 2. that he (she/it) might contain; imp. subj. 3rd pers. sing.

contuvierais that you (all) might contain; imp. subj. 2nd pers pl. / *contener.*

contuviéramos that we might contain; imp. subj. 1st pers. pl. / *contener.*

contuvieran that they might contain; imp. subj. 3rd pers. pl. / *contener.*

contuvieras that you might contain; imp. subj. 2nd pers. sing. / *contener.*

contuvieron they contained; past 3rd pers. pl. / *contener.*

contuviese 1. that I might contain; imp. subj. 1st pers. sing. / *contener.* 2. that he (she/it) might contain; imp. subj. 3rd pers. sing.

contuvieseis that you (all) might contain; imp. subj. 2nd pers pl. / *contener.*

contuviésemos that we might contain; imp. subj. 1st pers. pl. / *contener.*

contuviesen that they might contain; imp. subj. 3rd pers. pl. / *contener.*

contuvieses that you might contain; imp. subj. 2nd pers. sing. / *contener.*

contuvimos we contained; past 1st pers. pl. / *contener.*

contuviste you contained; past 2nd pers. sing. / *contener.*

contuvisteis you (all) contained; past 2nd pers. pl. / *contener.*

contuvo he (she/it) contained; past 3rd pers. sing. / *contener.*

convalecer to convalesce. irr.

convalezca 1. that I may convalesce; pres. subj. 1st pers. sing. / *convalecer* 2. that he (she/it) may convalesce; pres. subj. 3rd pers. sing. 3. let him (her/it) convalesce; impve. 3rd pers. sing.

convalezcáis that you (all) may convalesce; pres. subj. 2nd pers. pl. / *convalecer.*

convalezcamos 1. that we may convalesce; pres. subj. 1st pers. pl. / *convalecer.* 2. let us convalesce; impve. 1st pers. pl.

convalezcan 1. that they may convalesce; pres. subj. 3rd pers. pl. / *convalecer.* 2. let them convalesce; impve. 3rd pers. pl.

convalezcas that you may convalesce; pres. subj. 2nd pers. sing. / *convalecer.*

convalezco I convalesce; pres. ind. 1st pers. sing. / *convalecer.*

convalidar to confirm or to ratify. reg.

conven (you) agree; impve. 2nd pers. sing. / *convenir.*

convencer to convince. irr.

convendrá he (she/it) will agree; fut. 3rd pers. sing. / *convenir.*

convendrán they will agree; fut. 3rd pers. pl. / *convenir.*

convendrás you will agree; fut. 2nd pers. sing. / *convenir.*

convendré I shall agree; fut. 1st pers. sing. / *convenir.*

convendréis you (all) will agree; fut. 2nd pers. pl. / *convenir.*

convendremos we shall agree; fut. 1st pers. pl. / *convenir.*

convendría 1. I should agree; cond. 1st pers. sing. / *convenir.* 2. he (she/it) would agree; cond. 3rd pers. sing.

convendríais you (all) would agree; cond. 2nd pers. pl. / *convenir.*

convendríamos we should agree; cond. 1st pers. pl. / *convenir.*

convendrían they would agree; cond. 3rd pers. pl. / *convenir.*

convendrías you would agree; cond. 2nd pers. sing. / *convenir.*

convénete (you) come to an agreement; impve. 2nd pers. sing. / *convenirse.*

convenga 1. that I may agree; pres. subj. 1st pers. sing. / *convenir.* 2. that he (she/it) may agree; pres. subj. 3rd pers. sing. 3. let him (her/it) agree; impve. 3rd pers. sing.

convengáis that you (all) may agree; pres. subj. 2nd pers. pl. / *convenir.*

convengámonos let us come to an agreement; impve. 1st pers. pl. / *convenirse.*

convengamos 1. that we may agree; pres. subj. 1st pers. pl. / *convenir.* 2. let us agree; impve. 1st pers. pl.

convengan 1. that they may agree; pres. subj. 3rd pers. pl. / *convenir.* 2. let them agree; impve. 3rd pers. pl.

convénganse let them come to an agreement; impve. 3rd pers. pl. / *convenirse.*

convengas that you may agree; pres. subj. 2nd pers. sing. / *convenir.*

convéngase let him (her/it) come to an agreement; impve. 3rd pers. sing. / *convenirse.*

convengo I agree; pres. ind. 1st pers. sing. / *convenir.*

conveníos (you all) come to an agreement; impve. 2nd pers. pl. / *convenirse.*

convenir to agree or to be suitable. irr.

convenirse to come to an agreement. irr.

convenza 1. that I may convince; pres. subj. 1st pers. sing. / *convencer.* 2. that he (she/it) may convince; pres. subj. 3rd pers. sing. 3. let him (her/it) convince; impve. 3rd pers. sing.

convenzáis that you (all) may convince; pres. subj. 2nd pers. pl. / *convencer.*

convenzamos 1. that we may convince; pres. subj. 1st pers. pl. / *convencer.* 2. let us convince; impve. 1st pers. pl.

convenzan 1. that they may convince; pres. subj. 3rd pers. pl. / *convencer.* 2. let them convince; impve. 3rd pers. pl.

convenzas that you may convince; pres. subj. 2nd pers. sing. / *convencer.*

convenzo I convince; pres. ind. 1st pers. sing. / *convencer.*

converger to converge. irr.

convergir to converge. irr.

converja 1. that I may converge; pres. subj. 1st pers. sing. / *converger.* 2. that he (she/it) may converge; pres. subj. 3rd pers. sing. 3. let him (her/it) converge; impve. 3rd pers. sing.

converjáis that you (all) may converge; pres. subj. 2nd pers. pl. / *converger.*

converjamos 1. that we may converge; pres. subj. 1st pers. pl. / *converger.* 2. let us converge; impve. 1st pers. pl.

converjan 1. that they may converge; pres. subj. 3rd pers. pl. / *converger.* 2. let them converge; impve. 3rd pers. pl.

converjas that you may converge; pres. subj. 2nd pers. sing. / *converger.*

converjo I converge; pres. ind. 1st pers. sing. / *converger.*

conversar to converse or to dwell. reg.

convertíos (you all) change; impve. 2nd pers. pl. / *convertirse.*

convertir to convert or to change. irr

convertirse to change. irr.

convicto convicted; past part. / *convencer.*

convidándose offering one's services; pres. part. / *convidarse.*

convidaos (you all) offer your services; impve. 2nd pers. pl. / *convidarse.*

convidar to invite. reg.

convidarse to offer one's services. reg.

convídate (you) offer your services; impve. 2nd pers. sing. / *convidarse.*

convidémonos let us offer our services; impve. 1st pers. pl. / *convidarse*.

convídense let them offer their services; impve. 3rd pers. pl. / *convidarse*.

convídese let him (her/it) offer his (her/it's) services; impve. 3rd pers. sing. / *convidarse*.

conviene he (she/it) agrees; pres. ind. 3rd pers. sing. / *convenir*.

convienen they agree; pres. ind. 3rd pers. pl. / *convenir*.

convienes you agree; pres. ind. 2nd pers. sing. / *convenir*.

convierta 1. that I may convert; pres. subj. 1st pers. sing. / *convertir*. 2. that he (she/it) may convert; pres. subj. 3rd pers. sing. 3. let him (her/it) convert; impve. 3rd pers. sing.

conviertan 1. that they may convert; pres. subj. 3rd pers. pl. / *convertir*. 2. let them convert; impve. 3rd pers. pl.

conviértanse let them change; impve. 3rd pers. pl. / *convertirse*.

conviertas that you may convert; pres. subj. 2nd pers. sing. / *convertir*.

conviértase let him (her/it) change; impve. 3rd pers. sing. / *convertirse*.

convierte 1. he (she/it) converts; pres. ind. 3rd pers. sing. / *convertir*. 2. (you) convert; impve. 2nd pers. sing.

convierten they convert; pres. ind. 3rd pers. pl. / *convertir*.

conviertes you convert; pres.ind. 2nd pers. sing. / *convertir*.

conviértete (you) change; impve. 2nd pers. sing. / *convertirse*.

convierto I convert; pres. ind. 1st pers. sing. / *convertir*.

convine I agreed; pres. ind. 1st pers. sing. / *convenir*.

conviniendo agreeing; pres. part. / *convenir*.

conviniéndose coming to an agreement; pres. part. / *convenirse*.

conviniera 1. that I might agree; imp. subj. 1st pers. sing. / *convenir*. 2. that he (she/it) might agree; imp. subj. 3rd pers. sing.

convinierais that you (all) might agree; imp. subj. 2nd pers pl. / *convenir*.

conviniéramos that we might agree; imp. subj. 1st pers. pl. / *convenir*.

convinieran that they might agree; imp. subj. 3rd pers. pl. / *convenir*.

convinieras that you might agree; imp. subj. 2nd pers. sing. / *convenir*.

convinieron they agreed; past 3rd pers. pl. / *convenir*.

conviniese 1. that I might agree; imp. subj. 1st pers. sing. / *convenir*. 2. that he (she/it) might agree; imp. subj. 3rd pers. sing.

convinieseis that you (all) might agree; imp. subj. 2nd pers pl. / *convenir*.

conviniésemos that we might agree; imp. subj. 1st pers. pl. / *convenir*.

conviniesen that they might agree; imp. subj. 3rd pers. pl. / *convenir*.

convinieses that you might agree; imp. subj. 2nd pers. sing. / *convenir*.

convinimos we agreed; past 1st pers. pl. / *convenir*.

conviniste you agreed; past 2nd pers. sing. / *convenir*.

convinisteis you (all) agreed; past 2nd pers. pl. / *convenir*.

convino he (she/it) agreed; past 3rd pers. sing. / *convenir*.

convirtáis that you (all) may convert; pres. subj. 2nd pers. pl. / *convertir*.

convirtámonos let us change; impve. 1st pers. pl. / *convertirse*.

convirtamos 1. that we may convert; pres. subj. 1st pers. pl. / *convertir*. 2. let us convert; impve. 1st pers. pl.

convirtiendo converting; pres. part. / *convertir*.

convirtiéndose changing; pres. part. / *convertirse*.

convirtiera 1. that I might convert; imp. subj. 1st pers. sing. / *convertir*. 2. that he (she/it) might convert; imp. subj. 3rd pers. sing.

convirtierais that you (all) might convert; imp. subj. 2nd pers pl. / *convertir*.

convirtiéramos that we might convert; imp. subj. 1st pers. pl. / *convertir*.

convirtieran that they might convert; imp. subj. 3rd pers. pl. / *convertir*.

convirtieras that you might convert; imp. subj. 2nd pers. sing. / *convertir*.

convirtieron they converted; past 3rd pers. pl. / *convertir*.

convirtiese 1. that I might convert; imp. subj. 1st pers. sing. / *convertir*. 2. that he (she/it) might convert; imp. subj. 3rd pers. sing.

convirtieseis that you (all) might convert; imp. subj. 2nd pers pl. / *convertir*.

convirtiésemos that we might convert; imp. subj. 1st pers. pl. / *convertir*.

convirtiesen that they might convert; imp. subj. 3rd pers. pl. / *convertir*.

convirtieses that you might convert; imp. subj. 2nd pers. sing. / *convertir*.

convirtió he (she/it) converted; past 3rd pers. sing. / *convertir*.

convivir to coexist or to live together. reg.

convocar to convoke or to assemble. irr.

convoque 1. that I may convoke; pres. subj. 1st pers. sing. / *convocar*. 2. that he (she/it) may convoke; pres. subj. 3rd pers. sing. 3. let him (her/it) convoke; impve. 3rd pers. sing.

convoqué I convoked; past 1st pers. sing. / *convocar*.

convoquéis that you (all) may convoke; pres. subj. 2nd pers. pl. / *convocar*.

convoquemos 1. that we may convoke; pres. subj. 1st pers. pl. / *convocar*. 2. let us convoke; impve. 1st pers. pl.

convoquen 1. that they may convoke; pres. subj. 3rd pers. pl. / *convocar*. 2. let them convoke; impve. 3rd pers. pl.

convoques that you may convoke; pres. subj. 2nd pers. sing. / *convocar*.

convoyar to convoy or to escort. reg.

convulsionar to convulse. reg.
cooperar to cooperate. reg.
coordinar to coordinate. reg.
copar to take by surprise. reg.
copiar to copy. reg.
copulándose copulating; pres. part. / *copularse.*
copulaos (you all) copulate; impve. 2nd pers. pl. / *copularse.*
copular to copulate. reg.
copularse to copulate. reg.
copúlate (you) copulate; impve. 2nd pers. sing. / *copularse.*
copulémonos let us copulate; impve. 1st pers. pl. / *copularse.*
copúlense let them copulate; impve. 3rd pers. pl. / *copularse.*
copúlese let him (her/it) copulate; impve. 3rd pers. sing. / *copularse.*
coquetear to flirt or to act coquettishly. reg.
corcovar to bend. reg.
corcovear to buck or to leap. reg.
corcusir to mend roughly. reg.
corear to chorus. reg.
cornear to butt or to gore. reg.
coronar to crown or to climax. reg.
corrámonos let us slip through; impve. 1st pers. pl. / *correrse.*
córranse let them slip through; impve. 3rd pers. pl. / *correrse.*
córrase let him (her/it) slip through; impve. 3rd pers. sing. / *correrse.*
corregíos (you all) mend your way; impve. 2nd pers. pl. / *corregirse.*
corregir to correct. irr.
corregirse to mend one's way. irr.
correlacionar to correlate. reg.
correos (you all) slip through; impve. 2nd pers. pl. / *correrse.*
correr to run or to embarras. reg.
correrse to slip through or to be embarrassed. reg.
correspondámonos let us agree; impve. 1st pers. pl. / *corresponderse.*
correspóndanse let them agree; impve. 3rd pers. pl. / *corresponderse.*
correspóndase let him (her/it) agree; impve. 3rd pers. sing. / *corresponderse.*
correspondeos (you all) agree; impve. 2nd pers. pl. / *corresponderse.*
corresponder to correspond or to return. reg.
corresponderse to agree or to correspond. reg.
correspóndete (you) agree; impve. 2nd pers. sing. / *corresponderse.*
correspondiéndose agreeing; pres. part. / *corresponderse.*
córrete (you) slip through; impve. 2nd pers. sing. / *correrse.*
corretear to run around or to chase. reg.
corriéndose slipping through; pres. part. / *correrse.*

corrige 1. he (she/it) corrects; pres. ind. 3rd pers. sing. / *corregir.* 2. (you) correct; impve. 2nd pers. sing.
corrigen they correct; pres. ind. 3rd pers. pl. / *corregir.*
corriges you correct; pres. ind. 2nd pers. sing. / *corregir.*
corrígete (you) mend your ways; impve. 2nd pers. sing. / *corregirse.*
corrigiendo correcting; pres. part. / *corregir.*
corrigiéndose mending one's ways; pres. part. / *corregirse.*
corrigiera 1. that I might correct; imp. subj. 1st pers. sing. / *corregir.* 2. that he (she/it) might correct; imp. subj. 3rd pers. sing.
corrigierais that you (all) might correct; imp. subj. 2nd pers pl. / *corregir.*
corrigiéramos that we might correct; imp. subj. 1st pers. pl. / *corregir.*
corrigieran that they might correct; imp. subj. 3rd pers. pl. / *corregir.*
corrigieras that you might correct; imp. subj. 2nd pers. sing. / *corregir.*
corrigieron they corrected; past 3rd pers. pl. / *corregir.*
corrigiese 1. that I might correct; imp. subj. 1st pers. sing. / *corregir.* 2. that he (she/it) might correct; imp. subj. 3rd pers. sing.
corrigieseis that you (all) might correct; imp. subj. 2nd pers pl. / *corregir.*
corrigiésemos that we might correct; imp. subj. 1st pers. pl. / *corregir.*
corrigiesen that they might correct; imp. subj. 3rd pers. pl. / *corregir.*
corrigieses that you might correct; imp. subj. 2nd pers. sing. / *corregir.*
corrigió he (she/it) corrected; past 3rd pers. sing. / *corregir.*
corrija 1. that I may correct; pres. subj. 1st pers. sing. / *corregir.* 2. that he (she/it) may correct; pres. subj. 3rd pers. sing. 3. let him (her/it) correct; impve. 3rd pers. sing.
corrijáis that you (all) may correct; pres. subj. 2nd pers. pl. / *corregir.*
corrijámonos let us mend our way; impve. 1st pers. pl. / *corregirse.*
corrijamos 1. that we may correct; pres. subj. 1st pers. pl. / *corregir.* 2. let us correct; impve. 1st pers. pl.
corrijan 1. that they may correct; pres. subj. 3rd pers. pl. / *corregir.* 2. let them correct; impve. 3rd pers. pl.
corríjanse let them mend their way; impve. 3rd pers. pl. / *corregirse.*
corrijas that you may correct; pres. subj. 2nd pers. sing. / *corregir.*
corríjase let him (her/it) mend his (her/it's) way; impve. 3rd pers. sing. / *corregirse.*
corrijo I correct; pres. ind. 1st pers. sing. / *corregir.*
corroborar to corroborate. reg.
corroer to corrode. irr.
corroído corroded; past part. / *corroer.*

corrompámonos let us rot; impve. 1st pers. pl. / *corromperse*.

corrómpanse let them rot; impve. 3rd pers. pl. / *corromperse*.

corrómpase let him (her/it) rot; impve. 3rd pers. sing. / *corromperse*.

corrompeos (you all) rot; impve. 2nd pers. pl. / *corromperse*.

corromper to corrupt. reg. except pp.

corromperse to rot. reg.

corrómpete (you) rot; impve. 2nd pers. sing. / *corromperse*.

corrompiéndose rotting; pres. part. / *corromperse*.

corroto corrupted; past part. / *corromper*.

corroyendo corroding; pres. part. / *corroer*.

corroyera that it might corrode; imp. subj. 3rd pers. sing. / *corroer*.

corroyeran that they might corrode; imp. subj. 3rd pers. pl. / *corroer*.

corroyeron they corroded; past 3rd pers. pl. / *corroer*.

corroyese that it might corrode; imp. subj. 3rd pers. sing. / *corroer*.

corroyesen that they might corrode; imp. subj. 3rd pers. pl. / *corroer*.

corroyó it corroded; past 3rd pers. sing. / *corroer*.

corsear to privateer. reg.

cortándose becoming speechless; pres. part. / *cortarse*.

cortaos (you all) become speechless; impve. 2nd pers. pl. / *cortarse*.

cortar to cut. reg.

cortarse to become speechless. reg.

córtate (you) become speechless; impve. 2nd pers. sing. / *cortarse*.

cortejar to court or to woo. reg.

cortémonos let us become speechless; impve. 1st pers. pl. / *cortarse*.

córtense let them become speechless; impve. 3rd pers. pl. / *cortarse*.

córtese let him (her/it) become speechless; impve. 3rd pers. sing. / *cortarse*.

coruscar to glow or to shine. irr.

corusque 1. that it may glow; pres. subj. 3rd pers. sing. / *coruscar*. 2. let it glow; impve. 3rd pers. sing.

corusquen 1. that they may glow; pres. subj. 3rd pers. pl. / *coruscar*. 2. let them glow; impve. 3rd pers. pl.

coscándose shrugging; pres. part. / *coscarse*.

coscaos (you all) shrug; impve. 2nd pers. pl. / *coscarse*.

coscarse to shrug. reg.

cóscate (you) shrug; impve. 2nd pers. sing. / *coscarse*.

coscémonos let us shrug; impve. 1st pers. pl. / *coscarse*.

cóscense let them shrug; impve. 3rd pers. pl. / *coscarse*.

cóscese let him (her/it) shrug; impve. 3rd pers. sing. / *coscarse*.

cosechar to reap or harvest. reg.

coser to sew. reg.

cosquillar to tickle. reg.

cosquillear to tickle. reg.

costar to cost. irr.

costear to pay the cost of or to navigate along the coast. reg.

cotejar to compare or to collate. reg.

cotice 1. that I may quote (prices); pres. subj. 1st pers. sing. / *cotizar*. 2. that he (she/it) may quote (prices); pres. subj. 3rd pers. sing. 3. let him (her/it) quote (prices); impve. 3rd pers. sing.

coticé I quoted (prices); past 1st pers. sing. / *cotizar*.

coticéis that you (all) may quote (prices); pres. subj. 2nd pers. pl. / *cotizar*.

coticémonos let us be esteemed; impve. 1st pers. pl. / *cotizarse*.

coticemos 1. that we may quote (prices); pres. subj. 1st pers. pl. / *cotizar*. 2. let us quote (prices); impve. 1st pers. pl.

coticen 1. that they may quote (prices); pres. subj. 3rd pers. pl. / *cotizar*. 2. let them quote (prices); impve. 3rd pers. pl.

cotícense let them be esteemed; impve. 3rd pers. pl. / *cotizarse*.

cotices that you may quote (prices); pres. subj. 2nd pers. sing. / *cotizar*.

cotícese let him (her/it) be esteemed; impve. 3rd pers. sing. / *cotizarse*.

cotizándose being esteemed; pres. part. / *cotizarse*.

cotizaos (you all) be esteemed; impve. 2nd pers. pl. / *cotizarse*.

cotizar to quote (prices) or to prorate or to pay dues. irr.

cotizarse to be esteemed. irr.

cotízate (you) be esteemed; impve. 2nd pers. sing. / *cotizarse*.

cotorrear to chatter or to gossip. reg.

cozáis that I may boil; pres. subj. 1st pers. sing. / *cocer*.

cozámonos let us suffer intensely; impve. 1st pers. pl. / *cocerse*.

cozamos 1. that we may boil; pres. subj. 1st pers. pl. / *cocer*. 2. let us boil; impve. 1st pers. pl.

craquear to crack. reg.

crascitar to caw. reg.

creámonos let us believe ourselves to be; impve. 1st pers. pl. / *creerse*.

créanse let them believe themselves to be; impve. 3rd pers. pl. / *creerse*.

crear to create. reg.

créase let him (her/it) believe himself (herself/itself) to be; impve. 3rd pers. sing. / *creerse*.

creceos (you all) swell with importance; impve. 2nd pers. pl. / *crecerse*.

crecer to grow. reg.

crecerse to swell with importance. irr.

crécete (you) swell with importance; impve. 2nd pers. sing. / *crecerse*.

creciéndose swelling with importance; pres. part. / *crecerse*.

creeos (you all) believe yourselves to be; impve. 2nd pers. pl. / *creerse*.

creer to believe or to think. irr.

creerse to believe oneself to be. irr.

créete (you) believe yourself to be; impve. 2nd pers. sing. / *creerse*.

creí I believed; past 1st pers. sing. / *creer*.

creído believed; past part. / *creer*.

creímos we believed; past 1st pers. pl. / *creer*.

creíste you believed; past 2nd pers. sing. / *creer*.

creísteis you (all) believed; past 2nd pers. pl. / *creer*.

crepitar to crackle or to creak. reg.

creyendo believing; pres. part. / *creer*.

creyéndose believing oneself to be; pres. part. / *creerse*.

creyera 1. that I might believe; imp. subj. 1st pers. sing. / *creer*. 2. that he (she/it) might believe; imp. subj. 3rd pers. sing.

creyerais that you (all) might believe; imp. subj. 2nd pers pl. / *creer*.

creyéramos that we might believe; imp. subj. 1st pers. pl. / *creer*.

creyeran that they might believe; imp. subj. 3rd pers. pl. / *creer*.

creyeras that you might believe; imp. subj. 2nd pers. sing. / *creer*.

creyeron they believed; past 3rd pers. pl. / *creer*.

creyese 1. that I might believe; imp. subj. 1st pers. sing. / *creer*. 2. that he (she/it) might blieve; imp. subj. 3rd pers. sing.

creyeseis that you (all) might believe; imp. subj. 2nd pers pl. / *creer*.

creyésemos that we might believe; imp. subj. 1st pers. pl. / *creer*.

creyesen that they might believe; imp. subj. 3rd pers. pl. / *creer*.

creyeses that you might believe; imp. subj. 2nd pers. sing. / *creer*.

creyó he (she/it) believed; past 3rd pers. sing. / *creer*.

crezca 1. that I may grow; pres. subj. 1st pers. sing. / *crecer*. 2. that he (she/it) may grow; pres. subj. 3rd pers. sing. 3. let him (her/it) grow; impve. 3rd pers. sing.

crezcáis that you (all) may grow; pres. subj. 2nd pers. pl. / *crecer*.

crezcámonos let us swell with importance; impve. 1st pers. pl. / *crecerse*.

crezcamos 1. that I may grow; pres. subj. 1st pers. sing. / *crecer*. 2. let us grow; impve. 1st pers. pl.

crezcan 1. that they may grow; pres. subj. 3rd pers. pl. / *crecer*. 2. let them grow; impve. 3rd pers. pl.

crézcanse let them swell with importance; impve. 3rd pers. pl. / *crecerse*.

crezcas that you may grow; pres. subj. 2nd pers. sing. / *crecer*.

crézcase let him (her/it) swell with importance; impve. 3rd pers. sing. / *crecerse*.

crezco I grow; pres. ind. 1st pers. sing. / *crecer*.

cría 1. he (she/it) breeds; pres. ind. 3rd pers. sing. / *criar* 2. (you) breed; impve. 2nd pers. sing.

crían they breed; pres. ind. 3rd pers. pl. / *criar*.

criándose growing up; pres. part. / *criarse*.

criaos (you all) grow up; impve. 2nd pers. pl. / *criarse*.

criar to breed or to rear. irr.

criarse to grow up. irr.

crías you breed; pres.ind. 2nd pers. sing. / *criar*.

críate (you) grow up; impve. 2nd pers. sing. / *criarse*.

cribar to sift. reg.

críe 1. that I may breed; pres. subj. 1st pers. sing. / *criar*. 2. that he (she/it) may breed; pres. subj. 3rd pers. sing. 3. let him (her/it) breed; impve. 3rd pers. sing.

criémonos let us grow up; impve. 1st pers. pl. / *criarse*.

críen 1. that they may breed; pres. subj. 3rd pers. pl. / *criar*. 2. let them breed; impve. 3rd pers. pl.

críense let them grow up; impve. 3rd pers. pl. / *criarse*.

críes that you may breed; pres. subj. 2nd pers. sing. / *criar*.

críese let him (her/it) grow up; impve. 3rd pers. sing. / *criarse*.

criminar to incriminate or to censure. reg.

crío I breed; pres. ind. 1st pers. sing. / *criar*.

crispándose twitching; pres. part. / *crisparse*.

crispaos (you all) twitch; impve. 2nd pers. pl. / *crisparse*.

crispar to contract (as muscles). reg.

crisparse to twitch. reg.

críspate (you) twitch; impve. 2nd pers. sing. / *crisparse*.

crispémonos let us twitch; impve. 1st pers. pl. / *crisparse*.

críspense let them twitch; impve. 3rd pers. pl. / *crisparse*.

críspese let him (her/it) twitch; impve. 3rd pers. sing. / *crisparse*.

cristalice 1. that I may crystallize; pres. subj. 1st pers. sing. / *cristalizar*. 2. that he (she/it) may crystallize; pres. subj. 3rd pers. sing. 3. let him (her/it) crystallize; impve. 3rd pers. sing.

cristalicé I crystallized; past 1st pers. sing. / *cristalizar*.

cristalicéis that you (all) may crystallize; pres. subj. 2nd pers. pl. / *cristalizar*.

cristalicemos 1. that we may crystallize; pres. subj. 1st pers. pl. / *cristalizar*. 2. let us crystallize; impve. 1st pers. pl.

cristalicen 1. that they may crystallize; pres. subj. 3rd pers. pl. / *cristalizar*. 2. let them crystallize; impve. 3rd pers. pl.

cristalices that you may crystallize; pres. subj. 2nd pers. sing. / *cristalizar*.

cristalizar to crystallize. irr.

cristianar to christen. reg.

cristianice 1. that I may christianize; pres. subj. 1st pers. sing. / *cristianizar*. 2. that he (she/it) may christianize; pres. subj. 3rd pers. sing. 3. let him (her/it) christianize; impve. 3rd pers. sing.

cristianicé I christianized; past 1st pers. sing. / *cristianizar*.

cristianicéis that you (all) may christianize; pres. subj. 2nd pers. pl. / *cristianizar*.

cristianicemos 1. that we may christianize; pres. subj. 1st pers. pl. / *cristianizar*. 2. let us christianize; impve. 1st pers. pl.

cristianicen 1. that they may christianize; pres. subj. 3rd pers. pl. / *cristianizar*. 2. let them christianize; impve. 3rd pers. pl.

cristianices that you may christianize; pres. subj. 2nd pers. sing. / *cristianizar*.

cristianizar to christianize. irr.

criticar to criticize. irr.

critique 1. that I may criticize; pres. subj. 1st pers. sing. / *criticar*. 2. that he (she/it) may criticize; pres. subj. 3rd pers. sing. 3. let him (her/it) criticize; impve. 3rd pers. sing.

critiqué I criticized; past 1st pers. sing. / *criticar*.

critiquéis that you (all) may criticize; pres. subj. 2nd pers. pl. / *criticar*.

critiquemos 1. that we may criticize; pres. subj. 1st pers. pl. / *criticar*. 2. let us criticize; impve. 1st pers. pl.

critiquen 1. that they may criticize; pres. subj. 3rd pers. pl. / *criticar* 2. let them criticize; impve. 3rd pers. pl.

critiques that you may criticize; pres. subj. 2nd pers. sing. / *criticar*.

critiquice 1. that I may be over critical; pres. subj. 1st pers. sing. / *critiquizar*. 2. that he (she/it) may be over critical; pres. subj. 3rd pers. sing. 3. let him (her/it) be over critical; impve. 3rd pers. sing.

critiquicé I was over critical; past 1st pers. sing. / *critiquizar*.

critiquicéis that you (all) may be over critical; pres. subj. 2nd pers. pl. / *critiquizar*.

critiquicemos 1. that we may be over critical; pres. subj. 1st pers. pl. / *critiquizar*. 2. let us be over critical; impve. 1st pers. pl.

critiquicen 1. that they may be over critical; pres. subj. 3rd pers. pl. / *critiquizar*. 2. let them be over critical; impve. 3rd pers. pl.

critiquices that you may be over critical; pres. subj. 2nd pers. sing. / *critiquizar*.

critiquizar to be over critical. irr.

croar to croak. reg.

cromar to chrome plate. reg.

cronometrar to time (sports). reg.

cruce 1. that I may cross; pres. subj. 1st pers. sing. / *cruzar*. 2. that he (she/it) may cross; pres. subj. 3rd pers. sing. 3. let him (her/it) cross; impve. 3rd pers. sing.

crucé I crossed; past 1st pers. sing. / *cruzar*.

crucéis that you (all) may cross; pres. subj. 2nd pers. pl. / *cruzar*.

crucémonos let us cross paths; impve. 1st pers. pl. / *cruzarse*.

crucemos 1. that we may cross; pres. subj. 1st pers. pl. / *cruzar*. 2. let us cross; impve. 1st pers. pl.

crucen 1. that they may cross; pres. subj. 3rd pers. pl. / *cruzar*. 2. let them cross; impve. 3rd pers. pl.

crúcense let them cross paths; impve. 3rd pers. pl. / *cruzarse*.

cruces that you may cross; pres. subj. 2nd pers. sing. / *cruzar*.

crúcese let him (her/it) cross paths; impve. 3rd pers. sing. / *cruzarse*.

crucificar to crucify. irr.

crucifique 1. that I may crucify; pres. subj. 1st pers. sing. / *crucificar*. 2. that he (she/it) may crucify; pres. subj. 3rd pers. sing. 3. let him (her/it) crucify; impve. 3rd pers. sing.

crucifiqué I crucified; past 1st pers. sing. / *crucificar*.

crucifiquéis that you (all) may crucify; pres. subj. 2nd pers. pl. / *crucificar*.

crucifiquemos 1. that we may crucify; pres. subj. 1st pers. pl. / *crucificar*. 2. let us crucify; impve. 1st pers. pl.

crucifiquen 1. that they may crucify; pres. subj. 3rd pers. pl. / *crucificar* 2. let them crucify; impve. 3rd pers. pl.

crucifiques that you may crucify; pres. subj. 2nd pers. sing. / *crucificar*.

crujir to creak or to gnash teeth. reg.

cruzándose crossing paths; pres. part. / *cruzarse*.

cruzaos (you all) cross paths; impve. 2nd pers. pl. / *cruzarse*.

cruzar to cross or to cruise. irr.

cruzarse to cross paths. irr.

crúzate (you) cross paths; impve. 2nd pers. sing. / *cruzarse*.

cuadrándose squaring one's shoulders; pres. part. / *cuadrarse*.

cuadraos (you all) square your shoulders; impve. 2nd pers. pl. / *cuadrarse*.

cuadrar to square or to fit. reg. ar-conju.

cuadrarse to square one's shoulders. reg. ar-conju.

cuádrate (you) square your shoulders; impve. 2nd pers. sing. / *cuadrarse*.

cuadrémonos let us square our shoulders; impve. 1st pers. pl. / *cuadrarse*.

cuádrense let them square their shoulders; impve. 3rd pers. pl. / *cuadrarse*.

cuádrese let him (her/it) square his (her/it's) shoulders; impve. 3rd pers. sing. / *cuadrarse*.

cuadricular to mark off in squares. reg. ar-conju.

cuadruplicándose quadrupling; pres. part. / *cuadruplicarse*.

cuadruplicaos (you all) quadruple; impve. 2nd pers. pl. / *cuadruplicarse*.

cuadruplicar to quadruple. irr.

cuadruplicarse to quadruple. irr.

cuadruplícate (you) quadruple; impve. 2nd pers. sing. / *cuadruplicarse*.

cuadruplique 1. that I may quadruple; pres. subj. 1st pers. sing. / *cuadruplicar*. 2. that he (she/it) may quadruple; pres. subj. 3rd pers. sing. 3. let him (her/it) quadruple; impve. 3rd pers. sing.

cuadrupliqué I quadrupled; past 1st pers. sing. / *cuadruplicar.*

cuadrupliquéis that you (all) may quadruple; pres. subj. 2nd pers. pl. / *cuadruplicar.*

cuadrupliquémonos let us quadruple; impve. 1st pers. pl. / *cuadruplicarse.*

cuadrupliquemos 1. that we may quadruple; pres. subj. 1st pers. pl. / *cuadruplicar.* 2. let us quadruple; impve. 1st pers. pl.

cuadrupliquen 1. that they may quadruple; pres. subj. 3rd pers. pl. / *cuadruplicar.* 2. let them quadruple: impve. 3rd pers. pl.

cuadruplíquense let them quadruple; impve. 3rd pers. pl. / *cuadruplicarse.*

cuadrupliques that you may quadruple; pres. subj. 2nd pers. sing. / *cuadruplicar.*

cuadruplíquese let him (her/it) quadruple; impve. 3rd pers. sing. / *cuadruplicarse.*

cuajándose curdling; pres. part. / *cuajarse.*

cuajar to coagulate or to jell. reg. ar-conju.

cuajarse to curdle or to become crowded. reg. ar-conju.

cuájense let them curdle; impve. 3rd pers. pl. / *cuajarse.*

cuájese let it curdle; impve. 3rd pers. sing. / *cuajarse.*

cuantía 1. he (she/it) appraises; pres. ind. 3rd pers. sing. / *cuantiar.* 2. (you) appraise; impve. 2nd pers. sing.

cuantían they appraise; pres. ind. 3rd pers. pl. / *cuantiar.*

cuantiar to appraise. irr.

cuantías you appraise; pres. ind. 2nd pers. sing. / *cuantiar.*

cuantíe 1. that I may appraise; pres. subj. 1st pers. sing. / *cuantiar.* 2. that he (she/it) may appraise; pres. subj. 3rd pers. sing. 3. let him (her/it) appraise; impve. 3rd pers. sing.

cuantíen 1. that they may appraise; pres. subj. 3rd pers. pl. / *cuantiar.* 2. let them appraise; impve. 3rd pers. pl.

cuantíes that you may appraise; pres. subj. 2nd pers. sing. / *cuantiar.*

cuantío I appraise; pres. ind. 1st pers. sing. / *cuantiar.*

cuarteándose cracking; pres. part. / *cuartearse.*

cuarteaos (you all) crack; impve. 2nd pers. pl. / *cuartearse.*

cuartear to quarter or to dodge. reg.

cuartearse to crack or split. reg.

cuartéate (you) crack; impve 2nd pers. sing. / *cuartearse.*

cuarteémonos let us crack; impve. 1st pers. pl. / *cuartearse.*

cuartéense let them crack; impve. 3rd pers. pl. / *cuartearse.*

cuartéese let him (her/it) crack; impve. 3rd pers. sing. / *cuartearse.*

cubicar to determine the volume of. irr.

cubierto covered; past part. / *cubrir.*

cubique 1. that I may determine the volume of; pres. subj. 1st pers. sing. / *cubicar.* 2. that he (she/it) may determine the volume of; pres. subj. 3rd pers. sing. 3. let him (her/it) determine the volume of; impve. 3rd pers. sing.

cubiqué I determined the volume of; past 1st pers. sing. / *cubicar.*

cubiquéis that you (all) may determine the volume of; pres. subj. 2nd pers. pl. / *cubicar.*

cubiquemos 1. that we may determine the volume of; pres. subj. 1st pers. pl. / *cubicar.* 2. let us determine the volume of; impve. 1st pers. pl.

cubiquen 1. that they may determine the volume of; pres. subj. 3rd pers. pl. / *cubicar.* 2. let them determine the volume of; impve. 3rd pers. pl.

cubiques that you may determine the volume of; pres. subj. 2nd pers. sing. / *cubicar.*

cubrámonos let us put on our hats; impve. 1st pers. pl. / *cubrirse.*

cúbranse let them put on their hats; impve. 3rd pers. pl. / *cubrirse.*

cúbrase let him (her) put on his (her) hat; impve. 3rd pers. sing. / *cubrirse.*

cúbrete (you) put on your hat; impve. 2nd pers. sing. / *cubrirse.*

cubriéndose putting on one's hat; pres. part. / *cubrirse.*

cubríos (you all) put on your hats; impve. 2nd pers. pl. / *cubrirse.*

cubrir to cover or to protect. reg. except pp.

cubrirse to put on one's hat. reg.

cucar to wink. reg.

cucharear to spoon out. reg.

cuchichear to whisper. reg.

cuchuchear to whisper. reg.

cuece 1. he (she/it) boils; pres. ind. 3rd pers. sing. / *cocer.* 2. (you) boil; impve. 2nd pers. sing.

cuecen they boil; pres. ind. 3rd pers. pl. / *cocer.*

cueces you boil; pres. ind. 2nd pers. sing. / *cocer.*

cuécete (you) suffer intensley; impve. 2nd pers. sing. / *cocerse.*

cuela 1. he (she/it) strains; pres. ind. 3rd pers. sing. / *colar.* 2. (you) strain; impve. 2nd pers. sing.

cuelan they strain; pres. ind. 3rd pers. pl. / *colar.*

cuelas you strain; pres. ind. 2nd pers. sing. / *colar.*

cuélate (you) slip in; impve. 2nd pers. sing. / *colarse.*

cuele 1. that I may strain; pres. subj. 1st pers. sing. / *colar.* 2. that he (she/it) may strain; pres. subj. 3rd pers. sing. 3. let him (her/it) strain; impve. 3rd pers. sing.

cuelen 1. that they may strain; pres. subj. 3rd pers. pl. / *colar.* 2. let them strain; impve. 3rd pers. pl.

cuélense let them slip in; impve. 3rd pers. pl. / *colarse.*

cueles that you may strain; pres. subj. 2nd pers. sing. / *colar.*

cuélese let him (her/it) slip in; impve. 3rd pers. sing. / *colarse.*

cuelga 1. he (she/it) hangs; pres. ind. 3rd pers. sing. / *colgar.* 2. (you) hang; impve. 2nd pers. sing.

cuelgan they hang; pres. ind. 3rd pers. pl. / *colgar*.

cuelgas you hang; pres. ind. 2nd pers. sing. / *colgar*.

cuelgo I hang; pres. ind. 1st pers. sing. / *colgar*.

cuelgue 1. that I may hang; pres. subj. 1st pers. sing. / *colgar*. 2. that he (she/it) may hang; pres. subj. 3rd pers. sing. 3. let him (her/it) hang; impve. 3rd pers. sing.

cuelguen 1. that they may hang; pres. subj. 3rd pers. pl. / *colgar*. 2. let them hang; impve. 3rd pers. pl.

cuelgues that you may hang; pres. subj. 2nd pers. sing. / *colgar*.

cuelo I strain; pres. ind. 1st pers. sing. / *colar*.

cuenta 1. he (she/it) counts; pres. ind. 3rd pers. sing. / *contar*. 2. (you) count; impve. 2nd pers. sing.

cuentan they count; pres. ind. 3rd pers. pl. / *contar*.

cuentas you count; pres. ind. 2nd pers. sing. / *contar*.

cuente 1. that I may count; pres. subj. 1st pers. sing. / *contar*. 2. that he (she/it) may count; pres. subj. 3rd pers. sing. 3. let him (her/it) count; impve. 3rd pers. sing.

cuenten 1. that they may count; pres. subj. 3rd pers. pl. / *contar*. 2. let them count; impve. 3rd pers. pl.

cuentes that you may count; pres. subj. 2nd pers. sing. / *contar*.

cuento I count; pres. ind. 1st pers. sing. / *contar*.

cuerear to whip. reg.

cuerpear to dodge. reg.

cuesta 1. he (she/it) costs; pres. ind. 3rd pers. sing. / *costar*. 2. (you) cost; impve. 2nd pers. sing.

cuestan they cost; pres. ind. 3rd pers. pl. / *costar*.

cuestas you cost; pres. ind. 2nd pers. sing. / *costar*.

cueste 1. that I may cost; pres. subj. 1st pers. sing. / *costar*. 2. that he (she/it) may cost; pres. subj. 3rd pers. sing. 3. let him (her/it) cost; impve. 3rd pers. sing.

cuesten 1. that they may cost; pres. subj. 3rd pers. pl. / *costar*. 2. let them cost; impve. 3rd pers. pl.

cuestes that you may cost; pres. subj. 2nd pers. sing. / *costar*.

cuestionar to question or to dispute. reg.

cuesto I cost; pres. ind. 1st pers. sing. / *costar*.

cueza 1. that I may boil; pres. subj. 1st pers. sing. / *cocer*. 2. that he (she/it) may boil; pres. subj. 3rd pers. sing. 3. let him (her/it) boil; impve. 3rd pers. sing.

cuezan 1. that they may boil; pres. subj. 3rd pers. pl. / *cocer*. 2. let them boil; impve. 3rd pers. pl.

cuézanse let them suffer intensley; impve. 3rd pers. pl. / *cocerse*.

cuezas that you may boil; pres. subj. 2nd pers. sing. / *cocer*.

cuézase let him (her/it) suffer intensley; impve. 3rd pers. sing. / *cocerse*.

cuezo I boil; pres. ind. 1st pers. sing. / *cocer*.

cuidándose looking after oneself; pres. part. / *cuidarse*.

cuidaos (you all) look after yourselves; impve. 2nd pers. pl. / *cuidarse*.

cuidar to take care of. reg.

cuidarse to look after oneself. reg.

cuídate (you) look after yourself; impve. 2nd pers. sing. / *cuidarse*.

cuidémonos let us look after ourselves; impve. 1st pers. pl. / *cuidarse*.

cuídense let them look after themselves; impve. 3rd pers. pl. / *cuidarse*.

cuídese let him (her/it) look after himself (herself/itself); impve. 3rd pers. sing. / *cuidarse*.

culebrear to wriggle or zigzag. reg.

culminar to culminate. reg.

culpándose taking the blame; pres. part. / *culparse*.

culpaos (you all) take the blame; impve. 2nd pers. pl. / *culparse*.

culpar to blame or to accuse. reg.

culparse to take the blame. reg.

cúlpate (you) take the blame; impve. 2nd pers. sing. / *culparse*.

culpémonos let us take the blame; impve. 1st pers. pl. / *culparse*.

cúlpense let them take the blame; impve. 3rd pers. pl. / *culparse*.

cúlpese let him (her/it) take the blame; impve. 3rd pers. sing. / *culparse*.

cultivar to cultivate. reg.

culturar to cultivate. reg.

cúmplanse let them come true; impve. 3rd pers. pl. / *cumplirse*.

cúmplase let it come true; impve. 3rd pers. sing. / *cumplirse*.

cumpliéndose coming true; pres. part. / *cumplirse*.

cumplimentar to compliment. reg.

cumplir to fulfil or to fall due. reg.

cumplirse to come true. reg.

cumular to accumulate. reg.

cundir to spread. reg.

cupe I fitted; past 1st pers. sing. / *caber*.

cupiera 1. that I might fit; imp. subj. 1st pers. sing. / *caber*. 2. that he (she/it) might fit; imp. subj. 3rd pers. sing.

cupierais that you (all) might fit; imp. subj. 2nd pers pl. / *caber*.

cupiéramos that we might fit; imp. subj. 1st pers. pl. / *caber*.

cupieran that they might fit; imp. subj. 3rd pers. pl. / *caber*.

cupieras that you might fit; imp. subj. 2nd pers. sing. / *caber*.

cupieron they fitted; past 3rd pers. pl. / *caber*.

cupiese 1. that I might fit; imp. subj. 1st pers. sing. / *caber*. 2. that he (she/it) might fit; imp. subj. 3rd pers. sing.

cupieseis that you (all) might fit; imp. subj. 2nd pers pl. / *caber*.

cupiésemos that we might fit; imp. subj. 1st pers. pl. / *caber*.

cupiesen that they might fit; imp. subj. 3rd pers. pl. / *caber*.

cupieses that you might fit; imp. subj. 2nd pers. sing. / *caber*

cupimos we fitted; past 1st pers. pl. / *caber*.

cupiste you fitted; past 2nd pers. sing. / *caber.*
cupisteis you (all) fitted; past 2nd pers. pl. / *caber.*
cupo he (she/it) fitted; past 3rd pers. sing. / *caber.*
curándose undergoing treatment; pres. part. / *curarse.*
curaos (you all) undergo treatment; impve. 2nd pers. pl. / *curarse.*
curar to cure or to heal. reg.
curarse to undergo treatment. reg.
cúrate (you) undergo treatment; impve. 2nd pers. sing. / *curarse.*
curémonos let us undergo treatment; impve. 1st pers. pl. / *curarse.*
cúrense let them undergo treatment; impve. 3rd pers. pl. / *curarse.*
cúrese let him (her/it) undergo treatment; impve. 3rd pers. sing. / *curarse.*
curiosear to snoop or to pry. reg.
cursar to frequent or to study. reg.
curtámonos let us get sunburned; impve. 1st pers. pl. / *curtirse.*
cúrtanse let them get sunburned; impve. 3rd pers. pl. / *curtirse.*
cúrtase let him (her/it) get sunburned; impve. 3rd pers. sing. / *curtirse.*
cúrtete (you) get sunburned; impve. 2nd pers. sing. / *curtirse.*
curtiéndose getting sunburned; pres. part. / *curtirse.*
curtíos (you all) get sunburned; impve. 2nd pers. pl. / *curtirse.*
curtir to tan or to harden. reg.
curtirse to get sunburned. reg.
curvar to curve or to bend. reg.
curvear to curve. reg.
cusir to sew poorly. reg.
custodiar to guard. reg.
cutir to knock. reg.

CH

chacolotear to clatter. reg.
chacotear to frolic or to banter. reg.
chacharear to chatter. reg.
chafallar to patch up or to botch. reg.
chafar to flatten or to muss. reg.
chafarrinar to blotch or to taint. reg.
chaflanar to bevel. reg.
chalándose being crazy; pres. part. / *chalarse.*
chalanear to trade shrewdly. reg.
chalaos (you all) be crazy; impve. 2nd pers. pl. / *chalarse.*
chalar to drive crazy. reg.
chalarse to be crazy. reg.
chálate (you) be crazy; impve. 2nd pers. sing. / *chalarse.*
chalémonos let us be crazy; impve. 1st pers. pl. / *chalarse.*
chálense let them be crazy; impve. 3rd pers. pl. / *chalarse.*

chálese let him (her/it) be crazy; impve. 3rd pers. sing. / *chalarse.*
chamar to swap. reg.
chamorrar to crop (hair). reg.
champurrar to mix (drinks). reg.
champurrear to mix (drinks). reg.
chamuscándose getting seared; pres. part. / *chamuscarse.*
chamuscaos (you all) get seared; impve. 2nd pers. pl. / *chamuscarse.*
chamuscar to scortch. irr.
chamuscarse to get seared. irr.
chamúscate (you) get seared; impve. 2nd pers. sing. / *chamuscarse.*
chamusque 1. that I may scortch; pres. subj. 1st pers. sing. / *chamuscar.* 2. that he (she/it) may scortch; pres. subj. 3rd pers. sing. 3. let him (her/it) scortch; impve. 3rd pers. sing.
chamusqué I scortched; past 1st pers. sing. / *chamuscar.*
chamusquéis that you (all) may scortch; pres. subj. 2nd pers. pl. / *chamuscar.*
chamusquémonos let us get seared; impve. 1st pers. pl. / *chamuscarse.*
chamusquemos 1. that we may scortch; pres. subj. 1st pers. pl. / *chamuscar.* 2. let us scortch; impve. 1st pers. pl.
chamusquen 1. that they may scortch; pres. subj. 3rd pers. pl. / *chamuscar.* 2. let them scortch; impve. 3rd pers. pl.
chamúsquense let them get seared; impve. 3rd pers. pl. / *chamuscarse.*
chamusques that you may scortch; pres. subj. 2nd pers. sing. / *chamuscar.*
chamúsquese let him (her/it) get seared; impve. 3rd pers. sing. / *chamuscarse.*
chanceándose jesting; pres. part. / *chancearse.*
chanceaos (you all) jest; impve. 2nd pers. pl. / *chancearse.*
chancear to joke or to fool. reg.
chancearse to jest. reg..
chancéate (you) jest; impve. 2nd pers. sing. / *chancearse.*
chanceémonos let us jest; impve. 1st pers. pl. / *chancearse.*
chancéense let them jest; impve. 3rd pers. pl. / *chancearse.*
chancéese let him (her/it) jest; impve. 3rd pers. sing. / *chancearse.*
chantajear to blackmail. reg.
chantándose standing pat (cards); pres. part. / *chantarse.*
chantaos (you all) stand pat (cards); impve. 2nd pers. pl. / *chantarse.*
chantar to put on or to tell to someone's face. reg.
chantarse to stand pat (cards). reg.
chántate (you) stand pat (cards); impve. 2nd pers. sing. / *chantarse.*
chantémonos let us stand pat (cards); impve. 1st pers. pl. / *chantarse.*

chántense let them stand pat (cards); impve. 3rd pers. pl. / *chantarse.*

chántese let him (her/it) stand pat (cards); impve. 3rd pers. sing. / *chantarse.*

chapalear to splash or to paddle. reg.

chapar to plate or coat. reg.

chaparrear to rain heavily. reg.

chapeándose padding one's nest; pres. part. / *chapearse.*

chapeaos (you all) pad your nest; impve. 2nd pers. pl. / *chapearse.*

chapear to plate or veneer. reg.

chapearse to pad one's nest. reg.

chapéate (you) pad your nest; impve. 2nd pers. sing. / *chapearse.*

chapeémonos let us pad our nest; impve. 1st pers. pl. / *chapearse.*

chapéense let them pad their nest; impve. 3rd pers. pl. / *chapearse.*

chapéese let him (her/it) pad his (her/it's) nest; impve. 3rd pers. sing. / *chapearse.*

chapotear to sponge down or to moisten. reg.

chapuce 1. that I may duck; pres. subj. 1st pers. sing. / *chapuzar.* 2. that he (she/it) may duck; pres. subj. 3rd pers. sing. 3. let him (her/it) duck; impve. 3rd pers. sing.

chapucé I ducked; past 1st pers. sing. / *chapuzar.*

chapucear to bungle or to botch. reg.

chapucéis that you (all) may duck; pres. subj. 2nd pers. pl. / *chapuzar.*

chapucemos 1. that we may duck; pres. subj. 1st pers. pl. / *chapuzar.* 2. let us duck; impve. 1st pers. pl.

chapucen 1. that they may duck; pres. subj. 3rd pers. pl. / *chapuzar.* 2. let them duck; impve. 3rd pers. pl.

chapuces that you may duck; pres. subj. 2nd pers. sing. / *chapuzar.*

chapurrar to speak brokenly or to jabber. reg.

chapurrear to speak badly or to mix (drinks). reg.

chapuzar to duck or to dive. irr.

chaquetear to turn tail. reg.

charlar to chatter. reg.

charolar to varnish or to polish. reg.

chascar to click (tongue) or to chew noisily. irr.

chasque 1. that I may click (tongue); pres. subj. 1st pers. sing. / *chascar.* 2. that he (she/it) may click (tongue); pres. subj. 3rd pers. sing. 3. let him (her/it) click (tongue); impve. 3rd pers. sing.

chasqué I clicked (tongue); past 1st pers. sing. / *chascar.*

chasqueándose being disappointed; pres. part. / *chasquearse.*

chasqueaos (you all) be disappointed; impve. 2nd pers. pl. / *chasquearse.*

chasquear to trick or to disappoint. reg.

chasquearse to be disappointed. reg.

chasquéate (you) be disappointed; impve. 2nd pers. sing. / *chasquearse.*

chasquéemonos let us be disappointed; impve. 1st pers. pl. / *chasquearse.*

chasquéense let them be disappointed; impve. 3rd pers. pl. / *chasquearse.*

chasquéese let him (her/it) be disappointed; impve. 3rd pers. sing. / *chasquearse.*

chasquéis that you (all) may click (tongue); pres. subj. 2nd pers. pl. / *chascar.*

chasquemos 1. that we may click (tongue); pres. subj. 1st pers. pl. / *chascar.* 2. let us click (tongue); impve. 1st pers. pl.

chasquen 1. that they may click (tongue); pres. subj. 3rd pers. pl. / *chascar.* 2. let them click (tongue); impve. 3rd pers. pl.

chasques that you may click (tongue); pres. subj. 2nd pers. sing. / *chascar.*

chicoleándose having a good time; pres. part. / *chicolearse.*

chicoleaos (you all) have a good time; impve. 2nd pers. pl. / *chicolearse.*

chicolear to pay compliments. reg.

chicolearse to have a good time. reg.

chicoléate (you) have a good time; impve. 2nd pers. sing. / *chicolearse.*

chicoleémonos let us have a good time; impve. 1st pers. pl. / *chicolearse.*

chicoléense let them have a good time; impve. 3rd pers. pl. / *chicolearse.*

chicoléese let him (her/it) have a good time; impve. 3rd pers. sing. / *chicolearse.*

chicotear to whip or to quarrel. reg.

chichear to hiss. reg.

chiflándose becoming unbalanced; pres. part. / *chiflarse.*

chiflaos (you all) become unbalanced; impve. 2nd pers. pl. / *chiflarse.*

chiflar to whistle at or to jeer. reg.

chiflarse to become unbalanced or crazy. reg.

chíflate (you) become unbalanced; impve. 2nd pers. sing. / *chiflarse.*

chiflémonos let us become unbalanced; impve. 1st pers. pl. / *chiflarse.*

chíflense let them become unbalanced; impve. 3rd pers. pl. / *chiflarse.*

chíflese let him (her/it) become unbalanced; impve. 3rd pers. sing. / *chiflarse.*

chillándose being offended; pres. part. / *chillarse.*

chillaos (you all) be offended; impve. 2nd pers. pl. / *chillarse.*

chillar to scream. reg.

chillarse to be offended. reg.

chíllate (you) be offended; impve. 2nd pers. sing. / *chillarse.*

chillémonos let us be offended; impve. 1st pers. pl. / *chillarse.*

chíllense let them be offended; impve. 3rd pers. pl. / *chillarse.*

chíllese let him (her/it) be offended; impve. 3rd pers. sing. / *chillarse.*

chinchándose getting fed up; pres. part. / *chincharse.*

chinchaos (you all) get fed up; impve. 2nd pers. pl. / *chincharse.*

chinchar to pester. reg.
chincharse to get fed up. reg.
chínchate (you) get fed up; impve. 2nd pers. sing. /
 chincharse.
chinchémonos let us get fed up; impve. 1st pers. pl. /
 chincharse.
chínchense let them get fed up; impve. 3rd pers. pl. /
 chincharse.
chínchese let him (her/it) get fed up; impve. 3rd pers.
 sing. / chincharse.
chiquear to fondle. reg.
chirlar to yell. reg.
chirría 1. he (she/it) squeaks; pres. ind. 3rd pers.
 sing. / chirriar. 2. (you) squeak; impve. 2nd pers.
 sing.
chirrían they squeak; pres. ind. 3rd pers. pl. /
 chirriar.
chirriar to squeak or sizzle. irr.
chirrías you squeak; pres. ind. 2nd pers. sing. /
 chirriar.
chirríe 1. that I may squeak; pres. subj. 1st pers. sing.
 / chirriar. 2. that he (she/it) may squeak; pres. subj.
 3rd pers. sing. 3. let him (her/it) squeak; impve. 3rd
 pers. sing.
chirríen 1. that they may squeak; pres. subj. 3rd pers.
 pl. / chirriar. 2. let them squeak; impve. 3rd pers. pl.
chirríes that you may squeak; pres. subj. 2nd pers.
 sing. / chirriar.
chirrío I squeak; pres. ind. 1st pers. sing. / chirriar.
chismear to gossip or to tattle. reg.
chismorrear to gossip or tattle. reg.
chispear to sparkle. reg.
chisporrotear to sputter or to throw off sparks. reg.
chistar to say a word. reg.
chocar to collide or to surprise. irr.
chocarrear to joke or to clown. reg.
chochear to dote. reg.
choque 1. that I may collide; pres. subj. 1st pers. sing.
 / chocar. 2. that he (she/it) may collide; pres. subj.
 3rd pers. sing. 3. let him (her/it) collide; impve. 3rd
 pers. sing.
choqué I collided; past 1st pers. sing. / chocar.
choquéis that you (all) may collide; pres. subj. 2nd
 pers. pl. / chocar.
choquemos 1. that we may collide; pres. subj. 1st
 pers. pl. / chocar. 2. let us collide; impve. 1st pers. pl.
choquen 1. that they may collide; pres. subj. 3rd pers.
 pl. / chocar. 2. let them collide; impve. 3rd pers. pl.
choques that you may collide; pres. subj. 2nd pers.
 sing. / chocar.
chorrear to drip or to gush. reg.
choteándose teasing; pres. part. / chotearse.
choteaos (you all) tease; impve. 2nd pers. pl. /
 chotearse.
chotear to make fun of. reg.

chotearse to tease. reg.
chotéate (you) tease; impve. 2nd pers. sing. /
 chotearse.
choteémonos let us tease; impve. 1st pers. pl. /
 chotearse.
chotéense let them tease; impve. 3rd pers. pl. /
 chotearse.
chotéese let him (her/it) tease; impve. 3rd pers. sing.
 / chotearse.
chuchear to whisper. reg.
chufándose scoffing; pres. part. / chufarse.
chufaos (you all) scoff; impve. 2nd pers. pl. /
 chufarse.
chufar to mock or to scorn. reg.
chufarse to scoff. reg.
chúfate (you) scoff; impve. 2nd pers. sing. / chufarse.
chufémonos let us scoff; impve. 1st pers. pl. /
 chufarse.
chúfense let them scoff; impve. 3rd pers. pl. /
 chufarse.
chúfese let him (her/it) scoff; impve. 3rd pers. sing. /
 chufarse.
chulear to make fun of kindly. reg.
chupándose shriveling up; pres. part. / chuparse.
chupaos (you all) shrivel up; impve. 2nd pers. pl. /
 chuparse.
chupar to suck or to sip. reg.
chuparse to shrivel up. reg.
chúpate (you) shrivel up; impve. 2nd pers. sing. /
 chuparse.
chupémonos let us shrivel up; impve. 1st pers. pl. /
 chuparse.
chúpense let them shrivel up; impve. 3rd pers. pl. /
 chuparse.
chúpese let him (her/it) shrivel up; impve. 3rd pers.
 sing. / chuparse.
churrasquear to barbecue. reg.
churruscar to frizzle or to burn. irr.
churrusque 1. that I may frizzle; pres. subj. 1st pers.
 sing. / churruscar. 2. that he (she/it) may frizzle;
 pres. subj. 3rd pers. sing. 3. let him (her/it) frizzle;
 impve. 3rd pers. sing.
churrusqué I frizzled; past 1st pers. sing. /
 churruscar.
churrusquéis that you (all) may frizzle; pres. subj.
 2nd pers. pl. / churruscar.
churrusquemos 1. that we may frizzle; pres. subj. 1st
 pers. pl. / churruscar. 2. let us frizzle; impve. 1st
 pers. pl.
churrusquen 1. that they may frizzle; pres. subj. 3rd
 pers. pl. / churruscar. 2. let them frizzle; impve. 3rd
 pers. pl.
churrusques that you may frizzle; pres. subj. 2nd
 pers. sing. / churruscar.
chutar to shoot (in sports). reg.

D

dallar to mow. reg.

damnificar to hurt or to damage. irr.

damnifique 1. that I may hurt; pres. subj. 1st pers. sing. / *damnificar*. 2. that he (she/it) may hurt; pres. subj. 3rd pers. sing. 3. let him (her/it) hurt; impve. 3rd pers. sing.

damnifiqué I hurt; past 1st pers. sing. / *damnificar*.

damnifiquéis that you (all) may hurt; pres. subj. 2nd pers. pl. / *damnificar*.

damnifiquemos 1. that we may hurt; pres. subj. 1st pers. pl. / *damnificar*. 2. let us hurt; impve. 1st pers. pl.

damnifiquen 1. that they may hurt; pres. subj. 3rd pers. pl. / *damnificar*. 2. let us hurt; impve. 3rd pers. pl.

damnifiques that you may hurt; pres. subj. 2nd pers. sing. / *damnificar*.

dance 1. that I may dance; pres. subj. 1st pers. sing. / *danzar*. 2. that he (she/it) may dance; pres. subj. 3rd pers. sing. 3. let him (her/it) dance; impve. 3rd pers. sing.

dancé I danced; past 1st pers. sing. / *danzar*.

dancéis that you (all) may dance; pres. subj. 2nd pers. pl. / *danzar*.

dancemos 1. that we may dance; pres. subj. 1st pers. pl. / *danzar*. 2. let us dance; impve. 1st pers. pl.

dancen 1. that they may dance; pres. subj. 3rd pers. pl. / *danzar*. 2. let them dance; impve. 3rd pers. pl.

dances that you may dance; pres. subj. 2nd pers. sing. / *danzar*.

dándose giving up; pres. part. / *darse*.

danzar to dance. irr.

dañándose spoiling; pres. part. / *dañarse*.

dañaos (you all) spoil; impve. 2nd pers. pl. / *dañarse*.

dañar to damage or to harm. reg.

dañarse to spoil or to rot. reg.

dáñate (you) spoil; impve. 2nd pers. sing. / *dañarse*.

dañémonos let us spoil; impve. 1st pers. pl. / *dañarse*.

dáñense let them spoil; impve. 3rd pers. pl. / *dañarse*.

dáñese let him (her/it) spoil; impve. 3rd pers. sing. / *dañarse*.

daos (you all) give up; impve. 2nd pers. pl. / *darse*.

dar to give or to strike. irr.

darse to give up or to surrender. irr.

datar to date. reg.

date (you) give up; impve. 2nd pers. sing. / *darse*.

dé 1. that I may give; pres. subj. 1st pers. sing. / *dar*. 2. that he (she/it) may give; pres. subj. 3rd pers. sing. 3. let him (her/it) give; impve. 3rd pers. sing.

debatámonos let us struggle; impve. 1st pers. pl. / *debatirse*.

debátanse let them struggle; impve. 3rd pers. pl. / *debatirse*.

debátase let him (her/it) struggle; impve. 3rd pers. sing. / *debatirse*.

debátete (you) struggle; impve. 2nd pers. sing. / *debatirse*.

debatiéndose struggling; pres. part. / *debatirse*.

debatíos (you all) struggle; impve. 2nd pers. pl. / *debatirse*.

debatir to debate. reg.

debatirse to struggle. reg.

debelar to subdue. reg.

deber to owe or to ought. reg.

debilitándose becoming weak; pres. part. / *debilitarse*.

debilitaos (you all) become weak; impve. 2nd pers. pl. / *debilitarse*.

debilitar to debilitate or to weaken. reg.

debilitarse to become weak. reg.

debilítate (you) become weak; impve. 2nd pers. sing. / *debilitarse*.

debilitémonos let us become weak; impve. 1st pers. pl. / *debilitarse*.

debilítense let them become weak; impve. 3rd pers. pl. / *debilitarse*.

debilítese let him (her/it) become weak; impve. 3rd pers. sing. / *debilitarse*.

debitar to debit. reg.

debutar to make a debut or to begin. reg.

decaer to decay or to decline. irr.

decaído decayed; past part. / *decaer*.

decaiga 1. that I may decay; pres. subj. 1st pers. sing. / *decaer*. 2. that he (she/it) may decay; pres. subj. 3rd pers. sing. 3. let him (her/it) decay; impve. 3rd pers. sing.

decaigáis that you (all) may decay; pres. subj. 2nd pers. pl. / *decaer*.

decaigamos 1. that we may decay; pres. subj. 1st pers. pl. / *decaer*. 2. let us decay; impve. 1st pers. pl.

decaigan 1. that they may decay; pres. subj. 3rd pers. pl. / *decaer*. 2. let them decay; impve. 3rd pers. pl.

decaigas that you may decay; pres. subj. 2nd pers. sing. / *decaer*.

decaigo I decay; pres. ind. 1st pers. sing. / *decaer*.

decalvar to crop or to shave. reg.

decampar to decamp. reg.

decantar to decant or to exaggerate. reg.

decapitar to decapitate. reg.

decayendo decaying; pres. part. / *decaer*.

decayera 1. that I might decay; imp. subj. 1st pers. sing. / *decaer*. 2. that he (she/it) might decay; imp. subj. 3rd pers. sing.

decayerais that you (all) might decay; imp. subj. 2nd pers pl. / *decaer*.

decayéramos that we might decay; imp. subj. 1st pers. pl. / *decaer*.

decayeran that they might decay; imp. subj. 3rd pers. pl. / *decaer*.

decayeras that you might decay; imp. subj. 2nd pers. sing. / *decaer*.

decayeron they decayed; past 3rd pers. pl. / *decaer*.

decayese 1. that I might decay; imp. subj. 1st pers. sing. / *decaer*. 2. that he (she/it) might decay; imp. subj. 3rd pers. sing.

decayeseis that you (all) might decay; imp. subj. 2nd pers pl. / *decaer*.

decayésemos that we might decay; imp. subj. 1st pers. pl. / *decaer.*

decayesen that they might decay; imp. subj. 3rd pers. pl. / *decaer.*

decayeses that you might decay; imp. subj. 2nd pers. sing. / *decaer.*

decayó he (she/it) decayed; past 3rd pers. sing. / *decaer.*

decentándose getting bedsores; pres. part. / *decentarse.*

decentaos (you all) get bedsores; impve. 2nd pers. pl. / *decentarse.*

decentar to start on. irr.

decentarse to get bedsores. irr.

decentémonos let us get bedsores; impve. 1st pers. pl. / *decentarse.*

decepcionar to disappoint or to disillusion. reg.

decidámonos let us decide; impve. 1st pers. pl. / *decidirse.*

decídanse let them decide; impve. 3rd pers. pl. / *decidirse.*

decídase let him (her/it) decide; impve. 3rd pers. sing. / *decidirse.*

decídete (you) decide; impve. 2nd pers. sing. / *decidirse.*

decidiéndose deciding; pres. part. / *decidirse.*

decidíos (you all) decide; impve. 2nd pers. pl. / *decidirse.*

decidir to decide. reg.

decidirse to decide. reg.

decienta 1. he (she/it) starts on; pres. ind. 3rd pers. sing. / *decentar.* 2. (you) start on; impve. 2nd pers. sing.

decientan they start on; pres. ind. 3rd pers. pl. / *decentar.*

decientas you start on; pres. ind. 2nd pers. sing. / *decentar.*

deciéntate (you) get bedsores; impve. 2nd pers. sing. / *decentarse.*

deciente 1. that I may start on; pres. subj. 1st pers. sing. / *decentar.* 2. that he (she/it) may start on; pres. subj. 3rd pers. sing. 3. let him (her/it) start on; impve. 3rd pers. sing.

decienten 1. that they may start on; pres. subj. 3rd pers. pl. / *decentar.* 2. let them start on; impve. 3rd pers. pl.

deciéntense let them get bedsores; impve. 3rd pers. pl. / *decentarse.*

decientes that you may start on; pres. subj. 2nd pers. sing. / *decentar.*

deciéntese let him (her/it) get bedsores; impve. 3rd pers. sing. / *decentarse.*

deciento I start on; pres. ind. 1st pers. sing. / *decentar.*

decir to say. irr.

declamar to declaim or to recite. reg.

declarándose breaking out; pres. part. / *declararse.*

declaraos (you all) break out; impve. 2nd pers. pl. / *declararse.*

declarar to declare. reg.

declararse to break out. reg.

declárate (you) break out; impve. 2nd pers. sing. / *declararse.*

declarémonos let us break out; impve. 1st pers. pl. / *declararse.*

declárense let them break out; impve. 3rd pers. pl. / *declararse.*

declárese let him (her/it) break out; impve. 3rd pers. sing. / *declararse.*

declinar to decline. reg.

decomisar to confiscate. reg.

decorar to decorate or to memorize. reg.

decrecer to decrease. irr.

decrepitar to crackle with heat. reg.

decretar to decree. reg.

decrezca 1. that I may decrease; pres. subj. 1st pers. sing. / *decrecer.* 2. that he (she/it) may decrease; pres. subj. 3rd pers. sing. 3. let him (her/it) decrease; impve. 3rd pers. sing.

decrezcáis that you (all) may decrease; pres. subj. 2nd pers. pl. / *decrecer.*

decrezcamos 1. that we may decrease; pres. subj. 1st pers. pl. / *decrecer.* 2. let us decrease; impve. 1st pers. pl.

decrezcan 1. that they may decrease; pres. subj. 3rd pers. pl. / *decrecer.* 2. let them decrease; impve. 3rd pers. pl.

decrezcas that you may decrease; pres. subj. 2nd pers. sing. / *decrecer.*

decrezco I decrease; pres. ind. 1st pers. sing. / *decrecer.*

decuplar to multiply by ten. reg.

decuplicar to multiply by ten. irr.

decuplique 1. that I may multiply by ten; pres. subj. 1st pers. sing. / *decuplicar.* 2. that he (she/it) may multiply by ten; pres. subj. 3rd pers. sing. 3. let him (her/it) multiply by ten; impve. 3rd pers. sing.

decupliqué I multiplied by ten; past 1st pers. sing. / *decuplicar.*

decupliquéis that you (all) may multiply by ten; pres. subj. 2nd pers. pl. / *decuplicar.*

decupliquemos 1. that we may multiply by ten; pres. subj. 1st pers. pl. / *decuplicar.* 2. let us multiply by ten; impve. 1st pers. pl.

decupliquen 1. that they may multiply by ten; pres. subj. 3rd pers. pl. / *decuplicar.* 2. let them multiply by ten; impve. 3rd pers. pl.

decupliques that you may multiply by ten; pres. subj. 2nd pers. sing. / *decuplicar.*

dedicándose being dedicated; pres. part. / *dedicarse.*

dedicaos (you all) be dedicated; impve. 2nd pers. pl. / *dedicarse.*

dedicar to dedicate. irr.

dedicarse to be dedicated. irr.

dedícate (you) be dedicated; impve. 2nd pers. sing. / *dedicarse.*

dedique 1. that I may dedicate; pres. subj. 1st pers. sing. / *dedicar.* 2. that he (she/it) may dedicate; pres. subj. 3rd pers. sing. 3. let him (her/it) dedicate; impve. 3rd pers. sing.

dediqué I dedicated; past 1st pers. sing. / *dedicar.*

dediquéis that you (all) may dedicate; pres. subj. 2nd pers. pl. / *dedicar.*

dediquémonos let us be dedicated; impve. 1st pers. pl. / *dedicarse.*

dediquemos 1. that we may dedicate; pres. subj. 1st pers. pl. / *dedicar.* 2. let us dedicate; impve. 1st pers. pl.

dediquen 1. that they may dedicate; pres. subj. 3rd pers. pl. / *dedicar.* 2. let them dedicate; impve. 3rd pers. pl.

dedíquense let them be dedicated; impve. 3rd pers. pl. / *dedicarse.*

dediques that you may dedicate; pres. subj. 2nd pers. sing. / *dedicar.*

dedíquese let him (her/it) be dedicated; impve. 3rd pers. sing. / *dedicarse.*

deducir to deduce. irr.

deduje I deduced; past 1st pers. sing. / *deducir.*

dedujera 1. that I might deduce; imp. subj. 1st pers. sing. / *deducir.* 2. that he (she/it) might deduce; imp. subj. 3rd pers. sing.

dedujerais that you (all) might deduce; imp. subj. 2nd pers pl. / *deducir.*

dedujéramos that we might deduce; imp. subj. 1st pers. pl. / *deducir.*

dedujeran that they might deduce; imp. subj. 3rd pers. pl. / *deducir.*

dedujeras that you might deduce; imp. subj. 2nd pers. sing. / *deducir.*

dedujeron they deduced; past 3rd pers. pl. / *deducir.*

dedujese 1. that I might deduce; imp. subj. 1st pers. sing. / *deducir.* 2. that he (she/it) might deduce; imp. subj. 3rd pers. sing.

dedujeseis that you (all) might deduce; imp. subj. 2nd pers pl. / *deducir.*

dedujésemos that we might deduce; imp. subj. 1st pers. pl. / *deducir.*

dedujesen that they might deduce; imp. subj. 3rd pers. pl. / *deducir.*

dedujeses that you might deduce; imp. subj. 2nd pers. sing. / *deducir.*

dedujimos we deduced; past 1st pers. pl. / *deducir.*

dedujiste you deduced; past 2nd pers. sing. / *deducir.*

dedujisteis you (all) deduced; past 2nd pers. pl. / *deducir.*

dedujo he (she/it) deduced; past 3rd pers. sing. / *deducir.*

deduzca 1. that I may deduce; pres. subj. 1st pers. sing. / *deducir.* 2. that he (she/it) may deduce; pres. subj. 3rd pers. sing. 3. let him (her/it) deduce; impve. 3rd pers. sing.

deduzcáis that you (all) may deduce; pres. subj. 2nd pers. pl. / *deducir.*

deduzcamos 1. that we may deduce; pres. subj. 1st pers. pl. / *deducir.* 2. let us deduce; impve. 1st pers. pl.

deduzcan 1. that they may deduce; pres. subj. 3rd pers. pl. / *deducir.* 2. let them deduce; impve. 3rd pers. pl.

deduzcas that you may deduce; pres. subj. 2nd pers. sing. / *deducir.*

deduzco I deduce; pres. ind. 1st pers. sing. / *deducir.*

defalcar to embezzle. irr.

defalque 1. that I may embezzle; pres. subj. 1st pers. sing. / *defalcar.* 2. that he (she/it) may embezzle; pres. subj. 3rd pers. sing. 3. let him (her/it) embezzle; impve. 3rd pers. sing.

defalqué I embezzled; past 1st pers. sing. / *defalcar.*

defalquéis that you (all) may embezzle; pres. subj. 2nd pers. pl. / *defalcar.*

defalquemos 1. that we may embezzle; pres. subj. 1st pers. pl. / *defalcar.* 2. let us embezzle; impve. 1st pers. pl.

defalquen 1. that they may embezzle; pres. subj. 3rd pers. pl. / *defalcar.* 2. let them embezzle; impve. 3rd pers. pl.

defalques that you may embezzle; pres. subj. 2nd pers. sing. / *defalcar.*

defecar to defecate or to purify. irr.

defeccionar to desert. reg.

defender to defend or to resist. irr.

defeque 1. that I may defecate; pres. subj. 1st pers. sing. / *defecar.* 2. that he (she/it) may defecate; pres. subj. 3rd pers. sing. 3. let him (her/it) defecate; impve. 3rd pers. sing.

defequé I defecated; past 1st pers. sing. / *defecar.*

defequéis that you (all) may defecate; pres. subj. 2nd pers. pl. / *defecar.*

defequemos 1. that we may defecate; pres. subj. 1st pers. pl. / *defecar.* 2. let us defecate; impve. 1st pers. pl.

defequen 1. that they may defecate; pres. subj. 3rd pers. pl. / *defecar.* 2. let them defecate; impve. 3rd pers. pl.

defeques that you may defecate; pres. subj. 2nd pers. sing. / *defecar.*

deferir to defer. irr.

defienda 1. that I may defend; pres. subj. 1st pers. sing. / *defender.* 2. that he (she/it) may defend; pres. subj. 3rd pers. sing. 3. let him (her/it) defend; impve. 3rd pers. sing.

defiendan 1. that they may defend; pres. subj. 3rd pers. pl. / *defender.* 2. let them defend; impve. 3rd pers. pl.

defiendas that you may defend; pres. subj. 2nd pers. sing. / *defender.*

defiende 1. he (she/it) defends; pres. ind. 3rd pers. sing. / *defender.* 2. (you) defend; impve. 2nd pers. sing.

defienden they defend; pres. ind. 3rd pers. pl. / *defender.*

defiendes you defend; pres. ind. 2nd pers. sing. / *defender.*

defiendo I defend; pres. ind. 1st pers. sing. / *defender.*

defiera 1. that I may defer; pres. subj. 1st pers. sing. / *deferir.* 2. that he (she/it) may defer; pres. subj. 3rd pers. sing. 3. let him (her/it) defer; impve. 3rd pers. sing.

defieran 1. that they may defer; pres. subj. 3rd pers. pl. / *deferir.* 2. let them defer; impve. 3rd pers. pl.

defieras that you may defer; pres. subj. 2nd pers. sing. / *deferir.*

defiere 1. he (she/it) defers; pres. ind. 3rd pers. sing. / *deferir.* 2. (you) defer; impve. 2nd pers. sing.

defieren they defer; pres. ind. 3rd pers. pl. / *deferir.*

defieres you defer; pres. ind. 2nd pers. sing. / *deferir.*

defiero I defer; pres. ind. 1st pers. sing. / *deferir.*

definir to define or to determine. reg.

deflagrar to burn quickly. reg.

deformándose losing its shape; pres. part. / *deformarse.*

deformaos (you all) lose your shape; impve. 2nd pers. pl. / *deformarse.*

deformar to deform. reg.

deformarse to lose its shape or form. reg.

defórmate (you) lose your shape; impve. 2nd pers. sing. / *deformarse.*

deformémonos let us lose our shape; impve. 1st pers. pl. / *deformarse.*

defórmense let them lose their shape; impve. 3rd pers. pl. / *deformarse.*

defórmese let him (her/it) lose his (her/its) shape; impve. 3rd pers. sing. / *deformarse.*

defraudar to defraud or to disappoint. reg.

degenerar to degenerate. reg.

deglutir to swallow. reg.

degollar to behead. irr.

degradar to degrade or to debase. reg.

degüella 1. he (she/it) beheads; pres. ind. 3rd pers. sing. / *degollar* 2. (you) behead; impve. 2nd pers. sing.

degüellan they behead; pres. ind. 3rd pers. pl. / *degollar.*

degüellas you behead; pres. ind. 2nd pers. sing. / *degollar.*

degüelle 1. that I may behead; pres. subj. 1st pers. sing. / *degollar.* 2. that he (she/it) may behead; pres. subj. 3rd pers. sing. 3. let him (her/it) behead; impve. 3rd pers. sing.

degüellen 1. that they may behead; pres. subj. 3rd pers. pl. / *degollar.* 2. let them behead; impve. 3rd pers. pl.

degüelles that you may behead; pres. subj. 2nd pers. sing. / *degollar.*

degüello I behead; pres. ind. 1st pers. sing. / *degollar.*

degustar to taste or to sample. reg.

deificar to deify. irr.

deifique 1. that I may deify; pres. subj. 1st pers. sing. / *deificar.* 2. that he (she/it) may deify; pres. subj. 3rd pers. sing. 3. let him (her/it) deify; impve. 3rd pers. sing.

deifiqué I deified; past 1st pers. sing. / *deificar.*

deifiquéis that you (all) may deify; pres. subj. 2nd pers. pl. / *deificar.*

deifiquemos 1. that we may deify; pres. subj. 1st pers. pl. / *deificar.* 2. let us deify; impve. 1st pers. pl.

deifiquen 1. that they may deify; pres. subj. 3rd pers. pl. / *deificar.* 2. let them deify; impve. 3rd pers. pl.

deifiques that you may deify; pres. subj. 2nd pers. sing. / *deificar.*

deis that you (all) may give; pres. subj. 2nd pers. pl. / *dar.*

dejándose being slipshod; pres. part. / *dejarse.*

dejaos (you all) be slipshod; impve. 2nd pers. pl. / *dejarse.*

dejar to leave or to permit. reg.

dejarse to be slipshod. reg.

déjate (you) be slipshod; impve. 2nd pers. sing. / *dejarse.*

dejémonos let us be slipshod; impve. 1st pers. pl. / *dejarse.*

déjense let them be slipshod; impve. 3rd pers. pl. / *dejarse.*

déjese let him (her/it) be slipshod; impve. 3rd pers. sing. / *dejarse.*

delatar to denounce or to betray. reg.

delegar to delegate. irr.

delegue 1. that I may delegate; pres. subj. 1st pers. sing. / *delegar.* 2. that he (she/it) may delegate; pres. subj. 3rd pers. sing. 3. let him (her/it) delegate; impve. 3rd pers. sing.

delegué I delegated; past 1st pers. sing. / *delegar.*

deleguéis that you (all) may delegate; pres. subj. 2nd pers. pl. / *delegar.*

deleguemos 1. that we may delegate; pres. subj. 1st pers. pl. / *delegar.* 2. let us delegate; impve. 1st pers. pl.

deleguen 1. that they may delegate; pres. subj. 3rd pers. pl. / *delegar.* 2. let them delegate; impve. 3rd pers. pl.

delegues that you may delegate; pres. subj. 2nd pers. sing. / *delegar.*

deleitándose delighting; pres. part. / *deleitarse.*

deleitaos (you all) delight; impve. 2nd pers. pl. / *deleitarse.*

deleitar to delight. reg.

deleitarse to delight. reg.

deleítate (you) delight; impve. 2nd pers. sing. / *deleitarse.*

deleitémonos let us delight; impve. 1st pers. pl. / *deleitarse.*

deleítense let them delight; impve. 3rd pers. pl. / *deleitarse.*

deleítese let him (her/it) delight; impve. 3rd pers. sing. / *deleitarse.*

deletrear to spell or to decipher. reg.

deliberar to deliberate. reg.

delimitar to delimit. reg.

delinca 1. that I may transgress; pres. subj. 1st pers. sing. / *delinquir.* 2. that he (she/it) may transgress; pres. subj. 3rd pers. sing. 3. let him (her/it) transgress; impve. 3rd pers. sing.

delincáis that you (all) may transgress; pres. subj. 2nd pers. pl. / *delinquir.*

delincamos 1. that we may transgress; pres. subj. 1st pers. pl. / *delinquir* 2. let us transgress; impve. 1st pers. pl.

delincan 1. that they may transgress; pres. subj. 3rd pers. pl. / *delinquir.* 2. let them transgress; impve. 3rd pers. pl.

delincas that you may transgress; pres. subj. 2nd pers. sing. / *delinquir*.

delinco I transgress; pres. ind. 1st pers. sing. / *delinquir*.

delinear to delineate. reg.

delinquir to transgress. irr.

delirar to be delirious or to rave. reg.

deludir to delude. reg.

demacrándose wasting away; pres. part. / *demacrarse*.

demacraos (you all) waste away; impve. 2nd pers. pl. / *demacrarse*.

demacrar to emaciate. reg.

demacrarse to waste away. reg.

demácrate (you) waste away; impve. 2nd pers. sing. / *demacrarse*.

demacrémonos let us waste away; impve. 1st pers. pl. / *demacrarse*.

demácrense let them waste away; impve. 3rd pers. pl. / *demacrarse*.

demácrese let him (her/it) waste away; impve. 3rd pers. sing. / *demacrarse*.

demandar to demand. reg.

demarcar to demarcate or to fix the limits of. irr.

demarque 1. that I may demarcate; pres. subj. 1st pers. sing. / *demarcar*. 2. that he (she/it) may demarcate; pres. subj. 3rd pers. sing. 3. let him (her/it) demarcate; impve. 3rd pers. sing.

demarqué I demarcated; past 1st pers. sing. / *demarcar*.

demarquéis that you (all) may demarcate; pres. subj. 2nd pers. pl. / *demarcar*.

demarquemos 1. that we may demarcate; pres. subj. 1st pers. pl. / *demarcar*. 2. let us demarcate; impve. 1st pers. pl.

demarquen 1. that they may demarcate; pres. subj. 3rd pers. pl. / *demarcar* 2. let them demarcate; impve. 3rd pers. pl.

demarques that you may demarcate; pres. subj. 2nd pers. sing. / *demarcar*.

demasiándose going too far; pres. part. / *demasiarse*.

demasiaos (you all) go too far; impve. 2nd pers. pl. / *demasiarse*.

demasiarse to go too far. reg.

demasíate (you) go too far; impve. 2nd pers. sing. / *demasiarse*.

demasiémonos let us go too far; impve. 1st pers. pl. / *demasiarse*.

demasíense let them go too far; impve. 3rd pers. pl. / *demasiarse*.

demasíese let him (her/it) go too far; impve. 3rd pers. sing. / *demasiarse*.

demediar to cut in half. reg.

dementar to drive mad. reg.

democratice 1. that I may democratize; pres. subj. 1st pers. sing. / *democratizar*. 2. that he (she/it) may democratize; pres. subj. 3rd pers. sing. 3. let him (her/it) democratize; impve. 3rd pers. sing.

democraticé I democratized; past 1st pers. sing. / *democratizar*.

democraticéis that you (all) may democratize; pres. subj. 2nd pers. pl. / *democratizar*.

democraticemos 1. that we may democratize; pres. subj. 1st pers. pl. / *democratizar*. 2. let us democratize; impve. 1st pers. pl.

democraticen 1. that they may democratize; pres. subj. 3rd pers. pl. / *democratizar*. 2. let them democratize; impve. 3rd pers. pl.

democratices that you may democratize; pres. subj. 2nd pers. sing. / *democratizar*.

democratizar to democratize. irr.

demoler to demolish. irr.

démonos let us give up; impve. 1st pers. pl. / *darse*.

demorándose lingering; pres. part. / *demorarse*.

demoraos (you all) linger; impve. 2nd pers. pl. / *demorarse*.

demorar to delay. reg.

demorarse to linger or to tarry. reg.

demórate (you) linger; impve. 2nd pers. sing. / *demorarse*.

demorémonos let us linger; impve. 1st pers. pl. / *demorarse*.

demórense let them linger; impve. 3rd pers. pl. / *demorarse*.

demórese let him (her/it) linger; impve. 3rd pers. sing. / *demorarse*.

demos 1. that we may give; pres. subj. 1st pers. pl. / *dar*. 2. let us give; impve. 1st pers. pl.

demostrar to demonstrate or to prove. irr.

demovilice 1. that I may demobilize; pres. subj. 1st pers. sing. / *demovilizar*. 2. that he (she/it) may demobilize; pres. subj. 3rd pers. sing. 3. let him (her/it) demobilize; impve. 3rd pers. sing.

demovilicé I demobilized; past 1st pers. sing. / *demovilizar*.

demovilicéis that you (all) may demobilize; pres. subj. 2nd pers. pl. / *demovilizar*.

demovilicemos 1. that we may demobilize; pres. subj. 1st pers. pl. / *demovilizar*. 2. let us demobilize; impve. 1st pers. pl.

demovilicen 1. that they may demobilize; pres. subj. 3rd pers. pl. / *demovilizar*. 2. let them demobilize; impve. 3rd pers. pl.

demovilices that you may demobilize; pres. subj. 2nd pers. sing. / *demovilizar*.

demovilizar to demobilize. irr.

demudándose turning pale; pres. part. / *demudarse*.

demudaos (you all) turn pale; impve. 2nd pers. pl. / *demudarse*.

demudar to alter or to disguise. reg.

demudarse to turn pale. reg.

demúdate (you) turn pale; impve. 2nd pers. sing. / *demudarse*.

demudémonos let us turn pale; impve. 1st pers. pl. / *demudarse*.

demúdense let them turn pale; impve. 3rd pers. pl. / *demudarse*.

demúdese let him (her/it) turn pale; impve. 3rd pers. sing. / *demudarse*.

demuela 1. that I may demolish; pres. subj. 1st pers. sing. / *demoler.* 2. that he (she/it) may demolish; pres. subj. 3rd pers. sing. 3. let him (her/it) demolish; impve. 3rd pers. sing.

demuelan 1. that they may demolish; pres. subj. 3rd pers. pl. / *demoler.* 2. let them demolish; impve. 3rd pers. pl.

demuelas that you may demolish; pres. subj. 2nd pers. sing. / *demoler.*

demuele 1. he (she/it) demolishes; pres. ind. 3rd pers. sing. / *demoler.* 2. (you) demolish; impve. 2nd pers. sing.

demuelen they demolish; pres. ind. 3rd pers. pl. / *demoler.*

demueles you demolish; pres. ind. 2nd pers. sing. / *demoler.*

demuelo I demolish; pres. ind. 1st pers. sing. / *demoler.*

demuestra 1. he (she/it) demonstrates; pres. ind. 3rd pers. sing. / *demostrar.* 2. (you) demonstrate; impve. 2nd pers. sing.

demuestran they demonstrate; pres. ind. 3rd pers. pl. / *demostrar.*

demuestras you demonstrate; pres. ind. 2nd pers. sing. / *demostrar.*

demuestre 1. that I may demonstrate; pres. subj. 1st pers. sing. / *demostrar.* 2. that he (she/it) may demonstrate; pres. subj. 3rd pers. sing. 3. let him (her/it) demonstrate; impve. 3rd pers. sing.

demuestren 1. that they may demonstrate; pres. subj. 3rd pers. pl. / *demostrar.* 2. let them demonstrate; impve. 3rd pers. pl.

demuestres that you may demonstrate; pres. subj. 2nd pers. sing. / *demostrar.*

demuestro I demonstrate; pres. ind. 1st pers. sing. / *demostrar.*

den 1. that they may give; pres. subj. 3rd pers. pl. / *dar.* 2. let them give; impve. 3rd pers. pl.

denegar to deny. irr.

denegrecer to blacken. irr.

denegrezca 1. that I may blacken; pres. subj. 1st pers. sing. / *denegrecer.* 2. that he (she/it) may blacken; pres. subj. 3rd pers. sing. 3. let him (her/it) blacken; impve. 3rd pers. sing.

denegrezcáis that you (all) may blacken; pres. subj. 2nd pers. pl. / *denegrecer.*

denegrezcamos 1. that we may blacken; pres. subj. 1st pers. pl. / *denegrecer.* 2. let us blacken; impve. 1st pers. pl.

denegrezcan 1. that they may blacken; pres. subj. 3rd pers. pl. / *denegrecer* 2. let them blacken; impve. 3rd pers. pl.

denegrezcas that you may blacken; pres. subj. 2nd pers. sing. / *denegrecer.*

denegrezco I blacken; pres. ind. 1st pers. sing. / *denegrecer.*

denegué I denied; past 1st pers. sing. / *denegar.*

deneguéis that you (all) may deny; pres. subj. 2nd pers. pl. / *denegar.*

deneguemos 1. that we may deny; pres. subj. 1st pers. pl. / *denegar.* 2. let us deny; impve. 1st pers. pl.

deniega 1. he (she/it) denies; pres. ind. 3rd pers. sing. / *denegar.* 2. (you) deny; impve. 2nd pers. sing.

deniegan they deny; pres. ind. 3rd pers. pl. / *denegar.*

deniegas you deny; pres. ind. 2nd pers. sing. / *denegar.*

deniego I deny; pres. ind. 1st pers. sing. / *denegar.*

deniegue 1. that I may deny; pres. subj. 1st pers. sing. / *denegar.* 2. that he (she/it) may deny; pres. subj. 3rd pers. sing. 3. let him (her/it) deny; impve. 3rd pers. sing.

denieguen 1. that they may deny; pres. subj. 3rd pers. pl. / *denegar.* 2. let them deny; impve. 3rd pers. pl.

deniegues that you may deny; pres. subj. 2nd pers. sing. / *denegar.*

denigrar to defame or to malign. reg.

denominar to name. reg.

denostar to insult. irr.

denotar to denote or to indicate. reg.

dense let them give up; impve. 3rd pers. pl. / *darse.*

densificar to densify. irr.

densifique 1. that I may densify; pres. subj. 1st pers. sing. / *densificar.* 2. that he (she/it) may densify; pres. subj. 3rd pers. sing. 3. let him (her/it) densify; impve. 3rd pers. sing.

densifiqué I densified; past 1st pers. sing. / *densificar.*

densifiquéis that you (all) may densify; pres. subj. 2nd pers. pl. / *densificar.*

densifiquemos 1. that we may densify; pres. subj. 1st pers. pl. / *densificar.* 2. let us densify; impve. 1st pers. pl.

densifiquen 1. that they may densify; pres. subj. 3rd pers. pl. / *densificar* 2. let them densify; impve. 3rd pers. pl.

densifiques that you may densify; pres. subj. 2nd pers. sing. / *densificar.*

dentar to teethe or to indent. irr.

dentellar to chatter (teeth). reg.

dentellear to nibble. reg.

denudándose being stripped bare; pres. part. / *denudarse.*

denudaos (you all) be stripped bare; impve. 2nd pers. pl. / *denudarse.*

denudar to denude or lay bare. reg.

denudarse to be stripped bare. reg.

denúdate (you) be stripped bare; impve. 2nd pers. sing. / *denudarse.*

denudémonos let us be stripped bare; impve. 1st pers. pl. / *denudarse.*

denúdense let them be stripped bare; impve. 3rd pers. pl. / *denudarse.*

denúdese let him (her/it) be stripped bare; impve. 3rd pers. sing. / *denudarse.*

denuesta 1. he (she/it) insults; pres. ind. 3rd pers. sing. / *denostar.* 2. (you) insult; impve. 2nd pers. sing.

denuestan they insult; pres. ind. 3rd pers. pl. / *denostar.*

denuestas you insult; pres. ind. 2nd pers. sing. / *denostar.*

denueste 1. that I may insult; pres. subj. 1st pers. sing. / *denostar*. 2. that he (she/it) may insult; pres. subj. 3rd pers. sing. 3. let him (her/it) insult; impve. 3rd pers. sing.

denuesten 1. that they may insult; pres. subj. 3rd pers. pl. / *denostar*. 2. let them insult; impve. 3rd pers. pl.

denuestes that you may insult; pres. subj. 2nd pers. sing. / *denostar*.

denuesto I insult; pres. ind. 1st pers. sing. / *denostar*.

denunciar to denounce or to proclaim. reg.

deparar to offer or to provide. reg.

departir to talk. reg.

depauperar to impoverish or to weaken. reg.

depender to depend. reg.

depilar to depilate. reg.

deplorar to deplore or to regret. reg.

depon (you) depose; impve. 2nd pers. sing. / *deponer*.

depondrá he (she/it) will depose; fut. 3rd pers. sing. / *deponer*.

depondrán they will depose; fut. 3rd pers. pl. / *deponer*.

depondrás you will depose; fut. 2nd pers. sing. / *deponer*.

depondré I shall depose; fut. 1st pers. sing. / *deponer*.

depondréis you (all) will depose; fut. 2nd pers. pl. / *deponer*.

depondremos we shall depose; fut. 1st pers. pl. / *deponer*.

depondría 1. I should depose; cond. 1st pers. sing. / *deponer*. 2. he (she/it) would depose; cond. 3rd pers. sing.

depondríais you (all) would depose; cond. 2nd pers. pl. / *deponer*.

depondríamos we should depose; cond. 1st pers. pl. / *deponer*.

depondrían they would depose; cond. 3rd pers. pl. / *deponer*.

depondrías you would depose; cond. 2nd pers. sing. / *deponer*.

deponer to depose or to defecate. irr.

deponga 1. that I may depose; pres. subj. 1st pers. sing. / *deponer*. 2. that he (she/it) may depose; pres. subj. 3rd pers. sing. 3. let him (her/it) depose; impve. 3rd pers. sing.

depongáis that you (all) may depose; pres. subj. 2nd pers. pl. / *deponer*.

depongamos 1. that we may depose; pres. subj. 1st pers. pl. / *deponer*. 2. let us depose; impve. 1st pers. pl.

depongan 1. that they may depose; pres. subj. 3rd pers. pl. / *deponer*. 2. let them depose; impve. 3rd pers. pl.

depongas that you may depose; pres. subj. 2nd pers. sing. / *deponer*.

depongo I depose; pres. ind. 1st pers. sing. / *deponer*.

deportar to deport. reg.

depositándose settling (as sediment); pres. part. / *depositarse*.

depositar to deposit. reg.

depositarse to settle (as sediment). reg.

deposítense let them settle (as sediment); impve. 3rd pers. pl. / *depositarse*.

deposítese let it settle (as sediment); impve. 3rd pers. sing. / *depositarse*.

depravar to deprave or corrupt. reg.

deprecar to entreat. irr.

depreciar to depreciate. reg.

depredar to depredate or to rob. reg.

depreque 1. that I may entreat; pres. subj. 1st pers. sing. / *deprecar*. 2. that he (she/it) may entreat; pres. subj. 3rd pers. sing. 3. let him (her/it) entreat; impve. 3rd pers. sing.

deprequé I entreated; past 1st pers. sing. / *deprecar*.

deprequéis that you (all) may entreat; pres. subj. 2nd pers. pl. / *deprecar*.

deprequemos 1. that we may entreat; pres. subj. 1st pers. pl. / *deprecar*. 2. let us entreat; impve. 1st pers. pl.

deprequen 1. that they may entreat; pres. subj. 3rd pers. pl. / *deprecar*. 2. let them entreat; impve. 3rd pers. pl.

depreques that you may entreat; pres. subj. 2nd pers. sing. / *deprecar*.

deprimir to depress. reg.

depuesto deposed; past part. / *deponer*.

depurar to purify. reg.

depuse I deposed; past 1st pers. sing. / *deponer*.

depusiera 1. that I might depose; imp. subj. 1st pers. sing. / *deponer*. 2. that he (she/it) might depose; imp. subj. 3rd pers. sing.

depusierais that you (all) might depose; imp. subj. 2nd pers pl. / *deponer*.

depusiéramos that we might depose; imp. subj. 1st pers. pl. / *deponer*.

depusieran that they might depose; imp. subj. 3rd pers. pl. / *deponer*.

depusieras that you might depose; imp. subj. 2nd pers. sing. / *deponer*.

depusieron they deposed; past 3rd pers. pl. / *deponer*.

depusiese 1. that I might depose; imp. subj. 1st pers. sing. / *deponer*. 2. that he (she/it) might depose; imp. subj. 3rd pers. sing.

depusieseis that you (all) might depose; imp. subj. 2nd pers pl. / *deponer*.

depusiésemos that we might depose; imp. subj. 1st pers. pl. / *deponer*.

depusiesen that they might depose; imp. subj. 3rd pers. pl. / *deponer*.

depusieses that you might depose; imp. subj. 2nd pers. sing. / *deponer*.

depusimos we deposed; past 1st pers. pl. / *deponer*.

depusiste you deposed; past 2nd pers. sing. / *deponer*.

depusisteis you (all) deposed; past 2nd pers. pl. / *deponer*.

depuso he (she/it) deposed; past 3rd pers. sing. / *deponer*

derivándose deriving; pres. part. / *derivarse*.

derivaos (you all) derive; impve. 2nd pers. pl. / *derivarse.*

derivar to derive or to direct. reg.

derivarse to derive or to drift. reg.

derívate (you) derive; impve. 2nd pers. sing. / *derivarse.*

derivémonos let us derive; impve. 1st pers. pl. / *derivarse.*

derívense let them derive; impve. 3rd pers. pl. / *derivarse.*

derívese let him (her/it) derive; impve. 3rd pers. sing. / *derivarse.*

derogar to derogate or to revoke. irr.

derogue 1. that I may derogate; pres. subj. 1st pers. sing. / *derogar.* 2. that he (she/it) may derogate; pres. subj. 3rd pers. sing. 3. let him (her/it) derogate; impve. 3rd pers. sing.

derogué I derogated; past 1st pers. sing. / *derogar.*

deroguéis that you (all) may derogate; pres. subj. 2nd pers. pl. / *derogar.*

deroguemos 1. that we may derogate; pres. subj. 1st pers. pl. / *derogar.* 2. let us derogate; impve. 1st pers. pl.

deroguen 1. that they may derogate; pres. subj. 3rd pers. pl. / *derogar.* 2. let them derogate; impve. 3rd pers. pl.

derogues that you may derogate; pres. subj. 2nd pers. sing. / *derogar.*

derrabar to cut the tail of or to dock. reg.

derramándose overflowing; pres. part. / *derramarse.*

derramaos (you all) overflow; impve. 2nd pers. pl. / *derramarse.*

derramar to spill. reg.

derramarse to overflow. reg.

derrámate (you) overflow; impve. 2nd pers. sing. / *derramarse.*

derramémonos let us overflow; impve. 1st pers. pl. / *derramarse.*

derrámense let them overflow; impve. 3rd pers. pl. / *derramarse.*

derrámese let him (her/it) overflow; impve. 3rd pers. sing. / *derramarse.*

derrelicto forsook; past part. / *derrelinquir*

derrelinca 1. that I may forsake; pres. subj. 1st pers. sing. / *derrelinquir.* 2. that he (she/it) may forsake; pres. subj. 3rd pers. sing. 3. let him (her/it) forsake; impve. 3rd pers. sing.

derrelincáis that you (all) may forsake; pres. subj. 2nd pers. pl. / *derrelinquir.*

derrelincamos 1. that we may forsake; pres. subj. 1st pers. pl. / *derrelinquir* 2. let us forsake; impve. 1st pers. pl.

derrelincan 1. that they may forsake; pres. subj. 3rd pers. pl. / *derrelinquir.* 2. let them forsake; impve. 3rd pers. pl.

derrelincas that you may forsake; pres. subj. 2nd pers. sing. / *derrelinquir.*

derrelinco I forsake; pres. ind. 1st pers. sing. / *derrelinquir.*

derrengar to cripple or to break the back of. irr.

derrengué I crippled; past 1st pers. sing. / *derrengar.*

derrenguéis that you (all) may cripple; pres. subj. 2nd pers. pl. / *derrengar.*

derrenguemos 1. that we may cripple; pres. subj. 1st pers. pl. / *derrengar.* 2. let us cripple; impve. 1st pers. pl.

derretíos (you all) fall apart; impve. 2nd pers. pl. / *derretirse.*

derretir to melt. irr.

derretirse to fall apart. irr.

derribándose lying down; pres. part. / *derribarse.*

derribaos (you all) lie down; impve. 2nd pers. pl. / *derribarse.*

derribar to demolish. reg.

derribarse to lie down. reg.

derríbate (you) lie down; impve. 2nd pers. sing. / *derribarse.*

derribémonos let us lie down; impve. 1st pers. pl. / *derribarse.*

derríbense let them lie down; impve. 3rd pers. pl. / *derribarse.*

derríbese let him (her/it) lie down; impve. 3rd pers. sing. / *derribarse.*

derrienga 1. he (she/it) cripples; pres. ind. 3rd pers. sing. / *derrengar.* 2. (you) cripple; impve. 2nd pers. sing.

derriengan they cripple; pres. ind. 3rd pers. pl. / *derrengar.*

derriengas you cripple; pres. ind. 2nd pers. sing. / *derrengar.*

derriengo I cripple; pres. ind. 1st pers. sing. / *derrengar.*

derriengue 1. that I may cripple; pres. subj. 1st pers. sing. / *derrengar.* 2. that he (she/it) may cripple; pres. subj. 3rd pers. sing. 3. let him (her/it) cripple; impve. 3rd pers. sing.

derrienguen 1. that they may cripple; pres. subj. 3rd pers. pl. / *derrengar.* 2. let them cripple; impve. 3rd pers. pl.

derriengues that you may cripple; pres. subj. 2nd pers. sing. / *derrengar.*

derrita 1. that I may melt; pres. subj. 1st pers. sing. / *derretir.* 2. that he (she/it) may melt; pres. subj. 3rd pers. sing. 3. let him (her/it) melt; impve. 3rd pers. sing.

derritáis that you (all) may melt; pres. subj. 2nd pers. pl. / *derretir.*

derritámonos let us fall apart; impve. 1st pers. pl. / *derretirse.*

derritamos 1. that we may melt; pres. subj. 1st pers. pl. / *derretir.* 2. let us melt; impve. 1st pers. pl.

derritan 1. that they may melt; pres. subj. 3rd pers. pl. / *derretir.* 2. let them melt; impve. 3rd pers. pl.

derrítanse let them fall apart; impve. 3rd pers. pl. / *derretirse.*

derritas that you may melt; pres. subj. 2nd pers. sing. / *derretir.*

derrítase let him (her/it) fall apart; impve. 3rd pers. sing. / *derretirse.*

derrite 1. he (she/it) melts; pres. ind. 3rd pers. sing. / *derretir.* 2. (you) melt; impve. 2nd pers. sing.

derriten they melt; pres. ind. 3rd pers. pl. / *derretir.*

derrites you melt; pres. ind. 2nd pers. sing. / *derretir.*

derrítete (you) fall apart; impve. 2nd pers. sing. / *derretirse.*

derritiendo melting; pres. part. / *derretir.*

derritiéndose falling apart; pres. part. / *derretirse.*

derritiera 1. that I might melt; imp. subj. 1st pers. sing. / *derretir.* 2. that he (she/it) might melt; imp. subj. 3rd pers. sing.

derritierais that you (all) might melt; imp. subj. 2nd pers pl. / *derretir.*

derritiéramos that we might melt; imp. subj. 1st pers. pl. / *derretir.*

derritieran that they might melt; imp. subj. 3rd pers. pl. / *derretir.*

derritieras that you might melt; imp. subj. 2nd pers. sing. / *derretir.*

derritieron they melted; past 3rd pers. pl. / *derretir.*

derritiese 1. that I might melt; imp. subj. 1st pers. sing. / *derretir.* 2. that he (she/it) might melt; imp. subj. 3rd pers. sing.

derritieseis that you (all) might melt; imp. subj. 2nd pers pl. / *derretir.*

derritiésemos that we might melt; imp. subj. 1st pers. pl. / *derretir.*

derritiesen that they might melt; imp. subj. 3rd pers. pl. / *derretir.*

derritieses that you might melt; imp. subj. 2nd pers. sing. / *derretir.*

derritió he (she/it) melted; past 3rd pers. sing. / *derretir.*

derrito I melt; pres. ind. 1st pers. sing. / *derretir.*

derrocar to throw down. irr.

derrochar to waste. reg.

derroque 1. that I may throw down; pres. subj. 1st pers. sing. / *derrocar.* 2. that he (she/it) may throw down; pres. subj. 3rd pers. sing. 3. let him (her/it) throw down; impve. 3rd pers. sing.

derroqué I threw down; past 1st pers. sing. / *derrocar.*

derroquéis that you (all) may throw down; pres. subj. 2nd pers. pl. / *derrocar.*

derroquemos 1. that we may throw down; pres. subj. 1st pers. pl. / *derrocar.* 2. let us throw down; impve. 1st pers. pl.

derroquen 1. that they may throw down; pres. subj. 3rd pers. pl. / *derrocar.* 2. let them throw down; impve. 3rd pers. pl.

derroques that you may throw down; pres. subj. 2nd pers. sing. / *derrocar.*

derrotándose straying off course (boat); pres. part. / *derrotarse.*

derrotar to defeat or to squander. reg.

derrotarse to stray off course (boat). reg.

derrótense let them stray off course (boat); impve. 3rd pers. pl. / *derrotarse.*

derrótese let it stray off course (boat); impve. 3rd pers. sing. / *derrotarse.*

derrubiar to erode. reg.

derruir to ruin or to destroy. irr.

derrumbándose crumbling; pres. part. / *derrumbarse.*

derrumbaos (you all) crumble; impve. 2nd pers. pl. / *derrumbarse.*

derrumbar to fling down. reg.

derrumbarse to crumble. reg.

derrúmbate (you) crumble; impve. 2nd pers. sing. / *derrumbarse.*

derrumbémonos let us crumble; impve. 1st pers. pl. / *derrumbarse.*

derrúmbense let them crumble; impve. 3rd pers. pl. / *derrumbarse.*

derrúmbese let him (her/it) crumble; impve. 3rd pers. sing. / *derrumbarse.*

derruya 1. that I may ruin; pres. subj. 1st pers. sing. / *derruir.* 2. that he (she/it) may ruin; pres. subj. 3rd pers. sing. 3. let him (her/it) ruin; impve. 3rd pers. sing.

derruyáis that you (all) may ruin; pres. subj. 2nd pers. pl. / *derruir.*

derruyamos 1. that we may ruin; pres. subj. 1st pers. pl. / *derruir.* 2. let us ruin; impve. 1st pers. pl.

derruyan 1. that they may ruin; pres. subj. 3rd pers. pl. / *derruir.* 2. let them ruin; impve. 3rd pers. pl.

derruyas that you may ruin; pres. subj. 2nd pers. sing. / *derruir.*

derruye 1. he (she/it) ruins; pres. ind. 3rd pers. sing. / *derruir.* 2. (you) ruin; impve. 2nd pers. sing.

derruyen they ruin; pres. ind. 3rd pers. pl. / *derruir.*

derruyendo ruining; pres. part. / *derruir.*

derruyera 1. that I might ruin; imp. subj. 1st pers. sing. / *derruir.* 2. that he (she/it) might ruin; imp. subj. 3rd pers. sing.

derruyerais that you (all) might ruin; imp. subj. 2nd pers pl. / *derruir.*

derruyéramos that we might ruin; imp. subj. 1st pers. pl. / *derruir.*

derruyeran that they might ruin; imp. subj. 3rd pers. pl. / *derruir.*

derruyeras that you might ruin; imp. subj. 2nd pers. sing. / *derruir.*

derruyeron they ruined; past 3rd pers. pl. / *derruir.*

derruyes you ruin; pres. ind. 2nd pers. sing. / *derruir.*

derruyese 1. that I might ruin; imp. subj. 1st pers. sing. / *derruir.* 2. that he (she/it) might ruin; imp. subj. 3rd pers. sing.

derruyeseis that you (all) might ruin; imp. subj. 2nd pers pl. / *derruir.*

derruyésemos that we might ruin; imp. subj. 1st pers. pl. / *derruir.*

derruyesen that they might ruin; imp. subj. 3rd pers. pl. / *derruir.*

derruyeses that you might ruin; imp. subj. 2nd pers. sing. / *derruir.*

derruyo I ruin; pres. ind. 1st pers. sing. / *derruir.*

derruyó he (she/it) ruined; past 3rd pers. sing. / *derruir.*

des that you may give; pres. subj. 2nd pers. sing. / *dar.*

desabarrancar to pull out of. irr.

desabarranque 1. that I may pull out of; pres. subj. 1st pers. sing. / *desabarrancar*. 2. that he (she/it) may pull out of; pres. subj. 3rd pers. sing. 3. let him (her/it) pull out of; impve. 3rd pers. sing.

desabarranqué I pulled out of; past 1st pers. sing. / *desabarrancar*.

desabarranquéis that you (all) may pull out of; pres. subj. 2nd pers. pl. / *desabarrancar*.

desabarranquemos 1. that we may pull out of; pres. subj. 1st pers. pl. / *desabarrancar*. 2. let us pull out of; impve. 1st pers. pl.

desabarranquen 1. that they may pull out of; pres. subj. 3rd pers. pl. / *desabarrancar*. 2. let them pull out of; impve. 3rd pers. pl.

desabarranques that you may pull out of; pres. subj. 2nd pers. sing. / *desabarrancar*.

desabastecer to cut off supplies from. irr.

desabastezca 1. that I may cut off supplies from; pres. subj. 1st pers. sing. / *desabastecer*. 2. that he (she/it) may cut off supplies from; pres. subj. 3rd pers. sing. 3. let him (her/it) cut off supplies from; impve. 3rd pers. sing.

desabastezcáis that you (all) may cut off supplies from; pres. subj. 2nd pers. pl. / *desabastecer*.

desabastezcamos 1. that we may cut off supplies from; pres. subj. 1st pers. pl. / *desabastecer*. 2. let us cut off supplies from; impve. 1st pers. pl.

desabastezcan 1. that they may cut off supplies from; pres. subj. 3rd pers. pl. / *desabastecer*. 2. let them cut off supplies from; impve. 3rd pers. pl.

desabastezcas that you may cut off supplies from; pres. subj. 2nd pers. sing. / *desabastecer*.

desabastezco I cut off supplies from; pres. ind. 1st pers. sing. / *desabastecer*.

desabollar to remove the dents from. reg.

desabonándose canceling one's subscription; pres. part. / *desabonarse*.

desabonaos (you all) cancel your subscription; impve. 2nd pers. pl. / *desabonarse*.

desabonarse to cancel one's subscription. reg.

desabónate (you) cancel your subscription; impve. 2nd pers. sing. / *desabonarse*.

desabonémonos let us cancel our subscription; impve. 1st pers. pl. / *desabonarse*.

desabónense let them cancel their subscription; impve. 3rd pers. pl. / *desabonarse*.

desabónese let him (her/it) cancel his (her/its) subscription; impve. 3rd pers. sing. / *desabonarse*.

desabotonar to unbutton or to blossom. reg.

desabrigándose uncovering oneself; pres. part. / *desabrigarse*.

desabrigaos (you all) uncover yourselves; impve. 2nd pers. pl. / *desabrigarse*.

desabrigar to uncover or to expose. irr.

desabrigarse to uncover oneself. irr.

desabrígate (you) uncover yourself; impve. 2nd pers. sing. / *desabrigarse*.

desabrigue 1. that I may uncover; pres. subj. 1st pers. sing. / *desabrigar*. 2. that he (she/it) may uncover; pres. subj. 3rd pers. sing. 3. let him (her/it) uncover; impve. 3rd pers. sing.

desabrigué I uncovered; past 1st pers. sing. / *desabrigar*.

desabriguéis that you (all) may uncover; pres. subj. 2nd pers. pl. / *desabrigar*.

desabriguémonos let us uncover ourselves; impve. 1st pers. pl. / *desabrigarse*.

desabriguemos 1. that we may uncover; pres. subj. 1st pers. pl. / *desabrigar*. 2. let us uncover; impve. 1st pers. pl.

desabriguen 1. that they may uncover; pres. subj. 3rd pers. pl. / *desabrigar* 2. let them uncover; impve. 3rd pers. pl.

desabríguense let them uncover themselves; impve. 3rd pers. pl. / *desabrigarse*.

desabrigues that you may uncover; pres. subj. 2nd pers. sing. / *desabrigar*.

desabríguese let him (her/it) uncover himself (herself/itself); impve. 3rd pers. sing. / *desabrigarse*.

desabrir to taint (food) or to vex. reg.

desabrochándose unburdening oneself; pres. part. / *desabrocharse*.

desabrochaos (you all) unburden yourselves; impve. 2nd pers. pl. / *desabrocharse*.

desabrochar to unbutton. reg.

desabrocharse to unburden oneself. reg.

desabróchate (you) unburden yourself; impve. 2nd pers. sing. / *desabrocharse*.

desabrochémonos let us unburden ourselves; impve. 1st pers. pl. / *desabrocharse*.

desabróchense let them unburden themselves; impve. 3rd pers. pl. / *desabrocharse*.

desabróchese let him (her/it) unburden himself (herself/itself); impve. 3rd pers. sing. / *desabrocharse*.

desacalorándose cooling off; pres. part. / *desacalorarse*.

desacaloraos (you all) cool off; impve. 2nd pers. pl. / *desacalorarse*.

desacalorarse to cool off. reg.

desacalórate (you) cool off; impve. 2nd pers. sing. / *desacalorarse*.

desacalorémonos let us cool off; impve. 1st pers. pl. / *desacalorarse*.

desacalórense let them cool off; impve. 3rd pers. pl. / *desacalorarse*.

desacalórese let him (her/it) cool off; impve. 3rd pers. sing. / *desacalorarse*.

desacatar to behave disrespectfully. reg.

desacerbar to mitigate or to temper. reg.

desacertar to err. irr.

desacierta 1. he (she/it) errs; pres. ind. 3rd pers. sing. / *desacertar*. 2. (you) err; impve. 2nd pers. sing.

desaciertan they err; pres. ind. 3rd pers. pl. / *desacertar*.

desaciertas you err; pres. ind. 2nd pers. sing. / *desacertar*.

desacierte 1. that I may err; pres. subj. 1st pers. sing. / *desacertar*. 2. that he (she/it) may err; pres. subj. 3rd pers. sing. 3. let him (her/it) err; impve. 3rd pers. sing.

desacierten 1. that they may err; pres. subj. 3rd pers. pl. / *desacertar*. 2. let them err; impve. 3rd pers. pl.

desaciertes that you may err; pres. subj. 2nd pers. sing. / *desacertar*.

desacierto I err; pres. ind. 1st pers. sing. / *desacertar*.

desacomodándose losing one's job; pres. part. / *desacomodarse*.

desacomodaos (you all) lose your jobs; impve. 2nd pers. pl. / *desacomodarse*.

desacomodar to inconvenience or to dismiss. reg.

desacomodarse to lose one's job. reg.

desacomódate (you) lose your job; impve. 2nd pers. sing. / *desacomodarse*.

desacomodémonos let us lose our jobs; impve. 1st pers. pl. / *desacomodarse*.

desacomódense let them lose their jobs; impve. 3rd pers. pl. / *desacomodarse*.

desacomódese let him (her) lose his (her) job; impve. 3rd pers. sing. / *desacomodarse*.

desaconsejar to dissuade. reg.

desacoplar to uncouple. reg.

desacordándose being forgetful; pres. part. / *desacordarse*.

desacordaos (you all) be forgetful; impve. 2nd pers. pl. / *desacordarse*.

desacordar to put out of tune. irr.

desacordarse to be forgetful. irr.

desacordémonos let us be forgetful; impve. 1st pers. pl. / *desacordarse*.

desacostumbrándose becoming unaccustomed; pres. part. / *desacostumbrarse*.

desacostumbraos (you all) become unaccustomed; impve. 2nd pers. pl. / *desacostumbrarse*.

desacostumbrar to break a habit. reg.

desacostumbrarse to become unaccustomed. reg.

desacostúmbrate (you) become unaccustomed; impve. 2nd pers. sing. / *desacostumbrarse*.

desacostumbrémonos let us become unaccustomed; impve. 1st pers. pl. / *desacostumbrarse*.

desacostúmbrense let them become unaccustomed; impve. 3rd pers. pl. / *desacostumbrarse*.

desacostúmbrese let him (her/it) become unaccustomed; impve. 3rd pers. sing. / *desacostumbrarse*.

desacotar to lay open (ground) or to remove (a restriction). reg.

desacreditar to discredit. reg.

desactivar to deactivate. reg.

desacuerda 1. he (she/it) puts out of tune; pres. ind. 3rd pers. sing. / *desacordar*. 2. (you) put out of tune; impve. 2nd pers. sing.

desacuerdan they put out of tune; pres. ind. 3rd pers. pl. / *desacordar*.

desacuerdas you put out of tune; pres. ind. 2nd pers. sing. / *desacordar*.

desacuérdate (you) be forgetful; impve. 2nd pers. sing. / *desacordarse*.

desacuerde 1. that I may put out of tune; pres. subj. 1st pers. sing. / *desacordar*. 2. that he (she/it) may put out of tune; pres. subj. 3rd pers. sing. 3. let him (her/it) put out of tune; impve. 3rd pers. sing.

desacuerden 1. that they may put out of tune; pres. subj. 3rd pers. pl. / *desacordar*. 2. let them put out of tune; impve. 3rd pers. pl.

desacuérdense let them be forgetful; impve. 3rd pers. pl. / *desacordarse*.

desacuerdes that you may put out of tune; pres. subj. 2nd pers. sing. / *desacordar*.

desacuérdese let him (her/it) be forgetful; impve. 3rd pers. sing. / *desacordarse*.

desacuerdo I put out of tune; pres. ind. 1st pers. sing. / *desacordar*.

desadvertir to overlook. irr.

desadvierta 1. that I may overlook; pres. subj. 1st pers. sing. / *desadvertir*. 2. that he (she/it) may overlook; pres. subj. 3rd pers. sing. 3. let him (her/it) overlook; impve. 3rd pers. sing.

desadviertan 1. that they may overlook; pres. subj. 3rd pers. pl. / *desadvertir*. 2. let them overlook; impve. 3rd pers. pl.

desadviertas that you may overlook; pres. subj. 2nd pers. sing. / *desadvertir*.

desadvierte 1. he (she/it) overlooks; pres. ind. 3rd pers. sing. / *desadvertir*. 2. (you) overlook; impve. 2nd pers. sing.

desadvierten they overlook; pres. ind. 3rd pers. pl. / *desadvertir*.

desadviertes you overlook; pres. ind. 2nd pers. sing. / *desadvertir*.

desadvierto I overlook; pres. ind. 1st pers. sing. / *desadvertir*.

desadvirtáis that you (all) may overlook; pres. subj. 2nd pers. pl. / *desavertir*.

desadvirtamos 1. that we may overlook; pres. subj. 1st pers. pl. / *desadvertir* 2. let us overlook; impve. 1st pers. pl.

desadvirtiendo overlooking; pres. part. / *desadvertir*.

desadvirtiera 1. that I might overlook; imp. subj. 1st pers. sing. / *desadvertir*. 2. that he (she/it) might overlook; imp. subj. 3rd pers. sing.

desadvirtierais that you (all) might overlook; imp. subj. 2nd pers pl. / *desadvertir*.

desadvirtiéramos that we might overlook; imp. subj. 1st pers. pl. / *desadvertir*.

desadvirtieran that they might overlook; imp. subj. 3rd pers. pl. / *desadvertir*.

desadvirtieras that you might overlook; imp. subj. 2nd pers. sing. / *desadvertir*.

desadvirtieron they overlooked; past 3rd pers. pl. / *desadvertir*.

desadvirtiese 1. that I might overlook; imp. subj. 1st pers. sing. / *desadvertir*. 2. that he (she/it) might overlook; imp. subj. 3rd pers. sing.

desadvirtieseis that you (all) might overlook; imp. subj. 2nd pers pl. / *desadvertir*.

desadvirtiésemos that we might overlook; imp. subj. 1st pers. pl. / *desadvertir*.

desadvirtiesen that they might overlook; imp. subj. 3rd pers. pl. / *desadvertir.*

desadvirtieses that you might overlook; imp. subj. 2nd pers. sing. / *desadvertir.*

desadvirtió he (she/it) overlooked; past 3rd pers. sing. / *desadvertir.*

desaferrar to loosen or to persuade. reg.

desafía 1. he (she/it) challenges; pres. ind. 3rd pers. sing. / *desafiar.* 2. (you) challenge; impve. 2nd pers. sing.

desafían they challenge; pres. ind. 3rd pers. pl. / *desafiar.*

desafiar to challenge or to defy. irr.

desafías you challenge; pres. ind. 2nd pers. sing. / *desafiar.*

desaficionándose losing one's liking for; pres. part. / *desaficionarse.*

desaficionaos (you all) lose your liking for; impve. 2nd pers. pl. / *desaficionarse.*

desaficionar to disaffect or to stop the desire to. reg.

desaficionarse to lose one's liking for. reg.

desaficiónate (you) lose your liking for; impve. 2nd pers. sing. / *desaficionarse.*

desaficionémonos let us lose our liking for; impve. 1st pers. pl. / *desaficionarse.*

desaficiónense let them lose their liking for; impve. 3rd pers. pl. / *desaficionarse.*

desaficiónese let him (her/it) lose his (her/its) liking for; impve. 3rd pers. sing. / *desaficionarse.*

desafíe 1. that I may challenge; pres. subj. 1st pers. sing. / *desafiar.* 2. that he (she/it) may challenge; pres. subj. 3rd pers. sing. 3. let him (her/it) challenge; impve. 3rd pers. sing.

desafíen 1. that they may challenge; pres. subj. 3rd pers. pl. / *desafiar* 2. let them challenge; impve. 3rd pers. pl.

desafíes that you may challenge; pres. subj. 2nd pers. sing. / *desafiar.*

desafilar to blunt or to dull. reg.

desafinándose getting out of tune; pres. part. / *desafinarse.*

desafinaos (you all) get out of tune; impve. 2nd pers. pl. / *desafinarse.*

desafinar to be discordant. reg.

desafinarse to get out of tune. reg.

desafínate (you) get out of tune; impve. 2nd pers. sing. / *desafinarse.*

desafinémonos let us get out of tune; impve. 1st pers. pl. / *desafinarse.*

desafínense let them get out of tune; impve. 3rd pers. pl. / *desafinarse.*

desafínese let him (her/it) get out of tune; impve. 3rd pers. sing. / *desafinarse.*

desafío I challenge; pres. ind. 1st pers. sing. / *desafiar.*

desaforándose overstepping the mark; pres. part. / *desaforarse.*

desaforaos (you all) overstep the mark; impve. 2nd pers. pl. / *desaforarse.*

desaforar to encroach on the rights of. irr.

desaforarse to overstep the mark. irr.

desaforémonos let us overstep the mark; impve. 1st pers. pl. / *desaforarse.*

desafuera 1. he (she/it) encroaches on the rights of; pres. ind. 3rd pers. sing. / *desaforar.* 2. (you) encroach on the rights of; impve. 2nd pers. sing.

desafueran they encroach on the rights of; pres. ind. 3rd pers. pl. / *desaforar.*

desafueras you encroach on the rights of; pres. ind. 2nd pers. sing. / *desaforar.*

desafuérate (you) overstep the mark; impve. 2nd pers. sing. / *desaforarse.*

desafuere 1. that I may encroach on the rights of; pres. subj. 1st pers. sing. / *desaforar.* 2. that he (she/it) may encroach on the rights of; pres. subj. 3rd pers. sing. 3. let him (her/it) encroach on the rights of; impve. 3rd pers. sing.

desafueren 1. that they may encroach on the rights of; pres. subj. 3rd pers. pl. / *desaforar.* 2. let them encroach on the rights of; impve. 3rd pers. pl.

desafuérense let them overstep the mark; impve. 3rd pers. pl. / *desaforarse.*

desafueres that you may encroach on the rights of; pres. subj. 2nd pers. sing. / *desaforar.*

desafuérese let him (her/it) overstep the mark; impve. 3rd pers. sing. / *desaforarse.*

desafuero I encroach on the rights of; pres. ind. 1st pers. sing. / *desaforar.*

desagradar to displease. reg.

desagradecer to be ungrateful. irr.

desagradezca 1. that I may be ungrateful; pres. subj. 1st pers. sing. / *desagradecer.* 2. that he (she/it) may be ungrateful; pres. subj. 3rd pers. sing. 3. let him (her/it) be ungrateful; impve. 3rd pers. sing.

desagradezcáis that you (all) may be ungrateful; pres. subj. 2nd pers. pl. / *desagradecer.*

desagradezcamos 1. that we may be ungrateful; pres. subj. 1st pers. pl. / *desagradecer.* 2. let us be ungrateful; impve. 1st pers. pl.

desagradezcan 1. that they may be ungrateful; pres. subj. 3rd pers. pl. / *desagradecer.* 2. let them be ungrateful; impve. 3rd pers. pl.

desagradezcas that you may be ungrateful; pres. subj. 2nd pers. sing. / *desagradecer.*

desagradezco I am ungrateful; pres. ind. 1st pers. sing. / *desagradecer.*

desagraviar to make amends to. reg.

desagregándose disintegrating; pres. part. / *desagregarse.*

desagregaos (you all) disintegrate; impve. 2nd pers. pl. / *desagregarse.*

desagregar to separate or to disintegrate. irr.

desagregarse to disintegrate. irr.

desagrégate (you) disintegrate; impve. 2nd pers. sing. / *desagregarse.*

desagregue 1. that I may separate; pres. subj. 1st pers. sing. / *desagregar.* 2. that he (she/it) may separate; pres. subj. 3rd pers. sing. 3. let him (her/it) separate; impve. 3rd pers. sing.

desagregué I separated; past 1st pers. sing. / *desagregar.*

desagreguéis that you (all) may separate; pres. subj. 2nd pers. pl. / *desagregar.*

desagreguémonos let us disintegrate; impve. 1st pers. pl. / *desagregarse.*

desagreguemos 1. that we may separate; pres. subj. 1st pers. pl. / *desagregar.* 2. let us separate; impve. 1st pers. pl.

desagreguen 1. that they may separate; pres. subj. 3rd pers. pl. / *desagregar.* 2. let them separate; impve. 3rd pers. pl.

desagréguense let them disintegrate; impve. 3rd pers. pl. / *desagregarse.*

desagregues that you may separate; pres. subj. 2nd pers. sing. / *desagregar.*

desagréguese let him (her/it) disintegrate; impve. 3rd pers. sing. / *desagregarse.*

desaguar to drain. irr.

desagüe 1. that I may drain; pres. subj. 1st pers. sing. / *desaguar.* 2. that he (she/it) may drain; pres. subj. 3rd pers. sing. 3. let him (her/it) drain; impve. 3rd pers. sing.

desagüé I drained; past 1st pers. sing. / *desaguar.*

desagüéis that you (all) may drain; pres. subj. 2nd pers. pl. / *desaguar.*

desagüemos 1. that we may drain; pres. subj. 1st pers. pl. / *desaguar.* 2. let us drain; impve. 1st pers. pl.

desagüen 1. that they may drain; pres. subj. 3rd pers. pl. / *desaguar.* 2. let them drain; impve. 3rd pers. pl.

desagües that you may drain; pres. subj. 2nd pers. sing. / *desaguar.*

desahogándose finding relief; pres. part. / *desahogarse.*

desahogaos (you all) find relief; impve. 2nd pers. pl. / *desahogarse.*

desahogar to relieve or ease from pain. irr.

desahogarse to find relief or release. irr.

desahógate (you) find relief; impve. 2nd pers. sing. / *desahogarse.*

desahogue 1. that I may relieve; pres. subj. 1st pers. sing. / *desahogar.* 2. that he (she/it) may relieve; pres. subj. 3rd pers. sing. 3. let him (her/it) relieve; impve. 3rd pers. sing.

desahogué I relieved; past 1st pers. sing. / *desahogar.*

desahoguéis that you (all) may relieve; pres. subj. 2nd pers. pl. / *desahogar.*

desahoguémonos let us find relief; impve. 1st pers. pl. / *desahogarse.*

desahoguemos 1. that we may relieve; pres. subj. 1st pers. pl. / *desahogar.* 2. let us relieve; impve. 1st pers. pl.

desahoguen 1. that they may relieve; pres. subj. 3rd pers. pl. / *desahogar.* 2. let them relieve; impve. 3rd pers. pl.

desahóguense let them find relief; impve. 3rd pers. pl. / *desahogarse.*

desahogues that you may relieve; pres. subj. 2nd pers. sing. / *desahogar.*

desahóguese let him (her/it) find relief; impve. 3rd pers. sing. / *desahogarse.*

desahuciándose despairing; pres. part. / *desahuciarse.*

desahuciaos (you all) despair; impve. 2nd pers. pl. / *desahuciarse.*

desahuciar to declare incurable or to evict. reg.

desahuciarse to despair. reg.

desahucíate (you) despair; impve. 2nd pers. sing. / *desahuciarse.*

desahuciémonos let us despair; impve. 1st pers. pl. / *desahuciarse.*

desahucíense let them despair; impve. 3rd pers. pl. / *desahuciarse.*

desahucíese let him (her/it) despair; impve. 3rd pers. sing. / *desahuciarse.*

desahumar to clear of smoke. reg.

desairar to slight. reg.

desajustándose disagreeing; pres. part. / *desajustarse.*

desajustaos (you all) disagree; impve. 2nd pers. pl. / *desajustarse.*

desajustar to disarrange. reg.

desajustarse to disagree. reg.

desajústate (you) disagree; impve. 2nd pers. sing. / *desajustarse.*

desajustémonos let us disagree; impve. 1st pers. pl. / *desajustarse.*

desajústense let them disagree; impve. 3rd pers. pl. / *desajustarse.*

desajústese let him (her/it) disagree; impve. 3rd pers. sing. / *desajustarse.*

desalándose hastening; pres. part. / *desalarse.*

desalaos (you all) hasten; impve. 2nd pers. pl. / *desalarse.*

desalar to desalt. reg.

desalar to clip the wings of or to rush or to yearn. reg.

desalarse to hasten. reg.

desálate (you) hasten; impve. 2nd pers. sing. / *desalarse.*

desalémonos let us hasten; impve. 1st pers. pl. / *desalarse.*

desálense let them hasten; impve. 3rd pers. pl. / *desalarse.*

desalentándose getting discouraged; pres. part. / *desalentarse.*

desalentaos (you all) get discouraged; impve. 2nd pers. pl. / *desalentarse.*

desalentar to discourage or to make breathless. irr.

desalentarse to get discouraged. irr.

desalentémonos let us get discouraged; impve. 1st pers. pl. / *desalentarse.*

desálese let him (her/it) hasten; impve. 3rd pers. sing. / *desalarse.*

desalienta 1. he (she/it) discourages; pres. ind. 3rd pers. sing. / *desalentar.* 2. (you) discourage; impve. 2nd pers. sing.

desalientan they discourage; pres. ind. 3rd pers. pl. / *desalentar.*

desalientas you discourage; pres. ind. 2nd pers. sing. / *desalentar.*

desaliéntate (you) get discouraged; impve. 2nd pers. sing. / *desalentarse*.

desaliente 1. that I may discourage; pres. subj. 1st pers. sing. / *desalentar*. 2. that he (she/it) may discourage; pres. subj. 3rd pers. sing. 3. let him (her/it) discourage; impve. 3rd pers. sing.

desalienten 1. that they may discourage; pres. subj. 3rd pers. pl. / *desalentar*. 2. let them discourage; impve. 3rd pers. pl.

desaliéntense let them get discouraged; impve. 3rd pers. pl. / *desalentarse*.

desalientes that you may discourage; pres. subj. 2nd pers. sing. / *desalentar*.

desaliéntese let him (her/it) get discouraged; impve. 3rd pers. sing. / *desalentarse*.

desaliento I discourage; pres. ind. 1st pers. sing. / *desalentar*.

desalinear to put out of alignment. reg.

desaliñar to disarrange. reg.

desalivar to salivate. reg.

desalmándose being eager; pres. part. / *desalmarse*.

desalmaos (you all) be eager; impve. 2nd pers. pl. / *desalmarse*.

desalmar to weaken. reg.

desalmarse to be eager. reg.

desálmate (you) be eager; impve. 2nd pers. sing. / *desalmarse*.

desalmémonos let us be eager; impve. 1st pers. pl. / *desalmarse*.

desálmense let them be eager; impve. 3rd pers. pl. / *desalmarse*.

desálmese let him (her/it) be eager; impve. 3rd pers. sing. / *desalmarse*.

desalojar to dislodge or to evict. reg.

desalquilar to discontinue the rental of. reg.

desalterar to allay or to assuage. reg.

desamar to dislike. reg.

desamarrar to untie. reg.

desamistándose quarreling; pres. part. / *desamistarse*.

desamistaos (you all) quarrel; impve. 2nd pers. pl. / *desamistarse*.

desamistarse to quarrel. reg.

desamístate (you) quarrel; impve. 2nd pers. sing. / *desamistarse*.

desamistémonos let us quarrel; impve. 1st pers. pl. / *desamistarse*.

desamístense let them quarrel; impve. 3rd pers. pl. / *desamistarse*.

desamístese let him (her/it) quarrel; impve. 3rd pers. sing. / *desamistarse*.

desamorar to alienate. reg.

desamortice 1. that I may disentail; pres. subj. 1st pers. sing. / *desamortizar*. 2. that he (she/it) may disentail; pres. subj. 3rd pers. sing. 3. let him (her/it) disentail; impve. 3rd pers. sing.

desamorticé I disentailed; past 1st pers. sing. / *desamortizar*.

desamorticéis that you (all) may disentail; pres. subj. 2nd pers. pl. / *desamortizar*.

desamorticemos 1. that we may disentail; pres. subj. 1st pers. pl. / *desamortizar*. 2. let us disentail; impve. 1st pers. pl.

desamorticen 1. that they may disentail; pres. subj. 3rd pers. pl. / *desamortizar*. 2. let them disentail; impve. 3rd pers. pl.

desamortices that you may disentail; pres. subj. 2nd pers. sing. / *desamortizar*.

desamortizar to disentail. irr.

desamparar to abandon or forsake. reg.

desamueblar to strip of furniture. reg.

desandar to retrace. irr.

desanduve I retraced; past 1st pers. sing. / *desandar*.

desanduviera 1. that I might retrace; imp. subj. 1st pers. sing. / *desandar*. 2. that he (she/it) might retrace; imp. subj. 3rd pers. sing.

desanduvierais that you (all) might retrace; imp. subj. 2nd pers pl. / *desandar*.

desanduviéramos that we might retrace; imp. subj. 1st pers. pl. / *desandar*.

desanduvieran that they might retrace; imp. subj. 3rd pers. pl. / *desandar*.

desanduvieras that you might retrace; imp. subj. 2nd pers. sing. / *desandar*.

desanduvieron they retraced; past 3rd pers. pl. / *desandar*.

desanduviese 1. that I might retrace; imp. subj. 1st pers. sing. / *desandar*. 2. that he (she/it) might retrace; imp. subj. 3rd pers. sing.

desanduvieseis that you (all) might retrace; imp. subj. 2nd pers pl. / *desandar*.

desanduviésemos that we might retrace; imp. subj. 1st pers. pl. / *desandar*.

desanduviesen that they might retrace; imp. subj. 3rd pers. pl. / *desandar*.

desanduvieses that you might retrace; imp. subj. 2nd pers. sing. / *desandar*.

desanduvimos we retraced; past 1st pers. pl. / *desandar*.

desanduviste you retraced; past 2nd pers. sing. / *desandar*.

desanduvisteis you (all) retraced; past 2nd pers. pl. / *desandar*.

desanduvo he (she/it) retraced; past 3rd per. sing. / *desandar*.

desangrándose losing blood; pres. part. / *desangrarse*.

desangraos (you all) lose blood; impve. 2nd pers. pl. / *desangrarse*.

desangrar to bleed heavily or to drain. reg.

desangrarse to lose blood. reg.

desángrate (you) lose blood; impve. 2nd pers. sing. / *desangrarse*.

desangrémonos let us lose blood; impve. 1st pers. pl. / *desangrarse*.

desángrense let them lose blood; impve. 3rd pers. pl. / *desangrarse*.

desángrese let him (her/it) lose blood; impve. 3rd pers. sing. / *desangrarse*.

desanimándose becoming discouraged; pres. part. / *desanimarse.*

desanimaos (you all) become discouraged; impve. 2nd pers. pl. / *desanimarse.*

desanimar to dishearten. reg.

desanimarse to become discouraged. reg.

desanímate (you) become discouraged; impve. 2nd pers. sing. / *desanimarse.*

desanimémonos let us become discouraged; impve. 1st pers. pl. / *desanimarse.*

desanímense let them become discouraged; impve. 3rd pers. pl. / *desanimarse.*

desanímese let him (her/it) become discouraged; impve. 3rd pers. sing. / *desanimarse.*

desanublándose clearing up (weather); pres. part. / *desanublarse.*

desanublar to clarify. reg.

desanublarse to clear up (weather). reg.

desanúblese let it clear up (weather); impve. 3rd pers. sing. / *desanublarse.*

desanudar to untie. reg.

desañudar to untie. reg.

desapadrinar to disapprove of. reg.

desapareceos (you all) vanish; impve. 2nd pers. pl. / *desaparecerse.*

desaparecer to disappear. irr.

desaparecerse to vanish. irr.

desaparécete (you) vanish; impve. 2nd pers. sing. / *desaparecerse.*

desapareciéndose vanishing; pres. part. / *desaparecerse.*

desaparejar to unharness. reg.

desaparezca 1. that I may disappear; pres. subj. 1st pers. sing. / *desaparecer.* 2. that he (she/it) may disappear; pres. subj. 3rd pers. sing. 3. let him (her/it) disappear; impve. 3rd pers. sing.

desaparezcáis that you (all) may disappear; pres. subj. 2nd pers. pl. / *desaparecer.*

desaparezcámonos let us vanish; impve. 1st pers. pl. / *desaparecerse.*

desaparezcamos 1. that we may disappear; pres. subj. 1st pers. pl. / *desaparecer.* 2. let us disappear; impve. 1st pers. pl.

desaparezcan 1. that they may disappear; pres. subj. 3rd pers. pl. / *desaparecer.* 2. let them disappear; impve. 3rd pers. pl.

desaparézcanse let them vanish; impve. 3rd pers. pl. / *desaparecerse.*

desaparezcas that you may disappear; pres. subj. 2nd pers. sing. / *desaparecer.*

desaparézcase let him (her/it) vanish; impve. 3rd pers. sing. / *desaparecerse.*

desaparezco I disappear; pres. ind. 1st pers. sing. / *desaparecer.*

desaparroquiándose losing trade; pres. part. / *desaparroquiarse.*

desaparroquiaos (you all) lose trade; impve. 2nd pers. pl. / *desaparroquiarse.*

desaparroquiar to take customers away from. reg.

desaparroquiarse to lose trade. reg.

desaparroquíate (you) lose trade; impve. 2nd pers. sing. / *desaparroquiarse.*

desaparroquiémonos let us lose trade; impve. 1st pers. pl. / *desaparroquiarse.*

desaparroquíense let them lose trade; impve. 3rd pers. pl. / *desaparroquiarse.*

desaparroquíese let him (her/it) lose trade; impve. 3rd pers. sing. / *desaparroquiarse.*

desapasionándose becoming indifferent; pres. part. / *desapasionarse.*

desapasionaos (you all) become indifferent; impve. 2nd pers. pl. / *desapasionarse.*

desapasionar to make objective. reg.

desapasionarse to become indifferent. reg.

desapasiónate (you) become indifferent; impve. 2nd pers. sing. / *desapasionarse.*

desapasionémonos let us become indifferent; impve. 1st pers. pl. / *desapasionarse.*

desapasiónense let them become indifferent; impve. 3rd pers. pl. / *desapasionarse.*

desapasiónese let him (her/it) become indifferent; impve. 3rd pers. sing. / *desapasionarse.*

desapegándose dissociating oneself; pres. part. / *desapegarse.*

desapegaos (you all) dissociate yourselves; impve. 2nd pers. pl. / *desapegarse.*

desapegarse to dissociate oneself. irr.

desapégate (you) dissociate yourself; impve. 2nd pers. sing. / *desapegarse.*

desapegue 1. that I may dissociate myself; pres. subj. 1st pers. sing. / *desapegarse.* 2. that he (she/it) may dissociate himself (herself/itself); pres. subj. 3rd pers. sing.

desapegué I dissociated myself; past 1st pers. sing. / *desapegarse.*

desapeguéis that you (all) may dissociate yourselves; pres. subj. 2nd pers. pl. / *desapegarse.*

desapeguémonos let us dissociate ourselves; impve. 1st pers. pl. / *desapegarse.*

desapeguemos that we may dissociate ourselves; pres. subj. 1st pers. pl. / *desapegarse.*

desapeguen that they may dissociate themselves; pres. subj. 3rd pers. pl. / *desapegarse.*

desapéguense let them dissociate themselves; impve. 3rd pers. pl. / *desapegarse.*

desapegues that you may dissociate yourself; pres. subj. 2nd pers. sing. / *desapegarse.*

desapéguese let him (her/it) dissociate himself (herself/itself); impve. 3rd pers. sing. / *desapegarse.*

desaplicándose being idle; pres. part. / *desaplicarse.*

desaplicaos (you all) be idle; impve. 2nd pers. pl. / *desaplicarse.*

desaplicar to make idle. irr.

desaplicarse to be idle. irr.

desaplícate (you) be idle; impve. 2nd pers. sing. / *desaplicarse.*

desaplique 1. that I may make idle; pres. subj. 1st pers. sing. / *desaplicar.* 2. that he (she/it) may make idle; pres. subj. 3rd pers. sing. 3. let him (her/it) make idle; impve. 3rd pers. sing.

desapliqué I made idle; past 1st pers. sing. / *desaplicar.*

desapliquéis that you (all) may make idle; pres. subj. 2nd pers. pl. / *desaplicar.*

desapliquémonos let us be idle; impve. 1st pers. pl. / *desaplicarse.*

desapliquemos 1. that we may make idle; pres. subj. 1st pers. pl. / *desaplicar* 2. let us make idle; impve. 1st pers. pl.

desapliquen 1. that they may make idle; pres. subj. 3rd pers. pl. / *desaplicar.* 2. let them make idle; impve. 3rd pers. pl.

desaplíquense let them be idle; impve. 3rd pers. pl. / *desaplicarse.*

desapliques that you may make idle; pres. subj. 2nd pers. sing. / *desaplicar.*

desaplíquese let him (her/it) be idle; impve. 3rd pers. sing. / *desaplicarse.*

desapoderar to disposses. reg.

desaposesionar to dispossess. reg.

desapreciar to underestimate. reg.

desaprender to unlearn. reg.

desaprensar to take the shine off or to free. reg.

desaprobar to disapprove. irr.

desapropiándose surrendering; pres. part. / *desapropiarse.*

desapropiaos (you all) surrender; impve. 2nd pers. pl. / *desapropiarse.*

desapropiar to take from. reg.

desapropiarse to surrender. reg.

desapropíate (you) surrender; impve. 2nd pers. sing. / *desapropiarse.*

desapropiémonos let us surrender; impve. 1st pers. pl. / *desapropiarse.*

desapropíense let them surrender; impve. 3rd pers. pl. / *desapropiarse.*

desapropíese let him (her/it) surrender; impve. 3rd pers. sing. / *desapropiarse.*

desaprovechar to waste or misuse. reg.

desaprueba 1. he (she/it) disapproves; pres. ind. 3rd pers. sing. / *desaprobar.* 2. (you) disapprove; impve. 2nd pers. sing.

desaprueban they disapprove; pres. ind. 3rd pers. pl. / *desaprobar.*

desapruebas you disapprove; pres. ind. 2nd pers. sing. / *desaprobar.*

desapruebe 1. that I may disapprove; pres. subj. 1st pers. sing. / *desaprobar.* 2. that he (she/it) may disapprove; pres. subj. 3rd pers. sing. 3. let him (her/it) disapprove; impve. 3rd pers. sing.

desaprueben 1. that they may disapprove; pres. subj. 3rd pers. pl. / *desaprobar.* 2. let them disapprove; impve. 3rd pers. pl.

desapruebes that you may disapprove; pres. subj. 2nd pers. sing. / *desaprobar.*

desapruebo I disapprove; pres. ind. 1st pers. sing. / *desaprobar.*

desapuntalar to remove the supports of. reg.

desapuntar to unstitch or to make one lose aim. reg.

desarbolar to unmast. reg.

desarmándose disarming; pres. part. / *desarmarse.*

desarmaos (you all) disarm; impve. 2nd pers. pl. / *desarmarse.*

desarmar to disarm or to take apart. reg.

desarmarse to disarm. reg.

desármate (you) disarm; impve. 2nd pers. sing. / *desarmarse.*

desarmémonos let us disarm; impve. 1st pers. pl. / *desarmarse.*

desármense let them disarm; impve. 3rd pers. pl. / *desarmarse.*

desármese let him (her/it) disarm; impve. 3rd pers. sing. / *desarmarse.*

desarraigar to uproot or to expel. irr.

desarraigue 1. that I may uproot; pres. subj. 1st pers. sing. / *desarraigar.* 2. that he (she/it) may uproot; pres. subj. 3rd pers. sing. 3. let him (her/it) uproot; impve. 3rd pers. sing.

desarraigué I uprooted; past 1st pers. sing. / *desarraigar.*

desarraiguéis that you (all) may uproot; pres. subj. 2nd pers. pl. / *desarraigar.*

desarraiguemos 1. that we may uproot; pres. subj. 1st pers. pl. / *desarraigar.* 2. let us uproot; impve. 1st pers. pl.

desarraiguen 1. that they may uproot; pres. subj. 3rd pers. pl. / *desarraigar* 2. let them uproot; impve. 3rd pers. pl.

desarraigues that you may uproot; pres. subj. 2nd pers. sing. / *desarraigar.*

desarrebujar to disentangle. reg.

desarreglar to disarrange or to upset. reg.

desarrimar to separate or to dissuade. reg.

desarrollándose growing; pres. part. / *desarrollarse.*

desarrollaos (you all) grow; impve. 2nd pers. pl. / *desarrollarse.*

desarrollar to unroll or to develop. reg.

desarrollarse to grow or to happen. reg.

desarróllate (you) grow; impve. 2nd pers. sing. / *desarrollarse.*

desarrollémonos let us grow; impve. 1st pers. pl. / *desarrollarse.*

desarróllense let them grow; impve. 3rd pers. pl. / *desarrollarse.*

desarróllese let him (her/it) grow; impve. 3rd pers. sing. / *desarrollarse.*

desarropar to undress. reg.

desarrugar to unwrinkle. irr.

desarrugue 1. that I may unwrinkle; pres. subj. 1st pers. sing. / *desarrugar.* 2. that he (she/it) may unwrinkle; pres. subj. 3rd pers. sing. 3. let him (her/it) unwrinkle; impve. 3rd pers. sing.

desarrugué I unwrinkled; past 1st pers. sing. / *desarrugar.*

desarruguéis that you (all) may unwrinkle; pres. subj. 2nd pers. pl. / *desarrugar.*

desarruguemos 1. that we may unwrinkle; pres. subj. 1st pers. pl. / *desarrugar* 2. let us unwrinkle; impve. 1st pers. pl.

desarruguen 1. that they may unwrinkle; pres. subj. 3rd pers. pl. / *desarrugar*. 2. let them unwrinkle; impve. 3rd pers. pl.

desarrugues that you may unwrinkle; pres. subj. 2nd pers. sing. / *desarrugar*.

desarticular to dislocate. reg.

desasear to mess up. reg.

desásete (you) get rid (of); impve. 2nd pers. sing. / *desasirse*.

desasga 1. that I may loosen; pres. subj. 1st pers. sing. / *desasir*. 2. that he (she/it) may loosen; pres. subj. 3rd pers. sing. 3. let him (her/it) loosen; impve. 3rd pers. sing.

desasgáis that you (all) may loosen; pres. subj. 2nd pers. pl. / *desasir*.

desasgámonos let us get rid (of); impve. 1st pers. pl. / *desasirse*.

desasgamos 1. that we may loosen; pres. subj. 1st pers. pl. / *desasir*. 2. let us loosen; impve. 1st pers. pl. / *desasirse*.

desasgan 1. that they may loosen; pres. subj. 3rd pers. pl. / *desasir*. 2. let them loosen; impve. 3rd pers. pl.

desásganse let them get rid (of); impve. 3rd pers. pl. / *desasirse*.

desasgas that you may loosen; pres. subj. 2nd pers. sing. / *desasir*.

desásgase let him (her/it) get rid (of); impve. 3rd pers. sing. / *desasirse*.

desasgo I loosen; pres. ind. 1st pers. sing. / *desasir*.

desasiéndose getting rid (of); pres. part. / *desasirse*.

desasíos (you all) get rid (of); impve. 2nd pers. pl. / *desasirse*.

desasir to loosen. irr.

desasirse to get rid (of). irr.

desasociar to dissociate. reg.

desasosegar to disquiet. irr.

desasosegué I disquieted; past 1st pers. sing. / *desasosegar*.

desasoseguéis that you (all) may disquiet; pres. subj. 2nd pers. pl. / *desasosegar*.

desasoseguemos 1. that we may disquiet; pres. subj. 1st pers. pl. / *desasosegar* 2. let us disquiet; impve. 1st pers. pl.

desasosiega 1. he (she/it) disquiets; pres. ind. 3rd pers. sing. / *desasosegar*. 2. (you) disquiet; impve. 2nd pers. sing.

desasosiegan they disquiet; pres. ind. 3rd pers. pl. / *desasosegar*.

desasosiegas you disquiet; pres. ind. 2nd pers. sing. / *desasosegar*.

desasosiego I disquiet; pres. ind. 1st pers. sing. / *desasosegar*.

desasosiegue 1. that I may disquiet; pres. subj. 1st pers. sing. / *desasosegar*. 2. that he (she/it) may disquiet; pres. subj. 3rd pers. sing. 3. let him (her/it) disquiet; impve. 3rd pers. sing.

desasosieguen 1. that they may disquiet; pres. subj. 3rd pers. pl. / *desasosegar*. 2. let them disquiet; impve. 3rd pers. pl.

desasosiegues that you may disquiet; pres. subj. 2nd pers. sing. / *desasosegar*.

desatándose breaking out; pres. part. / *desatarse*.

desataos (you all) break out; impve. 2nd pers. pl. / *desatarse*.

desatar to untie. reg.

desatarse to break out. reg.

desatascar to extricate or to unclog. irr.

desatasque 1. that I may extricate; pres. subj. 1st pers. sing. / *desatascar*. 2. that he (she/it) may extricate; pres. subj. 3rd pers. sing. 3. let him (her/it) extricate; impve. 3rd pers. sing.

desatasqué I extricated; past 1st pers. sing. / *desatascar*.

desatasquéis that you (all) may extricate; pres. subj. 2nd pers. pl. / *desatascar*.

desatasquemos 1. that we may extricate; pres. subj. 1st pers. pl. / *desatascar* 2. let us extricate; impve. 1st pers. pl.

desatasquen 1. that they may extricate; pres. subj. 3rd pers. pl. / *desatascar*. 2. let them extricate; impve. 3rd pers. pl.

desatasques that you may extricate; pres. subj. 2nd pers. sing. / *desatascar*.

desátate (you) break out; impve. 2nd pers. sing. / *desatarse*.

desatavía 1. he (she/it) strips of decorations; pres. ind. 3rd pers. sing. / *desataviar*. 2. (you) strip of decorations; impve. 2nd pers. sing.

desatavían they strip of decorations; pres. ind. 3rd pers. pl. / *desataviar*.

desataviar to strip of decorations. irr.

desatavías you strip of decorations; pres. ind. 2nd pers. sing. / *desataviar*.

desatavíe 1. that I may strip or decorations; pres. subj. 1st pers. sing. / *desataviar*. 2. that he (she/it) may strip of decorations; pres. subj. 3rd pers. sing. 3. let him (her/it) strip of decorations; impve. 3rd pers. sing.

desatavíen 1. that they may strip of decorations; pres. subj. 3rd pers. pl. / *desataviar*. 2. let them strip of decorations; impve. 3rd pers. pl.

desatavíes that you may strip of decorations; pres. subj. 2nd pers. sing. / *desataviar*.

desatavío I strip of decorations; pres. ind. 1st pers. sing. / *desataviar*.

desatémonos let us break out; impve. 1st pers. pl. / *desatarse*.

desatender to disregard. irr.

desátense let them break out; impve. 3rd pers. pl. / *desatarse*.

desátese let him (her/it) break out; impve. 3rd pers. sing. / *desatarse*.

desatienda 1. that I may disregard; pres. subj. 1st pers. sing. / *desatender*. 2. that he (she/it) may disregard; pres. subj. 3rd pers. sing. 3. let him (her/it) disregard; impve. 3rd pers. sing.

desatiendan 1. that they may disregard; pres. subj. 3rd pers. pl. / *desatender*. 2. let them disregard; impve. 3rd pers. pl.

desatiendas that you may disregard; pres. subj. 2nd pers. sing. / *desatender*.

desatiende 1. he (she/it) disregards; pres. ind. 3rd pers. sing. / *desatender*. 2. (you) disregard; impve. 2nd pers. sing.

desatienden they disregard; pres. ind. 3rd pers. pl. / *desatender*.

desatiendes you disregard; pres. ind. 2nd pers. sing. / *desatender*.

desatiendo I disregard; pres. ind. 1st pers. sing. / *desatender*.

desatinándose getting confused; pres. part. / *desatinarse*.

desatinaos (you all) get confused; impve. 2nd pers. pl. / *desatinarse*.

desatinar to talk or act foolishly. reg.

desatinarse to get confused. reg.

desatínate (you) get confused; impve. 2nd pers. sing. / *desatinarse*.

desatinémonos let us get confused; impve. 1st pers. pl. / *desatinarse*.

desatínense let them get confused; impve. 3rd pers. pl. / *desatinarse*.

desatínese let him (her/it) get confused; impve. 3rd pers. sing. / *desatinarse*.

desatornillar to unscrew. reg.

desatracar to cast off (boat). irr.

desatrancar to unbolt. irr.

desatranque 1. that I may unbolt; pres. subj. 1st pers. sing. / *desatrancar*. 2. that he (she/it) may unbolt; pres. subj. 3rd pers. sing. 3. let him (her/it) unbolt; impve. 3rd pers. sing.

desatranqué I unbolted; past 1st pers. sing. / *desatrancar*.

desatranquéis that you (all) may unbolt; pres. subj. 2nd pers. pl. / *desatrancar*.

desatranquemos 1. that we may unbolt; pres. subj. 1st pers. pl. / *desatrancar*. 2. let us unbolt; impve. 1st pers. pl.

desatranquen 1. that they may unblot; pres. subj. 3rd pers. pl. / *desatrancar* 2. let them unbolt; impve. 3rd pers. pl.

desatranques that you may unbolt; pres. subj. 2nd pers. sing. / *desatrancar*.

desatraque 1. that I may cast off (boat); pres. subj. 1st pers. sing. / *desatracar*. 2. that he (she/it) may cast off (boat); pres. subj. 3rd pers. sing. 3. let him (her/it) cast off (boat); impve. 3rd pers. sing.

desatraqué I cast off (boat); past 1st pers. sing. / *desatracar*.

desatraquéis that you (all) may cast off (boat); pres. subj. 2nd pers. pl. / *desatracar*.

desatraquemos 1. that we may cast off (boat); pres. subj. 1st pers. pl. / *desatracar*. 2. let us cast off (boat); impve. 1st pers. pl.

desatraquen 1. that they may cast off (boat); pres. subj. 3rd pers. pl. / *desatracar*. 2. let them cast off (boat); impve. 3rd pers. pl.

desatraques that you may cast off (boat); pres. subj. 2nd pers. sing. / *desatracar*.

desaturdir to bring to or to rouse. reg.

desautorice 1. that I may deprive of authority; pres. subj. 1st pers. sing. / *desautorizar*. 2. that he (she/it) may deprive of authority; pres. subj. 3rd pers. sing. 3. let him (her/it) deprive of authority; impve. 3rd pers. sing.

desautoricé I deprived of authority; past 1st pers. sing. / *desautorizar*.

desautoricéis that you (all) may deprive of authority; pres. subj. 2nd pers. pl. / *desautorizar*.

desautoricemos 1. that we may deprive of authority; pres. subj. 1st pers. pl. / *desautorizar*. 2. let us deprive of authority; impve. 1st pers. pl.

desautoricen 1. that they may deprive of authority; pres. subj. 3rd pers. pl. / *desautorizar*. 2. let them deprive of authority; impve. 3rd pers. pl.

desautorices that you may deprive of authority; pres. subj. 2nd pers. sing. / *desautorizar*.

desautorizar to deprive of authority. irr.

desavahándose cheering up; pres. part. / *desavaharse*.

desavahaos (you all) cheer up; impve. 2nd pers. pl. / *desavaharse*.

desavahar to air or to cool. reg.

desavaharse to cheer up. reg.

desaváhate (you) cheer up; impve. 2nd pers. sing. / *desavaharse*.

desavahémonos let us cheer up; impve. 1st pers. pl. / *desavaharse*.

desaváhense let them cheer up; impve. 3rd pers. pl. / *desavaharse*.

desaváhese let him (her/it) cheer up; impve. 3rd pers. sing. / *desavaharse*.

desaven (you) cause trouble with; impve. 2nd pers. sing. / *desavenir*.

desavendrá he (she/it) will cause trouble with; fut. 3rd pers. sing. / *desavenir*.

desavendrán they will cause trouble with; fut. 3rd pers. pl. / *desavenir*.

desavendrás you will cause trouble with; fut. 2nd pers. sing. / *desavenir*.

desavendré I shall cause trouble with; fut. 1st pers. sing. / *desavenir*.

desavendréis you (all) will cause trouble with; fut. 2nd pers. pl. / *desavenir*.

desavendremos we shall cause trouble with; fut. 1st pers. pl. / *desavenir*.

desavendría 1. I should cause trouble with; cond. 1st pers. sing. / *desavenir*. 2. he (she/it) would cause trouble with; cond. 3rd pers. sing.

desavendríais you (all) would cause trouble with; cond. 2nd pers. pl. / *desavenir*.

desavendríamos we should cause trouble with; cond. 1st pers. pl. / *desavenir*.

desavendrían they would cause trouble with; cond. 3rd pers. pl. / *desavenir*.

desavendrías you would cause trouble with; cond. 2nd pers. sing. / *desavenir*.

desavénete (you) disagree; impve. 2nd pers. sing. / *desavenirse*.

desavenga 1. that I may cause trouble with; pres. subj. 1st pers. sing. / *desavenir*. 2. that he (she/it) may cause trouble with; pres. subj. 3rd pers. sing. 3. let him (her/it)cause trouble with; impve. 3rd pers. sing.

desavengáis that you (all) may cause trouble with; pres. subj. 2nd pers. pl. / *desavenir*.

desavengámonos let us disagree; impve. 1st pers. pl. / *desavenirse*.

desavengamos 1. that we may cause trouble with; pres. subj. 1st pers. pl. / *desavenir*. 2. let us cause trouble with; impve. 1st pers. pl.

desavengan 1. that they may cause trouble with; pres. subj. 3rd pers. pl. / *desavenir*. 2. let them cause trouble with; impve. 3rd pers. pl.

desavénganse let them disagree; impve. 3rd pers. pl. / *desavenirse*.

desavengas that you may cause trouble with; pres. subj. 2nd pers. sing. / *desavenir*.

desavéngase let him (her/it) disagree; impve. 3rd pers. sing. / *desavenirse*.

desavengo I cause trouble with; pres. ind. 1st pers. sing. / *desavenir*.

desavveníos (you all) disagree; impve. 2nd pers. pl. / *desavenirse*.

desavenir to cause trouble with. irr.

desavenirse to disagree or quarrel. irr.

desavía 1. he (she/it) misleads; pres. ind. 3rd pers. sing. / *desaviar*. 2. (you) mislead; impve. 2nd pers. sing.

desavían they mislead; pres. ind. 3rd pers. pl. / *desaviar*.

desaviar to mislead or to deprive. irr.

desavías you mislead; pres. ind. 2nd pers. sing. / *desaviar*.

desavíe 1. that I may mislead; pres. subj. 1st pers. sing. / *desaviar*. 2. that he (she/it) may mislead; pres. subj. 3rd pers. sing. 3. let him (her/it) mislead; impve. 3rd pers. sing.

desavíen 1. that they may mislead; pres. subj. 3rd pers. pl. / *desaviar*. 2. let them mislead; impve. 3rd pers. pl.

desaviene he (she/it) causes trouble with; pres. ind. 3rd pers. sing. / *desavenir*.

desavienen they cause trouble with; pres. ind. 3rd pers. pl. / *desavenir*.

desavienes you cause trouble with; pres. ind. 2nd pers. sing. / *desavenir*.

desavíes that you may mislead; pres. subj. 2nd pers. sing. / *desaviar*.

desavine I caused trouble with; pres. ind. 1st pers. sing. / *desavenir*.

desaviniendo causing trouble with; pres. part. / *desavenir*.

desaviniéndose disagreeing; pres. part. / *desavenirse*.

desaviniera 1. that I might cause trouble with; imp. subj. 1st pers. sing. / *desavenir*. 2. that he (she/it) might cause trouble with; imp. subj. 3rd pers. sing.

desavinierais that you (all) might cause trouble with; imp. subj. 2nd pers pl. / *desavenir*.

desaviniéramos that we might cause trouble with; imp. subj. 1st pers. pl. / *desavenir*.

desavinieran that they might cause trouble with; imp. subj. 3rd pers. pl. / *desavenir*.

desavinieras that you might cause trouble with; imp. subj. 2nd pers. sing. / *desavenir*.

desavinieron they caused trouble with; past 3rd pers. pl. / *desavenir*.

desaviniese 1. that I might cause trouble with; imp. subj. 1st pers. sing. / *desavenir*. 2. that he (she/it) might cause trouble with; imp. subj. 3rd pers. sing.

desavinieseis that you (all) might cause trouble with; imp. subj. 2nd pers pl. / *desavenir*.

desaviniésemos that we might cause trouble with; imp. subj. 1st pers. pl. / *desavenir*.

desaviniesen that they might cause trouble with; imp. subj. 3rd pers. pl. / *desavenir*.

desavinieses that you might cause trouble with; imp. subj. 2nd pers. sing. / *desavenir*.

desavinimos we caused trouble with; past 1st pers. pl. / *desavenir*.

desaviniste you caused trouble with; past 2nd pers. sing. / *desavenir*.

desavinisteis you (all) caused trouble with; past 2nd pers. pl. / *desavenir*.

desavino he (she/it) caused trouble with; past 3rd pers. sing. / *desavenir*.

desavío I mislead; pres. ind. 1st pers. sing. / *desaviar*.

desayudar to hinder. reg.

desayunándose eating breakfast; pres. part. / *desayunarse*.

desayunaos (you all) eat breakfast; impve. 2nd pers. pl. / *desayunarse*.

desayunar to have breakfast. reg.

desayunarse to eat breakfast. reg.

desayúnate (you) eat breakfast; impve. 2nd pers. sing. / *desayunarse*.

desayunémonos let us eat breakfast; impve. 1st pers. pl. / *desayunarse*.

desayúnense let them eat breakfast; impve. 3rd pers. pl. / *desayunarse*.

desayúnese let him (her/it) eat breakfast; impve. 3rd pers. sing. / *desayunarse*.

desazonándose feeling indisposed; pres. part. / *desazonarse*.

desazonaos (you all) feel indisposed; impve. 2nd pers. pl. / *desazonarse*.

desazonar to make tasteless. reg.

desazonarse to feel indisposed or restless. reg.

desazónate (you) feel indisposed; impve. 2nd pers. sing. / *desazonarse*.

desazonémonos let us feel indisposed; impve. 1st pers. pl. / *desazonarse*.

desazónense let them feel indisposed; impve. 3rd pers. pl. / *desazonarse*.

desazónese let him (her/it) feel indisposed; impve. 3rd pers. sing. / *desazonarse*.

desbancar to supplant or to oust. irr.

desbandándose disbanding; pres. part. / *desbandarse*.

desbandaos (you all) disband; impve. 2nd pers. pl. / *desbandarse.*

desbandarse to disband or to desert. reg.

desbándate (you) disband; impve. 2nd pers. sing. / *desbandarse.*

desbandémonos let us disband; impve. 1st pers. pl. / *desbandarse.*

desbándense let them disband; impve. 3rd pers. pl. / *desbandarse.*

desbándese let him (her/it) disband; impve. 3rd pers. sing. / *desbandarse.*

desbanque 1. that I may supplant; pres. subj. 1st pers. sing. / *desbancar.* 2. that he (she/it) may supplant; pres. subj. 3rd pers. sing. 3. let him (her/it) supplant; impve. 3rd pers. sing.

desbanqué I supplanted; past 1st pers. sing. / *desbancar.*

desbanquéis that you (all) may supplant; pres. subj. 2nd pers. pl. / *desbancar.*

desbanquemos 1. that we may supplant; pres. subj. 1st pers. pl. / *desbancar.* 2. let us supplant; impve. 1st pers. pl.

desbanquen 1. that they may supplant; pres. subj. 3rd pers. pl. / *desbancar* 2. let them supplant; impve. 3rd pers. pl.

desbanques that you may supplant; pres. subj. 2nd pers. sing. / *desbancar.*

desbarajustar to throw into confusion. reg.

desbaratándose being unreasonable; pres. part. / *desbaratarse.*

desbarataos (you all) be unreasonable; impve. 2nd pers. pl. / *desbaratarse.*

desbaratar to destroy or to disperse. reg.

desbaratarse to be unreasonable. reg.

desbarátate (you) be unreasonable; impve. 2nd pers. sing. / *desbaratarse.*

desbaratémonos let us be unreasonable; impve. 1st pers. pl. / *desbaratarse.*

desbarátense let them be unreasonable; impve. 3rd pers. pl. / *desbaratarse.*

desbarátese let him (her/it) be unreasonable; impve. 3rd pers. sing. / *desbaratarse.*

desbarbar to shave or to trim. reg.

desbarrar to unbar or to slip away. reg.

desbarretar to unbolt. reg.

desbastar to rough in or to plane or to give social polish. reg.

desbocándose running wild; pres. part. / *desbocarse.*

desbocaos (you all) run wild; impve. 2nd pers. pl. / *desbocarse.*

desbocar to break the edge of or to run into. irr.

desbocarse to run wild. irr.

desbócate (you) run wild; impve. 2nd pers. sing. / *desbocarse.*

desboque 1. that I may break the edge of; pres. subj. 1st pers. sing. / *desbocar.* 2. that he (she/it) may break the edge of; pres. subj. 3rd pers. sing. 3. let him (her/it) break the edge of; impve. 3rd pers. sing.

desboqué I broke the edge of; past 1st pers. sing. / *desbocar.*

desboquéis that you (all) may break the edge of; pres. subj. 2nd pers. pl. / *desbocar.*

desboquémonos let us run wild; impve. 1st pers. pl. / *desbocarse.*

desboquemos 1. that we may break the edge of; pres. subj. 1st pers. pl. / *desbocar.* 2. let us break the edge of; impve. 1st pers. pl.

desboquen 1. that they may break the edge of; pres. subj. 3rd pers. pl. / *desbocar.* 2. let them break the edge of; impve. 3rd pers. pl.

desbóquense let them run wild; impve. 3rd pers. pl. / *desbocarse.*

desboques that you may break the edge of; pres. subj. 2nd pers. sing. / *desbocar.*

desbóquese let him (her/it) run wild; impve. 3rd pers. sing. / *desbocarse.*

desbordándose losing self-control; pres. part. / *desbordarse.*

desbordaos (you all) lose self-control; impve. 2nd pers. pl. / *desbordarse.*

desbordar to overflow. reg.

desbordarse to lose self-control. reg.

desbórdate (you) lose self-control; impve. 2nd pers. sing. / *desbordarse.*

desbordémonos let us lose self-control; impve. 1st pers. pl. / *desbordarse.*

desbórdense let them lose self-control; impve. 3rd pers. pl. / *desbordarse.*

desbórdese let him (her/it) lose self-control; impve. 3rd pers. sing. / *desbordarse.*

desbravándose calming down; pres. part. / *desbravarse.*

desbravaos (you all) calm down; impve. 2nd pers. pl. / *desbravarse.*

desbravar to break in or to tame. reg.

desbravarse to calm down. reg.

desbrávate (you) calm down; impve. 2nd pers. sing. / *desbravarse.*

desbravecer to break in or to tame. irr.

desbravémonos let us calm down; impve. 1st pers. pl. / *desbravarse.*

desbrávense let them calm down; impve. 3rd pers. pl. / *desbravarse.*

desbrávese let him (her/it) calm down; impve. 3rd pers. sing. / *desbravarse.*

desbravezca 1. that I may break in; pres. subj. 1st pers. sing. / *desbravecer.* 2. that he (she/it) may break in; pres. subj. 3rd pers. sing. 3. let him (her/it) break in; impve. 3rd pers. sing.

desbravezcáis that you (all) may break in; pres. subj. 2nd pers. pl. / *desbravecer.*

desbravezcamos 1. that we may break in; pres. subj. 1st pers. pl. / *desbravecer* 2. let us break in; impve. 1st pers. pl.

desbravezcan 1. that they may break in; pres. subj. 3rd pers. pl. / *desbravecer.* 2. let them break in; impve. 3rd pers. pl.

desbravezcas that you may break in; pres. subj. 2nd pers. sing. / *desbravecer.*

desbravezco I break in; pres. ind. 1st pers. sing. / *desbravecer.*

desbrazándose waving one's arms violently; pres. part. / *desbrazarse.*

desbrazaos (you all) wave your arms violently; impve. 2nd pers. pl. / *desbrazarse.*

desbrazarse to wave one's arms violently. reg.

desbrázate (you) wave your arms violently; impve. 2nd pers. sing. / *desbrazarse.*

desbrazémonos let us wave our arms violently; impve. 1st pers. pl. / *desbrazarse.*

desbrázense let them wave their arms violently; impve. 3rd pers. pl. / *desbrazarse.*

desbrázese let him (her/its) wave his (her/its) arms violently; impve. 3rd pers. sing. / *desbrazarse.*

desbridar to unbridle. reg.

desbroce 1. that I may clear of brush; pres. subj. 1st pers. sing. / *desbrozar.* 2. that he (she/it) may clear of brush; pres. subj. 3rd pers. sing. 3. let him (her/it) clear of brush; impve. 3rd pers. sing.

desbrocé I cleared of bursh; past 1st pers. sing. / *desbrozar.*

desbrocéis that you (all) may clear of brush; pres. subj. 2nd pers. pl. / *desbrozar.*

desbrocemos 1. that we may clear of brush; pres. subj. 1st pers. pl. / *desbrozar.* 2. let us clear of brush; impve. 1st pers. pl.

desbrocen 1. that they may clear of brush; pres. subj. 3rd pers. pl. / *desbrozar.* 2. let them clear of brush; impve. 3rd pers. pl.

desbroces that you may clear of brush; pres. subj. 2nd pers. sing. / *desbrozar.*

desbrozar to clear of brush. irr.

desbrujar to wear away. reg.

desbuchar to disgorge or to reveal (secrets). reg.

descabalar to break the completeness of. reg.

descabalgar to dismount. reg.

descabece 1. that I may behead; pres. subj. 1st pers. sing. / *descabezar.* 2. that he (she/it) may behead; pres. subj. 3rd pers. sing. 3. let him (her/it) behead; impve. 3rd pers. sing.

descabecé I beheaded; past 1st pers. sing. / *descabezar.*

descabecéis that you (all) may behead; pres. subj. 2nd pers. pl. / *descabezar.*

descabecémonos let us rack our brains; impve. 1st pers. pl. / *descabezarse.*

descabecemos 1. that we may behead; pres. subj. 1st pers. pl. / *descabezar.* 2. let us behead; impve. 1st pers. pl.

descabecen 1. that they may behead; pres. subj. 3rd pers. pl. / *descabezar.* 2. let them behead; impve. 3rd pers. pl.

descabécense let them rack their brains; impve. 3rd pers. pl. / *descabezarse.*

descabeces that you may behead; pres. subj. 2nd pers. sing. / *descabezar.*

descabécese let him (her/it) rack his (her/its) brains; impve. 3rd pers. sing. / *descabezarse.*

descabellar to dishevel or to kill with drive to the neck. reg.

descabezándose racking one's brains; pres. part. / *descabezarse.*

descabezaos (you all) rack your brains; impve. 2nd pers. pl. / *descabezarse.*

descabezar to behead. irr.

descabezarse to rack one's brains. irr.

descabézate (you) rack your brains; impve. 2nd pers. sing. / *descabezarse.*

descabúllamonos let us sneak away; impve. 1st pers. pl. / *descabullirse.*

descabúllanse let them sneak away; impve. 3rd pers. pl. / *descabullirse.*

descabúllase let him (her/it) sneak away; impve. 3rd pers. sing. / *descabullirse.*

descabulléndose sneaking away; pres. part. / *descabullirse.*

descabullera 1. that I might sneak away; imp. subj. 1st pers. sing. / *descabullirse.* 2. that he (she/it) might sneak away; imp. subj. 3rd pers. sing.

descabullerais that you (all) might sneak away; imp. subj. 2nd pers pl. / *descabullirse.*

descabulléramos that we might sneak away; imp. subj. 1st pers. pl. / *descabullirse.*

descabulleran that they might sneak away; imp. subj. 3rd pers. pl. / *descabullirse.*

descabulleras that you might sneak away; imp. subj. 2nd pers. sing. / *descabullirse.*

descabulleron they sneaked away; past 3rd pers. pl. / *descabullirse.*

descabullese 1. that I might sneak away; imp. subj. 1st pers. sing. / *descabullirse.* 2. that he (she/it) might sneak away; imp. subj. 3rd pers. sing.

descabulleseis that you (all) might sneak away; imp. subj. 2nd pers. pl. / *descabullirse.*

descabullésemos that we might sneak away; imp. subj. 1st pers. pl. / *descabullirse.*

descabullesen that they might sneak away; imp. subj. 3rd pers. pl. / *descabullirse.*

descabulleses that you might sneak away; imp. subj. 2nd pers. sing. / *descabullirse.*

descabúllete (you) sneak away; impve. 2nd pers. sing. / *descabullirse.*

descabulló he (she/it) sneaked away; past 3rd pers. sing. / *descabullirse.*

descabullos (you all) sneak away; impve. 2nd pers. pl. / *descabullirse.*

descaecer to decline or to languish. irr.

descaezca 1. that I may decline; pres. subj. 1st pers. sing. / *descaecer.* 2. that he (she/it) may decline; pres. subj. 3rd pers. sing. 3. let him (her/it) decline; impve. 3rd pers. sing.

descaezcáis that you (all) may decline; pres. subj. 2nd pers. pl. / *descaecer.*

descaezcamos 1. that we may decline; pres. subj. 1st pers. pl. / *descaecer.* 2. let us decline; impve. 1st pers. pl.

descaezcan 1. that they may decline; pres. subj. 3rd pers. pl. / *descaecer.* 2. let them decline; impve. 3rd pers. pl.

descaezcas that you may decline; pres. subj. 2nd pers. sing. / *descaecer.*

descaezco I decline; pres. ind. 1st pers. sing. / *descaecer.*

descalabrándose suffering a head wound; pres. part. / *descalabrarse.*

descalabraos (you all) suffer a head wound; impve. 2nd pers. pl. / *descalabrarse.*

descalabrar to hurt one's head. reg.

descalabrarse to suffer a head wound. reg.

descalábrate (you) suffer a head wound; impve. 2nd pers. sing. / *descalabrarse.*

descalabrémonos let us suffer a head wound; impve. 1st pers. pl. / *descalabrarse.*

descalábrense let them suffer a head wound; impve. 3rd pers. pl. / *descalabrarse.*

descalábrese let him (her/it) suffer a head wound; impve. 3rd pers. sing. / *descalabrarse.*

descalce 1. that I may remove my shoes; pres. subj. 1st pers. sing. / *descalzar.* 2. that he (she/it) may remove his (her/its) shoes; pres. subj. 3rd pers. sing.

descalcé I removed my shoes; past 1st pers. sing. / *descalzar.*

descalcéis that you (all) may remove your shoes; pres. subj. 2nd pers. pl. / *descalzar.*

descalcémonos let us remove our shoes; impve. 1st pers. pl. / *descalzar.*

descalcemos that we may remove our shoes; pres. subj. 1st pers. pl. / *descalzar.*

descalcen that they may remove their shoes; pres. subj. 3rd pers. pl. / *descalzar.*

descálcense let them remove their shoes; impve. 3rd pers. pl. / *descalzarse.*

descalces that you may remove your shoes; pres. subj. 2nd pers. sing. / *descalzar.*

descálcese let him (her/it) remove his (her/its) shoes; impve. 3rd pers. sing. / *descalzarse.*

descalificar to disqualify. irr.

descalifique 1. that I may disaualify; pres. subj. 1st pers. sing. / *descalificar.* 2. that he (she/it) may disqualify; pres. subj. 3rd pers. sing. 3. let him (her/it) disqualify; impve. 3rd pers. sing.

descalifiqué I disqualified; past 1st pers. sing. / *descalificar.*

descalifiquéis that you (all) may disqualify; pres. subj. 2nd pers. pl. / *descalificar.*

descalifiquemos 1. that we may disqualify; pres. subj. 1st pers. pl. / *descalificar.* 2. let us disqualify; impve. 1st pers. pl.

descalifiquen 1. that they may disqualify; pres. subj. 3rd pers. pl. / *descalificar.* 2. let them disqualify; impve. 3rd pers. pl.

descalifiques that you may disqualify; pres. subj. 2nd pers. sing. / *descalificar.*

descalzándose removing one's shoes; pres. part. / *descalzarse.*

descalzaos (you all) remove your shoes; impve. 2nd pers. pl. / *descalzarse.*

descalzar to remove one's shoes or to undermine. irr.

descalzarse to remove one's shoes. irr.

descálzate (you) remove your shoes; impve. 2nd pers. sing. / *descalzarse.*

descambiar to exchange (goods). reg.

descaminándose going astray; pres. part. / *descaminarse.*

descaminaos (you all) go astray; impve. 2nd pers. pl. / *descaminarse.*

descaminar to mislead. reg.

descaminarse to go astray. reg.

descamínate (you) go astray; impve. 2nd pers. sing. / *descaminarse.*

descaminémonos let us go astray; impve. 1st pers. pl. / *descaminarse.*

descamínense let them go astray; impve. 3rd pers. pl. / *descaminarse.*

descamínese let him (her/it) go astray; impve. 3rd pers. sing. / *descaminarse.*

descampar to stop raining and clear off. reg.

descansar to rest. reg.

descantear to smoothe the edges of. reg.

descantillar to pare. reg.

descantonar to chip off. reg.

descarándose acting impudently; pres. part. / *descararse.*

descaraos (you all) act impudently; impve. 2nd pers. pl. / *descararse.*

descararse to act impudently. reg.

descárate (you) act impudently; impve. 2nd pers. sing. / *descararse.*

descarémonos let us act impudently; impve. 1st pers. pl. / *descararse.*

descárense let them act impudently; impve. 3rd pers. pl. / *descararse.*

descárese let him (her/it) act impudently; impve. 3rd pers. sing. / *descararse.*

descargándose freeing oneself of; pres. part. / *descargarse.*

descargaos (you all) free yourselves 0f; impve. 2nd pers. pl. / *descargarse.*

descargar to discharge or to unload. irr.

descargarse to free oneself of. irr.

descárgate (you) free yourself of; impve. 2nd pers. sing. / *descargarse.*

descargue 1. that I may discharge; pres. subj. 1st pers. sing. / *descargar.* 2. that he (she/it) may discharge; pres. subj. 3rd pers. sing. 3. let him (her/it) discharge; impve. 3rd pers. sing.

descargué I discharged; past 1st pers. sing. / *descargar.*

descarguéis that you (all) may discharge; pres. subj. 2nd pers. pl. / *descargar.*

descarguémonos let us free ourselves of; impve. 1st pers. pl. / *descargarse.*

descarguemos 1. that we may discharge; pres. subj. 1st pers. pl. / *descargar.* 2. let us discharge; impve. 1st pers. pl.

descarguen 1. that they may discharge; pres. subj. 3rd pers. pl. / *descargar.* 2. let them discharge; impve. 3rd pers. pl.

descárguense let them free themselves of; impve. 3rd pers. pl. / *descargarse.*

descargues that you may discharge; pres. subj. 2nd pers. sing. / *descargar.*

descárguese let him (her/it) free himself (herself/itself) of; impve. 3rd pers. sing. / *descargarse.*

descarnándose losing weight; pres. part. / *descarnarse.*

descarnaos (you all) lose weight; impve. 2nd pers. pl. / *descarnarse.*

descarnar to remove the flesh from. reg.

descarnarse to lose weight. reg.

descárnate (you) lose weight; impve. 2nd pers. sing. / *descarnarse.*

descarnémonos let us lose weight; impve. 1st pers. pl. / *descarnarse.*

descárnense let them lose weight; impve. 3rd pers. pl. / *descarnarse.*

descárnese let him (her/it) lose weight; impve. 3rd pers. sing. / *descarnarse.*

descarría 1. he (she/it) misleads; pres. ind. 3rd pers. sing. / *descarriar.* 2. (you) mislead; impve. 2nd pers. sing.

descarrían they mislead; pres. ind. 3rd pers. pl. / *descarriar.*

descarriándose going astray; pres. part. / *descarriarse.*

descarriaos (you all) go astray; impve. 2nd pers. pl. / *descarriarse.*

descarriar to mislead. irr.

descarriarse to go astray. irr.

descarrías you mislead; pres. ind. 2nd pers. sing. / *descarriar.*

descarríate (you) go astray; impve. 2nd pers. sing. / *descarriarse.*

descarríe 1. that I may mislead; pres. subj. 1st pers. sing. / *descarriar.* 2. that he (she/it) may mislead; pres. subj. 3rd pers. sing. 3. let him (her/it) mislead; impve. 3rd pers. sing.

descarriémonos let us go astray; impve. 1st pers. pl. / *descarriarse.*

descarríen 1. that they may mislead; pres. subj. 3rd pers. pl. / *descarriar* 2. let them mislead; impve. 3rd pers. pl.

descarríense let them go astray; impve. 3rd pers. pl. / *descarriarse.*

descarríes that you may mislead; pres. subj. 2nd pers. sing. / *descarriar.*

descarríese let him (her/it) go astray; impve. 3rd pers. sing. / *descarriarse.*

descarrilándose going astray; pres. part. / *descarrilarse.*

descarrilaos (you all) go astray; impve. 2nd pers. pl. / *descarrilarse.*

descarrilar to derail. reg.

descarrilarse to go astray. reg.

descarrílate (you) go astray; impve. 2nd pers. sing. / *descarrilarse.*

descarrilémonos let us go astray; impve. 1st pers. pl. / *descarrilarse.*

descarrílense let them go astray; impve. 3rd pers. pl. / *descarrilarse.*

descarrílese let him (her/it) go astray; impve. 3rd pers. sing. / *descarrilarse.*

descarrío I mislead; pres. ind. 1st pers. sing. / *descarriar.*

descartándose shirking; pres. part. / *descartarse.*

descartaos (you all) shirk; impve. 2nd pers. pl. / *descartarse.*

descartar to discard. reg.

descartarse to shirk. reg.

descártate (you) shirk; impve. 2nd pers. sing. / *descartarse.*

descartémonos let us shirk; impve. 1st pers. pl. / *descartarse.*

descártense let them shirk; impve. 3rd pers. pl. / *descartarse.*

descártese let him (her/it) shirk; impve. 3rd pers. sing. / *descartarse.*

descasándose being deranged; pres. part. / *descasarse.*

descasaos (you all) be deranged; impve. 2nd pers. pl. / *descasarse.*

descasar to annul the marriage of. reg.

descasarse to be deranged. reg.

descásate (you) be deranged; impve. 2nd pers. sing. / *descasarse.*

descascándose shattering; pres. part. / *descascarse.*

descascaos (you all) shatter; impve. 2nd pers. pl. / *descascarse.*

descascar to shell or to peel. irr.

descascarándose chipping off; pres. part. / *descascararse.*

descascaraos (you all) chip off; impve. 2nd pers. pl. / *descascararse.*

descascarar to shell or to peel. reg.

descascararse to chip off. reg.

descascárate (you) chip off; impve. 2nd pers. sing. / *descascararse.*

descascarémonos let us chip off; impve. 1st pers. pl. / *descascararse.*

descascárense let them chip off; impve. 3rd pers. pl. / *descascararse.*

descascárese let him (her/it) chip off; impve. 3rd pers. sing. / *descascararse.*

descascarse to shatter. irr.

descáscate (you) shatter; impve. 2nd pers. sing. / *descascarse.*

descasémonos let us be deranged; impve. 1st pers. pl. / *descasarse.*

descásense let them be deranged; impve. 3rd pers. pl. / *descasarse.*

descásese let him (her/it) be deranged; impve. 3rd pers. sing. / *descasarse.*

descasque 1. that I may shell; pres. subj. 1st pers. sing. / *descascar.* 2. that he (she/it) may shell; pres. subj. 3rd pers. sing. 3. let him (her/it) shell; impve. 3rd pers. sing.

descasqué I shelled; past 1st pers. sing. / *descascar.*

descasquéis that you (all) may shell; pres. subj. 2nd pers. pl. / *descascar.*

descasquémonos let us shatter; impve. 1st pers. pl. / *descascarse.*

descasquemos 1. that we may shell; pres. subj. 1st pers. pl. / *descascar*. 2. let us shell; impve. 1st pers. pl.

descasquen 1. that they may shell; pres. subj. 3rd pers. pl. / *descascar*. 2. let them shell; impve. 3rd pers. pl.

descásquense let them shatter; impve. 3rd pers. pl. / *descascarse*.

descasques that you may shell; pres. subj. 2nd pers. sing. / *descascar*.

descásquese let him (her/it) shatter; impve. 3rd pers. sing. / *descascarse*.

descastándose losing one's natural affections; pres. part. / *descastarse*.

descastaos (you all) lose your natural affections; impve. 2nd pers. pl. / *descastarse*.

descastar to exterminate. reg.

descastarse to lose one's natural affections. reg.

descástate (you) lose your natural affections; impve. 2nd pers. sing. / *descastarse*.

descastémonos let us lose our natural affections; impve. 1st pers. pl. / *descastarse*.

descástense let them lose their natural affections; impve. 3rd pers. pl. / *descastarse*.

descástese let him (her/it) lose his (her/its) natural affections; impve. 3rd pers. sing. / *descastarse*.

descatolice 1. that I may cause to lapse; pres. subj. 1st pers. sing. / *descatolizar*. 2. that he (she/it) may cause to lapse; pres. subj. 3rd pers. sing. 3. let him (her/it) cause to lapse; impve. 3rd pers. sing.

descatolicé I caused to lapse; past 1st pers. sing. / *descatolizar*.

descatolicéis that you (all) may cause to lapse; pres. subj. 2nd pers. pl. / *descatolizar*.

descatolicémonos let us lapse; impve. 1st pers. pl. / *descatolizarse*.

descatolicemos 1. that we may cause to lapse; pres. subj. 1st pers. pl. / *descatolizar*. 2. let us cause to lapse; impve. 1st pers. pl.

descatolicen 1. that they may cause to lapse; pres. subj. 3rd pers. pl. / *descatolizar*. 2. let them cause to lapse; impve. 3rd pers. pl.

descatolícense let them lapse; impve. 3rd pers. pl. / *descatolizarse*.

descatolices that you may cause to lapse; pres. subj. 2nd pers. sing. / *descatolizar*.

descatolícese let him (her/it) lapse; impve. 3rd pers. sing. / *descatolizarse*.

descatolizándose lapsing; pres. part. / *descatolizarse*.

descatolizaos (you all) lapse; impve. 2nd pers. pl. / *descatolizarse*.

descatolizar to cause to lapse. irr.

descatolizarse to lapse. irr.

descatolízate (you) lapse; impve. 2nd pers. sing. / *descatolizarse*.

descender to descend or to originate. irr.

descentralice 1. that I may decentralize; pres. subj. 1st pers. sing. / *descentralizar*. 2. that he (she/it) may decentralize; pres. subj. 3rd pers. sing. 3. let him (her/it) decentralize; impve. 3rd pers. sing.

descentralicé I decentralized; past 1st pers. sing. / *descentralizar*.

descentralicéis that you (all) may decentralize; pres. subj. 2nd pers. pl. / *descentralizar*.

descentralicemos 1. that we may decentralize; pres. subj. 1st pers. pl. / *descentralizar*. 2. let us decentralize; impve. 1st pers. pl.

descentralicen 1. that they may decentralize; pres. subj. 3rd pers. pl. / *descentralizar*. 2. let them decentralize; impve. 3rd pers. pl.

descentralices that you may decentralize; pres. subj. 2nd pers. sing. / *descentralizar*.

descentralizar to decentralize. irr.

descentrándose being off center ; pres. part. / *descentrarse*.

descentraos (you all) be off center; impve. 2nd pers. pl. / *descentrarse*.

descentrar to put off center. reg.

descentrarse to be off center. reg.

descéntrate (you) be off center; impve. 2nd pers. sing. / *descentrarse*.

descentrémonos let us be off center; impve. 1st pers. pl. / *descentrarse*.

descéntrense let them be off center; impve. 3rd pers. pl. / *descentrarse*.

descéntrese let him (her/it) be off center; impve. 3rd pers. sing. / *descentrarse*.

desceñir to undergird. irr.

descepar to uproot or to get rid of. reg.

descercar to tear down the fences of. irr.

descerebrar to brain. reg.

descerque 1. that I may tear down the fences of; pres. subj. 1st pers. sing. / *descercar*. 2. that he (she/it) may tear down the fences of; pres. subj. 3rd pers. sing. 3. let him (her/it) tear down the fences of; impve. 3rd pers. sing.

descerqué I tore down the fences of; past 1st pers. sing. / *descercar*.

descerquéis that you (all) may tear down the fences of; pres. subj. 2nd pers. pl. / *descercar*.

descerquemos 1. that we may tear down the fences of; pres. subj. 1st pers. pl. / *descercar*. 2. let us tear down the fences of; impve. 1st pers. pl.

descerquen 1. that they may tear down the fences of; pres. subj. 3rd pers. pl. / *descercar*. 2. let them tear down the fences of; impve. 3rd pers. pl.

descerques that you may tear down the fences of; pres. subj. 2nd pers. sing. / *descercar*.

descerrajar to break the lock of or to shoot. reg.

descienda 1. that I may descend; pres. subj. 1st pers. sing. / *descender*. 2. that he (she/it) may descend; pres. subj. 3rd pers. sing. 3. let him (her/it) descend; impve. 3rd pers. sing.

desciendan 1. that they may descend; pres. subj. 3rd pers. pl. / *descender*. 2. let them descend; impve. 3rd pers. pl.

desciendas that you may descend; pres. subj. 2nd pers. sing. / *descender*.

desciende 1. he (she/it) descends; pres. ind. 3rd pers. sing. / *descender*. 2. (you) descend; impve. 2nd pers. sing.

descienden they descend; pres. ind. 3rd pers. pl. / *descender*.

desciendes you descend; pres. ind. 2nd pers. sing. / *descender*.

desciendo I descend; pres. ind. 1st pers. sing. / *descender*.

descifrar to decipher. reg.

descinchar to loosen the saddle straps of. reg.

desciña 1. that I may undergird; pres. subj. 1st pers. sing. / *desceñir*. 2. that he (she/it) may undergird; pres. subj. 3rd pers. sing. 3. let him (her/it) undergird; impve. 3rd pers. sing.

desciñáis that you (all) may undergird; pres. subj. 2nd pers. pl. / *desceñir*.

desciñamos 1. that we may undergird; pres. subj. 1st pers. pl. / *desceñir*. 2. let us undergird; impve. 1st pers. pl.

desciñan 1. that they may undergird; pres. subj. 3rd pers. pl. / *desceñir*. 2. let them undergird; impve. 3rd pers. pl.

desciñas that you may undergird; pres. subj. 2nd pers. sing. / *desceñir*.

desciñe 1. he (she/it) undergirds; pres. ind. 3rd pers. sing. / *desceñir*. 2. (you) undergird; impve. 2nd pers. sing.

desciñen they undergird; pres. ind. 3rd pers. pl. / *desceñir*.

desciñendo undergirding; pres. part. / *desceñir*.

desciñera 1. that I might undergird; imp. subj. 1st pers. sing. / *desceñir*. 2. that he (she/it) might undergird; imp. subj. 3rd pers. sing.

desciñerais that you (all) might undergird; imp. subj. 2nd pers pl. / *desceñir*.

desciñéramos that we might undergird; imp. subj. 1st pers. pl. / *desceñir*.

desciñeran that they might undergird; imp. subj. 3rd pers. pl. / *desceñir*.

desciñeras that you might undergird; imp. subj. 2nd pers. sing. / *desceñir*.

desciñeron they undergirded; past 3rd pers. pl. / *desceñir*.

desciñes you undergird; pres. ind. 2nd pers. sing. / *desceñir*.

desciñese 1. that I might undergird; imp. subj. 1st pers. sing. / *desceñir*. 2. that he (she/it) might undergird; imp. subj. 3rd pers. sing.

desciñeseis that you (all) might undergird; imp. subj. 2nd pers pl. / *desceñir*.

desciñésemos that we might undergird; imp. subj. 1st pers. pl. / *desceñir*.

desciñesen that they might undergird; imp. subj. 3rd pers. pl. / *desceñir*.

desciñeses that you might undergird; imp. subj. 2nd pers. sing. / *desceñir*.

desciño I undergird; pres. ind. 1st pers. sing. / *desceñir*.

desciñó he (she/it) undergirded; past 3rd pers. sing. / *desceñir*.

descivilice 1. that I may decivilize; pres. subj. 1st pers. sing. / *descivilizar*. 2. that he (she/it) may decivilize; pres. subj. 3rd pers. sing. 3. let him (her/it) decivilize; impve. 3rd pers. sing.

descivilicé I decivilized; past 1st pers. sing. / *descivilizar*.

descivilicéis that you (all) may decivilice; pres. subj. 2nd pers. pl. / *descivilizar*.

descivilicemos 1. that we may decivilize; pres. subj. 1st pers. pl. / *descivilizar*. 2. let us decivilize; impve. 1st pers. pl.

descivilicen 1. that they may decivilize; pres. subj. 3rd pers. pl. / *descivilizar*. 2. let them decivilize; impve. 3rd pers. pl.

descivilices that you may decivilize; pres. subj. 2nd pers. sing. / *descivilizar*.

descivilizar to decivilize or to barbarize. irr.

desclasificar to disqualify. irr.

desclasifique 1. that I may disqualify; pres. subj. 1st pers. sing. / *desclasificar*. 2. that he (she/it) may disqualify; pres. subj. 3rd pers. sing. 3. let him (her/it) disqualify; impve. 3rd pers. sing.

desclasifiqué I disqualified; past 1st pers. sing. / *desclasificar*.

desclasifiquéis that you (all) may disqualify; pres. subj. 2nd pers. pl. / *desclasificar*.

desclasifiquemos 1. that we may disqualify; pres. subj. 1st pers. pl. / *desclasificar*. 2. let us disqualify; impve. 1st pers. pl.

desclasifiquen 1. that they may disqualify; pres. subj. 3rd pers. pl. / *desclasificar*. 2. let them disqualify; impve. 3rd pers. pl.

desclasifiques that you may disqualify; pres. subj. 2nd pers. sing. / *desclasificar*.

desclavar to pull out the nails from. reg.

descoagular to dissolve a clot. reg.

descobijar to uncover. reg.

descocándose being impudent; pres. part. / *descocarse*.

descocaos (you all) be impudent; impve. 2nd pers. pl. / *descocarse*.

descocarse to be impudent. irr.

descócate (you) be impudent; impve. 2nd pers. sing. / *descocarse*.

descocer to digest. irr.

descogollar to prune a tree. reg.

descolar to dock or to snub. reg.

descolgándose falling down; pres. part. / *descolgarse*.

descolgaos (you all) fall down; impve. 2nd pers. pl. / *descolgarse*.

descolgar to take down. irr.

descolgarse to fall down. irr.

descolgué I took down; past 1st pers. sing. / *descolgar*.

descolguéis that you (all) may take down; pres. subj. 2nd pers. pl. / *descolgar*.

descolguémonos let us fall down; impve. 1st pers. pl. / *descolgarse*.

descolguemos 1. that we may take down; pres. subj. 1st pers. pl. / *descolgar*. 2. let them take down; impve. 1st pers. pl.

descolorándose fading; pres. part. / *descolorarse*.

descoloraos (you all) fade; impve. 2nd pers. pl. / *descolorarse*.

descolorar to discolor. reg.

descolorarse to fade. reg.

descolórate (you) fade; impve. 2nd pers. sing. / *descolorarse*.

descolorémonos let us fade; impve. 1st pers. pl. / *descolorarse*.

descolórense let them fade; impve. 3rd pers. pl. / *descolorarse*.

descolórese let him (her/it) fade; impve. 3rd pers. sing. / *descolorarse*.

descolorir to discolor. reg.

descollar to excel. irr.

descombrar to disencumber. reg.

descomedíos (you all) be rude; impve. 2nd pers. pl. / *descomedirse*.

descomedirse to be rude. irr.

descomida 1. that I may be rude; pres. subj. 1st pers. sing. / *descomedirse*. 2. that he (she/it) may be rude; pres. subj. 3rd pers. sing.

descomidáis that you (all) may be rude; pres. subj. 2nd pers. pl. / *descomedirse*.

descomidámonos let us be rude; impve. 1st pers. pl. / *descomedirse*.

descomidamos that we may be rude; pres. subj. 1st pers. pl. / *descomedirse*.

descomidan that they may be rude; pres. subj. 3rd pers. pl. / *descomedirse*.

descomídanse let them be rude; impve. 3rd pers. pl. / *descomedirse*.

descomidas that you may be rude; pres. subj. 2nd pers. sing. / *descomedirse*.

descomídase let him (her/it) be rude; impve. 3rd pers. pl. / *descomedirse*.

descomide he (she/it) is rude; pres. ind. 3rd pers. sing. / *descomedirse*.

descomiden they are rude; pres. ind. 3rd pers. pl. / *descomedirse*.

descomides you are rude; pres. ind. 2nd pers. sing. / *descomedirse*.

descomídete (you) be rude; impve. 2nd pers. sing. / *descomedirse*.

descomidiéndose being rude; pres. part. / *descomedirse*.

descomidiera 1. that I might be rude; imp. subj. 1st pers. sing. / *descomedirse*. 2. that he (she/it) might be rude; imp. subj. 3rd pers. sing.

descomidierais that you (all) might be rude; imp. subj. 2nd pers pl / *descomedirse*.

descomidiéramos that we might be rude; imp. subj. 1st pers. pl. / *descomedirse*.

descomidieran that they might be rude; imp. subj. 3rd pers. pl. / *descomedirse*.

descomidieras that you might be rude; imp. subj. 2nd pers. sing. / *descomedirse*.

descomidieron they were rude; past 3rd pers. pl. / *descomedirse*.

descomidiese 1. that I might be rude; imp. subj. 1st pers. sing. / *descomedirse*. 2. that he (she/it) might be rude; imp. subj. 3rd pers. sing.

descomidieseis that you (all) might be rude; imp. subj. 2nd pers pl. / *descomedirse*.

descomidiésemos that we might be rude; imp. subj. 1st pers. pl. / *descomedirse*.

descomidiesen that they might be rude; imp. subj. 3rd pers. pl. / *descomedirse*.

descomidieses that you might be rude; imp. subj. 2nd pers. sing. / *descomedirse*.

descomidió he (she/it) was rude; past 3rd pers sing. / *descomedirse*.

descomido I am rude; pres. ind. 1st pers. sing. / *descomedirse*.

descompaginar to disorganize or to confuse. reg.

descompletar to make incomplete. reg.

descompon (you) upset; impve. 2nd pers. sing. / *descomponer*.

descompondrá he (she/it) will upset; fut. 3rd pers. sing. / *descomponer*.

descompondrán they will upset; fut. 3rd pers. pl. / *descomponer*.

descompondrás you will upset; fut. 2nd pers. sing. / *descomponer*.

descompondré I shall upset; fut. 1st pers. sing. / *descomponer*.

descompondréis you (all) will upset; fut. 2nd pers. pl. / *descomponer*.

descompondremos we shall upset; fut. 1st pers. pl. / *descomponer*.

descompondría 1. I should upset; cond. 1st pers. sing. / *descomponer*. 2. he (she/it) would upset; cond. 3rd pers. sing.

descompondríais you (all) would upset; cond. 2nd pers. pl. / *descomponer*.

descompondríamos we should upset; cond. 1st pers. pl. / *descomponer*.

descompondrían they would upset; cond. 3rd pers. pl. / *descomponer*.

descompondrías you would upset; cond. 2nd pers. sing. / *descomponer*.

descomponer to upset. irr.

descomponerse to decompose or rot. irr.

descomponga 1. that I may upset; pres. subj. 1st pers. sing. / *descomponer*. 2. that he (she/it) may upset; pres. subj. 3rd pers. sing. 3. let him (her/it) upset; impve. 3rd pers. sing.

descompongáis that you (all) may upset; pres. subj. 2nd pers. pl. / *descomponer*.

descompongamos 1. that we may upset; pres. subj. 1st pers. pl. / *descomponer*. 2. let us upset; impve. 1st pers. pl.

descompongan 1. that they may upset; pres. subj. 3rd pers. pl. / *descomponer*. 2. let them upset; impve. 3rd pers. pl.

descompónganse let them decompose; impve. 3rd pers. pl. / *descomponerse*.

descompongas that you may upset; pres. subj. 2nd pers. sing. / *descomponer.*

descompóngase let it decompose; impve. 3rd pers. sing. / *descomponerse.*

descompongo I upset; pres. ind. 1st pers. sing. / *descomponer.*

descomponiendo upsetting; pres. part. / *descomponer.*

descomponiéndose decomposing; pres. part. / *descomponerse.*

descompuesto upset; past part. / *descomponer.*

descompuse I upset; past 1st pers. sing. / *descomponer.*

descompusiera 1. that I might upset; imp. subj. 1st pers. sing. / *descomponer.* 2. that he (she/it) might upset; imp. subj. 3rd pers. sing.

descompusierais that you (all) might upset; imp. subj. 2nd pers pl. / *descomponer.*

descompusiéramos that we might upset; imp. subj. 1st pers. pl. / *descomponer.*

descompusieran that they might upset; imp. subj. 3rd pers. pl. / *descomponer.*

descompusieras that you might upset; imp. subj. 2nd pers. sing. / *descomponer.*

descompusieron they upset; past 3rd pers. pl. / *descomponer.*

descompusiese 1. that I might upset; imp. subj. 1st pers. sing. / *descomponer.* 2. that he (she/it) might upset; imp. subj. 3rd pers. sing.

descompusieseis that you (all) might upset; imp. subj. 2nd pers pl. / *descomponer.*

descompusiésemos that we might upset; imp. subj. 1st pers. pl. / *descomponer.*

descompusiesen that they might upset; imp. subj. 3rd pers. pl. / *descomponer.*

descompusieses that you might upset; imp. subj. 2nd pers. sing. / *descomponer.*

descompusimos we upset; past 1st pers. pl. / *descomponer.*

descompusiste you upset; past 2nd pers. sing. / *descomponer.*

descompusisteis you (all) upset; past 2nd pers. pl. / *descomponer.*

descompuso he (she/it) upset; past 3rd pers. sing. / *descomponer.*

descomulgar to excommunicate. irr.

descomulgue 1. that I may excommunicate; pres. subj. 1st pers. sing. / *descomulgar.* 2. that he (she/it) may excommunicate; pres. subj. 3rd pers. sing. 3. let him (her/it) excommunicate; impve. 3rd pers. sing.

descomulgué I excommunicated; past 1st pers. sing. / *descomulgar.*

descomulguéis that you (all) may excommunicate; pres. subj. 2nd pers. pl. / *descomulgar.*

descomulguemos 1. that we may excommunicate; pres. subj. 1st pers. pl. / *descomulgar.* 2. let us excommunicate; impve. 1st pers. pl.

descomulguen 1. that they may excommunicate; pres. subj. 3rd pers. pl. / *descomulgar.* 2. let them excommunicate; impve. 3rd pers. pl.

descomulgues that you may excommunicate; pres. subj. 2nd pers. sing. / *descomulgar.*

desconceptúa 1. he (she/it) discredits; pres. ind. 3rd pers. sing. / *desconceptuar.* 2. (you) discredit; impve. 2nd pers. sing.

desconceptúan they discredit; pres. ind. 3rd pers. pl. / *desconceptuar.*

desconceptuar to discredit. irr.

desconceptúas you discredit; pres. ind. 2nd pers. sing. / *desconceptuar.*

desconceptúe 1. that I may discredit; pres. subj. 1st pers. sing. / *desconceptuar.* 2. that he (she/it) may discredit; pres. subj. 3rd pers. sing. 3. let him (her/it) discredit; impve. 3rd pers. sing.

desconceptúen 1. that they may discredit; pres. subj. 3rd pers. pl. / *desconceptuar.* 2. let them discredit; impve. 3rd pers. pl.

desconceptúes that you may discredit; pres. subj. 2nd pers. sing. / *desconceptuar.*

desconceptúo I discredit; pres. ind. 1st pers. sing. / *desconceptuar.*

desconcertándose getting upset; pres. part. / *desconcertarse.*

desconcertaos (you all) get upset; impve. 2nd pers. pl. / *desconcertarse.*

desconcertar to disconcert or to confuse. irr.

desconcertarse to get upset. irr.

desconcertémonos let us get upset; impve. 1st pers. pl. / *desconcertarse.*

desconcierta 1. he (she/it) disconcerts; pres. ind. 3rd pers. sing. / *desconcertar.* 2. (you) disconcert; impve. 2nd pers. sing.

desconciertan they disconcert; pres. ind. 3rd pers. pl. / *desconcertar.*

desconciertas you disconcert; pres. ind. 2nd pers. sing. / *desconcertar.*

desconciértate (you) get upset; impve. 2nd pers. sing. / *desconcertarse.*

desconcierte 1. that I may disconcert; pres. subj. 1st pers. sing. / *desconcertar.* 2. that he (she/it) may disconcert; pres. subj. 3rd pers. sing. 3. let him (her/it) disconcert; impve. 3rd pers. sing.

desconcierten 1. that they may disconcert; pres. subj. 3rd pers. pl. / *desconcertar.* 2. let them disconcert; impve. 3rd pers. pl.

desconciértense let them get upset; impve. 3rd pers. pl. / *desconcertarse.*

desconciertes that you may disconcert; pres. subj. 2nd pers. sing. / *desconcertar.*

desconciértese let him (her/it) get upset; impve. 3rd pers. sing. / *desconcertarse.*

desconcierto I disconcert; pres. ind. 1st pers. sing. / *desconcertar.*

desconchándose peeling off; pres. part. / *desconcharse.*

desconchaos (you all) peel off; impve. 2nd pers. pl. / *desconcharse.*

desconchar to scrape off. reg.

desconcharse to peel off. reg.

descónchate (you) peel off; impve. 2nd pers. sing. / *desconcharse.*

desconchémonos let us peel off; impve. 1st pers. pl. / *desconcharse*.

descónchense let them peel off; impve. 3rd pers. pl. / *desconcharse*.

descónchese let him (her/it) peel off; impve. 3rd pers. sing. / *desconcharse*.

desconectar to disconnect. reg.

desconfía 1. he (she/it) distrusts; pres. ind. 3rd pers. sing. / *desconfiar* 2. (you) distrust; impve. 2nd pers. sing.

desconfían they distrust; pres. ind. 3rd pers. pl. / *desconfiar*.

desconfiar to distrust. irr.

desconfías you distrust; pres. ind. 2nd pers. sing. / *desconfiar*.

desconfíe 1. that I may distrust; pres. subj. 1st pers. sing. / *desconfiar*. 2. that he (she/it) may distrust; pres. subj. 3rd pers. sing. 3. let him (her/it) distrust; impve. 3rd pers. sing.

desconfíen 1. that they may distrust; pres. subj. 3rd pers. pl. / *desconfiar*. 2. let them distrust; impve. 3rd pers. pl.

desconfíes that you may distrust; pres. subj. 2nd pers. sing. / *desconfiar*.

desconfío I distrust; pres. ind. 1st pers. sing. / *desconfiar*.

desconformar to disagree. reg.

descongelar to melt or to defrost. reg.

descongestionar to clear of congestion. reg.

descongojar to comfort. reg.

desconoceos (you all) be unrecognizable; impve. 2nd pers. pl. / *desconocerse*.

desconocer to fail to recognize. irr.

desconocerse to be unrecognizable. irr.

desconócete (you) be unrecognizable; impve. 2nd pers. sing. / *desconocerse*.

desconociéndose being unrecognizable; pres. part. / *desconocerse*.

desconozca 1. that I may fail to recognize; pres. subj. 1st pers. sing. / *desconocer*. 2. that he (she/it) may fail to recognize; pres. subj. 3rd pers. sing. 3. let him (her/it) fail to recognize; impve. 3rd pers. sing.

desconozcáis that you (all) may fail to recognize; pres. subj. 2nd pers. pl. / *desconocer*.

desconozcámonos let us be unrecognizable; impve. 1st pers. pl. / *desconocerse*.

desconozcamos 1. that we may fail to recognize; pres. subj. 1st pers. pl. / *desconocer*. 2. let us fail to recognize; impve. 1st pers. pl.

desconozcan 1. that they may fail to recognize; pres. subj. 3rd pers. pl. / *desconocer*. 2. let them fail to recognize; impve. 3rd pers. pl.

desconózcanse let them be unrecognizable; impve. 3rd pers. pl. / *desconocerse*.

desconozcas that you may fail to recognize; pres. subj. 2nd pers. sing. / *desconocer*.

desconózcase let him (her/it) be unrecognizable; impve. 3rd pers. sing. / *desconocerse*.

desconozco I fail to recognize; pres. ind. 1st pers. sing. / *desconocer*.

desconsolándose losing heart; pres. part. / *desconsolarse*.

desconsolaos (you all) lose heart; impve. 2nd pers. pl. / *desconsolarse*.

desconsolar to grieve. irr.

desconsolarse to lose heart. irr.

desconsolémonos let us lose heart; impve. 1st pers. pl. / *desconsolarse*.

desconsuela 1. he (she/it) grieves; pres. ind. 3rd pers. sing. / *desconsolar*. 2. (you) grieve; impve. 2nd pers. sing.

desconsuelan they grieve; pres. ind. 3rd pers. pl. / *desconsolar*.

desconsuelas you grieve; pres. ind. 2nd pers. sing. / *desconsolar*.

desconsuélate (you) lose heart; impve. 2nd pers. sing. / *desconsolarse*.

desconsuele 1. that I may grieve; pres. subj. 1st pers. sing. / *desconsolar*. 2. that he (she/it) may grieve; pres. subj. 3rd pers. sing. 3. let him (her/it) grieve; impve. 3rd pers. sing.

desconsuelen 1. that they may grieve; pres. subj. 3rd pers. pl. / *desconsolar* 2. let them grieve; impve. 3rd pers. pl.

desconsuélense let them lose heart; impve. 3rd pers. pl. / *desconsolarse*.

desconsueles that you may grieve; pres. subj. 2nd pers. sing. / *desconsolar*.

desconsuélese let him (her/it) lose heart; impve. 3rd pers. sing. / *desconsolarse*.

desconsuelo I grieve; pres. ind. 1st pers. sing. / *desconsolar*.

descontagiar to disinfect. reg.

descontaminar to decontaminate. reg.

descontar to discount or to deduct. irr.

descontentar to displease. reg.

descontinúa 1. he (she/it) discontinues; pres. ind. 3rd pers. sing. / *descontinuar*. 2. (you) discontinue; impve. 2nd pers. sing.

descontinúan they discontinue; pres. ind. 3rd pers. pl. / *descontinuar*.

descontinuar to discontinue. irr.

descontinúas you discontinue; pres. ind. 2nd pers. sing. / *descontinuar*.

descontinúe 1. that I may discontinue; pres. subj. 1st pers. sing. / *descontinuar* 2. that he (she/it) may discontinue; pres. subj. 3rd pers. sing. 3. let him (her/it) discontinue; impve. 3rd pers. sing.

descontinúen 1. that they may discontinue; pres. subj. 3rd pers. pl. / *descontinuar*. 2. let them discontinue; impve. 3rd pers. pl.

descontinúes that you may discontinue; pres. subj. 2nd pers. sing. / *descontinuar*.

descontinúo I discontinue; pres. ind. 1st pers. sing. / *descontinuar*.

descontrolar to decontrol. reg.

desconven (you) disagree; impve. 2nd pers. sing. / *desconvenir*.

desconvendrá he (she/it) will disagree; fut. 3rd pers. sing. / *desconvenir*.

desconvendrán they will disagree; fut. 3rd pers. pl. / *desconvenir.*

desconvendrás you will disagree; fut. 2nd pers. sing. / *desconvenir.*

desconvendré I shall disagree; fut. 1st pers. sing. / *desconvenir.*

desconvendréis you (all) will disagree; fut. 2nd pers. pl. / *desconvenir.*

desconvendremos we shall disagree; fut. 1st pers. pl. / *desconvenir.*

desconvendría 1. I should disagree; cond. 1st pers. sing. / *desconvenir.* 2. he (she/it) would disagree; cond. 3rd pers. sing.

desconvendríais you (all) would disagree; cond. 2nd pers. pl. / *desconvenir.*

desconvendríamos we should disagree; cond. 1st pers. pl. / *desconvenir.*

desconvendrían they would disagree; cond. 3rd pers. pl. / *desconvenir.*

desconvendrías you would disagree; cond. 2nd pers. sing. / *desconvenir.*

desconvénete (you) disagree; impve. 2nd pers. sing. / *desconvenirse.*

desconvenga 1. that I may disagree; pres. subj. 1st pers. sing. / *desconvenir.* 2. that he (she/it) may disagree; pres. subj. 3rd pers. sing. 3. let him (her/it) disagree; impve. 3rd pers. sing.

desconvengáis that you (all) may disagree; pres. subj. 2nd pers. pl. / *desconvenir.*

desconvengámonos let us disagree; impve. 1st pers. pl. / *desconvenirse.*

desconvengamos 1. that we may disagree; pres. subj. 1st pers. pl. / *desconvenir* 2. let us disagree; impve. 1st pers. pl.

desconvengan 1. that they may disagree; pres. subj. 3rd pers. pl. / *desconvenir.* 2. let them disagree; impve. 3rd pers. pl.

desconvénganse let them disagree; impve. 3rd pers. pl. / *desconvenirse.*

desconvengas that you may disagree; pres. subj. 2nd pers. sing. / *desconvenir.*

desconvéngase let him (her/it) disagree; impve. 3rd pers. sing. / *desconvenirse.*

desconvengo I disagree; pres. ind. 1st pers. sing. / *desconvenir.*

desconveníos (you all) disagree; impve. 2nd pers. pl. / *desconvenirse.*

desconvenir to disagree or to be mismatched. irr.

desconvenirse to disagree. irr.

desconviene he (she/it) disagrees; pres. ind. 3rd pers. sing. / *desconvenir.*

desconvienen they disagree; pres. ind. 3rd pers. pl. / *desconvenir.*

desconvienes you disagree; pres. ind. 2nd pers. sing. / *desconvenir.*

desconvine I disagreed; past 1st pers. sing. / *desconvenir.*

desconviniendo disagreeing; pres. part. / *desconvenir.*

desconviniéndose disagreeing; pres. part. / *desconvenirse.*

desconviniera 1. that I might disagree; imp. subj. 1st pers. sing. / *desconvenir.* 2. that he (she/it) might disagree; imp. subj. 3rd pers. sing.

desconvinierais that you (all) might disagree; imp. subj. 2nd pers pl. / *desconvenir.*

desconviniéramos that we might disagree; imp. subj. 1st pers. pl. / *desconvenir.*

desconvinieran that they might disagree; imp. subj. 3rd pers. pl. / *desconvenir.*

desconvinieras that you might disagree; imp. subj. 2nd pers. sing. / *desconvenir.*

desconvinieron they disagreed; past 3rd pers. pl. / *desconvenir.*

desconviniese 1. that I might disagree; imp. subj. 1st pers. sing. / *desconvenir.* 2. that he (she/it) might disagree; imp. subj. 3rd pers. sing.

desconvinieseis that you (all) might disagree; imp. subj. 2nd pers pl. / *desconvenir.*

desconviniésemos that we might disagree; imp. subj. 1st pers. pl. / *desconvenir.*

desconviniesen that they might disagree; imp. subj. 3rd pers. pl. / *desconvenir.*

desconvinieses that you might disagree; imp. subj. 2nd pers. sing. / *desconvenir.*

desconvinimos we disagreed; past 1st pers. pl. / *desconvenir.*

desconviniste you disagreed; past 2nd pers. sing. / *desconvenir.*

desconvinisteis you (all) disagreed; past 2nd pers. pl. / *desconvenir.*

desconvino he (she/it) disagreed; past 3rd pers. sing. / *desconvenir.*

descoque 1. that I may be impudent; pres. subj. 1st pers. sing. / *descocarse.* 2. that he (she/it) may be impudent; pres. subj. 3rd pers. sing.

descoqué I was impudent; past 1st pers. sing. / *descocarse.*

descoquéis that you (all) may be impudent; pres. subj. 2nd pers. pl. / *descocarse.*

descoquémonos let us be impudent; impve. 1st pers. pl. / *descocarse.*

descoquemos that we may be impudent; pres. subj. 1st pers. pl. / *descocarse.*

descoquen that they may be impudent; pres. subj. 3rd pers. pl. / *descocarse.*

descóquense let them be impudent; impve. 3rd pers. pl. / *descocarse.*

descoques that you may be impudent; pres. subj. 2nd pers. sing. / *descocarse.*

descóquese let him (her/it) be impudent; impve. 3rd pers. sing. / *descocarse.*

descorazonar to dishearten or to discourage. reg.

descorchándose uncorking; pres. part. / *descorcharse.*

descorchaos (you all) uncork; impve. 2nd pers. pl. / *descorcharse.*

descorchar to uncork. reg.

descorcharse to uncork. reg.

descórchate (you) uncork; impve. 2nd pers. sing. / *descorcharse.*

descorchémonos let us uncork; impve. 1st pers. pl. / *descorcharse.*

descórchense let them uncork; impve. 3rd pers. pl. / *descorcharse.*

descórchese let him (her/it) uncork; impve. 3rd pers. sing. / *descorcharse.*

descornar to dehorn. irr.

descorrer to go back over or to flow. reg.

descortece 1. that I may strip the bark from; pres. subj. 1st pers. sing. / *descortezar.* 2. that he (she/it) may strip the bark from; pres. subj. 3rd pers. sing. 3. let him (her/it) strip the bark from; impve. 3rd pers. sing.

descortecé I stripped the bark from; past 1st pers. sing. / *descortezar.*

descortecéis that you (all) may strip the bark from; pres. subj. 2nd pers. pl. / *descortezar.*

descortecemos 1. that we may strip the bark from; pres. subj. 1st pers. pl. / *descortezar.* 2. let us strip the bark from; impve. 1st pers. pl.

descortecen 1. that they may strip the bark from; pres. subj. 3rd pers. pl. / *descortezar.* 2. let them strip the bark from; impve. 3rd pers. pl.

descorteces that you may strip the bark from; pres. subj. 2nd pers. sing. / *descortezar.*

descortezar to strip the bark from or to civilize. irr.

descosámonos let us blab; impve. 1st pers. pl. / *descoserse.*

descósanse let them blab; impve. 3rd pers. pl. / *descoserse.*

descósase let him (her/it) blab; impve. 3rd pers. sing. / *descoserse.*

descoseos (you all) blab; impve. 2nd pers. pl. / *descoserse.*

descoser to rip or unstitch. reg.

descoserse to blab or prattle. reg.

descósete (you) blab; impve. 2nd pers. sing. / *descoserse.*

descosiéndose blabbing; pres. part. / *descoserse.*

descostrándose flaking; pres. part. / *descostrarse.*

descostrar to take the crust off. reg.

descostrarse to flake or to scale off. reg.

descóstrense let them flake; impve. 3rd pers. pl. / *descostrarse.*

descóstrese let it flake; impve. 3rd pers. sing. / *descostrarse.*

descotar to cut low in the neck (a dress). reg.

descoyuntándose getting out of joint; pres. part. / *descoyuntarse.*

descoyuntaos (you all) get out of joint; impve. 2nd pers. pl. / *descoyuntarse.*

descoyuntar to dislocate or to annoy. reg.

descoyuntarse to get out of joint. reg.

descoyúntate (you) get out of joint; impve. 2nd pers. sing. / *descoyuntarse.*

descoyuntémonos let us get out of joint; impve. 1st pers. pl. / *descoyuntarse.*

descoyúntense let them get out of joint; impve. 3rd pers. pl. / *descoyuntarse.*

descoyúntese let him (her/it) get out of joint; impve. 3rd pers. sing. / *descoyuntarse.*

descozáis that you (all) may digest; pres. subj. 2nd pers. pl. / *descocer.*

descozamos 1. that we may digest; pres. subj. 1st pers. pl. / *descocer.* 2. let us digest; impve. 1st pers. pl.

descreer to disbelieve. irr.

descreí I disbelieved; past 1st pers. sing. / *descreer.*

descreído disbelieved; past. part. / *descreer.*

descreímos we disbelieved; past 1st pers. pl. / *descreer.*

descreíste you disbelieved; past 2nd pers. sing. / *descreer.*

descreísteis you (all) disbelieved; past 2nd pers. pl. / *descreer.*

descreyendo disbelieving; pres. part. / *descreer.*

descreyera 1. that I might disbelieve; imp. subj. 1st pers. sing. / *descreer.* 2. that he (she/it) might disbelieve; imp. subj. 3rd pers. sing.

descreyerais that you (all) might disbelieve; imp. subj. 2nd pers pl. / *descreer.*

descreyéramos that we might disbelieve; imp. subj. 1st pers. pl. / *descreer.*

descreyeran that they might disbelieve; imp. subj. 3rd pers. pl. / *descreer.*

descreyeras that you might disbelieve; imp. subj. 2nd pers. sing. / *descreer.*

descreyeron they disbelieved; past 3rd pers. pl. / *descreer.*

descreyese 1. that I might disbelieve; imp. subj. 1st pers. sing. / *descreer.* 2. that he (she/it) might disbelieve; imp. subj. 3rd pers. sing.

descreyeseis that you (all) might disbelieve; imp. subj. 2nd pers pl. / *descreer.*

descreyésemos that we might disbelieve; imp. subj. 1st pers. pl. / *descreer.*

descreyesen that they might disbelieve; imp. subj. 3rd pers. pl. / *descreer.*

descreyeses that you might disbelieve; imp. subj. 2nd pers. sing. / *descreer.*

descreyó he (she/it) disbelieved; past 3rd pers. sing. / *descreer.*

describir to describe. reg.except for pp.

descrito described; past part. / *describir.*

descuajar to dissolve or to uproot. reg.

descuajaringándose collapsing; pres. part. / *descuajaringarse.*

descuajaringaos (you all) collapse; impve. 2nd pers. pl. / *descuajaringarse.*

descuajaringarse to collapse or to fall apart. irr.

descuajaríngate (you) collapse; impve. 2nd pers. sing. / *descuajaringarse.*

descuajaringue 1. that I may collapse; pres. subj. 1st pers. sing. / *descuajaringarse.* 2. that he (she/it) may collapse; pres. subj. 3rd pers. sing.

descuajaringué I collapsed; past 1st pers. sing. / *descuajaringarse.*

descuajaringuéis that you (all) may collapse; pres. subj. 2nd pers. pl. / *descuajaringarse.*

descuajaringuémonos let us collapse; impve. 1st pers. pl. / *descuajaringarse.*

descuajaringuemos that we may collapse; pres. subj. 1st pers. pl. / *descuajaringarse*.

descuajaringuen that they may collapse; pres. subj. 3rd pers. pl. / *descuajaringarse*.

descuajarínguense let them collapse; impve. 3rd pers. pl. / *descuajaringarse*.

descuajaringues that you may collapse; pres. subj. 2nd pers. sing. / *descuajaringarse*.

descuajarínguese let him (her/it) collapse; impve. 3rd pers. sing. / *descuajaringarse*.

descuartice 1. that I may quarter; pres. subj. 1st pers. sing. / *descuartizar*. 2. that he (she/it) may quarter; pres. subj. 3rd pers. sing. 3. let him (her/it) quarter; impve. 3rd pers. sing.

descuarticé I quartered; past 1st pers. sing. / *descuartizar*.

descuarticéis that you (all) may quarter; pres. subj. 2nd pers. pl. / *descuartizar*.

descuarticemos 1. that we may quarter; pres. subj. 1st pers. pl. / *descuartizar*. 2. let us quarter; impve. 1st pers. pl.

descuarticen 1. that they may quarter; pres. subj. 3rd pers. pl. / *descuartizar*. 2. let them quarter; impve. 3rd pers. pl.

descuartices that you may quarter; pres. subj. 2nd pers. sing. / *descuartizar*.

descuartizar to quarter or to carve. irr.

descubierto discovered; past part. / *descubrir*.

descubrámonos let us take off our hats; impve. 1st pers. pl. / *descubrirse*.

descúbranse let them take off their hats; impve. 3rd pers. pl. / *descubrirse*.

descúbrase let him (her/it) take off his (her/its) hat; impve. 3rd pers. sing. / *descubrirse*.

descúbrete (you) take off your hat; impve. 2nd pers. sing. / *descubrirse*.

descubriéndose taking off one's hat; pres. part. / *descubrirse*.

descubríos (you all) take off your hats; impve. 2nd pers. pl. / *descubrirse*.

descubrir to discover. reg. except for pp.

descubrirse to take off one's hat. reg. except for pp.

descuece 1. he (she/it) digests; pres. ind. 3rd pers. sing. / *descocer*. 2. (you) digest; impve. 2nd pers. sing.

descuecen they digest; pres. ind. 3rd pers. pl. / *descocer*.

descueces you digest; pres. ind. 2nd pers. sing. / *descocer*.

descuelga 1. he (she/it) takes down; pres. ind. 3rd pers. sing. / *descolgar*. 2. (you) take down; impve. 2nd pers. sing.

descuelgan they take down; pres. ind. 3rd pers. pl. / *descolgar*.

descuelgas you take down; pres. ind. 2nd pers. sing. / *descolgar*.

descuelgo I take down; pres. ind. 1st pers. sing. / *descolgar*.

descuelgue 1. that I may take down; pres. subj. 1st pers. sing. / *descolgar*. 2. that he (she/it) may take down; pres. subj. 3rd pers. sing. 3. let him (her/it) take down; impve. 3rd pers. sing.

descuelguen 1. that they may take down; pres. subj. 3rd pers. pl. / *descolgar*. 2. let them take down; impve. 3rd pers. pl.

descuélguense let them fall down; impve. 3rd pers. pl. / *descolgarse*.

descuelgues that you may take down; pres. subj. 2nd pers. sing. / *descolgar*.

descuélguese let him (her/it) fall down; impve. 3rd pers. sing. / *descolgarse*.

descuella 1. he (she/it) excels; pres. ind. 3rd pers. sing. / *descollar*. 2. (you) excel; impve. 2nd pers. sing.

descuellan they excel; pres. ind. 3rd pers. pl. / *descollar*.

descuellas you excel; pres. ind. 2nd pers. sing. / *descollar*.

descuelle 1. that I may excel; pres. subj. 1st pers. sing. / *descollar*. 2. that he (she/it) may excel; pres. subj. 3rd pers. sing. 3. let him (her/it) excel; impve. 3rd pers. sing.

descuellen 1. that they may excel; pres. subj. 3rd pers. pl. / *descollar*. 2. let them excel; impve. 3rd pers. pl.

descuelles that you may excel; pres. subj. 2nd pers. sing. / *descollar*.

descuello I excel; pres. ind. 1st pers. sing. / *descollar*.

descuenta 1. he (she/it) discounts; pres. ind. 3rd pers. sing. / *descontar*. 2. (you) discount; impve. 2nd pers. sing.

descuentan they discount; pres. ind. 3rd pers. pl. / *descontar*.

descuentas you discount; pres. ind. 2nd pers. sing. / *descontar*.

descuente 1. that I may discount; pres. subj. 1st pers. sing. / *descontar*. 2. that he (she/it) may discount; pres. subj. 3rd pers. sing. 3. let him (her/it) discount; impve. 3rd pers. sing.

descuenten 1. that they may discount; pres. subj. 3rd pers. pl. / *descontar* 2. let them discount; impve. 3rd pers. pl.

descuentes that you may discount; pres. subj. 2nd pers. sing. / *descontar*.

descuento I discount; pres. ind. 1st pers. sing. / *descontar*.

descuerna 1. he (she/it) dehorns; pres. ind. 3rd pers. sing. / *descornar*. 2. (you) dehorn; impve. 2nd pers. sing.

descuernan they dehorn; pres. ind. 3rd pers. pl. / *descornar*.

descuernas you dehorn; pres. ind. 2nd pers. sing. / *descornar*.

descuerne 1. that I may dehorn; pres. subj. 1st pers. sing. / *descornar*. 2. that he (she/it) may dehorn; pres. subj. 3rd pers. sing. 3. let him (her/it) dehorn; impve. 3rd pers. sing.

descuernen 1. that they may dehorn; pres. subj. 3rd pers. pl. / *descornar*. 2. let them dehorn; impve. 3rd pers. pl.

descuernes that you may dehorn; pres. subj. 2nd pers. sing. / *descornar.*

descuerno I dehorn; pres. ind. 1st pers. sing. / *descornar.*

descuerza 1. that I may digest; pres. subj. 1st pers. sing. / *descocer.* 2. that he (she/it) may digest; pres. subj. 3rd pers. sing. 3. let him (her/it) digest; impve. 3rd pers. sing.

descuerzan 1. that they may digest; pres. subj. 3rd pers. pl. / *descocer.* 2. let them digest; impve. 3rd pers. pl.

descuerzas that you may digest; pres. subj. 2nd pers. sing. / *descocer.*

descuerzo I digest; pres. ind. 1st pers. sing. / *descocer.*

descuidándose being careless; pres. part. / *descuidarse.*

descuidaos (you all) be careless; impve. 2nd pers. pl. / *descuidarse.*

descuidar to neglect. reg.

descuidarse to be careless. reg.

descuídate (you) be careless; impve. 2nd pers. sing. / *descuidarse.*

descuidémonos let us be careless; impve. 1st pers. pl. / *descuidarse.*

descuídense let them be careless; impve. 3rd pers. pl. / *descuidarse.*

descuídese let him (her/it) be careless; impve. 3rd pers. sing. / *descuidarse.*

desdecíos (you all) retract; impve. 2nd pers. pl. / *desdecirse.*

desdecir to degenerate. irr.

desdecirse to retract. irr.

desdeñándose being distainful; pres. part. / *desdeñarse.*

desdeñaos (you all) be distainful; impve. 2nd pers. pl. / *desdeñarse.*

desdeñar to distain. reg.

desdeñarse to be distainful. reg.

desdéñate (you) be distainful; impve. 2nd pers. sing. / *desdeñarse.*

desdeñémonos let us be distainful; impve. 1st pers. pl. / *desdeñarse.*

desdéñense let them be distainful; impve. 3rd pers. pl. / *desdeñarse.*

desdéñese let him (her/it) be distainful; impve. 3rd pers. sing. / *desdeñarse.*

desdi (you) degenerate; impve. 2nd pers. sing. / *desdecir.*

desdibujar to become blurred. reg.

desdice he (she/it) degenerates; pres. ind. 3rd pers. sing. / *desdecir.*

desdicen they degenerate; pres. ind. 3rd pers. pl. / *desdecir.*

desdices you degenerate; pres. ind. 2nd pers. sing. / *desdecir.*

desdiciendo degenerating; pres. part. / *desdecir.*

desdiciéndose retracting; pres. part. / *desdecirse.*

desdicho degenerated; past part. / *desdecir.*

desdíete (you) retract; impve. 2nd pers. sing. / *desdecirse.*

desdiga 1. that I may degenerate; pres. subj. 1st pers. sing. / *desdecir.* 2. that he (she/it) may degenerate; pres. subj. 3rd pers. sing. 3. let him (her/it) degenerate; impve. 3rd pers. sing.

desdigáis that you (all) may degenerate; pres. subj. 2nd pers. pl. / *desdecir.*

desdigámonos let us retract; impve. 1st pers. pl. / *desdecirse.*

desdigamos 1. that we may degenerate; pres. subj. 1st pers. pl. / *desdecir.* 2. let us degenerate; impve. 1st pers. pl.

desdigan 1. that they may degenerate; pres. subj. 3rd pers. pl. / *desdecir.* 2. let them degenerate; impve. 3rd pers. pl.

desdíganse let them retract; impve. 3rd pers. pl. / *desdecirse.*

desdigas that you may degenerate; pres. subj. 2nd pers. sing. / *desdecir.*

desdígase let him (her/it) retract; impve. 3rd pers. sing. / *desdecirse.*

desdigo I degenerate; pres. ind. 1st pers. sing. / *desdecir.*

desdije I degenerated; past 1st pers. sing. / *desdecir.*

desdijera 1. that I might degenerate; imp. subj. 1st pers. sing. / *desdecir.* 2. that he (she/it) might degenerate; imp. subj. 3rd pers. sing.

desdijerais that you (all) might degenerate; imp. subj. 2nd pers pl. / *desdecir.*

desdijéramos that we might degenerate; imp. subj. 1st pers. pl. / *desdecir.*

desdijeran that they might degenerate; imp. subj. 3rd pers. pl. / *desdecir.*

desdijeras that you might degenerate; imp. subj. 2nd pers. sing. / *desdecir.*

desdijeron they degenerated; past 3rd pers. pl. / *desdecir.*

desdijese 1. that I might degenerate; imp. subj. 1st pers. sing. / *desdecir.* 2. that he (she/it) might degenerate; imp. subj. 3rd pers. sing.

desdijeseis that you (all) might degenerate; imp. subj. 2nd pers pl. / *desdecir.*

desdijésemos that we might degenerate; imp. subj. 1st pers. pl. / *desdecir.*

desdijesen that they might degenerate; imp. subj. 3rd pers. pl. / *desdecir.*

desdijeses that you might degenerate; imp. subj. 2nd pers. sing. / *desdecir.*

desdijimos we degenerated; past 1st pers. pl. / *desdecir.*

desdijiste you degenerated; past 2nd pers. sing. / *desdecir.*

desdijisteis you (all) degenerated; past 2nd pers. pl. / *desdecir.*

desdijo he (she/it) degenerated; past 3rd pers. sing. / *desdecir.*

desdirá he (she/it) will degenerate; fut. 3rd pers. sing. / *desdecir.*

desdirán they will degenerate; fut. 3rd pers. pl. / *desdecir.*

desdirás you will degenerate; fut. 2nd pers. sing. / *desdecir.*

desdiré I shall degenerate; fut. 1st pers. sing. / *desdecir.*

desdiréis you (all) will degenerate; fut. 2nd pers. pl. / *desdecir.*

desdiremos we shall degenerate; fut. 1st pers. pl. / *desdecir.*

desdiría 1. I should degenerate; cond. 1st pers. sing. / *desdecir.* 2. he (she/it) would degenerate; cond. 3rd pers. sing.

desdiríais you (all) would degenerate; cond. 2nd pers. pl. / *desdecir.*

desdiríamos we should degenerate; cond. 1st pers. pl. / *desdecir.*

desdirían they would degenerate; cond. 3rd pers. pl. / *desdecir.*

desdirías you would degenerate; cond. 2nd pers. sing. / *desdecir.*

desdoblándose spreading out; pres. part. / *desdoblarse.*

desdoblaos (you all) spread out; impve. 2nd pers. pl. / *desdoblarse.*

desdoblar to unfold or to spread out. reg.

desdoblarse to spread out. reg.

desdóblate (you) spread out; impve. 2nd pers. sing. / *desdoblarse.*

desdoblémonos let us spread out; impve. 1st pers. pl. / *desdoblarse.*

desdóblense let them spread out; impve. 3rd pers. pl. / *desdoblarse.*

desdóblese let him (her/it) spread out; impve. 3rd pers. sing. / *desdoblarse.*

desdorar to tarnish or to dishonor. reg.

dése let him (her/it) give up; impve. 3rd pers. sing. / *darse.*

desear to desire or want. reg.

desecándose drying up; pres. part. / *desecarse.*

desecaos (you all) dry up; impve. 2nd pers. pl. / *desecarse.*

desecar to dry. irr.

desecarse to dry up. irr.

desécate (you) dry up; impve. 2nd pers. sing. / *desecarse.*

desechar to reject. reg.

desedificar to set a bad example for. irr.

desedifique 1. that I may set a bad example for; pres. subj. 1st pers. sing. / *desedificar.* 2. that he (she/it) may set a bad example for; pres. subj. 3rd pers. sing. 3. let him (her/it) set a bad example for; impve. 3rd pers. sing.

desedifiqué I set a bad example for; past 1st pers. sing. / *desedificar.*

desedifiquéis that you (all) may set bad example for; pres. subj. 2nd pers. pl. / *desedificar.*

desedifiquemos 1. that we may set a bad example for; pres. subj. 1st pers. pl. / *desedificar.* 2. let us set a bad example for; impve. 1st pers. pl.

desedifiquen 1. that they may set a bad example for; past 1st pers. sing. / *desedificar.*

desedifiques that you may set a bad example for; pres. subj. 2nd pers. sing. / *desedificar.*

desellar to unseal. reg.

desembalar to unpack. reg.

desembarace 1. that I may rid; pres. subj. 1st pers. sing. / *desembarazar.* 2. that he (she/it) may rid; pres. subj. 3rd pers. sing. 3. let him (her/it) rid; impve. 3rd pers. sing.

desembaracé I rid; past 1st pers. sing. / *desembarazar.*

desembaracéis that you (all) may rid; pres. subj. 2nd pers. pl. / *desembarazar.*

desembaracémonos let us get free; impve. 1st pers. pl. / *desembarazarse.*

desembaracemos 1. that we may rid; pres. subj. 1st pers. pl. / *desembarazar.* 2. let us rid; impve. 1st pers. pl.

desembaracen 1. that they may rid; pres. subj. 3rd pers. pl. / *desembarazar.* 2. let them rid; impve. 3rd pers. pl.

desembarácense let them get free; impve. 3rd pers. pl. / *desembarazarse.*

desembaraces that you may rid; pres. subj. 2nd pers. sing. / *desembarazar.*

desembarácese let him (her/it) get free; impve. 3rd pers. sing. / *desembarazarse.*

desembarazándose getting free; pres. part. / *desembarazarse.*

desembarazaos (you all) get free; impve. 2nd pers. pl. / *desembarazarse.*

desembarazar to rid or to free. irr.

desembarazarse to get free. irr.

desembarázate (you) get free; impve. 2nd pers. sing. / *desembarazarse.*

desembarcándose unloading; pres. part. / *desembarcarse.*

desembarcaos (you all) unload; impve. 2nd pers. pl. / *desembarcarse.*

desembarcar to disembark or to unload. irr.

desembarcarse to unload. irr.

desembárcate (you) unload; impve. 2nd pers. sing. / *desembarcarse.*

desembargar to lift the embargo on. irr.

desembargue 1. that I may lift the embargo on; pres. subj. 1st pers. sing. / *desembargar.* 2. that he (she/it) may lift the embargo on; pres. subj. 3rd pers. sing. 3. let him (her/it) lift the embargo on; impve. 3rd pers. sing.

desembargué I lifted the embargo on; past 1st pers. sing. / *desembargar.*

desembarguéis that you (all) may lift the embargo on; pres. subj. 2nd pers. pl. / *desembargar.*

desembarguemos 1. that we may lift the embargo on; pres. subj. 1st pers. pl. / *desembargar.* 2. let us lift the embargo on; impve. 1st pers. pl.

desembarguen 1. that they may lift the embargo on; pres. subj. 3rd pers. pl. / *desembargar.* 2. let them lift the embargo on; impve. 3rd pers. pl.

desembargues that you may lift the embargo on; pres. subj. 2nd pers. sing. / *desembargar.*

desembarque 1. that I may disembark; pres. subj. 1st pers. sing. / *desembarcar*. 2. that he (she/it) may disembark; pres. subj. 3rd pers. sing. 3. let him (her/it) disembark; impve. 3rd pers. sing.

desembarqué I disembarked; past 1st pers. sing. / *desembarcar*.

desembarquéis that you (all) may disembark; pres. subj. 2nd pers. pl. / *desembarcar*.

desembarquen let us unload; impve. 1st pers. pl. / *desembarcarse*.

desembarquemos 1. that we may disembark; pres. subj. 1st pers. pl. / *desembarcar*. 2. let us disembark; impve. 1st pers. pl.

desembarquen 1. that they may disembark; pres. subj. 3rd pers. pl. / *desembarcar*. 2. let them disembark; impve. 3rd pers. pl.

desembárquense let them unload; impve. 3rd pers. pl. / *desembarcarse*.

desembarques that you may disembark; pres. subj. 2nd pers. sing. / *desembarcar*.

desembárquese let him (her/it) unload; impve. 3rd pers. sing. / *desembarcarse*.

desembarrancar to float (as a grounded ship). irr.

desembarranque 1. that it may float (as a grounded ship); pres. subj. 3rd pers. sing. / *desembarrancar*. 2. let it float (as a grounded ship); impve. 3rd pers. sing.

desembarranquen 1. that they may float (as a grounded ship); pres. subj. 3rd pers. pl. / *desembarrancar*. 2. let them float (as a grounded ship); impve. 3rd pers. pl.

desembarrar to clean of mud. reg.

desembocar to flow into. irr.

desembolsar to disemburse or to pay out. reg.

desemboque 1. that it may flow into; pres. subj. 3rd pers. sing. / *desembocar* 2. let it flow into; impve. 3rd pers. sing.

desemboquen 1. that they may flow into; pres. subj. 3rd pers. pl. / *desembocar*. 2. let them flow into; impve. 3rd pers. pl.

desemborrachándose sobering up; pres. part. / *desemborracharse*.

desemborrachaos (you all) sober up; impve. 2nd pers. pl. / *desemborracharse*.

desemborrachar to sober up. reg.

desemborracharse to sober up. reg.

desemborráchate (you) sober up; impve. 2nd pers. sing. / *desemborracharse*.

desemborrachémonos let us sober up; impve. 1st pers. pl. / *desemborracharse*.

desemborráchense let them sober up; impve. 3rd pers. pl. / *desemborracharse*.

desemborráchese let him (her/it) sober up; impve. 3rd pers. sing. / *desemborracharse*.

desembotar to sharpen (wits). reg.

desembozar to unmuffle or to uncover. reg.

desembragar to disengage. irr.

desembrague 1. that I may disengage; pres. subj. 1st pers. sing. / *desembragar*. 2. that he (she/it) may disengage; pres. subj. 3rd pers. sing. 3. let him (her/it) disengage; impve. 3rd pers. sing.

desembragué I disengaged; past 1st pers. sing. / *desembragar*.

desembraguéis that you (all) may disengage; pres. subj. 2nd pers. pl. / *desembragar*.

desembraguemos 1. that we may disengage; pres. subj. 1st pers. pl. / *desembragar*. 2. let us disengage; impve. 1st pers. pl.

desembraguen 1. that they may disengage; pres. subj. 3rd pers. pl. / *desembragar*. 2. let them disengage; impve. 3rd pers. pl.

desembragues that you may disengage; pres. subj. 2nd pers. sing. / *desembragar*.

desembriagar to sober up. irr.

desembriague 1. that I may sober up; pres. subj. 1st pers. sing. / *desembriagar*. 2. that he (she/it) may sober up; pres. subj. 3rd pers. sing. 3. let him (her/it) sober up; impve. 3rd pers. sing.

desembriagué I sobered up; past 1st pers. sing. / *desembriagar*.

desembriaguéis that you (all) may sober up; pres. subj. 2nd pers. pl. / *desembriagar*.

desembriaguemos 1. that we may sober up; pres. subj. 1st pers. pl. / *desembriagar*. 2. let us sober up; impve. 1st pers. pl.

desembriaguen 1. that they may sober up; pres. subj. 3rd pers. pl. / *desembriagar*. 2. let them sober up; impve. 3rd pers. pl.

desembriagues that you may sober up; pres. subj. 2nd pers. sing. / *desembriagar*.

desembrollar to unravel. reg.

desembuchar to disgorge. reg.

desemejar to disfigure or to differ. reg.

desempacándose becoming calm; pres. part. / *desempacarse*.

desempacaos (you all) become calm; impve. 2nd pers. pl. / *desempacarse*.

desempacar to unpack. irr.

desempacarse to become calm. irr.

desempácate (you) become calm; impve. 2nd pers. sing. / *desempacarse*.

desempachándose casting off one's timidity; pres. part. / *desempacharse*.

desempachaos you (all) cast off your timidity; impve. 2nd pers. pl. / *desempacharse*.

desempachar to relieve of indigestion. reg.

desempacharse to cast off one's timidity. reg.

desempáchate (you) cast off your timidity; impve. 2nd pers. sing. / *desempacharse*.

desempachémonos let us cast off our timidity; impve. 1st pers. pl. / *desempacharse*.

desempáchense let them cast off their timidity; impve. 3rd pers. pl. / *desempacharse*.

desempáchese let him (her/it) cast off his (her/its) timidity; impve. 3rd pers. sing. / *desempacharse*.

desempapelar to take the paper off. reg.

desempaque 1. that I may unpack; pres. subj. 1st pers. sing. / *desempacar*. 2. that he (she/it) may unpack; pres. subj. 3rd pers. sing. 3. let him (her/it) unpack; impve. 3rd pers. sing.

desempaqué I unpacked; past 1st pers. sing. / *desempacar*.

desempaquéis that you (all) may unpack; pres. subj. 2nd pers. pl. / *desempacar.*

desempaquémonos let us become calm; impve. 1st pers. pl. / *desempacarse.*

desempaquemos 1. that we may unpack; pres. subj. 1st pers. pl. / *desempacar.* 2. let us unpack; impve. 1st pers. pl.

desempaquen 1. that they may unpack; pres. subj. 3rd pers. pl. / *desempacar.* 2. let them unpack; impve. 3rd pers. pl.

desempáquense let them become calm; impve. 3rd pers. pl. / *desempacarse.*

desempaques that you may unpack; pres. subj. 2nd pers. sing. / *desempacar.*

desempáquese let him (her/it) become calm; impve. 3rd pers. sing. / *desempacarse.*

desempaquetar to unpack or to unwrap. reg.

desemparejar to unnmatch. reg.

desempatar to break the tie in or to decide. reg.

desempeñar to redeem. reg.

desempolvándose brushing up; pres. part. / *desempolvarse.*

desempolvaos (you all) brush up; impve. 2nd pers. pl. / *desempolvarse.*

desempolvar to dust. reg.

desempolvarse to brush up. reg.

desempólvate (you) brush up; impve. 2nd pers. sing. / *desempolvarse.*

desempolvémonos let us brush up; impve. 1st pers. pl. / *desempolvarse.*

desempólvense let them brush up; impve. 3rd pers. pl. / *desempolvarse.*

desempólvese let him (her/it) brush up; impve. 3rd pers. sing. / *desempolvarse.*

desempolvorar to dust. reg.

desenamorar to disenchant. reg.

desencabestrar to disentangle from the halter. reg.

desencadenándose breaking loose; pres. part. / *desencadenarse.*

desencadenaos (you all) break loose; impve. 2nd pers. pl. / *desencadenarse.*

desencadenar to unchain. reg.

desencadenarse to break loose. reg.

desencadénate (you) break loose; impve. 2nd pers. sing. / *desencadenarse.*

desencadenémonos let us break loose; impve. 1st pers. pl. / *desencadenarse.*

desencadénense let them break loose; impve. 3rd pers. pl. / *desencadenarse.*

desencadénese let him (her/it) break loose; impve. 3rd pers. sing. / *desencadenarse.*

desencajándose looking distorted; pres. part. / *desencajarse.*

desencajar to disjoint. reg.

desencajarse to look distorted. reg.

desencájense let them look distorted; impve. 3rd pers. pl. / *desencajarse.*

desencájese let it look distorted; impve. 3rd pers. sing. / *desencajarse.*

desencajonar to unpack. reg.

desencallar to refloat. reg.

desencantar to disenchant or to disillusion. reg.

desencapotándose taking one's cloak off; pres. part. / *desencapotarse.*

desencapotaos (you all) take your cloaks off; impve. 2nd pers. pl. / *desencapotarse.*

desencapotarse to take one's cloak off. reg.

desencapótate (you) take your cloak off; impve. 2nd pers. sing. / *desencapotarse.*

desencapotémonos let us take our cloaks off; impve. 1st pers. pl. / *desencapotarse.*

desencapótense let them take their cloaks off; impve. 3rd pers. pl. / *desencapotarse.*

desencapótese let him (her/it) take his (her/its) cloak off; impve. 3rd pers. sing. / *desencapotarse.*

desencarcelar to set free. reg.

desencarnándose dying; pres. part. / *desencarnarse.*

desencarnaos (you all) die; impve. 2nd pers. pl. / *desencarnarse.*

desencarnar to disembody. reg.

desencarnarse to die. reg.

desencárnate (you) die; impve. 2nd pers. sing. / *desencarnarse.*

desencarnémonos let us die; impve. 1st pers. pl. / *desencarnarse.*

desencárnense let them die; impve. 3rd pers. pl. / *desencarnarse.*

desencárnese let him (her/it) die; impve. 3rd pers. sing. / *desencarnarse.*

desencogeos (you all) grow bold; impve. 2nd pers. pl. / *desencogerse.*

desencoger to unfold. irr.

desencogerse to grow bold. irr.

desencógete (you) grow bold; impve. 2nd pers. sing. / *desencogerse.*

desencogiéndose growing bolder; pres. part. / *desencogerse.*

desencoja 1. that I may unfold; pres. subj. 1st pers. sing. / *desencoger.* 2. that he (she/it) may unfold; pres. subj. 3rd pers. sing. 3. let him (her/it) unfold; impve. 3rd pers. sing.

desencojáis that you (all) may unfold; pres. subj. 2nd pers. pl. / *desencoger.*

desencojámonos let us grow bold; impve. 1st pers. pl. / *desencogerse.*

desencojamos 1. that we may unfold; pres. subj. 1st pers. pl. / *desencoger.* 2. let us unfold; impve. 1st pers. pl.

desencojan 1. that they may unfold; pres. subj. 3rd pers. pl. / *desencoger.* 2. let them unfold; impve. 3rd pers. pl.

desencójanse let them grow bold; impve. 3rd pers. pl. / *desencogerse.*

desencojas that you may unfold; pres. subj. 2nd pers. sing. / *desencoger.*

desencójase let him (her/it) grow bold; impve. 3rd pers. sing. / *desencogerse.*

desencojo I unfold; pres. ind. 1st pers. sing. / *desencoger.*

desencolerice 1. that I may calm down; pres. subj. 1st pers. sing. / *desencolerizarse.* 2. that he (she/it) may calm down; pres. subj. 3rd pers. sing.

desencolericé I calmed down; past 1st pers. sing. / *desencolerizarse.*

desencolericéis that you (all) may calm down; pres. subj. 2nd pers. pl. / *desencolerizarse.*

desencolericémonos let us calm down; impve. 1st pers. pl. / *desencolerizarse.*

desencolericemos that we may calm down; pres. subj. 1st pers. pl. / *desencolerizarse.*

desencolericen that they may calm down; pres. subj. 3rd pers. pl. / *desencolerizarse.*

desencolericense let them calm down; impve. 3rd pers. pl. / *desencolerizarse.*

desencolerices that you may calm down; pres. subj. 2nd pers. sing. / *desencolerizarse.*

desencolerícese let him (her/it) calm down; impve. 3rd pers. sing. / *desencolerizarse.*

desencolerizándose calming down; pres. part. / *desencolerizarse.*

desencolerizaos (you all) calm down; impve. 2nd pers. pl. / *desencolerizarse.*

desencolerizar to calm down. irr.

desencolerizarse to calm down. irr.

desencolerízate (you) calm down; impve. 2nd pers. sing. / *desencolerizarse.*

desenconándose subsiding; pres. part. / *desenconarse.*

desenconar to reduce or to appease. reg.

desenconarse to subside or to soften. reg.

desencónense let them subside; impve. 3rd pers. pl. / *desenconarse.*

desencónese let it subside; impve. 3rd pers. sing. / *desenconarse.*

desencordar to unstring. irr.

desencordelar to unfasten. reg.

desencorvar to straighten. reg.

desencuerda 1. he (she/it) unstrings; pres. ind. 3rd pers. sing. / *desencordar.* 2. (you) unstring; impve. 2nd pers. sing.

desencuerdan they unstring; pres. ind. 3rd pers. pl. / *desencordar.*

desencuerdas you unstring; pres. ind. 2nd pers. sing. / *desencordar.*

desencuerde 1. that I may unstring; pres. subj. 1st pers. sing. / *desencordar.* 2. that he (she/it) may unstring; pres. subj. 3rd pers. sing. 3. let him (her/it) unstring; impve. 3rd pers. sing.

desencuerden 1. that they may unstring; pres. subj. 3rd pers. pl. / *desencordar.* 2. let them unstring; impve. 3rd pers. pl.

desencuerdes that you may unstring; pres. subj. 2nd pers. sing. / *desencordar.*

desencuerdo I unstring; pres. ind. 1st pers. sing. / *desencordar.*

desenchufar to unplug or to disconnect. reg.

desendiosar to humble. reg.

desenfadándose cherring up; pres. part. / *desenfadarse.*

desenfadaos (you all) cheer up; impve. 2nd pers. pl. / *desenfadarse.*

desenfadar to appease or to calm. reg.

desenfadarse to cheer up. reg.

desenfádate (you) cheer up; impve. 2nd pers. sing. / *desenfadarse.*

desenfadémonos let us cheer up; impve. 1st pers. pl. / *desenfadarse.*

desenfádense let them cheer up; impve. 3rd pers. pl. / *desenfadarse.*

desenfádese let him (her/it) cheer up; impve. 3rd pers. sing. / *desenfadarse.*

desenfrenándose losing all restraint; pres. part. / *desenfrenarse.*

desenfrenaos (you all) lose all restraint; impve. 2nd pers. pl. / *desenfrenarse.*

desenfrenar to unbridle. reg.

desenfrenarse to lose all restraint. reg.

desenfrénate (you) lose all restraint; impve. 2nd pers. sing. / *desenfrenarse.*

desenfrenémonos let us lose all restraint; impve. 1st pers. pl. / *desenfrenarse.*

desenfrénense let them lose all restraint; impve. 3rd pers. pl. / *desenfrenarse.*

desenfrénese let him (her/it) lose all restraint; impve. 3rd pers. sing. / *desenfrenarse.*

desenganchar to unhook. reg.

desengañándose getting disillusioned; pres. part. / *desengañarse.*

desengañaos (you all) get disillusioned; impve. 2nd pers. pl. / *desengañarse.*

desengañar to undeceive or to disappoint. reg.

desengañarse to get disillusioned. reg.

desengáñate (you) get disillusioned; impve. 2nd pers. sing. / *desengañarse.*

desengañémonos let us get disillusioned; impve. 1st pers. pl. / *desengañarse.*

desengáñense let them get disillusioned; impve. 3rd pers. pl. / *desengañarse.*

desengáñese let him (her/it) get disillusioned; impve. 3rd pers. sing. / *desengañarse.*

desengranar to throw out of gear. reg.

desenhebrar to unthread. reg.

desenjaece 1. that I may unharness; pres. subj. 1st pers. sing. / *desenjaezar.* 2. that he (she/it) may unharness; pres. subj. 3rd pers. sing. 3. let him (her/it) unharness; impve. 3rd pers. sing.

desenjaecé I unharnessed; past 1st pers. sing. / *desenjaezar.*

desenjaecéis that you (all) may unharness; pres. subj. 2nd pers. pl. / *desenjaezar.*

desenjaecemos 1. that we may unharness; pres. subj. 1st pers. pl. / *desenjaezar.* 2. let us unharness; impve. 1st pers. pl.

desenjaecen 1. that they may unharness; pres. subj. 3rd pers. pl. / *desenjaezar.* 2. let them unharness; impve. 3rd pers. pl.

desenjaeces that you may unharness; pres. subj. 2nd pers. sing. / *desenjaezar.*

desenjaezar to unharness. irr.

desenjaular to uncage. reg.

desenlace 1. that I may untie; pres. subj. 1st pers. sing. / *desenlazar*. 2. that he (she/it) may untie; pres. subj. 3rd pers. sing. 3. let him (her/it) untie; impve. 3rd pers. sing.

desenlacé I untied; past 1st pers. sing. / *desenlazar*.

desenlacéis that you (all) may untie; pres. subj. 2nd pers. pl. / *desenlazar*.

desenlacémonos let us unfold (story); impve. 1st pers. pl. / *desenlazarse*.

desenlacemos 1. that we may untie; pres. subj. 1st pers. pl. / *desenlazar*. 2. let us untie; impve. 1st pers. pl.

desenlacen 1. that they may untie; pres. subj. 3rd pers. pl. / *desenlazar*. 2. let them untie; impve. 3rd pers. pl.

desenlácense let them unfold (story); impve. 3rd pers. pl. / *desenlazarse*.

desenlaces that you may untie; pres. subj. 2nd pers. sing. / *desenlazar*.

desenlácese let him (her/it) unfold (story); impve. 3rd pers. sing. / *desenlazarse*.

desenlazándose unfolding (story); pres. part. / *desenlazarse*.

desenlazaos (you all) unfold (story); impve. 2nd pers. pl. / *desenlazarse*.

desenlazar to untie or to unravel. irr.

desenlazarse to unfold (story). irr.

desenlázate (you) unfold (story); impve. 2nd pers. sing. / *desenlazarse*.

desenlodar to remove the mud from. reg.

desenmarañar to untangle. reg.

desenmascarándose unmasking; pres. part. / *desenmascararse*.

desenmascaraos (you all) unmask; impve. 2nd pers. pl. / *desenmascararse*.

desenmascarar to unmask. reg.

desenmascararse to unmask. reg.

desenmascárate (you) unmask; impve. 2nd pers. sing. / *desenmascararse*.

desenmascarémonos let us unmask; impve. 1st pers. pl. / *desenmascararse*.

desenmascárense let them unmask; impve. 3rd pers. pl. / *desenmascararse*.

desenmascárese let him (her/it) unmask; impve. 3rd pers. sing. / *desenmascararse*.

desenojándose calming down; pres. part. / *desenojarse*.

desenojaos (you all) calm down; impve. 2nd pers. pl. / *desenojarse*.

desenojar to calm the anger of. reg.

desenojarse to calm down. reg.

desenójate (you) calm down; impve. 2nd pers. sing. / *desenojarse*.

desenojémonos let us calm down; impve. 1st pers. pl. / *desenojarse*.

desenójense let them calm down; impve. 3rd pers. pl. / *desenojarse*.

desenójese let him (her/it) calm down; impve. 3rd pers. sing. / *desenojarse*.

desenredándose extricating oneself; pres. part. / *desenredarse*.

desenredaos (you all) extricate yourselves; impve. 2nd pers. pl. / *desenredarse*.

desenredar to disentangle. reg.

desenredarse to extricate oneself. reg.

desenrédate (you) extricate yourself; impve. 2nd pers. sing. / *desenredarse*.

desenredémonos let us extricate ourselves; impve. 1st pers. pl. / *desenredarse*.

desenrédense let them extricate themselves; impve. 3rd pers. pl. / *desenredarse*.

desenrédese let him (her/it) extricate himself (herself/itself); impve. 3rd pers. sing. / *desenredarse*.

desenrollar to unroll. reg.

desenroscar to untwist or to unscrew. irr.

desenrosque 1. that I may untwist; pres. subj. 1st pers. sing. / *desenroscar*. 2. that he (she/it) may untwist; pres. subj. 3rd pers. sing. 3. let him (her/it) untwist; impve. 3rd pers. sing.

desenrosqué I untwisted; past 1st pers. sing. / *desenroscar*.

desenrosquéis that you (all) may untwist; pres. subj. 2nd pers. pl. / *desenroscar*.

desenrosquemos 1. that we may untwist; pres. subj. 1st pers. pl. / *desenroscar*. 2. let us untwist; impve. 1st pers. pl.

desenrosquen 1. that they may untwist; pres. subj. 3rd pers. pl. / *desenroscar*. 2. let them untwist; impve. 3rd pers. pl.

desenrosques that you may untwist; pres. subj. 2nd pers. sing. / *desenroscar*.

desensartar to unstring or to unthread. reg.

desensillar to unsaddle. reg.

desentendámonos let us ignore; impve. 1st pers. pl. / *desentenderse*.

desentendeos (you all) ignore; impve. 2nd pers. pl. / *desentenderse*.

desentenderse to ignore or to pretend ignorance. irr.

desentendiéndose ignoring; pres. part. / *desentenderse*.

desenterrar to unearth. irr.

desentienda 1. that I may ignore; pres. subj. 1st pers. sing. / *desentenderse*. 2. that he (she/it) may ignore; pres. subj. 3rd pers. sing.

desentiendan that they may ignore; pres. subj. 3rd pers. pl. / *desentenderse*.

desentiéndanse let them ignore; impve. 3rd pers. pl. / *desentenderse*.

desentiendas that you may ignore; pres. subj. 2nd pers. sing. / *desentenderse*.

desentiéndase let him (her/it) ignore; impve. 3rd pers. sing. / *desentenderse*.

desentiende he (she/it) ignores; pres. ind. 3rd pers. sing. / *desentenderse*.

desentienden they ignore; pres. ind. 3rd pers. pl. / *desentenderse*.

desentiendes you ignore; pres. ind. 2nd pers. sing. / *desentenderse*.

desentiéndete (you) ignore; impve. 2nd pers. sing. / *desentenderse.*

desentiendo I ignore; past 1st pers. sing. / *desentenderse.*

desentierra 1. he (she/it) unearths; pres. ind. 3rd pers. sing. / *desenterrar* 2. (you) unearth; impve. 2nd pers. sing.

desentierran they unearth; pres. ind. 3rd pers. pl. / *desenterrar.*

desentierras you unearth; pres. ind. 2nd pers. sing. / *desenterrar.*

desentierre 1. that I may unearth; pres. subj. 1st pers. sing. / *desenterrar.* 2. that he (she/it) may unearth; pres. subj. 3rd pers. sing. 3. let him (her/it) unearth; impve. 3rd pers. sing.

desentierren 1. that they may unearth; pres. subj. 3rd pers. pl. / *desenterrar.* 2. let them unearth; impve. 3rd pers. pl.

desentierres that you may unearth; pres. subj. 2nd pers. sing. / *desenterrar.*

desentierro I unearth; pres. ind. 1st pers. sing. / *desenterrar.*

desentonándose behaving with impropriety; pres. part. / *desentonarse.*

desentonaos (you all) behave with impropriety; impve. 2nd pers. pl. / *desentonarse.*

desentonar to humble or to be out of tune. reg.

desentonarse to behave or to speak with impropriety. reg.

desentónate (you) behave with impropriety; impve. 2nd pers. sing. / *desentonarse.*

desentonémonos let us behave with impropriety; impve. 1st pers. pl. / *desentonarse.*

desentónense let them behave with impropriety; impve. 3rd pers. pl. / *desentonarse.*

desentónese let him (her/it) behave with impropriety; impve. 3rd pers. sing. / *desentonarse.*

desentrañándose giving one's best; pres. part. / *desentrañarse.*

desentrañaos (you all) give your best; impve. 2nd pers. pl. / *desentrañarse.*

desentrañar to eviscerate or to figure out. reg.

desentrañarse to give one's best. reg.

desentráñate (you) give your best; impve. 2nd pers. sing. / *desentrañarse.*

desentrañémonos let us give our best; impve. 1st pers. pl. / *desentrañarse.*

desentráñense let them give their best; impve. 3rd pers. pl. / *desentrañarse.*

desentráñese let him (her/it) give his (her/its) best; impve. 3rd pers. sing. / *desentrañarse.*

desenvainar to unsheathe. reg.

desenvolvámonos let us develope; impve. 1st pers. pl. / *desenvolverse.*

desenvolveos (you all) develope; impve. 2nd pers. pl. / *desenvolverse.*

desenvolver to unwrap or to unroll. irr.

desenvolverse to develope. irr.

desenvolviéndose developing; pres. part. / *desenvolverse.*

desenvuelto unwrapped; past part. / *desenvolver*

desenvuelva 1. that I may unwrap; pres. subj. 1st pers. sing. / *desenvolver.* 2. that he (she/it) may unwrap; pres. subj. 3rd pers. sing. 3. let him (her/it) unwrap; impve. 3rd pers. sing.

desenvuelvan 1. that they may unwrap; pres. subj. 3rd pers. pl. / *desenvolver.* 2. let them unwrap; impve. 3rd pers. pl.

desenvuélvanse let them develope; impve. 3rd pers. pl. / *desenvolverse.*

desenvuelvas that you may unwrap; pres. subj. 2nd pers. sing. / *desenvolver.*

desenvuélvase let him (her/it) develope; impve. 3rd pers. sing. / *desenvolverse.*

desenvuelve 1. he (she/it) unwraps; pres. ind. 3rd pers. sing. / *desenvolver.* 2. (you) unwrap; impve. 2nd pers. sing.

desenvuelven they unwrap; pres. ind. 3rd pers. pl. / *desenvolver.*

desenvuelves you unwrap; pres. ind. 2nd pers. sing. / *desenvolver.*

desenvuélvete (you) develope; impve. 2nd pers. sing. / *desenvolverse.*

desenvuelvo I unwrap; pres. ind. 1st pers. sing. / *desenvolver.*

deseque 1. that I may dry; pres. subj. 1st pers. sing. / *desecar.* 2. that he (she/it) may dry; pres. subj. 3rd pers. sing. 3. let him (her/it) dry; impve. 3rd pers. sing.

desequé I dried; past 1st pers. sing. / *desecar.*

desequéis that you (all) may dry; pres. subj. 2nd pers. pl. / *desecar.*

desequémonos let us dry up; impve. 1st pers. pl. / *desecarse.*

desequemos 1. that we may dry; pres. subj. 1st pers. pl. / *desecar.* 2. let us dry; impve. 1st pers. pl.

desequen 1. that they may dry; pres. subj. 3rd pers. pl. / *desecar.* 2. let them dry; impve. 3rd pers. pl.

deséquense let them dry up; impve. 3rd pers. pl. / *desecarse.*

deseques that you may dry; pres. subj. 2nd pers. sing. / *desecar.*

deséquese let him (her/it) dry up; impve. 3rd pers. sing. / *desecarse.*

desequilibrar to unbalance. reg.

desertar to desert. reg.

deservir to do a disservice to. irr.

deseslabonándose withdrawing; pres. part. / *deseslabonarse.*

deseslabonaos (you all) withdraw; impve. 2nd pers. pl. / *deseslabonarse.*

deseslabonar to unlink. reg.

deseslabonarse to withdraw. reg.

deseslabónate (you) withdraw; impve. 2nd pers. sing. / *deseslabonarse.*

deseslabonémonos let us withdraw; impve. 1st pers. pl. / *deseslabonarse.*

deseslabónense let them withdraw; impve. 3rd pers. pl. / *deseslabonarse.*

deseslabónese let him (her/it) withdraw; impve. 3rd pers. sing. / *deseslabonarse.*

desesperance 1. that I may discourage; pres. subj. 1st pers. sing. / *desesperanzar.* 2. that he (she/it) may discourage; pres. subj. 3rd pers. sing. 3. let him (her/it) discourage; impve. 3rd pers. sing.

desesperancé I discouraged; past 1st pers. sing. / *desesperanzar.*

desesperancéis that you (all) may discourage; pres. subj. 2nd pers. pl. / *desesperanzar.*

desesperancémonos let us lose hope; impve. 1st pers. pl. / *desesperanzarse.*

desesperancemos 1. that we may discourage; pres. subj. 1st pers. pl. / *desesperanzar.* 2. let us discourage; impve. 1st pers. pl.

desesperancen 1. that they may discourage; pres. subj. 3rd pers. pl. / *desesperanzar.* 2. let them discourage; impve. 3rd pers. pl.

desesperáncense let them lose hope; impve. 3rd pers. pl. / *desesperanzarse.*

desesperances that you may discourage; pres. subj. 2nd pers. sing. / *desesperanzar.*

desesperáncese let him (her/it) lose hope; impve. 3rd pers. sing. / *desesperanzarse.*

desesperándose becoming impatient; pres. part. / *desesperarse.*

desesperanzándose losing hope; pres. part. / *desesperanzarse.*

desesperanzaos (you all) lose hope; impve. 2nd pers. pl. / *desesperanzarse.*

desesperanzar to discourage. irr.

desesperanzarse to lose hope. irr.

desesperánzate (you) lose hope; impve. 2nd pers. sing. / *desesperanzarse.*

desesperaos (you all) become impatient; impve. 2nd pers. pl. / *desesperarse.*

desesperar to despair. reg.

desesperarse to become impatient. reg.

desespérate (you) become impatient; impve. 2nd pers. sing. / *desesperarse.*

desesperémonos let us become impatient; impve. 1st pers. pl. / *desesperarse.*

desespérense let them become impatient; impve. 3rd pers. pl. / *desesperarse.*

desespérese let him (her/it) become impatient; impve. 3rd pers. sing. / *desesperarse.*

desestimar to hold in low esteem. reg.

desfalcar to embezzle. irr.

desfalque 1. that I may embezzle; pres. subj. 1st pers. sing. / *desfalcar.* 2. that he (she/it) may embezzle; pres. subj. 3rd pers. sing. 3. let him (her/it) embezzle; impve. 3rd pers. sing.

desfalqué I embezzled; past 1st pers. sing. / *desfalcar.*

desfalquéis that you (all) may embezzle; pres. subj. 2nd pers. pl. / *desfalcar.*

desfalquemos 1. that we may embezzle; pres. subj. 1st pers. pl. / *desfalcar.* 2. let us embezzle; impve. 1st pers. pl.

desfalquen 1. that they may embezzle; pres. subj. 3rd pers. pl. / *desfalcar.* 2. let them embezzle. impve. 3rd pers. pl.

desfalques that you may embezzle; pres. subj. 2nd pers. sing. / *desfalcar.*

desfallecer to weaken or to faint. irr.

desfallezca 1. that I may weaken; pres. subj. 1st pers. sing. / *desfallecer.* 2. that he (she/it) may weaken; pres. subj. 3rd pers. sing. 3. let him (her/it) weaken; impve. 3rd pers. sing.

desfallezcáis that you (all) may weaken; pres. subj. 2nd pers. pl. / *desfallecer.*

desfallezcamos 1. that we may weaken; pres. subj. 1st pers. pl. / *desfallecer.* 2. let us weaken; impve. 1st pers. pl.

desfallezcan 1. that they may weaken; pres. subj. 3rd pers. pl. / *desfallecer.* 2. let them weaken. impve. 3rd pers. pl.

desfallezcas that you may weaken; pres. subj. 2nd pers. sing. / *desfallecer.*

desfallezco I weaken; pres. ind. 1st pers. sing. / *desfallecer.*

desfavorecer to disfavor. irr.

desfavorezca 1. that I may disfavor; pres. subj. 1st pers. sing. / *desfavorecer.* 2. that he (she/it) may disfavor; pres. subj. 3rd pers. sing. 3. let him (her/it) disfavor; impve. 3rd pers. sing.

desfavorezcáis that you (all) may disfavor; pres. subj. 2nd pers. pl. / *desfavorecer.*

desfavorezcamos 1. that we may disfavor; pres. subj. 1st pers. pl. / *desfavorecer.* 2. let us disfavor; impve. 1st pers. pl.

desfavorezcan 1. that they may disfavor; pres. subj. 3rd pers. pl. / *desfavorecer.* 2. let them disfavor; impve. 3rd pers. pl.

desfavorezcas that you may disfavor; pres. subj. 2nd pers. sing. / *desfavorecer.*

desfavorezco I disfavor; pres. ind. 1st pers. sing. / *desfavorecer.*

desfigurándose becoming distorted; pres. part. / *desfigurarse.*

desfiguraos (you all) become distorted; impve. 2nd pers. pl. / *desfigurarse.*

desfigurar to disfigure. reg.

desfigurarse to become distorted. reg.

desfigúrate (you) become distorted; impve. 2nd pers. sing. / *desfigurarse.*

desfigurémonos let us become distorted; impve. 1st pers. pl. / *desfigurarse.*

desfigúrense let them become distorted; impve. 3rd pers. pl. / *desfigurarse.*

desfigúrese let him (her/it) become distorted; impve. 3rd pers. sing. / *desfigurarse.*

desfilar to march in file. reg.

desflorar to deflower or to skim. reg.

desfloreceos (you all) fade; impve. 2nd pers. pl. / *desflorecerse.*

desflorecer to wither or to fade. irr.

desflorecerse to fade. irr.

desflorécete (you) fade; impve. 2nd pers. sing. / *desflorecerse.*

desfloreciéndose fading; pres. part. / *desflorecerse.*

desflorezca 1. that I may wither; pres. subj. 1st pers. sing. / *desflorecer.* 2. that he (she/it) may wither; pres. subj. 3rd pers. sing. 3. let him (her/it) wither; impve. 3rd pers. sing.

desflorezcáis that you (all) may wither; pres. subj. 2nd pers. pl. / *desflorecer*.

desflorezcámonos let us fade; impve. 1st pers. pl. / *desflorecerse*.

desflorezcamos 1. that we may wither; pres. subj. 1st pers. pl. / *desflorecer*. 2. let us wither; impve. 1st pers. pl.

desflorezcan 1. that they may wither; pres. subj. 3rd pers. pl. / *desflorecer* 2. let them wither; impve. 3rd pers. pl.

desflorézcanse let them fade; impve. 3rd pers. pl. / *desflorecerse*.

desflorezcas that you may wither; pres. subj. 2nd pers. sing. / *desflorecer*.

desflorézcase let him (her/it) fade; impve. 3rd pers. sing. / *desflorecerse*.

desflorezco I wither; pres. ind. 1st pers. sing. / *desflorecer*.

desfogándose venting one's anger; pres. part. / *desfogarse*.

desfogaos (you all) vent your anger; impve. 2nd pers. pl. / *desfogarse*.

desfogar to give vent to. irr.

desfogarse to vent one's anger. irr.

desfógate (you) vent your anger; impve. 2nd pers. sing. / *desfogarse*.

desfogue 1. that I may give vent to; pres. subj. 1st pers. sing. / *desfogar*. 2. that he (she/it) may give vent to; pres. subj. 3rd pers. sing. 3. let him (her/it) give vent to; impve. 3rd pers. sing.

desfogué I gave vent to; past 1st pers. sing. / *desfogar*.

desfoguéis that you (all) may give vent to; pres. subj. 2nd pers. pl. / *desfogar*.

desfoguémonos let us vent our anger; impve. 1st pers. pl. / *desfogarse*.

desfoguemos 1. that we may give vent to; pres. subj. 1st pers. pl. / *desfogar*. 2. let us give vent to; impve. 1st pers. pl.

desfoguen 1. that they may give vent to; pres. subj. 3rd pers. pl. / *desfogar*. 2. let them give vent to; impve. 3rd pers. pl.

desfóguense let them vent their anger; impve. 3rd pers. pl. / *desfogarse*.

desfogues that you may give vent to; pres. subj. 2nd pers. sing. / *desfogar*.

desfóguese let him (her/it) vent his (her/its) anger; impve. 3rd pers. sing. / *desfogarse*.

desfondándose going in over one's head; pres. part. / *desfondarse*.

desfondaos (you all) go in over your heads; impve. 2nd pers. pl. / *desfondarse*.

desfondar to stave in. reg.

desfondarse to go in over one's head. reg.

desfóndate (you) go in over your head; impve. 2nd pers. sing. / *desfondarse*.

desfondémonos let us go in over our heads; impve. 1st pers. pl. / *desfondarse*.

desfóndense let them go in over their heads; impve. 3rd pers. pl. / *desfondarse*.

desfóndese let him (her/it) go in over his (her/its) head; impve. 3rd pers. sing. / *desfondarse*.

desfrenar to take off the brakes. reg.

desgajándose breaking off; pres. part. / *desgajarse*.

desgajaos (you all) break off; impve. 2nd pers. pl. / *desgajarse*.

desgajar to tear. reg.

desgajarse to break off. reg.

desgájate (you) break off; impve. 2nd pers. sing. / *desgajarse*.

desgajémonos let us break off; impve. 1st pers. pl. / *desgajarse*.

desgájense let them break off; impve. 3rd pers. pl. / *desgajarse*.

desgájese let him (her/it) break off; impve. 3rd pers. sing. / *desgajarse*.

desganándose losing one's appetite; pres. part. / *desganarse*.

desganaos (you all) lose your appetites; impve. 2nd pers. pl. / *desganarse*.

desganar to dissuade. reg.

desganarse to lose one's appetite or interest. reg.

desgánate (you) lose your appetite; impve. 2nd pers. sing. / *desganarse*.

desganémonos let us lose our appetites; impve. 1st pers. pl. / *desganarse*.

desgánense let them lose their appetites; impve. 3rd pers. pl. / *desganarse*.

desgánese let him (her/it) lose his (her/its) appetite; impve. 3rd pers. sing. / *desganarse*.

desgañitándose yelling and bawling; pres. part. / *desgañitarse*.

desgañitaos (you all) yell and bawl; impve. 2nd pers. pl. / *desgañitarse*.

desgañitarse to yell and bawl. reg.

desgañítate (you) yell and bawl; impve. 2nd pers. sing. / *desgañitarse*.

desgañitémonos let us yell and bawl; impve. 1st pers. pl. / *desgañitarse*.

desgañítense let them yell and bawl; impve. 3rd pers. pl. / *desgañitarse*.

desgañítese let him (her/it) yell and bawl; impve. 3rd pers. sing. / *desgañitarse*.

desgargantándose shouting until blue in the face; pres. part. / *desgargantarse*.

desgargantaos (you all) shout until blue in the face; impve. 2nd pers. pl. / *desgargantarse*.

desgargantarse to shout until blue in the face. reg.

desgargántate (you) shout until blue in the face; impve. 2nd pers. sing. / *desgargantarse*.

desgargantémonos let us shout until blue in the face; impve. 1st pers. pl. / *desgargantarse*.

desgargántense let them shout until blue in the face; impve. 3rd pers. pl. / *desgargantarse*.

desgargántese let him (her/it) shout until blue in the face; impve. 3rd pers. sing. / *desgargantarse*.

desgaritándose giving up a job; pres. part. / *desgaritarse.*

desgaritaos (you all) give up a job; impve. 2nd pers. pl. / *desgaritarse.*

desgaritar to go astray. reg.

desgaritarse to give up a job. reg.

desgarítate (you) give up a job; impve. 2nd pers. sing. / *desgaritarse.*

desgaritémonos let us give up a job; impve. 1st pers. pl. / *desgaritarse.*

desgaritense let them give up a job; impve. 3rd pers. pl. / *desgaritarse.*

desgarítese let him (her/it) give up a job; impve. 3rd pers. sing. / *desgaritarse.*

desgarrándose retiring; pres. part. / *desgarrarse.*

desgarraos (you all) retire; impve. 2nd pers. pl. / *desgarrarse.*

desgarrar to tear or to cough up. reg.

desgarrarse to retire. reg.

desgárrate (you) retire; impve. 2nd pers. sing. / *desgarrarse.*

desgarrémonos let us retire; impve. 1st pers. pl. / *desgarrarse.*

desgárrense let them retire; impve. 3rd pers. pl. / *desgarrarse.*

desgárrese let him (her/it) retire; impve. 3rd pers. sing. / *desgarrarse.*

desgastándose losing one's vigor; pres. part. / *desgastarse.*

desgastaos (you all) lose your vigor; impve. 2nd pers. pl. / *desgastarse.*

desgastar to wear away or to consume. reg.

desgastarse to lose one's vigor. reg.

desgástate (you) lose your vigor; impve. 2nd pers. sing. / *desgastarse.*

desgastémonos let us lose our vigor; impve. 1st pers. pl. / *desgastarse.*

desgástense let them lose their vigor; impve. 3rd pers. pl. / *desgastarse.*

desgástese let him (her/it) lose his (her/its) vigor; impve. 3rd pers. sing. / *desgastarse.*

desgaznatándose yelling and screaming; pres. part. / *desgaznatarse.*

desgaznataos (you all) yell and scream; impve. 2nd pers. pl. / *desgaznatarse.*

desgaznatarse to yell and scream. reg.

desgaznátate (you) yell and scream; impve. 2nd pers. sing. / *desgaznatarse.*

desgaznatémonos let us yell and scream; impve. 1st pers. pl. / *desgaznatarse.*

desgaznátense let them yell and scream; impve. 3rd pers. pl. / *desgaznatarse.*

desgaznátese let him (her/it) yell and scream; impve. 3rd pers. sing. / *desgaznatarse.*

desglosar to separate into parts or divisions. reg.

desgobernar to misgovern or to dislocate. irr.

desgobierna 1. he (she/it) misgoverns; pres. ind. 3rd pers. sing. / *desgobernar.* 2. (you) misgovern; impve. 2nd pers. sing.

desgobiernan they misgovern; pres. ind. 3rd pers. pl. / *desgobernar.*

desgobiernas you misgovern; pres. ind. 2nd pers. sing. / *desgobernar.*

desgobierne 1. that I may misgovern; pres. subj. 1st pers. sing. / *desgobernar.* 2. that he (she/it) may misgovern; pres. subj. 3rd pers. sing. 3. let him (her/it) misgovern; impve. 3rd pers. sing.

desgobiernen 1. that they may misgovern; pres. subj. 3rd pers. pl. / *desgobernar.* 2. let them misgovern; impve. 3rd pers. pl.

desgobiernes that you may misgovern; pres. subj. 2nd pers. sing. / *desgobernar.*

desgobierno I misgovern; pres. ind. 1st pers. sing. / *desgobernar.*

desgonce 1. that I may unhinge; pres. subj. 1st pers. sing. / *desgonzar.* 2. that he (she/it) may unhinge; pres. subj. 3rd pers. sing. 3. let him (her/it) unhinge; impve. 3rd pers. sing.

desgoncé I unhinged; past 1st pers. sing. / *desgonzar.*

desgoncéis that you (all) may unhinge; pres. subj. 2nd pers. pl. / *desgonzar.*

desgoncemos 1. that we may unhinge; pres. subj. 1st pers. pl. / *desgonzar.* 2. let us unhinge; impve. 1st pers. pl.

desgoncen 1. that they may unhinge; pres. subj. 3rd pers. pl. / *desgonzar.* 2. let them unhinge; impve. 3rd pers. pl.

desgonces that you may unhinge; pres. subj. 2nd pers. sing. / *desgonzar.*

desgonzar to unhinge. irr.

desgoznándose gyrating; pres. part. / *desgoznarse.*

desgoznar to unhinge. reg.

desgoznarse to gyrate. reg.

desgóznense let them gyrate; impve. 3rd pers. pl. / *desgoznarse.*

desgóznese let it gyrate; impve. 3rd pers. sing. / *desgoznarse.*

desgraciándose declining; pres. part. / *desgraciarse.*

desgraciaos (you all) decline; impve. 2nd pers. pl. / *desgraciarse.*

desgraciar to displease or to spoil. reg.

desgraciarse to decline or to quarrel. reg.

desgráciate (you) decline; impve. 2nd pers. sing. / *desgraciarse.*

desgraciémonos let us decline; impve. 1st pers. pl. / *desgraciarse.*

desgracíense let them decline; impve. 3rd pers. pl. / *desgraciarse.*

desgracíese let him (her/it) decline; impve. 3rd pers. sing. / *desgraciarse.*

desgramar to remove grass from. reg.

desgranándose dropping off; pres. part. / *desgranarse..*

desgranaos (you all) drop off; impve. 2nd pers. pl. / *desgranarse .*

desgranar to thresh. reg.

desgranarse to drop off. reg.

desgránate (you) drop off; impve. 2nd pers. sing. / *desgranarse .*

desgranémonos let us drop off; impve. 1st pers. pl. / *desgranarse* .

desgránense let them drop off; impve. 3rd pers. pl. / *desgranarse* .

desgránese let him (her/it) drop off; impve. 3rd pers. sing. / *desgranarse* .

desgrasar to remove the grease from. reg.

desgravar to lower the tax on. reg.

desgreñar to dishevel. reg.

desguace 1. that I may hew; pres. subj. 1st pers. sing. / *desguazar*. 2. that he (she/it) may hew; pres. subj. 3rd pers. sing. 3. let him (her/it) hew; impve. 3rd pers. sing.

desguacé I hewed; past 1st pers. sing. / *desguazar*.

desguacéis that you (all) may hew; pres. subj. 2nd pers. pl. / *desguazar*.

desguacemos 1. that we may hew; pres. subj. 1st pers. pl. / *desguazar*. 2. let us hew; impve. 1st pers. pl.

desguacen 1. that they may hew; pres. subj. 3rd pers. pl. / *desguazar*. 2. let them hew; impve. 3rd pers. pl.

desguaces that you may hew; pres. subj. 2nd pers. sing. / *desguazar*.

desguarnecer to strip ornaments from. irr.

desguarnezca 1. that I may strip ornaments from; pres. subj. 1st pers. sing. / *desguarnecer*. 2. that he (she/it) may strip ornaments from; pres. subj. 3rd pers. sing. 3. let him (her/it) strip ornaments from; impve. 3rd pers. sing.

desguarnezcáis that you (all) may strip ornaments from; pres. subj. 2nd pers. pl. / *desguarnecer*.

desguarnezcamos 1. that we may strip ornaments from; pres. subj. 1st pers. pl. / *desguarnecer*. 2. let us strip ornaments from; impve. 1st pers. pl.

desguarnezcan 1. that they may strip ornaments from; pres. subj. 3rd pers. pl. / *desguarnecer*. 2. let them strip ornaments from; impve. 3rd pers. pl.

desguarnezcas that you may strip ornaments from; pres. subj. 2nd pers. sing. / *desguarnecer*.

desguarnezco I strip ornaments from; pres. ind. 1st pers. sing. / *desguarnecer*.

desguazar to hew or to dismantle. irr.

deshabitar to vacate. reg.

deshabituándose becoming unaccustomed; pres. part. / *deshabituarse*.

deshabituaos (you all) become unaccustomed; impve. 2nd pers. pl. / *deshabituarse*.

deshabituar to break a habit. reg.

deshabituarse to become unaccustomed. reg.

deshabitúate (you) become unaccustomed; impve. 2nd pers. sing. / *deshabituarse*.

deshabituémonos let us become unaccustomed; impve. 1st pers. pl. / *deshabituarse*.

deshabitúense let them become unaccustomed; impve. 3rd pers. pl. / *deshabituarse*.

deshabitúese let him (her/it) become unaccustomed; impve. 3rd pers. sing. / *deshabituarse*.

deshaceos (you all) melt; impve. 2nd pers. pl. / *deshacerse*.

deshacer to undo or to dissolve. irr.

deshacerse to melt or to get rid of. irr.

deshaciéndose melting; pres. part. / *deshacerse*.

deshaga 1. that I may undo; pres. subj. 1st pers. sing. / *deshacer*. 2. that he (she/it) may undo; pres. subj. 3rd pers. sing. 3. let him (her/it) undo; impve. 3rd pers. sing.

deshagáis that you (all) may undo; pres. subj. 2nd pers. pl. / *deshacer*.

deshagámonos let us melt; impve. 1st pers. pl. / *deshacerse*.

deshagamos 1. that we may undo; pres. subj. 1st pers. pl. / *deshacer*. 2. let us undo; impve. 1st pers. pl.

deshagan 1. that they may undo; pres. subj. 3rd pers. pl. / *deshacer*. 2. let them undo; impve. 3rd pers. pl.

desháganse let them melt; impve. 3rd pers. pl. / *deshacerse*.

deshagas that you may undo; pres. subj. 2nd pers. sing. / *deshacer*.

deshágase let it melt; impve. 3rd pers. sing. / *deshacerse*.

deshago I undo; pres. ind. 1st pers. sing. / *deshacer*.

deshará he (she/it) will undo; fut. 3rd pers. sing. / *deshacer*.

desharán they will undo; fut. 3rd pers. pl. / *deshacer*.

desharás you will undo; fut. 2nd pers. sing. / *deshacer*.

desharé I shall undo; fut. 1st pers. sing. / *deshacer*.

desharéis you (all) will undo; fut. 2nd pers. pl. / *deshacer*.

desharemos we shall undo; fut. 1st pers. pl. / *deshacer*.

desharía 1. I should undo; cond. 1st pers. sing. / *deshacer*. 2. he (she/it) would undo; cond. 3rd pers. sing.

desharíais you (all) would undo; cond. 2nd pers. pl. / *deshacer*.

desharíamos we should undo; cond. 1st pers. pl. / *deshacer*.

desharían they would undo; cond. 3rd pers. pl. / *deshacer*.

desharías you would undo; cond. 2nd pers. sing. / *deshacer*.

deshaz (you) undo; impve. 2nd pers. sing. / *deshacer*.

deshebillar to unbuckle. reg.

deshebrar to unravel. reg.

deshecho undid; past part. / *deshacer*.

deshelándose melting; pres. part. / *deshelarse*.

deshelar to thaw. irr.

deshelarse to melt. irr.

desherbar to weed. irr.

desheredándose betraying one's heritage; pres. part. / *desheredarse*.

desheredaos (you all) betray your heritage; impve. 2nd pers. pl. / *desheredarse*.

desheredar to disinherit. reg.

desheredarse to betray one's heritage. reg.

desherédate (you) betray your heritage; impve. 2nd pers. sing. / *desheredarse*.

desheredémonos let us betray our heritage; impve. 1st pers. pl. / *desheredarse*.

desherédense let them betray their heritage; impve.
3rd pers. pl. / *desheredarse.*

desherédese let him (her/it) betray his (her/its)
heritage; impve. 3rd pers. sing. / *desheredarse.*

desherrar to unchain or to unshoe. irr.

deshice I undid; past 1st pers. sing. / *deshacer.*

deshiciera 1. that I might undo; imp. subj. 1st pers.
sing. / *deshacer.* 2. that he (she/it) might undo; imp.
subj. 3rd pers. sing.

deshicierais that you (all) might undo; imp. subj. 2nd
pers pl. / *deshacer.*

deshiciéramos that we might undo; imp. subj. 1st
pers. pl. / *deshacer.*

deshicieran that they might undo; imp. subj. 3rd
pers. pl. / *deshacer.*

deshicieras that you might undo; imp. subj. 2nd pers.
sing. / *deshacer.*

deshicieron they undid; past 3rd pers. pl. / *deshacer.*

deshiciese 1. that I might undo; imp. subj. 1st pers.
sing. / *deshacer.* 2. that he (she/it) might undo; imp.
subj. 3rd pers. sing.

deshicieseis that you (all) might undo; imp. subj. 2nd
pers pl. / *deshacer.*

deshiciésemos that we might undo; imp. subj. 1st
pers. pl. / *deshacer.*

deshiciesen that they might undo; imp. subj. 3rd pers.
pl. / *deshacer.*

deshicieses that you might undo; imp. subj. 2nd pers.
sing. / *deshacer.*

deshicimos we undid; past 1st pers. pl. / *deshacer.*

deshiciste you undid ; past 2nd pers. sing. / *deshacer.*

deshicisteis you (all) undid; past 2nd pers. pl. /
deshacer.

deshidratar to dehydrate. reg.

deshiela it thaws; pres. ind. 3rd pers. sing. / *deshelar.*

deshiele 1. that it may thaw; pres. subj. 3rd pers. sing.
/ *deshelar.* 2. let it thaw; impve. 1st pers. sing.

deshielen 1. that they may thaw; pres. subj. 3rd pers.
pl. / *deshelar.* 2. let them thaw; impve. 3rd pers. pl.

deshiélense let them melt; impve. 3rd pers. pl. /
deshelarse.

deshiélese let it melt; impve. 3rd pers. sing. /
deshelarse.

deshierba 1. he (she/it) weeds; pres. ind. 3rd pers.
sing. / *desherbar.* 2. (you) weed; impve. 2nd pers.
sing.

deshierban they weed; pres. ind. 3rd pers. pl. /
desherbar.

deshierbas you weed; pres. ind. 2nd pers. sing. /
desherbar.

deshierbe 1. that I may weed; pres. subj. 1st pers.
sing. / *desherbar.* 2. that he (she/it) may weed; pres.
subj. 3rd pers. sing. 3. let him (her/it) weed; impve.
3rd pers. sing.

deshierben 1. that they may weed; pres. subj. 3rd
pers. pl. / *desherbar.* 2. let them weed; impve. 3rd
pers. pl.

deshierbes that you may weed; pres. subj. 2nd pers.
sing. / *desherbar.*

deshierbo I weed; pres. ind. 1st pers. sing. /
desherbar.

deshierra 1. he (she/it) unchains; pres. ind. 3rd pers.
sing. / *desherrar.* 2. (you) unchain; impve. 2nd pers.
sing.

deshierran they unchain; pres. ind. 3rd pers. pl. /
desherrar.

deshierras you unchain; pres. ind. 2nd pers. sing. /
desherrar.

deshierre 1. that I may unchain; pres. subj. 1st pers.
sing. / *desherrar.* 2. that he (she/it) may unchain;
pres. subj. 3rd pers. sing. 3. let him (her/it) unchain;
impve. 3rd pers. sing.

deshierren 1. that they may unchain; pres. subj. 3rd
pers. pl. / *desherrar.* 2. let them unchain; impve. 3rd
pers. pl.

deshierres that you may unchain; pres. subj. 2nd
pers. sing. / *desherrar.*

deshierro I unchain; pres. ind. 1st pers. sing. /
desherrar.

deshilachándose fraying; pres. part. / *deshilacharse.*

deshilachaos (you all) fray; impve. 2nd pers. pl. /
deshilacharse.

deshilachar to ravel. reg.

deshilacharse to fray. reg.

deshiláchate (you) fray; impve. 2nd pers. sing. /
deshilacharse.

deshilachémonos let us fray; impve. 1st pers. pl. /
deshilacharse.

deshiláchense let them fray; impve. 3rd pers. pl. /
deshilacharse.

deshiláchese let him (her/it) fray; impve. 3rd pers.
sing. / *deshilacharse.*

deshilándose fraying; pres. part. / *deshilarse.*

deshilaos (you all) fray; impve. 2nd pers. pl. /
deshilarse.

deshilar to unravel. reg.

deshilarse to fray. reg.

deshílate (you) fray; impve. 2nd pers. sing. /
deshilarse.

deshilémonos let us fray; impve. 1st pers. pl. /
deshilarse.

deshílense let them fray; impve. 3rd pers. pl. /
deshilarse.

deshílese let him (her/it) fray; impve. 3rd pers. sing. /
deshilarse.

deshilvanar to unbaste. reg.

deshinchándose going down; pres. part. /
deshincharse.

deshinchar to reduce the swelling. reg.

deshincharse to go down. reg.

deshínchense let them go down; impve. 3rd pers. pl. /
deshincharse.

deshínchese let it go down; impve. 3rd pers. sing. /
deshincharse.

deshipotecar to end the mortgage on. irr.

deshipoteque 1. that I may end the mortgage on;
pres. subj. 1st pers. sing. / *deshipotecar.* 2. that he
(she/it) may end the mortgage on; pres. subj. 3rd
pers. sing. 3. let him (her/it) end the mortgage on;
impve. 3rd pers. sing.

deshipotequé I ended the mortgage on; past 1st pers. sing. / *deshipotecar.*

deshipotequéis that you (all) may end the mortgage on; pres. subj. 2nd pers. pl. / *deshipotecar.*

deshipotequemos 1. that we may end the mortgage on; pres. subj. 1st pers. pl. / *deshipotecar.* 2. let us end the mortgage on; impve. 1st pers. pl.

deshipotequen 1. that they may end the mortgage on; pres. subj. 3rd pers. pl. / *deshipotecar.* 2. let them end the mortgage on; impve. 3rd pers. pl.

deshipoteques that you may end the mortgage on; pres. subj. 2nd pers. sing. / *deshipotecar.*

deshizo he (she/it) undid; past. ind. 3rd pers. sing. / deshacer.

deshojándose losing petals; pres. part. / *deshojarse.*

deshojar to strip leaves or pages. reg.

deshojarse to lose petals. reg.

deshójense let them lose petals; impve. 3rd pers. pl. / *deshojarse.*

deshójese let it lose petals; impve. 3rd pers. sing. / *deshojarse.*

deshollejar to pare or to husk. reg.

deshollinar to sweep (chimneys). reg.

deshonorar to dishonor. reg.

deshonrar to dishonor. reg.

deshuesa he (she/it) removes the bone from; pres. ind. 3rd pers. sing. / *desosar.*

deshuesan they remove the bone from; pres. ind. 3rd pers. pl. / *desosar.*

deshuesar to remove pits or stones. reg.

deshuesas you remove the bone from ; pres. ind. 2nd pers. sing. / *desosar.*

deshuese 1. that I may remove the bone from; pres. subj. 1st pers. sing. / *desosar.* 2. that he (she/it) may remove the bone from; pres. subj. 3rd pers. sing.

deshuesen that they may remove the bone from; pres. subj. 3rd pers. pl. / *desosar.*

deshueses that you may remove the bone from; pres. subj. 2nd pers. sing. / *desosar.*

deshueso I remove the bone from ; pres. ind. 1st pers. sing. / *desosar.*

deshumedecer to dehumidify. irr.

deshumedezca 1. that I may dehumidify; pres. subj. 1st pers. sing. / *deshumedecer.* 2. that he (she/it) may dehumidify; pres. subj. 3rd pers. sing. 3. let him (her/it) dehumidify; impve. 3rd pers. sing.

deshumedezcáis that you (all) may dehumidify; pres. subj. 2nd pers. pl. / *deshumedecer.*

deshumedezcamos 1. that we may dehumidify; pres. subj. 1st pers. pl. / *deshumedecer.* 2. let us dehumidify; impve. 1st pers. pl.

deshumedezcan 1. that they may dehumidify; pres. subj. 3rd pers. pl. / *deshumedecer.* 2. let them dehumidify; impve. 3rd pers. pl.

deshumedezcas that you may dehumidify; pres. subj. 2nd pers. sing. / *deshumedecer.*

deshumedezco I dehumidify; pres. ind. 1st pers. sing. / *deshumedecer.*

designar to designate or to design. reg.

desigualándose excelling; pres. part. / *desigualarse.*

desigualaos (you all) excel; impve. 2nd pers. pl. / *desigualarse.*

desigualar to make unequal. reg.

desigualarse to excel. reg.

desiguálate (you) excel; impve. 2nd pers. sing. / *desigualarse.*

desigualémonos let us excel; impve. 1st pers. pl. / *desigualarse.*

desiguálense let them excel; impve. 3rd pers. pl. / *desigualarse.*

desiguálese let him (her/it) excel; impve. 3rd pers. sing. / *desigualarse.*

desilusionándose becoming disillusioned; pres. part. / *desilusionarse.*

desilusionaos (you all) become disillusioned; impve. 2nd pers. pl. / *desilusionarse.*

desilusionar to disillusion. reg.

desilusionarse to become disillusioned. reg.

desilusiónate (you) become disillusioned; impve. 2nd pers. sing. / *desilusionarse.*

desilusionémonos let us become disillusioned; impve. 1st pers. pl. / *desilusionarse.*

desilusiónense let them become disillusioned; impve. 3rd pers. pl. / *desilusionarse.*

desilusiónese let him (her/it) become disillusioned; impve. 3rd pers. sing. / *desilusionarse.*

desimanar to demagnetize. reg.

desimantar to demagnetize. reg.

desimpresionar to undeceive. reg.

desinclinándose being unwilling; pres. part. / *desinclinarse.*

desinclinaos (you all) be unwilling; impve. 2nd pers. pl. / *desinclinarse.*

desinclinar to disincline. reg.

desinclinarse to be unwilling. reg.

desinclínate (you) be unwilling; impve. 2nd pers. sing. / *desinclinarse.*

desinclinémonos let us be unwilling; impve. 1st pers. pl. / *desinclinarse.*

desinclínense let them be unwilling; impve. 3rd pers. pl. / *desinclinarse.*

desinclínese let him (her/it) be unwilling; impve. 3rd pers. sing. / *desinclinarse.*

desinfectar to disinfect. reg.

desinficionar to disinfect. reg.

desinflamar to reduce the inflammation in. reg.

desinflar to deflate. reg.

desintegrándose disintegrating; pres. part. / *desintegrarse.*

desintegraos (you all) disintegrate; impve. 2nd pers. pl. / *desintegrarse.*

desintegrar to disintegrate. reg.

desintegrarse to disintegtate. reg.

desintégrate (you) disintegrate; impve. 2nd pers. sing. / *desintegrarse.*

desintegrémonos let us disintegrate; impve. 1st pers. pl. / *desintegrarse.*

desintégrense let them disintegrate; impve. 3rd pers. pl. / *desintegrarse.*

desintégrese let him (her/it) disintegrate; impve. 3rd pers. sing. / *desintegrarse.*

desinteresándose ‑losing interest; pres. part. / *desinteresarse.*

desinteresaos (you all) lose interest; impve. 2nd pers. pl. / *desinteresarse.*

desinteresarse to lose interest. reg.

desinterésate (you) lose interest; impve. 2nd pers. sing. / *desinteresarse.*

desinteresémonos let us lose interest; impve. 1st pers. pl. / *desinteresarse.*

desinterésense let them lose interest; impve. 3rd pers. pl. / *desinteresarse.*

desinterésese let him (her/it) lose interest; impve. 3rd pers. sing. / *desinteresarse.*

desirva 1. that I may do a disservice to; pres. subj. 1st pers. sing. / *deservir.* 2. that he (she/it) may do a disservice to; pres. subj. 3rd pers. sing. 3. let him (her/it) do a disservice to; impve. 3rd pers. sing.

desirváis that you (all) may do a disservice to; pres. subj. 2nd pers. pl. / *deservir.*

desirvamos 1. that we may do a disservice to; pres. subj. 1st pers. pl. / *deservir.* 2. let us do a disservice to; impve. 1st pers. pl.

desirvan 1. that they may do a disservice to; pres. subj. 3rd pers. pl. / *deservir.* 2. let them do a disservice to; impve. 3rd pers. pl.

desirvas that you may do a disservice to; pres. subj. 2nd pers. sing. / *deservir.*

desirve 1. he (she/it) does a disservice to; pres. ind. 3rd pers. sing. / *deservir.* 2. (you) do a disservice to; impve. 2nd pers. sing.

desirven they do a disservice to; pres. ind. 3rd pers. pl. / *deservir.*

desirves you do a disservice to; pres. ind. 2nd pers. sing. / *deservir.*

desirviendo doing a disservice to; pres. part. / *deservir.*

desirviera 1. that I might do a disservice to; imp. subj. 1st pers. sing. / *deservir.* 2. that he (she/it) might do a disservice to; imp. subj. 3rd pers. sing.

desirvierais that you (all) might do a disservice to; imp. subj. 2nd pers pl. / *deservir.*

desirviéramos that we might do a disservice to; imp. subj. 1st pers. pl. / *deservir.*

desirvieran that they might do a disservice to; imp. subj. 3rd pers. pl. / *deservir.*

desirvieras that you might do a disservice to; imp. subj. 2nd pers. sing. / *deservir.*

desirvieron they did a disservice to; past 3rd pers. pl. / *deservir.*

desirviese 1. that I might do a disservice to; imp. subj. 1st pers. sing. / *deservir.* 2. that he (she/it) might do a disservice to; imp. subj. 3rd pers. sing.

desirvieseis that you (all) might do a disservice to; imp. subj. 2nd pers pl. / *deservir.*

desirviésemos that we might do a disservice; imp. subj. 1st pers. pl. / *deservir.*

desirviesen that they might do a disservice; imp. subj. 3rd pers. pl. / *deservir.*

desirvieses that you might do a disservice; imp. subj. 2nd pers. sing. / *deservir.*

desirvió he (she/it) did a disservice; past. 3rd pers. sing. / *deservir.*

desirvo I do a disservice; pres. ind. 1st pers. sing. / *deservir.*

desistir to desist or stop. reg.

desjarretar to hamstring. reg.

desjuntándose severing; pres. part. / *desjuntarse.*

desjuntaos (you all) sever; impve. 2nd pers. pl. / *desjuntarse.*

desjuntar to divide or separate. reg.

desjuntarse to sever. reg.

desjúntate (you) sever; impve. 2nd pers. sing. / *desjuntarse.*

desjuntémonos let us sever; impve. 1st pers. pl. / *desjuntarse.*

desjúntense let them sever; impve. 3rd pers. pl. / *desjuntarse.*

desjúntese let him (her/it) sever; impve. 3rd pers. sing. / *desjuntarse.*

deslabonar to unlink. reg.

deslavar to wash superficially or to weaken. reg.

desleír to dissolve. irr.

desleírse to become diluted. irr.

deslenguándose blabbing; pres. part. / *deslenguarse.*

deslenguaos (you all) blab; impve. 2nd pers. pl. / *deslenguarse.*

deslenguar to cut the tongue out of. reg.

deslenguarse to blab. reg.

deslengúate (you) blab; impve. 2nd pers. sing. / *deslenguarse.*

deslenguémonos let us blab; impve. 1st pers. pl. / *deslenguarse.*

deslengúense let them blab; impve. 3rd pers. pl. / *deslenguarse.*

deslengúese let him (her/it) blab; impve. 3rd pers. sing. / *deslenguarse.*

deslía 1. that I may dissolve; pres. subj. 1st pers. sing. / *desleír.* 2. that he (she/it) may dissolve; pres. subj. 3rd pers. sing. 3. let him (her/it) dissolve; impve. 3rd pers. sing.

deslía he (she/it) unties; pres. ind. 3rd pers. sing. / *desliar.* 2. (you) untie; impve. 2nd pers. sing.

desliáis that you (all) may dissolve; pres. subj. 2nd pers. pl. / *desleír.*

desliamos 1. that we may dissolve; pres. subj. 1st pers. pl. / *desleír.* 2. let us dissolve; impve. 1st pers. pl.

deslían 1. that they may dissolve; pres. subj. 3rd pers. pl. / *desleír.* 2. let them dissolve; impve. 3rd pers. pl.

deslían they untie; pres. ind. 3rd pers. pl. / *desliar.*

desliánse let them become diluted; impve. 3rd pers. pl. / *desleírse.*

desliar to untie or to unroll. irr.

deslías that you may dissolve; pres. subj. 2nd pers. sing. / *desleír.*

deslías you untie; pres. ind. 2nd pers. sing. / *desliar.*

deslíase let it become diluted; impve. 3rd pers. sing. / *desleírse.*

deslice 1. that I may slip; pres. subj. 1st pers. sing. / *deslizar*. 2. that he (she/it) may slip; pres. subj. 3rd pers. sing. 3. let him (her/it) slip; impve. 3rd pers. sing.

deslicé I slipped; past 1st pers. sing. / *deslizar*.

deslicéis that you (all) may slip; pres. subj. 2nd pers. pl. / *deslizar*.

deslicémonos let us slip away; impve. 1st pers. pl. / *deslizarse*.

deslicemos 1. that we may slip; pres. subj. 1st pers. pl. / *deslizar*. 2. let us slip; impve. 1st pers. pl.

deslicen 1. that they may slip; pres. subj. 3rd pers. pl. / *deslizar*. 2. let them slip; impve. 3rd pers. pl.

deslícense let them slip away; impve. 3rd pers. pl. / *deslizarse*.

deslices that you may slip; pres. subj. 2nd pers. sing. / *deslizar*.

deslícese let him (her/it) slip away; impve. 3rd pers. sing. / *deslizarse*.

deslíe 1. he (she/it) dissolves; pres. ind. 3rd pers. sing. / *desleír*. 2. (you) dissolve; impve. 2nd pers. sing.

deslíe 1. that I may untie; pres. subj. 1st pers. sing. / *desliar*. 2. that he (she/it) may untie; pres. subj. 3rd pers. sing. 3. let him (her/it) untie; impve. 3rd pers. sing.

deslíen they dissolve; pres. ind. 3rd pers. pl. / *desleír*.

deslíen 1. that they may untie; pres. subj. 3rd pers. pl. / *desliar*. 2. let them untie; impve. 3rd pers. pl.

desliendo dissolving; pres. part. / *desleír*.

desliéndose becoming diluted; pres. part. / *desleírse*.

desliera 1. that I might dissolve; imp. subj. 1st pers. sing. / *desleír*. 2. that he (she/it) might dissolve; imp. subj. 3rd pers. sing.

deslierais that you (all) might dissolve; imp. subj. 2nd pers pl. / *desleír*.

desliéramos that we might dissolve; imp. subj. 1st pers. pl. / *desleír*.

deslieran that they might dissolve; imp. subj. 3rd pers. pl. / *desleír*.

deslieras that you might dissolve; imp. subj. 2nd pers. sing. / *desleír*.

deslieron they dissolved; past 3rd pers. pl. / *desleír*.

deslíes you dissolve; pres. ind. 2nd pers. sing. / *desleír*.

deslíes that you may untie; pres. subj. 2nd pers. sing. / *desliar*.

desliese 1. that I might dissolve; imp. subj. 1st pers. sing. / *desleír*. 2. that he (she/it) might dissolve; imp. subj. 3rd pers. sing.

deslieseis that you (all) might dissolve; imp. subj. 2nd pers pl. / *desleír*.

desliésemos that we might dissolve; imp. subj. 1st pers. pl. / *desleír*.

desliesen that they might dissolve; imp. subj. 3rd pers. pl. / *desleír*.

deslieses that you might dissolve; imp. subj. 2nd pers. sing. / *desleír*.

desligar to untie. irr.

desligue 1. that I may untie; pres. subj. 1st pers. sing. / *desligar*. 2. that he (she/it) may untie; pres. subj. 3rd pers. sing. 3. let him (her/it) untie; impve. 3rd pers. sing.

desligué I untied; past 1st pers. sing. / *desligar*.

desliguéis that you (all) may untie; pres. subj. 2nd pers. pl. / *desligar*.

desliguemos 1. that we may untie; pres. subj. 1st pers. pl. / *desligar*. 2. let us untie; impve. 1st pers. pl.

desliguen 1. that they may untie; pres. subj. 3rd pers. pl. / *desligar*. 2. let them untie; impve. 3rd pers. pl.

desligues that you may untie; pres. subj. 2nd pers. sing. / *desligar*.

deslindar to mark the boundries of. reg.

deslío I dissolve; pres. ind. 1st pers. sing. / *desleír*.

deslío I untie; pres. ind. 1st pers. sing. / *desliar*.

deslió he (she/it) dissolved; past 3rd pers. sing. / *desleír*.

deslizándose slipping away; pres. part. / *deslizarse*.

deslizaos (you all) slip away; impve. 2nd pers. pl. / *deslizarse*.

deslizar to slip or to slide. irr.

deslizarse to slip away. irr.

deslízate (you) slip away; impve. 2nd pers. sing. / *deslizarse*.

deslucir to tarnish or to discredit. irr.

deslumbrar to dazzle. reg.

deslustrar to tarnish. reg.

desluzca 1. that I may tarnish; pres. subj. 1st pers. sing. / *deslucir*. 2. that he (she/it) may tarnish; pres. subj. 3rd pers. sing. 3. let him (her/it) tarnish; impve. 3rd pers. sing.

desluzcáis that you (all) may tarnish; pres. subj. 2nd pers. pl. / *deslucir*.

desluzcamos 1. that we may tarnish; pres. subj. 1st pers. pl. / *deslucir*. 2. let us tarnish; impve. 1st pers. pl.

desluzcan 1. that they may tarnish; pres. subj. 3rd pers. pl. / *deslucir*. 2. let them tarnish; impve. 3rd pers. pl.

desluzcas that you may tarnish; pres. subj. 2nd pers. sing. / *deslucir*.

desluzco I tarnish; pres. ind. 1st pers. sing. / *deslucir*.

desmadejar to enervate or to weaken. reg.

desmagnetice 1. that I may demagnetize; pres. subj. 1st pers. sing. / *desmagnetizar*. 2. that he (she/it) may demagnetize; pres. subj. 3rd pers. sing. 3. let him (her/it) demagnetize; impve. 3rd pers. sing.

desmagneticé I demagnetized; past 1st pers. sing. / *desmagnetizar*.

desmagneticéis that you (all) may demagnetize; pres. subj. 2nd pers. pl. / *desmagnetizar*.

desmagneticemos 1. that we may demagnetize; pres. subj. 1st pers. pl. / *desmagnetizar*. 2. let us demagnetize; impve. 1st pers. pl.

desmagneticen 1. that they may demagnetize; pres. subj. 3rd pers. pl. / *desmagnetizar*. 2. let them demagnetize; impve. 3rd pers. pl.

desmagnetices that you may demagnetize; pres. subj. 2nd pers. sing. / *desmagnetizar*.

desmagnetizar to demagnetize. irr.

desmalecé I weeded; past 1st pers. sing. / *desmalezar.*

desmalecéis that you (all) may weed; pres. subj. 2nd pers. pl. / *desmalezar.*

desmalecemos 1. that we may weed; pres. subj. 1st pers. pl. / *desmalezar.* 2. let us weed; impve. 1st pers. pl.

desmalezar to weed. irr.

desmaliece 1. that I may weed; pres. subj. 1st pers. sing. / *desmalezar.* 2. that he (she/it) may weed; pres. subj. 3rd pers. sing. 3. let him (her/it) weed; impve. 3rd pers. sing.

desmaliecen 1. that they may weed; pres. subj. 3rd pers. pl. / *desmalezar.* 2. let them weed; impve. 3rd pers. pl.

desmalieces that you may weed; pres. subj. 2nd pers. sing. / *desmalezar.*

desmalieza 1. he (she/it) weeds; pres. ind. 3rd pers. sing. / *desmalezar.* 2. (you) weed; impve. 2nd pers. sing.

desmaliezan they weed; pres. ind. 3rd pers. pl. / *desmalezar.*

desmaliezas you weed; pres. ind. 2nd pers. sing. / *desmalezar.*

desmaliezo I weed; pres. ind. 1st pers. sing. / *desmalezar.*

desmanchar to clean (clothes). reg.

desmandándose being insubordinate; pres. part. / *desmandarse.*

desmandaos (you all) be insubordinate; impve. 2nd pers. pl. / *desmandarse.*

desmandar to countermand. reg.

desmandarse to be insubordinate. reg.

desmándate (you) be insubordinate; impve. 2nd pers. sing. / *desmandarse.*

desmandémonos let us be insubordinate; impve. 1st pers. pl. / *desmandarse.*

desmándense let them be insubordinate; impve. 3rd pers. pl. / *desmandarse.*

desmándese let him (her/it) be insubordinate; impve. 3rd pers. sing. / *desmandarse.*

desmantelándose falling into disrepair; pres. part. / *desmantelarse.*

desmantelar to dismantle. reg.

desmantelarse to fall into disrepair. reg.

desmantélense let them fall into disrepair; impve. 3rd pers. pl. / *desmantelarse.*

desmantélese let it fall into disrepair; impve. 3rd pers. sing. / *desmantelarse.*

desmarañar to disentangle. reg.

desmayándose fainting; pres. part. / *desmayarse.*

desmayaos (you all) faint; impve. 2nd pers. pl. / *desmayarse.*

desmayar to dismay. reg.

desmayarse to faint. reg.

desmáyate (you) faint; impve. 2nd pers. sing. / *desmayarse.*

desmayémonos let us faint; impve. 1st pers. pl. / *desmayarse.*

desmáyense let them faint; impve. 3rd pers. pl. / *desmayarse.*

desmáyese let him (her/it) faint; impve. 3rd pers. sing. / *desmayarse.*

desmedíos (you all) lose self control; impve. 2nd pers. pl. / *desmedirse.*

desmedirse to lose self control. irr.

desmedrándose deteriorating; pres. part. / *desmedrarse.*

desmedraos (you all) deteriorate; impve. 2nd pers. pl. / *desmedrarse.*

desmedrar to impair. reg.

desmedrarse to deteriorate. reg.

desmédrate (you) deteriorate; impve. 2nd pers. sing. / *desmedrarse.*

desmedrémonos let us deteriorate; impve. 1st pers. pl. / *desmedrarse.*

desmédrense let them deteriorate; impve. 3rd pers. pl. / *desmedrarse.*

desmédrese let him (her/it) deteriorate; impve. 3rd pers. sing. / *desmedrarse.*

desmejorándose getting worse; pres. part. / *desmejorarse.*

desmejoraos (you all) get worse; impve. 2nd pers. pl. / *desmejorarse.*

desmejorar to make worse. reg.

desmejorarse to get worse. reg.

desmejórate (you) get worse; impve. 2nd pers. sing. / *desmejorarse.*

desmejorémonos let us get worse; impve. 1st pers. pl. / *desmejorarse.*

desmejórense let them get worse; impve. 3rd pers. pl. / *desmejorarse.*

desmejórese let him (her/it) get worse; impve. 3rd pers. sing. / *desmejorarse.*

desmelenándose giving in; pres. part. / *desmelenarse.*

desmelenaos (you all) give in; impve. 2nd pers. pl. / *desmelenarse.*

desmelenar to dishevel. reg.

desmelenarse to give in. reg.

desmelénate (you) give in; impve. 2nd pers. sing. / *desmelenarse.*

desmelenémonos let us give in; impve. 1st pers. pl. / *desmelenarse.*

desmelénense let them give in; impve. 3rd pers. pl. / *desmelenarse.*

desmelénese let him (her/it) give in; impve. 3rd pers. sing. / *desmelenarse.*

desmembrándose disintegrating; pres. part. / *desmembrarse.*

desmembrar to dismember. irr.

desmembrarse to disintegrate. irr.

desmemoriándose losing one's memory; pres. part. / *desmemoriarse.*

desmemoriaos (you all) lose your memory; impve. 2nd pers. pl. / *desmemoriarse.*

desmemoriarse to lose one's memory. reg.

desmemoríate (you) lose your memory; impve. 2nd pers. sing. / *desmemoriarse.*

desmemoriémonos let us lose our memory; impve.
1st pers. pl. / *desmemoriarse.*
desmemoríense let them lose their memory; impve.
3rd pers. pl. / *desmemoriarse.*
desmemoríese let him (her/it) lose his (her/its)
memory; impve. 3rd pers. sing. / *desmemoriarse.*
desmenguar to diminish. irr.
desmengüe 1. that I may diminish; pres. subj. 1st
pers. sing. / *desmenguar.* 2. that he (she/it) may
diminish; pres. subj. 3rd pers. sing. 3. let him
(her/it) diminish; impve. 3rd pers. sing.
desmengüé I diminished; past 1st pers. sing. /
desmenguar.
desmengüéis that you (all) may diminish; pres. subj.
2nd pers. pl. / *desmenguar.*
desmengüemos 1. that we may diminish; pres. subj.
1st pers. pl. / *desmenguar.* 2. let us diminish; impve.
1st pers. pl.
desmengüen 1. that they may diminish; pres. subj.
3rd pers. pl. / *desmenguar.* 2. let them diminish;
impve. 3rd pers. pl.
desmengües that you may diminish; pres. subj. 2nd
pers. sing. / *desmenguar.*
desmentíos (you all) retract; impve. 2nd pers. pl. /
desmentirse.
desmentir to contradict or to disprove. irr.
desmentirse to retract. irr.
desmenuce 1. that I may crumble; pres. subj. 1st pers.
sing. / *desmenuzar.* 2. that he (she/it) may crumble;
pres. subj. 3rd pers. sing. 3. let him (her/it) crumble;
impve. 3rd pers. sing.
desmenucé I crumbled; past 1st pers. sing. /
desmenuzar.
desmenucéis that you (all) may crumble; pres. subj.
2nd pers. pl. / *desmenuzar.*
desmenucémonos let us fall to peices; impve. 1st
pers. pl. / *desmenuzarse.*
desmenucemos 1. that we may crumble; pres. subj.
1st pers. pl. / *desmenuzar.* 2. let us crumble; impve.
1st pers. pl.
desmenucen 1. that they may crumble; pres. subj. 3rd
pers. pl. / *desmenuzar.* 2. let them crumble; impve.
3rd pers. pl.
desmenúcense let them fall to peices; impve. 3rd
pers. pl. / *desmenuzarse.*
desmenuces that you may crumble; pres. subj. 2nd
pers. sing. / *desmenuzar.*
desmenúcese let him (her/it) fall to peices; impve.
3rd pers. sing. / *desmenuzarse.*
desmenuzándose falling to pieces; pres. part. /
desmenuzarse.
desmenuzaos (you all) fall to pieces; impve. 2nd
pers. pl. / *desmenuzarse.*
desmenuzar to crumble or to examine closely. irr.
desmenuzarse to fall to pieces. irr.
desmenúzate (you) fall to pieces; impve. 2nd pers.
sing. / *desmenuzarse.*
desmerecer to be unworthy of. irr.

desmerezca 1. that I may be unworthy of; pres. subj.
1st pers. sing. / *desmerecer.* 2. that he (she/it) may
be unworthy of; pres. subj. 3rd pers. sing. 3. let him
(her/it) be unworthy of; impve. 3rd pers. sing.
desmerezcáis that you (all) may be unworthy of;
pres. subj. 2nd pers. pl. / *desmerecer.*
desmerezcamos 1. that we may be unworthy of; pres.
subj. 1st pers. pl. / *desmerecer.* 2. let us be unworthy
of; impve. 1st pers. pl.
desmerezcan 1. that they may be unworthy of; pres.
subj. 3rd pers. pl. / *desmerecer.* 2. let them be
unworthy of; impve. 3rd pers. pl.
desmerezcas that you may be unworthy of; pres. subj.
2nd pers. sing. / *desmerecer.*
desmerezco I am unworthy of; pres. ind. 1st pers.
sing. / *desmerecer.*
desmesurándose being insolent; pres. part. /
desmesurarse.
desmesuraos (you all) are insolent; impve. 2nd pers.
pl. / *desmesurarse.*
desmesurar to exaggerate. reg.
desmesurarse to be insolent. reg.
desmesúrate (you) be insolent; impve. 2nd pers. sing.
/ *desmesurarse.*
desmesurémonos let us be insolent; impve. 1st pers.
pl. / *desmesurarse.*
desmesúrense let them be insolent; impve. 3rd pers.
pl. / *desmesurarse.*
desmesúrese let him (her/it) be insolent; impve. 3rd
pers. sing. / *desmesurarse.*
desmida 1. that I may lose self control; pres. subj. 1st
pers. sing. / *desmedirse.* 2. that he (she/it) may lose
self control; pres. subj. 3rd pers. sing.
desmidáis that you (all) may lose self control; pres.
subj. 2nd pers. pl. / *desmedirse.*
desmidámonos let us lose self control; impve. 1st
pers. pl. / *desmedirse.*
desmidamos that we may lose self control; pres. subj.
1st pers. pl. / *desmedirse.*
desmidan that they may lose self control; pres. subj.
3rd pers. pl. / *desmedirse.*
desmídanse let them lose self control; impve. 3rd
pers. pl. / *desmedirse.*
desmidas that you may lose self control; pres. subj.
2nd pers. sing. / *desmedirse.*
desmídase let him (her/it) lose self control; impve.
3rd pers. sing. / *desmedirse.*
desmide he (she/it) loses self control; pres. ind. 3rd
pers. sing. / *desmedirse.*
desmiden they lose self control; pres. ind. 3rd pers.
pl. / *desmedirse.*
desmides you lose self control; pres. ind. 2nd pers.
sing. / *desmedirse.*
desmídete (you) lose self control; impve. 2nd pers.
sing. / *desmedirse.*
desmidiéndose losing self control; pres. part. /
desmedirse.
desmidiera 1. that I might lose self control; imp. subj.
1st pers. sing. / *desmedirse.* 2. that he (she/it) might
lose self control; imp. subj. 3rd pers. sing.

desmidierais that you (all) might lose self control; imp. subj. 2nd pers pl. / *desmedirse.*

desmidiéramos that we might lose self control; imp. subj. 1st pers. pl. / *desmedirse.*

desmidieran that they might lose self control; imp. subj. 3rd pers. pl. / *desmedirse.*

desmidieras that you might lose self control; imp. subj. 2nd pers. sing. / *desmedirse.*

desmidieron they lost self control; past 3rd pers. pl. / *desmedirse.*

desmidiese 1. that I might lose self control; imp. subj. 1st pers. sing. / *desmedirse.* 2. that he (she/it) might lose self control; imp. subj. 3rd pers. sing.

desmidieseis that you (all) might lose self control; imp. subj. 2nd pers pl. / *desmedirse.*

desmidiésemos that we might lose self control; imp. subj. 1st pers. pl. / *desmedirse.*

desmidiesen that they might lose self control; imp. subj. 3rd pers. pl. / *desmedirse.*

desmidieses that you might lose self control; imp. subj. 2nd pers. sing. / *desmedirse.*

desmidió he (she/it) lost self control; past 3rd pers. sing. / *desmedirse.*

desmido I lose self control; pres. ind. 1st pers. sing. / *desmedirse.*

desmiembra 1. he (she/it) dismembers; pres. ind. 3rd pers. sing. / *desmembrar.* 2. (you) dismember; impve. 2nd pers. sing.

desmiembran they dismember; pres. ind. 3rd pers. pl. / *desmembrar.*

desmiembras you dismember; pres. ind. 2nd pers. sing. / *desmembrar.*

desmiémbrate (you) disintegrate; impve. 2nd pers. sing. / *desmembrarse.*

desmiembre 1. that I may dismember; pres. subj. 1st pers. sing. / *desmembrar.* 2. that he (she/it) may dismember; pres. subj. 3rd pers. sing. 3. let him (her/it) dismember; impve. 3rd pers. sing.

desmiembren that they may dismember; pres. subj. 3rd pers. pl. / *desmembrar.*

desmiémbrense let them disintegrate; impve. 3rd pers. pl. / *desmembrarse.*

desmiembres that you may dismember; pres. subj. 2nd pers. sing. / *desmembrar.*

desmiémbrese let him (her/it) disintegrate; impve. 3rd pers. sing. / *desmembrarse.*

desmiembro I dismember; pres. ind. 1st pers. sing. / *desmembrar.*

desmienta 1. that I may contradict; pres. subj. 1st pers. sing. / *desmentir.* 2. that he (she/it) may contradict; pres. subj. 3rd pers. sing. 3. let him (her/it) contradict; impve. 3rd pers. sing.

desmientan 1. that they may contradict; pres. subj. 3rd pers. pl. / *desmentir.* 2. let them contradict; impve. 3rd pers. pl.

desmiéntanse let them retract; impve. 3rd pers. pl. / *desmentirse.*

desmientas that you may contradict; pres. subj. 2nd pers. sing. / *desmentir.*

desmiéntase let him (her/it) retract; impve. 3rd pers. sing. / *desmentirse.*

desmiente 1. he (she/it) contradicts; pres. ind. 3rd pers. sing. / *desmentir.* 2. (you) contradict; impve. 2nd pers. sing.

desmienten they contradict; pres. ind. 3rd pers. pl. / *desmentir.*

desmientes you contradict; pres. ind. 2nd pers. sing. / *desmentir.*

desmiéntete (you) retract; impve. 2nd pers. sing. / *desmentirse.*

desmiento I contradict; pres. ind. 1st pers. sing. / *desmentir.*

desmigajándose crumbling; pres. part. / *desmigajarse.*

desmigajaos (you all) crumble; impve. 2nd pers. pl. / *desmigajarse.*

desmigajar to crumble. reg.

desmigajarse to crumble. reg.

desmigájate (you) crumble; impve. 2nd pers. sing. / *desmigajarse.*

desmigajémonos let us crumble; impve. 1st pers. pl. / *desmigajarse.*

desmigájense let them crumble; impve. 3rd pers. pl. / *desmigajarse.*

desmigájese let him (her/it) crumble; impve. 3rd pers. sing. / *desmigajarse.*

desmigar to crumble (bread). irr.

desmigue 1. that I may crumble (bread); pres. subj. 1st pers. sing. / *desmigar.* 2. that he (she/it) may crumble (bread); pres. subj. 3rd pers. sing. 3. let him (her/it) crumble (bread); impve. 3rd pers. sing.

desmigué I crumbled (bread); past 1st pers. sing. / *desmigar.*

desmiguéis that you (all) may crumble (bread); pres. subj. 2nd pers. pl. / *desmigar.*

desmiguemos 1. that we may crumble (bread); pres. subj. 1st pers. pl. / *desmigar.* 2. let us crumble (bread); impve. 1st pers. pl.

desmiguen 1. that they may crumble (bread); pres. subj. 3rd pers. pl. / *desmigar.* 2. let them crumble (bread); impve. 3rd pers. pl.

desmigues that you may crumble (bread); pres. subj. 2nd pers. sing. / *desmigar.*

desmilitarice 1. that I may demilitarize; pres. subj. 1st pers. sing. / *desmilitarizar.* 2. that he (she/it) may demilitarize; pres. subj. 3rd pers. sing. 3. let him (her/it) demilitarize; impve. 3rd pers. sing.

desmilitaricé I demilitarized; past 1st pers. sing. / *desmilitarizar.*

desmilitaricemos 1. that we may demilitarize; pres. subj. 1st pers. pl. / *desmilitarizar.* 2. let us demilitarize; impve. 1st pers. pl.

desmilitaricen 1. that they may demilitarize; pres. subj. 3rd pers. pl. / *desmilitarizar.* 2. let them demilitarize; impve. 3rd pers. pl.

desmilitarices that you may demilitarize; pres. subj. 2nd pers. sing. / *desmilitarizar.*

desmilitarizar to demilitarize. irr.

desmintáis that you (all) may contradict; pres. subj. 2nd pers. pl. / *desmentir.*

desmintámonos let us retract; impve. 1st pers. pl. / *desmentirse.*

desmintamos 1. that we may contradict; pres. subj. 1st pers. pl. / *desmentir*. 2. let us contradict; impve. 1st pers. pl.

desmintiendo contradicting; pres. part. / *desmentir*.

desmintiéndose retracting; pres. part. / *desmentirse*.

desmintiera 1. that I might contradict; imp. subj. 1st pers. sing. / *desmentir*. 2. that he (she/it) might contradict; imp. subj. 3rd pers. sing.

desmintierais that you (all) might contradict; imp. subj. 2nd pers pl. / *desmentir*.

desmintiéramos that we might contradict; imp. subj. 1st pers. pl. / *desmentir*.

desmintieran that they might contradict; imp. subj. 3rd pers. pl. / *desmentir*.

desmintieras that you might contradict; imp. subj. 2nd pers. sing. / *desmentir*.

desmintieron they contradicted; past 3rd pers. pl. / *desmentir*.

desmintiese 1. that I might contradict; imp. subj. 1st pers. sing. / *desmentir*. 2. that he (she/it) might contradict; imp. subj. 3rd pers. sing.

desmintieseis that you (all) might contradict; imp. subj. 2nd pers pl. / *desmentir*.

desmintiésemos that we might contradict; imp. subj. 1st pers. pl. / *desmentir*.

desmintiesen that they might contradict; imp. subj. 3rd pers. pl. / *desmentir*.

desmintieses that you might contradict; imp. subj. 2nd pers. sing. / *desmentir*.

desmintió he (she/it) contradicted; past. ind. 3rd pers. sing. / *desmentir*.

desmochar to cut off. reg.

desmonetice 1. that I may demonetize; pres. subj. 1st pers. sing. / *desmonetizar*. 2. that he (she/it) may demonetize; pres. subj. 3rd pers. sing. 3. let him (her/it) demonetize; impve. 3rd pers. sing.

desmoneticé I demonetized; past 1st pers. sing. / *desmonetizar*.

desmoneticéis that you (all) may demonetize; pres. subj. 2nd pers. pl. / *desmonetizar*.

desmoneticemos 1. that we may demonetize; pres. subj. 1st pers. pl. / *desmonetizar*. 2. let us demonetize; impve. 1st pers. pl.

desmoneticen 1. that they may demonetize; pres. subj. 3rd pers. pl. / *desmonetizar*. 2. let them demonetize; impve. 3rd pers. pl.

desmonetices that you may demonetize; pres. subj. 2nd pers. sing. / *desmonetizar*.

desmonetizar to demonetize or to deprive of money. reg.

desmontándose dismounting; pres. part. / *desmontarse*.

desmontaos (you all) dismount; impve. 2nd pers. pl. / *desmontarse*.

desmontar to dismount or to dismantle. reg.

desmontarse to dismount. reg.

desmóntate (you) dismount; impve. 2nd pers. sing. / *desmontarse*.

desmontémonos let us dismount; impve. 1st pers. pl. / *desmontarse*.

desmóntense let them dismount; impve. 3rd pers. pl. / *desmontarse*.

desmóntese let him (her/it) dismount; impve. 3rd pers. sing. / *desmontarse*.

desmoralice 1. that I may demoralize; pres. subj. 1st pers. sing. / *desmoralizar*. 2. that he (she/it) may demoralize; pres. subj. 3rd pers. sing. 3. let him (her/it) demoralize; impve. 3rd pers. sing.

desmoralicé I demoralized; past 1st pers. sing. / *desmoralizar*.

desmoralicéis that you (all) may demoralize; pres. subj. 2nd pers. pl. / *desmoralizar*.

desmoralicémonos let us become demoralized; impve. 1st pers. pl. / *desmoralizarse*.

desmoralicemos 1. that we may demoralize; pres. subj. 1st pers. pl. / *desmoralizar*. 2. let us demoralize; impve. 1st pers. pl.

desmoralicen 1. that they may demoralize; pres. subj. 3rd pers. pl. / *desmoralizar*. 2. let them demoralize; impve. 3rd pers. pl.

desmoralícense let them become demoralized; impve. 3rd pers. pl. / *desmoralizarse*.

desmoralices that you may demoralize; pres. subj. 2nd pers. sing. / *desmoralizarse*.

desmoralícese let him (her/it) become demoralized; impve. 3rd pers. sing. / *desmoralizarse*.

desmoralizándose becoming demoralized; pres. part. / *desmoralizarse*.

desmoralizaos (you all) become demoralized; impve. 2nd pers. pl. / *desmoralizarse*.

desmoralizar to demoralize. irr.

desmoralizarse to become demoralized. irr.

desmoralízate (you) become demoralized; impve. 2nd pers. sing. / *desmoralizarse*.

desmoronándose decaying; pres. part. / *desmoronarse*.

desmoronaos (you all) decay; impve. 2nd pers. pl. / *desmoronarse*.

desmoronar to crumble. reg.

desmoronarse to decay. reg.

desmorónate (you) decay; impve. 2nd pers. sing. / *desmoronarse*.

desmoronémonos let us decay; impve. 1st pers. pl. / *desmoronarse*.

desmorónense let them decay; impve. 3rd pers. pl. / *desmoronarse*.

desmorónese let him (her/it) decay; impve. 3rd pers. sing. / *desmoronarse*.

desmotar to gin (cotton). reg.

desmovilice 1. that I may demobilize; pres. subj. 1st pers. sing. / *desmovilizar*. 2. that he (she/it) may demobilize; pres. subj. 3rd pers. sing. 3. let him (her/it) demobilize; impve. 3rd pers. sing.

desmovilicé I demobilized; past 1st pers. sing. / *desmovilizar*.

desmovilicéis that you (all) may demobilize; pres. subj. 2nd pers. pl. / *desmovilizar*.

desmovilicemos 1. that we may demobilize; pres. subj. 1st pers. pl. / *desmovilizar*. 2. let us demobilize; impve. 1st pers. pl.

desmovilicen 1. that they may demobilize; pres. subj. 3rd pers. pl. / *desmovilizar*. 2. let them demobilize; impve. 3rd pers. pl.

desmovilices that you may demobilize; pres. subj. 2nd pers. sing. / *desmovilizar*.

desmovilizar to demobilize / *desmovilizar*.

desnatar to skim. reg.

desnaturalice 1. that I may denaturalize; pres. subj. 1st pers. sing. / *desnaturalizar*. 2. that he (she/it) may denaturalize; pres. subj. 3rd pers. sing. 3. let him (her/it) denaturalize; impve. 3rd pers. sing.

desnaturalicéis that you (all) may denaturalize; pres. subj. 2nd pers. pl. / *desnaturalizar*.

desnaturalicémonos let us become unnatural; impve. 1st pers. pl. / *desnaturalizarse*.

desnaturalicemos 1. that we may denaturalize; pres. subj. 1st pers. pl. / *desnaturalizar*. 2. let us denaturalize; impve. 1st pers. pl.

desnaturalicen 1. that they may denaturalize; pres. subj. 3rd pers. pl. / *desnaturalizar*. 2. let them denaturalize; impve. 3rd pers. pl.

desnaturalícense let them become unnatural; impve. 3rd pers. pl. / *desnaturalizarse*.

desnaturalices that you may denaturalize; pres. subj. 2nd pers. sing. / *desnaturalizar*.

desnaturalícese let him (her/it) become unnatural; impve. 3rd pers. sing. / *desnaturalizarse*.

desnaturalizándose becoming unnatural; pres. part. / *desnaturalizarse*.

desnaturalizaos you (all) become unnatural; past 2nd pers. pl. / *desnaturalizarse*.

desnaturalizar to denaturalize. irr.

desnaturalizarse to become unnatural. irr.

desnaturalízate (you) become unnatural; impve. 2nd pers. sing. / *desnaturalizarse*.

desnivelar to make uneven. reg.

desnucándose breaking one's neck; pres. part. / *desnucarse*.

desnucaos (you all) break your necks; impve. 2nd pers. pl. / *desnucarse*.

desnucar to break the neck of. irr.

desnucarse to break one's neck. irr.

desnúcate (you) break your neck; impve. 2nd pers. sing. / *desnucarse*.

desnudándose uncovering; pres. part. / *desnudarse*.

desnudaos (you all) uncover; impve. 2nd pers. pl. / *desnudarse*.

desnudar to undress. reg.

desnudarse to uncover. reg.

desnúdate (you) uncover; impve. 2nd pers. sing. / *desnudarse*.

desnudémonos let us uncover; impve. 1st pers. pl. / *desnudarse*.

desnúdense let them uncover; impve. 3rd pers. pl. / *desnudarse*.

desnúdese let him (her/it) uncover; impve. 3rd pers. sing. / *desnudarse*.

desnuque 1. that I may break the neck of; pres. subj. 1st pers. sing. / *desnucar*. 2. that he (she/it) may break the neck of; pres. subj. 3rd pers. sing. 3. let him (her/it) break the neck of; impve. 3rd pers. sing.

desnuqué I broke the neck of; past 1st pers. sing. / *desnucar*.

desnuquéis that you (all) may break the neck of; pres. subj. 2nd pers. pl. / *desnucar*.

desnuquémonos let us break our necks; impve. 1st pers. pl. / *desnucarse*.

desnuquemos 1. that we may break the neck of; pres. subj. 1st pers. pl. / *desnucar*. 2. let us break the neck of; impve. 1st pers. pl.

desnuquen 1. that they may break the neck of; pres. subj. 3rd pers. pl. / *desnucar*. 2. let them break the neck of; impve. 3rd pers. pl.

desnúquense let them break their necks; impve. 3rd pers. pl. / *desnucarse*.

desnuques that you may break the neck of; pres. subj. 2nd pers. sing. / *desnucar*.

desnúquese let him (her/it) break his (her/its) neck; impve. 3rd pers. sing. / *desnucarse*.

desobedecer to disobey. irr.

desobedezca 1. that I may disobey; pres. subj. 1st pers. sing. / *desobedecer*. 2. that he (she/it) may disobey; pres. subj. 3rd pers. sing. 3. let him (her/it) disobey; impve. 3rd pers. sing.

desobedezcáis that you (all) may disobey; pres. subj. 2nd pers. pl. / *desobedecer*.

desobedezcamos 1. that we may disobey; pres. subj. 1st pers. pl. / *desobedecer*. 2. let us disobey; impve. 1st pers. pl.

desobedezcan 1. that they may disobey; pres. subj. 3rd pers. pl. / *desobedecer*. 2. let them disobey; impve. 3rd pers. pl.

desobedezcas that you may disobey; pres. subj. 2nd pers. sing. / *desobedecer*.

desobedezco I disobey; pres. ind. 1st pers. sing. / *desobedecer*.

desobligar to release from an obligation. irr.

desobligue 1. that I may release from an obligation; pres. subj. 1st pers. sing. / *desobligar*. 2. that he (she/it) may release from an obligation; pres. subj. 3rd pers. sing. 3. let him (her/it) release from an obligation; impve. 3rd pers. sing.

desobligué I released from an obligation; past 1st pers. sing. / *desobligar*.

desobliguéis that you (all) may release from an obligation; pres. subj. 2nd pers. pl. / *desobligar*.

desobliguemos 1. that we may release from an obligation; pres. subj. 1st pers. pl. / *desobligar*. 2. let us release from an obligation; impve. 1st pers. pl.

desobliguen 1. that they may release from an obligation; pres. subj. 3rd pers. pl. / *desobligar*. 2. let them release from an obligation; impve. 3rd pers. pl.

desobligues that you may release from an obligation; pres. subj. 2nd pers. sing. / *desobligar*.

desocupándose getting out; pres. part. / *desocuparse*.

desocupaos you (all) get out; past 2nd pers. pl. / *desocuparse*.

desocupar to empty or to vacate. reg.

desocuparse to get out. reg.

desocúpate (you) get out; impve. 2nd pers. sing. / *desocuparse*.

desocupémonos let us get out; impve. 1st pers. pl. / *desocuparse*.

desocúpense let them get out; impve. 3rd pers. pl. / *desocuparse*.

desocúpese let him (her/it) get out; impve. 3rd pers. sing. / *desocuparse*.

desodorice 1. that I may deodorize; pres. subj. 1st pers. sing. / *desodorizar*. 2. that he (she/it) may deodorize; pres. subj. 3rd pers. sing. 3. let him (her/it) deodorize; impve. 3rd pers. sing.

desodoricé I deodorized; past 1st pers. sing. / *desodorizar*.

desodoricéis that you (all) may deodorize; pres. subj. 2nd pers. pl. / *desodorizar*.

desodoricemos 1. that we may deodorize; pres. subj. 1st pers. pl. / *desodorizar*. 2. let us deodorize; impve. 1st pers. pl.

desodoricen 1. that they may deodorize; pres. subj. 3rd pers. pl. / *desodorizar*. 2. let them deodorize; impve. 3rd pers. pl.

desodorices that you may deodorize; pres. subj. 2nd pers. sing. / *desodorizar*.

desodorizar to deodorize / *desodorizar*.

desoiga 1. that I may be deaf to; pres. subj. 1st pers. sing. / *desoír*. 2. that he (she/it) may be deaf to; pres. subj. 3rd pers. sing. 3. let him (her/it) be deaf to; impve. 3rd pers. sing.

desoigáis that you (all) may be deaf to; pres. subj. 2nd pers. pl. / *desoír*.

desoigamos 1. that we may be deaf to; pres. subj. 1st pers. pl. / *desoír*. 2. let us be deaf to; impve. 1st pers. pl.

desoigan 1. that they be deaf to; pres. subj. 3rd pers. pl. / *desoír*. 2. let them be deaf to; impve. 3rd pers. pl.

desoigas that you may be deaf to; pres. subj. 2nd pers. sing. / *desoír*.

desoigo I am deaf to; pres. ind. 1st pers. sing. / *desoír*.

desoír to be deaf to. irr.

desolándose grieving; pres. part. / *desolarse*.

desolaos (you all) grieve; impve. 2nd pers. pl. / *desolarse*.

desolar to desolate. irr.

desolarse to grieve. irr.

desolémonos let us grieve; impve. 1st pers. pl. / *desolarse*.

desollar to skin or to swindle. irr.

desordenándose living a disorderly life; pres. part. / *desordenarse*.

desordenaos (you all) live a disorderly life; impve. 2nd pers. pl. / *desordenarse*.

desordenar to disorder or to upset. reg.

desordenarse to live a disorderly life. reg.

desordénate (you) live a disorderly life; impve. 2nd pers. sing. / *desordenarse*.

desordenémonos let us live a disorderly life; impve. 1st pers. pl. / *desordenarse*.

desordénense let them live a disorderly life; impve. 3rd pers. pl. / *desordenarse*.

desordénese let him (her/it) live a disorderly life; impve. 3rd pers. sing. / *desordenarse*.

desorganice 1. that I may disorganize; pres. subj. 1st pers. sing. / *desorganizar*. 2. that he (she/it) may disorganize; pres. subj. 3rd pers. sing. 3. let him (her/it) disorganize; impve. 3rd pers. sing.

desorganicé I disorganized; past 1st pers. sing. / *desorganizar*.

desorganicéis that you (all) may disorganize; pres. subj. 2nd pers. pl. / *desorganizar*.

desorganicemos 1. that we may disorganize; pres. subj. 1st pers. pl. / *desorganizar*. 2. let us disorganize; impve. 1st pers. pl.

desorganicen 1. that they may disorganize; pres. subj. 3rd pers. pl. / *desorganizar*. 2. let them disorganize; impve. 3rd pers. pl.

desorganices that you may disorganize; pres. subj. 2nd pers. sing. / *desorganizar*.

desorganizar to disorganize. irr.

desorientándose getting lost; pres. part. / *desorientarse*.

desorientaos (you all) get lost; impve. 2nd pers. pl. / *desorientarse*.

desorientar to disorient. reg.

desorientarse to get lost. reg.

desoriéntate (you) get lost; impve. 2nd pers. sing. / *desorientarse*.

desorientémonos let us get lost; impve. 1st pers. pl. / *desorientarse*.

desoriéntense let them get lost; impve. 3rd pers. pl. / *desorientarse*.

desoriéntese let him (her/it) get lost; impve. 3rd pers. sing. / *desorientarse*.

desosar to remove the bone from. irr.

desovar to spawn. reg.

desovillar to unwind. reg.

desoye 1. he (she/it) is deaf to; pres. ind. 3rd pers. sing. / *desoír*. 2. (you) are deaf to; impve. 2nd pers. sing.

desoyen they are deaf to; pres. ind. 3rd pers. pl. / *desoír*.

desoyendo being deaf to; pres. part. / *desoír*.

desoyera 1. that I might be deaf to; imp. subj. 1st pers. sing. / *desoír*. 2. that he (she/it) might be deaf to; imp. subj. 3rd pers. sing.

desoyerais that you (all) might be deaf to; imp. subj. 2nd pers pl. / *desoír*.

desoyéramos that we might be deaf to; imp. subj. 1st pers. pl. / *desoír*.

desoyeran that they might be deaf to; imp. subj. 3rd pers. pl. / *desoír*.

desoyeras that you might be deaf to; imp. subj. 2nd pers. sing. / *desoír*.

desoyeron they were deaf to; past 3rd pers. pl. / *desoír*.

desoyes you be deaf to; pres. ind. 2nd pers. sing. / *desoír*.

desoyese 1. that I might be deaf to; imp. subj. 1st pers. sing. / *desoír*. 2. that he (she/it) might be deaf to; imp. subj. 3rd pers. sing.

desoyeseis that you (all) might be deaf to; imp. subj. 2nd pers pl. / *desoír*.

desoyésemos that we might be deaf to; imp. subj. 1st pers. pl. / *desoír*.

desoyesen that they might be deaf to; imp. subj. 3rd pers. pl. / *desoír*.

desoyeses that you might be deaf to; imp. subj. 2nd pers. sing. / *desoír*.

desoyó he (she/it) was deaf to; past 3rd pers. sing. / *desoír*.

despabilándose waking up; pres. part. / *despabilarse*.

despabilaos (you all) wake up; impve. 2nd pers. pl. / *despabilarse*.

despabilar to snuff (candle). reg.

despabilarse to wake up. reg.

despabílate (you) wake up; impve. 2nd pers. sing. / *despabilarse*.

despabilémonos let us wake up; impve. 1st pers. pl. / *despabilarse*.

despabílense let them wake up; impve. 3rd pers. pl. / *despabilarse*.

despabílese let him (her/it) wake up; impve. 3rd pers. sing. / *despabilarse*.

despachándose hurrying up; pres. part. / *despacharse*.

despachaos (you all) hurry up; impve. 2nd pers. pl. / *despacharse*.

despachar to dispatch. reg.

despacharse to hurry up. reg.

despáchate (you) hurry up; impve. 2nd pers. sing. / *despacharse*.

despachémonos let us hurry up; impve. 1st pers. pl. / *despacharse*.

despáchense let them hurry up; impve. 3rd pers. pl. / *despacharse*.

despáchese let him (her/it) hurry up; impve. 3rd pers. sing. / *despacharse*.

despachurrar to squash. reg.

despampanándose being convulsed (laughter); pres. part. / *despampanarse*.

despampanaos (you all) be convulsed (laughter); impve. 2nd pers. pl. / *despampanarse*.

despampanar to prune (vines). reg.

despampanarse to be convulsed (laughter). reg.

despampánate (you) be convulsed (laughter); impve. 2nd pers. sing. / *despampanarse*.

despampanémonos let us be convulsed (laughter); impve. 1st pers. pl. / *despampanarse*.

despampánense let them be convulsed (laughter); impve. 3rd pers. pl. / *despampanarse*.

despampánese let him (her/it) be convulsed (laughter); impve. 3rd pers. sing. / *despampanarse*.

desparejar to make uneven. reg.

desparpajándose ranting; pres. part. / *desparpajarse*.

desparpajaos (you all) rant; impve. 2nd pers. pl. / *desparpajarse*.

desparpajar to upset or to scatter. reg.

desparpajarse to rant. reg.

desparpájate (you) rant; impve. 2nd pers. sing. / *desparpajarse*.

desparpajémonos let us rant; impve. 1st pers. pl. / *desparpajarse*.

desparpájense let them rant; impve. 3rd pers. pl. / *desparpajarse*.

desparpájese let him (her/it) rant; impve. 3rd pers. sing. / *desparpajarse*.

desparramándose leading a reckless life; pres. part. / *desparramarse*.

desparramaos (you all) lead a reckless life; impve. 2nd pers. pl. / *desparramarse*.

desparramar to scatter or to squander. reg.

desparramarse to lead a reckless life. reg.

desparrámate (you) lead a reckless life; impve. 2nd pers. sing. / *desparramarse*.

desparramémonos let us lead a reckless life; impve. 1st pers. pl. / *desparramarse*.

desparrámense let them lead a reckless life; impve. 3rd pers. pl. / *desparramarse*.

desparrámese let him (her/it) lead a reckless life; impve. 3rd pers. sing. / *desparramarse*.

despartir to separate. reg.

despatarrándose sprawling; pres. part. / *despatarrarse*.

despatarraos (you all) sprawl; impve. 2nd pers. pl. / *despatarrarse*.

despatarrarse to sprawl. reg.

despatárrate (you) sprawl; impve. 2nd pers. sing. / *despatarrarse*.

despatarrémonos let us sprawl; impve. 1st pers. pl. / *despatarrarse*.

despatárrense let them sprawl; impve. 3rd pers. pl. / *despatarrarse*.

despatárrese let him (her/it) sprawl; impve. 3rd pers. sing. / *despatarrarse*.

despatillar to groove (wood) or to shave off (whiskers). reg.

despavesar to snuff. reg.

despeándose getting sore feet; pres. part. / *despearse*.

despeaos (you all) get sore feet; impve. 2nd pers. pl. / *despearse*.

despear to damage the feet of. reg.

despearse to get sore feet. reg.

despéate (you) get sore feet; impve. 2nd pers. sing. / *despearse*.

despechándose fretting; pres. part. / *despecharse*.

despechaos (you all) fret; impve. 2nd pers. pl. / *despecharse*.

despechar to spite or to enrage. reg.

despecharse to fret or to give up hope. reg.

despéchate (you) fret; impve. 2nd pers. sing. / *despecharse*.

despechémonos let us fret; impve. 1st pers. pl. / *despecharse*.

despéchense let them fret; impve. 3rd pers. pl. / *despecharse*.

despéchese let him (her/it) fret; impve. 3rd pers. sing. / *despecharse*.

despedace 1. that I may tear into pieces; pres. subj. 1st pers. sing. / *despedazar*. 2. that he (she/it) may tear into pieces; pres. subj. 3rd pers. sing. 3. let him (her/it) tear into pieces; impve. 3rd pers. sing.

despedacé I tore into pieces; past 1st pers. sing. / *despedazar*.

despedacéis that you (all) may tear into pieces; pres. subj. 2nd pers. pl. / *despedazar*.

despedacémonos de risa let us burst into fits of laughter; impve. 1st pers. pl. / *despedazarse de risa*.

despedacemos 1. that we may tear into pieces; pres. subj. 1st pers. pl. / *despedazar*. 2. let us tear into pieces; impve. 1st pers. pl.

despedacen 1. that they may tear into pieces; pres. subj. 3rd pers. pl. / *despedazar*. 2. let them tear into pieces; impve. 3rd pers. pl.

despedácense de risa let them burst into fits of laughter; impve. 3rd pers. pl. / *despedazarse de risa*.

despedaces that you may tear into pieces; pres. subj. 2nd pers. sing. / *despedazar*.

despedácese de risa let him (her/it) burst into fits of laughter; impve. 3rd pers. sing. / *despedazarse de risa*.

despedazándose de risa bursting into fits of laughter; pres. part. / *despedazarse de risa*.

despedazaos de risa (you all) burst into fits of laughter; impve. 2nd pers. pl. / *despedazarse de risa*.

despedazar to tear into pieces. irr.

despedazarse de risa to burst into fits of laughter. irr.

despedázate de risa (you) burst into fits of laughter; impve. 2nd pers. sing. / *despedazarse de risa*.

despedíos (you all) take leave; impve. 2nd pers. pl. / *despedirse*

despedir to dismiss or to give off. irr.

despedirse to take leave. irr.

despeémonos let us get sore feet; impve. 1st pers. pl. / *despearse*.

despéense let them get sore feet; impve. 3rd pers. pl. / *despearse*.

despéese let him (her/it) get sore feet; impve. 3rd pers. sing. / *despearse*.

despegándose coming loose; pres. part. / *despegarse*.

despegaos (you all) come loose; impve. 2nd pers. pl. / *despegarse*.

despegar to detach. irr

despegarse to come loose. irr.

despégate (you) come loose; impve. 2nd pers. sing. / *despegarse*.

despegue 1. that I may detach; pres. subj. 1st pers. sing. / *despegar*. 2. that he (she/it) may detach; pres. subj. 3rd pers. sing. 3. let him (her/it) detach; impve. 3rd pers. sing.

despegué I detached; past 1st pers. sing. / *despegar*.

despeguéis that you (all) may detach; pres. subj. 2nd pers. pl. / *despegar*.

despeguémonos let us come loose; impve. 1st pers. pl. / *despegarse*.

despeguemos 1. that we may detach; pres. subj. 1st pers. pl. / *despegar*. 2. let us detach; impve. 1st pers. pl.

despeguen 1. that they may detach; pres. subj. 3rd pers. pl. / *despegar*. 2. let them detach; impve. 3rd pers. pl.

despéguense let them come loose; impve. 3rd pers. pl. / *despegarse*.

despegues that you may detach; pres. subj. 2nd pers. sing. / *despegar*.

despéguese let him (her/it) come loose; impve. 3rd pers. sing. / *despegarse*.

despeinar to dishevel. reg.

despejándose being at ease; pres. part. / *despejarse*.

despejaos (you all) be at ease; impve. 2nd pers. pl. / *despejarse*.

despejar to clear. reg.

despejarse to be at ease. reg.

despéjate (you) be at ease; impve. 2nd pers. sing. / *despejarse*.

despejémonos let us be at ease; impve. 1st pers. pl. / *despejarse*.

despéjense let them be at ease; impve. 3rd pers. pl. / *despejarse*.

despéjese let him (her/it) be at ease; impve. 3rd pers. sing. / *despejarse*.

despeluce 1. that I may make the hair stand on end; pres. subj. 1st pers. sing. / *despeluzar*. 2. that he (she/it) may make the hair stand on end; pres. subj. 3rd pers. sing. 3. let him (her/it) make the hair stand on end; impve. 3rd pers. sing.

despelucé I made the hair stand on end; past 1st pers. sing. / *despeluzar*.

despelucéis that you (all) may make the hair stand on end; pres. subj. 2nd pers. pl. / *despeluzar*.

despelucemos 1. that we may make the hair stand on end; pres. subj. 1st pers. pl. / *despeluzar*. 2. let us make the hair stand on end; impve. 1st pers. pl.

despelucen 1. that they may make the hair stand on end; pres. subj. 3rd pers. pl. / *despeluzar*. 2. let them make the hair stand on end; impve. 3rd pers. pl.

despeluces that you may make the hair stand on end; pres. subj. 2nd pers. sing. / *despeluzar*.

despeluzar to make the hair stand on end. irr.

despeluznar to make the hair stand on end. reg.

despellejar to skin or flay. reg.

despenar to console or to kill. reg.

despeñándose falling headlong; pres. part. / *despeñarse*.

despeñaos (you all) fall headlong; impve. 2nd pers. pl. / *despeñarse*.

despeñar to throw over a cliff. reg.

despeñarse to fall headlong. reg.

despéñate (you) fall headlong; impve. 2nd pers. sing. / *despeñarse*.

despeñémonos let us fall headlong; impve. 1st pers. pl. / *despeñarse*.

despéñense let them fall headlong; impve. 3rd pers. pl. / *despeñarse*.

despéñese let him (her/it) fall headlong; impve. 3rd pers. sing. / *despeñarse*.

despepitándose screaming violently; pres. part. / *despepitarse*.

despepitaos (you all) scream violently; impve. 2nd pers. pl. / *despepitarse*.

despepitar to remove seeds from. reg.

despepitarse to scream violently. reg.

despepítate (you) scream violently; impve. 2nd pers. sing. / *despepitarse*.

despepitémonos let us scream violently; impve. 1st pers. pl. / *despepitarse*.

despepítense let them scream violently; impve. 3rd pers. pl. / *despepitarse*.

despepítese let him (her/it) scream violently; impve. 3rd pers. sing. / *despepitarse*.

despercudir to clean completely of grime. reg.

desperdiciar to waste or to lose. reg.

desperdigar to scatter. irr.

desperdigue 1. that I may scatter; pres. subj. 1st pers. sing. / *desperdigar*. 2. that he (she/it) may scatter; pres. subj. 3rd pers. sing. 3. let him (her/it) scatter; impve. 3rd pers. sing.

desperdigué I scattered; past 1st pers. sing. / *desperdigar*.

desperdiguéis that you (all) may scatter; pres. subj. 2nd pers. pl. / *desperdigar*.

desperdiguemos 1. that we may scatter; pres. subj. 1st pers. pl. / *desperdigar*. 2. let us scatter; impve. 1st pers. pl.

desperdiguen 1. that they may scatter; pres. subj. 3rd pers. pl. / *desperdigar*. 2. let them scatter; impve. 3rd pers. pl.

desperdigues that you may scatter; pres. subj. 2nd pers. sing. / *desperdigar*.

desperece 1. that I may stretch; pres. subj. 1st pers. sing. / *desperezarse*. 2. that he (she/it) may stretch; pres. subj. 3rd pers. sing.

desperecé I stretched; past 1st pers. sing. / *desperezarse*.

desperecéis that you (all) may stretch; pres. subj. 2nd pers. pl. / *desperezarse*.

desperecémonos let us stretch; impve. 1st pers. pl. / *desperezarse*.

desperecemos that we may stretch; pres. subj. 1st pers. pl. / *desperezarse*.

desperecen that they may stretch; pres. subj. 3rd pers. pl. / *desperezarse*.

desperécense let them stretch; impve. 3rd pers. pl. / *desperezarse*.

despereces that you may stretch; pres. subj. 2nd pers. sing. / *desperezarse*.

desperécese let him (her/it) stretch; impve. 3rd pers. sing. / *desperezarse*.

desperezándose stretching; pres. part. / *desperezarse*.

desperezaos (you all) stretch; impve. 2nd pers. pl. / *desperezarse*.

desperezarse to stretch. irr.

desperézate (you) stretch; impve. 2nd pers. sing. / *desperezarse*.

despernar to injure the legs of. irr.

despertándose waking up; pres. part. / *despertarse*.

despertaos (you all) wake up; impve. 2nd pers. pl. / *despertarse*.

despertar to awake. irr.

despertarse to wake up. irr.

despertémonos let us wake up; impve. 1st pers. pl. / *despertarse*.

despicándose having one's honor satisfied; pres. part. / *despicarse*.

despicaos (you all) have your honor satisfied; impve. 2nd pers. pl. / *despicarse*.

despicar to satisfy. irr.

despicarse to have one's honor satisfied. irr.

despícate (you) have your honor satisfied; impve. 2nd pers. sing. / *despicarse*.

despichar to dry out or to kick off. reg.

despida 1. that I may dismiss; pres. subj. 1st pers. sing. / *despedir*. 2. that he (she/it) may dismiss; pres. subj. 3rd pers. sing. 3. let him (her/it) dismiss; impve. 3rd pers. sing.

despidáis that you (all) may dismiss; pres. subj. 2nd pers. pl. / *despedir*.

despidámonos let us take leave; impve. 1st pers. pl. / *despedirse*.

despidamos 1. that we may dismiss; pres. subj. 1st pers. pl. / *despedir*. 2. let us dismiss; impve. 1st pers. pl.

despidan 1. that they may dismiss; pres. subj. 3rd pers. pl. / *despedir*. 2. let them dismiss; impve. 3rd pers. pl.

despídanse let them take leave; impve. 3rd pers. pl. / *despedirse*.

despidas that you may dismiss; pres. subj. 2nd pers. sing. / *despedir*.

despídase let him (her/it) take leave; impve. 3rd pers. sing. / *despedirse*.

despide 1. he (she/it) dismisses; pres. ind. 3rd pers. sing. / *despedir*. 2. (you) dismiss; impve. 2nd pers. sing.

despiden they dismiss; pres. ind. 3rd pers. pl. / *despedir*.

despides you dismiss; pres. ind. 2nd pers. sing. / *despedir*.

despídete (you) take leave; impve. 2nd pers. sing. / *despedirse*.

despidiendo dismissing; pres. part. / *despedir*.

despidiéndose taking leave; pres. part. / *despedirse*.

despidiera 1. that I might dismiss; imp. subj. 1st pers. sing. / *despedir*. 2. that he (she/it) might dismiss; imp. subj. 3rd pers. sing.

despidierais that you (all) might dismiss; imp. subj. 2nd pers pl. / *despedir*.

despidiéramos that we might dismiss; imp. subj. 1st pers. pl. / *despedir*.

despidieran that they might dismiss; imp. subj. 3rd pers. pl. / *despedir*.

despidieras that you might dismiss; imp. subj. 2nd pers. sing. / *despedir*.

despidieron they dismissed; past 3rd pers. pl. / *despedir*.

despidiese 1. that I might dismiss; imp. subj. 1st pers. sing. / *despedir*. 2. that he (she/it) might dismiss; imp. subj. 3rd pers. sing.

despidieseis that you (all) might dismiss; imp. subj. 2nd pers pl. / *despedir.*

despidiésemos that we might dismiss; imp. subj. 1st pers. pl. / *despedir.*

despidiesen that they might dismiss; imp. subj. 3rd pers. pl. / *despedir.*

despidieses that you might dismiss; imp. subj. 2nd pers. sing. / *despedir.*

despidió he (she/it) dismissed; past 3rd pers. sing. / *despedir.*

despido I dismiss; pres. ind. 1st pers. sing. / *despedir.*

despierna 1. he (she/it) injures the legs of; pres. ind. 3rd pers. sing. / *despernar.* 2. (you) injure the legs of; impve. 2nd pers. sing.

despiernan they injure the legs of; pres. ind. 3rd pers. pl. / *despernar.*

despiernas you injure the legs of; pres. ind. 2nd pers. sing. / *despernar.*

despierne 1. that I may injure the legs of; pres. subj. 1st pers. sing. / *despernar.* 2. that he (she/it) may injure the legs of; pres. subj. 3rd pers. sing. 3. let him (her/it) injure the legs of; impve. 3rd pers. sing.

despiernen 1. that they may injure the legs of; pres. subj. 3rd pers. pl. / *despernar.* 2. let them injure the legs of; impve. 3rd pers. pl.

despiernes that you may injure the legs of; pres. subj. 2nd pers. sing. / *despernar.*

despierno I injure the legs of; pres. ind. 1st pers. sing. / *despernar.*

despierta 1. he (she/it) awakes; pres. ind. 3rd pers. sing. / *despertar.* 2. (you) awake; impve. 2nd pers. sing.

despiertan they awake; pres. ind. 3rd pers. pl. / *despertar.*

despiertas you awake; pres. ind. 2nd pers. sing. / *despertar.*

despiértate (you) wake up; impve. 2nd pers. sing. / *despertarse.*

despierte 1. that I may awake; pres. subj. 1st pers. sing. / *despertar.* 2. that he (she/it) may awake; pres. subj. 3rd pers. sing. 3. let him (her/it) awake; impve. 3rd pers. sing.

despierten 1. that they may awake; pres. subj. 3rd pers. pl. / *despertar.* 2. let them awake; impve. 3rd pers. pl.

despiértense let them wake up; impve. 3rd pers. pl. / *despertarse.*

despiertes that you may awake; pres. subj. 2nd pers. sing. / *despertar.*

despiértese let him (her/it) wake up; impve. 3rd pers. sing. / *despertarse.*

despierto I awake; pres. ind. 1st pers. sing. / *despertar.*

despilfarrándose bluing it in (money); pres. part. / *despilfarrarse.*

despilfarraos (you all) blue it in (money); impve. 2nd pers. pl. / *despilfarrarse.*

despilfarrar to squander. reg.

despilfarrarse to blue it in (money). reg.

despilfárrate (you) blue it in (money); impve. 2nd pers. sing. / *despilfarrarse.*

despilfarrémonos let us blue it in (money); impve. 1st pers. pl. / *despilfarrarse.*

despilfárrense let them blue it in (money); impve. 3rd pers. pl. / *despilfarrarse.*

despilfárrese let him (her/it) blue it in (money); impve. 3rd pers. sing. / *despilfarrarse.*

despintándose fading; pres. part. / *despintarse.*

despintaos you (all) fade; past 2nd pers. pl. / *despintarse.*

despintar to strip the paint from. reg.

despintarse to fade. reg.

despíntate (you) fade; impve. 2nd pers. sing. / *despintarse.*

despintémonos let us fade; impve. 1st pers. pl. / *despintarse.*

despíntense let them fade; impve. 3rd pers. pl. / *despintarse.*

despíntese let him (her/it) fade; impve. 3rd pers. sing. / *despintarse.*

despiojar to delouse or to remove from one's lousy surroundings. reg.

despique 1. that I may satisfy; pres. subj. 1st pers. sing. / *despicar.* 2. that he (she/it) may satisfy; pres. subj. 3rd pers. sing. 3. let him (her/it) satisfy; impve. 3rd pers. sing.

despiqué I satisfied; past 1st pers. sing. / *despicar.*

despiquéis that you (all) may satisfy; pres. subj. 2nd pers. pl. / *despicar.*

despiquémonos let us have our honor satisfied; impve. 1st pers. pl. / *despicarse.*

despiquemos 1. that we may satisfy; pres. subj. 1st pers. pl. / *despicar.* 2. let us satisfy; impve. 1st pers. pl.

despiquen 1. that they may satisfy; pres. subj. 3rd pers. pl. / *despicar.* 2. let them satisfy; impve. 3rd pers. pl.

despíquense let them have their honor satisfied; impve. 3rd pers. pl. / *despicarse.*

despiques that you may satisfy; pres. subj. 2nd pers. sing. / *despicar.*

despíquese let him (her/it) have his (her/its) honor satisfied; impve. 3rd pers. sing. / *despicarse.*

despistándose getting muddled; pres. part. / *despistarse.*

despistaos (you all) get muddled; impve. 2nd pers. pl. / *despistarse.*

despistar to throw off the track. reg.

despistarse to get muddled. reg.

despístate (you) get muddled; impve. 2nd pers. sing. / *despistarse.*

despistémonos let us get muddled; impve. 1st pers. pl. / *despistarse.*

despístense let them get muddled; impve. 3rd pers. pl. / *despistarse.*

despístese let him (her/it) get muddled; impve. 3rd pers. sing. / *despistarse.*

despizcar to crush or to grind up. irr.

despizque 1. that I may crush; pres. subj. 1st pers. sing. / *despizcar.* 2. that he (she/it) may crush; pres. subj. 3rd pers. sing. 3. let him (her/it) crush; impve. 3rd pers. sing.

despizqué I crushed; past 1st pers. sing. / *despizcar*.

despizquéis that you (all) may crush; pres. subj. 2nd pers. pl. / *despizcar*.

despizquemos 1. that we may crush; pres. subj. 1st pers. pl. / *despizcar*. 2. let us crush; impve. 1st pers. pl.

despizquen 1. that they may crush; pres. subj. 3rd pers. pl. / *despizcar*. 2. let them crush; impve. 3rd pers. pl.

despizques that you may crush; pres. subj. 2nd pers. sing. / *despizcar*.

desplace 1. that I may displace; pres. subj. 1st pers. sing. / *desplazar*. 2. that he (she/it) may displace; pres. subj. 3rd pers. sing. 3. let him (her/it) displace; impve. 3rd pers. sing.

desplacé I displaced; past 1st pers. sing. / *desplazar*.

desplacéis that you (all) may displace; pres. subj. 2nd pers. pl. / *desplazar*.

desplacémonos let us move; impve. 1st pers. pl. / *desplazarse*.

desplacemos 1. that we may displace; pres. subj. 1st pers. pl. / *desplazar*. 2. let us displace; impve. 1st pers. pl.

desplacen 1. that they may displace; pres. subj. 3rd pers. pl. / *desplazar*. 2. let them displace; impve. 3rd pers. pl.

desplácense let them move; impve. 3rd pers. pl. / *desplazarse*.

desplacer to displease. irr.

desplaces that you may displace; pres. subj. 2nd pers. sing. / *desplazar*.

desplácese let him (her/it) move; impve. 3rd pers. sing. / *desplazarse*.

desplantándose losing one's stance; pres. part. / *desplantarse*.

desplantaos (you all) lose your stance; impve. 2nd pers. pl. / *desplantarse*.

desplantar to uproot. reg.

desplantarse to lose one's stance. reg.

desplántate (you) lose your stance; impve. 2nd pers. sing. / *desplantarse*.

desplantémonos let us lose our stance; impve. 1st pers. pl. / *desplantarse*.

desplántense let them lose their stance; impve. 3rd pers. pl. / *desplantarse*.

desplántese let him (her/it) lose his (her/its) stance; impve. 3rd pers. sing. / *desplantarse*.

desplazándose moving; pres. part. / *desplazarse*.

desplazaos (you all) move; impve. 2nd pers. pl. / *desplazarse*.

desplazar to displace. irr.

desplazarse to move. irr.

desplázate (you) move; impve. 2nd pers. sing. / *desplazarse*.

desplazca 1. that I may displease; pres. subj. 1st pers. sing. / *desplacer*. 2. that he (she/it) may displease; pres. subj. 3rd pers. sing. 3. let him (her/it) displease; impve. 3rd pers. sing.

desplazcáis that you (all) may displease; pres. subj. 2nd pers. pl. / *desplacer*.

desplazcamos 1. that we may displease; pres. subj. 1st pers. pl. / *desplacer*. 2. let us displease; impve. 1st pers. pl.

desplazcan 1. that they may displease; pres. subj. 3rd pers. pl. / *desplacer*. 2. let them displease; impve. 3rd pers. pl.

desplazcas that you may displease; pres. subj. 2nd pers. sing. / *desplacer*.

desplazco I displease; pres. ind. 1st pers. sing. / *desplacer*.

desplega that he (she/it) may; pres. subj. 3rd pers. sing. / *desplacer*.

desplegar to unfold. irr.

desplegarse to deploy. irr.

desplegue that he (she/it) may displease; pres. subj. 3rd pers. sing. / *desplacer*.

desplegué I unfolded; past 1st pers. sing. / *desplegar*.

despleguéis that you (all) may unfold; pres. subj. 2nd pers. pl. / *desplegar*.

despleguémonos let us deploy; impve. 1st pers. pl. / *desplegarse*.

despleguemos 1. that we may unfold; pres. subj. 1st pers. pl. / *desplegar*. 2. let us unfold; impve. 1st pers. pl.

despliega 1. he (she/it) unfolds; pres. ind. 3rd pers. sing. / *desplegar*. 2. (you) unfold; impve. 2nd pers. sing.

despliegan they unfold; pres. ind. 3rd pers. pl. / *desplegar*.

despliegas you unfold; pres. ind. 2nd pers. sing. / *desplegar*.

despliégate (you) deploy; impve. 2nd pers. sing. / *desplegarse*.

despliego I unfold; pres. ind. 1st pers. sing. / *desplegar*.

despliegue 1. that I may unfold; pres. subj. 1st pers. sing. / *desplegar*. 2. that he (she/it) may unfold; pres. subj. 3rd pers. sing. 3. let him (her/it) unfold; impve. 3rd pers. sing.

desplieguen 1. that they may unfold; pres. subj. 3rd pers. pl. / *desplegar*. 2. let them unfold; impve. 3rd pers. pl.

despliéguense let them deploy; impve. 3rd pers. pl. / *desplegarse*.

despliegues that you may unfold; pres. subj. 2nd pers. sing. / *desplegar*.

despliéguese let him (her/it) deploy; impve. 3rd pers. sing. / *desplegarse*.

desplomándose slumping; pres. part. / *desplomarse*.

desplomaos (you all) slump; impve. 2nd pers. pl. / *desplomarse*.

desplomar to put out of plumb. reg.

desplomarse to slump or to collapse. reg.

desplómate (you) slump; impve. 2nd pers. sing. / *desplomarse*.

desplomémonos let us slump; impve. 1st pers. pl. / *desplomarse*.

desplómense let them slump; impve. 3rd pers. pl. / *desplomarse*.

desplómese let him (her/it) slump; impve. 3rd pers. sing. / *desplomarse*.

desplugo he (she/it) displeased; past. 3rd pers. sing. / *desplacer.*

despluguiera that he (she/it) might displease; imp. subj. 3rd pers. sing. / *desplacer.*

despluguieron they displeased; past 3rd pers. pl. / *desplacer.*

despluguiese that he (she/it) might displease; imp. subj. 3rd pers. sing. / *desplacer.*

desplumándose molting; pres. part. / *desplumarse.*

desplumaos (you all) molt; impve. 2nd pers. pl. / *desplumarse.*

desplumar to pluck (fowl). reg.

desplumarse to molt. reg.

desplúmate (you) molt; impve. 2nd pers. sing. / *desplumarse.*

desplúmense let them molt; impve. 3rd pers. pl. / *desplumarse.*

desplúmese let him (her/it) molt; impve. 3rd pers. sing. / *desplumarse.*

despoblándose becoming depopulated; pres. part. / *despoblarse.*

despoblar to depopulate. irr.

despoblarse to become depopulated. irr.

despojándose undressing; pres. part. / *despojarse.*

despojaos (you all) undress; impve. 2nd pers. pl. / *despojarse.*

despojar to despoil. reg.

despojarse to undress. reg.

despójate (you) undress; impve. 2nd pers. sing. / *despojarse.*

despojémonos let us undress; impve. 1st pers. pl. / *despojarse.*

despójense let them undress; impve. 3rd pers. pl. / *despojarse.*

despójese let him (her) undress; impve. 3rd pers. sing. / *despojarse.*

despolvar to dust or to sprinkle. reg.

despopularice 1. that I may make unpopular; pres. subj. 1st pers. sing. / *despopularizar.* 2. that he (she/it) may make unpopular; pres. subj. 3rd pers. sing. 3. let him (her/it) make unpopular; impve. 3rd pers. sing.

despopularicé I made unpopular; past 1st pers. sing. / *despopularizar.*

despopularicéis that you (all) may make unpopular; pres. subj. 2nd pers. pl. / *despopularizar.*

despopularicemos 1. that we may make unpopular; pres. subj. 1st pers. pl. / *despopularizar.* 2. let us make unpopular; impve. 1st pers. pl.

despopularicen 1. that they may make unpopular; pres. subj. 3rd pers. pl. / *despopularizar.* 2. let them make unpopular; impve. 3rd pers. pl.

despopularices that you may make unpopular; pres. subj. 2nd pers. sing. / *despopularizar.*

despopularizar to make unpopular. irr.

desportillar to chip or to nick. reg.

desposándose getting engaged or married; pres. part. / *desposarse.*

desposaos (you all) get engaged or married; impve. 2nd pers. pl. / *desposarse.*

desposar to marry. reg.

desposarse to get engaged or married. reg.

despósate (you) get engaged or married; impve. 2nd pers. sing. / *desposarse.*

desposeámonos let us renounce our possessions; impve. 1st pers. pl. / *desposeerse.*

desposéanse let them renounce their possessions; impve. 3rd pers. pl. / *desposeerse.*

desposéase let him (her/it) renounce his (her/its) possessions; impve. 3rd pers. sing. / *desposeerse.*

desposeeos (you all) renounce your possessions; impve. 2nd pers. pl. / *desposeerse.*

desposeer to dispossess or to deprive. irr.

desposeerse to renounce one's possessions. irr.

desposéete (you) renounce your possessions; impve. 2nd pers. sing. / *desposeerse.*

desposeí I dispossessed; past 1st pers. sing. / *desposeer.*

desposeído dispossessed; past part. / *desposeer.*

desposeímos we dispossessed; past 1st pers. pl. / *desposeer.*

desposeíste you dispossessed; past 2nd pers. sing. / *desposeer.*

desposeísteis you (all) dispossessed; past 2nd pers. pl. / *desposeer.*

desposémonos let us get engaged or married; impve. 1st pers. pl. / *desposarse.*

despósense let them get engaged or married; impve. 3rd pers. pl. / *desposarse.*

despósese let him (her) get engaged or married; impve. 3rd pers. sing. / *desposarse.*

desposeyendo dispossessing; pres. part. / *desposeer.*

desposeyéndose renouncing one's possessions; pres. part. / *desposeer.*

desposeyera 1. that I might dispossess; imp. subj. 1st pers. sing. / *desposeer.* 2. that he (she/it) might disposses; imp. subj. 3rd pers. sing.

desposeyerais that you (all) might dispossess; imp. subj. 2nd pers pl. / *desposeer.*

desposeyéramos that we might dispossess; imp. subj. 1st pers. pl. / *desposeer.*

desposeyeran that they might dispossess; imp. subj. 3rd pers. pl. / *desposeer.*

desposeyeras that you might dispossess; imp. subj. 2nd pers. sing. / *desposeer.*

desposeyeron they dispossessed; past 3rd pers. pl. / *desposeer.*

desposeyese 1. that I might dispossess; imp. subj. 1st pers. sing. / *desposeer.* 2. that he (she/it) might dispossess; imp. subj. 3rd pers. sing.

desposeyeseis that you (all) might dispossess; imp. subj. 2nd pers pl. / *desposeer.*

desposeyésemos that we might dispossess; imp. subj. 1st pers. pl. / *desposeer.*

desposeyesen that they might dispossess; imp. subj. 3rd pers. pl. / *desposeer.*

desposeyeses that you might dispossess; imp. subj. 2nd pers. sing. / *desposeer.*

desposeyó he (she/it) dispossessed; past. ind. 3rd pers. sing. / *desposeer.*

despotice 1. that I may tyrannize; pres. subj. 1st pers. sing. / *despotizar*. 2. that he (she/it) may tyrannize; pres. subj. 3rd pers. sing. 3. let him (her/it) tyrannize; impve. 3rd pers. sing.

despoticé I tyrannized; past 1st pers. sing. / *despotizar. despotizar*.

despoticéis that you (all) may tyrannize; pres. subj. 2nd pers. pl. / *despotizar*.

despoticemos 1. that we may tyrannize; pres. subj. 1st pers. pl. / *despotizar*. 2. let us tyrannize; impve. 1st pers. pl.

despoticen 1. that they may tyrannize; pres. subj. 3rd pers. pl. / *despotizar*. 2. let them tyrannize; impve. 3rd pers. pl.

despotices that you may tyrannize; pres. subj. 2nd pers. sing. / *despotizar*.

despotizar to tyrannize. irr.

despotricar to rant or rave. irr.

despotrique 1. that I may rant; pres. subj. 1st pers. sing. / *despotricar*. 2. that he (she/it) may rant; pres. subj. 3rd pers. sing. 3. let him (her/it) rant; impve. 3rd pers. sing.

despotriqué I ranted; past 1st pers. sing. / *despotricar*.

despotriquéis that you (all) may rant; pres. subj. 2nd pers. pl. / *despotricar*.

despotriquemos 1. that we may rant; pres. subj. 1st pers. pl. / *despotricar*. 2. let us rant; impve. 1st pers. pl.

despotriquen 1. that they may rant; pres. subj. 3rd pers. pl. / *despotricar*. 2. let them rant; impve. 3rd pers. pl.

despotriques that you may rant; pres. subj. 2nd pers. sing. / *despotricar*.

despreciándose not deigning; pres. part. / *despreciarse*.

despreciaos (you all) don't deign; impve. 2nd pers. pl. / *despreciarse*.

despreciar to despise. reg.

despreciarse to not deign. reg.

despréciate (you) don't deign; impve. 2nd pers. sing. / *despreciarse*.

despreciémonos let us not deign; impve. 1st pers. pl. / *despreciarse*.

desprecíense let them not deign; impve. 3rd pers. pl. / *despreciarse*.

desprecíese let him (her/it) not deign; impve. 3rd pers. sing. / *despreciarse*.

desprendámonos let us come loose; impve. 1st pers. pl. / *desprenderse*.

despréndanse let them come loose; impve. 3rd pers. pl. / *desprenderse*.

despréndase let him (her/it) come loose; impve. 3rd pers. sing. / *desprenderse*.

desprendeos (you all) come loose; impve. 2nd pers. pl. / *desprenderse*.

desprender to unfasten. reg.

desprenderse to come loose. reg.

despréndete (you) come loose; impve. 2nd pers. sing. / *desprenderse*.

desprendiéndose coming loose; pres. part. / *desprenderse*.

despreocupándose forgetting one's worries; pres. part. / *despreocuparse*.

despreocupaos (you all) forget your worries; impve. 2nd pers. pl. / *despreocuparse*.

despreocuparse to forget one's worries. reg.

despreocúpate (you) forget your worries; impve. 2nd pers. sing. / *despreocuparse*.

despreocupémonos let us forget our worries; impve. 1st pers. pl. / *despreocuparse*.

despreocúpense let them forget their worries; impve. 3rd pers. pl. / *despreocuparse*.

despreocúpese let him (her/it) forget his (her/its) worries; impve. 3rd pers. sing. / *despreocuparse*.

desprestigiándose losing one's reputation; pres. part. / *desprestigiarse*.

desprestigiaos (you all) lose your reputations; impve. 2nd pers. pl. / *desprestigiarse*.

desprestigiar to discredit. reg.

desprestigiarse to lose one's reputation. reg.

desprestigíate (you) lose your reputation; impve. 2nd pers. sing. / *desprestigiarse*.

desprestigiémonos let us lose our reputation; impve. 1st pers. pl. / *desprestigiarse*.

desprestigíense let them lose their reputation; impve. 3rd pers. pl. / *desprestigiarse*.

desprestigíese let him (her/it) lose his (her/its) reputation; impve. 3rd pers. sing. / *desprestigiarse*.

desproveer to deprive of provisions. reg. except for pp.

desproveído deprived of provisions; past part. / *desproveer*.

desprovisto deprived of provisions; past part. / *desproveer*.

despuebla 1. he (she/it) depopulates; pres. ind. 3rd pers. sing. / *despoblar*. 2. (you) depopulate; impve. 2nd pers. sing.

despueblan they depopulate; pres. ind. 3rd pers. pl. / *despoblar*.

despueblas you depopulate; pres. ind. 2nd pers. sing. / *despoblar*.

despueble 1. that I may depopulate; pres. subj. 1st pers. sing. / *despoblar*. 2. that he (she/it) may depopulate; pres. subj. 3rd pers. sing. 3. let him (her/it) depopulate; impve. 3rd pers. sing.

despueblen 1. that they may depopulate; pres. subj. 3rd pers. pl. / *despoblar*. 2. let them depopulate; impve. 3rd pers. pl.

despuéblense let them become depopulated; impve. 3rd pers. pl. / *despoblarse*.

despuebles that you may depopulate; pres. subj. 2nd pers. sing. / *despoblar*.

despuéblese let it become depopulated; impve. 3rd pers. sing. / *despoblarse*.

despueblo I depopulate; pres. ind. 1st pers. sing. / *despoblar*.

despuntar to blunt or to sprout. reg.

desquiciándose collapsing; pres. part. / *desquiciarse*.

desquiciaos (you all) collapse; impve. 2nd pers. pl. / *desquiciarse*.

desquiciar to unhinge or to enrage. reg.

desquiciarse to collapse. reg.

desquicíate (you) collapse; impve. 2nd pers. sing. / *desquiciarse.*

desquiciémonos let us collapse; impve. 1st pers. pl. / *desquiciarse.*

desquicíense let them collapse; impve. 3rd pers. pl. / *desquiciarse.*

desquicíese let him (her/it) collapse; impve. 3rd pers. sing. / *desquiciarse.*

desquijarándose roaring; pres. part. / *desquijararse.*

desquijaraos (you all) roar; impve. 2nd pers. pl. / *desquijararse.*

desquijarar to break the jaw of. reg.

desquijararse to roar. reg.

desquijárate (you) roar; impve. 2nd pers. sing. / *desquijararse.*

desquijarémonos let us roar; impve. 1st pers. pl. / *desquijararse.*

desquijárense let them roar; impve. 3rd pers. pl. / *desquijararse.*

desquijárese let him (her/it) roar; impve. 3rd pers. sing. / *desquijararse.*

desquilatar to alloy or to devaluate. reg.

desquitándose getting even; pres. part. / *desquitarse.*

desquitaos (you all) get even; impve. 2nd pers. pl. / *desquitarse.*

desquitar to recoup. reg.

desquitarse to get even. reg.

desquítate (you) get even; impve. 2nd pers. sing. / *desquitarse.*

desquitémonos let us get even; impve. 1st pers. pl. / *desquitarse.*

desquítense let them get even; impve. 3rd pers. pl. / *desquitarse.*

desquítese let him (her/it) get even; impve. 3rd pers. sing. / *desquitarse.*

desrice 1. that I may uncurl; pres. subj. 1st pers. sing. / *desrizar.* 2. that he (she/it) may uncurl; pres. subj. 3rd pers. sing. 3. let him (her/it) uncurl; impve. 3rd pers. sing.

desricé I uncurled; past 1st pers. sing. / *desrizar.*

desricéis that you (all) may uncurl; pres. subj. 2nd pers. pl. / *desrizar.*

desricemos 1. that we may uncurl; pres. subj. 1st pers. pl. / *desrizar.* 2. let us uncurl; impve. 1st pers. pl.

desricen 1. that they may uncurl; pres. subj. 3rd pers. pl. / *desrizar.* 2. let them uncurl; impve. 3rd pers. pl.

desrices that you may uncurl; pres. subj. 2nd pers. sing. / *desrizar.*

desrielándose jumping the track; pres. part. / *desrielarse.*

desrielaos (you all) jump the track; impve. 2nd pers. pl. / *desrielarse.*

desrielarse to jump the track. reg.

desriélate (you) jump the track; impve. 2nd pers. sing. / *desrielarse.*

desrielémonos let us jump the track; impve. 1st pers. pl. / *desrielarse.*

desriélense let them jump the track; impve. 3rd pers. pl. / *desrielarse.*

desriélese let him (her/it) jump the track; impve. 3rd pers. sing. / *desrielarse.*

desrizar to uncurl. irr.

destacándose excelling; pres. part. / *destacarse.*

destacaos (you all) excel; impve. 2nd pers. pl. / *destacarse.*

destacar to detach. irr.

destacarse to excel. irr.

destácate (you) excel; impve. 2nd pers. sing. / *destacarse.*

destajar to let out work on piece rate or to cut (cards). reg.

destapándose getting uncovered; pres. part. / *destaparse.*

destapaos (you all) get uncovered; impve. 2nd pers. pl. / *destaparse.*

destapar to uncover. reg.

destaparse to get uncovered. reg.

destápate (you) get uncovered; impve. 2nd pers. sing. / *destaparse.*

destapémonos let us get uncovered; impve. 1st pers. pl. / *destaparse.*

destápense let them get uncovered; impve. 3rd pers. pl. / *destaparse.*

destápese let him (her/it) get uncovered; impve. 3rd pers. sing. / *destaparse.*

destaponar to uncork. reg.

destaque 1. that I may detach; pres. subj. 1st pers. sing. / *destacar.* 2. that he (she/it) may detach; pres. subj. 3rd pers. sing. 3. let him (her/it) detach; impve. 3rd pers. sing.

destaqué I detached; past 1st pers. sing. / *destacar.*

destaquéis that you (all) may detach; pres. subj. 2nd pers. pl. / *destacar.*

destaquémonos let us excel; impve. 1st pers. pl. / *destacarse.*

destaquemos 1. that we may detach; pres. subj. 1st pers. pl. / *destacar.* 2. let us detach; impve. 1st pers. pl.

destaquen 1. that they may detach; pres. subj. 3rd pers. pl. / *destacar.* 2. let them detach; impve. 3rd pers. pl.

destáquense let them excel; impve. 3rd pers. pl. / *destacarse.*

destaques that you may detach; pres. subj. 2nd pers. sing. / *destacar.*

destáquese let him (her/it) excel; impve. 3rd pers. sing. / *destacarse.*

destejer to unweave or to upset. reg.

destellar to flash or sparkle. reg.

destemplándose being indisposed; pres. part. / *destemplarse.*

destemplaos (you all) be indisposed; impve. 2nd pers. pl. / *destemplarse.*

destemplar to distemper or to put out of tune. reg.

destemplarse to be indisposed. reg.

destémplate (you) be indisposed; impve. 2nd pers. sing. / *destemplarse.*

destemplémonos let us be indisposed; impve. 1st pers. pl. / *destemplarse.*

destémplense let them be indisposed; impve. 3rd pers. pl. / *destemplarse.*

destémplese let him (her/it) be indisposed; impve. 3rd pers. sing. / *destemplarse.*

desteñir to fade. irr.

desteñirse to become discolored. irr.

desternillándose splitting one's sides with laughter; pres. part. / *desternillarse.*

desternillaos (you all) split your sides with laughter; impve. 2nd pers. pl. / *desternillarse.*

desternillarse to split one's sides with laughter. reg.

desterníllate (you) split your sides with laughter; impve. 2nd pers. sing. / *desternillarse.*

desternillémonos let us split our sides with laughter; impve. 1st pers. pl. / *desternillarse.*

desterníllense let them split their sides with laughter; impve. 3rd pers. pl. / *desternillarse.*

desterníllese let him (her/it) split his (her/its) sides with laughter; impve. 3rd pers. sing. / *desternillarse.*

desterrar to exile. irr.

destetar to wean. reg.

destierra 1. he (she/it) exiles; pres. ind. 3rd pers. sing. / *desterrar.* 2. (you) exile; impve. 2nd pers. sing.

destierran they exile; pres. ind. 3rd pers. pl. / *desterrar.*

destierras you exile; pres. ind. 2nd pers. sing. / *desterrar.*

destierre 1. that I may exile; pres. subj. 1st pers. sing. / *desterrar.* 2. that he (she/it) may exile; pres. subj. 3rd pers. sing. 3. let him (her/it) exile; impve. 3rd pers. sing.

destierren 1. that they may exile; pres. subj. 3rd pers. pl. / *desterrar.* 2. let them exile; impve. 3rd pers. pl.

destierres that you may exile; pres. subj. 2nd pers. sing. / *desterrar.*

destierro I exile; pres. ind. 1st pers. sing. / *desterrar.*

destilándose dripping; pres. part. / *destilarse.*

destilaos (you all) drip; impve. 2nd pers. pl. / *destilarse.*

destilar to distil. reg.

destilarse to drip. reg.

destílate (you) drip ; impve. 2nd pers. sing. / *destilarse.*

destilémonos let us drip; impve. 1st pers. pl. / *destilarse.*

destílense let them drip; impve. 3rd pers. pl. / *destilarse.*

destílese let him (her/it) drip; impve. 3rd pers. sing. / *destilarse.*

destinar to destine or to designate. reg.

destiña 1. that I may fade; pres. subj. 1st pers. sing. / *desteñir.* 2. that he (she/it) may fade; pres. subj. 3rd pers. sing. 3. let him (her/it) fade; impve. 3rd pers. sing.

destiñáis that you (all) may fade; pres. subj. 2nd pers. pl. / *desteñir.*

destiñamos 1. that we may fade; pres. subj. 1st pers. pl. / *desteñir.* 2. let us fade; impve. 1st pers. pl.

destiñan 1. that they may fade; pres. subj. 3rd pers. pl. / *desteñir.* 2. let them fade; impve. 3rd pers. pl.

destíñanse let them become discolored; impve. 3rd pers. pl. / *desteñirse.*

destiñas that you may fade; pres. subj. 2nd pers. sing. / *desteñir.*

destíñase let it become discolored; impve. 3rd pers. sing. / *desteñirse.*

destiñe 1. he (she/it) fades; pres. ind. 3rd pers. sing. / *desteñir.* 2. (you) fade; impve. 2nd pers. sing.

destiñen they fade; pres. ind. 3rd pers. pl. / *desteñir.*

destiñendo fading; pres. part. / *desteñir.*

destiñéndose becoming discolored; pres. part. / *desteñirse.*

destiñera 1. that I might fade; imp. subj. 1st pers. sing. / *desteñir.* 2. that he (she/it) might fade; imp. subj. 3rd pers. sing.

destiñerais that you (all) might fade; imp. subj. 2nd pers pl. / *desteñir.*

destiñéramos that we might fade; imp. subj. 1st pers. pl. / *desteñir.*

destiñeran that they might fade; imp. subj. 3rd pers. pl. / *desteñir.*

destiñeras that you might fade; imp. subj. 2nd pers. sing. / *desteñir.*

destiñeron they faded; past 3rd pers. pl. / *desteñir.*

destiñes you fade; pres. ind. 2nd pers. sing. / *desteñir.*

destiñese 1. that I might fade; imp. subj. 1st pers. sing. / *desteñir.* 2. that he (she/it) might fade; imp. subj. 3rd pers. sing.

destiñeseis that you (all) might fade; imp. subj. 2nd pers pl. / *desteñir.*

destiñésemos that we might fade; imp. subj. 1st pers. pl. / *desteñir.*

destiñesen that they might fade; imp. subj. 3rd pers. pl. / *desteñir.*

destiñeses that you might fade; imp. subj. 2nd pers. sing. / *desteñir.*

destiño I fade; pres. ind. 1st pers. sing. / *desteñir.*

destiñó he (she/it) faded; past 3rd pers. sing. / *desteñir.*

destituir to deprive. irr.

destituya 1. that I may deprive; pres. subj. 1st pers. sing. / *destituir.* 2. that he (she/it) may deprive; pres. subj. 3rd pers. sing. 3. let him (her/it) deprive; impve. 3rd pers. sing.

destituyáis that you (all) may deprive; pres. subj. 2nd pers. pl. / *destituir.*

destituyamos 1. that we may deprive; pres. subj. 1st pers. pl. / *destituir.* 2. let us deprive; impve. 1st pers. pl.

destituyan 1. that they may deprive; pres. subj. 3rd pers. pl. / *destituir.* 2. let them deprive; impve. 3rd pers. pl.

destituyas that you may deprive; pres. subj. 2nd pers. sing. / *destituir.*

destituye 1. he (she/it) deprives; pres. ind. 3rd pers. sing. / *destituir.* 2. (you) deprive; impve. 2nd pers. sing.

destituyen they deprive; pres. ind. 3rd pers. pl. / *destituir.*

destituyendo depriving; pres. part. / *destituir.*

destituyera 1. that I might deprive; imp. subj. 1st pers. sing. / *destituir.* 2. that he (she/it) might deprive; imp. subj. 3rd pers. sing.

destituyerais that you (all) might deprive; imp. subj. 2nd pers pl. / *destituir.*

destituyéramos that we might deprive; imp. subj. 1st pers. pl. / *destituir.*

destituyeran that they might deprive; imp. subj. 3rd pers. pl. / *destituir.*

destituyeras that you might deprive; imp. subj. 2nd pers. sing. / *destituir.*

destituyeron they deprived; past 3rd pers. pl. / *destituir.*

destituyes you deprive; pres. ind. 2nd pers. sing. / *destituir.*

destituyese 1. that I might deprive; imp. subj. 1st pers. sing. / *destituir.* 2. that he (she/it) might deprive; imp. subj. 3rd pers. sing.

destituyeseis that you (all) might deprive; imp. subj. 2nd pers pl. / *destituir.*

destituyésemos that we might deprive; imp. subj. 1st pers. pl. / *destituir.*

destituyesen that they might deprive; imp. subj. 3rd pers. pl. / *destituir.*

destituyeses that you might deprive; imp. subj. 2nd pers. sing. / *destituir.*

destituyo I deprive; pres. ind. 1st pers. sing. / *destituir.*

destituyó he (she/it) deprived; past 3rd pers. sing. / *destituir.*

destocar to remove the headgear of. irr.

destoque 1. that I may remove the headgear of; pres. subj. 1st pers. sing. / *destocar.* 2. that he (she/it) may remove the head gear of; pres. subj. 3rd pers. sing. 3. let him (her/it) remove the headgear of; impve. 3rd pers. sing.

destoqué I removed the headgear of; past 1st pers. sing. / *destocar.*

destoquéis that you (all) may remove the headgear of; pres. subj. 2nd pers. pl. / *destocar.*

destoquemos 1. that we may remove the headgear of; pres. subj. 1st pers. pl. / *destocar.* 2. let us remove the headgear of; impve. 1st pers. pl.

destoquen 1. that they may remove the headgear of; pres. subj. 3rd pers. pl. / *destocar.* 2. let them remove the headgear of; impve. 3rd pers. pl.

destoques that you may remove the headgear of; pres. subj. 2nd pers. sing. / *destocar.*

destorcer to untwist. irr.

destornillándose acting foolishly; pres. part. / *destornillarse.*

destornillaos (you all) act foolishly; impve. 2nd pers. pl. / *destornillarse.*

destornillar to unscrew. reg.

destornillarse to act foolishly. reg.

destorníllate (you) act foolishly; impve. 2nd pers. sing. / *destornillarse.*

destornillémonos let us act foolishly; impve. 1st pers. pl. / *destornillarse.*

destorníllense let them act foolishly; impve. 3rd pers. pl. / *destornillarse.*

destorníllese let him (her/it) act foolishly; impve. 3rd pers. sing. / *destornillarse.*

destorzáis that you (all) may untwist; pres. subj. 2nd pers. pl. / *destorcer.*

destorzamos 1. that we may untwist; pres. subj. 1st pers. pl. / *destorcer.* 2. let us untwist; impve. 1st pers. pl.

destrabar to unlock. reg.

destrejar to act with dexterity. reg.

destrence 1. that I may unbraid; pres. subj. 1st pers. sing. / *destrenzar.* 2. that he (she/it) may unbraid; pres. subj. 3rd pers. sing. 3. let him (her/it) unbraid; impve. 3rd pers. sing.

destrencé I unbraided; past 1st pers. sing. / *destrenzar.*

destrencéis that you (all) may unbraid; pres. subj. 2nd pers. pl. / *destrenzar.*

destrencemos 1. that we may unbraid; pres. subj. 1st pers. pl. / *destrenzar.* 2. let us unbraid; impve. 1st pers. pl.

destrencen 1. that they may unbraid; pres. subj. 3rd pers. pl. / *destrenzar.* 2. let them unbraid; impve. 3rd pers. pl.

destrences that you may unbraid; pres. subj. 2nd pers. sing. / *destrenzar.*

destrenzar to unbraid. irr.

destrice 1. that I may tear to shreds; pres. subj. 1st pers. sing. / *destrizar.* 2. that he (she/it) may tear to shreds; pres. subj. 3rd pers. sing. 3. let him (her/it) tear to shreds; impve. 3rd pers. sing.

destricé I tore to shreds; past 1st pers. sing. / *destrizar.*

destricéis that you (all) may tear to shreds; pres. subj. 2nd pers. pl. / *destrizar.*

destricémonos let us go to pieces; impve. 1st pers. pl. / *destrizarse.*

destricemos 1. that we may tear to shreds; pres. subj. 1st pers. pl. / *destrizar.* 2. let us tear to shreds; impve. 1st pers. pl.

destricen 1. that they may tear to shreds; pres. subj. 3rd pers. pl. / *destrizar.* 2. let them tear to shreds; impve. 3rd pers. pl.

destrícense let them go to pieces; impve. 3rd pers. pl. / *destrizarse.*

destrices that you may tear to shreds; pres. subj. 2nd pers. sing. / *destrizar.*

destrícese let him (her/it) go to pieces; impve. 3rd pers. sing. / *destrizarse.*

destripar to disembowel. reg.

destrizándose going to pieces; pres. part. / *destrizarse.*

destrizaos (you all) go to pieces; impve. 2nd pers. pl. / *destrizarse.*

destrizar to tear to shreds. irr.

destrizarse to go to pieces. irr.

destrízate (you) go to pieces; impve. 2nd pers. sing. / *destrizarse.*

destroce 1. that I may destroy; pres. subj. 1st pers. sing. / *destrozar*. 2. that he (she/it) may destroy; pres. subj. 3rd pers. sing. 3. let him (her/it) destroy; impve. 3rd pers. sing.

destrocé I destroyed; past 1st pers. sing. / *destrozar*.

destrocéis that you (all) may destroy; pres. subj. 2nd pers. pl. / *destrozar*.

destrocemos 1. that we may destroy; pres. subj. 1st pers. pl. / *destrozar*. 2. let us destroy; impve. 1st pers. pl.

destrocen 1. that they may destroy; pres. subj. 3rd pers. pl. / *destrozar*. 2. let them destroy; impve. 3rd pers. pl.

destroces that you may destroy; pres. subj. 2nd pers. sing. / *destrozar*.

destronar to dethrone. reg.

destroncándose coming apart; pres. part. / *destroncarse*.

destroncaos (you all) come apart; impve. 2nd pers. pl. / *destroncarse*.

destroncar to lop off. irr.

destroncarse to come apart. irr.

destróncate (you) come apart; impve. 2nd pers. sing. / *destroncarse*.

destronque 1. that I may lop off; pres. subj. 1st pers. sing. / *destroncar*. 2. that he (she/it) may lop off; pres. subj. 3rd pers. sing. 3. let him (her/it) lop off; impve. 3rd pers. sing.

destronqué I lopped off; past 1st pers. sing. / *destroncar*.

destronquéis that you (all) may lop off; pres. subj. 2nd pers. pl. / *destroncar*.

destronquémonos let us come apart; impve. 1st pers. pl. / *destroncarse*.

destronquemos 1. that we may lop off; pres. subj. 1st pers. pl. / *destroncar*. 2. let us lop off; impve. 1st pers. pl.

destronquen 1. that they may lop off; pres. subj. 3rd pers. pl. / *destroncar*. 2. let them lop off; impve. 3rd pers. pl.

destrónquense let them come apart; impve. 3rd pers. pl. / *destroncarse*.

destronques that you may lop off; pres. subj. 2nd pers. sing. / *destroncar*.

destrónquese let him (her/it) come apart; impve. 3rd pers. sing. / *destroncarse*.

destrozar to destroy. irr.

destruíos (you all) cancel out (math); impve. 2nd pers. pl. / *destruirse*.

destruir to destroy. irr.

destruirse to cancel out (math). irr.

destruya 1. that I may destroy; pres. subj. 1st pers. sing. / *destruir*. 2. that he (she/it) may destroy; pres. subj. 3rd pers. sing. 3. let him (her/it) destroy; impve. 3rd pers. sing.

destruyáis that you (all) may destroy; pres. subj. 2nd pers. pl. / *destruir*.

destruyámonos let us cancel out (math); impve. 1st pers. pl. / *destruirse*.

destruyamos 1. that we may destroy; pres. subj. 1st pers. pl. / *destruir*. 2. let us destroy; impve. 1st pers. pl.

destruyan 1. that they may destroy; pres. subj. 3rd pers. pl. / *destruir*. 2. let them destroy; impve. 3rd pers. pl.

destrúyanse let them cancel out (math); impve. 3rd pers. pl. / *destruirse*.

destruyas that you may destroy; pres. subj. 2nd pers. sing. / *destruir*.

destrúyase let him (her/it) cancel out (math); impve. 3rd pers. sing. / *destruirse*.

destruye 1. he (she/it) destroys; pres. ind. 3rd pers. sing. / *destruir*. 2. (you) destroy; impve. 2nd pers. sing.

destruyen they destroy; pres. ind. 3rd pers. pl. / *destruir*.

destruyendo destroying; pres. part. / *destruir*.

destruyéndose canceling out (math); pres. part. / *destruirse*.

destruyera 1. that I might destroy; imp. subj. 1st pers. sing. / *destruir*. 2. that he (she/it) might destroy; imp. subj. 3rd pers. sing.

destruyerais that you (all) might destroy; imp. subj. 2nd pers pl. / *destruir*.

destruyéramos that we might destroy; imp. subj. 1st pers. pl. / *destruir*.

destruyeran that they might destroy; imp. subj. 3rd pers. pl. / *destruir*.

destruyeras that you might destroy; imp. subj. 2nd pers. sing. / *destruir*.

destruyeron they destroyed; past 3rd pers. pl. / *destruir*.

destruyes you destroy; pres. ind. 2nd pers. sing. / *destruir*.

destruyese 1. that I might destroy; imp. subj. 1st pers. sing. / *destruir*. 2. that he (she/it) might destroy; imp. subj. 3rd pers. sing.

destruyeseis that you (all) might destroy; imp. subj. 2nd pers pl. / *destruir*.

destruyésemos that we might destroy; imp. subj. 1st pers. pl. / *destruir*.

destruyesen that they might destroy; imp. subj. 3rd pers. pl. / *destruir*.

destruyeses that you might destroy; imp. subj. 2nd pers. sing. / *destruir*.

destrúyete (you) cancel out (math); impve. 2nd pers. sing. / *destruirse*.

destruyo I destroy; pres. ind. 1st pers. sing. / *destruir*.

destruyó he (she/it) destroyed; past 3rd pers. sing. / *destruir*.

destuerce 1. he (she/it) untwists; pres. ind. 3rd pers. sing. / *destorcer*. 2. (you) untwist; impve. 2nd pers. sing.

destuercen they untwist; pres. ind. 3rd pers. pl. / *destorcer*.

destuerces you untwist; pres. ind. 2nd pers. sing. / *destorcer*.

destuerza 1. that I may untwist; pres. subj. 1st pers. sing. / *destorcer.* 2. that he (she/it) may untwist; pres. subj. 3rd pers. sing. 3. let him (her/it) untwist; impve. 3rd pers. sing.

destuerzan 1. that they may untwist; pres. subj. 3rd pers. pl. / *destorcer.* 2. let them untwist; impve. 3rd pers. pl.

destuerzas that you may untwist; pres. subj. 2nd pers. sing. / *destorcer.*

destuerzo I untwist; pres. ind. 1st pers. sing. / *destorcer.*

destusar to husk (corn). reg.

desudar to wipe the sweat off. reg.

desuela 1. he (she/it) desolates; pres. ind. 3rd pers. sing. / *desolar.* 2. (you) desolate; impve. 2nd pers. sing.

desuelan they desolate; pres. ind. 3rd pers. pl. / *desolar.*

desuelas you desolate; pres. ind. 2nd pers. sing. / *desolar.*

desuélate (you) grieve; impve. 2nd pers. sing. / *desolarse.*

desuele 1. that I may desolate; pres. subj. 1st pers. sing. / *desolar.* 2. that he (she/it) may desolate; pres. subj. 3rd pers. sing. 3. let him (her/it) desolate; impve. 3rd pers. sing.

desuelen 1. that they may desolate; pres. subj. 3rd pers. pl. / *desolar.* 2. let them desolate; impve. 3rd pers. pl.

desuélense let them grieve; impve. 3rd pers. pl. / *desolarse.*

desueles that you may desolate; pres. subj. 2nd pers. sing. / *desolar.*

desuélese let him (her/it) grieve; impve. 3rd pers. sing. / *desolarse.*

desuelo I desolate; pres. ind. 1st pers. sing. / *desolar.*

desuella 1. he (she/it) skins; pres. ind. 3rd pers. sing. / *desollar.* 2. (you) skin; impve. 2nd pers. sing.

desuellan they skin; pres. ind. 3rd pers. pl. / *desollar.*

desuellas you skin; pres. ind. 2nd pers. sing. / *desollar.*

desuelle 1. that I may skin; pres. subj. 1st pers. sing. / *desollar.* 2. that he (she/it) may skin; pres. subj. 3rd pers. sing. 3. let him (her/it) skin; impve. 3rd pers. sing.

desuellen 1. that they may skin; pres. subj. 3rd pers. pl. / *desollar.* 2. let them skin; impve. 3rd pers. pl.

desuelles that you may skin; pres. subj. 2nd pers. sing. / *desollar.*

desuello I skin; pres. ind. 1st pers. sing. / *desollar.*

desunámonos let us fall apart; impve. 1st pers. pl. / *desunirse.*

desúnanse let them fall apart; impve. 3rd pers. pl. / *desunirse.*

desúnase let him (her/it) fall apart; impve. 3rd pers. sing. / *desunirse.*

desuncir to unyoke. irr.

desúnete (you) fall apart; impve. 2nd pers. sing. / *desunirse.*

desuniéndose falling apart; pres. part. / *desunirse.*

desuníos (you all) fall apart; impve. 2nd pers. pl. / *desunirse.*

desunir to disunite. reg.

desunirse to fall apart. reg.

desunza 1. that I may unyoke; pres. subj. 1st pers. sing. / *desuncir.* 2. that he (she/it) may unyoke; pres. subj. 3rd pers. sing. 3. let him (her/it) unyoke; impve. 3rd pers. sing.

desunzáis that you (all) may unyoke; pres. subj. 2nd pers. pl. / *desuncir.*

desunzamos 1. that we may unyoke; pres. subj. 1st pers. pl. / *desuncir.* 2. let us unyoke; impve. 1st pers. pl.

desunzan 1. that they may unyoke; pres. subj. 3rd pers. pl. / *desuncir.* 2. let them unyoke; impve. 3rd pers. pl.

desunzas that you may unyoke; pres. subj. 2nd pers. sing. / *desuncir.*

desunzo I unyoke; pres. ind. 1st pers. sing. / *desuncir.*

desusándose becoming unused; pres. part. / *desusarse.*

desusaos (you all) become unused; impve. 2nd pers. pl. / *desusarse.*

desusar to disuse. reg.

desusarse to become unused. reg.

desúsate (you) become unused; impve. 2nd pers. sing. / *desusarse.*

desusémonos let us become unused; impve. 1st pers. pl. / *desusarse.*

desúsense let them become unused; impve. 3rd pers. pl. / *desusarse.*

desúsese let him (her/it) become unused; impve. 3rd pers. sing. / *desusarse.*

desvainar to shell (vegetables). reg.

desvalijar to steal (from a bag). reg.

desvalorar to devalue. reg.

desvalorice 1. that I may devaluate; pres. subj. 1st pers. sing. / *desvalorizar.* 2. that he (she/it) may devaluate; pres. subj. pres. subj. 3rd pers. sing. 3rd pers. sing; impve. 3rd pers. sing.

desvaloricé I devaluated; past 1st pers. sing.; past 1st pers. sing. / *desvalorizar.*

desvaloricéis that you (all) may devaluate; pres. subj. 2nd pers. pl. / *desvalorizar.*

desvaloricemos 1. that we may devaluate; pres. subj. 1st pers. pl. / *desvalorizar.* 2. let us devaluate; impve. 1st pers. pl.

desvaloricen 1. that they may devaluate; pres. subj. 3rd pers. pl. / *desvalorizar.* 2. let them devaluate; impve. 3rd pers. pl.

desvalorices that you may devaluate; pres. subj. 2nd pers. sing. / *desvalorizar.*

desvalorizar to devalue. irr.

desvaneceos (you all) disappear; impve. 2nd pers. pl. / *desvanecerse.*

desvanecer to fade. irr.

desvanecerse to disappear. irr.

desvanécete (you) disappear; impve. 2nd pers. sing. / *desvanecerse.*

desvaneciéndose disappearing; pres. part. / *desvanecerse.*

desvanezca 1. that I may fade; pres. subj. 1st pers. sing. / *desvanecer.* 2. that he (she/it) may fade; pres. subj. 3rd pers. sing. 3. let him (her/it) fade; impve. 3rd pers. sing.

desvanezcáis that you (all) may fade; pres. subj. 2nd pers. pl. / *desvanecer.*

desvanezcámonos let us disappear; impve. 1st pers. pl. / *desvanecerse.*

desvanezcamos 1. that we may fade; pres. subj. 1st pers. pl. / *desvanecer.* 2. let us fade; impve. 1st pers. pl.

desvanezcan 1. that they may fade; pres. subj. 3rd pers. pl. / *desvanecer.* 2. let them fade; impve. 3rd pers. pl.

desvanézcanse let them disappear; impve. 3rd pers. pl. / *desvanecerse.*

desvanezcas that you may fade; pres. subj. 2nd pers. sing. / *desvanecer.*

desvanézcase let him (her/it) disappear; impve. 3rd pers. sing. / *desvanecerse.*

desvanezco I fade; pres. ind. 1st pers. sing. / *desvanecer.*

desvarar to slip. reg.

desvaría 1. he (she/it) raves; pres. ind. 3rd pers. sing. / *desvariar.* 2. (you) rave; impve. 2nd pers. sing.

desvarían they rave; pres. ind. 3rd pers. pl. / *desvariar.*

desvariar to rave. irr.

desvarías you rave; pres. ind. 2nd pers. sing. / *desvariar.*

desvaríe 1. that I may rave; pres. subj. 1st pers. sing. / *desvariar.* 2. that he (she/it) may rave; pres. subj. 3rd pers. sing. 3. let him (her/it) rave; impve. 3rd pers. sing.

desvaríen 1. that they may rave; pres. subj. 3rd pers. pl. / *desvariar.* 2. let them rave; impve. 3rd pers. pl.

desvaríes that you may rave; pres. subj. 2nd pers. sing. / *desvariar.*

desvarío I rave; pres. ind. 1st pers. sing. / *desvariar.*

desvedar to remove a restriction from. reg.

desvelándose staying awake; pres. part. / *desvelarse.*

desvelaos (you all) stay awake; impve. 2nd pers. pl. / *desvelarse.*

desvelar to keep awake. reg.

desvelarse to stay awake. reg.

desvélate (you) stay awake; impve. 2nd pers. sing. / *desvelarse.*

desvelémonos let us stay awake; impve. 1st pers. pl. / *desvelarse.*

desvélense let them stay awake; impve. 3rd pers. pl. / *desvelarse.*

desvélese let him (her/it) stay awake; impve. 3rd pers. sing. / *desvelarse.*

desvencijándose falling apart; pres. part. / *desvencijarse.*

desvencijaos (you all) fall apart; impve. 2nd pers. pl. / *desvencijarse.*

desvencijar to loosen. reg.

desvencijarse to fall apart. reg.

desvencíjate (you) fall apart; impve. 2nd pers. sing. / *desvencijarse.*

desvencijémonos let us fall apart; impve. 1st pers. pl. / *desvencijarse.*

desvencíjense let them fall apart; impve. 3rd pers. pl. / *desvencijarse.*

desvencíjese let him (her/it) fall apart; impve. 3rd pers. sing. / *desvencijarse.*

desvendar to unbandage. reg.

desvergoncé I was shameless; past 1st pers. sing. / *desvergonzarse.*

desvergoncéis that you (all) may be shameless; pres. subj. 2nd pers. pl. / *desvergonzarse.*

desvergoncémonos let us be shameless; impve. 1st pers. pl. / *desvergonzarse.*

desvergoncemos that we may be shameless; pres. subj. 1st pers. pl. / *desvergonzarse.*

desvergonzarse to be shameless. irr.

desverguence 1. that I may be shameless; pres. subj. 1st pers. sing. / *desvergonzarse.* 2. that he (she/it) may be shameless; pres. subj. 3rd pers. sing.

desverguencen that they may be shameless; pres. subj. 3rd pers. pl. / *desvergonzarse.*

desverguéncense let them be shameless; impve. 3rd pers. pl. / *desvergonzarse.*

desverguences that you may be shameless; pres. subj. 2nd pers. sing. / *desvergonzarse.*

desverguéncese let him (her/it) be shameless; impve. 3rd pers. sing. / *desvergonzarse.*

desverguenza he (she/it) is shameless; pres. ind. 3rd pers. sing. / *desvergonzarse.*

desverguenzan they are shameless; pres. ind. 3rd pers. pl. / *desvergonzarse.*

desverguenzas you are shameless; pres. ind. 2nd pers. sing. / *desvergonzarse.*

desverguénzate (you) be shameless; impve. 2nd pers. sing. / *desvergonzarse.*

desverguenzo I am shameless; pres. ind. 1st pers. sing. / *desvergonzarse.*

desvestíos (you all) undress; impve. 2nd pers. pl. / *desvestirse.*

desvestir to undress. irr.

desvestirse to undress. irr.

desvía 1. he (she/it) deviates; pres. ind. 3rd pers. sing. / *desviar.* 2. (you) deviate; impve. 2nd pers. sing.

desvían they deviate; pres. ind. 3rd pers. pl. / *desviar.*

desviándose changing direction; pres. part. / *desviarse.*

desviaos (you all) change direction; impve. 2nd pers. pl. / *desviarse.*

desviar to deviate. irr.

desviarse to change direction. irr.

desvías you deviate; pres. ind. 2nd pers. sing. / *desviar.*

desvíate (you) change direction; impve. 2nd pers. sing. / *desviarse.*

desvíe 1. that I may deviate; pres. subj. 1st pers. sing. / *desviar*. 2. that he (she/it) may deviate; pres. subj. 3rd pers. sing. 3. let him (her/it) deviate; impve. 3rd pers. sing.

desviémonos let us change direction; impve. 1st pers. pl. / *desviarse*.

desvíen 1. that they may deviate; pres. subj. 3rd pers. pl. / *desviar*. 2. let them deviate; impve. 3rd pers. pl.

desvíense let them change direction; impve. 3rd pers. pl. / *desviarse*.

desvíes that you may deviate; pres. subj. 2nd pers. sing. / *desviar*.

desvíese let him (her/it) change direction; impve. 3rd pers. sing. / *desviarse*.

desvío I deviate; pres. ind. 1st pers. sing. / *desviar*.

desvirgar to deflower. irr.

desvirgue 1. that I may deflower; pres. subj. 1st pers. sing. / *desvirgar*. 2. that he (she/it) may deflower; pres. subj. 3rd pers. sing. 3. let him (her/it) deflower; impve. 3rd pers. sing.

desvirgué I deflowered; past 1st pers. sing. / *desvirgar*.

desvirguéis that you (all) may deflower; pres. subj. 2nd pers. pl. / *desvirgar*.

desvirguemos 1. that we may deflower; pres. subj. 1st pers. pl. / *desvirgar*. 2. let us deflower; impve. 1st pers. pl.

desvirguen 1. that they may deflower; pres. subj. 3rd pers. pl. / *desvirgar*. 2. let them deflower; impve. 3rd pers. pl.

desvirgues that you may deflower; pres. subj. 2nd pers. sing. / *desvirgar*.

desvirtúa 1. he (she/it) detracts from; pres. ind. 3rd pers. sing. / *desvirtuar*. 2. (you) detract from; impve. 2nd pers. sing.

desvirtúan they detract from; pres. ind. 3rd pers. pl. / *desvirtuar*.

desvirtuándose losing strength; pres. part. / *desvirtuarse*.

desvirtuaos (you all) lose strength; impve. 2nd pers. pl. / *desvirtuarse*.

desvirtuar to detract from. irr.

desvirtuarse to lose strength. irr.

desvirtúas you detract from; pres. ind. 2nd pers. sing. / *desvirtuar*.

desvirtúate (you) lose strength; impve. 2nd pers. sing. / *desvirtuarse*.

desvirtúe 1. that I may detract from; pres. subj. 1st pers. sing. / *desvirtuar*. 2. that he (she/it) may detract from; pres. subj. 3rd pers. sing. 3. let him (her/it) detract from; impve. 3rd pers. sing.

desvirtuémonos let us lose strength; impve. 1st pers. pl. / *desvirtuarse*.

desvirtúen 1. that they may detract from; pres. subj. 3rd pers. pl. / *desvirtuar*. 2. let them detract from; impve. 3rd pers. pl.

desvirtúense let them lose strength; impve. 3rd pers. pl. / *desvirtuarse*.

desvirtúes that you may detract from; pres. subj. 2nd pers. sing. / *desvirtuar*.

desvirtúese let him (her/it) lose strength; impve. 3rd pers. sing. / *desvirtuarse*.

desvirtúo I detract from; pres. ind. 1st pers. sing. / *desvirtuar*.

desvista 1. that I may undress; pres. subj. 1st pers. sing. / *desvestir*. 2. that he (she/it) may undress; pres. subj. 3rd pers. sing. 3. let him (her/it) undress; impve. 3rd pers. sing.

desvistáis that you (all) may undress; pres. subj. 2nd pers. pl. / *desvestir*.

desvistámonos let us undress; impve. 1st pers. pl. / *desvestirse*.

desvistamos 1. that we may undress; pres. subj. 1st pers. pl. / *desvestir*. 2. let us undress; impve. 1st pers. pl.

desvistan 1. that they may undress; pres. subj. 3rd pers. pl. / *desvestir*. 2. let them undress; impve. 3rd pers. pl.

desvístanse let them undress; impve. 3rd pers. pl. / *desvestirse*.

desvistas that you may undress; pres. subj. 2nd pers. sing. / *desvestir*.

desvístase let him (her/it) undress; impve. 3rd pers. sing. / *desvestir*.

desviste 1. he (she/it) undresses; pres. ind. 3rd pers. sing. / *desvestir*. 2. (you) undress; impve. 2nd pers. sing.

desvisten they undress; pres. ind. 3rd pers. pl. / *desvestir*.

desvistes you undress; pres. ind. 2nd pers. sing. / *desvestir*.

desvístete (you) undress; impve. 2nd pers. sing. / *desvestirse*.

desvistiendo undressing; pres. part. / *desvestir*.

desvistiéndose undressing; pres. part. / *desvestirse*.

desvistiera 1. that I might undress; imp. subj. 1st pers. sing. / *desvestir*. 2. that he (she/it) might undress; imp. subj. 3rd pers. sing.

desvistierais that you (all) might undress; imp. subj. 2nd pers pl. / *desvestir*.

desvistiéramos that we might undress; imp. subj. 1st pers. pl. / *desvestir*.

desvistieran that they might undress; imp. subj. 3rd pers. pl. / *desvestir*.

desvistieras that you might undress; imp. subj. 2nd pers. sing. / *desvestir*.

desvistieron they undressed; past 3rd pers. pl. / *desvestir*.

desvistiese 1. that I might undress; imp. subj. 1st pers. sing. / *desvestir*. 2. that he (she/it) might undress; imp. subj. 3rd pers. sing.

desvistieseis that you (all) might undress; imp. subj. 2nd pers pl. / *desvestir*.

desvistiésemos that we might undress; imp. subj. 1st pers. pl. / *desvestir*.

desvistiesen that they might undress; imp. subj. 3rd pers. pl. / *desvestir*.

desvistieses that you might undress; imp. subj. 2nd pers. sing. / *desvestir*.

desvistió he (she/it) undressed; past 3rd pers. sing. / *desvestir*.

desvisto I undress; pres. ind. 1st pers. sing. / *desvestir.*

desvivámonos let us long for; impve. 1st pers. pl. / *desvivirse.*

desvívanse let them long for; impve. 3rd pers. pl. / *desvivirse.*

desvívase let him (her/it) long for; impve. 3rd pers. sing. / *desvivirse.*

desvívete (you) long for; impve. 2nd pers. sing. / *desvivirse.*

desviviéndose longing for; pres. part. / *desvivirse.*

desvivíos (you all) long for; impve. 2nd pers. pl. / *desvivirse.*

desvivirse to long for. reg.

desvolver to change the shape of. irr.

desvuelto changed the shape of; past part. / *desvolver.*

desvuelva 1. that I may change the shape of; pres. subj. 1st pers. sing. / *desvolver.* 2. that he (she/it) may change the shape of; pres. subj. 3rd pers. sing. 3. let him (her/it) change the shape of; impve. 3rd pers. sing.

desvuelvan 1. that they may change the shape of; pres. subj. 3rd pers. pl. / *desvolver.* 2. let them change the shape of; impve. 3rd pers. pl.

desvuelvas that you may change the shape of; pres. subj. 2nd pers. sing. / *desvolver.*

desvuelve 1. he (she/it) changes the shape of; pres. ind. 3rd pers. sing. / *desvolver.* 2. (you) change the shape of; impve. 2nd pers. sing.

desvuelven they change the shape of; pres. ind. 3rd pers. pl. / *desvolver.*

desvuelves you change the shape of; pres. ind. 2nd pers. sing. / *desvolver.*

desvuelvo I change the shape of; pres. ind. 1st pers. sing. / *desvolver.*

desyerbar to weed. reg.

detallar to detail or to retail. reg.

detectar to detect. reg.

deten (you) detain; impve. 2nd pers. sing. / *detener.*

detendrá he (she/it) will detain; fut. 3rd pers. sing. / *detener.*

detendrán they will detain; fut. 3rd pers. pl. / *detener.*

detendrás you will detain; fut. 2nd pers. sing. / *detener.*

detendré I shall detain; fut. 1st pers. sing. / *detener.*

detendréis you (all) will detain; fut. 2nd pers. pl. / *detener.*

detendremos we shall detain; fut. 1st pers. pl. / *detener.*

detendría 1. I should detain; cond. 1st pers. sing. / *detener.* 2. he (she/it) would detain; cond. 3rd pers. sing.

detendríais you (all) would detain; cond. 2nd pers. pl. / *detener.*

detendríamos we should detain; cond. 1st pers. pl. / *detener.*

detendrían they would detain; cond. 3rd pers. pl. / *detener.*

detendrías you would detain; cond. 2nd pers. sing. / *detener.*

deteneos (you all) stop; impve. 2nd pers. pl. / *detenerse.*

detener to detain. irr.

detenerse to stop. irr.

deténete (you) stop; impve. 2nd pers. sing. / *detenerse.*

detenga 1. that I may detain; pres. subj. 1st pers. sing. / *detener.* 2. that he (she/it) may detain; pres. subj. 3rd pers. sing. 3. let him (her/it) detain; impve. 3rd pers. sing.

detengáis that you (all) may detain; pres. subj. 2nd pers. pl. / *detener.*

detengámonos let us stop; impve. 1st pers. pl. / *detenerse.*

detengamos 1. that we may detain; pres. subj. 1st pers. pl. / *detener.* 2. let us detain; impve. 1st pers. pl.

detengan 1. that they may detain; pres. subj. 3rd pers. pl. / *detener.* 2. let them detain; impve. 3rd pers. pl.

deténganse let them stop; impve. 3rd pers. pl. / *detenerse.*

detengas that you may detain; pres. subj. 2nd pers. sing. / *detener.*

deténgase let him (her/it) stop; impve. 3rd pers. sing. / *detenerse.*

detengo I detain; pres. ind. 1st pers. sing. / *detener.*

deteniendo detaining; pres. part. / *detener.*

deteniéndose stopping; pres. part. / *detenerse.*

detentar to keep unlawfully. reg.

deteriorándose deteriorating; pres. part. / *deteriorarse.*

deterioraos (you all) deteriorate; impve. 2nd pers. pl. / *deteriorarse.*

deteriorar to deteriorate. reg.

deteriorarse to deteriorate. reg.

deteriórate (you) deteriorate; impve. 2nd pers. sing. / *deteriorarse.*

deteriorémonos let us deteriorate; impve. 1st pers. pl. / *deteriorarse.*

deteriórense let them deteriorate; impve. 3rd pers. pl. / *deteriorarse.*

deteriórese let him (her/it) deteriorate; impve. 3rd pers. sing. / *deteriorarse.*

determinándose deciding; pres. part. / *determinarse.*

determinaos (you all) decide; impve. 2nd pers. pl. / *determinarse.*

determinar to determine. reg.

determinarse to decide. reg.

determínate (you) decide; impve. 2nd pers. sing. / *determinarse.*

determinémonos let us decide; impve. 1st pers. pl. / *determinarse.*

determínense let them decide; impve. 3rd pers. pl. / *determinarse.*

determínese let him (her/it) decide; impve. 3rd pers. sing. / *determinarse.*

detestar to detest. reg.

detiene he (she/it) detains; pres. ind. 3rd pers. sing. / *detener.*

detienen they detain; pres. ind. 3rd pers. pl. / *detener.*

detienes you detain; pres. ind. 2nd pers. sing. / *detener.*

detonar to detonate. reg.

detractar to detract or to defame. reg.

detraer to detract or to remove. irr.

detraiga 1. that I may detract; pres. subj. 1st pers. sing. / *detraer.* 2. that he (she/it) may detract; pres. subj. 3rd pers. sing. 3. let him (her/it) detract; impve. 3rd pers. sing.

detraigáis that you (all) may detract; pres. subj. 2nd pers. pl. / *detraer.*

detraigamos 1. that we may detract; pres. subj. 1st pers. pl. / *detraer.* 2. let us detract; impve. 1st pers. pl.

detraigan 1. that they may detract; pres. subj. 3rd pers. pl. / *detraer.* 2. let them detract; impve. 3rd pers. pl.

detraigas that you may detract; pres. subj. 2nd pers. sing. / *detraer.*

detraigo I detract; pres. ind. 1st pers. sing. / *detraer.*

detraje I detracted; past 1st pers. sing. / *detraer.*

detrajera 1. that I might detract; imp. subj. 1st pers. sing. / *detraer.* 2. that he (she/it) might detract; imp. subj. 3rd pers. sing.

detrajerais that you (all) might detract; imp. subj. 2nd pers pl. / *detraer.*

detrajéramos that we might detract; imp. subj. 1st pers. pl. / *detraer.*

detrajeran that they might detract; imp. subj. 3rd pers. pl. / *detraer.*

detrajeras that you might detract; imp. subj. 2nd pers. sing. / *detraer.*

detrajeron they detracted; past 3rd pers. pl. / *detraer.*

detrajese 1. that I might detract; imp. subj. 1st pers. sing. / *detraer.* 2. that he (she/it) might detract; imp. subj. 3rd pers. sing.

detrajeseis that you (all) might detract; imp. subj. 2nd pers pl. / *detraer.*

detrajésemos that we might detract; imp. subj. 1st pers. pl. / *detraer.*

detrajesen that they might detract; imp. subj. 3rd pers. pl. / *detraer.*

detrajeses that you might detract; imp. subj. 2nd pers. sing. / *detraer.*

detrajimos we detracted; past 1st pers. pl. / *detraer.*

detrajiste you detracted; past 2nd pers. sing. / *detraer.*

detrajisteis you (all) detracted; past 2nd pers. pl. / *detraer.*

detrajo he (she/it) detracted; past 3rd pers. sing. / *detraer.*

detrayendo detracting; pres. part. / *detraer.*

detuve I detained; past 1st pers. sing. / *detener.*

detuviera 1. that I might detain; imp. subj. 1st pers. sing. / *detener.* 2. that he (she/it) might detain; imp. subj. 3rd pers. sing.

detuvierais that you (all) might detain; imp. subj. 2nd pers pl. / *detener.*

detuviéramos that we might detain; imp. subj. 1st pers. pl. / *detener.*

detuvieran that they might detain; imp. subj. 3rd pers. pl. / *detener.*

detuvieras that you might detain; imp. subj. 2nd pers. sing. / *detener.*

detuvieron they detained; past 3rd pers. pl. / *detener.*

detuviese 1. that I might detain; imp. subj. 1st pers. sing. / *detener.* 2. that he (she/it) might detain; imp. subj. 3rd pers. sing.

detuvieseis that you (all) might detain; imp. subj. 2nd pers pl. / *detener.*

detuviésemos that we might detain; imp. subj. 1st pers. pl. / *detener.*

detuviesen that they might detain; imp. subj. 3rd pers. pl. / *detener.*

detuvieses that you might detain; imp. subj. 2nd pers. sing. / *detener.*

detuvimos we detained; past 1st pers. pl. / *detener.*

detuviste you detained; past 2nd pers. sing. / *detener.*

detuvisteis you (all) detained; past 2nd pers. pl. / *detener.*

detuvo he (she/it) detained; past 3rd pers. sing. / *detener.*

devanándose writhing; pres. part. / *devanarse.*

devanaos (you all) writhe; impve. 2nd pers. pl. / *devanarse.*

devanar to wind or to reel. reg.

devanarse to writhe. reg.

devánate (you) writhe; impve. 2nd pers. sing. / *devanarse.*

devanear to rave or to daydream. reg.

devanémonos let us writhe; impve. 1st pers. pl. / *devanarse.*

devánense let them writhe; impve. 3rd pers. pl. / *devanarse.*

devánese let him (her/it) writhe; impve. 3rd pers. sing. / *devanarse.*

devastar to devastate. reg.

deven (you) happen; impve. 2nd pers. sing. / *devenir.*

devendrá he (she/it) will happen; fut. 3rd pers. sing. / *devenir.*

devendrán they will happen; fut. 3rd pers. pl. / *devenir.*

devendrás you will happen; fut. 2nd pers. sing. / *devenir.*

devendré I shall happen; fut. 1st pers. sing. / *devenir.*

devendréis you (all) will happen; fut. 2nd pers. pl. / *devenir.*

devendremos we shall happen; fut. 1st pers. pl. / *devenir.*

devendría 1. I should happen; cond. 1st pers. sing. / *devenir.* 2. he (she/it) would happen; cond. 3rd pers. sing.

devendríais you (all) would happen; cond. 2nd pers. pl. / *devenir.*

devendríamos we should happen; cond. 1st pers. pl. / *devenir.*

devendrían they would happen; cond. 3rd pers. pl. / *devenir.*

devendrías you would happen; cond. 2nd pers. sing. / *devenir.*

devenga 1. that I may happen; pres. subj. 1st pers. sing. / *devenir*. 2. that he (she/it) may happen; pres. subj. 3rd pers. sing. 3. let him (her/it) happen; impve. 3rd pers. sing.

devengáis that you (all) may happen; pres. subj. 2nd pers. pl. / *devenir*.

devengamos 1. that we may happen; pres. subj. 1st pers. pl. / *devenir*. 2. let us happen; impve. 1st pers. pl.

devengan 1. that they may happen; pres. subj. 3rd pers. pl. / *devenir*. 2. let them happen; impve. 3rd pers. pl.

devengar to earn or to receive. irr.

devengas that you may happen; pres. subj. 2nd pers. sing. / *devenir*.

devengo I happen; pres. ind. 1st pers. sing. / *devenir*.

devengue 1. that I may earn; pres. subj. 1st pers. sing. / *devengar*. 2. that he (she/it) may earn; pres. subj. 3rd pers. sing. 3. let him (her/it) earn; impve. 3rd pers. sing.

devengué I earned; past 1st pers. sing. / *devengar*.

devenguéis that you (all) may earn; pres. subj. 2nd pers. pl. / *devengar*.

devenguemos 1. that we may earn; pres. subj. 1st pers. pl. / *devengar*. 2. let us earn; impve. 1st pers. pl.

devenguen 1. that they may earn; pres. subj. 3rd pers. pl. / *devengar*. 2. let them earn; impve. 3rd pers. pl.

devengues that you may earn; pres. subj. 2nd pers. sing. / *devengar*.

deviene he (she/it) happens; pres. ind. 3rd pers. sing. / *devenir*.

devienen they happen; pres. ind. 3rd pers. pl. / *devenir*.

devienes you happen; pres. ind. 2nd pers. sing. / *devenir*.

devine I happened; past 1st pers. sing. / *devenir*.

deviniendo happening; pres. part. / *devenir*.

deviniera 1. that I might happen; imp. subj. 1st pers. sing. / *devenir*. 2. that he (she/it) might happen; imp. subj. 3rd pers. sing.

devinierais that you (all) might happen; imp. subj. 2nd pers pl. / *devenir*.

deviniéramos that we might happen; imp. subj. 1st pers. pl. / *devenir*.

devinieran that they might happen; imp. subj. 3rd pers. pl. / *devenir*.

devinieras that you might happen; imp. subj. 2nd pers. sing. / *devenir*.

devinieron they happened; past 3rd pers. pl. / *devenir*.

deviniese 1. that I might happen; imp. subj. 1st pers. sing. / *devenir*. 2. that he (she/it) might happen; imp. subj. 3rd pers. sing.

devinieseis that you (all) might happen; imp. subj. 2nd pers pl. / *devenir*.

deviniésemos that we might happen; imp. subj. 1st pers. pl. / *devenir*.

deviniesen that they might happen; imp. subj. 3rd pers. pl. / *devenir*.

devinieses that you might happen; imp. subj. 2nd pers. sing. / *devenir*.

devinimos we happened; past 1st pers. pl. / *devenir*.

deviniste you happened; past 2nd pers. sing. / *devenir*.

devinisteis you (all) happened; past 2nd pers. pl. / *devenir*.

devino he (she/it) happened; past 3rd pers. sing. / *devenir*.

devolvámonos let us come back; impve. 1st pers. pl. / *devolverse*.

devolveos (you all) come back; impve. 2nd pers. pl. / *devolverse*.

devolver to return. irr.

devolverse to come back. irr.

devolviéndose coming back; pres. part. / *devolverse*.

devorar to devour. reg.

devuelto returned; past part. / *devolver*.

devuelva 1. that I may return; pres. subj. 1st pers. sing. / *devolver*. 2. that he (she/it) may return; pres. subj. 3rd pers. sing. 3. let him (her/it) return; impve. 3rd pers. sing.

devuelvan 1. that they may return; pres. subj. 3rd pers. pl. / *devolver*. 2. let them return; impve. 3rd pers. pl.

devuélvanse let them come back; impve. 3rd pers. pl. / *devolverse*.

devuelvas that you may return; pres. subj. 2nd pers. sing. / *devolver*.

devuélvase let him (her/it) come back; impve. 3rd pers. sing. / *devolverse*.

devuelve 1. he (she/it) returns; pres. ind. 3rd pers. sing. / *devolver*. 2. (you) return; impve. 2nd pers. sing.

devuelven they return; pres. ind. 3rd pers. pl. / *devolver*.

devuelves you return; pres. ind. 2nd pers. sing. / *devolver*.

devuélvete (you) come back; impve. 2nd pers. sing. / *devolverse*.

devuelvo I return; pres. ind. 1st pers. sing. / *devolver*.

di I gave; past 1st pers. sing. / *dar*.

di (you) say; impve. 2nd pers. sing. / *decir*.

dí I gave; past 1st pers. sing. / *dar*.

diagnosticar to diagnose. irr.

diagnostique 1. that I may diagnose; pres. subj. 1st pers. sing. / *diagnosticar*. 2. that he (she/it) may diagnose; pres. subj. 3rd pers. sing. 3. let him (her/it) diagnose; impve. 3rd pers. sing.

diagnostiqué I diagnosed; past 1st pers. sing. / *diagnosticar*.

diagnostiquéis that you (all) may diagnose; pres. subj. 2nd pers. pl. / *diagnosticar*.

diagnostiquemos 1. that we may diagnose; pres. subj. 1st pers. pl. / *diagnosticar*. 2. let us diagnose; impve. 1st pers. pl.

diagnostiquen 1. that they may diagnose; pres. subj. 3rd pers. pl. / *diagnosticar*. 2. let them diagnose; impve. 3rd pers. pl.

diagnostiques that you may diagnose; pres. subj. 2nd pers. sing. / *diagnosticar*.

dialogar to dialogue. irr.

dialogue 1. that I may dialogue; pres. subj. 1st pers. sing. / *dialogar*. 2. that he (she/it) may dialogue; pres. subj. 3rd pers. sing. 3. let him (her/it) dialogue; impve. 3rd pers. sing.

dialogué I dialogued; past 1st pers. sing. / *dialogar*.

dialoguéis that you (all) may dialogue; pres. subj. 2nd pers. pl. / *dialogar*.

dialoguemos 1. that we may dialogue; pres. subj. 1st pers. pl. / *dialogar*. 2. let us dialogue; impve. 1st pers. pl.

dialoguen 1. that they may dialogue; pres. subj. 3rd pers. pl. / *dialogar*. 2. let them dialogue; impve. 3rd pers. pl.

dialogues that you may dialogue; pres. subj. 2nd pers. sing. / *dialogar*.

dibujándose appearing; pres. part. / *dibujarse*.

dibujaos (you all) appear; impve. 2nd pers. pl. / *dibujarse*.

dibujar to draw. reg.

dibujarse to appear. reg.

dibújate (you) appear; impve. 2nd pers. sing. / *dibujarse*.

dibujémonos let us appear; impve. 1st pers. pl. / *dibujarse*.

dibújense let them appear; impve. 3rd pers. pl. / *dibujarse*.

dibújese let him (her/it) appear; impve. 3rd pers. sing. / *dibujarse*.

dice he (she/it) says; pres. ind. 3rd pers. sing. / *decir*.

dicen they say; pres. ind. 3rd pers. pl. / *decir*.

dices you say; pres. ind. 2nd pers. sing. / *decir*.

diciendo saying; pres. part. / *decir*.

dictaminar to pass judgement. reg.

dictar to dictate. reg.

dicho said; past part. / *decir*.

dienta 1. he (she/it) teethes; pres. ind. 3rd pers. sing. / *dentar*. 2. (you) teethe; impve. 2nd pers. sing.

dientan they teethe; pres. ind. 3rd pers. pl. / *dentar*.

dientas you teethe; pres. ind. 2nd pers. sing. / *dentar*.

diente 1. that I may teethe; pres. subj. 1st pers. sing. / *dentar*. 2. that he (she/it) may teethe; pres. subj. 3rd pers. sing. 3. let him (her/it) teethe; impve. 3rd pers. sing.

dienten 1. that they may teethe; pres. subj. 3rd pers. pl. / *dentar*. 2. let them teethe; impve. 3rd pers. pl.

dientes that you may teethe; pres. subj. 2nd pers. sing. / *dentar*.

diento I teethe; pres. ind. 1st pers. sing. / *dentar*.

diera 1. that I might give; imp. subj. 1st pers. sing. / *dar*. 2. that he (she/it) might give; imp. subj. 3rd pers. sing.

dierais that you (all) might give; imp. subj. 2nd pers pl. / *dar*.

diéramos that we might give; imp. subj. 1st pers. pl. / *dar*.

dieran that they might give; imp. subj. 3rd pers. pl. / *dar*.

dieras that you might give; imp. subj. 2nd pers. sing. / *dar*.

dieron they gave; past 3rd pers. pl. / *dar*.

diese 1. that I might give; imp. subj. 1st pers. sing. / *dar*. 2. that he (she/it) might give; imp. subj. 3rd pers. sing.

dieseis that you (all) might give; imp. subj. 2nd pers pl. / *dar*.

diésemos that we might give; imp. subj. 1st pers. pl. / *dar*.

diesen that they might give; imp. subj. 3rd pers. pl. / *dar*.

dieses that you might give; imp. subj. 2nd pers. sing. / *dar*.

dietándose dieting; pres. part. / *dietarse*.

dietaos (you all) diet; impve. 2nd pers. pl. / *dietarse*.

dietar to diet. reg.

dietarse to diet. reg.

diétate (you) diet; impve. 2nd pers. sing. / *dietarse*.

dietémonos let us diet; impve. 1st pers. pl. / *dietarse*.

diétense let them diet; impve. 3rd pers. pl. / *dietarse*.

diétese let him (her/it) diet; impve. 3rd pers. sing. / *dietarse*.

diezmar to decimate or to tithe. reg.

difamar to defame. reg.

diferenciándose differing; pres. part. / *diferenciarse*.

diferenciaos (you all) differ; impve. 2nd pers. pl. / *diferenciarse*.

diferenciar to differentiate. reg.

diferenciarse to differ. reg.

diferénciate (you) differ; impve. 2nd pers. sing. / *diferenciarse*.

diferenciémonos let us differ; impve. 1st pers. pl. / *diferenciarse*.

diferénciense let them differ; impve. 3rd pers. pl. / *diferenciarse*.

diferénciese let him (her/it) differ; impve. 3rd pers. sing. / *diferenciarse*.

diferíos (you all) differ; impve. 2nd pers. pl. / *diferirse*.

diferir to defer. irr.

diferirse to differ. irr.

dificultándose becoming difficult; pres. part. / *dificultarse*.

dificultaos (you all) become difficult; impve. 2nd pers. pl. / *dificultarse*.

dificultar to make difficult. reg.

dificultarse to become difficult. reg.

dificúltate (you) become difficult; impve. 2nd pers. sing. / *dificultarse*.

dificultémonos let us become difficult; impve. 1st pers. pl. / *dificultarse*.

dificúltense let them become difficult; impve. 3rd pers. pl. / *dificultarse*.

dificúltese let him (her/it) become difficult; impve. 3rd pers. sing. / *dificultarse*.

difiera 1. that I may defer; pres. subj. 1st pers. sing. / *diferir*. 2. that he (she/it) may defer; pres. subj. 3rd pers. sing. 3. let him (her/it) defer; impve. 3rd pers. sing.

difieran 1. that they may defer; pres. subj. 3rd pers. pl. / *diferir*. 2. let them defer; impve. 3rd pers. pl.

difiéranse let them differ; impve. 3rd pers. pl. / *diferirse.*

difieras that you may defer; pres. subj. 2nd pers. sing. / *diferir.*

difiérase let him (her/it) differ; impve. 3rd pers. sing. / *diferirse.*

difiere 1. he (she/it) defers; pres. ind. 3rd pers. sing. / *diferir.* 2. (you) defer; impve. 2nd pers. sing.

difieren they defer; pres. ind. 3rd pers. pl. / *diferir.*

difieres you defer; pres. ind. 2nd pers. sing. / *diferir.*

difiérete (you) differ; impve. 2nd pers. sing. / *diferirse.*

difiero I defer; pres. ind. 1st pers. sing. / *diferir.*

difiráis that you (all) may defer; pres. subj. 2nd pers. pl. / *diferir.*

difirámonos let us differ; impve. 1st pers. pl. / *diferirse.*

difiramos 1. that we may defer; pres. subj. 1st pers. pl. / *diferir.* 2. let us defer; impve. 1st pers. pl.

difiriendo deferring; pres. part. / *diferir.*

difiriéndose differing; pres. part. / *diferirse.*

difiriera 1. that I might defer; imp. subj. 1st pers. sing. / *diferir.* 2. that he (she/it) might defer; imp. subj. 3rd pers. sing.

difirierais that you (all) might defer; imp. subj. 2nd pers pl. / *diferir.*

difiriéramos that we might defer; imp. subj. 1st pers. pl. / *diferir.*

difirieran that they might defer; imp. subj. 3rd pers. pl. / *diferir.*

difirieras that you might defer; imp. subj. 2nd pers. sing. / *diferir.*

difirieron they deferred; past 3rd pers. pl. / *diferir.*

difiriese 1. that I might defer; imp. subj. 1st pers. sing. / *diferir.* 2. that he (she/it) might defer; imp. subj. 3rd pers. sing.

difirieseis that you (all) might defer; imp. subj. 2nd pers pl. / *diferir.*

difiriésemos that we might defer; imp. subj. 1st pers. pl. / *diferir.*

difiriesen that they might defer; imp. subj. 3rd pers. pl. / *diferir.*

difirieses that you might defer; imp. subj. 2nd pers. sing. / *diferir.*

difirió he (she/it) deferred; past 3rd pers. sing. / *diferir.*

difractar to diffract. reg.

difundir to diffuse or to spread. reg.

diga 1. that I may say; pres. subj. 1st pers. sing. / *decir.* 2. that he (she/it) may say; pres. subj. 3rd pers. sing. 3. let him (her/it) say; impve. 3rd pers. sing.

digáis that you (all) may say; pres. subj. 2nd pers. pl. / *decir.*

digamos 1. that we may say; pres. subj. 1st pers. pl. / *decir.* 2. let us say; impve. 1st pers. pl.

digan 1. that they may say; pres. subj. 3rd pers. pl. / *decir.* 2. let them say; impve. 3rd pers. pl.

digas that you may say; pres. subj. 2nd pers. sing. / *decir.*

digerir to digest. irr.

digiera 1. that I may digest; pres. subj. 1st pers. sing. / *digerir.* 2. that he (she/it) may digest; pres. subj. 3rd pers. sing. 3. let him (her/it) digest; impve. 3rd pers. sing.

digieran 1. that they may digest; pres. subj. 3rd pers. pl. / *digerir.* 2. let them digest; impve. 3rd pers. pl.

digieras that you may digest; pres. subj. 2nd pers. sing. / *digerir.*

digiere 1. he (she/it) digests; pres. ind. 3rd pers. sing. / *digerir.* 2. (you) digest; impve. 2nd pers. sing.

digieren they digest; pres. ind. 3rd pers. pl. / *digerir.*

digieres you digest; pres. ind. 2nd pers. sing. / *digerir.*

digiero I digest; pres. ind. 1st pers. sing. / *digerir.*

digiráis that you (all) may digest; pres. subj. 2nd pers. pl. / *digerir.*

digiramos 1. that we may digest; pres. subj. 1st pers. pl. / *digerir.* 2. let us digest; impve. 1st pers. pl.

digiriendo digesting; pres. part. / *digerir.*

digiriera 1. that I might digest; imp. subj. 1st pers. sing. / *digerir.* 2. that he (she/it) might digest; imp. subj. 3rd pers. sing.

digirierais that you (all) might digest; imp. subj. 2nd pers pl. / *digerir.*

digiriéramos that we might digest; imp. subj. 1st pers. pl. / *digerir.*

digirieran that they might digest; imp. subj. 3rd pers. pl. / *digerir.*

digirieras that you might digest; imp. subj. 2nd pers. sing. / *digerir.*

digirieron they digested; past 3rd pers. pl. / *digerir.*

digiriese 1. that I might digest; imp. subj. 1st pers. sing. / *digerir.* 2. that he (she/it) might digest; imp. subj. 3rd pers. sing.

digirieseis that you (all) might digest; imp. subj. 2nd pers pl. / *digerir.*

digiriésemos that we might digest; imp. subj. 1st pers. pl. / *digerir.*

digiriesen that they might digest; imp. subj. 3rd pers. pl. / *digerir.*

digirieses that you might digest; imp. subj. 2nd pers. sing. / *digerir.*

digirió he (she/it) digested; past 3rd pers. sing. / *digerir.*

dignándose deigning; pres. part. / *dignarse.*

dignaos (you all) deign; impve. 2nd pers. pl. / *dignarse.*

dignarse to deign or to condescend. reg.

dígnate (you) deign; impve. 2nd pers. sing. / *dignarse.*

dignémonos let us deign; impve. 1st pers. pl. / *dignarse.*

dígnense let them deign; impve. 3rd pers. pl. / *dignarse.*

dígnese let him (her/it) deign; impve. 3rd pers. sing. / *dignarse.*

dignificar to dignify. irr.

dignifique 1. that I may dignify; pres. subj. 1st pers. sing. / *dignificar.* 2. that he (she/it) may dignify; pres. subj. 3rd pers. sing. 3. let him (her/it) dignify; impve. 3rd pers. sing.

dignifiqué I dignified; past 1st pers. sing. / *dignificar*.

dignifiquéis that you (all) may dignify; pres. subj. 2nd pers. pl. / *dignificar*.

dignifiquemos 1. that we may dignify; pres. subj. 1st pers. pl. / *dignificar*. 2. let us dignify; impve. 1st pers. pl.

dignifiquen 1. that they may dignify; pres. subj. 3rd pers. pl. / *dignificar*. 2. let them dignify; impve. 3rd pers. pl.

dignifiques that you may dignify; pres. subj. 2nd pers. sing. / *dignificar*.

digo I say; pres. ind. 1st pers. sing. / *decir*.

dije I said; past 1st pers. sing. / *decir*.

dijera 1. that I might say; imp. subj. 1st pers. sing. / *decir*. 2. that he (she/it) might say; imp. subj. 3rd pers. sing.

dijerais that you (all) might say; imp. subj. 2nd pers pl. / *decir*.

dijéramos that we might say; imp. subj. 1st pers. pl. / *decir*.

dijeran that they might say; imp. subj. 3rd pers. pl. / *decir*.

dijeras that you might say; imp. subj. 2nd pers. sing. / *decir*.

dijeron they said; past 3rd pers. pl. / *decir*.

dijese 1. that I might say; imp. subj. 1st pers. sing. / *decir*. 2. that he (she/it) might say; imp. subj. 3rd pers. sing.

dijeseis that you (all) might say; imp. subj. 2nd pers pl. / *decir*.

dijésemos that we might say; imp. subj. 1st pers. pl. / *decir*.

dijesen that they might say; imp. subj. 3rd pers. pl. / *decir*.

dijeses that you might say; imp. subj. 2nd pers. sing. / *decir*.

dijimos we said; past 1st pers. pl. / *decir*.

dijiste you said; past 2nd pers. sing. / *decir*.

dijisteis you (all) said; past 2nd pers. pl. / *decir*.

dijo he (she/it) said; past 3rd pers. sing. / *decir*.

dilapidar to dilapidate. reg.

dilatándose expanding; pres. part. / *dilatarse*.

dilataos (you all) expand; impve. 2nd pers. pl. / *dilatarse*.

dilatar to dilate or to widen. reg.

dilatarse to expand. reg.

dilátate (you) expand; impve. 2nd pers. sing. / *dilatarse*.

dilatémonos let us expand; impve. 1st pers. pl. / *dilatarse*.

dilátense let them expand; impve. 3rd pers. pl. / *dilatarse*.

dilátese let him (her/it) expand; impve. 3rd pers. sing. / *dilatarse*.

diligenciar to expedite. reg.

dilucidar to elucidate. reg.

diluíos (you all) dilute; impve. 2nd pers. pl. / *diluirse*.

diluir to dilute. irr.

diluirse to dilute. irr.

diluviar to pour down rain. reg.

diluya 1. that I may dilute; pres. subj. 1st pers. sing. / *diluir*. 2. that he (she/it) may dilute; pres. subj. 3rd pers. sing. 3. let him (her/it) dilute; impve. 3rd pers. sing.

diluyáis that you (all) may dilute; pres. subj. 2nd pers. pl. / *diluir*.

diluyámonos let us dilute; impve. 1st pers. pl. / *diluirse*.

diluyamos 1. that we may dilute; pres. subj. 1st pers. pl. / *diluir*. 2. let us dilute; impve. 1st pers. pl.

diluyan 1. that they may dilute; pres. subj. 3rd pers. pl. / *diluir*. 2. let them dilute; impve. 3rd pers. pl.

dilúyanse let them dilute; impve. 3rd pers. pl. / *diluirse*.

diluyas that you may dilute; pres. subj. 2nd pers. sing. / *diluir*.

dilúyase let him (her/it) dilute; impve. 3rd pers. sing. / *diluirse*.

diluye 1. he (she/it) dilutes; pres. ind. 3rd pers. sing. / *diluir*. 2. (you) dilute; impve. 2nd pers. sing.

diluyen they dilute; pres. ind. 3rd pers. pl. / *diluir*.

diluyendo diluting; pres. part. / *diluir*.

diluyéndose diluting; pres. part. / *diluirse*.

diluyera 1. that I might dilute; imp. subj. 1st pers. sing. / *diluir*. 2. that he (she/it) might dilute; imp. subj. 3rd pers. sing.

diluyerais that you (all) might dilute; imp. subj. 2nd pers pl. / *diluir*.

diluyéramos that we might dilute; imp. subj. 1st pers. pl. / *diluir*.

diluyeran that they might dilute; imp. subj. 3rd pers. pl. / *diluir*.

diluyeras that you might dilute; imp. subj. 2nd pers. sing. / *diluir*.

diluyeron they diluted; past 3rd pers. pl. / *diluir*.

diluyes you dilute; pres. ind. 2nd pers. sing. / *diluir*.

diluyese 1. that I might dilute; imp. subj. 1st pers. sing. / *diluir*. 2. that he (she/it) might dilute; imp. subj. 3rd pers. sing.

diluyeseis that you (all) might dilute; imp. subj. 2nd pers pl. / *diluir*.

diluyésemos that we might dilute; imp. subj. 1st pers. pl. / *diluir*.

diluyesen that they might dilute; imp. subj. 3rd pers. pl. / *diluir*.

diluyeses that you might dilute; imp. subj. 2nd pers. sing. / *diluir*.

dilúyete (you) dilute; impve. 2nd pers. sing. / *diluirse*.

diluyo I dilute; pres. ind. 1st pers. sing. / *diluir*.

diluyó he (she/it) diluted; past 3rd pers. sing. / *diluir*.

dimanar to spring or to emanate. reg.

diminuíos (you all) diminish; impve. 2nd pers. pl. / *diminuirse*.

diminuir to diminish. irr.

diminuirse to diminish. irr.

diminuya 1. that I may diminish; pres. subj. 1st pers. sing. / *diminuir*. 2. that he (she/it) may diminish; pres. subj. 3rd pers. sing. 3. let him (her/it) diminish; impve. 3rd pers. sing.

diminuyáis that you (all) may diminish; pres. subj. 2nd pers. pl. / *diminuir.*

diminuyámonos let us diminish; impve. 1st pers. pl. / *diminuirse.*

diminuyamos 1. that we may diminish; pres. subj. 1st pers. pl. / *diminuir.* 2. let us diminish; impve. 1st pers. pl.

diminuyan 1. that they may diminish; pres. subj. 3rd pers. pl. / *diminuir.* 2. let them diminish; impve. 3rd pers. pl.

diminúyanse let them diminish; impve. 3rd pers. pl. / *diminuirse.*

diminuyas that you may diminish; pres. subj. 2nd pers. sing. / *diminuir.*

diminúyase let him (her/it) diminish; impve. 3rd pers. sing. / *diminuirse.*

diminuye 1. he (she/it) diminishes; pres. ind. 3rd pers. sing. / *diminuir.* 2. (you) diminish; impve. 2nd pers. sing.

diminuyen they diminish; pres. ind. 3rd pers. pl. / *diminuir.*

diminuyendo diminishing; pres. part. / *diminuir.*

diminuyéndose diminishing; pres. part. / *diminuirse.*

diminuyera 1. that I might diminish; imp. subj. 1st pers. sing. / *diminuir.* 2. that he (she/it) might diminish; imp. subj. 3rd pers. sing.

diminuyerais that you (all) might diminish; imp. subj. 2nd pers pl. / *diminuir.*

diminuyéramos that we might diminish; imp. subj. 1st pers. pl. / *diminuir.*

diminuyeran that they might diminish; imp. subj. 3rd pers. pl. / *diminuir.*

diminuyeras that you might diminish; imp. subj. 2nd pers. sing. / *diminuir.*

diminuyeron they diminished; past 3rd pers. pl. / *diminuir.*

diminuyes you diminish; pres. ind. 2nd pers. sing. / *diminuir.*

diminuyese 1. that I might diminish; imp. subj. 1st pers. sing. / *diminuir.* 2. that he (she/it) might diminish; imp. subj. 3rd pers. sing.

diminuyeseis that you (all) might diminish; imp. subj. 2nd pers pl. / *diminuir.*

diminuyésemos that we might diminish; imp. subj. 1st pers. pl. / *diminuir.*

diminuyesen that they might diminish; imp. subj. 3rd pers. pl. / *diminuir.*

diminuyeses that you might diminish; imp. subj. 2nd pers. sing. / *diminuir.*

diminúyete (you) diminish; impve. 2nd pers. sing. / *diminuirse.*

diminuyo I diminish; pres. ind. 1st pers. sing. / *diminuir.*

diminuyó he (she/it) diminished; past 3rd pers. sing. / *diminuir.*

dimitir to resign. reg.

dimos we gave; past 1st pers. pl. / *dar.*

dinamitar to dynamite. reg.

dio he (she/it) gave; past 3rd pers. sing. / *dar.*

dió he (she/it) gave; past 3rd pers. sing. / *dar.*

diplomándose being graduated; pres. part. / *diplomarse.*

diplomaos (you all) be graduated; impve. 2nd pers. pl. / *diplomarse.*

diplomarse to be graduated. reg.

diplómate (you) be graduated; impve. 2nd pers. sing. / *diplomarse.*

diplomémonos let us be graduated; impve. 1st pers. pl. / *diplomarse.*

diplómense let them be graduated; impve. 3rd pers. pl. / *diplomarse.*

diplómese let him (her/it) be graduated; impve. 3rd pers. sing. / *diplomarse.*

diptongándose dipthongizing; pres. part. / *diptongarse.*

diptongaos (you all) dipthongize; impve. 2nd pers. pl. / *diptongarse.*

diptongar to dipthongize. irr.

diptongarse to dipthongize. irr.

diptóngate (you) dipthongize; impve. 2nd pers. sing. / *diptongarse.*

diptongue 1. that I may dipthongize; pres. subj. 1st pers. sing. / *diptongar.* 2. that he (she/it) may dipthongize; pres. subj. 3rd pers. sing. 3. let him (her/it) dipthongize; impve. 3rd pers. sing.

diptongué I dipthongized; past 1st pers. sing. / *diptongar.*

diptonguéis that you (all) may dipthongize; pres. subj. 2nd pers. pl. / *diptongar.*

diptonguémonos let us dipthongize; impve. 1st pers. pl. / *diptongarse.*

diptonguemos 1. that we may dipthongize; pres. subj. 1st pers. pl. / *diptongar.* 2. let us dipthongize; impve. 1st pers. pl.

diptonguen 1. that they may dipthongize; pres. subj. 3rd pers. pl. / *diptongar.* 2. let them dipthongize; impve. 3rd pers. pl.

diptónguense let them dipthongize; impve. 3rd pers. pl. / *diptongarse.*

diptongues that you may dipthongize; pres. subj. 2nd pers. sing. / *diptongar.*

diptónguese let him (her/it) dipthongize; impve. 3rd pers. sing. / *diptongarse.*

diputar to depute or to deputize. reg.

dirá he (she/it) will say; fut. 3rd pers. sing. / *decir.*

dirán they will say; fut. 3rd pers. pl. / *decir.*

dirás you will say; fut. 2nd pers. sing. / *decir.*

diré I shall say; fut. 1st pers. sing. / *decir.*

diréis you (all) will say; fut. 2nd pers. pl. / *decir.*

diremos we shall say; fut. 1st pers. pl. / *decir.*

diría 1. I should say; cond. 1st pers. sing. / *decir.* 2. he (she/it) would say; cond. 3rd pers. sing.

diríais you (all) would say; cond. 2nd pers. pl. / *decir.*

diríamos we should say; cond. 1st pers. pl. / *decir.*

dirían they would say; cond. 3rd pers. pl. / *decir.*

dirías you would say; cond. 2nd pers. sing. / *decir.*

dirígete (you) address; impve. 2nd pers. sing. / *dirigirse.*

dirigiéndose addressing; pres. part. / *dirigirse.*

dirigios (you all) address; impve. 2nd pers. pl. / *dirigirse.*

dirigir to direct or to govern. irr.

dirigirse to address. irr.

dirija 1. that I may direct; pres. subj. 1st pers. sing. / *dirigir.* 2. that he (she/it) may direct; pres. subj. 3rd pers. sing. 3. let him (her/it) direct; impve. 3rd pers. sing.

dirijáis that you (all) may direct; pres. subj. 2nd pers. pl. / *dirigir.*

dirijámonos let us address; impve. 1st pers. pl. / *dirigirse.*

dirijamos 1. that we may direct; pres. subj. 1st pers. pl. / *dirigir.* 2. let us direct; impve. 1st pers. pl.

dirijan 1. that they may direct; pres. subj. 3rd pers. pl. / *dirigir.* 2. let them direct; impve. 3rd pers. pl.

diríjanse let them address; impve. 3rd pers. pl. / *dirigirse.*

dirijas that you may direct; pres. subj. 2nd pers. sing. / *dirigir.*

diríjase let him (her/it) address; impve. 3rd pers. sing. / *dirigirse.*

dirijo I direct; pres. ind. 1st pers. sing. / *dirigir.*

dirimir to settle or to annul. reg.

discernir to discern. irr.

discierna 1. that I may discern; pres. subj. 1st pers. sing. / *discernir.* 2. that he (she/it) may discern; pres. subj. 3rd pers. sing. 3. let him (her/it) discern; impve. 3rd pers. sing.

disciernan 1. that they may discern; pres. subj. 3rd pers. pl. / *discernir.* 2. let them discern; impve. 3rd pers. pl.

disciernas that you may discern; pres. subj. 2nd pers. sing. / *discernir.*

discierne 1. he (she/it) discerns; pres. ind. 3rd pers. sing. / *discernir.* 2. (you) discern; impve. 2nd pers. sing.

disciernen they discern; pres. ind. 3rd pers. pl. / *discernir.*

disciernes you discern; pres. ind. 2nd pers. sing. / *discernir.*

discierno I discern; pres. ind. 1st pers. sing. / *discernir.*

disciplinándose disciplining oneself; pres. part. / *disciplinarse.*

disciplinaos (you all) discipline yourselves; impve. 2nd pers. pl. / *disciplinarse.*

disciplinar to discipline. reg.

disciplinarse to discipline oneself. reg.

disciplínate (you) discipline yourself; impve. 2nd pers. sing. / *disciplinarse.*

disciplinémonos let us discipline ourselves; impve. 1st pers. pl. / *disciplinarse.*

disciplínense let them discipline themselves; impve. 3rd pers. pl. / *disciplinarse.*

disciplínese let him (her/it) discipline himself (herself/itself); impve. 3rd pers. sing. / *disciplinarse.*

discontinúa 1. he (she/it) discontinues; pres. ind. 3rd pers. sing. / *discontinuar.* 2. (you) discontinue; impve. 2nd pers. sing.

discontinúan they discontinue; pres. ind. 3rd pers. pl. / *discontinuar.*

discontinuar to discontinue. irr.

discontinúas you discontinue; pres. ind. 2nd pers. sing. / *discontinuar.*

discontinúe 1. that I may discontinue; pres. subj. 1st pers. sing. / *discontinuar.* 2. that he (she/it) may discontinue; pres. subj. 3rd pers. sing. 3. let him (her/it) discontinue; impve. 3rd pers. sing.

discontinúen 1. that they may discontinue; pres. subj. 3rd pers. pl. / *discontinuar.* 2. let them discontinue; impve. 3rd pers. pl.

discontinúes that you may discontinue; pres. subj. 2nd pers. sing. / *discontinuar.*

discontinúo I discontinue; pres. ind. 1st pers. sing. / *discontinuar.*

disconven (you) disagree; impve. 2nd pers. sing. / *disconvenir.*

disconvendrá he (she/it) will disagree; fut. 3rd pers. sing. / *disconvenir.*

disconvendrán they will disagree; fut. 3rd pers. pl. / *disconvenir.*

disconvendrás you will disagree; fut. 2nd pers. sing. / *disconvenir.*

disconvendré I shall disagree; fut. 1st pers. sing. / *disconvenir.*

disconvendréis you (all) will disagree; fut. 2nd pers. pl. / *disconvenir.*

disconvendremos we shall disagree; fut. 1st pers. pl. / *disconvenir.*

disconvendría 1. I should disagree; cond. 1st pers. sing. / *disconvenir.* 2. he (she/it) would disagree; cond. 3rd pers. sing.

disconvendríais you (all) would disagree; cond. 2nd pers. pl. / *disconvenir.*

disconvendríamos we should disagree; cond. 1st pers. pl. / *disconvenir.*

disconvendrían they would disagree; cond. 3rd pers. pl. / *disconvenir.*

disconvendrías you would disagree; cond. 2nd pers. sing. / *disconvenir.*

disconvenga 1. that I may disagree; pres. subj. 1st pers. sing. / *disconvenir.* 2. that he (she/it) may disagree; pres. subj. 3rd pers. sing. 3. let him (her/it) disagree; impve. 3rd pers. sing.

disconvengáis that you (all) may disagree; pres. subj. 2nd pers. pl. / *disconvenir.*

disconvengamos 1. that we may disagree; pres. subj. 1st pers. pl. / *disconvenir.* 2. let us disagree; impve. 1st pers. pl.

disconvengan 1. that they may disagree; pres. subj. 3rd pers. pl. / *disconvenir.* 2. let them disagree; impve. 3rd pers. pl.

disconvengas that you may disagree; pres. subj. 2nd pers. sing. / *disconvenir.*

disconvengo I disagree; pres. ind. 1st pers. sing. / *disconvenir.*

disconvenir to disagree. irr.

disconviene he (she/it) disagrees; pres. ind. 3rd pers. sing. / *disconvenir.*

disconvienen they disagree; pres. ind. 3rd pers. pl. / *disconvenir.*

disconvienes you disagree; pres. ind. 2nd pers. sing. / *disconvenir.*

disconvine I disagreed; past 1st pers. sing. / *disconvenir.*

disconviniendo disagreeing; pres. part. / *disconvenir.*

disconviniera 1. that I might disagree; imp. subj. 1st pers. sing. / *disconvenir.* 2. that he (she/it) might disagree; imp. subj. 3rd pers. sing.

disconvinierais that you (all) might disagree; imp. subj. 2nd pers pl. / *disconvenir.*

disconviniéramos that we might disagree; imp. subj. 1st pers. pl. / *disconvenir.*

disconvinieran that they might disagree; imp. subj. 3rd pers. pl. / *disconvenir.*

disconvinieras that you might disagree; imp. subj. 2nd pers. sing. / *disconvenir.*

disconvinieron they disagreed; past 3rd pers. pl. / *disconvenir.*

disconviniese 1. that I might disagree; imp. subj. 1st pers. sing. / *disconvenir.* 2. that he (she/it) might disagree; imp. subj. 3rd pers. sing.

disconvinieseis that you (all) might disagree; imp. subj. 2nd pers pl. / *disconvenir.*

disconviniésemos that we might disagree; imp. subj. 1st pers. pl. / *disconvenir.*

disconviniesen that they might disagree; imp. subj. 3rd pers. pl. / *disconvenir.*

disconvinieses that you might disagree; imp. subj. 2nd pers. sing. / *disconvenir.*

disconvinimos we disagreed; past 1st pers. pl. / *disconvenir.*

disconviniste you disagreed; past 2nd pers. sing. / *disconvenir.*

disconvinisteis you (all) disagreed; past 2nd pers. pl. / *disconvenir.*

disconvino he (she/it) disagreed; past 3rd pers. sing. / *disconvenir.*

discordar to disagree. irr.

discrepar to differ. reg.

discretear to attempt cleverness. reg.

discriminar to discriminate. reg.

discuerda 1. he (she/it) disagrees; pres. ind. 3rd pers. sing. / *discordar.* 2. (you) disagree; impve. 2nd pers. sing.

discuerdan they disagree; pres. ind. 3rd pers. pl. / *discordar.*

discuerdas you disagree; pres. ind. 2nd pers. sing. / *discordar.*

discuerde 1. that I may disagree; pres. subj. 1st pers. sing. / *discordar.* 2. that he (she/it) may disagree; pres. subj. 3rd pers. sing. 3. let him (her/it) disagree; impve. 3rd pers. sing.

discuerden 1. that they may disagree; pres. subj. 3rd pers. pl. / *discordar.* 2. let them disagree; impve. 3rd pers. pl.

discuerdes that you may disagree; pres. subj. 2nd pers. sing. / *discordar.*

discuerdo I disagree; pres. ind. 1st pers. sing. / *discordar.*

disculpándose apologizing; pres. part. / *disculparse.*

disculpaos (you all) apologize; impve. 2nd pers. pl. / *disculparse.*

disculpar to excuse. reg.

disculparse to apologize. reg.

discúlpate (you) apologize; impve. 2nd pers. sing. / *disculparse.*

disculpémonos let us apologize; impve. 1st pers. pl. / *disculparse.*

discúlpense let them apologize; impve. 3rd pers. pl. / *disculparse.*

discúlpese let him (her/it) apologize; impve. 3rd pers. sing. / *disculparse.*

discurrir to ramble or to contrive. reg.

discursear to make speeches. reg.

discutir to discuss. reg.

disecar to dissect. irr.

diseminándose spreading; pres. part. / *diseminarse.*

diseminaos (you all) spread; impve. 2nd pers. pl. / *diseminarse.*

diseminar to disseminate. reg.

diseminarse to spread. reg.

disemínate (you) spread; impve. 2nd pers. sing. / *diseminarse.*

diseminémonos let us spread; impve. 1st pers. pl. / *diseminarse.*

disemínense let them spread; impve. 3rd pers. pl. / *diseminarse.*

disemínese let him (her/it) spread; impve. 3rd pers. sing. / *diseminarse.*

disentir to dissent. irr.

diseñar to design. reg.

diseque 1. that I may dissect; pres. subj. 1st pers. sing. / *disecar.* 2. that he (she/it) may dissect; pres. subj. 3rd pers. sing. 3. let him (her/it) dissect; impve. 3rd pers. sing.

disequé I dissected; past 1st pers. sing. / *disecar.*

disequéis that you (all) may dissect; pres. subj. 2nd pers. pl. / *disecar.*

disequemos 1. that we may dissect; pres. subj. 1st pers. pl. / *disecar.* 2. let us dissect; impve. 1st pers. pl.

disequen 1. that they may dissect; pres. subj. 3rd pers. pl. / *disecar.* 2. let them dissect; impve. 3rd pers. pl.

diseques that you may dissect; pres. subj. 2nd pers. sing. / *disecar.*

disertar to discourse. reg.

disformar to deform. reg.

disfrace 1. that I may disguise; pres. subj. 1st pers. sing. / *disfrazar.* 2. that he (she/it) may disguise; pres. subj. 3rd pers. sing. 3. let him (her/it) disguise; impve. 3rd pers. sing.

disfracé I disguised; past 1st pers. sing. / *disfrazar.*

disfracéis that you (all) may disguise; pres. subj. 2nd pers. pl. / *disfrazar.*

disfracémonos let us masquerade; impve. 1st pers. pl. / *disfrazarse.*

disfracemos 1. that we may disguise; pres. subj. 1st pers. pl. / *disfrazar*. 2. let us disguise; impve. 1st pers. pl.

disfracen 1. that they may disguise; pres. subj. 3rd pers. pl. / *disfrazar*. 2. let them disguise; impve. 3rd pers. pl.

disfrácense let them masquerade; impve. 3rd pers. pl. / *disfrazarse*.

disfraces that you may disguise; pres. subj. 2nd pers. sing. / *disfrazar*.

disfrácese let him (her/it) masquerade; impve. 3rd pers. sing. / *disfrazarse*.

disfrazándose masquerading; pres. part. / *disfrazarse*.

disfrazaos (you all) masquerade; impve. 2nd pers. pl. / *disfrazarse*.

disfrazar to disguise. irr.

disfrazarse to masquerade. irr.

disfrázate (you) masquerade; impve. 2nd pers. sing. / *disfrazarse*.

disfrutar to enjoy. reg.

disgregándose disintegrating; pres. part. / *disgregarse*.

disgregaos (you all) disintegrate; impve. 2nd pers. pl. / *disgregarse*.

disgregar to disintegrate. irr.

disgregarse to disintegrate. irr.

disgrégate (you) disintegrate; impve. 2nd pers. sing. / *disgregarse*.

disgregue 1. that I may disintegrate; pres. subj. 1st pers. sing. / *disgregar*. 2. that he (she/it) may disintegrate; pres. subj. 3rd pers. sing. 3. let him (her/it) disintegrate; impve. 3rd pers. sing.

disgregué I disintegrated; past 1st pers. sing. / *disgregar*.

disgreguéis that you (all) may disintegrate; pres. subj. 2nd pers. pl. / *disgregar*.

disgreguémonos let us disintegrate; impve. 1st pers. pl. / *disgregarse*.

disgreguemos 1. that we may disintegrate; pres. subj. 1st pers. pl. / *disgregar*. 2. let us disintegrate; impve. 1st pers. pl.

disgreguen 1. that they may disintegrate; pres. subj. 3rd pers. pl. / *disgregar*. 2. let them disintegrate; impve. 3rd pers. pl.

disgréguense let them disintegrate; impve. 3rd pers. pl. / *disgregarse*.

disgregues that you may disintegrate; pres. subj. 2nd pers. sing. / *disgregar*.

disgréguese let him (her/it) disintegrate; impve. 3rd pers. sing. / *disgregarse*.

disgustándose quarreling; pres. part. / *disgustarse*.

disgustaos (you all) quarrel; impve. 2nd pers. pl. / *disgustarse*.

disgustar to displease. reg.

disgustarse to quarrel. reg.

disgústate (you) quarrel; impve. 2nd pers. sing. / *disgustarse*.

disgustémonos let us quarrel; impve. 1st pers. pl. / *disgustarse*.

disgústense let them quarrel; impve. 3rd pers. pl. / *disgustarse*.

disgústese let him (her/it) quarrel; impve. 3rd pers. sing. / *disgustarse*.

disidir to dissent. reg.

disienta 1. that I may dissent; pres. subj. 1st pers. sing. / *disentir*. 2. that he (she/it) may dissent; pres. subj. 3rd pers. sing. 3. let him (her/it) dissent; impve. 3rd pers. sing.

disientan 1. that they may dissent; pres. subj. 3rd pers. pl. / *disentir*. 2. let them dissent; impve. 3rd pers. pl.

disientas that you may dissent; pres. subj. 2nd pers. sing. / *disentir*.

disiente 1. he (she/it) dissents; pres. ind. 3rd pers. sing. / *disentir*. 2. (you) dissent; impve. 2nd pers. sing.

disienten they dissent; pres. ind. 3rd pers. pl. / *disentir*.

disientes you dissent; pres. ind. 2nd pers. sing. / *disentir*.

disiento I dissent; pres. ind. 1st pers. sing. / *disentir*.

disimilar to dissimulate. reg.

disimular to hide. reg.

disintáis that you (all) may dissent; pres. subj. 2nd pers. pl. / *disentir*.

disintamos 1. that we may dissent; pres. subj. 1st pers. pl. / *disentir*. 2. let us dissent; impve. 1st pers. pl.

disintiendo dissenting; pres. part. / *disentir*.

disintiera 1. that I might dissent; imp. subj. 1st pers. sing. / *disentir*. 2. that he (she/it) might dissent; imp. subj. 3rd pers. sing.

disintierais that you (all) might dissent; imp. subj. 2nd pers pl. / *disentir*.

disintiéramos that we might dissent; imp. subj. 1st pers. pl. / *disentir*.

disintieran that they might dissent; imp. subj. 3rd pers. pl. / *disentir*.

disintieras that you might dissent; imp. subj. 2nd pers. sing. / *disentir*.

disintieron they dissented; past 3rd pers. pl. / *disentir*.

disintiese 1. that I might dissent; imp. subj. 1st pers. sing. / *disentir*. 2. that he (she/it) might dissent; imp. subj. 3rd pers. sing.

disintieseis that you (all) might dissent; imp. subj. 2nd pers. pl. / *disentir*.

disintiésemos that we might dissent; imp. subj. 1st pers. pl. / *disentir*.

disintiesen that they might dissent; imp. subj. 3rd pers. pl. / *disentir*.

disintieses that you might dissent; imp. subj. 2nd pers. sing. / *disentir*.

disintió he (she/it) dissented; past 3rd pers. sing. / *disentir*.

disipándose vanishing; pres. part. / *disiparse*.

disipaos (you all) vanish; impve. 2nd pers. pl. / *disiparse*.

disipar to dissipate. reg.

disiparse to vanish. reg.

disípate (you) vanish; impve. 2nd pers. sing. / *disiparse*.

disgústese let him (her/it) quarrel; impve. 3rd pers. sing. / *disgustarse*.

disipémonos let us vanish; impve. 1st pers. pl. / *disiparse.*

disípense let them vanish; impve. 3rd pers. pl. / *disiparse.*

disípese let him (her/it) vanish; impve. 3rd pers. sing. / *disiparse.*

dislocándose becoming dislocated; pres. part. / *dislocarse.*

dislocaos (you all) become dislocated; impve. 2nd pers. pl. / *dislocarse.*

dislocar to dislocate. irr.

dislocarse to become dislocated. irr.

dislócate (you) become dislocated; impve. 2nd pers. sing. / *dislocarse.*

disloque 1. that I may dislocate; pres. subj. 1st pers. sing. / *dislocar.* 2. that he (she/it) may dislocate; pres. subj. 3rd pers. sing. 3. let him (her/it) dislocate; impve. 3rd pers. sing.

disloqué I dislocated; past 1st pers. sing. / *dislocar.*

disloquéis that you (all) may dislocate; pres. subj. 2nd pers. pl. / *dislocar.*

disloquémonos let us become dislocated; impve. 1st pers. pl. / *dislocarse.*

disloquemos 1. that we may dislocate; pres. subj. 1st pers. pl. / *dislocar.* 2. let us dislocate; impve. 1st pers. pl.

disloquen 1. that they may dislocate; pres. subj. 3rd pers. pl. / *dislocar.* 2. let them dislocate; impve. 3rd pers. pl.

dislóquense let them become dislocated; impve. 3rd pers. pl. / *dislocarse.*

disloques that you may dislocate; pres. subj. 2nd pers. sing. / *dislocar.*

dislóquese let him (her/it) become dislocated; impve. 3rd pers. sing. / *dislocarse.*

disminuíos (you all) decrease; impve. 2nd pers. pl. / *disminuirse.*

disminuir to diminish. irr.

disminuirse to decrease. irr.

disminuya 1. that I may diminish; pres. subj. 1st pers. sing. / *disminuir.* 2. that he (she/it) may diminish; pres. subj. 3rd pers. sing. 3. let him (her/it) diminish; impve. 3rd pers. sing.

disminuyáis that you (all) may diminish; pres. subj. 2nd pers. pl. / *disminuir.*

disminuyámonos let us decrease; impve. 1st pers. pl. / *disminuirse.*

disminuyamos 1. that we may diminish; pres. subj. 1st pers. pl. / *disminuir.* 2. let us diminish; impve. 1st pers. pl.

disminuyan 1. that they may diminish; pres. subj. 3rd pers. pl. / *disminuir.* 2. let them diminish; impve. 3rd pers. pl.

disminúyanse let them decrease; impve. 3rd pers. pl. / *disminuirse.*

disminuyas that you may diminish; pres. subj. 2nd pers. sing. / *disminuir.*

disminúyase let him (her/it) decrease; impve. 3rd pers. sing. / *disminuirse.*

disminuye 1. he (she/it) diminishes; pres. ind. 3rd pers. sing. / *disminuir.* 2. (you) diminish; impve. 2nd pers. sing.

disminuyen they diminish; pres. ind. 3rd pers. pl. / *disminuir.*

disminuyendo diminishing; pres. part. / *disminuir.*

disminuyéndose decreasing; pres. part. / *disminuirse.*

disminuyera 1. that I might diminish; imp. subj. 1st pers. sing. / *disminuir.* 2. that he (she/it) might diminish; imp. subj. 3rd pers. sing.

disminuyerais that you (all) might diminish; imp. subj. 2nd pers pl. / *disminuir.*

disminuyéramos that we might diminish; imp. subj. 1st pers. pl. / *disminuir.*

disminuyeran that they might diminish; imp. subj. 3rd pers. pl. / *disminuir.*

disminuyeras that you might diminish; imp. subj. 2nd pers. sing. / *disminuir.*

disminuyeron they diminished; past 3rd pers. pl. / *disminuir.*

disminuyes you diminish; pres. ind. 2nd pers. sing. / *disminuir.*

disminuyese 1. that I might diminish; imp. subj. 1st pers. sing. / *disminuir.* 2. that he (she/it) might diminish; imp. subj. 3rd pers. sing.

disminuyeseis that you (all) might diminish; imp. subj. 2nd pers pl. / *disminuir.*

disminuyésemos that we might diminish; imp. subj. 1st pers. pl. / *disminuir.*

disminuyesen that they might diminish; imp. subj. 3rd pers. pl. / *disminuir.*

disminuyeses that you might diminish; imp. subj. 2nd pers. sing. / *disminuir.*

disminúyete (you) decrease; impve. 2nd pers. sing. / *disminuirse.*

disminuyo I diminish; pres. ind. 1st pers. sing. / *disminuir.*

disminuyó he (she/it) diminished; past 3rd pers. sing. / *disminuir.*

disociándose dissociating; pres. part. / *disociarse.*

disociaos (you all) dissociate; impve. 2nd pers. pl. / *disociarse.*

disociar to dissociate. reg.

disociarse to dissociate. reg.

disóciate (you) dissociate; impve. 2nd pers. sing. / *disociarse.*

disociémonos let us dissociate; impve. 1st pers. pl. / *disociarse.*

disocíense let them dissociate; impve. 3rd pers. pl. / *disociarse.*

disocíese let him (her/it) dissociate; impve. 3rd pers. sing. / *disociarse.*

disolvámonos let us break up; impve. 1st pers. pl. / *disolverse.*

disolveos (you all) break up; impve. 2nd pers. pl. / *disolverse.*

disolver to dissolve. irr.

disolverse to break up. irr.

disolviéndose breaking up; pres. part. / *disolverse.*

disonar to be dissonant. irr.

disparándose darting off; pres. part. / *dispararse*.
disparaos (you all) dart off; impve. 2nd pers. pl. / *dispararse*.
disparar to shoot. reg.
dispararse to dart off. reg.
dispárate (you) dart off; impve. 2nd pers. sing. / *dispararse*.
disparémonos let us dart off; impve. 1st pers. pl. / *dispararse*.
dispárense let them dart off; impve. 3rd pers. pl. / *dispararse*.
dispárese let him (her/it) dart off; impve. 3rd pers. sing. / *dispararse*.
dispartar to talk nonsense. reg.
dispensar to dispense or to excuse. reg.
dispersándose dispersing; pres. part. / *dispersarse*.
dispersaos (you all) disperse; impve. 2nd pers. pl. / *dispersarse*.
dispersar to disperse. reg.
dispersarse to disperse. reg.
dispérsate (you) disperse; impve. 2nd pers. sing. / *dispersarse*.
dispersémonos let us disperse; impve. 1st pers. pl. / *dispersarse*.
dispérsense let them disperse; impve. 3rd pers. pl. / *dispersarse*.
dispérsese let him (her/it) disperse; impve. 3rd pers. sing. / *dispersarse*.
dispon (you) dispose; impve. 2nd pers. sing. / *disponer*.
dispondrá he (she/it) will dispose; fut. 3rd pers. sing. / *disponer*.
dispondrán they will dispose; fut. 3rd pers. pl. / *disponer*.
dispondrás you will dispose; fut. 2nd pers. sing. / *disponer*.
dispondré I shall dispose; fut. 1st pers. sing. / *disponer*.
dispondréis you (all) will dispose; fut. 2nd pers. pl. / *disponer*.
dispondremos we shall dispose; fut. 1st pers. pl. / *disponer*.
dispondría 1. I should dispose; cond. 1st pers. sing. / *disponer*. 2. he (she/it) would dispose; cond. 3rd pers. sing.
dispondríais you (all) would dispose; cond. 2nd pers. pl. / *disponer*.
dispondríamos we should dispose; cond. 1st pers. pl. / *disponer*.
dispondrían they would dispose; cond. 3rd pers. pl. / *disponer*.
dispondrías you would dispose; cond. 2nd pers. sing. / *disponer*.
disponeos (you all) get ready; impve. 2nd pers. pl. / *disponerse*.
disponer to dispose or to arrange. irr.
disponerse to get ready. irr.

disponga 1. that I may dispose; pres. subj. 1st pers. sing. / *disponer*. 2. that he (she/it) may dispose; pres. subj. 3rd pers. sing. 3. let him (her/it) dispose; impve. 3rd pers. sing.
dispongáis that you (all) may dispose; pres. subj. 2nd pers. pl. / *disponer*.
dispongámonos let us get ready; impve. 1st pers. pl. / *disponerse*.
dispongamos 1. that we may dispose; pres. subj. 1st pers. pl. / *disponer*. 2. let us dispose; impve. 1st pers. pl.
dispongan 1. that they may dispose; pres. subj. 3rd pers. pl. / *disponer*. 2. let them dispose; impve. 3rd pers. pl.
disponganse let them get ready; impve. 3rd pers. pl. / *disponerse*.
dispongas that you may dispose; pres. subj. 2nd pers. sing. / *disponer*.
dispóngase let him (her/it) get ready; impve. 3rd pers. sing. / *disponerse*.
dispongo I dispose; pres. ind. 1st pers. sing. / *disponer*.
disponiendo disposing; pres. part. / *disponer*.
disponiéndose getting ready; pres. part. / *disponerse*.
dispónte (you) get ready; impve. 2nd pers. sing. / *disponerse*.
dispuesto disposed; past part. / *disponer*.
dispuse I disposed; past 1st pers. sing. / *disponer*.
dispusiera 1. that I might dispose; imp. subj. 1st pers. sing. / *disponer*. 2. that he (she/it) might dispose; imp. subj. 3rd pers. sing.
dispusierais that you (all) might dispose; imp. subj. 2nd pers pl. / *disponer*.
dispusiéramos that we might dispose; imp. subj. 1st pers. pl. / *disponer*.
dispusieran that they might dispose; imp. subj. 3rd pers. pl. / *disponer*.
dispusieras that you might dispose; imp. subj. 2nd pers. sing. / *disponer*.
dispusieron they disposed; past 3rd pers. pl. / *disponer*.
dispusiese 1. that I might dispose; imp. subj. 1st pers. sing. / *disponer*. 2. that he (she/it) might dispose; imp. subj. 3rd pers. sing.
dispusieseis that you (all) might dispose; imp. subj. 2nd pers. pl. / *disponer*.
dispusiésemos that we might dispose; imp. subj. 1st pers. pl. / *disponer*.
dispusiesen that they might dispose; imp. subj. 3rd pers. pl. / *disponer*.
dispusieses that you might dispose; imp. subj. 2nd pers. sing. / *disponer*.
dispusimos we disposed; past 1st pers. pl. / *disponer*.
dispusiste you disposed; past 2nd pers. sing. / *disponer*.
dispusisteis you (all) disposed; past 2nd pers. pl. / *disponer*.
dispuso he (she/it) disposed; past 3rd pers. sing. / *disponer*.
disputar to dispute. reg.
distanciándose being aloof; pres. part. / *distanciarse*.

distanciaos (you all) be aloof; impve. 2nd pers. pl. / *distanciarse.*

distanciar to outdistance. reg.

distanciarse to be aloof. reg.

distancíate (you) be aloof; impve. 2nd pers. sing. / *distanciarse.*

distanciémonos let us be aloof; impve. 1st pers. pl. / *distanciarse.*

distancíense let them be aloof; impve. 3rd pers. pl. / *distanciarse.*

distancíese let him (her/it) be aloof; impve. 3rd pers. sing. / *distanciarse.*

distar to be distant. reg.

diste you gave; past 2nd pers. sing. / *dar.*

disteis you (all) gave; past 2nd pers. pl. / *dar.*

distendámonos let us expand; impve. 1st pers. pl. / *distenderse.*

distendeos (you all) expand; impve. 2nd pers. pl. / *distenderse.*

distender to distend. irr.

distenderse to expand. irr.

distendiéndose expanding; pres. part. / *distenderse.*

distienda 1. that I may distend; pres. subj. 1st sing. / *distender.* 2. that he (she/it) may distend; pres. subj. 3rd pers. sing. 3. let him (her/it) distend; impve. 3rd pers. sing.

distiendan 1. that they may distend; pres. subj. 3rd pers. pl. / *distender.* 2. let them distend; impve. 3rd pers. pl.

distiéndanse let them expand; impve. 3rd pers. pl. / *distenderse.*

distiendas that you may distend; pres. subj. 2nd pers. sing. / *distender.*

distiéndase let him (her/it) expand; impve. 3rd pers. sing. / *distenderse.*

distiende 1. he (she/it) distends; pres. ind. 3rd pers. sing. / *distender.* 2. (you) distend; impve. 2nd pers. sing.

distienden they distend; pres. ind. 3rd pers. pl. / *distender.*

distiendes you distend; pres. ind. 2nd pers. sing. / *distender.*

distiéndete (you) expand; impve. 2nd pers. sing. / *distenderse.*

distiendo I distend; pres. ind. 1st pers. sing. / *distender.*

distinga 1. that I may distinguish; pres. subj. 1st pers. sing. / *distinguir.* 2. that he (she/it) may distinguish; pres. subj. 3rd pers. sing. 3. let him (her/it) distinguish; impve. 3rd pers. sing.

distingáis that you (all) may distinguish; pres. subj. 2nd pers. pl. / *distinguir.*

distingámonos let us excel; impve. 1st pers. pl. / *distinguirse.*

distingamos 1. that we may distinguish; pres. subj. 1st pers. pl. / *distinguir.* 2. let us distinguish; impve. 1st pers. pl.

distingan 1. that they may distinguish; pres. subj. 3rd pers. pl. / *distinguir.* 2. let them distinguish; impve. 3rd pers. pl.

distínganse let them excel; impve. 3rd pers. pl. / *distinguirse.*

distingas that you may distinguish; pres. subj. 2nd pers. sing. / *distinguir.*

distíngase let him (her/it) excel; impve. 3rd pers. sing. / *distinguirse.*

distingo I distinguish; pres. ind. 1st pers. sing. / *distinguir.*

distínguete (you) excel; impve. 2nd pers. sing. / *distinguirse.*

distinguiéndose excelling; pres. part. / *distinguirse.*

distinguíos (you all) excel; impve. 2nd pers. pl. / *distinguirse.*

distinguir to distinguish. irr.

distinguirse to excel or to differ. irr.

distorsionar to distort. reg.

distraeos (you all) have a good time; impve. 2nd pers. pl. / *distraerse.*

distraer to distract. irr.

distraerse to have a good time. irr.

distráete (you) have a good time; impve. 2nd pers. sing. / *distraerse.*

distraiga 1. that I may distract; pres. subj. 1st pers. sing. / *distraer.* 2. that he (she/it) may distract; pres. subj. 3rd pers. sing. 3. let him (her/it) distract; impve. 3rd pers. sing.

distraigáis that you (all) may distract; pres. subj. 2nd pers. pl. / *distraer.*

distraigámonos let us have a good time; impve. 1st pers. pl. / *distraerse.*

distraigamos 1. that we may distract; pres. subj. 1st pers. pl. / *distraer.* 2. let us distract; impve. 1st pers. pl.

distraigan 1. that they may distract; pres. subj. 3rd pers. pl. / *distraer.* 2. let them distract; impve. 3rd pers. pl.

distraíganse let them have a good time; impve. 3rd pers. pl. / *distraerse.*

distraigas that you may distract; pres. subj. 2nd pers. sing. / *distraer.*

distraígase let him (her/it) have a good time; impve. 3rd pers. sing. / *distraerse.*

distraigo I distract; pres. ind. 1st pers. sing. / *distraer.*

distraje I distracted; past 1st pers. sing. / *distraer.*

distrajera 1. that I might distract; imp. subj. 1st pers. sing. / *distraer.* 2. that he (she/it) might distract; imp. subj. 3rd pers. sing.

distrajerais that you (all) might distract; imp. subj. 2nd pers pl. / *distraer.*

distrajéramos that we might distract; imp. subj. 1st pers. pl. / *distraer.*

distrajeran that they might distract; imp. subj. 3rd pers. pl. / *distraer.*

distrajeras that you might distract; imp. subj. 2nd pers. sing. / *distraer.*

distrajeron they distracted; past 3rd pers. pl. / *distraer.*

distrajese 1. that I might distract; imp. subj. 1st pers. sing. / *distraer.* 2. that he (she/it) might distract; imp. subj. 3rd pers. sing.

distrajeseis that you (all) might distract; imp. subj. 2nd pers pl. / *distraer.*

distrajésemos that we might distract; imp. subj. 1st pers. pl. / *distraer.*

distrajesen that they might distract; imp. subj. 3rd pers. pl. / *distraer.*

distrajeses that you might distract; imp. subj. 2nd pers. sing. / *distraer.*

distrajimos we distracted; past 1st pers. pl. / *distraer.*

distrajiste you distracted; past 2nd pers. sing. / *distraer.*

distrajisteis you (all) distracted; past 2nd pers. pl. / *distraer.*

distrajo he (she/it) distracted; past 3rd pers. sing. / *distraer.*

distrayendo distracting; pres. part. / *distraer.*

distrayéndose having a good time; pres. part. / *distraerse.*

distribuir to distribute. irr.

distribuya 1. that I may distribute; pres. subj. 1st pers. sing. / *distribuir.* 2. that he (she/it) may distribute; pres. subj. 3rd pers. sing. 3. let him (her/it) distribute; impve. 3rd pers. sing.

distribuyáis that you (all) may distribute; pres. subj. 2nd pers. pl. / *distribuir.*

distribuyamos 1. that we may distribute; pres. subj. 1st pers. pl. / *distribuir.* 2. let us distribute; impve. 1st pers. pl.

distribuyan 1. that they may distribute; pres. subj. 3rd pers. pl. / *distribuir.* 2. let them distribute; impve. 3rd pers. pl.

distribuyas that you may distribute; pres. subj. 2nd pers. sing. / *distribuir.*

distribuye 1. he (she/it) distributes; pres. ind. 3rd pers. sing. / *distribuir.* 2. (you) distribute; impve. 2nd pers. sing.

distribuyen they distribute; pres. ind. 3rd pers. pl. / *distribuir.*

distribuyendo distributing; pres. part. / *distribuir.*

distribuyera 1. that I might distribute; imp. subj. 1st pers. sing. / *distribuir.* 2. that he (she/it) might distribute; imp. subj. 3rd pers. sing.

distribuyerais that you (all) might distribute; imp. subj. 2nd pers pl. / *distribuir.*

distribuyéramos that we might distribute; imp. subj. 1st pers. pl. / *distribuir.*

distribuyeran that they might distribute; imp. subj. 3rd pers. pl. / *distribuir.*

distribuyeras that you might distribute; imp. subj. 2nd pers. sing. / *distribuir.*

distribuyeron they distributed; past 3rd pers. pl. / *distribuir.*

distribuyes you distribute; pres. ind. 2nd pers. sing. / *distribuir.*

distribuyese 1. that I might distribute; imp. subj. 1st pers. sing. / *distribuir.* 2. that he (she/it) might distribute; imp. subj. 3rd pers. sing.

distribuyeseis that you (all) might distribute; imp. subj. 2nd pers pl. / *distribuir.*

distribuyésemos that we might distribute; imp. subj. 1st pers. pl. / *distribuir.*

distribuyesen that they might distribute; imp. subj. 3rd pers. pl. / *distribuir.*

distribuyeses that you might distribute; imp. subj. 2nd pers. sing. / *distribuir.*

distribuyo I distribute; pres. ind. 1st pers. sing. / *distribuir.*

distribuyó he (she/it) distributed; past 3rd pers. sing. / *distribuir.*

disturbar to disturb. reg.

disuadir to dissuade. reg.

disuelto dissolved; past part. / *disolver.*

disuelva 1. that I may dissolve; pres. subj. 1st pers. sing. / *disolver.* 2. that he (she/it) may dissolve; pres. subj. 3rd pers. sing. 3. let him (her/it) dissolve; impve. 3rd pers. sing.

disuelvan 1. that they may dissolve; pres. subj. 3rd pers. pl. / *disolver.* 2. let them dissolve; impve. 3rd pers. pl.

disuélvanse let them break up; impve. 3rd pers. pl. / *disolverse.*

disuelvas that you may dissolve; pres. subj. 2nd pers. sing. / *disolver.*

disuélvase let him (her/it) break up; impve. 3rd pers. sing. / *disolverse.*

disuelve 1. he (she/it) dissolves; pres. ind. 3rd pers. sing. / *disolver.* 2. (you) dissolve; impve. 2nd pers. sing.

disuelven they dissolve; pres. ind. 3rd pers. pl. / *disolver.*

disuelves you dissolve; pres. ind. 2nd pers. sing. / *disolver.*

disuélvete (you) break up; impve. 2nd pers. sing. / *disolverse.*

disuelvo I dissolve; pres. ind. 1st pers. sing. / *disolver.*

disuena 1. he (she/it) is dissonant; pres. ind. 3rd pers. sing. / *disonar.* 2. (you) be dissonant; impve. 2nd pers. sing.

disuenan they are dissonant; pres. ind. 3rd pers. pl. / *disonar.*

disuenas you are dissonant; pres. ind. 2nd pers. sing. / *disonar.*

disuene 1. that I may be dissonant; pres. subj. 1st pers. sing. / *disonar.* 2. that he (she/it) may be dissonant; pres. subj. 3rd pers. sing. 3. let him (her/it) be dissonant; impve. 3rd pers. sing.

disuenen 1. that they may be dissonant; pres. subj. 3rd pers. pl. / *disonar.* 2. let them be dissonant; impve. 3rd pers. pl.

disuenes that you may be dissonant; pres. subj. 2nd pers. sing. / *disonar.*

disueno I am dissonant; pres. ind. 1st pers. sing. / *disonar.*

divagar to ramble or to digress. irr.

divague 1. that I may ramble; pres. subj. 1st pers. sing. / *divagar.* 2. that he (she/it) may ramble; pres. subj. 3rd pers. sing. 3. let him (her/it) ramble; impve. 3rd pers. sing.

divagué I rambled; past 1st pers. sing. / *divagar.*

divaguéis that you (all) may ramble; pres. subj. 2nd pers. pl. / *divagar.*

divaguemos 1. that we may ramble; pres. subj. 1st pers. pl. / *divagar*. 2. let us ramble; impve. 1st pers. pl.

divaguen 1. that they may ramble; pres. subj. 3rd pers. pl. / *divagar*. 2. let them ramble; impve. 3rd pers. pl.

divagues that you may ramble; pres. subj. 2nd pers. sing. / *divagar*.

divergir to diverge. irr.

diverja 1. that I may diverge; pres. subj. 1st pers. sing. / *divergir*. 2. that he (she/it) may diverge; pres. subj. 3rd pers. sing. 3. let him (her/it) diverge; impve. 3rd pers. sing.

diverjáis that you (all) may diverge; pres. subj. 2nd pers. pl. / *divergir*.

diverjamos 1. that we may diverge; pres. subj. 1st pers. pl. / *divergir*. 2. let us diverge; impve. 1st pers. pl.

diverjan 1. that they may diverge; pres. subj. 3rd pers. pl. / *divergir*. 2. let them diverge; impve. 3rd pers. pl.

diverjas that you may diverge; pres. subj. 2nd pers. sing. / *divergir*.

diverjo I diverge; pres. ind. 1st pers. sing. / *divergir*.

diversificándose diversifying; pres. part. / *diversificarse*.

diversificaos (you all) diversify; impve. 2nd pers. pl. / *diversificarse*.

diversificar to diversify. irr.

diversificarse to diversify. irr.

diversifícate (you) diversify; impve. 2nd pers. sing. / *diversificarse*.

diversifique 1. that I may diversify; pres. subj. 1st pers. sing. / *diversificar*. 2. that he (she/it) may diversify; pres. subj. 3rd pers. sing. 3. let him (her/it) diversify; impve. 3rd pers. sing.

diversifiqué I diversified; past 1st pers. sing. / *diversificar*.

diversifiquéis that you (all) may diversify; pres. subj. 2nd pers. pl. / *diversificar*.

diversifiquémonos let us diversify; impve. 1st pers. pl. / *diversificarse*.

diversifiquemos 1. that we may diversify; pres. subj. 1st pers. pl. / *diversificar*. 2. let us diversify; impve. 1st pers. pl.

diversifiquen 1. that they may diversify; pres. subj. 3rd pers. pl. / *diversificar*. 2. let them diversify; impve. 3rd pers. pl.

diversifíquense let them diversify; impve. 3rd pers. pl. / *diversificarse*.

diversifiques that you may diversify; pres. subj. 2nd pers. sing. / *diversificar*.

diversifíquese let him (her/it) diversify; impve. 3rd pers. sing. / *diversificarse*.

divertíos (you all) have fun; impve. 2nd pers. pl. / *divertirse*.

divertir to amuse or to divert. irr.

divertirse to have fun. irr.

dividámonos let us separate; impve. 1st pers. pl. / *dividirse*.

divídanse let them separate; impve. 3rd pers. pl. / *dividirse*.

divídase let him (her/it) separate; impve. 3rd pers. sing. / *dividirse*.

divídete (you) separate; impve. 2nd pers. sing. / *dividirse*.

dividiéndose separating; pres. part. / *dividirse*.

dividíos (you all) separate; impve. 2nd pers. pl. / *dividirse*.

dividir to divide. reg.

dividirse to separate. reg.

divierta 1. that I may amuse; pres. subj. 1st pers. sing. / *divertir*. 2. that he (she/it) may amuse; pres. subj. 3rd pers. sing. 3. let him (her/it) amuse; impve. 3rd pers. sing.

diviertan 1. that they may amuse; pres. subj. 3rd pers. pl. / *divertir*. 2. let them amuse; impve. 3rd pers. pl.

diviértanse let them have fun; impve. 3rd pers. pl. / *divertirse*.

diviertas that you may amuse; pres. subj. 2nd pers. sing. / *divertir*.

diviértase let him (her/i) have fun; impve. 3rd pers. sing. / *divertirse*.

divierte 1. he (she/it) amuses; pres. ind. 3rd pers. sing. / *divertir*. 2. (you) amuse; impve. 2nd pers. sing.

divierten they amuse; pres. ind. 3rd pers. pl. / *divertir*.

diviertes you amuse; pres. ind. 2nd pers. sing. / *divertir*.

diviértete (you) have fun; impve. 2nd pers. sing. / *divertirse*.

divierto I amuse; pres. ind. 1st pers. sing. / *divertir*.

divinice 1. that I may deify; pres. subj. 1st pers. sing. / *divinizar*. 2. that he (she/it) may deify; pres. subj. 3rd pers. sing. 3. let him (her/it) deify; impve. 3rd pers. sing.

divinicé I deified; past 1st pers. sing. / *divinizar*.

divinicéis that you (all) may deify; pres. subj. 2nd pers. pl. / *divinizar*.

divinicemos 1. that we may deify; pres. subj. 1st pers. pl. / *divinizar*. 2. let us deify; impve. 1st pers. pl.

divinicen 1. that they may deify; pres. subj. 3rd pers. pl. / *divinizar*. 2. let them deify; impve. 3rd pers. pl.

divinices that you may deify; pres. subj. 2nd pers. sing. / *divinizar*.

divinizar to deify. irr

divirtáis that you (all) may amuse; pres. subj. 2nd pers. pl. / *divertir*.

divirtámonos let us have fun; impve. 1st pers. pl. / *divertirse*.

divirtamos 1. that we may amuse; pres. subj. 1st pers. pl. / *divertir*. 2. let us amuse; impve. 1st pers. pl.

divirtiendo amusing; pres. part. / *divertir*.

divirtiéndose having fun; pres. part. / *divertirse*.

divirtiera 1. that I might amuse; imp. subj. 1st pers. sing. / *divertir*. 2. that he (she/it) might amuse; imp. subj. 3rd pers. sing.

divirtierais that you (all) might amuse; imp. subj. 2nd pers pl. / *divertir*.

divirtiéramos that we might amuse; imp. subj. 1st pers. pl. / *divertir*.

divirtieran that they might amuse; imp. subj. 3rd pers. pl. / *divertir*.

divirtieras that you might amuse; imp. subj. 2nd pers. sing. / *divertir*.

divirtieron they amused; past 3rd pers. pl. / *divertir*.

divirtiese 1. that I might amuse; imp. subj. 1st pers. sing. / *divertir*. 2. that he (she/it) might amuse; imp. subj. 3rd pers. sing.

divirtieseis that you (all) might amuse; imp. subj. 2nd pers pl. / *divertir*.

divirtiésemos that we might amuse; imp. subj. 1st pers. pl. / *divertir*.

divirtiesen that they might amuse; imp. subj. 3rd pers. pl. / *divertir*.

divirtieses that you might amuse; imp. subj. 2nd pers. sing. / *divertir*.

divirtió he (she/it) amused; past 3rd pers. sing. / *divertir*.

divisar to sight or to perceive. reg.

divorciándose getting a divorce; pres. part. / *divorciarse*.

divorciaos (you all) get a divorce; impve. 2nd pers. pl. / *divorciarse*.

divorciar to divorce. reg.

divorciarse to get a divorce. reg.

divorcíate (you) get a divorce; impve. 2nd pers. sing. / *divorciarse*.

divorciémonos let us get a divorce; impve. 1st pers. pl. / *divorciarse*.

divorcíense let them get a divorce; impve. 3rd pers. pl. / *divorciarse*.

divorcíese let him (her/it) get a divorce; impve. 3rd pers. sing. / *divorciarse*.

divulgar to divulge. irr.

divulgue 1. that I may divulge; pres. subj. 1st pers. sing. / *divulgar*. 2. that he (she/it) may divulge; pres. subj. 3rd pers. sing. 3. let him (her/it) divulge; impve. 3rd pers. sing.

divulgué I divulged; past 1st pers. sing. / *divulgar*.

divulguéis that you (all) may divulge; pres. subj. 2nd pers. pl. / *divulgar*.

divulguemos 1. that we may divulge; pres. subj. 1st pers. pl. / *divulgar*. 2. let us divulge; impve. 1st pers. pl.

divulguen 1. that they may divulge; pres. subj. 3rd pers. pl. / *divulgar*. 2. let them divulge; impve. 3rd pers. pl.

divulgues that you may divulge; pres. subj. 2nd pers. sing. / *divulgar*.

doblándose bending; pres. part. / *doblarse*.

doblaos (you all) bend; impve. 2nd pers. pl. / *doblarse*.

doblar to bend or to double. reg.

doblarse to bend or to stoop. reg.

dóblate (you) bend; impve. 2nd pers. sing. / *doblarse*.

doblegándose yielding; pres. part. / *doblegarse*.

doblegaos (you all) yield; impve. 2nd pers. pl. / *doblegarse*.

doblegar to fold or to bend. irr.

doblegarse to yield. irr.

doblégate (you) yield; impve. 2nd pers. sing. / *doblegarse*.

doblegue 1. that I may fold; pres. subj. 1st pers. sing. / *doblegar*. 2. that he (she/it) may fold; pres. subj. 3rd pers. sing. 3. let him (her/it) fold; impve. 3rd pers. sing.

doblegué I folded; past 1st pers. sing. / *doblegar*.

dobleguéis that you (all) may fold; pres. subj. 2nd pers. pl. / *doblegar*.

dobleguémonos let us yield; impve. 1st pers. pl. / *doblegarse*.

dobleguemos 1. that we may fold; pres. subj. 1st pers. pl. / *doblegar*. 2. let us fold; impve. 1st pers. pl.

dobleguen 1. that they may fold; pres. subj. 3rd pers. pl. / *doblegar*. 2. let them fold; impve. 3rd pers. pl.

dobléguense let them yield; impve. 3rd pers. pl. / *doblegarse*.

doblegues that you may fold; pres. subj. 2nd pers. sing. / *doblegar*.

dobléguese let him (her/it) yield; impve. 3rd pers. sing. / *doblegarse*.

doblémonos let us bend; impve. 1st pers. pl. / *doblarse*.

dóblense let them bend; impve. 3rd pers. pl. / *doblarse*.

dóblese let him (her/it) bend; impve. 3rd pers. sing. / *doblarse*.

doctorándose getting a doctor's degree; pres. part. / *doctorarse*.

doctoraos (you all) get a doctor's degree; impve. 2nd pers. pl. / *doctorarse*.

doctorar to confer a doctor's degree upon. reg.

doctorarse to get a doctor's degree. reg.

doctórate (you) get a doctor's degree; impve. 2nd pers. sing. / *doctorarse*.

doctorémonos let us get a doctor's degree; impve. 1st pers. pl. / *doctorarse*.

doctórense let them get a doctor's degree; impve. 3rd pers. pl. / *doctorarse*.

doctórese let him (her) get a doctor's degree; impve. 3rd pers. sing. / *doctorarse*.

doctrinar to indoctrinate or to instruct. reg.

documentar to document or to inform. reg.

dogmatice 1. that I may dogmatize; pres. subj. 1st pers. sing. / *dogmatizar*. 2. that he (she/it) may dogmatize; pres. subj. 3rd pers. sing. 3. let him (her/it) dogmatize; impve. 3rd pers. sing.

dogmaticé I dogmatized; past 1st pers. sing. / *dogmatizar*.

dogmaticéis that you (all) may dogmatize; pres. subj. 2nd pers. pl. / *dogmatizar*.

dogmaticemos 1. that we may dogmatize; pres. subj. 1st pers. pl. / *dogmatizar*. 2. let us dogmatize; impve. 1st pers. pl.

dogmaticen 1. that they may dogmatize; pres. subj. 3rd pers. pl. / *dogmatizar*. 2. let them dogmatize; impve. 3rd pers. pl.

dogmatices that you may dogmatize; pres. subj. 2nd pers. sing. / *dogmatizar*.

dogmatizar to dogmatize. irr.

dolámonos let us regret; impve. 1st pers. pl. / *dolerse.*

dolar to hew. irr.

doleos (you all) regret; impve. 2nd pers. pl. / *dolerse.*

doler to hurt or to ache. irr.

dolerse to regret. irr.

doliéndose regretting; pres. part. / *dolerse.*

domar to tame. reg.

domeñar to tame or to dominate. reg.

domesticar to domesticate. irr.

domestique 1. that I may domesticate; pres. subj. 1st pers. sing. / *domesticar.* 2. that he (she/it) may domesticate; pres. subj. 3rd pers. sing. 3. let him (her/it) domesticate; impve. 3rd pers. sing.

domestiqué I domesticated; past 1st pers. sing. / *domesticar.*

domestiquéis that you (all) may domesticate; pres. subj. 2nd pers. pl. / *domesticar.*

domestiquemos 1. that we may domesticate; pres. subj. 1st pers. pl. / *domesticar.* 2. let us domesticate; impve. 1st pers. pl.

domestiquen 1. that they may domesticate; pres. subj. 3rd pers. pl. / *domesticar.* 2. let them domesticate; impve. 3rd pers. pl.

domestiques that you may domesticate; pres. subj. 2nd pers. sing. / *domesticar.*

domiciliándose residing; pres. part. / *domiciliarse.*

domiciliaos (you all) reside; impve. 2nd pers. pl. / *domiciliarse.*

domiciliar to house. reg.

domiciliarse to reside. reg.

domicilíate (you) reside; impve. 2nd pers. sing. / *domiciliarse.*

domiciliémonos let us reside; impve. 1st pers. pl. / *domiciliarse.*

domicilíense let them reside; impve. 3rd pers. pl. / *domiciliarse.*

domicilíese let him (her/it) reside; impve. 3rd pers. sing. / *domiciliarse.*

dominándose controlling oneself; pres. part. / *dominarse.*

dominaos (you all) control yourselves; impve. 2nd pers. pl. / *dominarse.*

dominar to dominate. reg.

dominarse to control oneself. reg.

domínate (you) control yourself; impve. 2nd pers. sing. / *dominarse.*

dominémonos let us control ourselves; impve. 1st pers. pl. / *dominarse.*

domínense let them control themselves; impve. 3rd pers. pl. / *dominarse.*

domínese let him (her/it) control himself (herself/itself); impve. 3rd pers. sing. / *dominarse.*

donar to donate. reg.

doñear to woo. reg.

dorar to gild or to sugar-coat. reg.

dormíos (you all) fall asleep; impve. 2nd pers. pl. / *dormirse.*

dormir to sleep. irr.

dormirse to fall asleep. irr.

dormitar to doze. reg.

dosificar to dose. irr.

dosifique 1. that I may dose; pres. subj. 1st pers. sing. / *dosificar.* 2. that he (she/it) may dose; pres. subj. 3rd pers. sing. 3. let him (her/it) dose; impve. 3rd pers. sing.

dosifiqué I dosed; past 1st pers. sing. / *dosificar.*

dosifiquéis that you (all) may dose; pres. subj. 2nd pers. pl. / *dosificar.*

dosifiquemos 1. that we may dose; pres. subj. 1st pers. pl. / *dosificar.* 2. let us dose; impve. 1st pers. pl.

dosifiquen 1. that they may dose; pres. subj. 3rd pers. pl. / *dosificar.* 2. let them dose; impve. 3rd pers. pl.

dosifiques that you may dose; pres. subj. 2nd pers. sing. / *dosificar.*

dotar to endow or to equip. reg.

doy I give; pres. ind. 1st pers. sing. / *dar.*

dragar to dredge. irr.

dragonear to boast or to flirt. reg.

drague 1. that I may dredge; pres. subj. 1st pers. sing. / *dragar.* 2. that he (she/it) may dredge; pres. subj. 3rd pers. sing. 3. let him (her/it) dredge; impve. 3rd pers. sing.

dragué I dredged; past 1st pers. sing. / *dragar.*

draguéis that you (all) may dredge; pres. subj. 2nd pers. pl. / *dragar.*

draguemos 1. that we may dredge; pres. subj. 1st pers. pl. / *dragar.* 2. let us dredge; impve. 1st pers. pl.

draguen 1. that they may dredge; pres. subj. 3rd pers. pl. / *dragar.* 2. let them dredge; impve. 3rd pers. pl.

dragues that you may dredge; pres. subj. 2nd pers. sing. / *dragar.*

dramatice 1. that I may dramatize; pres. subj. 1st pers. sing. / *dramatizar.* 2. that he (she/it) may dramatize; pres. subj. 3rd pers. sing. 3. let him (her/it) dramatize; impve. 3rd pers. sing.

dramaticé I dramatized; past 1st pers. sing. / *dramatizar.*

dramaticéis that you (all) may dramatize; pres. subj. 2nd pers. pl. / *dramatizar.*

dramaticemos 1. that we may dramatize; pres. subj. 1st pers. pl. / *dramatizar.* 2. let us dramatize; impve. 1st pers. pl.

dramaticen 1. that they may dramatize; pres. subj. 3rd pers. pl. / *dramatizar.* 2. let them dramatize; impve. 3rd pers. pl.

dramatices that you may dramatize; pres. subj. 2nd pers. sing. / *dramatizar.*

dramatizar to dramatize. irr.

drenar to drain. reg.

driblar to dribble. reg.

duchándose taking a shower; pres. part. / *ducharse.*

duchaos (you all) take a shower; impve. 2nd pers. pl. / *ducharse.*

duchar to douche. reg.

ducharse to take a shower. reg.

dúchate (you) take a shower; impve. 2nd pers. sing. / *ducharse.*

duchémonos let us take a shower; impve. 1st pers. pl. / *ducharse.*

dúchense let them take a shower; impve. 3rd pers. pl. / *ducharse.*

dúchese let him (her/it) take a shower; impve. 3rd pers. sing. / *ducharse.*

dudar to doubt or to hesitate. reg.

duela 1. he (she/it) hews; pres. ind. 3rd pers. sing. / *dolar.* 2. (you) hew; impve. 2nd pers. sing.

duela 1. that I may hurt; pres. subj. 1st pers. sing. / *doler.* 2. that he (she/it) may hurt; pres. subj. 3rd pers. sing. 3. let him (her/it) hurt; impve. 3rd pers. sing.

duelan they hew; pres. ind. 3rd pers. pl. / *dolar.*

duelan 1. that they may hurt; pres. subj. 3rd pers. pl. / *doler.* 2. let them hurt; impve. 3rd pers. pl.

duélanse let them regret; impve. 3rd pers. pl. / *dolerse.*

duelas you hew; pres. ind. 2nd pers. sing. / *dolar.*

duelas that you may hurt; pres. subj. 2nd pers. sing. / *doler.*

duélase let him (her/it) regret; impve. 3rd pers. sing. / *dolerse.*

duele 1. that I may hew; pres. subj. 1st pers. sing. / *dolar.* 2. that he (she/it) may hew; pres. subj. 3rd pers. sing. 3. let him (her/it) hew; impve. 3rd pers. sing.

duele 1. he (she/it) hurts; pres. ind. 3rd pers. sing. / *doler.* 2. (you) hurt; impve. 2nd pers. sing.

duelen 1. that they may hew; pres. subj. 3rd pers. pl. / *dolar.* 2. let them hew; impve. 3rd pers. pl.

duelen they hurt; pres. ind. 3rd pers. pl. / *doler.*

dueles that you may hew; pres. subj. 2nd pers. sing. / *dolar.*

dueles you hurt; pres. ind. 2nd pers. sing. / *doler.*

duélete (you) regret; impve. 2nd pers. sing. / *dolerse.*

duelo I hew; pres. ind. 1st pers. sing. / *dolar.*

duelo I hurt; pres. ind. 1st pers. sing. / *doler.*

duerma 1. that I may sleep; pres. subj. 1st pers. sing. / *dormir.* 2. that he (she/it) may sleep; pres. subj. 3rd pers. sing. 3. let him (her/it) sleep; impve. 3rd pers. sing.

duerman 1. that they may sleep; pres. subj. 3rd pers. pl. / *dormir.* 2. let them sleep; impve. 3rd pers. pl.

duérmanse let them fall asleep; impve. 3rd pers. pl. / *dormirse.*

duermas that you may sleep; pres. subj. 2nd pers. sing. / *dormir.*

duérmase let him (her/it) fall asleep; impve. 3rd pers. sing. / *dormir.*

duerme 1. he (she/it) sleeps; pres. ind. 3rd pers. sing. / *dormir.* 2. (you) sleep; impve. 2nd pers. sing.

duermen they sleep; pres. ind. 3rd pers. pl. / *dormir.*

duermes you sleep; pres. ind. 2nd pers. sing. / *dormir.*

duérmete (you) fall asleep; impve. 2nd pers. sing. / *dormirse.*

duermo I sleep; pres. ind. 1st pers. sing. / *dormir.*

dulcificar to sweeten. irr.

dulcifique 1. that I may sweeten; pres. subj. 1st pers. sing. / *dulcificar.* 2. that he (she/it) may sweeten; pres. subj. 3rd pers. sing. 3. let him (her/it) sweeten; impve. 3rd pers. sing.

dulcifiqué I sweetened; past 1st pers. sing. / *dulcificar.*

dulcifiquéis that you (all) may sweeten; pres. subj. 2nd pers. pl. / *dulcificar.*

dulcifiquemos 1. that we may sweeten; pres. subj. 1st pers. pl. / *dulcificar.* 2. let us sweeten; impve. 1st pers. pl.

dulcifiquen 1. that they may sweeten; pres. subj. 3rd pers. pl. / *dulcificar.* 2. let them sweeten; impve. 3rd pers. pl.

dulcifiques that you may sweeten; pres. subj. 2nd pers. sing. / *dulcificar.*

duplicar to duplicate or to double. irr.

duplique 1. that I may duplicate; pres. subj. 1st pers. sing. / *duplicar.* 2. that he (she/it) may duplicate; pres. subj. 3rd pers. sing. 3. let him (her/it) duplicate; impve. 3rd pers. sing.

dupliqué I duplicated; past 1st pers. sing. / *duplicar.*

dupliquéis that you (all) may duplicate; pres. subj. 2nd pers. pl. / *duplicar.*

dupliquemos 1. that we may duplicate; pres. subj. 1st pers. pl. / *duplicar.* 2. let us duplicate; impve. 1st pers. pl.

dupliquen 1. that they may duplicate; pres. subj. 3rd pers. pl. / *duplicar.* 2. let them duplicate; impve. 3rd pers. pl.

dupliques that you may duplicate; pres. subj. 2nd pers. sing. / *duplicar.*

durar to last or to endure. reg.

durmáis that you (all) may sleep; pres. subj. 2nd pers. pl. / *dormir.*

durmámonos let us fall asleep; impve. 1st pers. pl. / *dormirse.*

durmamos 1. that we may sleep; pres. subj. 1st pers. pl. / *dormir.* 2. let us sleep; impve. 1st pers. pl.

durmiendo sleeping; pres. part. / *dormir.*

durmiéndose falling asleep; pres. part. / *dormirse.*

durmiera 1. that I might sleep; imp. subj. 1st pers. sing. / *dormir.* 2. that he (she/it) might sleep; imp. subj. 3rd pers. sing.

durmierais that you (all) might sleep; imp. subj. 2nd pers pl. / *dormir.*

durmiéramos that we might sleep; imp. subj. 1st pers. pl. / *dormir.*

durmieran that they might sleep; imp. subj. 3rd pers. pl. / *dormir.*

durmieras that you might sleep; imp. subj. 2nd pers. sing. / *dormir.*

durmieron they slept; past 3rd pers. pl. / *dormir.*

durmiese 1. that I might sleep; imp. subj. 1st pers. sing. / *dormir.* 2. that he (she/it) might sleep; imp. subj. 3rd pers. sing.

durmieseis that you (all) might sleep; imp. subj. 2nd pers pl. / *dormir.*

durmiésemos that we might sleep; imp. subj. 1st pers. pl. / *dormir.*

durmiesen that they might sleep; imp. subj. 3rd pers. pl. / *dormir.*

durmieses that you might sleep; imp. subj. 2nd pers. sing. / *dormir.*

durmió he (she/it) slept; past 3rd pers. sing. / *dormir.*

E

eclipsándose disappearing; pres. part. / *eclipsarse*.
eclipsaos (you all) disappear; impve. 2nd pers. pl. / *eclipsarse*.
eclipsar to eclipse. reg.
eclipsarse to disappear. reg.
eclípsate (you) disappear; impve. 2nd pers. sing. / *eclipsarse*.
eclipsémonos let us disappear; impve. 1st pers. pl. / *eclipsarse*.
eclípsense let them disappear; impve. 3rd pers. pl. / *eclipsarse*.
eclípsese let him (her/it) disappear; impve. 3rd pers. sing. / *eclipsarse*.
economice 1. that I may economize; pres. subj. 1st pers. sing. / *economizar*. 2. that he (she/it) may economize; pres. subj. 3rd pers. sing. 3. let him (her/it) economize; impve. 3rd pers. sing.
economicé I economized; past 1st pers. sing. / *economizar*.
economicéis that you (all) may economize; pres. subj. 2nd pers. pl. / *economizar*.
economicemos 1. that we may economize; pres. subj. 1st pers. pl. / *economizar*. 2. let us economize; impve. 1st pers. pl.
economicen 1. that they may economize; pres. subj. 3rd pers. pl. / *economizar*. 2. let them economize; impve. 3rd pers. pl.
economices that you may economize; pres. subj. 2nd pers. sing. / *economizar*.
economizar to economize. irr.
echándose lying down; pres. part. / *echarse*.
echaos (you all) lie down; impve. 2nd pers. pl. / *echarse*.
echar to throw. reg.
echarse to lie down. reg.
échate (you) lie down; impve. 2nd pers. sing. / *echarse*.
echémonos let us lie down; impve. 1st pers. pl. / *echarse*.
échense let them lie down; impve. 3rd pers. pl. / *echarse*.
échese let him (her/it) lie down; impve. 3rd pers. sing. / *echarse*.
edificar to build or to edify. irr.
edifique 1. that I may build; pres. subj. 1st pers. sing. / *edificar*. 2. that he (she/it) may build; pres. subj. 3rd pers. sing. 3. let him (her/it) build; impve. 3rd pers. sing.
edifiqué I built; past 1st pers. sing. / *edificar*.
edifiquéis that you (all) may build; pres. subj. 2nd pers. pl. / *edificar*.
edifiquemos 1. that we may build; pres. subj. 1st pers. pl. / *edificar*. 2. let us build; impve. 1st pers. pl.
edifiquen 1. that they may build; pres. subj. 3rd pers. pl. / *edificar*. 2. let them build; impve. 3rd pers. pl.
edifiques that you may build; pres. subj. 2nd pers. sing. / *edificar*.

editar to publish. reg.
educar to educate. irr.
educir to bring out or to educe. irr.
eduje I brought out; past 1st pers. sing. / *educir*.
edujera 1. that I might bring out; imp. subj. 1st pers. sing. / *educir*. 2. that he (she/it) might bring out; imp. subj. 3rd pers. sing.
edujerais that you (all) might bring out; imp. subj. 2nd pers pl. / *educir*.
edujéramos that we might bring out; imp. subj. 1st pers. pl. / *educir*.
edujeran that they might bring out; imp. subj. 3rd pers. pl. / *educir*.
edujeras that you might bring out; imp. subj. 2nd pers. sing. / *educir*.
edujeron they brought out; past 3rd pers. pl. / *educir*.
edujese 1. that I might bring out; imp. subj. 1st pers. sing. / *educir*. 2. that he (she/it) might bring out; imp. subj. 3rd pers. sing.
edujeseis that you (all) might bring out; imp. subj. 2nd pers pl. / *educir*.
edujésemos that we might bring out; imp. subj. 1st pers. pl. / *educir*.
edujesen that they might bring out; imp. subj. 3rd pers. pl. / *educir*.
edujeses that you might bring out; imp. subj. 2nd pers. sing. / *educir*.
edujimos we brought out; past 1st pers. pl. / *educir*.
edujiste you brought out; past 2nd pers. sing. / *educir*.
edujisteis you (all) brought out; past 2nd pers. pl. / *educir*.
edujo he (she/it) brought out; past 3rd pers. sing. / *educir*.
eduque 1. that I may educate; pres. subj. 1st pers. sing. / *educar*. 2. that he (she/it) may educate; pres. subj. 3rd pers. sing. 3. let him (her/it) educate; impve. 3rd pers. sing.
eduqué I educated; past 1st pers. sing. / *educar*.
eduquéis that you (all) may educate; pres. subj. 2nd pers. pl. / *educar*.
eduquemos 1. that we may educate; pres. subj. 1st pers. pl. / *educar*. 2. let us educate; impve. 1st pers. pl.
eduquen 1. that they may educate; pres. subj. 3rd pers. pl. / *educar*. 2. let them educate; impve. 3rd pers. pl.
eduques that you may educate; pres. subj. 2nd pers. sing. / *educar*.
eduzca 1. that I may bring out; pres. subj. 1st pers. sing. / *educir*. 2. that he (she/it) may bring out; pres. subj. 3rd pers. sing. 3. let him (her/it) bring out; impve. 3rd pers. sing.
eduzcáis that you (all) may bring out; pres. subj. 2nd pers. pl. / *educir*.
eduzcamos 1. that we may bring out; pres. subj. 1st pers. pl. / *educir*. 2. let us bring out; impve. 1st pers. pl.
eduzcan 1. that they may bring out; pres. subj. 3rd pers. pl. / *educir*. 2. let them bring out; impve. 3rd pers. pl.

eduzcas that you may bring out; pres. subj. 2nd pers. sing. / *educir*.

eduzco I bring out; pres. ind. 1st pers. sing. / *educir*.

efectúa 1. he (she/it) effects; pres. ind. 3rd pers. sing. / *efectuar*. 2. (you) effect; impve. 2nd pers. sing.

efectúan they effect; pres. ind. 3rd pers. pl. / *efectuar*.

efectuar to effect. irr.

efectúas you effect; pres. ind. 2nd pers. sing. / *efectuar*.

efectúe 1. that I may effect; pres. subj. 1st pers. sing. / *efectuar*. 2. that he (she/it) may effect; pres. subj. 3rd pers. sing. 3. let him (her/it) effect; impve. 3rd pers. sing.

efectúen 1. that they may effect; pres. subj. 3rd pers. pl. / *efectuar*. 2. let them effect; impve. 3rd pers. pl.

efectúes that you may effect; pres. subj. 2nd pers. sing. / *efectuar*.

efectúo I effect; pres. ind. 1st pers. sing. / *efectuar*.

egresar to graduate or to withdraw (money). reg.

ejecutar to execute. reg.

ejecutoriar to confirm. reg.

ejemplificar to exemplify. irr.

ejemplifique 1. that I may exemplify; pres. subj. 1st pers. sing. / *ejemplificar*. 2. that he (she/it) may exemplify; pres. subj. 3rd pers. sing. 3. let him (her/it) exemplify; impve. 3rd pers. sing.

ejemplifiqué I exemplified; past 1st pers. sing. / *ejemplificar*.

ejemplifiquéis that you (all) may exemplify; pres. subj. 2nd pers. pl. / *ejemplificar*.

ejemplifiquemos 1. that we may exemplify; pres. subj. 1st pers. pl. / *ejemplificar*. 2. let us exemplify; impve. 1st pers. pl.

ejemplifiquen 1. that they may exemplify; pres. subj. 3rd pers. pl. / *ejemplificar*. 2. let them exemplify; impve. 3rd pers. pl.

ejemplifiques that you may exemplify; pres. subj. 2nd pers. sing. / *ejemplificar*.

ejercer to practice or to exercise. irr.

ejercitándose becoming proficient; pres. part. / *ejercitarse*.

ejercitaos (you all) become proficient; impve. 2nd pers. pl. / *ejercitarse*.

ejercitar to exercise or to drill. reg.

ejercitarse to become proficient. reg.

ejercítate (you) become proficient; impve. 2nd pers. sing. / *ejercitarse*.

ejercitémonos let us become proficient; impve. 1st pers. pl. / *ejercitarse*.

ejercítense let them become proficient; impve. 3rd pers. pl. / *ejercitarse*.

ejercítese let him (her/it) become proficient; impve. 3rd pers. sing. / *ejercitarse*.

ejerza 1. that I may practice; pres. subj. 1st pers. sing. / *ejercer*. 2. that he (she/it) may practice; pres. subj. 3rd pers. sing. 3. let him (her/it) practice; impve. 3rd pers. sing.

ejerzáis that you (all) may practice; pres. subj. 2nd pers. pl. / *ejercer*.

ejerzamos 1. that we may practice; pres. subj. 1st pers. pl. / *ejercer*. 2. let us practice; impve. 1st pers. pl.

ejerzan 1. that they may practice; pres. subj. 3rd pers. pl. / *ejercer*. 2. let them practice; impve. 3rd pers. pl.

ejerzas that you may practice; pres. subj. 2nd pers. sing. / *ejercer*.

ejerzo I practice; pres. ind. 1st pers. sing. / *ejercer*.

elaborar to elaborate or to manufacture. reg.

electrice 1. that I may electrify; pres. subj. 1st pers. sing. / *electrizar*. 2. that he (she/it) may electrify; pres. subj. 3rd pers. sing. 3. let him (her/it) electrify; impve. 3rd pers. sing.

electricé I electrified; past 1st pers. sing. / *electrizar*.

electricéis that you (all) may electrify; pres. subj. 2nd pers. pl. / *electrizar*.

electricemos 1. that we may electrify; pres. subj. 1st pers. pl. / *electrizar*. 2. let us electrify; impve. 1st pers. pl.

electricen 1. that they may electrify; pres. subj. 3rd pers. pl. / *electrizar*. 2. let them electrify; impve. 3rd pers. pl.

electrícense let them become charged with electricity; impve. 3rd pers. pl. / *electrizarse*.

electrices that you may electrify; pres. subj. 2nd pers. sing. / *electrizar*.

electrícese let it become charged with electricity; impve. 3rd pers. sing. / *electrizarse*.

electrificar to electrify. irr.

electrifique 1. that I may electrify; pres. subj. 1st pers. sing. / *electrificar*. 2. that he (she/it) may electrify; pres. subj. 3rd pers. sing. 3. let him (her/it) electrify; impve. 3rd pers. sing.

electrifiqué I electrified; past 1st pers. sing. / *electrificar*.

electrifiquéis that you (all) may electrify; pres. subj. 2nd pers. pl. / *electrificar*.

electrifiquemos 1. that we may electrify; pres. subj. 1st pers. pl. / *electrificar*. 2. let us electrify; impve. 1st pers. pl.

electrifiquen 1. that they may electrify; pres. subj. 3rd pers. pl. / *electrificar*. 2. let them electrify; impve. 3rd pers. pl.

electrifiques that you may electrify; pres. subj. 2nd pers. sing. / *electrificar*.

electrizándose becoming charged with electricity; pres. part. / *electrizarse*.

electrizar to electrify or to thrill. irr.

electrizarse to become charged with electricty. irr.

electrocutar to electrocute. reg.

electrolice 1. that I may electrolyze; pres. subj. 1st pers. sing. / *electrolizar*. 2. that he (she/it) may electrolyze; pres. subj. 3rd pers. sing. 3. let him (her/it) electrolyze; impve. 3rd pers. sing.

electrolicé I electrolized; past 1st pers. sing. / *electrolizar*.

electrolicéis that you (all) may electrolyze; pres. subj. 2nd pers. pl. / *electrolizar*.

electrolicemos 1. that we may electrolyze; pres. subj. 1st pers. pl. / *electrolizar*. 2. let us electrolyze; impve. 1st pers. pl.

electrolicen 1. that they may electrolyze; pres. subj. 3rd pers. pl. / *electrolizar*. 2. let them electrolyze; impve. 3rd pers. pl.

electrolices that you may electrolyze; pres. subj. 2nd pers. sing. / *electrolizar*.

electrolizar to electrolyze. irr.

electroplatear to electroplate. reg.

elegir to elect. irr.

elevándose rising; pres. part. / *elevarse*.

elevaos (you all) rise; impve. 2nd pers. pl. / *elevarse*.

elevar to elevate. reg.

elevarse to rise or to soar. reg.

elévate (you) rise; impve. 2nd pers. sing. / *elevarse*.

elevémonos let us rise; impve. 1st pers. pl. / *elevarse*.

elévense let them rise; impve. 3rd pers. pl. / *elevarse*.

elévese let him (her/it) rise; impve. 3rd pers. sing. / *elevarse*.

elidir to elide. reg.

elige 1. he (she/it) elects; pres. ind. 3rd pers. sing. / *elegir*. 2. (you) elect; impve. 2nd pers. sing.

eligen they elect; pres. ind. 3rd pers. pl. / *elegir*.

eliges you elect; pres. ind. 2nd pers. sing. / *elegir*.

eligiendo electing; pres. part. / *elegir*.

eligiera 1. that I might elect; imp. subj. 1st pers. sing. / *elegir*. 2. that he (she/it) might elect; imp. subj. 3rd pers. sing.

eligierais that you (all) might elect; imp. subj. 2nd pers pl. / *elegir*.

eligiéramos that we might elect; imp. subj. 1st pers. pl. / *elegir*.

eligieran that they might elect; imp. subj. 3rd pers. pl. / *elegir*.

eligieras that you might elect; imp. subj. 2nd pers. sing. / *elegir*.

eligieron they elected; past 3rd pers. pl. / *elegir*.

eligiese 1. that I might elect; imp. subj. 1st pers. sing. / *elegir*. 2. that he (she/it) might elect; imp. subj. 3rd pers. sing.

eligieseis that you (all) might elect; imp. subj. 2nd pers pl. / *elegir*.

eligiésemos that we might elect; imp. subj. 1st pers. pl. / *elegir*.

eligiesen that they might elect; imp. subj. 3rd pers. pl. / *elegir*.

eligieses that you might elect; imp. subj. 2nd pers. sing. / *elegir*.

eligió he (she/it) elected; past 3rd pers. sing. / *elegir*.

elija 1. that I may elect; pres. subj. 1st pers. sing. / *elegir*. 2. that he (she/it) may elect; pres. subj. 3rd pers. sing. 3. let him (her/it) elect; impve. 3rd pers. sing.

elijáis that you (all) may elect; pres. subj. 2nd pers. pl. / *elegir*.

elijamos 1. that we may elect; pres. subj. 1st pers. pl. / *elegir*. 2. let us elect; impve. 1st pers. pl.

elijan 1. that they may elect; pres. subj. 3rd pers. pl. / *elegir*. 2. let them elect; impve. 3rd pers. pl.

elijas that you may elect; pres. subj. 2nd pers. sing. / *elegir*.

elijo I elect; pres. ind. 1st pers. sing. / *elegir*.

eliminar to eliminate. reg.

elogiar to praise. reg.

elucidar to elucidate. reg.

eludir to elude. reg.

emanar to emanate. reg.

emancipándose becoming free; pres. part. / *emanciparse*.

emancipaos (you all) become free; impve. 2nd pers. pl. / *emanciparse*.

emancipar to emancipate. reg.

emanciparse to become free. reg.

emancípate (you) become free; impve. 2nd pers. sing. / *emanciparse*.

emancipémonos let us become free; impve. 1st pers. pl. / *emanciparse*.

emancípense let them become free; impve. 3rd pers. pl. / *emanciparse*.

emancípese let him (her/it) become free; impve. 3rd pers. sing. / *emanciparse*.

emascular to emasculate. reg.

embadurnar to daub or to smear. reg.

embalándose rushing; pres. part. / *embalarse*.

embalaos (you all) rush; impve. 2nd pers. pl. / *embalarse*.

embalar to pack or to bale. reg.

embalarse to rush. reg.

embálate (you) rush; impve. 2nd pers. sing. / *embalarse*.

embaldosar to tile. reg.

embalémonos let us rush; impve. 1st pers. pl. / *embalarse*.

embálense let them rush; impve. 3rd pers. pl. / *embalarse*.

embálese let him (her/it) rush; impve. 3rd pers. sing. / *embalarse*.

embalsamar to embalm or to perfume. reg.

embalsándose damming up; pres. part. / *embalsarse*.

embalsaos (you all) dam up; impve. 2nd pers. pl. / *embalsarse*.

embalsar to put on a raft. reg.

embalsarse to dam up. reg.

embálsate (you) dam up; impve. 2nd pers. sing. / *embalsarse*.

embalsémonos let us dam up; impve. 1st pers. pl. / *embalsarse*.

embálsense let them dam up; impve. 3rd pers. pl. / *embalsarse*.

embálsese let him (her/it) dam up; impve. 3rd pers. sing. / *embalsarse*.

embanderar to decorate with flags. reg.

embarace 1. that I may embarrass; pres. subj. 1st pers. sing. / *embarazar*. 2. that he (she/it) may embarrass; pres. subj. 3rd pers. sing. 3. let him (her/it) embarrass; impve. 3rd pers. sing.

embaracé I embarrassed; past 1st pers. sing. / *embarazar*.

embaracéis that you (all) may embarrass; pres. subj. 2nd pers. pl. / *embarazar*.

embaracémonos let us become pregnant; impve. 1st pers. pl. / *embarazarse*.

embaracemos 1. that we may embarrass; pres. subj. 1st pers. pl. / *embarazar.* 2. let us embarrass; impve. 1st pers. pl.

embaracen 1. that they may embarrass; pres. subj. 3rd pers. pl. / *embarazar.* 2. let them embarrass; impve. 3rd pers. pl.

embarácense let them become pregnant; impve. 3rd pers. pl. / *embarazarse.*

embaraces that you may embarrass; pres. subj. 2nd pers. sing. / *embarazar.*

embarácese let (her/it) become pregnant; impve. 3rd pers. sing. / *embarazarse.*

embarazándose becoming pregnant; pres. part. / *embarazarse.*

embarazaos (you all) become pregnant; impve. 2nd pers. pl. / *embarazarse.*

embarazar to embarrass or to hinder. irr.

embarazarse to become pregnant. irr.

embarázate (you) become pregnant; impve. 2nd pers. sing. / *embarazarse.*

embarcándose sailing; pres. part. / *embarcarse.*

embarcaos (you all) sail; impve. 2nd pers. pl. / *embarcarse.*

embarcar to embark. irr.

embarcarse to sail. irr.

embárcate (you) sail; impve. 2nd pers. sing. / *embarcarse.*

embargar to embargo or to impede. irr.

embargue 1. that I may embargo; pres. subj. 1st pers. sing. / *embargar.* 2. that he (she/it) may embargo; pres. subj. 3rd pers. sing. 3. let him (her/it) embargo; impve. 3rd pers. sing.

embargué I embargoed; past 1st pers. sing. / *embargar.*

embarguéis that you (all) may embargo; pres. subj. 2nd pers. pl. / *embargar.*

embarguemos 1. that we may embargo; pres. subj. 1st pers. pl. / *embargar.* 2. let us embargo; impve. 1st pers. pl.

embarguen 1. that they may embargo; pres. subj. 3rd pers. pl. / *embargar.* 2. let them embargo; impve. 3rd pers. pl.

embargues that you may embargo; pres. subj. 2nd pers. sing. / *embargar.*

embarque 1. that I may embark; pres. subj. 1st pers. sing. / *embarcar.* 2. that he (she/it) may embark; pres. subj. 3rd pers. sing. 3. let him (her/it) embark; impve. 3rd pers. sing.

embarqué I embarked; past 1st pers. sing. / *embarcar.*

embarquéis that you (all) may embark; pres. subj. 2nd pers. pl. / *embarcar.*

embarquémonos let us sail; impve. 1st pers. pl. / *embarcarse.*

embarquemos 1. that we may embark; pres. subj. 1st pers. pl. / *embarcar.* 2. let us embark; impve. 1st pers. pl.

embarquen 1. that they may embark; pres. subj. 3rd pers. pl. / *embarcar.* 2. let them embark; impve. 3rd pers. pl.

embárquense let them sail; impve. 3rd pers. pl. / *embarcarse.*

embarques that you may embark; pres. subj. 2nd pers. sing. / *embarcar.*

embárquese let him (her/it) sail; impve. 3rd pers. sing. / *embarcarse.*

embarrancar to run aground or to run into a ditch. irr.

embarranque 1. that I may run aground; pres. subj. 1st pers. sing. / *embarrancar.* 2. that he (she/it) may run aground; pres. subj. 3rd pers. sing. 3. let him (her/it) run aground; impve. 3rd pers. sing.

embarranqué I ran aground; past 1st pers. sing. / *embarrancar.*

embarranquéis that you (all) may run aground; pres. subj. 2nd pers. pl. / *embarrancar.*

embarranquemos 1. that we may run aground; pres. subj. 1st pers. pl. / *embarrancar.* 2. let us run aground; impve. 1st pers. pl.

embarranquen 1. that they may run aground; pres. subj. 3rd pers. pl. / *embarrancar.* 2. let them run aground; impve. 3rd pers. pl.

embarranques that you may run aground; pres. subj. 2nd pers. sing. / *embarrancar.*

embarrar to smear with mud. reg.

embarullar to mess up. reg.

embastar to baste or to tack. reg.

embasteceos (you all) become coarse; impve. 2nd pers. pl. / *embastecerse.*

embastecer to get fat or flabby. irr.

embastecerse to become coarse. irr.

embastécete (you) become coarse; impve. 2nd pers. sing. / *embastecerse.*

embasteciéndose becoming coarse; pres. part. / *embastecerse.*

embastezca 1. that I may get fat; pres. subj. 1st pers. sing. / *embastecer.* 2. that he (she/it) may get fat; pres. subj. 3rd pers. sing. 3. let him (her/it) get fat; impve. 3rd pers. sing.

embastezcáis that you (all) may get fat; pres. subj. 2nd pers. pl. / *embastecer.*

embastezcámonos let us become coarse; impve. 1st pers. pl. / *embastecerse.*

embastezcamos 1. that we may get fat; pres. subj. 1st pers. pl. / *embastecer.* 2. let us get fat; impve. 1st pers. pl.

embastezcan 1. that they may get fat; pres. subj. 3rd pers. pl. / *embastecer.* 2. let them get fat; impve. 3rd pers. pl.

embastézcanse let them become coarse; impve. 3rd pers. pl. / *embastecerse.*

embastezcas that you may get fat; pres. subj. 2nd pers. sing. / *embastecer.*

embastézcase let him (her/it) become coarse; impve. 3rd pers. sing. / *embastecerse.*

embastezco I get fat; pres. ind. 1st pers. sing. / *embastecer.*

embaucar to deceive. irr.

embauque 1. that I may deceive; pres. subj. 1st pers. sing. / *embaucar.* 2. that he (she/it) may deceive; pres. subj. 3rd pers. sing. 3. let him (her/it) deceive; impve. 3rd pers. sing.

embauqué I deceived; past 1st pers. sing. / *embaucar.*

embauquéis that you (all) may deceive; pres. subj. 2nd pers. pl. / *embaucar.*

embauquemos 1. that we may deceive; pres. subj. 1st pers. pl. / *embaucar.* 2. let us deceive; impve. 1st pers. pl.

embauquen 1. that they may deceive; pres. subj. 3rd pers. pl. / *embaucar.* 2. let them deceive; impve. 3rd pers. pl.

embauques that you may deceive; pres. subj. 2nd pers. sing. / *embaucar.*

embebámonos let us be delighted; impve. 1st pers. pl. / *embeberse.*

embébanse let them be delighted; impve. 3rd pers. pl. / *embeberse.*

embébase let him (her/it) be delighted; impve. 3rd pers. sing. / *embeberse.*

embebecer to amuse or to charm. irr.

embebeos (you all) be delighted; impve. 2nd pers. pl. / *embeberse.*

embeber to drink or to absorb. reg.

embeberse to be delighted. reg.

embébete (you) be delighted; impve. 2nd pers. sing. / *embeberse.*

embebezca 1. that I may amuse; pres. subj. 1st pers. sing. / *embebecer.* 2. that he (she/it) may amuse; pres. subj. 3rd pers. sing. 3. let him (her/it) amuse; impve. 3rd pers. sing.

embebezcáis that you (all) may amuse; pres. subj. 2nd pers. pl. / *embebecer.*

embebezcamos 1. that we may amuse; pres. subj. 1st pers. pl. / *embebecer.* 2. let us amuse; impve. 1st pers. pl.

embebezcan 1. that they may amuse; pres. subj. 3rd pers. pl. / *embebecer.* 2. let them amuse; impve. 3rd pers. pl.

embebezcas that you may amuse; pres. subj. 2nd pers. sing. / *embebecer.*

embebezco I amuse; pres. ind. 1st pers. sing. / *embebecer.*

embebiéndose being delighted; pres. part. / *embeberse.*

embelecar to deceive. irr.

embeleque 1. that I may deceive; pres. subj. 1st pers. sing. / *embelecar.* 2. that he (she/it) may deceive; pres. subj. 3rd pers. sing. 3. let him (her/it) deceive; impve. 3rd pers. sing.

embelequé I deceived; past 1st pers. sing. / *embelecar.*

embelequéis that you (all) may deceive; pres. subj. 2nd pers. pl. / *embelecar.*

embelequemos 1. that we may deceive; pres. subj. 1st pers. pl. / *embelecar.* 2. let us deceive; impve. 1st pers. pl.

embelequen 1. that they may deceive; pres. subj. 3rd pers. pl. / *embelecar.* 2. let them deceive; impve. 3rd pers. pl.

embeleques that you may deceive; pres. subj. 2nd pers. sing. / *embelecar.*

embelesar to charm. reg.

embellecer to embellish. irr.

embellezca 1. that I may embellish; pres. subj. 1st pers. sing. / *embellecer.* 2. that he (she/it) may embellish; pres. subj. 3rd pers. sing. 3. let him (her/it) embellish; impve. 3rd pers. sing.

embellezcáis that you (all) may embellish; pres. subj. 2nd pers. pl. / *embellecer.*

embellezcamos 1. that we may embellish; pres. subj. 1st pers. pl. / *embellecer.* 2. let us embellish; impve. 1st pers. pl.

embellezcan 1. that they may embellish; pres. subj. 3rd pers. pl. / *embellecer.* 2. let them embellish; impve. 3rd pers. pl.

embellezcas that you may embellish; pres. subj. 2nd pers. sing. / *embellecer.*

embellezco I embellish; pres. ind. 1st pers. sing. / *embellecer.*

emberrenchinándose flying into a rage; pres. part. / *emberrenchinarse.*

emberrenchinaos (you all) fly into a rage; impve. 2nd pers. pl. / *emberrenchinarse.*

emberrenchinarse to fly into a rage. reg.

emberrenchínate (you) fly into a rage; impve. 2nd pers. sing. / *emberrenchinarse.*

emberrenchinémonos let us fly into a rage; impve. 1st pers. pl. / *emberrenchinarse.*

emberrenchínense let them fly into a rage; impve. 3rd pers. pl. / *emberrenchinarse.*

emberrenchínese let him (her/it) fly into a rage; impve. 3rd pers. sing. / *emberrenchinarse.*

emberrinchinándose flying into a rage; pres. part. / *emberrinchinarse.*

emberrinchinaos (you all) fly into a rage; impve. 2nd pers. pl. / *emberrinchinarse.*

emberrinchinarse to fly into a rage. reg.

emberrinchínate (you) fly into a rage; impve. 2nd pers. sing. / *emberrinchinarse.*

emberrinchinémonos let us fly into a rage; impve. 1st pers. pl. / *emberrinchinarse.*

emberrinchínense let them fly into a rage; impve. 3rd pers. pl. / *emberrinchinarse.*

emberrinchínese let him (her/it) fly into a rage; impve. 3rd pers. sing. / *emberrinchinarse.*

embestir to attack. irr.

embetunar to cover with pitch. reg.

embista 1. that I may attack; pres. subj. 1st pers. sing. / *embestir.* 2. that he (she/it) may attack; pres. subj. 3rd pers. sing. 3. let him (her/it) attack; impve. 3rd pers. sing.

embistáis that you (all) may attack; pres. subj. 2nd pers. pl. / *embestir.*

embistamos 1. that we may attack; pres. subj. 1st pers. pl. / *embestir.* 2. let us attack; impve. 1st pers. pl.

embistan 1. that they may attack; pres. subj. 3rd pers. pl. / *embestir.* 2. let them attack; impve. 3rd pers. pl.

embistas that you may attack; pres. subj. 2nd pers. sing. / *embestir.*

embiste 1. he (she/it) attacks; pres. ind. 3rd pers. sing. / *embestir.* 2. (you) attack; impve. 2nd pers. sing.

embisten they attack; pres. ind. 3rd pers. pl. / *embestir.*

embistes you attack; pres. ind. 2nd pers. sing. / *embestir.*

embistiendo attacking; pres. part. / *embestir.*

embistiera 1. that I might attack; imp. subj. 1st pers. sing. / *embestir.* 2. that he (she/it) might attack; imp. subj. 3rd pers. sing.

embistierais that you (all) might attack; imp. subj. 2nd pers pl. / *embestir.*

embistiéramos that we might attack; imp. subj. 1st pers. pl. / *embestir.*

embistieran that they might attack; imp. subj. 3rd pers. pl. / *embestir.*

embistieras that you might attack; imp. subj. 2nd pers. sing. / *embestir.*

embistieron they attacked; past 3rd pers. pl. / *embestir.*

embistiese 1. that I might attack; imp. subj. 1st pers. sing. / *embestir.* 2. that he (she/it) might attack; imp. subj. 3rd pers. sing.

embistieseis that you (all) might attack; imp. subj. 2nd pers pl. / *embestir.*

embistiésemos that we might attack; imp. subj. 1st pers. pl. / *embestir.*

embistiesen that they might attack; imp. subj. 3rd pers. pl. / *embestir.*

embistieses that you might attack; imp. subj. 2nd pers. sing. / *embestir.*

embistió he (she/it) attacked; past 3rd pers. sing. / *embestir.*

embisto I attack; pres. ind. 1st pers. sing. / *embestir.*

emblandeceos (you all) be moved with pity; impve. 2nd pers. pl. / *emblandecerse.*

emblandecer to soften. irr.

emblandecerse to be moved to pity. irr.

emblandécete (you) be moved with pity; impve. 2nd pers. sing. / *emblandecerse.*

emblandeciéndose being moved with pity; pres. part. / *emblandecerse.*

emblandezca 1. that I may soften; pres. subj. 1st pers. sing. / *emblandecer.* 2. that he (she/it) may soften; pres. subj. 3rd pers. sing. 3. let him (her/it) soften; impve. 3rd pers. sing.

emblandezcáis that you (all) may soften; pres. subj. 2nd pers. pl. / *emblandecer.*

emblandezcámonos let us be moved with pity; impve. 1st pers. pl. / *emblandecerse.*

emblandezcamos 1. that we may soften; pres. subj. 1st pers. pl. / *emblandecer.* 2. let us soften; impve. 1st pers. pl.

emblandezcan 1. that they may soften; pres. subj. 3rd pers. pl. / *emblandecer.* 2. let them soften; impve. 3rd pers. pl.

emblandézcanse let them be moved with pity; impve. 3rd pers. pl. / *emblandecerse.*

emblandezcas that you may soften; pres. subj. 2nd pers. sing. / *emblandecer.*

emblandézcase let him (her/it) be moved with pity; impve. 3rd pers. sing. / *emblandecerse.*

emblandezco I soften; pres. ind. 1st pers. sing. / *emblandecer.*

emblanquecer to whiten. irr.

emblanquezca 1. that I may whiten; pres. subj. 1st pers. sing. / *emblanquecer.* 2. that he (she/it) may whiten; pres. subj. 3rd pers. sing. 3. let him (her/it) whiten; impve. 3rd pers. sing.

emblanquezcáis that you (all) may whiten; pres. subj. 2nd pers. pl. / *emblanquecer.*

emblanquezcamos 1. that we may whiten; pres. subj. 1st pers. pl. / *emblanquecer.* 2. let us whiten; impve. 1st pers. pl.

emblanquezcan 1. that they may whiten; pres. subj. 3rd pers. pl. / *emblanquecer.* 2. let them whiten; impve. 3rd pers. pl.

emblanquezcas that you may whiten; pres. subj. 2nd pers. sing. / *emblanquecer.*

emblanquezco I whiten; pres. ind. 1st pers. sing. / *emblanquecer.*

embobándose being amazed; pres. part. / *embobarse.*

embobaos (you all) be amazed; impve. 2nd pers. pl. / *embobarse.*

embobar to amuse or to fascinate. reg.

embobarse to be amazed. reg.

embóbate (you) be amazed; impve. 2nd pers. sing. / *embobarse.*

embobecer to stupefy. irr.

embobémonos let us be amazed; impve. 1st pers. pl. / *embobarse.*

embóbense let them be amazed; impve. 3rd pers. pl. / *embobarse.*

embóbese let him (her/it) be amazed; impve. 3rd pers. sing. / *embobarse.*

embobezca 1. that I may stupefy; pres. subj. 1st pers. sing. / *embobecer.* 2. that he (she/it) may stupefy; pres. subj. 3rd pers. sing. 3. let him (her/it) stupefy; impve. 3rd pers. sing.

embobezcáis that you (all) may stupefy; pres. subj. 2nd pers. pl. / *embobecer.*

embobezcamos 1. that we may stupefy; pres. subj. 1st pers. pl. / *embobecer.* 2. let us stupefy; impve. 1st pers. pl.

embobezcan 1. that they may stupefy; pres. subj. 3rd pers. pl. / *embobecer.* 2. let them stupefy; impve. 3rd pers. pl.

embobezcas that you may stupefy; pres. subj. 2nd pers. sing. / *embobecer.*

embobezco I stupefy; pres. ind. 1st pers. sing. / *embobecer.*

embocar to put into the mouth. irr.

emboce 1. that I may muffle; pres. subj. 1st pers. sing. / *embozar.* 2. that he (she/it) may muffle; pres. subj. 3rd pers. sing. 3. let him (her/it) muffle; impve. 3rd pers. sing.

embocé I muffled; past 1st pers. sing. / *embozar.*

embocéis that you (all) may muffle; pres. subj. 2nd pers. pl. / *embozar.*

embocémonos let us muffle ourselves; impve. 1st pers. pl. / *embozarse.*

embocemos 1. that we may muffle; pres. subj. 1st pers. pl. / *embozar*. 2. let us muffle; impve. 1st pers. pl.

embocen 1. that they may muffle; pres. subj. 3rd pers. pl. / *embozar*. 2. let them muffle; impve. 3rd pers. pl.

embócense let them muffle themselves; impve. 3rd pers. pl. / *embozarse*.

emboces that you may muffle; pres. subj. 2nd pers. sing. / *embozar*.

embócese let him (her/it) muffle himself (herself/itself); impve. 3rd pers. sing. / *embozarse*.

embodegar to store in a cellar. reg.

embolándose getting drunk; pres. part. / *embolarse*.

embolaos (you all) get drunk; impve. 2nd pers. pl. / *embolarse*.

embolar to tip a bull's horns with wooden balls or to polish black. reg.

embolarse to get drunk. reg.

embólate (you) get drunk; impve. 2nd pers. sing. / *embolarse*.

embolémonos let us get drunk; impve. 1st pers. pl. / *embolarse*.

embólense let them get drunk; impve. 3rd pers. pl. / *embolarse*.

embólese let him (her/it) get drunk; impve. 3rd pers. sing. / *embolarse*.

embolsándose pocketing; pres. part. / *embolsarse*.

embolsaos (you all) pocket; impve. 2nd pers. pl. / *embolsarse*.

embolsar to put into a pocket or purse. reg.

embolsarse to pocket. reg.

embólsate (you) pocket; impve. 2nd pers. sing. / *embolsarse*.

embolsémonos let us pocket; impve. 1st pers. pl. / *embolsarse*.

embólsense let them pocket; impve. 3rd pers. pl. / *embolsarse*.

embólsese let him (her/it) pocket; impve. 3rd pers. sing. / *embolsarse*.

embonar to improve. reg.

emboque 1. that I may put into the mouth; pres. subj. 1st pers. sing. / *embocar*. 2. that he (she/it) may put in the mouth; pres. subj. 3rd pers. sing. 3. let him (her/it) put into the mouth; impve. 3rd pers. sing.

emboqué I put into the mouth; past 1st pers. sing. / *embocar*.

emboquéis that you (all) may put into the mouth; pres. subj. 2nd pers. pl. / *embocar*.

emboquemos 1. that we may put into the mouth; pres. subj. 1st pers. pl. / *embocar*. 2. let us put into the mouth; impve. 1st pers. pl.

emboquen 1. that they may put into the mouth; pres. subj. 3rd pers. pl. / *embocar*. 2. let them put into the mouth; impve. 3rd pers. pl.

emboques that you may put into the mouth; pres. subj. 2nd pers. sing. / *embocar*.

emboquillar to tip (cigarettes). reg.

emborrachándose getting drunk; pres. part. / *emborracharse*.

emborrachaos (you all) get drunk; impve. 2nd pers. pl. / *emborracharse*.

emborrachar to intoxicate. reg.

emborracharse to get drunk. reg.

emborráchate (you) get drunk; impve. 2nd pers. sing. / *emborracharse*.

emborrachémonos let us get drunk; impve. 1st pers. pl. / *emborracharse*.

emborráchense let them get drunk; impve. 3rd pers. pl. / *emborracharse*.

emborráchese let him (her/it) get drunk; impve. 3rd pers. sing. / *emborracharse*.

emborrar to pad. reg.

emborrascándose becoming stormy; pres. part. / *emborrascarse*.

emborrascaos (you all) become stormy; impve. 2nd pers. pl. / *emborrascarse*.

emborrascar to provoke or to anger. irr.

emborrascarse to become stormy. irr.

emborráscate (you) become stormy; impve. 2nd pers. sing. / *emborrascarse*.

emborrasque 1. that I may provoke; pres. subj. 1st pers. sing. / *emborrascar*. 2. that he (she/it) may provoke; pres. subj. 3rd pers. sing. 3. let him (her/it) provoke; impve. 3rd pers. sing.

emborrasqué I provoked; past 1st pers. sing. / *emborrascar*.

emborrasquéis that you (all) may provoke; pres. subj. 2nd pers. pl. / *emborrascar*.

emborrasquémonos let us become stormy; impve. 1st pers. pl. / *emborrascarse*.

emborrasquemos 1. that we may provoke; pres. subj. 1st pers. pl. / *emborrascar*. 2. let us provoke; impve. 1st pers. pl.

emborrasquen 1. that they may provoke; pres. subj. 3rd pers. pl. / *emborrascar*. 2. let them provoke; impve. 3rd pers. pl.

emborrásquense let them become stormy; impve. 3rd pers. pl. / *emborrascarse*.

emborrasques that you may provoke; pres. subj. 2nd pers. sing. / *emborrascar*.

emborrásquese let him (her/it) become stormy; impve. 3rd pers. sing. / *emborrascarse*.

emborronar to blot or to scribble. reg.

emboscándose going into the woods; pres. part. / *emboscarse*.

emboscaos (you all) go into the woods; impve. 2nd pers. pl. / *emboscarse*.

emboscar to ambush. irr.

emboscarse to go into the woods. irr.

embóscate (you) go into the woods; impve. 2nd pers. sing. / *emboscarse*.

embosque 1. that I may ambush; pres. subj. 1st pers. sing. / *emboscar*. 2. that he (she/it) may ambush; pres. subj. 3rd pers. sing. 3. let him (her/it) ambush; impve. 3rd pers. sing.

embosqué I ambushed; past 1st pers. sing. / *emboscar*.

embosquéis that you (all) may ambush; pres. subj. 2nd pers. pl. / *emboscar*.

embosquémonos let us go into the woods; impve. 1st pers. pl. / *emboscarse.*

embosquemos 1. that we may ambush; pres. subj. 1st pers. pl. / *emboscar.* 2. let us ambush; impve. 1st pers. pl.

embosquen 1. that they may ambush; pres. subj. 3rd pers. pl. / *emboscar.* 2. let them ambush; impve. 3rd pers. pl.

embósquense let them go into the woods; impve. 3rd pers. pl. / *emboscarse.*

embosques that you may ambush; pres. subj. 2nd pers. sing. / *emboscar.*

embósquese let him (her/it) go into the woods; impve. 3rd pers. sing. / *emboscarse.*

embotar to blunt. reg.

embotellar to bottle. reg.

embotijándose being in a rage; pres. part. / *embotijarse.*

embotijaos (you all) be in a rage; impve. 2nd pers. pl. / *embotijarse.*

embotijar to put into jars. reg.

embotijarse to be in a rage. reg.

embotíjate (you) be in a rage; impve. 2nd pers. sing. / *embotijarse.*

embotijémonos let us be in a rage; impve. 1st pers. pl. / *embotijarse.*

embotíjense let them be in a rage; impve. 3rd pers. pl. / *embotijarse.*

embotíjese let him (her/it) be in a rage; impve. 3rd pers. sing. / *embotijarse.*

embovedar to arch or to vault. reg.

embozalar to muzzle. reg.

embozándose muffling oneself; pres. part. / *embozarse.*

embozaos (you all) muffle yourselves; impve. 2nd pers. pl. / *embozarse.*

embozar to muffle or to disguise. irr.

embozarse to muffle oneself. irr.

embózate (you) muffle youself; impve. 2nd pers. sing. / *embozarse.*

embrace 1. that I may clasp; pres. subj. 1st pers. sing. / *embrazar.* 2. that he (she/it) may clasp; pres. subj. 3rd pers. sing. 3. let him (her/it) clasp; impve. 3rd pers. sing.

embracé I clasped; past 1st pers. sing. / *embrazar.*

embracéis that you (all) may clasp; pres. subj. 2nd pers. pl. / *embrazar.*

embracemos 1. that we may clasp; pres. subj. 1st pers. pl. / *embrazar.* 2. let us clasp; impve. 1st pers. pl.

embracen 1. that they may clasp; pres. subj. 3rd pers. pl. / *embrazar.* 2. let them clasp; impve. 3rd pers. pl.

embraces that you may clasp; pres. subj. 2nd pers. sing. / *embrazar.*

embragar to let out the clutch. irr.

embrague 1. that I may let out the clutch; pres. subj. 1st pers. sing. / *embragar.* 2. that he (she/it) may let out the clutch; pres. subj. 3rd pers. sing. 3. let him (her/it) let out the clutch; impve. 3rd pers. sing.

embragué I let out the clutch; past 1st pers. sing. / *embragar.*

embraguéis that you (all) may let out the clutch; pres. subj. 2nd pers. pl. / *embragar.*

embraguemos 1. that we may let out the clutch; pres. subj. 1st pers. pl. / *embragar.* 2. let us let out the clutch; impve. 1st pers. pl.

embraguen 1. that they may let out the clutch; pres. subj. 3rd pers. pl. / *embragar.* 2. let them let out the clutch; impve. 3rd pers. pl.

embragues that you may let out the clutch; pres. subj. 2nd pers. sing. / *embragar.*

embraveceos (you all) become enraged; impve. 2nd pers. pl. / *embravecerse.*

embravecer to enrage or to become strong. irr.

embravecerse to become enraged. irr.

embravécete (you) become enraged; impve. 2nd pers. sing. / *embravecerse.*

embraveciéndose becoming enraged; pres. part. / *embravecerse.*

embravezca 1. that I may enrage; pres. subj. 1st pers. sing. / *embravecer.* 2. that he (she/it) may enrage; pres. subj. 3rd pers. sing. 3. let him (her/it) enrage; impve. 3rd pers. sing.

embravezcáis that you (all) may enrage; pres. subj. 2nd pers. pl. / *embravecer.*

embravezcámonos let us become enraged; impve. 1st pers. pl. / *embravecerse.*

embravezcamos 1. that we may enrage; pres. subj. 1st pers. pl. / *embravecer.* 2. let us enrage; impve. 1st pers. pl.

embravezcan 1. that they may enrage; pres. subj. 3rd pers. pl. / *embravecer.* 2. let them enrage; impve. 3rd pers. pl.

embravézcanse let them become enraged; impve. 3rd pers. pl. / *embravecerse.*

embravezcas that you may enrage; pres. subj. 2nd pers. sing. / *embravecer.*

embravézcase let him (her/it) become enraged; impve. 3rd pers. sing. / *embravecerse.*

embravezco I enrage; pres. ind. 1st pers. sing. / *embravecer.*

embrazar to clasp or to engage (gears). irr.

embrear to coat with pitch. reg.

embriagándose getting drunk; pres. part. / *embriagarse.*

embriagaos (you all) get drunk; impve. 2nd pers. pl. / *embriagarse.*

embriagar to intoxicate. irr.

embriagarse to get drunk. irr.

embriágate (you) get drunk; impve. 2nd pers. sing. / *embriagarse.*

embriague 1. that I may intoxicate; pres. subj. 1st pers. sing. / *embriagar.* 2. that he (she/it) may intoxicate; pres. subj. 3rd pers. sing. 3. let him (her/it) intoxicate; impve. 3rd pers. sing.

embriagué I intoxicated; past 1st pers. sing. / *embriagarse.*

embriaguéis that you (all) may intoxicate; pres. subj. 2nd pers. pl. / *embriagar.*

embriaguémonos let us get drunk; impve. 1st pers. pl. / *embriagarse.*

embriaguemos 1. that we may intoxicate; pres. subj. 1st pers. pl. / *embriagar.* 2. let us intoxicate; impve. 1st pers. pl.

embriaguen 1. that they may intoxicate; pres. subj. 3rd pers. pl. / *embriagar.* 2. let them intoxicate; impve. 3rd pers. pl.

embriáguense let them get drunk; impve. 3rd pers. pl. / *embriagarse.*

embriagues that you may intoxicate; pres. subj. 2nd pers. sing. / *embriagar.*

embriáguese let him (her/it) get drunk; impve. 3rd pers. sing. / *embriagarse.*

embrocar to place upside down. irr.

embrollar to embroil or to entangle. reg.

embromándose being bothered; pres. part. / *embromarse.*

embromaos (you all) be bothered; impve. 2nd pers. pl. / *embromarse.*

embromar to tease or to bore. reg.

embromarse to be bothered. reg.

embrómate (you) be bothered; impve. 2nd pers. sing. / *embromarse.*

embromémonos let us be bothered; impve. 1st pers. pl. / *embromarse.*

embrómense let them be bothered; impve. 3rd pers. pl. / *embromarse.*

embrómese let him (her/it) be bothered; impve. 3rd pers. sing. / *embromarse.*

embroque 1. that I may place upside down; pres. subj. 1st pers. sing. / *embrocar.* 2. that he (she/it) may place upside down; pres. subj. 3rd pers. sing. 3. let him (her/it) place upside down; impve. 3rd pers. sing.

embroqué I placed upside down; past 1st pers. sing. / *embrocar.*

embroquéis that you (all) may place upside down; pres. subj. 2nd pers. pl. / *embrocar.*

embroquemos 1. that we may place upside down; pres. subj. 1st pers. pl. / *embrocar.* 2. let us place upside down; impve. 1st pers. pl.

embroquen 1. that they may place upside down; pres. subj. 3rd pers. pl. / *embrocar.* 2. let them place upside down; impve. 3rd pers. pl.

embroques that you may place upside down; pres. subj. 2nd pers. sing. / *embrocar.*

embrujar to bewitch or to charm. reg.

embrutecer to stupefy. irr.

embrutezca 1. that I may stupefy; pres. subj. 1st pers. sing. / *embrutecer.* 2. that he (she/it) may stupefy; pres. subj. 3rd pers. sing. 3. let him (her/it) stupefy; impve. 3rd pers. sing.

embrutezcáis that you (all) may stupefy; pres. subj. 2nd pers. pl. / *embrutecer.*

embrutezcamos 1. that we may stupefy; pres. subj. 1st pers. pl. / *embrutecer.* 2. let us stupefy; impve. 1st pers. pl.

embrutezcan 1. that they may stupefy; pres. subj. 3rd pers. pl. / *embrutecer.* 2. let them stupefy; impve. 3rd pers. pl.

embrutezcas that you may stupefy; pres. subj. 2nd pers. sing. / *embrutecer.*

embrutezco I stupefy; pres. ind. 1st pers. sing. / *embrutecer.*

embuchar to stuff. reg.

embutir to inlay or to stuff. reg.

emerger to emerge. irr.

emerja 1. that I may emerge; pres. subj. 1st pers. sing. / *emerger.* 2. that he (she/it) may emerge; pres. subj. 3rd pers. sing. 3. let him (her/it) emerge; impve. 3rd pers. sing.

emerjáis that you (all) may emerge; pres. subj. 2nd pers. pl. / *emerger.*

emerjamos 1. that we may emerge; pres. subj. 1st pers. pl. / *emerger.* 2. let us emerge; impve. 1st pers. pl.

emerjan 1. that they may emerge; pres. subj. 3rd pers. pl. / *emerger.* 2. let them emerge; impve. 3rd pers. pl.

emerjas that you may emerge; pres. subj. 2nd pers. sing. / *emerger.*

emerjo I emerge; pres. ind. 1st pers. sing. / *emerger.*

emigrar to emigrate. reg.

emitir to emit. reg.

emocionándose being stirred; pres. part. / *emocionarse.*

emocionaos (you all) be stirred; impve. 2nd pers. pl. / *emocionarse.*

emocionar to touch or to excite. reg.

emocionarse to be stirred. reg.

emociónate (you) be stirred; impve. 2nd pers. sing. / *emocionarse.*

emocionémonos let us be stirred; impve. 1st pers. pl. / *emocionarse.*

emociónense let them be stirred; impve. 3rd pers. pl. / *emocionarse.*

emociónese let him (her/it) be stirred; impve. 3rd pers. sing. / *emocionarse.*

empacándose getting angry; pres. part. / *empacarse.*

empacaos (you all) get angry; impve. 2nd pers. pl. / *empacarse.*

empacar to pack. irr.

empacarse to get angry. irr.

empácate (you) get angry; impve. 2nd pers. sing. / *empacarse.*

empachándose getting embarrassed; pres. part. / *empacharse.*

empachaos (you all) get embarrassed; impve. 2nd pers. pl. / *empacharse.*

empachar to stuff or to surfeit. reg.

empacharse to get embarrassed. reg.

empáchate (you) get embarrassed; impve. 2nd pers. sing. / *empacharse.*

empachémonos let us get embarrassed; impve. 1st pers. pl. / *empacharse.*

empáchense let them get embarrassed; impve. 3rd pers. pl. / *empacharse.*

empáchese let him (her/it) get embarrassed; impve. 3rd pers. sing. / *empacharse.*

empadronándose registering; pres. part. / *empadronarse.*

empadronaos (you all) register; impve. 2nd pers. pl. / *empadronarse.*

empadronar to register. reg.

empadronarse to register. reg.

empadrónate (you) register; impve. 2nd pers. sing. / *empadronarse.*

empadronémonos let us register; impve. 1st pers. pl. / *empadronarse.*

empadrónense let them register; impve. 3rd pers. pl. / *empadronarse.*

empadrónese let him (her/it) register; impve. 3rd pers. sing. / *empadronarse.*

empajar to cover with straw. reg.

empalagar to cloy or to bore. irr.

empalague 1. that I may bore; pres. subj. 1st pers. sing. / *empalagar.* 2. that he (she/it) may bore; pres. subj. 3rd pers. sing. 3. let him (her/it) bore; impve. 3rd pers. sing.

empalagué I bored; past 1st pers. sing. / *empalagar.*

empalaguéis that you (all) may bore; pres. subj. 2nd pers. pl. / *empalagar.*

empalaguemos 1. that we may bore; pres. subj. 1st pers. pl. / *empalagar.* 2. let us bore; impve. 1st pers. pl.

empalaguen 1. that they may bore; pres. subj. 3rd pers. pl. / *empalagar.* 2. let them bore; impve. 3rd pers. pl.

empalagues that you may bore; pres. subj. 2nd pers. sing. / *empalagar.*

empalar to impale. reg.

empalice 1. that I may fence; pres. subj. 1st pers. sing. / *empalizar.* 2. that he (she/it) may fence; pres. subj. 3rd pers. sing. 3. let him (her/it) fence; impve. 3rd pers. sing.

empalicé I fenced; past 1st pers. sing. / *empalizar.*

empalicéis that you (all) may fence; pres. subj. 2nd pers. pl. / *empalizar.*

empalicemos 1. that we may fence; pres. subj. 1st pers. pl. / *empalizar.* 2. let us fence; impve. 1st pers. pl.

empalicen 1. that they may fence; pres. subj. 3rd pers. pl. / *empalizar.* 2. let them fence; impve. 3rd pers. pl.

empalices that you may fence; pres. subj. 2nd pers. sing. / *empalizar.*

empalizar to fence. irr.

empalmar to splice. reg.

empanar to bread. reg.

empanice 1. that I may bread; pres. subj. 1st pers. sing. / *empanizar.* 2. that he (she/it) may bread; pres. subj. 3rd pers. sing. 3. let him (her/it) bread; impve. 3rd pers. sing.

empanicé I breaded; past 1st pers. sing. / *empanizar.*

empanicéis that you (all) may bread; pres. subj. 2nd pers. pl. / *empanizar.*

empanicemos 1. that we may bread; pres. subj. 1st pers. pl. / *empanizar.* 2. let us bread; impve. 1st pers. pl.

empanicen 1. that they may bread; pres. subj. 3rd pers. pl. / *empanizar.* 2. let them bread; impve. 3rd pers. pl.

empanices that you may bread; pres. subj. 2nd pers. sing. / *empanizar.*

empanizar to bread. irr.

empantanar to swamp. reg.

empañar to swaddle or to blur. reg.

empañetar to plaster. reg.

empapándose delving into; pres. part. / *empaparse.*

empapaos (you all) delve into; impve. 2nd pers. pl. / *empaparse.*

empapar to soak. reg.

empaparse to delve into. reg.

empápate (you) delve into; impve. 2nd pers. sing. / *empaparse.*

empapelar to paper. reg.

empapémonos let us delve into; impve. 1st pers. pl. / *empaparse.*

empápense let them delve into; impve. 3rd pers. pl. / *empaparse.*

empápese let him (her/it) delve into; impve. 3rd pers. sing. / *empaparse.*

empaque 1. that I may pack; pres. subj. 1st pers. sing. / *empacar.* 2. that he (she/it) may pack; pres. subj. 3rd pers. sing. 3. let him (her/it) pack; impve. 3rd pers. sing.

empaqué I packed; past 1st pers. sing. / *empacar.*

empaquéis that you (all) may pack; pres. subj. 2nd pers. pl. / *empacar.*

empaquémonos let us get angry; impve. 1st pers. pl. / *empacarse.*

empaquemos 1. that we may pack; pres. subj. 1st pers. pl. / *empacar.* 2. let us pack; impve. 1st pers. pl.

empaquen 1. that they may pack; pres. subj. 3rd pers. pl. / *empacar.* 2. let them pack; impve. 3rd pers. pl.

empáquense let them get angry; impve. 3rd pers. pl. / *empacarse.*

empaques that you may pack; pres. subj. 2nd pers. sing. / *empacar.*

empáquese let him (her/it) get angry; impve. 3rd pers. sing. / *empacarse.*

empaquetándose dressing up; pres. part. / *empaquetarse.*

empaquetaos (you all) dress up; impve. 2nd pers. pl. / *empaquetarse.*

empaquetar to pack. reg.

empaquetarse to dress up. reg.

empaquétate (you) dress up; impve. 2nd pers. sing. / *empaquetarse.*

empaquetémonos let us dress up; impve. 1st pers. pl. / *empaquetarse.*

empaquétense let them dress up; impve. 3rd pers. pl. / *empaquetarse.*

empaquétese let him (her/it) dress up; impve. 3rd pers. sing. / *empaquetarse.*

emparchar to put a plaster cast on. reg.

emparedar to confine or to wall in. reg.

emparejar to pair or to level. reg.

emparentar to become related by marriage. irr.

---

empanicen 1. that they may bread; pres. subj. 3rd pers. pl. / *empanizar.* 2. let them bread; impve. 3rd pers. pl.

empanices that you may bread; pres. subj. 2nd pers. sing. / *empanizar.*

emparienta 1. he (she/it) becomes related by marriage; pres. ind. 3rd pers. sing. / *emparentar*. 2. (you) become related by marriage; impve. 2nd pers. sing.

emparientan they become related by marriage; pres. ind. 3rd pers. pl. / *emparentar*.

emparientas you become related by marriage; pres. ind. 2nd pers. sing. / *emparentar*.

empariente 1. that I may become related by marriage; pres. subj. 1st pers. sing. / *emparentar*. 2. that he (she/it) may become related by marriage; pres. subj. 3rd pers. sing. 3. let him (her/it) become related by marriage; impve. 3rd pers. sing.

emparienten 1. that they may become related by marriage; pres. subj. 3rd pers. pl. / *emparentar*. 2. let them become related by marriage; impve. 3rd pers. pl.

emparientes that you may become related by marriage; pres. subj. 2nd pers. sing. / *emparentar*.

empariento I become related by marriage; pres. ind. 1st pers. sing. / *emparentar*.

empastándose getting lost in the pasture; pres. part. / *empastarse*.

empastaos (you all) get lost in the pasture; impve. 2nd pers. pl. / *empastarse*.

empastar to paste or to fill a tooth. reg.

empastarse to get lost in the pasture. reg.

empástate (you) get lost in the pasture; impve. 2nd pers. sing. / *empastarse*.

empastelar to botch or to compromise. reg.

empastémonos let us get lost in the pasture; impve. 1st pers. pl. / *empastarse*.

empástense let them get lost in the pasture; impve. 3rd pers. pl. / *empastarse*.

empástese let him (her/it) get lost in the pasture; impve. 3rd pers. sing. / *empastarse*.

empatándose tying (sports); pres. part. / *empatarse*.

empataos (you all) tie (sports); impve. 2nd pers. pl. / *empatarse*.

empatar to tie (vote reg.

empatarse to tie (sports). reg.

empátate (you) tie (sports); impve. 2nd pers. sing. / *empatarse*.

empatémonos let us tie (sports); impve. 1st pers. pl. / *empatarse*.

empátense let them tie (sports); impve. 3rd pers. pl. / *empatarse*.

empátese let him (her/it) tie (sports); impve. 3rd pers. sing. / *empatarse*.

empavesar to deck out with flags. reg.

empecé I began; past 1st pers. sing. / *empezar*.

empecéis that you (all) may begin; pres. subj. 2nd pers. pl. / *empezar*.

empecemos 1. that we may begin; pres. subj. 1st pers. pl. / *empezar*. 2. let us begin; impve. 1st pers. pl.

empecinándose being stubborn; pres. part. / *empecinarse*.

empecinaos (you all) be stubborn; impve. 2nd pers. pl. / *empecinarse*.

empecinarse to be stubborn or to persist. reg.

empecínate (you) be stubborn; impve. 2nd pers. sing. / *empecinarse*.

empecinémonos let us be stubborn; impve. 1st pers. pl. / *empecinarse*.

empecínense let them be stubborn; impve. 3rd pers. pl. / *empecinarse*.

empecínese let him (her/it) be stubborn; impve. 3rd pers. sing. / *empecinarse*.

empederniéndose becoming hardened; pres. part. / *empedernirse*.

empederníos (you all) become hardened; impve. 2nd pers. pl. / *empedernirse*.

empedernir to harden. irr. this verb is used only in the forms that have an i in the ending.

empedernirse to become hardened. irr.

empedrar to pave with stones. irr.

empegarse to coat with pitch. irr.

empegue 1. that I may coat with pitch; pres. subj. 1st pers. sing. / *empegarse*. 2. that he (she/it) may coat with pitch; pres. subj. 3rd pers. sing. 3. let him (her/it) coat with pitch; impve. 3rd pers. sing.

empegué I coated with pitch; past 1st pers. sing. / *empegarse*.

empeguéis that you (all) may coat with pitch; pres. subj. 2nd pers. pl. / *empegarse*.

empeguemos 1. that we may coat with pitch; pres. subj. 1st pers. pl. / *empegarse*. 2. let us coat with pitch; impve. 1st pers. pl.

empeguen 1. that they may coat with pitch; pres. subj. 3rd pers. pl. / *empegarse*. 2. let them coat with pitch; impve. 3rd pers. pl.

empegues that you may coat with pitch; pres. subj. 2nd pers. sing. / *empegarse*.

empelotándose getting tangled up; pres. part. / *empelotarse*.

empelotaos (you all) get tangled up; impve. 2nd pers. pl. / *empelotarse*.

empelotarse to get tangled up. reg.

empelótate (you) get tangled up; impve. 2nd pers. sing. / *empelotarse*.

empelotémonos let us get tangled up; impve. 1st pers. pl. / *empelotarse*.

empelótense let them get tangled up; impve. 3rd pers. pl. / *empelotarse*.

empelótese let him (her/it) get tangled up; impve. 3rd pers. sing. / *empelotarse*.

empellar to push. irr.

empellejar to cover with skins. reg.

empeñándose persisting; pres. part. / *empeñarse*.

empeñaos (you all) persist; impve. 2nd pers. pl. / *empeñarse*.

empeñar to pawn or to compel. reg.

empeñarse to persist. reg.

empéñate (you) persist; impve. 2nd pers. sing. / *empeñarse*.

empeñémonos let us persist; impve. 1st pers. pl. / *empeñarse*.

empéñense let them persist; impve. 3rd pers. pl. / *empeñarse*.

empéñese let him (her/it) persist; impve. 3rd pers. sing. / *empeñarse.*

empeorándose getting worse; pres. part. / *empeorarse.*

empeoraos (you all) get worse; impve. 2nd pers. pl. / *empeorarse.*

empeorar to make worse. reg.

empeorarse to get worse. reg.

empeórate (you) get worse; impve. 2nd pers. sing. / *empeorarse.*

empeorémonos let us get worse; impve. 1st pers. pl. / *empeorarse.*

empeórense let them get worse; impve. 3rd pers. pl. / *empeorarse.*

empeórese let him (her/it) get worse; impve. 3rd pers. sing. / *empeorarse.*

empequeñecer to belittle or to diminish. irr.

empequeñezca 1. that I may belittle; pres. subj. 1st pers. sing. / *empequeñecer.* 2. that he (she/it) may belittle; pres. subj. 3rd pers. sing. 3. let him (her/it) belittle; impve. 3rd pers. sing.

empequeñezcáis that you (all) may belittle; pres. subj. 2nd pers. pl. / *empequeñecer.*

empequeñezcamos 1. that we may belittle; pres. subj. 1st pers. pl. / *empequeñecer.* 2. let us belittle; impve. 1st pers. pl.

empequeñezcan 1. that they may belittle; pres. subj. 3rd pers. pl. / *empequeñecer.* 2. let them belittle; impve. 3rd pers. pl.

empequeñezcas that you may belittle; pres. subj. 2nd pers. sing. / *empequeñecer.*

empequeñezco I belittle; pres. ind. 1st pers. sing. / *empequeñecer.*

emperece 1. that I may make lazy; pres. subj. 1st pers. sing. / *emperezar.* 2. that he (she/it) may make lazy; pres. subj. 3rd pers. sing. 3. let him (her/it) make lazy; impve. 3rd pers. sing.

emperecé I made lazy; past 1st pers. sing. / *emperezar.*

emperecéis that you (all) may make lazy; pres. subj. 2nd pers. pl. / *emperezar.*

emperecémonos let us become lazy; impve. 1st pers. pl. / *emperezarse.*

emperecemos 1. that we may make lazy; pres. subj. 1st pers. pl. / *emperezar.* 2. let us make lazy; impve. 1st pers. pl.

emperecen 1. that they may make lazy; pres. subj. 3rd pers. pl. / *emperezar.* 2. let them make lazy; impve. 3rd pers. pl.

emperécense let them become lazy; impve. 3rd pers. pl. / *emperezarse.*

empereces that you may make lazy; pres. subj. 2nd pers. sing. / *emperezar.*

emperécese let him (her/it) become lazy; impve. 3rd pers. sing. / *emperezarse.*

emperezándose becoming lazy; pres. part. / *emperezarse.*

emperezaos (you all) become lazy; impve. 2nd pers. pl. / *emperezarse.*

emperezar to make lazy. irr.

emperezarse to become lazy. irr.

emperézate (you) become lazy; impve. 2nd pers. sing. / *emperezarse.*

emperifollándose dressing up; pres. part. / *emperifollarse.*

emperifollaos (you all) dress up; impve. 2nd pers. pl. / *emperifollarse.*

emperifollar to decorate. reg.

emperifollarse to dress up. reg.

emperifóllate (you) dress up; impve. 2nd pers. sing. / *emperifollarse.*

emperifollémonos let us dress up; impve. 1st pers. pl. / *emperifollarse.*

emperifóllense let them dress up; impve. 3rd pers. pl. / *emperifollarse.*

emperifóllese let him (her/it) dress up; impve. 3rd pers. sing. / *emperifollarse.*

emperrándose becoming stubborn; pres. part. / *emperrarse.*

emperraos (you all) become stubborn; impve. 2nd pers. pl. / *emperrarse.*

emperrarse to become stubborn. reg.

empérrate (you) become stubborn; impve. 2nd pers. sing. / *emperrarse.*

emperrémonos let us become stubborn; impve. 1st pers. pl. / *emperrarse.*

empérrense let them become stubborn; impve. 3rd pers. pl. / *emperrarse.*

empérrese let him (her/it) become stubborn; impve. 3rd pers. sing. / *emperrarse.*

empezar to begin. irr.

empicotar to pillory. reg.

empiece 1. that I may begin; pres. subj. 1st pers. sing. / *empezar.* 2. that he (she/it) may begin; pres. subj. 3rd pers. sing. 3. let him (her/it) begin; impve. 3rd pers. sing.

empiecen 1. that they may begin; pres. subj. 3rd pers. pl. / *empezar.* 2. let them begin; impve. 3rd pers. pl.

empieces that you may begin; pres. subj. 2nd pers. sing. / *empezar.*

empiedra 1. he (she/it) paves with stones; pres. ind. 3rd pers. sing. / *empedrar.* 2. (you) pave with stones; impve. 2nd pers. sing.

empiedran they pave with stones; pres. ind. 3rd pers. pl. / *empedrar.*

empiedras you pave with stones; pres. ind. 2nd pers. sing. / *empedrar.*

empiedre 1. that I may pave with stones; pres. subj. 1st pers. sing. / *empedrar.* 2. that he (she/it) may pave with stones; pres. subj. 3rd pers. sing. 3. let him (her/it) pave with stones; impve. 3rd pers. sing.

empiedren 1. that they may pave with stones; pres. subj. 3rd pers. pl. / *empedrar.* 2. let them pave with stones; impve. 3rd pers. pl.

empiedres that you may pave with stones; pres. subj. 2nd pers. sing. / *empedrar.*

empiedro I pave with stones; pres. ind. 1st pers. sing. / *empedrar.*

empiella 1. he (she/it) pushes; pres. ind. 3rd pers. sing. / *empellar.* 2. (you) push; impve. 2nd pers. sing.

empiellan they push; pres. ind. 3rd pers. pl. / *empellar.*

empiellas you push; pres. ind. 2nd pers. sing. / *empellar.*

empielle 1. that I may push; pres. subj. 1st pers. sing. / *empellar.* 2. that he (she/it) may push; pres. subj. 3rd pers. sing. 3. let him (her/it) push; impve. 3rd pers. sing.

empiellen 1. that they may push; pres. subj. 3rd pers. pl. / *empellar.* 2. let them push; impve. 3rd pers. pl.

empielles that you may push; pres. subj. 2nd pers. sing. / *empellar.*

empiello I push; pres. ind. 1st pers. sing. / *empellar.*

empieza 1. he (she/it) begins; pres. ind. 3rd pers. sing. / *empezar.* 2. (you) begin; impve. 2nd pers. sing.

empiezan they begin; pres. ind. 3rd pers. pl. / *empezar.*

empiezas you begin; pres. ind. 2nd pers. sing. / *empezar.*

empiezo I begin; pres. ind. 1st pers. sing. / *empezar.*

empilar to pile up. reg.

empinándose standing on tiptoes; pres. part. / *empinarse.*

empinaos (you all) stand on tiptoes; impve. 2nd pers. pl. / *empinarse.*

empinar to raise. reg.

empinarse to stand on tiptoes. reg.

empínate (you) stand on tiptoes; impve. 2nd pers. sing. / *empinarse.*

empinémonos let us stand on tiptoes; impve. 1st pers. pl. / *empinarse.*

empínense let them stand on tiptoes; impve. 3rd pers. pl. / *empinarse.*

empínese let him (her/it) stand on tiptoes; impve. 3rd pers. sing. / *empinarse.*

empizarrar to slate. reg.

emplace 1. that I may summon; pres. subj. 1st pers. sing. / *emplazar.* 2. that he (she/it) may summon; pres. subj. 3rd pers. sing. 3. let him (her/it) summon; impve. 3rd pers. sing.

emplacé I summoned; past 1st pers. sing. / *emplazar.*

emplacéis that you (all) may summon; pres. subj. 2nd pers. pl. / *emplazar.*

emplacemos 1. that we may summon; pres. subj. 1st pers. pl. / *emplazar.* 2. let us summon; impve. 1st pers. pl.

emplacen 1. that they may summon; pres. subj. 3rd pers. pl. / *emplazar.* 2. let them summon; impve. 3rd pers. pl.

emplaces that you may summon; pres. subj. 2nd pers. sing. / *emplazar.*

emplastándose getting all sticky; pres. part. / *emplastarse.*

emplastaos (you all) get all sticky; impve. 2nd pers. pl. / *emplastarse.*

emplastar to plaster. reg.

emplastarse to get all sticky. reg.

emplástate (you) get all sticky; impve. 2nd pers. sing. / *emplastarse.*

emplastecer to stop cracks before painting. irr.

emplastémonos let us get all sticky; impve. 1st pers. pl. / *emplastarse.*

emplástense let them get all sticky; impve. 3rd pers. pl. / *emplastarse.*

emplástese let him (her/it) get all sticky; impve. 3rd pers. sing. / *emplastarse.*

emplastezca 1. that I may stop cracks before painting; pres. subj. 1st pers. sing. / *emplastecer.* 2. that he (she/it) may stop cracks before painting; pres. subj. 3rd pers. sing. 3. let him (her/it) stop cracks before painting; impve. 3rd pers. sing.

emplastezcáis that you (all) may stop cracks before painting; pres. subj. 2nd pers. pl. / *emplastecer.*

emplastezcamos 1. that we may stop cracks before painting; pres. subj. 1st pers. pl. / *emplastecer.* 2. let us stop cracks before painting; impve. 1st pers. pl.

emplastezcan 1. that they may stop cracks before painting; pres. subj. 3rd pers. pl. / *emplastecer.* 2. let them stop cracks before painting; impve. 3rd pers. pl.

emplastezcas that you may stop cracks before painting; pres. subj. 2nd pers. sing. / *emplastecer.*

emplastezco I stop cracks before painting; pres. ind. 1st pers. sing. / *emplastecer.*

emplazar to summon. irr.

empleándose being employed; pres. part. / *emplearse.*

empleaos (you all) be employed; impve. 2nd pers. pl. / *emplearse.*

emplear to employ. reg.

emplearse to be employed. reg.

empléate (you) be employed; impve. 2nd pers. sing. / *emplearse.*

empleémonos let us be employed; impve. 1st pers. pl. / *emplearse.*

empléense let them be employed; impve. 3rd pers. pl. / *emplearse.*

empléese let him (her/it) be employed; impve. 3rd pers. sing. / *emplearse.*

emplomar to seal with lead. reg.

emplumándose growing feathers; pres. part. / *emplumarse.*

emplumaos (you all) grow feathers; impve. 2nd pers. pl. / *emplumarse.*

emplumar to feather. reg.

emlumarse to grow feathers. reg.

emplúmate (you) grow feathers; impve. 2nd pers. sing. / *emplumarse.*

emplumecer to grow feathers. irr.

emplumémonos let us grow feathers; impve. 1st pers. pl. / *emplumarse.*

emplúmense let them grow feathers; impve. 3rd pers. pl. / *emplumarse.*

emplúmese let him (her/it) grow feathers; impve. 3rd pers. sing. / *emplumarse.*

emplumezca 1. that I may grow feathers; pres. subj. 1st pers. sing. / *emplumecer.* 2. that he (she/it) may grow feathers; pres. subj. 3rd pers. sing. 3. let him (her/it) grow feathers; impve. 3rd pers. sing.

emplumezcáis that you (all) may grow feathers; pres. subj. 2nd pers. pl. / *emplumecer.*

emplumezcamos 1. that we may grow feathers; pres. subj. 1st pers. pl. / *emplumecer*. 2. let us grow feathers; impve. 1st pers. pl.

emplumezcan 1. that they may grow feathers; pres. subj. 3rd pers. pl. / *emplumecer*. 2. let them grow feathers; impve. 3rd pers. pl.

emplumezcas that you may grow feathers; pres. subj. 2nd pers. sing. / *emplumecer*.

emplumezco I grow feathers; pres. ind. 1st pers. sing. / *emplumecer*.

empobreceos (you all) become poor; impve. 2nd pers. pl. / *empobrecerse*.

empobrecer to impoverish. irr.

empobrecerse to become poor. irr.

empobrécete (you) become poor; impve. 2nd pers. sing. / *empobrecerse*.

empobreciéndose becoming poor; pres. part. / *empobrecerse*.

empobrezca 1. that I may impoverish; pres. subj. 1st pers. sing. / *empobrecer*. 2. that he (she/it) may impoverish; pres. subj. 3rd pers. sing. 3. let him (her/it) impoverish; impve. 3rd pers. sing.

empobrezcáis that you (all) may impoverish; pres. subj. 2nd pers. pl. / *empobrecer*.

empobrezcámonos let us become poor; impve. 1st pers. pl. / *empobrecerse*.

empobrezcamos 1. that we may impoverish; pres. subj. 1st pers. pl. / *empobrecer*. 2. let us impoverish; impve. 1st pers. pl.

empobrezcan 1. that they may impoverish; pres. subj. 3rd pers. pl. / *empobrecer*. 2. let them impoverish; impve. 3rd pers. pl.

empobrézcanse let them become poor; impve. 3rd pers. pl. / *empobrecerse*.

empobrezcas that you may impoverish; pres. subj. 2nd pers. sing. / *empobrecer*.

empobrézcase let him (her/it) become poor; impve. 3rd pers. sing. / *empobrecerse*.

empobrezco I impoverish; pres. ind. 1st pers. sing. / *empobrecer*.

empodreceos (you all) rot; impve. 2nd pers. pl. / *empodrecerse*.

empodrecer to rot. irr.

empodrecerse to rot. irr.

empodrécete (you) rot; impve. 2nd pers. sing. / *empodrecerse*.

empodreciéndose rotting; pres. part. / *empodrecerse*.

empodrezca 1. that I may rot; pres. subj. 1st pers. sing. / *empodrecer*. 2. that he (she/it) may rot; pres. subj. 3rd pers. sing. 3. let him (her/it) rot; impve. 3rd pers. sing.

empodrezcáis that you (all) may rot; pres. subj. 2nd pers. pl. / *empodrecer*.

empodrezcámonos let us rot; impve. 1st pers. pl. / *empodrecerse*.

empodrezcamos 1. that we may rot; pres. subj. 1st pers. pl. / *empodrecer*. 2. let us rot; impve. 1st pers. pl.

empodrezcan 1. that they may rot; pres. subj. 3rd pers. pl. / *empodrecer*. 2. let them rot; impve. 3rd pers. pl.

empodrézcanse let them rot; impve. 3rd pers. pl. / *empodrecerse*.

empodrezcas that you may rot; pres. subj. 2nd pers. sing. / *empodrecer*.

empodrézcase let him (her/it) rot; impve. 3rd pers. sing. / *empodrecerse*.

empodrezco I rot; pres. ind. 1st pers. sing. / *empodrecer*.

empolvándose being out of practice; pres. part. / *empolvarse*.

empolvaos (you all) be out of practice; impve. 2nd pers. pl. / *empolvarse*.

empolvar to powder or to cover with dust. reg.

empolvarse to be out of practice. reg.

empólvate (you) be out of practice; impve. 2nd pers. sing. / *empolvarse*.

empolvémonos let us be out of practice; impve. 1st pers. pl. / *empolvarse*.

empólvense let them be out of practice; impve. 3rd pers. pl. / *empolvarse*.

empólvese let him (her/it) be out of practice; impve. 3rd pers. sing. / *empolvarse*.

empollar to hatch or to brood. reg.

emponzoñar to poison. reg.

emporcar to soil. irr.

emporqué I soiled; past 1st pers. sing. / *emporcar*.

emporquéis that you (all) may soil; pres. subj. 2nd pers. pl. / *emporcar*.

emporquemos 1. that we may soil; pres. subj. 1st pers. pl. / *emporcar*. 2. let us soil; impve. 1st pers. pl.

empotrar to embed (wall). reg.

emprender to undertake. reg.

empreñar to impregnate. reg.

emprimar to prime. reg.

empuerca 1. he (she/it) soils; pres. ind. 3rd pers. sing. / *emporcar*. 2. (you) soil; impve. 2nd pers. sing.

empuercan they soil; pres. ind. 3rd pers. pl. / *emporcar*.

empuercas you soil; pres. ind. 2nd pers. sing. / *emporcar*.

empuerco I soil; pres. ind. 1st pers. sing. / *emporcar*.

empuerque 1. that I may soil; pres. subj. 1st pers. sing. / *emporcar*. 2. that he (she/it) may soil; pres. subj. 3rd pers. sing. 3. let him (her/it) soil; impve. 3rd pers. sing.

empuerquen 1. that they may soil; pres. subj. 3rd pers. pl. / *emporcar*. 2. let them soil; impve. 3rd pers. pl.

empuerques that you may soil; pres. subj. 2nd pers. sing. / *emporcar*.

empujar to push. reg.

empuñar to grasp. reg.

emular to emulate. reg.

emulsionar to emulsify. reg.

enajenándose being in a trance; pres. part. / *enajenarse*.

enajenaos (you all) be in a trance; impve. 2nd pers. pl. / *enajenarse*.

enajenar to alienate or to disposses. reg.

enajenarse to be in a trance. reg.

enajénate (you) be in a trance; impve. 2nd pers. sing. / *enajenarse.*

enajenémonos let us be in a trance; impve. 1st pers. pl. / *enajenarse.*

enajénense let them be in a trance; impve. 3rd pers. pl. / *enajenarse.*

enajénese let him (her/it) be in a trance; impve. 3rd pers. sing. / *enajenarse.*

enaltecer to praise or to exalt. irr.

enaltezca 1. that I may praise; pres. subj. 1st pers. sing. / *enaltecer.* 2. that he (she/it) may praise; pres. subj. 3rd pers. sing. 3. let him (her/it) praise; impve. 3rd pers. sing.

enaltezcáis that you (all) may praise; pres. subj. 2nd pers. pl. / *enaltecer.*

enaltezcamos 1. that we may praise; pres. subj. 1st pers. pl. / *enaltecer.* 2. let us praise; impve. 1st pers. pl.

enaltezcan 1. that they may praise; pres. subj. 3rd pers. pl. / *enaltecer.* 2. let them praise; impve. 3rd pers. pl.

enaltezcas that you may praise; pres. subj. 2nd pers. sing. / *enaltecer.*

enaltezco I praise; pres. ind. 1st pers. sing. / *enaltecer.*

enamorándose falling in love; pres. part. / *enamorarse.*

enamoraos (you all) fall in love; impve. 2nd pers. pl. / *enamorarse.*

enamorar to enamor or to make love. reg.

enamorarse to fall in love. reg.

enamórate (you) fall in love; impve. 2nd pers. sing. / *enamorarse.*

enamorémonos let us fall in love; impve. 1st pers. pl. / *enamorarse.*

enamórense let them fall in love; impve. 3rd pers. pl. / *enamorarse.*

enamórese let him (her/it) fall in love; impve. 3rd pers. sing. / *enamorarse.*

enarbolándose becoming angry; pres. part. / *enarbolarse.*

enarbolaos (you all) become angry; impve. 2nd pers. pl. / *enarbolarse.*

enarbolar to hoist. reg.

enarbolarse to become angry. reg.

enarbólate (you) become angry; impve. 2nd pers. sing. / *enarbolarse.*

enarbolémonos let us become angry; impve. 1st pers. pl. / *enarbolarse.*

enarbólense let them become angry; impve. 3rd pers. pl. / *enarbolarse.*

enarbólese let him (her/it) become angry; impve. 3rd pers. sing. / *enarbolarse.*

enarcar to arch. irr.

enardeceos (you all) become aroused; impve. 2nd pers. pl. / *enardecerse.*

enardecer to excite. irr.

enardecerse to become aroused or inflamed. irr.

enardécete (you) become aroused; impve. 2nd pers. sing. / *enardecerse.*

enardeciéndose becoming aroused; pres. part. / *enardecerse.*

enardezca 1. that I may excite; pres. subj. 1st pers. sing. / *enardecer.* 2. that he (she/it) may excite; pres. subj. 3rd pers. sing. 3. let him (her/it) excite; impve. 3rd pers. sing.

enardezcáis that you (all) may excite; pres. subj. 2nd pers. pl. / *enardecer.*

enardezcámonos let us become aroused; impve. 1st pers. pl. / *enardecerse.*

enardezcamos 1. that we may excite; pres. subj. 1st pers. pl. / *enardecer.* 2. let us excite; impve. 1st pers. pl.

enardezcan 1. that they may excite; pres. subj. 3rd pers. pl. / *enardecer.* 2. let them excite; impve. 3rd pers. pl.

enardézcanse let them become aroused; impve. 3rd pers. pl. / *enardecerse.*

enardezcas that you may excite; pres. subj. 2nd pers. sing. / *enardecer.*

enardézcase let him (her/it) become aroused; impve. 3rd pers. sing. / *enardecerse.*

enardezco I excite; pres. ind. 1st pers. sing. / *enardecer.*

enarenar to cover with sand. reg.

enarque 1. that I may arch; pres. subj. 1st pers. sing. / *enarcar.* 2. that he (she/it) may arch; pres. subj. 3rd pers. sing. 3. let him (her/it) arch; impve. 3rd pers. sing.

enarqué I arched; past 1st pers. sing. / *enarcar.*

enarquéis that you (all) may arch; pres. subj. 2nd pers. pl. / *enarcar.*

enarquemos 1. that we may arch; pres. subj. 1st pers. pl. / *enarcar.* 2. let us arch; impve. 1st pers. pl.

enarquen 1. that they may arch; pres. subj. 3rd pers. pl. / *enarcar.* 2. let them arch; impve. 3rd pers. pl.

enarques that you may arch; pres. subj. 2nd pers. sing. / *enarcar.*

encabece 1. that I may put a heading on; pres. subj. 1st pers. sing. / *encabezar.* 2. that he (she/it) may put a heading on; pres. subj. 3rd pers. sing. 3. let him (her/it) put a heading on; impve. 3rd pers. sing.

encabecé I put a heading on; past 1st pers. sing. / *encabezar.*

encabecéis that you (all) may put a heading on; pres. subj. 2nd pers. pl. / *encabezar.*

encabecemos 1. that we may put a heading on; pres. subj. 1st pers. pl. / *encabezar.* 2. let us put a heading on; impve. 1st pers. pl.

encabecen 1. that they may put a heading on; pres. subj. 3rd pers. pl. / *encabezar.* 2. let them put a heading on; impve. 3rd pers. pl.

encabeces that you may put a heading on; pres. subj. 2nd pers. sing. / *encabezar.*

encabestrar to put a halter on. reg.

encabezar to put a heading on. irr.

encabezonar to register or to take a census. reg.

encabritándose rearing on the hind legs; pres. part. / *encabritarse.*

encabritaos (you all) rear on the hind legs; impve. 2nd pers. pl. / *encabritarse.*

encabritarse to rear on the hind legs. reg.
encabrítate (you) rear on the hind legs; impve. 2nd pers. sing. / *encabritarse.*
encabritémonos let us rear on the hind legs; impve. 1st pers. pl. / *encabritarse.*
encabrítense let them rear on the hind legs; impve. 3rd pers. pl. / *encabritarse.*
encabrítese let him (her/it) rear on the hind legs; impve. 3rd pers. sing. / *encabritarse.*
encadenar to chain. reg.
encajándose squeezing into; pres. part. / *encajarse.*
encajaos (you all) squeeze into; impve. 2nd pers. pl. / *encajarse.*
encajar to insert. reg.
encajarse to squeeze into. reg.
encájate (you) squeeze into; impve. 2nd pers. sing. / *encajarse.*
encajémonos let us squeeze into; impve. 1st pers. pl. / *encajarse.*
encájense let them squeeze into; impve. 3rd pers. pl. / *encajarse.*
encájese let him (her/it) squeeze into; impve. 3rd pers. sing. / *encajarse.*
encajetillar to package. reg.
encajonándose narrowing; pres. part. / *encajonarse.*
encajonaos (you all) narrow; impve. 2nd pers. pl. / *encajonarse.*
encajonar to pack or to crate. reg.
encajonarse to narrow. reg.
encajónate (you) narrow; impve. 2nd pers. sing. / *encajonarse.*
encajonémonos let us narrow; impve. 1st pers. pl. / *encajonarse.*
encajónense let them narrow; impve. 3rd pers. pl. / *encajonarse.*
encajónese let him (her/it) narrow; impve. 3rd pers. sing. / *encajonarse.*
encalar to whitewash. reg.
encalvecer to get bald. irr.
encalvezca 1. that I may get bald; pres. subj. 1st pers. sing. / *encalvecer.* 2. that he (she/it) may get bald; pres. subj. 3rd pers. sing. 3. let him (her/it) get bald; impve. 3rd pers. sing.
encalvezcáis that you (all) may get bald; pres. subj. 2nd pers. pl. / *encalvecer.*
encalvezcamos 1. that we may get bald; pres. subj. 1st pers. pl. / *encalvecer.* 2. let us get bald; impve. 1st pers. pl.
encalvezcan 1. that they may get bald; pres. subj. 3rd pers. pl. / *encalvecer.* 2. let them get bald; impve. 3rd pers. pl.
encalvezcas that you may get bald; pres. subj. 2nd pers. sing. / *encalvecer.*
encalvezco I get bald; pres. ind. 1st pers. sing. / *encalvecer.*
encallar to run aground. reg.
encallecer to get calluses. irr.

encallezca 1. that I may get calluses; pres. subj. 1st pers. sing. / *encallecer.* 2. that he (she/it) may get calluses; pres. subj. 3rd pers. sing. 3. let him (her/it) get calluses; impve. 3rd pers. sing.
encallezcáis that you (all) may get calluses; pres. subj. 2nd pers. pl. / *encallecer.*
encallezcamos 1. that we may get calluses; pres. subj. 1st pers. pl. / *encallecer.* 2. let us get calluses; impve. 1st pers. pl.
encallezcan 1. that they may get calluses; pres. subj. 3rd pers. pl. / *encallecer.* 2. let them get calluses; impve. 3rd pers. pl.
encallezcas that you may get calluses; pres. subj. 2nd pers. sing. / *encallecer.*
encallezco I get calluses; pres. ind. 1st pers. sing. / *encallecer.*
encamándose taking to one's bed; pres. part. / *encamarse.*
encamaos (you all) take to your beds; impve. 2nd pers. pl. / *encamarse.*
encamarse to take to one's bed. reg.
encámate (you) take to your bed; impve. 2nd pers. sing. / *encamarse.*
encamémonos let us take to our bed; impve. 1st pers. pl. / *encamarse.*
encámense let them take to their beds; impve. 3rd pers. pl. / *encamarse.*
encámese let him (her/it) take to his (her/its) bed; impve. 3rd pers. sing. / *encamarse.*
encaminándose starting out; pres. part. / *encaminarse.*
encaminaos (you all) start out; impve. 2nd pers. pl. / *encaminarse.*
encaminar to direct or to guide. reg.
encaminarse to start out. reg.
encamínate (you) start out; impve. 2nd pers. sing. / *encaminarse.*
encaminémonos let us start out; impve. 1st pers. pl. / *encaminarse.*
encamínense let them start out; impve. 3rd pers. pl. / *encaminarse.*
encamínese let him (her/it) start out; impve. 3rd pers. sing. / *encaminarse.*
encamotándose becoming infatuated; pres. part. / *encamotarse.*
encamotaos (you all) become infatuated; impve. 2nd pers. pl. / *encamotarse.*
encamotarse to become infatuated. reg.
encamótate (you) become infatuated; impve. 2nd pers. sing. / *encamotarse.*
encamotémonos let us become infatuated; impve. 1st pers. pl. / *encamotarse.*
encamótense let them become infatuated; impve. 3rd pers. pl. / *encamotarse.*
encamótese let him (her/it) become infatuated; impve. 3rd pers. sing. / *encamotarse.*
encanalar to channel. reg.
encanalice 1. that I may channel; pres. subj. 1st pers. sing. / *encanalizar.* 2. that he (she/it) may channel; pres. subj. 3rd pers. sing. 3. let him (her/it) channel; impve. 3rd pers. sing.

encanalicé I channeled; past 1st pers. sing. / *encanalizar.*

encanalicéis that you (all) may channel; pres. subj. 2nd pers. pl. / *encanalizar.*

encanalicemos 1. that we may channel; pres. subj. 1st pers. pl. / *encanalizar.* 2. let us channel; impve. 1st pers. pl.

encanalicen 1. that they may channel; pres. subj. 3rd pers. pl. / *encanalizar.* 2. let them channel; impve. 3rd pers. pl.

encanalices that you may channel; pres. subj. 2nd pers. sing. / *encanalizar.*

encanalizar to channel. irr.

encanallándose becoming depraved; pres. part. / *encanallarse.*

encanallaos (you all) become depraved; impve. 2nd pers. pl. / *encanallarse.*

encanallar to corrupt. reg.

encanallarse to become depraved. reg.

encanállate (you) become depraved; impve. 2nd pers. sing. / *encanallarse.*

encanallémonos let us become depraved; impve. 1st pers. pl. / *encanallarse.*

encanállense let them become depraved; impve. 3rd pers. pl. / *encanallarse.*

encanállese let him (her/it) become depraved; impve. 3rd pers. sing. / *encanallarse.*

encandecer to make red hot. irr.

encandezca 1. that I may make red hot; pres. subj. 1st pers. sing. / *encandecer.* 2. that he (she/it) may make red hot; pres. subj. 3rd pers. sing. 3. let him (her/it) make red hot; impve. 3rd pers. sing.

encandezcáis that you (all) may make red hot; pres. subj. 2nd pers. pl. / *encandecer.*

encandezcamos 1. that we may make red hot; pres. subj. 1st pers. pl. / *encandecer.* 2. let us make red hot; impve. 1st pers. pl.

encandezcan 1. that they may make red hot; pres. subj. 3rd pers. pl. / *encandecer.* 2. let them make red hot; impve. 3rd pers. pl.

encandezcas that you may make red hot; pres. subj. 2nd pers. sing. / *encandecer.*

encandezco I make red hot; pres. ind. 1st pers. sing. / *encandecer.*

encandilándose lighting up; pres. part. / *encandilarse.*

encandilaos (you all) light up; impve. 2nd pers. pl. / *encandilarse.*

encandilar to dazzle. reg.

encandilarse to light up. reg.

encandílate (you) light up; impve. 2nd pers. sing. / *encandilarse.*

encandilémonos let us light up; impve. 1st pers. pl. / *encandilarse.*

encandílense let them light up; impve. 3rd pers. pl. / *encandilarse.*

encandílese let him (her/it) light up; impve. 3rd pers. sing. / *encandilarse.*

encanecer to turn gray. irr.

encanezca 1. that I may turn gray; pres. subj. 1st pers. sing. / *encanecer.* 2. that he (she/it) may turn gray; pres. subj. 3rd pers. sing. 3. let him (her/it) turn gray; impve. 3rd pers. sing.

encanezcáis that you (all) may turn gray; pres. subj. 2nd pers. pl. / *encanecer.*

encanezcamos 1. that we may turn gray; pres. subj. 1st pers. pl. / *encanecer.* 2. let us turn gray; impve. 1st pers. pl.

encanezcan 1. that they may turn gray; pres. subj. 3rd pers. pl. / *encanecer.* 2. let them turn gray; impve. 3rd pers. pl.

encanezcas that you may turn gray; pres. subj. 2nd pers. sing. / *encanecer.*

encanezco I turn gray; pres. ind. 1st pers. sing. / *encanecer.*

encanijándose becoming thin; pres. part. / *encanijarse.*

encanijaos (you all) become thin; impve. 2nd pers. pl. / *encanijarse.*

encanijarse to become thin. reg.

encaníjate (you) become thin; impve. 2nd pers. sing. / *encanijarse.*

encanijémonos let us become thin; impve. 1st pers. pl. / *encanijarse.*

encaníjense let them become thin; impve. 3rd pers. pl. / *encanijarse.*

encaníjese let him (her/it) become thin; impve. 3rd pers. sing. / *encanijarse.*

encantar to enchant or to charm. reg.

encapillar to confine in the death cell. reg.

encapotándose becoming cloudy; pres. part. / *encapotarse.*

encapotar to cloak or to veil. reg.

encapotarse to become cloudy. reg.

encapótense let them become cloudy; impve. 3rd pers. pl. / *encapotarse.*

encapótese let it become cloudy; impve. 3rd pers. sing. / *encapotarse.*

encaprichándose being stubborn; pres. part. / *encapricharse.*

encaprichaos (you all) be stubborn; impve. 2nd pers. pl. / *encapricharse.*

encapricharse to be stubborn. reg.

encapríchate (you) be stubborn; impve. 2nd pers. sing. / *encapricharse.*

encaprichémonos let us be stubborn; impve. 1st pers. pl. / *encapricharse.*

encapríchense let them be stubborn; impve. 3rd pers. pl. / *encapricharse.*

encapríchese let him (her/it) be stubborn; impve. 3rd pers. sing. / *encapricharse.*

encapuchar to cover with a hood. reg.

encaramándose climbing up; pres. part. / *encaramarse.*

encaramaos (you all) climb up; impve. 2nd pers. pl. / *encaramarse.*

encaramar to raise. reg.

encaramarse to climb up. reg.

encarámate (you) climb up; impve. 2nd pers. sing. / *encaramarse*.

encaramémonos let us climb up; impve. 1st pers. pl. / *encaramarse*.

encarámense let them climb up; impve. 3rd pers. pl. / *encaramarse*.

encarámese let him (her/it) climb up; impve. 3rd pers. sing. / *encaramarse*.

encarándose facing; pres. part. / *encararse*.

encaraos (you all) face; impve. 2nd pers. pl. / *encararse*.

encarar to aim or to point. reg.

encararse to face or to confront. reg.

encárate (you) face; impve. 2nd pers. sing. / *encararse*.

encarcelar to incarcerate or to imprison. reg.

encarecer to raise the price of. irr.

encarémonos let us face; impve. 1st pers. pl. / *encararse*.

encárense let them face; impve. 3rd pers. pl. / *encararse*.

encárese let him (her/it) face; impve. 3rd pers. sing. / *encararse*.

encarezca 1. that I may raise the peice of; pres. subj. 1st pers. sing. / *encarecer*. 2. that he (she/it) may raise the price of; pres. subj. 3rd pers. sing. 3. let him (her/it)ise the price of; impve. 3rd pers. sing.

encarezcáis that you (all) may raise the price of; pres. subj. 2nd pers. pl. / *encarecer*.

encarezcamos 1. that we may raise the price of; pres. subj. 1st pers. pl. / *encarecer*. 2. let us raise the price of; impve. 1st pers. pl.

encarezcan 1. that they may raise the price of; pres. subj. 3rd pers. pl. / *encarecer*. 2. let them raise the price of; impve. 3rd pers. pl.

encarezcas that you may raise the price of; pres. subj. 2nd pers. sing. / *encarecer*.

encarezco I raise the price of; pres. ind. 1st pers. sing. / *encarecer*.

encargándose taking charge; pres. part. / *encargarse*.

encargaos (you all) take charge; impve. 2nd pers. pl. / *encargarse*.

encargar to entrust. irr.

encargarse to take charge. irr.

encárgate (you) take charge; impve. 2nd pers. sing. / *encargarse*.

encargue 1. that I may entrust; pres. subj. 1st pers. sing. / *encargar*. 2. that he (she/it) may entrust; pres. subj. 3rd pers. sing. 3. let him (her/it) entrust; impve. 3rd pers. sing.

encargué I entrusted; past 1st pers. sing. / *encargar*.

encarguéis that you (all) may entrust; pres. subj. 2nd pers. pl. / *encargar*.

encarguémonos let us take charge; impve. 1st pers. pl. / *encargarse*.

encarguemos 1. that we may entrust; pres. subj. 1st pers. pl. / *encargar*. 2. let us entrust; impve. 1st pers. pl.

encarguen 1. that they may entrust; pres. subj. 3rd pers. pl. / *encrgar*. 2. let them entrust; impve. 3rd pers. pl.

encárguense let them take charge; impve. 3rd pers. pl. / *encargarse*.

encargues that you may entrust; pres. subj. 2nd pers. sing. / *encargar*.

encárguese let him (her/it) take charge; impve. 3rd pers. sing. / *encargarse*.

encariñándose becoming fond of; pres. part. / *encariñarse*.

encariñaos (you all) become fond of; impve. 2nd pers. pl. / *encariñarse*.

encariñar to inspire affection. reg.

encariñarse to become fond of. reg.

encaríñate (you) become fond of; impve. 2nd pers. sing. / *encariñarse*.

encariñémonos let us become fond of; impve. 1st pers. pl. / *encariñarse*.

encaríñense let them become fond of; impve. 3rd pers. pl. / *encariñarse*.

encaríñese let him (her/it) become fond of; impve. 3rd pers. sing. / *encariñarse*.

encarnándose mixing; pres. part. / *encarnarse*.

encarnaos (you all) mix; impve. 2nd pers. pl. / *encarnarse*.

encarnar to incarnate. reg.

encarnarse to mix or to fuse. reg.

encárnate (you) mix; impve. 2nd pers. sing. / *encarnarse*.

encarnecer to grow fat. irr.

encarnémonos let us mix; impve. 1st pers. pl. / *encarnarse*.

encárnense let them mix; impve. 3rd pers. pl. / *encarnarse*.

encárnese let him (her/it) mix; impve. 3rd pers. sing. / *encarnarse*.

encarnezca 1. that I may grow fat; pres. subj. 1st pers. sing. / *encarnecer*. 2. that he (she/it) may grow fat; pres. subj. 3rd pers. sing. 3. let him (her/it) grow fat; impve. 3rd pers. sing.

encarnezcáis that you (all) may grow fat; pres. subj. 2nd pers. pl. / *encarnecer*.

encarnezcamos 1. that we may grow fat; pres. subj. 1st pers. pl. / *encarnecer*. 2. let us grow fat; impve. 1st pers. pl.

encarnezcan 1. that they may grow fat; pres. subj. 3rd pers. pl. / *encarnecer*. 2. let them grow fat; impve. 3rd pers. pl.

encarnezcas that you may grow fat; pres. subj. 2nd pers. sing. / *encarnecer*.

encarnezco I grow fat; pres. ind. 1st pers. sing. / *encarnecer*.

encarnice 1. that I may infuriate; pres. subj. 1st pers. sing. / *encarnizar*. 2. that he (she/it) may infuriate; pres. subj. 3rd pers. sing. 3. let him (her/it) infuriate; impve. 3rd pers. sing.

encarnicé I infuriated; past 1st pers. sing. / *encarnizar*.

encarnicéis that you (all) may infuriate; pres. subj. 2nd pers. pl. / *encarnizar*.

encarnicémonos let us become bloodthirsty; impve. 1st pers. pl. / *encarnizarse*.

encarnicemos 1. that we may infuriate; pres. subj. 1st pers. pl. / *encarnizar*. 2. let us infuriate; impve. 1st pers. pl.

encarnicen 1. that they may infuriate; pres. subj. 3rd pers. pl. / *encarnizar*. 2. let them infuriate; impve. 3rd pers. pl.

encarnícense let them become bloodthirsty; impve. 3rd pers. pl. / *encarnizarse*.

encarnices that you may infuriate; pres. subj. 2nd pers. sing. / *encarnizar*.

encarnícese let him (her/it) become bloodthirsty; impve. 3rd pers. sing. / *encarnizarse*.

encarnizándose becoming bloodthirsty; pres. part. / *encarnizarse*.

encarnizaos (you all) become bloodthirsty; impve. 2nd pers. pl. / *encarnizarse*.

encarnizar to infuriate. irr.

encarnizarse to become bloodthirsty. irr.

encarnízate (you) become bloodthirsty; impve. 2nd pers. sing. / *encarnizarse*.

encarrilar to set right. reg.

encartándose being unable to discard (cards); pres. part. / *encartarse*.

encartaos (you all) be unable to discard (cards); impve. 2nd pers. pl. / *encartarse*.

encartar to enrole or to proscribe. reg.

encartarse to be unable to discard (cards). reg.

encártate (you) be unable to discard (cards); impve. 2nd pers. sing. / *encartarse*.

encartémonos let us be unable to discard (cards); impve. 1st pers. pl. / *encartarse*.

encártense let them be unable to discard (cards); impve. 3rd pers. pl. / *encartarse*.

encártese let him (her/it) be unable to discard (cards); impve. 3rd pers. sing. / *encartarse*.

encartonar to cover with cardboard. reg.

encasar to set bones. reg.

encasillar to pigeonhole. reg.

encasquetándose clapping on one's hat; pres. part. / *encasquetarse*.

encasquetaos (you all) clap on your hats; impve. 2nd pers. pl. / *encasquetarse*.

encasquetar to put on tight. reg.

encasquetarse to clap on one's hat. reg.

encasquétate (you) clap on your hat; impve. 2nd pers. sing. / *encasquetarse*.

encasquetémonos let us clap on our hats; impve. 1st pers. pl. / *encasquetarse*.

encasquétense let them clap on their hats; impve. 3rd pers. pl. / *encasquetarse*.

encasquétese let him (her) clap on his (her) hat; impve. 3rd pers. sing. / *encasquetarse*.

encastar to crossbreed. reg.

encastillándose withdrawing; pres. part. / *encastillarse*.

encastillaos (you all) withdraw; impve. 2nd pers. pl. / *encastillarse*.

encastillar to fortify. reg.

eastillarse to withdraw. reg.

encastíllate (you) withdraw; impve. 2nd pers. sing. / *encastillarse*.

encastillémonos let us withdraw; impve. 1st pers. pl. / *encastillarse*.

encastíllense let them withdraw; impve. 3rd pers. pl. / *encastillarse*.

encastíllese let him (her/it) withdraw; impve. 3rd pers. sing. / *encastillarse*.

encastrar to engage gears. reg.

encauce 1. that I may channel; pres. subj. 1st pers. sing. / *encauzar*. 2. that he (she/it) may channel; pres. subj. 3rd pers. sing. 3. let him (her/it) channel; impve. 3rd pers. sing.

encaucé I channeled; past 1st pers. sing. / *encauzar*.

encaucéis that you (all) may channel; pres. subj. 2nd pers. pl. / *encauzar*.

encaucemos 1. that we may channel; pres. subj. 1st pers. pl. / *encauzar*. 2. let us channel; impve. 1st pers. pl.

encaucen 1. that they may channel; pres. subj. 3rd pers. pl. / *encauzar*. 2. let them channel; impve. 3rd pers. pl.

encauces that you may channel; pres. subj. 2nd pers. sing. / *encauzar*.

encauchar to coat with rubber. reg.

encausar to indict. reg.

encauzar to channel or to direct. irr.

encelándose becoming jealous; pres. part. / *encelarse*.

encelaos (you all) become jealous; impve. 2nd pers. pl. / *encelarse*.

encelar to make jealous. reg.

encelarse to become jealous. reg.

encélate (you) become jealous; impve. 2nd pers. sing. / *encelarse*.

encelémonos let us become jealous; impve. 1st pers. pl. / *encelarse*.

encélense let them become jealous; impve. 3rd pers. pl. / *encelarse*.

encélese let him (her/it) become jealous; impve. 3rd pers. sing. / *encelarse*.

encenagándose getting into the mud; pres. part. / *encenagarse*.

encenagaos (you all) get into the mud; impve. 2nd pers. pl. / *encenagarse*.

encenagarse to get into the mud. irr.

encenágate (you) get into the mud; impve. 2nd pers. sing. / *encenagarse*.

encenague 1. that I may get into the mud; pres. subj. 1st pers. sing. / *encenagarse*. 2. that he (she/it) may get into the mud; pres. subj. 3rd pers. sing.

encenagué I got into the mud; past 1st pers. sing. / *encenagarse*.

encenaguéis that you (all) may get into the mud; pres. subj. 2nd pers. pl. / *encenagarse*.

encenaguémonos let us get into the mud; impve. 1st pers. pl. / *encenagarse*.

encenaguemos that we may get into the mud; pres. subj. 1st pers. pl. / *encenagarse*.

encenaguen that they may get into the mud; pres. subj. 3rd pers. pl. / *encenagarse*.

encenáguense let them get into the mud; impve. 3rd pers. pl. / *encenagarse.*

encenagues that you may get into the mud; pres. subj. 2nd pers. sing. / *encenagarse.*

encenáguese let him (her/it) get into the mud; impve. 3rd pers. sing. / *encenagarse.*

encendámonos let us blush; impve. 1st pers. pl. / *encenderse.*

encendeos (you all) blush; impve. 2nd pers. pl. / *encenderse.*

encender to ignite. irr.

encenderse to blush. irr.

encendiéndose blushing; pres. part. / *encenderse.*

encepándose taking root; pres. part. / *enceparse.*

encepaos (you all) take root; impve. 2nd pers. pl. / *enceparse.*

encepar to put in the stocks. reg.

enceparse to take root. reg.

encépate (you) take root; impve. 2nd pers. sing. / *enceparse.*

encepémonos let us take root; impve. 1st pers. pl. / *enceparse.*

encépense let them take root; impve. 3rd pers. pl. / *enceparse.*

encépese let him (her/it) take root; impve. 3rd pers. sing. / *enceparse.*

encerar to wax. reg.

encerrándose going into seclusion; pres. part. / *encerrarse.*

encerraos (you all) go into seclusion; impve. 2nd pers. pl. / *encerrarse.*

encerrar to lock up or to include. irr.

encerrarse to go into seclusion. irr.

encerrémonos let us go into seclusion; impve. 1st pers. pl. / *encerrarse.*

encienda 1. that I may ignite; pres. subj. 1st pers. sing. / *encender.* 2. that he (she/it) may ignite; pres. subj. 3rd pers. sing. 3. let him (her/it) ignite; impve. 3rd pers. sing.

enciendan 1. that they may ignite; pres. subj. 3rd pers. pl. / *encender.* 2. let them ignite; impve. 3rd pers. pl.

enciéndanse let them blush; impve. 3rd pers. pl. / *encenderse.*

enciendas that you may ignite; pres. subj. 2nd pers. sing. / *encender.*

enciéndase let him (her/it) blush; impve. 3rd pers. sing. / *encenderse.*

enciende 1. he (she/it) ignites; pres. ind. 3rd pers. sing. / *encender.* 2. (you) ignite; impve. 2nd pers. sing.

encienden they ignite; pres. ind. 3rd pers. pl. / *encender.*

enciendes you ignite; pres. ind. 2nd pers. sing. / *encender.*

enciéndete (you) blush; impve. 2nd pers. sing. / *encenderse.*

enciendo I ignite; pres. ind. 1st pers. sing. / *encender.*

encierra 1. he (she/it) locks up; pres. ind. 3rd pers. sing. / *encerrar.* 2. (you) lock up; impve. 2nd pers. sing.

encierran they lock up; pres. ind. 3rd pers. pl. / *encerrar.*

encierras you lock up; pres. ind. 2nd pers. sing. / *encerrar.*

enciérrate (you) go into seclusion; impve. 2nd pers. sing. / *encerrarse.*

encierre 1. that I may lock up; pres. subj. 1st pers. sing. / *encerrar.* 2. that he (she/it) may lock up; pres. subj. 3rd pers. sing. 3. let him (her/it) lock up; impve. 3rd pers. sing.

encierren 1. that they may lock up; pres. subj. 3rd pers. pl. / *encerrar.* 2. let them lock up; impve. 3rd pers. pl.

enciérrense let them go into seclusion; impve. 3rd pers. pl. / *encerrarse.*

encierres that you may lock up; pres. subj. 2nd pers. sing. / *encerrar.*

enciérrese let him (her/it) go into seclusion; impve. 3rd pers. sing. / *encerrarse.*

encierro I lock up; pres. ind. 1st pers. sing. / *encerrar.*

encintar to trim with ribbon or to curb. reg.

enclaustrar to cloister. reg.

enclavar to nail. reg.

enclavijar to pin or to peg. reg.

enclocándose brooding; pres. part. / *enclocarse.*

enclocaos (you all) brood; impve. 2nd pers. pl. / *enclocarse.*

enclocar to brood. irr.

enclocarse to brood. irr.

encloqué I brooded; past 1st pers. sing. / *enclocar.*

encloquéis that you (all) may brood; pres. subj. 2nd pers. pl. / *enclocar.*

encloquémonos let us brood; impve. 1st pers. pl. / *enclocarse.*

encloquemos 1. that we may brood; pres. subj. 1st pers. pl. / *enclocar.* 2. let us brood; impve. 1st pers. pl.

enclueca 1. he (she/it) broods; pres. ind. 3rd pers. sing. / *enclocar.* 2. (you) brood; impve. 2nd pers. sing.

encluecan they brood; pres. ind. 3rd pers. pl. / *enclocar.*

encluecas you brood; pres. ind. 2nd pers. sing. / *enclocar.*

encluécate (you) brood; impve. 2nd pers. sing. / *enclocarse.*

enclueco I brood; pres. ind. 1st pers. sing. / *enclocar.*

enclueque 1. that I may brood; pres. subj. 1st pers. sing. / *enclocar.* 2. that he (she/it) may brood; pres. subj. 3rd pers. sing. 3. let him (her/it) brood; impve. 3rd pers. sing.

encluequen 1. that they may brood; pres. subj. 3rd pers. pl. / *enclocar.* 2. let them brood; impve. 3rd pers. pl.

encluéquense let them brood; impve. 3rd pers. pl. / *enclocarse.*

enclueques that you may brood; pres. subj. 2nd pers. sing. / *enclocar.*

encluéquese let him (her/it) brood; impve. 3rd pers. sing. / *enclocarse*.

encobándose brooding; pres. part. / *encobarse*.

encobaos (you all) brood; impve. 2nd pers. pl. / *encobarse*.

encobar to brood. reg.

encobarse to brood. reg.

encóbate (you) brood; impve. 2nd pers. sing. / *encobarse*.

encobémonos let us brood; impve. 1st pers. pl. / *encobarse*.

encóbense let them brood; impve. 3rd pers. pl. / *encobarse*.

encóbese let him (her/it) brood; impve. 3rd pers. sing. / *encobarse*.

encocorar to annoy. reg.

encofrar to build a form for concrete. reg.

encogeos (you all) shrivel; impve. 2nd pers. pl. / *encogerse*.

encoger to shrink. irr.

encogerse to shrivel. irr.

encógete (you) shrivel; impve. 2nd pers. sing. / *encogerse*.

encogiéndose shriveling; pres. part. / *encogerse*.

encoja 1. that I may shrink; pres. subj. 1st pers. sing. / *encoger*. 2. that he (she/it) may shrink; pres. subj. 3rd pers. sing. 3. let him (her/it) shrink; impve. 3rd pers. sing.

encojáis that you (all) may shrink; pres. subj. 2nd pers. pl. / *encoger*.

encojámonos let us shrivel; impve. 1st pers. pl. / *encogerse*.

encojamos 1. that we may shrink; pres. subj. 1st pers. pl. / *encoger*. 2. let us shrink; impve. 1st pers. pl.

encojan 1. that they may shrink; pres. subj. 3rd pers. pl. / *encoger*. 2. let them shrink; impve. 3rd pers. pl.

encojándose going lame; pres. part. / *encojarse*.

encójanse let them shrivel; impve. 3rd pers. pl. / *encogerse*.

encojaos (you all) go lame; impve. 2nd pers. pl. / *encojarse*.

encojar to cripple. reg.

encojarse to go lame. reg.

encojas that you may shrink; pres. subj. 2nd pers. sing. / *encoger*.

encójase let him (her/it) shrivel; impve. 3rd pers. sing. / *encogerse*.

encójate (you) go lame; impve. 2nd pers. sing. / *encojarse*.

encojémonos let us go lame; impve. 1st pers. pl. / *encojarse*.

encójense let them go lame; impve. 3rd pers. pl. / *encojarse*.

encójese let him (her/it) go lame; impve. 3rd pers. sing. / *encojarse*.

encojo I shrink; pres. ind. 1st pers. sing. / *encoger*.

encolar to glue. reg.

encolerice 1. that I may anger; pres. subj. 1st pers. sing. / *encolerizar*. 2. that he (she/it) may anger; pres. subj. 3rd pers. sing. 3. let him (her/it) anger; impve. 3rd pers. sing.

encolericé I angered; past 1st pers. sing. / *encolerizar*.

encolericéis that you (all) may anger; pres. subj. 2nd pers. pl. / *encolerizar*.

encolericémonos let us become angry; impve. 1st pers. pl. / *encolerizarse*.

encolericemos 1. that we may anger; pres. subj. 1st pers. pl. / *encolerizar*. 2. let us anger; impve. 1st pers. pl.

encolericen 1. that they may anger; pres. subj. 3rd pers. pl. / *encolerizar*. 2. let them anger; impve. 3rd pers. pl.

encolerícense let them become angry; impve. 3rd pers. pl. / *encolerizarse*.

encolerices that you may anger; pres. subj. 2nd pers. sing. / *encolerizar*.

encolerícese let him (her/it) become angry; impve. 3rd pers. sing. / *encolerizarse*.

encolerizándose becoming angry; pres. part. / *encolerizarse*.

encolerizaos (you all) become angry; impve. 2nd pers. pl. / *encolerizarse*.

encolerizar to anger. irr.

encolerizarse to become angry. irr.

encolerízate (you) become angry; impve. 2nd pers. sing. / *encolerizarse*.

encomendándose sending regards; pres. part. / *encomendarse*.

encomendaos (you all) send regards; impve. 2nd pers. pl. / *encomendarse*.

encomendar to entrust. irr.

encomendarse to send regards. irr.

encomendémonos let us send regards; impve. 1st pers. pl. / *encomendarse*.

encomiar to extole or to praise. reg.

encomienda 1. he (she/it) entrusts; pres. ind. 3rd pers. sing. / *encomendar*. 2. (you) entrust; impve. 2nd pers. sing.

encomiendan they entrust; pres. ind. 3rd pers. pl. / *encomendar*.

encomiendas you entrust; pres. ind. 2nd pers. sing. / *encomendar*.

encomiéndate (you) send regards; impve. 2nd pers. sing. / *encomendarse*.

encomiende 1. that I may entrust; pres. subj. 1st pers. sing. / *encomendar*. 2. that he (she/it) may entrust; pres. subj. 3rd pers. sing. 3. let him (her/it) entrust; impve. 3rd pers. sing.

encomienden 1. that they may entrust; pres. subj. 3rd pers. pl. / *encomendar*. 2. let them entrust; impve. 3rd pers. pl.

encomiéndense let them send regards; impve. 3rd pers. pl. / *encomendarse*.

encomiendes that you may entrust; pres. subj. 2nd pers. sing. / *encomendar*.

encomiéndese let him (her/it) send regards; impve. 3rd pers. sing. / *encomendarse*.

encomiendo I entrust; pres. ind. 1st pers. sing. / *encomendar.*

enconándose festering; pres. part. / *enconarse.*

enconaos (you all) fester; impve. 2nd pers. pl. / *enconarse.*

enconar to inflame or to irritate. reg.

enconarse to fester. reg.

encónate (you) fester; impve. 2nd pers. sing. / *enconarse.*

enconémonos let us fester; impve. 1st pers. pl. / *enconarse.*

encónense let them fester; impve. 3rd pers. pl. / *enconarse.*

encónese let him (her/it) fester; impve. 3rd pers. sing. / *enconarse.*

encontrándose being found; pres. part. / *encontrarse.*

encontraos (you all) be found; impve. 2nd pers. pl. / *encontrarse.*

encontrar to meet or to encounter. irr.

encontrarse to be found. irr.

encontrémonos let us be found; impve. 1st pers. pl. / *encontrarse.*

encopetándose becoming conceited; pres. part. / *encopetarse.*

encopetaos (you all) become conceited; impve. 2nd pers. pl. / *encopetarse.*

encopetar to arrange hair high on the head. reg.

encopetarse to become conceited. reg.

encopétate (you) become conceited; impve. 2nd pers. sing. / *encopetarse.*

encopetémonos let us become conceited; impve. 1st pers. pl. / *encopetarse.*

encopétense let them become conceited; impve. 3rd pers. pl. / *encopetarse.*

encopétese let him (her/it) become conceited; impve. 3rd pers. sing. / *encopetarse.*

encorajándose being in a rage; pres. part. / *encorajarse.*

encorajaos (you all) be in a rage; impve. 2nd pers. pl. / *encorajarse.*

encorajar to give courage. reg.

encorajarse to be in a rage. reg.

encorájate (you) be in a rage; impve. 2nd pers. sing. / *encorajarse.*

encorajémonos let us be in a rage; impve. 1st pers. pl. / *encorajarse.*

encorájense let them be in a rage; impve. 3rd pers. pl. / *encorajarse.*

encorájese let him (her/it) be in a rage; impve. 3rd pers. sing. / *encorajarse.*

encorándose healing over; pres. part. / *encorarse.*

encoraos (you all) heal over; impve. 2nd pers. pl. / *encorarse.*

encorar to cover with leather. irr.

encorarse to heal over. irr.

encorchar to hive or to cork. reg.

encorchetar to fasten with hooks and eyes. reg.

encordar to string. irr.

encordelar to string. reg.

encordonar to tie with string. reg.

encorémonos let us heal over; impve. 1st pers. pl. / *encorarse.*

encornudar to cuckold or to grow horns. reg.

encorrear to strap. reg.

encorvándose stooping; pres. part. / *encorvarse.*

encorvaos (you all) stoop; impve. 2nd pers. pl. / *encorvarse.*

encorvar to bend. reg.

encorvarse to stoop. reg.

encórvate (you) stoop; impve. 2nd pers. sing. / *encorvarse.*

encorvémonos let us stoop; impve. 1st pers. pl. / *encorvarse.*

encórvense let them stoop; impve. 3rd pers. pl. / *encorvarse.*

encórvese let him (her/it) stoop; impve. 3rd pers. sing. / *encorvarse.*

encostrar to encrust. reg.

encovar to put in the cellar. irr.

encrasar to thicken or to fertilize. reg.

encrespándose becoming rough; pres. part. / *encresparse.*

encrespaos (you all) become rough; impve. 2nd pers. pl. / *encresparse.*

encrespar to curl. reg.

encresparse to become rough. reg.

encréspate (you) become rough; impve. 2nd pers. sing. / *encresparse.*

encrespémonos let us become rough; impve. 1st pers. pl. / *encresparse.*

encréspense let them become rough; impve. 3rd pers. pl. / *encresparse.*

encréspese let him (her/it) become rough; impve. 3rd pers. sing. / *encresparse.*

encristalar to glaze. reg.

encrudecer to make rough and raw. irr.

encrudezca 1. that I may make rough and raw; pres. subj. 1st pers. sing. / *encrudecer.* 2. that he (she/it) may make rough and raw; pres. subj. 3rd pers. sing. 3. let him (her/it) make rough and raw; impve. 3rd pers. sing.

encrudezcáis that you (all) may make rough and raw; pres. subj. 2nd pers. pl. / *encrudecer.*

encrudezcamos 1. that we may make rough and raw; pres. subj. 1st pers. pl. / *encrudecer.* 2. let us make rough and raw; impve. 1st pers. pl.

encrudezcan 1. that they may make rough and raw; pres. subj. 3rd pers. pl. / *encrudecer.* 2. let them make rough and raw; impve. 3rd pers. pl.

encrudezcas that you may make rough and raw; pres. subj. 2nd pers. sing. / *encrudecer.*

encrudezco I make rough and raw; pres. ind. 1st pers. sing. / *encrudecer.*

encuadernar to bind (books). reg.

encuadrar to frame. reg.

encubar to barrel. reg.

encubierto covered; past part. / *encubrir.*

encubrir to cover or to hide. reg. except for pp.

encuentra 1. he (she/it) meets; pres. ind. 3rd pers. sing. / *encontrar*. 2. (you) meet; impve. 2nd pers. sing.

encuentran they meet; pres. ind. 3rd pers. pl. / *encontrar*.

encuentras you meet; pres. ind. 2nd pers. sing. / *encontrar*.

encuéntrate (you) be found; impve. 2nd pers. sing. / *encontrarse*.

encuentre 1. that I may meet; pres. subj. 1st pers. sing. / *encontrar*. 2. that he (she/it) may meet; pres. subj. 3rd pers. sing. 3. let him (her/it) meet; impve. 3rd pers. sing.

encuentren 1. that they may meet; pres. subj. 3rd pers. pl. / *encontrar*. 2. let them meet; impve. 3rd pers. pl.

encuéntrense let them be found; impve. 3rd pers. pl. / *encontrarse*.

encuentres that you may meet; pres. subj. 2nd pers. sing. / *encontrar*.

encuéntrese let him (her/it) be found; impve. 3rd pers. sing. / *encontrarse*.

encuentro I meet; pres. ind. 1st pers. sing. / *encontrar*.

encuera 1. he (she/it) covers with leather; pres. ind. 3rd pers. sing. / *encorar*. 2. (you) cover with leather; impve. 2nd pers. sing.

encueran they cover with leather; pres. ind. 3rd pers. pl. / *encorar*.

encuerándose stripping; pres. part. / *encuerarse*.

encueraos (you all) strip; impve. 2nd pers. pl. / *encuerarse*.

encuerar to strip of clothes or money. reg.

encuerarse to strip. reg.

encueras you cover with leather; pres. ind. 2nd pers. sing. / *encorar*.

encuérate (you) heal over; impve. 2nd pers. sing. / *encorarse*.

encuérate (you) strip; impve. 2nd pers. sing. / *encuerarse*.

encuerda 1. he (she/it) strings; pres. ind. 3rd pers. sing. / *encordar*. 2. (you) string; impve. 2nd pers. sing.

encuerdan they string; pres. ind. 3rd pers. pl. / *encordar*.

encuerdas you string; pres. ind. 2nd pers. sing. / *encordar*.

encuerde 1. that I may string; pres. subj. 1st pers. sing. / *encordar*. 2. that he (she/it) may string; pres. subj. 3rd pers. sing. 3. let him (her/it) string; impve. 3rd pers. sing.

encuerden 1. that they may string; pres. subj. 3rd pers. pl. / *encordar*. 2. let them string; impve. 3rd pers. pl.

encuerdes that you may string; pres. subj. 2nd pers. sing. / *encordar*.

encuerdo I string; pres. ind. 1st pers. sing. / *encordar*.

encuere 1. that I may cover with leather; pres. subj. 1st pers. sing. / *encorar*. 2. that he (she/it) may cover with leather; pres. subj. 3rd pers. sing. 3. let him (her/it) cover with leather; impve. 3rd pers. sing.

encuerémonos let us strip; impve. 1st pers. pl. / *encuerarse*.

encueren 1. that they may cover with leather; pres. subj. 3rd pers. pl. / *encorar*. 2. let them cover with leather; impve. 3rd pers. pl.

encuérense let them heal over; impve. 3rd pers. pl. / *encorarse*.

encuérense let them strip; impve. 3rd pers. pl. / *encuerarse*.

encueres that you may cover with leather; pres. subj. 2nd pers. sing. / *encorar*.

encuérese let him (her/it) heal over; impve. 3rd pers. sing. / *encorarse*.

encuérese let him (her/it) strip; impve. 3rd pers. sing. / *encuerarse*.

encuero I cover with leather; pres. ind. 1st pers. sing. / *encorar*.

encueva 1. he (she/it) puts in the cellar; pres. ind. 3rd pers. sing. / *encovar*. 2. (you) put in the cellar; impve. 2nd pers. sing.

encuevan they put in the cellar; pres. ind. 3rd pers. pl. / *encovar*.

encuevas you put in the cellar; pres. ind. 2nd pers. sing. / *encovar*.

encueve 1. that I may put in the cellar; pres. subj. 1st pers. sing. / *encovar*. 2. that he (she/it) may put in the cellar; pres. subj. 3rd pers. sing. 3. let him (her/it) put in the cellar; impve. 3rd pers. sing.

encueven 1. that they may put in the cellar; pres. subj. 3rd pers. pl. / *encovar*. 2. let them put in the cellar; impve. 3rd pers. pl.

encueves that you may put in the cellar; pres. subj. 2nd pers. sing. / *encovar*.

encuevo I put in the cellar; pres. ind. 1st pers. sing. / *encovar*.

encumbrándose becoming proud; pres. part. / *encumbrarse*.

encumbraos (you all) become proud; impve. 2nd pers. pl. / *encumbrarse*.

encumbrar to raise. reg.

encumbrarse to become proud. reg.

encúmbrate (you) become proud; impve. 2nd pers. sing. / *encumbrarse*.

encumbrémonos let us become proud; impve. 1st pers. pl. / *encumbrarse*.

encúmbrense let them become proud; impve. 3rd pers. pl. / *encumbrarse*.

encúmbrese let him (her/it) become proud; impve. 3rd pers. sing. / *encumbrarse*.

encurtir to pickle. reg.

enchapar to veneer. reg.

encharcándose being inundated; pres. part. / *encharcarse*.

encharcaos (you all) be inundated; impve. 2nd pers. pl. / *encharcarse*.

encharcar to flood. irr.

encharcarse to be inundated. irr.

enchárcate (you) be inundated; impve. 2nd pers. sing. / *encharcarse*.

encharque 1. that I may flood; pres. subj. 1st pers. sing. / *encharcar*. 2. that he (she/it) may flood; pres. subj. 3rd pers. sing. 3. let him (her/it) flood; impve. 3rd pers. sing.

encharqué I flooded; past 1st pers. sing. / *encharcar*.

encharquéis that you (all) may flood; pres. subj. 2nd pers. pl. / *encharcar*.

encharquémonos let us be inundated; impve. 1st pers. pl. / *encharcarse*.

encharquemos 1. that we may flood; pres. subj. 1st pers. pl. / *encharcar*. 2. let us flood; impve. 1st pers. pl.

encharquen 1. that they may flood; pres. subj. 3rd pers. pl. / *encharcar*. 2. let them flood; impve. 3rd pers. pl.

enchárquense let them be inundated; impve. 3rd pers. pl. / *encharcarse*.

encharques that you may flood; pres. subj. 2nd pers. sing. / *encharcar*.

enchárquese let him (her/it) be inundated; impve. 3rd pers. sing. / *encharcarse*.

enchilar to put chili on. reg.

enchuecándose getting bent; pres. part. / *enchuecarse*.

enchuecaos (you all) get bent; impve. 2nd pers. pl. / *enchuecarse*.

enchuecar to bend or twist. irr.

enchuecarse to get bent. irr.

enchuécate (you) get bent; impve. 2nd pers. sing. / *enchuecarse*.

enchueque 1. that I may bend; pres. subj. 1st pers. sing. / *enchuecar*. 2. that he (she/it) may bend; pres. subj. 3rd pers. sing. 3. let him (her/it) bend; impve. 3rd pers. sing.

enchuequé I bent; past 1st pers. sing. / *enchuecar*.

enchuequéis that you (all) may bend; pres. subj. 2nd pers. pl. / *enchuecarse*.

enchuequémonos let us get bent; impve. 1st pers. pl. / *enchuecarse*.

enchuequemos 1. that we may bend; pres. subj. 1st pers. pl. / *enchuecar*. 2. let us bend; impve. 1st pers. pl.

enchuequen 1. that they may bend; pres. subj. 3rd pers. pl. / *enchuecar*. 2. let them bend; impve. 3rd pers. pl.

enchuéquense let them get bent; impve. 3rd pers. pl. / *enchuecarse*.

enchueques that you may bend; pres. subj. 2nd pers. sing. / *enchuecar*.

enchuéquese let him (her/it) get bent; impve. 3rd pers. sing. / *enchuecarse*.

enchufar to plug in. reg.

endechándose grieving; pres. part. / *endecharse*.

endechaos (you all) grieve; impve. 2nd pers. pl. / *endecharse*.

endechar to bewail or to grieve. reg.

endecharse to grieve. reg.

endéchate (you) grieve; impve. 2nd pers. sing. / *endecharse*.

endechémonos let us grieve; impve. 1st pers. pl. / *endecharse*.

endéchense let them grieve; impve. 3rd pers. pl. / *endecharse*.

endéchese let him (her/it) grieve; impve. 3rd pers. sing. / *endecharse*.

endemoniar to irritate. reg.

endentándose meshing; pres. part. / *endentarse*.

endentaos (you all) mesh; impve. 2nd pers. pl. / *endentarse*.

endentar to indent. irr.

endentarse to mesh. irr.

endentecer to teethe. irr.

endentémonos let us mesh; impve. 1st pers. pl. / *endentarse*.

endentezca 1. that I may teethe; pres. subj. 1st pers. sing. / *endentecer*. 2. that he (she/it) may teethe; pres. subj. 3rd pers. sing. 3. let him (her/it) teethe; impve. 3rd pers. sing.

endentezcáis that you (all) may teethe; pres. subj. 2nd pers. pl. / *endentecer*.

endentezcamos 1. that we may teethe; pres. subj. 1st pers. pl. / *endentecer*. 2. let us teethe; impve. 1st pers. pl.

endentezcan 1. that they may teethe; pres. subj. 3rd pers. pl. / *endentecer*. 2. let them teethe; impve. 3rd pers. pl.

endentezcas that you may teethe; pres. subj. 2nd pers. sing. / *endentecer*.

endentezco I teethe; pres. ind. 1st pers. sing. / *endentecer*.

enderece 1. that I may straighten; pres. subj. 1st pers. sing. / *enderezar*. 2. that he (she/it) may straighten; pres. subj. 3rd pers. sing. 3. let him (her/it) straighten; impve. 3rd pers. sing.

enderecé I straightened; past 1st pers. sing. / *enderezar*.

enderecéis that you (all) may straighten; pres. subj. 2nd pers. pl. / *enderezar*.

enderecémonos let us straighten up; impve. 1st pers. pl. / *enderezarse*.

enderecemos 1. that we may strighten; pres. subj. 1st pers. pl. / *enderezar*. 2. let us straighten; impve. 1st pers. pl.

enderecen 1. that they may straighten; pres. subj. 3rd pers. pl. / *enderezar*. 2. let them straighten; impve. 3rd pers. pl.

enderécense let them straighten up; impve. 3rd pers. pl. / *enderezarse*.

endereces that you may straighten; pres. subj. 2nd pers. sing. / *enderezar*.

enderécese let him (her/it) straighten up; impve. 3rd pers. sing. / *enderezarse*.

enderezándose straightening up; pres. part. / *enderezarse*.

enderezaos (you all) straighten up; impve. 2nd pers. pl. / *enderezarse*.

enderezar to straighten. irr.

enderezarse to straighten up. irr.

enderézate (you) straighten up; impve. 2nd pers. sing. / *enderezarse*.

endeudándose getting into debt; pres. part. / *endeudarse*.

endeudaos (you all) get into debt; impve. 2nd pers. pl. / *endeudarse*.

endeudarse to get into debt. reg.

endeúdate (you) get into debt; impve. 2nd pers. sing. / *endeudarse*.

endeudémonos let us get into debt; impve. 1st pers. pl. / *endeudarse*.

endeúdense let them get into debt; impve. 3rd pers. pl. / *endeudarse*.

endeúdese let him (her/it) get into debt; impve. 3rd pers. sing. / *endeudarse*.

endiablándose becoming furious; pres. part. / *endiablarse*.

endiablaos (you all) become furious; impve. 2nd pers. pl. / *endiablarse*.

endiablar to corrupt. reg.

endiablarse to become furious. reg.

endiáblate (you) become furious; impve. 2nd pers. sing. / *endiablarse*.

endiablémonos let us become furious; impve. 1st pers. pl. / *endiablarse*.

endiáblense let them become furious; impve. 3rd pers. pl. / *endiablarse*.

endiáblese let him (her/it) become furious; impve. 3rd pers. sing. / *endiablarse*.

endienta 1. he (she/it) indents; pres. ind. 3rd pers. sing. / *endentar*. 2. (you) indent; impve. 2nd pers. sing.

endientan they indent; pres. ind. 3rd pers. pl. / *endentar*.

endientas you indent; pres. ind. 2nd pers. sing. / *endentar*.

endiéntate (you) mesh; impve. 2nd pers. sing. / *endentarse*.

endiente 1. that I may indent; pres. subj. 1st pers. sing. / *endentar*. 2. that he (she/it) may indent; pres. subj. 3rd pers. sing. 3. let him (her/it) indent; impve. 3rd pers. sing.

endienten 1. that they may indent; pres. subj. 3rd pers. pl. / *endentar*. 2. let them indent; impve. 3rd pers. pl.

endiéntense let them mesh; impve. 3rd pers. pl. / *endentarse*.

endientes that you may indent; pres. subj. 2nd pers. sing. / *endentar*.

endiéntese let him (her/it) mesh; impve. 3rd pers. sing. / *endentarse*.

endiento I indent; pres. ind. 1st pers. sing. / *endentar*.

endilgar to direct or to help. irr.

endilgue 1. that I may direct; pres. subj. 1st pers. sing. / *endilgar*. 2. that he (she/it) may direct; pres. subj. 3rd pers. sing. 3. let him (her/it) direct; impve. 3rd pers. sing.

endilgué I directed; past 1st pers. sing. / *endilgar*.

endilguéis that you (all) may direct; pres. subj. 2nd pers. pl. / *endilgar*.

endilguemos 1. that we may direct; pres. subj. 1st pers. pl. / *endilgar*. 2. let us direct; impve. 1st pers. pl.

endilguen 1. that they may direct; pres. subj. 3rd pers. pl. / *endilgar*. 2. let them direct; impve. 3rd pers. pl.

endilgues that you may direct; pres. subj. 2nd pers. sing. / *endilgar*.

endiosándose becoming haughty; pres. part. / *endiosarse*.

endiosaos (you all) become haughty; impve. 2nd pers. pl. / *endiosarse*.

endiosar to deify. reg.

endiosarse to become haughty. reg.

endiósate (you) become haughty; impve. 2nd pers. sing. / *endiosarse*.

endiosémonos let us become haughty; impve. 1st pers. pl. / *endiosarse*.

endiósense let them become haughty; impve. 3rd pers. pl. / *endiosarse*.

endiósese let him (her/it) become haughty; impve. 3rd pers. sing. / *endiosarse*.

endomingándose putting on one's sunday best; pres. part. / *endomingarse*.

endomingaos (you all) put on your sunday best; impve. 2nd pers. pl. / *endomingarse*.

endomingarse to put on one's sunday best. irr.

endomíngate (you) put on your sunday best; impve. 2nd pers. sing. / *endomingarse*.

endomingue 1. that I may put on my sunday best; pres. subj. 1st pers. sing. / *endomingarse*. 2. that he (she/it) may put on his (her/its) sunday best; pres. subj. 3rd pers. sing.

endomingué I put on my sunday best; past 1st pers. sing. / *endomingarse*.

endominguéis that you (all) may put on your sunday best; pres. subj. 2nd pers. pl. / *endomingarse*.

endominguémonos let us put on our sunday best; impve. 1st pers. pl. / *endomingarse*.

endominguemos that we may put on our sunday best; pres. subj. 1st pers. pl. / *endomingarse*.

endominguen that they may put on their sunday best; pres. subj. 3rd pers. pl. / *endomingarse*.

endomínguense let them put on their sunday best; impve. 3rd pers. pl. / *endomingarse*.

endomingues that you may put on your sunday best; pres. subj. 2nd pers. sing. / *endomingarse*.

endomínguese let him (her/it) put on his (her/its) sunday best; impve. 3rd pers. sing. / *endomingarse*.

endorsar to endorse. reg.

endosar to endorse. reg.

endulce 1. that I may sweeten; pres. subj. 1st pers. sing. / *endulzar*. 2. that he (she/it) may sweeten; pres. subj. 3rd pers. sing. 3. let him (her/it) sweeten; impve. 3rd pers. sing.

endulcé I sweetened; past 1st pers. sing. / *endulzar*.

endulcéis that you (all) may sweeten; pres. subj. 2nd pers. pl. / *endulzar*.

endulcemos 1. that we may sweeten; pres. subj. 1st pers. pl. / *endulzar*. 2. let us sweeten; impve. 1st pers. pl.

endulcen 1. that they may sweeten; pres. subj. 3rd pers. pl. / *endulzar*. 2. let them sweeten; impve. 3rd pers. pl.

endulces that you may sweeten; pres. subj. 2nd pers. sing. / *endulzar.*

endulzar to sweeten. irr.

endurar to endure. reg.

endureceos (you all) become cruel; impve. 2nd pers. pl. / *endurecerse.*

endurecer to harden. irr.

endurecerse to become cruel. irr.

endurécete (you) become cruel; impve. 2nd pers. sing. / *endurecerse.*

endureciéndose becoming cruel; pres. part. / *endurecerse.*

endurezca 1. that I may harden; pres. subj. 1st pers. sing. / *endurecer.* 2. that he (she/it) may harden; pres. subj. 3rd pers. sing. 3. let him (her/it) harden; impve. 3rd pers. sing.

endurezcáis that you (all) may harden; pres. subj. 2nd pers. pl. / *endurecer.*

endurezcámonos let us become cruel; impve. 1st pers. pl. / *endurecerse.*

endurezcamos 1. that we may harden; pres. subj. 1st pers. pl. / *endurecer.* 2. let us harden; impve. 1st pers. pl.

endurezcan 1. that they may harden; pres. subj. 3rd pers. pl. / *endurecer.* 2. let them harden; impve. 3rd pers. pl.

endurézcanse let them become cruel; impve. 3rd pers. pl. / *endurecerse.*

endurezcas that you may harden; pres. subj. 2nd pers. sing. / *endurecer.*

endurézcase let him (her/it) become cruel; impve. 3rd pers. sing. / *endurecerse.*

endurezco I harden; pres. ind. 1st pers. sing. / *endurecer.*

enemistándose becoming enemies; pres. part. / *enemistarse.*

enemistaos (you all) become enemies; impve. 2nd pers. pl. / *enemistarse.*

enemistar to estrange. reg.

enemistarse to become enemies. reg.

enemístate (you) become enemies; impve. 2nd pers. sing. / *enemistarse.*

enemistémonos let us become enemies; impve. 1st pers. pl. / *enemistarse.*

enemístense let them become enemies; impve. 3rd pers. pl. / *enemistarse.*

enemístese let him (her/it) become enemies; impve. 3rd pers. sing. / *enemistarse.*

enervándose becoming effeminate; pres. part. / *enervarse.*

enervaos (you all) become effeminate; impve. 2nd pers. pl. / *enervarse.*

enervar to enervate or to weaken. reg.

enervarse to become effeminate. reg.

enérvate (you) become effeminate; impve. 2nd pers. sing. / *enervarse.*

enervémonos let us become effeminate; impve. 1st pers. pl. / *enervarse.*

enérvense let them become effeminate; impve. 3rd pers. pl. / *enervarse.*

enérvese let him (her/it) become effeminate; impve. 3rd pers. sing. / *enervarse.*

enfadándose becoming annoyed; pres. part. / *enfadarse.*

enfadaos (you all) become annoyed; impve. 2nd pers. pl. / *enfadarse.*

enfadar to anger. reg.

enfadarse to become annoyed. reg.

enfádate (you) become annoyed; impve. 2nd pers. sing. / *enfadarse.*

enfadémonos let us become annoyed; impve. 1st pers. pl. / *enfadarse.*

enfádense let them become annoyed; impve. 3rd pers. pl. / *enfadarse.*

enfádese let him (her/it) become annoyed; impve. 3rd pers. sing. / *enfadarse.*

enfangándose sinking in the mud; pres. part. / *enfangarse.*

enfangaos (you all) sink in the mud; impve. 2nd pers. pl. / *enfangarse.*

enfangar to soil with mud. irr.

enfangarse to sink in the mud. irr.

enfángate (you) sink in the mud; impve. 2nd pers. sing. / *enfangarse.*

enfangue 1. that I may soil with mud; pres. subj. 1st pers. sing. / *enfangar.* 2. that he (she/it) may soil with mud; pres. subj. 3rd pers. sing. 3. let him (her/it) soil with mud; impve. 3rd pers. sing.

enfangué I soiled with mud; past 1st pers. sing. / *enfangar.*

enfanguéis that you (all) may soil with mud; pres. subj. 2nd pers. pl. / *enfangar.*

enfanguémonos let us sink in the mud; impve. 1st pers. pl. / *enfangarse.*

enfanguemos 1. that we may soil with mud; pres. subj. 1st pers. pl. / *enfangar.* 2. let us soil with mud; impve. 1st pers. pl.

enfanguen 1. that they may soil with mud; pres. subj. 3rd pers. pl. / *enfangar.* 2. let them soil with mud; impve. 3rd pers. pl.

enfánguense let them sink in the mud; impve. 3rd pers. pl. / *enfangarse.*

enfangues that you may soil with mud; pres. subj. 2nd pers. sing. / *enfangar.*

enfánguese let him (her/it) sink in the mud; impve. 3rd pers. sing. / *enfangarse.*

enfardar to bale. reg.

enfardelar to bale. reg.

enfermándose becoming sick; pres. part. / *enfermarse.*

enfermaos (you all) become sick; impve. 2nd pers. pl. / *enfermarse.*

enfermar to make sick. reg.

enfermarse to become sick. reg.

enférmate (you) become sick; impve. 2nd pers. sing. / *enfermarse.*

enfermémonos let us become sick; impve. 1st pers. pl. / *enfermarse.*

enférmense let them become sick; impve. 3rd pers. pl. / *enfermarse.*

enférmese let him (her/it) become sick; impve. 3rd pers. sing. / *enfermarse.*

enfeudar to enfeoff or to invest with a right or estate. reg.

enfilar to line up. reg.

enflacar to get thin. reg.

enflaqueceos (you all) become discouraged; impve. 2nd pers. pl. / *enflaquecerse.*

enflaquecer to weaken. irr.

enflaquecerse to become discouraged. irr.

enflaquécete (you) become discouraged; impve. 2nd pers. sing. / *enflaquecerse.*

enflaqueciéndose becoming discouraged; pres. part. / *enflaquecerse.*

enflaquezca 1. that I may weaken; pres. subj. 1st pers. sing. / *enflaquecer.* 2. that he (she/it) may weaken; pres. subj. 3rd pers. sing. 3. let him (her/it) weaken; impve. 3rd pers. sing.

enflaquezcáis that you (all) may weaken; pres. subj. 2nd pers. pl. / *enflaquecer.*

enflaquezcámonos let us become discouraged; impve. 1st pers. pl. / *enflaquecerse.*

enflaquezcamos 1. that we may weaken; pres. subj. 1st pers. pl. / *enflaquecer.* 2. let us weaken; impve. 1st pers. pl.

enflaquezcan 1. that they may weaken; pres. subj. 3rd pers. pl. / *enflaquecer.* 2. let them weaken; impve. 3rd pers. pl.

enflaquézcanse let them become discouraged; impve. 3rd pers. pl. / *enflaquecerse.*

enflaquezcas that you may weaken; pres. subj. 2nd pers. sing. / *enflaquecer.*

enflaquézcase let him (her/it) become discouraged; impve. 3rd pers. sing. / *enflaquecerse.*

enflaquezco I weaken; pres. ind. 1st pers. sing. / *enflaquecer.*

enfocar to focus. irr.

enfoque 1. that I may focus; pres. subj. 1st pers. sing. / *enfocar.* 2. that he (she/it) may focus; pres. subj. 3rd pers. sing. 3. let him (her/it) focus; impve. 3rd pers. sing.

enfoqué I focused; past 1st pers. sing. / *enfocar.*

enfoquéis that you (all) may focus; pres. subj. 2nd pers. pl. / *enfocar.*

enfoquemos 1. that we may focus; pres. subj. 1st pers. pl. / *enfocar.* 2. let us focus; impve. 1st pers. pl.

enfoquen 1. that they may focus; pres. subj. 3rd pers. pl. / *enfocar.* 2. let them focus; impve. 3rd pers. pl.

enfoques that you may focus; pres. subj. 2nd pers. sing. / *enfocar.*

enfoscándose becoming grumpy; pres. part. / *enfoscarse.*

enfoscaos (you all) become grumpy; impve. 2nd pers. pl. / *enfoscarse.*

enfoscar to fill in (with mortar). irr.

enfoscarse to become grumpy. irr.

enfóscate (you) become grumpy; impve. 2nd pers. sing. / *enfoscarse.*

enfosque 1. that I may fill in (with mortar); pres. subj. 1st pers. sing. / *enfoscar.* 2. that he (she/it) may fill in (with mortar); pres. subj. 3rd pers. sing. 3. let him (her/it) fill in (with mortar); impve. 3rd pers. sing.

enfosqué I filled in (with mortar); past 1st pers. sing. / *enfoscar.*

enfosquéis that you (all) may fill in (with mortar ; pres. subj. 2nd pers. pl. / *enfoscar.*

enfosquémonos let us become grumpy; impve. 1st pers. pl. / *enfoscarse.*

enfosquemos 1. that we may fill in (with mortar); pres. subj. 1st pers. pl. / *enfoscar.* 2. let us fill in (with mortar); impve. 1st pers. pl.

enfosquen 1. that they may fill in (with mortar); pres. subj. 3rd pers. pl. / *enfoscar.* 2. let them fill in (with mortar); impve. 3rd pers. pl.

enfósquense let them become grumpy; impve. 3rd pers. pl. / *enfoscarse.*

enfosques that you may fill in (with mortar); pres. subj. 2nd pers. sing. / *enfoscar.*

enfósquese let him (her/it) become grumpy; impve. 3rd pers. sing. / *enfoscarse.*

enfrascándose becoming deeply involved; pres. part. / *enfrascarse.*

enfrascaos (you all) become deeply involved; impve. 2nd pers. pl. / *enfrascarse.*

enfrascar to bottle. irr.

enfrascarse to become deeply involved. irr.

enfráscate (you) become deeply involved; impve. 2nd pers. sing. / *enfrascarse.*

enfrasque 1. that I may bottle; pres. subj. 1st pers. sing. / *enfrascar.* 2. that he (she/it) may bottle; pres. subj. 3rd pers. sing. 3. let him (her/it) bottle; impve. 3rd pers. sing.

enfrasqué I bottled; past 1st pers. sing. / *enfrascar.*

enfrasquéis that you (all) may bottle; pres. subj. 2nd pers. pl. / *enfrascar.*

enfrasquémonos let us become deeply involved; impve. 1st pers. pl. / *enfrascarse.*

enfrasquemos 1. that we may bottle; pres. subj. 1st pers. pl. / *enfrascar.* 2. let us bottle; impve. 1st pers. pl.

enfrasquen 1. that they may bottle; pres. subj. 3rd pers. pl. / *enfrascar.* 2. let them bottle; impve. 3rd pers. pl.

enfrasquense let them become deeply involved; impve. 3rd pers. pl. / *enfrascarse.*

enfrasques that you may bottle; pres. subj. 2nd pers. sing. / *enfrascar.*

enfrásquese let him (her/it) become deeply involved; impve. 3rd pers. sing. / *enfrascarse.*

enfrenar to restrain or to bridle. reg.

enfrentándose opposing; pres. part. / *enfrentarse.*

enfrentaos (you all) oppose; impve. 2nd pers. pl. / *enfrentarse.*

enfrentar to confront. reg.

enfrentarse to face or to oppose. reg.

enfréntate (you) oppose; impve. 2nd pers. sing. / *enfrentarse.*

enfrentémonos let us oppose; impve. 1st pers. pl. / *enfrentarse.*

enfréntense let them oppose; impve. 3rd pers. pl. / *enfrentarse.*

enfréntese let him (her/it) oppose; impve. 3rd pers. sing. / *enfrentarse.*

enfría 1. he (she/it) cools; pres. ind. 3rd pers. sing. / *enfriar.* 2. (you) cool; impve. 2nd pers. sing.

enfrían they cool; pres. ind. 3rd pers. pl. / *enfriar.*

enfriándose cooling off; pres. part. / *enfriarse.*

enfriaos (you all) cool off; impve. 2nd pers. pl. / *enfriarse.*

enfriar to cool. irr.

enfriarse to cool off. irr.

enfrías you cool; pres. ind. 2nd pers. sing. / *enfriar.*

enfríate (you) cool off; impve. 2nd pers. sing. / *enfriarse.*

enfríe 1. that I may cool; pres. subj. 1st pers. sing. / *enfriar.* 2. that he (she/it) may cool; pres. subj. 3rd pers. sing. 3. let him (her/it) cool; impve. 3rd pers. sing.

enfriémonos let us cool off; impve. 1st pers. pl. / *enfriarse.*

enfríen 1. that they may cool; pres. subj. 3rd pers. pl. / *enfriar.* 2. let them cool; impve. 3rd pers. pl.

enfríense let them cool off; impve. 3rd pers. pl. / *enfriarse.*

enfríes that you may cool; pres. subj. 2nd pers. sing. / *enfriar.*

enfríese let him (her/it) cool off; impve. 3rd pers. sing. / *enfriarse.*

enfrío I cool; pres. ind. 1st pers. sing. / *enfriar.*

enfundar to sheathe. reg.

enfureceos (you all) rage; impve. 2nd pers. pl. / *enfurecerse.*

enfurecer to infuriate. irr.

enfurecerse to rage. irr.

enfurécete (you) rage; impve. 2nd pers. sing. / *enfurecerse.*

enfureciéndose raging; pres. part. / *enfurecerse.*

enfurezca 1. that I may infuriate; pres. subj. 1st pers. sing. / *enfurecer.* 2. that he (she/it) may infuriate; pres. subj. 3rd pers. sing. 3. let him (her/it) infuriate; impve. 3rd pers. sing.

enfurezcáis that you (all) may infuriate; pres. subj. 2nd pers. pl. / *enfurecer.*

enfurezcámonos let us rage; impve. 1st pers. pl. / *enfurecerse.*

enfurezcamos 1. that we may infuriate; pres. subj. 1st pers. pl. / *enfurecer.* 2. let us infuriate; impve. 1st pers. pl.

enfurezcan 1. that they may infuriate; pres. subj. 3rd pers. pl. / *enfurecer.* 2. let them infuriate; impve. 3rd pers. pl.

enfurézcanse let them rage; impve. 3rd pers. pl. / *enfurecerse.*

enfurezcas that you may infuriate; pres. subj. 2nd pers. sing. / *enfurecer.*

enfurézcase let him (her/it) rage; impve. 3rd pers. sing. / *enfurecerse.*

enfurezco I infuriate; pres. ind. 1st pers. sing. / *enfurecer.*

enfurruñándose pouting; pres. part. / *enfurruñarse.*

enfurruñaos (you all) pout; impve. 2nd pers. pl. / *enfurruñarse.*

enfurruñarse to pout. reg.

enfurrúñate (you) pout; impve. 2nd pers. sing. / *enfurruñarse.*

enfurruñémonos let us pout; impve. 1st pers. pl. / *enfurruñarse.*

enfurrúñense let them pout; impve. 3rd pers. pl. / *enfurruñarse.*

enfurrúñese let him (her/it) pout; impve. 3rd pers. sing. / *enfurruñarse.*

enfurtir to full or to mill clothes. reg.

engalanándose dressing up; pres. part. / *engalanarse.*

engalanaos (you all) dress up; impve. 2nd pers. pl. / *engalanarse.*

engalanar to adorn. reg.

engalanarse to dress up. reg.

engalánate (you) dress up; impve. 2nd pers. sing. / *engalanarse.*

engalanémonos let us dress up; impve. 1st pers. pl. / *engalanarse.*

engalánense let them dress up; impve. 3rd pers. pl. / *engalanarse.*

engalánese let him (her/it) dress up; impve. 3rd pers. sing. / *engalanarse.*

enganchándose engaging; pres. part. / *engancharse.*

enganchaos (you all) engage; impve. 2nd pers. pl. / *engancharse.*

enganchar to hook. reg.

engancharse to engage. reg.

engánchate (you) engage; impve. 2nd pers. sing. / *engancharse.*

enganchémonos let us engage; impve. 1st pers. pl. / *engancharse.*

engánchense let them engage; impve. 3rd pers. pl. / *engancharse.*

engánchese let him (her/it) engage; impve. 3rd pers. sing. / *engancharse.*

engañándose being mistaken; pres. part. / *engañarse.*

engañaos (you all) be mistaken; impve. 2nd pers. pl. / *engañarse.*

engañar to deceive. reg.

engañarse to be mistaken. reg.

engáñate (you) be mistaken; impve. 2nd pers. sing. / *engañarse.*

engañémonos let us be mistaken; impve. 1st pers. pl. / *engañarse.*

engáñense let them be mistaken; impve. 3rd pers. pl. / *engañarse.*

engáñese let him (her/it) be mistaken; impve. 3rd pers. sing. / *engañarse.*

engarce 1. that I may link; pres. subj. 1st pers. sing. / *engarzar.* 2. that he (she/it) may link; pres. subj. 3rd pers. sing. 3. let him (her/it) link; impve. 3rd pers. sing.

engarcé I linked; past 1st pers. sing. / *engarzar.*

engarcéis that you (all) may link; pres. subj. 2nd pers. pl. / *engarzar.*

engarcemos 1. that we may link; pres. subj. 1st pers. pl. / *engarzar*. 2. let us link; impve. 1st pers. pl.

engarcen 1. that they may link; pres. subj. 3rd pers. pl. / *engarzar*. 2. let them link; impve. 3rd pers. pl.

engarces that you may link; pres. subj. 2nd pers. sing. / *engarzar*.

engarrotar to garrote. reg.

engarzar to link or to thread. irr.

engastar to mount jewels or to chase. reg.

engatusar to coax. reg.

engazar to curl. reg.

engendrar to engender or to beget. reg.

englobar to lump together. reg.

engolfándose going deeply into; pres. part. / *engolfarse*.

engolfaos (you all) go deeply into; impve. 2nd pers. pl. / *engolfarse*.

engolfar to go far out to sea. reg.

engolfarse to go deeply into. reg.

engólfate (you) go deeply into; impve. 2nd pers. sing. / *engolfarse*.

engolfémonos let us go deeply into; impve. 1st pers. pl. / *engolfarse*.

engólfense let them go deeply into; impve. 3rd pers. pl. / *engolfarse*.

engólfese let him (her/it) go deeply into; impve. 3rd pers. sing. / *engolfarse*.

engolosinándose taking a liking; pres. part. / *engolosinarse*.

engolosinaos (you all) take a liking; impve. 2nd pers. pl. / *engolosinarse*.

engolosinar to allure. reg.

engolosinarse to take a liking. reg.

engolosínate (you) take a liking; impve. 2nd pers. sing. / *engolosinarse*.

engolosinémonos let us take a liking; impve. 1st pers. pl. / *engolosinarse*.

engolosínense let them take a liking; impve. 3rd pers. pl. / *engolosinarse*.

engolosínese let him (her/it) take a liking; impve. 3rd pers. sing. / *engolosinarse*.

engomar to gum or to rubberize. reg.

engordándose getting fat; pres. part. / *engordarse*.

engordaos (you all) get fat; impve. 2nd pers. pl. / *engordarse*.

engordar to fatten. reg.

engordarse to get fat. reg.

engórdate (you) get fat; impve. 2nd pers. sing. / *engordarse*.

engordémonos let us get fat; impve. 1st pers. pl. / *engordarse*.

engórdense let them get fat; impve. 3rd pers. pl. / *engordarse*.

engórdese let him (her/it) get fat; impve. 3rd pers. sing. / *engordarse*.

engoznar to hinge. reg.

engranar to throw in gear. reg.

engrandecer to enlarge or to augment. irr.

engrandezca 1. that I may enlarge; pres. subj. 1st pers. sing. / *engrandecer*. 2. that he (she/it) may enlarge; pres. subj. 3rd pers. sing. 3. let him (her/it) enlarge; impve. 3rd pers. sing.

engrandezcáis that you (all) may enlarge; pres. subj. 2nd pers. pl. / *engrandecer*.

engrandezcamos 1. that we may enlarge; pres. subj. 1st pers. pl. / *engrandecer*. 2. let us enlarge; impve. 1st pers. pl.

engrandezcan 1. that they may enlarge; pres. subj. 3rd pers. pl. / *engrandecer*. 2. let them enlarge; impve. 3rd pers. pl.

engrandezcas that you may enlarge; pres. subj. 2nd pers. sing. / *engrandecer*.

engrandezco I enlarge; pres. ind. 1st pers. sing. / *engrandecer*.

engrapar to cramp with irons. reg.

engrasar to lubricate. reg.

engreíos (you all) become vain; impve. 2nd pers. pl. / *engreírse*.

engreír to make conceited. irr.

engreírse to become vain. irr.

engría 1. that I may make conceited; pres. subj. 1st pers. sing. / *engreír*. 2. that he (she/it) may make conceited; pres. subj. 3rd pers. sing. 3. let him (her/it) make conceited; impve. 3rd pers. sing.

engriáis that you (all) may make conceited; pres. subj. 2nd pers. pl. / *engreír*.

engriámonos let us become vain; impve. 1st pers. pl. / *engreírse*.

engriamos 1. that we may make conceited; pres. subj. 1st pers. pl. / *engreír*. 2. let us make conceited; impve. 1st pers. pl.

engrían 1. that they may make conceited; pres. subj. 3rd pers. pl. / *engreír*. 2. let them make conceited; impve. 3rd pers. pl.

engríanse let them become vain; impve. 3rd pers. pl. / *engreírse*.

engrías that you may make conceited; pres. subj. 2nd pers. sing. / *engreír*.

engríase let him (her/it) become vain; impve. 3rd pers. sing. / *engreírse*.

engríe 1. he (she/it) makes conceited; pres. ind. 3rd pers. sing. / *engreír*. 2. (you) make conceited; impve. 2nd pers. sing.

engríen they make conceited; pres. ind. 3rd pers. pl. / *engreír*.

engriendo making conceited; pres. part. / *engreír*.

engriéndose becoming vain; pres. part. / *engreírse*.

engriera 1. that I might make conceited; imp. subj. 1st pers. sing. / *engreír*. 2. that he (she/it) might make conceited; imp. subj. 3rd pers. sing.

engrierais that you (all) might make conceited; imp. subj. 2nd pers pl. / *engreír*.

engriéramos that we might make conceited; imp. subj. 1st pers. pl. / *engreír*.

engrieran that they might make conceited; imp. subj. 3rd pers. pl. / *engreír*.

engrieras that you might make conceited; imp. subj. 2nd pers. sing. / *engreír*.

engrieron they made conceited; past 3rd pers. pl. / *engreír.*

engríes you make conceited; pres. ind. 2nd pers. sing. / *engreír.*

engriese 1. that I might make conceited; imp. subj. 1st pers. sing. / *engreír.* 2. that he (she/it) might make conceited; imp. subj. 3rd pers. sing.

engrieseis that you (all) might make conceited; imp. subj. 2nd pers pl. / *engreír.*

engriésemos that we might make conceited; imp. subj. 1st pers. pl. / *engreír.*

engriesen that they might make conceited; imp. subj. 3rd pers. pl. / *engreír.*

engrieses that you might make conceited; imp. subj. 2nd pers. sing. / *engreír.*

engríete (you) become vain; impve. 2nd pers. sing. / *engreírse.*

engrío I make conceited; pres. ind. 1st pers. sing. / *engreír.*

engrió he (she/it) made conceited; past 3rd pers. sing. / *engreír.*

engrosándose broadening; pres. part. / *engrosarse.*

engrosaos (you all) broaden; impve. 2nd pers. pl. / *engrosarse.*

engrosar to enlarge. irr.

engrosarse to broaden. irr.

engrosémonos let us broaden; impve. 1st pers. pl. / *engrosarse.*

engrudar to paste or to glue. reg.

engruesa 1. he (she/it) enlarges; pres. ind. 3rd pers. sing. / *engrosar.* 2. (you) enlarge; impve. 2nd pers. sing.

engruesan they enlarge; pres. ind. 3rd pers. pl. / *engrosar.*

engruesar to get fat. reg.

engruesas you enlarge; pres. ind. 2nd pers. sing. / *engrosar.*

engruésate (you) broaden; impve. 2nd pers. sing. / *engrosarse.*

engruese 1. that I may enlarge; pres. subj. 1st pers. sing. / *engrosar.* 2. that he (she/it) may enlarge; pres. subj. 3rd pers. sing. 3. let him (her/it) enlarge; impve. 3rd pers. sing.

engruesen 1. that they may enlarge; pres. subj. 3rd pers. pl. / *engrosar.* 2. let them enlarge; impve. 3rd pers. pl.

engruésense let them broaden; impve. 3rd pers. pl. / *engrosarse.*

engrueses that you may enlarge; pres. subj. 2nd pers. sing. / *engrosar.*

engruésese let him (her/it) broaden; impve. 3rd pers. sing. / *engrosarse.*

engrueso I enlarge; pres. ind. 1st pers. sing. / *engrosar.*

enguantar to glove. reg.

enguirnaldar to garland. reg.

engullendo gobbling; pres. part. / *engullir.*

engullera 1. that I might gobble; imp. subj. 1st pers. sing. / *engullir.* 2. that he (she/it) might gobble; imp. subj. 3rd pers. sing.

engullerais that you (all) might gobble; imp. subj. 2nd pers pl. / *engullir.*

engulléramos that we might gobble; imp. subj. 1st pers. pl. / *engullir.*

engulleran that they might gobble; imp. subj. 3rd pers. pl. / *engullir.*

engulleras that you might gobble; imp. subj. 2nd pers. sing. / *engullir.*

engulleron they gobbled; past 3rd pers. pl. / *engullir.*

engullese 1. that I might gobble; imp. subj. 1st pers. sing. / *engullir.* 2. that he (she/it) might gobble; imp. subj. 3rd pers. sing.

engulleseis that you (all) might gobble; imp. subj. 2nd pers pl. / *engullir.*

engullésemos that we might gobble; imp. subj. 1st pers. pl. / *engullir.*

engullesen that they might gobble; imp. subj. 3rd pers. pl. / *engullir.*

engulleses that you might gobble; imp. subj. 2nd pers. sing. / *engullir.*

engullir to gobble. irr.

engulló he (she/it) gobbled; past 3rd pers. sing. / *engullir.*

enhebrar to thread. reg.

enherbolar to poison (with herbs). reg.

enhestándose standing upright; pres. part. / *enhestarse.*

enhestaos (you all) stand upright; impve. 2nd pers. pl. / *enhestarse.*

enhestar to erect or to hoist. irr.

enhestarse to stand upright. irr.

enhestémonos let us stand upright; impve. 1st pers. pl. / *enhestarse.*

enhiesta 1. he (she/it) erects; pres. ind. 3rd pers. sing. / *enhestar.* 2. (you) erect; impve. 2nd pers. sing.

enhiestan they erect; pres. ind. 3rd pers. pl. / *enhestar.*

enhiestas you erect; pres. ind. 2nd pers. sing. / *enhestar.*

enhiéstate (you) stand upright; impve. 2nd pers. sing. / *enhestarse.*

enhieste 1. that I may erect; pres. subj. 1st pers. sing. / *enhestar.* 2. that he (she/it) may erect; pres. subj. 3rd pers. sing. 3. let him (her/it) erect; impve. 3rd pers. sing.

enhiesten 1. that they may erect; pres. subj. 3rd pers. pl. / *enhestar.* 2. let them erect; impve. 3rd pers. pl.

enhiéstense let them stand upright; impve. 3rd pers. pl. / *enhestarse.*

enhiestes that you may erect; pres. subj. 2nd pers. sing. / *enhestar.*

enhiéstese let him (her/it) stand upright; impve. 3rd pers. sing. / *enhestarse.*

enhiesto I erect; pres. ind. 1st pers. sing. / *enhestar.*

enhilar to thread. reg.

enhuerar to addle. reg.

enjabonar to soap. reg.

enjaece 1. that I may harness; pres. subj. 1st pers. sing. / *enjaezar*. 2. that he (she/it) may harness; pres. subj. 3rd pers. sing. 3. let him (her/it) harness; impve. 3rd pers. sing.

enjaecé I harnessed; past 1st pers. sing. / *enjaezar*.

enjaecéis that you (all) may harness; pres. subj. 2nd pers. pl. / *enjaezar*.

enjaecemos 1. that we may harness; pres. subj. 1st pers. pl. / *enjaezar*. 2. let us harness; impve. 1st pers. pl.

enjaecen 1. that they may harness; pres. subj. 3rd pers. pl. / *enjaezar*. 2. let them harness; impve. 3rd pers. pl.

enjaeces that you may harness; pres. subj. 2nd pers. sing. / *enjaezar*.

enjaezar to harness. irr.

enjaguar to rinse. irr.

enjagüe 1. that I may rinse; pres. subj. 1st pers. sing. / *enjaguar*. 2. that he (she/it) may rinse; pres. subj. 3rd pers. sing. 3. let him (her/it) rinse; impve. 3rd pers. sing.

enjagüé I rinsed; past 1st pers. sing. / *enjaguar*.

enjagüéis that you (all) may rinse; pres. subj. 2nd pers. pl. / *enjaguar*.

enjagüemos 1. that we may rinse; pres. subj. 1st pers. pl. / *enjaguar*. 2. let us rinse; impve. 1st pers. pl.

enjagüen 1. that they may rinse; pres. subj. 3rd pers. pl. / *enjaguar*. 2. let them rinse; impve. 3rd pers. pl.

enjagües that you may rinse; pres. subj. 2nd pers. sing. / *enjaguar*.

enjalbegándose painting one's face; pres. part. / *enjalbegarse*.

enjalbegaos (you all) paint your faces; impve. 2nd pers. pl. / *enjalbegarse*.

enjalbegar to whitewash. irr.

enjalbegarse to paint one's face. irr.

enjalbégate (you) paint your face; impve. 2nd pers. sing. / *enjalbegarse*.

enjalbegue 1. that I may whitewash; pres. subj. 1st pers. sing. / *enjalbegar*. 2. that he (she/it) may whitewash; pres. subj. 3rd pers. sing. 3. let him (her/it) whitewash; impve. 3rd pers. sing.

enjalbegué I whitewashed; past 1st pers. sing. / *enjalbegar*.

enjalbeguéis that you (all) may whitewash; pres. subj. 2nd pers. pl. / *enjalbegar*.

enjalbeguémonos let us paint our faces; impve. 1st pers. pl. / *enjalbegarse*.

enjalbeguemos 1. that we may whitewash; pres. subj. 1st pers. pl. / *enjalbegar*. 2. let us whitewash; impve. 1st pers. pl.

enjalbeguen 1. that they may whitewash; pres. subj. 3rd pers. pl. / *enjalbegar*. 2. let them whitewash; impve. 3rd pers. pl.

enjalbéguense let them paint their faces; impve. 3rd pers. pl. / *enjalbegarse*.

enjalbegues that you may whitewash; pres. subj. 2nd pers. sing. / *enjalbegar*.

enjalbéguese let him (her/it) paint his (her/its) face; impve. 3rd pers. sing. / *enjalbegarse*.

enjambrar to empty a bee hive or to swarm. reg.

enjarciar to rig (a ship). reg.

enjardinar to set out. reg.

enjaretar to run through the hem. reg.

enjaular to cage. reg.

enjergar to start up (something). irr.

enjergue 1. that I may start up (something); pres. subj. 1st pers. sing. / *enjergar*. 2. that he (she/it) may start up (something); pres. subj. 3rd pers. sing. 3. let him (her/it) start up (something); impve. 3rd pers. sing.

enjergué I started up (something); past 1st pers. sing. / *enjergar*.

enjerguéis that you (all) may start up (something); pres. subj. 2nd pers. pl. / *enjergar*.

enjerguemos 1. that we may start up (something); pres. subj. 1st pers. pl. / *enjergar*. 2. let us start up (something); impve. 1st pers. pl.

enjerguen 1. that they may start up (something); pres. subj. 3rd pers. pl. / *enjergar*. 2. let them start up (something); impve. 3rd pers. pl.

enjergues that you may start up (something); pres. subj. 2nd pers. sing. / *enjergar*.

enjertar to engraft. reg.

enjoyar to bejewel. reg.

enjuagar to rinse. irr.

enjuague 1. that I may rinse; pres. subj. 1st pers. sing. / *enjuagar*. 2. that he (she/it) may rinse; pres. subj. 3rd pers. sing. 3. let him (her/it) rinse; impve. 3rd pers. sing.

enjuagué I rinsed; past 1st pers. sing. / *enjuagar*.

enjuaguéis that you (all) may rinse; pres. subj. 2nd pers. pl. / *enjuagar*.

enjuaguemos 1. that we may rinse; pres. subj. 1st pers. pl. / *enjuagar*. 2. let us rinse; impve. 1st pers. pl.

enjuaguen 1. that they may rinse; pres. subj. 3rd pers. pl. / *enjuagar*. 2. let them rinse; impve. 3rd pers. pl.

enjuagues that you may rinse; pres. subj. 2nd pers. sing. / *enjuagar*.

enjugándose taking off weight; pres. part. / *enjugarse*.

enjugaos (you all) take off weight; impve. 2nd pers. pl. / *enjugarse*.

enjugar to dry. irr.

enjugarse to take off weight. irr.

enjúgate (you) take off weight; impve. 2nd pers. sing. / *enjugarse*.

enjugue 1. that I may dry; pres. subj. 1st pers. sing. / *enjugar*. 2. that he (she/it) may dry; pres. subj. 3rd pers. sing. 3. let him (her/it) dry; impve. 3rd pers. sing.

enjugué I dried; past 1st pers. sing. / *enjugar*.

enjuguéis that you (all) may dry; pres. subj. 2nd pers. pl. / *enjugar*.

enjuguémonos let us take off weight; impve. 1st pers. pl. / *enjugarse*.

enjuguemos 1. that we may dry; pres. subj. 1st pers. pl. / *enjugar*. 2. let us dry; impve. 1st pers. pl.

enjuguen 1. that they may dry; pres. subj. 3rd pers. pl. / *enjugar*. 2. let them dry; impve. 3rd pers. pl.

enjúguense let them take off weight; impve. 3rd pers. pl. / *enjugarse*.

enjugues that you may dry; pres. subj. 2nd pers. sing. / *enjugar.*

enjúguese let him (her/it) take off weight; impve. 3rd pers. sing. / *enjugarse.*

enjuiciar indict. reg.

enlabiar to wheedle. reg.

enlace 1. that I may join; pres. subj. 1st pers. sing. / *enlazar.* 2. that he (she/it) may join; pres. subj. 3rd pers. sing. 3. let him (her/it) join; impve. 3rd pers. sing.

enlacé I joined; past 1st pers. sing. / *enlazar.*

enlacéis that you (all) may join; pres. subj. 2nd pers. pl. / *enlazar.*

enlacémonos let us be joined in marriage; impve. 1st pers. pl. / *enlazarse.*

enlacemos 1. that we may join; pres. subj. 1st pers. pl. / *enlazar.* 2. let us join; impve. 1st pers. pl.

enlacen 1. that they may join; pres. subj. 3rd pers. pl. / *enlazar.* 2. let them join; impve. 3rd pers. pl.

enlácense let them be joined in marriage; impve. 3rd pers. pl. / *enlazarse.*

enlaces that you may join; pres. subj. 2nd pers. sing. / *enlazar.*

enlácese let him (her/it) be joined in marriage; impve. 3rd pers. sing. / *enlazarse.*

enladrillar to pave with bricks. reg.

enlatar to can. reg.

enlazándose being joined in marriage; pres. part. / *enlazarse.*

enlazaos (you all) be joined in marriage; impve. 2nd pers. pl. / *enlazarse.*

enlazar to join. irr.

enlazarse to be joined in marriage. irr.

enlázate (you) be joined in marriage; impve. 2nd pers. sing. / *enlazarse.*

enlistonar to lath. reg.

enlodándose getting muddy; pres. part. / *enlodarse.*

enlodaos (you all) get muddy; impve. 2nd pers. pl. / *enlodarse.*

enlodar to cover with mud. reg.

enlodarse to get muddy. reg.

enlódate (you) get muddy; impve. 2nd pers. sing. / *enlodarse.*

enlodémonos let us get muddy; impve. 1st pers. pl. / *enlodarse.*

enlódense let them get muddy; impve. 3rd pers. pl. / *enlodarse.*

enlódese let him (her/it) get muddy; impve. 3rd pers. sing. / *enlodarse.*

enloqueceos (you all) go crazy; impve. 2nd pers. pl. / *enloquecerse.*

enloquecer to drive insane. irr.

enloquecerse to go crazy. irr.

enloquécete (you) go crazy; impve. 2nd pers. sing. / *enloquecerse.*

enloqueciéndose going crazy; pres. part. / *enloquecerse.*

enloquezca 1. that I may drive insane; pres. subj. 1st pers. sing. / *enloquecer.* 2. that he (she/it) may drive insane; pres. subj. 3rd pers. sing. 3. let him (her/it) drive insane; impve. 3rd pers. sing.

enloquezcáis that you (all) may drive insane; pres. subj. 2nd pers. pl. / *enloquecer.*

enloquezcámonos let us go crazy; impve. 1st pers. pl. / *enloquecerse.*

enloquezcamos 1. that we may drive insane; pres. subj. 1st pers. pl. / *enloquecer.* 2. let us drive insane; impve. 1st pers. pl.

enloquezcan 1. that they may drive insane; pres. subj. 3rd pers. pl. / *enloquecer.* 2. let them drive insane; impve. 3rd pers. pl.

enloquézcanse let them go crazy; impve. 3rd pers. pl. / *enloquecerse.*

enloquezcas that you may drive insane; pres. subj. 2nd pers. sing. / *enloquecer.*

enloquézcase let him (her/it) go crazy; impve. 3rd pers. sing. / *enloquecerse.*

enloquezco I drive insane; pres. ind. 1st pers. sing. / *enloquecer.*

enlosar to tile. reg.

enlucir to plaster or to polish. irr.

enlutándose wearing mourning; pres. part. / *enlutarse.*

enlutaos (you all) wear mourning; impve. 2nd pers. pl. / *enlutarse.*

enlutar to put into mourning. reg.

enlutarse to wear mourning. reg.

enlútate (you) wear mourning; impve. 2nd pers. sing. / *enlutarse.*

enlutémonos let us wear mourning; impve. 1st pers. pl. / *enlutarse.*

enlútense let them wear mourning; impve. 3rd pers. pl. / *enlutarse.*

enlútese let him (her/it) wear mourning; impve. 3rd pers. sing. / *enlutarse.*

enluzca 1. that I may plaster; pres. subj. 1st pers. sing. / *enlucir.* 2. that he (she/it) may plaster; pres. subj. 3rd pers. sing. 3. let him (her/it) plaster; impve. 3rd pers. sing.

enluzcáis that you (all) may plaster; pres. subj. 2nd pers. pl. / *enlucir.*

enluzcamos 1. that we may plaster; pres. subj. 1st pers. pl. / *enlucir.* 2. let us plaster; impve. 1st pers. pl.

enluzcan 1. that they may plaster; pres. subj. 3rd pers. pl. / *enlucir.* 2. let them plaster; impve. 3rd pers. pl.

enluzcas that you may plaster; pres. subj. 2nd pers. sing. / *enlucir.*

enluzco I plaster; pres. ind. 1st pers. sing. / *enlucir.*

enllantar to put a tire on. reg.

enmaderar to board up. reg.

enmagreceos (you all) grow thin; impve. 2nd pers. pl. / *enmagrecerse.*

enmagrecer to make thin. irr.

enmagrecerse to grow thin. irr.

enmagrécete (you) grow thin; impve. 2nd pers. sing. / *enmagrecerse.*

enmagreciéndose growing thin; pres. part. / *enmagrecerse.*

enmagrezca 1. that I may make thin; pres. subj. 1st pers. sing. / *enmagrecer.* 2. that he (she/it) may make thin; pres. subj. 3rd pers. sing. 3. let him (her/it) make thin; impve. 3rd pers. sing.

enmagrezcáis that you (all) may make thin; pres. subj. 2nd pers. pl. / *enmagrecer.*

enmagrezcámonos let us grow thin; impve. 1st pers. pl. / *enmagrecerse.*

enmagrezcamos 1. that we may make thin; pres. subj. 1st pers. pl. / *enmagrecer.* 2. let us make thin; impve. 1st pers. pl.

enmagrezcan 1. that they may make thin; pres. subj. 3rd pers. pl. / *enmagrecer.* 2. let them make thin; impve. 3rd pers. pl.

enmagrézcanse let them grow thin; impve. 3rd pers. pl. / *enmagrecerse.*

enmagrezcas that you may make thin; pres. subj. 2nd pers. sing. / *enmagrecer.*

enmagrézcase let him (her/it) grow thin; impve. 3rd pers. sing. / *enmagrecerse.*

enmagrezco I make thin; pres. ind. 1st pers. sing. / *enmagrecer.*

enmantecar to butter. irr.

enmanteque 1. that I may butter; pres. subj. 1st pers. sing. / *enmantecar.* 2. that he (she/it) may butter; pres. subj. 3rd pers. sing. 3. let him (her/it) butter; impve. 3rd pers. sing.

enmantequé I buttered; past 1st pers. sing. / *enmantecar.*

enmantequéis that you (all) may butter; pres. subj. 2nd pers. pl. / *enmantecar.*

enmantequemos 1. that we may butter; pres. subj. 1st pers. pl. / *enmantecar.* 2. let us butter; impve. 1st pers. pl.

enmantequen 1. that they may butter; pres. subj. 3rd pers. pl. / *enmantecar.* 2. let them butter; impve. 3rd pers. pl.

enmanteques that you may butter; pres. subj. 2nd pers. sing. / *enmantecar.*

enmarañar to entangle. reg.

enmarcar to frame. reg.

enmascarándose masquerading; pres. part. / *enmascararse.*

enmascaraos (you all) masquerade; impve. 2nd pers. pl. / *enmascararse.*

enmascarar to mask. reg.

enmascararse to masquerade. reg.

enmascárate (you) masquerade; impve. 2nd pers. sing. / *enmascararse.*

enmascarémonos let us masquerade; impve. 1st pers. pl. / *enmascararse.*

enmascárense let them masquerade; impve. 3rd pers. pl. / *enmascararse.*

enmascárese let him (her/it) masquerade; impve. 3rd pers. sing. / *enmascararse.*

enmasillar to putty. reg.

enmelar to cover with honey. irr.

enmendándose reforming; pres. part. / *enmendarse.*

enmendaos (you all) reform; impve. 2nd pers. pl. / *enmendarse.*

enmendar to amend or to correct. irr.

enmendarse to reform. irr.

enmendémonos let us reform; impve. 1st pers. pl. / *enmendarse.*

enmiela 1. he (she/it) covers with honey; pres. ind. 3rd pers. sing. / *enmelar.* 2. (you) cover with honey; impve. 2nd pers. sing.

enmielan they cover with honey; pres. ind. 3rd pers. pl. / *enmelar.*

enmielas you cover with honey; pres. ind. 2nd pers. sing. / *enmelar.*

enmiele 1. that I may cover with honey; pres. subj. 1st pers. sing. / *enmelar.* 2. that he (she/it) may cover with honey; pres. subj. 3rd pers. sing. 3. let him (her/it) cover with honey; impve. 3rd pers. sing.

enmielen 1. that they may cover with honey; pres. subj. 3rd pers. pl. / *enmelar.* 2. let them cover with honey; impve. 3rd pers. pl.

enmieles that you may cover with honey; pres. subj. 2nd pers. sing. / *enmelar.*

enmielo I cover with honey; pres. ind. 1st pers. sing. / *enmelar.*

enmienda 1. he (she/it) amends; pres. ind. 3rd pers. sing. / *enmendar.* 2. (you) amend; impve. 2nd pers. sing.

enmiendan they amend; pres. ind. 3rd pers. pl. / *enmendar.*

enmiendas you amend; pres. ind. 2nd pers. sing. / *enmendar.*

enmiéndate (you) reform; impve. 2nd pers. sing. / *enmendarse.*

enmiende 1. that I may amend; pres. subj. 1st pers. sing. / *enmendar.* 2. that he (she/it) may amend; pres. subj. 3rd pers. sing. 3. let him (her/it) amend; impve. 3rd pers. sing.

enmienden 1. that they may amend; pres. subj. 3rd pers. pl. / *enmendar.* 2. let them amend; impve. 3rd pers. pl.

enmiéndense let them reform; impve. 3rd pers. pl. / *enmendarse.*

enmiendes that you may amend; pres. subj. 2nd pers. sing. / *enmendar.*

enmiéndese let him (her/it) reform; impve. 3rd pers. sing. / *enmendarse.*

enmiendo I amend; pres. ind. 1st pers. sing. / *enmendar.*

enmoheceos (you all) become rusty; impve. 2nd pers. pl. / *enmohecerse.*

enmohecer to mold or to rust. irr.

enmohecerse to become rusty. irr.

enmohécete (you) become rusty; impve. 2nd pers. sing. / *enmohecerse.*

enmoheciéndose becoming rusty; pres. part. / *enmohecerse.*

enmohezca 1. that I may mold; pres. subj. 1st pers. sing. / *enmohecer.* 2. that he (she/it) may mold; pres. subj. 3rd pers. sing. 3. let him (her/it) mold; impve. 3rd pers. sing.

enmohezcáis that you (all) may mold; pres. subj. 2nd pers. pl. / *enmohecer.*

enmohezcámonos let us become rusty; impve. 1st pers. pl. / *enmohecerse.*

enmohezcamos 1. that we may mold; pres. subj. 1st pers. pl. / *enmohecer.* 2. let us mold; impve. 1st pers. pl.

enmohezcan 1. that they may mold; pres. subj. 3rd pers. pl. / *enmohecer.* 2. let them mold; impve. 3rd pers. pl.

enmohézcanse let them become rusty; impve. 3rd pers. pl. / *enmohecerse.*

enmohezcas that you may mold; pres. subj. 2nd pers. sing. / *enmohecer.*

enmohézcase let him (her/it) become rusty; impve. 3rd pers. sing. / *enmohecerse.*

enmohezco I mold; pres. ind. 1st pers. sing. / *enmohecer.*

enmollecer to soften or to mollify. irr.

enmollezca 1. that I may soften; pres. subj. 1st pers. sing. / *enmollecer.* 2. that he (she/it) may soften; pres. subj. 3rd pers. sing. 3. let him (her/it) soften; impve. 3rd pers. sing.

enmollezcáis that you (all) may soften; pres. subj. 2nd pers. pl. / *enmollecer.*

enmollezcamos 1. that we may soften; pres. subj. 1st pers. pl. / *enmollecer.* 2. let us soften; impve. 1st pers. pl.

enmollezcan 1. that they may soften; pres. subj. 3rd pers. pl. / *enmollecer.* 2. let them soften; impve. 3rd pers. pl.

enmollezcas that you may soften; pres. subj. 2nd pers. sing. / *enmollecer.*

enmollezco I soften; pres. ind. 1st pers. sing. / *enmollecer.*

enmudecer to silence. irr.

enmudezca 1. that I may silence; pres. subj. 1st pers. sing. / *enmudecer.* 2. that he (she/it) may silence; pres. subj. 3rd pers. sing. 3. let him (her/it) silence; impve. 3rd pers. sing.

enmudezcáis that you (all) may silence; pres. subj. 2nd pers. pl. / *enmudecer.*

enmudezcamos 1. that we may silence; pres. subj. 1st pers. pl. / *enmudecer.* 2. let us silence; impve. 1st pers. pl.

enmudezcan 1. that they may silence; pres. subj. 3rd pers. pl. / *enmudecer.* 2. let them silence; impve. 3rd pers. pl.

enmudezcas that you may silence; pres. subj. 2nd pers. sing. / *enmudecer.*

enmudezco I silence; pres. ind. 1st pers. sing. / *enmudecer.*

ennegreceos (you all) become dark; impve. 2nd pers. pl. / *ennegrecerse.*

ennegrecer to blacken. irr.

ennegrecerse to become dark. irr.

ennegrécete (you) become dark; impve. 2nd pers. sing. / *ennegrecerse.*

ennegreciéndose becoming dark; pres. part. / *ennegrecerse.*

ennegrezca 1. that I may blacken; pres. subj. 1st pers. sing. / *ennegrecer.* 2. that he (she/it) may blacken; pres. subj. 3rd pers. sing. 3. let him (her/it) blacken; impve. 3rd pers. sing.

ennegrezcáis that you (all) may blacken; pres. subj. 2nd pers. pl. / *ennegrecer.*

ennegrezcámonos let us become dark; impve. 1st pers. pl. / *ennegrecerse.*

ennegrezcamos 1. that we may blacken; pres. subj. 1st pers. pl. / *ennegrecer.* 2. let us blacken; impve. 1st pers. pl.

ennegrezcan 1. that they may blacken; pres. subj. 3rd pers. pl. / *ennegrecer.* 2. let them blacken; impve. 3rd pers. pl.

ennegrézcanse let them become dark; impve. 3rd pers. pl. / *ennegrecerse.*

ennegrezcas that you may blacken; pres. subj. 2nd pers. sing. / *ennegrecer.*

ennegrézcase let him (her/it) become dark; impve. 3rd pers. sing. / *ennegrecerse.*

ennegrezco I blacken; pres. ind. 1st pers. sing. / *ennegrecer.*

ennobleceos (you all) become ennobled; impve. 2nd pers. pl. / *ennoblecerse.*

ennoblecer to ennoble. irr.

ennoblecerse to become ennobled. irr.

ennoblécete (you) become ennobled; impve. 2nd pers. sing. / *ennoblecerse.*

ennobleciéndose becoming ennobled; pres. part. / *ennoblecerse.*

ennoblezca 1. that I may ennoble; pres. subj. 1st pers. sing. / *ennoblecer.* 2. that he (she/it) may ennoble; pres. subj. 3rd pers. sing. 3. let him (her/it) ennoble; impve. 3rd pers. sing.

ennoblezcáis that you (all) may ennoble; pres. subj. 2nd pers. pl. / *ennoblecer.*

ennoblezcámonos let us become ennobled; impve. 1st pers. pl. / *ennoblecerse.*

ennoblezcamos 1. that we may ennoble; pres. subj. 1st pers. pl. / *ennoblecer.* 2. let us ennoble; impve. 1st pers. pl.

ennoblezcan 1. that they may ennoble; pres. subj. 3rd pers. pl. / *ennoblecer.* 2. let them ennoble; impve. 3rd pers. pl.

ennoblézcanse let them become ennobled; impve. 3rd pers. pl. / *ennoblecerse.*

ennoblezcas that you may ennoble; pres. subj. 2nd pers. sing. / *ennoblecer.*

ennoblézcase let him (her/it) become ennobled; impve. 3rd pers. sing. / *ennoblecerse.*

ennoblezco I ennoble; pres. ind. 1st pers. sing. / *ennoblecer.*

enojándose becoming angry; pres. part. / *enojarse.*

enojaos (you all) become angry; impve. 2nd pers. pl. / *enojarse.*

enojar to annoy. reg.

enojarse to become angry. reg.

enójate (you) become angry; impve. 2nd pers. sing. / *enojarse.*

enojémonos let us become angry; impve. 1st pers. pl. / *enojarse.*

enójense let them become angry; impve. 3rd pers. pl. / *enojarse.*

enójese let him (her/it) become angry; impve. 3rd pers. sing. / *enojarse.*

enorgulleceos (you all) be proud; impve. 2nd pers. pl. / *enorgullecerse.*

enorgullecer to fill with pride. irr.

enorgullecerse to be proud. irr.

enorgullécete (you) be proud; impve. 2nd pers. sing. / *enorgullecerse.*

enorgulleciendo filling with pride; pres. part. / *enorgullecer.*

enorgulleciéndose being proud; pres. part. / *enorgullecerse.*

enorgullezca 1. that I may fill with pride; pres. subj. 1st pers. sing. / *enorgullecer.* 2. that he (she/it) may fill with pride; pres. subj. 3rd pers. sing. 3. let him (her/it) fill with pride; impve. 3rd pers. sing.

enorgullezcáis that you (all) may fill with pride; pres. subj. 2nd pers. pl. / *enorgullecer.*

enorgullezcámonos let us be proud; impve. 1st pers. pl. / *enorgullecerse.*

enorgullezcamos 1. that we may fill with pride; pres. subj. 1st pers. pl. / *enorgullecer.* 2. let us fill with pride; impve. 1st pers. pl.

enorgullezcan 1. that they may fill with pride; pres. subj. 3rd pers. pl. / *enorgullecer.* 2. let them fill with pride; impve. 3rd pers. pl.

enorgullézcanse let them be proud; impve. 3rd pers. pl. / *enorgullecerse.*

enorgullezcas that you may fill with pride; pres. subj. 2nd pers. sing. / *enorgullecer.*

enorgullézcase let him (her/it) be proud; impve. 3rd pers. sing. / *enorgullecerse.*

enorgullezco I fill with pride; pres. ind. 1st pers. sing. / *enorgullecer.*

enquiciar to put on hinges. reg.

enquillotrar to fall in love. reg.

enrabiándose becoming enraged; pres. part. / *enrabiarse.*

enrabiaos (you all) become enraged; impve. 2nd pers. pl. / *enrabiarse.*

enrabiar to enrage. reg.

enrabiarse to become enraged. reg.

enrabíate (you) become enraged; impve. 2nd pers. sing. / *enrabiarse.*

enrabiémonos let us become enraged; impve. 1st pers. pl. / *enrabiarse.*

enrabíense let them become enraged; impve. 3rd pers. pl. / *enrabiarse.*

enrabíese let him (her/it) become enraged; impve. 3rd pers. sing. / *enrabiarse.*

enraice 1. that I may take root; pres. subj. 1st pers. sing. / *enraizar.* 2. that he (she/it) may take root; pres. subj. 3rd pers. sing. 3. let him (her/it) take root; impve. 3rd pers. sing.

enraicé I took root; past 1st pers. sing. / *enraizar.*

enraicéis that you (all) may take root; pres. subj. 2nd pers. pl. / *enraizar.*

enraicemos 1. that we may take root; pres. subj. 1st pers. pl. / *enraizar.* 2. let us take root; impve. 1st pers. pl.

enraicen 1. that they may take root; pres. subj. 3rd pers. pl. / *enraizar.* 2. let them take root; impve. 3rd pers. pl.

enraices that you may take root; pres. subj. 2nd pers. sing. / *enraizar.*

enraizar to take root. irr.

enramar to branch or to decorate with branches. reg.

enranciándose becoming rancid; pres. part. / *enranciarse.*

enranciar to make rancid. reg.

enranciarse to become rancid. reg.

enranciense let them become rancid; impve. 3rd pers. pl. / *enranciarse.*

enranciese let it become rancid; impve. 3rd pers. sing. / *enranciarse.*

enrareceos (you all) become rare; impve. 2nd pers. pl. / *enrarecerse.*

enrarecer to rarefy. irr.

enrarecerse to become rare. irr.

enrarécete (you) become rare; impve. 2nd pers. sing. / *enrarecerse.*

enrareciéndose becoming rare; pres. part. / *enrarecerse.*

enrarezca 1. that I may rarefy; pres. subj. 1st pers. sing. / *enrarecer.* 2. that he (she/it) may rarefy; pres. subj. 3rd pers. sing. 3. let him (her/it) rarefy; impve. 3rd pers. sing.

enrarezcáis that you (all) may rarefy; pres. subj. 2nd pers. pl. / *enrarecer.*

enrarezcámonos let us become rare; impve. 1st pers. pl. / *enrarecerse.*

enrarezcamos 1. that we may rarefy; pres. subj. 1st pers. pl. / *enrarecer.* 2. let us rarefy; impve. 1st pers. pl.

enrarezcan 1. that they may rarefy; pres. subj. 3rd pers. pl. / *enrarecer.* 2. let them rarefy; impve. 3rd pers. pl.

enrarézcanse let them become rare; impve. 3rd pers. pl. / *enrarecerse.*

enrarezcas that you may rarefy; pres. subj. 2nd pers. sing. / *enrarecer.*

enrarézcase let him (her/it) become rare; impve. 3rd pers. sing. / *enrarecerse.*

enrarezco I rarefy; pres. ind. 1st pers. sing. / *enrarecer.*

enredándose having an affair; pres. part. / *enredarse.*

enredaos (you all) have an affair; impve. 2nd pers. pl. / *enredarse.*

enredar to entangle. reg.

enredarse to have an affair. reg.

enrédate (you) have an affair; impve. 2nd pers. sing. / *enredarse.*

enredémonos let us have an affair; impve. 1st pers. pl. / *enredarse.*

enrédense let them have an affair; impve. 3rd pers. pl. / *enredarse.*

enrédese let him (her/it) have an affair; impve. 3rd pers. sing. / *enredarse.*

enrejar to put grillwork over. reg.

enría 1. he (she/it) soaks; pres. ind. 3rd pers. sing. / *enriar.* 2. (you) soak; impve. 2nd pers. sing.

enrían they soak; pres. ind. 3rd pers. pl. / *enriar.*

enriar to ret or to soak. irr.

enrías you soak; pres. ind. 2nd pers. sing. / *enriar.*

enríe 1. that I may soak; pres. subj. 1st pers. sing. / *enriar.* 2. that he (she/it) may soak; pres. subj. 3rd pers. sing. 3. let him (her/it) soak; impve. 3rd pers. sing.

enrielar to cast into ingots. reg.

enríen 1. that they may soak; pres. subj. 3rd pers. pl. / *enriar.* 2. let them soak; impve. 3rd pers. pl.

enríes that you may soak; pres. subj. 2nd pers. sing. / *enriar.*

enrío I soak; pres. ind. 1st pers. sing. / *enriar.*

enriqueceos (you all) become rich; impve. 2nd pers. pl. / *enriquecerse.*

enriquecer to enrich. irr.

enriquecerse to become rich. irr.

enriquécete (you) become rich; impve. 2nd pers. sing. / *enriquecerse.*

enriqueciéndose becoming rich; pres. part. / *enriquecerse.*

enriquezca 1. that I may enrich; pres. subj. 1st pers. sing. / *enriquecer.* 2. that he (she/it) may enrich; pres. subj. 3rd pers. sing. 3. let him (her/it) enrich; impve. 3rd pers. sing.

enriquezcáis that you (all) may enrich; pres. subj. 2nd pers. pl. / *enriquecer.*

enriquezcámonos let us become rich; impve. 1st pers. pl. / *enriquecerse.*

enriquezcamos 1. that we may enrich; pres. subj. 1st pers. pl. / *enriquecer.* 2. let us enrich; impve. 1st pers. pl.

enriquezcan 1. that they may enrich; pres. subj. 3rd pers. pl. / *enriquecer.* 2. let them enrich; impve. 3rd pers. pl.

enriquézcanse let them become rich; impve. 3rd pers. pl. / *enriquecerse.*

enriquezcas that you may enrich; pres. subj. 2nd pers. sing. / *enriquecer.*

enriquézcase let him (her/it) become rich; impve. 3rd pers. sing. / *enriquecerse.*

enriquezco I enrich; pres. ind. 1st pers. sing. / *enriquecer.*

enriscándose taking refuge in the rocks; pres. part. / *enriscarse.*

enriscaos (you all) take refuge in the rocks; impve. 2nd pers. pl. / *enriscarse.*

enriscar to raise. irr.

enriscarse to take refuge in the rocks. irr.

enríscate (you) take refuge in the rocks; impve. 2nd pers. sing. / *enriscarse.*

enrisque 1. that I may raise; pres. subj. 1st pers. sing. / *enriscar.* 2. that he (she/it) may raise; pres. subj. 3rd pers. sing. 3. let him (her/it) raise; impve. 3rd pers. sing.

enrisqué I raised; past 1st pers. sing. / *enriscar.*

enrisquéis that you (all) may raise; pres. subj. 2nd pers. pl. / *enriscar.*

enrisquémonos let us take refuge in the rocks; impve. 1st pers. pl. / *enriscarse.*

enrisquemos 1. that we may raise; pres. subj. 1st pers. pl. / *enriscar.* 2. let us raise; impve. 1st pers. pl.

enrisquen 1. that they may raise; pres. subj. 3rd pers. pl. / *enriscar.* 2. let them raise; impve. 3rd pers. pl.

enrísquense let them take refuge in the rocks; impve. 3rd pers. pl. / *enriscarse.*

enrisques that you may raise; pres. subj. 2nd pers. sing. / *enriscar.*

enrísquese let him (her/it) take refuge in the rocks; impve. 3rd pers. sing. / *enriscarse.*

enristrar to straighten out (a difficulty). reg.

enrizar to curl. reg.

enrocar to castle (chess). irr.

enrojándose reddening; pres. part. / *enrojarse.*

enrojaos (you all) redden; impve. 2nd pers. pl. / *enrojarse.*

enrojar to redden. reg.

enrojarse to redden. reg.

enrójate (you) redden; impve. 2nd pers. sing. / *enrojarse.*

enrojeceos (you all) blush; impve. 2nd pers. pl. / *enrojecerse.*

enrojecer to flush. irr.

enrojecerse to blush. irr.

enrojécete (you) blush; impve. 2nd pers. sing. / *enrojecerse.*

enrojeciéndose blushing; pres. part. / *enrojecerse.*

enrojémonos let us redden; impve. 1st pers. pl. / *enrojarse.*

enrójense let them redden; impve. 3rd pers. pl. / *enrojarse.*

enrójese let him (her/it) redden; impve. 3rd pers. sing. / *enrojarse.*

enrojezca 1. that I may flush; pres. subj. 1st pers. sing. / *enrojecer.* 2. that he (she/it) may flush; pres. subj. 3rd pers. sing. 3. let him (her/it) flush; impve. 3rd pers. sing.

enrojezcáis that you (all) may flush; pres. subj. 2nd pers. pl. / *enrojecer.*

enrojezcámonos let us blush; impve. 1st pers. pl. / *enrojecerse.*

enrojezcamos 1. that we may flush; pres. subj. 1st pers. pl. / *enrojecer.* 2. let us flush; impve. 1st pers. pl.

enrojezcan 1. that they may flush; pres. subj. 3rd pers. pl. / *enrojecer.* 2. let them flush; impve. 3rd pers. pl.

enrojézcanse let them blush; impve. 3rd pers. pl. / *enrojecerse.*

enrojezcas that you may flush; pres. subj. 2nd pers. sing. / *enrojecer.*

enrojézcase let him (her/it) blush; impve. 3rd pers. sing. / *enrojecerse.*

enrojezco I flush; pres. ind. 1st pers. sing. / *enrojecer*

enrolar to enlist. reg.

enrollar to roll up. reg.

enromar to blunt. reg.

enronqueceos (you all) become hoarse; impve. 2nd pers. pl. / *enronquecerse.*

enronquecer to make hoarse. irr.

enronquecerse to become hoarse. irr.

enronquécete (you) become hoarse; impve. 2nd pers. sing. / *enronquecerse.*

enronqueciéndose becoming hoarse; pres. part. / *enronquecerse.*

enronquezca 1. that I may make hoarse; pres. subj. 1st pers. sing. / *enronquecer.* 2. that he (she/it) may make hoarse; pres. subj. 3rd pers. sing. 3. let him (her/it) make hoarse; impve. 3rd pers. sing.

enronquezcáis that you (all) may make hoarse; pres. subj. 2nd pers. pl. / *enronquecer.*

enronquezcámonos let us become hoarse; impve. 1st pers. pl. / *enronquecerse.*

enronquezcamos 1. that we may make hoarse; pres. subj. 1st pers. pl. / *enronquecer.* 2. let us make hoarse; impve. 1st pers. pl.

enronquezcan 1. that they may make hoarse; pres. subj. 3rd pers. pl. / *enronquecer.* 2. let them make hoarse; impve. 3rd pers. pl.

enronquézcanse let them become hoarse; impve. 3rd pers. pl. / *enronquecerse.*

enronquezcas that you may make hoarse; pres. subj. 2nd pers. sing. / *enronquecer.*

enronquézcase let him (her/it) become hoarse; impve. 3rd pers. sing. / *enronquecerse.*

enronquezco I make hoarse; pres. ind. 1st pers. sing. / *enronquecer.*

enroque 1. that I may castle (chess); pres. subj. 1st pers. sing. / *enrocar.* 2. that he (she/it) may castle (chess); pres. subj. 3rd pers. sing. 3. let him (her/it) castle (chess); impve. 3rd pers. sing.

enroqué I castled (chess); past 1st pers. sing. / *enrocar.*

enroquéis that you (all) may castle (chess); pres. subj. 2nd pers. pl. / *enrocar.*

enroquemos 1. that we may castle (chess); pres. subj. 1st pers. pl. / *enrocar.* 2. let us castle (chess); impve. 1st pers. pl.

enroquen 1. that they may castle (chess); pres. subj. 3rd pers. pl. / *enrocar.* 2. let them castle (chess); impve. 3rd pers. pl.

enroques that you may castle (chess); pres. subj. 2nd pers. sing. / *enrocar.*

enroscándose coiling; pres. part. / *enroscarse.*

enroscaos (you all) coil; impve. 2nd pers. pl. / *enroscarse.*

enroscar to twist. irr.

enroscarse to coil. irr.

enróscate (you) coil; impve. 2nd pers. sing. / *enroscarse.*

enrosque 1. that I may twist; pres. subj. 1st pers. sing. / *enroscar.* 2. that he (she/it) may twist; pres. subj. 3rd pers. sing. 3. let him (her/it) twist; impve. 3rd pers. sing.

enrosqué I twisted; past 1st pers. sing. / *enroscar.*

enrosquéis that you (all) may twist; pres. subj. 2nd pers. pl. / *enroscar.*

enrosquémonos let us coil; impve. 1st pers. pl. / *enroscarse.*

enrosquemos 1. that we may twist; pres. subj. 1st pers. pl. / *enroscar.* 2. let us twist; impve. 1st pers. pl.

enrosquen 1. that they may twist; pres. subj. 3rd pers. pl. / *enroscar.* 2. let them twist; impve. 3rd pers. pl.

enrósquense let them coil; impve. 3rd pers. pl. / *enroscarse.*

enrosques that you may twist; pres. subj. 2nd pers. sing. / *enroscar.*

enrósquese let him (her/it) coil; impve. 3rd pers. sing. / *enroscarse.*

enrubiar to bleach (hair). reg.

ensacar to sack. irr.

ensalce 1. that I may exalt; pres. subj. 1st pers. sing. / *ensalzar.* 2. that he (she/it) may exalt; pres. subj. 3rd pers. sing. 3. let him (her/it) exalt; impve. 3rd pers. sing.

ensalcé I exalted; past 1st pers. sing. / *ensalzar.*

ensalcéis that you (all) may exalt; pres. subj. 2nd pers. pl. / *ensalzar.*

ensalcémonos let us boast; impve. 1st pers. pl. / *ensalzarse.*

ensalcemos 1. that we may exalt; pres. subj. 1st pers. pl. / *ensalzar.* 2. let us exalt; impve. 1st pers. pl.

ensalcen 1. that they may exalt; pres. subj. 3rd pers. pl. / *ensalzar.* 2. let them exalt; impve. 3rd pers. pl.

ensálcense let them boast; impve. 3rd pers. pl. / *ensalzarse.*

ensalces that you may exalt; pres. subj. 2nd pers. sing. / *ensalzar.*

ensálcese let him (her/it) boast; impve. 3rd pers. sing. / *ensalzarse.*

ensalmar to set bones. reg.

ensalzándose boasting; pres. part. / *ensalzarse.*

ensalzaos (you all) boast; impve. 2nd pers. pl. / *ensalzarse.*

ensalzar to exalt. irr.

ensalzarse to boast. irr.

ensálzate (you) boast; impve. 2nd pers. sing. / *ensalzarse.*

ensamblar to join. reg.

ensanchándose expanding; pres. part. / *ensancharse.*

ensanchaos (you all) expand; impve. 2nd pers. pl. / *ensancharse.*

ensanchar to widen. reg.

ensancharse to expand. reg.

ensánchate (you) expand; impve. 2nd pers. sing. / *ensancharse.*

ensanchémonos let us expand; impve. 1st pers. pl. / *ensancharse.*

ensánchense let them expand; impve. 3rd pers. pl. / *ensancharse.*

ensánchese let him (her/it) expand; impve. 3rd pers. sing. / *ensancharse.*

ensandecer to grow crazy. irr.

ensandezca 1. that I may grow crazy; pres. subj. 1st pers. sing. / *ensandecer*. 2. that he (she/it) may grow crazy; pres. subj. 3rd pers. sing. 3. let him (her/it) grow crazy; impve. 3rd pers. sing.

ensandezcáis that you (all) may grow crazy; pres. subj. 2nd pers. pl. / *ensandecer*.

ensandezcamos 1. that we may grow crazy; pres. subj. 1st pers. pl. / *ensandecer*. 2. let us grow crazy; impve. 1st pers. pl.

ensandezcan 1. that they may grow crazy; pres. subj. 3rd pers. pl. / *ensandecer*. 2. let them grow crazy; impve. 3rd pers. pl.

ensandezcas that you may grow crazy; pres. subj. 2nd pers. sing. / *ensandecer*.

ensandezco I grow crazy; pres. ind. 1st pers. sing. / *ensandecer*.

ensangrentándose raging; pres. part. / *ensangrentarse*.

ensangrentaos (you all) rage; impve. 2nd pers. pl. / *ensangrentarse*.

ensangrentar to stain with blood. irr.

ensangrentarse to rage. irr.

ensangrentémonos let us rage; impve. 1st pers. pl. / *ensangrentarse*.

ensangrienta 1. he (she/it) stains with blood; pres. ind. 3rd pers. sing. / *ensangrentar*. 2. (you) stain with blood; impve. 2nd pers. sing.

ensangrientan they stain with blood; pres. ind. 3rd pers. pl. / *ensangrentar*.

ensangrientas you stain with blood; pres. ind. 2nd pers. sing. / *ensangrentar*.

ensangriéntate (you) rage; impve. 2nd pers. sing. / *ensangrentarse*.

ensangriente 1. that I may stain with blood; pres. subj. 1st pers. sing. / *ensangrentar*. 2. that he (she/it) may stain with blood; pres. subj. 3rd pers. sing. 3. let him (her/it) stain with blood; impve. 3rd pers. sing.

ensangrienten 1. that they may stain with blood; pres. subj. 3rd pers. pl. / *ensangrentar*. 2. let them stain with blood; impve. 3rd pers. pl.

ensangriéntense let them rage; impve. 3rd pers. pl. / *ensangrentarse*.

ensangrientes that you may stain with blood; pres. subj. 2nd pers. sing. / *ensangrentar*.

ensangriéntese let him (her/it) rage; impve. 3rd pers. sing. / *ensangrentarse*.

ensangriento I stain with blood; pres. ind. 1st pers. sing. / *ensangrentar*.

ensañándose being ruthless; pres. part. / *ensañarse*.

ensañaos (you all) be ruthless; impve. 2nd pers. pl. / *ensañarse*.

ensañar to irritate. reg.

ensañarse to be ruthless. reg.

ensáñate (you) be ruthless; impve. 2nd pers. sing. / *ensañarse*.

ensañémonos let us be ruthless; impve. 1st pers. pl. / *ensañarse*.

ensáñense let them be ruthless; impve. 3rd pers. pl. / *ensañarse*.

ensáñese let him (her/it) be ruthless; impve. 3rd pers. sing. / *ensañarse*.

ensaque 1. that I may sack; pres. subj. 1st pers. sing. / *ensacar*. 2. that he (she/it) may sack; pres. subj. 3rd pers. sing. 3. let him (her/it) sack; impve. 3rd pers. sing.

ensaqué I sacked; past 1st pers. sing. / *ensacar*.

ensaquéis that you (all) may sack; pres. subj. 2nd pers. pl. / *ensacar*.

ensaquemos 1. that we may sack; pres. subj. 1st pers. pl. / *ensacar*. 2. let us sack; impve. 1st pers. pl.

ensaquen 1. that they may sack; pres. subj. 3rd pers. pl. / *ensacar*. 2. let them sack; impve. 3rd pers. pl.

ensaques that you may sack; pres. subj. 2nd pers. sing. / *ensacar*.

ensartándose falling into a trap; pres. part. / *ensartarse*.

ensartaos (you all) fall into a trap; impve. 2nd pers. pl. / *ensartarse*.

ensartar to string or thread. reg.

ensartarse to fall into a trap. reg.

ensártate (you) fall into a trap; impve. 2nd pers. sing. / *ensartarse*.

ensartémonos let us fall into a trap; impve. 1st pers. pl. / *ensartarse*.

ensártense let them fall into a trap; impve. 3rd pers. pl. / *ensartarse*.

ensártese let him (her/it) fall into a trap; impve. 3rd pers. sing. / *ensartarse*.

ensayándose practicing; pres. part. / *ensayarse*.

ensayaos (you all) practice; impve. 2nd pers. pl. / *ensayarse*.

ensayar to try. reg.

ensayarse to practice. reg.

ensáyate (you) practice; impve. 2nd pers. sing. / *ensayarse*.

ensayémonos let us practice; impve. 1st pers. pl. / *ensayarse*.

ensáyense let them practice; impve. 3rd pers. pl. / *ensayarse*.

ensáyese let him (her/it) practice; impve. 3rd pers. sing. / *ensayarse*.

ensebar to grease. reg.

enseñándose teaching oneself; pres. part. / *enseñarse*.

enseñaos (you all) teach yourselves; impve. 2nd pers. pl. / *enseñarse*.

enseñar to teach. reg.

enseñarse to teach oneself. reg.

enséñate (you) teach yourself; impve. 2nd pers. sing. / *enseñarse*.

enseñémonos let us teach ourselves; impve. 1st pers. pl. / *enseñarse*.

enséñense let them teach themselves; impve. 3rd pers. pl. / *enseñarse*.

enséñese let him (her/it) teach himself (herself/itself); impve. 3rd pers. sing. / *enseñarse*.

enseñoreándose taking possession; pres. part. / *enseñorearse*.

enseñoreaos (you all) take possession; impve. 2nd pers. pl. / *enseñorearse*.

enseñorear to domineer. reg.

enseñorearse to take possession. reg.

enseñoréate (you) take possession; impve. 2nd pers. sing. / *enseñorearse*.

enseñoreémonos let us take possession; impve. 1st pers. pl. / *enseñorearse*.

enseñoréense let them take possession; impve. 3rd pers. pl. / *enseñorearse*.

enseñoréese let him (her/it) take possession; impve. 3rd pers. sing. / *enseñorearse*.

enseriándose becoming sober; pres. part. / *enseriarse*.

enseriaos (you all) become sober; impve. 2nd pers. pl. / *enseriarse*.

enseriarse to become sober. reg.

enseríate (you) become sober; impve. 2nd pers. sing. / *enseriarse*.

enseriémonos let us become sober; impve. 1st pers. pl. / *enseriarse*.

enseríense let them become sober; impve. 3rd pers. pl. / *enseriarse*.

enseríese let him (her/it) become sober; impve. 3rd pers. sing. / *enseriarse*.

ensilar to put into a silo. reg.

ensillar to saddle. reg.

ensimismándose becoming absorbed in thought; pres. part. / *ensimismarse*.

ensimismaos (you all) become absorbed in thought; impve. 2nd pers. pl. / *ensimismarse*.

ensimismarse to become absorbed in thought. reg.

ensimísmate (you) become absorbed in thought; impve. 2nd pers. sing. / *ensimismarse*.

ensimismémonos let us become absorbed in thought; impve. 1st pers. pl. / *ensimismarse*.

ensimísmense let them become absorbed in thought; impve. 3rd pers. pl. / *ensimismarse*.

ensimísmese let him (her/it) become absorbed in thought; impve. 3rd pers. sing. / *ensimismarse*.

ensoberbeceos (you all) become proud; impve. 2nd pers. pl. / *ensoberbecerse*.

ensoberbecer to make proud. irr.

ensoberbecerse to become proud. irr.

ensoberbécete (you) become proud; impve. 2nd pers. sing. / *ensoberbecerse*.

ensoberbeciéndose becoming proud; pres. part. / *ensoberbecerse*.

ensoberbezca 1. that I may make proud; pres. subj. 1st pers. sing. / *ensoberbecer*. 2. that he (she/it) may make proud; pres. subj. 3rd pers. sing. 3. let him (her/it) make proud; impve. 3rd pers. sing.

ensoberbezcáis that you (all) may make proud; pres. subj. 2nd pers. pl. / *ensoberbecer*.

ensoberbezcámonos let us become proud; impve. 1st pers. pl. / *ensoberbecerse*.

ensoberbezcamos 1. that we may make proud; pres. subj. 1st pers. pl. / *ensoberbecer*. 2. let us make proud; impve. 1st pers. pl.

ensoberbezcan 1. that they may make proud; pres. subj. 3rd pers. pl. / *ensoberbecer*. 2. let them make proud; impve. 3rd pers. pl.

ensoberbézcanse let them become proud; impve. 3rd pers. pl. / *ensoberbecerse*.

ensoberbezcas that you may make proud; pres. subj. 2nd pers. sing. / *ensoberbecer*.

ensoberbézcase let him (her/it) become proud; impve. 3rd pers. sing. / *ensoberbecerse*.

ensoberbezco I make proud; pres. ind. 1st pers. sing. / *ensoberbecer*.

ensombrecer to darken. irr.

ensombrezca 1. that I may darken; pres. subj. 1st pers. sing. / *ensombrecer*. 2. that he (she/it) may darken; pres. subj. 3rd pers. sing. 3. let him (her/it) darken; impve. 3rd pers. sing.

ensombrezcáis that you (all) may darken; pres. subj. 2nd pers. pl. / *ensombrecer*.

ensombrezcamos 1. that we may darken; pres. subj. 1st pers. pl. / *ensombrecer*. 2. let us darken; impve. 1st pers. pl.

ensombrezcan 1. that they may darken; pres. subj. 3rd pers. pl. / *ensombrecer*. 2. let them darken; impve. 3rd pers. pl.

ensombrezcas that you may darken; pres. subj. 2nd pers. sing. / *ensombrecer*.

ensombrezco I darken; pres. ind. 1st pers. sing. / *ensombrecer*.

ensopar to soak. reg.

ensordecer to deafen. irr.

ensordezca 1. that I may deafen; pres. subj. 1st pers. sing. / *ensordecer*. 2. that he (she/it) may deafen; pres. subj. 3rd pers. sing. 3. let him (her/it) deafen; impve. 3rd pers. sing.

ensordezcáis that you (all) may deafen; pres. subj. 2nd pers. pl. / *ensordecer*.

ensordezcamos 1. that we may deafen; pres. subj. 1st pers. pl. / *ensordecer*. 2. let us deafen; impve. 1st pers. pl.

ensordezcan 1. that they may deafen; pres. subj. 3rd pers. pl. / *ensordecer*. 2. let them deafen; impve. 3rd pers. pl.

ensordezcas that you may deafen; pres. subj. 2nd pers. sing. / *ensordecer*.

ensordezco I deafen; pres. ind. 1st pers. sing. / *ensordecer*.

ensortijándose curling; pres. part. / *ensortijarse*.

ensortijaos (you all) curl; impve. 2nd pers. pl. / *ensortijarse*.

ensortijar to curl. reg.

ensortijarse to curl. reg.

ensortíjate (you) curl; impve. 2nd pers. sing. / *ensortijarse*.

ensortijémonos let us curl; impve. 1st pers. pl. / *ensortijarse*.

ensortíjense let them curl; impve. 3rd pers. pl. / *ensortijarse*.

ensortíjese let him (her/it) curl; impve. 3rd pers. sing. / *ensortijarse*.

ensuciándose accepting bribes; pres. part. / *ensuciarse*.

ensuciaos (you all) accept bribes; impve. 2nd pers. pl. / *ensuciarse*.

ensuciar to soil. reg.

ensuciarse to accept bribes. reg.
ensucíate (you) accept bribes; impve. 2nd pers. sing. / *ensuciarse.*
ensuciémonos let us accept bribes; impve. 1st pers. pl. / *ensuciarse.*
ensucíense let them accept bribes; impve. 3rd pers. pl. / *ensuciarse.*
ensucíese let him (her/it) accept bribes; impve. 3rd pers. sing. / *ensuciarse.*
entablándose settling; pres. part. / *entablarse.*
entablaos (you all) settle; impve. 2nd pers. pl. / *entablarse.*
entablar to board up. reg.
entablarse to settle. reg.
entáblate (you) settle; impve. 2nd pers. sing. / *entablarse.*
entablémonos let us settle; impve. 1st pers. pl. / *entablarse.*
entáblense let them settle; impve. 3rd pers. pl. / *entablarse.*
entáblese let him (her/it) settle; impve. 3rd pers. sing. / *entablarse.*
entablillar to splint. reg.
entalegar to bag or to hoard. irr.
entalegue 1. that I may hoard; pres. subj. 1st pers. sing. / *entalegar.* 2. that he (she/it) may hoard; pres. subj. 3rd pers. sing. 3. let him (her/it) hoard; impve. 3rd pers. sing.
entalegué I hoarded; past 1st pers. sing. / *entalegar.*
entaleguéis that you (all) may hoard; pres. subj. 2nd pers. pl. / *entalegar.*
entaleguemos 1. that we may hoard; pres. subj. 1st pers. pl. / *entalegar.* 2. let us hoard; impve. 1st pers. pl.
entaleguen 1. that they may hoard; pres. subj. 3rd pers. pl. / *entalegar.* 2. let them hoard; impve. 3rd pers. pl.
entalegues that you may hoard; pres. subj. 2nd pers. sing. / *entalegar.*
entallar to carve or to fit closely. reg.
entapice 1. that I may hang with tapestry; pres. subj. 1st pers. sing. / *entapizar.* 2. that he (she/it) may hang with tapestry; pres. subj. 3rd pers. sing. 3. let him (her/it) hang with tapestry; impve. 3rd pers. sing.
entapicé I hung with tapestry; past 1st pers. sing. / *entapizar.*
entapicéis that you (all) may hang with tapestry; pres. subj. 2nd pers. pl. / *entapizar.*
entapicemos 1. that we may hang with tapestry; pres. subj. 1st pers. pl. / *entapizar.* 2. let us hang with tapestry; impve. 1st pers. pl.
entapicen 1. that they may hang with tapestry; pres. subj. 3rd pers. pl. / *entapizar.* 2. let them hang with tapestry; impve. 3rd pers. pl.
entapices that you may hang with tapestry; pres. subj. 2nd pers. sing. / *entapizar.*
entapizar to hang with tapestry. irr.
entarimar to floor (boards). reg.
entendámonos let us be understood; impve. 1st pers. pl. / *entenderse.*

entendeos (you all) be understood; impve. 2nd pers. pl. / *entenderse.*
entender to understand. irr.
entenderse to be understood. irr.
entendiéndose being understood; pres. part. / *entenderse.*
enterándose finding out; pres. part. / *enterarse.*
enteraos (you all) find out; impve. 2nd pers. pl. / *enterarse.*
enterar to inform. reg.
enterarse to find out. reg.
entérate (you) find out; impve. 2nd pers. sing. / *enterarse.*
enterémonos let us find out; impve. 1st pers. pl. / *enterarse.*
entérense let them find out; impve. 3rd pers. pl. / *enterarse.*
entérese let him (her/it) find out; impve. 3rd pers. sing. / *enterarse.*
enterneceos (you all) become tender; impve. 2nd pers. pl. / *enternecerse.*
enternecer to soften. irr.
enternecerse to become tender. irr.
enternécete (you) become tender; impve. 2nd pers. sing. / *enternecerse.*
enterneciéndose becoming tender; pres. part. / *enternecerse.*
enternezca 1. that I may soften; pres. subj. 1st pers. sing. / *enternecer.* 2. that he (she/it) may soften; pres. subj. 3rd pers. sing. 3. let him (her/it) soften; impve. 3rd pers. sing.
enternezcáis that you (all) may soften; pres. subj. 2nd pers. pl. / *enternecer.*
enternezcámonos let us become tender; impve. 1st pers. pl. / *enternecerse.*
enternezcamos 1. that we may soften; pres. subj. 1st pers. pl. / *enternecer.* 2. let us soften; impve. 1st pers. pl.
enternezcan 1. that they may soften; pres. subj. 3rd pers. pl. / *enternecer.* 2. let them soften; impve. 3rd pers. pl.
enternézcanse let them become tender; impve. 3rd pers. pl. / *enternecerse.*
enternezcas that you may soften; pres. subj. 2nd pers. sing. / *enternecer.*
enternézcase let him (her/it) become tender; impve. 3rd pers. sing. / *enternecerse.*
enternezco I soften; pres. ind. 1st pers. sing. / *enternecer.*
enterrar to bury. irr.
entesar to stretch. irr.
entibar to prop or to lean. reg.
entibiándose cooling off; pres. part. / *entibiarse.*
entibiaos (you all) cool off; impve. 2nd pers. pl. / *entibiarse.*
entibiar to make lukewarm. reg.
entibiarse to cool off. reg.
entibíate (you) cool off; impve. 2nd pers. sing. / *entibiarse.*

entibiémonos let us cool off; impve. 1st pers. pl. / *entibiarse.*

entibíense let them cool off; impve. 3rd pers. pl. / *entibiarse.*

entibíese let him (her/it) cool off; impve. 3rd pers. sing. / *entibiarse.*

entienda 1. that I may understand; pres. subj. 1st pers. sing. / *entender.* 2. that he (she/it) may understand; pres. subj. 3rd pers. sing. 3. let him (her/it) understand; impve. 3rd pers. sing.

entiendan 1. that they may understand; pres. subj. 3rd pers. pl. / *entender.* 2. let them understand; impve. 3rd pers. pl.

entiéndanse let them be understood; impve. 3rd pers. pl. / *entenderse.*

entiendas that you may understand; pres. subj. 2nd pers. sing. / *entender.*

entiéndase let him (her/it) be understood / *entenderse.* ; impve. 3rd pers. sing. /

entiende 1. he (she/it) understands; pres. ind. 3rd pers. sing. / *entender.* 2. (you) understand; impve. 2nd pers. sing.

entienden they understand; pres. ind. 3rd pers. pl. / *entender.*

entiendes you understand; pres. ind. 2nd pers. sing. / *entender.*

entiéndete (you) be understood; impve. 2nd pers. sing. / *entenderse.*

entiendo I understand; pres. ind. 1st pers. sing. / *entender.*

entierra 1. he (she/it) buries; pres. ind. 3rd pers. sing. / *enterrar.* 2. (you) bury; impve. 2nd pers. sing.

entierran they bury; pres. ind. 3rd pers. pl. / *enterrar.*

entierras you bury; pres. ind. 2nd pers. sing. / *enterrar.*

entierre 1. that I may bury; pres. subj. 1st pers. sing. / *enterrar.* 2. that he (she/it) may bury; pres. subj. 3rd pers. sing. 3. let him (her/it) bury; impve. 3rd pers. sing.

entierren 1. that they may bury; pres. subj. 3rd pers. pl. / *enterrar.* 2. let them bury; impve. 3rd pers. pl.

entierres that you may bury; pres. subj. 2nd pers. sing. / *enterrar.*

entierro I bury; pres. ind. 1st pers. sing. / *enterrar.*

entiesa 1. he (she/it) stretches; pres. ind. 3rd pers. sing. / *entesar.* 2. (you) stretch; impve. 2nd pers. sing.

entiesan they stretch; pres. ind. 3rd pers. pl. / *entesar.*

entiesas you stretch; pres. ind. 2nd pers. sing. / *entesar.*

entiese 1. that I may stretch; pres. subj. 1st pers. sing. / *entesar.* 2. that he (she/it) may stretch; pres. subj. 3rd pers. sing. 3. let him (her/it) stretch; impve. 3rd pers. sing.

entiesen 1. that they may stretch; pres. subj. 3rd pers. pl. / *entesar.* 2. let them stretch; impve. 3rd pers. pl.

entieses that you may stretch; pres. subj. 2nd pers. sing. / *entesar.*

entieso I stretch; pres. ind. 1st pers. sing. / *entesar.*

entintar to ink. reg.

entoldándose becoming cloudy; pres. part. / *entoldarse.*

entoldar to cover with an awning. reg.

entoldarse to become cloudy. reg.

entóldense let them become cloudy; impve. 3rd pers. pl. / *entoldarse.*

entóldese let it become cloudy; impve. 3rd pers. sing. / *entoldarse.*

entonándose putting on airs; pres. part. / *entonarse.*

entonaos (you all) put on airs; impve. 2nd pers. pl. / *entonarse.*

entonar to intone. reg.

entonarse to put on airs. reg.

entónate (you) put on airs; impve. 2nd pers. sing. / *entonarse.*

entonémonos let us put on airs; impve. 1st pers. pl. / *entonarse.*

entónense let them put on airs; impve. 3rd pers. pl. / *entonarse.*

entónese let him (her/it) put on airs; impve. 3rd pers. sing. / *entonarse.*

entonteceos (you all) grow stupid; impve. 2nd pers. pl. / *entontecerse.*

entontecer to make foolish. irr.

entontecerse to grow stupid. irr.

entontécete (you) grow stupid; impve. 2nd pers. sing. / *entontecerse.*

entonteciéndose growing stupid; pres. part. / *entontecerse.*

entontezca 1. that I may make foolish; pres. subj. 1st pers. sing. / *entontecer.* 2. that he (she/it) may make foolish; pres. subj. 3rd pers. sing. 3. let him (her/it) make foolish; impve. 3rd pers. sing.

entontezcáis that you (all) may make foolish; pres. subj. 2nd pers. pl. / *entontecer.*

entontezcámonos let us grow stupid; impve. 1st pers. pl. / *entontecerse.*

entontezcamos 1. that we may make foolish; pres. subj. 1st pers. pl. / *entontecer.* 2. let us make foolish; impve. 1st pers. pl.

entontezcan 1. that they may make foolish; pres. subj. 3rd pers. pl. / *entontecer.* 2. let them make foolish; impve. 3rd pers. pl.

entontézcanse let them grow stupid; impve. 3rd pers. pl. / *entontecerse.*

entontezcas that you may make foolish; pres. subj. 2nd pers. sing. / *entontecer.*

entontézcase let him (her/it) grow stupid; impve. 3rd pers. sing. / *entontecerse.*

entontezco I make foolish; pres. ind. 1st pers. sing. / *entontecer.*

entorchar to braid. reg.

entornar to half open. reg.

entornillar to thread (a screw). reg.

entorpeceos (you all) stick; impve. 2nd pers. pl. / *entorpecerse.*

entorpecer to benumb. irr.

entorpecerse to stick or to jam. irr.

entorpécete (you) stick; impve. 2nd pers. sing. / *entorpecerse.*

entorpeciéndose sticking; pres. part. / *entorpecerse.*

entorpezca 1. that I may benumb; pres. subj. 1st pers. sing. / *entorpecer*. 2. that he (she/it) may benumb; pres. subj. 3rd pers. sing. 3. let him (her/it) benumb; impve. 3rd pers. sing.

entorpezcáis that you (all) may benumb; pres. subj. 2nd pers. pl. / *entorpecer*.

entorpezcámonos let us stick; impve. 1st pers. pl. / *entorpecerse*.

entorpezcamos 1. that we may benumb; pres. subj. 1st pers. pl. / *entorpecer*. 2. let us benumb; impve. 1st pers. pl.

entorpezcan 1. that they may benumb; pres. subj. 3rd pers. pl. / *entorpecer*. 2. let them benumb; impve. 3rd pers. pl.

entorpézcanse let them stick; impve. 3rd pers. pl. / *entorpecerse*.

entorpezcas that you may benumb; pres. subj. 2nd pers. sing. / *entorpecer*.

entorpézcase let him (her/it) stick; impve. 3rd pers. sing. / *entorpecerse*.

entorpezco I benumb; pres. ind. 1st pers. sing. / *entorpecer*.

entortar to bend. irr.

entosigar to poison. irr.

entosigue 1. that I may poison; pres. subj. 1st pers. sing. / *entosigar*. 2. that he (she/it) may poison; pres. subj. 3rd pers. sing. 3. let him (her/it) poison; impve. 3rd pers. sing.

entosigué I poisoned; past 1st pers. sing. / *entosigar*.

entosiguéis that you (all) may poison; pres. subj. 2nd pers. pl. / *entosigar*.

entosiguemos 1. that we may poison; pres. subj. 1st pers. pl. / *entosigar*. 2. let us poison; impve. 1st pers. pl.

entosiguen 1. that they may poison; pres. subj. 3rd pers. pl. / *entosigar*. 2. let them poison; impve. 3rd pers. pl.

entosigues that you may poison; pres. subj. 2nd pers. sing. / *entosigar*.

entrampándose falling in debt; pres. part. / *entramparse*.

entrampaos (you all) fall in debt; impve. 2nd pers. pl. / *entramparse*.

entrampar to trap. reg.

entramparse to fall into debt. reg.

entrámpate (you) fall in debt; impve. 2nd pers. sing. / *entramparse*.

entrampémonos let us fall in debt; impve. 1st pers. pl. / *entramparse*.

entrámpense let them fall in debt; impve. 3rd pers. pl. / *entramparse*.

entrámpese let him (her/it) fall in debt; impve. 3rd pers. sing. / *entramparse*.

entrándose slipping in; pres. part. / *entrarse*.

entrañándose becoming closely attached; pres. part. / *entrañarse*.

entrañaos (you all) become closely attached; impve. 2nd pers. pl. / *entrañarse*.

entrañar to contain. reg.

entrañarse to become closely attached. reg.

entráñate (you) become closely attached; impve. 2nd pers. sing. / *entrañarse*.

entrañémonos let us become closely attached; impve. 1st pers. pl. / *entrañarse*.

entráñense let them become closely attached; impve. 3rd pers. pl. / *entrañarse*.

entráñese let him (her/it) become closely attached; impve. 3rd pers. sing. / *entrañarse*.

entraos (you all) slip in; impve. 2nd pers. pl. / *entrarse*.

entrar to enter. reg.

entrarse to slip in. reg.

éntrate (you) slip in; impve. 2nd pers. sing. / *entrarse*.

entreabierto half opened; past part. / *entreabrir*.

entreabrir to half open. reg. except for pp.

entrecoger to catch. irr.

entrecoja 1. that I may catch; pres. subj. 1st pers. sing. / *entrecoger*. 2. that he (she/it) may catch; pres. subj. 3rd pers. sing. 3. let him (her/it) catch; impve. 3rd pers. sing.

entrecojáis that you (all) may catch; pres. subj. 2nd pers. pl. / *entrecoger*.

entrecojamos 1. that we may catch; pres. subj. 1st pers. pl. / *entrecoger*. 2. let us catch; impve. 1st pers. pl.

entrecojan 1. that they may catch; pres. subj. 3rd pers. pl. / *entrecoger*. 2. let them catch; impve. 3rd pers. pl.

entrecojas that you may catch; pres. subj. 2nd pers. sing. / *entrecoger*.

entrecojo I catch; pres. ind. 1st pers. sing. / *entrecoger*.

entrecortar to cut halfway. reg.

entrecruce 1. that I may interweave; pres. subj. 1st pers. sing. / *entrecruzar*. 2. that he (she/it) may interweave; pres. subj. 3rd pers. sing. 3. let him (her/it) interweave; impve. 3rd pers. sing.

entrecrucé I interwove; past 1st pers. sing. / *entrecruzar*.

entrecrucéis that you (all) may interweave; pres. subj. 2nd pers. pl. / *entrecruzar*.

entrecrucémonos let us cross; impve. 1st pers. pl. / *entrecruzarse*.

entrecrucemos 1. that we may interweave; pres. subj. 1st pers. pl. / *entrecruzar*. 2. let us interweave; impve. 1st pers. pl.

entrecrucen 1. that they may interweave; pres. subj. 3rd pers. pl. / *entrecruzar*. 2. let them interweave; impve. 3rd pers. pl.

entrecrúcense let them cross; impve. 3rd pers. pl. / *entrecruzarse*.

entrecruces that you may interweave; pres. subj. 2nd pers. sing. / *entrecruzar*.

entrecrúcese let him (her/it) cross; impve. 3rd pers. sing. / *entrecruzarse*.

entrecruzándose crossing; pres. part. / *entrecruzarse*.

entrecruzaos (you all) cross; impve. 2nd pers. pl. / *entrecruzarse*.

entrecruzar to interweave. irr.

entrecruzarse to cross. irr.

entrecrúzate (you) cross; impve. 2nd pers. sing. / *entrecruzarse.*

entregándose surrendering; pres. part. / *entregarse.*

entregaos (you all) surrender; impve. 2nd pers. pl. / *entregarse.*

entregar to deliver. irr.

entregarse to surrender. irr.

entrégate (you) surrender; impve. 2nd pers. sing. / *entregarse.*

entregue 1. that I may deliver; pres. subj. 1st pers. sing. / *entregar.* 2. that he (she/it) may deliver; pres. subj. 3rd pers. sing. 3. let him (her/it) deliver; impve. 3rd pers. sing.

entregué I delivered; past 1st pers. sing. / *entregar.*

entreguéis that you (all) may deliver; pres. subj. 2nd pers. pl. / *entregar.*

entreguémonos let us surrender; impve. 1st pers. pl. / *entregarse.*

entreguemos 1. that we may deliver; pres. subj. 1st pers. pl. / *entregar.* 2. let us deliver; impve. 1st pers. pl.

entreguen 1. that they may deliver; pres. subj. 3rd pers. pl. / *entregar.* 2. let them deliver; impve. 3rd pers. pl.

entréguense let them surrender; impve. 3rd pers. pl. / *entregarse.*

entregues that you may deliver; pres. subj. 2nd pers. sing. / *entregar.*

entréguese let him (her/it) surrender; impve. 3rd pers. sing. / *entregarse.*

entrelace 1. that I may interlace; pres. subj. 1st pers. sing. / *entrelazar.* 2. that he (she/it) may interlace; pres. subj. 3rd pers. sing. 3. let him (her/it) interlace; impve. 3rd pers. sing.

entrelacé I interlaced; past 1st pers. sing. / *entrelazar.*

entrelacéis that you (all) may interlace; pres. subj. 2nd pers. pl. / *entrelazar.*

entrelacemos 1. that we may interlace; pres. subj. 1st pers. pl. / *entrelazar.* 2. let us interlace; impve. 1st pers. pl.

entrelacen 1. that they may interlace; pres. subj. 3rd pers. pl. / *entrelazar.* 2. let them interlace; impve. 3rd pers. pl.

entrelaces that you may interlace; pres. subj. 2nd pers. sing. / *entrelazar.*

entrelazar to interlace. irr.

entrelucir to show through. irr.

entreluzca 1. that I may show through; pres. subj. 1st pers. sing. / *entrelucir.* 2. that he (she/it) may show through; pres. subj. 3rd pers. sing. 3. let him (her/it) show through; impve. 3rd pers. sing.

entreluzcáis that you (all) may show through; pres. subj. 2nd pers. pl. / *entrelucir.*

entreluzcamos 1. that we may show through; pres. subj. 1st pers. pl. / *entrelucir.* 2. let us show through; impve. 1st pers. pl.

entreluzcan 1. that they may show through; pres. subj. 3rd pers. pl. / *entrelucir.* 2. let them show through; impve. 3rd pers. pl.

entreluzcas that you may show through; pres. subj. 2nd pers. sing. / *entrelucir.*

entreluzco I show through; pres. ind. 1st pers. sing. / *entrelucir.*

entremetámonos let us meddle; impve. 1st pers. pl. / *entremeterse.*

entremétanse let them meddle; impve. 3rd pers. pl. / *entremeterse.*

entremétase let him (her/it) meddle; impve. 3rd pers. sing. / *entremeterse.*

entremeteos (you all) meddle; impve. 2nd pers. pl. / *entremeterse.*

entremeter to insert. reg.

entremeterse to meddle. reg.

entremétete (you) meddle; impve. 2nd pers. sing. / *entremeterse.*

entremetiéndose meddling; pres. part. / *entremeterse.*

entremezclándose intermingling; pres. part. / *entremezclarse.*

entremezclaos (you all) intermingle; impve. 2nd pers. pl. / *entremezclarse.*

entremezclar to intermingle. reg.

entremezclarse to intermingle. reg.

entremézclate (you) intermingle; impve. 2nd pers. sing. / *entremezclarse.*

entremezclémonos let us intermingle; impve. 1st pers. pl. / *entremezclarse.*

entremézclense let them intermingle; impve. 3rd pers. pl. / *entremezclarse.*

entremézclese let him (her/it) intermingle; impve. 3rd pers. sing. / *entremezclarse.*

entrémonos let us slip in; impve. 1st pers. pl. / *entrarse.*

entrenándose training; pres. part. / *entrenarse.*

entrenaos (you all) train; impve. 2nd pers. pl. / *entrenarse.*

entrenar to train or to coach. reg.

entrenarse to train. reg.

entrénate (you) train; impve. 2nd pers. sing. / *entrenarse.*

entrenémonos let us train; impve. 1st pers. pl. / *entrenarse.*

entrénense let them train; impve. 3rd pers. pl. / *entrenarse.*

entrénese let him (her/it) train; impve. 3rd pers. sing. / *entrenarse.*

éntrense let them slip in; impve. 3rd pers. pl. / *entrarse.*

entreoiga 1. that I may barely hear; pres. subj. 1st pers. sing. / *entreoir.* 2. that he (she/it) may barely hear; pres. subj. 3rd pers. sing. 3. let him (her/it) barely hear; impve. 3rd pers. sing.

entreoigáis that you (all) may barely hear; pres. subj. 2nd pers. pl. / *entreoir.*

entreoigamos 1. that we may barely hear; pres. subj. 1st pers. pl. / *entreoir.* 2. let us barely hear; impve. 1st pers. pl.

entreoigan 1. that they may barely hear; pres. subj. 3rd pers. pl. / *entreoir.* 2. let them barely hear; impve. 3rd pers. pl.

entreoigas that you may barely hear; pres. subj. 2nd pers. sing. / *entreoir.*

entreoigo I barely hear; pres. ind. 1st pers. sing. / *entreoir*.

entreoir to barely hear. irr.

entreoye 1. he (she/it) barely hears; pres. ind. 3rd pers. sing. / *entreoir*. 2. (you) barely hear; impve. 2nd pers. sing.

entreoyen they barely hear; pres. ind. 3rd pers. pl. / *entreoir*.

entreoyendo barely hearing; pres. part. / *entreoir*.

entreoyera 1. that I might barely hear; imp. subj. 1st pers. sing. / *entreoir*. 2. that he (she/it) might barely hear; imp. subj. 3rd pers. sing.

entreoyerais that you (all) might barely hear; imp. subj. 2nd pers pl. / *entreoir*.

entreoyéramos that we might barely hear; imp. subj. 1st pers. pl. / *entreoir*.

entreoyeran that they might barely hear; imp. subj. 3rd pers. pl. / *entreoir*.

entreoyeras that you might barely hear; imp. subj. 2nd pers. sing. / *entreoir*.

entreoyeron they barely heard; past 3rd pers. pl. / *entreoir*.

entreoyes you barely hear; pres. ind. 2nd pers. sing. / *entreoir*.

entreoyese 1. that I might barely hear; imp. subj. 1st pers. sing. / *entreoir*. 2. that he (she/it) might barely hear; imp. subj. 3rd pers. sing.

entreoyeseis that you (all) might barely hear; imp. subj. 2nd pers pl. / *entreoir*.

entreoyésemos that we might barely hear; imp. subj. 1st pers. pl. / *entreoir*.

entreoyesen that they might barely hear; imp. subj. 3rd pers. pl. / *entreoir*.

entreoyeses that you might barely hear; imp. subj. 2nd pers. sing. / *entreoir*.

entreoyó he (she/it) barely heard; past. ind. 3rd pers. sing. / *entreoir*.

entrepareceos (you all) show through; impve. 2nd pers. pl. / *entreparecerse*.

entreparecerse to show through. irr.

entreparécete (you) show through; impve. 2nd pers. sing. / *entreparecerse*.

entrepareciéndose showing through; pres. part. / *entreparecerse*.

entreparezca 1. that I may show through; pres. subj. 1st pers. sing. / *entreparecerse*. 2. that he (she/it) may show through; pres. subj. 3rd pers. sing.

entreparezcáis that you (all) may show through; pres. subj. 2nd pers. pl. / *entreparecerse*.

entreparezcámonos let us show through; impve. 1st pers. pl. / *entreparecerse*.

entreparezcamos that we may show through; pres. subj. 1st pers. pl. / *entreparecerse*.

entreparezcan that they may show through; pres. subj. 3rd pers. pl. / *entreparecerse*.

entreparézcanse let them show through; impve. 3rd pers. pl. / *entreparecerse*.

entreparezcas that you may show through; pres. subj. 2nd pers. sing. / *entreparecerse*.

entreparézcase let him (her/it) show through; impve. 3rd pers. sing. / *entreparecerse*.

entreparezco I show through; pres. ind. 1st pers. sing. / *entreparecerse*.

entrepon (you) interpose; impve. 2nd pers. sing. / *entreponer*.

entrepondrá he (she/it) will interpose; fut. 3rd pers. sing. / *entreponer*.

entrepondrán they will interpose; fut. 3rd pers. pl. / *entreponer*.

entrepondrás you will interpose; fut. 2nd pers. sing. / *entreponer*.

entrepondré I shall interpose; fut. 1st pers. sing. / *entreponer*.

entrepondréis you (all) will interpose; fut. 2nd pers. pl. / *entreponer*.

entrepondremos we shall interpose; fut. 1st pers. pl. / *entreponer*.

entrepondría 1. I should interpose; cond. 1st pers. sing. / *entreponer*. 2. he (she/it) would interpose; cond. 3rd pers. sing..

entrepondríais you (all) would interpose; cond. 2nd pers. pl. / *entreponer*.

entrepondríamos we should interpose; cond. 1st pers. pl. / *entreponer*.

entrepondrían they would interpose; cond. 3rd pers. pl. / *entreponer*.

entrepondrías you would interpose; cond. 2nd pers. sing. / *entreponer*.

entreponer to interpose. irr.

entreponga 1. that I may interpose; pres. subj. 1st pers. sing. / *entreponer*. 2. that he (she/it) may interpose; pres. subj. 3rd pers. sing. 3. let him (her/it) interpose; impve. 3rd pers. sing.

entrepongáis that you (all) may interpose; pres. subj. 2nd pers. pl. / *entreponer*.

entrepongamos 1. that we may interpose; pres. subj. 1st pers. pl. / *entreponer*. 2. let us interpose; impve. 1st pers. pl.

entrepongan 1. that they may interpose; pres. subj. 3rd pers. pl. / *entreponer*. 2. let them interpose. impve. 3rd pers. pl.

entrepongas that you may interpose; pres. subj. 2nd pers. sing. / *entreponer*.

entrepongo I interpose; pres. ind. 1st pers. sing. / *entreponer*.

entrepuesto interposed; past part. / *entreponer*.

entrepuse I interposed; past 1st pers. sing. / *entreponer*.

entrepusiera 1. that I might interpose; imp. subj. 1st pers. sing. / *entreponer*. 2. that he (she/it) might interpose; imp. subj. 3rd pers. sing.

entrepusierais that you (all) might interpose; imp. subj. 2nd pers pl. / *entreponer*.

entrepusiéramos that we might interpose; imp. subj. 1st pers. pl. / *entreponer*.

entrepusieran that they might interpose; imp. subj. 3rd pers. pl. / *entreponer*.

entrepusieras that you might interpose; imp. subj. 2nd pers. sing. / *entreponer*.

entrepusieron they interposed; past 3rd pers. pl. / *entreponer*.

entrepusiese 1. that I might interpose; imp. subj. 1st pers. sing. / *entreponer*. 2. that he (she/it) might interpose; imp. subj. 3rd pers. sing.

entrepusieseis that you (all) might interpose; imp. subj. 2nd pers pl. / *entreponer*.

entrepusiésemos that we might interpose; imp. subj. 1st pers. pl. / *entreponer*.

entrepusiesen that they might interpose; imp. subj. 3rd pers. pl. / *entreponer*.

entrepusieses that you might interpose; imp. subj. 2nd pers. sing. / *entreponer*.

entrepusimos we interposed; past 1st pers. pl. / *entreponer*.

entrepusiste you interposed; past 2nd pers. sing. / *entreponer*.

entrepusisteis you (all) interposed; past 2nd pers. pl. / *entreponer*.

entrepuso he (she/it) interposed; past 3rd pers. sing. / *entreponer*.

entresacar to pick out. irr.

entresaque 1. that I may pick out; pres. subj. 1st pers. sing. / *entresacar*. 2. that he (she/it) may pick out; pres. subj. 3rd pers. sing. 3. let him (her/it) pick out; impve. 3rd pers. sing.

entresaqué I picked out; past 1st pers. sing. / *entresacar*.

entresaquéis that you (all) may pick out; pres. subj. 2nd pers. pl. / *entresacar*.

entresaquemos 1. that we may pick out; pres. subj. 1st pers. pl. / *entresacar*. 2. let us pick out; impve. 1st pers. pl.

entresaquen 1. that they may pick out; pres. subj. 3rd pers. pl. / *entresacar*. 2. let them pick out; impve. 3rd pers. pl.

entresaques that you may pick out; pres. subj. 2nd pers. sing. / *entresacar*.

éntrese let him (her/it) slip in; impve. 3rd pers. sing. / *entrarse*.

entretallándose fitting together; pres. part. / *entretallarse*.

entretallaos (you all) fit together; impve. 2nd pers. pl. / *entretallarse*.

entretallar to sculpture in bas-relief. reg.

entretallarse to fit together. reg.

entretállate (you) fit together; impve. 2nd pers. sing. / *entretallarse*.

entretallémonos let us fit together; impve. 1st pers. pl. / *entretallarse*.

entretállense let them fit together; impve. 3rd pers. pl. / *entretallarse*.

entretállese let him (her/it) fit together; impve. 3rd pers. sing. / *entretallarse*.

entretejer to interweave. reg.

entreten (you) entertain; impve. 2nd pers. sing. / *entretener*.

entretendrá he (she/it) will entertain; fut. 3rd pers. sing. / *entretener*.

entretendrán they will entertain; fut. 3rd pers. pl. / *entretener*.

entretendrás you will entertain; fut. 2nd pers. sing. / *entretener*.

entretendré I shall entertain; fut. 1st pers. sing. / *entretener*.

entretendréis you (all) will entertain; fut. 2nd pers. pl. / *entretener*.

entretendremos we shall entertain; fut. 1st pers. pl. / *entretener*.

entretendría 1. I should entertain; cond. 1st pers. sing. / *entretener*. 2. he (she/it) would entertain; cond. 3rd pers. sing.

entretendríais you (all) would entertain; cond. 2nd pers. pl. / *entretener*.

entretendríamos we should entertain; cond. 1st pers. pl. / *entretener*.

entretendrían they would entertain; cond. 3rd pers. pl. / *entretener*.

entretendrías you would entertain; cond. 2nd pers. sing. / *entretener*.

entreteneos (you all) amuse yourselves; impve. 2nd pers. pl. / *entretenerse*.

entretener to entertain or to delay. irr.

entretenerse to amuse oneself. irr.

entreténete (you) amuse yourself; impve. 2nd pers. sing. / *entretenerse*.

entreteniéndose amusing oneself; pres. part. / *entretenerse*.

entretenga 1. that I may entertain; pres. subj. 1st pers. sing. / *entretener*. 2. that he (she/it) may entertain; pres. subj. 3rd pers. sing. 3. let him (her/it) entertain; impve. 3rd pers. sing.

entretengáis that you (all) may entertain; pres. subj. 2nd pers. pl. / *entretener*.

entretengámonos let us amuse ourselves; impve. 1st pers. pl. / *entretenerse*.

entretengamos 1. that we may entertain; pres. subj. 1st pers. pl. / *entretener*. 2. let us entertain; impve. 1st pers. pl.

entretengan 1. that they may entertain; pres. subj. 3rd pers. pl. / *entretener*. 2. let them entertain; impve. 3rd pers. pl.

entreténganse let them amuse themselves; impve. 3rd pers. pl. / *entretenerse*.

entretengas that you may entertain; pres. subj. 2nd pers. sing. / *entretener*.

entreténgase let him (her/it) amuse himself (herself/itself); impve. 3rd pers. sing. / *entretenerse*.

entretengo I entertain; pres. ind. 1st pers. sing. / *entretener*.

entretiene 1. he (she/it) entertains; pres. ind. 3rd pers. sing. / *entretener*. 2. (you) entertain; impve. 2nd pers. sing.

entretienen they entertain; pres. ind. 3rd pers. pl. / *entretener*.

entretienes you entertain; pres. ind. 2nd pers. sing. / *entretener*.

entretuve I entertained; past 1st pers. sing. / *entretener*.

entretuviera 1. that I might entertain; imp. subj. 1st pers. sing. / *entretener*. 2. that he (she/it) might entertain; imp. subj. 3rd pers. sing.

entretuvierais that you (all) might entertain; imp. subj. 2nd pers pl. / *entretener*.

entretuviéramos that we might entertain; imp. subj. 1st pers. pl. / *entretener.*

entretuvieran that they might entertain; imp. subj. 3rd pers. pl. / *entretener.*

entretuvieras that you might entertain; imp. subj. 2nd pers. sing. / *entretener.*

entretuvieron they entertained; past 3rd pers. pl. / *entretener.*

entretuviese 1. that I might entertain; imp. subj. 1st pers. sing. / *entretener.* 2. that he (she/it) might entertain; imp. subj. 3rd pers. sing.

entretuvieseis that you (all) might entertain; imp. subj. 2nd pers pl. / *entretener.*

entretuviésemos that we might entertain; imp. subj. 1st pers. pl. / *entretener.*

entretuviesen that they might entertain; imp. subj. 3rd pers. pl. / *entretener.*

entretuvieses that you might entertain; imp. subj. 2nd pers. sing. / *entretener.*

entretuvimos we entertained; past 1st pers. pl. / *entretener.*

entretuviste you entertained; past 2nd pers. sing. / *entretener.*

entretuvisteis you (all) entertained; past 2nd pers. pl. / *entretener.*

entretuvo he (she/it) entertained; past 3rd pers. sing. / *entretener.*

entrevea 1. that I may glimpse; pres. subj. 1st pers. sing. / *entrever.* 2. that he (she/it) may glimpse; pres. subj. 3rd pers. sing. 3. let him (her/it) glimpse; impve. 3rd pers. sing.

entreveáis that you (all) may glimpse; pres. subj. 2nd pers. pl. / *entrever.*

entreveamos 1. that we may glimpse; pres. subj. 1st pers. pl. / *entrever.* 2. let us glimpse; impve. 1st pers. pl.

entrevean 1. that they may glimpse; pres. subj. 3rd pers. pl. / *entrever.* 2. let them glimpse; impve. 3rd pers. pl.

entreveas that you may glimpse; pres. subj. 2nd pers. sing. / *entrever.*

entreveía 1. I was glimpsing; imp. ind. 1st pers. sing. / *entrever.* 2. he (she/it) was glimpsing; imp. ind. 3rd pers. sing.

entreveíais you (all) were glimpsing; imp. ind. 2nd pers. pl. / *entrever.*

entreveíamos we were glimpsing; imp. ind. 1st pers. pl. / *entrever.*

entreveían they were glimpsing; imp. ind. 3rd pers. pl. / *entrever.*

entreveías you were glimpsing; imp. ind. 2nd pers. sing. / *entrever.*

entrevenándose spreading through the veins; pres. part. / *entrevenarse.*

entrevenaos (you all) spread through the veins; impve. 2nd pers. pl. / *entrevenarse.*

entrevenarse to spread through the veins. reg.

entrevénate (you) spread through the veins; impve. 2nd pers. sing. / *entrevenarse.*

entrevenémonos let us spread through the veins; impve. 1st pers. pl. / *entrevenarse.*

entrevénense let them spread through the veins; impve. 3rd pers. pl. / *entrevenarse.*

entrevénese let him (her/it) spread through the veins; impve. 3rd pers. sing. / *entrevenarse.*

entreveo I glimpse; pres. ind. 1st pers. sing. / *entrever.*

entrever to glimpse. irr.

entreverar to intermingle. reg.

entrevi I glimpsed; past 1st pers. sing. / *entrever.*

entrevio he (she/it) glimpsed; past 3rd pers. sing. / *entrever.*

entrevistándose being interviewed; pres. part. / *entrevistarse.*

entrevistaos (you all) be interviewed; impve. 2nd pers. pl. / *entrevistarse.*

entrevistar to interview. reg.

entrevistarse to be interviewed. reg.

entrevístate (you) be interviewed; impve. 2nd pers. sing. / *entrevistarse.*

entrevistémonos let us be interviewed; impve. 1st pers. pl. / *entrevistarse.*

entrevístense let them be interviewed; impve. 3rd pers. pl. / *entrevistarse.*

entrevístese let him (her/it) be interviewed; impve. 3rd pers. sing. / *entrevistarse.*

entrevisto glimpsed; past part. / *entrever.*

entristeceos (you all) grieve; impve. 2nd pers. pl. / *entristecerse.*

entristecer to sadden. irr.

entristecerse to grieve. irr.

entristécete (you) grieve; impve. 2nd pers. sing. / *entristecerse.*

entristeciéndose grieving; pres. part. / *entristecerse.*

entristezca 1. that I may sadden; pres. subj. 1st pers. sing. / *entristecer.* 2. that he (she/it) may sadden; pres. subj. 3rd pers. sing. 3. let him (her/it) sadden; impve. 3rd pers. sing.

entristezcáis that you (all) may sadden; pres. subj. 2nd pers. pl. / *entristecer.*

entristezcámonos let us grieve; impve. 1st pers. pl. / *entristecerse.*

entristezcamos 1. that we may sadden; pres. subj. 1st pers. pl. / *entristecer.* 2. let us sadden; impve. 1st pers. pl.

entristezcan 1. that they may sadden; pres. subj. 3rd pers. pl. / *entristecer.* 2. let them sadden; impve. 3rd pers. pl.

entristézcanse let them grieve; impve. 3rd pers. pl. / *entristecerse.*

entristezcas that you may sadden; pres. subj. 2nd pers. sing. / *entristecer.*

entristézcase let him (her/it) grieve; impve. 3rd pers. sing. / *entristecerse.*

entristezco I sadden; pres. ind. 1st pers. sing. / *entristecer.*

entrometer to insert. reg.

entronar to enthrone. reg.

entroncándose being connected; pres. part. / *entroncarse.*

entroncaos (you all) be connected; impve. 2nd pers. pl. / *entroncarse.*

entroncar to be related. irr.

entroncarse to be connected. irr.

entróncate (you) be connected; impve. 2nd pers. sing. / *entroncarse.*

entronice 1. that I may enthrone; pres. subj. 1st pers. sing. / *entronizar.* 2. that he (she/it) may enthrone; pres. subj. 3rd pers. sing. 3. let him (her/it) enthrone; impve. 3rd pers. sing.

entronicé I enthroned; past 1st pers. sing. / *entronizar.*

entronicéis that you (all) may enthrone; pres. subj. 2nd pers. pl. / *entronizar.*

entronicemos 1. that we may enthrone; pres. subj. 1st pers. pl. / *entronizar.* 2. let us enthrone; impve. 1st pers. pl.

entronicen 1. that they may enthrone; pres. subj. 3rd pers. pl. / *entronizar.* 2. let them enthrone; impve. 3rd pers. pl.

entronices that you may enthrone; pres. subj. 2nd pers. sing. / *entronizar.*

entronizar to enthrone. irr.

entronque 1. that I may be related; pres. subj. 1st pers. sing. / *entroncar.* 2. that he (she/it) may be related; pres. subj. 3rd pers. sing. 3. let him (her/it) be related; impve. 3rd pers. sing.

entronqué I was related; past 1st pers. sing. / *entroncar.*

entronquéis that you (all) may be related; pres. subj. 2nd pers. pl. / *entroncar.*

entronquémonos let us be connected; impve. 1st pers. pl. / *entroncarse.*

entronquemos 1. that we may be related; pres. subj. 1st pers. pl. / *entroncar.* 2. let us be related; impve. 1st pers. pl.

entronquen 1. that they may be related; pres. subj. 3rd pers. pl. / *entroncar.* 2. let them be related; impve. 3rd pers. pl.

entrónquense let them be connected; impve. 3rd pers. pl. / *entroncarse.*

entronques that you may be related; pres. subj. 2nd pers. sing. / *entroncar.*

entrónquese let him (her/it) be connected; impve. 3rd pers. sing. / *entroncarse.*

entruchar to lure. reg.

entubar to pipe. reg.

entuerta 1. he (she/it) bends; pres. ind. 3rd pers. sing. / *entortar.* 2. (you) bend; impve. 2nd pers. sing.

entuertan they bend; pres. ind. 3rd pers. pl. / *entortar.*

entuertas you bend; pres. ind. 2nd pers. sing. / *entortar.*

entuerte 1. that I may bend; pres. subj. 1st pers. sing. / *entortar.* 2. that he (she/it) may bend; pres. subj. 3rd pers. sing. 3. let him (her/it) bend; impve. 3rd pers. sing.

entuerten 1. that they may bend; pres. subj. 3rd pers. pl. / *entortar.* 2. let them bend; impve. 3rd pers. pl.

entuertes that you may bend; pres. subj. 2nd pers. sing. / *entortar.*

entuerto I bend; pres. ind. 1st pers. sing. / *entortar.*

entulleceos (you all) be crippled; impve. 2nd pers. pl. / *entullecerse.*

entullecerse to be crippled. irr.

entullécete (you) be crippled; impve. 2nd pers. sing. / *entullecerse.*

entulleciéndose being crippled; pres. part. / *entullecerse.*

entullezca 1. that I may be crippled; pres. subj. 1st pers. sing. / *entullecerse.* 2. that he (she/it) may be crippled; pres. subj. 3rd pers. sing.

entullezcáis that you (all) may be crippled; pres. subj. 2nd pers. pl. / *entullecerse.*

entullezcámonos let us be crippled; impve. 1st pers. pl. / *entullecerse.*

entullezcamos that we may be crippled; pres. subj. 1st pers. pl. / *entullecerse.*

entullezcan that they may be crippled; pres. subj. 3rd pers. pl. / *entullecerse.*

entullézcanse let them be crippled; impve. 3rd pers. pl. / *entullecerse.*

entullezcas that you may be crippled; pres. subj. 2nd pers. sing. / *entullecerse.*

entullézcase let him (her/it) be crippled; impve. 3rd pers. sing. / *entullecerse.*

entullezco I am crippled; past 1st pers. sing. / *entullecerse.*

entumámonos let us get numb; impve. 1st pers. pl. / *entumirse.*

entúmanse let them get numb; impve. 3rd pers. pl. / *entumirse.*

entúmase let him (her/it) get numb; impve. 3rd pers. sing. / *entumirse.*

entumeceos (you all) swell; impve. 2nd pers. pl. / *entumecerse.*

entumecer to make numb. irr.

entumecerse to swell. irr.

entumécete (you) swell; impve. 2nd pers. sing. / *entumecerse.*

entumeciéndose swelling; pres. part. / *entumecerse.*

entúmete (you) get numb; impve. 2nd pers. sing. / *entumirse.*

entumezca 1. that I may make numb; pres. subj. 1st pers. sing. / *entumecer.* 2. that he (she/it) may make numb; pres. subj. 3rd pers. sing. 3. let him (her/it) make numb; impve. 3rd pers. sing.

entumezcáis that you (all) may make numb; pres. subj. 2nd pers. pl. / *entumecer.*

entumezcámonos let us swell; impve. 1st pers. pl. / *entumecerse.*

entumezcamos 1. that we may make numb; pres. subj. 1st pers. pl. / *entumecer.* 2. let us make numb; impve. 1st pers. pl.

entumezcan 1. that they may make numb; pres. subj. 3rd pers. pl. / *entumecer.* 2. let them make numb; impve. 3rd pers. pl.

entumézcanse let them swell; impve. 3rd pers. pl. / *entumecerse.*

entumezcas that you may make numb; pres. subj. 2nd pers. sing. / *entumecer.*

entumézcase let him (her/it) swell; impve. 3rd pers. sing. / *entumecerse.*

entumezco I make numb; pres. ind. 1st pers. sing. /
entumecer.
entumiéndose getting numb; pres. part. / *entumirse.*
entumíos (you all) get numb; impve. 2nd pers. pl. /
entumirse.
entumirse to get numb. reg.
entupir to compress or to block. reg.
enturbiándose getting muddy; pres. part. /
enturbiarse.
enturbiaos (you all) get muddy; impve. 2nd pers. pl. /
enturbiarse.
enturbiar to muddy. reg.
enturbiarse to get muddy. reg.
enturbíate (you) get muddy; impve. 2nd pers. sing. /
enturbiarse.
enturbiémonos let us get muddy; impve. 1st pers. pl.
/ *enturbiarse.*
enturbíense let them get muddy; impve. 3rd pers. pl.
/ *enturbiarse.*
enturbíese let him (her/it) get muddy; impve. 3rd
pers. sing. / *enturbiarse.*
entusiasmándose being enthusiastic; pres. part. /
entusiasmarse.
entusiasmaos (you all) be enthusiastic; impve. 2nd
pers. pl. / *entusiasmarse.*
entusiasmar to make enthusiastic. reg.
entusiasmarse to be enthusiastic. reg.
entusiásmate (you) be enthusiastic; impve. 2nd pers.
sing. / *entusiasmarse.*
entusiasmémonos let us be enthusiastic; impve. 1st
pers. pl. / *entusiasmarse.*
entusiásmense let them be enthusiastic; impve. 3rd
pers. pl. / *entusiasmarse.*
entusiásmese let him (her/it) be enthusiastic; impve.
3rd pers. sing. / *entusiasmarse.*
enumerar to enumerate. reg.
enunciar to enunciate. reg.
envainar to sheathe. reg.
envalentonándose getting bold; pres. part. /
envalentonarse.
envalentonaos (you all) get bold; impve. 2nd pers. pl.
/ *envalentonarse.*
envalentonar to encourage. reg.
envalentonarse to get bold. reg.
envalentónate (you) get bold; impve. 2nd pers. sing. /
envalentonarse.
envalentonémonos let us get bold; impve. 1st pers.
pl. / *envalentonarse.*
envalentónense let them get bold; impve. 3rd pers.
pl. / *envalentonarse.*
envalentónese let him (her/it) get bold; impve. 3rd
pers. sing. / *envalentonarse.*
envaneceos (you all) become vain; impve. 2nd pers.
pl. / *envanecerse.*
envanecer to make vain. irr.
envanecerse to become vain. irr.
envanécete (you) become vain; impve. 2nd pers. sing.
/ *envanecerse.*
envaneciéndose becoming vain; pres. part. /
envanecerse.

envanezca 1. that I may make vain; pres. subj. 1st
pers. sing. / *envanecer.* 2. that he (she/it) may make
vain; pres. subj. 3rd pers. sing. 3. let him (her/it)
make vain; impve. 3rd pers. sing.
envanezcáis that you (all) may make vain; pres. subj.
2nd pers. pl. / *envanecer.*
envanezcámonos let us become vain; impve. 1st pers.
pl. / *envanecerse.*
envanezcamos 1. that we may make vain; pres. subj.
1st pers. pl. / *envanecer.* 2. let us make vain; impve.
1st pers. pl.
envanezcan 1. that they may make vain; pres. subj.
3rd pers. pl. / *envanecer.* 2. let them make vain;
impve. 3rd pers. pl.
envanézcanse let them become vain; impve. 3rd pers.
pl. / *envanecerse.*
envanezcas that you may make vain; pres. subj. 2nd
pers. sing. / *envanecer.*
envanézcase let him (her/it) become vain; impve. 3rd
pers. sing. / *envanecerse.*
envanezco I make vain; pres. ind. 1st pers. sing. /
envanecer.
envarándose becoming numb; pres. part. / *envararse.*
envaraos (you all) become numb; impve. 2nd pers.
pl. / *envararse.*
envarar to be numb. reg.
envararse to become numb. reg.
envárate (you) become numb; impve. 2nd pers. sing.
/ *envararse.*
envarémonos let us become numb; impve. 1st pers.
pl. / *envararse.*
envárense let them become numb; impve. 3rd pers.
pl. / *envararse.*
envárese let him (her/it) become numb; impve. 3rd
pers. sing. / *envararse.*
envasar to pack or to bottle. reg.
envejeceos (you all) grow old; impve. 2nd pers. pl. /
envejecerse.
envejecer to make old. irr.
envejecerse to grow old. irr.
envejécete (you) grow old; impve. 2nd pers. sing. /
envejecerse.
envejeciéndose growing old; pres. part. / *envejecerse.*
envejezca 1. that I may make old; pres. subj. 1st pers.
sing. / *envejecer.* 2. that he (she/it) may make old;
pres. subj. 3rd pers. sing. 3. let him (her/it) make
old; impve. 3rd pers. sing.
envejezcáis that you (all) may make old; pres. subj.
2nd pers. pl. / *envejecer.*
envejezcámonos let us grow old; impve. 1st pers. pl. /
envejecerse.
envejezcamos 1. that we may make old; pres. subj. 1st
pers. pl. / *envejecer.* 2. let us make old; impve. 1st
pers. pl.
envejezcan 1. that they may make old; pres. subj. 3rd
pers. pl. / *envejecer.* 2. let them make old; impve.
3rd pers. pl.
envejézcanse let them grow old; impve. 3rd pers. pl. /
envejecerse.
envejezcas that you may make old; pres. subj. 2nd
pers. sing. / *envejecer.*

envejézcase let him (her/it) grow old; impve. 3rd pers. sing. / *envejecerse.*

envejezco I make old; pres. ind. 1st pers. sing. / *envejecer.*

envenenar to poison. reg.

enverdeceos (you all) turn green; impve. 2nd pers. pl. / *enverdecerse.*

enverdecer to turn green. irr.

enverdecerse to turn green. irr.

enverdécete (you) turn green; impve. 2nd pers. sing. / *enverdecerse.*

enverdeciéndose turning green; pres. part. / *enverdecerse.*

enverdezca 1. that I may turn green; pres. subj. 1st pers. sing. / *enverdecer.* 2. that he (she/it) may turn green; pres. subj. 3rd pers. sing. 3. let him (her/it) turn green; impve. 3rd pers. sing.

enverdezcáis that you (all) may turn green; pres. subj. 2nd pers. pl. / *enverdecer.*

enverdezcámonos let us turn green; impve. 1st pers. pl. / *enverdecerse.*

enverdezcamos 1. that we may turn green; pres. subj. 1st pers. pl. / *enverdecer.* 2. let us turn green; impve. 1st pers. pl.

enverdezcan 1. that they may turn green; pres. subj. 3rd pers. pl. / *enverdecer.* 2. let them turn green; impve. 3rd pers. pl.

enverdézcanse let them turn green; impve. 3rd pers. pl. / *enverdecerse.*

enverdezcas that you may turn green; pres. subj. 2nd pers. sing. / *enverdecer.*

enverdézcase let him (her/it) turn green; impve. 3rd pers. sing. / *enverdecerse.*

enverdezco I turn green; pres. ind. 1st pers. sing. / *enverdecer.*

envestir to invest. irr.

envía 1. he (she/it) sends; pres. ind. 3rd pers. sing. / *enviar.* 2. (you) send; impve. 2nd pers. sing.

envían they send; pres. ind. 3rd pers. pl. / *enviar.*

enviar to send. irr.

envías you send; pres. ind. 2nd pers. sing. / *enviar.*

enviciándose becoming addicted to; pres. part. / *enviciarse.*

enviciaos (you all) become addicted to; impve. 2nd pers. pl. / *enviciarse.*

enviciar to corrupt. reg.

enviciarse to become addicted to. reg.

enviciate (you) become addicted to; impve. 2nd pers. sing. / *enviciarse.*

enviciémonos let us become addicted to; impve. 1st pers. pl. / *enviciarse.*

envíciense let them become addicted to; impve. 3rd pers. pl. / *enviciarse.*

envíciese let him (her/it) become addicted to; impve. 3rd pers. sing. / *enviciarse.*

envidar to bid against. reg.

envidiar to envy. reg.

envíe 1. that I may send; pres. subj. 1st pers. sing. / *enviar.* 2. that he (she/it) may send; pres. subj. 3rd pers. sing. 3. let him (her/it) send; impve. 3rd pers. sing.

envíen 1. that they may send; pres. subj. 3rd pers. pl. / *enviar.* 2. let them send; impve. 3rd pers. pl.

envíes that you may send; pres. subj. 2nd pers. sing. / *enviar.*

envileceos (you all) be debased; impve. 2nd pers. pl. / *envilecerse.*

envilecer to revile. irr.

envilecerse to be debased. irr

envilécete (you) be debased; impve. 2nd pers. sing. / *envilecerse.*

envileciéndose being debased; pres. part. / *envilecerse.*

envilezca 1. that I may revile; pres. subj. 1st pers. sing. / *envilecer.* 2. that he (she/it) may revile; pres. subj. 3rd pers. sing. 3. let him (her/it) revile; impve. 3rd pers. sing.

envilezcáis that you (all) may revile; pres. subj. 2nd pers. pl. / *envilecer.*

envilezcámonos let us be debased; impve. 1st pers. pl. / *envilecerse.*

envilezcamos 1. that we may revile; pres. subj. 1st pers. pl. / *envilecer.* 2. let us revile; impve. 1st pers. pl.

envilezcan 1. that they may revile; pres. subj. 3rd pers. pl. / *envilecer.* 2. let them revile; impve. 3rd pers. pl.

envilézcanse let them be debased; impve. 3rd pers. pl. / *envilecerse.*

envilezcas that you may revile; pres. subj. 2nd pers. sing. / *envilecer.*

envilézcase let him (her/it) be debased; impve. 3rd pers. sing. / *envilecerse.*

envilezco I revile; pres. ind. 1st pers. sing. / *envilecer.*

envío I send; pres. ind. 1st pers. sing. / *enviar.*

envista 1. that I may invest; pres. subj. 1st pers. sing. / *envestir.* 2. that he (she/it) may invest; pres. subj. 3rd pers. sing. 3. let him (her/it) invest; impve. 3rd pers. sing.

envistáis that you (all) may invest; pres. subj. 2nd pers. pl. / *envestir.*

envistamos 1. that we may invest; pres. subj. 1st pers. pl. / *envestir.* 2. let us invest; impve. 1st pers. pl.

envistan 1. that they may invest; pres. subj. 3rd pers. pl. / *envestir.* 2. let them invest; impve. 3rd pers. pl.

envistas that you may invest; pres. subj. 2nd pers. sing. / *envestir.*

enviste 1. he (she/it) invests; pres. ind. 3rd pers. sing. / *envestir.* 2. (you) invest; impve. 2nd pers. sing.

envisten they invest; pres. ind. 3rd pers. pl. / *envestir.*

envistes you invest; pres. ind. 2nd pers. sing. / *envestir.*

envistiendo investing; pres. part. / *envestir.*

envistiera 1. that I might invest; imp. subj. 1st pers. sing. / *envestir.* 2. that he (she/it) might invest; imp. subj. 3rd pers. sing.

envistierais that you (all) might invest; imp. subj. 2nd pers pl. / *envestir.*

envistiéramos that we might invest; imp. subj. 1st pers. pl. / *envestir*.

envistieran that they might invest; imp. subj. 3rd pers. pl. / *envestir*.

envistieras that you might invest; imp. subj. 2nd pers. sing. / *envestir*.

envistieron they invested; past 3rd pers. pl. / *envestir*.

envistiese 1. that I might invest; imp. subj. 1st pers. sing. / *envestir*. 2. that he (she/it) might invest; imp. subj. 3rd pers. sing.

envistieseis that you (all) might invest; imp. subj. 2nd pers pl. / *envestir*.

envistiésemos that we might invest; imp. subj. 1st pers. pl. / *envistir*.

envistiesen that they might invest; imp. subj. 3rd pers. pl. / *envestir*.

envistieses that you might invest; imp. subj. 2nd pers. sing. / *envestir*.

envistió he (she/it) invested; past 3rd pers. sing. / *envestir*.

envisto I invest; pres. ind. 1st pers. sing. / *envestir*.

enviudar to be widowed. reg.

envolvámonos let us become involved; impve. 1st pers. pl. / *envolverse*.

envolveos (you all) become involved; impve. 2nd pers. pl. / *envolverse*.

envolver to wrap. irr.

envolverse to become involved. irr.

envolviéndose becoming involved; pres. part. / *envolverse*.

envuelto wrapped; past part. / *envolver*.

envuelva 1. that I may wrap; pres. subj. 1st pers. sing. / *envolver*. 2. that he (she/it) may wrap; pres. subj. 3rd pers. sing. 3. let him (her/it) wrap; impve. 3rd pers. sing.

envuelvan 1. that they may wrap; pres. subj. 3rd pers. pl. / *envolver*. 2. let them wrap; impve. 3rd pers. pl.

envuélvanse let them become involved; impve. 3rd pers. pl. / *envolverse*.

envuelvas that you may wrap; pres. subj. 2nd pers. sing. / *envolver*.

envuélvase let him (her/it) become involved; impve. 3rd pers. sing. / *envolverse*.

envuelve 1. he (she/it) wraps; pres. ind. 3rd pers. sing. / *envolver*. 2. (you) wrap; impve. 2nd pers. sing.

envuelven they wrap; pres. ind. 3rd pers. pl. / *envolver*.

envuelves you wrap; pres. ind. 2nd pers. sing. / *envolver*.

envuélvete (you) become involved; impve. 2nd pers. sing. / *envolverse*.

envuelvo I wrap; pres. ind. 1st pers. sing. / *envolver*.

enyesar to plaster. reg.

enyugar to yoke. irr.

enyugue 1. that I may yoke; pres. subj. 1st pers. sing. / *enyugar*. 2. that he (she/it) may yoke; pres. subj. 3rd pers. sing. 3. let him (her/it) yoke; impve. 3rd pers. sing.

enyugué I yoked; past 1st pers. sing. / *enyugar*.

enyuguéis that you (all) may yoke; pres. subj. 2nd pers. pl. / *enyugar*.

enyuguemos 1. that we may yoke; pres. subj. 1st pers. pl. / *enyugar*. 2. let us yoke; impve. 1st pers. pl.

enyuguen 1. that they may yoke; pres. subj. 3rd pers. pl. / *enyugar*. 2. let them yoke; impve. 3rd pers. pl.

enyugues that you may yoke; pres. subj. 2nd pers. sing. / *enyugar*.

enzainándose looking askanse; pres. part. / *enzainarse*.

enzainaos (you all) look askanse; impve. 2nd pers. pl. / *enzainarse*.

enzainarse to look askance. reg.

enzaínate (you) look askanse; impve. 2nd pers. sing. / *enzainarse*.

enzainémonos let us look askanse; impve. 1st pers. pl. / *enzainarse*.

enzaínense let them look askanse; impve. 3rd pers. pl. / *enzainarse*.

enzaínese let him (her/it) look askanse; impve. 3rd pers. sing. / *enzainarse*.

enzolvándose getting clogged; pres. part. / *enzolvarse*.

enzolvaos (you all) get clogged; impve. 2nd pers. pl. / *enzolvarse*.

enzolvar to clog. reg.

enzolvarse to get clogged. reg.

enzólvate (you) get clogged; impve. 2nd pers. sing. / *enzolvarse*.

enzolvémonos let us get clogged; impve. 1st pers. pl. / *enzolvarse*.

enzólvense let them get clogged; impve. 3rd pers. pl. / *enzolvarse*.

enzólvese let him (her/it) get clogged; impve. 3rd pers. sing. / *enzolvarse*.

enzunchar to bind with hoops. reg.

epilogar to sum up. irr.

epilogue 1. that I may sum up; pres. subj. 1st pers. sing. / *epilogar*. 2. that he (she/it) may sum up; pres. subj. 3rd pers. sing. 3. let him (her/it) sum up; impve. 3rd pers. sing.

epilogué I summed up; past 1st pers. sing. / *epilogar*.

epiloguéis that you (all) may sum up; pres. subj. 2nd pers. pl. / *epilogar*.

epiloguemos 1. that we may sum up; pres. subj. 1st pers. pl. / *epilogar*. 2. let us sum up; impve. 1st pers. pl.

epiloguen 1. that they may sum up; pres. subj. 3rd pers. pl. / *epilogar*. 2. let them sum up; impve. 3rd pers. pl.

epilogués that you may sum up; pres. subj. 2nd pers. sing. / *epilogar*.

epitomar to epitomize. reg.

equilibrándose counterbalancing; pres. part. / *equilibrarse*.

equilibraos (you all) counterbalance; impve. 2nd pers. pl. / *equilibrarse*.

equilibrar to balance. reg.

equilibrarse to counterbalance. reg.

equilíbrate (you) counterbalance; impve. 2nd pers. sing. / *equilibrarse.*

equilibrémonos let us counterbalance; impve. 1st pers. pl. / *equilibrarse.*

equilíbrense let them counterbalance; impve. 3rd pers. pl. / *equilibrarse.*

equilíbrese let him (her/it) counterbalance; impve. 3rd pers. sing. / *equilibrarse.*

equipar to equip. reg.

equiparar to compare. reg.

equival (you) be equivalent; impve. 2nd pers. sing. / *equivaler.*

equivaldrá he (she/it) will be equivalent; fut. 3rd pers. sing. / *equivaler.*

equivaldrán they will be equivalent; fut. 3rd pers. pl. / *equivaler.*

equivaldrás you will be equivalent; fut. 2nd pers. sing. / *equivaler.*

equivaldré I shall be equivalent; fut. 1st pers. sing. / *equivaler.*

equivaldréis you (all) will be equivalent; fut. 2nd pers. pl. / *equivaler.*

equivaldremos we shall be equivalent; fut. 1st pers. pl. / *equivaler.*

equivaldría 1. I should be equivalent; cond. 1st pers. sing. / *equivaler.* 2. he (she/it) would be equivalent; cond. 3rd pers. sing.

equivaldríais you (all) would be equivalent; cond. 2nd pers. pl. / *equivaler.*

equivaldríamos we should be equivalent; cond. 1st pers. pl. / *equivaler.*

equivaldrían they would be equivalent; cond. 3rd pers. pl. / *equivaler.*

equivaldrías you would be equivalent; cond. 2nd pers. sing. / *equivaler.*

equivaler to be equivalent. irr.

equivalga 1. that I may be equivalent; pres. subj. 1st pers. sing. / *equivaler.* 2. that he (she/it) may be equivalent; pres. subj. 3rd pers. sing. 3. let him (her/it) be equivalent; impve. 3rd pers. sing.

equivalgáis that you (all) may be equivalent; pres. subj. 2nd pers. pl. / *equivaler.*

equivalgamos 1. that we may be equivalent; pres. subj. 1st pers. pl. / *equivaler.* 2. let us be equivalent; impve. 1st pers. pl.

equivalgan 1. that they may be equivalent; pres. subj. 3rd pers. pl. / *equivaler.* 2. let them be equivalent; impve. 3rd pers. pl.

equivalgas that you may be equivalent; pres. subj. 2nd pers. sing. / *equivaler.*

equivalgo I am equivalent; pres. ind. 1st pers. sing. / *equivaler.*

equivocándose being mistaken; pres. part. / *equivocarse.*

equivocaos (you all) be mistaken; impve. 2nd pers. pl. / *equivocarse.*

equivocar to mistake. irr.

equivocarse to be mistaken. irr.

equivócate (you) be mistaken; impve. 2nd pers. sing. / *equivocarse.*

equivoque 1. that I may mistake; pres. subj. 1st pers. sing. / *equivocar.* 2. that he (she/it) may mistake; pres. subj. 3rd pers. sing. 3. let him (her/it) mistake; impve. 3rd pers. sing.

equivoqué I mistook; past 1st pers. sing. / *equivocar.*

equivoquéis that you (all) may mistake; pres. subj. 2nd pers. pl. / *equivocar.*

equivoquémonos let us be mistaken; impve. 1st pers. pl. / *equivocarse.*

equivoquemos 1. that we may mistake; pres. subj. 1st pers. pl. / *equivocar.* 2. let us mistake; impve. 1st pers. pl.

equivoquen 1. that they may mistake; pres. subj. 3rd pers. pl. / *equivocar.* 2. let them mistake; impve. 3rd pers. pl.

equivóquense let them be mistaken; impve. 3rd pers. pl. / *equivocarse.*

equivoques that you may mistake; pres. subj. 2nd pers. sing. / *equivocar.*

equivóquese let him (her/it) be mistaken; impve. 3rd pers. sing. / *equivocarse.*

era 1. I was being; imp. ind. 1st pers. sing. / *ser.* 2. he (she/it) was being; imp. ind. 3rd pers. sing.

eradicar to eradicate. irr.

eradique 1. that I may eradicate; pres. subj. 1st pers. sing. / *eradicar.* 2. that he (she/it) may eradicate; pres. subj. 3rd pers. sing. 3. let him (her/it) eradicate; impve. 3rd pers. sing.

eradiqué I eradicated; past 1st pers. sing. / *eradicar.*

eradiquéis that you (all) may eradicate; pres. subj. 2nd pers. pl. / *eradicar.*

eradiquemos 1. that we may eradicate; pres. subj. 1st pers. pl. / *eradicar.* 2. let us eradicate; impve. 1st pers. pl.

eradiquen 1. that they may eradicate; pres. subj. 3rd pers. pl. / *eradicar.* 2. let them eradicate; impve. 3rd pers. pl.

eradiques that you may eradicate; pres. subj. 2nd pers. sing. / *eradicar.*

erais you (all) were being; imp. ind. 2nd pers. pl. / *ser.*

éramos we were being; imp. ind. 1st pers. pl. / *ser.*

eran they were being; imp. ind. 3rd pers. pl. / *ser.*

eras you were being; imp. ind. 2nd pers. sing. / *ser.*

eres you be; pres. ind. 2nd pers. sing. / *ser.*

ergotice 1. that I may argue; pres. subj. 1st pers. sing. / *ergotizar.* 2. that he (she/it) may argue; pres. subj. 3rd pers. sing. 3. let him (her/it) argue; impve. 3rd pers. sing.

ergoticé I argued; past 1st pers. sing. / *ergotizar.*

ergoticéis that you (all) may argue; pres. subj. 2nd pers. pl. / *ergotizar.*

ergoticemos 1. that we may argue; pres. subj. 1st pers. pl. / *ergotizar.* 2. let us argue; impve. 1st pers. pl.

ergoticen 1. that they may argue; pres. subj. 3rd pers. pl. / *ergotizar.* 2. let them argue; impve. 3rd pers. pl.

ergotices that you may argue; pres. subj. 2nd pers. sing. / *ergotizar.*

ergotizar to argue. irr.

erguíos (you all) staighten; impve. 2nd pers. pl. / *erguirse*.

erguir to erect. irr.

erguirse to straighten. irr.

erice 1. that I may set on end; pres. subj. 1st pers. sing. / *erizar*. 2. that he (she/it) may set on end; pres. subj. 3rd pers. sing. 3. let him (her/it) set on end; impve. 3rd pers. sing.

ericé I set on end; past 1st pers. sing. / *erizar*.

ericéis that you (all) may set on end; pres. subj. 2nd pers. pl. / *erizar*.

ericémonos let us bristle; impve. 1st pers. pl. / *erizarse*.

ericemos 1. that we may set on end; pres. subj. 1st pers. pl. / *erizar*. 2. let us set on end; impve. 1st pers. pl.

ericen 1. that they may set on end; pres. subj. 3rd pers. pl. / *erizar*. 2. let them set on end; impve. 3rd pers. pl.

erícense let them bristle; impve. 3rd pers. pl. / *erizarse*.

erices that you may set on end; pres. subj. 2nd pers. sing. / *erizar*.

erícese let him (her/it) bristle; impve. 3rd pers. sing. / *erizarse*.

erigir to erect or to establish. irr.

erija 1. that I may erect; pres. subj. 1st pers. sing. / *erigir*. 2. that he (she/it) may erect; pres. subj. 3rd pers. sing. 3. let him (her/it) erect; impve. 3rd pers. sing.

erijáis that you (all) may erect; pres. subj. 2nd pers. pl. / *erigir*.

erijamos 1. that we may erect; pres. subj. 1st pers. pl. / *erigir*. 2. let us erect; impve. 1st pers. pl.

erijan 1. that they may erect; pres. subj. 3rd pers. pl. / *erigir*. 2. let them erect; impve. 3rd pers. pl.

erijas that you may erect; pres. subj. 2nd pers. sing. / *erigir*.

erijo I erect; pres. ind. 1st pers. sing. / *erigir*.

erizándose bristling; pres. part. / *erizarse*.

erizaos (you all) bristle; impve. 2nd pers. pl. / *erizarse*.

erizar to set on end. irr.

erizarse to bristle. irr.

erízate (you) bristle; impve. 2nd pers. sing. / *erizarse*.

erogar to divide. irr.

erogue 1. that I may divide; pres. subj. 1st pers. sing. / *erogar*. 2. that he (she/it) may divide; pres. subj. 3rd pers. sing. 3. let him (her/it) divide; impve. 3rd pers. sing.

erogué I divided; past 1st pers. sing. / *erogar*.

eroguéis that you (all) may divide; pres. subj. 2nd pers. pl. / *erogar*.

eroguemos 1. that we may divide; pres. subj. 1st pers. pl. / *erogar*. 2. let us divide; impve. 1st pers. pl.

eroguen 1. that they may divide; pres. subj. 3rd pers. pl. / *erogar*. 2. let them divide; impve. 3rd pers. pl.

erogues that you may divide; pres. subj. 2nd pers. sing. / *erogar*.

erradicar to eradicate. irr.

erradique 1. that I may eradicate; pres. subj. 1st pers. sing. / *erradicar*. 2. that he (she/it) may eradicate; pres. subj. 3rd pers. sing. 3. let him (her/it) eradicate; impve. 3rd pers. sing.

erradiqué I eradicated; past 1st pers. sing. / *erradicar*.

erradiquéis that you (all) may eradicate; pres. subj. 2nd pers. pl. / *erradicar*.

erradiquemos 1. that we may eradicate; pres. subj. 1st pers. pl. / *erradicar*. 2. let us eradicate; impve. 1st pers. pl.

erradiquen 1. that they may eradicate; pres. subj. 3rd pers. pl. / *erradicar*. 2. let them eradicate; impve. 3rd pers. pl.

erradiques that you may eradicate; pres. subj. 2nd pers. sing. / *erradicar*.

errándose wandering; pres. part. / *errarse*.

erraos (you all) wander; impve. 2nd pers. pl. / *errarse*.

errar to err or to miss. irr.

errarse to wander. irr.

errémonos let us wander; impve. 1st pers. pl. / *errarse*.

eructar to belch. reg.

erumpir to erupt. reg.

erutar to belch. reg.

es he (she/it) is; pres. ind. 3rd pers. sing. / *ser*.

esboce 1. that I may sketch; pres. subj. 1st pers. sing. / *esbozar*. 2. that he (she/it) may sketch; pres. subj. 3rd pers. sing. 3. let him (her/it) sketch; impve. 3rd pers. sing.

esbocé I sketched; past 1st pers. sing. / *esbozar*.

esbocéis that you (all) may sketch; pres. subj. 2nd pers. pl. / *esbozar*.

esbocemos 1. that we may sketch; pres. subj. 1st pers. pl. / *esbozar*. 2. let us sketch; impve. 1st pers. pl.

esbocen 1. that they may sketch; pres. subj. 3rd pers. pl. / *esbozar*. 2. let them sketch; impve. 3rd pers. pl.

esboces that you may sketch; pres. subj. 2nd pers. sing. / *esbozar*.

esbozar to sketch. irr.

escabechar to pickle. reg.

escabullámonos let us slip away; impve. 1st pers. pl. / *escabullirse*.

escabúllanse let them slip away; impve. 3rd pers. pl. / *escabullirse*.

escabúllase let him (her/it) slip away; impve. 3rd pers. sing. / *escabullirse*.

escabulléndose slipping away; pres. part. / *escabullirse*.

escabullera 1. that I might slip away; imp. subj. 1st pers. sing. / *escabullirse*. 2. that he (she/it) might slip away; imp. subj. 3rd pers. sing.

escabullerais that you (all) might slip away; imp. subj. 2nd pers pl. / *escabullirse*.

escabulléramos that we might slip away; imp. subj. 1st pers. pl. / *escabullirse*.

escabulleran that they might slip away; imp. subj. 3rd pers. pl. / *escabullirse*.

escabulleras that you might slip away; imp. subj. 2nd pers. sing. / *escabullirse*.

escabulleron they slipped away; past 3rd pers. pl. / *escabullirse*.

escabullese 1. that I might slip away; imp. subj. 1st pers. sing. / *escabullirse*. 2. that he (she/it) might slip away; imp. subj. 3rd pers. sing.

escabulleseis that you (all) might slip away; imp. subj. 2nd pers pl. / *escabullirse*.

escabullésemos that we might slip away; imp. subj. 1st pers. pl. / *escabullirse*.

escabullesen that they might slip away; imp. subj. 3rd pers. pl. / *escabullirse*.

escabulleses that you might slip away; imp. subj. 2nd pers. sing. / *escabullirse*.

escabúllete (you) slip away; impve. 2nd pers. sing. / *escabullirse*.

escabullirse to slip away or to escape. irr.

escabulló he (she/it) slipped away; past 3rd pers. sing. / *escabullirse*.

escabullos (you all) slip away; impve. 2nd pers. pl. / *escabullirse*.

escalar to climb. reg.

escaldándose being vexed; pres. part. / *escaldarse*.

escaldaos (you all) be vexed; impve. 2nd pers. pl. / *escaldarse*.

escaldar to scald. reg.

escaldarse to be vexed. reg.

escáldate (you) be vexed; impve. 2nd pers. sing. / *escaldarse*.

escaldémonos let us be vexed; impve. 1st pers. pl. / *escaldarse*.

escáldense let them be vexed; impve. 3rd pers. pl. / *escaldarse*.

escáldese let him (her/it) be vexed; impve. 3rd pers. sing. / *escaldarse*.

escalfar to poach (eggs). reg.

escalofría he (she/it) becomes chilled; pres. ind. 3rd pers. sing. / *escalofriarse*.

escalofrían they become chilled; pres. ind. 3rd pers. pl. / *escalofriarse*.

escalofriándose becoming chilled; pres. part. / *escalofriarse*.

escalofriaos (you all) become chilled; impve. 2nd pers. pl. / *escalofriarse*.

escalofriarse to become chilled. irr.

escalofrías you become chilled; pres. ind. 2nd pers. sing. / *escalofriarse*.

escalofríate (you) become chilled; impve. 2nd pers. sing. / *escalofriarse*.

escalofríe 1. that I may become chilled; pres. subj. 1st pers. sing. / *escalofriarse*. 2. that he (she/it) may become chilled; pres. subj. 3rd pers. sing.

escalofriémonos let us become chilled; impve. 1st pers. pl. / *escalofriarse*.

escalofríen that they may become chilled; pres. subj. 3rd pers. pl. / *escalofriarse*.

escalofríense let them become chilled; impve. 3rd pers. pl. / *escalofriarse*.

escalofríes that you may become chilled; pres. subj. 2nd pers. sing. / *escalofriarse*.

escalofríese let him (her/it) become chilled; impve. 3rd pers. sing. / *escalofriarse*.

escalofrío I become chilled; pres. ind. 1st pers. sing. / *escalofriarse*.

escalonándose rising in terraces; pres. part. / *escalonarse*.

escalonar to arrange in steps. reg.

escalonarse to rise in terraces. reg.

escalónense let them rise in terraces; impve. 3rd pers. pl. / *escalonarse*.

escalónese let it rise in terraces; impve. 3rd pers. sing. / *escalonarse*.

escalpar to scalp. reg.

escamándose becoming wary; pres. part. / *escamarse*.

escamaos (you all) become wary; impve. 2nd pers. pl. / *escamarse*.

escamar to scale (a fish). reg.

escamarse to become wary. reg.

escámate (you) become wary; impve. 2nd pers. sing. / *escamarse*.

escamémonos let us become wary; impve. 1st pers. pl. / *escamarse*.

escámense let them become wary; impve. 3rd pers. pl. / *escamarse*.

escámese let him (her/it) become wary; impve. 3rd pers. sing. / *escamarse*.

escamondar to prune. reg.

escamotar to whisk away. reg.

escamotear to palm away. reg.

escampar to clear or to stop raining. reg.

escanciar to pour out (wine). reg.

escandalice 1. that I may scandalize; pres. subj. 1st pers. sing. / *escandalizar*. 2. that he (she/it) may scandalize; pres. subj. 3rd pers. sing. 3. let him (her/it) scandalize; impve. 3rd pers. sing.

escandalicé I scandalized; past 1st pers. sing. / *escandalizar*.

escandalicéis that you (all) may scandalize; pres. subj. 2nd pers. pl. / *escandalizar*.

escandalicémonos let us be shocked; impve. 1st pers. pl. / *escandalizarse*.

escandalicemos 1. that we may scandalize; pres. subj. 1st pers. pl. / *escandalizar*. 2. let us scandalize; impve. 1st pers. pl.

escandalicen 1. that they may scandalize; pres. subj. 3rd pers. pl. / *escandalizar*. 2. let them scandalize; impve. 3rd pers. pl.

escandalícense let them be shocked; impve. 3rd pers. pl. / *escandalizarse*.

escandalices that you may scandalize; pres. subj. 2nd pers. sing. / *escandalizar*.

escandalícese let him (her/it) be shocked; impve. 3rd pers. sing. / *escandalizarse*.

escandalizándose being shocked; pres. part. / *escandalizarse*.

escandalizaos (you all) be shocked; impve. 2nd pers. pl. / *escandalizarse*.

escandalizar to scandalize. irr

escandalizarse to be shocked. irr.

escandalízate (you) be shocked; impve. 2nd pers. sing. / *escandalizarse*.

escandir to scan (verse). reg.

escantillar to gauge. reg.

escapándose running away; pres. part. / *escaparse*.

escapaos (you all) run away; impve. 2nd pers. pl. / *escaparse*.

escapar to escape. reg.

escaparse to run away. reg.

escápate (you) run away; impve. 2nd pers. sing. / *escaparse*.

escapémonos let us run away; impve. 1st pers. pl. / *escaparse*.

escápense let them run away; impve. 3rd pers. pl. / *escaparse*.

escápese let him (her/it) run away; impve. 3rd pers. sing. / *escaparse*.

escaramuce 1. that I may skirmish; pres. subj. 1st pers. sing. / *escaramuzar*. 2. that he (she/it) may skirmish; pres. subj. 3rd pers. sing. 3. let him (her/it) skirmish; impve. 3rd pers. sing.

escaramucé I skirmished; past 1st pers. sing. / *escaramuzar*.

escaramucear to skirmish. reg.

escaramucéis that you (all) may skirmish; pres. subj. 2nd pers. pl. / *escaramuzar*.

escaramucemos 1. that we may skirmish; pres. subj. 1st pers. pl. / *escaramuzar*. 2. let us skirmish; impve. 1st pers. pl.

escaramucen 1. that they may skirmish; pres. subj. 3rd pers. pl. / *escaramuzar*. 2. let them skirmish; impve. 3rd pers. pl.

escaramuces that you may skirmish; pres. subj. 2nd pers. sing. / *escaramuzar*.

escaramuzar to skirmish. irr.

escarbar to scrape. reg.

escarcear to prance. reg.

escarchar to freeze or to frost a cake. reg.

escardar to weed. reg.

escardillar to weed. reg.

escariar to ream. reg.

escarmentar to punish severely. irr.

escarmienta 1. he (she/it) punishes severely; pres. ind. 3rd pers. sing. / *escarmentar*. 2. (you) punish severely; impve. 2nd pers. sing.

escarmientan they punish severely; pres. ind. 3rd pers. pl. / *escarmentar*.

escarmientas you punish severely; pres. ind. 2nd pers. sing. / *escarmentar*.

escarmiente 1. that I may punish severely; pres. subj. 1st pers. sing. / *escarmentar*. 2. that he (she/it) may punish severely; pres. subj. 3rd pers. sing. 3. let him (her/it) punish severely; impve. 3rd pers. sing.

escarmienten 1. that they may punish severely; pres. subj. 3rd pers. pl. / *escarmentar*. 2. let them punish severely; impve. 3rd pers. pl.

escarmientes that you may punish severely; pres. subj. 2nd pers. sing. / *escarmentar*.

escarmiento I punish severely; pres. ind. 1st pers. sing. / *escarmentar*.

escarnecer to mock or to jeer. irr.

escarnezca 1. that I may mock; pres. subj. 1st pers. sing. / *escarnecer*. 2. that he (she/it) may mock; pres. subj. 3rd pers. sing. 3. let him (her/it) mock; impve. 3rd pers. sing.

escarnezcáis that you (all) may mock; pres. subj. 2nd pers. pl. / *escarnecer*.

escarnezcamos 1. that we may mock; pres. subj. 1st pers. pl. / *escarnecer*. 2. let us mock; impve. 1st pers. pl.

escarnezcan 1. that they may mock; pres. subj. 3rd pers. pl. / *escarnecer*. 2. let them mock; impve. 3rd pers. pl.

escarnezcas that you may mock; pres. subj. 2nd pers. sing. / *escarnecer*.

escarnezco I mock; pres. ind. 1st pers. sing. / *escarnecer*.

escasear to skimp on. reg.

escatimar to curtail. reg.

escayolar to put in plaster. reg.

escenificar to dramatize. irr.

escenifique 1. that I may dramatize; pres. subj. 1st pers. sing. / *escenificar*. 2. that he (she/it) may dramatize; pres. subj. 3rd pers. sing. 3. let him (her/it) dramatize; impve. 3rd pers. sing.

escenifiqué I dramatized; past 1st pers. sing. / *escenificar*.

escenifiquéis that you (all) may dramatize; pres. subj. 2nd pers. pl. / *escenificar*.

escenifiquemos 1. that we may dramatize; pres. subj. 1st pers. pl. / *escenificar*. 2. let us dramatize; impve. 1st pers. pl.

escenifiquen 1. that they may dramatize; pres. subj. 3rd pers. pl. / *escenificar*. 2. let them dramatize; impve. 3rd pers. pl.

escenifiques that you may dramatize; pres. subj. 2nd pers. sing. / *escenificar*.

esclarecer to illuminate. irr.

esclarezca 1. that I may illuminate; pres. subj. 1st pers. sing. / *esclarecer*. 2. that he (she/it) may illuminate; pres. subj. 3rd pers. sing. 3. let him (her/it) illuminate; impve. 3rd pers. sing.

esclarezcáis that you (all) may illuminate; pres. subj. 2nd pers. pl. / *esclarecer*.

esclarezcamos 1. that we may illuminate; pres. subj. 1st pers. pl. / *esclarecer*. 2. let us illuminate; impve. 1st pers. pl.

esclarezcan 1. that they may illuminate; pres. subj. 3rd pers. pl. / *esclarecer*. 2. let them illuminate; impve. 3rd pers. pl.

esclarezcas that you may illuminate; pres. subj. 2nd pers. sing. / *esclarecer*.

esclarezco I illuminate; pres. ind. 1st pers. sing. / *esclarecer*.

esclavice 1. that I may enslave; pres. subj. 1st pers. sing. / *esclavizar*. 2. that he (she/it) may enslave; pres. subj. 3rd pers. sing. 3. let him (her/it) enslave; impve. 3rd pers. sing.

esclavicé I enslaved; past 1st pers. sing. / *esclavizar*.

esclavicéis that you (all) may enslave; pres. subj. 2nd pers. pl. / *esclavizar*.

esclavicemos 1. that we may enslave; pres. subj. 1st pers. pl. / *esclavizar*. 2. let us enslave; impve. 1st pers. pl.

esclavicen 1. that they may enslave; pres. subj. 3rd pers. pl. / *esclavizar*. 2. let them enslave; impve. 3rd pers. pl.

esclavices that you may enslave; pres. subj. 2nd pers. sing. / *esclavizar*.

esclavizar to enslave. irr.

escobar to sweep. reg.

escobillar to brush. reg.

escocer to sting or to irritate. irr.

escoger to choose. irr.

escoja 1. that I may choose; pres. subj. 1st pers. sing. / *escoger*. 2. that he (she/it) may choose; pres. subj. 3rd pers. sing. 3. let him (her/it) choose; impve. 3rd pers. sing.

escojáis that you (all) may choose; pres. subj. 2nd pers. pl. / *escoger*.

escojamos 1. that we may choose; pres. subj. 1st pers. pl. / *escoger*. 2. let us choose; impve. 1st pers. pl.

escojan 1. that they may choose; pres. subj. 3rd pers. pl. / *escoger*. 2. let them choose; impve. 3rd pers. pl.

escojas that you may choose; pres. subj. 2nd pers. sing. / *escoger*.

escojo I choose; pres. ind. 1st pers. sing. / *escoger*.

escoltar to escort. reg.

escombrar to clean up. reg.

escondámonos let us hide; impve. 1st pers. pl. / *esconderse*.

escóndanse let them hide; impve. 3rd pers. pl. / *esconderse*.

escóndase let him (her/it) hide; impve. 3rd pers. sing. / *esconderse*.

escondeos (you all) hide; impve. 2nd pers. pl. / *esconderse*.

esconder to conceal. reg.

esconderse to hide. reg.

escóndete (you) hide; impve. 2nd pers. sing. / *esconderse*.

escondiéndose hiding; pres. part. / *esconderse*.

escorar to prop or to list (boat). reg.

escorce 1. that I may foreshorten; pres. subj. 1st pers. sing. / *escorzar*. 2. that he (she/it) may foreshorten; pres. subj. 3rd pers. sing. 3. let him (her/it) foreshorten; impve. 3rd pers. sing.

escorcé I foreshortened; past 1st pers. sing. / *escorzar*.

escorcéis that you (all) may foreshorten; pres. subj. 2nd pers. pl. / *escorzar*.

escorcemos 1. that we may foreshorten; pres. subj. 1st pers. pl. / *escorzar*. 2. let us foreshorten; impve. 1st pers. pl.

escorcen 1. that they may foreshorten; pres. subj. 3rd pers. pl. / *escorzar*. 2. let them foreshorten; impve. 3rd pers. pl.

escorces that you may foreshorten; pres. subj. 2nd pers. sing. / *escorzar*.

escorchar to flay (hides). reg.

escorzar to foreshorten. irr.

escotar to cut to fit. reg.

escozáis that you (all) may sting; pres. subj. 2nd pers. pl. / *escocer*.

escozamos 1. that we may sting; pres. subj. 1st pers. pl. / *escocer*. 2. let us sting; impve. 1st pers. pl.

escribámonos let us carry on correspondence; impve. 1st pers. pl. / *escribirse*.

escríbanse let them carry on correspondence; impve. 3rd pers. pl. / *escribirse*.

escríbase let him (her/it) carry on correspondence; impve. 3rd pers. sing. / *escribirse*.

escríbete (you) carry on correspondence; impve. 2nd pers. sing. / *escribirse*.

escribiéndose carrying on correspondence; pres. part. / *escribirse*.

escribíos (you all) carry on correspondence; impve. 2nd pers. pl. / *escribirse*.

escribir to write. reg. except for pp.

escribirse to carry on correspondence. reg.

escrito written; past part. / *escribir*.

escrupulice 1. that I may scruple; pres. subj. 1st pers. sing. / *escrupulizar*. 2. that he (she/it) may scruple; pres. subj. 3rd pers. sing. 3. let him (her/it) scruple; impve. 3rd pers. sing.

escrupulicé I scrupled; past 1st pers. sing. / *escrupulizar*.

escrupulicéis that you (all) may scruple; pres. subj. 2nd pers. pl. / *escrupulizar*.

escrupulicemos 1. that we may scruple; pres. subj. 1st pers. pl. / *escrupulizar*. 2. let us scruple; impve. 1st pers. pl.

escrupulicen 1. that they may scruple; pres. subj. 3rd pers. pl. / *escrupulizar*. 2. let them scruple; impve. 3rd pers. pl.

escrupulices that you may scruple; pres. subj. 2nd pers. sing. / *escrupulizar*.

escrupulizar to scruple. irr.

escrutar to scrutinize or to count votes. reg.

escuchándose speaking with affectation; pres. part. / *escucharse*.

escuchaos (you all) speak with affectation; impve. 2nd pers. pl. / *escucharse*.

escuchar to listen. reg.

escucharse to speak with affectation. reg.

escúchate (you) speak with affectation; impve. 2nd pers. sing. / *escucharse*.

escuchémonos let us speak with affectation; impve. 1st pers. pl. / *escucharse*.

escúchense let them speak with affectation; impve. 3rd pers. pl. / *escucharse*.

escúchese let him (her/it) speak with affectation; impve. 3rd pers. sing. / *escucharse*.

escudar to shield. reg.

escudriñar to scrutinize. reg.

escuece 1. he (she/it) stings; pres. ind. 3rd pers. sing. / *escocer*. 2. (you) sting; impve. 2nd pers. sing.

escuecen they sting; pres. ind. 3rd pers. pl. / *escocer*.

escueces you sting; pres. ind. 2nd pers. sing. / *escocer*.

escueza 1. that I may sting; pres. subj. 1st pers. sing. / *escocer.* 2. that he (she/it) may sting; pres. subj. 3rd pers. sing. 3. let him (her/it) sting; impve. 3rd pers. sing.

escuezan 1. that they may sting; pres. subj. 3rd pers. pl. / *escocer.* 2. let them sting; impve. 3rd pers. pl.

escuezas that you may sting; pres. subj. 2nd pers. sing. / *escocer.*

escuezo I sting; pres. ind. 1st pers. sing. / *escocer.*

esculcar to search. irr.

esculpir to sculpture. reg.

esculque 1. that I may search; pres. subj. 1st pers. sing. / *esculcar.* 2. that he (she/it) may search; pres. subj. 3rd pers. sing. 3. let him (her/it) search; impve. 3rd pers. sing.

esculqué I searched; past 1st pers. sing. / *esculcar.*

esculquéis that you (all) may search; pres. subj. 2nd pers. pl. / *esculcar.*

esculquemos 1. that we may search; pres. subj. 1st pers. pl. / *esculcar.* 2. let us search; impve. 1st pers. pl.

esculquen 1. that they may search; pres. subj. 3rd pers. pl. / *esculcar.* 2. let them search; impve. 3rd pers. pl.

esculques that you may search; pres. subj. 2nd pers. sing. / *esculcar.*

escullámonos let us slip away; impve. 1st pers. pl. / *escullirse.*

escúllanse let them slip away; impve. 3rd pers. pl. / *escullirse.*

escúllase let him (her/it) slip away; impve. 3rd pers. sing. / *escullirse.*

escúllete (you) slip away; impve. 2nd pers. sing. / *escullirse.*

esculliéndose slipping away; pres. part. / *escullirse.*

escullíos (you all) slip away; impve. 2nd pers. pl. / *escullirse.*

escullirse to slip away. reg.

escupir to spit. reg.

escúrranse let them ooze out; impve. 3rd pers. pl. / *escurrirse.*

escúrrase let it ooze out; impve. 3rd pers. sing. / *escurrirse.*

escurriéndose oozing out; pres. part. / *escurrirse.*

escurrir to drain or to drip. reg.

escurrirse to ooze out. reg.

esforcé I strengthened; past 1st pers. sing. / *esforzar.*

esforcéis that you (all) may strengthen; pres. subj. 2nd pers. pl. / *esforzar.*

esforcémonos let us try hard; impve. 1st pers. pl. / *esforzarse.*

esforcemos 1. that we may strengthen; pres. subj. 1st pers. pl. / *esforzar.* 2. let us strengthen; impve. 1st pers. pl.

esforzándose trying hard; pres. part. / *esforzarse.*

esforzaos (you all) try hard; impve. 2nd pers. pl. / *esforzarse.*

esforzar to strengthen. irr.

esforzarse to try hard. irr.

esfuerce 1. that I may strengthen; pres. subj. 1st pers. sing. / *esforzar.* 2. that he (she/it) may strengthen; pres. subj. 3rd pers. sing. 3. let him (her/it) strengthen; impve. 3rd pers. sing.

esfuercen 1. that they may strengthen; pres. subj. 3rd pers. pl. / *esforzar.* 2. let them strengthen; impve. 3rd pers. pl.

esfuércense let them try hard; impve. 3rd pers. pl. / *esforzarse.*

esfuerces that you may strengthen; pres. subj. 2nd pers. sing. / *esforzar.*

esfuércese let him (her/it) try hard; impve. 3rd pers. sing. / *esforzarse.*

esfuerza 1. he (she/it) strengthens; pres. ind. 3rd pers. sing. / *esforzar.* 2. (you) strengthen; impve. 2nd pers. sing.

esfuerzan they strengthen; pres. ind. 3rd pers. pl. / *esforzar.*

esfuerzas you strengthen; pres. ind. 2nd pers. sing. / *esforzar.*

esfuérzate (you) try hard; impve. 2nd pers. sing. / *esforzarse.*

esfuerzo I strengthen; pres. ind. 1st pers. sing. / *esforzar.*

esfumándose vanishing; pres. part. / *esfumarse.*

esfumaos (you all) vanish; impve. 2nd pers. pl. / *esfumarse.*

esfumar to shade or to blur. reg.

esfumarse to vanish. reg.

esfúmate (you) vanish; impve. 2nd pers. sing. / *esfumarse.*

esfumémonos let us vanish; impve. 1st pers. pl. / *esfumarse.*

esfúmense let them vanish; impve. 3rd pers. pl. / *esfumarse.*

esfúmese let him (her/it) vanish; impve. 3rd pers. sing. / *esfumarse.*

esgrimir to fence or to wield. reg.

eslabonar to link. reg.

esmaltar to enamel. reg.

esmerándose striving; pres. part. / *esmerarse.*

esmeraos (you all) strive; impve. 2nd pers. pl. / *esmerarse.*

esmerar to polish. reg.

esmerarse to strive. reg.

esmérate (you) strive; impve. 2nd pers. sing. / *esmerarse.*

esmerémonos let us strive; impve. 1st pers. pl. / *esmerarse.*

esmérense let them strive; impve. 3rd pers. pl. / *esmerarse.*

esmérese let him (her/it) strive; impve. 3rd pers. sing. / *esmerarse.*

esmerilar to burnish. reg.

espabilándose looking lively; pres. part. / *espabilarse.*

espabilaos (you all) look lively; impve. 2nd pers. pl. / *espabilarse.*

espabilar to snuff (a candle). reg.

espabilarse to look lively. reg.

espabílate (you) look lively; impve. 2nd pers. sing. / *espabilarse.*

espabilémonos let us look lively; impve. 1st pers. pl. / *espabilarse.*

espabílense let them look lively; impve. 3rd pers. pl. / *espabilarse.*

espabílese let him (her/it) look lively; impve. 3rd pers. sing. / *espabilarse.*

espacía 1.he (she/it) spaces out; pres. ind. 3rd pers. sing. / *espaciar.* 2. (you) space out; impve. 2nd pers. sing.

espacían they space out; pres. ind. 3rd pers. pl. / *espaciar.*

espaciándose relaxing; pres. part. / *espaciarse.*

espaciaos (you all) relax; impve. 2nd pers. pl. / *espaciarse.*

espaciar to space out. reg.

espaciarse to relax. reg.

espacías you space out; pres. ind. 2nd pers. sing. / *espaciar.*

espacíate (you) relax; impve. 2nd pers. sing. / *espaciarse.*

espacíe 1. that I may space out; pres. subj. 1st pers. sing. / *espaciar.* 2. that he (she/it) may space out; pres. subj. 3rd pers. sing. 3. let him (her/it) space out; impve. 3rd pers. sing.

espaciémonos let us relax; impve. 1st pers. pl. / *espaciarse.*

espacíen 1. that they may space out; pres. subj. 3rd pers. pl. / *espaciar.* 2. let them space out; impve. 3rd pers. pl.

espacíense let them relax; impve. 3rd pers. pl. / *espaciarse.*

espacíes that you may space out; pres. subj. 2nd pers. sing. / *espaciar.*

espacíese let him (her/it) relax; impve. 3rd pers. sing. / *espaciarse.*

espacío I space out; pres. ind. 1st pers. sing. / *espaciar.*

espantándose being astonished; pres. part. / *espantarse.*

espantaos (you all) be astonished; impve. 2nd pers. pl. / *espantarse.*

espantar to frighten. reg.

espantarse to be astonished. reg.

espántate (you) be astonished; impve. 2nd pers. sing. / *espantarse.*

espantémonos let us be astonished; impve. 1st pers. pl. / *espantarse.*

espántense let them be astonished; impve. 3rd pers. pl. / *espantarse.*

espántese let him (her/it) be astonished; impve. 3rd pers. sing. / *espantarse.*

espárcete (you) amuse yourself; impve. 2nd pers. sing. / *esparcirse.*

esparciéndose amusing oneself; pres. part. / *esparcirse.*

esparcíos (you all) amuse yourselves; impve. 2nd pers. pl. / *esparcirse.*

esparcir to scatter. irr.

esparcirse to amuse oneself. irr.

esparza 1. that I may scatter; pres. subj. 1st pers. sing. / *esparcir.* 2. that he (she/it) may scatter; pres. subj. 3rd pers. sing. 3. let him (her/it) scatter; impve. 3rd pers. sing.

esparzáis that you (all) may scatter; pres. subj. 2nd pers. pl. / *esparcir.*

esparzámonos let us amuse ourselves; impve. 1st pers. pl. / *esparcirse.*

esparzamos 1. that we may scatter; pres. subj. 1st pers. pl. / *esparcir.* 2. let us scatter; impve. 1st pers. pl.

esparzan 1. that they may scatter; pres. subj. 3rd pers. pl. / *esparcir.* 2. let them scatter; impve. 3rd pers. pl.

espárzanse let them amuse themselves; impve. 3rd pers. pl. / *esparcirse.*

esparzas that you may scatter; pres. subj. 2nd pers. sing. / *esparcir.*

espárzase let him (her/it) amuse himself (herself/itself); impve. 3rd pers. sing. / *esparcirse.*

esparzo I scatter; pres. ind. 1st pers. sing. / *esparcir.*

especialice 1. that I may specialize; pres. subj. 1st pers. sing. / *especializar.* 2. that he (she/it) may specialize; pres. subj. 3rd pers. sing. 3. let him (her/it) specialize; impve. 3rd pers. sing.

especialicé I specialized; past 1st pers. sing. / *especializar.*

especialicéis that you (all) may specialize; pres. subj. 2nd pers. pl. / *especializar.*

especialicémonos let us specialize; impve. 1st pers. pl. / *especializarse.*

especialicemos 1. that we may specialize; pres. subj. 1st pers. pl. / *especializar.* 2. let us specialize; impve. 1st pers. pl.

especialicen 1. that they may specialize; pres. subj. 3rd pers. pl. / *especializar.* 2. let them specialize; impve. 3rd pers. pl.

especialícense let them specialize; impve. 3rd pers. pl. / *especializarse.*

especialices that you may specialize; pres. subj. 2nd pers. sing. / *especializar.*

especialícese let him (her/it) specialize; impve. 3rd pers. sing. / *especializarse.*

especializándose specializing; pres. part. / *especializarse.*

especializaos (you all) specialize; impve. 2nd pers. pl. / *especializarse.*

especializar to specialize. irr.

especializarse to specialize. irr.

especialízate (you) specialize; impve. 2nd pers. sing. / *especializarse.*

especiar to spice. reg.

especificar to specify. irr.

especifique 1. that I may specify; pres. subj. 1st pers. sing. / *especificar.* 2. that he (she/it) may specify; pres. subj. 3rd pers. sing. 3. let him (her/it) specify; impve. 3rd pers. sing.

especifiqué I specified; past 1st pers. sing. / *especificar.*

especifiquéis that you (all) may specify; pres. subj. 2nd pers. pl. / *especificar.*

especifiquemos 1. that we may specify; pres. subj. 1st pers. pl. / *especificar.* 2. let us specify; impve. 1st pers. pl.

especifiquen 1. that they may specify; pres. subj. 3rd pers. pl. / *especificar.* 2. let them specify; impve. 3rd pers. pl.

especifiques that you may specify; pres. subj. 2nd pers. sing. / *especificar.*

especular to speculate. reg.

espeluznándose being terrified; pres. part. / *espeluznarse.*

espeluznaos (you all) be terrified; impve. 2nd pers. pl. / *espeluznarse.*

espeluznar to terrify. reg.

espeluznarse to be terrified. reg.

espelúznate (you) be terrified; impve. 2nd pers. sing. / *espeluznarse.*

espeluznémonos let us be terrified; impve. 1st pers. pl. / *espeluznarse.*

espelúznense let them be terrified; impve. 3rd pers. pl. / *espeluznarse.*

espelúznese let him (her/it) be terrified; impve. 3rd pers. sing. / *espeluznarse.*

esperance 1. that I may give hope; pres. subj. 1st pers. sing. / *esperanzar.* 2. that he (she/it) may give hope; pres. subj. 3rd pers. sing. 3. let him (her/it) give hope; impve. 3rd pers. sing.

esperancé I gave hope; past 1st pers. sing. / *esperanzar.*

esperancéis that you (all) may give hope; pres. subj. 2nd pers. pl. / *esperanzar.*

esperancemos 1. that we may give hope; pres. subj. 1st pers. pl. / *esperanzar.* 2. let us give hope; impve. 1st pers. pl.

esperancen 1. that they may give hope; pres. subj. 3rd pers. pl. / *esperanzar.* 2. let them give hope; impve. 3rd pers. pl.

esperances that you may give hope; pres. subj. 2nd pers. sing. / *esperanzar.*

esperándose waiting; pres. part. / *esperarse.*

esperanzar to give hope. irr.

esperaos (you all) wait; impve. 2nd pers. pl. / *esperarse.*

esperar to hope. reg.

esperarse to wait. reg.

espérate (you) wait; impve. 2nd pers. sing. / *esperarse.*

esperece 1. that I may stretch; pres. subj. 1st pers. sing. / *esperezarse.* 2. that he (she/it) may stretch; pres. subj. 3rd pers. sing.

esperecé I stretched; past 1st pers. sing. / *esperezarse.*

esperecéis that you (all) may stretch; pres. subj. 2nd pers. pl. / *esperezarse.*

esperecémonos let us stretch; impve. 1st pers. pl. / *esperezarse.*

esperecemos that we may stretch; pres. subj. 1st pers. pl. / *esperezarse.*

esperecen that they may stretch; pres. subj. 3rd pers. pl. / *esperezarse.*

esperécense let them stretch; impve. 3rd pers. pl. / *esperezarse.*

espereces that you may stretch; pres. subj. 2nd pers. sing. / *esperezarse.*

esperécese let him (her/it) stretch; impve. 3rd pers. sing. / *esperezarse.*

esperémonos let us wait; impve. 1st pers. pl. / *esperarse.*

espérense let them wait; impve. 3rd pers. pl. / *esperarse.*

espérese let him (her/it) wait; impve. 3rd pers. sing. / *esperarse.*

esperezándose stretching; pres. part. / *esperezarse.*

esperezaos (you all) stretch; impve. 2nd pers. pl. / *esperezarse.*

esperezarse to stretch (one's arms and legs). irr.

esperézate (you) stretch; impve. 2nd pers. sing. / *esperezarse.*

espesándose becoming thick; pres. part. / *espesarse.*

espesaos (you all) become thick; impve. 2nd pers. pl. / *espesarse.*

espesar to thicken. reg.

espesarse to become thick. reg.

espésate (you) become thick; impve. 2nd pers. sing. / *espesarse.*

espesémonos let us become thick; impve. 1st pers. pl. / *espesarse.*

espésense let them become thick; impve. 3rd pers. pl. / *espesarse.*

espésese let him (her/it) become thick; impve. 3rd pers. sing. / *espesarse.*

espetándose becoming stiff; pres. part. / *espetarse.*

espetaos (you all) become stiff; impve. 2nd pers. pl. / *espetarse.*

espetar to spit or to skewer. reg.

espetarse to become stiff or formal. reg.

espétate (you) become stiff; impve. 2nd pers. sing. / *espetarse.*

espetémonos let us become stiff; impve. 1st pers. pl. / *espetarse.*

espétense let them become stiff; impve. 3rd pers. pl. / *espetarse.*

espétese let him (her/it) become stiff; impve. 3rd pers. sing. / *espetarse.*

espía 1. he (she/it) spies; pres. ind. 3rd pers. sing. / *espiar.* 2. (you) spy; impve. 2nd pers. sing.

espían they spy; pres. ind. 3rd pers. pl. / *espiar.*

espiándose getting lame (horses); pres. part. / *espiarse.*

espiar to spy. irr.

espiarse to get lame (horses). irr.

espías you spy; pres. ind. 2nd pers. sing. / *espiar.*

espichar to prick or to die. reg.

espíe 1. that I may spy; pres. subj. 1st pers. sing. / *espiar.* 2. that he (she/it) may spy; pres. subj. 3rd pers. sing. 3. let him (her/it) spy; impve. 3rd pers. sing.

espíen 1. that they may spy; pres. subj. 3rd pers. pl. / *espiar.* 2. let them spy; impve. 3rd pers. pl.

espíense let them get lame (horses); impve. 3rd pers. pl. / *espiarse.*

espíes that you may spy; pres. subj. 2nd pers. sing. / *espiar.*

espíese let it get lame (horse); impve. 3rd pers. sing. / *espiarse.*

espigándose growing tall; pres. part. / *espigarse.*

espigaos (you all) grow tall; impve. 2nd pers. pl. / *espigarse.*

espigar to glean. irr.

espigarse to grow tall. irr.

espígate (you) grow tall; impve. 2nd pers. sing. / *espigarse.*

espigue 1. that I may glean; pres. subj. 1st pers. sing. / *espigar.* 2. that he (she/it) may glean; pres. subj. 3rd pers. sing. 3. let him (her/it) glean; impve. 3rd pers. sing.

espigué I gleaned; past 1st pers. sing. / *espigar.*

espiguéis that you (all) may glean; pres. subj. 2nd pers. pl. / *espigar.*

espiguémonos let us grow tall; impve. 1st pers. pl. / *espigarse.*

espiguemos 1. that we may glean; pres. subj. 1st pers. pl. / *espigar.* 2. let us glean; impve. 1st pers. pl.

espiguen 1. that they may glean; pres. subj. 3rd pers. pl. / *espigar.* 2. let them glean; impve. 3rd pers. pl.

espíguense let them grow tall; impve. 3rd pers. pl. / *espigarse.*

espigues that you may glean; pres. subj. 2nd pers. sing. / *espigar.*

espíguese let him (her/it) grow tall; impve. 3rd pers. sing. / *espigarse.*

espinar to prick. reg.

espío I spy; pres. ind. 1st pers. sing. / *espiar.*

espirar to exhale or to expire. reg.

espiritándose getting agitated; pres. part. / *espiritarse.*

espiritaos (you all) get agitated; impve. 2nd pers. pl. / *espiritarse.*

espiritar to possess with the devil. reg.

espiritarse to get agitated. reg.

espirítate (you) get agitated; impve. 2nd pers. sing. / *espiritarse.*

espiritémonos let us get agitated; impve. 1st pers. pl. / *espiritarse.*

espirítense let them get agitated; impve. 3rd pers. pl. / *espiritarse.*

espirítese let him (her/it) get agitated; impve. 3rd pers. sing. / *espiritarse.*

espitar to tap (a barrel). reg.

espolear to spur. reg.

espolvorear to powder. reg.

esponjándose swelling with pride; pres. part. / *esponjarse.*

esponjaos (you all) swell with pride; impve. 2nd pers. pl. / *esponjarse.*

esponjar to make spongy. reg.

esponjarse to swell with pride. reg.

espónjate (you) swell with pride; impve. 2nd pers. sing. / *esponjarse.*

esponjémonos let us swell with pride; impve. 1st pers. pl. / *esponjarse.*

espónjense let them swell with pride; impve. 3rd pers. pl. / *esponjarse.*

espónjese let him (her/it) swell with pride; impve. 3rd pers. sing. / *esponjarse.*

espontaneándose owning up; pres. part. / *espontanearse.*

espontaneaos (you all) own up; impve. 2nd pers. pl. / *espontanearse.*

espontanearse to own up. reg.

espontanéate (you) own up; impve. 2nd pers. sing. / *espontanearse.*

espontaneémonos let us own up; impve. 1st pers. pl. / *espontanearse.*

espontanéense let them own up; impve. 3rd pers. pl. / *espontanearse.*

espontanéese let him (her/it) own up; impve. 3rd pers. sing. / *espontanearse.*

espulgar to delouse. irr.

espulgue 1. that I may delouse; pres. subj. 1st pers. sing. / *espulgar.* 2. that he (she/it) may delouse; pres. subj. 3rd pers. sing. 3. let him (her/it) delouse; impve. 3rd pers. sing.

espulgué I deloused; past 1st pers. sing. / *espulgar.*

espulguéis that you (all) may delouse; pres. subj. 2nd pers. pl. / *espulgar.*

espulguemos 1. that we may delouse; pres. subj. 1st pers. pl. / *espulgar.* 2. let us delouse; impve. 1st pers. pl.

espulguen 1. that they may delouse; pres. subj. 3rd pers. pl. / *espulgar.* 2. let them delouse; impve. 3rd pers. pl.

espulgues that you may delouse; pres. subj. 2nd pers. sing. / *espulgar.*

espumar to skim. reg.

esputar to expectorate. reg.

esquía 1. he (she/it) skis; pres. ind. 3rd pers. sing. / *esquiar.* 2. (you) ski; impve. 2nd pers. sing.

esquían they ski; pres. ind. 3rd pers. pl. / *esquiar.*

esquiar to ski. irr.

esquías you ski; pres. ind. 2nd pers. sing. / *esquiar.*

esquiciar to sketch. reg.

esquíe 1. that I may ski; pres. subj. 1st pers. sing. / *esquiar.* 2. that he (she/it) may ski; pres. subj. 3rd pers. sing. 3. let him (her/it) ski; impve. 3rd pers. sing.

esquíen 1. that they may ski; pres. subj. 3rd pers. pl. / *esquiar.* 2. let them ski; impve. 3rd pers. pl.

esquíes that you may ski; pres. subj. 2nd pers. sing. / *esquiar.*

esquilar to shear. reg.

esquilmar to harvest or to impoverish. reg.

esquío I ski; pres. ind. 1st pers. sing. / *esquiar.*

esquivándose withdrawing; pres. part. / *esquivarse.*

esquivaos (you all) withdraw; impve. 2nd pers. pl. / *esquivarse.*

esquivar to avoid. reg.

esquivarse to withdraw. reg.

esquívate (you) withdraw; impve. 2nd pers. sing. / *esquivarse.*

esquivémonos let us withdraw; impve. 1st pers. pl. / *esquivarse.*

esquívense let them withdraw; impve. 3rd pers. pl. / *esquivarse.*

esquívese let him (her/it) withdraw; impve. 3rd pers. sing. / *esquivarse.*

está he (she/it) is; pres. ind. 3rd pers. sing. / *estar.*

estabilice 1. that I may stabilize; pres. subj. 1st pers. sing. / *estabilizar.* 2. that he (she/it) may stabilize; pres. subj. 3rd pers. sing. 3. let him (her/it) stabilize; impve. 3rd pers. sing.

estabilicé I stabilized; past 1st pers. sing. / *estabilizar.*

estabilicéis that you (all) may stabilize; pres. subj. 2nd pers. pl. / *estabilizar.*

estabilicemos 1. that we may stabilize; pres. subj. 1st pers. pl. / *estabilizar.* 2. let us stabilize; impve. 1st pers. pl.

estabilicen 1. that they may stabilize; pres. subj. 3rd pers. pl. / *estabilizar.* 2. let them stabilize; impve. 3rd pers. pl.

estabilices that you may stabilize; pres. subj. 2nd pers. sing. / *estabilizar.*

estabilizar to stabilize. irr.

estableceos (you all) settle; impve. 2nd pers. pl. / *establecerse.*

establecer to establish. irr.

establecerse to settle. irr.

establécete (you) settle; impve. 2nd pers. sing. / *establecerse.*

estableciéndose settling; pres. part. / *establecerse.*

establezca 1. that I may establish; pres. subj. 1st pers. sing. / *establecer.* 2. that he (she/it) may establish; pres. subj. 3rd pers. sing. 3. let him (her/it) establish; impve. 3rd pers. sing.

establezcáis that you (all) may establish; pres. subj. 2nd pers. pl. / *establecer.*

establezcámonos let us settle; impve. 1st pers. pl. / *establecerse.*

establezcamos 1. that we may establish; pres. subj. 1st pers. pl. / *establecer.* 2. let us establish; impve. 1st pers. pl.

establezcan 1. that they may establish; pres. subj. 3rd pers. pl. / *establecer.* 2. let them establish; impve. 3rd pers. pl.

establézcanse let them settle; impve. 3rd pers. pl. / *establecerse.*

establezcas that you may establish; pres. subj. 2nd pers. sing. / *establecer.*

establézcase let him (her/it) settle; impve. 3rd pers. sing. / *establecerse.*

establezco I establish; pres. ind. 1st pers. sing. / *establecer.*

estacándose remaining stiff; pres. part. / *estacarse.*

estacaos (you all) remain stiff; impve. 2nd pers. pl. / *estacarse.*

estacar to stake. irr.

estacarse to remain stiff. irr.

estácate (you) remain stiff; impve. 2nd pers. sing. / *estacarse.*

estacionándose parking; pres. part. / *estacionarse.*

estacionaos (you all) park; impve. 2nd pers. pl. / *estacionarse.*

estacionar to station or to place. reg.

estacionarse to park. reg.

estaciónate (you) park; impve. 2nd pers. sing. / *estacionarse.*

estacionémonos let us park; impve. 1st pers. pl. / *estacionarse.*

estaciónense let them park; impve. 3rd pers. pl. / *estacionarse.*

estaciónese let him (her/it) park; impve. 3rd pers. sing. / *estacionarse.*

estafar to swindle. reg.

estallar to explode. reg.

estampar to stamp or to print. reg.

están they are; pres. ind. 3rd pers. pl. / *estar.*

estancándose becoming stagnant; pres. part. / *estancarse.*

estancaos (you all) become stagnant; impve. 2nd pers. pl. / *estancarse.*

estancar to stop. irr.

estancarse to become stagnant. irr.

estáncate (you) become stagnant; impve. 2nd pers. sing. / *estancarse.*

estandardice 1. that I may standardize; pres. subj. 1st pers. sing. / *estandardizar.* 2. that he (she/it) may standardize; pres. subj. 3rd pers. sing. 3. let him (her/it) standardize; impve. 3rd pers. sing.

estandardicé I standardized; past 1st pers. sing. / *estandardizar.*

estandardicéis that you (all) may standardize; pres. subj. 2nd pers. pl. / *estandardizar.*

estandardicemos 1. that we may standardize; pres. subj. 1st pers. pl. / *estandardizar.* 2. let us standardize; impve. 1st pers. pl.

estandardicen 1. that they may standardize; pres. subj. 3rd pers. pl. / *estandardizar.* 2. let them standardize; impve. 3rd pers. pl.

estandardices that you may standardize; pres. subj. 2nd pers. sing. / *estandardizar.*

estandardizar to standardize. irr.

estandarice 1. that I may standardize; pres. subj. 1st pers. sing. / *estandarizar.* 2. that he (she/it) may standardize; pres. subj. 3rd pers. sing. 3. let him (her/it) standardize; impve. 3rd pers. sing.

estandaricé I standardized; past 1st pers. sing. / *estandarizar.*

estandaricéis that you (all) may standardize; pres. subj. 2nd pers. pl. / *estandarizar.*

estandaricemos 1. that we may standardize; pres. subj. 1st pers. pl. / *estandarizar.* 2. let us standardize; impve. 1st pers. pl.

estandaricen 1. that they may standardize; pres. subj. 3rd pers. pl. / *estandarizar.* 2. let them standardize; impve. 3rd pers. pl.

estandarices that you may standardize; pres. subj. 2nd pers. sing. / *estandarizar.*

estandarizar to standardize. irr.

estándose remaining; pres. part. / *estarse.*

estanque 1. that I may stop; pres. subj. 1st pers. sing. / *estancar*. 2. that he (she/it) may stop; pres. subj. 3rd pers. sing. 3. let him (her/it) stop; impve. 3rd pers. sing.

estanqué I stopped; past 1st pers. sing. / *estancar*.

estanquéis that you (all) may stop; pres. subj. 2nd pers. pl. / *estancar*.

estanquémonos let us become stagnant; impve. 1st pers. pl. / *estancarse*.

estanquemos 1. that we may stop; pres. subj. 1st pers. pl. / *estancar*. 2. let us stop; impve. 1st pers. pl.

estanquen 1. that they may stop; pres. subj. 3rd pers. pl. / *estancar*. 2. let them stop; impve. 3rd pers. pl.

estánquense let them become stagnant; impve. 3rd pers. pl. / *estancarse*.

estanques that you may stop; pres. subj. 2nd pers. sing. / *estancar*.

estánquese let him (her/it) become stagnant; impve. 3rd pers. sing. / *estancarse*.

estañar to tin or to solder. reg.

estaos (you all) remain; impve. 2nd pers. pl. / *estarse*.

estaque 1. that I may stake; pres. subj. 1st pers. sing. / *estacar*. 2. that he (she/it) may stake; pres. subj. 3rd pers. sing. 3. let him (her/it) stake; impve. 3rd pers. sing.

estaqué I staked; past 1st pers. sing. / *estacar*.

estaquéis that you (all) may stake; pres. subj. 2nd pers. pl. / *estacar*.

estaquémonos let us remain stiff; impve. 1st pers. pl. / *estacarse*.

estaquemos 1. that we may stake; pres. subj. 1st pers. pl. / *estacar*. 2. let us stake; impve. 1st pers. pl.

estaquen 1. that they may stake; pres. subj. 3rd pers. pl. / *estacar*. 2. let them stake; impve. 3rd pers. pl.

estáquense let them remain stiff; impve. 3rd pers. pl. / *estacarse*.

estaques that you may stake; pres. subj. 2nd pers. sing. / *estacar*.

estáquese let him (her/it) remain stiff; impve. 3rd pers. sing. / *estacarse*.

estar to be. irr.

estarcir to stencil. reg.

estarse to remain. irr.

estás you be; pres. ind. 2nd pers. sing. / *estar*.

estáte (you) remain; impve. 2nd pers. sing. / *estarse*.

estatuir to establish or to ordain. irr.

estatuya 1. that I may establish; pres. subj. 1st pers. sing. / *estatuir*. 2. that he (she/it) may establish; pres. subj. 3rd pers. sing. 3. let him (her/it) establish; impve. 3rd pers. sing.

estatuyáis that you (all) may establish; pres. subj. 2nd pers. pl. / *estatuir*.

estatuyamos 1. that we may establish; pres. subj. 1st pers. pl. / *estatuir*. 2. let us establish; impve. 1st pers. pl.

estatuyan 1. that they may establish; pres. subj. 3rd pers. pl. / *estatuir*. 2. let them establish; impve. 3rd pers. pl.

estatuyas that you may establish; pres. subj. 2nd pers. sing. / *estatuir*.

estatuye 1. he (she/it) establishes; pres. ind. 3rd pers. sing. / *estatuir*. 2. (you) establish; impve. 2nd pers. sing.

estatuyen they establish; pres. ind. 3rd pers. pl. / *estatuir*.

estatuyendo establishing; pres. part. / *estatuir*.

estatuyera 1. that I might establish; imp. subj. 1st pers. sing. / *estatuir*. 2. that he (she/it) might establish; imp. subj. 3rd pers. sing.

estatuyerais that you (all) might establish; imp. subj. 2nd pers pl. / *estatuir*.

estatuyéramos that we might establish; imp. subj. 1st pers. pl. / *estatuir*.

estatuyeran that they might establish; imp. subj. 3rd pers. pl. / *estatuir*.

estatuyeras that you might establish; imp. subj. 2nd pers. sing. / *estatuir*.

estatuyeron they established; past 3rd pers. pl. / *estatuir*.

estatuyes you establish; pres. ind. 2nd pers. sing. / *estatuir*.

estatuyese 1. that I might establish; imp. subj. 1st pers. sing. / *estatuir*. 2. that he (she/it) might establish; imp. subj. 3rd pers. sing.

estatuyeseis that you (all) might establish; imp. subj. 2nd pers. pl. / *estatuir*.

estatuyésemos that we might establish; imp. subj. 1st pers. pl. / *estatuir*.

estatuyesen that they might establish; imp. subj. 3rd pers. pl. / *estatuir*.

estatuyeses that you might establish; imp. subj. 2nd pers. sing. / *estatuir*.

estatuyo I establish; pres. ind. 1st pers. sing. / *estatuir*.

estatuyó he (she/it) established; past 3rd pers. sing. / *estatuir*.

esté 1. that I may be; pres. subj. 1st pers. sing. / *estar*. 2. that he (she/it) may be; pres. subj. 3rd pers. sing. 3. let him (her/it) be; impve. 3rd pers. sing.

estémonos let us remain; impve. 1st pers. pl. / *estarse*.

estén 1. that they may be; pres. subj. 3rd pers. pl. / *estar*. 2. let them be; impve. 3rd pers. pl.

esténse let them remain; impve. 3rd pers. pl. / *estarse*.

esterar to cover with matting. reg.

estercolar to fertilize. irr.

estercuela 1. he (she/it) fertilizes; pres. ind. 3rd pers. sing. / *estercolar*. 2. (you) fertilize; impve. 2nd pers. sing.

estercuelan they fertilize; pres. ind. 3rd pers. pl. / *estercolar*.

estercuelas you fertilize; pres. ind. 2nd pers. sing. / *estercolar*.

estercuele 1. that I may fertilize; pres. subj. 1st pers. sing. / *estercolar*. 2. that he (she/it) may fertilize; pres. subj. 3rd pers. sing. 3. let him (her/it) fertilize; impve. 3rd pers. sing.

estercuelen 1. that they may fertilize; pres. subj. 3rd pers. pl. / *estercolar*. 2. let them fertilize; impve. 3rd pers. pl.

estercueles that you may fertilize; pres. subj. 2nd pers. sing. / *estercolar*.

estercuelo I fertilize; pres. ind. 1st pers. sing. / *estercolar*.

estereotipar to stereotype. reg.

esterilice 1. that I may sterilize; pres. subj. 1st pers. sing. / *esterilizar*. 2. that he (she/it) may sterilize; pres. subj. 3rd pers. sing. 3. let him (her/it) sterilize; impve. 3rd pers. sing.

esterilicé I sterilized; past 1st pers. sing. / *esterilizar*.

esterilicéis that you (all) may sterilize; pres. subj. 2nd pers. pl. / *esterilizar*.

esterilicemos 1. that we may sterilize; pres. subj. 1st pers. pl. / *esterilizar*. 2. let us sterilize; impve. 1st pers. pl.

esterilicen 1. that they may sterilize; pres. subj. 3rd pers. pl. / *esterilizar*. 2. let them sterilize; impve. 3rd pers. pl.

esterilices that you may sterilize; pres. subj. 2nd pers. sing. / *esterilizar*.

esterilizar to sterilize. irr.

estés that you may be; pres. subj. 2nd pers. sing. / *estar*.

estése let him (her/it) remain; impve. 3rd pers. sing. / *estarse*.

estibar to pack or to stow. reg.

estigmatice 1. that I may stigmatize; pres. subj. 1st pers. sing. / *estigmatizar*. 2. that he (she/it) may stigmatize; pres. subj. 3rd pers. sing. 3. let him (her/it) stigmatize; impve. 3rd pers. sing.

estigmaticé I stigmatized; past 1st pers. sing. / *estigmatizar*.

estigmaticéis that you (all) may stigmatize; pres. subj. 2nd pers. pl. / *estigmatizar*.

estigmaticemos 1. that we may stigmatize; pres. subj. 1st pers. pl. / *estigmatizar*. 2. let us stigmatize; impve. 1st pers. pl.

estigmaticen 1. that they may stigmatize; pres. subj. 3rd pers. pl. / *estigmatizar*. 2. let them stigmatize; impve. 3rd pers. pl.

estigmatices that you may stigmatize; pres. subj. 2nd pers. sing. / *estigmatizar*.

estigmatizar to stigmatize. irr.

estilándose being in style; pres. part. / *estilarse*.

estilaos (you all) be in style; impve. 2nd pers. pl. / *estilarse*.

estilar to use. reg.

estilarse to be in style. reg.

estílate (you) be in style; impve. 2nd pers. sing. / *estilarse*.

estilémonos let us be in style; impve. 1st pers. pl. / *estilarse*.

estílense let them be in style; impve. 3rd pers. pl. / *estilarse*.

estílese let him (her/it) be in style; impve. 3rd pers. sing. / *estilarse*.

estilice 1. that I may stylize; pres. subj. 1st pers. sing. / *estilizar*. 2. that he (she/it) may stylize; pres. subj. 3rd pers. sing. 3. let him (her/it) stylize; impve. 3rd pers. sing.

estilicé I stylized; past 1st pers. sing. / *estilizar*.

estilicéis that you (all) may stylize; pres. subj. 2nd pers. pl. / *estilizar*.

estilicemos 1. that we may stylize; pres. subj. 1st pers. pl. / *estilizar*. 2. let us stylize; impve. 1st pers. pl.

estilicen 1. that they may stylize; pres. subj. 3rd pers. pl. / *estilizar*. 2. let them stylize; impve. 3rd pers. pl.

estilices that you may stylize; pres. subj. 2nd pers. sing. / *estilizar*.

estilizar to stylize. irr.

estimar to esteem. reg.

estimular to stimulate. reg.

estipular to stipulate. reg.

estirándose stretching out; pres. part. / *estirarse*.

estiraos (you all) stretch out; impve. 2nd pers. pl. / *estirarse*.

estirar to stretch. reg.

estirarse to stretch out. reg.

estírate (you) stretch out; impve. 2nd pers. sing. / *estirarse*.

estirémonos let us stretch out; impve. 1st pers. pl. / *estirarse*.

estírense let them stretch out; impve. 3rd pers. pl. / *estirarse*.

estírese let him (her/it) stretch out; impve. 3rd pers. sing. / *estirarse*.

estofar to quilt or to stew. reg.

estomagar to upset the stomach. irr.

estomague 1. that I may upset the stomach; pres. subj. 1st pers. sing. / *estomagar*. 2. that he (she/it) may upset the stomach; pres. subj. 3rd pers. sing. 3. let him (her/it) upset the stomach; impve. 3rd pers. sing.

estomagué I upset the stomach; past 1st pers. sing. / *estomagar*.

estomaguéis that you (all) may upset the stomach; pres. subj. 2nd pers. pl. / *estomagar*.

estomaguemos 1. that we may upset the stomach; pres. subj. 1st pers. pl. / *estomagar*. 2. let us upset the stomach; impve. 1st pers. pl.

estomaguen 1. that they may upset the stomach; pres. subj. 3rd pers. pl. / *estomagar*. 2. let them upset the stomach; impve. 3rd pers. pl.

estomagues that you may upset the stomach; pres. subj. 2nd pers. sing. / *estomagar*.

estoquear to pierce with a rapier. reg.

estorbar to hinder. reg.

estornudar to sneeze. reg.

estoy I am; pres. ind. 1st pers. sing. / *estar*.

estragar to corrupt. irr.

estrague 1. that I may corrupt; pres. subj. 1st pers. sing. / *estragar*. 2. that he (she/it) may corrupt; pres. subj. 3rd pers. sing. 3. let him (her/it) corrupt; impve. 3rd pers. sing.

estragué I corrupted; past 1st pers. sing. / *estragar*.

estraguéis that you (all) may corrupt; pres. subj. 2nd pers. pl. / *estragar*.

estraguemos 1. that we may corrupt; pres. subj. 1st pers. pl. / *estragar*. 2. let us corrupt; impve. 1st pers. pl.

estraguen 1. that they may corrupt; pres. subj. 3rd pers. pl. / *estragar*. 2. let them corrupt; impve. 3rd pers. pl.

estragues that you may corrupt; pres. subj. 2nd pers. sing. / *estragar*.

estrangular to strangle. reg.

estratificándose stratifying; pres. part. / *estratificarse*.

estratificaos (you all) stratify; impve. 2nd pers. pl. / *estratificarse*.

estratificar to stratify. irr.

estratificarse to stratify. irr.

estratifícate (you) stratify; impve. 2nd pers. sing. / *estratificarse*.

estratifique 1. that I may stratify; pres. subj. 1st pers. sing. / *estratificar*. 2. that he (she/it) may stratify; pres. subj. 3rd pers. sing. 3. let him (her/it) stratify; impve. 3rd pers. sing.

estratifiqué I stratified; past 1st pers. sing. / *estratificar*.

estratifiquéis that you (all) may stratify; pres. subj. 2nd pers. pl. / *estratificar*.

estratifiquémonos let us stratify; impve. 1st pers. pl. / *estratificarse*.

estratifiquemos 1. that we may stratify; pres. subj. 1st pers. pl. / *estratificar*. 2. let us stratify; impve. 1st pers. pl.

estratifiquen 1. that they may stratify; pres. subj. 3rd pers. pl. / *estratificar*. 2. let them stratify; impve. 3rd pers. pl.

estratifíquense let them stratify; impve. 3rd pers. pl. / *estratificarse*.

estratifiques that you may stratify; pres. subj. 2nd pers. sing. / *estratificar*.

estratifíquese let him (her/it) stratify; impve. 3rd pers. sing. / *estratificarse*.

estrechándose becoming narrow; pres. part. / *estrecharse*.

estrechaos (you all) become narrow; impve. 2nd pers. pl. / *estrecharse*.

estrechar to tighten. reg.

estrecharse to become narrow. reg.

estréchate (you) become narrow; impve. 2nd pers. sing. / *estrecharse*.

estrechémonos let us become narrow; impve. 1st pers. pl. / *estrecharse*.

estréchense let them become narrow; impve. 3rd pers. pl. / *estrecharse*.

estréchese let him (her/it) become narrow; impve. 3rd pers. sing. / *estrecharse*.

estregar to rub or to scrub. irr.

estregué I rubbed; past 1st pers. sing. / *estregar*.

estreguéis that you (all) may rub; pres. subj. 2nd pers. pl. / *estregar*.

estreguemos 1. that we may rub; pres. subj. 1st pers. pl. / *estregar*. 2. let us rub; impve. 1st pers. pl.

estrellándose shattering; pres. part. / *estrellarse*.

estrellaos (you all) shatter; impve. 2nd pers. pl. / *estrellarse*.

estrellar to star or to dash to pieces. reg.

estrellarse to shatter. reg.

estréllate (you) shatter; impve. 2nd pers. sing. / *estrellarse*.

estrellémonos let us shatter; impve. 1st pers. pl. / *estrellarse*.

estréllense let them shatter; impve. 3rd pers. pl. / *estrellarse*.

estréllese let him (her/it) shatter; impve. 3rd pers. sing. / *estrellarse*.

estremeceos (you all) tremble; impve. 2nd pers. pl. / *estremecerse*.

estremecer to shake. irr.

estremecerse to tremble. irr.

estremécete (you) tremble; impve. 2nd pers. sing. / *estremecerse*.

estremeciéndose trembling; pres. part. / *estremecerse*.

estremezca 1. that I may shake; pres. subj. 1st pers. sing. / *estremecer*. 2. that he (she/it) may shake; pres. subj. 3rd pers. sing. 3. let him (her/it) shake; impve. 3rd pers. sing.

estremezcáis that you (all) may shake; pres. subj. 2nd pers. pl. / *estremecer*.

estremezcámonos let us tremble; impve. 1st pers. pl. / *estremecerse*.

estremezcamos 1. that we may shake; pres. subj. 1st pers. pl. / *estremecer*. 2. let us shake; impve. 1st pers. pl.

estremezcan 1. that they may shake; pres. subj. 3rd pers. pl. / *estremecer*. 2. let them shake; impve. 3rd pers. pl.

estremézcanse let them tremble; impve. 3rd pers. pl. / *estremecerse*.

estremezcas that you may shake; pres. subj. 2nd pers. sing. / *estremecer*.

estremézcase let him (her/it) tremble; impve. 3rd pers. sing. / *estremecerse*.

estremezco I shake; pres. ind. 1st pers. sing. / *estremecer*.

estrenándose appearing for the first time; pres. part. / *estrenarse*.

estrenaos (you all) appear for the first time; impve. 2nd pers. pl. / *estrenarse*.

estrenar to use for the first time. reg.

estrenarse to appear for the first time. reg.

estrénate (you) appear for the first time; impve. 2nd pers. sing. / *estrenarse*.

estrenémonos let us appear for the first time; impve. 1st pers. pl. / *estrenarse*.

estrénense let them appear for the first time; impve. 3rd pers. pl. / *estrenarse*.

estrénese let him (her/it) appear for the first time; impve. 3rd pers. sing. / *estrenarse*.

estreñíos (you all) become constipated; impve. 2nd pers. pl. / *estreñirse*.

estreñir to constipate. irr.

estreñirse to become constipated. irr.

estría 1. he (she/it) grooves; pres. ind. 3rd pers. sing. / *estriar*. 2. (you) groove; impve. 2nd pers. sing.

estrían they groove; pres. ind. 3rd pers. pl. / *estriar*.

estriar to groove. irr.

estrías you groove; pres. ind. 2nd pers. sing. / *estriar*.

estribar to rest. reg.

estríe 1. that I may groove; pres. subj. 1st pers. sing. / *estriar*. 2. that he (she/it) may groove; pres. subj. 3rd pers. sing. 3. let him (her/it) groove; impve. 3rd pers. sing.

estriega 1. he (she/it) rubs; pres. ind. 3rd pers. sing. / *estregar*. 2. (you) rub; impve. 2nd pers. sing.

estriegan they rub; pres. ind. 3rd pers. pl. / *estregar*.

estriegas you rub; pres. ind. 2nd pers. sing. / *estregar*.

estriego I rub; pres. ind. 1st pers. sing. / *estregar*.

estriegue 1. that I may rub; pres. subj. 1st pers. sing. / *estregar*. 2. that he (she/it) may rub; pres. subj. 3rd pers. sing. 3. let him (her/it) rub; impve. 3rd pers. sing.

estrieguen 1. that they may rub; pres. subj. 3rd pers. pl. / *estregar*. 2. let them rub; impve. 3rd pers. pl.

estriegues that you may rub; pres. subj. 2nd pers. sing. / *estregar*.

estríen 1. that they may groove; pres. subj. 3rd pers. pl. / *estriar*. 2. let them groove; impve. 3rd pers. pl.

estríes that you may groove; pres. subj. 2nd pers. sing. / *estriar*.

estriña 1. that it may constipate; pres. subj. 3rd pers. sing. / *estreñir*. 2. let it constipate; impve. 3rd pers. sing.

estriñámonos let us become constipated; impve. 1st pers. pl. / *estreñirse*.

estriñan 1. that they may constipate; pres. subj. 3rd pers. pl. / *estreñir*. 2. let them constipate; impve. 3rd pers. pl.

estríñanse let them become constipated; impve. 3rd pers. pl. / *estreñirse*.

estríñase let him (her/it) become constipated; impve. 3rd pers. sing. / *estreñirse*.

estriñe it constipates; pres. ind. 3rd pers. sing. / *estreñir*.

estriñen they constipate; pres. ind. 3rd pers. pl. / *estreñir*.

estriñendo constipating; pres. part. / *estreñir*.

estriñéndose becoming constipated; pres. part. / *estreñirse*.

estriñera that it might constipate; imp. subj. 3rd pers. sing. / *estreñir*.

estriñeran that they might constipate; imp. subj. 3rd pers. pl. / *estreñir*.

estriñeron they constipated; past 3rd pers. pl. / *estreñir*.

estriñese that it might constipate; imp. subj. 3rd pers. sing. / *estreñir*.

estriñesen that they might constipate; imp. subj. 3rd pers. pl. / *estreñir*.

estríñete (you) become constipated; impve. 2nd pers. sing. / *estreñirse*.

estriñó it constipated; past 3rd pers. sing. / *estreñir*.

estrío I groove; pres. ind. 1st pers. sing. / *estriar*.

estropeándose spoiling; pres. part. / *estropearse*.

estropeaos (you all) spoil; impve. 2nd pers. pl. / *estropearse*.

estropear to cripple. reg.

estropearse to spoil. reg.

estropéate (you) spoil; impve. 2nd pers. sing. / *estropearse*.

estropeémonos let us spoil; impve. 1st pers. pl. / *estropearse*.

estropéense let them spoil; impve. 3rd pers. pl. / *estropearse*.

estropéese let him (her/it) spoil; impve. 3rd pers. sing. / *estropearse*.

estrujar to squeeze. reg.

estucar to stucco. irr.

estudiar to study. reg.

estuprar to rape. reg.

estuque 1. that I may stucco; pres. subj. 1st pers. sing. / *estucar*. 2. that he (she/it) may stucco; pres. subj. 3rd pers. sing. 3. let him (her/it) stucco; impve. 3rd pers. sing.

estuqué I stuccoed; past 1st pers. sing. / *estucar*.

estuquéis that you (all) may stucco; subj. 2nd pers. pl. / *estucar*.

estuquemos 1. that we may stucco; pres. subj. 1st pers. pl. / *estucar*. 2. let us stucco; impve. 1st pers. pl.

estuquen 1. that they may stucco; pres. subj. 3rd pers. pl. / *estucar*. 2. let them stucco; impve. 3rd pers. pl.

estuques that you may stucco; pres. subj. 2nd pers. sing. / *estucar*.

estuve I was; past 1st pers. sing. / *estar*.

estuviera 1. that I might be; imp. subj. 1st pers. sing. / *estar*. 2. that he (she/it) might be; imp. subj. 3rd pers. sing.

estuvierais that you (all) might be; imp. subj. 2nd pers pl. / *estar*.

estuviéramos that we might be; imp. subj. 1st pers. pl. / *estar*.

estuvieran that they might be; imp. subj. 3rd pers. pl. / *estar*.

estuvieras that you might be; imp. subj. 2nd pers. sing. / *estar*.

estuvieron they were; past 3rd pers. pl. / *estar*.

estuviese 1. that I might be; imp. subj. 1st pers. sing. / *estar*. 2. that he (she/it) might be; imp. subj. 3rd pers. sing.

estuvieseis that you (all) might be; imp. subj. 2nd pers pl. / *estar*.

estuviésemos that we might be; imp. subj. 1st pers. pl. / *estar*.

estuviesen that they might be; imp. subj. 3rd pers. pl. / *estar*.

estuvieses that you might be; imp. subj. 2nd pers. sing. / *estar*.

estuvimos we were; past 1st pers. pl. / *estar*.

estuviste you were; past 2nd pers. sing. / *estar*.

estuvisteis you (all) were; past 2nd pers. pl. / *estar*.

estuvo he (she/it) was; past 3rd pers. sing. / *estar*.

eternice 1. that I may make eternal; pres. subj. 1st pers. sing. / *eternizar*. 2. that he (she/it) may make eternal; pres. subj. 3rd pers. sing. 3. let him (her/it) make eternal; impve. 3rd pers. sing.

eternicé I made eternal; past 1st pers. sing. / *eternizar*.

eternicéis that you (all) may make eternal; pres. subj. 2nd pers. pl. / *eternizar*.

eternicémonos let us go on forever; impve. 1st pers. pl. / *eternizarse.*

eternicemos 1. that we may make eternal; pres. subj. 1st pers. pl. / *eternizar.* 2. let us make eternal; impve. 1st pers. pl.

eternicen 1. that they may make eternal; pres. subj. 3rd pers. pl. / *eternizar.* 2. let them make eternal; impve. 3rd pers. pl.

eternícense let them go on forever; impve. 3rd pers. pl. / *eternizarse.*

eternices that you may make eternal; pres. subj. 2nd pers. sing. / *eternizar.*

eternícese let him (her/it) go on forever; impve. 3rd pers. sing. / *eternizarse.*

eternizándose going on forever; pres. part. / *eternizarse.*

eternizaos (you all) go on forever; impve. 2nd pers. pl. / *eternizarse.*

eternizar to make eternal. irr.

eternizarse to go on forever. irr.

eternízate (you) go on forever; impve. 2nd pers. sing. / *eternizarse.*

europeice 1. that I may europeanize; pres. subj. 1st pers. sing. / *europeizar.* 2. that he (she/it) may europeanize; pres. subj. 3rd pers. sing. 3. let him (her/it) europeanize; impve. 3rd pers. sing.

europeicé I europeanized; past 1st pers. sing. / *europeizar.*

europeicéis that you (all) may europeanize; pres. subj. 2nd pers. pl. / *europeizar.*

europeicemos 1. that we may europeanize; pres. subj. 1st pers. pl. / *europeizar.* 2. let us europeanize; impve. 1st pers. pl.

europeicen 1. that they may europeanize; pres. subj. 3rd pers. pl. / *europeizar.* 2. let them europeanize; impve. 3rd pers. pl.

europeices that you may europeanize; pres. subj. 2nd pers. sing. / *europeizar.*

europeizar to europeanize. irr.

evacúa 1. he (she/it) evacuates; pres. ind. 3rd pers. sing. / *evacuar.* 2. (you) evacuate; impve. 2nd pers. sing.

evacúan they evacuate; pres. ind. 3rd pers. pl. / *evacuar.*

evacuar to evacuate. irr.

evacúas you evacuate; pres. ind. 2nd pers. sing. / *evacuar.*

evacúe 1. that I may evacuate; pres. subj. 1st pers. sing. / *evacuar.* 2. that he (she/it) may evacuate; pres. subj. 3rd pers. sing. 3. let him (her/it) evacuate; impve. 3rd pers. sing.

evacúen 1. that they may evacuate; pres. subj. 3rd pers. pl. / *evacuar.* 2. let them evacuate; impve. 3rd pers. pl.

evacúes that you may evacuate; pres. subj. 2nd pers. sing. / *evacuar.*

evacúo I evacuate; pres. ind. 1st pers. sing. / *evacuar.*

evadámonos let us escape; impve. 1st pers. pl. / *evadirse.*

evádanse let them escape; impve. 3rd pers. pl. / *evadirse.*

evádase let him (her/it) escape; impve. 3rd pers. sing. / *evadirse.*

evádete (you) escape; impve. 2nd pers. sing. / *evadirse.*

evadiéndose escaping; pres. part. / *evadirse.*

evadíos (you all) escape; impve. 2nd pers. pl. / *evadirse.*

evadir to evade. reg.

evadirse to escape. reg.

evalúa 1. he (she/it) evaluates; pres. ind. 3rd pers. sing. / *evaluar.* 2. (you) evaluate; impve. 2nd pers. sing.

evalúan they evaluate; pres. ind. 3rd pers. pl. / *evaluar.*

evaluar to evaluate. irr.

evalúas you evaluate; pres. ind. 2nd pers. sing. / *evaluar.*

evalúe 1. that I may evaluate; pres. subj. 1st pers. sing. / *evaluar.* 2. that he (she/it) may evaluate; pres. subj. 3rd pers. sing. 3. let him (her/it) evaluate; impve. 3rd pers. sing.

evalúen 1. that they may evaluate; pres. subj. 3rd pers. pl. / *evaluar.* 2. let them evaluate; impve. 3rd pers. pl.

evalúes that you may evaluate; pres. subj. 2nd pers. sing. / *evaluar.*

evalúo I evaluate; pres. ind. 1st pers. sing. / *evaluar.*

evangelice 1. that I may evangelize; pres. subj. 1st pers. sing. / *evangelizar.* 2. that he (she/it) may evangelize; pres. subj. 3rd pers. sing. 3. let him (her/it) evangelize; impve. 3rd pers. sing.

evangelicé I evangelized; past 1st pers. sing. / *evangelizar.*

evangelicéis that you (all) may evangelize; pres. subj. 2nd pers. pl. / *evangelizar.*

evangelicemos 1. that we may evangelize; pres. subj. 1st pers. pl. / *evangelizar.* 2. let us evangelize; impve. 1st pers. pl.

evangelicen 1. that they may evangelize; pres. subj. 3rd pers. pl. / *evangelizar.* 2. let them evangelize; impve. 3rd pers. pl.

evangelices that you may evangelize; pres. subj. 2nd pers. sing. / *evangelizar.*

evangelizar to evangelize. irr.

evaporándose disappearing; pres. part. / *evaporarse.*

evaporaos (you all) disappear; impve. 2nd pers. pl. / *evaporarse.*

evaporar to evaporate. reg.

evaporarse to disappear. reg.

evapórate (you) disappear; impve. 2nd pers. sing. / *evaporarse.*

evaporémonos let us disappear; impve. 1st pers. pl. / *evaporarse.*

evapórense let them disappear; impve. 3rd pers. pl. / *evaporarse.*

evapórese let him (her/it) disappear; impve. 3rd pers. sing. / *evaporarse.*

evaporice 1. that I may vaporize; pres. subj. 1st pers. sing. / *evaporizar.* 2. that he (she/it) may vaporize; pres. subj. 3rd pers. sing. 3. let him (her/it) vaporize; impve. 3rd pers. sing.

evaporicé I vaporized; past 1st pers. sing. / *evaporizar*.

evaporicéis that you (all) may vaporize; pres. subj. 2nd pers. pl. / *evaporizar*.

evaporicemos 1. that we may vaporize; pres. subj. 1st pers. pl. / *evaporizar*. 2. let us vaporize; impve. 1st pers. pl.

evaporicen 1. that they may vaporize; pres. subj. 3rd pers. pl. / *evaporizar*. 2. let them vaporize; impve. 3rd pers. pl.

evaporices that you may vaporize; pres. subj. 2nd pers. sing. / *evaporizar*.

evaporizar to vaporize. irr.

evidenciándose being evident; pres. part. / *evidenciarse*.

evidenciaos (you all) be evident; impve. 2nd pers. pl. / *evidenciarse*.

evidenciar to make evident. reg.

evidenciarse to be evident. reg.

evidencíate (you) be evident; impve. 2nd pers. sing. / *evidenciarse*.

evidenciémonos let us be evident; impve. 1st pers. pl. / *evidenciarse*.

evidencíense let them be evident; impve. 3rd pers. pl. / *evidenciarse*.

evidencíese let him (her/it) be evident; impve. 3rd pers. sing. / *evidenciarse*.

eviscerar to eviscerate. reg.

evitar to avoid. reg.

evocar to evoke. irr.

evolucionar to evolve. reg.

evoque 1. that I may evoke; pres. subj. 1st pers. sing. / *evocar*. 2. that he (she/it) may evoke; pres. subj. 3rd pers. sing. 3. let him (her/it) evoke; impve. 3rd pers. sing.

evoqué I evoked; past 1st pers. sing. / *evocar*.

evoquéis that you (all) may evoke; pres. subj. 2nd pers. pl. / *evocar*.

evoquemos 1. that we may evoke; pres. subj. 1st pers. pl. / *evocar*. 2. let us evoke; impve. 1st pers. pl.

evoquen 1. that they may evoke; pres. subj. 3rd pers. pl. / *evocar*. 2. let them evoke; impve. 3rd pers. pl.

evoques that you may evoke; pres. subj. 2nd pers. sing. / *evocar*.

exacerbándose becoming irritated; pres. part. / *exacerbarse*.

exacerbaos (you all) become irritated; impve. 2nd pers. pl. / *exacerbarse*.

exacerbar to exasperate. reg.

exacerbarse to become irritated. reg.

exacérbate (you) become irritated; impve. 2nd pers. sing. / *exacerbarse*.

exacerbémonos let us become irritated; impve. 1st pers. pl. / *exacerbarse*.

exacérbense let them become irritated; impve. 3rd pers. pl. / *exacerbarse*.

exacérbese let him (her/it) become irritated; impve. 3rd pers. sing. / *exacerbarse*.

exagerar to exaggerate. reg.

exaltándose becoming excited; pres. part. / *exaltarse*.

exaltaos (you all) become excited; impve. 2nd pers. pl. / *exaltarse*.

exaltar to exalt. reg.

exaltarse to become excited. reg.

exáltate (you) become excited; impve. 2nd pers. sing. / *exaltarse*.

exaltémonos let us become excited; impve. 1st pers. pl. / *exaltarse*.

exáltense let them become excited; impve. 3rd pers. pl. / *exaltarse*.

exáltese let him (her/it) become excited; impve. 3rd pers. sing. / *exaltarse*.

examinándose taking an examination; pres. part. / *examinarse*.

examinaos (you all) take an examination; impve. 2nd pers. pl. / *examinarse*.

examinar to examine. reg.

examinarse to take an examination. reg.

examínate (you) take an examination; impve. 2nd pers. sing. / *examinarse*.

examinémonos let us take an examination; impve. 1st pers. pl. / *examinarse*.

examínense let them take an examination; impve. 3rd pers. pl. / *examinarse*.

examínese let him (her/it) take an examination; impve. 3rd pers. sing. / *examinarse*.

exasperándose becoming intense; pres. part. / *exasperarse*.

exasperaos (you all) become intense; impve. 2nd pers. pl. / *exasperarse*.

exasperar to exasperate. reg.

exasperarse to become intense. reg.

exaspérate (you) become intense; impve. 2nd pers. sing. / *exasperarse*.

exasperémonos let us become intense; impve. 1st pers. pl. / *exasperarse*.

exaspérense let them become intense; impve. 3rd pers. pl. / *exasperarse*.

exaspérese let him (her/it) become intense; impve. 3rd pers. sing. / *exasperarse*.

excarcelar to release from prison. reg.

excavar to excavate. reg.

excedámonos let us overstep the limit; impve. 1st pers. pl. / *excederse*.

excédanse let them overstep the limit; impve. 3rd pers. pl. / *excederse*.

excédase let him (her/it) overstep the limit; impve. 3rd pers. sing. / *excederse*.

excedeos (you all) overstep the limit; impve. 2nd pers. pl. / *excederse*.

exceder to exceed. reg.

excederse to overstep the limit. reg.

excédete (you) overstep the limit; impve. 2nd pers. sing. / *excederse*.

excediéndose overstepping the limit; pres. part. / *excederse*.

exceptúa 1. he (she/it) excepts; pres. ind. 3rd pers. sing. / *exceptuar*. 2. (you) except; impve. 2nd pers. sing.

exceptúan they except; pres. ind. 3rd pers. pl. / *exceptuar.*

exceptuar to except. irr.

exceptúas you except; pres. ind. 2nd pers. sing. / *exceptuar.*

exceptúe 1. that I may except; pres. subj. 1st pers. sing. / *exceptuar.* 2. that he (she/it) may except; pres. subj. 3rd pers. sing. 3. let him (her/it) except; impve. 3rd pers. sing.

exceptúen 1. that they may except; pres. subj. 3rd pers. pl. / *exceptuar.* 2. let them except; impve. 3rd pers. pl.

exceptúes that you may except; pres. subj. 2nd pers. sing. / *exceptuar.*

exceptúo I except; pres. ind. 1st pers. sing. / *exceptuar.*

excitándose becoming excited; pres. part. / *excitarse.*

excitaos (you all) become excited; impve. 2nd pers. pl. / *excitarse.*

excitar to excite. reg.

excitarse to become excited. reg.

excítate (you) become excited; impve. 2nd pers. sing. / *excitarse.*

excitémonos let us become excited; impve. 1st pers. pl. / *excitarse.*

excítense let them become excited; impve. 3rd pers. pl. / *excitarse.*

excítese let him (her/it) become excited; impve. 3rd pers. sing. / *excitarse.*

exclamar to exclaim. reg.

exclaustrar to secularize a monk. reg.

excluir to exclude. irr.

excluso excluded; past part. / *excluir.*

excluya 1. that I may exclude; pres. subj. 1st pers. sing. / *excluir.* 2. that he (she/it) may exclude; pres. subj. 3rd pers. sing. 3. let him (her/it) exclude; impve. 3rd pers. sing.

excluyáis that you (all) may exclude; pres. subj. 2nd pers. pl. / *excluir.*

excluyamos 1. that we may exclude; pres. subj. 1st pers. pl. / *excluir.* 2. let us exclude; impve. 1st pers. pl.

excluyan 1. that they may exclude; pres. subj. 3rd pers. pl. / *excluir.* 2. let them exclude; impve. 3rd pers. pl.

excluyas that you may exclude; pres. subj. 2nd pers. sing. / *excluir.*

excluye 1. he (she/it) excludes; pres. ind. 3rd pers. sing. / *excluir.* 2. (you) exclude; impve. 2nd pers. sing.

excluyen they exclude; pres. ind. 3rd pers. pl. / *excluir.*

excluyendo excluding; pres. part. / *excluir.*

excluyera 1. that I might exclude; imp. subj. 1st pers. sing. / *excluir.* 2. that he (she/it) might exclude; imp. subj. 3rd pers. sing.

excluyerais that you (all) might exclude; imp. subj. 2nd pers pl. / *excluir.*

excluyéramos that we might exclude; imp. subj. 1st pers. pl. / *excluir.*

excluyeran that they might exclude; imp. subj. 3rd pers. pl. / *excluir.*

excluyeras that you might exclude; imp. subj. 2nd pers. sing. / *excluir.*

excluyeron they excluded; past 3rd pers. pl. / *excluir.*

excluyes you exclude; pres. ind. 2nd pers. sing. / *excluir.*

excluyese 1. that I might exclude; imp. subj. 1st pers. sing. / *excluir.* 2. that he (she/it) might exclude; imp. subj. 3rd pers. sing.

excluyeseis that you (all) might exclude; imp. subj. 2nd pers pl. / *excluir.*

excluyésemos that we might exclude; imp. subj. 1st pers. pl. / *excluir.*

excluyesen that they might exclude; imp. subj. 3rd pers. pl. / *excluir.*

excluyeses that you might exclude; imp. subj. 2nd pers. sing. / *excluir.*

excluyo I exclude; pres. ind. 1st pers. sing. / *excluir.*

excluyó he (she/it) excluded; past 3rd pers. sing. / *excluir.*

excomulgar to excommunicate. irr.

excomulgue 1. that I may excommunicate; pres. subj. 1st pers. sing. / *excomulgar.* 2. that he (she/it) may excommunicate; pres. subj. 3rd pers. sing. 3. let him (her/it) excommunicate; impve. 3rd pers. sing.

excomulgué I excommunicated; past 1st pers. sing. / *excomulgar.*

excomulguéis that you (all) may excommunicate; pres. subj. 2nd pers. pl. / *excomulgar.*

excomulguemos 1. that we may excommunicate; pres. subj. 1st pers. pl. / *excomulgar.* 2. let us excommunicate; impve. 1st pers. pl.

excomulguen 1. that they may excommunicate; pres. subj. 3rd pers. pl. / *excomulgar.* 2. let them excommunicate; impve. 3rd pers. pl.

excomulgues that you may excommunicate; pres. subj. 2nd pers. sing. / *excomulgar.*

excomunicar to excommunicate. irr.

excomunique 1. that I may excommunicate; pres. subj. 1st pers. sing. / *excomunicar.* 2. that he (she/it) may excommunicate; pres. subj. 3rd pers. sing. 3. let him (her/it) excommunicate; impve. 3rd pers. sing.

excomuniqué I excommunicated; past 1st pers. sing. / *excomunicar.*

excomuniquéis that you (all) may excommunicate; pres. subj. 2nd pers. pl. / *excomunicar.*

excomuniquemos 1. that we may excommunicate; pres. subj. 1st pers. pl. / *excomunicar.* 2. let us excommunicate; impve. 1st pers. pl.

excomuniquen 1. that they may excommunicate; pres. subj. 3rd pers. pl. / *excomunicar.* 2. let them excommunicate; impve. 3rd pers. pl.

excomuniques that you may excommunicate; pres. subj. 2nd pers. sing. / *excomunicar.*

excoriándose skinning; pres. part. / *excoriarse.*

excoriaos (you all) skin; impve. 2nd pers. pl. / *excoriarse.*

excoriar to skin. reg.

excoriarse to skin. reg.

excoríate (you) skin; impve. 2nd pers. sing. / *excoriarse*.

excoriémonos let us skin; impve. 1st pers. pl. / *excoriarse*.

excoríense let them skin; impve. 3rd pers. pl. / *excoriarse*.

excoríese let him (her/it) skin; impve. 3rd pers. sing. / *excoriarse*.

excrementar to move the bowels. reg.

excretar to excrete. reg.

exculpar to exculpate. reg.

excusándose apologizing; pres. part. / *excusarse*.

excusaos (you all) apologize; impve. 2nd pers. pl. / *excusarse*.

excusar to excuse. reg.

excusarse to apologize. reg.

excúsate (you) apologize; impve. 2nd pers. sing. / *excusarse*.

excusémonos let us apologize; impve. 1st pers. pl. / *excusarse*.

excúsense let them apologize; impve. 3rd pers. pl. / *excusarse*.

excúsese let him (her/it) apologize; impve. 3rd pers. sing. / *excusarse*.

execrar to execrate. reg.

exencionar to exempt. reg.

exentar to exempt. reg.

exhalándose evaporating; pres. part. / *exhalarse*.

exhalaos (you all) evaporate; impve. 2nd pers. pl. / *exhalarse*.

exhalar to exhale. reg.

exhalarse to evaporate. reg.

exhálate (you) evaporate; impve. 2nd pers. sing. / *exhalarse*.

exhalémonos let us evaporate; impve. 1st pers. pl. / *exhalarse*.

exhálense let them evaporate; impve. 3rd pers. pl. / *exhalarse*.

exhálese let him (her/it) evaporate; impve. 3rd pers. sing. / *exhalarse*.

exheredar to disinherit. reg.

exhibámonos let us show off; impve. 1st pers. pl. / *exhibirse*.

exhíbanse let them show off; impve. 3rd pers. pl. / *exhibirse*.

exhíbase let him (her/it) show off; impve. 3rd pers. sing. / *exhibirse*.

exhíbete (you) show off; impve. 2nd pers. sing. / *exhibirse*.

exhibiéndose showing off; pres. part. / *exhibirse*.

exhibíos (you all) show off; impve. 2nd pers. pl. / *exhibirse*.

exhibir to exhibit. reg.

exhibirse to show off. reg.

exhortar to exhort. reg.

exhumar to exhume. reg.

exigir to demand. irr.

exija 1. that I may demand; pres. subj. 1st pers. sing. / *exigir*. 2. that he (she/it) may demand; pres. subj. 3rd pers. sing. 3. let him (her/it) demand; impve. 3rd pers. sing.

exijáis that you (all) may demand; pres. subj. 2nd pers. pl. / *exigir*.

exijamos 1. that we may demand; pres. subj. 1st pers. pl. / *exigir*. 2. let us demand; impve. 1st pers. pl.

exijan 1. that they may demand; pres. subj. 3rd pers. pl. / *exigir*. 2. let them demand; impve. 3rd pers. pl.

exijas that you may demand; pres. subj. 2nd pers. sing. / *exigir*.

exijo I demand; pres. ind. 1st pers. sing. / *exigir*.

exilar to exile. reg.

exiliar to exile. reg.

eximámonos let us avoid; impve. 1st pers. pl. / *eximirse*.

exímanse let them avoid; impve. 3rd pers. pl. / *eximirse*.

exímase let him (her/it) avoid; impve. 3rd pers. sing. / *eximirse*.

exímete (you) avoid; impve. 2nd pers. sing. / *eximirse*.

eximiéndose avoiding; pres. part. / *eximirse*.

exímíos (you all) avoid; impve. 2nd pers. pl. / *eximirse*.

eximir to exempt. reg.

eximirse to avoid. reg.

existir to exist. reg.

exonerándose defecating; pres. part. / *exonerarse*.

exoneraos (you all) defecate; impve. 2nd pers. pl. / *exonerarse*.

exonerar to exonerate. reg.

exonerarse to defecate. reg.

exonérate (you) defecate; impve. 2nd pers. sing. / *exonerarse*.

exonerémonos let us defecate; impve. 1st pers. pl. / *exonerarse*.

exonérense let them defecate; impve. 3rd pers. pl. / *exonerarse*.

exonérese let him (her/it) defecate; impve. 3rd pers. sing. / *exonerarse*.

exorcice 1. that I may exorcise; pres. subj. 1st pers. sing. / *exorcizar*. 2. that he (she/it) may exorcise; pres. subj. 3rd pers. sing. 3. let him (her/it) exorcise; impve. 3rd pers. sing.

exorcicé I exorcised; past 1st pers. sing. / *exorcizar*.

exorcicéis that you (all) may exorcise; pres. subj. 2nd pers. pl. / *exorcizar*.

exorcicemos 1. that we may exorcise; pres. subj. 1st pers. pl. / *exorcizar*. 2. let us exorcise; impve. 1st pers. pl.

exorcicen 1. that they may exorcise; pres. subj. 3rd pers. pl. / *exorcizar*. 2. let them exorcise; impve. 3rd pers. pl.

exorcices that you may exorcise; pres. subj. 2nd pers. sing. / *exorcizar*.

exorcizar to exorcise. irr.

exornar to adorn. reg.

expandir to expand. reg.

expansionándose becoming expansive; pres. part. / *expansionarse*.

expansionaos (you all) become expansive; impve. 2nd pers. pl. / *expansionarse*.

expansionarse to become expansive. reg.

expansiónate (you) become expansive; impve. 2nd pers. sing. / *expansionarse*.

expansionémonos let us become expansive; impve. 1st pers. pl. / *expansionarse*.

expansiónense let them become expansive; impve. 3rd pers. pl. / *expansionarse*.

expansiónese let him (her/it) become expansive; impve. 3rd pers. sing. / *expansionarse*.

expatriándose settling abroad; pres. part. / *expatriarse*.

expatriaos (you all) settle abroad; impve. 2nd pers. pl. / *expatriarse*.

expatriar to expatriate. reg.

expatriarse to settle abroad. reg.

expatríate (you) settle abroad; impve. 2nd pers. sing. / *expatriarse*.

expatriémonos let us settle abroad; impve. 1st pers. pl. / *expatriarse*.

expatríense let them settle abroad; impve. 3rd pers. pl. / *expatriarse*.

expatríese let him (her/it) settle abroad; impve. 3rd pers. sing. / *expatriarse*.

expectorar to expectorate. reg.

expedir to expedite. irr.

expeditar to expedite. reg.

expeler to expel. reg -er conju.

expender to expend. reg.

experimentar to experiment or to experience. reg.

expía 1. he (she/it) expiates; pres. ind. 3rd pers. sing. / *expiar*. 2. (you) expiate; impve. 2nd pers. sing.

expían they expiate; pres. ind. 3rd pers. pl. / *expiar*.

expiar to expiate or to atone for. irr.

expías you expiate; pres. ind. 2nd pers. sing. / *expiar*.

expida 1. that I may expedite; pres. subj. 1st pers. sing. / *expedir*. 2. that he (she/it) may expedite; pres. subj. 3rd pers. sing. 3. let him (her/it) expedite; impve. 3rd pers. sing.

expidáis that you (all) may expedite; pres. subj. 2nd pers. pl. / *expedir*.

expidamos 1. that we may expedite; pres. subj. 1st pers. pl. / *expedir*. 2. let us expedite; impve. 1st pers. pl.

expidan 1. that they may expedite; pres. subj. 3rd pers. pl. / *expedir*. 2. let them expedite; impve. 3rd pers. pl.

expidas that you may expedite; pres. subj. 2nd pers. sing. / *expedir*.

expide 1. he (she/it) expedites; pres. ind. 3rd pers. sing. / *expedir*. 2. (you) expedite; impve. 2nd pers. sing.

expiden they expedite; pres. ind. 3rd pers. pl. / *expedir*.

expides you expedite; pres. ind. 2nd pers. sing. / *expedir*.

expidiendo expediting; pres. part. / *expedir*.

expidiera 1. that I might expedite; imp. subj. 1st pers. sing. / *expedir*. 2. that he (she/it) might expedite; imp. subj. 3rd pers. sing.

expidierais that you (all) might expedite; imp. subj. 2nd pers pl. / *expedir*.

expidiéramos that we might expedite; imp. subj. 1st pers. pl. / *expedir*.

expidieran that they might expedite; imp. subj. 3rd pers. pl. / *expedir*.

expidieras that you might expedite; imp. subj. 2nd pers. sing. / *expedir*.

expidieron they expedited; past 3rd pers. pl. / *expedir*.

expidiese 1. that I might expedite; imp. subj. 1st pers. sing. / *expedir*. 2. that he (she/it) might expedite; imp. subj. 3rd pers. sing.

expidieseis that you (all) might expedite; imp. subj. 2nd pers pl. / *expedir*.

expidiésemos that we might expedite; imp. subj. 1st pers. pl. / *expedir*.

expidiesen that they might expedite; imp. subj. 3rd pers. pl. / *expedir*.

expidieses that you might expedite; imp. subj. 2nd pers. sing. / *expedir*.

expidió he (she/it) expedited; past 3rd pers. sing. / *expedir*.

expido I expedite; pres. ind. 1st pers. sing. / *expedir*.

expíe 1. that I may expiate; pres. subj. 1st pers. sing. / *expiar*. 2. that he (she/it) may expiate; pres. subj. 3rd pers. sing. 3. let him (her/it) expiate; impve. 3rd pers. sing.

expíen 1. that they may expiate; pres. subj. 3rd pers. pl. / *expiar*. 2. let them expiate; impve. 3rd pers. pl.

expíes that you may expiate; pres. subj. 2nd pers. sing. / *expiar*.

expío I expiate; pres. ind. 1st pers. sing. / *expiar*.

expirar to expire. reg.

explanar to explain or to level. reg.

explayándose going on and on; pres. part. / *explayarse*.

explayaos (you all) go on and on; impve. 2nd pers. pl. / *explayarse*.

explayar to extend. reg.

explayarse to go on and on. reg.

expláyate (you) go on and on; impve. 2nd pers. sing. / *explayarse*.

explayémonos let us go on and on; impve. 1st pers. pl. / *explayarse*.

expláyense let them go on and on; impve. 3rd pers. pl. / *explayarse*.

expláyese let him (her/it) go on and on; impve. 3rd pers. sing. / *explayarse*.

explicándose understanding; pres. part. / *explicarse*.

explicaos (you all) understand; impve. 2nd pers. pl. / *explicarse*.

explicar to explain. irr.

explicarse to understand. irr.

explícate (you) understand; impve. 2nd pers. sing. / *explicarse*.

explique 1. that I may explain; pres. subj. 1st pers. sing. / *explicar*. 2. that he (she/it) may explain; pres. subj. 3rd pers. sing. 3. let him (her/it) explain; impve. 3rd pers. sing.

expliqué I explained; past 1st pers. sing. / *explicar*.

expliquéis that you (all) may explain; pres. subj. 2nd pers. pl. / *explicar*.

expliquémonos let us understand; impve. 1st pers. pl. / *explicarse*.

expliquemos 1. that we may explain; pres. subj. 1st pers. pl. / *explicar*. 2. let us explain; impve. 1st pers. pl.

expliquen 1. that they may explain; pres. subj. 3rd pers. pl. / *explicar*. 2. let them explain; impve. 3rd pers. pl.

explíquense let them understand; impve. 3rd pers. pl. / *explicarse*.

expliques that you may explain; pres. subj. 2nd pers. sing. / *explicar*.

explíquese let him (her/it) understand; impve. 3rd pers. sing. / *explicarse*.

explorar to explore. reg.

explotar to exploit or to explode. reg.

expon (you) expose; impve. 2nd pers. sing. / *exponer*.

expondrá he (she/it) will expose; fut. 3rd pers. sing. / *exponer*.

expondrán they will expose; fut. 3rd pers. pl. / *exponer*.

expondrás you will expose; fut. 2nd pers. sing. / *exponer*.

expondré I shall expose; fut. 1st pers. sing. / *exponer*.

expondréis you (all) will expose; fut. 2nd pers. pl. / *exponer*.

expondremos we shall expose; fut. 1st pers. pl. / *exponer*.

expondría 1. I should expose; cond. 1st pers. sing. / *exponer*. 2. he (she/it) would expose; cond. 3rd pers. sing.

expondríais you (all) would expose; cond. 2nd pers. pl. / *exponer*.

expondríamos we should expose; cond. 1st pers. pl. / *exponer*.

expondrían they would expose; cond. 3rd pers. pl. / *exponer*.

expondrías you would expose; cond. 2nd pers. sing. / *exponer*.

exponeos (you all) run a risk; impve. 2nd pers. pl. / *exponerse*.

exponer to expose. irr.

exponerse to run a risk. irr.

exponga 1. that I may expose; pres. subj. 1st pers. sing. / *exponer*. 2. that he (she/it) may expose; pres. subj. 3rd pers. sing. 3. let him (her/it) expose; impve. 3rd pers. sing.

expongáis that you (all) may expose; pres. subj. 2nd pers. pl. / *exponer*.

expongámonos let us run a risk; impve. 1st pers. pl. / *exponerse*.

expongamos 1. that we may expose; pres. subj. 1st pers. pl. / *exponer*. 2. let us expose; impve. 1st pers. pl.

expongan 1. that they may expose; pres. subj. 3rd pers. pl. / *exponer*. 2. let them expose; impve. 3rd pers. pl.

expónganse let them run a risk; impve. 3rd pers. pl. / *exponerse*.

expongas that you may expose; pres. subj. 2nd pers. sing. / *exponer*.

expóngase let him (her/it) run a risk; impve. 3rd pers. sing. / *exponerse*.

expongo I expose; pres. ind. 1st pers. sing. / *exponer*.

exponiendo exposing; pres. part. / *exponer*.

exponiéndose running a risk; pres. part. / *exponerse*.

expónte (you) run a risk; impve. 2nd pers. sing. / *exponerse*.

exportar to export. reg.

expresándose speaking; pres. part. / *expresarse*.

expresaos (you all) speak; impve. 2nd pers. pl. / *expresarse*.

expresar to express. reg.

expresarse to speak. reg.

exprésate (you) speak; impve. 2nd pers. sing. / *expresarse*.

expresémonos let us speak; impve. 1st pers. pl. / *expresarse*.

exprésense let them speak; impve. 3rd pers. pl. / *expresarse*.

exprésese let him (her/it) speak; impve. 3rd pers. sing. / *expresarse*.

exprimir to squeeze out. reg.

expropiar to expropriate. reg.

expuesto exposed; past part. / *exponer*.

expugnar to take by storm. reg.

expulsar to expel. reg.

expurgar to expurgate. irr.

expurgue 1. that I may expurgate; pres. subj. 1st pers. sing. / *expurgar*. 2. that he (she/it) may expurgate; pres. subj. 3rd pers. sing. 3. let him (her/it) expurgate; impve. 3rd pers. sing.

expurgué I expurgated; past 1st pers. sing. / *expurgar*.

expurguéis that you (all) may expurgate; pres. subj. 2nd pers. pl. / *expurgar*.

expurguemos 1. that we may expurgate; pres. subj. 1st pers. pl. / *expurgar*. 2. let us expurgate; impve. 1st pers. pl.

expurguen 1. that they may expurgate; pres. subj. 3rd pers. pl. / *expurgar*. 2. let them expurgate; impve. 3rd pers. pl.

expurgues that you may expurgate; pres. subj. 2nd pers. sing. / *expurgar*.

expuse I exposed; past 1st pers. sing. / *exponer*.

expusiera 1. that I might expose; imp. subj. 1st pers. sing. / *exponer*. 2. that he (she/it) might expose; imp. subj. 3rd pers. sing.

expusierais that you (all) might expose; imp. subj. 2nd pers pl. / *exponer*.

expusiéramos that we might expose; imp. subj. 1st pers. pl. / *exponer*.

expusieran that they might expose; imp. subj. 3rd pers. pl. / *exponer*.

expusieras that you might expose; imp. subj. 2nd pers. sing. / *exponer.*

expusieron they exposed; past 3rd pers. pl. / *exponer.*

expusiese 1. that I might expose; imp. subj. 1st pers. sing. / *exponer.* 2. that he (she/it) might expose; imp. subj. 3rd pers. sing.

expusieseis that you (all) might expose; imp. subj. 2nd pers pl. / *exponer.*

expusiésemos that we might expose; imp. subj. 1st pers. pl. / *exponer.*

expusiesen that they might expose; imp. subj. 3rd pers. pl. / *exponer.*

expusieses that you might expose; imp. subj. 2nd pers. sing. / *exponer.*

expusimos we exposed; past 1st pers. pl. / *exponer.*

expusiste you exposed; past 2nd pers. sing. / *exponer.*

expusisteis you (all) exposed; past 2nd pers. pl. / *exponer.*

expuso he (she/it) exposed; past 3rd pers. sing. / *exponer.*

extasía 1. he (she/it) delights; pres. ind. 3rd pers. sing. / *extasiar.* 2. (you) delight; impve. 2nd pers. sing.

extasían they delight; pres. ind. 3rd pers. pl. / *extasiar.*

extasiándose being in ecstasy; pres. part. / *extasiarse.*

extasiaos (you all) be in ecstasy; impve. 2nd pers. pl. / *extasiarse.*

extasiar to delight. irr.

extasiarse to be in ecstasy. irr.

extasías you delight; pres. ind. 2nd pers. sing. / *extasiar.*

extasíate (you) be in ecstasy; impve. 2nd pers. sing. / *extasiarse.*

extasíe 1. that I may delight; pres. subj. 1st pers. sing. / *extasiar.* 2. that he (she/it) may delight; pres. subj. 3rd pers. sing. 3. let him (her/it) delight; impve. 3rd pers. sing.

extasiémonos let us be in ecstasy; impve. 1st pers. pl. / *extasiarse.*

extasíen 1. that they may delight; pres. subj. 3rd pers. pl. / *extasiar.* 2. let them delight; impve. 3rd pers. pl.

extasíense let them be in ecstasy; impve. 3rd pers. pl. / *extasiarse.*

extasíes that you may delight; pres. subj. 2nd pers. sing. / *extasiar.*

extasíese let him (her/it) be in ecstasy; impve. 3rd pers. sing. / *extasiarse.*

extasío I delight; pres. ind. 1st pers. sing. / *extasiar.*

extendámonos let us spread; impve. 1st pers. pl. / *extenderse.*

extendeos (you all) spread; impve. 2nd pers. pl. / *extenderse.*

extender to extend. irr.

extenderse to spread. irr.

extendiéndose spreading; pres. part. / *extenderse.*

extenúa 1. he (she/it) weakens; pres. ind. 3rd pers. sing. / *extenuar.* 2. (you) weaken; impve. 2nd pers. sing.

extenúan they weaken; pres. ind. 3rd pers. pl. / *extenuar.*

extenuándose languishing; pres. part. / *extenuarse.*

extenuaos (you all) languish; impve. 2nd pers. pl. / *extenuarse.*

extenuar to weaken. irr.

extenuarse to languish. irr.

extenúas you weaken; pres. ind. 2nd pers. sing. / *extenuar.*

extenúate (you) languish; impve. 2nd pers. sing. / *extenuarse.*

extenúe 1. that I may weaken; pres. subj. 1st pers. sing. / *extenuar.* 2. that he (she/it) may weaken; pres. subj. 3rd pers. sing. 3. let him (her/it) weaken; impve. 3rd pers. sing.

extenuémonos let us languish; impve. 1st pers. pl. / *extenuarse.*

extenúen 1. that they may weaken; pres. subj. 3rd pers. pl. / *extenuar.* 2. let them weaken; impve. 3rd pers. pl.

extenúense let them languish; impve. 3rd pers. pl. / *extenuarse.*

extenúes that you may weaken; pres. subj. 2nd pers. sing. / *extenuar.*

extenúese let him (her/it) languish; impve. 3rd pers. sing. / *extenuarse.*

extenúo I weaken; pres. ind. 1st pers. sing. / *extenuar.*

exteriorice 1. that I may make manifest; pres. subj. 1st pers. sing. / *exteriorizar.* 2. that he (she/it) may make manifest; pres. subj. 3rd pers. sing. 3. let him (her/it) make manifest; impve. 3rd pers. sing.

exterioricé I made manifest; past 1st pers. sing. / *exteriorizar.*

exterioricéis that you (all) may make manifest; pres. subj. 2nd pers. pl. / *exteriorizar.*

exterioricémonos let us unbusom ourselves; impve. 1st pers. pl. / *exteriorizarse.*

exterioricemos 1. that we may make manifest; pres. subj. 1st pers. pl. / *exteriorizar.* 2. let us make manifest; impve. 1st pers. pl.

exterioricen 1. that they may make manifest; pres. subj. 3rd pers. pl. / *exteriorizar.* 2. let them make manifest; impve. 3rd pers. pl.

exteriorícense let them unbusom themselves; impve. 3rd pers. pl. / *exteriorizarse.*

exteriorices that you may make manifest; pres. subj. 2nd pers. sing. / *exteriorizar.*

exteriorícese let him (her/it) unbusom himself (herself/ itself); impve. 3rd pers. sing. / *exteriorizarse.*

exteriorizándose unbusoming oneself; pres. part. / *exteriorizarse.*

exteriorizaos (you all) unbusom yourselves; impve. 2nd pers. pl. / *exteriorizarse.*

exteriorizar to make manifest. irr.

exteriorizarse to unbusom oneself. irr.

exteriorízate (you) unbusom yourself; impve. 2nd pers. sing. / *exteriorizarse.*

exterminar to exterminate. reg.

extienda 1. that I may extend; pres. subj. 1st pers. sing. / *extender*. 2. that he (she/it) may extend; pres. subj. 3rd pers. sing. 3. let him (her/it) extend; impve. 3rd pers. sing.

extiendan 1. that they may extend; pres. subj. 3rd pers. pl. / *extender*. 2. let them extend; impve. 3rd pers. pl.

extiéndanse let them spread; impve. 3rd pers. pl. / *extenderse*.

extiendas that you may extend; pres. subj. 2nd pers. sing. / *extender*.

extiéndase let him (her/it) spread; impve. 3rd pers. sing. / *extenderse*.

extiende 1. he (she/it) extends; pres. ind. 3rd pers. sing. / *extender*. 2. (you) extend; impve. 2nd pers. sing.

extienden they extend; pres. ind. 3rd pers. pl. / *extender*.

extiendes you extend; pres. ind. 2nd pers. sing. / *extender*.

extiéndete (you) spread; impve. 2nd pers. sing. / *extenderse*.

extiendo I extend; pres. ind. 1st pers. sing. / *extender*.

extinga 1. that I may extinguish; pres. subj. 1st pers. sing. / *extinguir*. 2. that he (she/it) may extinguish; pres. subj. 3rd pers. sing. 3. let him (her/it) extinguish; impve. 3rd pers. sing.

extingáis that you (all) may extinguish; pres. subj. 2nd pers. pl. / *extinguir*.

extingamos 1. that we may extinguish; pres. subj. 1st pers. pl. / *extinguir*. 2. let us extinguish; impve. 1st pers. pl.

extingan 1. that they may extinguish; pres. subj. 3rd pers. pl. / *extinguir*. 2. let them extinguish; impve. 3rd pers. pl.

extingas that you may extinguish; pres. subj. 2nd pers. sing. / *extinguir*.

extingo I extinguish; pres. ind. 1st pers. sing. / *extinguir*.

extinguir to extinguish. irr.

extirpar to extirpate or to eradicate. reg.

extorsionar to extort. reg.

extractar to abstract. reg.

extraer to extract. irr.

extraiga 1. that I may extract; pres. subj. 1st pers. sing. / *extraer*. 2. that he (she/it) may extract; pres. subj. 3rd pers. sing. 3. let him (her/it) extract; impve. 3rd pers. sing.

extraigáis that you (all) may extract; pres. subj. 2nd pers. pl. / *extraer*.

extraigamos 1. that we may extract; pres. subj. 1st pers. pl. / *extraer*. 2. let us extract; impve. 1st pers. pl.

extraigan 1. that they may extract; pres. subj. 3rd pers. pl. / *extraer*. 2. let them extract; impve. 3rd pers. pl.

extraigas that you may extract; pres. subj. 2nd pers. sing. / *extraer*.

extraigo I extract; pres. ind. 1st pers. sing. / *extraer*.

extraje I extracted; past 1st pers. sing. / *extraer*.

extrajera 1. that I might extract; imp. subj. 1st pers. sing. / *extraer*. 2. that he (she/it) might extract; imp. subj. 3rd pers. sing.

extrajerais that you (all) might extract; imp. subj. 2nd pers pl. / *extraer*.

extrajéramos that we might extract; imp. subj. 1st pers. pl. / *extraer*.

extrajeran that they might extract; imp. subj. 3rd pers. pl. / *extraer*.

extrajeras that you might extract; imp. subj. 2nd pers. sing. / *extraer*.

extrajeron they extracted; past 3rd pers. pl. / *extraer*.

extrajese 1. that I might extract; imp. subj. 1st pers. sing. / *extraer*. 2. that he (she/it) might extract; imp. subj. 3rd pers. sing.

extrajeseis that you (all) might extract; imp. subj. 2nd pers pl. / *extraer*.

extrajésemos that we might extract; imp. subj. 1st pers. pl. / *extraer*.

extrajesen that they might extract; imp. subj. 3rd pers. pl. / *extraer*.

extrajeses that you might extract; imp. subj. 2nd pers. sing. / *extraer*.

extrajimos we extracted; past 1st pers. pl. / *extraer*.

extrajiste you extracted; past 2nd pers. sing. / *extraer*.

extrajisteis you (all) extracted; past 2nd pers. pl. / *extraer*.

extrajo he (she/it) extracted; past 3rd pers. sing. / *extraer*.

extralimitándose overstepping authority; pres. part. / *extralimitarse*.

extralimitaos (you all) overstep authority; impve. 2nd pers. pl. / *extralimitarse*.

extralimitarse to overstep authority. reg.

extralimítate (you) overstep authority; impve. 2nd pers. sing. / *extralimitarse*.

extralimitémonos let us overstep authority; impve. 1st pers. pl. / *extralimitarse*.

extralimítense let them overstep authority; impve. 3rd pers. pl. / *extralimitarse*.

extralimítese let him (her/it) overstep authority; impve. 3rd pers. sing. / *extralimitarse*.

extrañándose being surprised; pres. part. / *extrañarse*.

extrañaos (you all) be surprised; impve. 2nd pers. pl. / *extrañarse*.

extrañar to banish. reg.

extrañarse to be surprised. reg.

extráñate (you) be surprised; impve. 2nd pers. sing. / *extrañarse*.

extrañémonos let us be surprised; impve. 1st pers. pl. / *extrañarse*.

extráñense let them be surprised; impve. 3rd pers. pl. / *extrañarse*.

extráñese let him (her/it) be surprised; impve. 3rd pers. sing. / *extrañarse*.

extravía 1. he (she/it) leads astray; pres. ind. 3rd pers. sing. / *extraviar*. 2. (you) lead astray; impve. 2nd pers. sing.

extravían they lead astray; pres. ind. 3rd pers. pl. / *extraviar*.

extraviándose getting lost; pres. part. / *extraviarse*.

extraviaos (you all) get lost; impve. 2nd pers. pl. / *extraviarse*.

extraviar to lead astray. irr.

extraviarse to get lost. irr.

extravías you lead astray; pres. ind. 2nd pers. sing. / *extraviar*.

extravíate (you) get lost; impve. 2nd pers. sing. / *extraviarse*.

extravíe 1. that I may lead astray; pres. subj. 1st pers. sing. / *extraviar*. 2. that he (she/it) may lead astray; pres. subj. 3rd pers. sing. 3. let him (her/it) lead astray; impve. 3rd pers. sing.

extraviémonos let us get lost; impve. 1st pers. pl. / *extraviarse*.

extravíen 1. that they may lead astray; pres. subj. 3rd pers. pl. / *extraviar*. 2. let them lead astray; impve. 3rd pers. pl.

extravíense let them get lost; impve. 3rd pers. pl. / *extraviarse*.

extravíes that you may lead astray; pres. subj. 2nd pers. sing. / *extraviar*.

extravíese let him (her/it) get lost; impve. 3rd pers. sing. / *extraviarse*.

extravío I lead astray; pres. ind. 1st pers. sing. / *extraviar*.

extrayendo extracting; pres. part. / *extraer*.

extremándose taking special pains; pres. part. / *extremarse*.

extremaos (you all) take special pains; impve. 2nd pers. pl. / *extremarse*.

extremar to carry to extreme. reg.

extremarse to take special pains. reg.

extrémate (you) take special pains; impve. 2nd pers. sing. / *extremarse*.

extremémonos let us take special pains; impve. 1st pers. pl. / *extremarse*.

extrémense let them take special pains; impve. 3rd pers. pl. / *extremarse*.

extrémese let him (her/it) take special pains; impve. 3rd pers. sing. / *extremarse*.

exudar to exude. reg.

exultar to exult. reg.

eyacular to ejaculate. reg.

F

fabricar to fabricate. irr.

fabrique 1. that I may fabricate; pres. subj. 1st pers. sing. / *fabricar*. 2. that he (she/it) may fabricate; pres. subj. 3rd pers. sing. 3. let him (her/it) fabricate; impve. 3rd pers. sing.

fabriqué I fabricated; past 1st pers. sing. / *fabricar*.

fabriquéis that you (all) may fabricate; pres. subj. 2nd pers. pl. / *fabricar*.

fabriquemos 1. that we may fabricate; pres. subj. 1st pers. pl. / *fabricar*. 2. let us fabricate; impve. 1st pers. pl.

fabriquen 1. that they may fabricate; pres. subj. 3rd pers. pl. / *fabricar*. 2. let them fabricate; impve. 3rd pers. pl.

fabriques that you may fabricate; pres. subj. 2nd pers. sing. / *fabricar*.

facilitar to facilitate. reg.

factorice 1. that I may factor; pres. subj. 1st pers. sing. / *factorizar*. 2. that he (she/it) may factor; pres. subj. 3rd pers. sing. 3. let him (her/it) factor; impve. 3rd pers. sing.

factoricé I factored; past 1st pers. sing. / *factorizar*.

factoricéis that you (all) may factor; pres. subj. 2nd pers. pl. / *factorizar*.

factoricemos 1. that we may factor; pres. subj. 1st pers. pl. / *factorizar*. 2. let us factor; impve. 1st pers. pl.

factoricen 1. that they may factor; pres. subj. 3rd pers. pl. / *factorizar*. 2. let them factor; impve. 3rd pers. pl.

factorices that you may factor; pres. subj. 2nd pers. sing. / *factorizar*.

factorizar to factor. irr.

facturar to invoice. reg.

facultar to authorize. reg.

fachendear to brag. reg.

fajándose fighting; pres. part. / *fajarse*.

fajaos (you all) fight; impve. 2nd pers. pl. / *fajarse*.

fajar to girdle. reg.

fajarse to fight. reg.

fájate (you) fight; impve. 2nd pers. sing. / *fajarse*.

fajémonos let us fight; impve. 1st pers. pl. / *fajarse*.

fájense let them fight; impve. 3rd pers. pl. / *fajarse*.

fájese let him (her/it) fight; impve. 3rd pers. sing. / *fajarse*.

faldear to skirt (a hill). reg.

falsear to falsify or to weaken. reg.

falsificar to falsify. irr.

falsifique 1. that I may falsify; pres. subj. 1st pers. sing. / *falsificar*. 2. that he (she/it) may falsify; pres. subj. 3rd pers. sing. 3. let him (her/it) falsify; impve. 3rd pers. sing.

falsifiqué I falsified; past 1st pers. sing. / *falsificar*.

falsifiquéis that you (all) may falsify; pres. subj. 2nd pers. pl. / *falsificar*.

falsifiquemos 1. that we may falsify; pres. subj. 1st pers. pl. / *falsificar*. 2. let us falsify; impve. 1st pers. pl.

falsifiquen 1. that they may falsify; pres. subj. 3rd pers. pl. / *falsificar*. 2. let them falsify; impve. 3rd pers. pl.

falsifiques that you may falsify; pres. subj. 2nd pers. sing. / *falsificar*.

faltar to be lacking or to offend. reg.

fallar to fail or to render a verdict. reg.

fallecer to die. irr.

fallezca 1. that I may die; pres. subj. 1st pers. sing. / *fallecer*. 2. that he (she/it) may die; pres. subj. 3rd pers. sing. 3. let him (her/it) die; impve. 3rd pers. sing.

fallezcáis that you (all) may die; pres. subj. 2nd pers. pl. / *fallecer*.

fallezcamos 1. that we may die; pres. subj. 1st pers. pl. / *fallecer*. 2. let us die; impve. 1st pers. pl.

fallezcan 1. that they may die; pres. subj. 3rd pers. pl. / *fallecer*. 2. let them die; impve. 3rd pers. pl.

fallezcas that you may die; pres. subj. 2nd pers. sing. / *fallecer*.

fallezco I die; pres. ind. 1st pers. sing. / *fallecer*.

familiarice 1. that I may familiarize; pres. subj. 1st pers. sing. / *familiarizar*. 2. that he (she/it) may familiarize; pres. subj. 3rd pers. sing. 3. let him (her/it) familiarize; impve. 3rd pers. sing.

familiaricé I familiarized; past 1st pers. sing. / *familiarizar*.

familiaricéis that you (all) may familiarize; pres. subj. 2nd pers. pl. / *familiarizar*.

familiaricémonos let us become familiar; impve. 1st pers. pl. / *familiarizarse*.

familiaricemos 1. that we may familiarize; pres. subj. 1st pers. pl. / *familiarizar*. 2. let us familiarize; impve. 1st pers. pl.

familiaricen 1. that they may familiarize; pres. subj. 3rd pers. pl. / *familiarizar*. 2. let them familiarize; impve. 3rd pers. pl.

familiarícense let them become familiar; impve. 3rd pers. pl. / *familiarizarse*.

familiarices that you may familiarize; pres. subj. 2nd pers. sing. / *familiarizar*.

familiarícese let him (her/it) become familiar; impve. 3rd pers. sing. / *familiarizarse*.

familiarizándose becoming familiar; pres. part. / *familiarizarse*.

familiarizaos (you all) become familiar; impve. 2nd pers. pl. / *familiarizarse*.

familiarizar to familiarize. irr.

familiarizarse to become familiar. irr.

familiarízate (you) become familiar; impve. 2nd pers. sing. / *familiarizarse*.

fanfarronear to boast. reg.

fantasear to daydream or to imagine. reg.

farfullar to sputter or to stumble through. reg.

farolear to boast. reg.

fascinar to fascinate. reg.

fastidiar to annoy. reg.

fatigándose getting tired; pres. part. / *fatigarse*.

fatigaos (you all) get tired; impve. 2nd pers. pl. / *fatigarse*.

fatigar to fatigue. irr.

fatigarse to get tired. irr.

fatígate (you) get tired; impve. 2nd pers. sing. / *fatigarse*.

fatigue 1. that I may fatigue; pres. subj. 1st pers. sing. / *fatigar*. 2. that he (she/it) may fatigue; pres. subj. 3rd pers. sing. 3. let him (her/it) fatigue; impve. 3rd pers. sing.

fatigué I fatigued; past 1st pers. sing. / *fatigar*.

fatiguéis that you (all) may fatigue; pres. subj. 2nd pers. pl. / *fatigar*.

fatiguémonos let us get tired; impve. 1st pers. pl. / *fatigarse*.

fatiguemos 1. that we may fatigue; pres. subj. 1st pers. pl. / *fatigar*. 2. let us fatigue; impve. 1st pers. pl.

fatiguen 1. that they may fatigue; pres. subj. 3rd pers. pl. / *fatigar*. 2. let them fatigue; impve. 3rd pers. pl.

fatíguense let them get tired; impve. 3rd pers. pl. / *fatigarse*.

fatigues that you may fatigue; pres. subj. 2nd pers. sing. / *fatigar*.

fatíguese let him (her/it) get tired; impve. 3rd pers. sing. / *fatigarse*.

favoreceos (you all) avail yourselves; impve. 2nd pers. pl. / *favorecerse*.

favorecer to favor. irr.

favorecerse to avail oneself. irr.

favorécete (you) avail yourself; impve. 2nd pers. sing. / *favorecerse*.

favoreciéndose availing oneself; pres. part. / *favorecerse*.

favorezca 1. that I may favor; pres. subj. 1st pers. sing. / *favorecer*. 2. that he (she/it) may favor; pres. subj. 3rd pers. sing. 3. let him (her/it) favor; impve. 3rd pers. sing.

favorezcáis that you (all) may favor; pres. subj. 2nd pers. pl. / *favorecer*.

favorezcámonos let us avail ourselves; impve. 1st pers. pl. / *favorecerse*.

favorezcamos 1. that we may favor; pres. subj. 1st pers. pl. / *favorecer*. 2. let us favor; impve. 1st pers. pl.

favorezcan 1. that they may favor; pres. subj. 3rd pers. pl. / *favorecer*. 2. let them favor; impve. 3rd pers. pl.

favorézcanse let them avail themselves; impve. 3rd pers. pl. / *favorecerse*.

favorezcas that you may favor; pres. subj. 2nd pers. sing. / *favorecer*.

favorézcase let him (her/it) avail himself (herself/itself) ; impve. 3rd pers. sing. / *favorecerse*.

favorezco I favor; pres. ind. 1st pers. sing. / *favorecer*.

fecundar to fertilize. reg.

fechar to date. reg.

federar to federate. reg.

felicitar to congratulate. reg.

fenecer to finish or to die. irr.

fenezca 1. that I may finish; pres. subj. 1st pers. sing. / *fenecer*. 2. that he (she/it) may finish; pres. subj. 3rd pers. sing. 3. let him (her/it) finish; impve. 3rd pers. sing.

fenezcáis that you (all) may finish; pres. subj. 2nd pers. pl. / *fenecer*.

fenezcamos 1. that we may finish; pres. subj. 1st pers. pl. / *fenecer*. 2. let us finish; impve. 1st pers. pl.

fenezcan 1. that they may finish; pres. subj. 3rd pers. pl. / *fenecer*. 2. let them finish; impve. 3rd pers. pl.

fenezcas that you may finish; pres. subj. 2nd pers. sing. / *fenecer*.

fenezco I finish; pres. ind. 1st pers. sing. / *fenecer*.

feriar to buy or to quit work. reg.

fermentar to ferment. reg.

ferrar to cover with iron. irr.

fertilice 1. that I may fertilize; pres. subj. 1st pers. sing. / *fertilizar*. 2. that he (she/it) may fertilize; pres. subj. 3rd pers. sing. 3. let him (her/it) fertilize; impve. 3rd pers. sing.

fertilicé I fertilized; past 1st pers. sing. / *fertilizar*.

fertilicéis that you (all) may fertilize; pres. subj. 2nd pers. pl. / *fertilizar*.

fertilicemos 1. that we may fertilize; pres. subj. 1st pers. pl. / *fertilizar*. 2. let us fertilize; impve. 1st pers. pl.

fertilicen 1. that they may fertilize; pres. subj. 3rd pers. pl. / *fertilizar*. 2. let them fertilize; impve. 3rd pers. pl.

fertilices that you may fertilize; pres. subj. 2nd pers. sing. / *fertilizar*.

fertilizar to fertilize. irr.

festear to pay court. reg.

festejar to entertain. reg.

festinar to hasten. reg.

festonar to wreathe. reg.

festonear to festoon. reg.

fía 1. he (she/it) guarantees; pres. ind. 3rd pers. sing. / *fiar*. 2. (you) guarantee; impve. 2nd pers. sing.

fían they guarantee; pres. ind. 3rd pers. pl. / *fiar*.

fiándose trusting; pres. part. / *fiarse*.

fiaos (you all) trust; impve. 2nd pers. pl. / *fiarse*.

fiar to guarantee. irr.

fiarse to trust. irr.

fías you guarantee; pres. ind. 2nd pers. sing. / *fiar*.

fíate (you) trust; impve. 2nd pers. sing. / *fiarse*.

fichar to peg (a person) or to move (in dominoes). reg.

fíe 1. that I may guarantee; pres. subj. 1st pers. sing. / *fiar*. 2. that he (she/it) may guarantee; pres. subj. 3rd pers. sing. 3. let him (her/it) guarantee; impve. 3rd pers. sing.

fiémonos let us trust; impve. 1st pers. pl. / *fiarse*.

fíen 1. that they may guarantee; pres. subj. 3rd pers. pl. / *fiar*. 2. let them guarantee; impve. 3rd pers. pl.

fiense let them trust; impve. 3rd pers. pl. / *fiarse*.

fierra 1. he (she/it) covers with iron; pres. ind. 3rd pers. sing. / *ferrar*. 2. (you) cover with iron; impve. 2nd pers. sing.

fierran they cover with iron; pres. ind. 3rd pers. pl. / *ferrar*.

fierras you cover with iron; pres. ind. 2nd pers. sing. / *ferrar*.

fierre 1. that I may cover with iron; pres. subj. 1st pers. sing. / *ferrar*. 2. that he (she/it) may cover with iron; pres. subj. 3rd pers. sing. 3. let him (her/it) cover with iron; impve. 3rd pers. sing.

fierren 1. that they may cover with iron; pres. subj. 3rd pers. pl. / *ferrar*. 2. let them cover with iron; impve. 3rd pers. pl.

fierres that you may cover with iron; pres. subj. 2nd pers. sing. / *ferrar*.

fierro I cover with iron; pres. ind. 1st pers. sing. / *ferrar*.

fíes that you may guarantee; pres. subj. 2nd pers. sing. / *fiar*.

fíese let him (her/it) trust; impve. 3rd pers. sing. / *fiarse*.

figurándose imagining; pres. part. / *figurarse*.

figuraos (you all) imagine; impve. 2nd pers. pl. / *figurarse*.

figurar to figure. reg.

figurarse to imagine. reg.

figúrate (you) imagine; impve. 2nd pers. sing. / *figurarse*.

figurémonos let us imagine; impve. 1st pers. pl. / *figurarse*.

figúrense let them imagine; impve. 3rd pers. pl. / *figurarse*.

figúrese let him (her/it) imagine; impve. 3rd pers. sing. / *figurarse*.

fijándose settling; pres. part. / *fijarse*.

fijaos (you all) settle; impve. 2nd pers. pl. / *fijarse*.

fijar to fix. reg.

fijarse to settle. reg.

fíjate (you) settle; impve. 2nd pers. sing. / *fijarse*.

fijémonos let us settle; impve. 1st pers. pl. / *fijarse*.

fíjense let them settle; impve. 3rd pers. pl. / *fijarse*.

fíjese let him (her/it) settle; impve. 3rd pers. sing. / *fijarse*.

filmar to film. reg.

filosofar to philosophize. reg.

filtrándose seeping through; pres. part. / *filtrarse*.

filtrar to filter. reg.

filtrarse to seep through. reg.

fíltrense let them seep through; impve. 3rd pers. pl. / *filtrarse*.

fíltrese let it seep through; impve. 3rd pers. sing. / *filtrarse*.

finalice 1. that I may finish; pres. subj. 1st pers. sing. / *finalizar*. 2. that he (she/it) may finish; pres. subj. 3rd pers. sing. 3. let him (her/it) finish; impve. 3rd pers. sing.

finalicé I finished; past 1st pers. sing. / *finalizar*.

finalicéis that you (all) may finish; pres. subj. 2nd pers. pl. / *finalizar*.

finalicemos 1. that we may finish; pres. subj. 1st pers. pl. / *finalizar*. 2. let us finish; impve. 1st pers. pl.

finalicen 1. that they may finish; pres. subj. 3rd pers. pl. / *finalizar*. 2. let them finish; impve. 3rd pers. pl.

finalices that you may finish; pres. subj. 2nd pers. sing. / *finalizar*.

finalizar to finish. irr.

financiar to finance. reg.

finándose longing for; pres. part. / *finarse*.

finaos (you all) long for; impve. 2nd pers. pl. / *finarse*.

finar to die. reg.

finarse to long for. reg.

fínate (you) long for; impve. 2nd pers. sing. / *finarse*.
fincándose residing; pres. part. / *fincarse*.
fincaos (you all) reside; impve. 2nd pers. pl. / *fincarse*.
fincar to buy real estate. irr.
fincarse to reside. irr.
fíncate (you) reside; impve. 2nd pers. sing. / *fincarse*.
finémonos let us long for; impve. 1st pers. pl. / *finarse*.
fínense let them long for; impve. 3rd pers. pl. / *finarse*.
fínese let him (her/it) long for; impve. 3rd pers. sing. / *finarse*.
fíngete (you) pretend to be; impve. 2nd pers. sing. / *fingirse*.
fingiéndose pretending to be; pres. part. / *fingirse*.
fingíos (you all) pretend to be; impve. 2nd pers. pl. / *fingirse*.
fingir to feign. irr.
fingirse to pretend to be. irr.
finiquitar to settle an account. reg.
finja 1. that I may feign; pres. subj. 1st pers. sing. / *fingir*. 2. that he (she/it) may feign; pres. subj. 3rd pers. sing. 3. let him (her/it) feign; impve. 3rd pers. sing.
finjáis that you (all) may feign; pres. subj. 2nd pers. pl. / *fingir*.
finjámonos let us pretend to be; impve. 1st pers. pl. / *fingirse*.
finjamos 1. that we may feign; pres. subj. 1st pers. pl. / *fingir*. 2. let us feign; impve. 1st pers. pl.
finjan 1. that they may feign; pres. subj. 3rd pers. pl. / *fingir*. 2. let them feign; impve. 3rd pers. pl.
finjanse let them pretend to be; impve. 3rd pers. pl. / *fingirse*.
finjas that you may feign; pres. subj. 2nd pers. sing. / *fingir*.
finjase let him (her/it) pretend to be; impve. 3rd pers. sing. / *fingirse*.
finjo I feign; pres. ind. 1st pers. sing. / *fingir*.
finque 1. that I may buy real estate; pres. subj. 1st pers. sing. / *fincar*. 2. that he (she/it) may buy real estate; pres. subj. 3rd pers. sing. 3. let him (her/it) buy real estate; impve. 3rd pers. sing.
finqué I bought real estate; past 1st pers. sing. / *fincar*.
finquéis that you (all) may buy real estate; pres. subj. 2nd pers. pl. / *fincar*.
finquémonos let us reside; impve. 1st pers. pl. / *fincarse*.
finquemos 1. that we may buy real estate; pres. subj. 1st pers. pl. / *fincar*. 2. let us buy real estate; impve. 1st pers. pl.
finquen 1. that they may buy real estate; pres. subj. 3rd pers. pl. / *fincar*. 2. let them buy real estate; impve. 3rd pers. pl.
finquense let them reside; impve. 3rd pers. pl. / *fincarse*.
finques that you may buy real estate; pres. subj. 2nd pers. sing. / *fincar*.

fínquese let him (her/it) reside; impve. 3rd pers. sing. / *fincarse*.
fío I guarantee; pres. ind. 1st pers. sing. / *fiar*.
firmar to sign. reg.
fiscalice 1. that I may audit; pres. subj. 1st pers. sing. / *fiscalizar*. 2. that he (she/it) may audit; pres. subj. 3rd pers. sing. 3. let him (her/it) audit; impve. 3rd pers. sing.
fiscalicé I audited; past 1st pers. sing. / *fiscalizar*.
fiscalicéis that you (all) may audit; pres. subj. 2nd pers. pl. / *fiscalizar*.
fiscalicemos 1. that we may audit; pres. subj. 1st pers. pl. / *fiscalizar*. 2. let us audit; impve. 1st pers. pl.
fiscalicen 1. that they may audit; pres. subj. 3rd pers. pl. / *fiscalizar*. 2. let them audit; impve. 3rd pers. pl.
fiscalices that you may audit; pres. subj. 2nd pers. sing. / *fiscalizar*.
fiscalizar to audit or to criticize. irr.
fisgándose mocking; pres. part. / *fisgarse*.
fisgaos (you all) mock; impve. 2nd pers. pl. / *fisgarse*.
fisgar to pry. irr.
fisgarse to mock. irr.
físgate (you) mock; impve. 2nd pers. sing. / *fisgarse*.
fisgonear to pry. reg.
fisgue 1. that I may pry; pres. subj. 1st pers. sing. / *fisgar*. 2. that he (she/it) may pry; pres. subj. 3rd pers. sing. 3. let him (her/it) pry; impve. 3rd pers. sing.
fisgué I pried; past 1st pers. sing. / *fisgar*.
fisguéis that you (all) may pry; pres. subj. 2nd pers. pl. / *fisgar*.
fisguémonos let us mock; impve. 1st pers. pl. / *fisgarse*.
fisguemos 1. that we may pry; pres. subj. 1st pers. pl. / *fisgar*. 2. let us pry; impve. 1st pers. pl.
fisguen 1. that they may pry; pres. subj. 3rd pers. pl. / *fisgar*. 2. let them pry; impve. 3rd pers. pl.
físguense let them mock; impve. 3rd pers. pl. / *fisgarse*.
fisgues that you may pry; pres. subj. 2nd pers. sing. / *fisgar*.
físguese let him (her/it) mock; impve. 3rd pers. sing. / *fisgarse*.
flagelar to flagellate or to whip. reg.
flagrar to blaze. reg.
flamear to flame. reg.
flanquear to flank. reg.
flaquear to flag or to weaken. reg.
flechar to shoot (an arrow). reg.
fletándose getting out; pres. part. / *fletarse*.
fletaos (you all) get out; impve. 2nd pers. pl. / *fletarse*.
fletar to charter (a boat). reg.
fletarse to get out. reg.
flétate (you) get out; impve. 2nd pers. sing. / *fletarse*.
fletémonos let us get out; impve. 1st pers. pl. / *fletarse*.
flétense let them get out; impve. 3rd pers. pl. / *fletarse*.

flétese let him (her/it) get out; impve. 3rd pers. sing. / *fletarse*.
flexionar to flex or to bend. reg.
flirtear to flirt. reg.
flojear to slacken or to be lazy. reg.
florar to flower. reg.
floreándose shining; pres. part. / *florearse*.
floreaos (you all) shine; impve. 2nd pers. pl. / *florearse*.
florear to decorate with flowers or to pay compliments. reg.
florearse to shine or to excel. reg.
floréate (you) shine; impve. 2nd pers. sing. / *florearse*.
florecer to flower or to flourish. irr.
florecerse to become mouldy. irr.
floreciéndose becoming mouldy; pres. part. / *florecerse*.
floreémonos let us shine; impve. 1st pers. pl. / *florearse*.
floréense let them shine; impve. 3rd pers. pl. / *florearse*.
floréese let him (her/it) shine; impve. 3rd pers. sing. / *florearse*.
floretear to decorate with flowers or to fence. reg.
florezca 1. that I may flourish; pres. subj. 1st pers. sing. / *florecer*. 2. that he (she/it) may flourish; pres. subj. 3rd pers. sing. 3. let him (her/it) flourish; impve. 3rd pers. sing.
florezcáis that you (all) may flourish; pres. subj. 2nd pers. pl. / *florecer*.
florezcamos 1. that we may flourish; pres. subj. 1st pers. pl. / *florecer*. 2. let us flourish; impve. 1st pers. pl.
florezcan 1. that they may flourish; pres. subj. 3rd pers. pl. / *florecer*. 2. let them flourish; impve. 3rd pers. pl.
florézcanse let them become moldy; impve. 3rd pers. pl. / *florecerse*.
florezcas that you may flower; pres. subj. 2nd pers. sing. / *florecer*.
florézcase let it become moldy; impve. 3rd pers. sing. / *florecerse*.
florezco I flourish; pres. ind. 1st pers. sing. / *florecer*.
flotar to float. reg.
fluctúa 1. he (she/it) fluctuates; pres. ind. 3rd pers. sing. / *fluctuar*. 2. (you) fluctuate; impve. 2nd pers. sing.
fluctúan they fluctuate; pres. ind. 3rd pers. pl. / *fluctuar*.
fluctuar to fluctuate. irr.
fluctúas you fluctuate; pres. ind. 2nd pers. sing. / *fluctuar*.
fluctúe 1. that I may fluctuate; pres. subj. 1st pers. sing. / *fluctuar*. 2. that he (she/it) may fluctuate; pres. subj. 3rd pers. sing. 3. let him (her/it) fluctuate; impve. 3rd pers. sing.
fluctúen 1. that they may fluctuate; pres. subj. 3rd pers. pl. / *fluctuar*. 2. let them fluctuate; impve. 3rd pers. pl.

fluctúes that you may fluctuate; pres. subj. 2nd pers. sing. / *fluctuar*.
fluctúo I fluctuate; pres. ind. 1st pers. sing. / *fluctuar*.
fluir to flow. irr.
fluya 1. that it may flow; pres. subj. 3rd pers. sing. / *fluir*. 2. let it flow; impve. 3rd pers. sing.
fluyan 1. that they may flow; pres. subj. 3rd pers. pl. / *fluir*. 2. let them flow; impve. 3rd pers. pl.
fluye it flows; pres. ind. 3rd pers. sing. / *fluir*.
fluyen they flow; pres. ind. 3rd pers. pl. / *fluir*.
fluyendo flowing; pres. part. / *fluir*.
fluyera that it might flow; imp. subj. 3rd pers. sing. / *fluir*.
fluyeran that they might flow; imp. subj. 3rd pers. pl. / *fluir*.
fluyeron they flowed; past 3rd pers. pl. / *fluir*.
fluyese that it might flow; imp. subj. 3rd pers. sing. / *fluir*.
fluyesen that they might flow; imp. subj. 3rd pers. pl. / *fluir*.
fluyó it flowed; past 3rd pers. sing. / *fluir*.
follar to foliate. reg.
follar to blow (bellows). irr.
fomentar to foment or to encourage. reg.
fondeándose saving up for the future; pres. part. / *fondearse*.
fondeaos (you all) save up for the future; impve. 2nd pers. pl. / *fondearse*.
fondear to cast anchor or to sound. reg.
fondearse to save up for the future. reg.
fondéate (you) save up for the future; impve. 2nd pers. sing. / *fondearse*.
fondeémonos let us save up for the future; impve. 1st pers. pl. / *fondearse*.
fondéense let them save up for the future; impve. 3rd pers. pl. / *fondearse*.
fondéese let him (her/it) save up for the future; impve. 3rd pers. sing. / *fondearse*.
forcé I forced; past 1st pers. sing. / *forzar*.
forcéis that you (all) may force; pres. subj. 2nd pers. pl. / *forzar*.
forcejar to struggle. reg.
forcejear to strive. reg.
forcemos 1. that we may force; pres. subj. 1st pers. pl. / *forzar*. 2. let us force; impve. 1st pers. pl.
forjar to forge. reg.
formalice 1. that I may formalize; pres. subj. 1st pers. sing. / *formalizar*. 2. that he (she/it) may formalize; pres. subj. 3rd pers. sing. 3. let him (her/it) formalize; impve. 3rd pers. sing.
formalicé I formalized; past 1st pers. sing. / *formalizar*.
formalicéis that you (all) may formalize; pres. subj. 2nd pers. pl. / *formalizar*.
formalicémonos let us become serious; impve. 1st pers. pl. / *formalizarse*.
formalicemos 1. that we may formalize; pres. subj. 1st pers. pl. / *formalizar*. 2. let us formalize; impve. 1st pers. pl.

formalicen 1. that they may formalize; pres. subj. 3rd pers. pl. / *formalizar.* 2. let them formalize; impve. 3rd pers. pl.

formalícense let them become serious; impve. 3rd pers. pl. / *formalizarse.*

formalices that you may formalize; pres. subj. 2nd pers. sing. / *formalizar.*

formalícese let him (her/it) become serious; impve. 3rd pers. sing. / *formalizarse.*

formalizándose becoming serious; pres. part. / *formalizarse.*

formalizaos (you all) become serious; impve. 2nd pers. pl. / *formalizarse.*

formalizar to formalize. irr.

formalizarse to become serious. irr.

formalízate (you) become serious; impve. 2nd pers. sing. / *formalizarse.*

formándose becoming educated; pres. part. / *formarse.*

formaos (you all) become educated; impve. 2nd pers. pl. / *formarse.*

formar to form. reg.

formarse to become educated. reg.

fórmate (you) become educated; impve. 2nd pers. sing. / *formarse.*

formémonos let us become educated; impve. 1st pers. pl. / *formarse.*

fórmense let them become educated; impve. 3rd pers. pl. / *formarse.*

fórmese let him (her/it) become educated; impve. 3rd pers. sing. / *formarse.*

formular to formulate. reg.

fornicar to fornicate. irr.

fornique 1. that I may fornicate; pres. subj. 1st pers. sing. / *fornicar.* 2. that he (she/it) may fornicate; pres. subj. 3rd pers. sing. 3. let him (her/it) fornicate; impve. 3rd pers. sing.

forniqué I fornicated; past 1st pers. sing. / *fornicar.*

forniquéis that you (all) may fornicate; pres. subj. 2nd pers. pl. / *fornicar.*

forniquemos 1. that we may fornicate; pres. subj. 1st pers. pl. / *fornicar.* 2. let us fornicate; impve. 1st pers. pl.

forniquen 1. that they may fornicate; pres. subj. 3rd pers. pl. / *fornicar.* 2. let them fornicate; impve. 3rd pers. pl.

forniques that you may fornicate; pres. subj. 2nd pers. sing. / *fornicar.*

forrajear to forage. reg.

forrándose eating well; pres. part. / *forrarse.*

forraos (you all) eat well; impve. 2nd pers. pl. / *forrarse.*

forrar to line or to cover. reg.

forrarse to eat well. reg.

fórrate (you) eat well; impve. 2nd pers. sing. / *forrarse.*

forrémonos let us eat well; impve. 1st pers. pl. / *forrarse.*

fórrense let them eat well; impve. 3rd pers. pl. / *forrarse.*

fórrese let him (her/it) eat well; impve. 3rd pers. sing. / *forrarse.*

fortalecer to fortify. irr.

fortalezca 1. that I may fortify; pres. subj. 1st pers. sing. / *fortalecer.* 2. that he (she/it) may fortify; pres. subj. 3rd pers. sing. 3. let him (her/it) fortify; impve. 3rd pers. sing.

fortalezcáis that you (all) may fortify; pres. subj. 2nd pers. pl. / *fortalecer.*

fortalezcamos 1. that we may fortify; pres. subj. 1st pers. pl. / *fortalecer.* 2. let us fortify; impve. 1st pers. pl.

fortalezcan 1. that they may fortify; pres. subj. 3rd pers. pl. / *fortalecer.* 2. let them fortify; impve. 3rd pers. pl.

fortalezcas that you may fortify; pres. subj. 2nd pers. sing. / *fortalecer.*

fortalezco I fortify; pres. ind. 1st pers. sing. / *fortalecer.*

fortificar to fortify. irr.

fortifique 1. that I may fortify; pres. subj. 1st pers. sing. / *fortificar.* 2. that he (she/it) may fortify; pres. subj. 3rd pers. sing. 3. let him (her/it) fortify; impve. 3rd pers. sing.

fortifiqué I fortified; past 1st pers. sing. / *fortificar.*

fortifiquéis that you (all) may fortify; pres. subj. 2nd pers. pl. / *fortificar.*

fortifiquemos 1. that we may fortify; pres. subj. 1st pers. pl. / *fortificar.* 2. let us fortify; impve. 1st pers. pl.

fortifiquen 1. that they may fortify; pres. subj. 3rd pers. pl. / *fortificar.* 2. let them fortify; impve. 3rd pers. pl.

fortifiques that you may fortify; pres. subj. 2nd pers. sing. / *fortificar.*

forzar to force. irr.

fosforecer to glow. irr.

fosforescer to be phosphorescent. reg.

fosforezca 1. that I may glow; pres. subj. 1st pers. sing. / *fosforecer.* 2. that he (she/it) may glow; pres. subj. 3rd pers. sing. 3. let him (her/it) glow; impve. 3rd pers. sing.

fosforezcáis that you (all) may glow; pres. subj. 2nd pers. pl. / *fosforecer.*

fosforezcamos 1. that we may glow; pres. subj. 1st pers. pl. / *fosforecer.* 2. let us glow; impve. 1st pers. pl.

fosforezcan 1. that they may glow; pres. subj. 3rd pers. pl. / *fosforecer.* 2. let them glow; impve. 3rd pers. pl.

fosforezcas that you may glow; pres. subj. 2nd pers. sing. / *fosforecer.*

fosforezco I glow; pres. ind. 1st pers. sing. / *fosforecer.*

fosilice 1. that I may fossilize; pres. subj. 1st pers. sing. / *fosilizar.* 2. that he (she/it) may fossilize; pres. subj. 3rd pers. sing. 3. let him (her/it) fossilize; impve. 3rd pers. sing.

fosilicé I fossilized; past 1st pers. sing. / *fosilizar.*

fosilicéis that you (all) may fossilize; pres. subj. 2nd pers. pl. / *fosilizar.*

fosilicémonos let us become fossilized; impve. 1st pers. pl. / *fosilizarse.*

fosilicemos 1. that we may fossilize; pres. subj. 1st pers. pl. / *fosilizar.* 2. let us fossilize; impve. 1st pers. pl.

fosilicen 1. that they may fossilize; pres. subj. 3rd pers. pl. / *fosilizar.* 2. let them fossilize; impve. 3rd pers. pl.

fosilícense let them become fossilized; impve. 3rd pers. pl. / *fosilizarse.*

fosilices that you may fossilize; pres. subj. 2nd pers. sing. / *fosilizar.*

fosilícese let him (her/it) become fossilized; impve. 3rd pers. sing. / *fosilizarse.*

fosilizándose becoming fossilized; pres. part. / *fosilizarse.*

fosilizaos (you all) become fossilized; impve. 2nd pers. pl. / *fosilizarse.*

fosilizar to fossilize. irr.

fosilizarse to become fossilized. irr.

fosilízate (you) become fossilized; impve. 2nd pers. sing. / *fosilizarse.*

fotograbar to photoengrave. reg.

fotografía 1. he (she/it) photographs; pres. ind. 3rd pers. sing. / *photografiar.* 2. (you) photograph; impve. 2nd pers. sing.

fotografían they photograph; pres. ind. 3rd pers. pl. / *photografiar.*

fotografiar to photograph. irr.

fotografías you photograph; pres. ind. 2nd pers. sing. / *photografiar.*

fotografie 1. that I may photograph; pres. subj. 1st pers. sing. / *photografiar.* 2. that he (she/it) may photograph; pres. subj. 3rd pers. sing. 3. let him (her/it) photograph; impve. 3rd pers. sing.

fotografíen 1. that they may photograph; pres. subj. 3rd pers. pl. / *photografiar.* 2. let them photograph; impve. 3rd pers. pl.

fotografíes that you may photograph; pres. subj. 2nd pers. sing. / *photografiar.*

fotografío I photograph; pres. ind. 1st pers. sing. / *photografiar.*

fotostatar to photostat. reg.

fracasar to fail. reg.

fraccionar to divide into fractions. reg.

fracturándose fracturing; pres. part. / *fracturarse.*

fracturaos (you all) fracture; impve. 2nd pers. pl. / *fracturarse.*

fracturar to fracture. reg.

fracturarse to fracture. reg.

fractúrate (you) fracture; impve. 2nd pers. sing. / *fracturarse.*

fracturémonos let us fracture; impve. 1st pers. pl. / *fracturarse.*

fractúrense let them fracture; impve. 3rd pers. pl. / *fracturarse.*

fractúrese let him (her/it) fracture; impve. 3rd pers. sing. / *fracturarse.*

fragmentar to fragment. reg.

fraguar to forge. irr.

fragüe 1. that I may forge; pres. subj. 1st pers. sing. / *fraguar.* 2. that he (she/it) may forge; pres. subj. 3rd pers. sing. 3. let him (her/it) forge; impve. 3rd pers. sing.

fragüé I forged; past 1st pers. sing. / *fraguar.*

fragüéis that you (all) may forge; pres. subj. 2nd pers. pl. / *fraguar.*

fragüemos 1. that we may forge; pres. subj. 1st pers. pl. / *fraguar.* 2. let us forge; impve. 1st pers. pl.

fragüen 1. that they may forge; pres. subj. 3rd pers. pl. / *fraguar.* 2. let them forge; impve. 3rd pers. pl.

fragües that you may forge; pres. subj. 2nd pers. sing. / *fraguar.*

franqueándose unbosoming oneself; pres. part. / *franquearse.*

franqueaos (you all) unbosom yourselves; impve. 2nd pers. pl. / *franquearse.*

franquear to exempt. reg.

franquearse to unbosom oneself. reg.

franquéate (you) unbosom yourself; impve. 2nd pers. sing. / *franquearse.*

franqueémonos let us unbosom ourselves; impve. 1st pers. pl. / *franquearse.*

franquéense let them unbosom themselves; impve. 3rd pers. pl. / *franquearse.*

franquéese let him (her/it) unbosom himself (herself/itself); impve. 3rd pers. sing. / *franquearse.*

frasear to phrase. reg.

fraternice 1. that I may fraternize; pres. subj. 1st pers. sing. / *fraternizar.* 2. that he (she/it) may fraternize; pres. subj. 3rd pers. sing. 3. let him (her/it) fraternize; impve. 3rd pers. sing.

fraternicé I fraternized; past 1st pers. sing. / *fraternizar.*

fraternicéis that you (all) may fraternize; pres. subj. 2nd pers. pl. / *fraternizar.*

fraternicemos 1. that we may fraternize; pres. subj. 1st pers. pl. / *fraternizar.* 2. let us fraternize; impve. 1st pers. pl.

fraternicen 1. that they may fraternize; pres. subj. 3rd pers. pl. / *fraternizar.* 2. let them fraternize; impve. 3rd pers. pl.

fraternices that you may fraternize; pres. subj. 2nd pers. sing. / *fraternizar.*

fraternizar to fraternize. irr.

frece 1. that I may spawn; pres. subj. 1st pers. sing. / *frezar.* 2. that he (she/it) may spawn; pres. subj. 3rd pers. sing. 3. let him (her/it) spawn; impve. 3rd pers. sing.

frecé I spawned; past 1st pers. sing. / *frezar.*

frecéis that you (all) may spawn; pres. subj. 2nd pers. pl. / *frezar.*

frecemos 1. that we may spawn; pres. subj. 1st pers. pl. / *frezar.* 2. let us spawn; impve. 1st pers. pl.

frecen 1. that they may spawn; pres. subj. 3rd pers. pl. / *frezar.* 2. let them spawn; impve. 3rd pers. pl.

freces that you may spawn; pres. subj. 2nd pers. sing. / *frezar.*

frecuentar to frequent. reg.

fregar to scrub. irr.

fregué I scrubbed; past 1st pers. sing. / *fregar.*

freguéis that you (all) may scrub; pres. subj. 2nd pers. pl. / *fregar.*

freguemos 1. that we may scrub; pres. subj. 1st pers. pl. / *fregar.* 2. let us scrub; impve. 1st pers. pl.

freír to fry. irr.

frenar to brake. reg.

fresar to mill. reg.

frezar to spawn. irr.

fría 1. that I may fry; pres. subj. 1st pers. sing. / *freír.* 2. that he (she/it) may fry; pres. subj. 3rd pers. sing. 3. let him (her/it) fry; impve. 3rd pers. sing.

friáis that you (all) may fry; pres. subj. 2nd pers. pl. / *freír.*

friamos 1. that we may fry; pres. subj. 1st pers. pl. / *freír.* 2. let us fry; impve. 1st pers. pl.

frían 1. that they may fry; pres. subj. 3rd pers. pl. / *freír.* 2. let them fry; impve. 3rd pers. pl.

frías that you may fry; pres. subj. 2nd pers. sing. / *freír.*

friccionar to rub. reg.

fríe 1. he (she/it) fries; pres. ind. 3rd pers. sing. / *freír.* 2. (you) fry; impve. 2nd pers. sing.

friega 1. he (she/it) scrubs; pres. ind. 3rd pers. sing. / *fregar.* 2. (you) scrub; impve. 2nd pers. sing.

friegan they scrub; pres. ind. 3rd pers. pl. / *fregar.*

friegas you scrub; pres. ind. 2nd pers. sing. / *fregar.*

friego I scrub; pres. ind. 1st pers. sing. / *fregar.*

friegue 1. that I may scrub; pres. subj. 1st pers. sing. / *fregar.* 2. that he (she/it) may scrub; pres. subj. 3rd pers. sing. 3. let him (her/it) scrub; impve. 3rd pers. sing.

frieguen 1. that they may scrub; pres. subj. 3rd pers. pl. / *fregar.* 2. let them scrub; impve. 3rd pers. pl.

friegues that you may scrub; pres. subj. 2nd pers. sing. / *fregar.*

fríen they fry; pres. ind. 3rd pers. pl. / *freír.*

friendo frying; pres. part. / *freír.*

friera 1. that I might fry; imp. subj. 1st pers. sing. / *freír.* 2. that he (she/it) might fry; imp. subj. 3rd pers. sing.

frierais that you (all) might fry; imp. subj. 2nd pers pl. / *freír.*

friéramos that we might fry; imp. subj. 1st pers. pl. / *freír.*

frieran that they might fry; imp. subj. 3rd pers. pl. / *freír.*

frieras that you might fry; imp. subj. 2nd pers. sing. / *freír.*

frieron they fried; past 3rd pers. pl. / *freír.*

fríes you fry; pres. ind. 2nd pers. sing. / *freír.*

friese 1. that I might fry; imp. subj. 1st pers. sing. / *freír.* 2. that he (she/it) might fry; imp. subj. 3rd pers. sing.

frieseis that you (all) might fry; imp. subj. 2nd pers pl. / *freír.*

friésemos that we might fry; imp. subj. 1st pers. pl. / *freír.*

friesen that they might fry; imp. subj. 3rd pers. pl. / *freír.*

frieses that you might fry; imp. subj. 2nd pers. sing. / *freír.*

frío I fry; pres. ind. 1st pers. sing. / *freír.*

frió he (she/it) fried; past 3rd pers. sing. / *freír.*

frisar to frieze or to tease. reg.

frito fried; past part. / *freír.*

frotar to rub. reg.

fructificar to bear fruit. irr.

fructifique 1. that I may bear fruit; pres. subj. 1st pers. sing. / *fructificar.* 2. that he (she/it) may bear fruit; pres. subj. 3rd pers. sing. 3. let him (her/it) bear fruit; impve. 3rd pers. sing.

fructifiqué I bore friut; past 1st pers. sing. / *fructificar.*

fructifiquéis that you (all) may bear fruit; pres. subj. 2nd pers. pl. / *fructificar.*

fructifiquemos 1. that we may bear fruit; pres. subj. 1st pers. pl. / *fructificar.* 2. let us bear fruit; impve. 1st pers. pl.

fructifiquen 1. that they may bear fruit; pres. subj. 3rd pers. pl. / *fructificar.* 2. let them bear fruit; impve. 3rd pers. pl.

fructifiques that you may bear fruit; pres. subj. 2nd pers. sing. / *fructificar.*

fruir to be gratified. irr.

frúncete (you) frown; impve. 2nd pers. sing. / *fruncirse.*

frunciéndose frowning; pres. part. / *fruncirse.*

fruncíos (you all) frown; impve. 2nd pers. pl. / *fruncirse.*

fruncir to wrinkle. irr.

fruncirse to frown. irr.

frunza 1. that I may wrinkle; pres. subj. 1st pers. sing. / *fruncir.* 2. that he (she/it) may wrinkle; pres. subj. 3rd pers. sing. 3. let him (her/it) wrinkle; impve. 3rd pers. sing.

frunzáis that you (all) may wrinkle; pres. subj. 2nd pers. pl. / *fruncir.*

frunzámonos let us frown; impve. 1st pers. pl. / *fruncirse.*

frunzamos 1. that we may wrinkle; pres. subj. 1st pers. pl. / *fruncir.* 2. let us wrinkle; impve. 1st pers. pl.

frunzan 1. that they may wrinkle; pres. subj. 3rd pers. pl. / *fruncir.* 2. let them wrinkle; impve. 3rd pers. pl.

frúnzanse let them frown; impve. 3rd pers. pl. / *fruncirse.*

frunzas that you may wrinkle; pres. subj. 2nd pers. sing. / *fruncir.*

frúnzase let him (her/it) frown; impve. 3rd pers. sing. / *fruncirse.*

frunzo I wrinkle; pres. ind. 1st pers. sing. / *fruncir.*

frustrándose miscarrying; pres. part. / *frustrarse.*

frustraos (you all) miscarry; impve. 2nd pers. pl. / *frustrarse.*

frustrar to frustrate. reg.

frustrarse to miscarry. reg.

frústrate (you) miscarry; impve. 2nd pers. sing. / *frustrarse.*

frustrémonos let us miscarry; impve. 1st pers. pl. / *frustrarse*.

frústrense let them miscarry; impve. 3rd pers. pl. / *frustrarse*.

frústrese let him (her/it) miscarry; impve. 3rd pers. sing. / *frustrarse*.

frutar to yield fruit. reg.

fruya 1. that I may be gratified; pres. subj. 1st pers. sing. / *fruir*. 2. that he (she/it) may be gratified; pres. subj. 3rd pers. sing. 3. let him (her/it) be gratified; impve. 3rd pers. sing.

fruyáis that you (all) may be gratified; pres. subj. 2nd pers. pl. / *fruir*.

fruyamos 1. that we may be gratified; pres. subj. 1st pers. pl. / *fruir*. 2. let us be gratified; impve. 1st pers. pl.

fruyan 1. that they may be gratified; pres. subj. 3rd pers. pl. / *fruir*. 2. let them be gratified; impve. 3rd pers. pl.

fruyas that you may be gratified; pres. subj. 2nd pers. sing. / *fruir*.

fruye 1. he (she/it) is gratified; pres. ind. 3rd pers. sing. / *fruir*. 2. (you) be gratified; impve. 2nd pers. sing.

fruyen they are gratified; pres. ind. 3rd pers. pl. / *fruir*.

fruyendo being gratified; pres. part. / *fruir*.

fruyera 1. that I might be gratified; imp. subj. 1st pers. sing. / *fruir*. 2. that he (she/it) might be gratified; imp. subj. 3rd pers. sing.

fruyerais that you (all) might be gratified; imp. subj. 2nd pers pl. / *fruir*.

fruyéramos that we might be gratified; imp. subj. 1st pers. pl. / *fruir*.

fruyeran that they might be gratified; imp. subj. 3rd pers. pl. / *fruir*.

fruyeras that you might be gratified; imp. subj. 2nd pers. sing. / *fruir*.

fruyeron they were gratified; past 3rd pers. pl. / *fruir*.

fruyes you are gratified; pres. ind. 2nd pers. sing. / *fruir*.

fruyese 1. that I might be gratified; imp. subj. 1st pers. sing. / *fruir*. 2. that he (she/it) might be gratified; imp. subj. 3rd pers. sing.

fruyeseis that you (all) might be gratified; imp. subj. 2nd pers pl. / *fruir*.

fruyésemos that we might be gratified; imp. subj. 1st pers. pl. / *fruir*.

fruyesen that they might be gratified; imp. subj. 3rd pers. pl. / *fruir*.

fruyeses that you might be gratified; imp. subj. 2nd pers. sing. / *fruir*.

fruyo I am gratified; pres. ind. 1st pers. sing. / *fruir*.

fruyó he (she/it) was gratified; past 3rd pers. sing. / *fruir*.

fucilar to flash. reg.

fue he (she/it) went; past 3rd pers. sing. / *ir*.

fue he (she/it) was; past 3rd pers. sing. / *ser*.

fué he (she/it) went; past 3rd pers. sing. / *ir*.

fué he (she/it) was; past 3rd pers. sing. / *ser*.

fuella 1. he (she/it) blows (bellows); pres. ind. 3rd pers. sing. / *follar*. 2. (you) blow (bellows); impve. 2nd pers. sing.

fuellan they blow (bellows); pres. ind. 3rd pers. pl. / *follar*.

fuellas you blow (bellows); pres. ind. 2nd pers. sing. / *follar*.

fuelle 1. that I may blow (bellows); pres. subj. 1st pers. sing. / *follar*. 2. that he (she/it) may blow (bellows); pres. subj. 3rd pers. sing. 3. let him (her/it) blow (bellows); impve. 3rd pers. sing.

fuellen 1. that they may blow (bellows); pres. subj. 3rd pers. pl. / *follar*. 2. let them blow (bellows); impve. 3rd pers. pl.

fuelles that you may blow (bellows); pres. subj. 2nd pers. sing. / *follar*.

fuello I blow (bellows); pres. ind. 1st pers. sing. / *follar*.

fuera 1. that I might go; imp. subj. 1st pers. sing. / *ir*. 2. that he (she/it) might go; imp. subj. 3rd pers. sing.

fuera 1. that I might be; imp. subj. 1st pers. sing. / *ser*. 2. that he (she/it) might be; imp. subj. 3rd pers. sing.

fuerais that you (all) might go; imp. subj. 2nd pers pl. / *ir*.

fuerais that you (all) might be; imp. subj. 2nd pers pl. / *ser*.

fuéramos that we might go; imp. subj. 1st pers. pl. / *ir*.

fuéramos that we might be; imp. subj. 1st pers. pl. / *ser*.

fueran that they might go; imp. subj. 3rd pers. pl. / *ir*.

fueran that they might be; imp. subj. 3rd pers. pl. / *ser*.

fueras that you might go; imp. subj. 2nd pers. sing. / *ir*.

fueras that you might be; imp. subj. 2nd pers. sing. / *ser*.

fuerce 1. that I may force; pres. subj. 1st pers. sing. / *forzar*. 2. that he (she/it) may force; pres. subj. 3rd pers. sing. 3. let him (her/it) force; impve. 3rd pers. sing.

fuercen 1. that they may force; pres. subj. 3rd pers. pl. / *forzar*. 2. let them force; impve. 3rd pers. pl.

fuerces that you may force; pres. subj. 2nd pers. sing. / *forzar*.

fueron they went; past 3rd pers. pl. / *ir*.

fueron they were; past 3rd pers. pl. / *ser*.

fuerza 1. he (she/it) forces; pres. ind. 3rd pers. sing. / *forzar*. 2. (you) force; impve. 2nd pers. sing.

fuerzan they force; pres. ind. 3rd pers. pl. / *forzar*.

fuerzas you force; pres. ind. 2nd pers. sing. / *forzar*.

fuerzo I force; pres. ind. 1st pers. sing. / *forzar*.

fuese 1. that I might go; imp. subj. 1st pers. sing. / *ir*. 2. that he (she/it) might go; imp. subj. 3rd pers. sing.

fuese 1. that I might be; imp. subj. 1st pers. sing. / *ser*. 2. that he (she/it) might be; imp. subj. 3rd pers. sing.

fueseis that you (all) might go; imp. subj. 2nd pers pl. / *ir*.

fueseis that you (all) might be; imp. subj. 2nd pers pl. / *ser*.

fuésemos that we might go; imp. subj. 1st pers. pl. / *ir*.

fuésemos that we might be; imp. subj. 1st pers. pl. / *ser.*

fuesen that they might go; imp. subj. 3rd pers. pl. / *ir.*

fuesen that they might be; imp. subj. 3rd pers. pl. / *ser.*

fueses that you might go; imp. subj. 2nd pers. sing. / *ir.*

fueses that you might be; imp. subj. 2nd pers. sing. / *ser.*

fugándose fleeing; pres. part. / *fugarse.*

fugaos (you all) flee; impve. 2nd pers. pl. / *fugarse.*

fugarse to flee. irr.

fúgate (you) flee; impve. 2nd pers. sing. / *fugarse.*

fugue 1. that I may flee; pres. subj. 1st pers. sing. / *fugarse.* 2. that he (she/it) may flee; pres. subj. 3rd pers. sing.

fugué I fled; past 1st pers. sing. / *fugarse.*

fuguéis that you (all) may flee; pres. subj. 2nd pers. pl. / *fugarse.*

fuguémonos let us flee; impve. 1st pers. pl. / *fugarse.*

fuguemos that we may flee; pres. subj. 1st pers. pl. / *fugarse.*

fuguen that they may flee; pres. subj. 3rd pers. pl. / *fugarse.*

fúguense let them flee; impve. 3rd pers. pl. / *fugarse.*

fugues that you may flee; pres. subj. 2nd pers. sing. / *fugarse.*

fúguese let him (her/it) flee; impve. 3rd pers. sing. / *fugarse.*

fui I went; past 1st pers. sing. / *ir.*

fui I was; past 1st pers. sing. / *ser.*

fuí I went; past 1st pers. sing. / *ir.*

fuí I was; past 1st pers. sing. / *ser.*

fuimos we went; past 1st pers. pl. / *ir.*

fuimos we were; past 1st pers. pl. / *ser.*

fuiste you went; past 2nd pers. sing. / *ir.*

fuiste you were; past 2nd pers. sing. / *ser.*

fuisteis you (all) went; past 2nd pers. pl. / *ir.*

fuisteis you (all) were; past 2nd pers. pl. / *ser.*

fulgir to flash. reg.

fulgurar to shine. reg.

fulminar to strike as with lightening and thunder. reg.

fumándose wasting; pres. part. / *fumarse.*

fumaos (you all) waste; impve. 2nd pers. pl. / *fumarse.*

fumar to smoke. reg.

fumarse to waste. reg.

fúmate (you) waste; impve. 2nd pers. sing. / *fumarse.*

fumémonos let us waste; impve. 1st pers. pl. / *fumarse.*

fúmense let them waste; impve. 3rd pers. pl. / *fumarse.*

fúmese let him (her/it) waste; impve. 3rd pers. sing. / *fumarse.*

fumigar to fumigate. irr.

fumigue 1. that I may fumigate; pres. subj. 1st pers. sing. / *fumigar.* 2. that he (she/it) may fumigate; pres. subj. 3rd pers. sing. 3. let him (her/it) fumigate; impve. 3rd pers. sing.

fumigué I fumigated; past 1st pers. sing. / *fumigar.*

fumiguéis that you (all) may fumigate; pres. subj. 2nd pers. pl. / *fumigar.*

fumiguemos 1. that we may fumigate; pres. subj. 1st pers. pl. / *fumigar.* 2. let us fumigate; impve. 1st pers. pl.

fumiguen 1. that they may fumigate; pres. subj. 3rd pers. pl. / *fumigar.* 2. let them fumigate; impve. 3rd pers. pl.

fumigues that you may fumigate; pres. subj. 2nd pers. sing. / *fumigar.*

funcionar to function. reg.

fundamentar to lay the foundation of. reg.

fundámonos let us melt; impve. 1st pers. pl. / *fundirse.*

fúndanse let them melt; impve. 3rd pers. pl. / *fundirse.*

fundar to found or to establish. reg.

fúndase let him (her/it) melt; impve. 3rd pers. sing. / *fundirse.*

fúndete (you) melt; impve. 2nd pers. sing. / *fundirse.*

fundiéndose melting; pres. part. / *fundirse.*

fundíos (you all) melt; impve. 2nd pers. pl. / *fundirse.*

fundir to fuse. reg.

fundirse to melt. reg.

fungir to function. irr.

funja 1. that I may function; pres. subj. 1st pers. sing. / *fungir.* 2. that he (she/it) may function; pres. subj. 3rd pers. sing. 3. let him (her/it) function; impve. 3rd pers. sing.

funjáis that you (all) may function; pres. subj. 2nd pers. pl. / *fungir.*

funjamos 1. that we may function; pres. subj. 1st pers. pl. / *fungir.* 2. let us function; impve. 1st pers. pl.

funjan 1. that they may function; pres. subj. 3rd pers. pl. / *fungir.* 2. let them function; impve. 3rd pers. pl.

funjas that you may function; pres. subj. 2nd pers. sing. / *fungir.*

funjo I function; pres. ind. 1st pers. sing. / *fungir.*

fusilar to shoot. reg.

fusionar to fuse or to merge. reg.

fustigar to lash. irr.

fustigue 1. that I may lash; pres. subj. 1st pers. sing. / *fustigar.* 2. that he (she/it) may lash; pres. subj. 3rd pers. sing. 3. let him (her/it) lash; impve. 3rd pers. sing.

fustigué I lashed; past 1st pers. sing. / *fustigar.*

fustiguéis that you (all) may lash; pres. subj. 2nd pers. pl. / *fustigar.*

fustiguemos 1. that we may lash; pres. subj. 1st pers. pl. / *fustigar.* 2. let us lash; impve. 1st pers. pl.

fustiguen 1. that they may lash; pres. subj. 3rd pers. pl. / *fustigar.* 2. let them lash; impve. 3rd pers. pl.

fustigues that you may lash; pres. subj. 2nd pers. sing. / *fustigar.*

G

gafar to hook or to claw. reg.
gaguear to stutter. reg.
galantear to court or to woo. reg.
galardonar to reward. reg.
galonear to braid. reg.
galopar to gallop. reg.
galopear to gallop. reg.
galvanice 1. that I may galvanize; pres. subj. 1st pers. sing. / *galvanizar*. 2. that he (she/it) may galvanize; pres. subj. 3rd pers. sing. 3. let him (her/it) galvanize; impve. 3rd pers. sing.
galvanicé I galvanized; past 1st pers. sing. / *galvanizar*.
galvanicéis that you (all) may galvanize; pres. subj. 2nd pers. pl. / *galvanizar*.
galvanicemos 1. that we may galvanize; pres. subj. 1st pers. pl. / *galvanizar*. 2. let us galvanize; impve. 1st pers. pl.
galvanicen 1. that they may galvanize; pres. subj. 3rd pers. pl. / *galvanizar*. 2. let them galvanize; impve. 3rd pers. pl.
galvanices that you may galvanize; pres. subj. 2nd pers. sing. / *galvanizar*.
galvanizar to galvanize. irr.
gallardeándose being elegant; pres. part. / *gallardearse*.
gallardeaos (you all) be elegant; impve. 2nd pers. pl. / *gallardearse*.
gallardear to be gallant. reg.
gallardearse to be elegant. reg.
gallardéate (you) be elegant; impve. 2nd pers. sing. / *gallardearse*.
gallardeémonos let us be elegant; impve. 1st pers. pl. / *gallardearse*.
gallardéense let them be elegant; impve. 3rd pers. pl. / *gallardearse*.
gallardéese let him (her/it) be elegant; impve. 3rd pers. sing. / *gallardearse*.
gallear to bluster. reg.
ganándose earning; pres. part. / *ganarse*.
ganaos (you all) earn; impve. 2nd pers. pl. / *ganarse*.
ganar to win or to gain. reg.
ganarse to earn. reg.
gánate (you) earn; impve. 2nd pers. sing. / *ganarse*.
gandulear to loaf. reg.
ganémonos let us earn; impve. 1st pers. pl. / *ganarse*.
gánense let them earn; impve. 3rd pers. pl. / *ganarse*.
gánese let him (her/it) earn; impve. 3rd pers. sing. / *ganarse*.
gangrenándose becoming gangrenous; pres. part. / *gangrenarse*.
gangrenaos (you all) become gangrenous; impve. 2nd pers. pl. / *gangrenarse*.
gangrenar to cause gangrene. reg.
gangrenarse to become gangrenous. reg.

gangrénate (you) become gangrenous; impve. 2nd pers. sing. / *gangrenarse*.
gangrenémonos let us become gangrenous; impve. 1st pers. pl. / *gangrenarse*.
gangrénense let them become gangrenous; impve. 3rd pers. pl. / *gangrenarse*.
gangrénese let him (her/it) become gangrenous; impve. 3rd pers. sing. / *gangrenarse*.
ganguear to snivel. reg.
gañendo yelping; pres. part. / *gañir*.
gañera 1. that I might yelp; imp. subj. 1st pers. sing. / *gañir*. 2. that he (she/it) might yelp; imp. subj. 3rd pers. sing.
gañerais that you (all) might yelp; imp. subj. 2nd pers pl. / *gañir*.
gañéramos that we might yelp; imp. subj. 1st pers. pl. / *gañir*.
gañeran that they might yelp; imp. subj. 3rd pers. pl. / *gañir*.
gañeras that you might yelp; imp. subj. 2nd pers. sing. / *gañir*.
gañeron they yelped; past 3rd pers. pl. / *gañir*.
gañese 1. that I might yelp; imp. subj. 1st pers. sing. / *gañir*. 2. that he (she/it) might yelp; imp. subj. 3rd pers. sing.
gañeseis that you (all) might yelp; imp. subj. 2nd pers pl. / *gañir*.
gañésemos that we might yelp; imp. subj. 1st pers. pl. / *gañir*.
gañesen that they might yelp; imp. subj. 3rd pers. pl. / *gañir*.
gañeses that you might yelp; imp. subj. 2nd pers. sing. / *gañir*.
gañir to yelp. irr.
gañó he (she/it) yelped; past 3rd pers. sing. / *gañir*.
garabatear to scrawl or to hook. reg.
garantice 1. that I may guarantee; pres. subj. 1st pers. sing. / *garantizar*. 2. that he (she/it) may guarantee; pres. subj. 3rd pers. sing. 3. let him (her/it) guarantee; impve. 3rd pers. sing.
garanticé I guaranteed; past 1st pers. sing. / *garantizar*.
garanticéis that you (all) may guarantee; pres. subj. 2nd pers. pl. / *garantizar*.
garanticemos 1. that we may guarantee; pres. subj. 1st pers. pl. / *garantizar*. 2. let us guarantee; impve. 1st pers. pl.
garanticen 1. that they may guarantee; pres. subj. 3rd pers. pl. / *garantizar*. 2. let them guarantee; impve. 3rd pers. pl.
garantices that you may guarantee; pres. subj. 2nd pers. sing. / *garantizar*.
garantir to guarantee. used only in those forms where I is present in the verb ending.
garantizar to guarantee. irr.
garapiñar to sugar-coat. reg.
garbear to put on airs. reg.
gargajear to clear one's throat. reg.
gargantear to warble. reg.
gargarear to gargle. reg.

gargarice 1. that I may gargle; pres. subj. 1st pers. sing. / *gargarizar*. 2. that he (she/it) may gargle; pres. subj. 3rd pers. sing. 3. let him (her/it) gargle; impve. 3rd pers. sing.

gargaricé I gargled; past 1st pers. sing. / *gargarizar*.

gargaricéis that you (all) may gargle; pres. subj. 2nd pers. pl. / *gargarizar*.

gargaricemos 1. that we may gargle; pres. subj. 1st pers. pl. / *gargarizar*. 2. let us gargle; impve. 1st pers. pl.

gargaricen 1. that they may gargle; pres. subj. 3rd pers. pl. / *gargarizar*. 2. let them gargle; impve. 3rd pers. pl.

gargarices that you may gargle; pres. subj. 2nd pers. sing. / *gargarizar*.

gargarizar to gargle. irr.

garrafiñar to grab. reg.

garramar to pinch or to steal. reg.

garrapatear to scribble. reg.

gasificar to gasify. irr.

gasifique 1. that I may gasify; pres. subj. 1st pers. sing. / *gasificar*. 2. that he (she/it) may gasify; pres. subj. 3rd pers. sing. 3. let him (her/it) gasify; impve. 3rd pers. sing.

gasifiqué I gasified; past 1st pers. sing. / *gasificar*.

gasifiquéis that you (all) may gasify; pres. subj. 2nd pers. pl. / *gasificar*.

gasifiquemos 1. that we may gasify; pres. subj. 1st pers. pl. / *gasificar*. 2. let us gasify; impve. 1st pers. pl.

gasifiquen 1. that they may gasify; pres. subj. 3rd pers. pl. / *gasificar*. 2. let them gasify; impve. 3rd pers. pl.

gasifiques that you may gasify; pres. subj. 2nd pers. sing. / *gasificar*.

gastándose wearing out; pres. part. / *gastarse*.

gastaos (you all) wear out; impve. 2nd pers. pl. / *gastarse*.

gastar to spend. reg.

gastarse to wear out. reg.

gástate (you) wear out; impve. 2nd pers. sing. / *gastarse*.

gastémonos let us wear out; impve. 1st pers. pl. / *gastarse*.

gástense let them wear out; impve. 3rd pers. pl. / *gastarse*.

gástese let him (her/it) wear out; impve. 3rd pers. sing. / *gastarse*.

gatear to creep or to steal. reg.

geminar to geminate. reg.

gemir to moan. irr.

generalice 1. that I may generalize; pres. subj. 1st pers. sing. / *generalizar*. 2. that he (she it) may generalize; pres. subj. 3rd pers. sing. 3. let him (her/it) generalize; impve. 3rd pers. sing.

generalicé I generalized; past 1st pers. sing. / *generalizar*.

generalicéis that you (all) may generalize; pres. subj. 2nd pers. pl. / *generalizar*.

generalicémonos let us spread; impve. 1st pers. pl. / *generalizarse*.

generalicemos 1. that we may generalize; pres. subj. 1st pers. pl. / *generalizar*. 2. let us generalize; impve. 1st pers. pl.

generalicen 1. that they may generalize; pres. subj. 3rd pers. pl. / *generalizar*. 2. let them generalize; impve. 3rd pers. pl.

generalícense let them spread; impve. 3rd pers. pl. / *generalizarse*.

generalices that you may generalize; pres. subj. 2nd pers. sing. / *generalizar*.

generalícese let him (her/it) spread; impve. 3rd pers. sing. / *generalizarse*.

generalizándose spreading; pres. part. / *generalizarse*.

generalizaos (you all) spread; impve. 2nd pers. pl. / *generalizarse*.

generalizar to generalize. irr.

generalizarse to spread. irr.

generalízate (you) spread; impve. 2nd pers. sing. / *generalizarse*.

generar to generate. reg.

germinar to germinate. reg.

gesticular to gesticulate. reg.

gestionar to negotiate. reg.

gima 1. that I may moan; pres. subj. 1st pers. sing. / *gemir*. 2. that he (she/it) may moan; pres. subj. 3rd pers. sing. 3. let him (her/it) moan; impve. 3rd pers. sing.

gimáis that you (all) may moan; pres. subj. 2nd pers. pl. / *gemir*.

gimamos 1. that we may moan; pres. subj. 1st pers. pl. / *gemir*. 2. let us moan; impve. 1st pers. pl.

giman 1. that they may moan; pres. subj. 3rd pers. pl. / *gemir*. 2. let them moan; impve. 3rd pers. pl.

gimas that you may moan; pres. subj. 2nd pers. sing. / *gemir*.

gime 1. he (she/it) moans; pres. ind. 3rd pers. sing. / *gemir*. 2. (you) moan; impve. 2nd pers. sing.

gimen they moan; pres. ind. 3rd pers. pl. / *gemir*.

gimes you moan; pres. ind. 2nd pers. sing. / *gemir*.

gimiendo moaning; pres. part. / *gemir*.

gimiera 1. that I might moan; imp. subj. 1st pers. sing. / *gemir*. 2. that he (she/it) might moan; imp. subj. 3rd pers. sing.

gimierais that you (all) might moan; imp. subj. 2nd pers pl. / *gemir*.

gimiéramos that we might moan; imp. subj. 1st pers. pl. / *gemir*.

gimieran that they might moan; imp. subj. 3rd pers. pl. / *gemir*.

gimieras that you might moan; imp. subj. 2nd pers. sing. / *gemir*.

gimieron they moaned; past 3rd pers. pl. / *gemir*.

gimiese 1. that I might moan; imp. subj. 1st pers. sing. / *gemir*. 2. that he (she/it) might moan; imp. subj. 3rd pers. sing.

gimieseis that you (all) might moan; imp. subj. 2nd pers pl. / *gemir*.

gimiésemos that we might moan; imp. subj. 1st pers. pl. / *gemir.*

gimiesen that they might moan; imp. subj. 3rd pers. pl. / *gemir.*

gimieses that you might moan; imp. subj. 2nd pers. sing. / *gemir.*

gimió he (she/it) moaned; past 3rd pers. sing / *gemir.*

gimo I moan; pres. ind. 1st pers. sing. / *gemir.*

gimotear to whine. reg.

girar to revolve or to draw (checks). reg.

gitanear to live like a gipsy. reg.

glasear to glaze (paper etc.). reg.

gloría he (she/it) glories; pres. ind. 3rd pers. sing. / *gloriarse.*

glorían they glory; pres. ind. 3rd pers. pl. / *gloriarse.*

gloriándose glorying; pres. part. / *gloriarse.*

gloriaos (you all) glory; impve. 2nd pers. pl. / *gloriarse.*

gloriarse to glory. irr.

glorías you glory; pres. ind. 2nd pers. sing. / *gloriarse.*

gloríate (you) glory; impve. 2nd pers. sing. / *gloriarse.*

gloríe 1. that I may glory; pres. subj. 1st pers. sing. / *gloriarse.* 2. that he (she/it) may glory; pres. subj. 3rd pers. sing.

gloriémonos let us glory; impve. 1st pers. pl. / *gloriarse.*

gloríen that they may glory; pres. subj. 3rd pers. pl. / *gloriarse.*

gloríense let them glory; impve. 3rd pers. pl. / *gloriarse.*

gloríes that you may glory; pres. subj. 2nd pers. sing. / *gloriarse.*

gloríese let him (her/it) glory; impve. 3rd pers. sing. / *gloriarse.*

glorificándose winning glory; pres. part. / *glorificarse.*

glorificaos (you all) win glory; impve. 2nd pers. pl. / *glorificarse.*

glorificar to glorify. irr.

glorificarse to win glory. irr.

glorifícate (you) win glory; impve. 2nd pers. sing. / *glorificarse.*

glorifique 1. that I may glorify; pres. subj. 1st pers. sing. / *glorificar.* 2. that he (she/it) may glorify; pres. subj. 3rd pers. sing. 3. let him (her/it) glorify; impve. 3rd pers. sing.

glorifiqué I glorified; past 1st pers. sing. / *glorificar.*

glorifiquéis that you (all) may glorify; pres. subj. 2nd pers. pl. / *glorificar.*

glorifiquémonos let us win glory; impve. 1st pers. pl. / *glorificarse.*

glorifiquemos 1. that we may glorify; pres. subj. 1st pers. pl. / *glorificar.* 2. let us glorify; impve. 1st pers. pl.

glorifiquen 1. that they may glorify; pres. subj. 3rd pers. pl. / *glorificar.* 2. let them glorify; impve. 3rd pers. pl.

glorifíquense let them win glory; impve. 3rd pers. pl. / *glorificarse.*

glorifiques that you may glorify; pres. subj. 2nd pers. sing. / *glorificar.*

glorifíquese let him (her/it) win glory; impve. 3rd pers. sing. / *glorificarse.*

glorío I glory; pres. ind. 1st pers. sing. / *gloriarse.*

glosar to gloss or to comment on. reg.

glotonear to gormandize. reg.

gluglutear to gobble (as a turkey). reg.

gobernar to govern. irr.

gobierna 1. he (she/it) governs; pres. ind. 3rd pers. sing. / *gobernar.* 2. (you) govern; impve. 2nd pers. sing.

gobiernan they govern; pres. ind. 3rd pers. pl. / *gobernar.*

gobiernas you govern; pres. ind. 2nd pers. sing. / *gobernar.*

gobierne 1. that I may govern; pres. subj. 1st pers. sing. / *gobernar.* 2. that he (she/it) may govern; pres. subj. 3rd pers. sing. 3. let him (her/it) govern; impve. 3rd pers. sing.

gobiernen 1. that they may govern; pres. subj. 3rd pers. pl. / *gobernar.* 2. let them govern; impve. 3rd pers. pl.

gobiernes that you may govern; pres. subj. 2nd pers. sing. / *gobernar.*

gobierno I govern; pres. ind. 1st pers. sing. / *gobernar.*

goce 1. that I may enjoy; pres. subj. 1st pers. sing. / *gozar.* 2. that he (she/it) may enjoy; pres. subj. 3rd pers. sing. 3. let him (her/it) enjoy; impve. 3rd pers. sing.

gocé I enjoyed; past 1st pers. sing. / *gozar.*

gocéis that you (all) may enjoy; pres. subj. 2nd pers. pl. / *gozar.*

gocémonos let us rejoice; impve. 1st pers. pl. / *gozarse.*

gocemos 1. that we may enjoy; pres. subj. 1st pers. pl. / *gozar.* 2. let us enjoy; impve. 1st pers. pl.

gocen 1. that they may enjoy; pres. subj. 3rd pers. pl. / *gozar.* 2. let them enjoy; impve. 3rd pers. pl.

gócense let them rejoice; impve. 3rd pers. pl. / *gozarse.*

goces that you may enjoy; pres. subj. 2nd pers. sing. / *gozar.*

gócese let him (her/it) rejoice; impve. 3rd pers. sing. / *gozarse.*

golpear to beat or to knock. reg.

golpetear to pound. reg.

gorgotear to gurgle. reg.

gorjeándose gurgling; pres. part. / *gorjearse.*

gorjeaos (you all) gurgle; impve. 2nd pers. pl. / *gorjearse.*

gorjear to warble. reg.

gorjearse to gurgle. reg.

gorjéate (you) gurgle; impve. 2nd pers. sing. / *gorjearse.*

gorjeémonos let us gurgle; impve. 1st pers. pl. / *gorjearse.*

gorjéense let them gurgle; impve. 3rd pers. pl. / *gorjearse.*

gorjéese let him (her/it) gurgle; impve. 3rd pers. sing. / *gorjearse.*

gorrear to sponge. reg.

gorronear to sponge. reg.
goteándose leaking; pres. part. / *gotearse*.
goteaos (you all) leak; impve. 2nd pers. pl. / *gotearse*.
gotear to drip. reg.
gotearse to leak. reg.
gotéate (you) leak; impve. 2nd pers. sing. / *gotearse*.
goteémonos let us leak; impve. 1st pers. pl. / *gotearse*.
gotéense let them leak; impve. 3rd pers. pl. / *gotearse*.
gotéese let him (her/it) leak; impve. 3rd pers. sing. / *gotearse*.
gozándose rejoicing; pres. part. / *gozarse*.
gozaos (you all) rejoice; impve. 2nd pers. pl. / *gozarse*.
gozar to enjoy. irr.
gozarse to rejoice. irr.
gózate (you) rejoice; impve. 2nd pers. sing. / *gozarse*.
grabándose being engraved; pres. part. / *grabarse*.
grabaos (you all) be engraved; impve. 2nd pers. pl. / *grabarse*.
grabar to engrave. reg.
grabarse to be engraved. reg.
grábate (you) be engraved; impve. 2nd pers. sing. / *grabarse*.
grabémonos let us be engraved; impve. 1st pers. pl. / *grabarse*.
grábense let them be engraved; impve. 3rd pers. pl. / *grabarse*.
grábese let him (her/it) be engraved; impve. 3rd pers. sing. / *grabarse*.
gracejar to be a charmer. reg.
gradar to harrow. reg.
gradúa 1. he (she/it) graduates; pres. ind. 3rd pers. sing. / *graduar*. 2. (you) graduate; impve. 2nd pers. sing.
gradúan they graduate; pres. ind. 3rd pers. pl. / *graduar*.
graduándose graduating; pres. part. / *graduarse*.
graduaos (you all) graduate; impve. 2nd pers. pl. / *graduarse*.
graduar to graduate. irr.
graduarse to graduate. irr.
gradúas you graduate; pres. ind. 2nd pers. sing. / *graduar*.
gradúate (you) graduate; impve. 2nd pers. sing. / *graduarse*.
gradúe 1. that I may graduate; pres. subj. 1st pers. sing. / *graduar*. 2. that he (she/it) may graduate; pres. subj. 3rd pers. sing. 3. let him (her/it) graduate; impve. 3rd pers. sing.
graduémonos let us graduate; impve. 1st pers. pl. / *graduarse*.
gradúen 1. that they may graduate; pres. subj. 3rd pers. pl. / *graduar*. 2. let them graduate; impve. 3rd pers. pl.
gradúense let them graduate; impve. 3rd pers. pl. / *graduarse*.
gradúes that you may graduate; pres. subj. 2nd pers. sing. / *graduar*.
gradúese let him (her/it) graduate; impve. 3rd pers. sing. / *graduarse*.

gradúo I graduate; pres. ind. 1st pers. sing. / *graduar*.
granar to go to seed. reg.
granear to sow or to stipple. reg.
granice 1. that I may hail; pres. subj. 1st pers. sing. / *granizar*. 2. that he (she/it) may hail; pres. subj. 3rd pers. sing. 3. let him (her/it) hail; impve. 3rd pers. sing.
granicé I hailed; past 1st pers. sing. / *granizar*.
granicéis that you (all) may hail; pres. subj. 2nd pers. pl. / *granizar*.
granicemos 1. that we may hail; pres. subj. 1st pers. pl. / *granizar*. 2. let us hail; impve. 1st pers. pl.
granicen 1. that they may hail; pres. subj. 3rd pers. pl. / *granizar*. 2. let them hail; impve. 3rd pers. pl.
granices that you may hail; pres. subj. 2nd pers. sing. / *granizar*.
granizar to hail. irr.
granjeándose winning over; pres. part. / *granjearse*.
granjeaos (you all) win over; impve. 2nd pers. pl. / *granjearse*.
granjear to win or to earn. reg.
granjearse to win over. reg.
granjéate (you) win over; impve. 2nd pers. sing. / *granjearse*.
granjeémonos let us win over; impve. 1st pers. pl. / *granjearse*.
granjéense let them win over; impve. 3rd pers. pl. / *granjearse*.
granjéese let him (her/it) win over; impve. 3rd pers. sing. / *granjearse*.
granulándose becoming granulated; pres. part. / *granularse*.
granular to granulate. reg.
granularse to become granulated. reg.
granúlense let them become granulated; impve. 3rd pers. pl. / *granularse*.
granúlese let it become granulated; impve. 3rd pers. sing. / *granularse*.
gratificar to gratify. irr.
gratifique 1. that I may gratify; pres. subj. 1st pers. sing. / *gratificar*. 2. that he (she/it) may gratify; pres. subj. 3rd pers. sing. 3. let him (her/it) gratify; impve. 3rd pers. sing.
gratifiqué I gratified; past 1st pers. sing. / *gratificar*.
gratifiquéis that you (all) may gratify; pres. subj. 2nd pers. pl. / *gratificar*.
gratifiquemos 1. that we may gratify; pres. subj. 1st pers. pl. / *gratificar*. 2. let us gratify; impve. 1st pers. pl.
gratifiquen 1. that they may gratify; pres. subj. 3rd pers. pl. / *gratificar*. 2. let them gratify; impve. 3rd pers. pl.
gratifiques that you may gratify; pres. subj. 2nd pers. sing. / *gratificar*.
gratulándose rejoicing; pres. part. / *gratularse*.
gratulaos (you all) rejoice; impve. 2nd pers. pl. / *gratularse*.
gratular to congratulate. reg.
gratularse to rejoice. reg.

gratúlate (you) rejoice; impve. 2nd pers. sing. / *gratularse*.

gratulémonos let us rejoice; impve. 1st pers. pl. / *gratularse*.

gratúlense let them rejoice; impve. 3rd pers. pl. / *gratularse*.

gratúlese let him (her/it) rejoice; impve. 3rd pers. sing. / *gratularse*.

gravar to burden. reg.

gravitar to gravitate. reg.

graznar to caw or to croak. reg.

grietar to crack. reg.

gritar to shout. reg.

gruñendo grunting; pres. part. / *gruñir*.

gruñera 1. that I might grunt; imp. subj. 1st pers. sing. / *gruñir*. 2. that he (she/it) might grunt; imp. subj. 3rd pers. sing.

gruñerais that you (all) might grunt; imp. subj. 2nd pers pl. / *gruñir*.

gruñéramos that we might grunt; imp. subj. 1st pers. pl. / *gruñir*.

gruñeran that they might grunt; imp. subj. 3rd pers. pl. / *gruñir*.

gruñeras that you might grunt; imp. subj. 2nd pers. sing. / *gruñir*.

gruñeron they grunted; past 3rd pers. pl. / *gruñir*.

gruñese 1. that I might grunt; imp. subj. 1st pers. sing. / *gruñir*. 2. that he (she/it) might grunt; imp. subj. 3rd pers. sing.

gruñeseis that you (all) might grunt; imp. subj. 2nd pers pl. / *gruñir*.

gruñésemos that we might grunt; imp. subj. 1st pers. pl. / *gruñir*.

gruñesen that they might grunt; imp. subj. 3rd pers. pl. / *gruñir*.

gruñeses that you might grunt; imp. subj. 2nd pers. sing. / *gruñir*.

gruñir to grunt. irr.

gruñó he (she/it) grunted; past 3rd pers. sing. / *gruñir*.

guachapear to kick or to rattle. reg.

guadañar to mow. reg.

guapear to bluster. reg.

guardándose avoiding; pres. part. / *guardarse*.

guardaos (you all) avoid; impve. 2nd pers. pl. / *guardarse*.

guardar to guard. reg.

guardarse to avoid. reg.

guárdate (you) avoid; impve. 2nd pers. sing. / *guardarse*.

guardémonos let us avoid; impve. 1st pers. pl. / *guardarse*.

guárdense let them avoid; impve. 3rd pers. pl. / *guardarse*.

guárdese let him (her/it) avoid; impve. 3rd pers. sing. / *guardarse*.

guareceos (you all) take refuge; impve. 2nd pers. pl. / *guarecerse*.

guarecer to shelter. irr.

guarecerse to take refuge. irr.

guarécete (you) take refuge; impve. 2nd pers. sing. / *guarecerse*.

guareciéndose taking refuge; pres. part. / *guarecerse*.

guarezca 1. that I may shelter; pres. subj. 1st pers. sing. / *guarecer*. 2. that he (she/it) may shelter; pres. subj. 3rd pers. sing. 3. let him (her/it) shelter; impve. 3rd pers. sing.

guarezcáis that you (all) may shelter; pres. subj. 2nd pers. pl. / *guarecer*.

guarezcámonos let us take refuge; impve. 1st pers. pl. / *guarecerse*.

guarezcamos 1. that we may shelter; pres. subj. 1st pers. pl. / *guarecer*. 2. let us shelter; impve. 1st pers. pl.

guarezcan 1. that they may shelter; pres. subj. 3rd pers. pl. / *guarecer*. 2. let them shelter; impve. 3rd pers. pl.

guarézcanse let them take refuge; impve. 3rd pers. pl. / *guarecerse*.

guarezcas that you may shelter; pres. subj. 2nd pers. sing. / *guarecer*.

guarézcase let him (her/it) take refuge; impve. 3rd pers. sing. / *guarecerse*.

guarezco I shelter; pres. ind. 1st pers. sing. / *guarecer*.

guarnecer to garnish. irr.

guarnezca 1. that I may garnish; pres. subj. 1st pers. sing. / *guarnecer*. 2. that he (she/it) may garnish; pres. subj. 3rd pers. sing. 3. let him (her/it) garnish; impve. 3rd pers. sing.

guarnezcáis that you (all) may garnish; pres. subj. 2nd pers. pl. / *guarnecer*.

guarnezcamos 1. that we may garnish; pres. subj. 1st pers. pl. / *guarnecer*. 2. let us garnish; impve. 1st pers. pl.

guarnezcan 1. that they may garnish; pres. subj. 3rd pers. pl. / *guarnecer*. 2. let them garnish; impve. 3rd pers. pl.

guarnezcas that you may garnish; pres. subj. 2nd pers. sing. / *guarnecer*.

guarnezco I garnish; pres. ind. 1st pers. sing. / *guarnecer*.

guarnicionar to garrison. reg.

guerrear to war. reg.

guerrillear to wage guerrilla warfare. reg.

guía 1. he (she/it) guides; pres. ind. 3rd pers. sing. / *guiar*. 2. (you) guide; impve. 2nd pers. sing.

guían they guide; pres. ind. 3rd pers. pl. / *guiar*.

guiándose being guided; pres. part. / *guiarse*.

guiaos (you all) be guided; impve. 2nd pers. pl. / *guiarse*.

guiar to guide. irr.

guiarse to be guided. irr.

guías you guide; pres. ind. 2nd pers. sing. / *guiar*.

guíate (you) be guided; impve. 2nd pers. sing. / *guiarse*.

guíe 1. that I may guide; pres. subj. 1st pers. sing. / *guiar*. 2. that he (she/it) may guide; pres. subj. 3rd pers. sing. 3. let him (her/it) guide; impve. 3rd pers. sing.

guiémonos let us be guided; impve. 1st pers. pl. / *guiarse*.

guíen 1. that they may guide; pres. subj. 3rd pers. pl. / *guiar*. 2. let them guide; impve. 3rd pers. pl.

guíense let them be guided; impve. 3rd pers. pl. / *guiarse*.

guíes that you may guide; pres. subj. 2nd pers. sing. / *guiar*.

guíese let him (her/it) be guided; impve. 3rd pers. sing. / *guiarse*.

guillotinar to guillotine. reg.

guinchar to goad. reg.

guindar to hoist. reg.

guiñar to wink or to yaw. reg.

guío I guide; pres. ind. 1st pers. sing. / *guiar*.

guisar to cook. reg.

guitarrear to strum a guitar. reg.

gulusmear to hang around food. reg.

gusanear to teem. reg.

gustar to taste or to please. reg.

H

ha he (she/it) has; pres. ind. 3rd pers. sing. / *haber*.

haber to have. irr.

habilitar to habilitate or to qualify. reg.

habitar to inhabit. reg.

habitúa 1. he (she/it) accustoms; pres. ind. 3rd pers. sing. / *habituar*. 2. (you) accustom; impve. 2nd pers. sing.

habitúan they accustom; pres. ind. 3rd pers. pl. / *habituar*.

habituándose becoming accustomed; pres. part. / *habituarse*.

habituaos (you all) become accustomed; impve. 2nd pers. pl. / *habituarse*.

habituar to accustom. irr.

habituarse to become accustomed. irr.

habitúas you accustom; pres. ind. 2nd pers. sing. / *habituar*.

habitúate (you) become accustomed; impve. 2nd pers. sing. / *habituarse*.

habitúe 1. that I may accustom; pres. subj. 1st pers. sing. / *habituar*. 2. that he (she/it) may accustom; pres. subj. 3rd pers. sing. 3. let him (her/it) accustom; impve. 3rd pers. sing.

habituémonos let us become accustomed; impve. 1st pers. pl. / *habituarse*.

habitúen 1. that they may accustom; pres. subj. 3rd pers. pl. / *habituar*. 2. let them accustom; impve. 3rd pers. pl.

habitúense let them become accustomed; impve. 3rd pers. pl. / *habituarse*.

habitúes that you may accustom; pres. subj. 2nd pers. sing. / *habituar*.

habitúese let him (her/it) become accustomed; impve. 3rd pers. sing. / *habituarse*.

habitúo I accustom; pres. ind. 1st pers. sing. / *habituar*.

hablándose being on speaking terms; pres. part. / *hablarse*.

hablaos (you all) be on speaking terms; impve. 2nd pers. pl. / *hablarse*.

hablar to speak or to talk. reg.

hablarse to be on speaking terms. reg.

háblate (you) be on speaking terms; impve. 2nd pers. sing. / *hablarse*.

hablémonos let us be on speaking terms; impve. 1st pers. pl. / *hablarse*.

háblense let them be on speaking terms; impve. 3rd pers. pl. / *hablarse*.

háblese let him (her/it) be on speaking terms; impve. 3rd pers. sing. / *hablarse*.

habrá he (she/it) will have; fut. 3rd pers. sing. / *haber*.

habrán they will have; fut. 3rd pers. pl. / *haber*.

habrás you will have; fut. 2nd pers. sing. / *haber*.

habré I shall have; fut. 1st pers. sing. / *haber*.

habréis you (all) will have; fut. 2nd pers. pl. / *haber*.

habremos we shall have; fut. 1st pers. pl. / *haber*.

habría 1. I should have; cond. 1st pers. sing. / *haber*. 2. he (she/it) would have; cond. 3rd pers. sing.

habríais you (all) would have; cond. 2nd pers. pl. / *haber*.

habríamos we should have; cond. 1st pers. pl. / *haber*.

habrían they would have; cond. 3rd pers. pl. / *haber*.

habrías you would have; cond. 2nd pers. sing. / *haber*.

hacendándose buying property; pres. part. / *hacendarse*.

hacendaos (you all) buy property; impve. 2nd pers. pl. / *hacendarse*.

hacendar to transfer property. irr.

hacendarse to buy property. irr.

hacendémonos let us buy property; impve. 1st pers. pl. / *hacendarse*.

haceos (you all) become; impve. 2nd pers. pl. / *hacerse*.

hacer to do or to make. irr.

hacerse to become. irr.

hacienda 1. he (she/it) transfers property; pres. ind. 3rd pers. sing. / *hacendar*. 2. (you) transfer property; impve. 2nd pers. sing.

haciendan they transfer property; pres. ind. 3rd pers. pl. / *hacendar*.

haciendas you transfer property; pres. ind. 2nd pers. sing. / *hacendar*.

haciéndate (you) buy property; impve. 2nd pers. sing. / *hacendarse*.

haciende 1. that I may transfer property; pres. subj. 1st pers. sing. / *hacendar*. 2. that he (she/it) may transfer property; pres. subj. 3rd pers. sing. 3. let him (her/it) transfer property; impve. 3rd pers. sing.

hacienden 1. that they may transfer property; pres. subj. 3rd pers. pl. / *hacendar*. 2. let them transfer property; impve. 3rd pers. pl.

haciéndense let them buy property; impve. 3rd pers. pl. / *hacendarse*.

haciendes that you may transfer property; pres. subj. 2nd pers. sing. / *hacendar*.

haciéndese let him (her/it) buy property; impve. 3rd pers. sing. / *hacendarse.*

haciendo I transfer property; pres. ind. 1st pers. sing. / *hacendar.*

haciéndose becoming; pres. part. / *hacerse.*

hacinar to stack. reg.

hachar to hew. reg.

hachear to chop. reg.

hadar to foretell. reg.

haga 1. that I may do; pres. subj. 1st pers. sing. / *hacer.* 2. that he (she/it) may do; pres. subj. 3rd pers. sing. 3. let him (her/it) do; impve. 3rd pers. sing.

hagáis that you (all) may do; pres. subj. 2nd pers. pl. / *hacer.*

hagámonos let us become; impve. 1st pers. pl. / *hacerse.*

hagamos 1. that we may do; pres. subj. 1st pers. pl. / *hacer.* 2. let us do; impve. 1st pers. pl.

hagan 1. that they may do; pres. subj. 3rd pers. pl. / *hacer.* 2. let them do; impve. 3rd pers. pl.

háganse let them become; impve. 3rd pers. pl. / *hacerse.*

hagas that you may do; pres. subj. 2nd pers. sing. / *hacer.*

hágase let him (her/it) become; impve. 3rd pers. sing. / *hacerse.*

hago I do; pres. ind. 1st pers. sing. / *hacer.*

halagar to flatter. irr.

halague 1. that I may flatter; pres. subj. 1st pers. sing. / *halagar.* 2. that he (she/it) may flatter; pres. subj. 3rd pers. sing. 3. let him (her/it) flatter; impve. 3rd pers. sing.

halagué I flattered; past 1st pers. sing. / *halagar.*

halaguéis that you (all) may flatter; pres. subj. 2nd pers. pl. / *halagar.*

halaguemos 1. that we may flatter; pres. subj. 1st pers. pl. / *halagar.* 2. let us flatter; impve. 1st pers. pl.

halaguen 1. that they may flatter; pres. subj. 3rd pers. pl. / *halagar.* 2. let them flatter; impve. 3rd pers. pl.

halagues that you may flatter; pres. subj. 2nd pers. sing. / *halagar.*

halar to pull. reg.

halconear to be brazen. reg.

hallándose getting along; pres. part. / *hallarse.*

hallaos (you all) get along; impve. 2nd pers. pl. / *hallarse.*

hallar to find. reg.

hallarse to get along. reg.

hállate (you) get along; impve. 2nd pers. sing. / *hallarse.*

hallémonos let us get along; impve. 1st pers. pl. / *hallarse.*

hállense let them get along; impve. 3rd pers. pl. / *hallarse.*

hállese let him (her/it) get along; impve. 3rd pers. sing. / *hallarse.*

hamacar to swing. irr.

hamaque 1. that I may swing; pres. subj. 1st pers. sing. / *hamacar.* 2. that he (she/it) may swing; pres. subj. 3rd pers. sing. 3. let him (her/it) swing; impve. 3rd pers. sing.

hamaqué I swung; past 1st pers. sing. / *hamacar.*

hamaquéis that you (all) may swing; pres. subj. 2nd pers. pl. / *hamacar.*

hamaquemos 1. that we may swing; pres. subj. 1st pers. pl. / *hamacar.* 2. let us swing; impve. 1st pers. pl.

hamaquen 1. that they may swing; pres. subj. 3rd pers. pl. / *hamacar.* 2. let them swing; impve. 3rd pers. pl.

hamaques that you may swing; pres. subj. 2nd pers. sing. / *hamacar.*

hambrear to starve. reg.

han they have; pres. ind. 3rd pers. pl. / *haber.*

hará he (she/it) will do; fut. 3rd pers. sing. / *hacer.*

haraganear to loaf. reg.

harán they will do; fut. 3rd pers. pl. / *hacer.*

harás you will do; fut. 2nd pers. sing. / *hacer.*

haré I shall do; fut. 1st pers. sing. / *hacer.*

haréis you (all) will do; fut. 2nd pers. pl. / *hacer.*

haremos we shall do; fut. 1st pers. pl. / *hacer.*

haría 1. I should do; cond. 1st pers. sing. / *hacer.* 2. he (she/it) would do; cond. 3rd pers. sing.

haríais you (all) would do; cond. 2nd pers. pl. / *hacer.*

haríamos we should do; cond. 1st pers. pl. / *hacer.*

harían they would do; cond. 3rd pers. pl. / *hacer.*

harías you would do; cond. 2nd pers. sing. / *hacer.*

hartándose overeating; pres. part. / *hartarse.*

hartaos (you all) overeat; impve. 2nd pers. pl. / *hartarse.*

hartar to satiate or to glut. reg.

hartarse to overeat. reg.

hártate (you) overeat; impve. 2nd pers. sing. / *hartarse.*

hartémonos let us overeat; impve. 1st pers. pl. / *hartarse.*

hártense let them overeat; impve. 3rd pers. pl. / *hartarse.*

hártese let him (her/it) overeat; impve. 3rd pers. sing. / *hartarse.*

has you have; pres. ind. 2nd pers. sing. / *haber.*

hastía 1. he (she/it) surfeits; pres. ind. 3rd pers. sing. / *hastiar.* 2. (you) surfeit; impve. 2nd pers. sing.

hastían they surfeit; pres. ind. 3rd pers. pl. / *hastiar.*

hastiar to surfeit. irr.

hastías you surfeit; pres. ind. 2nd pers. sing. / *hastiar.*

hastíe 1. that I may surfeit; pres. subj. 1st pers. sing. / *hastiar.* 2. that he (she/it) may surfeit; pres. subj. 3rd pers. sing. 3. let him (her/it) surfeit; impve. 3rd pers. sing.

hastíen 1. that they may surfeit; pres. subj. 3rd pers. pl. / *hastiar.* 2. let them surfeit; impve. 3rd pers. pl.

hastíes that you may surfeit; pres. subj. 2nd pers. sing. / *hastiar.*

hastío I surfeit; pres. ind. 1st pers. sing. / *hastiar.*

hatear to pack up. reg.

hay there is or there are; pres. ind. 3rd pers. sing. or pl. / *haber.*

haya 1. that I may have; pres. subj. 1st pers. sing. / *haber.* 2. that he (she/it) may have; pres. subj. 3rd pers. sing. 3. let him (her/it) have; impve. 3rd pers. sing.

hayáis that you (all) may have; pres. subj. 2nd pers. pl. / *haber.*

hayamos 1. that we may have; pres. subj. 1st pers. pl. / *haber.* 2. let us have; impve. 1st pers. pl.

hayan 1. that they may have; pres. subj. 3rd pers. pl. / *haber.* 2. let them have; impve. 3rd pers. pl.

hayas that you may have; pres. subj. 2nd pers. sing. / *haber.*

haz (you) do; impve. 2nd pers. sing. / *hacer.*

he 1. I have; pres. ind. 1st pers. sing. / *haber.* 2. (you) have; impve. 2nd pers. sing.

hebraice 1. that I may judaize; pres. subj. 1st pers. sing. / *hebraizar.* 2. that he (she/it) may judaize; pres. subj. 3rd pers. sing. 3. let him (her/it) judaize; impve. 3rd pers. sing.

hebraicé I judaized; past 1st pers. sing. / *hebraizar.*

hebraicéis that you (all) may judaize; pres. subj. 2nd pers. pl. / *hebraizar.*

hebraicemos 1. that we may judaize; pres. subj. 1st pers. pl. / *hebraizar.* 2. let us judaize; impve. 1st pers. pl.

hebraicen 1. that they may judaize; pres. subj. 3rd pers. pl. / *hebraizar.* 2. let them judaize; impve. 3rd pers. pl.

hebraices that you may judaize; pres. subj. 2nd pers. sing. / *hebraizar.*

hebraizar to judaize. irr.

hechice 1. that I may bewitch; pres. subj. 1st pers. sing. / *hechizar.* 2. that he (she/it) may bewitch; pres. subj. 3rd pers. sing. 3. let him (her/it) bewitch; impve. 3rd pers. sing.

hechicé I bewitched; past 1st pers. sing. / *hechizar.*

hechicéis that you (all) may bewitch; pres. subj. 2nd pers. pl. / *hechizar.*

hechicemos 1. that we may bewitch; pres. subj. 1st pers. pl. / *hechizar.* 2. let us bewitch; impve. 1st pers. pl.

hechicen 1. that they may bewitch; pres. subj. 3rd pers. pl. / *hechizar.* 2. let them bewitch; impve. 3rd pers. pl.

hechices that you may bewitch; pres. subj. 2nd pers. sing. / *hechizar.*

hechizar to bewitch. irr.

hecho done or made; past part. / *hacer.*

heder to stink. irr.

helándose being frost-bitten; pres. part. / *helarse.*

helar to freeze. irr.

helarse to be frost-bitten. irr.

hemos we have; pres. ind. 1st pers. pl. / *haber.*

henchíos (you all) overeat; impve. 2nd pers. pl. / *henchirse.*

henchir to stuff. irr.

henchirse to overeat. irr.

hender to split. irr.

heñir to knead. irr.

herbajar to graze. reg.

herbajear to graze. reg.

herborice 1. that I may herbalize; pres. subj. 1st pers. sing. / *herborizar.* 2. that he (she/it) may herbalize; pres. subj. 3rd pers. sing. 3. let him (her/it) herbalize; impve. 3rd pers. sing.

herboricé I herbalized; past 1st pers. sing. / *herborizar.*

herboricéis that you (all) may herbalize; pres. subj. 2nd pers. pl. / *herborizar.*

herboricemos 1. that we may herbalize; pres. subj. 1st pers. pl. / *herborizar.* 2. let us herbalize; impve. 1st pers. pl.

herboricen 1. that they may herbalize; pres. subj. 3rd pers. pl. / *herborizar.* 2. let them herbalize; impve. 3rd pers. pl.

herborices that you may herbalize; pres. subj. 2nd pers. sing. / *herborizar.*

herborizar to herbalize. irr.

heredar to inherit. reg.

herir to wound. irr.

hermanándose becoming brothers; pres. part. / *hermanarse.*

hermanaos (you all) become brothers; impve. 2nd pers. pl. / *hermanarse.*

hermanar to match. reg.

hermanarse to become brothers. reg.

hermánate (you) become brothers; impve. 2nd pers. sing. / *hermanarse.*

hermanear to treat as a brother. reg.

hermanémonos let us become brothers; impve. 1st pers. pl. / *hermanarse.*

hermánense let them become brothers; impve. 3rd pers. pl. / *hermanarse.*

hermánese let him (it) become brothers / *hermanarse.*

hermosear to beautify. reg.

herrar to shoe (a horse) or to brand. irr.

herventar to boil. reg.

hervir to boil. irr.

hesitar to hesitate. reg.

hibernar to hibernate. reg.

hice I did; past 1st pers. sing. / *hacer.*

hiciera 1. that I might do; imp. subj. 1st pers. sing. / *hacer.* 2. that he (she/it) might do; imp. subj. 3rd pers. sing.

hicierais that you (all) might do; imp. subj. 2nd pers pl. / *hacer.*

hiciéramos that we might do; imp. subj. 1st pers. pl. / *hacer.*

hicieran that they might do; imp. subj. 3rd pers. pl. / *hacer.*

hicieras that you might do; imp. subj. 2nd pers. sing. / *hacer.*

hicieron they did; past 3rd pers. pl. / *hacer.*

hiciese 1. that I might do; imp. subj. 1st pers. sing. / *hacer.* 2. that he (she/it) might do; imp. subj. 3rd pers. sing.

hicieseis that you (all) might do; imp. subj. 2nd pers pl. / *hacer.*

hiciésemos that we might do; imp. subj. 1st pers. pl. / *hacer.*

hiciesen that they might do; imp. subj. 3rd pers. pl. / *hacer.*

hicieses that you might do; imp. subj. 2nd pers. sing. / *hacer.*

hicimos we did; past 1st pers. pl. / *hacer.*

hiciste you did; past 2nd pers. sing. / *hacer.*

hicisteis you (all) did; past 2nd pers. pl. / *hacer.*

hidratar to hydrate. reg.

hidrogenar to hydrogenate. reg.

hieda 1. that I may stink; pres. subj. 1st pers. sing. / *heder.* 2. that he (she/it) may stink; pres. subj. 3rd pers. sing. 3. let him (her/it) stink; impve. 3rd pers. sing.

hiedan 1. that they may stink; pres. subj. 3rd pers. pl. / *heder.* 2. let them stink; impve. 3rd pers. pl.

hiedas that you may stink; pres. subj. 2nd pers. sing. / *heder.*

hiede 1. he (she/it) stinks; pres. ind. 3rd pers. sing. / *heder.* 2. (you) stink; impve. 2nd pers. sing.

hieden they stink; pres. ind. 3rd pers. pl. / *heder.*

hiedes you stink; pres. ind. 2nd pers. sing. / *heder.*

hiedo I stink; pres. ind. 1st pers. sing. / *heder.*

hiela he (she/it) freezes; pres. ind. 3rd pers. sing. / *helar.*

hiélase let him (her/it) be frost-bitten; impve. 3rd pers. sing. / *helarse.*

hiele 1. that I may freeze; pres. subj. 1st pers. sing. / *helar.* 2. that he (she/it) may freeze; pres. subj. 3rd pers. sing. 3. let him (her/it) freeze; impve. 3rd pers. sing.

hienda 1. that I may split; pres. subj. 1st pers. sing. / *hender.* 2. that he (she/it) may split; pres. subj. 3rd pers. sing. 3. let him (her/it) split; impve. 3rd pers. sing.

hiendan 1. that they may split; pres. subj. 3rd pers. pl. / *hender.* 2. let them split; impve. 3rd pers. pl.

hiendas that you may split; pres. subj. 2nd pers. sing. / *hender.*

hiende 1. he (she/it) splits; pres. ind. 3rd pers. sing. / *hender.* 2. (you) split; impve. 2nd pers. sing.

hienden they split; pres. ind. 3rd pers. pl. / *hender.*

hiendes you split; pres. ind. 2nd pers. sing. / *hender.*

hiendo I split; pres. ind. 1st pers. sing. / *hender.*

hiera 1. that I may wound; pres. subj. 1st pers. sing. / *herir.* 2. that he (she/it) may wound; pres. subj. 3rd pers. sing. 3. let him (her/it) wound; impve. 3rd pers. sing.

hieran 1. that they may wound; pres. subj. 3rd pers. pl. / *herir.* 2. let them wound; impve. 3rd pers. pl.

hieras that you may wound; pres. subj. 2nd pers. sing. / *herir.*

hiere 1. he (she/it) wounds; pres. ind. 3rd pers. sing. / *herir.* 2. (you) wound; impve. 2nd pers. sing.

hieren they wound; pres. ind. 3rd pers. pl. / *herir.*

hieres you wound; pres. ind. 2nd pers. sing. / *herir.*

hiero I wound; pres. ind. 1st pers. sing. / *herir.*

hierra 1. he (she/it) shoes (a horse); pres. ind. 3rd pers. sing. / *herrar.* 2. (you) shoe (a horse); impve. 2nd pers. sing.

hierran they shoe (a horse); pres. ind. 3rd pers. pl. / *herrar.*

hierras you shoe (a horse); pres. ind. 2nd pers. sing. / *herrar.*

hierre 1. that I may shoe (a horse); pres. subj. 1st pers. sing. / *herrar.* 2. that he (she/it) may shoe (a horse); pres. subj. 3rd pers. sing. 3. let him (her/it) shoe (a horse); impve. 3rd pers. sing.

hierren 1. that they may shoe (a horse); pres. subj. 3rd pers. pl. / *herrar.* 2. let them shoe (a horse); impve. 3rd pers. pl.

hierres that you may shoe (a horse); pres. subj. 2nd pers. sing. / *herrar.*

hierro I shoe (a horse); pres. ind. 1st pers. sing. / *herrar.*

hierva 1. that I may boil; pres. subj. 1st pers. sing. / *hervir.* 2. that he (she/it) may boil; pres. subj. 3rd pers. sing. 3. let him (her/it) boil; impve. 3rd pers. sing.

hiervan 1. that they may boil; pres. subj. 3rd pers. pl. / *hervir.* 2. let them boil; impve. 3rd pers. pl.

hiervas that you may boil; pres. subj. 2nd pers. sing. / *hervir.*

hierve 1. he (she/it) boils; pres. ind. 3rd pers. sing. / *hervir.* 2. (you) boil; impve. 2nd pers. sing.

hierven they boil; pres. ind. 3rd pers. pl. / *hervir.*

hierves you boil; pres. ind. 2nd pers. sing. / *hervir.*

hiervo I boil; pres. ind. 1st pers. sing. / *hervir.*

hilar to spin. reg.

hilvanar to baste or to tack. reg.

hincándose kneeling; pres. part. / *hincarse.*

hincaos (you all) kneel; impve. 2nd pers. pl. / *hincarse.*

hincar to drive. irr.

hincarse to kneel. irr.

híncate (you) kneel; impve. 2nd pers. sing. / *hincarse.*

hincha 1. that I may stuff; pres. subj. 1st pers. sing. / *henchir.* 2. that he (she/it) may stuff; pres. subj. 3rd pers. sing. 3. let him (her/it) stuff; impve. 3rd pers. sing.

hincháis that you (all) may stuff; pres. subj. 2nd pers. pl. / *henchir.*

hinchámonos let us overeat; impve. 1st pers. pl. / *henchirse.*

hinchamos 1. that we may stuff; pres. subj. 1st pers. pl. / *henchir.* 2. let us stuff; impve. 1st pers. pl.

hinchan 1. that they may stuff; pres. subj. 3rd pers. pl. / *henchir.* 2. let them stuff; impve. 3rd pers. pl.

hinchándose swelling up; pres. part. / *hincharse.*

hínchanse let them overeat; impve. 3rd pers. pl. / *henchirse.*

hinchaos (you all) swell up; impve. 2nd pers. pl. / *hincharse.*

hinchar to swell. reg.

hincharse to swell up. reg.

hinchas that you may stuff; pres. subj. 2nd pers. sing. / *henchir.*

hínchase let him (her/it) overeat; impve. 3rd pers. sing. / *henchirse.*

hínchate (you) swell up; impve. 2nd pers. sing. / *hincharse.*

hinche 1. he (she/it) stuffs; pres. ind. 3rd pers. sing. / *henchir.* 2. (you) stuff; impve. 2nd pers. sing.

hinchémonos let us swell up; impve. 1st pers. pl. / *hincharse.*

hinchen they stuff; pres. ind. 3rd pers. pl. / *henchir.*

hínchense let them swell up; impve. 3rd pers. pl. / *hincharse.*

hinches you stuff; pres. ind. 2nd pers. sing. / *henchir.*

hínchese let him (her/it) swell up; impve. 3rd pers. sing. / *hincharse.*

hínchete (you) overeat; impve. 2nd pers. sing. / *henchirse.*

hinchiendo stuffing; pres. part. / *henchir.*

hinchiéndose overeating; pres. part. / *henchirse.*

hinchiera 1. that I might stuff; imp. subj. 1st pers. sing. / *henchir.* 2. that he (she/it) might stuff; imp. subj. 3rd pers. sing.

hinchierais that you (all) might stuff; imp. subj. 2nd pers pl. / *henchir.*

hinchiéramos that we might stuff; imp. subj. 1st pers. pl. / *henchir.*

hinchieran that they might stuff; imp. subj. 3rd pers. pl. / *henchir.*

hinchieras that you might stuff; imp. subj. 2nd pers. sing. / *henchir.*

hinchieron they stuffed; past 3rd pers. pl. / *henchir.*

hinchiese 1. that I might stuff; imp. subj. 1st pers. sing. / *henchir.* 2. that he (she/it) might stuff; imp. subj. 3rd pers. sing.

hinchieseis that you (all) might stuff; imp. subj. 2nd pers pl. / *henchir.*

hinchiésemos that we might stuff; imp. subj. 1st pers. pl. / *henchir.*

hinchiesen that they might stuff; imp. subj. 3rd pers. pl. / *henchir.*

hinchieses that you might stuff; imp. subj. 2nd pers. sing. / *henchir.*

hinchió he (she/it) stuffed; past 3rd pers. sing. / *henchir.*

hincho I stuff; pres. ind. 1st pers. sing. / *henchir.*

hinque 1. that I may drive; pres. subj. 1st pers. sing. / *hincar.* 2. that he (she/it) may drive; pres. subj. 3rd pers. sing. 3. let him (her/it) drive; impve. 3rd pers. sing.

hinqué I drove; past 1st pers. sing. / *hincar.*

hinquéis that you (all) may drive; pres. subj. 2nd pers. pl. / *hincar.*

hinquémonos let them kneel; impve. 3rd pers. pl. / *hincarse.*

hinquemos 1. that we may drive; pres. subj. 1st pers. pl. / *hincar.* 2. let us drive; impve. 1st pers. pl.

hinquen 1. that they may drive; pres. subj. 3rd pers. pl. / *hincar.* 2. let them drive; impve. 3rd pers. pl.

hínquense let them kneel; impve. 3rd pers. pl. / *hincarse.*

hinques that you may drive; pres. subj. 2nd pers. sing. / *hincar.*

hínquese let him (her/it) kneel; impve. 3rd pers. sing. / *hincarse.*

hiña 1. that I may knead; pres. subj. 1st pers. sing. / *heñir.* 2. that he (she/it) may knead; pres. subj. 3rd pers. sing. 3. let him (her/it) knead; impve. 3rd pers. sing.

hiñáis that you (all) may knead; pres. subj. 2nd pers. pl. / *heñir.*

hiñamos 1. that we may knead; pres. subj. 1st pers. pl. / *heñir.* 2. let us knead; impve. 1st pers. pl.

hiñan 1. that they may knead; pres. subj. 3rd pers. pl. / *heñir.* 2. let them knead; impve. 3rd pers. pl.

hiñas that you may knead; pres. subj. 2nd pers. sing. / *heñir.*

hiñe 1. he (she/it) kneads; pres. ind. 3rd pers. sing. / *heñir.* 2. (you) knead; impve. 2nd pers. sing.

hiñen they knead; pres. ind. 3rd pers. pl. / *heñir.*

hiñendo kneading; pres. part. / *heñir.*

hiñera 1. that I might knead; imp. subj. 1st pers. sing. / *heñir.* 2. that he (she/it) might knead; imp. subj. 3rd pers. sing.

hiñerais that you (all) might knead; imp. subj. 2nd pers pl. / *heñir.*

hiñéramos that we might knead; imp. subj. 1st pers. pl. / *heñir.*

hiñeran that they might knead; imp. subj. 3rd pers. pl. / *heñir.*

hiñeras that you might knead; imp. subj. 2nd pers. sing. / *heñir.*

hiñeron they kneaded; past 3rd pers. pl. / *heñir.*

hiñes you knead; pres. ind. 2nd pers. sing. / *heñir.*

hiñese 1. that I might knead; imp. subj. 1st pers. sing. / *heñir.* 2. that he (she/it) might knead; imp. subj. 3rd pers. sing.

hiñeseis that you (all) might knead; imp. subj. 2nd pers pl. / *heñir.*

hiñésemos that we might knead; imp. subj. 1st pers. pl. / *heñir.*

hiñesen that they might knead; imp. subj. 3rd pers. pl. / *heñir.*

hiñeses that you might knead; imp. subj. 2nd pers. sing. / *heñir.*

hiño I knead; pres. ind. 1st pers. sing. / *heñir.*

hiñó he (she/it) kneaded; past 3rd pers. sing. / *heñir.*

hipar to hiccup. reg.

hipnotice 1. that I may hypnotize; pres. subj. 1st pers. sing. / *hipnotizar.* 2. that he (she/it) may hypnotize; pres. subj. 3rd pers. sing. 3. let him (her/it) hypnotize; impve. 3rd pers. sing.

hipnoticé I hypnotized; past 1st pers. sing. / *hipnotizar.*

hipnoticéis that you (all) may hypnotize; pres. subj. 2nd pers. pl. / *hipnotizar.*

hipnoticemos 1. that we may hypnotize; pres. subj. 1st pers. pl. / *hipnotizar.* 2. let us hypnotize; impve. 1st pers. pl.

hipnoticen 1. that they may hypnotize; pres. subj. 3rd pers. pl. / *hipnotizar.* 2. let them hypnotize; impve. 3rd pers. pl.

hipnotices that you may hypnotize; pres. subj. 2nd pers. sing. / *hipnotizar.*

hipnotizar to hypnotize. irr.

hipotecar to mortgage. irr.

hipoteque 1. that I may mortgage; pres. subj. 1st pers. sing. / *hipotecar.* 2. that he (she/it) may mortgage; pres. subj. 3rd pers. sing. 3. let him (her/it) mortgage; impve. 3rd pers. sing.

hipotequé I mortgaged; past 1st pers. sing. / *hipotecar.*

hipotequéis that you (all) may mortgage; pres. subj. 2nd pers. pl. / *hipotecar.*

hipotequemos 1. that we may mortgage; pres. subj. 1st pers. pl. / *hipotecar.* 2. let us mortgage; impve. 1st pers. pl.

hipotequen 1. that they may mortgage; pres. subj. 3rd pers. pl. / *hipotecar.* 2. let them mortgage; impve. 3rd pers. pl.

hipoteques that you may mortgage; pres. subj. 2nd pers. sing. / *hipotecar.*

hiráis that you (all) may wound; pres. subj. 2nd pers. pl. / *herir.*

hiramos 1. that we may wound; pres. subj. 1st pers. pl. / *herir.* 2. let us wound; impve. 1st pers. pl.

hiriendo wounding; pres. part. / *herir.*

hiriera 1. that I might wound; imp. subj. 1st pers. sing. / *herir.* 2. that he (she/it) might wound; imp. subj. 3rd pers. sing.

hirierais that you (all) might wound; imp. subj. 2nd pers pl. / *herir.*

hiriéramos that we might wound; imp. subj. 1st pers. pl. / *herir.*

hirieran that they might wound; imp. subj. 3rd pers. pl. / *herir.*

hirieras that you might wound; imp. subj. 2nd pers. sing. / *herir.*

hirieron they wounded; past 3rd pers. pl. / *herir.*

hiriese 1. that I might wound; imp. subj. 1st pers. sing. / *herir.* 2. that he (she/it) might wound; imp. subj. 3rd pers. sing.

hirieseis that you (all) might wound; imp. subj. 2nd pers pl. / *herir.*

hiriésemos that we might wound; imp. subj. 1st pers. pl. / *herir.*

hiriesen that they might wound; imp. subj. 3rd pers. pl. / *herir.*

hirieses that you might wound; imp. subj. 2nd pers. sing. / *herir.*

hirió he (she/it) wounded; past 3rd pers. sing. / *herir.*

hirváis that you (all) may boil; pres. subj. 2nd pers. pl. / *hervir.*

hirvamos 1. that we may boil; pres. subj. 1st pers. pl. / *hervir.* 2. let us boil; impve. 1st pers. pl.

hirviendo boiling; pres. part. / *hervir.*

hirviera 1. that I might boil; imp. subj. 1st pers. sing. / *hervir.* 2. that he (she/it) might boil; imp. subj. 3rd pers. sing.

hirvierais that you (all) might boil; imp. subj. 2nd pers pl. / *hervir.*

hirviéramos that we might boil; imp. subj. 1st pers. pl. / *hervir.*

hirvieran that they might boil; imp. subj. 3rd pers. pl. / *hervir.*

hirvieras that you might boil; imp. subj. 2nd pers. sing. / *hervir.*

hirvieron they boiled; past 3rd pers. pl. / *hervir.*

hirviese 1. that I might boil; imp. subj. 1st pers. sing. / *hervir.* 2. that he (she/it) might boil; imp. subj. 3rd pers. sing.

hirvieseis that you (all) might boil; imp. subj. 2nd pers pl. / *hervir.*

hirviésemos that we might boil; imp. subj. 1st pers. pl. / *hervir.*

hirviesen that they might boil; imp. subj. 3rd pers. pl. / *hervir.*

hirvieses that you might boil; imp. subj. 2nd pers. sing. / *hervir.*

hirvió he (she/it) boiled; past 3rd pers. sing. / *hervir.*

hisopar to asperse. reg.

hisopear to asperse. reg.

hispanice 1. that I may hispanicize; pres. subj. 1st pers. sing. / *hispanizar.* 2. that he (she/it) may hispanicize; pres. subj. 3rd pers. sing. 3. let him (her/it) hispanicize; impve. 3rd pers. sing.

hispanicé I hispanicized; past 1st pers. sing. / *hispanizar.*

hispanicéis that you (all) may hispanicize; pres. subj. 2nd pers. pl. / *hispanizar.*

hispanicemos 1. that we may hispanicize; pres. subj. 1st pers. pl. / *hispanizar.* 2. let us hispanicize; impve. 1st pers. pl.

hispanicen 1. that they may hispanicize; pres. subj. 3rd pers. pl. / *hispanizar.* 2. let them hispanicize; impve. 3rd pers. pl.

hispanices that you may hispanicize; pres. subj. 2nd pers. sing. / *hispanizar.*

hispanizar to hispanicize. irr.

historiar to write the history of. reg.

hizo he (she/it) did; past 3rd pers. sing. / *hacer.*

hoce 1. that I may root up; pres. subj. 1st pers. sing. / *hozar.* 2. that he (she/it) may root up; pres. subj. 3rd pers. sing. 3. let him (her/it) root up; impve. 3rd pers. sing.

hocé I rooted up; past 1st pers. sing. / *hozar.*

hocéis that you (all) may root up; pres. subj. 2nd pers. pl. / *hozar.*

hocemos 1. that we may root up; pres. subj. 1st pers. pl. / *hozar.* 2. let us root up; impve. 1st pers. pl.

hocen 1. that they may root up; pres. subj. 3rd pers. pl. / *hozar.* 2. let them root up; impve. 3rd pers. pl.

hoces that you may root up; pres. subj. 2nd pers. sing. / *hozar.*

hocicar to root or to run up against a difficulty. irr.

hocique 1. that I may root; pres. subj. 1st pers. sing. / *hocicar.* 2. that he (she/it) may root; pres. subj. 3rd pers. sing. 3. let him (her/it) root; impve. 3rd pers. sing.

hociqué I rooted; past 1st pers. sing. / *hocicar.*

hociquéis that you (all) may root; pres. subj. 2nd pers. pl. / *hocicar.*

hociquemos 1. that we may root; pres. subj. 1st pers. pl. / *hocicar.* 2. let us root; impve. 1st pers. pl.

hociquen 1. that they may root; pres. subj. 3rd pers. pl. / *hocicar.* 2. let them root; impve. 3rd pers. pl.

hociques that you may root; pres. subj. 2nd pers. sing. / *hocicar.*

hojear to turn the pages of. reg.

holgándose being glad; pres. part. / *holgarse.*

holgaos (you all) be glad; impve. 2nd pers. pl. / *holgarse.*

holgar to rest. irr.

holgarse to be glad. irr.

holgazanear to idle or to loiter. reg.

holgué I rested; past 1st pers. sing. / *holgar.*

holguéis that you (all) may rest; pres. subj. 2nd pers. pl. / *holgar.*

holguémonos let us be glad; impve. 1st pers. pl. / *holgarse.*

holguemos 1. that we may rest; pres. subj. 1st pers. pl. / *holgar.* 2. let us rest; impve. 1st pers. pl.

hollar to tread on. irr.

hombreándose vying; pres. part. / *hombrearse.*

hombreaos (you all) vie; impve. 2nd pers. pl. / *hombrearse.*

hombrear to shoulder. reg.

hombrearse to vie. reg.

hombréate (you) vie; impve. 2nd pers. sing. / *hombrearse.*

hombreémonos let us vie; impve. 1st pers. pl. / *hombrearse.*

hombréense let them vie; impve. 3rd pers. pl. / *hombrearse.*

hombréese let him (her/it) vie; impve. 3rd pers. sing. / *hombrearse.*

homogeneice 1. that I may homogenize; pres. subj. 1st pers. sing. / *homogeneizar.* 2. that he (she/it) may homogenize; pres. subj. 3rd pers. sing. 3. let him (her/it) homogenize; impve. 3rd pers. sing.

homogeneicé I homogenized; past 1st pers. sing. / *homogeneizar.*

homogeneicéis that you (all) may homogenize; pres. subj. 2nd pers. pl. / *homogeneizar.*

homogeneicemos 1. that we may homogenize; pres. subj. 1st pers. pl. / *homogeneizar.* 2. let us homogenize; impve. 1st pers. pl.

homogeneicen 1. that they may homogenize; pres. subj. 3rd pers. pl. / *homogeneizar.* 2. let them homogenize; impve. 3rd pers. pl.

homogeneices that you may homogenize; pres. subj. 2nd pers. sing. / *homogeneizar.*

homogeneizar to homogenize. irr.

homogenice 1. that I may homogenize; pres. subj. 1st pers. sing. / *homogenizar.* 2. that he (she/it) may homogenize; pres. subj. 3rd pers. sing. 3. let him (her/it) homogenize; impve. 3rd pers. sing.

homogenicé I homogenized; past 1st pers. sing. / *homogenizar.*

homogenicéis that you (all) may homogenize; pres. subj. 2nd pers. pl. / *homogenizar.*

homogenicemos 1. that we may homogenize; pres. subj. 1st pers. pl. / *homogenizar.* 2. let us homogenize; impve. 1st pers. pl.

homogenicen 1. that they may homogenize; pres. subj. 3rd pers. pl. / *homogenizar.* 2. let them homogenize; impve. 3rd pers. pl.

homogenices that you may homogenize; pres. subj. 2nd pers. sing. / *homogenizar.*

homogenizar to homogenize. irr.

homologar to validate. irr.

homologue 1. that I may validate; pres. subj. 1st pers. sing. / *homologar.* 2. that he (she/it) may validate; pres. subj. 3rd pers. sing. 3. let him (her/it) validate; impve. 3rd pers. sing.

homologué I validated; past 1st pers. sing. / *homologar.*

homologuéis that you (all) may validate; pres. subj. 2nd pers. pl. / *homologar.*

homologuemos 1. that we may validate; pres. subj. 1st pers. pl. / *homologar.* 2. let us validate; impve. 1st pers. pl.

homologuen 1. that they may validate; pres. subj. 3rd pers. pl. / *homologar.* 2. let them validate; impve. 3rd pers. pl.

homologues that you may validate; pres. subj. 2nd pers. sing. / *homologar.*

hondear to sound (water). reg.

honrándose being honored; pres. part. / *honrarse.*

honraos (you all) be honored; impve. 2nd pers. pl. / *honrarse.*

honrar to honor. reg.

honrarse to be honored. reg.

hónrate (you) be honored; impve. 2nd pers. sing. / *honrarse.*

honrémonos let us be honored; impve. 1st pers. pl. / *honrarse.*

hónrense let them be honored; impve. 3rd pers. pl. / *honrarse.*

hónrese let him (her/it) be honored; impve. 3rd pers. sing. / *honrarse.*

horadar to perforate. reg.

hormiguear to swarm or to itch. reg.

hornear to bake. reg.

horripilar to horrify. reg.

horrorice 1. that I may horrify; pres. subj. 1st pers. sing. / *horrorizar.* 2. that he (she/it) may horrify; pres. subj. 3rd pers. sing. 3. let him (her/it) horrify; impve. 3rd pers. sing.

horroricé I horrified; past 1st pers. sing. / *horrorizar.*

horroricéis that you (all) may horrify; pres. subj. 2nd pers. pl. / *horrorizar.*

horroricemos 1. that we may horrify; pres. subj. 1st pers. pl. / *horrorizar.* 2. let us horrify; impve. 1st pers. pl.

horroricen 1. that they may horrify; pres. subj. 3rd pers. pl. / *horrorizar.* 2. let them horrify; impve. 3rd pers. pl.

horrorices that you may horrify; pres. subj. 2nd pers. sing. / *horrorizar.*

horrorizar to horrify. irr.

hospedándose staying; pres. part. / *hospedarse.*

hospedaos (you all) stay; impve. 2nd pers. pl. / *hospedarse.*

hospedar to lodge. reg.
hospedarse to stay. reg.
hospédate (you) stay; impve. 2nd pers. sing. / *hospedarse*.
hospedémonos let us stay; impve. 1st pers. pl. / *hospedarse*.
hospédense let them stay; impve. 3rd pers. pl. / *hospedarse*.
hospédese let him (her/it) stay; impve. 3rd pers. sing. / *hospedarse*.
hospitalice 1. that I may hospitalize; pres. subj. 1st pers. sing. / *hospitalizar*. 2. that he (she/it) may hospitalize; pres. subj. 3rd pers. sing. 3. let him (her/it) hospitalize; impve. 3rd pers. sing.
hospitalicé I hospitalized; past 1st pers. sing. / *hospitalizar*.
hospitalicéis that you (all) may hospitalize; pres. subj. 2nd pers. pl. / *hospitalizar*.
hospitalicemos 1. that we may hospitalize; pres. subj. 1st pers. pl. / *hospitalizar*. 2. let us hospitalize; impve. 1st pers. pl.
hospitalicen 1. that they may hospitalize; pres. subj. 3rd pers. pl. / *hospitalizar*. 2. let them hospitalize; impve. 3rd pers. pl.
hospitalices that you may hospitalize; pres. subj. 2nd pers. sing. / *hospitalizar*.
hospitalizar to hospitalize. irr.
hostigar to harass. irr.
hostigue 1. that I may harass; pres. subj. 1st pers. sing. / *hostigar*. 2. that he (she/it) may harass; pres. subj. 3rd pers. sing. 3. let him (her/it) harass; impve. 3rd pers. sing.
hostigué I harassed; past 1st pers. sing. / *hostigar*.
hostiguéis that you (all) may harass; pres. subj. 2nd pers. pl. / *hostigar*.
hostiguemos 1. that we may harass; pres. subj. 1st pers. pl. / *hostigar*. 2. let us harass; impve. 1st pers. pl.
hostiguen 1. that they may harass; pres. subj. 3rd pers. pl. / *hostigar*. 2. let them harass; impve. 3rd pers. pl.
hostigues that you may harass; pres. subj. 2nd pers. sing. / *hostigar*.
hostilice 1. that I may harass; pres. subj. 1st pers. sing. / *hostilizar*. 2. that he (she/it) may harass; pres. subj. 3rd pers. sing. 3. let him (her/it) harass; impve. 3rd pers. sing.
hostilicé I harassed; past 1st pers. sing. / *hostilizar*.
hostilicéis that you (all) may harass; pres. subj. 2nd pers. pl. / *hostilizar*.
hostilicemos 1. that we may harass; pres. subj. 1st pers. pl. / *hostilizar*. 2. let us harass; impve. 1st pers. pl.
hostilicen 1. that they may harass; pres. subj. 3rd pers. pl. / *hostilizar*. 2. let them harass; impve. 3rd pers. pl.
hostilices that you may harass; pres. subj. 2nd pers. sing. / *hostilizar*.
hostilizar to harass. irr.
hozar to root up. irr.
hube I had; past 1st pers. sing. / *haber*.

hubiera 1. that I might have; imp. subj. 1st pers. sing. / *haber*. 2. that he (she/it) might have; imp. subj. 3rd pers. sing.
hubierais that you (all) might have; imp. subj. 2nd pers pl. / *haber*.
hubiéramos that we might have; imp. subj. 1st pers. pl. / *haber*.
hubieran that they might have; imp. subj. 3rd pers. pl. / *haber*.
hubieras that you might have; imp. subj. 2nd pers. sing. / *haber*.
hubieron they had; past 3rd pers. pl. / *haber. haber*.
hubiese 1. that I might have; imp. subj. 1st pers. sing. / *haber*. 2. that he (she/it) might have; imp. subj. 3rd pers. sing.
hubieseis that you (all) might have; imp. subj. 2nd pers pl. / *haber*.
hubiésemos that we might have; imp. subj. 1st pers. pl. / *haber*.
hubiesen that they might have; imp. subj. 3rd pers. pl. / *haber*.
hubieses that you might have; imp. subj. 2nd pers. sing. / *haber*.
hubimos we had; past 1st pers. pl. / *haber*.
hubiste you had; past 2nd pers. sing. / *haber*.
hubisteis you (all) had; past 2nd pers. pl. / *haber*.
hubo he (she/it) had; past 3rd pers. sing. / *haber*.
huela 1. that I may smell; pres. subj. 1st pers. sing. / *oler*. 2. that he (she/it) may smell; pres. subj. 3rd pers. sing. 3. let him (her/it) smell; impve. 3rd pers. sing.
huelan 1. that they may smell; pres. subj. 3rd pers. pl. / *oler*. 2. let them smell; impve. 3rd pers. pl.
huelas that you may smell; pres. subj. 2nd pers. sing. / *oler*.
huele 1. he (she/it) smells; pres. ind. 3rd pers. sing. / *oler*. 2. (you) smell; impve. 2nd pers. sing.
huelen they smell; pres. ind. 3rd pers. pl. / *oler*.
hueles you smell; pres. ind. 2nd pers. sing. / *oler*.
huelga 1. he (she/it) rests; pres. ind. 3rd pers. sing. / *holgar*. 2. (you) rest; impve. 2nd pers. sing.
huelgan they rest; pres. ind. 3rd pers. pl. / *holgar*.
huelgas you rest; pres. ind. 2nd pers. sing. / *holgar*.
huélgate (you) be glad; impve. 2nd pers. sing. / *holgarse*.
huelgo I rest; pres. ind. 1st pers. sing. / *holgar*.
huelgue 1. that I may rest; pres. subj. 1st pers. sing. / *holgar*. 2. that he (she/it) may rest; pres. subj. 3rd pers. sing. 3. let him (her/it) rest; impve. 3rd pers. sing.
huelguen 1. that they may rest; pres. subj. 3rd pers. pl. / *holgar*. 2. let them rest; impve. 3rd pers. pl.
huélguense let them be glad; impve. 3rd pers. pl. / *holgarse*.
huelgues that you may rest; pres. subj. 2nd pers. sing. / *holgar*.
huélguese let him (her/it) be glad; impve. 3rd pers. sing. / *holgarse*.
huelo I smell; pres. ind. 1st pers. sing. / *oler*.

huella 1. he (she/it) treads on; pres. ind. 3rd pers. sing. / *hollar*. 2. (you) tread on; impve. 2nd pers. sing.

huellan they tread on; pres. ind. 3rd pers. pl. / *hollar*.

huellas you tread on; pres. ind. 2nd pers. sing. / *hollar*.

huelle 1. that I may tread on; pres. subj. 1st pers. sing. / *hollar*. 2. that he (she/it) may tread on; pres. subj. 3rd pers. sing. 3. let him (her/it) tread on; impve. 3rd pers. sing.

huellen 1. that they may tread on; pres. subj. 3rd pers. pl. / *hollar*. 2. let them tread on; impve. 3rd pers. pl.

huelles that you may tread on; pres. subj. 2nd pers. sing. / *hollar*.

huello I tread on; pres. ind. 1st pers. sing. / *hollar*.

huíos (you all) flee; impve. 2nd pers. pl. / *huirse*.

huir to flee. irr.

huirse to flee. irr.

humanar to humanize. reg.

humanice 1. that I may humanize; pres. subj. 1st pers. sing. / *humanizar*. 2. that he (she/it) may humanize; pres. subj. 3rd pers. sing. 3. let him (her/it) humanize; impve. 3rd pers. sing.

humanicé I humanized; past 1st pers. sing. / *humanizar*.

humanicéis that you (all) may humanize; pres. subj. 2nd pers. pl. / *humanizar*.

humanicémonos let us become more humane; impve. 1st pers. pl. / *humanizarse*.

humanicemos 1. that we may humanize; pres. subj. 1st pers. pl. / *humanizar*. 2. let us humanize; impve. 1st pers. pl.

humanicen 1. that they may humanize; pres. subj. 3rd pers. pl. / *humanizar*. 2. let them humanize; impve. 3rd pers. pl.

humanícense let them become more humane; impve. 3rd pers. pl. / *humanizarse*.

humanices that you may humanize; pres. subj. 2nd pers. sing. / *humanizar*.

humanícese let him (her/it) become more humane; impve. 3rd pers. sing. / *humanizarse*.

humanizándose becoming more humane; pres. part. / *humanizarse*.

humanizaos (you all) become more humane; impve. 2nd pers. pl. / *humanizarse*.

humanizar to humanize. irr.

humanizarse to become more humane or to soften. irr.

humanízate (you) become more humane; impve. 2nd pers. sing. / *humanizarse*.

humear to smoke. reg.

humedecer to moisten. irr.

humedezca 1. that I may moisten; pres. subj. 1st pers. sing. / *humedecer*. 2. that he (she/it) may moisten; pres. subj. 3rd pers. sing. 3. let him (her/it) moisten; impve. 3rd pers. sing.

humedezcáis that you (all) may moisten; pres. subj. 2nd pers. pl. / *humedecer*.

humedezcamos 1. that we may moisten; pres. subj. 1st pers. pl. / *humedecer*. 2. let us moisten; impve. 1st pers. pl.

humedezcan 1. that they may moisten; pres. subj. 3rd pers. pl. / *humedecer*. 2. let them moisten; impve. 3rd pers. pl.

humedezcas that you may moisten; pres. subj. 2nd pers. sing. / *humedecer*.

humedezco I moisten; pres. ind. 1st pers. sing. / *humedecer*.

humidificar to humidify. irr.

humidifique 1. that I may humidify; pres. subj. 1st pers. sing. / *humidificar*. 2. that he (she/it) may humidify; pres. subj. 3rd pers. sing. 3. let him (her/it) humidify; impve. 3rd pers. sing.

humidifiqué I humidified; past 1st pers. sing. / *humidificar*.

humidifiquéis that you (all) may humidify; pres. subj. 2nd pers. pl. / *humidificar*.

humidifiquemos 1. that we may humidify; pres. subj. 1st pers. pl. / *humidificar*. 2. let us humidify; impve. 1st pers. pl.

humidifiquen 1. that they may humidify; pres. subj. 3rd pers. pl. / *humidificar*. 2. let them humidify; impve. 3rd pers. pl.

humidifiques that you may humidify; pres. subj. 2nd pers. sing. / *humidificar*.

humillándose humbling oneself; pres. part. / *humillarse*.

humillaos (you all) humble yourselves; impve. 2nd pers. pl. / *humillarse*.

humillar to humiliate. reg.

humillarse to humble oneself. reg.

humíllate (you) humble yourself; impve. 2nd pers. sing. / *humillarse*.

humillémonos let us humble ourselves; impve. 1st pers. pl. / *humillarse*.

humíllense let them humble themselves; impve. 3rd pers. pl. / *humillarse*.

humíllese let him (her/it) humble himself (herself/itself); impve. 3rd pers. sing. / *humillarse*.

hundámonos let us collapse; impve. 1st pers. pl. / *hundirse*.

húndanse let them collapse; impve. 3rd pers. pl. / *hundirse*.

húndase let him (her/it) collapse; impve. 3rd pers. sing. / *hundirse*.

húndete (you) collapse; impve. 2nd pers. sing. / *hundirse*.

hundiéndose collapsing; pres. part. / *hundirse*.

hundíos (you all) collapse; impve. 2nd pers. pl. / *hundirse*.

hundir to sink. reg.

hundirse to collapse. reg.

hurgar to poke. irr.

hurgonear to stir or to meddle. reg.

hurgue 1. that I may poke; pres. subj. 1st pers. sing. / *hurgar*. 2. that he (she/it) may poke; pres. subj. 3rd pers. sing. 3. let him (her/it) poke; impve. 3rd pers. sing.

hurgué I poked; past 1st pers. sing. / *hurgar*.

hurguéis that you (all) may poke; pres. subj. 2nd pers. pl. / *hurgar.*

hurguemos 1. that we may poke; pres. subj. 1st pers. pl. / *hurgar.* 2. let us poke; impve. 1st pers. pl.

hurguen 1. that they may poke; pres. subj. 3rd pers. pl. / *hurgar.* 2. let them poke; impve. 3rd pers. pl.

hurgues that you may poke; pres. subj. 2nd pers. sing. / *hurgar.*

huronear to pry. reg.

hurtándose withdrawing; pres. part. / *hurtarse.*

hurtaos (you all) withdraw; impve. 2nd pers. pl. / *hurtarse.*

hurtar to steal. reg.

hurtarse to withdraw. reg.

húrtate (you) withdraw; impve. 2nd pers. sing. / *hurtarse.*

hurtémonos let us withdraw; impve. 1st pers. pl. / *hurtarse.*

húrtense let them withdraw; impve. 3rd pers. pl. / *hurtarse.*

húrtese let him (her/it) withdraw; impve. 3rd pers. sing. / *hurtarse.*

husmear to scent. reg.

huya 1. that I may flee; pres. subj. 1st pers. sing. / *huir.* 2. that he (she/it) may flee; pres. subj. 3rd pers. sing. 3. let him (her/it) flee; impve. 3rd pers. sing.

huyáis that you (all) may flee; pres. subj. 2nd pers. pl. / *huir.*

huyámonos let us flee; impve. 1st pers. pl. / *huirse.*

huyamos 1. that we may flee; pres. subj. 1st pers. pl. / *huir.* 2. let us flee; impve. 1st pers. pl.

huyan 1. that they may flee; pres. subj. 3rd pers. pl. / *huir.* 2. let them flee; impve. 3rd pers. pl.

húyanse let them flee; impve. 3rd pers. pl. / *huirse.*

huyas that you may flee; pres. subj. 2nd pers. sing. / *huir.*

húyase let him (her/it) flee; impve. 3rd pers. sing. / *huirse.*

huye 1. he (she/it) flees; pres. ind. 3rd pers. sing. / *huir.* 2. (you) flee; impve. 2nd pers. sing.

huyen they flee; pres. ind. 3rd pers. pl. / *huir.*

huyendo fleeing; pres. part. / *huir.*

huyéndose fleeing; pres. part. / *huirse.*

huyera 1. that I might flee; imp. subj. 1st pers. sing. / *huir.* 2. that he (she/it) might flee; imp. subj. 3rd pers. sing.

huyerais that you (all) might flee; imp. subj. 2nd pers pl. / *huir.*

huyéramos that we might flee; imp. subj. 1st pers. pl. / *huir.*

huyeran that they might flee; imp. subj. 3rd pers. pl. / *huir.*

huyeras that you might flee; imp. subj. 2nd pers. sing. / *huir.*

huyeron they fled; past 3rd pers. pl. / *huir.*

huyes you flee; pres. ind. 2nd pers. sing. / *huir.*

huyese 1. that I might flee; imp. subj. 1st pers. sing. / *huir.* 2. that he (she/it) might flee; imp. subj. 3rd pers. sing.

huyeseis that you (all) might flee; imp. subj. 2nd pers pl. / *huir.*

huyésemos that we might flee; imp. subj. 1st pers. pl. / *huir.*

huyesen that they might flee; imp. subj. 3rd pers. pl. / *huir.*

huyeses that you might flee; imp. subj. 2nd pers. sing. / *huir.*

húyete (you) flee; impve. 2nd pers. sing. / *huirse.*

huyo I flee; pres. ind. 1st pers. sing. / *huir.*

huyó he (she/it) fled; past 3rd pers. sing. / *huir.*

I

iba 1. I was going; imp. ind. 1st pers. sing. / *ir.* 2. he (she/it) was going; imp. ind. 3rd pers. sing.

ibais you (all) were going; imp. ind. 2nd pers. pl. / *ir.*

ibamos we were going; imp. ind. 1st pers. pl. / *ir.*

iban they were going; imp. ind. 3rd pers. pl. / *ir.*

ibas you were going; imp. ind. 2nd pers. sing. / *ir.*

ice 1. that I may hoist; pres. subj. 1st pers. sing. / *izar.* 2. that he (she/it) may hoist; pres. subj. 3rd pers. sing. 3. let him (her/it) hoist; impve. 3rd pers. sing.

icé I hoisted; past 1st pers. sing. / *izar.*

icéis that you (all) may hoist; pres. subj. 2nd pers. pl. / *izar.*

icemos 1. that we may hoist; pres. subj. 1st pers. pl. / *izar.* 2. let us hoist; impve. 1st pers. pl.

icen 1. that they may hoist; pres. subj. 3rd pers. pl. / *izar.* 2. let them hoist; impve. 3rd pers. pl.

ices that you may hoist; pres. subj. 2nd pers. sing. / *izar.*

id (you all) go; impve. 2nd pers. pl. / *ir.*

idealice 1. that I may idealize; pres. subj. 1st pers. sing. / *idealizar.* 2. that he (she/it) may idealize; pres. subj. 3rd pers. sing. 3. let him (her/it) idealize; impve. 3rd pers. sing.

idealicé I idealized; past 1st pers. sing. / *idealizar.*

idealicéis that you (all) may idealize; pres. subj. 2nd pers. pl. / *idealizar.*

idealicemos 1. that we may idealize; pres. subj. 1st pers. pl. / *idealizar.* 2. let us idealize; impve. 1st pers. pl.

idealicen 1. that they may idealize; pres. subj. 3rd pers. pl. / *idealizar.* 2. let them idealize; impve. 3rd pers. pl.

idealices that you may idealize; pres. subj. 2nd pers. sing. / *idealizar.*

idealizar to idealize. irr.

idear to plan. reg.

identificándose identifying oneself; pres. part. / *identificarse.*

identificaos (you all) identify yourselves; impve. 2nd pers. pl. / *identificarse.*

identificar to identify. irr.

identificarse to identify oneself. irr.

identifícate (you) identify yourself; impve. 2nd pers. sing. / *identificarse.*

identifique 1. that I may identify; pres. subj. 1st pers. sing. / *identificar*. 2. that he (she/it) may identify; pres. subj. 3rd pers. sing. 3. let him (her/it) identify; impve. 3rd pers. sing.

identifiqué I identified; past 1st pers. sing. / *identificar*.

identifiquéis that you (all) may identify; pres. subj. 2nd pers. pl. / *identificar*.

identifiquémonos let us identify ourselves; impve. 1st pers. pl. / *identificarse*.

identifiquemos 1. that we may identify; pres. subj. 1st pers. pl. / *identificar*. 2. let us identify; impve. 1st pers. pl.

identifiquen 1. that they may identify; pres. subj. 3rd pers. pl. / *identificar*. 2. let them identify; impve. 3rd pers. pl.

identifíquense let them identify themselves; impve. 3rd pers. pl. / *identificarse*.

identifiques that you may identify; pres. subj. 2nd pers. sing. / *identificar*.

identifíquese let him (her/it) identify himself (herself/itself); impve. 3rd pers. sing. / *identificarse*.

idiotice 1. that I may stupefy; pres. subj. 1st pers. sing. / *idiotizar*. 2. that he (she/it) may stupefy; pres. subj. 3rd pers. sing. 3. let him (her/it) stupefy; impve. 3rd pers. sing.

idioticé I stupefied; past 1st pers. sing. / *idiotizar*.

idioticéis that you (all) may stupefy; pres. subj. 2nd pers. pl. / *idiotizar*.

idioticemos 1. that we may stupefy; pres. subj. 1st pers. pl. / *idiotizar*. 2. let us stupefy; impve. 1st pers. pl.

idioticen 1. that they may stupefy; pres. subj. 3rd pers. pl. / *idiotizar*. 2. let them stupefy; impve. 3rd pers. pl.

idiotices that you may stupefy; pres. subj. 2nd pers. sing. / *idiotizar*.

idiotizar to stupefy. irr.

ido went; past part. / *ir*.

idolatrar to idolize. reg.

idos (you all) go away; impve. 2nd pers. pl. / *irse*.

ignifugar to flame-proof. irr.

ignifugue 1. that I may flame-proof; pres. subj. 1st pers. sing. / *ignifugar*. 2. that he (she/it) may flame-proof; pres. subj. 3rd pers. sing. 3. let him (her/it) flame-proof; impve. 3rd pers. sing.

ignifugué I flame-proofed; past 1st pers. sing. / *ignifugar*.

ignifuguéis that you (all) may flame-proof; pres. subj. 2nd pers. pl. / *ignifugar*.

ignifuguemos 1. that we may flame-proof; pres. subj. 1st pers. pl. / *ignifugar*. 2. let us flame-proof; impve. 1st pers. pl.

ignifuguen 1. that they may flame-proof; pres. subj. 3rd pers. pl. / *ignifugar*. 2. let them flame-proof; impve. 3rd pers. pl.

ignifugues that you may flame-proof; pres. subj. 2nd pers. sing. / *ignifugar*.

ignorar to be ignorant of. reg.

igualándose being equal; pres. part. / *igualarse*.

igualaos (you all) be equal; impve. 2nd pers. pl. / *igualarse*.

igualar to make equal. reg.

igualarse to be equal. reg.

iguálate (you) be equal; impve. 2nd pers. sing. / *igualarse*.

igualémonos let us be equal; impve. 1st pers. pl. / *igualarse*.

iguálense let them be equal; impve. 3rd pers. pl. / *igualarse*.

iguálese let him (her/it) be equal; impve. 3rd pers. sing. / *igualarse*.

ijadear to pant. reg.

iludir to delude or to mislead. reg.

iluminar to illuminate. reg.

ilusionándose becoming hopeful; pres. part. / *ilusionarse*.

ilusionaos (you all) become hopeful; impve. 2nd pers. pl. / *ilusionarse*.

ilusionar to give illusions to. reg.

ilusionarse to become hopeful. reg.

ilusiónate (you) become hopeful; impve. 2nd pers. sing. / *ilusionarse*.

ilusionémonos let us become hopeful; impve. 1st pers. pl. / *ilusionarse*.

ilusiónense let them become hopeful; impve. 3rd pers. pl. / *ilusionarse*.

ilusiónese let him (her/it) become hopeful; impve. 3rd pers. sing. / *ilusionarse*.

ilustrar to illustrate. reg.

imaginar to imagine. reg.

imanar to magnetize. reg.

imantar to magnetize. reg.

imbuir to imbue. irr.

imbuya 1. that I may imbue; pres. subj. 1st pers. sing. / *imbuir*. 2. that he (she/it) may imbue; pres. subj. 3rd pers. sing. 3. let him (her/it) imbue; impve. 3rd pers. sing.

imbuyáis that you (all) may imbue; pres. subj. 2nd pers. pl. / *imbuir*.

imbuyamos 1. that we may imbue; pres. subj. 1st pers. pl. / *imbuir*. 2. let us imbue; impve. 1st pers. pl.

imbuyan 1. that they may imbue; pres. subj. 3rd pers. pl. / *imbuir*. 2. let them imbue; impve. 3rd pers. pl.

imbuyas that you may imbue; pres. subj. 2nd pers. sing. / *imbuir*.

imbuye 1. he (she/it) imbues; pres. ind. 3rd pers. sing. / *imbuir*. 2. (you) imbue; impve. 2nd pers. sing.

imbuyen they imbue; pres. ind. 3rd pers. pl. / *imbuir*.

imbuyendo imbuing; pres. part. / *imbuir*.

imbuyera 1. that I might imbue; imp. subj. 1st pers. sing. / *imbuir*. 2. that he (she/it) might imbue; imp. subj. 3rd pers. sing.

imbuyerais that you (all) might imbue; imp. subj. 2nd pers pl. / *imbuir*.

imbuyéramos that we might imbue; imp. subj. 1st pers. pl. / *imbuir*.

imbuyeran that they might imbue; imp. subj. 3rd pers. pl. / *imbuir*.

imbuyeras that you might imbue; imp. subj. 2nd pers. sing. / *imbuir.*

imbuyeron they imbued; past 3rd pers. pl. / *imbuir.*

imbuyes you imbue; pres. ind. 2nd pers. sing. / *imbuir.*

imbuyese 1. that I might imbue; imp. subj. 1st pers. sing. / *imbuir.* 2. that he (she/it) might imbue; imp. subj. 3rd pers. sing.

imbuyeseis that you (all) might imbue; imp. subj. 2nd pers pl. / *imbuir.*

imbuyésemos that we might imbue; imp. subj. 1st pers. pl. / *imbuir.*

imbuyesen that they might imbue; imp. subj. 3rd pers. pl. / *imbuir.*

imbuyeses that you might imbue; imp. subj. 2nd pers. sing. / *imbuir.*

imbuyo I imbue; pres. ind. 1st pers. sing. / *imbuir.*

imbuyó he (she/it) imbued; past 3rd pers. sing. / *imbuir.*

imitar to imitate. reg.

impacientándose losing patience; pres. part. / *impacientarse.*

impacientaos (you all) lose patience; impve. 2nd pers. pl. / *impacientarse.*

impacientar to make impatient. reg.

impacientarse to lose patience. reg.

impaciéntate (you) lose patience; impve. 2nd pers. sing. / *impacientarse.*

impacientémonos let us lose patience; impve. 1st pers. pl. / *impacientarse.*

impaciéntense let them lose patience; impve. 3rd pers. pl. / *impacientarse.*

impaciéntese let him (her/it) lose patience; impve. 3rd pers. sing. / *impacientarse.*

impartir to impart. reg.

impedir to impede or to prevent. irr.

impeler to impel or to propel. reg.

imperar to rule. reg.

impermeabilice 1. that I may waterproof; pres. subj. 1st pers. sing. / *impermeabilizar.* 2. that he (she/it) may waterproof; pres. subj. 3rd pers. sing. 3. let him (her/it) waterproof; impve. 3rd pers. sing.

impermeabilicé I waterproofed; past 1st pers. sing. / *impermeabilizar.*

impermeabilicéis that you (all) may waterproof; pres. subj. 2nd pers. pl. / *impermeabilizar.*

impermeabilicemos 1. that we may waterproof; pres. subj. 1st pers. pl. / *impermeabilizar.* 2. let us waterproof; impve. 1st pers. pl.

impermeabilicen 1. that they may waterproof; pres. subj. 3rd pers. pl. / *impermeabilizar.* 2. let them waterproof; impve. 3rd pers. pl.

impermeabilices that you may waterproof; pres. subj. 2nd pers. sing. / *impermeabilizar.*

impermeabilizar to waterproof. irr.

impetrar to entreat. reg.

impida 1. that I may impede; pres. subj. 1st pers. sing. / *impedir.* 2. that he (she/it) may impede; pres. subj. 3rd pers. sing. 3. let him (her/it) impede; impve. 3rd pers. sing.

impidáis that you (all) may impede; pres. subj. 2nd pers. pl. / *impedir.*

impidamos 1. that we may impede; pres. subj. 1st pers. pl. / *impedir.* 2. let us impede; impve. 1st pers. pl.

impidan 1. that they may impede; pres. subj. 3rd pers. pl. / *impedir.* 2. let them impede; impve. 3rd pers. pl.

impidas that you may impede; pres. subj. 2nd pers. sing. / *impedir.*

impide 1. he (she/it) impedes; pres. ind. 3rd pers. sing. / *impedir.* 2. (you) impede; impve. 2nd pers. sing.

impiden they impede; pres. ind. 3rd pers. pl. / *impedir.*

impides you impede; pres. ind. 2nd pers. sing. / *impedir.*

impidiendo impeding; pres. part. / *impedir.*

impidiera 1. that I might impede; imp. subj. 1st pers. sing. / *impedir.* 2. that he (she/it) might impede; imp. subj. 3rd pers. sing.

impidierais that you (all) might impede; imp. subj. 2nd pers pl. / *impedir.*

impidiéramos that we might impede; imp. subj. 1st pers. pl. / *impedir.*

impidieran that they might impede; imp. subj. 3rd pers. pl. / *impedir.*

impidieras that you might impede; imp. subj. 2nd pers. sing. / *impedir.*

impidieron they impeded; past 3rd pers. pl. / *impedir.*

impidiese 1. that I might impede; imp. subj. 1st pers. sing. / *impedir.* 2. that he (she/it) might impede; imp. subj. 3rd pers. sing.

impidieseis that you (all) might impede; imp. subj. 2nd pers pl. / *impedir.*

impidiésemos that we might impede; imp. subj. 1st pers. pl. / *impedir.*

impidiesen that they might impede; imp. subj. 3rd pers. pl. / *impedir.*

impidieses that you might impede; imp. subj. 2nd pers. sing. / *impedir.*

impidió he (she/it) impeded; past 3rd pers. sing. / *impedir.*

impido I impede; pres. ind. 1st pers. sing. / *impedir.*

implantar to implant. reg.

implicar to imply or to implicate. irr.

implique 1. that I may imply; pres. subj. 1st pers. sing. / *implicar.* 2. that he (she/it) may imply; pres. subj. 3rd pers. sing. 3. let him (her/it) imply; impve. 3rd pers. sing.

impliqué I implied; past 1st pers. sing. / *implicar.*

impliquéis that you (all) may imply; pres. subj. 2nd pers. pl. / *implicar.*

impliquemos 1. that we may imply; pres. subj. 1st pers. pl. / *implicar.* 2. let us imply; impve. 1st pers. pl.

impliquen 1. that they may imply; pres. subj. 3rd pers. pl. / *implicar.* 2. let them imply; impve. 3rd pers. pl.

impliques that you may imply; pres. subj. 2nd pers. sing. / *implicar.*
implorar to implore. reg.
impon (you) impose; impve. 2nd pers. sing. / *imponer.*
impondrá he (she/it) will impose; fut. 3rd pers. sing. / *imponer.*
impondrán they will impose; fut. 3rd pers. pl. / *imponer.*
impondrás you will impose; fut. 2nd pers. sing. / *imponer.*
impondré I shall impose; fut. 1st pers. sing. / *imponer.*
impondréis you (all) will impose; fut. 2nd pers. pl. / *imponer.*
impondremos we shall impose; fut. 1st pers. pl. / *imponer.*
impondría 1. I should impose; cond. 1st pers. sing. / *imponer.* 2. he (she/it) would impose; cond. 3rd pers. sing.
impondríais you (all) would impose; cond. 2nd pers. pl. / *imponer.*
impondríamos we should impose; cond. 1st pers. pl. / *imponer.*
impondrían they would impose; cond. 3rd pers. pl. / *imponer.*
impondrías you would impose; cond. 2nd pers. sing. / *imponer.*
imponeos (you all) dominate; impve. 2nd pers. pl. / *imponerse.*
imponer to impose. irr.
imponerse to dominate. irr.
imponga 1. that I may impose; pres. subj. 1st pers. sing. / *imponer.* 2. that he (she/it) may impose; pres. subj. 3rd pers. sing. 3. let him (her/it) impose; impve. 3rd pers. sing.
impongáis that you (all) may impose; pres. subj. 2nd pers. pl. / *imponer.*
impongámonos let us dominate; impve. 1st pers. pl. / *imponerse.*
impongamos 1. that we may impose; pres. subj. 1st pers. pl. / *imponer.* 2. let us impose; impve. 1st pers. pl.
impongan 1. that they may impose; pres. subj. 3rd pers. pl. / *imponer.* 2. let them impose; impve. 3rd pers. pl.
impónganse let them dominate; impve. 3rd pers. pl. / *imponerse.*
impongas that you may impose; pres. subj. 2nd pers. sing. / *imponer.*
impóngase let him (her/it) dominate; impve. 3rd pers. sing. / *imponerse.*
impongo I impose; pres. ind. 1st pers. sing. / *imponer.*
imponiendo imposing; pres. part. / *imponer.*
imponiéndose dominating; pres. part. / *imponerse.*
imponte (you) dominate; impve. 2nd pers. sing. / *imponerse.*
importar to import or to matter. reg.
importunar to importune or to nag. reg.

imposibilitándose becoming unable; pres. part. / *imposibilitarse.*
imposibilitaos (you all) become unable; impve. 2nd pers. pl. / *imposibilitarse.*
imposibilitar to make impossible. reg.
imposibilitarse to become unable. reg.
imposibilítate (you) become unable; impve. 2nd pers. sing. / *imposibilitarse.*
imposibilitémonos let us become unable; impve. 1st pers. pl. / *imposibilitarse.*
imposibilítense let them become unable; impve. 3rd pers. pl. / *imposibilitarse.*
imposibilítese let him (her/it) become unable; impve. 3rd pers. sing. / *imposibilitarse.*
imprecar to imprecate or to curse. irr.
impregnándose becoming impregnated; pres. part. / *impregnarse.*
impregnaos (you all) become impregnated; impve. 2nd pers. pl. / *impregnarse.*
impregnar to impregnate. reg.
impregnarse to become impregnated. reg.
imprégnate (you) become impregnated; impve. 2nd pers. sing. / *impregnarse.*
impregnémonos let us become impregnated; impve. 1st pers. pl. / *impregnarse.*
imprégnense let them become impregnated; impve. 3rd pers. pl. / *impregnarse.*
imprégnese let him (her/it) become impregnated; impve. 3rd pers. sing. / *impregnarse.*
impreque 1. that I may imprecate; pres. subj. 1st pers. sing. / *imprecar.* 2. that he (she/it) may imprecate; pres. subj. 3rd pers. sing. 3. let him (her/it) imprecate; impve. 3rd pers. sing.
imprequé I imprecated; past 1st pers. sing. / *imprecar.*
imprequéis that you (all) may imprecate; pres. subj. 2nd pers. pl. / *imprecar.*
imprequemos 1. that we may imprecate; pres. subj. 1st pers. pl. / *imprecar.* 2. let us imprecate; impve. 1st pers. pl.
imprequen 1. that they may imprecate; pres. subj. 3rd pers. pl. / *imprecar.* 2. let them imprecate; impve. 3rd pers. pl.
impreques that you may imprecate; pres. subj. 2nd pers. sing. / *imprecar.*
impresionándose being stirred; pres. part. / *impresionarse.*
impresionaos (you all) be stirred; impve. 2nd pers. pl. / *impresionarse.*
impresionar to impress. reg.
impresionarse to be stirred. reg.
impresiónate (you) be stirred; impve. 2nd pers. sing. / *impresionarse.*
impresionémonos let us be stirred; impve. 1st pers. pl. / *impresionarse.*
impresiónense let them be stirred; impve. 3rd pers. pl. / *impresionarse.*
impresiónese let him (her/it) be stirred; impve. 3rd pers. sing. / *impresionarse.*
impreso printed; past part. / *imprimir.*

imprimir to print or to impress. reg.
improbar to disapprove. reg.
improvisar to improvise. reg.
impuesto imposed; past part. / *imponer.*
impugnar to impugn or to oppose. reg.
impulsar to impel. reg.
impuse I imposed; past 1st pers. sing. / *imponer.*
impusiera 1. that I might impose; imp. subj. 1st pers. sing. / *imponer.* 2. that he (she/it) might impose; imp. subj. 3rd pers. sing.
impusierais that you (all) might impose; imp. subj. 2nd pers pl. / *imponer.*
impusiéramos that we might impose; imp. subj. 1st pers. pl. / *imponer.*
impusieran that they might impose; imp. subj. 3rd pers. pl. / *imponer.*
impusieras that you might impose; imp. subj. 2nd pers. sing. / *imponer.*
impusieron they imposed; past 3rd pers. pl. / *imponer.*
impusiese 1. that I might impose; imp. subj. 1st pers. sing. / *imponer.* 2. that he (she/it) might impose; imp. subj. 3rd pers. sing.
impusieseis that you (all) might impose; imp. subj. 2nd pers pl. / *imponer.*
impusiésemos that we might impose; imp. subj. 1st pers. pl. / *imponer.*
impusiesen that they might impose; imp. subj. 3rd pers. pl. / *imponer.*
impusieses that you might impose; imp. subj. 2nd pers. sing. / *imponer.*
impusimos we imposed; past 1st pers. pl. / *imponer.*
impusiste you imposed; past 2nd pers. sing. / *imponer.*
impusisteis you (all) imposed; past 2nd pers. pl. / *imponer.*
impuso he (she/it) imposed; past 3rd pers. sing. / *imponer.*
imputar to impute. reg.
inaugurar to inaugurate. reg.
incapacitar to incapacitate. reg.
incautándose seizing; pres. part. / *incautarse.*
incautaos (you all) seize; impve. 2nd pers. pl. / *incautarse.*
incautarse to seize. reg.
incaútate (you) seize; impve. 2nd pers. sing. / *incautarse.*
incautémonos let us seize; impve. 1st pers. pl. / *incautarse.*
incaútense let them seize; impve. 3rd pers. pl. / *incautarse.*
incaútese let him (her/it) seize; impve. 3rd pers. sing. / *incautarse.*
incendiándose catching fire; pres. part. / *incendiarse.*
incendiaos (you all) catch fire; impve. 2nd pers. pl. / *incendiarse.*
incendiar to set on fire. reg.
incendiarse to catch fire. reg.
incendíate (you) catch fire; impve. 2nd pers. sing. / *incendiarse.*

incendiémonos let us catch fire; impve. 1st pers. pl. / *incendiarse.*
incendíense let them catch fire; impve. 3rd pers. pl. / *incendiarse.*
incendíese let him (her/it) catch fire; impve. 3rd pers. sing. / *incendiarse.*
incensar to flatter or to incense. irr.
incidir to fall into or to make an incision. reg.
inciensa 1. he (she/it) flatters; pres. ind. 3rd pers. sing. / *incensar.* 2. (you) flatter; impve. 2nd pers. sing.
inciensan they flatter; pres. ind. 3rd pers. pl. / *incensar.*
inciensas you flatter; pres. ind. 2nd pers. sing. / *incensar.*
inciense 1. that I may flatter; pres. subj. 1st pers. sing. / *incensar.* 2. that he (she/it) may flatter; pres. subj. 3rd pers. sing. 3. let him (her/it) flatter; impve. 3rd pers. sing.
inciensen 1. that they may flatter; pres. subj. 3rd pers. pl. / *incensar.* 2. let them flatter; impve. 3rd pers. pl.
incienses that you may flatter; pres. subj. 2nd pers. sing. / *incensar.*
incienso I flatter; pres. ind. 1st pers. sing. / *incensar.*
incinerar to incinerate. reg.
incitar to incite. reg.
inclinándose bowing; pres. part. / *inclinarse*
inclinaos (you all) bow; impve. 2nd pers. pl. / *inclinarse.*
inclinar to incline. reg.
inclinarse to bow. reg.
inclínate (you) bow; impve. 2nd pers. sing. / *inclinarse.*
inclinémonos let us bow; impve. 1st pers. pl. / *inclinarse.*
inclínense let them bow; impve. 3rd pers. pl. / *inclinarse.*
inclínese let him (her/it) bow; impve. 3rd pers. sing. / *inclinarse.*
incluir to include. irr.
incluya 1. that I may include; pres. subj. 1st pers. sing. / *incluir.* 2. that he (she/it) may include; pres. subj. 3rd pers. sing. 3. let him (her/it) include; impve. 3rd pers. sing.
incluyáis that you (all) may include; pres. subj. 2nd pers. pl. / *incluir.*
incluyamos 1. that we may include; pres. subj. 1st pers. pl. / *incluir.* 2. let us include; impve. 1st pers. pl.
incluyan 1. that they may include; pres. subj. 3rd pers. pl. / *incluir.* 2. let them include; impve. 3rd pers. pl.
incluyas that you may include; pres. subj. 2nd pers. sing. / *incluir.*
incluye 1. he (she/it) includes; pres. ind. 3rd pers. sing. / *incluir.* 2. (you) include; impve. 2nd pers. sing.
incluyen they include; pres. ind. 3rd pers. pl. / *incluir.*
incluyendo including; pres. part. / *incluir.*

incluyera 1. that I might include; imp. subj. 1st pers. sing. / *incluir*. 2. that he (she/it) might include; imp. subj. 3rd pers. sing.

incluyerais that you (all) might include; imp. subj. 2nd pers pl. / *incluir*.

incluyéramos that we might include; imp. subj. 1st pers. pl. / *incluir*.

incluyeran that they might include; imp. subj. 3rd pers. pl. / *incluir*.

incluyeras that you might include; imp. subj. 2nd pers. sing. / *incluir*.

incluyeron they included; past 3rd pers. pl. / *incluir*.

incluyes you include; pres. ind. 2nd pers. sing. / *incluir*.

incluyese 1. that I might include; imp. subj. 1st pers. sing. / *incluir*. 2. that he (she/it) might include; imp. subj. 3rd pers. sing.

incluyeseis that you (all) might include; imp. subj. 2nd pers pl. / *incluir*.

incluyésemos that we might include; imp. subj. 1st pers. pl. / *incluir*.

incluyesen that they might include; imp. subj. 3rd pers. pl. / *incluir*.

incluyeses that you might include; imp. subj. 2nd pers. sing. / *incluir*.

incluyo I include; pres. ind. 1st pers. sing. / *incluir*.

incluyó he (she/it) included; past 3rd pers. sing. / *incluir*.

incomodándose getting angry; pres. part. / *incomodarse*.

incomodaos (you all) get angry; impve. 2nd pers. pl. / *incomodarse*.

incomodar to inconvenience. reg.

incomodarse to get angry. reg.

incomódate (you) get angry; impve. 2nd pers. sing. / *incomodarse*.

incomodémonos let us get angry; impve. 1st pers. pl. / *incomodarse*.

incomódense let them get angry; impve. 3rd pers. pl. / *incomodarse*.

incomódese let him (her/it) get angry; impve. 3rd pers. sing. / *incomodarse*.

incomunicar to isolate. irr.

incomunique 1. that I may isolate; pres. subj. 1st pers. sing. / *incomunicar*. 2. that he (she/it) may isolate; pres. subj. 3rd pers. sing. 3. let him (her/it) isolate; impve. 3rd pers. sing.

incomuniqué I isolated; past 1st pers. sing. / *incomunicar*.

incomuniquéis that you (all) may isolate; pres. subj. 2nd pers. pl. / *incomunicar*.

incomuniquemos 1. that we may isolate; pres. subj. 1st pers. pl. / *incomunicar*. 2. let us isolate; impve. 1st pers. pl.

incomuniquen 1. that they may isolate; pres. subj. 3rd pers. pl. / *incomunicar*. 2. let them isolate; impve. 3rd pers. pl.

incomuniques that you may isolate; pres. subj. 2nd pers. sing. / *incomunicar*.

incorporándose joining; pres. part. / *incorporarse*.

incorporaos (you all) join; impve. 2nd pers. pl. / *incorporarse*.

incorporar to incorporate. reg.

incorporarse to join or to sit up. reg.

incorpórate (you) join; impve. 2nd pers. sing. / *incorporarse*.

incorporémonos let us join; impve. 1st pers. pl. / *incorporarse*.

incorpórense let them join; impve. 3rd pers. pl. / *incorporarse*.

incorpórese let him (her/it) join; impve. 3rd pers. sing. / *incorporarse*.

incrementar to increase. reg.

increpar to scold. reg.

incriminar to incriminate. reg.

incrustar to encrust or to inlay. reg.

incubar to incubate or to hatch. reg.

inculcándose being stubborn; pres. part. / *inculcarse*.

inculcaos (you all) be stubborn; impve. 2nd pers. pl. / *inculcarse*.

inculcar to inculcate. irr.

inculcarse to be stubborn. irr.

incúlcate (you) be stubborn; impve. 2nd pers. sing. / *inculcarse*.

inculpar to accuse. reg.

inculque 1. that I may inculcate; pres. subj. 1st pers. sing. / *inculcar*. 2. that he (she/it) may inculcate; pres. subj. 3rd pers. sing. 3. let him (her/it) inculcate; impve. 3rd pers. sing.

inculqué I inculcated; past 1st pers. sing. / *inculcar*.

inculquéis that you (all) may inculcate; pres. subj. 2nd pers. pl. / *inculcar*.

inculquémonos let us be stubborn; impve. 1st pers. pl. / *inculcarse*.

inculquemos 1. that we may inculcate; pres. subj. 1st pers. pl. / *inculcar*. 2. let us inculcate; impve. 1st pers. pl.

inculquen 1. that they may inculcate; pres. subj. 3rd pers. pl. / *inculcar*. 2. let them inculcate; impve. 3rd pers. pl.

incúlquense let them be stubborn; impve. 3rd pers. pl. / *inculcarse*.

inculques that you may inculcate; pres. subj. 2nd pers. sing. / *inculcar*.

incúlquese let him (her/it) be stubborn; impve. 3rd pers. sing. / *inculcarse*.

incumbir to be incumbent or to pertain. reg.

incurrir to incur or to fall into. reg.

indagar to investigate. irr.

indague 1. that I may investigate; pres. subj. 1st pers. sing. / *indagar*. 2. that he (she/it) may investigate; pres. subj. 3rd pers. sing. 3. let him (her/it) investigate; impve. 3rd pers. sing.

indagué I investigated; past 1st pers. sing. / *indagar*.

indaguéis that you (all) may investigate; pres. subj. 2nd pers. pl. / *indagar*.

indaguemos 1. that we may investigate; pres. subj. 1st pers. pl. / *indagar*. 2. let us investigate; impve. 1st pers. pl.

indaguen 1. that they may investigate; pres. subj. 3rd pers. pl. / *indagar*. 2. let them investigate; impve. 3rd pers. pl.

indagues that you may investigate; pres. subj. 2nd pers. sing. / *indagar*.

indemnice 1. that I may indemnify; pres. subj. 1st pers. sing. / *indemnizar*. 2. that he (she/it) may indemnify; pres. subj. 3rd pers. sing. 3. let him (her/it) indemnify; impve. 3rd pers. sing.

indemnicé I indemnified; past 1st pers. sing. / *indemnizar*.

indemnicéis that you (all) may indemnify; pres. subj. 2nd pers. pl. / *indemnizar*.

indemnicemos 1. that we may indemnify; pres. subj. 1st pers. pl. / *indemnizar*. 2. let us indemnify; impve. 1st pers. pl.

indemnicen 1. that they may indemnify; pres. subj. 3rd pers. pl. / *indemnizar*. 2. let them indemnify; impve. 3rd pers. pl.

indemnices that you may indemnify; pres. subj. 2nd pers. sing. / *indemnizar*.

indemnizar to indemnify. irr.

independice 1. that I may grant independence to; pres. subj. 1st pers. sing. / *independizar*. 2. that he (she/it) may grant independence to; pres. subj. 3rd pers. sing. 3. let him (her/it) grant independence to; impve. 3rd pers. sing.

independicé I granted independence to; past 1st pers. sing. / *independizar*.

independicéis that you (all) may grant independence to; pres. subj. 2nd pers. pl. / *independizar*

independicémonos let us become independent; impve. 1st pers. pl. / *independizarse*.

independicemos 1. that we may grant independence to; pres. subj. 1st pers. pl. / *independizar*. 2. let us grant independence to; impve. 1st pers. pl.

independicen 1. that they may grant independence to; pres. subj. 3rd pers. pl. / *independizar*. 2. let them grant independence to; impve. 3rd pers. pl.

independícense let them become independent; impve. 3rd pers. pl. / *independizarse*.

independices that you may grant independence to; pres. subj. 2nd pers. sing. / *independizar*.

independícese let him (her/it) become independent; impve. 3rd pers. sing. / *independizarse*.

independizándose becoming independent; pres. part. / *independizarse*.

independizaos (you all) become independent; impve. 2nd pers. pl. / *independizarse*.

independizar to grant independence to. irr.

independizarse to become independent. irr.

independízate (you) become independent; impve. 2nd pers. sing. / *independizarse*.

indicar to indicate. irr.

indigestándose causing indigestion; pres. part. / *indigestarse*.

indigestaos (you all) cause indigestion; impve. 2nd pers. pl. / *indigestarse*.

indigestarse to cause indigestion. reg.

indigéstate (you) cause indigestion; impve. 2nd pers. sing. / *indigestarse*.

indigestémonos let us cause indigestion; impve. 1st pers. pl. / *indigestarse*.

indigéstense let them cause indigestion; impve. 3rd pers. pl. / *indigestarse*.

indigéstese let him (her/it) cause indigestion; impve. 3rd pers. sing. / *indigestarse*.

indignándose becoming indignant; pres. part. / *indignarse*.

indignaos (you all) become indignant; impve. 2nd pers. pl. / *indignarse*.

indignar to anger. reg.

indignarse to become indignant. reg.

indígnate (you) become indignant; impve. 2nd pers. sing. / *indignarse*.

indignémonos let us become indignant; impve. 1st pers. pl. / *indignarse*.

indígnense let them become indignant; impve. 3rd pers. pl. / *indignarse*.

indígnese let him (her/it) become indignant; impve. 3rd pers. sing. / *indignarse*.

indique 1. that I may indicate; pres. subj. 1st pers. sing. / *indicar*. 2. that he (she/it) may indicate; pres. subj. 3rd pers. sing. 3. let him (her/it) indicate; impve. 3rd pers. sing.

indiqué I indicated; past 1st pers. sing. / *indicar*.

indiquéis that you (all) may indicate; pres. subj. 2nd pers. pl. / *indicar*.

indiquemos 1. that we may indicate; pres. subj. 1st pers. pl. / *indicar*. 2. let us indicate; impve. 1st pers. pl.

indiquen 1. that they may indicate; pres. subj. 3rd pers. pl. / *indicar*. 2. let them indicate; impve. 3rd pers. pl.

indiques that you may indicate; pres. subj. 2nd pers. sing. / *indicar*.

indisciplinándose rebeling; pres. part. / *indisciplinarse*.

indisciplinaos (you all) rebel; impve. 2nd pers. pl. / *indisciplinarse*.

indisciplinarse to rebel. reg.

indisciplínate (you) rebel; impve. 2nd pers. sing. / *indisciplinarse*.

indisciplinémonos let us rebel; impve. 1st pers. pl. / *indisciplinarse*.

indisciplínense let them rebel; impve. 3rd pers. pl. / *indisciplinarse*.

indisciplínese let him (her/it) rebel; impve. 3rd pers. sing. / *indisciplinarse*.

indispon (you) indispose; impve. 2nd pers. sing. / *indisponer*.

indispondrá he (she/it) will indispose; fut. 3rd pers. sing. / *indisponer*.

indispondrán they will indispose; fut. 3rd pers. pl. / *indisponer*.

indispondrás you will indispose; fut. 2nd pers. sing. / *indisponer*.

indispondré I shall indispose; fut. 1st pers. sing. / *indisponer*.

indispondréis you (all) will indispose; fut. 2nd pers. pl. / *indisponer*.

indispondremos we shall indispose; fut. 1st pers. pl. / *indisponer.*

indispondría 1. I should indispose; cond. 1st pers. sing. / *indisponer.* 2. he (she/it) would indispose; cond. 3rd pers. sing.

indispondríais you (all) would indispose; cond. 2nd pers. pl. / *indisponer.*

indispondríamos we should indispose; cond. 1st pers. pl. / *indisponer.*

indispondrían they would indispose; cond. 3rd pers. pl. / *indisponer.*

indispondrías you would indispose; cond. 2nd pers. sing. / *indisponer.*

indisponeos (you all) become ill; impve. 2nd pers. pl. / *indisponerse.*

indisponer to indispose. irr.

indisponerse to become ill. irr.

indisponga 1. that I may indispose; pres. subj. 1st pers. sing. / *indisponer.* 2. that he (she/it) may indispose; pres. subj. 3rd pers. sing. 3. let him (her/it) indispose; impve. 3rd pers. sing.

indispongáis that you (all) may indispose; pres. subj. 2nd pers. pl. / *indisponer.*

indispongámonos let us become ill; impve. 1st pers. pl. / *indisponerse.*

indispongamos 1. that we may indispose; pres. subj. 1st pers. pl. / *indisponer.* 2. let us indispose; impve. 1st pers. pl.

indispongan 1. that they may indispose; pres. subj. 3rd pers. pl. / *indisponer.* 2. let them indispose; impve. 3rd pers. pl.

indispónganse let them become ill; impve. 3rd pers. pl. / *indisponerse.*

indispongas that you may indispose; pres. subj. 2nd pers. sing. / *indisponer.*

indispóngase let him (her/it) become ill; impve. 3rd pers. sing. / *indisponerse.*

indispongo I indispose; pres. ind. 1st pers. sing. / *indisponer.*

indisponiendo indisposing; pres. part. / *indisponer.*

indisponiéndose becoming ill; pres. part. / *indisponerse.*

indisponte (you) become ill; impve. 2nd pers. sing. / *indisponerse.*

indispuesto indisposed; past part. / *indisponer.*

indispuse I indisposed; past 1st pers. sing. / *indisponer.*

indispusiera 1. that I might indispose; imp. subj. 1st pers. sing. / *indisponer.* 2. that he (she/it) might indispose; imp. subj. 3rd pers. sing.

indispusierais that you (all) might indispose; imp. subj. 2nd pers pl. / *indisponer.*

indispusiéramos that we might indispose; imp. subj. 1st pers. pl. / *indisponer.*

indispusieran that they might indispose; imp. subj. 3rd pers. pl. / *indisponer.*

indispusieras that you might indispose; imp. subj. 2nd pers. sing. / *indisponer.*

indispusieron they indisposed; past 3rd pers. pl. / *indisponer.*

indispusiese 1. that I might indispose; imp. subj. 1st pers. sing. / *indisponer.* 2. that he (she/it) might indispose; imp. subj. 3rd pers. sing.

indispusieseis that you (all) might indispose; imp. subj. 2nd pers pl. / *indisponer.*

indispusiésemos that we might indispose; imp. subj. 1st pers. pl. / *indisponer.*

indispusiesen that they might indispose; imp. subj. 3rd pers. pl. / *indisponer.*

indispusieses that you might indispose; imp. subj. 2nd pers. sing. / *indisponer.*

indispusimos we indisposed; past 1st pers. pl. / *indisponer.*

indispusiste you indisposed; past 2nd pers. sing. / *indisponer.*

indispusisteis you (all) indisposed; past 2nd pers. pl. / *indisponer.*

indispuso he (she/it) indisposed; past 3rd pers. sing. / _indisponer.*

individualice 1. that I may individualize; pres. subj. 1st pers. sing. / *individualizar.* 2. that he (she/it) may individualize; pres. subj. 3rd pers. sing. 3. let him (her/it) individualize; impve. 3rd pers. sing.

individualicé I individualized; past 1st pers. sing. / *individualizar.*

individualicéis that you (all) may individualize; pres. subj. 2nd pers. pl. / *individualizar.*

individualicemos 1. that we may individualize; pres. subj. 1st pers. pl. / *individualizar.* 2. let us individualize; impve. 1st pers. pl.

individualicen 1. that they may individualize; pres. subj. 3rd pers. pl. / *individualizar.* 2. let them idndividualize; impve. 3rd pers. pl.

individualices that you may individualize; pres. subj. 2nd pers. sing. / *individualizar.*

individualizar to individualize. irr.

inducir to induce or to persuade. irr.

induje I induced; past 1st pers. sing. / *inducir.*

indujera 1. that I might induce; imp. subj. 1st pers. sing. / *inducir.* 2. that he (she/it) might induce; imp. subj. 3rd pers. sing.

indujerais that you (all) might induce; imp. subj. 2nd pers pl. / *inducir.*

indujéramos that we might induce; imp. subj. 1st pers. pl. / *inducir.*

indujeran that they might induce; imp. subj. 3rd pers. pl. / *inducir.*

indujeras that you might induce; imp. subj. 2nd pers. sing. / *inducir.*

indujeron they induced; past 3rd pers. pl. / *inducir.*

indujese 1. that I might induce; imp. subj. 1st pers. sing. / *inducir.* 2. that he (she/it) might induce; imp. subj. 3rd pers. sing.

indujeseis that you (all) might induce; imp. subj. 2nd pers pl. / *inducir.*

indujésemos that we might induce; imp. subj. 1st pers. pl. / *inducir.*

indujesen that they might induce; imp. subj. 3rd pers. pl. / *inducir.*

indujeses that you might induce; imp. subj. 2nd pers. sing. / *inducir.*

indujimos we induced; past 1st pers. pl. / *inducir*.

indujiste you induced; past 2nd pers. sing. / *inducir*.

indujisteis you (all) induced; past 2nd pers. pl. / *inducir*.

indujo he (she/it) induced; past 3rd pers. sing. / *inducir*.

indultar to pardon. reg.

industrialice 1. that I may industrialize; pres. subj. 1st pers. sing. / *industrializar*. 2. that he (she/it) may industrialize; pres. subj. 3rd pers. sing. 3. let him (her/it) industrialize; impve. 3rd pers. sing.

industrialicé I industrialized; past 1st pers. sing. / *industrializar*.

industrialicéis that you (all) may industrialize; pres. subj. 2nd pers. pl. / *industrializar*.

industrialicemos 1. that we may industrialize; pres. subj. 1st pers. pl. / *industrializar*. 2. let us industrialize; impve. 1st pers. pl.

industrialicen 1. that they may industrialize; pres. subj. 3rd pers. pl. / *industrializar*. 2. let them industrialize; impve. 3rd pers. pl.

industrialices that you may industrialize; pres. subj. 2nd pers. sing. / *industrializar*.

industrializar to industrialize. irr.

industriándose finding a way; pres. part. / *industriarse*.

industriaos (you all) find a way; impve. 2nd pers. pl. / *industriarse*.

industriarse to find a way. reg.

industríate (you) find a way; impve. 2nd pers. sing. / *industriarse*.

industriémonos let us find a way; impve. 1st pers. pl. / *industriarse*.

industríense let them find a way; impve. 3rd pers. pl. / *industriarse*.

industríese let him (her/it) find a way; impve. 3rd pers. sing. / *industriarse*.

induzca 1. that I may induce; pres. subj. 1st pers. sing. / *inducir*. 2. that he (she/it) may induce; pres. subj. 3rd pers. sing. 3. let him (her/it) induce; impve. 3rd pers. sing.

induzcáis that you (all) may induce; pres. subj. 2nd pers. pl. / *inducir*.

induzcamos 1. that we may induce; pres. subj. 1st pers. pl. / *inducir*. 2. let us induce; impve. 1st pers. pl.

induzcan 1. that they may induce; pres. subj. 3rd pers. pl. / *inducir*. 2. let them induce; impve. 3rd pers. pl.

induzcas that you may induce; pres. subj. 2nd pers. sing. / *inducir*.

induzco I induce; pres. ind. 1st pers. sing. / *inducir*.

infamar to defame. reg.

infatuándose becoming vain; pres. part. / *infatuarse*.

infatuaos (you all) become vain; impve. 2nd pers. pl. / *infatuarse*.

infatuar to make vain. reg.

infatuarse to become vain. reg.

infatúate (you) become vain; impve. 2nd pers. sing. / *infatuarse*.

infatuémonos let us become vain; impve. 1st pers. pl. / *infatuarse*.

infatúense let them become vain; impve. 3rd pers. pl. / *infatuarse*.

infatúese let him (her/it) become vain; impve. 3rd pers. sing. / *infatuarse*.

infectándose becoming infected; pres. part. / *infectarse*.

infectaos (you all) become infected; impve. 2nd pers. pl. / *infectarse*.

infectar to infect. reg.

infectarse to become infected. reg.

inféctate (you) become infected; impve. 2nd pers. sing. / *infectarse*.

infectémonos let us become infected; impve. 1st pers. pl. / *infectarse*.

inféctense let them become infected; impve. 3rd pers. pl. / *infectarse*.

inféctese let him (her/it) become infected; impve. 3rd pers. sing. / *infectarse*.

inferíos (you all) follow; impve. 2nd pers. pl. / *inferirse*.

inferir to infer. irr.

inferirse to follow. irr.

infernar to upset. irr.

infestar to infest. reg.

inficionar to infect. reg._ -ar conju.

infiera 1. that I may infer; pres. subj. 1st pers. sing. / *inferir*. 2. that he (she/it) may infer; pres. subj. 3rd pers. sing. 3. let him (her/it) infer; impve. 3rd pers. sing.

infieran 1. that they may infer; pres. subj. 3rd pers. pl. / *inferir*. 2. let them infer; impve. 3rd pers. pl.

infiéranse let them follow; impve. 3rd pers. pl. / *inferirse*.

infieras that you may infer; pres. subj. 2nd pers. sing. / *inferir*.

infiérase let him (her/it) follow; impve. 3rd pers. sing. / *inferirse*.

infiere 1. he (she/it) infers; pres. ind. 3rd pers. sing. / *inferir*. 2. (you) infer; impve. 2nd pers. sing.

infieren they infer; pres. ind. 3rd pers. pl. / *inferir*.

infieres you infer; pres. ind. 2nd pers. sing. / *inferir*.

infiérete (you) follow; impve. 2nd pers. sing. / *inferirse*.

infierna 1. he (she/it) upsets; pres. ind. 3rd pers. sing. / *infernar*. 2. (you) upset; impve. 2nd pers. sing.

infiernan they upset; pres. ind. 3rd pers. pl. / *infernar*.

infiernas you upset; pres. ind. 2nd pers. sing. / *infernar*.

infierne 1. that I may upset; pres. subj. 1st pers. sing. / *infernar*. 2. that he (she/it) may upset; pres. subj. 3rd pers. sing. 3. let him (her/it) upset; impve. 3rd pers. sing.

infiernen 1. that they may upset; pres. subj. 3rd pers. pl. / *infernar*. 2. let them upset; impve. 3rd pers. pl.

infiernes that you may upset; pres. subj. 2nd pers. sing. / *infernar*.

infierno I upset; pres. ind. 1st pers. sing. / *infernar*.

infiero I infer; pres. ind. 1st pers. sing. / *inferir.*
infiltrándose filtering through; pres. part. / *infiltrarse.*
infiltraos (you all) filter through; impve. 2nd pers. pl. / *infiltrarse.*
infiltrar to infiltrate. reg.
infiltrarse to filter through. reg.
infíltrate (you) filter through; impve. 2nd pers. sing. / *infiltrarse.*
infiltrémonos let us filter through; impve. 1st pers. pl. / *infiltrarse.*
infíltrense let them filter through; impve. 3rd pers. pl. / *infiltrarse.*
infíltrese let him (her/it) filter through; impve. 3rd pers. sing. / *infiltrarse.*
infiráis that you (all) may infer; pres. subj. 2nd pers. pl. / *inferir.*
infirámonos let us follow; impve. 1st pers. pl. / *inferirse.*
infiramos 1. that we may infer; pres. subj. 1st pers. pl. / *inferir.* 2. let us infer; impve. 1st pers. pl.
infiriendo inferring; pres. part. / *inferir.*
infiriéndose following; pres. part. / *inferirse.*
infiriera 1. that I might infer; imp. subj. 1st pers. sing. / *inferir.* 2. that he (she/it) might infer; imp. subj. 3rd pers. sing.
infirierais that you (all) might infer; imp. subj. 2nd pers pl. / *inferir.*
infiriéramos that we might infer; imp. subj. 1st pers. pl. / *inferir.*
infirieran that they might infer; imp. subj. 3rd pers. pl. / *inferir.*
infirieras that you might infer; imp. subj. 2nd pers. sing. / *inferir.*
infirieron they inferred; past 3rd pers. pl. / *inferir.*
infiriese 1. that I might infer; imp. subj. 1st pers. sing. / *inferir.* 2. that he (she/it) might infer; imp. subj. 3rd pers. sing.
infirieseis that you (all) might infer; imp. subj. 2nd pers pl. / *inferir.*
infiriésemos that we might infer; imp. subj. 1st pers. pl. / *inferir.*
infiriesen that they might infer; imp. subj. 3rd pers. pl. / *inferir.*
infirieses that you might infer; imp. subj. 2nd pers. sing. / *inferir.*
infirió he (she/it) inferred; past 3rd pers. sing. / *inferir.*
inflamándose catching on fire; pres. part. / *inflamarse.*
inflamaos (you all) catch on fire; impve. 2nd pers. pl. / *inflamarse.*
inflamar to inflame. reg.
inflamarse to catch on fire. reg.
inflámate (you) catch on fire; impve. 2nd pers. sing. / *inflamarse.*
inflamémonos let us catch on fire; impve. 1st pers. pl. / *inflamarse.*
inflámense let them catch on fire; impve. 3rd pers. pl. / *inflamarse.*

inflámese let him (her/it) catch on fire; impve. 3rd pers. sing. / *inflamarse.*
inflándose becoming inflated; pres. part. / *inflarse.*
inflaos (you all) become inflated; impve. 2nd pers. pl. / *inflarse.*
inflar to inflate. reg.
inflarse to become inflated. reg.
ínflate (you) become inflated; impve. 2nd pers. sing. / *inflarse.*
inflémonos let us become inflated; impve. 1st pers. pl. / *inflarse.*
ínflense let them become inflated; impve. 3rd pers. pl. / *inflarse.*
ínflese let him (her/it) become inflated; impve. 3rd pers. sing. / *inflarse.*
inflexionar to inflect. reg.
infligir to inflict. irr.
inflija 1. that I may inflict; pres. subj. 1st pers. sing. / *infligir.* 2. that he (she/it) may inflict; pres. subj. 3rd pers. sing. 3. let him (her/it) inflict; impve. 3rd pers. sing.
inflijáis that you (all) may inflict; pres. subj. 2nd pers. pl. / *infligir.*
inflijamos 1. that we may inflict; pres. subj. 1st pers. pl. / *infligir.* 2. let us inflict; impve. 1st pers. pl.
inflijan 1. that they may inflict; pres. subj. 3rd pers. pl. / *infligir.* 2. let them inflict; impve. 3rd pers. pl.
inflijas that you may inflict; pres. subj. 2nd pers. sing. / *infligir.*
inflijo I inflict; pres. ind. 1st pers. sing. / *infligir.*
influenciar to influence. reg.
influir to influence. irr.
influya 1. that I may influence; pres. subj. 1st pers. sing. / *influir.* 2. that he (she/it) may influence; pres. subj. 3rd pers. sing. 3. let him (her/it) influence; impve. 3rd pers. sing.
influyáis that you (all) may influence; pres. subj. 2nd pers. pl. / *influir.*
influyamos 1. that we may influence; pres. subj. 1st pers. pl. / *influir.* 2. let us influence; impve. 1st pers. pl.
influyan 1. that they may influence; pres. subj. 3rd pers. pl. / *influir.* 2. let them influence; impve. 3rd pers. pl.
influyas that you may influence; pres. subj. 2nd pers. sing. / *influir.*
influye 1. he (she/it) influences; pres. ind. 3rd pers. sing. / *influir.* 2. (you) influence; impve. 2nd pers. sing.
influyen they influence; pres. ind. 3rd pers. pl. / *influir.*
influyendo influencing; pres. part. / *influir.*
influyera 1. that I might influence; imp. subj. 1st pers. sing. / *influir.* 2. that he (she/it) might influence; imp. subj. 3rd pers. sing.
influyerais that you (all) might influence; imp. subj. 2nd pers pl. / *influir.*
influyéramos that we might influence; imp. subj. 1st pers. pl. / *influir.*
influyeran that they might influence; imp. subj. 3rd pers. pl. / *influir.*

influyeras that you might influence; imp. subj. 2nd pers. sing. / *influir*.

influyeron they influenced; past 3rd pers. pl. / *influir*.

influyes you influence; pres. ind. 2nd pers. sing. / *influir*.

influyese 1. that I might influence; imp. subj. 1st pers. sing. / *influir*. 2. that he (she/it) might influence; imp. subj. 3rd pers. sing.

influyeseis that you (all) might influence; imp. subj. 2nd pers pl. / *influir*.

influyésemos that we might influence; imp. subj. 1st pers. pl. / *influir*.

influyesen that they might influence; imp. subj. 3rd pers. pl. / *influir*.

influyeses that you might influence; imp. subj. 2nd pers. sing. / *influir*.

influyo I influence; pres. ind. 1st pers. sing. / *influir*.

influyó he (she/it) influenced; past 3rd pers. sing. / *influir*.

informándose finding out; pres. part. / *informarse*.

informaos (you all) find out; impve. 2nd pers. pl. / *informarse*.

informar to inform. reg.

informarse to find out. reg.

infórmate (you) find out; impve. 2nd pers. sing. / *informarse*.

informémonos let us find out; impve. 1st pers. pl. / *informarse*.

infórmense let them find out; impve. 3rd pers. pl. / *informarse*.

infórmese let him (her/it) find out; impve. 3rd pers. sing. / *informarse*.

infringir to infringe. irr.

infrinja 1. that I may infringe; pres. subj. 1st pers. sing. / *infringir*. 2. that he (she/it) may infringe; pres. subj. 3rd pers. sing. 3. let him (her/it) infringe; impve. 3rd pers. sing.

infrinjáis that you (all) may infringe; pres. subj. 2nd pers. pl. / *infringir*.

infrinjamos 1. that we may infringe; pres. subj. 1st pers. pl. / *infringir*. 2. let us infringe; impve. 1st pers. pl.

infrinjan 1. that they may infringe; pres. subj. 3rd pers. pl. / *infringir*. 2. let them infringe; impve. 3rd pers. pl.

infrinjas that you may infringe; pres. subj. 2nd pers. sing. / *infringir*.

infrinjo I infringe; pres. ind. 1st pers. sing. / *infringir*.

infundir to infuse. reg.

ingeniándose managing; pres. part. / *ingeniarse*.

ingeniaos (you all) manage; impve. 2nd pers. pl. / *ingeniarse*.

ingeniar to contrive. reg.

ingeniarse to manage. reg.

ingeníate (you) manage; impve. 2nd pers. sing. / *ingeniarse*.

ingeniémonos let us manage; impve. 1st pers. pl. / *ingeniarse*.

ingeníense let them manage; impve. 3rd pers. pl. / *ingeiarse*.

ingeníese let him (her/it) manage; impve. 3rd pers. sing. / *ingeniarse*.

ingeríos (you all) mix; impve. 2nd pers. pl. / *ingerirse*.

ingerir to ingest or to consume. irr.

ingerirse to mix or to meddle. irr.

ingiera 1. that I may ingest; pres. subj. 1st pers. sing. / *ingerir*. 2. that he (she/it) may ingest; pres. subj. 3rd pers. sing. 3. let him (her/it) ingest; impve. 3rd pers. sing.

ingieran 1. that they may ingest; pres. subj. 3rd pers. pl. / *ingerir*. 2. let them ingest; impve. 3rd pers. pl.

ingiéranse let them mix; impve. 3rd pers. pl. / *ingerirse*.

ingieras that you may ingest; pres. subj. 2nd pers. sing. / *ingerir*.

ingiérase let him (her/it) mix; impve. 3rd pers. sing. / *ingerirse*.

ingiere 1. he (she/it) ingests; pres. ind. 3rd pers. sing. / *ingerir*. 2. (you) ingest; impve. 2nd pers. sing.

ingieren they ingest; pres. ind. 3rd pers. pl. / *ingerir*.

ingieres you ingest; pres. ind. 2nd pers. sing. / *ingerir*.

ingiérete (you) mix; impve. 2nd pers. sing. / *ingerirse*.

ingiero I ingest; pres. ind. 1st pers. sing. / *ingerir*.

ingiráis that you (all) may ingest; pres. subj. 2nd pers. pl. / *ingerir*.

ingirámonos let us mix; impve. 1st pers. pl. / *ingerirse*.

ingiramos 1. that we may ingest; pres. subj. 1st pers. pl. / *ingerir*. 2. let us ingest; impve. 1st pers. pl.

ingiriendo ingesting; pres. part. / *ingerir*.

ingiriéndose mixing; pres. part. / *ingerirse*.

ingiriera 1. that I might ingest; imp. subj. 1st pers. sing. / *ingerir* 2. that he (she/it) might ingest; imp. subj. 3rd pers. sing.

ingirierais that you (all) might ingest; imp. subj. 2nd pers pl. / *ingerir*.

ingiriéramos that we might ingest; imp. subj. 1st pers. pl. / *ingerir*.

ingirieran that they might ingest; imp. subj. 3rd pers. pl. / *ingerir*.

ingirieras that you might ingest; imp. subj. 2nd pers. sing. / *ingerir*.

ingirieron they ingested; past 3rd pers. pl. / *ingerir*.

ingiriese 1. that I might ingest; imp. subj. 1st pers. sing. / *ingerir*. 2. that he (she/it) might ingest; imp. subj. 3rd pers. sing.

ingirieseis that you (all) might ingest; imp. subj. 2nd pers pl. / *ingerir*.

ingiriésemos that we might ingest; imp. subj. 1st pers. pl. / *ingerir*.

ingiriesen that they might ingest; imp. subj. 3rd pers. pl. / *ingerir*.

ingirieses that you might ingest; imp. subj. 2nd pers. sing. / *ingerir*.

ingirió he (she/it) ingested; past 3rd pers. sing. / *ingerir*.

inglesar to anglicize. reg.

ingresándose enlisting; pres. part. / *ingresarse*.

ingresaos (you all) enlist; impve. 2nd pers. pl. / *ingresarse*.

ingresar to enter or to deposit. reg.

ingresarse to enlist. reg.
ingrésate (you) enlist; impve. 2nd pers. sing. / *ingresarse.*
ingresémonos let us enlist; impve. 1st pers. pl. / *ingresarse.*
ingrésense let them enlist; impve. 3rd pers. pl. / *ingresarse.*
ingrésese let him (her/it) enlist; impve. 3rd pers. sing. / *ingresarse.*
inhabilitar to disqualify or to incapacitate. reg.
inhalar to inhale. reg.
inhibámonos let us keep out; impve. 1st pers. pl. / *inhibirse.*
inhíbanse let them keep out; impve. 3rd pers. pl. / *inhibirse.*
inhíbase let him (her/it) keep out; impve. 3rd pers. sing. / *inhibirse.*
inhíbete (you) keep out; impve. 2nd pers. sing. / *inhibirse.*
inhibiéndose keeping out; pres. part. / *inhibirse.*
inhibíos (you all) keep out; impve. 2nd pers. pl. / *inhibirse.*
inhibir to inhibit. reg.
inhibirse to keep out. reg.
inhumar to bury. reg.
iniciándose being initiated; pres. part. / *iniciarse.*
iniciaos (you all) be initiated; impve. 2nd pers. pl. / *iniciarse.*
iniciar to initiate. reg.
iniciarse to be initiated. reg.
inicíate (you) be initiated; impve. 2nd pers. sing. / *iniciarse.*
iniciémonos let us be initiated; impve. 1st pers. pl. / *iniciarse.*
inicíense let them be initiated; impve. 3rd pers. pl. / *iniciarse.*
inicíese let him (her/it) be initiated; impve. 3rd pers. sing. / *iniciarse.*
injeríos (you all) interfere; impve. 2nd pers. pl. / *injerirse.*
injerir to insert. irr.
injerirse to interfere. irr.
injertar to graft. reg.
injiera 1. that I may insert; pres. subj. 1st pers. sing. / *injerir.* 2. that he (she/it) may insert; pres. subj. 3rd pers. sing. 3. let him (her/it) insert; impve. 3rd pers. sing.
injieran 1. that they may insert; pres. subj. 3rd pers. pl. / *injerir.* 2. let them insert; impve. 3rd pers. pl.
injiéranse let them interfere; impve. 3rd pers. pl. / *injerirse.*
injieras that you may insert; pres. subj. 2nd pers. sing. / *injerir.*
injiérase let him (her/it) interfere; impve. 3rd pers. sing. / *injerirse.*
injiere 1. he (she/it) inserts; pres. ind. 3rd pers. sing. / *injerir.* 2. (you) insert; impve. 2nd pers. sing.
injieren they insert; pres. ind. 3rd pers. pl. / *injerir.*
injieres you insert; pres. ind. 2nd pers. sing. / *injerir.*

injiérete (you) interfere; impve. 2nd pers. sing. / *injerirse.*
injiero I insert; pres. ind. 1st pers. sing. / *injerir.*
injiráis that you (all) may insert; pres. subj. 2nd pers. pl. / *injerir.*
injirámonos let us interfere; impve. 1st pers. pl. / *injerirse.*
injiramos 1. that we may insert; pres. subj. 1st pers. pl. / *injerir.* 2. let us insert; impve. 1st pers. pl.
injiriendo inserting; pres. part. / *injerir.*
injiriéndose interfering; pres. part. / *injerirse.*
injiriera 1. that I might insert; imp. subj. 1st pers. sing. / *injerir.* 2. that he (she/it) might insert; imp. subj. 3rd pers. sing.
injirierais that you (all) might insert; imp. subj. 2nd pers pl. / *injerir.*
injiriéramos that we might insert; imp. subj. 1st pers. pl. / *injerir.*
injirieran that they might insert; imp. subj. 3rd pers. pl. / *injerir.*
injirieras that you might insert; imp. subj. 2nd pers. sing. / *injerir.*
injirieron they inserted; past 3rd pers. pl. / *injerir.*
injiriese 1. that I might insert; imp. subj. 1st pers. sing. / *injerir.* 2. that he (she/it) might insert; imp. subj. 3rd pers. sing.
injiriesis that you (all) might insert; imp. subj. 2nd pers pl. / *injerir.*
injiriésemos that we might insert; imp. subj. 1st pers. pl. / *injerir.*
injiriesen that they might insert; imp. subj. 3rd pers. pl. / *injerir.*
injirieses that you might insert; imp. subj. 2nd pers. sing. / *injerir.*
injirió he (she/it) inserted; past 3rd pers. sing. / *injerir.*
injuriar to insult. reg.
inmérgete (you) be immersed; impve. 2nd pers. sing. / *inmergirse.*
inmergiéndose being immersed; pres. part. / *inmergirse.*
inmergíos (you all) be immersed; impve. 2nd pers. pl. / *inmergirse.*
inmergir to immerse. irr.
inmergirse to be immersed. irr.
inmerja 1. that I may immerse; pres. subj. 1st pers. sing. / *inmergir.* 2. that he (she/it) may immerse; pres. subj. 3rd pers. sing. 3. let him (her/it) immerse; impve. 3rd pers. sing.
inmerjáis that you (all) may immerse; pres. subj. 2nd pers. pl. / *inmergir.*
inmerjámonos let us be immersed; impve. 1st pers. pl. / *inmergirse.*
inmerjamos 1. that we may immerse; pres. subj. 1st pers. pl. / *inmergir.* 2. let us immerse; impve. 1st pers. pl.
inmerjan 1. that they may immerse; pres. subj. 3rd pers. pl. / *inmergir.* 2. let them immerse; impve. 3rd pers. pl.
inmérjanse let them be immersed; impve. 3rd pers. pl. / *inmergirse.*

inmerjas that you may immerse; pres. subj. 2nd pers. sing. / *inmergir.*

inmérjase let him (her/it) be immersed; impve. 3rd pers. sing. / *inmergirse.*

inmerjo I immerse; pres. ind. 1st pers. sing. / *inmergir.*

inmigrar to immigrate. reg.

inmiscuíos (you all) meddle; impve. 2nd pers. pl. / *inmiscuirse.*

inmiscuir to mix. irr.

inmiscuirse to meddle. irr.

inmiscuya 1. that I may mix; pres. subj. 1st pers. sing. / *inmiscuir.* 2. that he (she/it) may mix; pres. subj. 3rd pers. sing. 3. let him (her/it) mix; impve. 3rd pers. sing.

inmiscuyáis that you (all) may mix; pres. subj. 2nd pers. pl. / *inmiscuir.*

inmiscuyámonos let us meddle; impve. 1st pers. pl. / *inmiscuirse.*

inmiscuyamos 1. that we may mix; pres. subj. 1st pers. pl. / *inmiscuir.* 2. let us mix; impve. 1st pers. pl.

inmiscuyan 1. that they may mix; pres. subj. 3rd pers. pl. / *inmiscuir.* 2. let them mix; impve. 3rd pers. pl.

inmiscúyanse let them meddle; impve. 3rd pers. pl. / *inmiscuirse.*

inmiscuyas that you may mix; pres. subj. 2nd pers. sing. / *inmiscuir.*

inmiscúyase let him (her/it) meddle; impve. 3rd pers. sing. / *inmiscuirse.*

inmiscuye 1. he (she/it) mixes; pres. ind. 3rd pers. sing. / *inmiscuir.* 2. (you) mix; impve. 2nd pers. sing.

inmiscuyen they mix; pres. ind. 3rd pers. pl. / *inmiscuir.*

inmiscuyendo mixing; pres. part. / *inmiscuir.*

inmiscuyéndose meddling; pres. part. / *inmiscuirse.*

inmiscuyera 1. that I might mix; imp. subj. 1st pers. sing. / *inmiscuir.* 2. that he (she/it) might mix; imp. subj. 3rd pers. sing.

inmiscuyerais that you (all) might mix; imp. subj. 2nd pers pl. / *inmiscuir.*

inmiscuyéramos that we might mix; imp. subj. 1st pers. pl. / *inmiscuir.*

inmiscuyeran that they might mix; imp. subj. 3rd pers. pl. / *inmiscuir.*

inmiscuyeras that you might mix; imp. subj. 2nd pers. sing. / *inmiscuir.*

inmiscuyeron they mixed; past 3rd pers. pl. / *inmiscuir.*

inmiscuyes you mix; pres. ind. 2nd pers. sing. / *inmiscuir.*

inmiscuyese 1. that I might mix; imp. subj. 1st pers. sing. / *inmiscuir.* 2. that he (she/it) might mix; imp. subj. 3rd pers. sing.

inmiscuyeseis that you (all) might mix; imp. subj. 2nd pers pl. / *inmiscuir.*

inmiscuyésemos that we might mix; imp. subj. 1st pers. pl. / *inmiscuir.*

inmiscuyesen that they might mix; imp. subj. 3rd pers. pl. / *inmiscuir.*

inmiscuyeses that you might mix; imp. subj. 2nd pers. sing. / *inmiscuir.*

inmiscúyete (you) meddle; impve. 2nd pers. sing. / *inmiscuirse.*

inmiscuyo I mix; pres. ind. 1st pers. sing. / *inmiscuir.*

inmiscuyó he (she/it) mixed; past 3rd pers. sing. / *inmiscuir.*

inmolar to sacrifice. reg.

inmortalice 1. that I may immortalize; pres. subj. 1st pers. sing. / *inmortalizar.* 2. that he (she/it) may immortalize; pres. subj. 3rd pers. sing. 3. let him (her/it) immortalize; impve. 3rd pers. sing.

inmortalicé I immortalized; past 1st pers. sing. / *inmortalizar.*

inmortalicéis that you (all) may immortalize; pres. subj. 2nd pers. pl. / *inmortalizar.*

inmortalicemos 1. that we may immortalize; pres. subj. 1st pers. pl. / *inmortalizar.* 2. let us immortalize; impve. 1st pers. pl.

inmortalicen 1. that they may immortalize; pres. subj. 3rd pers. pl. / *inmortalizar.* 2. let them immortalize; impve. 3rd pers. pl.

inmortalices that you may immortalize; pres. subj. 2nd pers. sing. / *inmortalizar.*

inmortalizar to immortalize. irr.

inmovilice 1. that I may immobilize; pres. subj. 1st pers. sing. / *inmovilizar.* 2. that he (she/it) may immobilize; pres. subj. 3rd pers. sing. 3. let him (her/it) immobilize; impve. 3rd pers. sing.

inmovilicé I immobilized; past 1st pers. sing. / *inmovilizar.*

inmovilicéis that you (all) may immobilize; pres. subj. 2nd pers. pl. / *inmovilizar.*

inmovilicemos 1. that we may immobilize; pres. subj. 1st pers. pl. / *inmovilizar.* 2. let us immobilize; impve. 1st pers. pl.

inmovilicen 1. that they may immobilize; pres. subj. 3rd pers. pl. / *inmovilizar.* 2. let them immobilize; impve. 3rd pers. pl.

inmovilices that you may immobilize; pres. subj. 2nd pers. sing. / *inmovilizar.*

inmovilizar to immobilize. irr.

inmunice 1. that I may immunize; pres. subj. 1st pers. sing. / *inmunizar.* 2. that he (she/it) may immunize; pres. subj. 3rd pers. sing. 3. let him (her/it) immunize; impve. 3rd pers. sing.

inmunicé I immunized; past 1st pers. sing. / *inmunizar.*

inmunicéis that you (all) may immunize; pres. subj. 2nd pers. pl. / *inmunizar.*

inmunicemos 1. that we may immunize; pres. subj. 1st pers. pl. / *inmunizar.* 2. let us immunize; impve. 1st pers. pl.

inmunicen 1.that they may immunize; pres. subj. 3rd pers. pl. / *inmunizar.* 2. let them immunize; impve. 3rd pers. pl.

inmunices that you may immunize; pres. subj. 2nd pers. sing. / *inmunizar.*

inmunizar to immunize. irr.

inmutándose changing countenance; pres. part. / *inmutarse.*

inmutaos (you all) change countenance; impve. 2nd pers. pl. / *inmutarse.*

inmutar to alter or to change. reg.

inmutarse to change countenance. reg.

inmútate (you) change countenance; impve. 2nd pers. sing. / *inmutarse*.

inmutémonos let us change countenance; impve. 1st pers. pl. / *inmutarse*.

inmútense let them change countenance; impve. 3rd pers. pl. / *inmutarse*.

inmútese let him (her/it) change countenance; impve. 3rd pers. sing. / *inmutarse*.

innovar to innovate. reg.

inocular to inoculate. reg.

inquiera 1. that I may inquire; pres. subj. 1st pers. sing. / *inquirir*. 2. that he (she/it) may inquire; pres. subj. 3rd pers. sing. 3. let him (her/it) inquire; impve. 3rd pers. sing.

inquieran 1. that they may inquire; pres. subj. 3rd pers. pl. / *inquirir*. 2. let them inquire; impve. 3rd pers. pl.

inquieras that you may inquire; pres. subj. 2nd pers. sing. / *inquirir*.

inquiere 1. he (she/it) inquires; pres. ind. 3rd pers. sing. / *inquirir*. 2. (you) inquire; impve. 2nd pers. sing.

inquieren they inquire; pres. ind. 3rd pers. pl. / *inquirir*.

inquieres you inquire; pres. ind. 2nd pers. sing. / *inquirir*.

inquiero I inquire; pres. ind. 1st pers. sing. / *inquirir*.

inquietándose becoming disturbed; pres. part. / *inquietarse*.

inquietaos (you all) become disturbed; impve. 2nd pers. pl. / *inquietarse*.

inquietar to worry or to disturb. reg.

inquietarse to become disturbed. reg.

inquiétate (you) become disturbed; impve. 2nd pers. sing. / *inquietarse*.

inquietémonos let us become disturbed; impve. 1st pers. pl. / *inquietarse*.

inquiétense let them become disturbed; impve. 3rd pers. pl. / *inquietarse*.

inquiétese let him (her/it) become disturbed; impve. 3rd pers. sing. / *inquietarse*.

inquirir to inquire. irr.

inscribámonos let us register; impve. 1st pers. pl. / *inscribirse*.

inscríbanse let them register; impve. 3rd pers. pl. / *inscribirse*.

inscríbase let him (her/it) register; impve. 3rd pers. sing. / *inscribirse*.

inscríbete (you) register; impve. 2nd pers. sing. / *inscribirse*.

inscribiéndose registering; pres. part. / *inscribirse*.

inscribíos (you all) register; impve. 2nd pers. pl. / *inscribirse*.

inscribir to inscribe. reg. except for pp.

inscribirse to register. reg. except for pp.

inscripto inscribed; past part. / *inscribir*.

inscrito inscribed; past part. / *inscribir*.

inseminar to inseminate. reg.

insensibilice 1. that I may make insensible; pres. subj. 1st pers. sing. / *insensibilizar*. 2. that he (she/it) may make insensible; pres. subj. 3rd pers. sing. 3. let him (her/it) make insensible; impve. 3rd pers. sing.

insensibilicé I made insensible; past 1st pers. sing. / *insensibilizar*.

insensibilicéis that you (all) may make insensible; pres. subj. 2nd pers. pl. / *insensibilizar*.

insensibilicemos 1. that we may make insensible; pres. subj. 1st pers. pl. / *insensibilizar*. 2. let us make insensible; impve. 1st pers. pl.

insensibilicen 1. that they may make insensible; pres. subj. 3rd pers. pl. / *insensibilizar*. 2. let them make insensible; impve. 3rd pers. pl.

insensibilices that you may make insensible; pres. subj. 2nd pers. sing. / *insensibilizar*.

insensibilizar to make insensible. irr.

insertar to insert. reg.

inserto inserted; past part. / *insertar*.

insinúa 1. he (she/it) insinuates; pres. ind. 3rd pers. sing. / *insinuar* 2. (you) insinuate; impve. 2nd pers. sing.

insinúan they insinuate; pres. ind. 3rd pers. pl. / *insinuar*.

insinuándose slipping in; pres. part. / *insinuarse*.

insinuaos (you all) slip in; impve. 2nd pers. pl. / *insinuarse*.

insinuar to insinuate. irr.

insinuarse to slip in. irr.

insinúas you insinuate; pres. ind. 2nd pers. sing. / *insinuar*.

insinúate (you) slip in; impve. 2nd pers. sing. / *insinuarse*.

insinúe 1. that I may insinuate; pres. subj. 1st pers. sing. / *insinuar*. 2. that he (she/it) may insinuate; pres. subj. 3rd pers. sing. 3. let him (her/it) insinuate; impve. 3rd pers. sing.

insinuémonos let us slip in; impve. 1st pers. pl. / *insinuarse*.

insinúen 1. that they may insinuate; pres. subj. 3rd pers. pl. / *insinuar*. 2. let them insinuate; impve. 3rd pers. pl.

insinúense let them slip in; impve. 3rd pers. pl. / *insinuarse*.

insinúes that you may insinuate; pres. subj. 2nd pers. sing. / *insinuar*.

insinúese let him (her/it) slip in; impve. 3rd pers. sing. / *insinuarse*.

insinúo I insinuate; pres. ind. 1st pers. sing. / *insinuar*.

insistir to insist. reg.

insolándose getting sun-stroke; pres. part. / *insolarse*.

insolaos (you all) get sun-stroke; impve. 2nd pers. pl. / *insolarse*.

insolar to insolate or to expose to the sun. reg.

insolarse to get sun-stroke. reg.

insólate (you) get sun-stroke; impve. 2nd pers. sing. / *insolarse*.

insolémonos let us get sun-stroke; impve. 1st pers. pl. / *insolarse*.

insólense let them get sun-stroke; impve. 3rd pers. pl. / *insolarse.*

insolentándose becoming insolent; pres. part. / *insolentarse.*

insolentaos (you all) become insolent; impve. 2nd pers. pl. / *insolentarse.*

insolentar to make insolent. reg.

insolentarse to become insolent. reg.

insoléntate (you) become insolent; impve. 2nd pers. sing. / *insolentarse.*

insolentémonos let us become insolent; impve. 1st pers. pl. / *insolentarse.*

insoléntense let them become insolent; impve. 3rd pers. pl. / *insolentarse.*

insoléntese let him (her/it) become insolent; impve. 3rd pers. sing. / *insolentarse.*

insólese let him (her/it) get sun-stroke; impve. 3rd pers. sing. / *insolarse.*

inspeccionar to inspect. reg.

inspirándose being inspired; pres. part. / *inspirarse.*

inspiraos (you all) be inspired; impve. 2nd pers. pl. / *inspirarse.*

inspirar to inspire or to inhale. reg.

inspirarse to be inspired. reg.

inspírate (you) be inspired; impve. 2nd pers. sing. / *inspirarse.*

inspirémonos let us be inspired; impve. 1st pers. pl. / *inspirarse.*

inspírense let them be inspired; impve. 3rd pers. pl. / *inspirarse.*

inspírese let him (her/it) be inspired; impve. 3rd pers. sing. / *inspirarse.*

instalar to install. reg.

instar to urge. reg.

instaurar to restore. reg.

instigar to instigate. irr.

instigue 1. that I may instigate; pres. subj. 1st pers. sing. / *instigar.* 2. that he (she/it) may instigate; pres. subj. 3rd pers. sing. 3. let him (her/it) instigate; impve. 3rd pers. sing.

instigué I instigated; past 1st pers. sing. / *instigar.*

instiguéis that you (all) may instigate; pres. subj. 2nd pers. pl. / *instigar.*

instiguemos 1. that we may instigate; pres. subj. 1st pers. pl. / *instigar.* 2. let us instigate; impve. 1st pers. pl.

instiguen 1. that they may instigate; pres. subj. 3rd pers. pl. / *instigar.* 2. let them instigate; impve. 3rd pers. pl.

instigues that you may instigate; pres. subj. 2nd pers. sing. / *instigar.*

instilar to instill. reg.

instituir to institute. irr.

instituya 1. that I may institute; pres. subj. 1st pers. sing. / *instituir.* 2. that he (she/it) may institute; pres. subj. 3rd pers. sing. 3. let him (her/it) institute; impve. 3rd pers. sing.

instituyáis that you (all) may institute; pres. subj. 2nd pers. pl. / *instituir.*

instituyamos 1. that we may institute; pres. subj. 1st pers. pl. / *instituir.* 2. let us institute; impve. 1st pers. pl.

instituyan 1. that they may institute; pres. subj. 3rd pers. pl. / *instituir.* 2. let them institute; impve. 3rd pers. pl.

instituyas that you may institute; pres. subj. 2nd pers. sing. / *instituir.*

instituye 1. he (she/it) institutes; pres. ind. 3rd pers. sing. / *instituir.* 2. (you) institute; impve. 2nd pers. sing.

instituyen they institute; pres. ind. 3rd pers. pl. / *instituir.*

instituyendo instituting; pres. part. / *instituir.*

instituyera 1. that I might institute; imp. subj. 1st pers. sing. / *instituir.* 2. that he (she/it) might institute; imp. subj. 3rd pers. sing.

instituyerais that you (all) might institute; imp. subj. 2nd pers pl. / *instituir.*

instituyéramos that we might institute; imp. subj. 1st pers. pl. / *instituir.*

instituyeran that they might institute; imp. subj. 3rd pers. pl. / *instituir.*

instituyeras that you might institute; imp. subj. 2nd pers. sing. / *instituir.*

instituyeron they instituted; past 3rd pers. pl. / *instituir.*

instituyes you institute; pres. ind. 2nd pers. sing. / *instituir.*

instituyese 1. that I might institute; imp. subj. 1st pers. sing. / *instituir.* 2. that he (she/it) might institute; imp. subj. 3rd pers. sing.

instituyeseis that you (all) might institute; imp. subj. 2nd pers pl. / *instituir.*

instituyésemos that we might institute; imp. subj. 1st pers. pl. / *instituir.*

instituyesen that they might institute; imp. subj. 3rd pers. pl. / *instituir.*

instituyeses that you might institute; imp. subj. 2nd pers. sing. / *instituir.*

instituyo I institute; pres. ind. 1st pers. sing. / *instituir.*

instituyó he (she/it) instituted; past 3rd pers. sing. / *instituir.*

instruir to instruct. irr.

instrumentar to provide instrumentation for. reg.

instruya 1. that I may instruct; pres. subj. 1st pers. sing. / *instruir.* 2. that he (she/it) may instruct; pres. subj. 3rd pers. sing. 3. let him (her/it) instruct; impve. 3rd pers. sing.

instruyáis that you (all) may instruct; pres. subj. 2nd pers. pl. / *instruir.*

instruyamos 1. that we may instruct; pres. subj. 1st pers. pl. / *instruir.* 2. let us instruct; impve. 1st pers. pl.

instruyan 1. that they may instruct; pres. subj. 3rd pers. pl. / *instruir.* 2. let them instruct; impve. 3rd pers. pl.

instruyas that you may instruct; pres. subj. 2nd pers. sing. / *instruir.*

instruye 1. he (she/it) instructs; pres. ind. 3rd pers. sing. / *instruir.* 2. (you) instruct; impve. 2nd pers. sing.

instruyen they instruct; pres. ind. 3rd pers. pl. / *instruir.*

instruyendo instructing; pres. part. / *instruir.*

instruyera 1. that I might instruct; imp. subj. 1st pers. sing. / *instruir.* 2. that he (she/it) might instruct; imp. subj. 3rd pers. sing.

instruyerais that you (all) might instruct; imp. subj. 2nd pers pl. / *instruir.*

instruyéramos that we might instruct; imp. subj. 1st pers. pl. / *instruir.*

instruyeran that they might instruct; imp. subj. 3rd pers. pl. / *instruir.*

instruyeras that you might instruct; imp. subj. 2nd pers. sing. / *instruir.*

instruyeron they instructed; past 3rd pers. pl. / *instruir.*

instruyes you instruct; pres. ind. 2nd pers. sing. / *instruir.*

instruyese 1. that I might instruct; imp. subj. 1st pers. sing. / *instruir.* 2. that he (she/it) might instruct; imp. subj. 3rd pers. sing.

instruyeseis that you (all) might instruct; imp. subj. 2nd pers pl. / *instruir.*

instruyésemos that we might instruct; imp. subj. 1st pers. pl. / *instruir.*

instruyesen that they might instruct; imp. subj. 3rd pers. pl. / *instruir.*

instruyeses that you might instruct; imp. subj. 2nd pers. sing. / *instruir.*

instruyo I instruct; pres. ind. 1st pers. sing. / *instruir.*

instruyó he (she/it) instructed; past 3rd pers. sing. / *instruir.*

insubordinándose rebelling; pres. part. / *insubordinarse.*

insubordinaos (you all) rebel; impve. 2nd pers. pl. / *insubordinarse.*

insubordinar to incite to insubordination. reg.

insubordinarse to rebel. reg.

insubordínate (you) rebel; impve. 2nd pers. sing. / *insubordinarse.*

insubordinémonos let us rebel; impve. 1st pers. pl. / *insubordinarse.*

insubordínense let them rebel; impve. 3rd pers. pl. / *insubordinarse.*

insubordínese let him (her/it) rebel; impve. 3rd pers. sing. / *insubordinarse.*

insultándose being seized with a fit; pres. part. / *insultarse.*

insultaos (you all) be seized with a fit; impve. 2nd pers. pl. / *insultarse.*

insultar to insult. reg.

insultarse to be seized with a fit. reg.

insúltate (you) be seized with a fit; impve. 2nd pers. sing. / *insultarse.*

insultémonos let us be seized with a fit; impve. 1st pers. pl. / *insultarse.*

insúltense let them be seized with a fit; impve. 3rd pers. pl. / *insultarse.*

insúltese let him (her/it) be seized with a fit; impve. 3rd pers. sing. / *insultarse.*

insurreccionándose revolting; pres. part. / *insurreccionarse.*

insurreccionaos (you all) revolt; impve. 2nd pers. pl. / *insurreccionarse.*

insurreccionar to incite to rebel. reg.

insurreccionarse to revolt. reg.

insurrecciónate (you) revolt; impve. 2nd pers. sing. / *insurreccionarse.*

insurreccionémonos let us revolt; impve. 1st pers. pl. / *insurreccionarse.*

insurrecciónense let them revolt; impve. 3rd pers. pl. / *insurreccionarse.*

insurrecciónese let him (her/it) revolt; impve. 3rd pers. sing. / *insurreccionarse.*

integrar to integrate. reg.

intensar to intensify. reg.

intensificar to intensify. irr.

intensifique 1. that I may intensify; pres. subj. 1st pers. sing. / *intensificar.* 2. that he (she/it) may intensify; pres. subj. 3rd pers. sing. 3. let him (her/it) intensify; impve. 3rd pers. sing.

intensifiqué I intensified; past 1st pers. sing. / *intensificar.*

intensifiquéis that you (all) may intensify; pres. subj. 2nd pers. pl. / *intensificar.*

intensifiquemos 1. that we may intensify; pres. subj. 1st pers. pl. / *intensificar.* 2. let us intensify; impve. 1st pers. pl.

intensifiquen 1. that they may intensify; pres. subj. 3rd pers. pl. / *intensificar.* 2. let them intensify; impve. 3rd pers. pl.

intensifiques that you may intensify; pres. subj. 2nd pers. sing. / *intensificar.*

intentar to try. reg.

intercalar to intercalate or to place between. reg.

intercambiar to interchange. reg.

interceder to intercede. reg.

interceptar to intercept. reg.

intercomunicándose intercommunicating; pres. part. / *intercomunicarse.*

intercomunicaos (you all) intercommunicate; impve. 2nd pers. pl. / *intercomunicarse.*

intercomunicarse to intercommunicate. irr.

intercomunícate (you) intercommunicate; impve. 2nd pers. pl. / *intercomunicarse.*

intercomunique 1. that I may intercommunicate; pres. subj. 1st pers. sing. / *intercomunicarse.* 2. that he (she/it) may intercommunicate; pres. subj. 3rd pers. sing.

intercomuniqué I intercommunicated; past 1st pers. sing. / *intercomunicarse.*

intercomuniquéis that you (all) may intercommunicate; pres. subj. 2nd pers. pl. / *intercomunicarse.*

intercomuniquémonos let us intercommunicate; impve. 1st pers. pl. / *intercomunicarse.*

intercomuniquemos that we may intercommunicate; pres. subj. 1st pers. pl. / *intercomunicarse.*

intercomuniquen that they may intercommunicate; pres. subj. 3rd pers. pl. / *intercomunicarse.*

intercomuníquense let them intercommunicate; impve. 3rd pers. pl. / *intercomunicarse.*

intercomuniques that you may intercommunicate; pres. subj. 2nd pers. sing. / *intercomunicarse.*

intercomuníquese let him (her/it) intercommunicate; impve. 3rd pers. sing. / *intercomunicarse.*

interdecir to interdict. irr.

interdi (you) interdict; impve. 2nd pers. sing. / *interdecir.*

interdice he (she/it) interdicts; pres. ind. 3rd pers. sing. / *interdecir.*

interdicen they interdict; pres. ind. 3rd pers. pl. / *interdecir.*

interdices you interdict; pres. ind. 2nd pers. sing. / *interdecir.*

interdiciendo interdicting; pres. part. / *interdecir.*

interdicho interdicted; past part. / *interdecir.*

interdiga 1. that I may interdict; pres. subj. 1st pers. sing. / *interdecir.* 2. that he (she/it) may interdict; pres. subj. 3rd pers. sing. 3. let him (her/it) interdict; impve. 3rd pers. sing.

interdigáis that you (all) may interdict; pres. subj. 2nd pers. pl. / *interdecir.*

interdigamos 1. that we may interdict; pres. subj. 1st pers. pl. / *interdecir.* 2. let us interdict; impve. 1st pers. pl.

interdigan 1. that they may interdict; pres. subj. 3rd pers. pl. / *interdecir.* 2. let them interdict; impve. 3rd pers. pl.

interdigas that you may interdict; pres. subj. 2nd pers. sing. / *interdecir.*

interdigo I interdict; pres. ind. 1st pers. sing. / *interdecir.*

interdije I interdicted; past 1st pers. sing. / *interdecir.*

interdijera 1. that I might interdict; imp. subj. 1st pers. sing. / *interdecir.* 2. that he (she/it) might interdict; imp. subj. 3rd pers. sing.

interdijerais that you (all) might interdict; imp. subj. 2nd pers pl. / *interdecir.*

interdijéramos that we might interdict; imp. subj. 1st pers. pl. / *interdecir.*

interdijeran that they might interdict; imp. subj. 3rd pers. pl. / *interdecir.*

interdijeras that you might interdict; imp. subj. 2nd pers. sing. / *interdecir.*

interdijeron they interdicted; past 3rd pers. pl. / *interdecir.*

interdijese 1. that I might interdict; imp. subj. 1st pers. sing. / *interdecir.* 2. that he (she/it) might interdict; imp. subj. 3rd pers. sing.

interdijeseis that you (all) might interdict; imp. subj. 2nd pers pl. / *interdecir.*

interdijésemos that we might interdict; imp. subj. 1st pers. pl. / *interdecir.*

interdijesen that they might interdict; imp. subj. 3rd pers. pl. / *interdecir.*

interdijeses that you might interdict; imp. subj. 2nd pers. sing. / *interdecir.*

interdijimos we interdicted; past 1st pers. pl. / *interdecir.*

interdijiste you interdicted; past 2nd pers. sing. / *interdecir.*

interdijisteis you (all) interdicted; past 2nd pers. pl. / *interdecir.*

interdijo he (she/it) interdicted; past 3rd pers. sing. / *interdecir.*

interdirá he (she/it) will interdict; fut. 3rd pers. sing. / *interdecir.*

interdirán they will interdict; fut. 3rd pers. pl. / *interdecir.*

interdirás you will interdict; fut. 2nd pers. sing. / *interdecir.*

interdiré I shall interdict; fut. 1st pers. sing. / *interdecir.*

interdiréis you (all) will interdict; fut. 2nd pers. pl. / *interdecir.*

interdiremos we shall interdict; fut. 1st pers. pl. / *interdecir.*

interdiría 1. I should interdict; cond. 1st pers. sing. / *interdecir.* 2. he (she/it) would interdict; cond. 3rd pers. sing.

interdiríais you (all) would interdict; cond. 2nd pers. pl. / *interdecir.*

interdiríamos we should interdict; cond. 1st pers. pl. / *interdecir.*

interdirían they would interdict; cond. 3rd pers. pl. / *interdecir.*

interdirías you would interdict; cond. 2nd pers. sing. / *interdecir.*

interesándose being interested; pres. part. / *interesarse.*

interesaos (you all) be interested; impve. 2nd pers. pl. / *interesarse.*

interesar to interest. reg.

interesarse to be interested. reg.

interésate (you) be interested; impve. 2nd pers. sing. / *interesarse.*

interesémonos let us be interested; impve. 1st pers. pl. / *interesarse.*

interésense let them be interested; impve. 3rd pers. pl. / *interesarse.*

interésese let him (her/it) be interested; impve. 3rd pers. sing. / *interesarse.*

interferir to interfere. irr.

interfiera 1. that I may interfere; pres. subj. 1st pers. sing. / *interferir.* 2. that he (she/it) may interfere; pres. subj. 3rd pers. sing. 3. let him (her/it) interfere; impve. 3rd pers. sing.

interfieran 1. that they may interfere; pres. subj. 3rd pers. pl. / *interferir.* 2. let them interfere; impve. 3rd pers. pl.

interfieras that you may interfere; pres. subj. 2nd pers. sing. / *interferir.*

interfiere 1. he (she/it) interferes; pres. ind. 3rd pers. sing. / *interferir.* 2. (you) interfere; impve. 2nd pers. sing.

interfieren they interfere; pres. ind. 3rd pers. pl. / *interferir.*

interfieres you interfere; pres. ind. 2nd pers. sing. / *interferir.*

interfiero I interfere; pres. ind. 1st pers. sing. / *interferir.*

interfiráis that you (all) may interfere; pres. subj. 2nd pers. pl. / *interferir.*

interfiramos 1. that we may interfere; pres. subj. 1st pers. pl. / *interferir.* 2. let us interfere; impve. 1st pers. pl.

interfiriendo interfering; pres. part. / *interferir.*

interfiriera 1. that I might interfere; imp. subj. 1st pers. sing. / *interferir.* 2. that he (she/it) might interfere; imp. subj. 3rd pers. sing.

interfirierais that you (all) might interfere; imp. subj. 2nd pers pl. / *interferir.*

interfiriéramos that we might interfere; imp. subj. 1st pers. pl. / *interferir.*

interfirieran that they might interfere; imp. subj. 3rd pers. pl. / *interferir.*

interfirieras that you might interfere; imp. subj. 2nd pers. sing. / *interferir.*

interfirieron they interfered; past 3rd pers. pl. / *interferir.*

interfiriese 1. that I might interfere; imp. subj. 1st pers. sing. / *interferir.* 2. that he (she/it) might interfere; imp. subj. 3rd pers. sing.

interfirieseis that you (all) might interfere; imp. subj. 2nd pers pl. / *interferir.*

interfiriésemos that we might interfere; imp. subj. 1st pers. pl. / *interferir.*

interfiriesen that they might interfere; imp. subj. 3rd pers. pl. / *interferir.*

interfirieses that you might interfere; imp. subj. 2nd pers. sing. / *interferir.*

interfirió he (she/it) interfered; past 3rd pers. sing. / *interferir.*

interfoliar to interleave. reg.

interiorice 1. that I may familiarize; pres. subj. 1st pers. sing. / *interiorizar.* 2. that he (she/it) may familiarize; pres. subj. 3rd pers. sing. 3. let him (her/it) familiarize; impve. 3rd pers. sing.

interioricé I familiarized; past 1st pers. sing. / *interiorizar.*

interioricéis that you (all) may familiarize; pres. subj. 2nd pers. pl. / *interiorizar.*

interioricemos 1. that we may familiarize; pres. subj. 1st pers. pl. / *interiorizar.* 2. let us familiarize; impve. 1st pers. pl.

interioricen 1. that they may familiarize; pres. subj. 3rd pers. pl. / *interiorizar.* 2. let them familiarize; impve. 3rd pers. pl.

interiorices that you may familiarize; pres. subj. 2nd pers. sing. / *interiorizar.*

interiorizar to familiarize. irr.

interlinear to interline. reg.

intermediar to interpose. reg.

internacionalice 1. that I may internationalize; pres. subj. 1st pers. sing. / *internacionalizar.* 2. that he (she/it) may internationalize; pres. subj. 3rd pers. sing. 3. let him (her/it) internationalize; impve. 3rd pers. sing.

internacionalicé I internationalized; past 1st pers. sing. / *internacionalizar.*

internacionalicéis that you (all) may internationalize; pres. subj. 2nd pers. pl. / *internacionalizar.*

internacionalicemos 1. that we may internationalize; pres. subj. 1st pers. pl. / *internacionalizar.* 2. let us internationalize; impve. 1st pers. pl.

internacionalicen 1. that they may internationalize; pres. subj. 3rd pers. pl. / *internacionalizar.* 2. let them internationalize; impve. 3rd pers. pl.

internacionalices that you may internationalize; pres. subj. 2nd pers. sing. / *internacionalizar.*

internacionalizar to internationalize. irr.

internándose penetrating; pres. part. / *internarse.*

internaos (you all) penetrate; impve. 2nd pers. pl. / *internarse.*

internar to intern. reg.

internarse to penetrate. reg.

intérnate (you) penetrate; impve. 2nd pers. sing. / *internarse.*

internémonos let us penetrate; impve. 1st pers. pl. / *internarse.*

intérnense let them penetrate; impve. 3rd pers. pl. / *internarse.*

intérnese let him (her/it) penetrate; impve. 3rd pers. sing. / *internarse.*

interpaginar to interpage. reg.

interpelar to interrogate. reg.

interpolar to interpolate. reg.

interpon (you) interpose; impve. 2nd pers. sing. / *interponer.*

interpondrá he (she/it) will interpose; fut. 3rd pers. sing. / *interponer.*

interpondrán they will interpose; fut. 3rd pers. pl. / *interponer.*

interpondrás you will interpose; fut. 2nd pers. sing. / *interponer.*

interpondré I shall interpose; fut. 1st pers. sing. / *interponer.*

interpondréis you (all) will interpose; fut. 2nd pers. pl. / *interponer.*

interpondremos we shall interpose; fut. 1st pers. pl. / *interponer.*

interpondría 1. I should interpose; cond. 1st pers. sing. / *interponer.* 2. he (she/it) would interpose; cond. 3rd pers. sing.

interpondríais you (all) would interpose; cond. 2nd pers. pl. / *interponer.*

interpondríamos we should interpose; cond. 1st pers. pl. / *interponer.*

interpondrían they would interpose; cond. 3rd pers. pl. / *interponer.*

interpondrías you would interpose; cond. 2nd pers. sing. / *interponer.*

interponeos (you all) intervene; impve. 2nd pers. pl. / *interponerse.*

interponer to interpose. irr.
interponerse to intervene. irr.
interponga 1. that I may interpose; pres. subj. 1st pers. sing. / *interponer.* 2. that he (she/it) may interpose; pres. subj. 3rd pers. sing. 3. let him (her/it) interpose; impve. 3rd pers. sing.
interpongáis that you (all) may interpose; pres. subj. 2nd pers. pl. / *interponer.*
interpongámonos let us intervene; impve. 1st pers. pl. / *interponerse.*
interpongamos 1. that we may interpose; pres. subj. 1st pers. pl. / *interponer.* 2. let us interpose; impve. 1st pers. pl.
interpongan 1. that they may interpose; pres. subj. 3rd pers. pl. / *interponer.* 2. let them interpose; impve. 3rd pers. pl.
interpónganse let them intervene; impve. 3rd pers. pl. / *interponerse.*
interpongas that you may interpose; pres. subj. 2nd pers. sing. / *interponer.*
interpóngase let him (her/it) intervene; impve. 3rd pers. sing. / *interponerse.*
interpongo I interpose; pres. ind. 1st pers. sing. / *interponer.*
interponiendo interposing; pres. part. / *interponer.*
interponiéndose intervening; pres. part. / *interponerse.*
interponte (you) intervene; impve. 2nd pers. sing. / *interponerse.*
interpretar to interpret. reg.
interpuesto interposed; past part. / *interponer.*
interpuse I interposed; past 1st pers. sing. / *interponer.*
interpusiera 1. that I might interpose; imp. subj. 1st pers. sing. / *interponer.* 2. that he (she/it) might interpose; imp. subj. 3rd pers. sing.
interpusierais that you (all) might interpose; imp. subj. 2nd pers pl. / *interponer.*
interpusiéramos that we might interpose; imp. subj. 1st pers. pl. / *interponer.*
interpusieran that they might interpose; imp. subj. 3rd pers. pl. / *interponer.*
interpusieras that you might interpose; imp. subj. 2nd pers. sing. / *interponer.*
interpusieron they interposed; past 3rd pers. pl. / *interponer.*
interpusiese 1. that I might interpose; imp. subj. 1st pers. sing. / *interponer.* 2. that he (she/it) might interpose; imp. subj. 3rd pers. sing.
interpusieseis that you (all) might interpose; imp. subj. 2nd pers pl. / *interponer.*
interpusiésemos that we might interpose; imp. subj. 1st pers. pl. / *interponer.*
interpusiesen that they might interpose; imp. subj. 3rd pers. pl. / *interponer.*
interpusieses that you might interpose; imp. subj. 2nd pers. sing. / *interponer.*
interpusimos we interposed; past 1st pers. pl. / *interponer.*
interpusiste you interposed; past 2nd pers. sing. / *interponer.*

interpusisteis you (all) interposed; past 2nd pers. pl. / *interponer.*
interpuso he (she/it) interposed; past 3rd pers. sing. / *interponer.*
interrogar to interrogate. irr.
interrogue 1. that I may interrogate; pres. subj. 1st pers. sing. / *interrogar.* 2. that he (she/it) may interrogate; pres. subj. 3rd pers. sing. 3. let him (her/it) interrogate; impve. 3rd pers. sing.
interrogué I interrogated; past 1st pers. sing. / *interrogar.*
interroguéis that you (all) may interrogate; pres. subj. 2nd pers. pl. / *interrogar.*
interroguemos 1. that we may interrogate; pres. subj. 1st pers. pl. / *interrogar.* 2. let us interrogate; impve. 1st pers. pl.
interroguen 1. that they may interrogate; pres. subj. 3rd pers. pl. / *interrogar.* 2. let them interrogate; impve. 3rd pers. pl.
interrogues that you may interrogate; pres. subj. 2nd pers. sing. / *interrogar.*
interrumpir to interrupt. reg.
intersecándose intersecting; pres. part. / *intersecarse.*
intersecaos (you all) intersect; impve. 2nd pers. pl. / *intersecarse.*
intersecarse to intersect. reg.
intersécate (you) intersect; impve. 2nd pers. sing. / *intersecarse.*
intersecémonos let us intersect; impve. 1st pers. pl. / *intersecarse.*
intersécense let them intersect; impve. 3rd pers. pl. / *intersecarse.*
intersécese let him (her/it) intersect; impve. 3rd pers. sing. / *intersecarse.*
interven (you) intervene; impve. 2nd pers. sing. / *intervenir.*
intervendrá he (she/it) will intervene; fut. 3rd pers. sing. / *intervenir.*
intervendrán they will intervene; fut. 3rd pers. pl. / *intervenir.*
intervendrás you will intervene; fut. 2nd pers. sing. / *intervenir.*
intervendré I shall intervene; fut. 1st pers. sing. / *intervenir.*
intervendréis you (all) will intervene; fut. 2nd pers. pl. / *intervenir.*
intervendremos we shall intervene; fut. 1st pers. pl. / *intervenir.*
intervendría 1. I should intervene; cond. 1st pers. sing. / *intervenir.* 2. he (she/it) would intervene; cond. 3rd pers. sing.
intervendríais you (all) would intervene; cond. 2nd pers. pl. / *intervenir.*
intervendríamos we should intervene; cond. 1st pers. pl. / *intervenir.*
intervendrían they would intervene; cond. 3rd pers. pl. / *intervenir.*
intervendrías you would intervene; cond. 2nd pers. sing. / *intervenir.*

intervenga 1. that I may intervene; pres. subj. 1st pers. sing. / *intervenir*. 2. that he (she/it) may intervene; pres. subj. 3rd pers. sing. 3. let him (her/it) intervene; impve. 3rd pers. sing.

intervengáis that you (all) may intervene; pres. subj. 2nd pers. pl. / *intervenir*.

intervengamos 1. that we may intervene; pres. subj. 1st pers. pl. / *intervenir*. 2. let us intervene; impve. 1st pers. pl.

intervengan 1. that they may intervene; pres. subj. 3rd pers. pl. / *intervenir*. 2. let them intervene; impve. 3rd pers. pl.

intervengas that you may intervene; pres. subj. 2nd pers. sing. / *intervenir*.

intervengo I intervene; pres. ind. 1st pers. sing. / *intervenir*.

intervenir to intervene. irr.

interviene he (she/it) intervenes; pres. ind. 3rd pers. sing. / *intervenir*.

intervienen they intervene; pres. ind. 3rd pers. pl. / *intervenir*.

intervienes you intervene; pres. ind. 2nd pers. sing. / *intervenir*.

intervievar to have a meeting. reg.

interviewar to interview. reg.

intervine I intervened; past 1st pers. sing. / *intervenir*.

interviniendo intervening; pres. part. / *intervenir*.

interviniera 1. that I might intervene; imp. subj. 1st pers. sing. / *intervenir*. 2. that he (she/it) might intervene; imp. subj. 3rd pers. sing.

intervinierais that you (all) might intervene; imp. subj. 2nd pers pl. / *intervenir*.

interviniéramos that we might intervene; imp. subj. 1st pers. pl. / *intervenir*.

intervinieran that they might intervene; imp. subj. 3rd pers. pl. / *intervenir*.

intervinieras that you might intervene; imp. subj. 2nd pers. sing. / *intervenir*.

intervinieron they intervened; past 3rd pers. pl. / *intervenir*.

interviniese 1. that I might intervene; imp. subj. 1st pers. sing. / *intervenir*. 2. that he (she/it) might intervene; imp. subj. 3rd pers. sing.

intervinieseis that you (all) might intervene; imp. subj. 2nd pers pl. / *intervenir*.

interviniésemos that we might intervene; imp. subj. 1st pers. pl. / *intervenir*.

interviniesen that they might intervene; imp. subj. 3rd pers. pl. / *intervenir*.

intervinieses that you might intervene; imp. subj. 2nd pers. sing. / *intervenir*.

intervinimos we intervened; past 1st pers. pl. / *intervenir*.

interviniste you intervened; past 2nd pers. sing. / *intervenir*.

intervinisteis you (all) intervened; past 2nd pers. pl. / *intervenir*.

intervino he (she/it) intervened; past 3rd pers. sing. / *intervenir*.

intimándose becoming intimate; pres. part. / *intimarse*.

intimaos (you all) become intimate; impve. 2nd pers. pl. / *intimarse*.

intimar to intimate or to hint. reg.

intimarse to become intimate. reg.

intímate (you) become intimate; impve. 2nd pers. sing. / *intimarse*.

intimémonos let us become intimate; impve. 1st pers. pl. / *intimarse*.

intímense let them become intimate; impve. 3rd pers. pl. / *intimarse*.

intímese let him (her/it) become intimate; impve. 3rd pers. sing. / *intimarse*.

intimidándose losing courage; pres. part. / *intimidarse*.

intimidaos (you all) lose courage; impve. 2nd pers. pl. / *intimidarse*.

intimidar to intimidate. reg.

intimidarse to lose courage. reg.

intimídate (you) lose courage; impve. 2nd pers. sing. / *intimidarse*.

intimidémonos let us lose courage; impve. 1st pers. pl. / *intimidarse*.

intimídense let them lose courage; impve. 3rd pers. pl. / *intimidarse*.

intimídese let him (her/it) lose courage; impve. 3rd pers. sing. / *intimidarse*.

intitulándose being called; pres. part. / *intitularse*.

intitulaos (you all) be called; impve. 2nd pers. pl. / *intitularse*.

intitular to entitle. reg.

intitularse to be called. reg.

intitúlate (you) be called; impve. 2nd pers. sing. / *intitularse*.

intitulémonos let us be called; impve. 1st pers. pl. / *intitularse*.

intitúlense let them be called; impve. 3rd pers. pl. / *intitularse*.

intitúlese let him (her/it) be called; impve. 3rd pers. sing. / *intitularse*.

intoxicar to intoxicate. irr.

intoxique 1. that I may intoxicate; pres. subj. 1st pers. sing. / *intoxicar*. 2. that he (she/it) may intoxicate; pres. subj. 3rd pers. sing. 3. let him (her/it) intoxicate; impve. 3rd pers. sing.

intoxiqué I intoxicated; past 1st pers. sing. / *intoxicar*.

intoxiquéis that you (all) may intoxicate; pres. subj. 2nd pers. pl. / *intoxicar*.

intoxiquemos 1. that we may intoxicate; pres. subj. 1st pers. pl. / *intoxicar*. 2. let us intoxicate; impve. 1st pers. pl.

intoxiquen 1. that they may intoxicate; pres. subj. 3rd pers. pl. / *intoxicar*. 2. let them intoxicate; impve. 3rd pers. pl.

intoxiques that you may intoxicate; pres. subj. 2nd pers. sing. / *intoxicar*.

intranquilice 1. that I may worry; pres. subj. 1st pers. sing. / *intranquilizar*. 2. that he (she/it) may worry; pres. subj. 3rd pers. sing. 3. let him (her/it) worry; impve. 3rd pers. sing.

intranquilicé I worried; past 1st pers. sing. / *intranquilizar.*

intranquilicéis that you (all) may worry; pres. subj. 2nd pers. pl. / *intranquilizar.*

intranquilicémonos let us worry; impve. 1st pers. pl. / *intranquilizarse.*

intranquilicemos 1. that we may worry; pres. subj. 1st pers. pl. / *intranquilizar.* 2. let us worry; impve. 1st pers. pl.

intranquilicen 1. that they may worry; pres. subj. 3rd pers. pl. / *intranquilizar.* 2. let them worry; impve. 3rd pers. pl.

intranquilícense let them worry; impve. 3rd pers. pl. / *intranquilizarse.*

intranquilices that you may worry; pres. subj. 2nd pers. sing. / *intranquilizar.*

intranquilícese let him (her/it) worry; impve. 3rd pers. sing. / *intranquilizarse.*

intranquilizándose worrying; pres. part. / *intranquilizarse.*

intranquilizaos (you all) worry; impve. 2nd pers. pl. / *intranquilizarse.*

intranquilizar to worry. irr.

intranquilizarse to worry. irr.

intranquilízate (you) worry; impve. 2nd pers. sing. / *intranquilizarse.*

intrigar to intrigue. irr.

intrigue 1. that I may intrigue; pres. subj. 1st pers. sing. / *intrigar.* 2. that he (she/it) may intrigue; pres. subj. 3rd pers. sing. 3. let him (her/it) intrigue; impve. 3rd pers. sing.

intrigué I intrigued; past 1st pers. sing. / *intrigar.*

intriguéis that you (all) may intrigue; pres. subj. 2nd pers. pl. / *intrigar.*

intriguemos 1. that we may intrigue; pres. subj. 1st pers. pl. / *intrigar.* 2. let us intrigue; impve. 1st pers. pl.

intriguen 1. that they may intrigue; pres. subj. 3rd pers. pl. / *intrigar.* 2. let them intrigue; impve. 3rd pers. pl.

intrigues that you may intrigue; pres. subj. 2nd pers. sing. / *intrigar.*

intrincar to complicate. irr.

intrinque 1. that I may complicate; pres. subj. 1st pers. sing. / *intrincar.* 2. that he (she/it) may complicate; pres. subj. 3rd pers. sing. 3. let him (her/it) complicate; impve. 3rd pers. sing.

intrinqué I complicated; past 1st pers. sing. / *intrincar.*

intrinquéis that you (all) may complicate; pres. subj. 2nd pers. pl. / *intrincar.*

intrinquemos 1. that we may complicate; pres. subj. 1st pers. pl. / *intrincar.* 2. let us complicate; impve. 1st pers. pl.

intrinquen 1. that they may complicate; pres. subj. 3rd pers. pl. / *intrincar.* 2. let them complicate; impve. 3rd pers. pl.

intrinques that you may complicate; pres. subj. 2nd pers. sing. / *intrincar.*

introdúcete (you) interfere; impve. 2nd pers. sing. / *introducirse.*

introduciéndose interfering; pres. part. / *introducirse.*

introducíos (you all) interfere; impve. 2nd pers. pl. / *introducirse.*

introducir to introduce. irr.

introducirse to interfere. irr.

introduje I introduced; past 1st pers. sing. / *introducir.*

introdujera 1. that I might introduce; imp. subj. 1st pers. sing. / *introducir.* 2. that he (she/it) might introduce; imp. subj. 3rd pers. sing.

introdujerais that you (all) might introduce; imp. subj. 2nd pers pl. / *introducir.*

introdujéramos that we might introduce; imp. subj. 1st pers. pl. / *introducir.*

introdujeran that they might introduce; imp. subj. 3rd pers. pl. / *introducir.*

introdujeras that you might introduce; imp. subj. 2nd pers. sing. / *introducir.*

introdujeron they introduced; past 3rd pers. pl. / *introducir.*

introdujese 1. that I might introduce; imp. subj. 1st pers. sing. / *introducir.* 2. that he (she/it) might introduce; imp. subj. 3rd pers. sing.

introdujeseis that you (all) might introduce; imp. subj. 2nd pers pl. / *introducir.*

introdujésemos that we might introduce; imp. subj. 1st pers. pl. / *introducir.*

introdujesen that they might introduce; imp. subj. 3rd pers. pl. / *introducir.*

introdujeses that you might introduce; imp. subj. 2nd pers. sing. / *introducir.*

introdujimos we introduced; past 1st pers. pl. / *introducir.*

introdujiste you introduced; past 2nd pers. sing. / *introducir.*

introdujisteis you (all) introduced; past 2nd pers. pl. / *introducir.*

introdujo he (she/it) introduced; past 3rd pers. sing. / *introducir.*

introduzca 1. that I may introduce; pres. subj. 1st pers. sing. / *introducir.* 2. that he (she/it) may introduce; pres. subj. 3rd pers. sing. 3. let him (her/it) introduce; impve. 3rd pers. sing.

introduzcáis that you (all) may introduce; pres. subj. 2nd pers. pl. / *introducir.*

introduzcámonos let us interfere; impve. 1st pers. pl. / *introducirse.*

introduzcamos 1. that we may introduce; pres. subj. 1st pers. pl. / *introducir.* 2. let us introduce; impve. 1st pers. pl.

introduzcan 1. that they may introduce; pres. subj. 3rd pers. pl. / *introducir.* 2. let them introduce; impve. 3rd pers. pl.

introdúzcanse let them interfere; impve. 3rd pers. pl. / *introducirse.*

introduzcas that you may introduce; pres. subj. 2nd pers. sing. / *introducir.*

introdúzcase let him (her/it) interfere; impve. 3rd pers. sing. / *introducirse.*

introduzco I introduce; pres. ind. 1st pers. sing. / *introducir.*

intrusear to intrude. reg.

intuir to sense by intuition. irr.

intuya 1. that I may sense by intuition; pres. subj. 1st pers. sing. / *intuir*. 2. that he (she/it) may sense by intuition; pres. subj. 3rd pers. sing. 3. let him (her/it) sense by intuition; impve. 3rd pers. sing.

intuyáis that you (all) may sense by intuition; pres. subj. 2nd pers. pl. / *intuir*.

intuyamos 1. that we may sense by intuition; pres. subj. 1st pers. pl. / *intuir*. 2. let us sense by intuition; impve. 1st pers. pl.

intuyan 1. that they may sense by intuition; pres. subj. 3rd pers. pl. / *intuir*. 2. let them sense by intuition; impve. 3rd pers. pl.

intuyas that you may sense by intuition; pres. subj. 2nd pers. sing. / *intuir*.

intuye 1. he (she/it) senses by intuition; pres. ind. 3rd pers. sing. / *intuir*. 2. (you) sense by intuition; impve. 2nd pers. sing.

intuyen they sense by intuition; pres. ind. 3rd pers. pl. / *intuir*.

intuyendo sensing by intuition; pres. part. / *intuir*.

intuyera 1. that I might sense by intuition; imp. subj. 1st pers. sing. / *intuir*. 2. that he (she/it) might sense by intuition; imp. subj. 3rd pers. sing.

intuyerais that you (all) might sense by intuition; imp. subj. 2nd pers pl. / *intuir*.

intuyéramos that we might sense by intuition; imp. subj. 1st pers. pl. / *intuir*.

intuyeran that they might sense by intuition; imp. subj. 3rd pers. pl. / *intuir*.

intuyeras that you might sense by intuition; imp. subj. 2nd pers. sing. / *intuir*.

intuyeron they sensed by intuition; past 3rd pers. pl. / *intuir*.

intuyes you sense by intuition; pres. ind. 2nd pers. sing. / *intuir*.

intuyese 1. that I might sense by intuition; imp. subj. 1st pers. sing. / *intuir*. 2. that he (she/it) might sense by intuition; imp. subj. 3rd pers. sing.

intuyeseis that you (all) might sense by intuition; imp. subj. 2nd pers pl. / *intuir*.

intuyésemos that we might sense by intuition; imp. subj. 1st pers. pl. / *intuir*.

intuyesen that they might sense by intuition; imp. subj. 3rd pers. pl. / *intuir*.

intuyeses that you might sense by intuition; imp. subj. 2nd pers. sing. / *intuir*.

intuyo I sense by intuition; pres. ind. 1st pers. sing. / *intuir*.

intuyó he (she/it) sensed by intuition; past 3rd pers. sing. / *intuir*.

inundar to inundate or to flood. reg.

inutilice 1. that I may make useless; pres. subj. 1st pers. sing. / *inutilizar*. 2. that he (she/it) may make useless; pres. subj. 3rd pers. sing. 3. let him (her/it) make useless; impve. 3rd pers. sing.

inutilicé I made useless; past 1st pers. sing. / *inutilizar*.

inutilicéis that you (all) may make useless; pres. subj. 2nd pers. pl. / *inutilizar*.

inutilicémonos let us become useless; impve. 1st pers. pl. / *inutilizarse*.

inutilicemos 1. that we may make useless; pres. subj. 1st pers. pl. / *inutilizar*. 2. let us make useless; impve. 1st pers. pl.

inutilicen 1. that they may make useless; pres. subj. 3rd pers. pl. / *inutilizar*. 2. let them make useless; impve. 3rd pers. pl.

inutilícense let them become useless; impve. 3rd pers. pl. / *inutilizarse*.

inutilices that you may make useless; pres. subj. 2nd pers. sing. / *inutilizar*.

inutilícese let him (her/it) become useless; impve. 3rd pers. sing. / *inutilizarse*.

inutilizándose becoming useless; pres. part. / *inutilizarse*.

inutilizaos (you all) become useless; impve. 2nd pers. pl. / *inutilizarse*.

inutilizar to make useless. irr.

inutilizarse to become useless. irr.

inutilízate (you) become useless; impve. 2nd pers. sing. / *inutilizarse*.

invadir to invade. reg.

invalidar to invalidate. reg.

inventar to invent. reg.

inventaría 1. he (she/it) inventories; pres. ind. 3rd pers. sing. / *inventariar*. 2. (you) inventory; impve. 2nd pers. sing.

inventarían they inventory; pres. ind. 3rd pers. pl. / *inventariar*.

inventariar to inventory. irr.

inventarías you inventory; pres. ind. 2nd pers. sing. / *inventariar*.

inventaríe 1. that I may inventory; pres. subj. 1st pers. sing. / *inventariar*. 2. that he (she/it) may inventory; pres. subj. 3rd pers. sing. 3. let him (her/it) inventory; impve. 3rd pers. sing.

inventaríen 1. that they may inventory; pres. subj. 3rd pers. pl. / *inventariar*. 2. let them inventory; impve. 3rd pers. pl.

inventaríes that you may inventory; pres. subj. 2nd pers. sing. / *inventariar*.

inventarío I inventory; pres. ind. 1st pers. sing. / *inventariar*.

invernar to winter. irr.

invertir to invert or to invest. irr.

investigar to investigate. irr.

investigue 1. that I may investigate; pres. subj. 1st pers. sing. / *investigar*. 2. that he (she/it) may investigate; pres. subj. 3rd pers. sing. 3. let him (her/it) investigate; impve. 3rd pers. sing.

investigué I investigated; past 1st pers. sing. / *investigar*.

investiguéis that you (all) may investigate; pres. subj. 2nd pers. pl. / *investigar*.

investiguemos 1. that we may investigate; pres. subj. 1st pers. pl. / *investigar*. 2. let us investigate; impve. 1st pers. pl.

investiguen 1. that they may investigate; pres. subj. 3rd pers. pl. / *investigar*. 2. let them investigate; impve. 3rd pers. pl.

investigues that you may investigate; pres. subj. 2nd pers. sing. / *investigar.*

investir to invest or to endow. irr.

inveterándose getting old; pres. part. / *inveterarse.*

inveteraos (you all) get old; impve. 2nd pers. pl. / *inveterarse.*

inveterarse to get old. reg.

invetérate (you) get old; impve. 2nd pers. sing. / *inveterarse.*

inveterémonos let us get old; impve. 1st pers. pl. / *inveterarse.*

invetérense let them get old; impve. 3rd pers. pl. / *inveterarse.*

invetérese let him (her/it) get old; impve. 3rd pers. sing. / *inveterarse.*

invierna 1. he (she/it) winters; pres. ind. 3rd pers. sing. / *invernar.* 2. (you) winter; impve. 2nd pers. sing.

inviernan they winter; pres. ind. 3rd pers. pl. / *invernar.*

inviernas you winter; pres. ind. 2nd pers. sing. / *invernar.*

invierne 1. that I may winter; pres. subj. 1st pers. sing. / *invernar.* 2. that he (she/it) may winter; pres. subj. 3rd pers. sing. 3. let him (her/it) winter; impve. 3rd pers. sing.

inviernen 1. that they may winter; pres. subj. 3rd pers. pl. / *invernar.* 2. let them winter; impve. 3rd pers. pl.

inviernes that you may winter; pres. subj. 2nd pers. sing. / *invernar.*

invierno I winter; pres. ind. 1st pers. sing. / *invernar.*

invierta 1. that I may invert; pres. subj. 1st pers. sing. / *invertir.* 2. that he (she/it) may invert; pres. subj. 3rd pers. sing. 3. let him (her/it) invert; impve. 3rd pers. sing.

inviertan 1. that they may invert; pres. subj. 3rd pers. pl. / *invertir.* 2. let them invert; impve. 3rd pers. pl.

inviertas that you may invert; pres. subj. 2nd pers. sing. / *invertir.*

invierte 1. he (she/it) inverts; pres. ind. 3rd pers. sing. / *invertir.* 2. (you) invert; impve. 2nd pers. sing.

invierten they invert; pres. ind. 3rd pers. pl. / *invertir.*

inviertes you invert; pres. ind. 2nd pers. sing. / *invertir.*

invierto I invert; pres. ind. 1st pers. sing. / *invertir.*

invirtáis that you (all) may invert; pres. subj. 2nd pers. pl. / *invertir.*

invirtamos 1. that we may invert; pres. subj. 1st pers. pl. / *invertir.* 2. let us invert; impve. 1st pers. pl.

invirtiendo inverting; pres. part. / *invertir.*

invirtiera 1. that I might invert; imp. subj. 1st pers. sing. / *invertir.* 2. that he (she/it) might invert; imp. subj. 3rd pers. sing.

invirtierais that you (all) might invert; imp. subj. 2nd pers pl. / *invertir.*

invirtiéramos that we might invert; imp. subj. 1st pers. pl. / *invertir.*

invirtieran that they might invert; imp. subj. 3rd pers. pl. / *invertir.*

invirtieras that you might invert; imp. subj. 2nd pers. sing. / *invertir.*

invirtieron they inverted; past 3rd pers. pl. / *invertir.*

invirtiese 1. that I might invert; imp. subj. 1st pers. sing. / *invertir.* 2. that he (she/it) might invert; imp. subj. 3rd pers. sing.

invirtieseis that you (all) might invert; imp. subj. 2nd pers pl. / *invertir.*

invirtiésemos that we might invert; imp. subj. 1st pers. pl. / *invertir.*

invirtiesen that they might invert; imp. subj. 3rd pers. pl. / *invertir.*

invirtieses that you might invert; imp. subj. 2nd pers. sing. / *invertir.*

invirtió he (she/it) inverted; past 3rd pers. sing. / *invertir.*

invista 1. that I may invest; pres. subj. 1st pers. sing. / *investir.* 2. that he (she/it) may invest; pres. subj. 3rd pers. sing. 3. let him (her/it) invest; impve. 3rd pers. sing.

invistáis that you (all) may invest; pres. subj. 2nd pers. pl. / *investir.*

invistamos 1. that we may invest; pres. subj. 1st pers. pl. / *investir.* 2. let us invest; impve. 1st pers. pl.

invistan 1. that they may invest; pres. subj. 3rd pers. pl. / *investir.* 2. let them invest; impve. 3rd pers. pl.

invistas that you may invest; pres. subj. 2nd pers. sing. / *investir.*

inviste 1. he (she/it) invests; pres. ind. 3rd pers. sing. / *investir.* 2. (you) invest; impve. 2nd pers. sing.

invisten they invest; pres. ind. 3rd pers. pl. / *investir.*

invistes you invest; pres. ind. 2nd pers. sing. / *investir.*

invistiendo investing; pres. part. / *investir.*

invistiera 1. that I might invest; imp. subj. 1st pers. sing. / *investir.* 2. that he (she/it) might invest; imp. subj. 3rd pers. sing.

invistierais that you (all) might invest; imp. subj. 2nd pers pl. / *investir.*

invistiéramos that we might invest; imp. subj. 1st pers. pl. / *investir.*

invistieran that they might invest; imp. subj. 3rd pers. pl. / *investir.*

invistieras that you might invest; imp. subj. 2nd pers. sing. / *investir.*

invistieron they invested; past 3rd pers. pl. / *investir.*

invistiese 1. that I might invest; imp. subj. 1st pers. sing. / *investir.* 2. that he (she/it) might invest; imp. subj. 3rd pers. sing.

invistieseis that you (all) might invest; imp. subj. 2nd pers pl. / *investir.*

invistiésemos that we might invest; imp. subj. 1st pers. pl. / *investir.*

invistiesen that they might invest; imp. subj. 3rd pers. pl. / *investir.*

invistieses that you might invest; imp. subj. 2nd pers. sing. / *investir.*

invistió he (she/it) invested; past 3rd pers. sing. / *investir.*

invisto I invest; pres. ind. 1st pers. sing. / *investir.*

invitar to invite. reg.

invocar to invoke. irr.
involucrar to involve. reg.
invoque 1. that I may invoke; pres. subj. 1st pers.
sing. / *invocar*. 2. that he (she/it) may invoke; pres.
subj. 3rd pers. sing. 3. let him (her/it) invoke; impve.
3rd pers. sing.
invoqué I invoked; past 1st pers. sing. / *invocar*.
invoquéis that you (all) may invoke; pres. subj. 2nd
pers. pl. / *invocar*.
invoquemos 1. that we may invoke; pres. subj. 1st
pers. pl. / *invocar*. 2. let us invoke; impve. 1st pers.
pl.
invoquen 1. that they may invoke; pres. subj. 3rd
pers. pl. / *invocar*. 2. let them invoke; impve. 3rd
pers. pl.
invoques that you may invoke; pres. subj. 2nd pers.
sing. / *invocar*.
inyectar to inject. reg.
ir to go. irr.
irga 1. that I may erect; pres. subj. 1st pers. sing. /
erguir. 2. that he (she/it) may erect; pres. subj. 3rd
pers. sing. 3. let him (her/it) erect; impve. 3rd pers.
sing.
irgáis that you (all) may erect; pres. subj. 2nd pers.
pl. / *erguir*.
irgámonos let us straighten; impve. 1st pers. pl. /
erguirse.
irgamos 1. that we may erect; pres. subj. 1st pers. pl.
/ *erguir*. 2. let us erect; impve. 1st pers. pl.
irgan 1. that they may erect; pres. subj. 3rd pers. pl. /
erguir. 2. let them erect; impve. 3rd pers. pl.
írganse let them straighten; impve. 3rd pers. pl. /
erguirse.
irgas that you may erect; pres. subj. 2nd pers. sing. /
erguir.
írgase let him (her/it) straighten; impve. 3rd pers.
sing. / *erguirse*.
irgo I erect; pres. ind. 1st pers. sing. / *erguir*.
irgue 1. he (she/it) erects; pres. ind. 3rd pers. sing. /
erguir. 2. (you) erect; impve. 2nd pers. sing.
irguen they erect; pres. ind. 3rd pers. pl. / *erguir*.
irgues you erect; pres. ind. 2nd pers. sing. / *erguir*.
írguete (you) straighten; impve. 2nd pers. sing. /
erguirse.
irguiendo erecting; pres. part. / *erguir*.
irguiéndose straightening; pres. part. / *erguirse*.
irguiera 1. that I might erect; imp. subj. 1st pers.
sing. / *erguir*. 2. that he (she/it) might erect; imp.
subj. 3rd pers. sing.
irguierais that you (all) might erect; imp. subj. 2nd
pers pl. / *erguir*.
irguiéramos that we might erect; imp. subj. 1st pers.
pl. / *erguir*.
irguieran that they might erect; imp. subj. 3rd pers.
pl. / *erguir*.
irguieras that you might erect; imp. subj. 2nd pers.
sing. / *erguir*.
irguieron they erected; past 3rd pers. pl. / *erguir*.

irguiese 1. that I might erect; imp. subj. 1st pers. sing.
/ *erguir*. 2. that he (she/it) might erect; imp. subj. 3rd
pers. sing.
irguieseis that you (all) might erect; imp. subj. 2nd
pers pl. / *erguir*.
irguiésemos that we might erect; imp. subj. 1st pers.
pl. / *erguir*.
irguiesen that they might erect; imp. subj. 3rd pers.
pl. / *erguir*.
irguieses that you might erect; imp. subj. 2nd pers.
sing. / *erguir*.
irguió he (she/it) erected; past 3rd pers. sing. / *erguir*.
ironice 1. that I may be ironic; pres. subj. 1st pers.
sing. / *ironizar*. 2. that he (she/it) may be ironic;
pres. subj. 3rd pers. sing. 3. let him (her/it) be
ironic; impve. 3rd pers. sing.
ironicé I was ironic; past 1st pers. sing. / *ironizar*.
ironicéis that you (all) may be ironic; pres. subj. 2nd
pers. pl. / *ironizar*.
ironicemos 1. that we may be ironic; pres. subj. 1st
pers. pl. / *ironizar*. 2. let us be ironic; impve. 1st
pers. pl.
ironicen 1. that they may be ironic; pres. subj. 3rd
pers. pl. / *ironizar*. 2. let them be ironic; impve. 3rd
pers. pl.
ironices that you may be ironic; pres. subj. 2nd pers.
sing. / *ironizar*.
ironizar to be ironic. irr.
irradiar to radiate. reg.
irrigar to irrigate. irr.
irrigue 1. that I may irrigate; pres. subj. 1st pers. sing.
/ *irrigar*. 2. that he (she/it) may irrigate; pres. subj.
3rd pers. sing. 3. let him (her/it) irrigate; impve. 3rd
pers. sing.
irrigué I irrigated; past 1st pers. sing. / *irrigar*.
irriguéis that you (all) may irrigate; pres. subj. 2nd
pers. pl. / *irrigar*.
irriguemos 1. that we may irrigate; pres. subj. 1st
pers. pl. / *irrigar*. 2. let us irrigate; impve. 1st pers. pl.
irriguen 1. that they may irrigate; pres. subj. 3rd
pers. pl. / *irrigar*. 2. let them irrigate; impve. 3rd
pers. pl.
irrigues that you may irrigate; pres. subj. 2nd pers.
sing. / *irrigar*.
irritándose becoming irritated; pres. part. / *irritarse*.
irritaos (you all) become irritated; impve. 2nd pers.
pl. / *irritarse*.
irritar to irritate. reg.
irritarse to become irritated. reg.
irrítate (you) become irritated; impve. 2nd pers.
sing. / *irritarse*.
irritémonos let us become irritated; impve. 1st pers.
pl. / *irritarse*.
irrítense let them become irritated; impve. 3rd pers.
pl. / *irritarse*.
irrítese let him (her/it) become irritated; impve. 3rd
pers. sing. / *irritarse*.
irruir to invade. irr.
irrumpir to burst. reg.

irruya 1. that I may invade; pres. subj. 1st pers. sing. / *irruir*. 2. that he (she/it) may invade; pres. subj. 3rd pers. sing. 3. let him (her/it) invade; impve. 3rd pers. sing.
irruyáis that you (all) may invade; pres. subj. 2nd pers. pl. / *irruir*.
irruyamos 1. that we may invade; pres. subj. 1st pers. pl. / *irruir*. 2. let us invade; impve. 1st pers. pl.
irruyan 1. that they may invade; pres. subj. 3rd pers. pl. / *irruir*. 2. let them invade; impve. 3rd pers. pl.
irruyas that you may invade; pres. subj. 2nd pers. sing. / *irruir*.
irruye 1. he (she/it) invades; pres. ind. 3rd pers. sing. / *irruir*. 2. (you) invade; impve. 2nd pers. sing.
irruyen they invade; pres. ind. 3rd pers. pl. / *irruir*.
irruyendo invading; pres. part. / *irruir*.
irruyera 1. that I might invade; imp. subj. 1st pers. sing. / *irruir*. 2. that he (she/it) might invade; imp. subj. 3rd pers. sing.
irruyerais that you (all) might invade; imp. subj. 2nd pers pl. / *irruir*.
irruyéramos that we might invade; imp. subj. 1st pers. pl. / *irruir*.
irruyeran that they might invade; imp. subj. 3rd pers. pl. / *irruir*.
irruyeras that you might invade; imp. subj. 2nd pers. sing. / *irruir*.
irruyeron they invaded; past 3rd pers. pl. / *irruir*.
irruyes you invade; pres. ind. 2nd pers. sing. / *irruir*.
irruyese 1. that I might invade; imp. subj. 1st pers. sing. / *irruir*. 2. that he (she/it) might invade; imp. subj. 3rd pers. sing.
irruyeseis that you (all) might invade; imp. subj. 2nd pers pl. / *irruir*.
irruyésemos that we might invade; imp. subj. 1st pers. pl. / *irruir*.
irruyesen that they might invade; imp. subj. 3rd pers. pl. / *irruir*.
irruyeses that you might invade; imp. subj. 2nd pers. sing. / *irruir*.
irruyo I invade; pres. ind. 1st pers. sing. / *irruir*.
irruyó he (she/it) invaded; past 3rd pers. sing. / *irruir*.
irse to go away. irr.
iterar to iterate. reg.
izar to hoist. irr.
izquierdear to go wrong. reg.

J

jabonar to soap or to scold. reg.
jacarear to sing gay ballads. reg.
jactándose boasting; pres. part. / *jactarse*.
jactaos (you all) boast; impve. 2nd pers. pl. / *jactarse*.
jactarse to boast. reg.
jáctate (you) boast; impve. 2nd pers. sing. / *jactarse*.
jactémonos let us boast; impve. 1st pers. pl. / *jactarse*.
jáctense let them boast; impve. 3rd pers. pl. / *jactarse*.
jáctese let him (her/it) boast; impve. 3rd pers. sing. / *jactarse*.

jadear to pant. reg.
jalándose getting drunk; pres. part. / *jalarse*.
jalaos (you all) get drunk; impve. 2nd pers. pl. / *jalarse*.
jalar to pull or to woo. reg.
jalarse to get drunk. reg.
jálate (you) get drunk; impve. 2nd pers. sing. / *jalarse*.
jaleándose having noisy fun; pres. part. / *jalearse*.
jaleaos (you all) have noisy fun; impve. 2nd pers. pl. / *jalearse*.
jalear to spur on. reg.-ar conju.
jalearse to have noisy fun. reg.
jaléate (you) have noisy fun; impve. 2nd pers. sing. / *jalearse*.
jaleémonos let us have noisy fun; impve. 1st pers. pl. / *jalearse*.
jaléense let them have noisy fun; impve. 3rd pers. pl. / *jalearse*.
jaléese let him (her/it) have noisy fun; impve. 3rd pers. sing. / *jalearse*.
jalémonos let us get drunk; impve. 1st pers. pl. / *jalarse*.
jálense let them get drunk; impve. 3rd pers. pl. / *jalarse*.
jálese let him (her/it) get drunk; impve. 3rd pers. sing. / *jalarse*.
jalonar to mark. reg.
jalonear to pull. reg.
jamar to gorge. reg.
jaquear to check (chess) or to bully. reg.
jaspear to vein or to marble. reg.
jeringar to squirt. irr.
jeringue 1. that I may squirt; pres. subj. 1st pers. sing. / *jeringar*. 2. that he (she/it) may squirt; pres. subj. 3rd pers. sing. 3. let him (her/it) squirt; impve. 3rd pers. sing.
jeringué I squirted; past 1st pers. sing. / *jeringar*.
jeringuéis that you (all) may squirt; pres. subj. 2nd pers. pl. / *jeringar*.
jeringuemos 1. that we may squirt; pres. subj. 1st pers. pl. / *jeringar*. 2. let us squirt; impve. 1st pers. pl.
jeringuen 1. that they may squirt; pres. subj. 3rd pers. pl. / *jeringar*. 2. let them squirt; impve. 3rd pers. pl.
jeringues that you may squirt; pres. subj. 2nd pers. sing. / *jeringar*.
jineteándose showing off; pres. part. / *jinetearse*.
jineteaos (you all) show off; impve. 2nd pers. pl. / *jinetearse*.
jinetear to ride horseback. reg.
jinetearse to show off. reg.
jinetéate (you) show off; impve. 2nd pers. sing. / *jinetearse*.
jineteémonos let us show off; impve. 1st pers. pl. / *jinetearse*.
jinetéense let them show off; impve. 3rd pers. pl. / *jinetearse*.
jinetéese let him (her/it) show off; impve. 3rd pers. sing. / *jinetearse*.
jinglar to sway. reg.

jorobar to bother. reg.
jubilándose being pensioned; pres. part. / *jubilarse.*
jubilaos (you all) be pensioned; impve. 2nd pers. pl. / *jubilarse.*
jilar to retire. reg.
jubilarse to be pensioned. reg.
jubílate (you) be pensioned; impve. 2nd pers. sing. / *jubilarse.*
jubilémonos let us be pensioned; impve. 1st pers. pl. / *jubilarse.*
jubílense let them be pensioned; impve. 3rd pers. pl. / *jubilarse.*
jubílese let him (her/it) be pensioned; impve. 3rd pers. sing. / *jubilarse.*
judaice 1. that I may judaize; pres. subj. 1st pers. sing. / *judaizar.* 2.that he (she/it) may judaize; pres. subj. 3rd pers. sing. 3. let him (her/it) judaize; impve. 3rd pers. sing.
judaicé I judaized; past 1st pers. sing. / *judaizar.*
judaicéis that you (all) may judaize; pres. subj. 2nd pers. pl. / *judaizar.*
judaicemos 1. that we may judaize; pres. subj. 1st pers. pl. / *judaizar.* 2. let us judaize; impve. 1st pers. pl.
judaicen 1. that they may judaize; pres. subj. 3rd pers. pl. / *judaizar.* 2. let them judaize; impve. 3rd pers. pl.
judaices that you may judaize; pres. subj. 2nd pers. sing. / *judaizar.*
judaizar to judaize. irr.
juega 1. he (she/it) plays; pres. ind. 3rd pers. sing. / *jugar.* 2. (you) play; impve. 2nd pers. sing.
juegan they play; pres. ind. 3rd pers. pl. / *jugar.*
juegas you play; pres. ind. 2nd pers. sing. / *jugar.*
juégate (you) gamble; impve. 2nd pers. sing. / *jugarse.*
juego I play; pres. ind. 1st pers. sing. / *jugar.*
juegue 1. that I may play; pres. subj. 1st pers. sing. / *jugar.* 2. that he (she/it) may play; pres. subj. 3rd pers. sing. 3. let him (her/it) play; impve. 3rd pers. sing.
jueguen 1. that they may play; pres. subj. 3rd pers. pl. / *jugar.* 2. let them play; impve. 3rd pers. pl.
juéguense let them gamble; impve. 3rd pers. pl. / *jugarse.*
juegues that you may play; pres. subj. 2nd pers. sing. / *jugar.*
juéguese let him (her/it) gamble; impve. 3rd pers. sing. / *jugarse.*
jugándose gambling; pres. part. / *jugarse.*
jugaos (you all) gamble; impve. 2nd pers. pl. / *jugarse.*
jugar to play. irr.
jugarse to gamble. irr.
jugué I played; past 1st pers. sing. / *jugar.*
juguéis that you (all) may play; pres. subj. 2nd pers. pl. / *jugar.*
juguémonos let us gamble; impve. 1st pers. pl. / *jugarse.*
juguemos 1. that we may play; pres. subj. 1st pers. pl. / *jugar.* 2. let us play; impve. 1st pers. pl.

juguetear to play around. reg.
juntándose assembling; pres. part. / *juntarse.*
juntaos (you all) assemble; impve. 2nd pers. pl. / *juntarse.*
juntar to join. reg.
juntarse to assemble. reg.
júntate (you) assemble; impve. 2nd pers. sing. / *juntarse.*
juntémonos let us assemble; impve. 1st pers. pl. / *juntarse.*
júntense let them assemble; impve. 3rd pers. pl. / *juntarse.*
júntese let him (her/it) assemble; impve. 3rd pers. sing. / *juntarse.*
juramentándose taking an oath; pres. part. / *juramentarse.*
juramentaos (you all) take an oath; impve. 2nd pers. pl. / *juramentarse.*
juramentar to swear in. reg.
juramentarse to take an oath. reg.
juraméntate (you) take an oath; impve. 2nd pers. sing. / *juramentarse.*
juramentémonos let us take an oath; impve. 1st pers. pl. / *juramentarse.*
juraméntense let them take an oath; impve. 3rd pers. pl. / *juramentarse.*
juraméntese let him (her/it) take an oath; impve. 3rd pers. sing. / *juramentarse.*
jurándose cursing; pres. part. / *jurarse.*
juraos (you all) curse; impve. 2nd pers. pl. / *jurarse.*
jurar to swear. reg.
jurarse to curse. reg.
júrate (you) curse; impve. 2nd pers. sing. / *jurarse.*
jurémonos let us curse; impve. 1st pers. pl. / *jurarse.*
júrense let them curse; impve. 3rd pers. pl. / *jurarse.*
júrese let him (her/it) curse; impve. 3rd pers. sing. / *jurarse.*
justar to joust or to tilt. reg.
justificar to justify. irr.
justifique 1. that I may justify; pres. subj. 1st pers. sing. / *justificar.* 2. that he (she/it) may justify; pres. subj. 3rd pers. sing. 3. let him (her/it) justify; impve. 3rd pers. sing.
justifiqué I justified; past 1st pers. sing. / *justificar.*
justifiquéis that you (all) may justify; pres. subj. 2nd pers. pl. / *justificar.*
justifiquemos 1. that we may justify; pres. subj. 1st pers. pl. / *justificar.* 2. let us justify; impve. 1st pers. pl.
justifiquen 1. that they may justify; pres. subj. 3rd pers. pl. / *justificar.* 2. let them justify; impve. 3rd pers. pl.
justifiques that you may justify; pres. subj. 2nd pers. sing. / *justificar.*
juzgar to judge. irr.
juzgue 1. that I may judge; pres. subj. 1st pers. sing. / *juzgar.* 2. that he (she/it) may judge; pres. subj. 3rd pers. sing. 3. let him (her/it) judge; impve. 3rd pers. sing.
juzgué I judged; past 1st pers. sing. / *juzgar.*

juzguéis that you (all) may judge; pres. subj. 2nd pers. pl. / *juzgar.*

juzguemos 1. that we may judge; pres. subj. 1st pers. pl. / *juzgar.* 2. let us judge; impve. 1st pers. pl.

juzguen 1. that they may judge; pres. subj. 3rd pers. pl. / *juzgar.* 2. let them judge; impve. 3rd pers. pl.

juzgues that you may judge; pres. subj. 2nd pers. sing. / *juzgar.*

L

laborar to work. reg.

laborear to work (a mine). reg.

labrar to till or to work. reg.

lace 1. that I may lasso; pres. subj. 1st pers. sing. / *lazar.* 2. that he (she/it) may lasso; pres. subj. 3rd pers. sing. 3. let him (her/it) lasso; impve. 3rd pers. sing.

lacé I lassoed; past 1st pers. sing. / *lazar.*

lacear to adorn or to lasso. reg.

lacéis that you (all) may lasso; pres. subj. 2nd pers. pl. / *lazar.*

lacemos 1. that we may lasso; pres. subj. 1st pers. pl. / *lazar.* 2. let us lasso; impve. 1st pers. pl.

lacen 1. that they may lasso; pres. subj. 3rd pers. pl. / *lazar.* 2. let them lasso; impve. 3rd pers. pl.

lacerar to lacerate. reg.

laces that you may lasso; pres. subj. 2nd pers. sing. / *lazar.*

lacrándose being stricken; pres. part. / *lacrarse.*

lacraos (you all) be stricken; impve. 2nd pers. pl. / *lacrarse.*

lacrar to impair the health of. reg.

lacrarse to be stricken. reg.

lácrate (you) be stricken; impve. 2nd pers. sing. / *lacrarse.*

lacrémonos let us be stricken; impve. 1st pers. pl. / *lacrarse.*

lácrense let them be stricken; impve. 3rd pers. pl. / *lacrarse.*

lácrese let him (her/it) be stricken; impve. 3rd pers. sing. / *lacrarse.*

lactar to suckle or to nurse. reg.

ladeándose swaying; pres. part. / *ladearse.*

ladeaos (you all) sway; impve. 2nd pers. pl. / *ladearse.*

ladear to tilt. reg.

ladearse to sway. reg.

ladéate (you) sway; impve. 2nd pers. sing. / *ladearse.*

ladeémonos let us sway; impve. 1st pers. pl. / *ladearse.*

ladéense let them sway; impve. 3rd pers. pl. / *ladearse.*

ladéese let him (her/it) sway; impve. 3rd pers. sing. / *ladearse.*

ladrar to bark. reg.

ladrillar to brick. reg.

ladronear to thieve. reg.

lagrimar to weep. reg.

lagrimear to shed tears. reg.

laicice 1. that I may secularize; pres. subj. 1st pers. sing. / *laicizar.* 2. that he (she/it) may secularize; pres. subj. 3rd pers. sing. 3. let him (her/it) secularize; impve. 3rd pers. sing.

laicicé I secularized; past 1st pers. sing. / *laicizar.*

laicicéis that you (all) may secularize; pres. subj. 2nd pers. pl. / *laicizar.*

laicicemos 1. that we may secularize; pres. subj. 1st pers. pl. / *laicizar.* 2. let us secularize; impve. 1st pers. pl.

laicicen 1. that they may secularize; pres. subj. 3rd pers. pl. / *laicizar.* 2. let them secularize; impve. 3rd pers. pl.

laicices that you may secularize; pres. subj. 2nd pers. sing. / *laicizar.*

laicizar to secularize. irr.

lamentándose moaning; pres. part. / *lamentarse.*

lamentaos (you all) moan; impve. 2nd pers. pl. / *lamentarse.*

lamentar to lament. reg.

lamentarse to moan or to complain. reg.

laméntate (you) moan; impve. 2nd pers. sing. / *lamentarse.*

lamentémonos let us moan; impve. 1st pers. pl. / *lamentarse.*

laméntense let them moan; impve. 3rd pers. pl. / *lamentarse.*

laméntese let him (her/it) moan; impve. 3rd pers. sing. / *lamentarse.*

lamer to lick or to lap. reg.

laminar to laminate. reg.

lampacear to mop or to swab. reg.

lampear to shovel. reg.

lance 1. that I may hurl; pres. subj. 1st pers. sing. / *lanzar.* 2. that he (she/it) may hurl; pres. subj. 3rd pers. sing. 3. let him (her/it) hurl; impve. 3rd pers. sing.

lancé I hurled; past 1st pers. sing. / *lanzar.*

lancear to lance or to spear. reg.

lancéis that you (all) may hurl; pres. subj. 2nd pers. pl. / *lanzar.*

lancémonos let us rush; impve. 1st pers. pl. / *lanzarse.*

lancemos 1. that we may hurl; pres. subj. 1st pers. pl. / *lanzar.* 2. let us hurl; impve. 1st pers. pl.

lancen 1. that they may hurl; pres. subj. 3rd pers. pl. / *lanzar.* 2. let them hurl; impve. 3rd pers. pl.

láncense let them rush; impve. 3rd pers. pl. / *lanzarse.*

lances that you may hurl; pres. subj. 2nd pers. sing. / *lanzar.*

láncese let him (her/it) rush; impve. 3rd pers. sing. / *lanzarse.*

languidecer to languish. irr.

languidezca 1. that I may languish; pres. subj. 1st pers. sing. / *languidecer.* 2. that he (she/it) may languish; pres. subj. 3rd pers. sing. 3. let him (her/it) languish; impve. 3rd pers. sing.

languidezcáis that you (all) may languish; pres. subj. 2nd pers. pl. / *languidecer.*

languidezcamos 1. that we may languish; pres. subj. 1st pers. pl. / *languidecer*. 2. let us languish; impve. 1st pers. pl.

languidezcan 1. that they may languish; pres. subj. 3rd pers. pl. / *languidecer*. 2. let them languish; impve. 3rd pers. pl.

languidezcas that you may languish; pres. subj. 2nd pers. sing. / *languidecer*.

languidezco I languish; pres. ind. 1st pers. sing. / *languidecer*.

lanzándose rushing; pres. part. / *lanzarse*.

lanzaos (you all) rush; impve. 2nd pers. pl. / *lanzarse*.

lanzar to hurl. irr.

lanzarse to rush or to fling oneself. irr.

lánzate (you) rush; impve. 2nd pers. sing. / *lanzarse*.

lapidar to stone. reg.

laquear to lacquer. reg.

lardar to baste. reg.

lardear to grease or to lard. reg.

largándose going away; pres. part. / *largarse*.

largaos (you all) go away; impve. 2nd pers. pl. / *largarse*.

largar to loosen. irr.

largarse to go away. irr.

lárgate (you) go away; impve. 2nd pers. sing. / *largarse*.

largue 1. that I may loosen; pres. subj. 1st pers. sing. / *largar*. 2. that he (she/it) may loosen; pres. subj. 3rd pers. sing. 3. let him (her/it) loosen; impve. 3rd pers. sing.

largué I loosened; past 1st pers. sing. / *largar*.

larguéis that you (all) may loosen; pres. subj. 2nd pers. pl. / *largar*.

larguémonos let us go away; impve. 1st pers. pl. / *largarse*.

larguemos 1. that we may loosen; pres. subj. 1st pers. pl. / *largar*. 2. let us loosen; impve. 1st pers. pl.

larguen 1. that they may loosen; pres. subj. 3rd pers. pl. / *largar*. 2. let them loosen; impve. 3rd pers. pl.

lárguense let them go away; impve. 3rd pers. pl. / *largarse*.

largues that you may loosen; pres. subj. 2nd pers. sing. / *largar*.

lárguese let him (her/it) go away; impve. 3rd pers. sing. / *largarse*.

lastar to pay or to suffer for another. reg.

lastimándose getting hurt; pres. part. / *lastimarse*.

lastimaos (you all) get hurt; impve. 2nd pers. pl. / *lastimarse*.

lastimar to hurt. reg.

lastimarse to get hurt. reg.

lastímate (you) get hurt; impve. 2nd pers. sing. / *lastimarse*.

lastimémonos let us get hurt; impve. 1st pers. pl. / *lastimarse*.

lastímense let them get hurt; impve. 3rd pers. pl. / *lastimarse*.

lastímese let him (her/it) get hurt; impve. 3rd pers. sing. / *lastimarse*.

lastrar to ballast. reg.

latinice 1. that I may latinize; pres. subj. 1st pers. sing. / *latinizar*. 2. that he (she/it) may latinize; pres. subj. 3rd pers. sing. 3. let him (her/it) latinize; impve. 3rd pers. sing.

latinicé I latinized; past 1st pers. sing. / *latinizar*.

latinicéis that you (all) may latinize; pres. subj. 2nd pers. pl. / *latinizar*.

latinicemos 1. that we may latinize; pres. subj. 1st pers. pl. / *latinizar*. 2. let us latinize; impve. 1st pers. pl.

latinicen 1. that they may latinize; pres. subj. 3rd pers. pl. / *latinizar*. 2. let them latinize; impve. 3rd pers. pl.

latinices that you may latinize; pres. subj. 2nd pers. sing. / *latinizar*.

latinizar to latinize. irr.

latir to beat or to throb. reg.

laurear to honor. reg.

lavándose washing oneself; pres. part. / *lavarse*.

lavaos (you all) wash yourselves; impve. 2nd pers. pl. / *lavarse*.

lavar to wash. reg.

lavarse to wash oneself. reg.

lávate (you) wash yourself; impve. 2nd pers. sing. / *lavarse*.

lavémonos let us wash ourselves; impve. 1st pers. pl. / *lavarse*.

lávense let them wash themselves; impve. 3rd pers. pl. / *lavarse*.

lávese let him (her/it) wash himself (herself/itself); impve. 3rd pers. sing. / *lavarse*.

laxándose slackening; pres. part. / *laxarse*.

laxaos (you all) slacken; impve. 2nd pers. pl. / *laxarse*.

laxar to loosen. reg.

laxarse to slacken. reg.

láxate (you) slacken; impve. 2nd pers. sing. / *laxarse*.

laxémonos let us slacken; impve. 1st pers. pl. / *laxarse*.

láxense let them slacken; impve. 3rd pers. pl. / *laxarse*.

láxese let him (her/it) slacken; impve. 3rd pers. sing. / *laxarse*.

lazar to lasso. irr.

lechar to milk. reg..

leer to read. irr.

legalice 1. that I may legalize; pres. subj. 1st pers. sing. / *legalizar*. 2. that he (she/it) may legalize; pres. subj. 3rd pers. sing. 3. let him (her/it) legalize; impve. 3rd pers. sing.

legalicé I legalized; past 1st pers. sing. / *legalizar*.

legalicéis that you (all) may legalize; pres. subj. 2nd pers. pl. / *legalizar*.

legalicemos 1. that we may legalize; pres. subj. 1st pers. pl. / *legalizar*. 2. let us legalize; impve. 1st pers. pl.

legalicen 1. that they may legalize; pres. subj. 3rd pers. pl. / *legalizar*. 2. let them legalize; impve. 3rd pers. pl.

legalices that you may legalize; pres. subj. 2nd pers. sing. / *legalizar.*

legalizar to legalize. irr.

legar to bequeath. irr.

legislar to legislate. reg.

legitimar to legitimize. reg.

legrar to scrape. reg.

legue 1. that I may bequeath; pres. subj. 1st pers. sing. / *legar.* 2. that he (she/it) may bequeath; pres. subj. 3rd pers. sing. 3. let him (her/it) bequeath; impve. 3rd pers. sing.

legué I bequeathed; past 1st pers. sing. / *legar.*

leguéis that you (all) may bequeath; pres. subj. 2nd pers. pl. / *legar.*

leguemos 1. that we may bequeath; pres. subj. 1st pers. pl. / *legar.* 2. let us bequeath; impve. 1st pers. pl.

leguen 1. that they may bequeath; pres. subj. 3rd pers. pl. / *legar.* 2. let them bequeath; impve. 3rd pers. pl.

legues that you may bequeath; pres. subj. 2nd pers. sing. / *legar.*

leí I read; past 1st pers. sing. / *leer.*

leído read; past part. / *leer.*

leímos we read; past 1st pers. pl. / *leer.*

leíste you read; past 2nd pers. sing. / *leer.*

leísteis you (all) read; past 2nd pers. pl. / *leer.*

lenificar to soothe. irr.

lenifique 1. that I may soothe; pres. subj. 1st pers. sing. / *lenificar.* 2. that he (she/it) may soothe; pres. subj. 3rd pers. sing. 3. let him (her/it) soothe; impve. 3rd pers. sing.

lenifiqué I soothed; past 1st pers. sing. / *lenificar.*

lenifiquéis that you (all) may soothe; pres. subj. 2nd pers. pl. / *lenificar.*

lenifiquemos 1. that we may soothe; pres. subj. 1st pers. pl. / *lenificar.* 2. let us soothe; impve. 1st pers. pl.

lenifiquen 1. that they may soothe; pres. subj. 3rd pers. pl. / *lenificar.* 2. let them soothe; impve. 3rd pers. pl.

lenifiques that you may soothe; pres. subj. 2nd pers. sing. / *lenificar.*

lesionar to injure. reg.

letificar to animate or to cheer. reg.

letifique 1. that I may animate; pres. subj. 1st pers. sing. / *letificar.* 2. that he (she/it) may animate; pres. subj. 3rd pers. sing. 3. let him (her/it) animate; impve. 3rd pers. sing.

letifiqué I animated; past 1st pers. sing. / *letificar.*

letifiquéis that you (all) may animate; pres. subj. 2nd pers. pl. / *letificar.*

letifiquemos 1. that we may animate; pres. subj. 1st pers. pl. / *letificar.* 2. let us animate; impve. 1st pers. pl.

letifiquen 1. that they may animate; pres. subj. 3rd pers. pl. / *letificar.* 2. let them animate; impve. 3rd pers. pl.

letifiques that you may animate; pres. subj. 2nd pers. sing. / *letificar.*

leudándose fermenting; pres. part. / *leudarse.*

leudar to leaven. reg.

leudarse to ferment. reg.

leúdense let them ferment; impve. 3rd pers. pl. / *leudarse.*

leúdese let it ferment; impve. 3rd pers. sing. / *leudarse.*

levándose setting sail; pres. part. / *levarse.*

levantándose getting up; pres. part. / *levantarse.*

levantaos (you all) get up; impve. 2nd pers. pl. / *levantarse.*

levantar to raise. reg.

levantarse to get up. reg.

levántate (you) get up; impve. 2nd pers. sing. / *levantarse.*

levantémonos let us get up; impve. 1st pers. pl. / *levantarse.*

levántense let them get up; impve. 3rd pers. pl. / *levantarse.*

levántese let him (her/it) get up; impve. 3rd pers. sing. / *levantarse.*

levaos (you all) set sail; impve. 2nd pers. pl. / *levarse.*

levar to weigh anchor. reg.

levarse to set sail. reg.

lévate (you) set sail; impve. 2nd pers. sing. / *levarse.*

levémonos let us set sail; impve. 1st pers. pl. / *levarse.*

lévense let them set sail; impve. 3rd pers. pl. / *levarse.*

lévese let him (her/it) set sail; impve. 3rd pers. sing. / *levarse.*

leyendo reading; pres. part. / *leer.*

leyera 1. that I might read; imp. subj. 1st pers. sing. / *leer.* 2. that he (she/it) might read; imp. subj. 3rd pers. sing.

leyerais that you (all) might read; imp. subj. 2nd pers pl. / *leer.*

leyéramos that we might read; imp. subj. 1st pers. pl. / *leer.*

leyeran that they might read; imp. subj. 3rd pers. pl. / *leer.*

leyeras that you might read; imp. subj. 2nd pers. sing. / *leer.*

leyeron they read; past 3rd pers. pl. / *leer.*

leyese 1. that I might read; imp. subj. 1st pers. sing. / *leer.* 2. that he (she/it) might read; imp. subj. 3rd pers. sing.

leyeseis that you (all) might read; imp. subj. 2nd pers pl. / *leer.*

leyésemos that we might read; imp. subj. 1st pers. pl. / *leer.*

leyesen that they might read; imp. subj. 3rd pers. pl. / *leer.*

leyeses that you might read; imp. subj. 2nd pers. sing. / *leer.*

leyó he (she/it) read; past 3rd pers. sing. / *leer.*

lía 1. he (she/it) ties; pres. ind. 3rd pers. sing. / *liar.* 2. (you) tie; impve. 2nd pers. sing.

lían they tie; pres. ind. 3rd pers. pl. / *liar.*

liándose coming together; pres. part. / *liarse.*

liaos (you all) come together; impve. 2nd pers. pl. / *liarse.*

liar to tie or to bind. irr.

liarse to come together. irr.

lías you tie; pres. ind. 2nd-pers. sing. / *liar.*

líate (you) come together; impve. 2nd pers. sing. / *liarse.*

libar to taste. reg.

liberalice 1. that I may liberalize; pres. subj. 1st pers. sing. / *liberalizar.* 2. that he (she/it) may liberalize; pres. subj. 3rd pers. sing. 3. let him (her/it) liberalize; impve. 3rd pers. sing.

liberalicé I liberalized; past 1st pers. sing. / *liberalizar.*

liberalicéis that you (all) may liberalize; pres. subj. 2nd pers. pl. / *liberalizar.*

liberalicemos 1. that we may liberalize; pres. subj. 1st pers. pl. / *liberalizar.* 2. let us liberalize; impve. 1st pers. pl.

liberalicen 1. that they may liberalize; pres. subj. 3rd pers. pl. / *liberalizar.* 2. let them liberalize; impve. 3rd pers. pl.

liberalices that you may liberalize; pres. subj. 2nd pers. sing. / *liberalizar.*

liberalizar to liberalize. irr.

liberar to liberate. reg.

libertándose getting free; pres. part. / *libertarse.*

libertaos (you all) get free; impve. 2nd pers. pl. / *libertarse.*

libertar to get free. reg.

libertarse to get free. reg.

libértate (you) get free; impve. 2nd pers. sing. / *libertarse.*

libertémonos let us get free; impve. 1st pers. pl. / *libertarse.*

libértense let them get free; impve. 3rd pers. pl. / *libertarse.*

libértese let him (her/it) get free; impve. 3rd pers. sing. / *libertarse.*

librándose escaping; pres. part. / *librarse.*

libraos (you all) escape; impve. 2nd pers. pl. / *librarse.*

librar to free or to deliver. reg.

librarse to escape. reg.

líbrate (you) escape; impve. 2nd pers. sing. / *librarse.*

librémonos let us escape; impve. 1st pers. pl. / *librarse.*

líbrense let them escape; impve. 3rd pers. pl. / *librarse.*

líbrese let him (her/it) escape; impve. 3rd pers. sing. / *librarse.*

licenciándose graduating; pres. part. / *licenciarse.*

licenciaos (you all) graduate; impve. 2nd pers. pl. / *licenciarse.*

licenciar to license. reg.

licenciarse to graduate. reg.

licénciate (you) graduate; impve. 2nd pers. sing. / *licenciarse.*

licenciémonos let us graduate; impve. 1st pers. pl. / *licenciarse.*

licéncíense let them graduate; impve. 3rd pers. pl. / *licenciarse.*

licencíese let him (her/it) graduate; impve. 3rd pers. sing. / *licenciarse.*

licitar to bid for. reg.

licuar to liquefy. reg.

licuefaceos (you all) liquefy; impve. 2nd pers. pl. / *licuefacerse.*

licuefacer to liquefy. irr.

licuefacerse to liquefy. irr.

licuefaciéndose liquefying; pres. part. / *licuefacerse.*

licuefaga 1. that I may liquefy; pres. subj. 1st pers. sing. / *licuefacer.* 2. that he (she/it) may liquefy; pres. subj. 3rd pers. sing. 3. let him (her/it) liquefy; impve. 3rd pers. sing.

licuefagáis that you (all) may liquefy; pres. subj. 2nd pers. pl. / *licuefacer.*

licuefagámonos let us liquefy; impve. 1st pers. pl. / *licuefacerse.*

licuefagamos 1. that we may liquefy; pres. subj. 1st pers. pl. / *licuefacer.* 2. let us liquefy; impve. 1st pers. pl.

licuefagan 1. that they may liquefy; pres. subj. 3rd pers. pl. / *licuefacer.* 2. let them liquefy; impve. 3rd pers. pl.

licuefáganse let them liquefy; impve. 3rd pers. pl. / *licuefacerse.*

licuefagas that you may liquefy; pres. subj. 2nd pers. sing. / *licuefacer.*

licuefágase let him (her/it) liquefy; impve. 3rd pers. sing. / *licuefacerse.*

licuefago I liquefy; pres. ind. 1st pers. sing. / *licuefacer.*

licuefará he (she/it) will liquefy; fut. 3rd pers. sing. / *licuefacer.*

licuefarán they will liquefy; fut. 3rd pers. pl. / *licuefacer.*

licuefarás you will liquefy; fut. 2nd pers. sing. / *licuefacer.*

licuefaré I shall liquefy; fut. 1st pers. sing. / *licuefacer.*

licuefaréis you (all) will liquefy; fut. 2nd pers. pl. / *licuefacer.*

licuefaremos we shall liquefy; fut. 1st pers. pl. / *licuefacer.*

licuefaría 1. I should liquefy; cond. 1st pers. sing. / *licuefacer.* 2. he (she/it) would liquefy; cond. 3rd pers. sing.

licuefaríais you (all) would liquefy; cond. 2nd pers. pl. / *licuefacer.*

licuefaríamos we should liquefy; cond. 1st pers. pl. / *licuefacer.*

licuefarían they would liquefy; cond. 3rd pers. pl. / *licuefacer.*

licuefarías you would liquefy; cond. 2nd pers. sing. / *licuefacer.*

licuefaz (you) liquefy; impve. 2nd pers. sing. / *licuefacer.*

licuefázete (you) liquefy; impve. 2nd pers. sing. / *licuefacerse.*

licuefecho liquefied; past part. / *licuefacer.*

licuefice I liquefied; past 1st pers. sing. / *licuefacer.*

licueficiera 1. that I might liquefy; imp. subj. 1st pers. sing. / *licuefacer.* 2. that he (she/it) might liquefy; imp. subj. 3rd pers. sing.

licueficierais that you (all) might liquefy; imp. subj. 2nd pers pl. / *licuefacer.*

licueficiéramos that we might liquefy; imp. subj. 1st pers. pl. / *licuefacer.*

licueficieran that they might liquefy; imp. subj. 3rd pers. pl. / *licuefacer.*

licueficieras that you might liquefy; imp. subj. 2nd pers. sing. / *licuefacer.*

licueficieron they liquefied; past 3rd pers. pl. / *licuefacer.*

licueficiese 1. that I might liquefy; imp. subj. 1st pers. sing. / *licuefacer.* 2. that he (she/it) might liquefy; imp. subj. 3rd pers. sing.

licueficieseis that you (all) might liquefy; imp. subj. 2nd pers pl. / *licuefacer.*

licueficiésemos that we might liquefy; imp. subj. 1st pers. pl. / *licuefacer.*

licueficiesen that they might liquefy; imp. subj. 3rd pers. pl. / *licuefacer.*

licueficieses that you might liquefy; imp. subj. 2nd pers. sing. / *licuefacer.*

licueficimos we liquefied; past 1st pers. pl. / *licuefacer.*

licueficiste you liquefied; past 2nd pers. sing. / *licuefacer.*

licueficisteis you (all) liquefied; past 2nd pers. pl. / *licuefacer.*

licuefizo he (she/it) liquefied; past 3rd pers. sing. / *licuefacer.*

liderear to lead. reg.

lidiar to fight. reg.

líe 1. that I may tie; pres. subj. 1st pers. sing. / *liar.* 2. that he (she/it) may tie; pres. subj. 3rd pers. sing. 3. let him (her/it) tie; impve. 3rd pers. sing.

liémonos let us come together; impve. 1st pers. pl. / *liarse.*

líen 1. that they may tie; pres. subj. 3rd pers. pl. / *liar.* 2. let them tie; impve. 3rd pers. pl.

líense let them come together; impve. 3rd pers. pl. / *liarse.*

líes that you may tie; pres. subj. 2nd pers. sing. / *liar.*

líese let him (her/it) come together; impve. 3rd pers. sing. / *liarse.*

ligándose forming an alliance; pres. part. / *ligarse.*

ligaos (you all) form an alliance; impve. 2nd pers. pl. / *ligarse.*

ligar to bind or to tie. irr.

ligarse to form an alliance. irr.

lígate (you) form an alliance; impve. 2nd pers. sing. / *ligarse.*

ligue 1. that I may bind; pres. subj. 1st pers. sing. / *ligar.* 2. that he (she/it) may bind; pres. subj. 3rd pers. sing. 3. let him (her/it) bind; impve. 3rd pers. sing.

ligué I bound; past 1st pers. sing. / *ligar.*

liguéis that you (all) may bind; pres. subj. 2nd pers. pl. / *ligar.*

liguémonos let us form an alliance; impve. 1st pers. pl. / *ligarse.*

liguemos 1. that we may bind; pres. subj. 1st pers. pl. / *ligar.* 2. let us bind; impve. 1st pers. pl.

liguen 1. that they may bind; pres. subj. 3rd pers. pl. / *ligar.* 2. let them bind; impve. 3rd pers. pl.

líguense let them form an alliance; impve. 3rd pers. pl. / *ligarse.*

ligues that you may bind; pres. subj. 2nd pers. sing. / *ligar.*

líguese let him (her/it) form an alliance; impve. 3rd pers. sing. / *ligarse.*

lijar to sandpaper. reg.

limar to file or to smooth. reg.

limitar to limit. reg.

limosnear to beg alms. reg.

limpiar to clean. reg.

lincear to see through. reg.

linchar to lynch. reg.

lindar to bordar or to adjoin. reg.

linear to outline. reg.

lío I tie; pres. ind. 1st pers. sing. / *liar.*

liquidar to liquidate. reg.

lisiándose becoming crippled; pres. part. / *lisiarse.*

lisiaos (you all) become crippled; impve. 2nd pers. pl. / *lisiarse.*

lisiar to cripple. reg.

lisiarse to become crippled. reg.

lisíate (you) become crippled; impve. 2nd pers. sing. / *lisiarse.*

lisiémonos let us become crippled; impve. 1st pers. pl. / *lisiarse.*

lisíense let them become crippled; impve. 3rd pers. pl. / *lisiarse.*

lisíese let him (her/it) become crippled; impve. 3rd pers. sing. / *lisiarse.*

lisonjear to flatter. reg.

listar to list. reg.

litigar to litigate. irr.

litigue 1. that I may litigate; pres. subj. 1st pers. sing. / *litigar.* 2. that he (she/it) may litigate; pres. subj. 3rd pers. sing. 3. let him (her/it) litigate; impve. 3rd pers. sing.

litigué I litigated; past 1st pers. sing. / *litigar.*

litiguéis that you (all) may litigate; pres. subj. 2nd pers. pl. / *litigar.*

litiguemos 1. that we may litigate; pres. subj. 1st pers. pl. / *litigar.* 2. let us litigate; impve. 1st pers. pl.

litiguen 1. that they may litigate; pres. subj. 3rd pers. pl. / *litigar.* 2. let them litigate; impve. 3rd pers. pl.

litigues that you may litigate; pres. subj. 2nd pers. sing. / *litigar.*

litografía 1. he (she/it) lithographs; pres. ind. 3rd pers. sing. / *litografiar.* 2. (you) lithograph; impve. 2nd pers. sing.

litografían they lithograph; pres. ind. 3rd pers. pl. / *litografiar.*

litografiar to lithograph. irr.

litografías you lithograph; pres. ind. 2nd pers. sing. / *litografiar.*

litografíe 1. that I may lithograph; pres. subj. 1st pers. sing. / *litografiar*. 2. that he (she/it) may lithograph; pres. subj. 3rd pers. sing. 3. let him (her/it) lithograph; impve. 3rd pers. sing.

litografíen 1. that they may lithograph; pres. subj. 3rd pers. pl. / *litografiar*. 2. let them lithograph; impve. 3rd pers. pl.

litografíes that you may lithograph; pres. subj. 2nd pers. sing. / *litografiar*.

litografío I lithograph; pres. ind. 1st pers. sing. / *litografiar*.

lividecer to turn livid. irr.

lividezca 1. that I may turn livid; pres. subj. 1st pers. sing. / *lividecer*. 2. that he (she/it) may turn livid; pres. subj. 3rd pers. sing. 3. let him (her/it) turn livid; impve. 3rd pers. sing.

lividezcáis that you (all) may turn livid; pres. subj. 2nd pers. pl. / *lividecer*.

lividezcamos 1. that we may turn livid; pres. subj. 1st pers. pl. / *lividecer*. 2. let us turn livid; impve. 1st pers. pl.

lividezcan 1. that they may turn livid; pres. subj. 3rd pers. pl. / *lividecer*. 2. let them turn livid; impve. 3rd pers. pl.

lividezcas that you may turn livid; pres. subj. 2nd pers. sing. / *lividecer*.

lividezco I turn livid; pres. ind. 1st pers. sing. / *lividecer*.

loar to praise. reg.

localice 1. that I may localize; pres. subj. 1st pers. sing. / *localizar*. 2. that he (she/it) may localize; pres. subj. 3rd pers. sing. 3. let him (her/it) localize; impve. 3rd pers. sing.

localicé I localized; past 1st pers. sing. / *localizar*.

localicéis that you (all) may localize; pres. subj. 2nd pers. pl. / *localizar*.

localicemos 1. that we may localize; pres. subj. 1st pers. pl. / *localizar*. 2. let us localize; impve. 1st pers. pl.

localicen 1. that they may localize; pres. subj. 3rd pers. pl. / *localizar*. 2. let them localize; impve. 3rd pers. pl.

localices that you may localize; pres. subj. 2nd pers. sing. / *localizar*.

localizar to localize. irr.

lográndose being successful; pres. part. / *lograrse*.

lograos (you all) be successful; impve. 2nd pers. pl. / *lograrse*.

lograr to gain. reg.

lograrse to be successful. reg.

lógrate (you) be successful; impve. 2nd pers. sing. / *lograrse*.

lograr to profiteer. reg.

logrémonos let us be successful; impve. 1st pers. pl. / *lograrse*.

lógrense let them be successful; impve. 3rd pers. pl. / *lograrse*.

lógrese let him (her/it) be successful; impve. 3rd pers. sing. / *lograrse*.

loquear to act foolishly. reg.

losar to tile. reg.

lotear to subdivide. reg.

lozaneándose being lusty; pres. part. / *lozanearse*.

lozaneaos (you all) be lusty; impve. 2nd pers. pl. / *lozanearse*.

lozanear to luxuriate. reg.

lozanearse to be lusty. reg.

lozanéate (you) be lusty; impve. 2nd pers. sing. / *lozanearse*.

lozaneémonos let us be lusty; impve. 1st pers. pl. / *lozanearse*.

lozanéense let them be lusty; impve. 3rd pers. pl. / *lozanearse*.

lozanéese let him (her/it) be lusty; impve. 3rd pers. sing. / *lozanearse*.

lubricar to lubricate. irr.

lubrique 1. that I may lubricate; pres. subj. 1st pers. sing. / *lubricar*. 2. that he (she/it) may lubricate; pres. subj. 3rd pers. sing. 3. let him (her/it) lubricate; impve. 3rd pers. sing.

lubriqué I lubricated; past 1st pers. sing. / *lubricar*.

lubriquéis that you (all) may lubricate; pres. subj. 2nd pers. pl. / *lubricar*.

lubriquemos 1. that we may lubricate; pres. subj. 1st pers. pl. / *lubricar*. 2. let us lubricate; impve. 1st pers. pl.

lubriquen 1. that they may lubricate; pres. subj. 3rd pers. pl. / *lubricar*. 2. let them lubricate; impve. 3rd pers. pl.

lubriques that you may lubricate; pres. subj. 2nd pers. sing. / *lubricar*.

lúcete (you) dress up; impve. 2nd pers. sing. / *lucirse*.

luciéndose dressing up; pres. part. / *lucirse*.

lucíos (you all) dress up; impve. 2nd pers. pl. / *lucirse*.

lucir to shine. irr.

lucirse to dress up. irr.

lucrándose making a profit; pres. part. / *lucrarse*.

lucraos (you all) make a profit; impve. 2nd pers. pl. / *lucrarse*.

lucrar to obtain. reg.

lucrarse to make a profit. reg.

lúcrate (you) make a profit; impve. 2nd pers. sing. / *lucrarse*.

lucrémonos let us make a profit; impve. 1st pers. pl. / *lucrarse*.

lúcrense let them make a profit; impve. 3rd pers. pl. / *lucrarse*.

lúcrese let him (her/it) make a profit; impve. 3rd pers. sing. / *lucrarse*.

lucubrar to lucubrate. reg.

luchar to wrestle. reg.

lujuriar to be lustful. reg.

lustrar to polish or to roam. reg.

luzca 1. that I may shine; pres. subj. 1st pers. sing. / *lucir*. 2. that he (she/it) may shine; pres. subj. 3rd pers. sing. 3. let him (her/it) shine; impve. 3rd pers. sing.

luzcáis that you (all) may shine; pres. subj. 2nd pers. pl. / *lucir*.

luzcámonos let us dress up; impve. 1st pers. pl. / *lucirse*.

luzcamos 1. that we may shine; pres. subj. 1st pers. pl. / *lucir*. 2. let us shine; impve. 1st pers. pl.

luzcan 1. that they may shine; pres. subj. 3rd pers. pl. / *lucir*. 2. let them shine; impve. 3rd pers. pl.

lúzcanse let them dress up; impve. 3rd pers. pl. / *lucirse*.

luzcas that you may shine; pres. subj. 2nd pers. sing. / *lucir*.

lúzcase let him (her/it) dress up; impve. 3rd pers. sing. / *lucirse*.

luzco I shine; pres. ind. 1st pers. sing. / *lucir*.

LL

llagar to wound. irr.

llague 1. that I may wound; pres. subj. 1st pers. sing. / *llagar*. 2. that he (she/it) may wound; pres. subj. 3rd pers. sing. 3. let him (her/it) wound; impve. 3rd pers. sing.

llagué I wounded; past 1st pers. sing. / *llagar*.

llaguéis that you (all) may wound; pres. subj. 2nd pers. pl. / *llagar*.

llaguemos 1. that we may wound; pres. subj. 1st pers. pl. / *llagar*. 2. let us wound; impve. 1st pers. pl.

llaguen 1. that they may wound; pres. subj. 3rd pers. pl. / *llagar*. 2. let them wound; impve. 3rd pers. pl.

llagues that you may wound; pres. subj. 2nd pers. sing. / *llagar*.

llamándose being named; pres. part. / *llamarse*.

llamaos (you all) be named; impve. 2nd pers. pl. / *llamarse*.

llamar to call or to knock. reg.

llamarse to be named. reg.

llámate (you) be named; impve. 2nd pers. sing. / *llamarse*.

llamear to flame. reg.

llamémonos let us be named; impve. 1st pers. pl. / *llamarse*.

llámense let them be named; impve. 3rd pers. pl. / *llamarse*.

llámese let him (her/it) be named; impve. 3rd pers. sing. / *llamarse*.

llegándose approaching; pres. part. / *llegarse*.

llegaos (you all) approach; impve. 2nd pers. pl. / *llegarse*.

llegar to arrive. irr.

llegarse to approach. irr.

llégate (you) approach; impve. 2nd pers. sing. / *llegarse*.

llegue 1. that I may arrive; pres. subj. 1st pers. sing. / *llegar*. 2. that he (she/it) may arrive; pres. subj. 3rd pers. sing. 3. let him (her/it) arrive; impve. 3rd pers. sing.

llegué I arrived; past 1st pers. sing. / *llegar*.

lleguéis that you (all) may arrive; pres. subj. 2nd pers. pl. / *llegar*.

lleguémonos let us approach; impve. 1st pers. pl. / *llegarse*.

lleguemos 1. that we may arrive; pres. subj. 1st pers. pl. / *llegar*. 2. let us arrive; impve. 1st pers. pl.

lleguen 1. that they may arrive; pres. subj. 3rd pers. pl. / *llegar*. 2. let them arrive; impve. 3rd pers. pl.

lléguense let them approach; impve. 3rd pers. pl. / *llegarse*.

llegues that you may arrive; pres. subj. 2nd pers. sing. / *llegar*.

lléguese let him (her/it) approach; impve. 3rd pers. sing. / *llegarse*.

llenándose getting full; pres. part. / *llenarse*.

llenaos (you all) get full; impve. 2nd pers. pl. / *llenarse*.

llenar to fill. reg.

llenarse to get full. reg.

llénate (you) get full; impve. 2nd pers. sing. / *llenarse*.

llenémonos let us get full; impve. 1st pers. pl. / *llenarse*.

llénense let them get full; impve. 3rd pers. pl. / *llenarse*.

llénese let him (her/it) get full; impve. 3rd pers. sing. / *llenarse*.

llevándose taking away; pres. part. / *llevarse*.

llevaos (you all) take away; impve. 2nd pers. pl. / *llevarse*.

llevar to carry. reg.

llevarse to take away. reg.

llévate (you) take away; impve. 2nd pers. sing. / *llevarse*.

llevémonos let us take away; impve. 1st pers. pl. / *llevarse*.

llévense let them take away; impve. 3rd pers. pl. / *llevarse*.

llévese let him (her/it) take away; impve. 3rd pers. sing. / *llevarse*.

llorar to weep. reg.

lloriquear to whimper. reg.

llover to rain. irr.

lloverse to leak. irr.

lloviznar to drizzle. reg.

llueva 1. that it may rain; pres. subj. 3rd pers. sing. / *llover*. 2. let it rain; impve. 3rd pers. sing.

lluévase let it leak; impve. 3rd pers. sing. / *lloverse*.

llueve it rains; pres. ind. 3rd pers. sing. / *llover*.

M

macadamice 1. that I may macadamize; pres. subj. 1st pers. sing. / *macadamizar*. 2. that he (she/it) may macadamize; pres. subj. 3rd pers. sing. 3. let him (her/it) macadamize; impve. 3rd pers. sing.

macadamicé I macadamized; past 1st pers. sing. / *macadamizar*.

macadamicéis that you (all) may macadamize; pres. subj. 2nd pers. pl. / *macadamizar*.

macadamicemos 1. that we may macadamize; pres. subj. 1st pers. pl. / *macadamizar*. 2. let us macadamize; impve. 1st pers. pl.

macadamicen 1. that they may macadamize; pres. subj. 3rd pers. pl. / *macadamizar*. 2. let them macadamize; impve. 3rd pers. pl.

macadamices that you may macadamize; pres. subj. 2nd pers. sing. / *macadamizar*.

macadamizar to macadamize. irr.

macándose beginning to rot (fruit); pres. part. / *macarse*.

macarse to begin to rot (fruit). reg.

macear to hammer or to be a bore. reg.

mácense let them begin to rot (fruit); impve. 3rd pers. pl. / *macarse*.

macerar to macerate. reg.

mácese let it begin to rot (fruit); impve. 3rd pers. sing. / *macarse*.

macice 1. that I may fill up; pres. subj. 1st pers. sing. / *macizar*. 2. that he (she/it) may fill up; pres. subj. 3rd pers. sing. 3. let him (her/it) fill up; impve. 3rd pers. sing.

macicé I filled up; past 1st pers. sing. / *macizar*.

macicéis that you (all) may fill up; pres. subj. 2nd pers. pl. / *macizar*.

macicemos 1. that we may fill up; pres. subj. 1st pers. pl. / *macizar*. 2. let us fill up; impve. 1st pers. pl.

macicen 1. that they may fill up; pres. subj. 3rd pers. pl. / *macizar*. 2. let them fill up; impve. 3rd pers. pl.

macices that you may fill up; pres. subj. 2nd pers. sing. / *macizar*.

macizar to fill up. irr.

machacar to crush or to insist. irr.

machándose getting drunk; pres. part. / *macharse*.

machaos (you all) get drunk; impve. 2nd pers. pl. / *macharse*.

machaque 1. that I may crush; pres. subj. 1st pers. sing. / *machacar*. 2. that he (she/it) may crush; pres. subj. 3rd pers. sing. 3. let him (her/it) crush; impve. 3rd pers. sing.

machaqué I crushed; past 1st pers. sing. / *machacar*.

machaquéis that you (all) may crush; pres. subj. 2nd pers. pl. / *machacar*.

machaquemos 1. that we may crush; pres. subj. 1st pers. pl. / *machacar*. 2. let us crush; impve. 1st pers. pl.

machaquen 1. that they may crush; pres. subj. 3rd pers. pl. / *machacar*. 2. let them crush; impve. 3rd pers. pl.

machaques that you may crush; pres. subj. 2nd pers. sing. / *machacar*.

machar to crush. reg.

macharse to get drunk. reg.

máchate (you) get drunk; impve. 2nd pers. sing. / *macharse*.

machémonos let us get drunk; impve. 1st pers. pl. / *macharse*.

máchense let them get drunk; impve. 3rd pers. pl. / *macharse*.

máchese let him (her/it) get drunk; impve. 3rd pers. sing. / *macharse*.

machihembrar to dovetail. reg.

machucar to pound. irr.

machuque 1. that I may pound; pres. subj. 1st pers. sing. / *machucar*. 2. that he (she/it) may pound; pres. subj. 3rd pers. sing. 3. let him (her/it) pound; impve. 3rd pers. sing.

machuqué I pounded; past 1st pers. sing. / *machucar*.

machuquéis that you (all) may pound; pres. subj. 2nd pers. pl. / *machucar*.

machuquemos 1. that we may pound; pres. subj. 1st pers. pl. / *machucar*. 2. let us pound; impve. 1st pers. pl.

machuquen 1. that they may pound; pres. subj. 3rd pers. pl. / *machucar*. 2. let them pound; impve. 3rd pers. pl.

machuques that you may pound; pres. subj. 2nd pers. sing. / *machucar*.

madrugándose being ahead of others; pres. part. / *madrugarse*.

madrugaos (you all) be ahead of others; impve. 2nd pers. pl. / *madrugarse*.

madrugar to get up early. irr.

madrugarse to be ahead of others. irr.

madrúgate (you) be ahead of others; impve. 2nd pers. sing. / *madrugarse*.

madrugue 1. that I may get up early; pres. subj. 1st pers. sing. / *madrugar*. 2. that he (she/it) may get up early; pres. subj. 3rd pers. sing. 3. let him (her/it) get up early; impve. 3rd pers. sing.

madrugué I got up early; past 1st pers. sing. / *madrugar*.

madruguéis that you (all) may get up early; pres. subj. 2nd pers. pl. / *madrugar*.

madruguémonos let us be ahead of others; impve. 1st pers. pl. / *madrugarse*.

madruguemos 1. that we may get up early; pres. subj. 1st pers. pl. / *madrugar*. 2. let us get up early; impve. 1st pers. pl.

madruguen 1. that they may get up early; pres. subj. 3rd pers. pl. / *madrugar*. 2. let them get up early; impve. 3rd pers. pl.

madrúguense let them be ahead of others; impve. 3rd pers. pl. / *madrugarse*.

madrugues that you may get up early; pres. subj. 2nd pers. sing. / *madrugar*.

madrúguese let him (her/it) be ahead of others; impve. 3rd pers. sing. / *madrugarse*.

madurándose maturing; pres. part. / *madurarse*.

maduraos (you all) mature; impve. 2nd pers. pl. / *madurarse.*

madurar to ripen. reg.

madurarse to mature. reg.

madúrate (you) mature; impve. 2nd pers. sing. / *madurarse.*

madurémonos let us mature; impve. 1st pers. pl. / *madurarse.*

madúrense let them mature; impve. 3rd pers. pl. / *madurarse.*

madúrese let him (her/it) mature; impve. 3rd pers. sing. / *madurarse.*

maestrear to take charge of. reg.

magnetice 1. that I may magnetize; pres. subj. 1st pers. sing. / *magnetizar.* 2. that he (she/it) may magnetize; pres. subj. 3rd pers. sing. 3. let him (her/it) magnetize; impve. 3rd pers. sing.

magneticé I magnetized; past 1st pers. sing. / *magnetizar.*

magneticéis that you (all) may magnetize; pres. subj. 2nd pers. pl. / *magnetizar.*

magneticemos 1. that we may magnetize; pres. subj. 1st pers. pl. / *magnetizar.* 2. let us magnetize; impve. 1st pers. pl.

magneticen 1. that they may magnetize; pres. subj. 3rd pers. pl. / *magnetizar.* 2. let them magnetize; impve. 3rd pers. pl.

magnetices that you may magnetize; pres. subj. 2nd pers. sing. / *magnetizar.*

magnetizar to magnetize. irr.

magnificar to magnify. irr.

magnifique 1. that I may magnify; pres. subj. 1st pers. sing. / *magnificar.* 2. that he (she/it) may magnify; pres. subj. 3rd pers. sing. 3. let him (her/it) magnify; impve. 3rd pers. sing.

magnifiqué I magnified; past 1st pers. sing. / *magnificar.*

magnifiquéis that you (all) may magnify; pres. subj. 2nd pers. pl. / *magnificar.*

magnifiquemos 1. that we may magnify; pres. subj. 1st pers. pl. / *magnificar.* 2. let us magnify; impve. 1st pers. pl.

magnifiquen 1. that they may magnify; pres. subj. 3rd pers. pl. / *magnificar.* 2. let them magnify; impve. 3rd pers. pl.

magnifiques that you may magnify; pres. subj. 2nd pers. sing. / *magnificar.*

magullar to bruise. reg.

majar to pound. reg.

malbaratar to undersell or to squander. reg.

malcría 1. he (she/it) spoils; pres. ind. 3rd pers. sing. / *malcriar.* 2. (you) spoil; impve. 2nd pers. sing.

malcrían they spoil; pres. ind. 3rd pers. pl. / *malcriar.*

malcriar to spoil or to pamper. irr.

malcrías you spoil; pres. ind. 2nd pers. sing. / *malcriar.*

malcríe 1. that I may spoil; pres. subj. 1st pers. sing. / *malcriar.* 2. that he (she/it) may spoil; pres. subj. 3rd pers. sing. 3. let him (her/it) spoil; impve. 3rd pers. sing.

malcríen 1. that they may spoil; pres. subj. 3rd pers. pl. / *malcriar.* 2. let them spoil; impve. 3rd pers. pl.

malcríes that you may spoil; pres. subj. 2nd pers. sing. / *malcriar.*

malcrío I spoil; pres. ind. 1st pers. sing. / *malcriar.*

maldecir to curse. irr.

maldi (you) curse; impve. 2nd pers. sing. / *maldecir.*

maldice he (she/it) curses; pres. ind. 3rd pers. sing. / *maldecir.*

maldicen they curse; pres. ind. 3rd pers. pl. / *maldecir.*

maldices you curse; pres. ind. 2nd pers. sing. / *maldecir.*

maldiciendo cursing; pres. part. / *maldecir.*

maldiga 1. that I may curse; pres. subj. 1st pers. sing. / *maldecir.* 2. that he (she/it) may curse; pres. subj. 3rd pers. sing. 3. let him (her/it) curse; impve. 3rd pers. sing.

maldigáis that you (all) may curse; pres. subj. 2nd pers. pl. / *maldecir.*

maldigamos 1. that we may curse; pres. subj. 1st pers. pl. / *maldecir.* 2. let us curse; impve. 1st pers. pl.

maldigan 1. that they may curse; pres. subj. 3rd pers. pl. / *maldecir.* 2. let them curse; impve. 3rd pers. pl.

maldigas that you may curse; pres. subj. 2nd pers. sing. / *maldecir.*

maldigo I curse; pres. ind. 1st pers. sing. / *maldecir.*

maldije I cursed; past 1st pers. sing. / *maldecir.*

maldijera 1. that I might curse; imp. subj. 1st pers. sing. / *maldecir.* 2. that he (she/it) might curse; imp. subj. 3rd pers. sing.

maldijerais that you (all) might curse; imp. subj. 2nd pers pl. / *maldecir.*

maldijéramos that we might curse; imp. subj. 1st pers. pl. / *maldecir.*

maldijeran that they might curse; imp. subj. 3rd pers. pl. / *maldecir.*

maldijeras that you might curse; imp. subj. 2nd pers. sing. / *maldecir.*

maldijeron they cursed; past 3rd pers. pl. / *maldecir.*

maldijese 1. that I might curse; imp. subj. 1st pers. sing. / *maldecir.* 2. that he (she/it) might curse; imp. subj. 3rd pers. sing.

maldijeseis that you (all) might curse; imp. subj. 2nd pers pl. / *maldecir.*

maldijésemos that we might curse; imp. subj. 1st pers. pl. / *maldecir.*

maldijesen that they might curse; imp. subj. 3rd pers. pl. / *maldecir.*

maldijeses that you might curse; imp. subj. 2nd pers. sing. / *maldecir.*

maldijimos we cursed; past 1st pers. pl. / *maldecir.*

maldijiste you cursed; past 2nd pers. sing. / *maldecir.*

maldijisteis you (all) cursed; past 2nd pers. pl. / *maldecir.*

maldijo he (she/it) cursed; past 3rd pers. sing. / *maldecir.*

maldirá he (she/it) will curse; fut. 3rd pers. sing. / *maldecir.*

maldirán they will curse; fut. 3rd pers. pl. / *maldecir.*

maldirás you will curse; fut. 2nd pers. sing. / *maldecir.*

maldiré I shall curse; fut. 1st pers. sing. / *maldecir.*

maldiréis you (all) will curse; fut. 2nd pers. pl. / *maldecir.*

maldiremos we shall curse; fut. 1st pers. pl. / *maldecir.*

maldiría 1. I should curse; cond. 1st pers. sing. / *maldecir.* 2. he (she/it) would curse; cond. 3rd pers. sing.

maldiríais you (all) would curse; cond. 2nd pers. pl. / *maldecir.*

maldiríamos we should curse; cond. 1st pers. pl. / *maldecir.*

maldirían they would curse; cond. 3rd pers. pl. / *maldecir.*

maldirías you would curse; cond. 2nd pers. sing. / *maldecir.*

maldito cursed; past part. / *maldecir.*

malear to corrpt. reg.

maleficiar to harm or to curse. reg.

malgastar to squander. reg.

maliciándose going wrong; pres. part. / *maliciarse.*

maliciaos (you all) go wrong; impve. 2nd pers. pl. / *maliciarse.*

maliciar to suspect. reg.

maliciarse to go wrong. reg.

maliciate (you) go wrong; impve. 2nd pers. sing. / *maliciarse.*

maliciémonos let us go wrong; impve. 1st pers. pl. / *maliciarse.*

maliciense let them go wrong; impve. 3rd pers. pl. / *maliciarse.*

maliciese let him (her/it) go wrong; impve. 3rd pers. sing. / *maliciarse.*

malignándose spoiling; pres. part. / *malignarse.*

malignaos (you all) spoil; impve. 2nd pers. pl. / *malignarse.*

malignar to deprave. reg.

malignarse to spoil. reg.

malígnate (you) spoil; impve. 2nd pers. sing. / *malignarse.*

malignémonos let us spoil; impve. 1st pers. pl. / *malignarse.*

malígnense let them spoil; impve. 3rd pers. pl. / *malignarse.*

malígnese let him (her/it) spoil; impve. 3rd pers. sing. / *malignarse.*

malmeter to estrange or to waste. reg.

malográndose failing; pres. part. / *malograrse.*

malograos (you all) fail; impve. 2nd pers. pl. / *malograrse.*

malograr to waste. reg.

malograrse to fail. reg.

malógrate (you) fail; impve. 2nd pers. sing. / *malograrse.*

malogrémonos let us fail; impve. 1st pers. pl. / *malograrse.*

malógrense let them fail; impve. 3rd pers. pl. / *malograrse.*

malógrese let him (her/it) fail; impve. 3rd pers. sing. / *malograrse.*

malpagar to underpay. irr.

malpague 1. that I may underpay; pres. subj. 1st pers. sing. / *malpagar.* 2. that he (she/it) may underpay; pres. subj. 3rd pers. sing. 3. let him (her/it) underpay; impve. 3rd pers. sing.

malpagué I underpaid; past 1st pers. sing. / *malpagar.*

malpaguéis that you (all) may underpay; pres. subj. 2nd pers. pl. / *malpagar.*

malpaguemos 1. that we may underpay; pres. subj. 1st pers. pl. / *malpagar.* 2. let us underpay; impve. 1st pers. pl.

malpaguen 1. that they may underpay; pres. subj. 3rd pers. pl. / *malpagar.* 2. let them underpay; impve. 3rd pers. pl.

malpagues that you may underpay; pres. subj. 2nd pers. sing. / *malpagar.*

malparar to hurt. reg.

malparir to miscarry. reg.

malquerer to dislike. irr.

malquerrá he (she/it) will dislike; fut. 3rd pers. sing. / *malquerer.*

malquerrán they will dislike; fut. 3rd pers. pl. / *malquerer.*

malquerrás you will dislike; fut. 2nd pers. sing. / *malquerer.*

malquerré I shall dislike; fut. 1st pers. sing. / *malquerer.*

malquerréis you (all) will dislike; fut. 2nd pers. pl. / *malquerer.*

malquerremos we shall dislike; fut. 1st pers. pl. / *malquerer.*

malquerría 1. I should dislike; cond. 1st pers. sing. / *malquerer.* 2. he (she/it) would dislike; cond. 3rd pers. sing.

malquerríais you (all) would dislike; cond. 2nd pers. pl. / *malquerer.*

malquerríamos we should dislike; cond. 1st pers. pl. / *malquerer.*

malquerrían they would dislike; cond. 3rd pers. pl. / *malquerer.*

malquerrías you would dislike; cond. 2nd pers. sing. / *malquerer.*

malquiera 1. that I may dislike; pres. subj. 1st pers. sing. / *malquerer.* 2. that he (she/it) may dislike; pres. subj. 3rd pers. sing. 3. let him (her/it) dislike; impve. 3rd pers. sing.

malquieran 1. that they may dislike; pres. subj. 3rd pers. pl. / *malquerer.* 2. let them dislike; impve. 3rd pers. pl.

malquieras that you may dislike; pres. subj. 2nd pers. sing. / *malquerer.*

malquiere 1. he (she/it) dislikes; pres. ind. 3rd pers. sing. / *malquerer.* 2. (you) dislike; impve. 2nd pers. sing.

malquieren they dislike; pres. ind. 3rd pers. pl. / *malquerer.*

malquieres you dislike; pres. ind. 2nd pers. sing. / *malquerer.*

malquiero I dislike; pres. ind. 1st pers. sing. / *malquerer.*

malquise I disliked; past 1st pers. sing. / *malquerer.*

malquisiera 1. that I might dislike; imp. subj. 1st pers. sing. / *malquerer.* 2. that he (she/it) might dislike; imp. subj. 3rd pers. sing.

malquisierais that you (all) might dislike; imp. subj. 2nd pers pl. / *malquerer.*

malquisiéramos that we might dislike; imp. subj. 1st pers. pl. / *malquerer.*

malquisieran that they might dislike; imp. subj. 3rd pers. pl. / *malquerer.*

malquisieras that you might dislike; imp. subj. 2nd pers. sing. / *malquerer.*

malquisieron they disliked; past 3rd pers. pl. / *malquerer.*

malquisiese 1. that I might dislike; imp. subj. 1st pers. sing. / *malquerer.* 2. that he (she/it) might dislike; imp. subj. 3rd pers. sing.

malquisieseis that you (all) might dislike; imp. subj. 2nd pers pl. / *malquerer.*

malquisiésemos that we might dislike; imp. subj. 1st pers. pl. / *malquerer.*

malquisiesen that they might dislike; imp. subj. 3rd pers. pl. / *malquerer.*

malquisieses that you might dislike; imp. subj. 2nd pers. sing. / *malquerer.*

malquisimos we disliked; past 1st pers. pl. / *malquerer.*

malquisiste you disliked; past 2nd pers. sing. / *malquerer.*

malquisisteis you (all) disliked; past 2nd pers. pl. / *malquerer.*

malquiso he (she/it) disliked; past 3rd pers. sing. / *malquerer.*

malquistar to alienate. reg.

maltraer to mistreat. irr.

maltraiga 1. that I may mistreat; pres. subj. 1st pers. sing. / *maltraer.* 2. that he (she/it) may mistreat; pres. subj. 3rd pers. sing. 3. let him (her/it) mistreat; impve. 3rd pers. sing.

maltraigáis that you (all) may mistreat; pres. subj. 2nd pers. pl. / *maltraer.*

maltraigamos 1. that we may mistreat; pres. subj. 1st pers. pl. / *maltraer.* 2. let us mistreat; impve. 1st pers. pl.

maltraigan 1. that they may mistreat; pres. subj. 3rd pers. pl. / *maltraer.* 2. let them mistreat; impve. 3rd pers. pl.

maltraigas that you may mistreat; pres. subj. 2nd pers. sing. / *maltraer.*

maltraigo I mistreat; pres. ind. 1st pers. sing. / *maltraer.*

maltraje I mistreated; past 1st pers. sing. / *maltraer.*

maltrajera 1. that I might mistreat; imp. subj. 1st pers. sing. / *maltraer.* 2. that he (she/it) might mistreat; imp. subj. 3rd pers. sing.

maltrajerais that you (all) might mistreat; imp. subj. 2nd pers pl. / *maltraer.*

maltrajéramos that we might mistreat; imp. subj. 1st pers. pl. / *maltraer.*

maltrajeran that they might mistreat; imp. subj. 3rd pers. pl. / *maltraer.*

maltrajeras that you might mistreat; imp. subj. 2nd pers. sing. / *maltraer.*

maltrajeron they mistreated; past 3rd pers. pl. / *maltraer.*

maltrajese 1. that I might mistreat; imp. subj. 1st pers. sing. / *maltraer.* 2. that he (she/it) might mistreat; imp. subj. 3rd pers. sing.

maltrajeseis that you (all) might mistreat; imp. subj. 2nd pers pl. / *maltraer.*

maltrajésemos that we might mistreat; imp. subj. 1st pers. pl. / *maltraer.*

maltrajesen that they might mistreat; imp. subj. 3rd pers. pl. / *maltraer.*

maltrajeses that you might mistreat; imp. subj. 2nd pers. sing. / *maltraer.*

maltrajimos we mistreated; past 1st pers. pl. / *malquerer.*

maltrajiste you mistreated; past 2nd pers. sing. / *malquerer.*

maltrajisteis you (all) mistreated; past 2nd pers. pl. / *malquerer.*

maltrajo he (she/it) mistreated; past 3rd pers. sing. / *maltraer.*

maltratar to treat badly. reg.

maltrayendo mistreating; pres. part. / *maltraer.*

malvender to sell at a loss. reg.

malversar to misappropriate. reg.

mamándose getting drunk; pres. part. / *mamarse.*

mamaos (you all) get drunk; impve. 2nd pers. pl. / *mamarse.*

mamar to suck. reg.

mamarse to get drunk. reg.

mámate (you) get drunk; impve. 2nd pers. sing. / *mamarse.*

mamémonos let us get drunk; impve. 1st pers. pl. / *mamarse.*

mámense let them get drunk; impve. 3rd pers. pl. / *mamarse.*

mámese let him (her/it) get drunk; impve. 3rd pers. sing. / *mamarse.*

manar to flow out. reg.

mancar to maim. irr.

mancillar to stain or to blot. reg.

mancomunándose acting together; pres. part. / *mancomunarse.*

mancomunaos (you all) act together; impve. 2nd pers. pl. / *mancomunarse.*

mancomunar to associate or to unite. reg.

mancomunarse to act together. reg.

mancomúnate (you) act together; impve. 2nd pers. sing. / *mancomunarse.*

mancomunémonos let us act together; impve. 1st pers. pl. / *mancomunarse.*

mancomúnense let them act together; impve. 3rd pers. pl. / *mancomunarse.*

mancomúnese let him (her/it) act together; impve. 3rd pers. sing. / *mancomunarse*.

manchar to stain or to spot. reg.

mandándose interconnecting; pres. part. / *mandarse*.

mandaos (you all) interconnect; impve. 2nd pers. pl. / *mandarse*.

mandar to command or to rule. reg.

mandarse to interconnect. reg.

mándate (you) interconnect; impve. 2nd pers. sing. / *mandarse*.

mandémonos let us interconnect; impve. 1st pers. pl. / *mandarse*.

mándense let them interconnect; impve. 3rd pers. pl. / *mandarse*.

mándese let him (her/it) interconnect; impve. 3rd pers. sing. / *mandarse*.

manducar to eat up. irr.

manduque 1. that I may eat up; pres. subj. 1st pers. sing. / *manducar*. 2. that he (she/it) may eat up; pres. subj. 3rd pers. sing. 3. let him (her/it) eat up; impve. 3rd pers. sing.

manduqué I ate up; past 1st pers. sing. / *manducar*.

manduquéis that you (all) may eat up; pres. subj. 2nd pers. pl. / *manducar*.

manduquemos 1. that we may eat up; pres. subj. 1st pers. pl. / *manducar*. 2. let us eat up; impve. 1st pers. pl.

manduquen 1. that they may eat up; pres. subj. 3rd pers. pl. / *manducar*. 2. let them eat up; impve. 3rd pers. pl.

manduques that you may eat up; pres. subj. 2nd pers. sing. / *manducar*.

maneándose getting tangled up; pres. part. / *manearse*.

maneaos (you all) get tangled up; impve. 2nd pers. pl. / *manearse*.

manear to hobble. reg.

manearse to get tangled up. reg.

manéate (you) get tangled up; impve. 2nd pers. sing. / *manearse*.

maneémonos let us get tangled up; impve. 1st pers. pl. / *manearse*.

manéense let them get tangled up; impve. 3rd pers. pl. / *manearse*.

manéese let him (her/it) get tangled up; impve. 3rd pers. sing. / *manearse*.

manejándose behaving; pres. part. / *manejarse*.

manejaos (you all) behave; impve. 2nd pers. pl. / *manejarse*.

manejar to manage. reg.

manejarse to behave. reg.

manéjate (you) behave; impve. 2nd pers. sing. / *manejarse*.

manejémonos let us behave; impve. 1st pers. pl. / *manejarse*.

manéjense let them behave; impve. 3rd pers. pl. / *manejarse*.

manéjese let him (her/it) behave; impve. 3rd pers. sing. / *manejarse*.

mangonear to meddle. reg.

maniatar to manacle. reg.

manicurar to manicure. reg.

manifestar to manifest. irr.

manifiesta 1. he (she/it) manifests; pres. ind. 3rd pers. sing. / *manifestar*. 2. (you) manifest; impve. 2nd pers. sing.

manifiestan they manifest; pres. ind. 3rd pers. pl. / *manifestar*.

manifiestas you manifest; pres. ind. 2nd pers. sing. / *manifestar*.

manifieste 1. that I may manifest; pres. subj. 1st pers. sing. / *manifestar*. 2. that he (she/it) may manifest; pres. subj. 3rd pers. sing. 3. let him (her/it) manifest; impve. 3rd pers. sing.

manifiesten 1. that they may manifest; pres. subj. 3rd pers. pl. / *manifestar*. 2. let them manifest; impve. 3rd pers. pl.

manifiestes that you may manifest; pres. subj. 2nd pers. sing. / *manifestar*.

manifiesto I manifest; pres. ind. 1st pers. sing. / *manifestar*.

maniobrar to maneuver. reg.

manipular to manipulate. reg.

manosear to handle or to touch. reg.

manotear to slap or to gesticulate. reg.

manque 1. that I may maim; pres. subj. 1st pers. sing. / *mancar*. 2. that he (she/it) may maim; pres. subj. 3rd pers. sing. 3. let him (her/it) maim; impve. 3rd pers. sing.

manqué I maimed; past 1st pers. sing. / *mancar*.

manquear to feign a limp. reg.

manquéis that you (all) may maim; pres. subj. 2nd pers. pl. / *mancar*.

manquemos 1. that we may maim; pres. subj. 1st pers. pl. / *mancar*. 2. let us maim; impve. 1st pers. pl.

manquen 1. that they may maim; pres. subj. 3rd pers. pl. / *mancar*. 2. let them maim; impve. 3rd pers. pl.

manques that you may maim; pres. subj. 2nd pers. sing. / *mancar*.

mantear to toss in a blanket. reg.

manten (you) maintain; impve. 2nd pers. sing. / *mantener*.

mantendrá he (she/it) will maintain; fut. 3rd pers. sing. / *mantener*.

mantendrán they will maintain; fut. 3rd pers. pl. / *mantener*.

mantendrás you will maintain; fut. 2nd pers. sing. / *mantener*.

mantendré I shall maintain; fut. 1st pers. sing. / *mantener*.

mantendréis you (all) will maintain; fut. 2nd pers. pl. / *mantener*.

mantendremos we shall maintain; fut. 1st pers. pl. / *mantener*.

mantendría 1. I should maintain; cond. 1st pers. sing. / *mantener*. 2. he (she/it) would maintain; cond. 3rd pers. sing.

mantendríais you (all) would maintain; cond. 2nd pers. pl. / *mantener*.

mantendríamos we should maintain; cond. 1st pers. pl. / *mantener.*

mantendrían they would maintain; cond. 3rd pers. pl. / *mantener.*

mantendrías you would maintain; cond. 2nd pers. sing. / *mantener.*

manteneos (you all) continue; impve. 2nd pers. pl. / *mantenerse.*

mantener to maintain. irr.

mantenerse to continue. irr.

manténete (you) continue; impve. 2nd pers. sing. / *mantenerse.*

mantenga 1. that I may maintain; pres. subj. 1st pers. sing. / *mantener.* 2. that he (she/it) may maintain; pres. subj. 3rd pers. sing. 3. let him (her/it) maintain; impve. 3rd pers. sing.

mantengáis that you (all) may maintain; pres. subj. 2nd pers. pl. / *mantener.*

mantengámonos let us continue; impve. 1st pers. pl. / *mantenerse.*

mantengamos 1. that we may maintain; pres. subj. 1st pers. pl. / *mantener.* 2. let us maintain; impve. 1st pers. pl.

mantengan 1. that they may maintain; pres. subj. 3rd pers. pl. / *mantener.* 2. let them maintain; impve. 3rd pers. pl.

manténganse let them continue; impve. 3rd pers. pl. / *mantenerse.*

mantengas that you may maintain; pres. subj. 2nd pers. sing. / *mantener.*

manténgase let him (her/it) continue; impve. 3rd pers. sing. / *mantenerse.*

mantengo I maintain; pres. ind. 1st pers. sing. / *mantener.*

manteniéndose continuing; pres. part. / *mantenerse.*

mantiene he (she/it) maintains; pres. ind. 3rd pers. sing. / *mantener.*

mantienen they maintain; pres. ind. 3rd pers. pl. / *mantener.*

mantienes you maintain; pres. ind. 2nd pers. sing. / *mantener.*

mantuve I maintained; past 1st pers. sing. / *mantener.*

mantuviera 1. that I might maintain; imp. subj. 1st pers. sing. / *mantener.* 2. that he (she/it) might maintain; imp. subj. 3rd pers. sing.

mantuvierais that you (all) might maintain; imp. subj. 2nd pers pl. / *mantener.*

mantuviéramos that we might maintain; imp. subj. 1st pers. pl. / *mantener.*

mantuvieran that they might maintain; imp. subj. 3rd pers. pl. / *mantener.*

mantuvieras that you might maintain; imp. subj. 2nd pers. sing. / *mantener.*

mantuvieron they maintained; past 3rd pers. pl. / *mantener.*

mantuviese 1. that I might maintain; imp. subj. 1st pers. sing. / *mantener.* 2. that he (she/it) might maintain; imp. subj. 3rd pers. sing.

mantuvieseis that you (all) might maintain; imp. subj. 2nd pers pl. / *mantener.*

mantuviésemos that we might maintain; imp. subj. 1st pers. pl. / *mantener.*

mantuviesen that they might maintain; imp. subj. 3rd pers. pl. / *mantener.*

mantuvieses that you might maintain; imp. subj. 2nd pers. sing. / *mantener.*

mantuvimos we maintained; past 1st pers. pl. / *mantener.*

mantuviste you maintained; past 2nd pers. sing. / *mantener.*

mantuvisteis you (all) maintained; past 2nd pers. pl. / *mantener.*

mantuvo he (she/it) maintained; past 3rd pers. sing. / *mantener.*

manufacturar to manufacture. reg.

manumitir to manumit. reg.

mañanear to rise early. reg.

mañear to wangle. reg.

maquillándose putting on one's makeup; pres. part. / *maquillarse.*

maquillaos (you all) put on your makeup; impve. 2nd pers. pl. / *maquillarse.*

maquillar to make up. reg.

maquillarse to put on one's makeup. reg.

maquíllate (you) put on your makeup; impve. 2nd pers. sing. / *maquillarse.*

maquillémonos let us put on our makeup; impve. 1st pers. pl. / *maquillarse.*

maquíllense let them put on their makeup; impve. 3rd pers. pl. / *maquillarse.*

maquíllese let him (her) put on his (her) makeup / *maquillarse.*

maquinar to plot or to scheme. reg.

maravillándose marvelling; pres. part. / *maravillarse.*

maravillaos (you all) marvel; impve. 2nd pers. pl. / *maravillarse.*

maravillar to amaze. reg.

maravillarse to marvel. reg.

maravíllate (you) marvel; impve. 2nd pers. sing. / *maravillarse.*

maravillémonos let us marvel; impve. 1st pers. pl. / *maravillarse.*

maravíllense let them marvel; impve. 3rd pers. pl. / *maravillarse.*

maravíllese let him (her/it) marvel; impve. 3rd pers. sing. / *maravillarse.*

marcar to mark. irr.

marchándose going away; pres. part. / *marcharse.*

marchaos (you all) go away; impve. 2nd pers. pl. / *marcharse.*

marchar to march. reg.

marcharse to go away. reg.

márchate (you) go away; impve. 2nd pers. sing. / *marcharse.*

marchémonos let us go away; impve. 1st pers. pl. / *marcharse.*

márchense let them go away; impve. 3rd pers. pl. / *marcharse.*

márchese let him (her/it) go away; impve. 3rd pers. sing. / *marcharse.*

marchitándose fading; pres. part. / *marchitarse.*
marchitaos (you all) fade; impve. 2nd pers. pl. / *marchitarse.*
marchitar to wither. reg.
marchitarse to fade. reg.
marchítate (you) fade; impve. 2nd pers. sing. / *marchitarse.*
marchitémonos let us fade; impve. 1st pers. pl. / *marchitarse.*
marchítense let them fade; impve. 3rd pers. pl. / *marchitarse.*
marchítese let him (her/it) fade; impve. 3rd pers. sing. / *marchitarse.*
mareándose getting seasick; pres. part. / *marearse.*
mareaos (you all) get seasick; impve. 2nd pers. pl. / *marearse.*
marear to navigate. reg.
marearse to get seasick. reg.
maréate (you) get seasick; impve. 2nd pers. sing. / *marearse.*
mareémonos let us get seasick; impve. 1st pers. pl. / *marearse.*
maréense let them get seasick; impve. 3rd pers. pl. / *marearse.*
maréese let him (her/it) get seasick; impve. 3rd pers. sing. / *marearse.*
marginar to write in the margin. reg.
marinar to marinate. reg.
mariposear to flit. reg.
marque 1. that I may mark; pres. subj. 1st pers. sing. / *marcar.* 2. that he (she/it) may mark; pres. subj. 3rd pers. sing. 3. let him (her/it) mark; impve. 3rd pers. sing.
marqué I marked; past 1st pers. sing. / *marcar.*
marquéis that you (all) may mark; pres. subj. 2nd pers. pl. / *marcar.*
marquemos 1. that we may mark; pres. subj. 1st pers. pl. / *marcar.* 2. let us mark; impve. 1st pers. pl.
marquen 1. that they may mark; pres. subj. 3rd pers. pl. / *marcar.* 2. let them mark; impve. 3rd pers. pl.
marques that you may mark; pres. subj. 2nd pers. sing. / *marcar.*
marrar to fail. reg.
martillar to hammer. reg.
martillear to hammer. reg.
martirice 1. that I may martyr; pres. subj. 1st pers. sing. / *martirizar.* 2. that he (she/it) may martyr; pres. subj. 3rd pers. sing. 3. let him (her/it) martyr; impve. 3rd pers. sing.
martiricé I martyred; past 1st pers. sing. / *martirizar.*
martiricéis that you (all) may martyr; pres. subj. 2nd pers. pl. / *martirizar.*
martiricemos 1. that we may martyr; pres. subj. 1st pers. pl. / *martirizar.* 2. let us martyr; impve. 1st pers. pl.
martiricen 1. that they may martyr; pres. subj. 3rd pers. pl. / *martirizar.* 2. let them martyr; impve. 3rd pers. pl.
martirices that you may martyr; pres. subj. 2nd pers. sing. / *martirizar.*

martirizar to martyr. irr.
masacrar to massacre. reg.
masajear to massage. reg.
masar to knead. reg.
mascándose fraying; pres. part. / *mascarse.*
mascaos (you all) fray; impve. 2nd pers. pl. / *mascarse.*
mascar to chew. irr.
mascarse to fray. irr.
máscate (you) fray; impve. 2nd pers. sing. / *mascarse.*
mascullar to mumble. reg.
masque 1. that I may chew; pres. subj. 1st pers. sing. / *mascar.* 2. that he (she/it) may chew; pres. subj. 3rd pers. sing. 3. let him (her/it) chew; impve. 3rd pers. sing.
masqué I chewed; past 1st pers. sing. / *mascar.*
masquéis that you (all) may chew; pres. subj. 2nd pers. pl. / *mascar.*
masquémonos let us fray; impve. 1st pers. pl. / *mascarse.*
masquemos 1. that we may chew; pres. subj. 1st pers. pl. / *mascar.* 2. let us chew; impve. 1st pers. pl.
masquen 1. that they may chew; pres. subj. 3rd pers. pl. / *mascar.* 2. let them chew; impve. 3rd pers. pl.
másquense let them fray; impve. 3rd pers. pl. / *mascarse.*
masques that you may chew; pres. subj. 2nd pers. sing. / *mascar.*
másquese let him (her/it) fray; impve. 3rd pers. sing. / *mascarse.*
masticar to masticate or to chew. irr.
mastique 1. that I may masticate; pres. subj. 1st pers. sing. / *masticar.* 2. that he (she/it) may masticate; pres. subj. 3rd pers. sing. 3. let him (her/it) masticate; impve. 3rd pers. sing.
mastiqué I masticated; past 1st pers. sing. / *masticar.*
mastiquéis that you (all) may masticate; pres. subj. 2nd pers. pl. / *masticar.*
mastiquemos 1. that we may masticate; pres. subj. 1st pers. pl. / *masticar.* 2. let us masticate; impve. 1st pers. pl.
mastiquen 1. that they may masticate; pres. subj. 3rd pers. pl. / *masticar.* 2. let them masticate; impve. 3rd pers. pl.
mastiques that you may masticate; pres. subj. 2nd pers. sing. / *masticar.*
masturbándose masturbating; pres. part. / *masturbarse.*
masturbaos (you all) masturbate; impve. 2nd pers. pl. / *masturbarse.*
masturbarse to masturbate. reg.
mastúrbate (you) masturbate; impve. 2nd pers. sing. / *masturbarse.*
masturbémonos let us masturbate; impve. 1st pers. pl. / *masturbarse.*
mastúrbense let them masturbate; impve. 3rd pers. pl. / *masturbarse.*
mastúrbese let him (her/it) masturbate; impve. 3rd pers. sing. / *masturbarse.*
matándose committing suicide; pres. part. / *matarse.*

mataos (you all) commit suicide; impve. 2nd pers. pl. / *matarse*.

mataperrear to roam the streets committing mischief. reg.

matar to kill. reg.

matarse to commit suicide. reg.

mátate (you) commit suicide; impve. 2nd pers. sing. / *matarse*.

matear to plant seeds. reg.

matémonos let us commit suicide; impve. 1st pers. pl. / *matarse*.

mátense let them commit suicide; impve. 3rd pers. pl. / *matarse*.

materialice 1. that I may materialize; pres. subj. 1st pers. sing. / *materializar*. 2. that he (she/it) may materialize; pres. subj. 3rd pers. sing. 3. let him (her/it) materialize; impve. 3rd pers. sing.

materialicé I materialized; past 1st pers. sing. / *materializar*.

materialicéis that you (all) may materialize; pres. subj. 2nd pers. pl. / *materializar*.

materialicemos 1. that we may materialize; pres. subj. 1st pers. pl. / *materializar*. 2. let us materialize; impve. 1st pers. pl.

materialicen 1. that they may materialize; pres. subj. 3rd pers. pl. / *materializar*. 2. let them materialize; impve. 3rd pers. pl.

materialices that you may materialize; pres. subj. 2nd pers. sing. / *materializar*.

materializar to materialize. irr.

mátese let him (her/it) commit suicide; impve. 3rd pers. sing. / *matarse*.

matice 1. that I may tint; pres. subj. 1st pers. sing. / *matizar*. 2. that he (she/it) may tint; pres. subj. 3rd pers. sing. 3. let him (her/it) tint; impve. 3rd pers. sing.

maticé I tinted; past 1st pers. sing. / *matizar*.

maticéis that you (all) may tint; pres. subj. 2nd pers. pl. / *matizar*.

maticemos 1. that we may tint; pres. subj. 1st pers. pl. / *matizar*. 2. let us tint; impve. 1st pers. pl.

maticen 1. that they may tint; pres. subj. 3rd pers. pl. / *matizar*. 2. let them tint; impve. 3rd pers. pl.

matices that you may tint; pres. subj. 2nd pers. sing. / *matizar*.

matizar to shade or to tint. irr.

matraquear to jeer. reg.

matriculándose registering; pres. part. / *matricularse*.

matriculaos (you all) register; impve. 2nd pers. pl. / *matricularse*.

matricular to matriculate. reg.

matricularse to register. reg.

matricúlate (you) register; impve. 2nd pers. sing. / *matricularse*.

matriculémonos let us register; impve. 1st pers. pl. / *matricularse*.

matricúlense let them register; impve. 3rd pers. pl. / *matricularse*.

matricúlese let him (her/it) register; impve. 3rd pers. sing. / *matricularse*.

matutear to smuggle. reg.

maúlla 1. he (she/it) meows; pres. ind. 3rd pers. sing. / *maullar*. 2. (you) meow; impve. 2nd pers. sing.

maúllan they meow; pres. ind. 3rd pers. pl. / *maullar*.

maullar to meow. irr.

maúllas you meow; pres. ind. 2nd pers. sing. / *maullar*.

maúlle 1. that I may meow; pres. subj. 1st pers. sing. / *maullar*. 2. that he (she/it) may meow; pres. subj. 3rd pers. sing. 3. let him (her/it) meow; impve. 3rd pers. sing.

maúllen 1. that they may meow; pres. subj. 3rd pers. pl. / *maullar*. 2. let them meow; impve. 3rd pers. pl.

maúlles that you may meow; pres. subj. 2nd pers. sing. / *maullar*.

maúllo I meow; pres. ind. 1st pers. sing. / *maullar*.

mayar to meow. reg.

mayorear to wholesale. reg.

meándose urinating; pres. part. / *mearse*.

meaos (you all) urinate; impve. 2nd pers. pl. / *mearse*.

mear to urinate. reg.

mearse to urinate. reg.

méate (you) urinate; impve. 2nd pers. sing. / *mearse*.

mecanice 1. that I may mechanize; pres. subj. 1st pers. sing. / *mecanizar*. 2. that he (she/it) may mechanize; pres. subj. 3rd pers. sing. 3. let him (her/it) mechanize; impve. 3rd pers. sing.

mecanicé I mechanized; past 1st pers. sing. / *mecanizar*.

mecanicéis that you (all) may mechanize; pres. subj. 2nd pers. pl. / *mecanizar*.

mecanicémonos let us mechanize; impve. 1st pers. pl. / *mecanizarse*.

mecanicemos 1. that we may mechanize; pres. subj. 1st pers. pl. / *mecanizar*. 2. let us mechanize; impve. 1st pers. pl.

mecanicen 1. that they may mechanize; pres. subj. 3rd pers. pl. / *mecanizar*. 2. let them mechanize; impve. 3rd pers. pl.

mecanícense let them mechanize; impve. 3rd pers. pl. / *mecanizarse*.

mecanices that you may mechanize; pres. subj. 2nd pers. sing. / *mecanizar*.

mecanícese let him (her/it) mechanize; impve. 3rd pers. sing. / *mecanizarse*.

mecanizándose mechanizing; pres. part. / *mecanizarse*.

mecanizaos (you all) mechanize; impve. 2nd pers. pl. / *mecanizarse*.

mecanizar to mechanize. irr.

mecanizarse to mechanize. irr.

mecanízate (you) mechanize; impve. 2nd pers. sing. / *mecanizarse*.

mecanografía 1. he (she/it) types; pres. ind. 3rd pers. sing. / *mecanografiar*. 2. (you) type; impve. 2nd pers. sing.

mecanografían they type; pres. ind. 3rd pers. pl. / *mecanografiar*.

mecanografiar to type. irr.

mecanografías you type; pres. ind. 2nd pers. sing. / *mecanografiar*.

mecanografie 1. that I may type; pres. subj. 1st pers. sing. / *mecanografiar*. 2. that he (she/it) may type; pres. subj. 3rd pers. sing. 3. let him (her/it) type; impve. 3rd pers. sing.

mecanografíen 1. that they may type; pres. subj. 3rd pers. pl. / *mecanografiar*. 2. let them type; impve. 3rd pers. pl.

mecanografíes that you may type; pres. subj. 2nd pers. sing. / *mecanografiar*.

mecanografío I type; pres. ind. 1st pers. sing. / *mecanografiar*.

meceos (you all) swing; impve. 2nd pers. pl. / *mecerse*.

mecer to swing or to rock. irr.

mecerse to swing. irr.

mécete (you) swing; impve. 2nd pers. sing. / *mecerse*.

meciéndose swinging; pres. part. / *mecerse*.

mechar to lard. reg.

mediar to mediate or to be in the middle. reg.

mediatice 1. that I may control; pres. subj. 1st pers. sing. / *mediatizar*. 2. that he (she/it) may control; pres. subj. 3rd pers. sing. 3. let him (her/it) control; impve. 3rd pers. sing.

mediaticé I controlled; past 1st pers. sing. / *mediatizar*.

mediaticéis that you (all) may control; pres. subj. 2nd pers. pl. / *mediatizar*.

mediaticemos 1. that we may control; pres. subj. 1st pers. pl. / *mediatizar*. 2. let us control; impve. 1st pers. pl.

mediaticen 1. that they may control; pres. subj. 3rd pers. pl. / *mediatizar*. 2. let them control; impve. 3rd pers. pl.

mediatices that you may control; pres. subj. 2nd pers. sing. / *mediatizar*.

mediatizar to control. irr.

medicinándose taking medicine; pres. part. / *medicinarse*.

medicinaos (you all) take medicine; impve. 2nd pers. pl. / *medicinarse*.

medicinar to medicate. reg.

medicinarse to take medicine. reg.

medicínate (you) take medicine; impve. 2nd pers. sing. / *medicinarse*.

medicinémonos let us take medicine; impve. 1st pers. pl. / *medicinarse*.

medicínense let them take medicine; impve. 3rd pers. pl. / *medicinarse*.

medicínese let him (her/it) take medicine; impve. 3rd pers. sing. / *medicinarse*.

medíos (you all) act with moderation; impve. 2nd pers. pl. / *medirse*.

medir to measure. irr.

medirse to act with moderation. irr.

meditar to meditate. reg.

medrar to thrive. reg.

meémonos let us urinate; impve. 1st pers. pl. / *mearse*.

méense let them urinate; impve. 3rd pers. pl. / *mearse*.

méese let him (her/it) urinate; impve. 3rd pers. sing. / *mearse*.

mejorándose recovering; pres. part. / *mejorarse*.

mejoraos (you all) recover; impve. 2nd pers. pl. / *mejorarse*.

mejorar to improve. reg.

mejorarse to recover. reg.

mejórate (you) recover; impve. 2nd pers. sing. / *mejorarse*.

mejorémonos let us recover; impve. 1st pers. pl. / *mejorarse*.

mejórense let them recover; impve. 3rd pers. pl. / *mejorarse*.

mejórese let him (her/it) recover; impve. 3rd pers. sing. / *mejorarse*.

melancolice 1. that I may make melancholy; pres. subj. 1st pers. sing. / *melancolizar*. 2. that he (she/it) may make melancholy; pres. subj. 3rd pers. sing. 3. let him (her/it) make melancholy; impve. 3rd pers. sing.

melancolicé I made melancholy; past 1st pers. sing. / *melancolizar*.

melancolicéis that you (all) may make melancholy; pres. subj. 2nd pers. pl. / *melancolizar*.

melancolicémonos let us get melancholy; impve. 1st pers. pl. / *melancolizarse*.

melancolicemos 1. that we may make melancholy; pres. subj. 1st pers. pl. / *melancolizar*. 2. let us make melancholy; impve. 1st pers. pl.

melancolicen 1. that they may make melancholy; pres. subj. 3rd pers. pl. / *melancolizar*. 2. let them make melancholy; impve. 3rd pers. pl.

melancolícense let them get melancholy; impve. 3rd pers. pl. / *melancolizarse*.

melancolices that you may make melancholy; pres. subj. 2nd pers. sing. / *melancolizar*.

melancolícese let him (her/it) get melancholy; impve. 3rd pers. sing. / *melancolizarse*.

melancolizándose getting melancholy; pres. part. / *melancolizarse*.

melancolizaos (you all) get melancholy; impve. 2nd pers. pl. / *melancolizarse*.

melancolizar to make melancholy. irr.

melancolizarse to get melancholy. irr.

melancolízate (you) get melancholy; impve. 2nd pers. sing. / *melancolizarse*.

melindrear to be finicky. reg.

mellar to notch. reg.

memorice 1. that I may memorize; pres. subj. 1st pers. sing. / *memorizar*. 2. that he (she/it) may memorize; pres. subj. 3rd pers. sing. 3. let him (her/it) memorize; impve. 3rd pers. sing.

memoricé I memorized; past 1st pers. sing. / *memorizar*.

memoricéis that you (all) may memorize; pres. subj. 2nd pers. pl. / *memorizar*.

memoricemos 1. that we may memorize; pres. subj. 1st pers. pl. / *memorizar*. 2. let us memorize; impve. 1st pers. pl.

memoricen 1. that they may memorize; pres. subj. 3rd pers. pl. / *memorizar*. 2. let them memorize; impve. 3rd pers. pl.

memorices that you may memorize; pres. subj. 2nd pers. sing. / *memorizar*.

memorizar to memorize. irr.

mencionar to mention. reg.

mendigar to beg. irr.

mendigue 1. that I may beg; pres. subj. 1st pers. sing. / *mendigar*. 2. that he (she/it) may beg; pres. subj. 3rd pers. sing. 3. let him (her/it) beg; impve. 3rd pers. sing.

mendigué I begged; past 1st pers. sing. / *mendigar*.

mendiguéis that you (all) may beg; pres. subj. 2nd pers. pl. / *mendigar*.

mendiguemos 1. that we may beg; pres. subj. 1st pers. pl. / *mendigar*. 2. let us beg; impve. 1st pers. pl.

mendiguen 1. that they may beg; pres. subj. 3rd pers. pl. / *mendigar*. 2. let them beg; impve. 3rd pers. pl.

mendigues that you may beg; pres. subj. 2nd pers. sing. / *mendigar*.

meneándose wiggling; pres. part. / *menearse*.

meneaos (you all) wiggle; impve. 2nd pers. pl. / *menearse*.

menear to shake. reg.

menearse to wiggle or to wag. reg.

menéate (you) wiggle; impve. 2nd pers. sing. / *menearse*.

meneémonos let us wiggle; impve. 1st pers. pl. / *menearse*.

menéense let them wiggle; impve. 3rd pers. pl. / *menearse*.

menéese let him (her/it) wiggle; impve. 3rd pers. sing. / *menearse*.

menguar to decrease. irr.

mengüe 1. that I may decrease; pres. subj. 1st pers. sing. / *menguar*. 2. that he (she/it) may decrease; pres. subj. 3rd pers. sing. 3. let him (her/it) decrease; impve. 3rd pers. sing.

mengüé I decreased; past 1st pers. sing. / *menguar*.

mengüéis that you (all) may decrease; pres. subj. 2nd pers. pl. / *menguar*.

mengüemos 1. that we may decrease; pres. subj. 1st pers. pl. / *menguar*. 2. let us decrease; impve. 1st pers. pl.

mengüen 1. that they may decrease; pres. subj. 3rd pers. pl. / *menguar*. 2. let them decrease; impve. 3rd pers. pl.

mengües that you may decrease; pres. subj. 2nd pers. sing. / *menguar*.

menoscabar to lessen. reg.

menospreciar to underrate. reg.

menstrúa 1. she menstruates; pres. ind. 3rd pers. sing. / *menstruar*. 2. (you) menstrate; impve. 2nd pers. sing.

menstrúan they menstruate; pres. ind. 3rd pers. pl. / *menstruar*.

menstruar to menstruate. irr.

menstrúas you menstruate; pres. ind. 2nd pers. sing. / *menstruar*.

menstrúe 1. that I may menstruate; pres. subj. 1st pers. sing. / *menstruar*. 2. that she may menstruate; pres. subj. 3rd pers. sing. 3. let her menstruate; impve. 3rd pers. sing.

menstrúen 1. that they may menstruate; pres. subj. 3rd pers. pl. / *menstruar*. 2. let them menstruate; impve. 3rd pers. pl.

menstrúes that you may menstruate; pres. subj. 2nd pers. sing. / *menstruar*.

menstrúo I menstruate; pres. ind. 1st pers. sing. / *menstruar*.

mentar to mention. irr.

mentir to lie. irr.

menudear to happen frequently or to repeat. reg.

mercar to buy. irr.

mercerice 1. that I may mercerize; pres. subj. 1st pers. sing. / *mercerizar*. 2. that he (she/it) may mercerize; pres. subj. 3rd pers. sing. 3. let him (her/it) mercerize; impve. 3rd pers. sing.

mercericé I mercerized; past 1st pers. sing. / *mercerizar*.

mercericéis that you (all) may mercerize; pres. subj. 2nd pers. pl. / *mercerizar*.

mercericemos 1. that we may mercerize; pres. subj. 1st pers. pl. / *mercerizar*. 2. let us mercerize; impve. 1st pers. pl.

mercericen 1. that they may mercerize; pres. subj. 3rd pers. pl. / *mercerizar*. 2. let them mercerize; impve. 3rd pers. pl.

mercerices that you may mercerize; pres. subj. 2nd pers. sing. / *mercerizar*.

mercerizar to mercerize. irr.

merecer to deserve. irr.

merendar to have a snack. irr.

merezca 1. that I may deserve; pres. subj. 1st pers. sing. / *merecer*. 2. that he (she/it) may deserve; pres. subj. 3rd pers. sing. 3. let him (her/it) deserve; impve. 3rd pers. sing.

merezcáis that you (all) may deserve; pres. subj. 2nd pers. pl. / *merecer*.

merezcamos 1. that we may deserve; pres. subj. 1st pers. pl. / *merecer*. 2. let us deserve; impve. 1st pers. pl.

merezcan 1. that they may deserve; pres. subj. 3rd pers. pl. / *merecer*. 2. let them deserve; impve. 3rd pers. pl.

merezcas that you may deserve; pres. subj. 2nd pers. sing. / *merecer*.

merezco I deserve; pres. ind. 1st pers. sing. / *merecer*.

merienda 1. he (she/it) has a snack; pres. ind. 3rd pers. sing. / *merendar*. 2. (you) have a snack; impve. 2nd pers. sing.

meriendan they have a snack; pres. ind. 3rd pers. pl. / *merendar*.

meriendas you have a snack; pres. ind. 2nd pers. sing. / *merendar*.

meriende 1. that I may have a snack; pres. subj. 1st pers. sing. / *merendar*. 2. that he (she/it) may have a snack; pres. subj. 3rd pers. sing. 3. let him (her/it) have a snack; impve. 3rd pers. sing.

merienden 1. that they may have a snack; pres. subj. 3rd pers. pl. / *merendar*. 2. let them have a snack; impve. 3rd pers. pl.

meriendes that you may have a snack; pres. subj. 2nd pers. sing. / *merendar*.

meriendo I have a snack; pres. ind. 1st pers. sing. / *merendar*.

mermándose dwindling; pres. part. / *mermarse*.

mermaos (you all) dwindle; impve. 2nd pers. pl. / *mermarse*.

mermar to diminish. reg.

mermarse to dwindle. reg.

mérmate (you) dwindle; impve. 2nd pers. sing. / *mermarse*.

mermémonos let us dwindle; impve. 1st pers. pl. / *mermarse*.

mérmense let them dwindle; impve. 3rd pers. pl. / *mermarse*.

mérmese let him (her/it) dwindle; impve. 3rd pers. sing. / *mermarse*.

merodear to maraud or to forage. reg.

merque 1. that I may buy; pres. subj. 1st pers. sing. / *mercar*. 2. that he (she/it) may buy; pres. subj. 3rd pers. sing. 3. let him (her/it) buy; impve. 3rd pers. sing.

merqué I bought; past 1st pers. sing. / *mercar*.

merquéis that you (all) may buy; pres. subj. 2nd pers. pl. / *mercar*.

merquemos 1. that we may buy; pres. subj. 1st pers. pl. / *mercar*. 2. let us buy; impve. 1st pers. pl.

merquen 1. that they may buy; pres. subj. 3rd pers. pl. / *mercar*. 2. let them buy; impve. 3rd pers. pl.

merques that you may buy; pres. subj. 2nd pers. sing. / *mercar*.

mesándose tearing out one's hair; pres. part. / *mesarse*.

mesaos (you all) tear out your hair; impve. 2nd pers. pl. / *mesarse*.

mesar to tear out one's hair. reg.

mesarse to tear out one's hair. reg.

mésate (you) tear out your hair; impve. 2nd pers. sing. / *mesarse*.

mesémonos let us tear out our hair; impve. 1st pers. pl. / *mesarse*.

mésense let them tear out their hair; impve. 3rd pers. pl. / *mesarse*.

mésese let him (her/it) tear out his (her/its) hair; impve. 3rd pers. sing. / *mesarse*.

mesurándose controlling oneself; pres. part. / *mesurarse*.

mesuraos (you all) control yourselves; impve. 2nd pers. pl. / *mesurarse*.

mesurar to temper. reg.

mesurarse to control oneself. reg.

mesúrate (you) control yourself; impve. 2nd pers. sing. / *mesurarse*.

mesurémonos let us control ourselves; impve. 1st pers. pl. / *mesurarse*.

mesúrense let them control themselves; impve. 3rd pers. pl. / *mesurarse*.

mesúrese let him (her/it) control himself (herself/itself); impve. 3rd pers. sing. / *mesurarse*.

metalice 1. that I may be dominated by the love of money; pres. subj. 1st pers. sing. / *metalizarse*. 2. that he (she/it) may be dominated by the love of money; pres. subj. 3rd pers. sing.

metalicé I was dominated by the love of money; past 1st pers. sing. / *metalizarse*.

metalicéis that you (all) may be dominated by the love of money; pres. subj. 2nd pers. pl. / *metalizarse*.

metalicémonos let us be dominated by the love of money; impve. 1st pers. pl. / *metalizarse*.

metalicemos that we may be dominated by the love of money; pres. subj. 1st pers. pl. / *metalizarse*.

metalicen that they may be dominated by the love of money; pres. subj. 3rd pers. pl. / *metalizarse*.

metalícense let them be dominated by the love of money; impve. 3rd pers. pl. / *metalizarse*.

metalices that you may be dominated by the love of money; pres. subj. 2nd pers. sing. / *metalizarse*.

metalícese let him (her/it) be dominated by the love of money; impve. 3rd pers. sing. / *metalizarse*.

metalizándose being dominated by the love of money; pres. part. / *metalizarse*.

metalizaos (you all) be dominated by the love of money; impve. 2nd pers. pl. / *metalizarse*.

metalizarse to be dominated by the love of money. irr.

metalízate (you) be dominated by the love of money; impve. 2nd pers. sing. / *metalizarse*.

metámonos let us meddle; impve. 1st pers. pl. / *meterse*.

metamorfosear to metamorphose. reg.

métanse let them meddle; impve. 3rd pers. pl. / *meterse*.

métase let him (her/it) meddle; impve. 3rd pers. sing. / *meterse*.

meteos (you all) meddle; impve. 2nd pers. pl. / *meterse*.

meter to put in. reg.

meterse to meddle. reg.

métete (you) meddle; impve. 2nd pers. sing. / *meterse*.

metiéndose meddling; pres. part. / *meterse*.

meza 1. that I may swing; pres. subj. 1st pers. sing. / *mecer*. 2. that he (she/it) may swing; pres. subj. 3rd pers. sing. 3. let him (her/it) swing; impve. 3rd pers. sing.

mezáis that you (all) may swing; pres. subj. 2nd pers. pl. / *mecer*.

mezámonos let us swing; impve. 1st pers. pl. / *mecerse*.

mezamos 1. that we may swing; pres. subj. 1st pers. pl. / *mecer*. 2. let us swing; impve. 1st pers. pl.

mezan 1. that they may swing; pres. subj. 3rd pers. pl. / *mecer*. 2. let them swing; impve. 3rd pers. pl.

mézanse let them swing; impve. 3rd pers. pl. / *mecerse*.

mezas that you may swing; pres. subj. 2nd pers. sing. / *mecer*.

mézase let him (her/it) swing; impve. 3rd pers. sing. / *mecerse*.

mezclándose mingling; pres. part. / *mezclarse*.

mezclaos (you all) mingle; impve. 2nd pers. pl. / *mezclarse*.

mezclar to mix. reg.

mezclarse to mingle. reg.

mézclate (you) mingle; impve. 2nd pers. sing. / *mezclarse*.

mezclémonos let us mingle; impve. 1st pers. pl. / *mezclarse*.

mézclense let them mingle; impve. 3rd pers. pl. / *mezclarse*.

mézclese let him (her/it) mingle; impve. 3rd pers. sing. / *mezclarse*.

mezo I swing; pres. ind. 1st pers. sing. / *mecer*.

mía 1. he (she/it) meows; pres. ind. 3rd pers. sing. / *miar*. 2. (you) meow; impve. 2nd pers. sing.

mían they meow; pres. ind. 3rd pers. pl. / *miar*.

miar to meow. irr.

mías you meow; pres. ind. 2nd pers. sing. / *miar*.

mida 1. that I may measure; pres. subj. 1st pers. sing. / *medir*. 2. that he (she/it) may measure; pres. subj. 3rd pers. sing. 3. let him (her/it) measure; impve. 3rd pers. sing.

midáis that you (all) may measure; pres. subj. 2nd pers. pl. / *medir*.

midámonos let us act with moderation; impve. 1st pers. pl. / *medirse*.

midamos 1. that we may measure; pres. subj. 1st pers. pl. / *medir*. 2. let us measure; impve. 1st pers. pl.

midan 1. that they may measure; pres. subj. 3rd pers. pl. / *medir*. 2. let them measure; impve. 3rd pers. pl.

mídanse let them act with moderation; impve. 3rd pers. pl. / *medirse*.

midas that you may measure; pres. subj. 2nd pers. sing. / *medir*.

mídase let him (her/it) act with moderation; impve. 3rd pers. sing. / *medirse*.

mide 1. he (she/it) measures; pres. ind. 3rd pers. sing. / *medir*. 2. (you) measure; impve. 2nd pers. sing.

miden they measure; pres. ind. 3rd pers. pl. / *medir*.

mides you measure; pres. ind. 2nd pers. sing. / *medir*.

mídete (you) act with moderation; impve. 2nd pers. sing. / *medirse*.

midiendo measuring; pres. part. / *medir*.

midiéndose acting with moderation; pres. part. / *medirse*.

midiera 1. that I might measure; imp. subj. 1st pers. sing. / *medir*. 2. that he (she/it) might measure; imp. subj. 3rd pers. sing.

midierais that you (all) might measure; imp. subj. 2nd pers pl. / *medir*.

midiéramos that we might measure; imp. subj. 1st pers. pl. / *medir*.

midieran that they might measure; imp. subj. 3rd pers. pl. / *medir*.

midieras that you might measure; imp. subj. 2nd pers. sing. / *medir*.

midieron they measured; past 3rd pers. pl. / *medir*.

midiese 1. that I might measure; imp. subj. 1st pers. sing. / *medir*. 2. that he (she/it) might measure; imp. subj. 3rd pers. sing.

midieseis that you (all) might measure; imp. subj. 2nd pers pl. / *medir*.

midiésemos that we might measure; imp. subj. 1st pers. pl. / *medir*.

midiesen that they might measure; imp. subj. 3rd pers. pl. / *medir*.

midieses that you might measure; imp. subj. 2nd pers. sing. / *medir*.

midió he (she/it) measured; past 3rd pers. sing. / *medir*.

mido I measure; pres. ind. 1st pers. sing. / *medir*.

míe 1. that I may meow; pres. subj. 1st pers. sing. / *miar*. 2. that he (she/it) may meow; pres. subj. 3rd pers. sing. 3. let him (her/it) meow; impve. 3rd pers. sing.

míen 1. that they may meow; pres. subj. 3rd pers. pl. / *miar*. 2. let them meow; impve. 3rd pers. pl.

mienta 1. he (she/it) mentions; pres. ind. 3rd pers. sing. / *mentar*. 2. (you) mention; impve. 2nd pers. sing.

mienta 1. that I may lie; pres. subj. 1st pers. sing. / *mentir*. 2. that he (she/it) may lie; pres. subj. 3rd pers. sing. 3. let him (her/it) lie; impve. 3rd pers. sing.

mientan they mention; pres. ind. 3rd pers. pl. / *mentar*.

mientan 1. that they may lie; pres. subj. 3rd pers. pl. / *mentir*. 2. let them lie; impve. 3rd pers. pl.

mientas you mention; pres. ind. 2nd pers. sing. / *mentar*.

mientas that you may lie; pres. subj. 2nd pers. sing. / *mentir*.

miente 1. that I may mention; pres. subj. 1st pers. sing. / *mentar*. 2. that he (she/it) may mention; pres. subj. 3rd pers. sing. 3. let him (her/it) mention; impve. 3rd pers. sing.

miente 1. he (she/it) lies; pres. ind. 3rd pers. sing. / *mentir*. 2. (you) lie; impve. 2nd pers. sing.

mienten 1. that they may mention; pres. subj. 3rd pers. pl. / *mentar*. 2. let them mention; impve. 3rd pers. pl.

mienten they lie; pres. ind. 3rd pers. pl. / *mentir*.

mientes that you may mention; pres. subj. 2nd pers. sing. / *mentar*.

mientes you lie; pres. ind. 2nd pers. sing. / *mentir*.

miento I mention; pres. ind. 1st pers. sing. / *mentar*.

miento I lie; pres. ind. 1st pers. sing. / *mentir*.

míes that you may meow; pres. subj. 2nd pers. sing. / *miar*.

migar to crumble. irr.

migue 1. that I may crumble; pres. subj. 1st pers. sing. / *migar*. 2. that he (she/it) may crumble; pres. subj. 3rd pers. sing. 3. let him (her/it) crumble; impve. 3rd pers. sing.

migué I crumbled; past 1st pers. sing. / *migar*.

miguéis that you (all) may crumble; pres. subj. 2nd pers. pl. / *migar*.

miguemos 1. that we may crumble; pres. subj. 1st pers. pl. / *migar*. 2. let us crumble; impve. 1st pers. pl.

miguen 1. that they may crumble; pres. subj. 3rd pers. pl. / *migar*. 2. let them crumble; impve. 3rd pers. pl.

migues that you may crumble; pres. subj. 2nd pers. sing. / *migar*.

militar to serve in the military or to militate. reg.

militarice 1. that I may militarize; pres. subj. 1st pers. sing. / *militarizar*. 2. that he (she/it) may militarize; pres. subj. 3rd pers. sing. 3. let him (her/it) militarize; impve. 3rd pers. sing.

militaricé I militarized; past 1st pers. sing. / *militarizar*.

militaricéis that you (all) may militarize; pres. subj. 2nd pers. pl. / *militarizar*.

militaricemos 1. that we may militarize; pres. subj. 1st pers. pl. / *militarizar*. 2. let us militarize; impve. 1st pers. pl.

militaricen 1. that they may militarize; pres. subj. 3rd pers. pl. / *militarizar*. 2. let them militarize; impve. 3rd pers. pl.

militarices that you may militarize; pres. subj. 2nd pers. sing. / *militarizar*.

militarizar to militarize. irr.

mimar to pamper. reg.

mimbreándose bending; pres. part. / *mimbrearse*.

mimbreaos (you all) bend; impve. 2nd pers. pl. / *mimbrearse*.

mimbrear to sway. reg.

mimbrearse to bend. reg.

mimbréate (you) bend; impve. 2nd pers. sing. / *mimbrearse*.

mimbreémonos let us bend; impve. 1st pers. pl. / *mimbrearse*.

mimbréense let them bend; impve. 3rd pers. pl. / *mimbrearse*.

mimbréese let him (her/it) bend; impve. 3rd pers. sing. / *mimbrearse*.

mimeografía 1. he (she/it) mimeographs; pres. ind. 3rd pers. sing. / *mimeografiar*. 2. (you) mimeograph; impve. 2nd pers. sing.

mimeografían they mimeograph; pres. ind. 3rd pers. pl. / *mimeografiar*.

mimeografiar to mimeograph. irr.

mimeografías you mimeograph; pres. ind. 2nd pers. sing. / *mimeografiar*.

mimeografíe 1. that I may mimeograph; pres. subj. 1st pers. sing. / *mimeografiar*. 2. that he (she/it) may mimeograph; pres. subj. 3rd pers. sing. 3. let him (her/it) mimeograph; impve. 3rd pers. sing.

mimeografíen 1. that they may mimeograph; pres. subj. 3rd pers. pl. / *mimeografiar*. 2. let them mimeograph; impve. 3rd pers. pl.

mimeografíes that you may mimeograph; pres. subj. 2nd pers. sing. / *mimeografiar*.

mimeografío I mimeograph; pres. ind. 1st pers. sing. / *mimeografiar*.

minar to mine. reg.

miniar to illuminate or to paint in miniature. reg.

ministrar to minister. reg.

minorar to diminish. reg.

mintáis that you (all) may lie; pres. subj. 2nd pers. pl. / *mentir*.

mintamos 1. that we may lie; pres. subj. 1st pers. pl. / *mentir*. 2. let us lie; impve. 1st pers. pl.

mintiendo lying; pres. part. / *mentir*.

mintiera 1. that I might lie; imp. subj. 1st pers. sing. / *mentir*. 2. that he (she/it) might lie; imp. subj. 3rd pers. sing.

mintierais that you (all) might lie; imp. subj. 2nd pers pl. / *mentir*.

mintiéramos that we might lie; imp. subj. 1st pers. pl. / *mentir*.

mintieran that they might lie; imp. subj. 3rd pers. pl. / *mentir*.

mintieras that you might lie; imp. subj. 2nd pers. sing. / *mentir*.

mintieron they lied; past 3rd pers. pl. / *mentir*.

mintiese 1. that I might lie; imp. subj. 1st pers. sing. / *mentir*. 2. that he (she/it) might lie; imp. subj. 3rd pers. sing.

mintieseis that you (all) might lie; imp. subj. 2nd pers pl. / *mentir*.

mintiésemos that we might lie; imp. subj. 1st pers. pl. / *mentir*.

mintiesen that they might lie; imp. subj. 3rd pers. pl. / *mentir*.

mintieses that you might lie; imp. subj. 2nd pers. sing. / *mentir*.

mintió he (she/it) lied; past 3rd pers. sing. / *mentir*.

minutar to make a first draft of. reg.

mío I meow; pres. ind. 1st pers. sing. / *miar*.

mirándose following the example; pres. part. / *mirarse*.

miraos (you all) follow the example; impve. 2nd pers. pl. / *mirarse*.

mirar to look at. reg.

mirarse to follow the example. reg.

mírate (you) follow the example; impve. 2nd pers. sing. / *mirarse*.

mirémonos let us follow the example; impve. 1st pers. pl. / *mirarse*.

mírense let them follow the example; impve. 3rd pers. pl. / *mirarse*.

mírese let him (her/it) follow the example; impve. 3rd pers. sing. / *mirarse*.

mirlándose putting on airs; pres. part. / *mirlarse*.

mirlaos (you all) put on airs; impve. 2nd pers. pl. / *mirlarse*.

mirlarse to put on airs. reg.

mírlate (you) put on airs; impve. 2nd pers. sing. / *mirlarse*.

mirlémonos let us put on airs; impve. 1st pers. pl. / *mirlarse*.

mírlense let them put on airs; impve. 3rd pers. pl. / *mirlarse*.

mírlese let him (her/it) put on airs; impve. 3rd pers. sing. / *mirlarse*.

misar to hear mass. reg.

misonar to preach or to spread. reg.
mistar to mumble. reg.
mistificar to deceive. irr.
mistifique 1. that I may deceive; pres. subj. 1st pers. sing. / *mistificar*. 2. that he (she/it) may deceive; pres. subj. 3rd pers. sing. 3. let him (her/it) deceive; impve. 3rd pers. sing.
mistifiqué I deceived; past 1st pers. sing. / *mistificar*.
mistifiquéis that you (all) may deceive; pres. subj. 2nd pers. pl. / *mistificar*.
mistifiquemos 1. that we may deceive; pres. subj. 1st pers. pl. / *mistificar*. 2. let us deceive; impve. 1st pers. pl.
mistifiquen 1. that they may deceive; pres. subj. 3rd pers. pl. / *mistificar*. 2. let them deceive; impve. 3rd pers. pl.
mistifiques that you may deceive; pres. subj. 2nd pers. sing. / *mistificar*.
mitigar to mitigate. irr.
mitigue 1. that I may mitigate; pres. subj. 1st pers. sing. / *mitigar*. 2. that he (she/it) may mitigate; pres. subj. 3rd pers. sing. 3. let him (her/it) mitigate; impve. 3rd pers. sing.
mitigué I mitigated; past 1st pers. sing. / *mitigar*.
mitiguéis that you (all) may mitigate; pres. subj. 2nd pers. pl. / *mitigar*.
mitiguemos 1. that we may mitigate; pres. subj. 1st pers. pl. / *mitigar*. 2. let us mitigate; impve. 1st pers. pl.
mitiguen 1. that they may mitigate; pres. subj. 3rd pers. pl. / *mitigar*. 2. let them mitigate; impve. 3rd pers. pl.
mitigues that you may mitigate; pres. subj. 2nd pers. sing. / *mitigar*.
mixtificar to mystify. irr.
mixtifique 1. that I may mystify; pres. subj. 1st pers. sing. / *mixtificar*. 2. that he (she/it) may mystify; pres. subj. 3rd pers. sing. 3. let him (her/it) mystify; impve. 3rd pers. sing.
mixtifiqué I mystified; past 1st pers. sing. / *mixtificar*.
mixtifiquéis that you (all) may mystify; pres. subj. 2nd pers. pl. / *mixtificar*.
mixtifiquemos 1. that we may mystify; pres. subj. 1st pers. pl. / *mixtificar*. 2. let us mystify; impve. 1st pers. pl.
mixtifiquen 1. that they may mystify; pres. subj. 3rd pers. pl. / *mixtificar*. 2. let them mystify; impve. 3rd pers. pl.
mixtifiques that you may mystify; pres. subj. 2nd pers. sing. / *mixtificar*.
mixturar to mix. reg.
moblar to furnish. irr.
mocear to sow wild oats. reg.
mochar to cut off. reg.
modelándose modeling oneself; pres. part. / *modelarse*.
modelaos (you all) model yourselves; impve. 2nd pers. pl. / *modelarse*.
modelar to model. reg.
modelarse to model oneself. reg.

modélate (you) model yourself; impve. 2nd pers. sing. / *modelarse*.
modelémonos let us model ourselves; impve. 1st pers. pl. / *modelarse*.
modélense let them model themselves; impve. 3rd pers. pl. / *modelarse*.
modélese let him (her/it) model himself (herself/itself); impve. 3rd pers. sing. / *modelarse*.
moderar to moderate. reg.
modernice 1. that I may modernize; pres. subj. 1st pers. sing. / *modernizar*. 2. that he (she/it) may modernize; pres. subj. 3rd pers. sing. 3. let him (her/it) modernize; impve. 3rd pers. sing.
modernicé I modernized; past 1st pers. sing. / *modernizar*.
modernicéis that you (all) may modernize; pres. subj. 2nd pers. pl. / *modernizar*.
modernicemos 1. that we may modernize; pres. subj. 1st pers. pl. / *modernizar*. 2. let us modernize; impve. 1st pers. pl.
modernicen 1. that they may modernize; pres. subj. 3rd pers. pl. / *modernizar*. 2. let them modernize; impve. 3rd pers. pl.
modernices that you may modernize; pres. subj. 2nd pers. sing. / *modernizar*.
modernizar to modernize. irr.
modificar to modify. irr.
modifique 1. that I may modify; pres. subj. 1st pers. sing. / *modificar*. 2. that he (she/it) may modify; pres. subj. 3rd pers. sing. 3. let him (her/it) modify; impve. 3rd pers. sing.
modifiqué I modified; past 1st pers. sing. / *modificar*.
modifiquéis that you (all) may modify; pres. subj. 2nd pers. pl. / *modificar*.
modifiquemos 1. that we may modify; pres. subj. 1st pers. pl. / *modificar*. 2. let us modify; impve. 1st pers. pl.
modifiquen 1. that they may modify; pres. subj. 3rd pers. pl. / *modificar*. 2. let them modify; impve. 3rd pers. pl.
modifiques that you may modify; pres. subj. 2nd pers. sing. / *modificar*.
modular to modulate. reg.
mofándose jeering; pres. part. / *mofarse*.
mofaos (you all) jeer; impve. 2nd pers. pl. / *mofarse*.
mofar to deride. reg.
mofarse to jeer. reg.
mófate (you) jeer; impve. 2nd pers. sing. / *mofarse*.
mofémonos let us jeer; impve. 1st pers. pl. / *mofarse*.
mófense let them jeer; impve. 3rd pers. pl. / *mofarse*.
mófese let him (her/it) jeer; impve. 3rd pers. sing. / *mofarse*.
mojándose getting wet; pres. part. / *mojarse*
mojaos (you all) get wet; impve. 2nd pers. pl. / *mojarse*.
mojar to wet. reg.
mojarse to get wet. reg.
mójate (you) get wet; impve. 2nd pers. sing. / *jojarse*.
mojémonos let us get wet; impve. 1st pers. pl. / *mojarse*.

mójense let them get wet; impve. 3rd pers. pl. /
mojarse.

mójese let him (her/it) get wet; impve. 3rd pers. sing.
/ *mojarse.*

moldar to mold or to shape. reg.

moldear to mold or to cast. reg.

moler to grind. irr.

molestándose being vexed; pres. part. / *molestarse.*

molestaos (you all) be vexed; impve. 2nd pers. pl. /
molestarse.

molestar to molest. reg.

molestarse to be vexed. reg.

moléstate (you) be vexed; impve. 2nd pers. sing. /
molestarse.

molestémonos let us be vexed; impve. 1st pers. pl. /
molestarse.

moléstense let them be vexed; impve. 3rd pers. pl. /
molestarse.

moléstese let him (her/it) be vexed; impve. 3rd pers.
sing. / *molestarse.*

molificar to mollify or to soften. irr.

molifique 1. that I may mollify; pres. subj. 1st pers.
sing. / *molificar.* 2. that he (she/it) may mollify; pres.
subj. 3rd pers. sing. 3. let him (her/it) mollify;
impve. 3rd pers. sing.

molifiqué I mollified; past 1st pers. sing. / *molificar.*

molifiquéis that you (all) may mollify; pres. subj. 2nd
pers. pl. / *molificar.*

molifiquemos 1. that we may mollify; pres. subj. 1st
pers. pl. / *molificar.* 2. let us mollify; impve. 1st pers.
pl.

molifiquen 1. that they may mollify; pres. subj. 3rd
pers. pl. / *molificar.* 2. let them mollify; impve. 3rd
pers. pl.

molifiques that you may mollify; pres. subj. 2nd pers.
sing. / *molificar.*

mollear to give or to be soft. reg.

momificándose mummifying; pres. part. /
momificarse.

momificaos (you all) mummify; impve. 2nd pers. pl. /
momificarse.

momificar to mummify. irr.

momificarse to mummify. irr.

momifícate (you) mummify; impve. 2nd pers. sing. /
momificarse.

momifique 1. that I may mummify; pres. subj. 1st
pers. sing. / *momificar.* 2. that he (she/it) may
mummify; pres. subj. 3rd pers. sing. 3. let him
(her/it) mummify; impve. 3rd pers. sing.

momifiqué I mummified; past 1st pers. sing. /
momificar.

momifiquéis that you (all) may mummify; pres. subj.
2nd pers. pl. / *momificar.*

momifiquémonos let us mummify; impve. 1st pers.
pl. / *momificarse.*

momifiquemos 1. that we may mummify; pres. subj.
1st pers. pl. / *momificar.* 2. let us mummify; impve.
1st pers. pl.

momifiquen 1. that they may mummify; pres. subj.
3rd pers. pl. / *momificar.* 2. let them mummify;
impve. 3rd pers. pl.

momifiquense let them mummify; impve. 3rd pers.
pl. / *momificarse.*

momifiques that you may mummify; pres. subj. 2nd
pers. sing. / *momificar.*

momifíquese let him (her/it) mummify; impve. 3rd
pers. sing. / *momificarse.*

mondar to peel or to clean. reg.

monear to act the fool. reg.

monetice 1. that I may monetize; pres. subj. 1st pers.
sing. / *monetizar.* 2. that he (she/it) may monetize;
pres. subj. 3rd pers. sing. 3. let him (her/it)
monetize; impve. 3rd pers. sing.

moneticé I monetized; past 1st pers. sing. / *monetizar.*

moneticéis that you (all) may monetize; pres. subj.
2nd pers. pl. / *monetizar.*

moneticemos 1. that we may monetize; pres. subj. 1st
pers. pl. / *monetizar.* 2. let us monetize; impve. 1st
pers. pl.

moneticen 1. that they may monetize; pres. subj. 3rd
pers. pl. / *monetizar.* 2. let them monetize; impve.
3rd pers. pl.

monetices that you may monetize; pres. subj. 2nd
pers. sing. / *monetizar.*

monetizar to monetize. irr.

monologar to soliloquize. irr.

monologue 1. that I may soliloquize; pres. subj. 1st
pers. sing. / *monologar.* 2. that he (she/it) may
soliloquize; pres. subj. 3rd pers. sing. 3. let him
(her/it) soliloquize; impve. 3rd pers. sing.

monologué I soliloquized; past 1st pers. sing. /
monologar.

monologuéis that you (all) may soliloquize; pres.
subj. 2nd pers. pl. / *monologar.*

monologuemos 1. that we may soliloquize; pres. subj.
1st pers. pl. / *monologar.* 2. let us soliloquize; impve.
1st pers. pl.

monologuen 1. that they may soliloquize; pres. subj.
3rd pers. pl. / *monologar.* 2. let them soliloquize;
impve. 3rd pers. pl.

monologues that you may soliloquize; pres. subj. 2nd
pers. sing. / *monologar.*

monopolice 1. that I may monopolize; pres. subj. 1st
pers. sing. / *monopolizar.* 2. that he (she/it) may
monopolize; pres. subj. 3rd pers. sing. 3. let him
(her/it) monopolize; impve. 3rd pers. sing.

monopolicé I monopolized; past 1st pers. sing. /
monopolizar.

monopolicéis that you (all) may monopolize; pres.
subj. 2nd pers. pl. / *monopolizar.*

monopolicemos 1. that we may monopolize; pres.
subj. 1st pers. pl. / *monopolizar.* 2. let us
monopolize; impve. 1st pers. pl.

monopolicen 1. that they may monopolize; pres. subj.
3rd pers. pl. / *monopolizar.* 2. let them monopolize;
impve. 3rd pers. pl.

monopolices that you may monopolize; pres. subj.
2nd pers. sing. / *monopolizar.*

monopolizar to monopolize. irr.

montar to mount or to ride. reg.
moquear to snivel. reg.
moquetear to snivel. reg.
moralice 1. that I may moralize; pres. subj. 1st pers. sing. / *moralizar*. 2. that he (she/it) may moralize; pres. subj. 3rd pers. sing. 3. let him (her/it) moralize; impve. 3rd pers. sing.
moralicé I moralized; past 1st pers. sing. / *moralizar*.
moralicéis that you (all) may moralize; pres. subj. 2nd pers. pl. / *moralizar*.
moralicemos 1. that we may moralize; pres. subj. 1st pers. pl. / *moralizar*. 2. let us moralize; impve. 1st pers. pl.
moralicen 1. that they may moralize; pres. subj. 3rd pers. pl. / *moralizar*. 2. let them moralize; impve. 3rd pers. pl.
moralices that you may moralize; pres. subj. 2nd pers. sing. / *moralizar*.
moralizar to moralize. irr.
morar to dwell. reg.
morder to bite. irr.
mordiscar to nibble. irr.
mordisque 1. that I may nibble; pres. subj. 1st pers. sing. / *mordiscar*. 2. that he (she/it) may nibble; pres. subj. 3rd pers. sing. 3. let him (her/it) nibble; impve. 3rd pers. sing.
mordisqué I nibbled; past 1st pers. sing. / *mordiscar*.
mordisquear to nibble. reg.
mordisquéis that you (all) may nibble; pres. subj. 2nd pers. pl. / *mordiscar*.
mordisquemos 1. that we may nibble; pres. subj. 1st pers. pl. / *mordiscar*. 2. let us nibble; impve. 1st pers. pl.
mordisquen 1. that they may nibble; pres. subj. 3rd pers. pl. / *mordiscar*. 2. let them nibble; impve. 3rd pers. pl.
mordisques that you may nibble; pres. subj. 2nd pers. sing. / *mordiscar*.
morigerar to moderate. reg.
moríos (you all) die out; impve. 2nd pers. pl. / *morirse*.
morir to die. irr.
morirse to die out. irr.
mortificándose doing penance; pres. part. / *mortificarse*.
mortificaos (you all) do penance; impve. 2nd pers. pl. / *mortificarse*.
mortificar to mortify. irr.
mortificarse to do penance. irr.
mortifícate (you) do penance; impve. 2nd pers. sing. / *mortificarse*.
mortifique 1. that I may mortify; pres. subj. 1st pers. sing. / *mortificar*. 2. that he (she/it) may mortify; pres. subj. 3rd pers. sing. 3. let him (her/it) mortify; impve. 3rd pers. sing.
mortifiqué I mortified; past 1st pers. sing. / *mortificar*.
mortifiquéis that you (all) may mortify; pres. subj. 2nd pers. pl. / *mortificar*.

mortifiquémonos let us do penance; impve. 1st pers. pl. / *mortificarse*.
mortifiquemos 1. that we may mortify; pres. subj. 1st pers. pl. / *mortificar*. 2. let us mortify; impve. 1st pers. pl.
mortifiquen 1. that they may mortify; pres. subj. 3rd pers. pl. / *mortificar*. 2. let them mortify; impve. 3rd pers. pl.
mortifiquense let them do penance; impve. 3rd pers. pl. / *mortificarse*.
mortifiques that you may mortify; pres. subj. 2nd pers. sing. / *mortificar*.
mortifíquese let him (her/it) do penance; impve. 3rd pers. sing. / *mortificarse*.
mosqueándose taking offense; pres. part. / *mosquearse*.
mosqueaos (you all) take offense; impve. 2nd pers. pl. / *mosquearse*.
mosquear to swat flies or to elude. reg.
mosquearse to take offense. reg.
mosquéate (you) take offense; impve. 2nd pers. sing. / *mosquearse*.
mosquéémonos let us take offense; impve. 1st pers. pl. / *mosquearse*.
mosquéense let them take offense; impve. 3rd pers. pl. / *mosquearse*.
mosquéese let him (her/it) take offense; impve. 3rd pers. sing. / *mosquearse*.
mostrándose appearing; pres. part. / *mostrase*.
mostraos (you all) appear; impve. 2nd pers. pl. / *mostrase*.
mostrar to show. irr.
mostrarse to appear. irr.
mostrémonos let us appear; impve. 1st pers. pl. / *mostrase*.
motear to speckle. reg.
motejar to ridicule. reg.
motilar to crop (hair). reg.
motivar to motivate. reg.
motorice 1. that I may motorize; pres. subj. 1st pers. sing. / *motorizar*. 2. that he (she/it) may motorize; pres. subj. 3rd pers. sing. 3. let him (her/it) motorize; impve. 3rd pers. sing.
motoricé I motorized; past 1st pers. sing. / *motorizar*.
motoricéis that you (all) may motorize; pres. subj. 2nd pers. pl. / *motorizar*.
motoricemos 1. that we may motorize; pres. subj. 1st pers. pl. / *motorizar*. 2. let us motorize; impve. 1st pers. pl.
motoricen 1. that they may motorize; pres. subj. 3rd pers. pl. / *motorizar*. 2. let them motorize; impve. 3rd pers. pl.
motorices that you may motorize; pres. subj. 2nd pers. sing. / *motorizar*.
motorizar to motorize. irr.
movámonos let us move; impve. 1st pers. pl. / *moverse*.
moveos (you all) move; impve. 2nd pers. pl. / *moverse*.
mover to move. irr.

moverse to move. irr.

moviéndose moving; pres. part. / *moverse.*

movilice 1. that I may mobilize; pres. subj. 1st pers. sing. / *movilizar.* 2. that he (she/it) may mobilize; pres. subj. 3rd pers. sing. 3. let him (her/it) mobilize; impve. 3rd pers. sing.

movilicé I mobilized; past 1st pers. sing. / *movilizar.*

movilicéis that you (all) may mobilize; pres. subj. 2nd pers. pl. / *movilizar.*

movilicémonos let us mobilize; impve. 1st pers. pl. / *movilizarse.*

movilicemos 1. that we may mobilize; pres. subj. 1st pers. pl. / *movilizar.* 2. let us mobilize; impve. 1st pers. pl.

movilicen 1. that they may mobilize; pres. subj. 3rd pers. pl. / *movilizar.* 2. let them mobilize; impve. 3rd pers. pl.

movilícense let them mobilize; impve. 3rd pers. pl. / *movilizarse.*

movilices that you may mobilize; pres. subj. 2nd pers. sing. / *movilizar.*

movilícese let him (her/it) mobilize; impve. 3rd pers. sing. / *movilizarse.*

movilizándose mobilizing; pres. part. / *movilizarse.*

movilizaos (you all) mobilize; impve. 2nd pers. pl. / *movilizarse.*

movilizar to mobilize. irr.

movilizarse to mobilize. irr.

movilízate (you) mobilize; impve. 2nd pers. sing. / *movilizarse.*

mudándose getting changed; pres. part. / *mudarse.*

mudaos (you all) get changed; impve. 2nd pers. pl. / *mudarse.*

mudar to change. reg.

mudarse to get changed. reg.

múdate (you) get changed; impve. 2nd pers. sing. / *mudarse.*

mudémonos let us get changed; impve. 1st pers. pl. / *mudarse.*

múdense let them get changed; impve. 3rd pers. pl. / *mudarse.*

múdese let him (her/it) get changed; impve. 3rd pers. sing. / *mudarse.*

muebla 1. he (she/it) furnishes; pres. ind. 3rd pers. sing. / *moblar.* 2. (you) furnish; impve. 2nd pers. sing.

mueblan they furnish; pres. ind. 3rd pers. pl. / *moblar.*

mueblas you furnish; pres. ind. 2nd pers. sing. / *moblar.*

mueble 1. that I may furnish; pres. subj. 1st pers. sing. / *moblar.* 2. that he (she/it) may furnish; pres. subj. 3rd pers. sing. 3. let him (her/it) furnish; impve. 3rd pers. sing.

mueblen 1. that they may furnish; pres. subj. 3rd pers. pl. / *moblar.* 2. let them furnish; impve. 3rd pers. pl.

muebles that you may furnish; pres. subj. 2nd pers. sing. / *moblar.*

mueblo I furnish; pres. ind. 1st pers. sing. / *moblar.*

muela 1. that I may grind; pres. subj. 1st pers. sing. / *moler.* 2. that he (she/it) may grind; pres. subj. 3rd pers. sing. 3. let him (her/it) grind; impve. 3rd pers. sing.

muelan 1. that they may grind; pres. subj. 3rd pers. pl. / *moler.* 2. let them grind; impve. 3rd pers. pl.

muelas that you may grind; pres. subj. 2nd pers. sing. / *moler.*

muele 1. he (she/it) grinds; pres. ind. 3rd pers. sing. / *moler.* 2. (you) grind; impve. 2nd pers. sing.

muelen they grind; pres. ind. 3rd pers. pl. / *moler.*

mueles you grind; pres. ind. 2nd pers. sing. / *moler.*

muelo I grind; pres. ind. 1st pers. sing. / *moler.*

muera 1. that I may die; pres. subj. 1st pers. sing. / *morir.* 2. that he (she/it) may die; pres. subj. 3rd pers. sing. 3. let him (her/it) die; impve. 3rd pers. sing.

mueran 1. that they may die; pres. subj. 3rd pers. pl. / *morir.* 2. let them die; impve. 3rd pers. pl.

muéranse let them die out; impve. 3rd pers. pl. / *morirse.*

mueras that you may die; pres. subj. 2nd pers. sing. / *morir.*

muérase let him (her/it) die out; impve. 3rd pers. sing. / *morirse.*

muerda 1. that I may bite; pres. subj. 1st pers. sing. / *morder.* 2. that he (she/it) may bite; pres. subj. 3rd pers. sing. 3. let him (her/it) bite; impve. 3rd pers. sing.

muerdan 1. that they may bite; pres. subj. 3rd pers. pl. / *morder.* 2. let them bite; impve. 3rd pers. pl.

muerdas that you may bite; pres. subj. 2nd pers. sing. / *morder.*

muerde 1. he (she/it) bites; pres. ind. 3rd pers. sing. / *morder.* 2. (you) bite; impve. 2nd pers. sing.

muerden they bite; pres. ind. 3rd pers. pl. / *morder.*

muerdes you bite; pres. ind. 2nd pers. sing. / *morder.*

muerdo I bite; pres. ind. 1st pers. sing. / *morder.*

muere 1. he (she/it) dies; pres. ind. 3rd pers. sing. / *morir.* 2. (you) die; impve. 2nd pers. sing.

mueren they die; pres. ind. 3rd pers. pl. / *morir.*

mueres you die; pres. ind. 2nd pers. sing. / *morir.*

muérete (you) die out; impve. 2nd pers. sing. / *morirse.*

muero I die; pres. ind. 1st pers. sing. / *morir.*

muerto died; past part. / *morir.*

muestra 1. he (she/it) shows; pres. ind. 3rd pers. sing. / *mostrar.* 2. (you) show; impve. 2nd pers. sing.

muestran they show; pres. ind. 3rd pers. pl. / *mostrar.*

muestras you show; pres. ind. 2nd pers. sing. / *mostrar.*

muéstrate (you) appear; impve. 2nd pers. sing. / *mostrarse.*

muestre 1. that I may show; pres. subj. 1st pers. sing. / *mostrar.* 2. that he (she/it) may show; pres. subj. 3rd pers. sing. 3. let him (her/it) show; impve. 3rd pers. sing.

muestren 1. that they may show; pres. subj. 3rd pers. pl. / *mostrar.* 2. let them show; impve. 3rd pers. pl.

muéstrense let them appear; impve. 3rd pers. pl. / *mostrarse*.

muestres that you may show; pres. subj. 2nd pers. sing. / *mostrar*.

muéstrese let him (her/it) appear; impve. 3rd pers. sing. / *mostrarse*.

muestro I show; pres. ind. 1st pers. sing. / *mostrar*.

mueva 1. that I may move; pres. subj. 1st pers. sing. / *mover*. 2. that he (she/it) may move; pres. subj. 3rd pers. sing. 3. let him (her/it) move; impve. 3rd pers. sing.

muevan 1. that they may move; pres. subj. 3rd pers. pl. / *mover*. 2. let them move; impve. 3rd pers. pl.

muévanse let them move; impve. 3rd pers. pl. / *moverse*.

muevas that you may move; pres. subj. 2nd pers. sing. / *mover*.

muévase let him (her/it) move; impve. 3rd pers. sing. / *moverse*.

mueve 1. he (she/it) moves; pres. ind. 3rd pers. sing. / *mover*. 2. (you) move; impve. 2nd pers. sing.

mueven they move; pres. ind. 3rd pers. pl. / *mover*.

mueves you move; pres. ind. 2nd pers. sing. / *mover*.

muévete (you) move; impve. 2nd pers. sing. / *moverse*.

muevo I move; pres. ind. 1st pers. sing. / *mover*.

mugir to moo. irr.

muja 1. that he (she/it) may moo; pres. subj. 3rd pers. sing. / *mugir*. 2. let him (her/it) moo; impve. 3rd pers. sing.

mujan 1. that they may moo; pres. subj. 3rd pers. pl. / *mugir*. 2. let them moo; impve. 3rd pers. pl.

multar to fine. reg.

multiplicándose multiplying; pres. part. / *multiplicarse*.

multiplicaos (you all) multiply; impve. 2nd pers. pl. / *multiplicarse*.

multiplicar to multiply. irr.

multiplicarse to multiply. irr.

multiplícate (you) multiply; impve. 2nd pers. sing. / *multiplicarse*.

multiplique 1. that I may multiply; pres. subj. 1st pers. sing. / *multiplicar*. 2. that he (she/it) may multiply; pres. subj. 3rd pers. sing. 3. let him (her/it) multiply; impve. 3rd pers. sing.

multipliqué I multiplied; past 1st pers. sing. / *multiplicar*.

multipliquéis that you (all) may multiply; pres. subj. 2nd pers. pl. / *multiplicar*.

multipliquémonos let us multiply; impve. 1st pers. pl. / *multiplicarse*.

multipliquemos 1. that we may multiply; pres. subj. 1st pers. pl. / *multiplicar*. 2. let us multiply; impve. 1st pers. pl.

multipliquen 1. that they may multiply; pres. subj. 3rd pers. pl. / *multiplicar*. 2. let them multiply; impve. 3rd pers. pl.

multiplíquense let them multiply; impve. 3rd pers. pl. / *multiplicarse*.

multipliques that you may multiply; pres. subj. 2nd pers. sing. / *multiplicar*.

multiplíquese let him (her/it) multiply; impve. 3rd pers. sing. / *multiplicarse*.

mullendo fluffing; pres. part. / *mullir*.

mullera 1. that I might fluff; imp. subj. 1st pers. sing. / *mullir*. 2. that he (she/it) might fluff; imp. subj. 3rd pers. sing.

mullerais that you (all) might fluff; imp. subj. 2nd pers pl. / *mullir*.

mulléramos that we might fluff; imp. subj. 1st pers. pl. / *mullir*.

mulleran that they might fluff; imp. subj. 3rd pers. pl. / *mullir*.

mulleras that you might fluff; imp. subj. 2nd pers. sing. / *mullir*.

mulleron they fluffed; past 3rd pers. pl. / *mullir*.

mullese 1. that I might fluff; imp. subj. 1st pers. sing. / *mullir*. 2. that he (she/it) might fluff; imp. subj. 3rd pers. sing.

mulleseis that you (all) might fluff; imp. subj. 2nd pers pl. / *mullir*.

mullésemos that we might fluff; imp. subj. 1st pers. pl. / *mullir*.

mullesen that they might fluff; imp. subj. 3rd pers. pl. / *mullir*.

mulleses that you might fluff; imp. subj. 2nd pers. sing. / *mullir*.

mullir to fluff. irr.

mulló he (she/it) fluffed; past 3rd pers. sing. / *mullir*.

municionar to supply munitions. reg.

municipalice 1. that I may municipalize; pres. subj. 1st pers. sing. / *municipalizar*. 2. that he (she/it) may municipalize; pres. subj. 3rd pers. sing. 3. let him (her/it) municipalize; impve. 3rd pers. sing.

municipalicé I municipalized; past 1st pers. sing. / *municipalizar*.

municipalicéis that you (all) may municipalize; pres. subj. 2nd pers. pl. / *municipalizar*.

municipalicemos 1. that we may municipalize; pres. subj. 1st pers. pl. / *municipalizar*. 2. let us municipalize; impve. 1st pers. pl.

municipalicen 1. that they may municipalize; pres. subj. 3rd pers. pl. / *municipalizar*. 2. let them municipalize; impve. 3rd pers. pl.

municipalices that you may municipalize; pres. subj. 2nd pers. sing. / *municipalizar*.

municipalizar to municipalize. irr.

muña 1. that I may summon; pres. subj. 1st pers. sing. / *muñir*. 2. that he (she/it) may summon; pres. subj. 3rd pers. sing. 3. let him (her/it) summon; impve. 3rd pers. sing.

muñáis that you (all) may summon; pres. subj. 2nd pers. pl. / *muñir*.

muñamos 1. that we may summon; pres. subj. 1st pers. pl. / *muñir*. 2. let us summon; impve. 1st pers. pl.

muñan 1. that they may summon; pres. subj. 3rd pers. pl. / *muñir*. 2. let them summon; impve. 3rd pers. pl.

muñas that you may summon; pres. subj. 2nd pers. sing. / *muñir*.

muñe 1. he (she/it) summons; pres. ind. 3rd pers. sing. / *muñir.* 2. (you) summon; impve. 2nd pers. sing.

muñen they summon; pres. ind. 3rd pers. pl. / *muñir.*

muñendo summoning; pres. part. / *muñir.*

muñera 1. that I might summon; imp. subj. 1st pers. sing. / *muñir.* 2. that he (she/it) might summon; imp. subj. 3rd pers. sing.

muñerais that you (all) might summon; imp. subj. 2nd pers pl. / *muñir.*

muñéramos that we might summon; imp. subj. 1st pers. pl. / *muñir.*

muñeran that they might summon; imp. subj. 3rd pers. pl. / *muñir.*

muñeras that you might summon; imp. subj. 2nd pers. sing. / *muñir.*

muñeron they summoned; past 3rd pers. pl. / *muñir.*

muñes you summon; pres. ind. 2nd pers. sing. / *muñir.*

muñese 1. that I might summon; imp. subj. 1st pers. sing. / *muñir.* 2. that he (she/it) might summon; imp. subj. 3rd pers. sing.

muñeseis that you (all) might summon; imp. subj. 2nd pers pl. / *muñir.*

muñésemos that we might summon; imp. subj. 1st pers. pl. / *muñir.*

muñesen that they might summon; imp. subj. 3rd pers. pl. / *muñir.*

muñeses that you might summon; imp. subj. 2nd pers. sing. / *muñir.*

muño I summon; pres. ind. 1st pers. sing. / *muñir.*

muñó he (she/it) summoned; past 3rd pers. sing. / *muñir.*

muráis that you (all) may die; pres. subj. 2nd pers. pl. / *morir.*

murámonos let us die out; impve. 1st pers. pl. / *morirse.*

muramos 1. that we may die; pres. subj. 1st pers. pl. / *morir.* 2. let us die; impve. 1st pers. pl.

muriendo dying; pres. part. / *morir.*

muriéndose dying out; pres. part. / *morirse.*

muriera 1. that I might die; imp. subj. 1st pers. sing. / *morir.* 2. that he (she/it) might die; imp. subj. 3rd pers. sing.

murierais that you (all) might die; imp. subj. 2nd pers pl. / *morir.*

muriéramos that we might die; imp. subj. 1st pers. pl. / *morir.*

murieran that they might die; imp. subj. 3rd pers. pl. / *morir.*

murieras that you might die; imp. subj. 2nd pers. sing. / *morir.*

murieron they died; past 3rd pers. pl. / *morir.*

muriese 1. that I might die; imp. subj. 1st pers. sing. / *morir.* 2. that he (she/it) might die; imp. subj. 3rd pers. sing.

murieseis that you (all) might die; imp. subj. 2nd pers pl. / *morir.*

muriésemos that we might die; imp. subj. 1st pers. pl. / *morir.*

muriesen that they might die; imp. subj. 3rd pers. pl. / *morir.*

murieses that you might die; imp. subj. 2nd pers. sing. / *morir.*

murió he (she/it) died; past 3rd pers. sing. / *morir.*

murmullar to murmur. reg.

murmurar to murmur or to gossip. reg.

musitar to mumble. reg.

mutilar to mutilate. reg.

N

naceos (you all) sprout; impve. 2nd pers. pl. / *nacerse.*

nacer to be born. irr.

nacerse to sprout or to split. irr.

nácete (you) sprout; impve. 2nd pers. sing. / *nacerse.*

naciéndose sprouting; pres. part. / *nacerse.*

nacionalice 1. that I may nationalize; pres. subj. 1st pers. sing. / *nacionalizar.* 2. that he (she/it) may nationalize; pres. subj. 3rd pers. sing. 3. let him (her/it) nationalize; impve. 3rd pers. sing.

nacionalicé I nationalized; past 1st pers. sing. / *nacionalizar.*

nacionalicéis that you (all) may nationalize; pres. subj. 2nd pers. pl. / *nacionalizar.*

nacionalicémonos let us become naturalized; impve. 1st pers. pl. / *nacionalizarse.*

nacionalicemos 1. that we may nationalize; pres. subj. 1st pers. pl. / *nacionalizar.* 2. let us nationalize; impve. 1st pers. pl.

nacionalicen 1. that they may nationalize; pres. subj. 3rd pers. pl. / *nacionalizar.* 2. let them nationalize; impve. 3rd pers. pl.

nacionalícense let them become naturalized; impve. 3rd pers. pl. / *nacionalizarse.*

nacionalices that you may nationalize; pres. subj. 2nd pers. sing. / *nacionalizar.*

nacionalícese let him (her/it) become naturalized; impve. 3rd pers. sing. / *nacionalizarse.*

nacionalizándose becoming naturalized; pres. part. / *nacionalizarse.*

nacionalizaos (you all) become naturalized; impve. 2nd pers. pl. / *nacionalizarse.*

nacionalizar to nationalize. irr.

nacionalizarse to become naturalized. irr.

nacionalízate (you) become naturalized; impve. 2nd pers. sing. / *nacionalizarse.*

nadar to swim. reg.

narcotice 1. that I may drug; pres. subj. 1st pers. sing. / *narcotizar.* 2. that he (she/it) may drug; pres. subj. 3rd pers. sing. 3. let him (her/it) drug; impve. 3rd pers. sing.

narcoticé I drugged; past 1st pers. sing. / *narcotizar.*

narcoticéis that you (all) may drug; pres. subj. 2nd pers. pl. / *narcotizar.*

narcoticemos 1. that we may drug; pres. subj. 1st pers. pl. / *narcotizar.* 2. let us drug; impve. 1st pers. pl.

narcoticen 1. that they may drug; pres. subj. 3rd pers. pl. / *narcotizar.* 2. let them drug; impve. 3rd pers. pl.

narcotices that you may drug; pres. subj. 2nd pers. sing. / *narcotizar.*

narcotizar to drug. irr.

narrar to narrate. reg.

nasalice 1. that I may nasalize; pres. subj. 1st pers. sing. / *nasalizar.* 2. that he (she/it) may nasalize; pres. subj. 3rd pers. sing. 3. let him (her/it) nasalize; impve. 3rd pers. sing.

nasalicé I nasalized; past 1st pers. sing. / *nasalizar.*

nasalicéis that you (all) may nasalize; pres. subj. 2nd pers. pl. / *nasalizar.*

nasalicemos 1. that we may nasalize; pres. subj. 1st pers. pl. / *nasalizar.* 2. let us nasalize; impve. 1st pers. pl.

nasalicen 1. that they may nasalize; pres. subj. 3rd pers. pl. / *nasalizar.* 2. let them nasalize; impve. 3rd pers. pl.

nasalices that you may nasalize; pres. subj. 2nd pers. sing. / *nasalizar.*

nasalizar to nasalize. irr.

naturalice 1. that I may naturalize; pres. subj. 1st pers. sing. / *naturalizar.* 2. that he (she/it) may naturalize; pres. subj. 3rd pers. sing. 3. let him (her/it) naturalize; impve. 3rd pers. sing.

naturalicé I naturalized; past 1st pers. sing. / *naturalizar.*

naturalicéis that you (all) may naturalize; pres. subj. 2nd pers. pl. / *naturalizar.*

naturalicémonos let us become naturalized; impve. 1st pers. pl. / *naturalizarse.*

naturalicemos 1. that we may naturalize; pres. subj. 1st pers. pl. / *naturalizar.* 2. let us naturalize; impve. 1st pers. pl.

naturalicen 1. that they may naturalize; pres. subj. 3rd pers. pl. / *naturalizar.* 2. let them naturalize; impve. 3rd pers. pl.

naturalícense let them become naturalized; impve. 3rd pers. pl. / *naturalizarse.*

naturalices that you may naturalize; pres. subj. 2nd pers. sing. / *naturalizar.*

naturalícese let him (her/it) become naturalized; impve. 3rd pers. sing. / *naturalizarse.*

naturalizándose becoming naturalized; pres. part. / *naturalizarse.*

naturalizaos (you all) become naturalized; impve. 2nd pers. pl. / *naturalizarse.*

naturalizar to naturalize. irr.

naturalizarse to become naturalized. irr.

naturalízate (you) become naturalized; impve. 2nd pers. sing. / *naturalizarse.*

naufragar to be shipwrecked. irr.

naufrague 1. that I may be shipwrecked; pres. subj. 1st pers. sing. / *naufragar.* 2. that he (she/it) may be shipwrecked; pres. subj. 3rd pers. sing. 3. let him (her/it) be shipwrecked; impve. 3rd pers. sing.

naufragué I was shipwrecked; past 1st pers. sing. / *naufragar.*

naufraguéis that you (all) may be shipwrecked; pres. subj. 2nd pers. pl. / *naufragar.*

naufraguemos 1. that we may be shipwrecked; pres. subj. 1st pers. pl. / *naufragar.* 2. let us be shipwrecked; impve. 1st pers. pl.

naufraguen 1. that they may be shipwrecked; pres. subj. 3rd pers. pl. / *naufragar.* 2. let them be shipwrecked; impve. 3rd pers. pl.

naufragues that you may be shipwrecked; pres. subj. 2nd pers. sing. / *naufragar.*

navegar to navigate. irr.

navegue 1. that I may navigate; pres. subj. 1st pers. sing. / *navegar.* 2. that he (she/it) may navigate; pres. subj. 3rd pers. sing. 3. let him (her/it) navigate; impve. 3rd pers. sing.

navegué I navigated; past 1st pers. sing. / *navegar.*

naveguéis that you (all) may navigate; pres. subj. 2nd pers. pl. / *navegar.*

naveguemos 1. that we may navigate; pres. subj. 1st pers. pl. / *navegar.* 2. let us navigate; impve. 1st pers. pl.

naveguen 1. that they may navigate; pres. subj. 3rd pers. pl. / *navegar.* 2. let them navigate; impve. 3rd pers. pl.

navegues that you may navigate; pres. subj. 2nd pers. sing. / *navegar.*

nazca 1. that I may be born; pres. subj. 1st pers. sing. / *nacer.* 2. that he (she/it) may be born; pres. subj. 3rd pers. sing. 3. let him (her/it) be born; impve. 3rd pers. sing.

nazcáis that you (all) may be born; pres. subj. 2nd pers. pl. / *nacer.*

nazcámonos let us sprout; impve. 1st pers. pl. / *nacerse.*

nazcamos 1. that we may be born; pres. subj. 1st pers. pl. / *nacer.* 2. let us be born; impve. 1st pers. pl.

nazcan 1. that they may be born; pres. subj. 3rd pers. pl. / *nacer.* 2. let them be born; impve. 3rd pers. pl.

názcanse let them sprout; impve. 3rd pers. pl. / *nacerse.*

nazcas that you may be born; pres. subj. 2nd pers. sing. / *nacer.*

názcase let him (her/it) sprout; impve. 3rd pers. sing. / *nacerse.*

nazco I am born; pres. ind. 1st pers. sing. / *nacer.*

necear to speak foolishly. reg.

necesitándose being necessary; pres. part. / *necesitarse.*

necesitaos (you all) be necessary; impve. 2nd pers. pl. / *necesitarse.*

necesitar to need. reg.

necesitarse to be necessary. reg.

necesítate (you) be necessary; impve. 2nd pers. sing. / *necesitarse.*

necesitémonos let us be necessary; impve. 1st pers. pl. / *necesitarse.*

necesítense let them be necessary; impve. 3rd pers. pl. / *necesitarse.*

necesítese let him (her/it) be necessary; impve. 3rd pers. sing. / *necesitarse.*

negándose refusing; pres. part. / *negarse.*

negaos (you all) refuse; impve. 2nd pers. pl. / *negarse.*

negar to deny. irr.

negarse to refuse. irr.

negociar to negotiate. reg.

negrear to look black. reg.

negrecer to turn black. irr.

negrezca 1. that I may turn black; pres. subj. 1st pers. sing. / *negrecer.* 2. that he (she/it) may turn black; pres. subj. 3rd pers. sing. 3. let him (her/it) turn black; impve. 3rd pers. sing.

negrezcáis that you (all) may turn black; pres. subj. 2nd pers. pl. / *negrecer.*

negrezcamos 1. that we may turn black; pres. subj. 1st pers. pl. / *negrecer.* 2. let us turn black; impve. 1st pers. pl.

negrezcan 1. that they may turn black; pres. subj. 3rd pers. pl. / *negrecer.* 2. let them turn black; impve. 3rd pers. pl.

negrezcas that you may turn black; pres. subj. 2nd pers. sing. / *negrecer.*

negrezco I turn black; pres. ind. 1st pers. sing. / *negrecer.*

negué I denied; past 1st pers. sing. / *negar.*

neguéis that you (all) may deny; pres. subj. 2nd pers. pl. / *negar.*

neguémonos let us refuse; impve. 1st pers. pl. / *negarse.*

neguemos 1. that we may deny; pres. subj. 1st pers. pl. / *negar.* 2. let us deny; impve. 1st pers. pl.

neutralice 1. that I may neutralize; pres. subj. 1st pers. sing. / *neutralizar.* 2. that he (she/it) may neutralize; pres. subj. 3rd pers. sing. 3. let him (her/it) neutralize; impve. 3rd pers. sing.

neutralicé I neutralized; past 1st pers. sing. / *neutralizar.*

neutralicéis that you (all) may neutralize; pres. subj. 2nd pers. pl. / *neutralizar.*

neutralicemos 1. that we may neutralize; pres. subj. 1st pers. pl. / *neutralizar.* 2. let us neutralize; impve. 1st pers. pl.

neutralicen 1. that they may neutralize; pres. subj. 3rd pers. pl. / *neutralizar.* 2. let them neutralize; impve. 3rd pers. pl.

neutralices that you may neutralize; pres. subj. 2nd pers. sing. / *neutralizar.*

neutralizar to neutralize. irr.

nevar to snow. irr.

neviscar to snow lightly. irr.

nevisque 1. that it may snow lightly; pres. subj. 3rd pers. sing. / *neviscar.* 2. let it snow lightly; impve. 3rd pers. sing.

nevisquen 1. that they may snow lightly; pres. subj. 3rd pers. pl. / *neviscar.* 2. let them snow lightly; impve. 3rd pers. pl.

niega 1. he (she/it) denies; pres. ind. 3rd pers. sing. / *negar.* 2. (you) deny; impve. 2nd pers. sing.

niegan they deny; pres. ind. 3rd pers. pl. / *negar.*

niegas you deny; pres. ind. 2nd pers. sing. / *negar.*

niégate (you) refuse; impve. 2nd pers. sing. / *negarse.*

niego I deny; pres. ind. 1st pers. sing. / *negar.*

niegue 1. that I may deny; pres. subj. 1st pers. sing. / *negar.* 2. that he (she/it) may deny; pres. subj. 3rd pers. sing. 3. let him (her/it) deny; impve. 3rd pers. sing.

nieguen 1. that they may deny; pres. subj. 3rd pers. pl. / *negar.* 2. let them deny; impve. 3rd pers. pl.

niéguense let them refuse; impve. 3rd pers. pl. / *negarse.*

niegues that you may deny; pres. subj. 2nd pers. sing. / *negar.*

niéguese let him (her/it) refuse; impve. 3rd pers. sing. / *negarse.*

nieva it snows; pres. ind. 3rd pers. sing. / *nevar.*

nieve 1. that it may snow; pres. subj. 3rd pers. sing. / *nevar.* 2. let it snow; impve. 3rd pers. sing.

niquelar to nickel-plate. reg.

nivelándose coming level; pres. part. / *nivelarse.*

nivelaos (you all) come level; impve. 2nd pers. pl. / *nivelarse.*

nivelar to level. reg.

nivelarse to come level. reg.

nivélate (you) come level; impve. 2nd pers. sing. / *nivelarse.*

nivelémonos let us come level; impve. 1st pers. pl. / *nivelarse.*

nivélense let them come level; impve. 3rd pers. pl. / *nivelarse.*

nivélese let him (her/it) come level; impve. 3rd pers. sing. / *nivelarse.*

nombrar to name or to nominate. reg.

nominar to nominate. reg.

noquear to knock out. reg.

normalice 1. that I may normalize; pres. subj. 1st pers. sing. / *normalizar.* 2. that he (she/it) may normalize; pres. subj. 3rd pers. sing. 3. let him (her/it) normalize; impve. 3rd pers. sing.

normalicé I normalized; past 1st pers. sing. / *normalizar.*

normalicéis that you (all) may normalize; pres. subj. 2nd pers. pl. / *normalizar.*

normalicemos 1. that we may normalize; pres. subj. 1st pers. pl. / *normalizar.* 2. let us normalize; impve. 1st pers. pl.

normalicen 1. that they may normalize; pres. subj. 3rd pers. pl. / *normalizar.* 2. let them normalize; impve. 3rd pers. pl.

normalices that you may normalize; pres. subj. 2nd pers. sing. / *normalizar.*

normalizar to normalize. irr.

notándose being noticeable; pres. part. / *notarse.*

notaos (you all) be noticeable; impve. 2nd pers. pl. / *notarse.*

notar to note. reg.

notarice 1. that I may notarize; pres. subj. 1st pers. sing. / *notarizar.* 2. that he (she/it) may notarize; pres. subj. 3rd pers. sing. 3. let him (her/it) notarize; impve. 3rd pers. sing.

notaricé I notarized; past 1st pers. sing. / *notarizar.*

notaricéis that you (all) may notarize; pres. subj. 2nd pers. pl. / *notarizar.*

notaricemos 1. that we may notarize; pres. subj. 1st pers. pl. / *notarizar.* 2. let us notarize; impve. 1st pers. pl.

notaricen 1. that they may notarize; pres. subj. 3rd pers. pl. / *notarizar.* 2. let them notarize; impve. 3rd pers. pl.

notarices that you may notarize; pres. subj. 2nd pers. sing. / *notarizar.*

notarizar to notarize. irr.

notarse to be noticeable. reg.

nótate (you) be noticeable; impve. 2nd pers. sing. / *notarse.*

notémonos let us be noticeable; impve. 1st pers. pl. / *notarse.*

nótense let them be noticeable; impve. 3rd pers. pl. / *notarse.*

nótese let him (her/it) be noticeable; impve. 3rd pers. sing. / *notarse.*

noticiar to notify. reg.

notificar to notify. irr.

notifique 1. that I may notify; pres. subj. 1st pers. sing. / *notificar.* 2. that he (she/it) may notify; pres. subj. 3rd pers. sing. 3. let him (her/it) notify; impve. 3rd pers. sing.

notifiqué I notified; past 1st pers. sing. / *notificar.*

notifiquéis that you (all) may notify; pres. subj. 2nd pers. pl. / *notificar.*

notifiquemos 1. that we may notify; pres. subj. 1st pers. pl. / *notificar.* 2. let us notify; impve. 1st pers. pl.

notifiquen 1. that they may notify; pres. subj. 3rd pers. pl. / *notificar.* 2. let them notify; impve. 3rd pers. pl.

notifiques that you may notify; pres. subj. 2nd pers. sing. / *notificar.*

novelar to romance. reg.

nublándose becoming cloudy; pres. part. / *nublarse.*

nublar to cloud or to darken. reg.

nublarse to become cloudy. reg.

núblense let them become cloudy; impve. 3rd pers. pl. / *nublarse.*

núblese let it become cloudy; impve. 3rd pers. sing. / *nublarse.*

numerar to number. reg.

nutrir to nourish. reg.

O

obcecándose being obsessed; pres. part. / *obcecarse.*

obcecaos (you all) be obsessed; impve. 2nd pers. pl. / *obcecarse.*

obcecar to blind. irr.

obcecarse to be obsessed. irr.

obcécate (you) be obsessed; impve. 2nd pers. sing. / *obcecarse.*

obceque 1. that I may blind; pres. subj. 1st pers. sing. / *obcecar.* 2. that he (she/it) may blind; pres. subj. 3rd pers. sing. 3. let him (her/it) blind; impve. 3rd pers. sing.

obcequé I blinded; past 1st pers. sing. / *obcecar.*

obcequéis that you (all) may blind; pres. subj. 2nd pers. pl. / *obcecar.*

obcequémonos let us be obsessed; impve. 1st pers. pl. / *obcecarse.*

obcequemos 1. that we may blind; pres. subj. 1st pers. pl. / *obcecar.* 2. let us blind; impve. 1st pers. pl.

obcequen 1. that they may blind; pres. subj. 3rd pers. pl. / *obcecar.* 2. let them blind; impve. 3rd pers. pl.

obcéquense let them be obsessed; impve. 3rd pers. pl. / *obcecarse.*

obceques that you may blind; pres. subj. 2nd pers. sing. / *obcecar.*

obcéquese let him (her/it) be obsessed; impve. 3rd pers. sing. / *obcecarse.*

obedecer to obey. irr.

obedezca 1. that I may obey; pres. subj. 1st pers. sing. / *obedecer.* 2. that he (she/it) may obey; pres. subj. 3rd pers. sing. 3. let him (her/it) obey; impve. 3rd pers. sing.

obedezcáis that you (all) may obey; pres. subj. 2nd pers. pl. / *obedecer.*

obedezcamos 1. that we may obey; pres. subj. 1st pers. pl. / *obedecer.* 2. let us obey; impve. 1st pers. pl.

obedezcan 1. that they may obey; pres. subj. 3rd pers. pl. / *obedecer.* 2. let them obey; impve. 3rd pers. pl.

obedezcas that you may obey; pres. subj. 2nd pers. sing. / *obedecer.*

obedezco I obey; pres. ind. 1st pers. sing. / *obedecer.*

objetar to object. reg.

oblicuar to slant. reg.

obligándose binding oneself; pres. part. / *obligarse.*

obligaos (you all) bind yourselves; impve. 2nd pers. pl. / *obligarse.*

obligar to oblige. irr.

obligarse to bind oneself. irr.

oblígate (you) bind yourself; impve. 2nd pers. sing. / *obligarse.*

obligue 1. that I may oblige; pres. subj. 1st pers. sing. / *obligar.* 2. that he (she/it) may oblige; pres. subj. 3rd pers. sing. 3. let him (her/it) oblige; impve. 3rd pers. sing.

obligué I obliged; past 1st pers. sing. / *obligar.*

obliguéis that you (all) may oblige; pres. subj. 2nd pers. pl. / *obligar.*

obliguémonos let us bind ourselves; impve. 1st pers. pl. / *obligarse.*

obliguemos 1. that we may oblige; pres. subj. 1st pers. pl. / *obligar.* 2. let us oblige; impve. 1st pers. pl.

obliguen 1. that they may oblige; pres. subj. 3rd pers. pl. / *obligar.* 2. let them oblige; impve. 3rd pers. pl.

oblíguense let them bind themselves; impve. 3rd pers. pl. / *obligarse.*

obligues that you may oblige; pres. subj. 2nd pers. sing. / *obligar.*

oblíguese let him (her/it) bind himself (herself/itself); impve. 3rd pers. sing. / *obligarse.*

obliterar to obliterate. reg.

obrar to work. reg.

obscurecer to obscure. irr.

obscurecerse to get dark. irr.

obscureciéndose getting dark; pres. part. / *obscurecerse.*

obscurezca 1. that I may obscure; pres. subj. 1st pers. sing. / *obscurecer.* 2. that he (she/it) may obscure; pres. subj. 3rd pers. sing. 3. let him (her/it) obscure; impve. 3rd pers. sing.

obscurezcáis that you (all) may obscure; pres. subj. 2nd pers. pl. / *obscurecer.*

obscurezcamos 1. that we may obscure; pres. subj. 1st pers. pl. / *obscurecer.* 2. let us obscure; impve. 1st pers. pl.

obscurezcan 1. that they may obscure; pres. subj. 3rd pers. pl. / *obscurecer.* 2. let them obscure; impve. 3rd pers. pl.

obscurezcas that you may obscure; pres. subj. 2nd pers. sing. / *obscurecer.*

obscurézcase let it get dark; impve. 3rd pers. sing. / *obscurecerse.*

obscurezco I obscure; pres. ind. 1st pers. sing. / *obscurecer.*

obsequiar to court. reg.

observar to observe. reg.

obsesionar to obsess. reg.

obstar to obstruct. reg.

obstinándose persisting; pres. part. / *obstinarse.*

obstinaos (you all) persist; impve. 2nd pers. pl. / *obstinarse.*

obstinarse to persist. reg.

obstínate (you) persist; impve. 2nd pers. sing. / *obstinarse.*

obstinémonos let us persist; impve. 1st pers. pl. / *obstinarse.*

obstínense let them persist; impve. 3rd pers. pl. / *obstinarse.*

obstínese let him (her/it) persist; impve. 3rd pers. sing. / *obstinarse.*

obstruíos (you all) get stopped up; impve. 2nd pers. pl. / *obstruirse.*

obstruir to obstruct. irr.

obstruirse to get stopped up. irr.

obstruya 1. that I may obstruct; pres. subj. 1st pers. sing. / *obstruir.* 2. that he (she/it) may obstruct; pres. subj. 3rd pers. sing. 3. let him (her/it) obstruct; impve. 3rd pers. sing.

obstruyáis that you (all) may obstruct; pres. subj. 2nd pers. pl. / *obstruir.*

obstruyámonos let us get stopped up; impve. 1st pers. pl. / *obstruirse.*

obstruyamos 1. that we may obstruct; pres. subj. 1st pers. pl. / *obstruir.* 2. let us obstruct; impve. 1st pers. pl.

obstruyan 1. that they may obstruct; pres. subj. 3rd pers. pl. / *obstruir.* 2. let them obstruct; impve. 3rd pers. pl.

obstrúyanse let them get stopped up; impve. 3rd pers. pl. / *obstruirse.*

obstruyas that you may obstruct; pres. subj. 2nd pers. sing. / *obstruir.*

obstrúyase let him (her/it) get stopped up; impve. 3rd pers. sing. / *obstruirse.*

obstruye 1. he (she/it) obstructs; pres. ind. 3rd pers. sing. / *obstruir.* 2. (you) obstruct; impve. 2nd pers. sing.

obstruyen they obstruct; pres. ind. 3rd pers. pl. / *obstruir.*

obstruyendo obstructing; pres. part. / *obstruir.*

obstruyéndose getting stopped up; pres. part. / *obstruirse.*

obstruyera 1. that I might obstruct; imp. subj. 1st pers. sing. / *obstruir.* 2. that he (she/it) might obstruct; imp. subj. 3rd pers. sing.

obstruyerais that you (all) might obstruct; imp. subj. 2nd pers pl. / *obstruir.*

obstruyéramos that we might obstruct; imp. subj. 1st pers. pl. / *obstruir.*

obstruyeran that they might obstruct; imp. subj. 3rd pers. pl. / *obstruir.*

obstruyeras that you might obstruct; imp. subj. 2nd pers. sing. / *obstruir.*

obstruyeron they obstructed; past 3rd pers. pl. / *obstruir.*

obstruyes you obstruct; pres. ind. 2nd pers. sing. / *obstruir.*

obstruyese 1. that I might obstruct; imp. subj. 1st pers. sing. / *obstruir.* 2. that he (she/it) might obstruct; imp. subj. 3rd pers. sing.

obstruyeseis that you (all) might obstruct; imp. subj. 2nd pers pl. / *obstruir.*

obstruyésemos that we might obstruct; imp. subj. 1st pers. pl. / *obstruir.*

obstruyesen that they might obstruct; imp. subj. 3rd pers. pl. / *obstruir.*

obstruyeses that you might obstruct; imp. subj. 2nd pers. sing. / *obstruir.*

obstrúyete (you) get stopped up; impve. 2nd pers. sing. / *obstruirse.*

obstruyo I obstruct; pres. ind. 1st pers. sing. / *obstruir.*

obstruyó he (she/it) obstructed; past 3rd pers. sing. / *obstruir.*

obten (you) obtain; impve. 2nd pers. sing. / *obtener.*

obtendrá he (she/it) will obtain; fut. 3rd pers. sing. / *obtener.*

obtendrán they will obtain; fut. 3rd pers. pl. / *obtener.*

obtendrás you will obtain; fut. 2nd pers. sing. / *obtener.*

obtendré I shall obtain; fut. 1st pers. sing. / *obtener.*

obtendréis you (all) will obtain; fut. 2nd pers. pl. / *obtener.*

obtendremos we shall obtain; fut. 1st pers. pl. / *obtener.*

obtendría 1. I should obtain; cond. 1st pers. sing. / *obtener.* 2. he (she/it) would obtain; cond. 3rd pers. sing.

obtendríais you (all) would obtain; cond. 2nd pers. pl. / *obtener.*

obtendríamos we should obtain; cond. 1st pers. pl. / *obtener.*

obtendrían they would obtain; cond. 3rd pers. pl. / *obtener.*

obtendrías you would obtain; cond. 2nd pers. sing. / *obtener.*

obtener to obtain. irr.

obtenga 1. that I may obtain; pres. subj. 1st pers. sing. / *obtener.* 2. that he (she/it) may obtain; pres. subj. 3rd pers. sing. 3. let him (her/it) obtain; impve. 3rd pers. sing.

obtengáis that you (all) may obtain; pres. subj. 2nd pers. pl. / *obtener.*

obtengamos 1. that we may obtain; pres. subj. 1st pers. pl. / *obtener.* 2. let us obtain; impve. 1st pers. pl.

obtengan 1. that they may obtain; pres. subj. 3rd pers. pl. / *obtener.* 2. let them obtain; impve. 3rd pers. pl.

obtengas that you may obtain; pres. subj. 2nd pers. sing. / *obtener.*

obtengo I obtain; pres. ind. 1st pers. sing. / *obtener.*

obtiene he (she/it) obtains; pres. ind. 3rd pers. sing. / *obtener.*

obtienen they obtain; pres. ind. 3rd pers. pl. / *obtener.*

obtienes you obtain; pres. ind. 2nd pers. sing. / *obtener.*

obturar to stop up. reg.

obtuve I obtained; past 1st pers. sing. / *obtener.*

obtuviera 1. that I might obtain; imp. subj. 1st pers. sing. / *obtener.* 2. that he (she/it) might obtain; imp. subj. 3rd pers. sing.

obtuvierais that you (all) might obtain; imp. subj. 2nd pers pl. / *obtener.*

obtuviéramos that we might obtain; imp. subj. 1st pers. pl. / *obtener.*

obtuvieran that they might obtain; imp. subj. 3rd pers. pl. / *obtener.*

obtuvieras that you might obtain; imp. subj. 2nd pers. sing. / *obtener.*

obtuvieron they obtained; past 3rd pers. pl. / *obtener.*

obtuviese 1. that I might obtain; imp. subj. 1st pers. sing. / *obtener.* 2. that he (she/it) might obtain; imp. subj. 3rd pers. sing.

obtuvieseis that you (all) might obtain; imp. subj. 2nd pers pl. / *obtener.*

obtuviésemos that we might obtain; imp. subj. 1st pers. pl. / *obtener.*

obtuviesen that they might obtain; imp. subj. 3rd pers. pl. / *obtener.*

obtuvieses that you might obtain; imp. subj. 2nd pers. sing. / *obtener.*

obtuvimos we obtained; past 1st pers. pl. / *obtener.*

obtuviste you obtained; past 2nd pers. sing. / *obtener.*

obtuvisteis you (all) obtained; past 2nd pers. pl. / *obtener.*

obtuvo he (she/it) obtained; past 3rd pers. sing. / *obtener.*

obviar to obviate or to hinder. reg.

ocasionar to cause. reg.

occindentalice 1. that I may westernize; pres. subj. 1st pers. sing. / *occidentalizar.* 2. that he (she/it) may westernize; pres. subj. 3rd pers. sing. 3. let him (her/it) westernize; impve. 3rd pers. sing.

occindentalicé I westernized; past 1st pers. sing. / *occidentalizar.*

occindentalicéis that you (all) may westernize; pres. subj. 2nd pers. pl. / *occidentalizar.*

occindentalicemos 1. that we may westernize; pres. subj. 1st pers. pl. / *occidentalizar.* 2. let us westernize; impve. 1st pers. pl.

occindentalicen 1. that they may westernize; pres. subj. 3rd pers. pl. / *occidentalizar.* 2. let them westernize; impve. 3rd pers. pl.

occindentalices that you may westernize; pres. subj. 2nd pers. sing. / *occidentalizar.*

occindentalizar to westernize. irr.

ocluir to occlude. irr.

ocluya 1. that I may occlude; pres. subj. 1st pers. sing. / *ocluir.* 2. that he (she/it) may occlude; pres. subj. 3rd pers. sing. 3. let him (her/it) occlude; impve. 3rd pers. sing.

ocluyáis that you (all) may occlude; pres. subj. 2nd pers. pl. / *ocluir.*

ocluyamos 1. that we may occlude; pres. subj. 1st pers. pl. / *ocluir.* 2. let us occlude; impve. 1st pers. pl.

ocluyan 1. that they may occlude; pres. subj. 3rd pers. pl. / *ocluir.* 2. let them occlude; impve. 3rd pers. pl.

ocluyas that you may occlude; pres. subj. 2nd pers. sing. / *ocluir.*

ocluye 1. he (she/it) occludes; pres. ind. 3rd pers. sing. / *ocluir.* 2. (you) occlude; impve. 2nd pers. sing.

ocluyen they occlude; pres. ind. 3rd pers. pl. / *ocluir.*

ocluyendo occluding; pres. part. / *ocluir.*

ocluyera 1. that I might occlude; imp. subj. 1st pers. sing. / *ocluir.* 2. that he (she/it) might occlude; imp. subj. 3rd pers. sing.

ocluyerais that you (all) might occlude; imp. subj. 2nd pers pl. / *ocluir.*

ocluyéramos that we might occlude; imp. subj. 1st pers. pl. / *ocluir.*

ocluyeran that they might occlude; imp. subj. 3rd pers. pl. / *ocluir.*

ocluyeras that you might occlude; imp. subj. 2nd pers. sing. / *ocluir.*

ocluyeron they occluded; past 3rd pers. pl. / *ocluir.*

ocluyes you occlude; pres. ind. 2nd pers. sing. / *ocluir.*

ocluyese 1. that I might occlude; imp. subj. 1st pers. sing. / *ocluir.* 2. that he (she/it) might occlude; imp. subj. 3rd pers. sing.

ocluyeseis that you (all) might occlude; imp. subj. 2nd pers pl. / *ocluir.*

ocluyésemos that we might occlude; imp. subj. 1st pers. pl. / *ocluir.*

ocluyesen that they might occlude; imp. subj. 3rd pers. pl. / *ocluir.*

ocluyeses that you might occlude; imp. subj. 2nd pers. sing. / *ocluir.*

ocluyo I occlude; pres. ind. 1st pers. sing. / *ocluir.*

ocluyó he (she/it) occluded; past 3rd pers. sing. / *ocluir.*

ocultar to hide. reg.

ocupándose being busy; pres. part. / *ocuparse.*

ocupaos (you all) be busy; impve. 2nd pers. pl. / *ocuparse.*

ocupar to occupy. reg.

ocuparse to be busy. reg.

ocúpate (you) be busy; impve. 2nd pers. sing. / *ocuparse.*

ocupémonos let us be busy; impve. 1st pers. pl. / *ocuparse.*

ocúpense let them be busy; impve. 3rd pers. pl. / *ocuparse.*

ocúpese let him (her/it) be busy; impve. 3rd pers. sing. / *ocuparse.*

ocurrámonos let us come to mind; impve. 1st pers. pl. / *ocurrirse.*

ocúrranse let them come to mind; impve. 3rd pers. pl. / *ocurrirse.*

ocúrrase let him (her/it) come to mind; impve. 3rd pers. sing. / *ocurrirse.*

ocúrrete (you) come to mind; impve. 2nd pers. sing. / *ocurrirse.*

ocurriéndose coming to mind; pres. part. / *ocurrirse.*

ocurríos (you all) come to mind; impve. 2nd pers. pl. / *ocurrirse.*

ocurrir to occur. reg.

ocurrirse to come to mind. reg.

odiar to hate. reg.

ofendámonos let us take offence; impve. 1st pers. pl. / *ofenderse.*

oféndanse let them take offence; impve. 3rd pers. pl. / *ofenderse.*

oféndase let him (her/it) take offence; impve. 3rd pers. sing. / *ofenderse.*

ofendeos (you all) take offence; impve. 2nd pers. pl. / *ofenderse.*

ofender to offend. reg.

ofenderse to take offence. reg.

oféndete (you) take offence; impve. 2nd pers. sing. / *ofenderse.*

ofendiéndose taking offence; pres. part. / *ofenderse.*

oficiar officiate. reg.

ofreceos (you all) happen; impve. 2nd pers. pl. / *ofrecerse.*

ofrecer to offer. irr.

ofrecerse to happen. irr.

ofrécete (you) happen; impve. 2nd pers. sing. / *ofrecerse.*

ofreciéndose happening; pres. part. / *ofrecerse.*

ofrendar to present. reg.

ofrezca 1. that I may offer; pres. subj. 1st pers. sing. / *ofrecer.* 2. that he (she/it) may offer; pres. subj. 3rd pers. sing. 3. let him (her/it) offer; impve. 3rd pers. sing.

ofrezcáis that you (all) may offer; pres. subj. 2nd pers. pl. / *ofrecer.*

ofrezcámonos let us happen; impve. 1st pers. pl. / *ofrecerse.*

ofrezcamos 1. that we may offer; pres. subj. 1st pers. pl. / *ofrecer.* 2. let us offer; impve. 1st pers. pl.

ofrezcan 1. that they may offer; pres. subj. 3rd pers. pl. / *ofrecer.* 2. let them offer; impve. 3rd pers. pl.

ofrézcanse let them happen; impve. 3rd pers. pl. / *ofrecerse.*

ofrezcas that you may offer; pres. subj. 2nd pers. sing. / *ofrecer.*

ofrézcase let him (her/it) happen; impve. 3rd pers. sing. / *ofrecerse.*

ofrezco I offer; pres. ind. 1st pers. sing. / *ofrecer.*

ofuscándose getting confused; pres. part. / *ofuscarse.*

ofuscaos (you all) get confused; impve. 2nd pers. pl. / *ofuscarse.*

ofuscar to darken or to bewilder. irr.

ofuscarse to get confused. irr.

ofúscate (you) get confused; impve. 2nd pers. sing. / *ofuscarse.*

ofusque 1. that I may darken; pres. subj. 1st pers. sing. / *ofuscar.* 2. that he (she/it) may darken; pres. subj. 3rd pers. sing. 3. let him (her/it) darken; impve. 3rd pers. sing.

ofusqué I darkened; past 1st pers. sing. / *ofuscar.*

ofusquéis that you (all) may darken; pres. subj. 2nd pers. pl. / *ofuscar.*

ofusquémonos let us get confused; impve. 1st pers. pl. / *ofuscarse.*

ofusquemos 1. that we may darken; pres. subj. 1st pers. pl. / *ofuscar.* 2. let us darken; impve. 1st pers. pl.

ofusquen 1. that they may darken; pres. subj. 3rd pers. pl. / *ofuscar.* 2. let them darken; impve. 3rd pers. pl.

ofúsquense let them get confused; impve. 3rd pers. pl. / *ofuscarse.*

ofusques that you may darken; pres. subj. 2nd pers. sing. / *ofuscar.*

ofúsquese let him (her/it) get confused; impve. 3rd pers. sing. / *ofuscarse.*

oiga 1. that I may hear; pres. subj. 1st pers. sing. / *oír.* 2. that he (she/it) may hear; pres. subj. 3rd pers. sing. 3. let him (her/it) hear; impve. 3rd pers. sing.

oigáis that you (all) may hear; pres. subj. 2nd pers. pl. / *oír.*

oigamos 1. that we may hear; pres. subj. 1st pers. pl. / *oír.* 2. let us hear; impve. 1st pers. pl.

oigan 1. that they may hear; pres. subj. 3rd pers. pl. / *oír.* 2. let them hear; impve. 3rd pers. pl.

oigas that you may hear; pres. subj. 2nd pers. sing. / *oír.*

oigo I hear; pres. ind. 1st pers. sing. / *oír.*

ojear to eye or to stare. reg.

oler to smell. irr.

olfatear to smell. reg.

oliscar to smell (out). irr.

olisque 1. that I may smell (out); pres. subj. 1st pers. sing. / *oliscar.* 2. that he (she/it) may smell (out); pres. subj. 3rd pers. sing. 3. let him (her/it) smell (out); impve. 3rd pers. sing.

olisqué I smelled (out); past 1st pers. sing. / *oliscar.*

olisquéis that you (all) may smell (out); pres. subj. 2nd pers. pl. / *oliscar.*

olisquemos 1. that we may smell (out); pres. subj. 1st pers. pl. / *oliscar*. 2. let us smell (out); impve. 1st pers. pl.

olisquen 1. that they may smell (out); pres. subj. 3rd pers. pl. / *oliscar*. 2. let them smell (out); impve. 3rd pers. pl.

olisques that you may smell (out); pres. subj. 2nd pers. sing. / *oliscar*.

olvidándose being forgotten; pres. part. / *olvidarse*.

olvidaos (you all) be forgotten; impve. 2nd pers. pl. / *olvidarse*.

olvidar to forget. reg.

olvidarse to be forgotten. reg.

olvídate (you) be forgotten; impve. 2nd pers. sing. / *olvidarse*.

olvidémonos let us be forgotten; impve. 1st pers. pl. / *olvidarse*.

olvídense let them be forgotten; impve. 3rd pers. pl. / *olvidarse*.

olvídese let him (her/it) be forgotten; impve. 3rd pers. sing. / *olvidarse*.

omitir to omit. reg.

ondear to wave. reg.

ondular to undulate or to wave. reg.

operar to operate. reg.

opinar to opine or to think. reg.

opon (you) oppose; impve. 2nd pers. sing. / *oponer*.

opondrá he (she/it) will oppose; fut. 3rd pers. sing. / *oponer*.

opondrán they will oppose; fut. 3rd pers. pl. / *oponer*.

opondrás you will oppose; fut. 2nd pers. sing. / *oponer*.

opondré I shall oppose; fut. 1st pers. sing. / *oponer*.

opondréis you (all) will oppose; fut. 2nd pers. pl. / *oponer*.

opondremos we shall oppose; fut. 1st pers. pl. / *oponer*.

opondría 1. I should oppose; cond. 1st pers. sing. / *oponer*. 2. he (she/it) would oppose; cond. 3rd pers. sing.

opondríais you (all) would oppose; cond. 2nd pers. pl. / *oponer*.

opondríamos we should oppose; cond. 1st pers. pl. / *oponer*.

opondrían they would oppose; cond. 3rd pers. pl. / *oponer*.

opondrías you would oppose; cond. 2nd pers. sing. / *oponer*.

oponeos (you all) disapprove; impve. 2nd pers. pl. / *oponerse*.

oponer to oppose. irr.

oponerse to disapprove. irr.

oponga 1. that I may oppose; pres. subj. 1st pers. sing. / *oponer*. 2. that he (she/it) may oppose; pres. subj. 3rd pers. sing. 3. let him (her/it) oppose; impve. 3rd pers. sing.

opongáis that you (all) may oppose; pres. subj. 2nd pers. pl. / *oponer*.

opongámonos let us disapprove; impve. 1st pers. pl. / *oponerse*.

opongamos 1. that we may oppose; pres. subj. 1st pers. pl. / *oponer*. 2. let us oppose; impve. 1st pers. pl.

opongan 1. that they may oppose; pres. subj. 3rd pers. pl. / *oponer*. 2. let them oppose; impve. 3rd pers. pl.

opónganse let them disapprove; impve. 3rd pers. pl. / *oponerse*.

opongas that you may oppose; pres. subj. 2nd pers. sing. / *oponer*.

opóngase let him (her/it) disapprove; impve. 3rd pers. sing. / *oponerse*.

opongo I oppose; pres. ind. 1st pers. sing. / *oponer*.

oponiendo opposing; pres. part. / *oponer*.

oponiéndose disapproving; pres. part. / *oponerse*.

oponte (you) disapprove; impve. 2nd pers. sing. / *oponerse*.

oprimir to opress. reg.

optar to choose. reg.

opuesto opposed; past part. / *oponer*.

opuse I opposed; past 1st pers. sing. / *oponer*.

opusiera 1. that I might oppose; imp. subj. 1st pers. sing. / *oponer*. 2. that he (she/it) might oppose; imp. subj. 3rd pers. sing.

opusierais that you (all) might oppose; imp. subj. 2nd pers pl. / *oponer*.

opusiéramos that we might oppose; imp. subj. 1st pers. pl. / *oponer*.

opusieran that they might oppose; imp. subj. 3rd pers. pl. / *oponer*.

opusieras that you might oppose; imp. subj. 2nd pers. sing. / *oponer*.

opusieron they opposed; past 3rd pers. pl. / *oponer*.

opusiese 1. that I might oppose; imp. subj. 1st pers. sing. / *oponer*. 2. that he (she/it) might oppose; imp. subj. 3rd pers. sing.

opusieseis that you (all) might oppose; imp. subj. 2nd pers pl. / *oponer*.

opusiésemos that we might oppose; imp. subj. 1st pers. pl. / *oponer*.

opusiesen that they might oppose; imp. subj. 3rd pers. pl. / *oponer*.

opusieses that you might oppose; imp. subj. 2nd pers. sing. / *oponer*.

opusimos we opposed; past 1st pers. pl. / *oponer*.

opusiste you opposed; past 2nd pers. sing. / *oponer*.

opusisteis you (all) opposed; past 2nd pers. pl. / *oponer*.

opuso he (she/it) opposed; past 3rd pers. sing. / *oponer*.

orar to pray. reg.

ordenar to arrange. reg.

ordeñar to milk. reg.

oreándose becoming aired; pres. part. / *orearse*.

orear to expose to air. reg.

orearse to become aired. reg.

oréense let them become aired; impve. 3rd pers. pl. / *orearse*.

oréese let it become aired; impve. 3rd pers. sing. / *orearse*.

organice 1. that I may organize; pres. subj. 1st pers. sing. / *organizar*. 2. that he (she/it) may organize; pres. subj. 3rd pers. sing. 3. let him (her/it) organize; impve. 3rd pers. sing.

organicé I organized; past 1st pers. sing. / *organizar*.

organicéis that you (all) may organize; pres. subj. 2nd pers. pl. / *organizar*.

organicemos 1. that we may organize; pres. subj. 1st pers. pl. / *organizar*. 2. let us organize; impve. 1st pers. pl.

organicen 1. that they may organize; pres. subj. 3rd pers. pl. / *organizar*. 2. let them organize; impve. 3rd pers. pl.

organices that you may organize; pres. subj. 2nd pers. sing. / *organizar*.

orientándose getting one's bearings; pres. part. / *orientarse*. *orientarse*.

orientaos (you all) get your bearings; impve. 2nd pers. pl. / *orientarse*.

orientar to orient. reg.

orientarse to get one's bearings. reg.

oriéntate (you) get your bearings; impve. 2nd pers. sing. / *orientarse*.

orientémonos let us get our bearings; impve. 1st pers. pl. / *orientarse*.

oriéntense let them get their bearings; impve. 3rd pers. pl. / *orientarse*.

oriéntese let him (her/it) get his (her/its) bearings; impve. 3rd pers. sing. / *orientarse*.

orificar to fill with gold. irr.

orifique 1. that I may fill with gold; pres. subj. 1st pers. sing. / *orificar*. 2. that he (she/it) may fill with gold; pres. subj. 3rd pers. sing. 3. let him (her/it) fill with gold; impve. 3rd pers. sing.

orifiqué I filled with gold; past 1st pers. sing. / *orificar*.

orifiquéis that you (all) may fill with gold; pres. subj. 2nd pers. pl. / *orificar*.

orifiquemos 1. that we may fill with gold; pres. subj. 1st pers. pl. / *orificar*. 2. let us fill with gold; impve. 1st pers. pl.

orifiquen 1. that they may fill with gold; pres. subj. 3rd pers. pl. / *orificar*. 2. let them fill with gold; impve. 3rd pers. pl.

orifiques that you may fill with gold; pres. subj. 2nd pers. sing. / *orificar*.

originándose originating; pres. part. / *originarse*.

originaos (you all) originate; impve. 2nd pers. pl. / *originarse*.

originar to originate. reg.

originarse to originate. reg.

originate (you) originate; impve. 2nd pers. sing. / *originarse*.

originémonos let us originate; impve. 1st pers. pl. / *originarse*.

orígínense let them originate; impve. 3rd pers. pl. / *originarse*.

orígínese let him (her/it) originate; impve. 3rd pers. sing. / *originarse*.

orillándose skirting the edge of; pres. part. / *orillarse*.

orillaos (you all) skirt the edge of; impve. 2nd pers. pl. / *orillarse*.

orillar to trim the edge. reg.

orillarse to skirt the edge of. reg.

oríllate (you) skirt the edge of; impve. 2nd pers. sing. / *orillarse*.

orillémonos let us skirt the edge of; impve. 1st pers. pl. / *orillarse*.

oríllense let them skirt the edge of; impve. 3rd pers. pl. / *orillarse*.

oríllese let him (her/it) skirt the edge of; impve. 3rd pers. sing. / *orillarse*.

orinar to urinate. reg.

orlar to border. reg.

ornamentar to ornament. reg.

ornar to adorn. reg.

orquestar to orchestrate. reg.

orzar to luff. reg.

osar to dare. reg.

oscilar to oscillate. reg.

oscurecer to darken or to obscure. irr.

oscurecerse to get cloudy. irr.

oscureciéndose getting cloudy; pres. part. / *oscurecerse*.

oscurezca 1. that I may darken; pres. subj. 1st pers. sing. / *oscurecer*. 2. that he (she/it) may darken; pres. subj. 3rd pers. sing. 3. let him (her/it) darken; impve. 3rd pers. sing.

oscurezcáis that you (all) may darken; pres. subj. 2nd pers. pl. / *oscurecer*.

oscurezcamos 1. that we may darken; pres. subj. 1st pers. pl. / *oscurecer*. 2. let us darken; impve. 1st pers. pl.

oscurezcan 1. that they may darken; pres. subj. 3rd pers. pl. / *oscurecer*. 2. let them darken; impve. 3rd pers. pl.

oscurézcanse let them get cloudy; impve. 3rd pers. pl. / *oscurecerse*.

oscurezcas that you may darken; pres. subj. 2nd pers. sing. / *oscurecer*.

oscurézcase let it get cloudy; impve. 3rd pers. sing. / *oscurecerse*.

oscurezco I darken; pres. ind. 1st pers. sing. / *oscurecer*.

osificándose becoming ossified; pres. part. / *osificarse*.

osificaos (you all) become ossified; impve. 2nd pers. pl. / *osificarse*.

osificarse to become ossified. irr.

osifícate (you) become ossified; impve. 2nd pers. sing. / *osificarse*.

osifique 1. that I may become ossified; pres. subj. 1st pers. sing. / *osificarse*. 2. that he (she/it) may become ossified; pres. subj. 3rd pers. sing.

osifiqué I became ossified; past 1st pers. sing. / *osificarse*.

osifiquéis that you (all) may become ossified; pres. subj. 2nd pers. pl. / *osificarse*.

osifiquémonos let us become ossified; impve. 1st pers. pl. / *osificarse*.

osifiquemos that we may become ossified; pres. subj. 1st pers. pl. / *osificarse*.
osifiquen that they may become ossified; pres. subj. 3rd pers. pl. / *osificarse*.
osifíquense let them become ossified; impve. 3rd pers. pl. / *osificarse*.
osifiques that you may become ossified; pres. subj. 2nd pers. sing. / *osificarse*.
osifíquese let him (her/it) become ossified; impve. 3rd pers. sing. / *osificarse*.
ostentar to show. reg.
otear to survey. reg.
otoñar to spend the autumn. reg.
otorgar to grant. irr.
otorgue 1. that I may grant; pres. subj. 1st pers. sing. / *otorgar*. 2. that he (she/it) may grant; pres. subj. 3rd pers. sing. 3. let him (her/it) grant; impve. 3rd pers. sing.
otorgué I granted; past 1st pers. sing. / *otorgar*.
otorguéis that you (all) may grant; pres. subj. 2nd pers. pl. / *otorgar*.
otorguemos 1. that we may grant; pres. subj. 1st pers. pl. / *otorgar*. 2. let us grant; impve. 1st pers. pl.
otorguen 1. that they may grant; pres. subj. 3rd pers. pl. / *otorgar*. 2. let them grant; impve. 3rd pers. pl.
otorgues that you may grant; pres. subj. 2nd pers. sing. / *otorgar*.
ovar to lay eggs. reg.
ovillándose curling up into a ball; pres. part. / *ovillarse*.
ovillaos (you all) curl up into a ball; impve. 2nd pers. pl. / *ovillarse*.
ovillar to form into a ball. reg.
ovillarse to curl up into a ball. reg.
ovíllate (you) curl up into a ball; impve. 2nd pers. sing. / *ovillarse*.
ovillémonos let us curl up into a ball; impve. 1st pers. pl. / *ovillarse*.
ovíllense let them curl up into a ball; impve. 3rd pers. pl. / *ovillarse*.
ovíllese let him (her/it) curl up into a ball; impve. 3rd pers. sing. / *ovillarse*.
oxidándose rusting; pres. part. / *oxidarse*.
oxidaos (you all) rust; impve. 2nd pers. pl. / *oxidarse*.
oxidar to oxidize. reg.
oxidarse to rust. reg.
oxídate (you) rust; impve. 2nd pers. sing. / *oxidarse*.
oxidémonos let us rust; impve. 1st pers. pl. / *oxidarse*.
oxídense let them rust; impve. 3rd pers. pl. / *oxidarse*.
oxídese let him (her/it) rust; impve. 3rd pers. sing. / *oxidarse*.
oxigenar to oxygenate. reg.
oye 1. he (she/it) hears; pres. ind. 3rd pers. sing. / *oír*. 2. (you) hear; impve. 2nd pers. sing.
oyen they hear; pres. ind. 3rd pers. pl. / *oír*.
oyendo hearing; pres. part. / *oír*.
oyera 1. that I might hear; imp. subj. 1st pers. sing. / *oír*. 2. that he (she/it) might hear; imp. subj. 3rd pers. sing.

oyerais that you (all) might hear; imp. subj. 2nd pers pl. / *oír*.
oyéramos that we might hear; imp. subj. 1st pers. pl. / *oír*.
oyeran that they might hear; imp. subj. 3rd pers. pl. / *oír*.
oyeras that you might hear; imp. subj. 2nd pers. sing. / *oír*.
oyeron they heard; past 3rd pers. pl. / *oír*.
oyes you hear; pres. ind. 2nd pers. sing. / *oír*.
oyese 1. that I might hear; imp. subj. 1st pers. sing. / *oír*. 2. that he (she/it) might hear; imp. subj. 3rd pers. sing.
oyeseis that you (all) might hear; imp. subj. 2nd pers pl. / *oír*.
oyésemos that we might hear; imp. subj. 1st pers. pl. / *oír*.
oyesen that they might hear; imp. subj. 3rd pers. pl. / *oír*.
oyeses that you might hear; imp. subj. 2nd pers. sing. / *oír*.
oyó he (she/it) heard; past 3rd pers. sing. / *oír*.

P

pacer to pasture. irr.
pacificándose calming down; pres. part. / *pacificarse*.
pacificaos (you all) calm down; impve. 2nd pers. pl. / *pacificarse*.
pacificar to pacify. irr.
pacificarse to calm down. irr.
pacifícate (you) calm down; impve. 2nd pers. sing. / *pacificarse*.
pacifique 1. that I may pacify; pres. subj. 1st pers. sing. / *pacificar*. 2. that he (she/it) may pacify; pres. subj. 3rd pers. sing. 3. let him (her/it) pacify; impve. 3rd pers. sing.
pacifiqué I pacified; past 1st pers. sing. / *pacificar*.
pacifiquéis that you (all) may pacify; pres. subj. 2nd pers. pl. / *pacificar*.
pacifiquémonos let us calm down; impve. 1st pers. pl. / *pacificarse*.
pacifiquemos 1. that we may pacify; pres. subj. 1st pers. pl. / *pacificar*. 2. let us pacify; impve. 1st pers. pl.
pacifiquen 1. that they may pacify; pres. subj. 3rd pers. pl. / *pacificar*. 2. let them pacify; impve. 3rd pers. pl.
pacifíquense let them calm down; impve. 3rd pers. pl. / *pacificarse*.
pacifiques that you may pacify; pres. subj. 2nd pers. sing. / *pacificar*.
pacifíquese let him (her/it) calm down; impve. 3rd pers. sing. / *pacificarse*.
pactar to agree to. reg.
padecer to suffer. irr.

padezca 1. that I may suffer; pres. subj. 1st pers. sing. / *padecer*. 2. that he (she/it) may suffer; pres. subj. 3rd pers. sing. 3. let him (her/it) suffer; impve. 3rd pers. sing.

padezcáis that you (all) may suffer; pres. subj. 2nd pers. pl. / *padecer*.

padezcamos 1. that we may suffer; pres. subj. 1st pers. pl. / *padecer*. 2. let us suffer; impve. 1st pers. pl.

padezcan 1. that they may suffer; pres. subj. 3rd pers. pl. / *padecer*. 2. let them suffer; impve. 3rd pers. pl.

padezcas that you may suffer; pres. subj. 2nd pers. sing. / *padecer*.

padezco I suffer; pres. ind. 1st pers. sing. / *padecer*.

pagándose de being pleased with; pres. part. / *pagarse de*.

pagaos de (you all) be pleased with; impve. 2nd pers. pl. / *pagarse de*.

pagar to pay. irr.

pagarse de to be pleased with. irr.

págate de (you) be pleased with; impve. 2nd pers. sing. / *pagarse de*.

paginar to page. reg.

pague 1. that I may pay; pres. subj. 1st pers. sing. / *pagar*. 2. that he (she/it) may pay; pres. subj. 3rd pers. sing. 3. let him (her/it) pay; impve. 3rd pers. sing.

pagué I paid; past 1st pers. sing. / *pagar*.

paguéis that you (all) may pay; pres. subj. 2nd pers. pl. / *pagar*.

paguémonos de let us be pleased with; impve. 1st pers. pl. / *pagarse de*.

paguemos 1. that we may pay; pres. subj. 1st pers. pl. / *pagar*. 2. let us pay; impve. 1st pers. pl.

paguen 1. that they may pay; pres. subj. 3rd pers. pl. / *pagar*. 2. let them pay; impve. 3rd pers. pl.

páguense de let them be pleased with; impve. 3rd pers. pl. / *pagarse de*.

pagues that you may pay; pres. subj. 2nd pers. sing. / *pagar*.

páguese de let him (her/it) be pleased with; impve. 3rd pers. sing. / *pagarse de*.

pairar to lie to with all sails set. reg.

pajarear to hunt birds. reg.

paladeándose relishing; pres. part. / *paladearse*.

paladeaos (you all) relish; impve. 2nd pers. pl. / *paladearse*.

paladear to taste with relish. reg.

paladearse to relish. reg.

paladéate (you) relish; impve. 2nd pers. sing. / *paladearse*.

paladeémonos let us relish; impve. 1st pers. pl. / *paladearse*.

paladéense let them relish; impve. 3rd pers. pl. / *paladearse*.

paladéese let him (her/it) relish; impve. 3rd pers. sing. / *paladearse*.

palanganeándose bragging; pres. part. / *palanganearse*.

palanganeaos (you all) brag; impve. 2nd pers. pl. / *palanganearse*.

palanganearse to brag. reg.

palanganéate (you) brag; impve. 2nd pers. sing. / *palanganearse*.

palanganeémonos let us brag; impve. 1st pers. pl. / *palanganéense*.

palanganéense let them brag; impve. 3rd pers. pl. / *palanganearse*.

palanganéese let him (her/it) brag; impve. 3rd pers. sing. / *palanganearse*.

palear to shovel. reg.

paletear to paddle ineffectively. reg.

paliar to palliate or to cloak. reg.

palidecer to turn pale. irr.

palidezca 1. that I may turn pale; pres. subj. 1st pers. sing. / *palidecer*. 2. that he (she/it) may turn pale; pres. subj. 3rd pers. sing. 3. let him (her/it) turn pale; impve. 3rd pers. sing.

palidezcáis that you (all) may turn pale; pres. subj. 2nd pers. pl. / *palidecer*.

palidezcamos 1. that we may turn pale; pres. subj. 1st pers. pl. / *palidecer*. 2. let us turn pale; impve. 1st pers. pl.

palidezcan 1. that they may turn pale; pres. subj. 3rd pers. pl. / *palidecer*. 2. let them turn pale; impve. 3rd pers. pl.

palidezcas that you may turn pale; pres. subj. 2nd pers. sing. / *palidecer*.

palidezco I turn pale; pres. ind. 1st pers. sing. / *palidecer*.

palmar to die. reg.

palmear to clap or to pat. reg.

palmotear to applaud. reg.

palpar to feel or to grope. reg.

palpitar to palpitate or to throb. reg.

pampear to travel through the pampas. reg.

pandeándose bulging; pres. part. / *pandearse*.

pandeaos (you all) bulge; impve. 2nd pers. pl. / *pandearse*.

pandear to warp. reg.

pandearse to bulge. reg.

pandéate (you) bulge; impve. 2nd pers. sing. / *pandearse*.

pandeémonos let us bulge; impve. 1st pers. pl. / *pandearse*.

pandéense let them bulge; impve. 3rd pers. pl. / *pandearse*.

pandéese let him (her/it) bulge; impve. 3rd pers. sing. / *pandearse*.

panderetear to play on the tambourine. reg.

papar to gulp down. reg.

papelear to rummage through papers. reg.

parafrasear to paraphrase. reg.

paralelar to parallel. reg.

paralice 1. that I may paralyze; pres. subj. 1st pers. sing. / *paralizar*. 2. that he (she/it) may paralyze; pres. subj. 3rd pers. sing. 3. let him (her/it) paralyze; impve. 3rd pers. sing.

paralicé I paralyzed; past 1st pers. sing. / *paralizar*.

paralicéis that you (all) may paralyze; pres. subj. 2nd pers. pl. / *paralizar*.

paralicemos 1. that we may paralyze; pres. subj. 1st pers. pl. / *paralizar*. 2. let us paralyze; impve. 1st pers. pl.

paralicen 1. that they may paralyze; pres. subj. 3rd pers. pl. / *paralizar*. 2. let them paralyze; impve. 3rd pers. pl.

paralices that you may paralyze; pres. subj. 2nd pers. sing. / *paralizar*.

paralizar to paralyze. irr.

paralogice 1. that I may confuse; pres. subj. 1st pers. sing. / *paralogizar*. 2. that he (she/it) may confuse; pres. subj. 3rd pers. sing. 3. let him (her/it) confuse; impve. 3rd pers. sing.

paralogicé I confused; past 1st pers. sing. / *paralogizar*.

paralogicéis that you (all) may confuse; pres. subj. 2nd pers. pl. / *paralogizar*.

paralogicemos 1. that we may confuse; pres. subj. 1st pers. pl. / *paralogizar*. 2. let us confuse; impve. 1st pers. pl.

paralogicen 1. that they may confuse; pres. subj. 3rd pers. pl. / *paralogizar*. 2. let them confuse; impve. 3rd pers. pl.

paralogices that you may confuse; pres. subj. 2nd pers. sing. / *paralogizar*.

paralogizar to confuse. irr.

paramentar to adorn. reg.

parándose halting; pres. part. / *pararse*.

parangonar to compare. reg.

paraos (you all) halt; impve. 2nd pers. pl. / *pararse*.

parapetándose taking cover behind a parapet; pres. part. / *parapetarse*.

parapetaos (you all) take cover behind a parapet; impve. 2nd pers. pl. / *parapetarse*.

parapetarse to take cover behind a parapet. reg.

parapétate (you) take cover behind a parapet; impve. 2nd pers. sing. / *parapetarse*.

parapetémonos let us take cover behind a parapet; impve. 1st pers. pl. / *parapetarse*.

parapétense let them take cover behind a parapet; impve. 3rd pers. pl. / *parapetarse*.

parapétese let him (her/it) take cover behind a parapet; impve. 3rd pers. sing. / *parapetarse*.

parar to stop. reg.

pararse to halt. reg.

párate (you) halt; impve. 2nd pers. sing. / *pararse*.

parcelar to parcel out. reg.

parchar to patch. reg.

pardear to appear dusky. reg.

parear to pair. reg.

pareceos (you all) look alike; impve. 2nd pers. pl. / *parecerse*.

parecer to appear or to seem. irr.

parecerse to look alike. irr.

parécete (you) look alike; impve. 2nd pers. sing. / *parecerse*.

pareciéndose looking alike; pres. part. / *parecerse*.

parémonos let us halt; impve. 1st pers. pl. / *pararse*.

párense let them halt; impve. 3rd pers. pl. / *pararse*.

párese let him (her/it) halt; impve. 3rd pers. sing. / *pararse*.

parezca 1. that I may appear; pres. subj. 1st pers. sing. / *parecer*. 2. that he (she/it) may appear; pres. subj. 3rd pers. sing. 3. let him (her/it) appear; impve. 3rd pers. sing.

parezcáis that you (all) may appear; pres. subj. 2nd pers. pl. / *parecer*.

parezcámonos let us look alike; impve. 1st pers. pl. / *parecerse*.

parezcamos 1. that we may appear; pres. subj. 1st pers. pl. / *parecer*. 2. let us appear; impve. 1st pers. pl.

parezcan 1. that they may appear; pres. subj. 3rd pers. pl. / *parecer*. 2. let them appear; impve. 3rd pers. pl.

parézcanse let them look alike; impve. 3rd pers. pl. / *parecerse*.

parezcas that you may appear; pres. subj. 2nd pers. sing. / *parecer*.

parézcase let him (her/it) look alike; impve. 3rd pers. sing. / *parecerse*.

parezco I appear; pres. ind. 1st pers. sing. / *parecer*.

parir to give birth. reg.

parlamentar to parley. reg.

parlar to talk. reg.

parlotear to babble. reg.

parodiar to parody. reg.

parpadear to blink. reg.

parpar to quack. reg.

parquear to park. reg.

parrandear to revel. reg.

partámonos let us be torn apart; impve. 1st pers. pl. / *partirse*.

pártanse let them be torn apart; impve. 3rd pers. pl. / *partirse*.

pártase let him (her/it) be torn apart; impve. 3rd pers. sing. / *partirse*.

pártete (you) be torn apart; impve. 2nd pers. sing. / *partirse*.

participar to participate. reg.

partiéndose being torn apart; pres. part. / *partirse*.

partíos (you all) be torn apart; impve. 2nd pers. pl. / *partirse*.

partir to divide or to depart. reg.

partirse to be torn apart. reg.

pasándose changing over; pres. part. / *pasarse*.

pasaos (you all) change over; impve. 2nd pers. pl. / *pasarse*.

pasar to pass. reg.

pasarse to change over. reg.

pásate (you) change over; impve. 2nd pers. sing. / *pasarse*.

paseándose taking a walk; pres. part. / *pasearse*.

paseaos (you all) take a walk; impve. 2nd pers. pl. / *pasearse*.

pasear to walk. reg.

pasearse to take a walk. reg.

paséate (you) take a walk; impve. 2nd pers. sing. / *pasearse*.

paseémonos let us take a walk; impve. 1st pers. pl. / *pasearse.*

paséense let them take a walk; impve. 3rd pers. pl. / *pasearse.*

paséese let him (her/it) take a walk; impve. 3rd pers. sing. / *pasearse.*

pasémonos let us change over; impve. 1st pers. pl. / *pasarse.*

pásense let them change over; impve. 3rd pers. pl. / *pasarse.*

pásese let him (her/it) change over; impve. 3rd pers. sing. / *pasarse.*

pasmándose being astounded; pres. part. / *pasmarse.*

pasmaos (you all) be astounded; impve. 2nd pers. pl. / *pasmarse.*

pasmar to stun. reg.

pasmarse to be astounded or to become rigid. reg.

pásmate (you) be astounded; impve. 2nd pers. sing. / *pasmarse.*

pasmémonos let us be astounded; impve. 1st pers. pl. / *pasmarse.*

pásmense let them be astounded; impve. 3rd pers. pl. / *pasmarse.*

pásmese let him (her/it) be astounded; impve. 3rd pers. sing. / *pasmarse.*

pasquinar to lampoon. reg.

pastar to pasture. reg.

pastear to graze. reg.

pasterice 1. that I may pasteurize; pres. subj. 1st pers. sing. / *pasterizar.* 2. that he (she/it) may pasteurize; pres. subj. 3rd pers. sing. 3. let him (her/it) pasteurize; impve. 3rd pers. sing.

pastericé I pasteurized; past 1st pers. sing. / *pasterizar.*

pastericéis that you (all) may pasteurize; pres. subj. 2nd pers. pl. / *pasterizar.*

pastericemos 1. that we may pasteurize; pres. subj. 1st pers. pl. / *pasterizar.* 2. let us pasteurize; impve. 1st pers. pl.

pastericen 1. that they may pasteurize; pres. subj. 3rd pers. pl. / *pasterizar.* 2. let them pasteurize; impve. 3rd pers. pl.

pasterices that you may pasteurize; pres. subj. 2nd pers. sing. / *pasterizar.*

pasterizar to pasteurize. irr.

pasteurice 1. that I may pasteurize; pres. subj. 1st pers. sing. / *pasteurizar.* 2. that he (she/it) may pasteurize; pres. subj. 3rd pers. sing. 3. let him (her/it) pasteurize; impve. 3rd pers. sing.

pasteuricé I pasteurized; past 1st pers. sing. / *pasteurizar.*

pasteuricéis that you (all) may pasteurize; pres. subj. 2nd pers. pl. / *pasteurizar.*

pasteuricemos 1. that we may pasteurize; pres. subj. 1st pers. pl. / *pasteurizar.* 2. let us pasteurize; impve. 1st pers. pl.

pasteuricen 1. that they may pasteurize; pres. subj. 3rd pers. pl. / *pasteurizar.* 2. let them pasteurize; impve. 3rd pers. pl.

pasteurices that you may pasteurize; pres. subj. 2nd pers. sing. / *pasteurizar.*

pasteurizar to pasteurize. irr.

pastorear to pasture. reg.

patalear to kick around. reg.

patear to kick or to stamp. reg.

patentar to patent. reg.

patentice 1. that I may reveal; pres. subj. 1st pers. sing. / *patentizar.* 2. that he (she/it) may reveal; pres. subj. 3rd pers. sing. 3. let him (her/it) reveal; impve. 3rd pers. sing.

patenticé I revealed; past 1st pers. sing. / *patentizar.*

patenticéis that you (all) may reveal; pres. subj. 2nd pers. pl. / *patentizar.*

patenticemos 1. that we may reveal; pres. subj. 1st pers. pl. / *patentizar.* 2. let us reveal; impve. 1st pers. pl.

patenticen 1. that they may reveal; pres. subj. 3rd pers. pl. / *patentizar.* 2. let them reveal; impve. 3rd pers. pl.

patentices that you may reveal; pres. subj. 2nd pers. sing. / *patentizar.*

patentizar to reveal. irr.

patinar to skate or to skid. reg.

patrocinar to patronize or to sponsor. reg.

patrullar to patrol. reg.

patullar to tramp about. reg.

pausar to pause. reg.

pavimentar to pave. reg.

pavoneándose showing off; pres. part. / *pavonearse.*

pavoneaos (you all) show off; impve. 2nd pers. pl. / *pavonearse.*

pavonear to strut. reg.

pavonearse to show off. reg.

pavonéate (you) show off; impve. 2nd pers. sing. / *pavonearse.*

pavoneémonos let us show off; impve. 1st pers. pl. / *pavonearse.*

pavonéense let them show off; impve. 3rd pers. pl. / *pavonearse.*

pavonéese let him (her/it) show off; impve. 3rd pers. sing. / *pavonearse.*

payasear to clown. reg.

pazca 1. that I may pasture; pres. subj. 1st pers. sing. / *pacer.* 2. that he (she/it) may pasture; pres. subj. 3rd pers. sing. 3. let him (her/it) pasture; impve. 3rd pers. sing.

pazcáis that you (all) may pasture; pres. subj. 2nd pers. pl. / *pacer.*

pazcamos 1. that we may pasture; pres. subj. 1st pers. pl. / *pacer.* 2. let us pasture; impve. 1st pers. pl.

pazcan 1. that they may pasture; pres. subj. 3rd pers. pl. / *pacer.* 2. let them pasture; impve. 3rd pers. pl.

pazcas that you may pasture; pres. subj. 2nd pers. sing. / *pacer.*

pazco I pasture; pres. ind. 1st pers. sing. / *pacer.*

pealar to lasso. reg.

pecar to sin. irr.

pechar to shove with the chest. reg.

pedalear to pedal. reg.

pedantear to act the pedant. reg.

pedir to ask or to beg. irr.
pegándose fighting; pres. part. / *pegarse.*
pegaos (you all) fight; impve. 2nd pers. pl. / *pegarse.*
pegar to fasten or to hit. irr.
pegarse to fight or to intrude. irr.
pégate (you) fight; impve. 2nd pers. sing. / *pegarse.*
pegue 1. that I may fasten; pres. subj. 1st pers. sing. / *pegar.* 2. that he (she/it) may fasten; pres. subj. 3rd pers. sing. 3. let him (her/it) fasten; impve. 3rd pers. sing.
pegué I fastened; past 1st pers. sing. / *pegar.*
peguéis that you (all) may fasten; pres. subj. 2nd pers. pl. / *pegar.*
peguémonos let us fight; impve. 1st pers. pl. / *pegarse.*
peguemos 1. that we may fasten; pres. subj. 1st pers. pl. / *pegar.* 2. let us fasten; impve. 1st pers. pl.
peguen 1. that they may fasten; pres. subj. 3rd pers. pl. / *pegar.* 2. let them fasten; impve. 3rd pers. pl.
péguense let them fight; impve. 3rd pers. pl. / *pegarse.*
pegues that you may fasten; pres. subj. 2nd pers. sing. / *pegar.*
péguese let him (her/it) fight; impve. 3rd pers. sing. / *pegarse.*
peinándose combing one's hair; pres. part. / *peinarse.*
peinaos (you all) comb your hair; impve. 2nd pers. pl. / *peinarse.*
peinar to comb. reg.
peinarse to comb one's hair. reg.
peínate (you) comb your hair; impve. 2nd pers. sing. / *peinarse.*
peinémonos let us comb our hair; impve. 1st pers. pl. / *peinarse.*
peínense let them comb their hair; impve. 3rd pers. pl. / *peinarse.*
peínese let him (her) comb his (her) hair / *peinarse.*
pelándose peeling off; pres. part. / *pelarse.*
pelaos (you all) peel off; impve. 2nd pers. pl. / *pelarse.*
pelar to cut the hair. reg.
pelarse to peel off. reg.
pelárselas de to be strongly affected by. reg.
pelárselas por to be eager to. reg.
pélate (you) peel off; impve. 2nd pers. sing. / *pelarse.*
peleándose scuffling; pres. part. / *pelearse.*
peleaos (you all) scuffle; impve. 2nd pers. pl. / *pelearse.*
pelear to fight or to quarrel. reg.
pelearse to scuffle. reg.
peléate (you) scuffle; impve. 2nd pers. sing. / *pelearse.*
pelechar to molt or to shed. reg.
peleémonos let us scuffle; impve. 1st pers. pl. / *pelearse.*
peléense let them scuffle; impve. 3rd pers. pl. / *pelearse.*
peléese let him (her/it) scuffle; impve. 3rd pers. sing. / *pelearse.*
pelémonos let us peel off; impve. 1st pers. pl. / *pelarse.*

pélense let them peel off; impve. 3rd pers. pl. / *pelarse.*
pélese let him (her/it) peel off; impve. 3rd pers. sing. / *pelarse.*
peligrar to be in danger. reg.
pelotear to knock a ball around or to audit. reg.
pellizcándose yearning; pres. part. / *pellizcarse.*
pellizcaos (you all) yearn; impve. 2nd pers. pl. / *pellizcarse.*
pellizcar to pinch or to nip. irr.
pellizcarse to yearn. irr.
pellízcate (you) yearn; impve. 2nd pers. sing. / *pellizcarse.*
pellizque 1. that I may pinch; pres. subj. 1st pers. sing. / *pellizcar.* 2. that he (she/it) may pinch; pres. subj. 3rd pers. sing. 3. let him (her/it) pinch; impve. 3rd pers. sing.
pellizqué I pinched; past 1st pers. sing. / *pellizcar.*
pellizquéis that you (all) may pinch; pres. subj. 2nd pers. pl. / *pellizcar.*
pellizquémonos let us yearn; impve. 1st pers. pl. / *pellizcarse.*
pellizquemos 1. that we may pinch; pres. subj. 1st pers. pl. / *pellizcar.* 2. let us pinch; impve. 1st pers. pl.
pellizquen 1. that they may pinch; pres. subj. 3rd pers. pl. / *pellizcar.* 2. let them pinch; impve. 3rd pers. pl.
pellízquense let them yearn; impve. 3rd pers. pl. / *pellizcarse.*
pellizques that you may pinch; pres. subj. 2nd pers. sing. / *pellizcar.*
pellízquese let him (her/it) yearn; impve. 3rd pers. sing. / *pellizcarse.*
penalice 1. that I may penalize; pres. subj. 1st pers. sing. / *penalizar.* 2. that he (she/it) may penalize; pres. subj. 3rd pers. sing. 3. let him (her/it) penalize; impve. 3rd pers. sing.
penalicé I penalized; past 1st pers. sing. / *penalizar.*
penalicéis that you (all) may penalize; pres. subj. 2nd pers. pl. / *penalizar.*
penalicemos 1. that we may penalize; pres. subj. 1st pers. pl. / *penalizar.* 2. let us penalize; impve. 1st pers. pl.
penalicen 1. that they may penalize; pres. subj. 3rd pers. pl. / *penalizar.* 2. let them penalize; impve. 3rd pers. pl.
penalices that you may penalize; pres. subj. 2nd pers. sing. / *penalizar.*
penalizar to penalize. irr.
penándose grieving; pres. part. / *penarse.*
penaos (you all) grieve; impve. 2nd pers. pl. / *penarse.*
penar to suffer or to chastize. reg.
penarse to grieve. reg.
pénate (you) grieve; impve. 2nd pers. sing. / *penarse.*
pendenciar to quarrel. reg.
pender to hang or to depend. reg.
penémonos let us grieve; impve. 1st pers. pl. / *penarse.*

pénense let them grieve; impve. 3rd pers. pl. / *penarse.*

pénese let him (her/it) grieve; impve. 3rd pers. sing. / *penarse.*

penetrar to penetrate. reg.

pensar to think or to intend. irr.

pensionar to pension. reg.

pepenar to pick up. reg.

peque 1. that I may sin ; pres. subj. 1st pers. sing. / *pecar.* 2. that he (she/it) may sin ; pres. subj. 3rd pers. sing. 3. let him (her/it) sin ; impve. 3rd pers. sing.

pequé I sinned; past 1st pers. sing. / *pecar.*

pequéis that you (all) may sin ; pres. subj. 2nd pers. pl. / *pecar.*

pequemos 1. that we may sin ; pres. subj. 1st pers. pl. / *pecar.* 2. let us sin ; impve. 1st pers. pl.

pequen 1. that they may sin ; pres. subj. 3rd pers. pl. / *pecar.* 2. let them sin ; impve. 3rd pers. pl.

peques that you may sin ; pres. subj. 2nd pers. sing. / *pecar.*

percatándose being wary; pres. part. / *percatarse.*

percataos (you all) be wary; impve. 2nd pers. pl. / *percatarse.*

percatar to perceive. reg.

percatarse to be wary. reg.

percátate (you) be wary; impve. 2nd pers. sing. / *percatarse.*

percatémonos let us be wary; impve. 1st pers. pl. / *percatarse.*

percátense let them be wary; impve. 3rd pers. pl. / *percatarse.*

percátese let him (her/it) be wary; impve. 3rd pers. sing. / *percatarse.*

percibir to perceive. reg.

percudámonos let us get grimy; impve. 1st pers. pl. / *percudirse.*

percúdanse let them get grimy; impve. 3rd pers. pl. / *percudirse.*

percúdase let him (her/it) get grimy; impve. 3rd pers. sing. / *percudirse.*

percúdete (you) get grimy; impve. 2nd pers. sing. / *percudirse.*

percudiéndose getting grimy; pres. part. / *percudirse.*

percudíos (you all) get grimy; impve. 2nd pers. pl. / *percudirse.*

percudir to tarnish. reg.

percudirse to get grimy. reg.

percutir to percuss. reg.

perdámonos let us get lost; impve. 1st pers. pl. / *perderse.*

perdeos (you all) get lost; impve. 2nd pers. pl. / *perderse.*

perder to lose. irr.

perderse to get lost. irr.

perdiéndose getting lost; pres. part. / *perderse.*

perdigar to brown. irr.

perdigue 1. that I may brown; pres. subj. 1st pers. sing. / *perdigar.* 2. that he (she/it) may brown; pres. subj. 3rd pers. sing. 3. let him (her/it) brown; impve. 3rd pers. sing.

perdigué I browned; past 1st pers. sing. / *perdigar.*

perdiguéis that you (all) may brown; pres. subj. 2nd pers. pl. / *perdigar.*

perdiguemos 1. that we may brown; pres. subj. 1st pers. pl. / *perdigar.* 2. let us brown; impve. 1st pers. pl.

perdiguen 1. that they may brown; pres. subj. 3rd pers. pl. / *perdigar.* 2. let them brown; impve. 3rd pers. pl.

perdigues that you may brown; pres. subj. 2nd pers. sing. / *perdigar.*

perdonar to pardon. reg.

perdurar to last or to endure. reg.

pereceos (you all) crave; impve. 2nd pers. pl. / *perecerse.*

perecer to perish. irr.

perecerse to crave or to pine. irr.

perécete (you) crave; impve. 2nd pers. sing. / *perecerse.*

pereciéndose craving; pres. part. / *perecerse.*

peregrinar to roam. reg.

perezca 1. that I may perish; pres. subj. 1st pers. sing. / *perecer.* 2. that he (she/it) may perish; pres. subj. 3rd pers. sing. 3. let him (her/it) perish; impve. 3rd pers. sing.

perezcáis that you (all) may perish; pres. subj. 2nd pers. pl. / *perecer.*

perezcámonos let us crave; impve. 1st pers. pl. / *perecerse.*

perezcamos 1. that we may perish; pres. subj. 1st pers. pl. / *perecer.* 2. let us perish; impve. 1st pers. pl.

perezcan 1. that they may perish; pres. subj. 3rd pers. pl. / *perecer.* 2. let them perish; impve. 3rd pers. pl.

perézcanse let them crave; impve. 3rd pers. pl. / *perecerse.*

perezcas that you may perish; pres. subj. 2nd pers. sing. / *perecer.*

perézcase let him (her/it) crave; impve. 3rd pers. sing. / *perecerse.*

perezco I perish; pres. ind. 1st pers. sing. / *perecer.*

perfeccionar to perfect. reg.

perfilándose being silhouetted; pres. part. / *perfilarse.*

perfilaos (you all) be silhouetted; impve. 2nd pers. pl. / *perfilarse.*

perfilar to profile or to outline. reg.

perfilarse to be silhouetted. reg.

perfílate (you) be silhouetted; impve. 2nd pers. sing. / *perfilarse.*

perfilémonos let us be silhouetted; impve. 1st pers. pl. / *perfilarse.*

perfílense let them be silhouetted; impve. 3rd pers. pl. / *perfilarse.*

perfílese let him (her/it) be silhouetted; impve. 3rd pers. sing. / *perfilarse.*

perforar to perforate or to drill. reg.

perfumar to perfume. reg.

pergeñar to sketch. reg.
perifonear to broadcast. reg.
perifrasear to paraphrase. reg.
perjudicar to harm. irr.
perjudique 1. that I may harm; pres. subj. 1st pers. sing. / *perjudicar*. 2. that he (she/it) may harm; pres. subj. 3rd pers. sing. 3. let him (her/it) harm; impve. 3rd pers. sing.
perjudiqué I harmed; past 1st pers. sing. / *perjudicar*.
perjudiquéis that you (all) may harm; pres. subj. 2nd pers. pl. / *perjudicar*.
perjudiquemos 1. that we may harm; pres. subj. 1st pers. pl. / *perjudicar*. 2. let us harm; impve. 1st pers. pl.
perjudiquen 1. that they may harm; pres. subj. 3rd pers. pl. / *perjudicar*. 2. let them harm; impve. 3rd pers. pl.
perjudiques that you may harm; pres. subj. 2nd pers. sing. / *perjudicar*.
perjurándose committing perjury; pres. part. / *perjurarse*.
perjuraos (you all) commit perjury; impve. 2nd pers. pl. / *perjurarse*.
perjurar to commit perjury. reg.
perjurarse to commit perjury. reg.
perjúrate (you) commit perjury; impve. 2nd pers. sing. / *perjurarse*.
perjurémonos let us commit perjury; impve. 1st pers. pl. / *perjurarse*.
perjúrense let them commit perjury; impve. 3rd pers. pl. / *perjurarse*.
perjúrese let him (her/it) commit perjury; impve. 3rd pers. sing. / *perjurarse*.
permanecer to remain. irr.
permanezca 1. that I may remain; pres. subj. 1st pers. sing. / *permanecer*. 2. that he (she/it) may remain; pres. subj. 3rd pers. sing. 3. let him (her/it) remain; impve. 3rd pers. sing.
permanezcáis that you (all) may remain; pres. subj. 2nd pers. pl. / *permanecer*.
permanezcamos 1. that we may remain; pres. subj. 1st pers. pl. / *permanecer*. 2. let us remain; impve. 1st pers. pl.
permanezcan 1. that they may remain; pres. subj. 3rd pers. pl. / *permanecer*. 2. let them remain; impve. 3rd pers. pl.
permanezcas that you may remain; pres. subj. 2nd pers. sing. / *permanecer*.
permanezco I remain; pres. ind. 1st pers. sing. / *permanecer*.
permitámonos let us take the liberty; impve. 1st pers. pl. / *permitirse*.
permítanse let them take the liberty; impve. 3rd pers. pl. / *permitirse*.
permítase let him (her/it) take the liberty; impve. 3rd pers. sing. / *permitirse*.
permítete (you) take the liberty; impve. 2nd pers. sing. / *permitirse*.
permitiéndose taking the liberty; pres. part. / *permitirse*.

permitíos (you all) take the liberty; impve. 2nd pers. pl. / *permitirse*.
permitir to permit. reg.
permitirse to take the liberty. reg.
permutar to exchange. reg.
pernear to kick. reg.
pernoctar to spend the night. reg.
perorar to make a speech. reg.
perpetrar to perpetrate. reg.
perpetúa 1. he (she/it) perpetuates; pres. ind. 3rd pers. sing. / *perpetuar*. 2. (you) perpetuate; impve. 2nd pers. sing.
perpetúan they perpetuate; pres. ind. 3rd pers. pl. / *perpetuar*.
perpetuar to perpetuate. irr.
perpetúas you perpetuate; pres. ind. 2nd pers. sing. / *perpetuar*.
perpetúe 1. that I may perpetuate; pres. subj. 1st pers. sing. / *perpetuar*. 2. that he (she/it) may perpetuate; pres. subj. 3rd pers. sing. 3. let him (her/it) perpetuate; impve. 3rd pers. sing.
perpetúen 1. that they may perpetuate; pres. subj. 3rd pers. pl. / *perpetuar*. 2. let them perpetuate; impve. 3rd pers. pl.
perpetúes that you may perpetuate; pres. subj. 2nd pers. sing. / *perpetuar*.
perpetúo I perpetuate; pres. ind. 1st pers. sing. / *perpetuar*.
perseguir to persecute. irr.
perseverar to persevere. reg.
persiga 1. that I may persecute; pres. subj. 1st pers. sing. / *perseguir*. 2. that he (she/it) may persecute; pres. subj. 3rd pers. sing. 3. let him (her/it) persecute; impve. 3rd pers. sing.
persigáis that you (all) may persecute; pres. subj. 2nd pers. pl. / *perseguir*.
persigamos 1. that we may persecute; pres. subj. 1st pers. pl. / *perseguir*. 2. let us persecute; impve. 1st pers. pl.
persigan 1. that they may persecute; pres. subj. 3rd pers. pl. / *perseguir*. 2. let them persecute; impve. 3rd pers. pl.
persigas that you may persecute; pres. subj. 2nd pers. sing. / *perseguir*.
persignándose making the sign of the cross; pres. part. / *persignarse*.
persignaos (you all) make the sign of the cross; impve. 2nd pers. pl. / *persignarse*.
persignarse to make the sign of the cross. reg.
persígnate (you) make the sign of the cross; impve. 2nd pers. sing. / *persignarse*.
persignémonos let us make the sign of the cross; impve. 1st pers. pl. / *persignarse*.
persígnense let them make the sign of the cross; impve. 3rd pers. pl. / *persignarse*.
persígnese let him (her) make the sign of the cross / *persignarse*.
persigo I persecute; pres. ind. 1st pers. sing. / *perseguir*.

persigue 1. he (she/it) persecutes; pres. ind. 3rd pers. sing. / *perseguir.* 2. (you) persecute; impve. 2nd pers. sing.

persiguen they persecute; pres. ind. 3rd pers. pl. / *perseguir.*

persigues you persecute; pres. ind. 2nd pers. sing. / *perseguir.*

persiguiendo persecuting; pres. part. / *perseguir.*

persiguiera 1. that I might persecute; imp. subj. 1st pers. sing. / *perseguir.* 2. that he (she/it) might persecute; imp. subj. 3rd pers. sing.

persiguierais that you (all) might persecute; imp. subj. 2nd pers pl. / *perseguir.*

persiguiéramos that we might persecute; imp. subj. 1st pers. pl. / *perseguir.*

persiguieran that they might persecute; imp. subj. 3rd pers. pl. / *perseguir.*

persiguieras that you might persecute; imp. subj. 2nd pers. sing. / *perseguir.*

persiguieron they persecuted; past 3rd pers. pl. / *perseguir.*

persiguiese 1. that I might persecute; imp. subj. 1st pers. sing. / *perseguir.* 2. that he (she/it) might persecute; imp. subj. 3rd pers. sing.

persiguieseis that you (all) might persecute; imp. subj. 2nd pers pl. / *perseguir.*

persiguiésemos that we might persecute; imp. subj. 1st pers. pl. / *perseguir.*

persiguiesen that they might persecute; imp. subj. 3rd pers. pl. / *perseguir.*

persiguieses that you might persecute; imp. subj. 2nd pers. sing. / *perseguir.*

persiguió he (she/it) persecuted; past 3rd pers. sing. / *perseguir.*

persistir to persist. reg.

personalice 1. that I may personalize; pres. subj. 1st pers. sing. / *personalizar.* 2. that he (she/it) may personalize; pres. subj. 3rd pers. sing. 3. let him (her/it) personalize; impve. 3rd pers. sing.

personalicé I personalized; past 1st pers. sing. / *personalizar.*

personalicéis that you (all) may personalize; pres. subj. 2nd pers. pl. / *personalizar.*

personalicemos 1. that we may personalize; pres. subj. 1st pers. pl. / *personalizar.* 2. let us personalize; impve. 1st pers. pl.

personalicen 1. that they may personalize; pres. subj. 3rd pers. pl. / *personalizar.* 2. let them personalize; impve. 3rd pers. pl.

personalices that you may personalize; pres. subj. 2nd pers. sing. / *personalizar.*

personalizar to personalize. irr.

personificar to personify. irr.

personifique 1. that I may personify; pres. subj. 1st pers. sing. / *personificar.* 2. that he (she/it) may personify; pres. subj. 3rd pers. sing. 3. let him (her/it) personify; impve. 3rd pers. sing.

personifiqué I personified; past 1st pers. sing. / *personificar.*

personifiquéis that you (all) may personify; pres. subj. 2nd pers. pl. / *personificar.*

personifiquemos 1. that we may personify; pres. subj. 1st pers. pl. / *personificar.* 2. let us personify; impve. 1st pers. pl.

personifiquen 1. that they may personify; pres. subj. 3rd pers. pl. / *personificar.* 2. let them personify; impve. 3rd pers. pl.

personifiques that you may personify; pres. subj. 2nd pers. sing. / *personificar.*

perspirar to perspire. reg.

persuadir to persuade. reg.

pertenecer to belong. irr.

pertenezca 1. that I may belong; pres. subj. 1st pers. sing. / *pertenecer.* 2. that he (she/it) may belong; pres. subj. 3rd pers. sing. 3. let him (her/it) belong; impve. 3rd pers. sing.

pertenezcáis that you (all) may belong; pres. subj. 2nd pers. pl. / *pertenecer.*

pertenezcamos 1. that we may belong; pres. subj. 1st pers. pl. / *pertenecer.* 2. let us belong; impve. 1st pers. pl.

pertenezcan 1. that they may belong; pres. subj. 3rd pers. pl. / *pertenecer.* 2. let them belong; impve. 3rd pers. pl.

pertenezcas that you may belong; pres. subj. 2nd pers. sing. / *pertenecer.*

pertenezco I belong; pres. ind. 1st pers. sing. / *pertenecer.*

pertrechar to equip. reg.

perturbar to perturb or to disturb. reg.

pervertir to pervert. irr.

pervertirse to become depraved. irr.

pervierta 1. that I may pervert; pres. subj. 1st pers. sing. / *pervertir.* 2. that he (she/it) may pervert; pres. subj. 3rd pers. sing. 3. let him (her/it) pervert; impve. 3rd pers. sing.

perviertan 1. that they may pervert; pres. subj. 3rd pers. pl. / *pervertir.* 2. let them pervert; impve. 3rd pers. pl.

perviértanse let them become depraved; impve. 3rd pers. pl. / *pervertirse.*

perviertas that you may pervert; pres. subj. 2nd pers. sing. / *pervertir.*

perviértase let him (her/it) become depraved; impve. 3rd pers. sing. / *pervertirse.*

pervierte 1. he (she/it) perverts; pres. ind. 3rd pers. sing. / *pervertir.* 2. (you) pervert; impve. 2nd pers. sing.

pervierten they pervert; pres. ind. 3rd pers. pl. / *pervertir.*

perviertes you pervert; pres. ind. 2nd pers. sing. / *pervertir.*

perviértete (you) become depraved; impve. 2nd pers. sing. / *pervertirse.*

pervierto I pervert; pres. ind. 1st pers. sing. / *pervertir.*

pervirtáis that you (all) may pervert; pres. subj. 2nd pers. pl. / *pervertir.*

pervirtámonos let them become depraved; impve. 3rd pers. pl. / *pervertirse.*

pervirtamos 1. that we may pervert; pres. subj. 1st pers. pl. / *pervertir*. 2. let us pervert; impve. 1st pers. pl.

pervirtiendo perverting; pres. part. / *pervertir*.

pervirtiéndose becoming depraved; pres. part. / *pervertirse*.

pervirtiera 1. that I might pervert; imp. subj. 1st pers. sing. / *pervertir*. 2. that he (she/it) might pervert; imp. subj. 3rd pers. sing.

pervirtierais that you (all) might pervert; imp. subj. 2nd pers pl. / *pervertir*.

pervirtiéramos that we might pervert; imp. subj. 1st pers. pl. / *pervertir*.

pervirtieran that they might pervert; imp. subj. 3rd pers. pl. / *pervertir*.

pervirtieras that you might pervert; imp. subj. 2nd pers. sing. / *pervertir*.

pervirtieron they perverted; past 3rd pers. pl. / *pervertir*.

pervirtiese 1. that I might pervert; imp. subj. 1st pers. sing. / *pervertir*. 2. that he (she/it) might pervert; imp. subj. 3rd pers. sing.

pervirtieseis that you (all) might pervert; imp. subj. 2nd pers pl. / *pervertir*.

pervirtiésemos that we might pervert; imp. subj. 1st pers. pl. / *pervertir*.

pervirtiesen that they might pervert; imp. subj. 3rd pers. pl. / *pervertir*.

pervirtieses that you might pervert; imp. subj. 2nd pers. sing. / *pervertir*.

pervirtió he (she/it) perverted; past 3rd pers. sing. / *pervertir*.

pesar to weigh. reg.

pescar to fish. irr.

pesque 1. that I may fish; pres. subj. 1st pers. sing. / *pescar*. 2. that he (she/it) may fish; pres. subj. 3rd pers. sing. 3. let him (her/it) fish; impve. 3rd pers. sing.

pesqué I fished; past 1st pers. sing. / *pescar*.

pesquéis that you (all) may fish; pres. subj. 2nd pers. pl. / *pescar*.

pesquemos 1. that we may fish; pres. subj. 1st pers. pl. / *pescar*. 2. let us fish; impve. 1st pers. pl.

pesquen 1. that they may fish; pres. subj. 3rd pers. pl. / *pescar*. 2. let them fish; impve. 3rd pers. pl.

pesques that you may fish; pres. subj. 2nd pers. sing. / *pescar*.

pesquisar to investigate. reg.

pestañear to blink. reg.

petrificándose petrifying; pres. part. / *petrificarse*.

petrificaos (you all) petrify; impve. 2nd pers. pl. / *petrificarse*.

petrificar to petrify. irr.

petrificarse to petrify. irr.

petrifícate (you) petrify; impve. 2nd pers. sing. / *petrificarse*.

petrifique 1. that I may petrify; pres. subj. 1st pers. sing. / *petrificar*. 2. that he (she/it) may petrify; pres. subj. 3rd pers. sing. 3. let him (her/it) petrify; impve. 3rd pers. sing.

petrifiqué I petrified; past 1st pers. sing. / *petrificar*.

petrifiquéis that you (all) may petrify; pres. subj. 2nd pers. pl. / *petrificar*.

petrifiquémonos let us petrify; impve. 1st pers. pl. / *petrificarse*.

petrifiquemos 1. that we may petrify; pres. subj. 1st pers. pl. / *petrificar*. 2. let us petrify; impve. 1st pers. pl.

petrifiquen 1. that they may petrify; pres. subj. 3rd pers. pl. / *petrificar*. 2. let them petrify; impve. 3rd pers. pl.

petrifíquense let them petrify; impve. 3rd pers. pl. / *petrificarse*.

petrifiques that you may petrify; pres. subj. 2nd pers. sing. / *petrificar*.

petrifíquese let him (her/it) petrify; impve. 3rd pers. sing. / *petrificarse*.

pía 1. he (she/it) chirps; pres. ind. 3rd pers. sing. / *piar*. 2. (you) chirp; impve. 2nd pers. sing.

piafar to paw or to stamp. reg.

pialar to lasso. reg.

pían they chirp; pres. ind. 3rd pers. pl. / *piar*.

piar to chirp or to peep. irr.

pías you chirp; pres. ind. 2nd pers. sing. / *piar*.

picándose being angry; pres. part. / *picarse*.

picanear to goad. reg.

picaos (you all) be angry; impve. 2nd pers. pl. / *picarse*.

picar to prick. irr.

picarse to be angry or to spoil. irr.

pícate (you) be angry; impve. 2nd pers. sing. / *picarse*.

picoteándose squabbling; pres. part. / *picotearse*.

picoteaos (you all) squabble; impve. 2nd pers. pl. / *picotearse*.

picotear to peck. reg.

picotearse to squabble (women). reg.

picotéate (you) squabble; impve. 2nd pers. sing. / *picotearse*.

picoteémonos let us squabble; impve. 1st pers. pl. / *picotearse*.

picotéense let them squabble; impve. 3rd pers. pl. / *picotearse*.

picotéese let him (her/it) squabble; impve. 3rd pers. sing. / *picotearse*.

pida 1. that I may ask; pres. subj. 1st pers. sing. / *pedir*. 2. that he (she/it) may ask; pres. subj. 3rd pers. sing. 3. let him (her/it) ask; impve. 3rd pers. sing.

pidáis that you (all) may ask; pres. subj. 2nd pers. pl. / *pedir*.

pidamos 1. that we may ask; pres. subj. 1st pers. pl. / *pedir*. 2. let us ask; impve. 1st pers. pl.

pidan 1. that they may ask; pres. subj. 3rd pers. pl. / *pedir*. 2. let them ask; impve. 3rd pers. pl.

pidas that you may ask; pres. subj. 2nd pers. sing. / *pedir*.

pide 1. he (she/it) asks; pres. ind. 3rd pers. sing. / *pedir*. 2. (you) ask; impve. 2nd pers. sing.

piden they ask; pres. ind. 3rd pers. pl. / *pedir*.

pides you ask; pres. ind. 2nd pers. sing. / *pedir*.

pidiendo asking; pres. part. / *pedir*.
pidiera 1. that I might ask; imp. subj. 1st pers. sing. / *pedir*. 2. that he (she/it) might ask; imp. subj. 3rd pers. sing.
pidierais that you (all) might ask; imp. subj. 2nd pers pl. / *pedir*.
pidiéramos that we might ask; imp. subj. 1st pers. pl. / *pedir*.
pidieran that they might ask; imp. subj. 3rd pers. pl. / *pedir*.
pidieras that you might ask; imp. subj. 2nd pers. sing. / *pedir*.
pidieron they asked; past 3rd pers. pl. / *pedir*.
pidiese 1. that I might ask; imp. subj. 1st pers. sing. / *pedir*. 2. that he (she/it) might ask; imp. subj. 3rd pers. sing.
pidieseis that you (all) might ask; imp. subj. 2nd pers pl. / *pedir*.
pidiésemos that we might ask; imp. subj. 1st pers. pl. / *pedir*.
pidiesen that they might ask; imp. subj. 3rd pers. pl. / *pedir*.
pidieses that you might ask; imp. subj. 2nd pers. sing. / *pedir*.
pidió he (she/it) asked; past 3rd pers. sing. / *pedir*.
pido I ask; pres. ind. 1st pers. sing. / *pedir*.
píe 1. that I may chirp; pres. subj. 1st pers. sing. / *piar*. 2. that he (she/it) may chirp; pres. subj. 3rd pers. sing. 3. let him (her/it) chirp; impve. 3rd pers. sing.
píen 1. that they may chirp; pres. subj. 3rd pers. pl. / *piar*. 2. let them chirp; impve. 3rd pers. pl.
piensa 1. he (she/it) thinks; pres. ind. 3rd pers. sing. / *pensar*. 2. (you) think; impve. 2nd pers. sing.
piensan they think; pres. ind. 3rd pers. pl. / *pensar*.
piensas you think; pres. ind. 2nd pers. sing. / *pensar*.
piense 1. that I may think; pres. subj. 1st pers. sing. / *pensar*. 2. that he (she/it) may think; pres. subj. 3rd pers. sing. 3. let him (her/it) think; impve. 3rd pers. sing.
piensen 1. that they may think; pres. subj. 3rd pers. pl. / *pensar*. 2. let them think; impve. 3rd pers. pl.
pienses that you may think; pres. subj. 2nd pers. sing. / *pensar*.
pienso I think; pres. ind. 1st pers. sing. / *pensar*.
pierda 1. that I may lose; pres. subj. 1st pers. sing. / *perder*. 2. that he (she/it) may lose; pres. subj. 3rd pers. sing. 3. let him (her/it) lose; impve. 3rd pers. sing.
pierdan 1. that they may lose; pres. subj. 3rd pers. pl. / *perder*. 2. let them lose; impve. 3rd pers. pl.
piérdanse let them get lost; impve. 3rd pers. pl. / *perderse*.
pierdas that you may lose; pres. subj. 2nd pers. sing. / *perder*.
piérdase let him (her/it) get lost; impve. 2nd pers. sing. / *perderse*.
pierde 1. he (she/it) loses; pres. ind. 3rd pers. sing. / *perder*. 2. (you) lose; impve. 2nd pers. sing.
pierden they lose; pres. ind. 3rd pers. pl. / *perder*.
pierdes you lose; pres. ind. 2nd pers. sing. / *perder*.

piérdete (you) get lost; impve. 2nd pers. sing. / *perderse*.
pierdo I lose; pres. ind. 1st pers. sing. / *perder*.
píes that you may chirp; pres. subj. 2nd pers. sing. / *piar*.
pifiar to miscue (billards) or to jeer. reg.
pignorar to pledge. reg.
pilotar to pilot. reg.
pilotear to pilot. reg.
pillar to pillage or to plunder. reg.
pincelar to paint. reg.
pinchar to prick. reg.
pindonguear to gad about. reg.
pingar to drip. reg.
pintándose putting on make-up; pres. part. / *pintarse*.
pintaos (you all) put on make-up; impve. 2nd pers. pl. / *pintarse*.
pintar to paint. reg.
pintarla to play a part. reg.
pintarrajar to daub. reg.
pintarrajear to daub. reg.
pintarse to put on make-up. reg.
píntate (you) put on make-up; impve. 2nd pers. sing. / *pintarse*.
pintear to drizzle. reg.
pintémonos let us put on make-up; impve. 1st pers. pl. / *pintarse*.
píntense let them put on make-up; impve. 3rd pers. pl. / *pintarse*.
píntese let him (her/it) put on make-up; impve. 3rd pers. sing. / *pintarse*.
pintonear to color with ripening. reg.
pintorreándose daubing make-up on; pres. part. / *pintorrearse*.
pintorreaos (you all) daub make-up on; impve. 2nd pers. pl. / *pintorrearse*.
pintorrear to daub. reg.
pintorrearse to daub make-up on. reg.
pintorréate (you) daub make-up on; impve. 2nd pers. sing. / *pintorrearse*.
pintorreémonos let us daub make-up on; impve. 1st pers. pl. / *pintorrearse*.
pintorréense let them daub make-up on; impve. 3rd pers. pl. / *pintorrearse*.
pintorréese let him (her/it) daub make-up on; impve. 3rd pers. sing. / *pintorrearse*.
pío I chirp; pres. ind. 1st pers. sing. / *piar*.
pipía 1. he (she/it) peeps; pres. ind. 3rd pers. sing. / *pipiar*. 2. (you) peep; impve. 2nd pers. sing.
pipían they peep; pres. ind. 3rd pers. pl. / *pipiar*.
pipiar to peep or chirp. irr.
pipías you peep; pres. ind. 2nd pers. sing. / *pipiar*.
pipíe 1. that I may peep; pres. subj. 1st pers. sing. / *pipiar*. 2. that he (she/it) may peep; pres. subj. 3rd pers. sing. 3. let him (her/it) peep; impve. 3rd pers. sing.
pipíen 1. that they may peep; pres. subj. 3rd pers. pl. / *pipiar*. 2. let them peep; impve. 3rd pers. pl.

pipíes that you may peep; pres. subj. 2nd pers. sing. / *pipiar*.

pipío I peep; pres. ind. 1st pers. sing. / *pipiar*.

pique 1. that I may prick; pres. subj. 1st pers. sing. / *picar*. 2. that he (she/it) may prick; pres. subj. 3rd pers. sing. 3. let him (her/it) prick; impve. 3rd pers. sing.

piqué I pricked; past 1st pers. sing. / *picar*.

piquéis that you (all) may prick; pres. subj. 2nd pers. pl. / *picar*.

piquémonos let us be angry; impve. 1st pers. pl. / *picarse*.

piquemos 1. that we may prick; pres. subj. 1st pers. pl. / *picar*. 2. let us prick; impve. 1st pers. pl.

piquen 1. that they may prick; pres. subj. 3rd pers. pl. / *picar*. 2. let them prick; impve. 3rd pers. pl.

píquense let them be angry; impve. 3rd pers. pl. / *picarse*.

piques that you may prick; pres. subj. 2nd pers. sing. / *picar*.

píquese let him (her/it) be angry; impve. 3rd pers. sing. / *picarse*.

piratear to pirate. reg.

piropear to flatter. reg.

pirrándose dying for; pres. part. / *pirrarse*.

pirraos (you all) die for; impve. 2nd pers. pl. / *pirrarse*.

pirrarse to die for or to pine for. reg.

pírrate (you) die for; impve. 2nd pers. sing. / *pirrarse*.

pirrémonos let us die for; impve. 1st pers. pl. / *pirrarse*.

pírrense let them die for; impve. 3rd pers. pl. / *pirrarse*.

pírrese let him (her/it) die for; impve. 3rd pers. sing. / *pirrarse*.

piruetear to pirouette. reg.

pisándose being deceived; pres. part. / *pisarse*.

pisaos (you all) be deceived; impve. 2nd pers. pl. / *pisarse*.

pisar to step on. reg.

pisarse to be deceived. reg.

písate (you) be deceived; impve. 2nd pers. sing. / *pisarse*.

pisémonos let us be deceived; impve. 1st pers. pl. / *pisarse*.

písense let them be deceived; impve. 3rd pers. pl. / *pisarse*.

písese let him (her/it) be deceived; impve. 3rd pers. sing. / *pisarse*.

pisonear to tamp down. reg.

pisotear to trample on. reg.

pistonear to knock (cylinder). reg.

pitar to whistle. reg.

piular to chirp. reg.

placer to please. irr.

plagándose becoming infested with; pres. part. / *plagarse*.

plagaos (you all) become infested with; impve. 2nd pers. pl. / *plagarse*.

plagar to plague. irr.

plagarse to become infested with. irr.

plágate (you) become infested with; impve. 2nd pers. sing. / *plagarse*.

plagiar to plagiarize. reg.

plague 1. that I may plague; pres. subj. 1st pers. sing. / *plagar*. 2. that he (she/it) may plague; pres. subj. 3rd pers. sing. 3. let him (her/it) plague; impve. 3rd pers. sing.

plagué I plagued; past 1st pers. sing. / *plagar*.

plaguéis that you (all) may plague; pres. subj. 2nd pers. pl. / *plagar*.

plaguémonos let us become infested with; impve. 1st pers. pl. / *plagarse*.

plaguemos 1. that we may plague; pres. subj. 1st pers. pl. / *plagar*. 2. let us plague; impve. 1st pers. pl.

plaguen 1. that they may plague; pres. subj. 3rd pers. pl. / *plagar*. 2. let them plague; impve. 3rd pers. pl.

pláguense let them become infested with; impve. 3rd pers. pl. / *plagarse*.

plagues that you may plague; pres. subj. 2nd pers. sing. / *plagar*.

pláguese let him (her/it) become infested with; impve. 3rd pers. sing. / *plagarse*.

planchar to iron or to press. reg.

planchear to plate. reg.

planear to plan or to glide. reg.

planificar to plan. irr.

planifique 1. that I may plan; pres. subj. 1st pers. sing. / *planificar*. 2. that he (she/it) may plan; pres. subj. 3rd pers. sing. 3. let him (her/it) plan; impve. 3rd pers. sing.

planifiqué I planned; past 1st pers. sing. / *planificar*.

planifiquéis that you (all) may plan; pres. subj. 2nd pers. pl. / *planificar*.

planifiquemos 1. that we may plan; pres. subj. 1st pers. pl. / *planificar*. 2. let us plan; impve. 1st pers. pl.

planifiquen 1. that they may plan; pres. subj. 3rd pers. pl. / *planificar*. 2. let them plan; impve. 3rd pers. pl.

planifiques that you may plan; pres. subj. 2nd pers. sing. / *planificar*.

plantándose standing firm; pres. part. / *plantarse*.

plantaos (you all) stand firm; impve. 2nd pers. pl. / *plantarse*.

plantar to plant. reg.

plantarse to stand firm. reg.

plántate (you) stand firm; impve. 2nd pers. sing. / *plantarse*.

plantear to plan or to state. reg.

plantémonos let us stand firm; impve. 1st pers. pl. / *plantarse*.

plántense let them stand firm; impve. 3rd pers. pl. / *plantarse*.

plántese let him (her/it) stand firm; impve. 3rd pers. sing. / *plantarse*.

plantificándose dashing; pres. part. / *plantificarse*.

plantificaos (you all) dash; impve. 2nd pers. pl. / *plantificarse*.

plantificar to establish. irr.

plantificarse to dash. irr.
plantifícate (you) dash; impve. 2nd pers. sing. /
  plantificarse.
plantifique 1. that I may establish; pres. subj. 1st
  pers. sing. / *plantificar.* 2. that he (she/it) may
  establish; pres. subj. 3rd pers. sing. 3. let him
  (her/it) establish; impve. 3rd pers. sing.
plantifiqué I established; past 1st pers. sing. /
  plantificar.
plantifiquéis that you (all) may establish; pres. subj.
  2nd pers. pl. / *plantificar.*
plantifiquémonos let us dash; impve. 1st pers. pl. /
  plantificarse.
plantifiquemos 1. that we may establish; pres. subj.
  1st pers. pl. / *plantificar.* 2. let us establish; impve.
  1st pers. pl.
plantifiquen 1. that they may establish; pres. subj.
  3rd pers. pl. / *plantificar.* 2. let them establish;
  impve. 3rd pers. pl.
plantifíquense let them dash; impve. 3rd pers. pl. /
  plantificarse.
plantifiques that you may establish; pres. subj. 2nd
  pers. sing. / *plantificar.*
plantifíquese let him (her/it) dash; impve. 3rd pers.
  sing. / *plantificarse.*
plantillar to sole shoes. reg.
plaña 1. that I may lament; pres. subj. 1st pers. sing. /
  plañir. 2. that he (she/it) may lament; pres. subj. 3rd
  pers. sing. 3. let him (her/it) lament; impve. 3rd
  pers. sing.
plañáis that you (all) may lament; pres. subj. 2nd
  pers. pl. / *plañir.*
plañamos 1. that we may lament; pres. subj. 1st pers.
  pl. / *plañir.* 2. let us lament; impve. 1st pers. pl.
plañan 1. that they may lament; pres. subj. 3rd pers.
  pl. / *plañir.* 2. let them lament; impve. 3rd pers. pl.
plañas that you may lament; pres. subj. 2nd pers.
  sing. / *plañir.*
plañe 1. he (she/it) laments; pres. ind. 3rd pers. sing.
  / *plañir.* 2. (you) lament; impve. 2nd pers. sing.
plañen they lament; pres. ind. 3rd pers. pl. / *plañir.*
plañendo lamenting; pres. part. / *plañir.*
plañera 1. that I might lament; imp. subj. 1st pers.
  sing. / *plañir.* 2. that he (she/it) might lament; imp.
  subj. 3rd pers. sing.
plañerais that you (all) might lament; imp. subj. 2nd
  pers pl. / *plañir.*
plañéramos that we might lament; imp. subj. 1st
  pers. pl. / *plañir.*
plañeran that they might lament; imp. subj. 3rd pers.
  pl. / *plañir.*
plañeras that you might lament; imp. subj. 2nd pers.
  sing. / *plañir.*
plañeron they lamented; past 3rd pers. pl. / *plañir.*
plañes you lament; pres. ind. 2nd pers. sing. / *plañir.*
plañese 1. that I might lament; imp. subj. 1st pers.
  sing. / *plañir.* 2. that he (she/it) might lament; imp.
  subj. 3rd pers. sing.
plañeseis that you (all) might lament; imp. subj. 2nd
  pers pl. / *plañir.*

plañésemos that we might lament; imp. subj. 1st pers.
  pl. / *plañir.*
plañesen that they might lament; imp. subj. 3rd pers.
  pl. / *plañir.*
plañeses that you might lament; imp. subj. 2nd pers.
  sing. / *plañir.*
plañir to lament or to grieve. irr.
plaño I lament; pres. ind. 1st pers. sing. / *plañir.*
plañó he (she/it) lamented; past 3rd pers. sing. /
  plañir.
plasmar to mold. reg.
platear to coat with silver. reg.
platicar to chat. irr.
platinar to plate with platinum. reg.
platique 1. that I may chat; pres. subj. 1st pers. sing. /
  platicar. 2. that he (she/it) may chat; pres. subj. 3rd
  pers. sing. 3. let him (her/it) chat; impve. 3rd pers.
  sing.
platiqué I chatted; past 1st pers. sing. / *platicar.*
platiquéis that you (all) may chat; pres. subj. 2nd
  pers. pl. / *platicar.*
platiquemos 1. that we may chat; pres. subj. 1st pers.
  pl. / *platicar.* 2. let us chat; impve. 1st pers. pl.
platiquen 1. that they may chat; pres. subj. 3rd pers.
  pl. / *platicar.* 2. let them chat; impve. 3rd pers. pl.
platiques that you may chat; pres. subj. 2nd pers.
  sing. / *platicar.*
plazca 1. that I may please; pres. subj. 1st pers. sing. /
  placer. 2. that he (she/it) may please; pres. subj. 3rd
  pers. sing. 3. let him (her/it) please; impve. 3rd pers.
  sing.
plazcáis that you (all) may please; pres. subj. 2nd
  pers. pl. / *placer.*
plazcamos 1. that we may please; pres. subj. 1st pers.
  pl. / *placer.* 2. let us please; impve. 1st pers. pl.
plazcan 1. that they may please; pres. subj. 3rd pers.
  pl. / *placer.* 2. let them please; impve. 3rd pers. pl.
plazcas that you may please; pres. subj. 2nd pers.
  sing. / *placer.*
plazco I please; pres. ind. 1st pers. sing. / *placer.*
plega that he (she/it) may please; pres. subj. 3rd pers.
  sing. / *placer.*
plegándose yielding; pres. part. / *plegarse.*
plegaos (you all) yield; impve. 2nd pers. pl. / *plegarse.*
plegar to fold. irr.
plegarse to yield. irr.
plegue that he (she/it) may please; pres. subj. 3rd
  pers. sing. / *placer.*
plegué I folded; past 1st pers. sing. / *plegar.*
pleguéis that you (all) may fold; pres. subj. 2nd pers.
  pl. / *plegar.*
pleguémonos let us yield; impve. 1st pers. pl. /
  plegarse.
pleguemos 1. that we may fold; pres. subj. 1st pers.
  pl. / *plegar.* 2. let us fold; impve. 1st pers. pl.
pleitear to fight in court. reg.
pliega 1. he (she/it) folds; pres. ind. 3rd pers. sing. /
  plegar. 2. (you) fold; impve. 2nd pers. sing.
pliegan they fold; pres. ind. 3rd pers. pl. / *plegar.*
pliegas you fold; pres. ind. 2nd pers. sing. / *plegar.*

pliégate (you) yield; impve. 2nd pers. sing. / *plegarse*.

pliego I fold; pres. ind. 1st pers. sing. / *plegar*.

pliegue 1. that I may fold; pres. subj. 1st pers. sing. / *plegar*. 2. that he (she/it) may fold; pres. subj. 3rd pers. sing. 3. let him (her/it) fold; impve. 3rd pers. sing.

plieguen 1. that they may fold; pres. subj. 3rd pers. pl. / *plegar*. 2. let them fold; impve. 3rd pers. pl.

pliéguense let them yield; impve. 3rd pers. pl. / *plegarse*.

pliegues that you may fold; pres. subj. 2nd pers. sing. / *plegar*.

pliéguese let him (her/it) yield; impve. 3rd pers. sing. / *plegarse*.

plisar to pleat. reg.

plomar to seal with lead. reg.

plugo he (she/it) pleased; past 3rd pers. sing. / *placer*.

pluguiera that he (she/it) might please; imp. subj. 3rd pers. sing. / *placer*.

pluguieron they pleased; past 3rd pers. pl. / *placer*.

pluguiese that he (she/it) might please; imp. subj. 3rd pers. sing. / *placer*.

pluralice 1. that I may make plural; pres. subj. 1st pers. sing. / *pluralizar*. 2. that he (she/it) may make plural; pres. subj. 3rd pers. sing. 3. let him (her/it) make plural; impve. 3rd pers. sing.

pluralicé I made plural; past 1st pers. sing. / *pluralizar*.

pluralicéis that you (all) may make plural; pres. subj. 2nd pers. pl. / *pluralizar*.

pluralicemos 1. that we may make plural; pres. subj. 1st pers. pl. / *pluralizar*. 2. let us make plural; impve. 1st pers. pl.

pluralicen 1. that they may make plural; pres. subj. 3rd pers. pl. / *pluralizar*. 2. let them make plural; impve. 3rd pers. pl.

pluralices that you may make plural; pres. subj. 2nd pers. sing. / *pluralizar*.

pluralizar to make plural. irr.

poblándose budding; pres. part. / *poblarse*.

poblar to populate. irr.

poblarse to bud or to leaf. irr.

podar to prune. reg.

poder to be able or can. irr.

podrá he (she/it) will be able; fut. 3rd pers. sing. / *poder*.

podrán they will be able; fut. 3rd pers. pl. / *poder*.

podrás you will be able; fut. 2nd pers. sing. / *poder*.

podré I shall be able; fut. 1st pers. sing. / *poder*.

podréis you (all) will be able; fut. 2nd pers. pl. / *poder*.

podremos we shall be able; fut. 1st pers. pl. / *poder*.

podría 1. I should be able; cond. 1st pers. sing. / *poder*. 2. he (she/it) would be able; cond. 3rd pers. sing.

podríais you (all) would be able; cond. 2nd pers. pl. / *poder*.

podríamos we should be able; cond. 1st pers. pl. / *poder*.

podrían they would be able; cond. 3rd pers. pl. / *poder*.

podrías you would be able; cond. 2nd pers. sing. / *poder*.

podrir to rot. irr.

podrirse to putrefy. irr.

poetice 1. that I may compose poetry; pres. subj. 1st pers. sing. / *poetizar*. 2. that he (she/it) may compose poetry; pres. subj. 3rd pers. sing. 3. let him (her/it) compose poetry; impve. 3rd pers. sing.

poeticé I composed poetry; past 1st pers. sing. / *poetizar*.

poeticéis that you (all) may compose poetry; pres. subj. 2nd pers. pl. / *poetizar*.

poeticemos 1. that we may compose poetry; pres. subj. 1st pers. pl. / *poetizar*. 2. let us compose poetry; impve. 1st pers. pl.

poeticen 1. that they may compose poetry; pres. subj. 3rd pers. pl. / *poetizar*. 2. let them compose poetry; impve. 3rd pers. pl.

poetices that you may compose poetry; pres. subj. 2nd pers. sing. / *poetizar*.

poetizar to compose poetry. irr.

polarice 1. that I may polarize; pres. subj. 1st pers. sing. / *polarizar*. 2. that he (she/it) may polarize; pres. subj. 3rd pers. sing. 3. let him (her/it) polarize; impve. 3rd pers. sing.

polaricé I polarized; past 1st pers. sing. / *polarizar*.

polaricéis that you (all) may polarize; pres. subj. 2nd pers. pl. / *polarizar*.

polaricemos 1. that we may polarize; pres. subj. 1st pers. pl. / *polarizar*. 2. let us polarize; impve. 1st pers. pl.

polaricen 1. that they may polarize; pres. subj. 3rd pers. pl. / *polarizar*. 2. let them polarize; impve. 3rd pers. pl.

polarices that you may polarize; pres. subj. 2nd pers. sing. / *polarizar*.

polarizar to polarize. irr.

policopiar to duplicate. reg.

polimerice 1. that I may polymerize; pres. subj. 1st pers. sing. / *polimerizar*. 2. that he (she/it) may polymerize; pres. subj. 3rd pers. sing. 3. let him (her/it) polymerize; impve. 3rd pers. sing.

polimericé I polymerized; past 1st pers. sing. / *polimerizar*.

polimericéis that you (all) may polymerize; pres. subj. 2nd pers. pl. / *polimerizar*.

polimericemos 1. that we may polymerize; pres. subj. 1st pers. pl. / *polimerizar*. 2. let us polymerize; impve. 1st pers. pl.

polimericen 1. that they may polymerize; pres. subj. 3rd pers. pl. / *polimerizar*. 2. let them polymerize; impve. 3rd pers. pl.

polimerices that you may polymerize; pres. subj. 2nd pers. sing. / *polimerizar*.

polimerizar to polymerize. irr.

polinice 1. that I may pollinate; pres. subj. 1st pers. sing. / *polinizar*. 2. that he (she/it) may pollinate; pres. subj. 3rd pers. sing. 3. let him (her/it) pollinate; impve. 3rd pers. sing.

polinicé I pollinated; past 1st pers. sing. / *polinizar.*

polinicéis that you (all) may pollinate; pres. subj. 2nd pers. pl. / *polinizar.*

polinicemos 1. that we may pollinate; pres. subj. 1st pers. pl. / *polinizar.* 2. let us pollinate; impve. 1st pers. pl.

polinicen 1. that they may pollinate; pres. subj. 3rd pers. pl. / *polinizar.* 2. let them pollinate; impve. 3rd pers. pl.

polinices that you may pollinate; pres. subj. 2nd pers. sing. / *polinizar.*

polinizar to pollinate. irr.

politiquear to talk politics. reg.

polvorear to powder. reg.

polvorice 1. that I may pulverize; pres. subj. 1st pers. sing. / *polvorizar.* 2. that he (she/it) may pulverize; pres. subj. 3rd pers. sing. 3. let him (her/it) pulverize; impve. 3rd pers. sing.

polvoricé I pulverized; past 1st pers. sing. / *polvorizar.*

polvoricéis that you (all) may pulverize; pres. subj. 2nd pers. pl. / *polvorizar.*

polvoricemos 1. that we may pulverize; pres. subj. 1st pers. pl. / *polvorizar.* 2. let us pulverize; impve. 1st pers. pl.

polvoricen 1. that they may pulverize; pres. subj. 3rd pers. pl. / *polvorizar.* 2. let them pulverize; impve. 3rd pers. pl.

polvorices that you may pulverize; pres. subj. 2nd pers. sing. / *polvorizar.*

polvorizar to pulverize. irr.

pon (you) put; impve. 2nd pers. sing. / *poner.*

ponderar to ponder or to weigh. reg.

pondrá he (she/it) will put; fut. 3rd pers. sing. / *poner.*

pondrán they will put; fut. 3rd pers. pl. / *poner.*

pondrás you will put; fut. 2nd pers. sing. / *poner.*

pondré I shall put; fut. 1st pers. sing. / *poner.*

pondréis you (all) will put; fut. 2nd pers. pl. / *poner.*

pondremos we shall put; fut. 1st pers. pl. / *poner.*

pondría 1. I should put; cond. 1st pers. sing. / *poner.* 2. he (she/it) would put; cond. 3rd pers. sing.

pondríais you (all) would put; cond. 2nd pers. pl. / *poner.*

pondríamos we should put; cond. 1st pers. pl. / *poner.*

pondrían they would put; cond. 3rd pers. pl. / *poner.*

pondrías you would put; cond. 2nd pers. sing. / *poner.*

poneos (you all) become; impve. 2nd pers. pl. / *ponerse.*

poner to put. irr.

ponerse to become. irr.

ponga 1. that I may put; pres. subj. 1st pers. sing. / *poner.* 2. that he (she/it) may put; pres. subj. 3rd pers. sing. 3. let him (her/it) put; impve. 3rd pers. sing.

pongáis that you (all) may put; pres. subj. 2nd pers. pl. / *poner.*

pongámonos let us become; impve. 1st pers. pl. / *ponerse.*

pongamos 1. that we may put; pres. subj. 1st pers. pl. / *poner.* 2. let us put; impve. 1st pers. pl.

pongan 1. that they may put; pres. subj. 3rd pers. pl. / *poner.* 2. let them put; impve. 3rd pers. pl.

pónganse let them become; impve. 3rd pers. pl. / *ponerse.*

pongas that you may put; pres. subj. 2nd pers. sing. / *poner.*

póngase let him (her/it) become; impve. 3rd pers. sing. / *ponerse.*

pongo I put; pres. ind. 1st pers. sing. / *poner.*

poniendo putting; pres. part. / *poner.*

poniéndose becoming; pres. part. / *ponerse.*

ponte (you) become; impve. 2nd pers. sing. / *ponerse.*

pontear to bridge. reg.

pontificar to pontificate. irr.

pontifique 1. that I may pontificate; pres. subj. 1st pers. sing. / *pontificar.* 2. that he (she/it) may pontificate; pres. subj. 3rd pers. sing. 3. let him (her/it) pontificate; impve. 3rd pers. sing.

pontifiqué I pontificated; past 1st pers. sing. / *pontificar.*

pontifiquéis that you (all) may pontificate; pres. subj. 2nd pers. pl. / *pontificar.*

pontifiquemos 1. that we may pontificate; pres. subj. 1st pers. pl. / *pontificar.* 2. let us pontificate; impve. 1st pers. pl.

pontifiquen 1. that they may pontiificate; pres. subj. 3rd pers. pl. / *pontificar.* 2. let them pontificate; impve. 3rd pers. pl.

pontifiques that you may pontficate; pres. subj. 2nd pers. sing. / *pontificar.*

popar to scorn or to fondle. reg.

popularice 1. that I may popularize; pres. subj. 1st pers. sing. / *popularizar.* 2. that he (she/it) may popularize; pres. subj. 3rd pers. sing. 3. let him (her/it) popularize; impve. 3rd pers. sing.

popularicé I popularized; past 1st pers. sing. / *popularizar.*

popularicéis that you (all) may popularize; pres. subj. 2nd pers. pl. / *popularizar.*

popularicemos 1. that we may popularize; pres. subj. 1st pers. pl. / *popularizar.* 2. let us popularize; impve. 1st pers. pl.

popularicen 1. that they may popularize; pres. subj. 3rd pers. pl. / *popularizar.* 2. let them popularize; impve. 3rd pers. pl.

popularices that you may popularize; pres. subj. 2nd pers. sing. / *popularizar.*

popularizar to popularize. irr.

pordiosear to beg. reg.

porfía 1. he (she/it) persists; pres. ind. 3rd pers. sing. / *porfiar.* 2. (you) persist; impve. 2nd pers. sing.

porfían they persist; pres. ind. 3rd pers. pl. / *porfiar.*

porfiar to persist or to contend. irr.

porfías you persist; pres. ind. 2nd pers. sing. / *porfiar.*

porfíe 1. that I may persist; pres. subj. 1st pers. sing. / *porfiar.* 2. that he (she/it) may persist; pres. subj. 3rd pers. sing. 3. let him (her/it) persist; impve. 3rd pers. sing.

porfíen 1. that they may persist; pres. subj. 3rd pers. pl. / *porfiar.* 2. let them persist; impve. 3rd pers. pl.

porfíes that you may persist; pres. subj. 2nd pers. sing. / *porfiar.*

porfío I persist; pres. ind. 1st pers. sing. / *porfiar.*

pormenorice 1. that I may detail; pres. subj. 1st pers. sing. / *pormenorizar.* 2. that he (she/it) may detail; pres. subj. 3rd pers. sing. 3. let him (her/it) detail; impve. 3rd pers. sing.

pormenoricé I detailed; past 1st pers. sing. / *pormenorizar.*

pormenoricéis that you (all) may detail; pres. subj. 2nd pers. pl. / *pormenorizar.*

pormenoricemos 1. that we may detail; pres. subj. 1st pers. pl. / *pormenorizar.* 2. let us detail; impve. 1st pers. pl.

pormenoricen 1. that they may detail; pres. subj. 3rd pers. pl. / *pormenorizar.* 2. let them detail; impve. 3rd pers. pl.

pormenorices that you may detail; pres. subj. 2nd pers. sing. / *pormenorizar.*

pormenorizar to detail. irr.

portándose behaving; pres. part. / *portarse.*

portaos (you all) behave; impve. 2nd pers. pl. / *portarse.*

portar to carry. reg.

portarse to behave. reg.

pórtate (you) behave; impve. 2nd pers. sing. / *portarse.*

porteándose migrating (birds); pres. part. / *portearse.*

portear to carry or to slam. reg.

portearse to migrate (birds). reg.

portéense let them migrate (birds); impve. 3rd pers. pl. / *portearse.*

portéese let him (her/it) migrate (birds); impve. 3rd pers. sing. / *portearse.*

portémonos let us behave; impve. 1st pers. pl. / *portarse.*

pórtense let them behave; impve. 3rd pers. pl. / *portarse.*

pórtese let him (her/it) behave; impve. 3rd pers. sing. / *portarse.*

posándose settling; pres. part. / *posarse.*

posaos (you all) settle; impve. 2nd pers. pl. / *posarse.*

posar to rest or to lodge. reg.

posarse to settle. reg.

pósate (you) settle; impve. 2nd pers. sing. / *posarse.*

poseámonos let us be self-possessed; impve. 1st pers. pl. / *poseerse.*

poséanse let them be self-possessed; impve. 3rd pers. pl. / *poseerse.*

poséase let him (her/it) be self-possessed; impve. 3rd pers. sing. / *poseerse.*

poseeos (you all) be self-possessed; impve. 2nd pers. pl. / *poseerse.*

poseer to possess. irr.

poseerse to be self-possessed. irr.

poséete (you) be self-possessed; impve. 2nd pers. sing. / *poseerse.*

poseí I possessed; past 1st pers. sing. / *poseer.*

poseído possessed; past part. / *poseer.*

poseímos we possessed; past 1st pers. pl. / *poseer.*

poseíste you possessed; past 2nd pers. sing. / *poseer.*

poseísteis you (all) possessed; past 2nd pers. pl. / *poseer.*

posémonos let us settle; impve. 1st pers. pl. / *posarse.*

pósense let them settle; impve. 3rd pers. pl. / *posarse.*

pósese let him (her/it) settle; impve. 3rd pers. sing. / *posarse.*

posesionándose seizing control; pres. part. / *posesionarse.*

posesionaos (you all) seize control; impve. 2nd pers. pl. / *posesionarse.*

posesionar to give possession. reg.

posesionarse to seize control. reg.

posesiónate (you) seize control; impve. 2nd pers. sing. / *posesionarse.*

posesionémonos let us seize control; impve. 1st pers. pl. / *posesionarse.*

posesiónense let them seize control; impve. 3rd pers. pl. / *posesionarse.*

posesiónese let him (her/it) seize control; impve. 3rd pers. sing. / *posesionarse.*

poseyendo possessing; pres. part. / *poseer.*

poseyéndose being self-possessed; pres. part. / *poseerse.*

poseyera 1. that I might possess; imp. subj. 1st pers. sing. / *poseer.* 2. that he (she/it) might possess; imp. subj. 3rd pers. sing.

poseyerais that you (all) might possess; imp. subj. 2nd pers pl. / *poseer.*

poseyéramos that we might possess; imp. subj. 1st pers. pl. / *poseer.*

poseyeran that they might possess; imp. subj. 3rd pers. pl. / *poseer.*

poseyeras that you might possess; imp. subj. 2nd pers. sing. / *poseer.*

poseyeron they possessed; past 3rd pers. pl. / *poseer.*

poseyese 1. that I might possess; imp. subj. 1st pers. sing. / *poseer.* 2. that he (she/it) might possess; imp. subj. 3rd pers. sing.

poseyeseis that you (all) might possess; imp. subj. 2nd pers pl. / *poseer.*

poseyésemos that we might possess; imp. subj. 1st pers. pl. / *poseer.*

poseyesen that they might possess; imp. subj. 3rd pers. pl. / *poseer.*

poseyeses that you might possess; imp. subj. 2nd pers. sing. / *poseer.*

poseyó he (she/it) possessed; past 3rd pers. sing. / *poseer.*

posfechar to postdate. reg.

posibilitar to make possible. reg.

pospon (you) postpone; impve. 2nd pers. sing. / *posponer.*

pospondrá he (she/it) will postpone; fut. 3rd pers. sing. / *posponer*.

pospondrán they will postpone; fut. 3rd pers. pl. / *posponer*.

pospondrás you will postpone; fut. 2nd pers. sing. / *posponer*.

pospondré I shall postpone; fut. 1st pers. sing. / *posponer*.

pospondréis you (all) will postpone; fut. 2nd pers. pl. / *posponer*.

pospondremos we shall postpone; fut. 1st pers. pl. / *posponer*.

pospondría 1. I should postpone; cond. 1st pers. sing. / *posponer*. 2. he (she/it) would postpone; cond. 3rd pers. sing.

pospondríais you (all) would postpone; cond. 2nd pers. pl. / *posponer*.

pospondríamos we should postpone; cond. 1st pers. pl. / *posponer*.

pospondrían they would postpone; cond. 3rd pers. pl. / *posponer*.

pospondrías you would postpone; cond. 2nd pers. sing. / *posponer*.

posponer to postpone. irr.

posponga 1. that I may postpone; pres. subj. 1st pers. sing. / *posponer*. 2. that he (she/it) may postpone; pres. subj. 3rd pers. sing. 3. let him (her/it) postpone; impve. 3rd pers. sing.

pospongáis that you (all) may postpone; pres. subj. 2nd pers. pl. / *posponer*.

pospongamos 1. that we may postpone; pres. subj. 1st pers. pl. / *posponer*. 2. let us postpone; impve. 1st pers. pl.

pospongan 1. that they may postpone; pres. subj. 3rd pers. pl. / *posponer*. 2. let them postpone; impve. 3rd pers. pl.

pospongas that you may postpone; pres. subj. 2nd pers. sing. / *posponer*.

pospongo I postpone; pres. ind. 1st pers. sing. / *posponer*.

pospuesto postponed; past part. / *posponer*.

pospuse I postponed; past 1st pers. sing. / *posponer*.

pospusiera 1. that I might postpone; imp. subj. 1st pers. sing. / *posponer*. 2. that he (she/it) might postpone; imp. subj. 3rd pers. sing.

pospusierais that you (all) might postpone; imp. subj. 2nd pers pl. / *posponer*.

pospusiéramos that we might postpone; imp. subj. 1st pers. pl. / *posponer*.

pospusieran that they might postpone; imp. subj. 3rd pers. pl. / *posponer*.

pospusieras that you might postpone; imp. subj. 2nd pers. sing. / *posponer*.

pospusieron they postponed; past 3rd pers. pl. / *posponer*.

pospusiese 1. that I might postpone; imp. subj. 1st pers. sing. / *posponer*. 2. that he (she/it) might postpone; imp. subj. 3rd pers. sing.

pospusieseis that you (all) might postpone; imp. subj. 2nd pers pl. / *posponer*.

pospusiésemos that we might postpone; imp. subj. 1st pers. pl. / *posponer*.

pospusiesen that they might postpone; imp. subj. 3rd pers. pl. / *posponer*.

pospusieses that you might postpone; imp. subj. 2nd pers. sing. / *posponer*.

pospusimos we postponed; past 1st pers. pl. / *posponer*.

pospusiste you postponed; past 2nd pers. sing. / *posponer*.

pospusisteis you (all) postponed; past 2nd pers. pl. / *posponer*.

pospuso he (she/it) postponed; past 3rd pers. sing. / *posponer*.

postergar to delay. irr.

postergue 1. that I may delay; pres. subj. 1st pers. sing. / *postergar*. 2. that he (she/it) may delay; pres. subj. 3rd pers. sing. 3. let him (her/it) delay; impve. 3rd pers. sing.

postergué I delayed; past 1st pers. sing. / *postergar*.

posterguéis that you (all) may delay; pres. subj. 2nd pers. pl. / *postergar*.

posterguemos 1. that we may delay; pres. subj. 1st pers. pl. / *postergar*. 2. let us delay; impve. 1st pers. pl.

posterguen 1. that they may delay; pres. subj. 3rd pers. pl. / *postergar*. 2. let them delay; impve. 3rd pers. pl.

postergues that you may delay; pres. subj. 2nd pers. sing. / *postergar*.

postrándose kneeling down; pres. part. / *postrarse*.

postraos (you all) kneel down; impve. 2nd pers. pl. / *postrarse*.

postrar to prostrate. reg.

postrarse to kneel down. reg.

póstrate (you) kneel down; impve. 2nd pers. sing. / *postrarse*.

postrémonos let us kneel down; impve. 1st pers. pl. / *postrarse*.

póstrense let them kneel down; impve. 3rd pers. pl. / *postrarse*.

póstrese let him (her/it) kneel down; impve. 3rd pers. sing. / *postrarse*.

postular to postulate. reg.

potenciar to utilize or to exploit. reg.

practicar to practice. irr.

practique 1. that I may practice; pres. subj. 1st pers. sing. / *practicar*. 2. that he (she/it) may practice; pres. subj. 3rd pers. sing. 3. let him (her/it) practice; impve. 3rd pers. sing.

practiqué I practiced; past 1st pers. sing. / *practicar*.

practiquéis that you (all) may practice; pres. subj. 2nd pers. pl. / *practicar*.

practiquemos 1. that we may practice; pres. subj. 1st pers. pl. / *practicar*. 2. let us practice; impve. 1st pers. pl.

practiquen 1. that they may practice; pres. subj. 3rd pers. pl. / *practicar*. 2. let them practice; impve. 3rd pers. pl.

practiques that you may practice; pres. subj. 2nd pers. sing. / *practicar*.

precaucionándose taking precautions; pres. part. / *precaucionarse.*

precaucionaos (you all) take precautions; impve. 2nd pers. pl. / *precaucionarse.*

precaucionarse to take precautions. reg.

precauciónate (you) take precautions; impve. 2nd pers. sing. / *precaucionarse.*

precaucionémonos let us take precautions; impve. 1st pers. pl. / *precaucionarse.*

precauciónense let them take precautions; impve. 3rd pers. pl. / *precaucionarse.*

precauciónese let him (her/it) take precautions; impve. 3rd pers. sing. / *precaucionarse.*

precavámonos let us guard against; impve. 1st pers. pl. / *precaverse.*

precávanse let them guard against; impve. 3rd pers. pl. / *precaverse.*

precávase let him (her/it) guard against; impve. 3rd pers. sing. / *precaverse.*

precaveos (you all) guard against; impve. 2nd pers. pl. / *precaverse.*

precaver to prevent. reg.

precaverse to guard against. reg.

precávete (you) guard against; impve. 2nd pers. sing. / *precaverse.*

precaviéndose guarding against; pres. part. / *precaverse.*

preceder to precede. reg.

preceptúa 1. he (she/it) rules on; pres. ind. 3rd pers. sing. / *preceptuar.* 2. (you) rule on; impve. 2nd pers. sing.

preceptúan they rule on; pres. ind. 3rd pers. pl. / *preceptuar.*

preceptuar to rule on. irr.

preceptúas you rule on; pres. ind. 2nd pers. sing. / *preceptuar.*

preceptúe 1. that I may rule on; pres. subj. 1st pers. sing. / *preceptuar.* 2. that he (she/it) may rule on; pres. subj. 3rd pers. sing. 3. let him (her/it) rule on; impve. 3rd pers. sing.

preceptúen 1. that they may rule on; pres. subj. 3rd pers. pl. / *preceptuar.* 2. let them rule on; impve. 3rd pers. pl.

preceptúes that you may rule on; pres. subj. 2nd pers. sing. / *preceptuar.*

preceptúo I rule on; pres. ind. 1st pers. sing. / *preceptuar.*

preciándose taking pride; pres. part. / *preciarse.*

preciaos (you all) take pride; impve. 2nd pers. pl. / *preciarse.*

preciar to appraise. reg.

preciarse to take pride. reg.

precíate (you) take pride; impve. 2nd pers. sing. / *preciarse.*

preciémonos let us take pride; impve. 1st pers. pl. / *preciarse.*

precíense let them take pride; impve. 3rd pers. pl. / *preciarse.*

precíese let him (her/it) take pride; impve. 3rd pers. sing. / *preciarse.*

precintar to strap. reg.

precipitándose rushing headlong; pres. part. / *precipitarse.*

precipitaos (you all) rush headlong; impve. 2nd pers. pl. / *precipitarse.*

precipitar to precipitate. reg.

precipitarse to rush headlong. reg.

precipítate (you) rush headlong; impve. 2nd pers. sing. / *precipitarse.*

precipitémonos let us rush headlong; impve. 1st pers. pl. / *precipitarse.*

precipítense let them rush headlong; impve. 3rd pers. pl. / *precipitarse.*

precipítese let him (her/it) rush headlong; impve. 3rd pers. sing. / *precipitarse.*

precisar to determine precisely. reg.

preconcebir to preconceive. irr.

preconciba 1. that I may preconceive; pres. subj. 1st pers. sing. / *preconcebir.* 2. that he (she/it) may preconceive; pres. subj. 3rd pers. sing. 3. let him (her/it) preconceive; impve. 3rd pers. sing.

preconcibáis that you (all) may preconceive; pres. subj. 2nd pers. pl. / *preconcebir.*

preconcibamos 1. that we may preconceive; pres. subj. 1st pers. pl. / *preconcebir.* 2. let us preconceive; impve. 1st pers. pl.

preconciban 1. that they may preconceive; pres. subj. 3rd pers. pl. / *preconcebir.* 2. let them preconceive; impve. 3rd pers. pl.

preconcibas that you may preconceive; pres. subj. 2nd pers. sing. / *preconcebir.*

preconcibe 1. he (she/it) preconceives; pres. ind. 3rd pers. sing. / *preconcebir.* 2. (you) preconceive; impve. 2nd pers. sing.

preconciben they preconceive; pres. ind. 3rd pers. pl. / *preconcebir.*

preconcibes you preconceive; pres. ind. 2nd pers. sing. / *preconcebir.*

preconcibiendo preconceiving; pres. part. / *preconcebir.*

preconcibiera 1. that I might preconceive; imp. subj. 1st pers. sing. / *preconcebir.* 2. that he (she/it) might preconceive; imp. subj. 3rd pers. sing.

preconcibierais that you (all) might preconceive; imp. subj. 2nd pers pl / *preconcebir.*

preconcibiéramos that we might preconceive; imp. subj. 1st pers. pl. / *preconcebir.*

preconcibieran that they might preconceive; imp. subj. 3rd pers. pl. / *preconcebir.*

preconcibieras that you might preconceive; imp. subj. 2nd pers. sing. / *preconcebir.*

preconcibieron they preconceived; past 3rd pers. pl. / *preconcebir.*

preconcibiese 1. that I might preconceive; imp. subj. 1st pers. sing. / *preconcebir.* 2. that he (she/it) might preconceive; imp. subj. 3rd pers. sing.

preconcibieseis that you (all) might preconceive; imp. subj. 2nd pers pl. / *preconcebir.*

preconcibiésemos that we might preconceive; imp. subj. 1st pers. pl. / *preconcebir.*

preconcibiesen that they might preconceive; imp. subj. 3rd pers. pl. / *preconcebir*.

preconcibieses that you might preconceive; imp. subj. 2nd pers. sing. / *preconcebir*.

preconcibió he (she/it) preconceived; past 3rd pers. sing. / *preconcebir*.

preconcibo I preconceive; pres. ind. 1st pers. sing. / *preconcebir*.

preconice 1. that I may proclaim; pres. subj. 1st pers. sing. / *preconizar*. 2. that he (she/it) may proclaim; pres. subj. 3rd pers. sing. 3. let him (her/it) proclaim; impve. 3rd pers. sing.

preconicé I proclaimed; past 1st pers. sing. / *preconizar*.

preconicéis that you (all) may proclaim; pres. subj. 2nd pers. pl. / *preconizar*.

preconicemos 1. that we may proclaim; pres. subj. 1st pers. pl. / *preconizar*. 2. let us proclaim; impve. 1st pers. pl.

preconicen 1. that they may proclaim; pres. subj. 3rd pers. pl. / *preconizar*. 2. let them proclaim; impve. 3rd pers. pl.

preconices that you may proclaim; pres. subj. 2nd pers. sing. / *preconizar*.

preconizar to proclaim. irr.

preconocer to foreknow. irr.

preconozca 1. that I may foreknow; pres. subj. 1st pers. sing. / *preconocer*. 2. that he (she/it) may foreknow; pres. subj. 3rd pers. sing. 3. let him (her/it) foreknow; impve. 3rd pers. sing.

preconozcáis that you (all) may foreknow; pres. subj. 2nd pers. pl. / *preconocer*.

preconozcamos 1. that we may foreknow; pres. subj. 1st pers. pl. / *preconocer*. 2. let us foreknow; impve. 1st pers. pl.

preconozcan 1. that they may foreknow; pres. subj. 3rd pers. pl. / *preconocer*. 2. let them foreknow; impve. 3rd pers. pl.

preconozcas that you may foreknow; pres. subj. 2nd pers. sing. / *preconocer*.

preconozco I foreknow; pres. ind. 1st pers. sing. / *preconocer*.

predecir to predict. irr.

predestinar to predestine. reg.

predeterminar to predetermine. reg.

predi (you) predict; impve. 2nd pers. sing. / *predecir*.

predicar to preach. irr.

predice he (she/it) predicts; pres. ind. 3rd pers. sing. / *predecir*.

predicen they predict; pres. ind. 3rd pers. pl. / *predecir*.

predices you predict; pres. ind. 2nd pers. sing. / *predecir*.

prediciendo predicting; pres. part. / *predecir*.

predicho predicted; past part. / *predecir*.

prediga 1. that I may predict; pres. subj. 1st pers. sing. / *predecir*. 2. that he (she/it) may predict; pres. subj. 3rd pers. sing. 3. let him (her/it) predict; impve. 3rd pers. sing.

predigáis that you (all) may predict; pres. subj. 2nd pers. pl. / *predecir*.

predigamos 1. that we may predict; pres. subj. 1st pers. pl. / *predecir*. 2. let us predict; impve. 1st pers. pl.

predigan 1. that they may predict; pres. subj. 3rd pers. pl. / *predecir*. 2. let them predict; impve. 3rd pers. pl.

predigas that you may predict; pres. subj. 2nd pers. sing. / *predecir*.

predigo I predict; pres. ind. 1st pers. sing. / *predecir*.

predije I predicted; past 1st pers. sing. / *predecir*.

predijera 1. that I might predict; imp. subj. 1st pers. sing. / *predecir*. 2. that he (she/it) might predict; imp. subj. 3rd pers. sing.

predijerais that you (all) might predict; imp. subj. 2nd pers pl. / *predecir*.

predijéramos that we might predict; imp. subj. 1st pers. pl. / *predecir*.

predijeran that they might predict; imp. subj. 3rd pers. pl. / *predecir*.

predijeras that you might predict; imp. subj. 2nd pers. sing. / *predecir*.

predijeron they predicted; past 3rd pers. pl. / *predecir*.

predijese 1. that I might predict; imp. subj. 1st pers. sing. / *predecir*. 2. that he (she/it) might predict; imp. subj. 3rd pers. sing.

predijeseis that you (all) might predict; imp. subj. 2nd pers pl. / *predecir*.

predijésemos that we might predict; imp. subj. 1st pers. pl. / *predecir*.

predijesen that they might predict; imp. subj. 3rd pers. pl. / *predecir*.

predijeses that you might predict; imp. subj. 2nd pers. sing. / *predecir*.

predijimos we predicted; past 1st pers. pl. / *predecir*.

predijiste you predicted; past 2nd pers. sing. / *predecir*.

predijisteis you (all) predicted; past 2nd pers. pl. / *predecir*.

predijo he (she/it) predicted; past 3rd pers. sing. / *predecir*.

predique 1. that I may preach; pres. subj. 1st pers. sing. / *predicar*. 2. that he (she/it) may preach; pres. subj. 3rd pers. sing. 3. let him (her/it) preach; impve. 3rd pers. sing.

prediqué I preached; past 1st pers. sing. / *predicar*.

prediquéis that you (all) may preach; pres. subj. 2nd pers. pl. / *predicar*.

prediquemos 1. that we may preach; pres. subj. 1st pers. pl. / *predicar*. 2. let us preach; impve. 1st pers. pl.

prediquen 1. that they may preach; pres. subj. 3rd pers. pl. / *predicar*. 2. let them preach; impve. 3rd pers. pl.

prediques that you may preach; pres. subj. 2nd pers. sing. / *predicar*.

predirá he (she/it) will predict; fut. 3rd pers. sing. / *predecir*.

predirán they will predict; fut. 3rd pers. pl. / *predecir*.

predirás you will predict; fut. 2nd pers. sing. / *predecir*.

predíré I shall predict; fut. 1st pers. sing. / *predecir.*

predíréis you (all) will predict; fut. 2nd pers. pl. / *predecir.*

prediremos we shall predict; fut. 1st pers. pl. / *predecir.*

prediría 1. I should predict; cond. 1st pers. sing. / *predecir.* 2. he (she/it) would predict; cond. 3rd pers. sing.

prediríais you (all) would predict; cond. 2nd pers. pl. / *predecir.*

prediríamos we should predict; cond. 1st pers. pl. / *predecir.*

predirían they would predict; cond. 3rd pers. pl. / *predecir.*

predirías you would predict; cond. 2nd pers. sing. / *predecir.*

predispon (you) predispose; impve. 2nd pers. sing. / *predisponer.*

predispondrá he (she/it) will predispose; fut. 3rd pers. sing. / *predisponer.*

predispondrán they will predispose; fut. 3rd pers. pl. / *predisponer.*

predispondrás you will predispose; fut. 2nd pers. sing. / *predisponer.*

predispondré I shall predispose; fut. 1st pers. sing. / *predisponer.*

predispondréis you (all) will predispose; fut. 2nd pers. pl. / *predisponer.*

predispondremos we shall predispose; fut. 1st pers. pl. / *predisponer.*

predispondría 1. I should predispose; cond. 1st pers. sing. / *predisponer.* 2. he (she/it) would predispose; cond. 3rd pers. sing.

predispondríais you (all) would predispose; cond. 2nd pers. pl. / *predisponer.*

predispondríamos we should predispose; cond. 1st pers. pl. / *predisponer.*

predispondrían they would predispose; cond. 3rd pers. pl. / *predisponer.*

predispondrías you would predispose; cond. 2nd pers. sing. / *predisponer.*

predisponer to predispose. irr.

predisponga 1. that I may predispose; pres. subj. 1st pers. sing. / *predisponer.* 2. that he (she/it) may predispose; pres. subj. 3rd pers. sing. 3. let him (her/it) predispose; impve. 3rd pers. sing.

predispongáis that you (all) may predispose; pres. subj. 2nd pers. pl. / *predisponer.*

predispongamos 1. that we may predispose; pres. subj. 1st pers. pl. / *predisponer.* 2. let us predispose; impve. 1st pers. pl.

predispongan 1. that they may predispose; pres. subj. 3rd pers. pl. / *predisponer.* 2. let them predispose; impve. 3rd pers. pl.

predispongas that you may predispose; pres. subj. 2nd pers. sing. / *predisponer.*

predispongo I predispose; pres. ind. 1st pers. sing. / *predisponer.*

predispuesto predisposed; past part. / *predisponer.*

predispuse I predisposed; past 1st pers. sing. / *predisponer.*

predispusiera 1. that I might predispose; imp. subj. 1st pers. sing. / *predisponer.* 2. that he (she/it) might predispose; imp. subj. 3rd pers. sing.

predispusierais that you (all) might predispose; imp. subj. 2nd pers pl. / *predisponer.*

predispusiéramos that we might predispose; imp. subj. 1st pers. pl. / *predisponer.*

predispusieran that they might predispose; imp. subj. 3rd pers. pl. / *predisponer.*

predispusieras that you might predispose; imp. subj. 2nd pers. sing. / *predisponer.*

predispusieron they predisposed; past 3rd pers. pl. / *predisponer.*

predispusiese 1. that I might predispose; imp. subj. 1st pers. sing. / *predisponer.* 2. that he (she/it) might predispose; imp. subj. 3rd pers. sing.

predispusieseis that you (all) might predispose; imp. subj. 2nd pers pl. / *predisponer.*

predispusiésemos that we might predispose; imp. subj. 1st pers. pl. / *predisponer.*

predispusiesen that they might predispose; imp. subj. 3rd pers. pl. / *predisponer.*

predispusieses that you might predispose; imp. subj. 2nd pers. sing. / *predisponer.*

predispusimos we predisposed; past 1st pers. pl. / *predisponer.*

predispusiste you predisposed; past 2nd pers. sing. / *predisponer.*

predispusisteis you (all) predisposed; past 2nd pers. pl. / *predisponer.*

predispuso he (she/it) predisposed; past 3rd pers. sing. / *predisponer.*

predominar to predominate. reg.

preexistir to preexist. reg.

prefabricar to prefabricate. irr.

prefabrique 1. that I may prefabricate; pres. subj. 1st pers. sing. / *prefabricar.* 2. that he (she/it) may prefabricate; pres. subj. 3rd pers. sing. 3. let him (her/it) prefabricate; impve. 3rd pers. sing.

prefabriqué I prefabricated; past 1st pers. sing. / *prefabricar.*

prefabriquéis that you (all) may prefabricate; pres. subj. 2nd pers. pl. / *prefabricar.*

prefabriquemos 1. that we may prefabricate; pres. subj. 1st pers. pl. / *prefabricar.* 2. let us prefabricate; impve. 1st pers. pl.

prefabriquen 1. that they may prefabricate; pres. subj. 3rd pers. pl. / *prefabricar.* 2. let them prefabricate; impve. 3rd pers. pl.

prefabriques that you may prefabricate; pres. subj. 2nd pers. sing. / *prefabricar.*

preferir to prefer. irr.

prefiera 1. that I may prefer; pres. subj. 1st pers. sing. / *preferir.* 2. that he (she/it) may prefer; pres. subj. 3rd pers. sing. 3. let him (her/it) prefer; impve. 3rd pers. sing.

prefieran 1. that they may prefer; pres. subj. 3rd pers. pl. / *preferir.* 2. let them prefer; impve. 3rd pers. pl.

prefieras that you may prefer; pres. subj. 2nd pers. sing. / *preferir.*

prefiere 1. he (she/it) prefers; pres. ind. 3rd pers. sing. / *preferir*. 2. (you) prefer; impve. 2nd pers. sing.

prefieren they prefer; pres. ind. 3rd pers. pl. / *preferir*.

prefieres you prefer; pres. ind. 2nd pers. sing. / *preferir*.

prefiero I prefer; pres. ind. 1st pers. sing. / *preferir*.

prefijar to prefix. reg.

prefiráis that you (all) may prefer; pres. subj. 2nd pers. pl. / *preferir*.

prefiramos 1. that we may prefer; pres. subj. 1st pers. pl. / *preferir*. 2. let us prefer; impve. 1st pers. pl.

prefiriendo preferring; pres. part. / *preferir*.

prefiriera 1. that I might prefer; imp. subj. 1st pers. sing. / *preferir*. 2. that he (she/it) might prefer; imp. subj. 3rd pers. sing.

prefirierais that you (all) might prefer; imp. subj. 2nd pers pl. / *preferir*.

prefiriéramos that we might prefer; imp. subj. 1st pers. pl. / *preferir*.

prefirieran that they might prefer; imp. subj. 3rd pers. pl. / *preferir*.

prefirieras that you might prefer; imp. subj. 2nd pers. sing. / *preferir*.

prefirieron they preferred; past 3rd pers. pl. / *preferir*.

prefiriese 1. that I might prefer; imp. subj. 1st pers. sing. / *preferir*. 2. that he (she/it) might prefer; imp. subj. 3rd pers. sing.

prefirieseis that you (all) might prefer; imp. subj. 2nd pers pl. / *preferir*.

prefiriésemos that we might prefer; imp. subj. 1st pers. pl. / *preferir*.

prefiriesen that they might prefer; imp. subj. 3rd pers. pl. / *preferir*.

prefirieses that you might prefer; imp. subj. 2nd pers. sing. / *preferir*.

prefirió he (she/it) preferred; past 3rd pers. sing. / *preferir*.

pregonar to proclaim. reg.

preguntándose wondering; pres. part. / *preguntarse*.

preguntaos (you all) wonder; impve. 2nd pers. pl. / *preguntarse*.

preguntar to ask. reg.

preguntarse to wonder. reg.

pregúntate (you) wonder; impve. 2nd pers. sing. / *preguntarse*.

preguntémonos let us wonder; impve. 1st pers. pl. / *preguntarse*.

pregúntense let them wonder; impve. 3rd pers. pl. / *preguntarse*.

pregúntese let him (her/it) wonder; impve. 3rd pers. sing. / *preguntarse*.

prejuiciar to prejudice. reg.

prejuzgar to prejudge. irr.

prejuzgue 1. that I may prejudge; pres. subj. 1st pers. sing. / *prejuzgar*. 2. that he (she/it) may prejudge; pres. subj. 3rd pers. sing. 3. let him (her/it) prejudge; impve. 3rd pers. sing.

prejuzgué I prejudged; past 1st pers. sing. / *prejuzgar*.

prejuzguéis that you (all) may prejudge; pres. subj. 2nd pers. pl. / *prejuzgar*.

prejuzguemos 1. that we may prejudge; pres. subj. 1st pers. pl. / *prejuzgar*. 2. let us prejudge; impve. 1st pers. pl.

prejuzguen 1. that they may prejudge; pres. subj. 3rd pers. pl. / *prejuzgar*. 2. let them prejudge; impve. 3rd pers. pl.

prejuzgues that you may prejudge; pres. subj. 2nd pers. sing. / *prejuzgar*.

preludiar to prelude. reg.

premeditar to premeditate. reg.

premiar to reward. reg.

prendámonos let us dress up ; impve. 1st pers. pl. / *prenderse*.

prendándose taking a fancy to; pres. part. / *prendarse*.

préndanse let them dress up ; impve. 3rd pers. pl. / *prenderse*.

prendaos (you all) take a fancy to; impve. 2nd pers. pl. / *prendarse*.

prendar to pawn. reg.

prendarse to take a fancy to. reg.

préndase let him (her/it) dress up ; impve. 3rd pers. sing. / *prenderse*.

préndate (you) take a fancy to; impve. 2nd pers. sing. / *prendarse*.

prendémonos let us take a fancy to; impve. 1st pers. pl. / *prendarse*.

préndense let them take a fancy to; impve. 3rd pers. pl. / *prendarse*.

prendeos (you all) dress up ; impve. 2nd pers. pl. / *prenderse*.

prender to seize or to catch. reg.

prenderse to dress up. reg.

préndese let him (her/it) take a fancy to; impve. 3rd pers. sing. / *prendarse*.

préndete (you) dress up ; impve. 2nd pers. sing. / *prenderse*.

prendiéndose dressing up ; pres. part. / *prenderse*.

prensar to press. reg.

preñar to make pregnant. reg.

preocupándose being preoccupied; pres. part. / *preocuparse*.

preocupaos (you all) be preoccupied; impve. 2nd pers. pl. / *preocuparse*.

preocupar to preoccupy or to worry. reg.

preocuparse to be preoccupied. reg.

preocúpate (you) be preoccupied; impve. 2nd pers. sing. / *preocuparse*.

preocupémonos let us be preoccupied; impve. 1st pers. pl. / *preocuparse*.

preocúpense let them be preoccupied; impve. 3rd pers. pl. / *preocuparse*.

preocúpese let him (her/it) be preoccupied; impve. 3rd pers. sing. / *preocuparse*.

preordinar to preordain. reg.

preparándose getting ready; pres. part. / *prepararse*.

preparaos (you all) get ready; impve. 2nd pers. pl. / *prepararse*.

preparar to prepare. reg.
prepararse to get ready. reg.
prepárate (you) get ready; impve. 2nd pers. sing. / *prepararse.*
preparémonos let us get ready; impve. 1st pers. pl. / *prepararse.*
prepárense let them get ready; impve. 3rd pers. pl. / *prepararse.*
prepárese let him (her/it) get ready; impve. 3rd pers. sing. / *prepararse.*
prepon (you) prefer; impve. 2nd pers. sing. / *preponer.*
preponderar to prevail. reg.
prepondrá he (she/it) will prefer; fut. 3rd pers. sing. / *preponer.*
prepondrán they will prefer; fut. 3rd pers. pl. / *preponer.*
prepondrás you will prefer; fut. 2nd pers. sing. / *preponer.*
prepondré I shall prefer; fut. 1st pers. sing. / *preponer.*
prepondréis you (all) will prefer; fut. 2nd pers. pl. / *preponer.*
prepondremos we shall prefer; fut. 1st pers. pl. / *preponer.*
prepondría 1. I should prefer; cond. 1st pers. sing. / *preponer.* 2. he (she/it) would prefer; cond. 3rd pers. sing.
prepondríais you (all) would prefer; cond. 2nd pers. pl. / *preponer.*
prepondríamos we should prefer; cond. 1st pers. pl. / *preponer.*
prepondrían they would prefer; cond. 3rd pers. pl. / *preponer.*
prepondrías you would prefer; cond. 2nd pers. sing. / *preponer.*
preponga 1. that I may prefer; pres. subj. 1st pers. sing. / *preponer.* 2. that he (she/it) may prefer; pres. subj. 3rd pers. sing. 3. let him (her/it) prefer; impve. 3rd pers. sing.
prepongáis that you (all) may prefer; pres. subj. 2nd pers. pl. / *preponer.*
prepongamos 1. that we may prefer; pres. subj. 1st pers. pl. / *preponer.* 2. let us prefer; impve. 1st pers. pl.
prepongan 1. that they may prefer; pres. subj. 3rd pers. pl. / *preponer.* 2. let them prefer; impve. 3rd pers. pl.
prepongas that you may prefer; pres. subj. 2nd pers. sing. / *preponer.*
prepongo I prefer; pres. ind. 1st pers. sing. / *preponer.*
preposterar to reverse. reg.
prepuesto preferred; past part. / *preponer.*
prepuse I preferred; past 1st pers. sing. / *preponer.*
prepusiera 1. that I might prefer; imp. subj. 1st pers. sing. / *preponer.* 2. that he (she/it) might prefer; imp. subj. 3rd pers. sing.
prepusierais that you (all) might prefer; imp. subj. 2nd pers pl. / *preponer.*

prepusiéramos that we might prefer; imp. subj. 1st pers. pl. / *preponer.*
prepusieran that they might prefer; imp. subj. 3rd pers. pl. / *preponer.*
prepusieras that you might prefer; imp. subj. 2nd pers. sing. / *preponer.*
prepusieron they preferred; past 3rd pers. pl. / *preponer.*
prepusiese 1. that I might prefer; imp. subj. 1st pers. sing. / *preponer.* 2. that he (she/it) might prefer; imp. subj. 3rd pers. sing.
prepusieseis that you (all) might prefer; imp. subj. 2nd pers pl. / *preponer.*
prepusiésemos that we might prefer; imp. subj. 1st pers. pl. / *preponer.*
prepusiesen that they might prefer; imp. subj. 3rd pers. pl. / *preponer.*
prepusieses that you might prefer; imp. subj. 2nd pers. sing. / *preponer.*
prepusimos we preferred; past 1st pers. pl. / *preponer.*
prepusiste you preferred; past 2nd pers. sing. / *preponer.*
prepusisteis you (all) preferred; past 2nd pers. pl. / *preponer.*
prepuso he (she/it) preferred; past 3rd pers. sing. / *preponer.*
presagiar to foretell. reg.
prescindir to disregard. reg.
prescribir to prescribe. reg. except for pp.
prescripto prescribed; past part. / *prescribir.*
prescrito prescribed; past part. / *prescribir.*
presenciar to witness. reg.
presentándose appearing; pres. part. / *presentarse.*
presentaos (you all) appear; impve. 2nd pers. pl. / *presentarse.*
presentar to present. reg.
presentarse to appear. reg.
preséntate (you) appear; impve. 2nd pers. sing. / *presentarse.*
presentémonos let us appear; impve. 1st pers. pl. / *presentarse.*
preséntense let them appear; impve. 3rd pers. pl. / *presentarse.*
preséntese let him (her/it) appear; impve. 3rd pers. sing. / *presentarse.*
presentir to have a premonition. irr.
preservar to preserve. reg.
presidir to preside. reg.
presienta 1. that I may have a premonition; pres. subj. 1st pers. sing. / *presentir.* 2. that he (she/it) may have a premonition; pres. subj. 3rd pers. sing. 3. let him (her/it) have a premonition; impve. 3rd pers. sing.
presientan 1. that they may have a premonition; pres. subj. 3rd pers. pl. / *presentir.* 2. let them have a premonition; impve. 3rd pers. pl.
presientas that you may have a premonition; pres. subj. 2nd pers. sing. / *presentir.*

presiente 1. he (she/it) has a premonition; pres. ind. 3rd pers. sing. / *presentir*. 2. (you) have a premonition; impve. 2nd pers. sing.

presienten they have a premonition; pres. ind. 3rd pers. pl. / *presentir*.

presientes you have a premonition; pres. ind. 2nd pers. sing. / *presentir*.

presiento I have a premonition; pres. ind. 1st pers. sing. / *presentir*.

presintáis that you (all) may have a premonition; pres. subj. 2nd pers. pl. / *presentir*.

presintamos 1. that we may have a premonition; pres. subj. 1st pers. pl. / *presentir*. 2. let us have a premonition; impve. 1st pers. pl.

presintiendo having a premonition; pres. part. / *presentir*.

presintiera 1. that I might have a premonition; imp. subj. 1st pers. sing. / *presentir*. 2. that he (she/it) might have a premonition; imp. subj. 3rd pers. sing.

presintierais that you (all) might have a premonition; imp. subj. 2nd pers pl. / *presentir*.

presintiéramos that we might have a premonition; imp. subj. 1st pers. pl. / *presentir*.

presintieran that they might have a premonition; imp. subj. 3rd pers. pl. / *presentir*.

presintieras that you might have a premonition; imp. subj. 2nd pers. sing. / *presentir*.

presintieron they had a premonition; past 3rd pers. pl. / *presentir*.

presintiese 1. that I might have a premonition; imp. subj. 1st pers. sing. / *presentir*. 2. that he (she/it) might have a premonition; imp. subj. 3rd pers. sing.

presintieseis that you (all) might have a premonition; imp. subj. 2nd pers pl. / *presentir*.

presintiésemos that we might have a premonition; imp. subj. 1st pers. pl. / *presentir*.

presintiesen that they might have a premonition; imp. subj. 3rd pers. pl. / *presentir*.

presintieses that you might have a premonition; imp. subj. 2nd pers. sing. / *presentir*.

presintió he (she/it) had a premonition; past 3rd pers. sing. / *presentir*.

presionar to press. reg.

prestándose lending oneself; pres. part. / *prestarse*.

prestaos (you all) lend yourselves; impve. 2nd pers. pl. / *prestarse*.

prestar to lend. reg.

prestarse to lend oneself. reg.

préstate (you) lend yourself; impve. 2nd pers. sing. / *prestarse*.

prestémonos let us lend ourselves; impve. 1st pers. pl. / *prestarse*.

préstense let them lend themselves; impve. 3rd pers. pl. / *prestarse*.

préstese let him (her/it) lend himself (herself/itself); impve. 3rd pers. sing. / *prestarse*.

presumir to presume. reg.

presupon (you) presuppose; impve. 2nd pers. sing. / *presuponer*.

presupondrá he (she/it) will presuppose; fut. 3rd pers. sing. / *presuponer*.

presupondrán they will presuppose; fut. 3rd pers. pl. / *presuponer*.

presupondrás you will presuppose; fut. 2nd pers. sing. / *presuponer*.

presupondré I shall presuppose; fut. 1st pers. sing. / *presuponer*.

presupondréis you (all) will presuppose; fut. 2nd pers. pl. / *presuponer*.

presupondremos we shall presuppose; fut. 1st pers. pl. / *presuponer*.

presupondría 1. I should presuppose; cond. 1st pers. sing. / *presuponer*. 2. he (she/it) would presuppose; cond. 3rd pers. sing.

presupondríais you (all) would presuppose; cond. 2nd pers. pl. / *presuponer*.

presupondríamos we should presuppose; cond. 1st pers. pl. / *presuponer*.

presupondrían they would presuppose; cond. 3rd pers. pl. / *presuponer*.

presupondrías you would presuppose; cond. 2nd pers. sing. / *presuponer*.

presuponer to presuppose or to estimate. irr.

presuponga 1. that I may presuppose; pres. subj. 1st pers. sing. / *presuponer*. 2. that he (she/it) may presuppose; pres. subj. 3rd pers. sing. 3. let him (her/it) presuppose; impve. 3rd pers. sing.

presupongáis that you (all) may presuppose; pres. subj. 2nd pers. pl. / *presuponer*.

presupongamos 1. that we may presuppose; pres. subj. 1st pers. pl. / *presuponer*. 2. let us presuppose; impve. 1st pers. pl.

presupongan 1. that they may presuppose; pres. subj. 3rd pers. pl. / *presuponer*. 2. let them presuppose; impve. 3rd pers. pl.

presupongas that you may presuppose; pres. subj. 2nd pers. sing. / *presuponer*.

presupongo I presuppose; pres. ind. 1st pers. sing. / *presuponer*.

presupuesto presupposed; past part. / *presuponer*.

presupuse I presupposed; past 1st pers. sing. / *presuponer*.

presupusiera 1. that I might presuppose; imp. subj. 1st pers. sing. / *presuponer*. 2. that he (she/it) might presuppose; imp. subj. 3rd pers. sing.

presupusierais that you (all) might presuppose; imp. subj. 2nd pers pl. / *presuponer*.

presupusiéramos that we might presuppose; imp. subj. 1st pers. pl. / *presuponer*.

presupusieran that they might presuppose; imp. subj. 3rd pers. pl. / *presuponer*.

presupusieras that you might presuppose; imp. subj. 2nd pers. sing. / *presuponer*.

presupusieron they presupposed; past 3rd pers. pl. / *presuponer*.

presupusiese 1. that I might presuppose; imp. subj. 1st pers. sing. / *presuponer*. 2. that he (she/it) might presuppose; imp. subj. 3rd pers. sing.

presupusieseis that you (all) might presuppose; imp. subj. 2nd pers pl. / *presuponer*.

presupusiésemos that we might presuppose; imp. subj. 1st pers. pl. / *presuponer*.

presupusiesen that they might presuppose; imp. subj. 3rd pers. pl. / *presuponer.*

presupusieses that you might presuppose; imp. subj. 2nd pers. sing. / *presuponer.*

presupusimos we presupposed; past 1st pers. pl. / *presuponer.*

presupusiste you presupposed; past 2nd pers. sing. / *presuponer.*

presupusisteis you (all) presupposed; past 2nd pers. pl. / *presuponer.*

presupuso he (she/it) presupposed; past 3rd pers. sing. / *presuponer.*

pretender to pretend. reg.

preterir to ignore. irr. used only in inf. and pp.

pretextar to give as a pretext. reg.

preval (you) prevail; impve. 2nd pers. sing. / *prevaler.*

prevaldrá he (she/it) will prevail; fut. 3rd pers. sing. / *prevaler.*

prevaldrán they will prevail; fut. 3rd pers. pl. / *prevaler.*

prevaldrás you will prevail; fut. 2nd pers. sing. / *prevaler.*

prevaldré I shall prevail; fut. 1st pers. sing. / *prevaler.*

prevaldréis you (all) will prevail; fut. 2nd pers. pl. / *prevaler.*

prevaldremos we shall prevail; fut. 1st pers. pl. / *prevaler.*

prevaldría 1. I should prevail; cond. 1st pers. sing. / *prevaler.* 2. he (she/it) would prevail; cond. 3rd pers. sing.

prevaldríais you (all) would prevail; cond. 2nd pers. pl. / *prevaler.*

prevaldríamos we should prevail; cond. 1st pers. pl. / *prevaler.*

prevaldrían they would prevail; cond. 3rd pers. pl. / *prevaler.*

prevaldrías you would prevail; cond. 2nd pers. sing. / *prevaler.*

prevalecer to prevail. irr.

prevaleos (you all) take advantage; impve. 2nd pers. pl. / *prevalerse.*

prevaler to prevail. irr.

prevalerse to take advantage. irr.

preválete (you) take advantage; impve. 2nd pers. sing. / *prevalerse.*

prevalezca 1. that I may prevail; pres. subj. 1st pers. sing. / *prevalecer.* 2. that he (she/it) may prevail; pres. subj. 3rd pers. sing. 3. let him (her/it) prevail; impve. 3rd pers. sing.

prevalezcáis that you (all) may prevail; pres. subj. 2nd pers. pl. / *prevalecer.*

prevalezcamos 1. that we may prevail; pres. subj. 1st pers. pl. / *prevalecer.* 2. let us prevail; impve. 1st pers. pl.

prevalezcan 1. that they may prevail; pres. subj. 3rd pers. pl. / *prevalecer.* 2. let them prevail; impve. 3rd pers. pl.

prevalezcas that you may prevail; pres. subj. 2nd pers. sing. / *prevalecer.*

prevalezco I prevail; pres. ind. 1st pers. sing. / *prevalecer.*

prevalga 1. that I may prevail; pres. subj. 1st pers. sing. / *prevaler.* 2. that he (she/it) may prevail; pres. subj. 3rd pers. sing. 3. let him (her/it) prevail; impve. 3rd pers. sing.

prevalgáis that you (all) may prevail; pres. subj. 2nd pers. pl. / *prevaler.*

prevalgámonos let us take advantage; impve. 1st pers. pl. / *prevalerse.*

prevalgamos 1. that we may prevail; pres. subj. 1st pers. pl. / *prevaler.* 2. let us prevail; impve. 1st pers. pl.

prevalgan 1. that they may prevail; pres. subj. 3rd pers. pl. / *prevaler.* 2. let them prevail; impve. 3rd pers. pl.

preválganse let them take advantage; impve. 3rd pers. pl. / *prevalerse.*

prevalgas that you may prevail; pres. subj. 2nd pers. sing. / *prevaler.*

preválgase let him (her/it) take advantage; impve. 3rd pers. sing. / *prevalerse.*

prevalgo I prevail; pres. ind. 1st pers. sing. / *prevaler.*

prevaliéndose taking advantage; pres. part. / *prevalerse.*

prevaricar to prevaricate. irr.

prevarique 1. that I may prevaricate; pres. subj. 1st pers. sing. / *prevaricar.* 2. that he (she/it) may prevaricate; pres. subj. 3rd pers. sing. 3. let him (her/it) prevaricate; impve. 3rd pers. sing.

prevariqué I prevaricated; past 1st pers. sing. / *prevaricar.*

prevariquéis that you (all) may prevaricate; pres. subj. 2nd pers. pl. / *prevaricar.*

prevariquemos 1. that we may prevaricate; pres. subj. 1st pers. pl. / *prevaricar.* 2. let us prevaricate; impve. 1st pers. pl.

prevariquen 1. that they may prevaricate; pres. subj. 3rd pers. pl. / *prevaricar.* 2. let them prevaricate; impve. 3rd pers. pl.

prevariques that you may prevaricate; pres. subj. 2nd pers. sing. / *prevaricar.*

prevea 1. that I may foresee; pres. subj. 1st pers. sing. / *prever.* 2. that he (she/it) may foresee; pres. subj. 3rd pers. sing. 3. let him (her/it) foresee; impve. 3rd pers. sing.

preveáis that you (all) may foresee; pres. subj. 2nd pers. pl. / *prever.*

preveamos 1. that we may foresee; pres. subj. 1st pers. pl. / *prever.* 2. let us foresee; impve. 1st pers. pl.

prevean 1. that they may foresee; pres. subj. 3rd pers. pl. / *prever.* 2. let them foresee; impve. 3rd pers. pl.

preveas that you may foresee; pres. subj. 2nd pers. sing. / *prever.*

preveía 1. I was foreseeing; imp. ind. 1st pers. sing. / *prever.* 2. he (she/it) was foreseeing; imp. ind. 3rd pers. sing.

preveíais you (all) were foreseeing; imp. ind. 2nd pers. pl. / *prever.*

preveíamos we were foreseeing; imp. ind. 1st pers. pl. / *prever.*

preveían they were foreseeing; imp. ind. 3rd pers. pl.
/ *prever.*

preveías you were foreseeing; imp. ind. 2nd pers.
sing. / *prever.*

preven (you) prepare; impve. 2nd pers. sing. /
prevenir.

prevendrá he (she/it) will prepare; fut. 3rd pers. sing.
/ *prevenir.*

prevendrán they will prepare; fut. 3rd pers. pl. /
prevenir.

prevendrás you will prepare; fut. 2nd pers. sing. /
prevenir.

prevendré I shall prepare; fut. 1st pers. sing. /
prevenir.

prevendréis you (all) will prepare; fut. 2nd pers. pl. /
prevenir.

prevendremos we shall prepare; fut. 1st pers. pl. /
prevenir.

prevendría 1. I should prepare; cond. 1st pers. sing. /
prevenir. 2. he (she/it) would prepare; cond. 3rd
pers. sing.

prevendríais you (all) would prepare; cond. 2nd
pers. pl. / *prevenir.*

prevendríamos we should prepare; cond. 1st pers. pl.
/ *prevenir.*

prevendrían they would prepare; cond. 3rd pers. pl. /
prevenir.

prevendrías you would prepare; cond. 2nd pers. sing.
/ *prevenir.*

prevénete (you) get prepared; impve. 2nd pers. sing.
/ *prevenirse.*

prevenga 1. that I may prepare; pres. subj. 1st pers.
sing. / *prevenir.* 2. that he (she/it) may prepare; pres.
subj. 3rd pers. sing. 3. let him (her/it) prepare;
impve. 3rd pers. sing.

prevengáis that you (all) may prepare; pres. subj.
2nd pers. pl. / *prevenir.*

prevengámonos let us get prepared; impve. 1st pers.
pl. / *prevenirse.*

prevengamos 1. that we may prepare; pres. subj. 1st
pers. pl. / *prevenir.* 2. let us prepare; impve. 1st pers.
pl.

prevengan 1. that they may prepare; pres. subj. 3rd
pers. pl. / *prevenir.* 2. let them prepare; impve. 3rd
pers. pl.

prevénganse let them get prepared; impve. 3rd pers.
pl. / *prevenirse.*

prevengas that you may prepare; pres. subj. 2nd
pers. sing. / *prevenir.*

prevéngase let him (her/it) get prepared; impve. 3rd
pers. sing. / *prevenirse.*

prevengo I prepare; pres. ind. 1st pers. sing. /
prevenir.

preveníos (you all) get prepared; impve. 2nd pers. pl.
/ *prevenirse.*

prevenir to prepare. irr.

prevenirse to get prepared. irr.

preveo I foresee; pres. ind. 1st pers. sing. / *prever.*

prever to foresee. irr.

previ I foresaw; past 1st pers. sing. / *prever.*

previene he (she/it) prepares; pres. ind. 3rd pers.
sing. / *prevenir.*

previenen they prepare; pres. ind. 3rd pers. pl. /
prevenir.

previenes you prepare; pres. ind. 2nd pers. sing. /
prevenir.

previne I prepared; past 1st pers. sing. / *prevenir.*

previniendo preparing; pres. part. / *prevenir.*

previniéndose getting prepared; pres. part. /
prevenirse.

previniera 1. that I might prepare; imp. subj. 1st
pers. sing. / *prevenir.* 2. that he (she/it) might
prepare; imp. subj. 3rd pers. sing.

previnierais that you (all) might prepare; imp. subj.
2nd pers pl. / *prevenir.*

previniéramos that we might prepare; imp. subj. 1st
pers. pl. / *prevenir.*

previnieran that they might prepare; imp. subj. 3rd
pers. pl. / *prevenir.*

previnieras that you might prepare; imp. subj. 2nd
pers. sing. / *prevenir.*

previnieron they prepared; past 3rd pers. pl. /
prevenir.

previniese 1. that I might prepare; imp. subj. 1st pers.
sing. / *prevenir.* 2. that he (she/it) might prepare;
imp. subj. 3rd pers. sing.

previnieseis that you (all) might prepare; imp. subj.
2nd pers pl. / *prevenir.*

previniésemos that we might prepare; imp. subj. 1st
pers. pl. / *prevenir.*

previniesen that they might prepare; imp. subj. 3rd
pers. pl. / *prevenir.*

previnieses that you might prepare; imp. subj. 2nd
pers. sing. / *prevenir.*

previnimos we prepared; past 1st pers. pl. / *prevenir.*

previniste you prepared; past 2nd pers. sing. /
prevenir.

previnisteis you (all) prepared; past 2nd pers. pl. /
prevenir.

previno he (she/it) prepared; past 3rd pers. sing. /
prevenir.

previo he (she/it) foresaw; past 3rd pers. sing. /
prever.

previsto foresaw; past part. / *prever.*

primar to excel. reg.

principar to begin. reg.

pringándose profiteering; pres. part. / *pringarse.*

pringaos (you all) profiteer; impve. 2nd pers. pl. /
pringarse.

pringar to dip in grease. irr.

pringarse to profiteer. irr.

príngate (you) profiteer; impve. 2nd pers. sing. /
pringarse.

pringue 1. that I may dip in grease; pres. subj. 1st
pers. sing. / *pringar.* 2. that he (she/it) may dip in
grease; pres. subj. 3rd pers. sing. 3. let him (her/it)
dip in grease; impve. 3rd pers. sing.

pringué I dipped in grease; past 1st pers. sing. /
pringar.

pringuéis that you (all) may dip in grease; pres. subj. 2nd pers. pl. / *pringar*.

pringuémonos let us profiteer; impve. 1st pers. pl. / *pringarse*.

pringuemos 1. that we may dip in grease; pres. subj. 1st pers. pl. / *pringar*. 2. let us dip in grease; impve. 1st pers. pl.

pringuen 1. that they may dip in grease; pres. subj. 3rd pers. pl. / *pringar*. 2. let them dip in grease; impve. 3rd pers. pl.

prínguense let them profiteer; impve. 3rd pers. pl. / *pringarse*.

pringues that you may dip in grease; pres. subj. 2nd pers. sing. / *pringar*.

prínguese let him (her/it) profiteer; impve. 3rd pers. sing. / *pringarse*.

privándose depriving oneself; pres. part. / *privarse*.

privaos (you all) deprive yourselves; impve. 2nd pers. pl. / *privarse*.

privar to deprive. reg.

privarse to deprive oneself. reg.

prívate (you) deprive yourself; impve. 2nd pers. sing. / *privarse*.

privémonos let us deprive ourselves; impve. 1st pers. pl. / *privarse*.

prívense let them deprive themselves; impve. 3rd pers. pl. / *privarse*.

prívese let him (her/it) deprive himself (herself/itself); impve. 3rd pers. sing. / *privarse*.

privilegiar to favor. reg.

probándose trying on; pres. part. / *probarse*.

probaos (you all) try on; impve. 2nd pers. pl. / *probarse*.

probar to prove. irr.

probarse to try on. irr.

probémonos let us try on; impve. 1st pers. pl. / *probarse*.

proceder to proceed. reg.

procesar to prosecute. reg.

proclamar to proclaim. reg.

procrear to procreate. reg.

procurar to procure or get. reg.

prodigar to lavish. irr.

prodigue 1. that I may lavish; pres. subj. 1st pers. sing. / *prodigar*. 2. that he (she/it) may lavish; pres. subj. 3rd pers. sing. 3. let him (her/it) lavish; impve. 3rd pers. sing.

prodigué I lavished; past 1st pers. sing. / *prodigar*.

prodiguéis that you (all) may lavish; pres. subj. 2nd pers. pl. / *prodigar*.

prodiguemos 1. that we may lavish; pres. subj. 1st pers. pl. / *prodigar*. 2. let us lavish; impve. 1st pers. pl.

prodiguen 1. that they may lavish; pres. subj. 3rd pers. pl. / *prodigar*. 2. let them lavish; impve. 3rd pers. pl.

prodigues that you may lavish; pres. subj. 2nd pers. sing. / *prodigar*.

prodúcete (you) explain yourself; impve. 2nd pers. sing. / *producirse*.

produciéndose explaining oneself; pres. part. / *producirse*.

producíos (you all) explain yourselves; impve. 2nd pers. pl. / *producirse*.

producir to produce. irr.

producirse to explain oneself. irr.

produje I produced; past 1st pers. sing. / *producir*.

produjera 1. that I might produce; imp. subj. 1st pers. sing. / *producir*. 2. that he (she/it) might produce; imp. subj. 3rd pers. sing.

produjerais that you (all) might produce; imp. subj. 2nd pers pl. / *producir*.

produjéramos that we might produce; imp. subj. 1st pers. pl. / *producir*.

produjeran that they might produce; imp. subj. 3rd pers. pl. / *producir*.

produjeras that you might produce; imp. subj. 2nd pers. sing. / *producir*.

produjeron they produced; past 3rd pers. pl. / *producir*.

produjese 1. that I might produce; imp. subj. 1st pers. sing. / *producir*. 2. that he (she/it) might produce; imp. subj. 3rd pers. sing.

produjeseis that you (all) might produce; imp. subj. 2nd pers pl. / *producir*.

produjésemos that we might produce; imp. subj. 1st pers. pl. / *producir*.

produjesen that they might produce; imp. subj. 3rd pers. pl. / *producir*.

produjeses that you might produce; imp. subj. 2nd pers. sing. / *producir*.

produjimos we produced; past 1st pers. pl. / *producir*.

produjiste you produced; past 2nd pers. sing. / *producir*.

produjisteis you (all) produced; past 2nd pers. pl. / *producir*.

produjo he (she/it) produced; past 3rd pers. sing. / *producir*.

produzca 1. that I may produce; pres. subj. 1st pers. sing. / *producir*. 2. that he (she/it) may produce; pres. subj. 3rd pers. sing. 3. let him (her/it) produce; impve. 3rd pers. sing.

produzcáis that you (all) may produce; pres. subj. 2nd pers. pl. / *producir*.

produzcámonos let us explain ourselves; impve. 1st pers. pl. / *producirse*.

produzcamos 1. that we may produce; pres. subj. 1st pers. pl. / *producir*. 2. let us produce; impve. 1st pers. pl.

produzcan 1. that they may produce; pres. subj. 3rd pers. pl. / *producir*. 2. let them produce; impve. 3rd pers. pl.

prodúzcanse let them explain themselves; impve. 3rd pers. pl. / *producirse*.

produzcas that you may produce; pres. subj. 2nd pers. sing. / *producir*.

prodúzcase let him (her/it) explain himself (herself/itself); impve. 3rd pers. sing. / *producirse*.

produzco I produce; pres. ind. 1st pers. sing. / *producir*.

profanar to profane. reg.

proferir to utter. irr.

profesar to profess. reg.

profetice 1. that I may prophesy; pres. subj. 1st pers. sing. / *profetizar*. 2. that he (she/it) may prophesy; pres. subj. 3rd pers. sing. 3. let him (her/it) prophesy; impve. 3rd pers. sing.

profeticé I prophesied; past 1st pers. sing. / *profetizar*.

profeticéis that you (all) may prophesy; pres. subj. 2nd pers. pl. / *profetizar*.

profeticemos 1. that we may prophesy; pres. subj. 1st pers. pl. / *profetizar*. 2. let us prophesy; impve. 1st pers. pl.

profeticen 1. that they may prophesy; pres. subj. 3rd pers. pl. / *profetizar*. 2. let them prophesy; impve. 3rd pers. pl.

profetices that you may prophesy; pres. subj. 2nd pers. sing. / *profetizar*.

profetizar to prophesy. irr.

profiera 1. that I may utter; pres. subj. 1st pers. sing. / *proferir*. 2. that he (she/it) may utter; pres. subj. 3rd pers. sing. 3. let him (her/it) utter; impve. 3rd pers. sing.

profieran 1. that they may utter; pres. subj. 3rd pers. pl. / *proferir*. 2. let them utter; impve. 3rd pers. pl.

profieras that you may utter; pres. subj. 2nd pers. sing. / *proferir*.

profiere 1. he (she/it) utters; pres. ind. 3rd pers. sing. / *proferir*. 2. (you) utter; impve. 2nd pers. sing.

profieren they utter; pres. ind. 3rd pers. pl. / *proferir*.

profieres you utter; pres. ind. 2nd pers. sing. / *proferir*.

profiero I utter; pres. ind. 1st pers. sing. / *proferir*.

profiráis that you (all) may utter; pres. subj. 2nd pers. pl. / *proferir*.

profiramos 1. that we may utter; pres. subj. 1st pers. pl. / *proferir*. 2. let us utter; impve. 1st pers. pl.

profiriendo uttering; pres. part. / *proferir*.

profiriera 1. that I might utter; imp. subj. 1st pers. sing. / *proferir*. 2. that he (she/it) might utter; imp. subj. 3rd pers. sing.

profirierais that you (all) might utter; imp. subj. 2nd pers pl. / *proferir*.

profiriéramos that we might utter; imp. subj. 1st pers. pl. / *proferir*.

profirieran that they might utter; imp. subj. 3rd pers. pl. / *proferir*.

profirieras that you might utter; imp. subj. 2nd pers. sing. / *proferir*.

profirieron they uttered; past 3rd pers. pl. / *proferir*.

profiriese 1. that I might utter; imp. subj. 1st pers. sing. / *proferir*. 2. that he (she/it) might utter; imp. subj. 3rd pers. sing.

profirieseis that you (all) might utter; imp. subj. 2nd pers pl. / *proferir*.

profiriésemos that we might utter; imp. subj. 1st pers. pl. / *proferir*.

profiriesen that they might utter; imp. subj. 3rd pers. pl. / *proferir*.

profirieses that you might utter; imp. subj. 2nd pers. sing. / *proferir*.

profirió he (she/it) uttered; past 3rd pers. sing. / *proferir*.

profundice 1. that I may deepen; pres. subj. 1st pers. sing. / *profundizar*. 2. that he (she/it) may deepen; pres. subj. 3rd pers. sing. 3. let him (her/it) deepen; impve. 3rd pers. sing.

profundicé I deepened; past 1st pers. sing. / *profundizar*.

profundicéis that you (all) may deepen; pres. subj. 2nd pers. pl. / *profundizar*.

profundicemos 1. that we may deepen; pres. subj. 1st pers. pl. / *profundizar*. 2. let us deepen; impve. 1st pers. pl.

profundicen 1. that they may deepen; pres. subj. 3rd pers. pl. / *profundizar*. 2. let them deepen; impve. 3rd pers. pl.

profundices that you may deepen; pres. subj. 2nd pers. sing. / *profundizar*.

profundizar to deepen. irr.

programar to program. reg.

progresar to progress. reg.

prohibir to prohibit. reg.

prohijar to adopt. reg.

prologar to preface. irr.

prologue 1. that I may preface; pres. subj. 1st pers. sing. / *prologar*. 2. that he (she/it) may preface; pres. subj. 3rd pers. sing. 3. let him (her/it) preface; impve. 3rd pers. sing.

prologué I prefaced; past 1st pers. sing. / *prologar*.

prologuéis that you (all) may preface; pres. subj. 2nd pers. pl. / *prologar*.

prologuemos 1. that we may preface; pres. subj. 1st pers. pl. / *prologar*. 2. let us preface; impve. 1st pers. pl.

prologuen 1. that they may preface; pres. subj. 3rd pers. pl. / *prologar*. 2. let them preface; impve. 3rd pers. pl.

prologues that you may preface; pres. subj. 2nd pers. sing. / *prologar*.

prolongándose extending; pres. part. / *prolongarse*.

prolongaos (you all) extend; impve. 2nd pers. pl. / *prolongarse*.

prolongar to prolong. irr.

prolongarse to extend. irr.

prolóngate (you) extend; impve. 2nd pers. sing. / *prolongarse*.

prolongue 1. that I may prolong; pres. subj. 1st pers. sing. / *prolongar*. 2. that he (she/it) may prolong; pres. subj. 3rd pers. sing. 3. let him (her/it) prolong; impve. 3rd pers. sing.

prolongué I prolonged; past 1st pers. sing. / *prolongar*.

prolonguéis that you (all) may prolong; pres. subj. 2nd pers. pl. / *prolongar*.

prolonguémonos let us extend; impve. 1st pers. pl. / *prolongarse*.

prolonguemos 1. that we may prolong; pres. subj. 1st pers. pl. / *prolongar*. 2. let us prolong; impve. 1st pers. pl.

prolonguen 1. that they may prolong; pres. subj. 3rd pers. pl. / *prolongar.* 2. let them prolong; impve. 3rd pers. pl.

prolónguense let them extend; impve. 3rd pers. pl. / *prolongarse.*

prolongues that you may prolong; pres. subj. 2nd pers. sing. / *prolongar.*

prolónguese let him (her/it) extend; impve. 3rd pers. sing. / *prolongarse.*

promediar to average or to mediate. reg.

prometámonos let us become engaged; impve. 1st pers. pl. / *prometerse.*

prométanse let them become engaged; impve. 3rd pers. pl. / *prometerse.*

prométase let him (her/it) become engaged; impve. 3rd pers. sing. / *prometerse.*

prometeos (you all) become engaged; impve. 2nd pers. pl. / *prometerse.*

prometer to promise. reg.

prometerse to become engaged. reg.

prométete (you) become engaged; impve. 2nd pers. sing. / *prometerse.*

prometiéndose becoming engaged; pres. part. / *prometerse.*

promover to promote. irr.

promueva 1. that I may promote; pres. subj. 1st pers. sing. / *promover.* 2. that he (she/it) may promote; pres. subj. 3rd pers. sing. 3. let him (her/it) promote; impve. 3rd pers. sing.

promuevan 1. that they may promote; pres. subj. 3rd pers. pl. / *promover.* 2. let them promote; impve. 3rd pers. pl.

promuevas that you may promote; pres. subj. 2nd pers. sing. / *promover.*

promueve 1. he (she/it) promotes; pres. ind. 3rd pers. sing. / *promover.* 2. (you) promote; impve. 2nd pers. sing.

promueven they promote; pres. ind. 3rd pers. pl. / *promover.*

promueves you promote; pres. ind. 2nd pers. sing. / *promover.*

promuevo I promote; pres. ind. 1st pers. sing. / *promover.*

promulgar to promulgate. irr.

promulgue 1. that I may promulgate; pres. subj. 1st pers. sing. / *promulgar.* 2. that he (she/it) may promulgate; pres. subj. 3rd pers. sing. 3. let him (her/it) promulgate; impve. 3rd pers. sing.

promulgué I promulgated; past 1st pers. sing. / *promulgar.*

promulguéis that you (all) may promulgate; pres. subj. 2nd pers. pl. / *promulgar.*

promulguemos 1. that we may promulgate; pres. subj. 1st pers. pl. / *promulgar.* 2. let us promulgate; impve. 1st pers. pl.

promulguen 1. that they may promulgate; pres. subj. 3rd pers. pl. / *promulgar.* 2. let them promulgate; impve. 3rd pers. pl.

promulgues that you may promulgate; pres. subj. 2nd pers. sing. / *promulgar.*

pronosticar to prognosticate. irr.

pronostique 1. that I may prognosticate; pres. subj. 1st pers. sing. / *pronosticar.* 2. that he (she/it) may prognosticate; pres. subj. 3rd pers. sing. 3. let him (her/it) prognosticate; impve. 3rd pers. sing.

pronostiqué I prognosticated; past 1st pers. sing. / *pronosticar.*

pronostiquéis that you (all) may prognosticate; pres. subj. 2nd pers. pl. / *pronosticar.*

pronostiquemos 1. that we may prognosticate; pres. subj. 1st pers. pl. / *pronosticar.* 2. let us prognosticate; impve. 1st pers. pl.

pronostiquen 1. that they may prognosticate; pres. subj. 3rd pers. pl. / *pronosticar.* 2. let them prognosticate; impve. 3rd pers. pl.

pronostiques that you may prognosticate; pres. subj. 2nd pers. sing. / *pronosticar.*

pronunciándose rebelling; pres. part. / *pronunciarse.*

pronunciaos (you all) rebel; impve. 2nd pers. pl. / *pronunciarse.*

pronunciar to pronounce. reg.

pronunciarse to rebel. reg.

pronúnciate (you) rebel; impve. 2nd pers. sing. / *pronunciarse.*

pronunciémonos let us rebel; impve. 1st pers. pl. / *pronunciarse.*

pronúnciense let them rebel; impve. 3rd pers. pl. / *pronunciarse.*

pronúnciese let him (her/it) rebel; impve. 3rd pers. sing. / *pronunciarse.*

propagar to propagate. irr.

propague 1. that I may propagate; pres. subj. 1st pers. sing. / *propagar.* 2. that he (she/it) may propagate; pres. subj. 3rd pers. sing. 3. let him (her/it) propagate; impve. 3rd pers. sing.

propagué I propagated; past 1st pers. sing. / *propagar.*

propaguéis that you (all) may propagate; pres. subj. 2nd pers. pl. / *propagar.*

propaguemos 1. that we may propagate; pres. subj. 1st pers. pl. / *propagar.* 2. let us propagate; impve. 1st pers. pl.

propaguen 1. that they may propagate; pres. subj. 3rd pers. pl. / *propagar.* 2. let them propagate; impve. 3rd pers. pl.

propagues that you may propagate; pres. subj. 2nd pers. sing. / *propagar.*

propalar to divulge. reg.

propasándose overstepping one's bounds; pres. part. / *propasarse.*

propasaos (you all) overstep your bounds; impve. 2nd pers. pl. / *propasarse.*

propasarse to overstep one's bounds. reg.

propásate (you) overstep your bounds; impve. 2nd pers. sing. / *propasarse.*

propasémonos let us overstep our bounds; impve. 1st pers. pl. / *propasarse.*

propásense let them overstep their bounds; impve. 3rd pers. pl. / *propasarse.*

propásese let him (her/it) overstep his (her/its) bounds; impve. 3rd pers. sing. / *propasarse.*

propender to be inclined. reg.

propiciar to propitiate. reg.
propinar to give a drink to. reg.
propon (you) propose; impve. 2nd pers. sing. / *proponer.*
propondrá he (she/it) will propose; fut. 3rd pers. sing. / *proponer.*
propondrán they will propose; fut. 3rd pers. pl. / *proponer.*
propondrás you will propose; fut. 2nd pers. sing. / *proponer.*
propondré I shall propose; fut. 1st pers. sing. / *proponer.*
propondréis you (all) will propose; fut. 2nd pers. pl. / *proponer.*
propondremos we shall propose; fut. 1st pers. pl. / *proponer.*
propondría 1. I should propose; cond. 1st pers. sing. / *proponer.* 2. he (she/it) would propose; cond. 3rd pers. sing.
propondríais you (all) would propose; cond. 2nd pers. pl. / *proponer.*
propondríamos we should propose; cond. 1st pers. pl. / *proponer.*
propondrían they would propose; cond. 3rd pers. pl. / *proponer.*
propondrías you would propose; cond. 2nd pers. sing. / *proponer.*
proponeos (you all) resolve; impve. 2nd pers. pl. / *proponerse.*
proponer to propose. irr.
proponerse to resolve. irr.
proponga 1. that I may propose; pres. subj. 1st pers. sing. / *proponer.* 2. that he (she/it) may propose; pres. subj. 3rd pers. sing. 3. let him (her/it) propose; impve. 3rd pers. sing.
propongáis that you (all) may propose; pres. subj. 2nd pers. pl. / *proponer.*
propongámonos let us resolve; impve. 1st pers. pl. / *proponerse.*
propongamos 1. that we may propose; pres. subj. 1st pers. pl. / *proponer.* 2. let us propose; impve. 1st pers. pl.
propongan 1. that they may propose; pres. subj. 3rd pers. pl. / *proponer.* 2. let them propose; impve. 3rd pers. pl.
propónganse let them resolve; impve. 3rd pers. pl. / *proponerse.*
propongas that you may propose; pres. subj. 2nd pers. sing. / *proponer.*
propóngase let him (her/it) resolve; impve. 3rd pers. sing. / *proponerse.*
propongo I propose; pres. ind. 1st pers. sing. / *proponer.*
proponiendo proposing; pres. part. / *proponer.*
proponiéndose resolving; pres. part. / *proponerse.*
proponte (you) resolve; impve. 2nd pers. sing. / *proponerse.*
proporcionar to proportion. reg.
propuesto proposed; past part. / *proponer.*
propugnar to champion. reg.

propulsar to propel. reg.
propuse I proposed; past 1st pers. sing. / *proponer.*
propusiera 1. that I might propose; imp. subj. 1st pers. sing. / *proponer.* 2. that he (she/it) might propose; imp. subj. 3rd pers. sing.
propusierais that you (all) might propose; imp. subj. 2nd pers pl. / *proponer.*
propusiéramos that we might propose; imp. subj. 1st pers. pl. / *proponer.*
propusieran that they might propose; imp. subj. 3rd pers. pl. / *proponer.*
propusieras that you might propose; imp. subj. 2nd pers. sing. / *proponer.*
propusieron they proposed; past 3rd pers. pl. / *proponer.*
propusiese 1. that I might propose; imp. subj. 1st pers. sing. / *proponer.* 2. that he (she/it) might propose; imp. subj. 3rd pers. sing.
propusieseis that you (all) might propose; imp. subj. 2nd pers pl. / *proponer.*
propusiésemos that we might propose; imp. subj. 1st pers. pl. / *proponer.*
propusiesen that they might propose; imp. subj. 3rd pers. pl. / *proponer.*
propusieses that you might propose; imp. subj. 2nd pers. sing. / *proponer.*
propusimos we proposed; past 1st pers. pl. / *proponer.*
propusiste you proposed; past 2nd pers. sing. / *proponer.*
propusisteis you (all) proposed; past 2nd pers. pl. / *proponer.*
propuso he (she/it) proposed; past 3rd pers. sing. / *proponer.*
prorratear to prorate. reg.
prorrogar to put off. irr.
prorrogue 1. that I may put off; pres. subj. 1st pers. sing. / *prorrogar.* 2. that he (she/it) may put off; pres. subj. 3rd pers. sing. 3. let him (her/it) put off; impve. 3rd pers. sing.
prorrogué I put off; past 1st pers. sing. / *prorrogar.*
prorroguéis that you (all) may put off; pres. subj. 2nd pers. pl. / *prorrogar.*
prorroguemos 1. that we may put off; pres. subj. 1st pers. pl. / *prorrogar.* 2. let us put off; impve. 1st pers. pl.
prorroguen 1. that they may put off; pres. subj. 3rd pers. pl. / *prorrogar.* 2. let them put off; impve. 3rd pers. pl.
prorrogues that you may put off; pres. subj. 2nd pers. sing. / *prorrogar.*
prorrumpir to break forth. reg.
proscribir to proscribe. reg. except for pp.
proscripto proscribed; past part. / *proscribir.*
proscrito proscribed; past part. / *proscribir.*
proseguir to continue. irr.
prosificar to turn poetry into prose. irr.

prosifique 1. that I may turn poetry into prose; pres. subj. 1st pers. sing. / *prosificar*. 2. that he (she/it) may turn poetry into prose; pres. subj. 3rd pers. sing. 3. let him (her/it) turn poetry into prose; impve. 3rd pers. sing.

prosifiqué I turned poetry into prose; past 1st pers. sing. / *prosificar*.

prosifiquéis that you (all) may turn poetry into prose; pres. subj. 2nd pers. pl. / *prosificar*.

prosifiquemos 1. that we may turn poetry into prose; pres. subj. 1st pers. pl. / *prosificar*. 2. let us turn poetry into prose; impve. 1st pers. pl.

prosifiquen 1. that they may turn poetry into prose; pres. subj. 3rd pers. pl. / *prosificar*. 2. let them turn poetry into prose; impve. 3rd pers. pl.

prosifiques that you may turn poetry into prose; pres. subj. 2nd pers. sing. / *prosificar*.

prosiga 1. that I may continue; pres. subj. 1st pers. sing. / *proseguir*. 2. that he (she/it) may continue; pres. subj. 3rd pers. sing. 3. let him (her/it) continue; impve. 3rd pers. sing.

prosigáis that you (all) may continue; pres. subj. 2nd pers. pl. / *proseguir*.

prosigamos 1. that we may continue; pres. subj. 1st pers. pl. / *proseguir*. 2. let us continue; impve. 1st pers. pl.

prosigan 1. that they may continue; pres. subj. 3rd pers. pl. / *proseguir*. 2. let them continue; impve. 3rd pers. pl.

prosigas that you may continue; pres. subj. 2nd pers. sing. / *proseguir*.

prosigo I continue; pres. ind. 1st pers. sing. / *proseguir*.

prosigue 1. he (she/it) continues; pres. ind. 3rd pers. sing. / *proseguir*. 2. (you) continue; impve. 2nd pers. sing.

prosiguen they continue; pres. ind. 3rd pers. pl. / *proseguir*.

prosigues you continue; pres. ind. 2nd pers. sing. / *proseguir*.

prosiguiendo continuing ; pres. part. / *proseguir*.

prosiguiera 1. that I might continue; imp. subj. 1st pers. sing. / *proseguir*. 2. that he (she/it) might continue; imp. subj. 3rd pers. sing.

prosiguierais that you (all) might continue; imp. subj. 2nd pers pl. / *proseguir*.

prosiguiéramos that we might continue; imp. subj. 1st pers. pl. / *proseguir*.

prosiguieran that they might continue; imp. subj. 3rd pers. pl. / *proseguir*.

prosiguieras that you might continue; imp. subj. 2nd pers. sing. / *proseguir*.

prosiguieron they continued; past 3rd pers. pl. / *proseguir*.

prosiguiese 1. that I might continue; imp. subj. 1st pers. sing. / *proseguir*. 2. that he (she/it) might continue; imp. subj. 3rd pers. sing.

prosiguieseis that you (all) might continue; imp. subj. 2nd pers pl. / *proseguir*.

prosiguiésemos that we might continue; imp. subj. 1st pers. pl. / *proseguir*.

prosiguiesen that they might continue; imp. subj. 3rd pers. pl. / *proseguir*.

prosiguieses that you might continue; imp. subj. 2nd pers. sing. / *proseguir*.

prosiguió he (she/it) continued; past 3rd pers. sing. / *proseguir*.

prosperar to prosper. reg.

prosternándose prostrating oneself; pres. part. / *prosternarse*.

prosternaos (you all) prostrate yourselves; impve. 2nd pers. pl. / *prosternarse*.

prosternarse to prostrate oneself. reg.

prostérnate (you) prostrate yourself; impve. 2nd pers. sing. / *prosternarse*.

prosternémonos let us prostrate ourselves; impve. 1st pers. pl. / *prosternarse*.

prostérnense let them prostrate themselves; impve. 3rd pers. pl. / *prosternarse*.

prostérnese let him (her/it) prostrate himself (herself/itself); impve. 3rd pers. sing. / *prosternarse*.

prostituir to prostitute. irr.

prostituya 1. that I may prostitute; pres. subj. 1st pers. sing. / *prostituir*. 2. that he (she/it) may prostitute; pres. subj. 3rd pers. sing. 3. let him (her/it) prostitute; impve. 3rd pers. sing.

prostituyáis that you (all) may prostitute; pres. subj. 2nd pers. pl. / *prostituir*.

prostituyamos 1. that we may prostitute; pres. subj. 1st pers. pl. / *prostituir*. 2. let us prostitute; impve. 1st pers. pl.

prostituyan 1. that they may prostitute; pres. subj. 3rd pers. pl. / *prostituir*. 2. let them prostitute; impve. 3rd pers. pl.

prostituyas that you may prostitute; pres. subj. 2nd pers. sing. / *prostituir*.

prostituye 1. he (she/it) prostitutes; pres. ind. 3rd pers. sing. / *prostituir*. 2. (you) prostitute; impve. 2nd pers. sing.

prostituyen they prostitute; pres. ind. 3rd pers. pl. / *prostituir*.

prostituyendo prostituting; pres. part. / *prostituir*.

prostituyera 1. that I might prostitute; imp. subj. 1st pers. sing. / *prostituir*. 2. that he (she/it) might prostitute; imp. subj. 3rd pers. sing.

prostituyerais that you (all) might prostitute; imp. subj. 2nd pers pl. / *prostituir*.

prostituyéramos that we might prostitute; imp. subj. 1st pers. pl. / *prostituir*.

prostituyeran that they might prostitute; imp. subj. 3rd pers. pl. / *prostituir*.

prostituyeras that you might prostitute; imp. subj. 2nd pers. sing. / *prostituir*.

prostituyeron they prostituted; past 3rd pers. pl. / *prostituir*.

prostituyes you prostitute; pres. ind. 2nd pers. sing. / *prostituir*.

prostituyese 1. that I might prostitute; imp. subj. 1st pers. sing. / *prostituir*. 2. that he (she/it) might prostitute; imp. subj. 3rd pers. sing.

prostituyeseis that you (all) might prostitute; imp. subj. 2nd pers pl. / *prostituir*.

prostituyésemos that we might prostitute; imp. subj. 1st pers. pl. / *prostituir*.

prostituyesen that they might prostitute; imp. subj. 3rd pers. pl. / *prostituir*.

prostituyeses that you might prostitute; imp. subj. 2nd pers. sing. / *prostituir*.

prostituyo I prostitute; pres. ind. 1st pers. sing. / *prostituir*.

prostituyó he (she/it) prostituted; past 3rd pers. sing. / *prostituir*.

protagonice 1. that I may star in a production; pres. subj. 1st pers. sing. / *protagonizar*. 2. that he (she/it) may star in a production; pres. subj. 3rd pers. sing. 3. let him (her/it) star in a production; impve. 3rd pers. sing.

protagonicé I starred in a production; past 1st pers. sing. / *protagonizar*.

protagonicéis that you (all) may star in a production; pres. subj. 2nd pers. pl. / *protagonizar*.

protagonicemos 1. that we may star in a production; pres. subj. 1st pers. pl. / *protagonizar*. 2. let us star in a production; impve. 1st pers. pl.

protagonicen 1. that they may star in a production; pres. subj. 3rd pers. pl. / *protagonizar*. 2. let them star in a production; impve. 3rd pers. pl.

protagonices that you may star in a production; pres. subj. 2nd pers. sing. / *protagonizar*.

protagonizar to star in a production. irr.

proteger to protect. irr.

proteja 1. that I may protect; pres. subj. 1st pers. sing. / *proteger*. 2. that he (she/it) may protect; pres. subj. 3rd pers. sing. 3. let him (her/it) protect; impve. 3rd pers. sing.

protejáis that you (all) may protect; pres. subj. 2nd pers. pl. / *proteger*.

protejamos 1. that we may protect; pres. subj. 1st pers. pl. / *proteger*. 2. let us protect; impve. 1st pers. pl.

protejan 1. that they may protect; pres. subj. 3rd pers. pl. / *proteger*. 2. let them protect; impve. 3rd pers. pl.

protejas that you may protect; pres. subj. 2nd pers. sing. / *proteger*.

protejo I protect; pres. ind. 1st pers. sing. / *proteger*.

protestar to protest. reg.

protocolice 1. that I may make official; pres. subj. 1st pers. sing. / *protocolizar*. 2. that he (she/it) may make official; pres. subj. 3rd pers. sing. 3. let him (her/it) make official; impve. 3rd pers. sing.

protocolicé I made official; past 1st pers. sing. / *protocolizar*.

protocolicéis that you (all) may make official; pres. subj. 2nd pers. pl. / *protocolizar*.

protocolicemos 1. that we may make official; pres. subj. 1st pers. pl. / *protocolizar*. 2. let us make official; impve. 1st pers. pl.

protocolicen 1. that they may make official; pres. subj. 3rd pers. pl. / *protocolizar*. 2. let them make official; impve. 3rd pers. pl.

protocolices that you may make official; pres. subj. 2nd pers. sing. / *protocolizar*.

protocolizar to make official. irr.

proveer to provide. irr.

proveí I provided; past 1st pers. sing. / *proveer*.

proveído provided; past part. / *proveer*.

proveímos we provided; past 1st pers. pl. / *proveer*.

proveíste you provided; past 2nd pers. sing. / *proveer*.

proveísteis you (all) provided; past 2nd pers. pl. / *proveer*.

proven (you) originate; impve. 2nd pers. sing. / *provenir*.

provendrá he (she/it) will originate; fut. 3rd pers. sing. / *provenir*.

provendrán they will originate; fut. 3rd pers. pl. / *provenir*.

provendrás you will originate; fut. 2nd pers. sing. / *provenir*.

provendré I shall originate; fut. 1st pers. sing. / *provenir*.

provendréis you (all) will originate; fut. 2nd pers. pl. / *provenir*.

provendremos we shall originate; fut. 1st pers. pl. / *provenir*.

provendría 1. I should originate; cond. 1st pers. sing. / *provenir*. 2. he (she/it) would originate; cond. 3rd pers. sing.

provendríais you (all) would originate; cond. 2nd pers. pl. / *provenir*.

provendríamos we should originate; cond. 1st pers. pl. / *provenir*.

provendrían they would originate; cond. 3rd pers. pl. / *provenir*.

provendrías you would originate; cond. 2nd pers. sing. / *provenir*.

provenga 1. that I may originate; pres. subj. 1st pers. sing. / *provenir*. 2. that he (she/it) may originate; pres. subj. 3rd pers. sing. 3. let him (her/it) originate; impve. 3rd pers. sing.

provengáis that you (all) may originate; pres. subj. 2nd pers. pl. / *provenir*.

provengamos 1. that we may originate; pres. subj. 1st pers. pl. / *provenir*. 2. let us originate; impve. 1st pers. pl.

provengan 1. that they may originate; pres. subj. 3rd pers. pl. / *provenir*. 2. let them originate; impve. 3rd pers. pl.

provengas that you may originate; pres. subj. 2nd pers. sing. / *provenir*.

provengo I originate; pres. ind. 1st pers. sing. / *provenir*.

provenir to originate. irr.

proveyendo providing; pres. part. / *proveer*.

proveyera 1. that I might provide; imp. subj. 1st pers. sing. / *proveer*. 2. that he (she/it) might provide; imp. subj. 3rd pers. sing.

proveyerais that you (all) might provide; imp. subj. 2nd pers pl. / *proveer*.

proveyéramos that we might provide; imp. subj. 1st pers. pl. / *proveer*.

proveyeran that they might provide; imp. subj. 3rd pers. pl. / *proveer*.

proveyeras that you might provide; imp. subj. 2nd pers. sing. / *proveer.*

proveyeron they provided; past 3rd pers. pl. / *proveer.*

proveyese 1. that I might provide; imp. subj. 1st pers. sing. / *proveer.* 2. that he (she/it) might provide; imp. subj. 3rd pers. sing.

proveyeseis that you (all) might provide; imp. subj. 2nd pers pl. / *proveer.*

proveyésemos that we might provide; imp. subj. 1st pers. pl. / *proveer.*

proveyesen that they might provide; imp. subj. 3rd pers. pl. / *proveer.*

proveyeses that you might provide; imp. subj. 2nd pers. sing. / *proveer.*

proveyó he (she/it) provided; past 3rd pers. sing. / *proveer.*

providenciar to take the necessary steps. reg.

proviene he (she/it) originates; pres. ind. 3rd pers. sing. / *provenir.*

provienen they originate; pres. ind. 3rd pers. pl. / *provenir.*

provienes you originate; pres. ind. 2nd pers. sing. / *provenir.*

provine I originated; past 1st pers. sing. / *provenir.*

proviniendo originating; pres. part. / *provenir.*

proviniera 1. that I might originate; imp. subj. 1st pers. sing. / *provenir.* 2. that he (she/it) might originate; imp. subj. 3rd pers. sing.

provinierais that you (all) might originate; imp. subj. 2nd pers pl. / *provenir.*

proviniéramos that we might originate; imp. subj. 1st pers. pl. / *provenir.*

provinieran that they might originate; imp. subj. 3rd pers. pl. / *provenir.*

provinieras that you might originate; imp. subj. 2nd pers. sing. / *provenir.*

provinieron they originated; past 3rd pers. pl. / *provenir.*

proviniese 1. that I might originate; imp. subj. 1st pers. sing. / *provenir.* 2. that he (she/it) might originate; imp. subj. 3rd pers. sing.

provinieseis that you (all) might originate; imp. subj. 2nd pers pl. / *provenir.*

proviniésemos that we might originate; imp. subj. 1st pers. pl. / *provenir.*

proviniesen that they might originate; imp. subj. 3rd pers. pl. / *provenir.*

provinieses that you might originate; imp. subj. 2nd pers. sing. / *provenir.*

provinimos we originated; past 1st pers. pl. / *provenir.*

proviniste you originated; past 2nd pers. sing. / *provenir.*

provinisteis you (all) originated; past 2nd pers. pl. / *provenir.*

provino he (she/it) originated; past 3rd pers. sing. / *provenir.*

provisto provided; past part. / *proveer.*

provocar to provoke. irr.

provoque 1. that I may provoke; pres. subj. 1st pers. sing. / *provocar.* 2. that he (she/it) may provoke; pres. subj. 3rd pers. sing. 3. let him (her/it) provoke; impve. 3rd pers. sing.

provoqué I provoked; past 1st pers. sing. / *provocar.*

provoquéis that you (all) may provoke; pres. subj. 2nd pers. pl. / *provocar.*

provoquemos 1. that we may provoke; pres. subj. 1st pers. pl. / *provocar.* 2. let us provoke; impve. 1st pers. pl.

provoquen 1. that they may provoke; pres. subj. 3rd pers. pl. / *provocar.* 2. let them provoke; impve. 3rd pers. pl.

provoques that you may provoke; pres. subj. 2nd pers. sing. / *provocar.*

proyectándose casting (as a shadow); pres. part. / *proyectarse.*

proyectaos (you all) cast (as a shadow); impve. 2nd pers. pl. / *proyectarse.*

proyectar to project. reg.

proyectarse to cast (as a shadow). reg.

proyéctate (you) cast (as a shadow); impve. 2nd pers. sing. / *proyectarse.*

proyectémonos let us cast (as a shadow); impve. 1st pers. pl. / *proyectarse.*

proyéctense let them cast (as a shadow); impve. 3rd pers. pl. / *proyectarse.*

proyéctese let him (her/it) cast (as a shadow); impve. 3rd pers. sing. / *proyectarse.*

prueba 1. he (she/it) proves; pres. ind. 3rd pers. sing. / *probar.* 2. (you) prove; impve. 2nd pers. sing.

prueban they prove; pres. ind. 3rd pers. pl. / *probar.*

pruebas you prove; pres. ind. 2nd pers. sing. / *probar.*

pruébate (you) try on; impve. 2nd pers. sing. / *probarse.*

pruebe 1. that I may prove; pres. subj. 1st pers. sing. / *probar.* 2. that he (she/it) may prove; pres. subj. 3rd pers. sing. 3. let him (her/it) prove; impve. 3rd pers. sing.

prueben 1. that they may prove; pres. subj. 3rd pers. pl. / *probar.* 2. let them prove; impve. 3rd pers. pl.

pruébense let them try on; impve. 3rd pers. pl. / *probarse.*

pruebes that you may prove; pres. subj. 2nd pers. sing. / *probar.*

pruébese let him (her/it) try on; impve. 3rd pers. sing. / *probarse.*

pruebo I prove; pres. ind. 1st pers. sing. / *probar.*

psicoanalice 1. that I may psychoanalyze; pres. subj. 1st pers. sing. / *psicoanalizar.* 2. that he (she/it) may psychoanalyze; pres. subj. 3rd pers. sing. 3. let him (her/it) psychoanalyze; impve. 3rd pers. sing.

psicoanalicé I psychoanalyzed; past 1st pers. sing. / *psicoanalizar.*

psicoanalicéis that you (all) may psychoanalyze; pres. subj. 2nd pers. pl. / *psicoanalizar.*

psicoanalicemos 1. that we may psychoanalyze; pres. subj. 1st pers. pl. / *psicoanalizar.* 2. let us psychoanalyze; impve. 1st pers. pl.

psicoanalicen 1. that they may psychoanalyze; pres. subj. 3rd pers. pl. / *psicoanalizar*. 2. let them psychoanalyze; impve. 3rd pers. pl.

psicoanalices that you may psychoanalyze; pres. subj. 2nd pers. sing. / *psicoanalizar*.

psicoanalizar to psychoanalyze. irr.

publicar to publish. irr.

publique 1. that I may publish; pres. subj. 1st pers. sing. / *publicar*. 2. that he (she/it) may publish; pres. subj. 3rd pers. sing. 3. let him (her/it) publish; impve. 3rd pers. sing.

publiqué I published; past 1st pers. sing. / *publicar*.

publiquéis that you (all) may publish; pres. subj. 2nd pers. pl. / *publicar*.

publiquemos 1. that we may publish; pres. subj. 1st pers. pl. / *publicar*. 2. let us publish; impve. 1st pers. pl.

publiquen 1. that they may publish; pres. subj. 3rd pers. pl. / *publicar*. 2. let them publish; impve. 3rd pers. pl.

publiques that you may publish; pres. subj. 2nd pers. sing. / *publicar*.

pude I was able; past 1st pers. sing. / *poder*.

pudelar to puddle. reg.

pudiendo being able; pres. part. / *poder*.

pudiera 1. that I might be able; imp. subj. 1st pers. sing. / *poder*. 2. that he (she/it) might be able; imp. subj. 3rd pers. sing.

pudierais that you (all) might be able; imp. subj. 2nd pers pl. / *poder*.

pudiéramos that we might be able; imp. subj. 1st pers. pl. / *poder*.

pudieran that they might be able; imp. subj. 3rd pers. pl. / *poder*.

pudieras that you might be able; imp. subj. 2nd pers. sing. / *poder*.

pudieron they were able; past 3rd pers. pl. / *poder*.

pudiese 1. that I might be able; imp. subj. 1st pers. sing. / *poder*. 2. that he (she/it) might be able; imp. subj. 3rd pers. sing.

pudieseis that you (all) might be able; imp. subj. 2nd pers pl. / *poder*.

pudiésemos that we might be able; imp. subj. 1st pers. pl. / *poder*.

pudiesen that they might be able; imp. subj. 3rd pers. pl. / *poder*.

pudieses that you might be able; imp. subj. 2nd pers. sing. / *poder*.

pudimos we were able; past 1st pers. pl. / *poder*.

pudiste you were able; past 2nd pers. sing. / *poder*.

pudisteis you (all) were able; past 2nd pers. pl. / *poder*.

pudo he (she/it) was able; past 3rd pers. sing. / *poder*.

pudra 1. that I may rot; pres. subj. 1st pers. sing. / *podrir/pudrir*. 2. that he (she/it) may rot; pres. subj. 3rd pers. sing. 3. let him (her/it) rot; impve. 3rd pers. sing.

pudráis that you (all) may rot; pres. subj. 2nd pers. pl. / *podrir/pudrir*.

pudrámonos let us rot; impve. 1st pers. pl. / *pudirse*.

pudramos 1. that we may rot; pres. subj. 1st pers. pl. / *podrir/pudrir*. 2. let us rot; impve. 1st pers. pl.

pudran 1. that they may rot; pres. subj. 3rd pers. pl. / *podrir/pudrir*. 2. let them rot; impve. 3rd pers. pl.

púdranse let them rot; impve. 3rd pers. pl. / *pudirse*.

pudras that you may rot; pres. subj. 2nd pers. sing. / *podrir/pudrir*.

púdrase let him (her/it) rot; impve. 3rd pers. sing. / *pudirse*.

pudre 1. he (she/it) rots; pres. ind. 3rd pers. sing. / *podrir/pudrir*. 2. (you) rot; impve. 2nd pers. sing.

pudren they rot; pres. ind. 3rd pers. pl. / *podrir/pudrir*.

pudres you rot; pres. ind. 2nd pers. sing. / *podrir/pudrir*.

púdrete (you) rot; impve. 2nd pers. sing. / *pudirse*.

pudriendo rotting; pres. part. / *podrir/pudrir*.

pudriéndose rotting; pres. part. / *pudrirse*.

pudriera 1. that I might rot; imp. subj. 1st pers. sing. / *podrir/pudrir*. 2. that he (she/it) might rot; imp. subj. 3rd pers. sing.

pudrierais that you (all) might rot; imp. subj. 2nd pers pl. / *podrir/pudrir*.

pudriéramos that we might rot; imp. subj. 1st pers. pl. / *podrir/pudrir*.

pudrieran that they might rot; imp. subj. 3rd pers. pl. / *podrir/pudrir*.

pudrieras that you might rot; imp. subj. 2nd pers. sing. / *podrir/pudrir*.

pudrieron they rotted; past 3rd pers. pl. / *podrir/pudrir*.

pudriese 1. that I might rot; imp. subj. 1st pers. sing. / *podrir/pudrir*. 2. that he (she/it) might rot; imp. subj. 3rd pers. sing.

pudrieseis that you (all) might rot; imp. subj. 2nd pers pl. / *podrir/pudrir*.

pudriésemos that we might rot; imp. subj. 1st pers. pl. / *podrir/pudrir*.

pudriesen that they might rot; imp. subj. 3rd pers. pl. / *podrir/pudrir*.

pudrieses that you might rot; imp. subj. 2nd pers. sing. / *podrir/pudrir*.

pudrió he (she/it) rotted; past 3rd pers. sing. / *podrir/pudrir*.

pudrir to rot. irr.

pudrirse to rot. irr.

pudro I rot; pres. ind. 1st pers. sing. / *podrir/pudrir*.

puebla 1. he (she/it) populates; pres. ind. 3rd pers. sing. / *poblar*. 2. (you) populate; impve. 2nd pers. sing.

pueblan they populate; pres. ind. 3rd pers. pl. / *poblar*.

pueblas you populate; pres. ind. 2nd pers. sing. / *poblar*.

puéblate (you) bud; impve. 2nd pers. sing. / *poblarse*.

pueble 1. that I may populate; pres. subj. 1st pers. sing. / *poblar*. 2. that he (she/it) may populate; pres. subj. 3rd pers. sing. 3. let him (her/it) populate; impve. 3rd pers. sing.

pueblen 1. that they may populate; pres. subj. 3rd pers. pl. / *poblar.* 2. let them populate; impve. 3rd pers. pl.

puéblense let them bud; impve. 3rd pers. pl. / *poblarse.*

puebles that you may populate; pres. subj. 2nd pers. sing. / *poblar.*

puéblese let him (her/it) bud; impve. 3rd pers. sing. / *poblarse.*

pueblo I populate; pres. ind. 1st pers. sing. / *poblar.*

pueda 1. that I may be able; pres. subj. 1st pers. sing. / *poder.* 2. that he (she/it) may be able; pres. subj. 3rd pers. sing. 3. let him (her/it) be able; impve. 3rd pers. sing.

puedan 1. that they may be able; pres. subj. 3rd pers. pl. / *poder.* 2. let them be able; impve. 3rd pers. pl.

puedas that you may be able; pres. subj. 2nd pers. sing. / *poder.*

puede 1. he (she/it) is able; pres. ind. 3rd pers. sing. / *poder.* 2. (you) be able; impve. 2nd pers. sing.

pueden they are able; pres. ind. 3rd pers. pl. / *poder.*

puedes you are able; pres. ind. 2nd pers. sing. / *poder.*

puedo I am able; pres. ind. 1st pers. sing. / *poder.*

puesto put; past part. / *poner.*

pugnar to struggle. reg.

pujar to push ahead or to falter. reg.

pulámonos let us get dressed up; impve. 1st pers. pl. / *pulirse.*

púlanse let them get dressed up; impve. 3rd pers. pl. / *pulirse.*

púlase let him (her/it) get dressed up; impve. 3rd pers. sing. / *pulirse.*

púlete (you) get dressed up; impve. 2nd pers. sing. / *pulirse.*

puliéndose getting dressed up; pres. part. / *pulirse.*

pulimentar to polish. reg.

pulíos (you all) get dressed up; impve. 2nd pers. pl. / *pulirse.*

pulir to polish. reg.

pulirse to get dressed up. reg.

pulsar to touch or to pulsate. reg.

pulsear to hand wrestle. reg.

pulular to swarm. reg.

pulverice 1. that I may pulverize; pres. subj. 1st pers. sing. / *pulverizar.* 2. that he (she/it) may pulverize; pres. subj. 3rd pers. sing. 3. let him (her/it) pulverize; impve. 3rd pers. sing.

pulvericé I pulverized; past 1st pers. sing. / *pulverizar.*

pulvericéis that you (all) may pulverize; pres. subj. 2nd pers. pl. / *pulverizar.*

pulvericemos 1. that we may pulverize; pres. subj. 1st pers. pl. / *pulverizar.* 2. let us pulverize; impve. 1st pers. pl.

pulvericen 1. that they may pulverize; pres. subj. 3rd pers. pl. / *pulverizar.* 2. let them pulverize; impve. 3rd pers. pl.

pulverices that you may pulverize; pres. subj. 2nd pers. sing. / *pulverizar.*

pulverizar to pulverize. irr.

punce 1. that I may prick; pres. subj. 1st pers. sing. / *punzar.* 2. that he (she/it) may prick; pres. subj. 3rd pers. sing. 3. let him (her/it) prick; impve. 3rd pers. sing.

puncé I pricked; past 1st pers. sing. / *punzar.*

puncéis that you (all) may prick; pres. subj. 2nd pers. pl. / *punzar.*

puncemos 1. that we may prick; pres. subj. 1st pers. pl. / *punzar.* 2. let us prick; impve. 1st pers. pl.

puncen 1. that they may prick; pres. subj. 3rd pers. pl. / *punzar.* 2. let them prick; impve. 3rd pers. pl.

punces that you may prick; pres. subj. 2nd pers. sing. / *punzar.*

pungir to prick. irr.

punja 1. that I may prick; pres. subj. 1st pers. sing. / *pungir.* 2. that he (she/it) may prick; pres. subj. 3rd pers. sing. 3. let him (her/it) prick; impve. 3rd pers. sing.

punjáis that you (all) may prick; pres. subj. 2nd pers. pl. / *pungir.*

punjamos 1. that we may prick; pres. subj. 1st pers. pl. / *pungir.* 2. let us prick; impve. 1st pers. pl.

punjan 1. that they may prick; pres. subj. 3rd pers. pl. / *pungir.* 2. let them prick; impve. 3rd pers. pl.

punjas that you may prick; pres. subj. 2nd pers. sing. / *pungir.*

punjo I prick; pres. ind. 1st pers. sing. / *pungir.*

puntear to dot or to play (a guitar). reg.

puntúa 1. he (she/it) punctuates; pres. ind. 3rd pers. sing. / *puntuar.* 2. (you) punctuate; impve. 2nd pers. sing.

puntualice 1. that I may fix in my mind; pres. subj. 1st pers. sing. / *puntualizar.* 2. that he (she/it) may fix in his (her/its) mind; pres. subj. 3rd pers. sing. 3. let him (her/it) fix in his (her/its) mind; impve. 3rd pers. sing.

puntualicé I fixed in my mind; past 1st pers. sing. / *puntualizar.*

puntualicéis that you (all) may fix in your mind; pres. subj. 2nd pers. pl. / *puntualizar.*

puntualicemos 1. that we may fix in our minds; pres. subj. 1st pers. pl. / *puntualizar.* 2. let us fix in our minds; impve. 1st pers. pl.

puntualicen 1. that they may fix in their minds; pres. subj. 3rd pers. pl. / *puntualizar.* 2. let them fix in their minds; impve. 3rd pers. pl.

puntualices that you may fix in your mind; pres. subj. 2nd pers. sing. / *puntualizar.*

puntualizar to fix in one's mind. irr.

puntúan they punctuate; pres. ind. 3rd pers. pl. / *puntuar.*

puntuar to punctuate. irr.

puntúas you punctuate; pres. ind. 2nd pers. sing. / *puntuar.*

puntúe 1. that I may punctuate; pres. subj. 1st pers. sing. / *puntuar.* 2. that he (she/it) may punctuate; pres. subj. 3rd pers. sing. 3. let him (her/it) punctuate; impve. 3rd pers. sing.

puntúen 1. that they may punctuate; pres. subj. 3rd pers. pl. / *puntuar.* 2. let them punctuate; impve. 3rd pers. pl.

puntúes that you may punctuate; pres. subj. 2nd pers. sing. / *puntuar.*

puntúo I punctuate; pres. ind. 1st pers. sing. / *puntuar.*

punzar to prick. irr.

purgándose taking a laxative; pres. part. / *purgarse.*

purgaos (you all) take a laxative; impve. 2nd pers. pl. / *purgarse.*

purgar to purge. irr.

purgarse to take a laxative. irr.

púrgate (you) take a laxative; impve. 2nd pers. sing. / *purgarse.*

purgue 1. that I may purge; pres. subj. 1st pers. sing. / *purgar.* 2. that he (she/it) may purge; pres. subj. 3rd pers. sing. 3. let him (her/it) purge; impve. 3rd pers. sing.

purgué I purged; past 1st pers. sing. / *purgar.*

purguéis that you (all) may purge; pres. subj. 2nd pers. pl. / *purgar.*

purguémonos let us take a laxative; impve. 1st pers. pl. / *purgarse.*

purguemos 1. that we may purge; pres. subj. 1st pers. pl. / *purgar.* 2. let us purge; impve. 1st pers. pl.

purguen 1. that they may purge; pres. subj. 3rd pers. pl. / *purgar.* 2. let them purge; impve. 3rd pers. pl.

púrguense let them take a laxative; impve. 3rd pers. pl. / *purgarse.*

purgues that you may purge; pres. subj. 2nd pers. sing. / *purgar.*

púrguese let him (her/it) take a laxative; impve. 3rd pers. sing. / *purgarse.*

purificar to purify. irr.

purifique 1. that I may purify; pres. subj. 1st pers. sing. / *purificar.* 2. that he (she/it) may purify; pres. subj. 3rd pers. sing. 3. let him (her/it) purify; impve. 3rd pers. sing.

purifiqué I purified; past 1st pers. sing. / *purificar.*

purifiquéis that you (all) may purify; pres. subj. 2nd pers. pl. / *purificar.*

purifiquemos 1. that we may purify; pres. subj. 1st pers. pl. / *purificar.* 2. let us purify; impve. 1st pers. pl.

purifiquen 1. that they may purify; pres. subj. 3rd pers. pl. / *purificar.* 2. let them purify; impve. 3rd pers. pl.

purifiques that you may purify; pres. subj. 2nd pers. sing. / *purificar.*

puse I put; pres. ind. 1st pers. sing. / *poner.*

pusiera 1. that I might put; imp. subj. 1st pers. sing. / *poner.* 2. that he (she/it) might put; imp. subj. 3rd pers. sing.

pusierais that you (all) might put; imp. subj. 2nd pers pl. / *poner.*

pusiéramos that we might put; imp. subj. 1st pers. pl. / *poner.*

pusieran that they might put; imp. subj. 3rd pers. pl. / *poner.*

pusieras that you might put; imp. subj. 2nd pers. sing. / *poner.*

pusieron they put; past 3rd pers. pl. / *poner.*

pusiese 1. that I might put; imp. subj. 1st pers. sing. / *poner.* 2. that he (she/it) might put; imp. subj. 3rd pers. sing.

pusieseis that you (all) might put; imp. subj. 2nd pers pl. / *poner.*

pusiésemos that we might put; imp. subj. 1st pers. pl. / *poner.*

pusiesen that they might put; imp. subj. 3rd pers. pl. / *poner.*

pusieses that you might put; imp. subj. 2nd pers. sing. / *poner.*

pusimos we put; past 1st pers. pl. / *poner.*

pusiste you put; past 2nd pers. sing. / *poner.*

pusisteis you (all) put; past 2nd pers. pl. / *poner.*

puso he (she/it) put; past 3rd pers. sing. / *poner.*

putear to whore. reg.

Q

quebrajar to split or to crack. reg.

quebrándose getting broken; pres. part. / *quebrarse.*

quebrantándose getting broken; pres. part. / *quebrantarse.*

quebrantaos (you all) get broken; impve. 2nd pers. pl. / *quebrantarse.*

quebrantar to break. reg.

quebrantarse to get broken. reg.

quebrántate (you) get broken; impve. 2nd pers. sing. / *quebrantarse.*

quebrantémonos let us get broken; impve. 1st pers. pl. / *quebrantarse.*

quebrántense let them get broken; impve. 3rd pers. pl. / *quebrantarse.*

quebrántese let him (her/it) get broken; impve. 3rd pers. sing. / *quebrantarse.*

quebraos (you all) get broken; impve. 2nd pers. pl. / *quebrarse.*

quebrar to break. irr.

quebrarse to get broken. irr.

quebrémonos let us get broken; impve. 1st pers. pl. / *quebrarse.*

quedándose staying; pres. part. / *quedarse.*

quedaos (you all) stay; impve. 2nd pers. pl. / *quedarse.*

quedar to remain or to become. reg.

quedarse to stay. reg.

quédate (you) stay; impve. 2nd pers. sing. / *quedarse.*

quedémonos let us stay; impve. 1st pers. pl. / *quedarse.*

quédense let them stay; impve. 3rd pers. pl. / *quedarse.*

quédese let him (her/it) stay; impve. 3rd pers. sing. / *quedarse.*

quejándose complaining; pres. part. / *quejarse.*

quejaos (you all) complain; impve. 2nd pers. pl. / *quejarse.*

quejarse to complain. reg.

quéjate (you) complain; impve. 2nd pers. sing. / *quejarse.*

quejémonos let us complain; impve. 1st pers. pl. / *quejarse.*

quéjense let them complain; impve. 3rd pers. pl. / *quejarse.*

quéjese let him (her/it) complain; impve. 3rd pers. sing. / *quejarse.*

quemándose being hot; pres. part. / *quemarse.*

quemaos (you all) be hot; impve. 2nd pers. pl. / *quemarse.*

quemar to burn. reg.

quemarse to be hot. reg.

quémate (you) be hot; impve. 2nd pers. sing. / *quemarse.*

quemémonos let us be hot; impve. 1st pers. pl. / *quemarse.*

quémense let them be hot; impve. 3rd pers. pl. / *quemarse.*

quémese let him (her/it) be hot; impve. 3rd pers. sing. / *quemarse.*

quepa 1. that I may fit; pres. subj. 1st pers. sing. / *caber.* 2. that he (she/it) may fit; pres. subj. 3rd pers. sing. 3. let him (her/it) fit; impve. 3rd pers. sing.

quepáis that you (all) may fit; pres. subj. 2nd pers. pl. / *caber.*

quepamos 1. that we may fit; pres. subj. 1st pers. pl. / *caber.* 2. let us fit; impve. 1st pers. pl.

quepan 1. that they may fit; pres. subj. 3rd pers. pl. / *caber.* 2. let them fit; impve. 3rd pers. pl.

quepas that you may fit; pres. subj. 2nd pers. sing. / *caber.*

quepo I fit; pres. ind. 1st pers. sing. / *caber.*

querámonos let us love each other; impve. 1st pers. pl. / *quererse.*

querellándose complaining; pres. part. / *querellarse.*

querellaos (you all) complain; impve. 2nd pers. pl. / *querellarse.*

querellarse to complain. reg.

queréllate (you) complain; impve. 2nd pers. sing. / *querellarse.*

querellémonos let us complain; impve. 1st pers. pl. / *querellarse.*

queréllense let them complain; impve. 3rd pers. pl. / *querellarse.*

queréllese let him (her/it) complain; impve. 3rd pers. sing. / *querellarse.*

quereos (you all) love each other; impve. 2nd pers. pl. / *quererse.*

querer to want or to love. irr.

quererse to love each other. irr.

queriéndose loving each other; pres. part. / *quererse.*

querrá he (she/it) will want; fut. 3rd pers. sing. / *querer.*

querrán they will want; fut. 3rd pers. pl. / *querer.*

querrás you will want; fut. 2nd pers. sing. / *querer.*

querré I shall want; fut. 1st pers. sing. / *querer.*

querréis you (all) will want; fut. 2nd pers. pl. / *querer.*

querremos we shall want; fut. 1st pers. pl. / *querer.*

querría 1. I should want; cond. 1st pers. sing. / *querer.* 2. he (she/it) would want; cond. 3rd pers. sing.

querríais you (all) would want; cond. 2nd pers. pl. / *querer.*

querríamos we should want; cond. 1st pers. pl. / *querer.*

querrían they would want; cond. 3rd pers. pl. / *querer.*

querrías you would want; cond. 2nd pers. sing. / *querer.*

quiebra 1. he (she/it) breaks; pres. ind. 3rd pers. sing. / *quebrar.* 2. (you) break; impve. 2nd pers. sing.

quiebran they break; pres. ind. 3rd pers. pl. / *quebrar.*

quiebras you break; pres. ind. 2nd pers. sing. / *quebrar.*

quiébrate (you) get broken; impve. 2nd pers. sing. / *quebrarse.*

quiebre 1. that I may break; pres. subj. 1st pers. sing. / *quebrar.* 2. that he (she/it) may break; pres. subj. 3rd pers. sing. 3. let him (her/it) break; impve. 3rd pers. sing.

quiebren 1. that they may break; pres. subj. 3rd pers. pl. / *quebrar.* 2. let them break; impve. 3rd pers. pl.

quiébrense let them get broken; impve. 3rd pers. pl. / *quebrarse.*

quiebres that you may break; pres. subj. 2nd pers. sing. / *quebrar.*

quiébrese let him (her/it) get broken; impve. 3rd pers. sing. / *quebrarse.*

quiebro I break; pres. ind. 1st pers. sing. / *quebrar.*

quiera 1. that I may want; pres. subj. 1st pers. sing. / *querer.* 2. that he (she/it) may want; pres. subj. 3rd pers. sing. 3. let him (her/it) want; impve. 3rd pers. sing.

quieran 1. that they may want; pres. subj. 3rd pers. pl. / *querer.* 2. let them want; impve. 3rd pers. pl.

quiéranse let them love each other; impve. 3rd pers. pl. / *quererse.*

quieras that you may want; pres. subj. 2nd pers. sing. / *querer.*

quiérase let him (her/it) love each other; impve. 3rd pers. sing. / *quererse.*

quiere 1. he (she/it) wants; pres. ind. 3rd pers. sing. / *querer.* 2. (you) want; impve. 2nd pers. sing.

quieren they want; pres. ind. 3rd pers. pl. / *querer.*

quieres you want; pres. ind. 2nd pers. sing. / *querer.*

quiérete (you) love each other; impve. 2nd pers. sing. / *quererse.*

quiero I want; pres. ind. 1st pers. sing. / *querer.*

quilatar to assay or to purify. reg.

quintaesenciar to purify. reg.

quintar to draft for the military. reg.

quintuplicar to multiply by five. irr.

quintuplique 1. that I may multiply by five; pres. subj. 1st pers. sing. / *quintuplicar.* 2. that he (she/it) may multiply by five; pres. subj. 3rd pers. sing. 3. let him (her/it) multiply by five; impve. 3rd pers. sing.

quintupliqué I multiplied by five; past 1st pers. sing. / *quintuplicar.*

quintupliquéis that you (all) may multiply by five; pres. subj. 2nd pers. pl. / *quintuplicar.*

quintupliquemos 1. that we may multiply by five; pres. subj. 1st pers. pl. / *quintuplicar*. 2. let us multiply by five; impve. 1st pers. pl.

quintupliquen 1. that they may multiply by five; pres. subj. 3rd pers. pl. / *quintuplicar*. 2. let them multiply by five; impve. 3rd pers. pl.

quintupliques that you may multiply by five; pres. subj. 2nd pers. sing. / *quintuplicar*.

quise I wanted; past 1st pers. sing. / *querer*.

quisiera 1. that I might want; imp. subj. 1st pers. sing. / *querer*. 2. that he (she/it) might want; imp. subj. 3rd pers. sing.

quisierais that you (all) might want; imp. subj. 2nd pers pl. / *querer*.

quisiéramos that we might want; imp. subj. 1st pers. pl. / *querer*.

quisieran that they might want; imp. subj. 3rd pers. pl. / *querer*.

quisieras that you might want; imp. subj. 2nd pers. sing. / *querer*.

quisieron they wanted; past 3rd pers. pl. / *querer*.

quisiese 1. that I might want; imp. subj. 1st pers. sing. / *querer*. 2. that he (she/it) might want; imp. subj. 3rd pers. sing.

quisieseis that you (all) might want; imp. subj. 2nd pers pl. / *querer*.

quisiésemos that we might want; imp. subj. 1st pers. pl. / *querer*.

quisiesen that they might want; imp. subj. 3rd pers. pl. / *querer*.

quisieses that you might want; imp. subj. 2nd pers. sing. / *querer*.

quisimos we wanted; past 1st pers. pl. / *querer*.

quisiste you wanted; past 2nd pers. sing. / *querer*.

quisisteis you (all) wanted; past 2nd pers. pl. / *querer*.

quiso he (she/it) wanted; past 3rd pers. sing. / *querer*.

quitándose taking off (clothes); pres. part. / *quitarse*.

quitaos (you all) take off (clothes); impve. 2nd pers. pl. / *quitarse*.

quitar to remove. reg.

quitarse to take off (clothes). reg.

quítate (you) take off (clothes); impve. 2nd pers. sing. / *quitarse*.

quitémonos let us take off (clothes); impve. 1st pers. pl. / *quitarse*.

quítense let them take off (clothes); impve. 3rd pers. pl. / *quitarse*.

quítese let him (her/it) take off (clothes); impve. 3rd pers. sing. / *quitarse*.

R

rabear to wag the tail. reg.

rabiar to rage or to have rabies. reg.

rabosear to fray. reg.

raciocinar to reason. reg.

racionar to ration. reg.

radiar to radiate or to broadcast. reg.

radicándose settling; pres. part. / *radicarse*.

radicaos (you all) settle; impve. 2nd pers. pl. / *radicarse*.

radicar to take root. irr.

radicarse to settle. irr.

radícate (you) settle; impve. 2nd pers. sing. / *radicarse*.

radiodifundir to broadcast. reg.

radiografía 1. he (she/it) x-rays; pres. ind. 3rd pers. sing. / *radiografiar*. 2. (you) x-ray; impve. 2nd pers. sing.

radiografían they x-ray; pres. ind. 3rd pers. pl. / *radiografiar*.

radiografiar to x-ray. irr.

radiografías you x-ray; pres. ind. 2nd pers. sing. / *radiografiar*.

radiografíe 1. that I may x-ray; pres. subj. 1st pers. sing. / *radiografiar*. 2. that he (she/it) may x-ray; pres. subj. 3rd pers. sing. 3. let him (her/it) x-ray; impve. 3rd pers. sing.

radiografíen 1. that they may x-ray; pres. subj. 3rd pers. pl. / *radiografiar*. 2. let them x-ray; impve. 3rd pers. pl.

radiografíes that you may x-ray; pres. subj. 2nd pers. sing. / *radiografiar*.

radiografío I x-ray; pres. ind. 1st pers. sing. / *radiografiar*.

radique 1. that I may take root; pres. subj. 1st pers. sing. / *radicar*. 2. that he (she/it) may take root; pres. subj. 3rd pers. sing. 3. let him (her/it) take root; impve. 3rd pers. sing.

radiqué I took root; past 1st pers. sing. / *radicar*.

radiquéis that you (all) may take root; pres. subj. 2nd pers. pl. / *radicar*.

radiquémonos let us settle; impve. 1st pers. pl. / *radicarse*.

radiquemos 1. that we may take root; pres. subj. 1st pers. pl. / *radicar*. 2. let us take root; impve. 1st pers. pl.

radiquen 1. that they may take root; pres. subj. 3rd pers. pl. / *radicar*. 2. let them take root; impve. 3rd pers. pl.

radíquense let them settle; impve. 3rd pers. pl. / *radicarse*.

radiques that you may take root; pres. subj. 2nd pers. sing. / *radicar*.

radíquese let him (her/it) settle; impve. 3rd pers. sing. / *radicarse*.

raeos (you all) become worn; impve. 2nd pers. pl. / *raerse*.

raer to scrape off. irr.

raerse to become worn. irr.

ráete (you) become worn; impve. 2nd pers. sing. / *raerse*.

raído scraped off; past part. / *raer*.

raiga 1. that I may scrape off; pres. subj. 1st pers. sing. / *raer*. 2. that he (she/it) may scrape off; pres. subj. 3rd pers. sing. 3. let him (her/it) scrape off; impve. 3rd pers. sing.

raigáis that you (all) may scrape off; pres. subj. 2nd pers. pl. / *raer*.

raigámonos let us become worn; impve. 1st pers. pl. / *raerse.*

raigamos 1. that we may scrape off; pres. subj. 1st pers. pl. / *raer.* 2. let us scrape off; impve. 1st pers. pl.

raigan 1. that they may scrape off; pres. subj. 3rd pers. pl. / *raer.* 2. let them scrape off; impve. 3rd pers. pl.

raíganse let them become worn; impve. 3rd pers. pl. / *raerse.*

raigas that you may scrape off; pres. subj. 2nd pers. sing. / *raer.*

raígase let him (her/it) become worn; impve. 3rd pers. sing. / *raerse.*

raigo I scrape off; pres. ind. 1st pers. sing. / *raer.*

rajándose quitting; pres. part. / *rajarse.*

rajaos (you all) quit; impve. 2nd pers. pl. / *rajarse.*

rajar to split. reg.

rajarse to quit. reg.

rájate (you) quit; impve. 2nd pers. sing. / *rajarse.*

rajémonos let us quit; impve. 1st pers. pl. / *rajarse.*

rájense let them quit; impve. 3rd pers. pl. / *rajarse.*

rájese let him (her/it) quit; impve. 3rd pers. sing. / *rajarse.*

ralear to thin out. reg.

rallar to grate or to annoy. reg.

ramificándose ramifying; pres. part. / *ramificarse.*

ramificaos (you all) ramify; impve. 2nd pers. pl. / *ramificarse.*

ramificarse to ramify or to branch off. irr.

ramifícate (you) ramify; impve. 2nd pers. sing. / *ramificarse.*

ramifique 1. that I may ramify; pres. subj. 1st pers. sing. / *ramificarse.* 2. that he (she/it) may ramify; pres. subj. 3rd pers. sing.

ramifiqué I ramified; past 1st pers. sing. / *ramificarse.*

ramifiquéis that you (all) may ramify; pres. subj. 2nd pers. pl. / *ramificarse.*

ramifiquémonos let us ramify; impve. 1st pers. pl. / *ramificarse.*

ramifiquemos that we may ramify; pres. subj. 1st pers. pl. / *ramificarse.*

ramifiquen that they may ramify; pres. subj. 3rd pers. pl. / *ramificarse.*

ramifíquense let them ramify; impve. 3rd pers. pl. / *ramificarse.*

ramifiques that you may ramify; pres. subj. 2nd pers. sing. / *ramificarse.*

ramifíquese let him (her/it) ramify; impve. 3rd pers. sing. / *ramificarse.*

ramonear to cut off twigs. reg.

ranciándose going rancid; pres. part. / *ranciarse.*

ranciarse to go rancid. reg.

ranciense let them go rancid; impve. 3rd pers. pl. / *ranciarse.*

rancíese let it go rancid; impve. 3rd pers. sing. / *ranciarse.*

rancheándose settling in huts; pres. part. / *ranchearse.*

rancheaos (you all) settle in huts; impve. 2nd pers. pl. / *ranchearse.*

ranchear to settle in huts. reg.

ranchearse to settle in huts. reg.

ranchéate (you) settle in huts; impve. 2nd pers. sing. / *ranchearse.*

rancheémonos let us settle in huts; impve. 1st pers. pl. / *ranchearse.*

ranchéense let them settle in huts; impve. 3rd pers. pl. / *ranchearse.*

ranchéese let him (her/it) settle in huts; impve. 3rd pers. sing. / *ranchearse.*

ranurar to groove. reg.

rapar to shave. reg.

rapiñar to plunder. reg.

raposear to be foxy. reg.

raptar to abduct. reg.

rarefacer to rarefy. irr.

rarefaga 1. that I may rarefy; pres. subj. 1st pers. sing. / *rarefacer.* 2. that he (she/it) may rarefy; pres. subj. 3rd pers. sing. 3. let him (her/it) rarefy; impve. 3rd pers. sing.

rarefagáis that you (all) may rarefy; pres. subj. 2nd pers. pl. / *rarefacer.*

rarefagamos 1. that we may rarefy; pres. subj. 1st pers. pl. / *rarefacer.* 2. let us rarefy; impve. 1st pers. pl.

rarefagan 1. that they may rarefy; pres. subj. 3rd pers. pl. / *rarefacer.* 2. let them rarefy; impve. 3rd pers. pl.

rarefagas that you may rarefy; pres. subj. 2nd pers. sing. / *rarefacer.*

rarefago I rarefy; pres. ind. 1st pers. sing. / *rarefacer.*

rarefará he (she/it) will rarefy; fut. 3rd pers. sing. / *rarefacer.*

rarefarán they will rarefy; fut. 3rd pers. pl. / *rarefacer.*

rarefarás you will rarefy; fut. 2nd pers. sing. / *rarefacer.*

rarefaré I shall rarefy; fut. 1st pers. sing. / *rarefacer.*

rarefaréis you (all) will rarefy; fut. 2nd pers. pl. / *rarefacer.*

rarefaremos we shall rarefy; fut. 1st pers. pl. / *rarefacer.*

rarefaría 1. I should rarefy; cond. 1st pers. sing. / *rarefacer.* 2. he (she/it) would rarefy; cond. 3rd pers. sing.

rarefaríais you (all) would rarefy; cond. 2nd pers. pl. / *rarefacer.*

rarefaríamos we should rarefy; cond. 1st pers. pl. / *rarefacer.*

rarefarían they would rarefy; cond. 3rd pers. pl. / *rarefacer.*

rarefarías you would rarefy; cond. 2nd pers. sing. / *rarefacer.*

rarefaz (you) rarefy; impve. 2nd pers. sing. / *rarefacer.*

rarefecho rarefied; past part. / *rarefacer.*

rarefice I rarefied; past 1st pers. sing. / *rarefacer.*

rareficiera 1. that I might rarefy; imp. subj. 1st pers. sing. / *rarefacer*. 2. that he (she/it) might rarefy; imp. subj. 3rd pers. sing.

rareficierais that you (all) might rarefy; imp. subj. 2nd pers pl. / *rarefacer*.

rareficiéramos that we might rarefy; imp. subj. 1st pers. pl. / *rarefacer*.

rareficieran that they might rarefy; imp. subj. 3rd pers. pl. / *rarefacer*.

rareficieras that you might rarefy; imp. subj. 2nd pers. sing. / *rarefacer*.

rareficieron they rarefied; past 3rd pers. pl. / *rarefacer*.

rareficiese 1. that I might rarefy; imp. subj. 1st pers. sing. / *rarefacer*. 2. that he (she/it) might rarefy; imp. subj. 3rd pers. sing.

rareficieseis that you (all) might rarefy; imp. subj. 2nd pers pl. / *rarefacer*.

rareficiésemos that we might rarefy; imp. subj. 1st pers. pl. / *rarefacer*.

rareficiesen that they might rarefy; imp. subj. 3rd pers. pl. / *rarefacer*.

rareficieses that you might rarefy; imp. subj. 2nd pers. sing. / *rarefacer*.

rareficimos we rarefied; past 1st pers. pl. / *rarefacer*.

rareficiste you rarefied; past 2nd pers. sing. / *rarefacer*.

rareficisteis you (all) rarefied; past 2nd pers. pl. / *rarefacer*.

rarefizo he (she/it) rarefied; past 3rd pers. sing. / *rarefacer*.

rarificar to rarefy. irr.

rarifique 1. that I may rarefy; pres. subj. 1st pers. sing. / *rarificar*. 2. that he (she/it) may rarefy; pres. subj. 3rd pers. sing. 3. let him (her/it) rarefy; impve. 3rd pers. sing.

rarifiqué I rarefied; past 1st pers. sing. / *rarificar*.

rarifiquéis that you (all) may rarefy; pres. subj. 2nd pers. pl. / *rarificar*.

rarifiquemos 1. that we may rarefy; pres. subj. 1st pers. pl. / *rarificar*. 2. let us rarefy; impve. 1st pers. pl.

rarifiquen 1. that they may rarefy; pres. subj. 3rd pers. pl. / *rarificar*. 2. let them rarefy; impve. 3rd pers. pl.

rarifiques that you may rarefy; pres. subj. 2nd pers. sing. / *rarificar*.

rasándose clearing; pres. part. / *rasarse*.

rasaos (you all) clear; impve. 2nd pers. pl. / *rasarse*.

rasar to skim or to level off. reg.

rasarse to clear. reg.

rásate (you) clear; impve. 2nd pers. sing. / *rasarse*.

rascándose getting drunk; pres. part. / *rascarse*.

rascaos (you all) get drunk; impve. 2nd pers. pl. / *rascarse*.

rascar to scratch. irr.

rascarse to get drunk. irr.

ráscate (you) get drunk; impve. 2nd pers. sing. / *rascarse*.

rasémonos let us clear; impve. 1st pers. pl. / *rasarse*.

rásense let them clear; impve. 3rd pers. pl. / *rasarse*.

rásese let him (her/it) clear; impve. 3rd pers. sing. / *rasarse*.

rasgándose getting torn; pres. part. / *rasgarse*.

rasgaos (you all) get torn; impve. 2nd pers. pl. / *rasgarse*.

rasgar to tear. irr.

rasgarse to get torn. irr.

rásgate (you) get torn; impve. 2nd pers. sing. / *rasgarse*.

rasgue 1. that I may tear; pres. subj. 1st pers. sing. / *rasgar*. 2. that he (she/it) may tear; pres. subj. 3rd pers. sing. 3. let him (her/it) tear; impve. 3rd pers. sing.

rasgué I tore; past 1st pers. sing. / *rasgar*.

rasguear to strum. reg.

rasguéis that you (all) may tear; pres. subj. 2nd pers. pl. / *rasgar*.

rasguémonos let us get torn; impve. 1st pers. pl. / *rasgarse*.

rasguemos 1. that we may tear; pres. subj. 1st pers. pl. / *rasgar*. 2. let us tear; impve. 1st pers. pl.

rasguen 1. that they may tear; pres. subj. 3rd pers. pl. / *rasgar*. 2. let them tear; impve. 3rd pers. pl.

rásguense let them get torn; impve. 3rd pers. pl. / *rasgarse*.

rasgues that you may tear; pres. subj. 2nd pers. sing. / *rasgar*.

rásguese let him (her/it) get torn; impve. 3rd pers. sing. / *rasgarse*.

rasguñar to scratch. reg.

raspar to rasp or to scrape. reg.

raspear to scratch (pen). reg.

rasque 1. that I may scratch; pres. subj. 1st pers. sing. / *rascar*. 2. that he (she/it) may scratch; pres. subj. 3rd pers. sing. 3. let him (her/it) scratch; impve. 3rd pers. sing.

rasqué I scratched; past 1st pers. sing. / *rascar*.

rasquéis that you (all) may scratch; pres. subj. 2nd pers. pl. / *rascar*.

rasquémonos let us get drunk; impve. 1st pers. pl. / *rascarse*.

rasquemos 1. that we may scratch; pres. subj. 1st pers. pl. / *rascar*. 2. let us scratch; impve. 1st pers. pl.

rasquen 1. that they may scratch; pres. subj. 3rd pers. pl. / *rascar*. 2. let them scratch; impve. 3rd pers. pl.

rásquense let them get drunk; impve. 3rd pers. pl. / *rascarse*.

rasques that you may scratch; pres. subj. 2nd pers. sing. / *rascar*.

rásquese let him (her/it) get drunk; impve. 3rd pers. sing. / *rascarse*.

rasquetear to scrape. reg.

rastrear to trail or to skim. reg.

rastrillar to comb. reg.

rasurándose shaving; pres. part. / *rasurarse*.

rasuraos (you all) shave; impve. 2nd pers. pl. / *rasurarse*.

rasurar to shave. reg.

rasurarse to shave. reg.

rasúrate (you) shave; impve. 2nd pers. sing. / *rasurarse*.

rasurémonos let us shave; impve. 1st pers. pl. / *rasurarse*.

rasúrense let them shave; impve. 3rd pers. pl. / *rasurarse*.

rasúrese let him (her/it) shave; impve. 3rd pers. sing. / *rasurarse*.

ratear to pick pockets. reg.

ratificar to ratify. irr.

ratifique 1. that I may ratify; pres. subj. 1st pers. sing. / *ratificar*. 2. that he (she/it) may ratify; pres. subj. 3rd pers. sing. 3. let him (her/it) ratify; impve. 3rd pers. sing.

ratifiqué I ratified; past 1st pers. sing. / *ratificar*.

ratifiquéis that you (all) may ratify; pres. subj. 2nd pers. pl. / *ratificar*.

ratifiquemos 1. that we may ratify; pres. subj. 1st pers. pl. / *ratificar*. 2. let us ratify; impve. 1st pers. pl.

ratifiquen 1. that they may ratify; pres. subj. 3rd pers. pl. / *ratificar*. 2. let them ratify; impve. 3rd pers. pl.

ratifiques that you may ratify; pres. subj. 2nd pers. sing. / *ratificar*.

ratonar to gnaw. reg.

rayar to draw lines on. reg.

rayendo scraping off; pres. part. / *raer*.

rayéndose becoming worn; pres. part. / *raerse*.

rayera 1. that I might scrape off; imp. subj. 1st pers. sing. / *raer*. 2. that he (she/it) might scrape off; imp. subj. 3rd pers. sing.

rayerais that you (all) might scrape off; imp. subj. 2nd pers pl. / *raer*.

rayéramos that we might scrape off; imp. subj. 1st pers. pl. / *raer*.

rayeran that they might scrape off; imp. subj. 3rd pers. pl. / *raer*.

rayeras that you might scrape off; imp. subj. 2nd pers. sing. / *raer*.

rayeron they scraped off; past 3rd pers. pl. / *raer*.

rayese 1. that I might scrape off; imp. subj. 1st pers. sing. / *raer*. 2. that he (she/it) might scrape off; imp. subj. 3rd pers. sing.

rayeseis that you (all) might scrape off; imp. subj. 2nd pers pl. / *raer*.

rayésemos that we might scrape off; imp. subj. 1st pers. pl. / *raer*.

rayesen that they might scrape off; imp. subj. 3rd pers. pl. / *raer*.

rayeses that you might scrape off; imp. subj. 2nd pers. sing. / *raer*.

rayo I scrape off; pres. ind. 1st pers. sing. / *raer*.

rayó he (she/it) scraped off; past 3rd pers. sing. / *raer*.

razonar to reason. reg.

reabierto reopened; past part. / *reabrir*.

reabrir to reopen. reg. except for pp.

reaccionar to react. reg.

reactivar to reactivate. reg.

reajustar to readjust. reg.

realce 1. that I may emboss; pres. subj. 1st pers. sing. / *realzar*. 2. that he (she/it) may emboss; pres. subj. 3rd pers. sing. 3. let him (her/it) emboss; impve. 3rd pers. sing.

realcé I embossed; past 1st pers. sing. / *realzar*.

realcéis that you (all) may emboss; pres. subj. 2nd pers. pl. / *realzar*.

realcemos 1. that we may emboss; pres. subj. 1st pers. pl. / *realzar*. 2. let us emboss; impve. 1st pers. pl.

realcen 1. that they may emboss; pres. subj. 3rd pers. pl. / *realzar*. 2. let them emboss; impve. 3rd pers. pl.

realces that you may emboss; pres. subj. 2nd pers. sing. / *realzar*.

realice 1. that I may realize; pres. subj. 1st pers. sing. / *realizar*. 2. that he (she/it) may realize; pres. subj. 3rd pers. sing. 3. let him (her/it) realize; impve. 3rd pers. sing.

realicé I realized; past 1st pers. sing. / *realizar*.

realicéis that you (all) may realize; pres. subj. 2nd pers. pl. / *realizar*.

realicémonos let us be fulfilled; impve. 1st pers. pl. / *realizarse*.

realicemos 1. that we may realize; pres. subj. 1st pers. pl. / *realizar*. 2. let us realize; impve. 1st pers. pl.

realicen 1. that they may realize; pres. subj. 3rd pers. pl. / *realizar*. 2. let them realize; impve. 3rd pers. pl.

realícense let them be fulfilled; impve. 3rd pers. pl. / *realizarse*.

realices that you may realize; pres. subj. 2nd pers. sing. / *realizar*.

realícese let him (her/it) be fulfilled; impve. 3rd pers. sing. / *realizarse*.

realizándose being fulfilled; pres. part. / *realizarse*.

realizaos (you all) be fulfilled; impve. 2nd pers. pl. / *realizarse*.

realizar to realize. irr.

realizarse to be fulfilled. irr.

realízate (you) be fulfilled; impve. 2nd pers. sing. / *realizarse*.

realzar to emboss. irr.

reanimándose reviving; pres. part. / *reanimarse*.

reanimaos (you all) revive; impve. 2nd pers. pl. / *reanimarse*.

reanimar to cheer. reg.

reanimarse to revive. reg.

reanímate (you) revive; impve. 2nd pers. sing. / *reanimarse*.

reanimémonos let us revive; impve. 1st pers. pl. / *reanimarse*.

reanímense let them revive; impve. 3rd pers. pl. / *reanimarse*.

reanímese let him (her/it) revive; impve. 3rd pers. sing. / *reanimarse*.

reanudar to resume or to renew. reg.

reaparecer to reappear. irr.

reaparezca 1. that I may reappear; pres. subj. 1st pers. sing. / *reaparecer.* 2. that he (she/it) may reappear; pres. subj. 3rd pers. sing. 3. let him (her/it) reappear; impve. 3rd pers. sing.

reaparezcáis that you (all) may reappear; pres. subj. 2nd pers. pl. / *reaparecer.*

reaparezcamos 1. that we may reappear; pres. subj. 1st pers. pl. / *reaparecer.* 2. let us reappear; impve. 1st pers. pl.

reaparezcan 1. that they may reappear; pres. subj. 3rd pers. pl. / *reaparecer.* 2. let them reappear; impve. 3rd pers. pl.

reaparezcas that you may reappear; pres. subj. 2nd pers. sing. / *reaparecer.*

reaparezco I reappear; pres. ind. 1st pers. sing. / *reaparecer.*

rearmándose rearming; pres. part. / *rearmarse.*

rearmaos (you all) rearm; impve. 2nd pers. pl. / *rearmarse.*

rearmar to rearm. reg.

rearmarse to rearm. reg.

reármate (you) rearm; impve. 2nd pers. sing. / *rearmarse.*

rearmémonos let us rearm; impve. 1st pers. pl. / *rearmarse.*

reármense let them rearm; impve. 3rd pers. pl. / *rearmarse.*

reármese let him (her/it) rearm; impve. 3rd pers. sing. / *rearmarse.*

reasumir to resume. reg.

reavivar to revive. reg.

rebajándose humbling oneself; pres. part. / *rebajarse.*

rebajaos (you all) humble yourselves; impve. 2nd pers. pl. / *rebajarse.*

rebajar to diminish. reg.

rebajarse to humble oneself. reg.

rebájate (you) humble yourself; impve. 2nd pers. sing. / *rebajarse.*

rebajémonos let us humble ourselves; impve. 1st pers. pl. / *rebajarse.*

rebájense let them humble themselves; impve. 3rd pers. pl. / *rebajarse.*

rebájese let him (her/it) humble himself (herself/itself); impve. 3rd pers. sing. / *rebajarse.*

rebalsándose getting blocked up; pres. part. / *rebalsarse.*

rebalsaos (you all) get blocked up; impve. 2nd pers. pl. / *rebalsarse.*

rebalsar to dam (a stream). reg.

rebalsarse to get blocked up. reg.

rebálsate (you) get blocked up; impve. 2nd pers. sing. / *rebalsarse.*

rebalsémonos let us get blocked up; impve. 1st pers. pl. / *rebalsarse.*

rebálsense let them get blocked up; impve. 3rd pers. pl. / *rebalsarse.*

rebálsese let him (her/it) get blocked up; impve. 3rd pers. sing. / *rebalsarse.*

rebanar to slice. reg.

rebañar to clean up. reg.

rebasar to exceed. reg.

rebatir to repel. reg.

rebelándose rebelling; pres. part. / *rebelarse.*

rebelaos (you all) rebel; impve. 2nd pers. pl. / *rebelarse.*

rebelarse to rebel. reg.

rebélate (you) rebel; impve. 2nd pers. sing. / *rebelarse.*

rebelémonos let us rebel; impve. 1st pers. pl. / *rebelarse.*

rebélense let them rebel; impve. 3rd pers. pl. / *rebelarse.*

rebélese let him (her/it) rebel; impve. 3rd pers. sing. / *rebelarse.*

reblandeceos (you all) soften; impve. 2nd pers. pl. / *reblandecerse.*

reblandecer to soften. irr.

reblandecerse to soften. irr.

reblandécete (you) soften; impve. 2nd pers. sing. / *reblandecerse.*

reblandeciéndose softening; pres. part. / *reblandecerse.*

reblandezca 1. that I may soften; pres. subj. 1st pers. sing. / *reblandecer.* 2. that he (she/it) may soften; pres. subj. 3rd pers. sing. 3. let him (her/it) soften; impve. 3rd pers. sing.

reblandezcáis that you (all) may soften; pres. subj. 2nd pers. pl. / *reblandecer.*

reblandezcámonos let us soften; impve. 1st pers. pl. / *reblandecerse.*

reblandezcamos 1. that we may soften; pres. subj. 1st pers. pl. / *reblandecer.* 2. let us soften; impve. 1st pers. pl.

reblandezcan 1. that they may soften; pres. subj. 3rd pers. pl. / *reblandecer.* 2. let them soften; impve. 3rd pers. pl.

reblandézcanse let them soften; impve. 3rd pers. pl. / *reblandecerse.*

reblandezcas that you may soften; pres. subj. 2nd pers. sing. / *reblandecer.*

reblandézcase let him (her/it) soften; impve. 3rd pers. sing. / *reblandecerse.*

reblandezco I soften; pres. ind. 1st pers. sing. / *reblandecer.*

reboce 1. that I may muffle up; pres. subj. 1st pers. sing. / *rebozar.* 2. that he (she/it) may muffle up; pres. subj. 3rd pers. sing. 3. let him (her/it) muffle up; impve. 3rd pers. sing.

rebocé I muffled up; past 1st pers. sing. / *rebozar.*

rebocéis that you (all) may muffle up; pres. subj. 2nd pers. pl. / *rebozar.*

rebocémonos let us muffle ourselves up; impve. 1st pers. pl. / *rebozar.*

rebocemos 1. that we may muffle up; pres. subj. 1st pers. pl. / *rebozar.* 2. let us muffle up; impve. 1st pers. pl.

rebocen 1. that they may muffle up; pres. subj. 3rd pers. pl. / *rebozar.* 2. let them muffle up; impve. 3rd pers. pl.

rebócense let them muffle themselves up; impve. 3rd pers. pl. / *rebozarse.*

reboces that you may muffle up; pres. subj. 2nd pers. sing. / *rebozar.*

rebócese let him (her) muffle himself (herself) up; impve. 3rd pers. sing. / *rebozarse.*

rebombar to resound. reg.

rebosándose overflowing; pres. part. / *rebosarse.*

rebosaos (you all) overflow; impve. 2nd pers. pl. / *rebosarse.*

rebosar to overflow. reg.

rebosarse to overflow. reg.

rebósate (you) overflow; impve. 2nd pers. sing. / *rebosarse.*

rebosémonos let us overflow; impve. 1st pers. pl. / *rebosarse.*

rebósense let them overflow; impve. 3rd pers. pl. / *rebosarse.*

rebósese let him (her/it) overflow; impve. 3rd pers. sing. / *rebosarse.*

rebotándose becoming upset; pres. part. / *rebotarse.*

rebotaos (you all) become upset; impve. 2nd pers. pl. / *rebotarse.*

rebotar to rebound. reg.

rebotarse to become upset. reg.

rebótate (you) become upset; impve. 2nd pers. sing. / *rebotarse.*

rebotémonos let us become upset; impve. 1st pers. pl. / *rebotarse.*

rebótense let them become upset; impve. 3rd pers. pl. / *rebotarse.*

rebótese let him (her/it) become upset; impve. 3rd pers. sing. / *rebotarse.*

rebozándose muffling oneself up; pres. part. / *rebozarse.*

rebozaos (you all) muffle yourselves up; impve. 2nd pers. pl. / *rebozarse.*

rebozar to muffle up. irr.

rebozarse to muffle oneself up. irr.

rebózate (you) muffle yourself up; impve. 2nd pers. sing. / *rebozarse.*

rebrotar to sprout. reg.

rebufar to blow and snort. reg.

rebujándose wrapping oneself up; pres. part. / *rebujarse.*

rebujaos (you all) wrap yourselves up; impve. 2nd pers. pl. / *rebujarse.*

rebujar to jumble up. reg.

rebujarse to wrap oneself up. reg.

rebújate (you) wrap yourself up; impve. 2nd pers. sing. / *rebujarse.*

rebujémonos let us wrap ourselves up; impve. 1st pers. pl. / *rebujarse.*

rebújense let them wrap themselves up; impve. 3rd pers. pl. / *rebujarse.*

rebújese let him (her/it) wrap himself (herself/itself) up; impve. 3rd pers. sing. / *rebujarse.*

rebullámonos let us stir; impve. 1st pers. pl. / *rebullirse.*

rebúllanse let them stir; impve. 3rd pers. pl. / *rebullirse.*

rebúllase let him (her/it) stir; impve. 3rd pers. sing. / *rebullirse.*

rebullendo stirring; pres. part. / *rebullir.*

rebulléndose stirring; pres. part. / *rebullirse.*

rebullera 1. that I might stir; imp. subj. 1st pers. sing. / *rebullir.* 2. that he (she/it) might stir; imp. subj. 3rd pers. sing.

rebullerais that you (all) might stir; imp. subj. 2nd pers pl. / *rebullir.*

rebulléramos that we might stir; imp. subj. 1st pers. pl. / *rebullir.*

rebulleran that they might stir; imp. subj. 3rd pers. pl. / *rebullir.*

rebulleras that you might stir; imp. subj. 2nd pers. sing. / *rebullir.*

rebulleron they stirred; past 3rd pers. pl. / *rebullir.*

rebullese 1. that I might stir; imp. subj. 1st pers. sing. / *rebullir.* 2. that he (she/it) might stir; imp. subj. 3rd pers. sing.

rebulleseis that you (all) might stir; imp. subj. 2nd pers pl. / *rebullir.*

rebullésemos that we might stir; imp. subj. 1st pers. pl. / *rebullir.*

rebullesen that they might stir; imp. subj. 3rd pers. pl. / *rebullir.*

rebulleses that you might stir; imp. subj. 2nd pers. sing. / *rebullir.*

rebúllete (you) stir; impve. 2nd pers. sing. / *rebullirse.*

rebullíos (you all) stir; impve. 2nd pers. pl. / *rebullirse.*

rebullir to stir. irr.

rebullirse to stir. irr.

rebulló he (she/it) stirred; past 3rd pers. sing. / *rebullir.*

rebumbar to whistle (bullet). reg.

rebuscar to search carefully. irr.

rebuscárselas to manage. reg.

rebusque 1. that I may search carefully; pres. subj. 1st pers. sing. / *rebuscar.* 2. that he (she/it) may search carefully; pres. subj. 3rd pers. sing. 3. let him (her/it) search carefully; impve. 3rd pers. sing.

rebusqué I searched carefully; past 1st pers. sing. / *rebuscar.*

rebusquéis that you (all) may search carefully; pres. subj. 2nd pers. pl. / *rebuscar.*

rebusquemos 1. that we may search carefully; pres. subj. 1st pers. pl. / *rebuscar.* 2. let us search carefully; impve. 1st pers. pl.

rebusquen 1. that they may search carefully; pres. subj. 3rd pers. pl. / *rebuscar.* 2. let them search carefully; impve. 3rd pers. pl.

rebusques that you may search carefully; pres. subj. 2nd pers. sing. / *rebuscar.*

rebuznar to bray. reg.

recabar to request. reg.

recaer to relapse. irr.

recaído relapsed; past part. / *recaer.*

recaiga 1. that I may relapse; pres. subj. 1st pers. sing. / *recaer*. 2. that he (she/it) may relapse; pres. subj. 3rd pers. sing. 3. let him (her/it) relapse; impve. 3rd pers. sing.

recaigáis that you (all) may relapse; pres. subj. 2nd pers. pl. / *recaer*.

recaigamos 1. that we may relapse; pres. subj. 1st pers. pl. / *recaer*. 2. let us relapse; impve. 1st pers. pl.

recaigan 1. that they may relapse; pres. subj. 3rd pers. pl. / *recaer*. 2. let them relapse; impve. 3rd pers. pl.

recaigas that you may relapse; pres. subj. 2nd pers. sing. / *recaer*.

recaigo I relapse; pres. ind. 1st pers. sing. / *recaer*.

recalar to soak or to reach land. reg.

recalcándose harping on; pres. part. / *recalcarse*.

recalcaos (you all) harp on; impve. 2nd pers. pl. / *recalcarse*.

recalcar to emphasize. irr.

recalcarse to harp on. irr.

recálcate (you) harp on; impve. 2nd pers. sing. / *recalcarse*.

recalcitrar to resist. reg.

recalentándose becoming overheated; pres. part. / *recalentarse*.

recaléntaos (you all) become overheated; impve. 2nd pers. pl. / *recalentarse*.

recalentarse to become overheated. irr.

recalentarse to become overheated. irr.

recalentémonos let us become overheated; impve. 1st pers. pl. / *recalentarse*.

recalienta 1. he (she/it) reheats; pres. ind. 3rd pers. sing. / *recalentar*. 2. (you) reheat; impve. 2nd pers. sing.

recalientan they reheat; pres. ind. 3rd pers. pl. / *recalentar*.

recalientas you reheat; pres. ind. 2nd pers. sing. / *recalentar*.

recaliéntate (you) become overheated; impve. 2nd pers. sing. / *recalentarse*.

recaliente 1. that I may reheat; pres. subj. 1st pers. sing. / *recalentar*. 2. that he (she/it) may reheat; pres. subj. 3rd pers. sing. 3. let him (her/it) reheat; impve. 3rd pers. sing.

recalienten 1. that they may reheat; pres. subj. 3rd pers. pl. / *recalentar*. 2. let them reheat; impve. 3rd pers. pl.

recaliéntense let them become overheated; impve. 3rd pers. pl. / *recalentarse*.

recalientes that you may reheat; pres. subj. 2nd pers. sing. / *recalentar*.

recaliéntese let him (her/it) become overheated; impve. 3rd pers. sing. / *recalentarse*.

recaliento I reheat; pres. ind. 1st pers. sing. / *recalentar*.

recalque 1. that I may emphasize; pres. subj. 1st pers. sing. / *recalcar*. 2. that he (she/it) may emphasize; pres. subj. 3rd pers. sing. 3. let him (her/it) emphasize; impve. 3rd pers. sing.

recalqué I emphasized; past 1st pers. sing. / *recalcar*.

recalquéis that you (all) may emphasize; pres. subj. 2nd pers. pl. / *recalcar*.

recalquémonos let us harp on; impve. 1st pers. pl. / *recalcarse*.

recalquemos 1. that we may emphasize; pres. subj. 1st pers. pl. / *recalcar*. 2. let us emphasize; impve. 1st pers. pl.

recalquen 1. that they may emphasize; pres. subj. 3rd pers. pl. / *recalcar*. 2. let them emphasize; impve. 3rd pers. pl.

recálquense let them harp on; impve. 3rd pers. pl. / *recalcarse*.

recalques that you may emphasize; pres. subj. 2nd pers. sing. / *recalcar*.

recálquese let him (her/it) harp on; impve. 3rd pers. sing. / *recalcarse*.

recamar to embroider. reg.

recambiar to exchange again. reg.

recapacitar to think through. reg.

recapitular to recapitulate. reg.

recargándose increasing in temperature; pres. part. / *recargarse*.

recargaos (you all) increase in temperature; impve. 2nd pers. pl. / *recargarse*.

recargar to reload or to overload. irr.

recargarse to increase in temperature. irr.

recárgate (you) increase in temperature; impve. 2nd pers. sing. / *recargarse*.

recargue 1. that I may reload; pres. subj. 1st pers. sing. / *recargar*. 2. that he (she/it) may reload; pres. subj. 3rd pers. sing. 3. let him (her/it) reload; impve. 3rd pers. sing.

recargué I reloaded; past 1st pers. sing. / *recargar*.

recarguéis that you (all) may reload; pres. subj. 2nd pers. pl. / *recargar*.

recarguémonos let us increase in temperature; impve. 1st pers. pl. / *recargarse*.

recarguemos 1. that we may reload; pres. subj. 1st pers. pl. / *recargar*. 2. let us reload; impve. 1st pers. pl.

recarguen 1. that they may reload; pres. subj. 3rd pers. pl. / *recargar*. 2. let them reload; impve. 3rd pers. pl.

recárguense let them increase in temperature; impve. 3rd pers. pl. / *recargarse*.

recargues that you may reload; pres. subj. 2nd pers. sing. / *recargar*.

recárguese let him (her/it) increase in temperature; impve. 3rd pers. sing. / *recargarse*.

recatándose being cautious; pres. part. / *recatarse*.

recataos (you all) be cautious; impve. 2nd pers. pl. / *recatarse*.

recatar to conceal. reg.

recatarse to be cautious. reg.

recátate (you) be cautious; impve. 2nd pers. sing. / *recatarse*.

recatémonos let us be cautious; impve. 1st pers. pl. / *recatarse*.

recátense let them be cautious; impve. 3rd pers. pl. / *recatarse*.

recátese let him (her/it) be cautious; impve. 3rd pers. sing. / *recatarse.*

recauchar to retread tires. reg.

recauchutar to retread tires. reg.

recaudar to collect rents or taxes. reg.

recayendo relapsing; pres. part. / *recaer.*

recayera 1. that I might relapse; imp. subj. 1st pers. sing. / *recaer.* 2. that he (she/it) might relapse; imp. subj. 3rd pers. sing.

recayerais that you (all) might relapse; imp. subj. 2nd pers pl. / *recaer.*

recayéramos that we might relapse; imp. subj. 1st pers. pl. / *recaer.*

recayeran that they might relapse; imp. subj. 3rd pers. pl. / *recaer.*

recayeras that you might relapse; imp. subj. 2nd pers. sing. / *recaer.*

recayeron they relapsed; past 3rd pers. pl. / *recaer.*

recayese 1. that I might relapse; imp. subj. 1st pers. sing. / *recaer.* 2. that he (she/it) might relapse; imp. subj. 3rd pers. sing.

recayeseis that you (all) might relapse; imp. subj. 2nd pers pl. / *recaer.*

recayésemos that we might relapse; imp. subj. 1st pers. pl. / *recaer.*

recayesen that they might relapse; imp. subj. 3rd pers. pl. / *recaer.*

recayeses that you might relapse; imp. subj. 2nd pers. sing. / *recaer.*

recayo I relapse; pres. ind. 1st pers. sing. / *recaer.*

recayó he (she/it) relapsed; past 3rd pers. sing. / *recaer.*

rece 1. that I may pray; pres. subj. 1st pers. sing. / *rezar.* 2. that he (she/it) may pray; pres. subj. 3rd pers. sing. 3. let him (her/it) pray; impve. 3rd pers. sing.

recé I prayed; past 1st pers. sing. / *rezar.*

recéis that you (all) may pray; pres. subj. 2nd pers. pl. / *rezar.*

recelándose distrusting; pres. part. / *recelarse.*

recelaos (you all) distrust; impve. 2nd pers. pl. / *recelarse.*

recelar to fear. reg.

recelarse to distrust. reg.

recélate (you) distrust; impve. 2nd pers. sing. / *recelarse.*

recelémonos let us distrust; impve. 1st pers. pl. / *recelarse.*

recélense let them distrust; impve. 3rd pers. pl. / *recelarse.*

recélese let him (her/it) distrust; impve. 3rd pers. sing. / *recelarse.*

recemos 1. that we may pray; pres. subj. 1st pers. pl. / *rezar.* 2. let us pray; impve. 1st pers. pl.

recen 1. that they may pray; pres. subj. 3rd pers. pl. / *rezar.* 2. let them pray; impve. 3rd pers. pl.

recentándose being renewed; pres. part. / *recentarse.*

recentaos (you all) be renewed; impve. 2nd pers. pl. / *recentarse.*

recentar to leaven. irr.

recentarse to be renewed. irr.

recentémonos let us be renewed; impve. 1st pers. pl. / *recentarse.*

receptar to receive. reg.

reces that you may pray; pres. subj. 2nd pers. sing. / *rezar.*

recetar to prescribe. reg.

recibámonos let us graduate; impve. 1st pers. pl. / *recibirse.*

recíbanse let them graduate; impve. 3rd pers. pl. / *recibirse.*

recíbase let him (her/it) graduate; impve. 3rd pers. sing. / *recibirse.*

recíbete (you) graduate; impve. 2nd pers. sing. / *recibirse.*

recibiéndose graduating; pres. part. / *recibirse.*

recíbios (you all) graduate; impve. 2nd pers. pl. / *recibirse.*

recibir to receive. reg.

recibirse to graduate. reg.

recienta 1. he (she/it) leavens; pres. ind. 3rd pers. sing. / *recentar.* 2. (you) leaven; impve. 2nd pers. sing.

recientan they leaven; pres. ind. 3rd pers. pl. / *recentar.*

recientas you leaven; pres. ind. 2nd pers. sing. / *recentar.*

reciéntate (you) be renewed; impve. 2nd pers. sing. / *recentarse.*

reciente 1. that I may leaven; pres. subj. 1st pers. sing. / *recentar.* 2. that he (she/it) may leaven; pres. subj. 3rd pers. sing. 3. let him (her/it) leaven; impve. 3rd pers. sing.

recienten 1. that they may leaven; pres. subj. 3rd pers. pl. / *recentar.* 2. let them leaven; impve. 3rd pers. pl.

reciéntense let them be renewed; impve. 3rd pers. pl. / *recentarse.*

recientes that you may leaven; pres. subj. 2nd pers. sing. / *recentar.*

reciéntese let him (her/it) be renewed; impve. 3rd pers. sing. / *recentarse.*

reciento I leaven; pres. ind. 1st pers. sing. / *recentar.*

reciprocándose matching; pres. part. / *reciprocarse.*

reciprocaos (you all) match; impve. 2nd pers. pl. / *reciprocarse.*

reciprocar to reciprocate. irr.

reciprocarse to match. irr.

reciprócate (you) match; impve. 2nd pers. sing. / *reciprocarse.*

reciproque 1. that I may reciprocate; pres. subj. 1st pers. sing. / *reciprocar.* 2. that he (she/it) may reciprocate; pres. subj. 3rd pers. sing. 3. let him (her/it) reciprocate; impve. 3rd pers. sing.

reciproqué I reciprocated; past 1st pers. sing. / *reciprocar.*

reciproquéis that you (all) may reciprocate; pres. subj. 2nd pers. pl. / *reciprocar.*

reciproquémonos let us match; impve. 1st pers. pl. / *reciprocarse.*

reciproquemos 1. that we may reciprocate; pres. subj. 1st pers. pl. / *reciprocar*. 2. let us reciprocate; impve. 1st pers. pl.

reciproquen 1. that they may reciprocate; pres. subj. 3rd pers. pl. / *reciprocar*. 2. let them reciprocate; impve. 3rd pers. pl.

reciproquense let them match; impve. 3rd pers. pl. / *reciprocarse*.

reciproques that you may reciprocate; pres. subj. 2nd pers. sing. / *reciprocar*.

reciproquese let him (her/it) match; impve. 3rd pers. sing. / *reciprocarse*.

recitar to recite. reg.

reclamar to claim. reg.

reclinándose leaning; pres. part. / *reclinarse*.

reclinaos (you all) lean; impve. 2nd pers. pl. / *reclinarse*.

reclinar to recline. reg.

reclinarse to lean. reg.

reclínate (you) lean; impve. 2nd pers. sing. / *reclinarse*.

reclinémonos let us lean; impve. 1st pers. pl. / *reclinarse*.

reclínense let them lean; impve. 3rd pers. pl. / *reclinarse*.

reclínese let him (her/it) lean; impve. 3rd pers. sing. / *reclinarse*.

recluíos (you all) isolate yourselves; impve. 2nd pers. pl. / *recluirse*.

recluir to seclude. irr.

recluirse to isolate oneself. irr.

reclutar to recruit. reg.

recluya 1. that I may seclude; pres. subj. 1st pers. sing. / *recluir*. 2. that he (she/it) may seclude; pres. subj. 3rd pers. sing. 3. let him (her/it) seclude; impve. 3rd pers. sing.

recluyáis that you (all) may seclude; pres. subj. 2nd pers. pl. / *recluir*.

recluyámonos let us isolate ourselves; impve. 1st pers. pl. / *recluirse*.

recluyamos 1. that we may seclude; pres. subj. 1st pers. pl. / *recluir*. 2. let us seclude; impve. 1st pers. pl.

recluyan 1. that they may seclude; pres. subj. 3rd pers. pl. / *recluir*. 2. let them seclude; impve. 3rd pers. pl.

reclúyanse let them isolate themselves; impve. 3rd pers. pl. / *recluirse*.

recluyas that you may seclude; pres. subj. 2nd pers. sing. / *recluir*.

reclúyase let him (her/it) isolate himself (herself/itself); impve. 3rd pers. sing. / *recluirse*.

recluye 1. he (she/it) secludes; pres. ind. 3rd pers. sing. / *recluir*. 2. (you) seclude; impve. 2nd pers. sing.

recluyen they seclude; pres. ind. 3rd pers. pl. / *recluir*.

recluyendo secluding; pres. part. / *recluir*.

recluyéndose isolating oneself; pres. part. / *recluirse*.

recluyera 1. that I might seclude; imp. subj. 1st pers. sing. / *recluir*. 2. that he (she/it) might seclude; imp. subj. 3rd pers. sing.

recluyerais that you (all) might seclude; imp. subj. 2nd pers pl. / *recluir*.

recluyéramos that we might seclude; imp. subj. 1st pers. pl. / *recluir*.

recluyeran that they might seclude; imp. subj. 3rd pers. pl. / *recluir*.

recluyeras that you might seclude; imp. subj. 2nd pers. sing. / *recluir*.

recluyeron they secluded; past 3rd pers. pl. / *recluir*.

recluyes you seclude; pres. ind. 2nd pers. sing. / *recluir*.

recluyese 1. that I might seclude; imp. subj. 1st pers. sing. / *recluir*. 2. that he (she/it) might seclude; imp. subj. 3rd pers. sing.

recluyeseis that you (all) might seclude; imp. subj. 2nd pers pl. / *recluir*.

recluyésemos that we might seclude; imp. subj. 1st pers. pl. / *recluir*.

recluyesen that they might seclude; imp. subj. 3rd pers. pl. / *recluir*.

recluyeses that you might seclude; imp. subj. 2nd pers. sing. / *recluir*.

reclúyete (you) isolate yourself; impve. 2nd pers. sing. / *recluirse*.

recluyo I seclude; pres. ind. 1st pers. sing. / *recluir*.

recluyó he (she/it) secluded; past 3rd pers. sing. / *recluir*.

recobrándose recuperating; pres. part. / *recobrarse*.

recobraos (you all) recuperate; impve. 2nd pers. pl. / *recobrarse*.

recobrar to recover. reg.

recobrarse to recuperate. reg.

recóbrate (you) recuperate; impve. 2nd pers. sing. / *recobrarse*.

recobrémonos let us recuperate; impve. 1st pers. pl. / *recobrarse*.

recóbrense let them recuperate; impve. 3rd pers. pl. / *recobrarse*.

recóbrese let him (her/it) recuperate; impve. 3rd pers. sing. / *recobrarse*.

recoceos (you all) be eaten up with passion; impve. 2nd pers. pl. / *recocerse*.

recocer to recook. irr.

recocerse to be eaten up with passion. irr.

recociéndose being eaten up with passion; pres. part. / *recocerse*.

recodándose twisting and turning; pres. part. / *recodarse*.

recodaos (you all) twist and turn; impve. 2nd pers. pl. / *recodarse*.

recodar to lean (on elbow). reg.

recodarse to twist and turn. reg.

recódate (you) twist and turn; impve. 2nd pers. sing. / *recodarse*.

recodémonos let us twist and turn; impve. 1st pers. pl. / *recodarse*.

recódense let them twist and turn; impve. 3rd pers. pl. / *recodarse*.

recódese let him (her/it) twist and turn; impve. 3rd pers. sing. / *recodarse*.

recogeos (you all) take shelter; impve. 2nd pers. pl. / *recogerse.*

recoger to pick up. irr.

recogerse to take shelter. irr.

recógete (you) take shelter; impve. 2nd pers. sing. / *recogerse.*

recogiéndose taking shelter; pres. part. / *recogerse.*

recoja 1. that I may pick up; pres. subj. 1st pers. sing. / *recoger.* 2. that he (she/it) may pick up; pres. subj. 3rd pers. sing. 3. let him (her/it) pick up; impve. 3rd pers. sing.

recojáis that you (all) may pick up; pres. subj. 2nd pers. pl. / *recoger.*

recojámonos let us take shelter; impve. 1st pers. pl. / *recogerse.*

recojamos 1. that we may pick up; pres. subj. 1st pers. pl. / *recoger.* 2. let us pick up; impve. 1st pers. pl.

recojan 1. that they may pick up; pres. subj. 3rd pers. pl. / *recoger.* 2. let them pick up; impve. 3rd pers. pl.

recójanse let them take shelter; impve. 3rd pers. pl. / *recogerse.*

recojas that you may pick up; pres. subj. 2nd pers. sing. / *recoger.*

recójase let him (her/it) take shelter; impve. 3rd pers. sing. / *recogerse.*

recojo I pick up; pres. ind. 1st pers. sing. / *recoger.*

recolectar to harvest. reg.

recomendar to recommend. irr.

recomienda 1. he (she/it) recommends; pres. ind. 3rd pers. sing. / *recomendar.* 2. (you) recommend; impve. 2nd pers. sing.

recomiendan they recommend; pres. ind. 3rd pers. pl. / *recomendar.*

recomiendas you recommend; pres. ind. 2nd pers. sing. / *recomendar.*

recomiende 1. that I may recommend; pres. subj. 1st pers. sing. / *recomendar.* 2. that he (she/it) may recommend; pres. subj. 3rd pers. sing. 3. let him (her/it) recommend; impve. 3rd pers. sing.

recomienden 1. that they may recommend; pres. subj. 3rd pers. pl. / *recomendar.* 2. let them recommend; impve. 3rd pers. pl.

recomiendes that you may recommend; pres. subj. 2nd pers. sing. / *recomendar.*

recomiendo I recommend; pres. ind. 1st pers. sing. / *recomendar.*

recompensar to recompense. reg.

recompon (you) repair; impve. 2nd pers. sing. / *recomponer.*

recompondrá he (she/it) will repair; fut. 3rd pers. sing. / *recomponer.*

recompondrán they will repair; fut. 3rd pers. pl. / *recomponer.*

recompondrás you will repair; fut. 2nd pers. sing. / *recomponer.*

recompondré I shall repair; fut. 1st pers. sing. / *recomponer.*

recompondréis you (all) will repair; fut. 2nd pers. pl. / *recomponer.*

recompondremos we shall repair; fut. 1st pers. pl. / *recomponer.*

recompondría 1. I should repair; cond. 1st pers. sing. / *recomponer.* 2. he (she/it) would repair; cond. 3rd pers. sing.

recompondríais you (all) would repair; cond. 2nd pers. pl. / *recomponer.*

recompondríamos we should repair; cond. 1st pers. pl. / *recomponer.*

recompondrían they would repair; cond. 3rd pers. pl. / *recomponer.*

recompondrías you would repair; cond. 2nd pers. sing. / *recomponer.*

recomponga 1. that I may repair; pres. subj. 1st pers. sing. / *recomponer.* 2. that he (she/it) may repair; pres. subj. 3rd pers. sing. 3. let him (her/it) repair; impve. 3rd pers. sing.

recompongáis that you (all) may repair; pres. subj. 2nd pers. pl. / *recomponer.*

recompongamos 1. that we may repair; pres. subj. 1st pers. pl. / *recomponer.* 2. let us repair; impve. 1st pers. pl.

recompongan 1. that they may repair; pres. subj. 3rd pers. pl. / *recomponer.* 2. let them repair; impve. 3rd pers. pl.

recompongas that you may repair; pres. subj. 2nd pers. sing. / *recomponer.*

recompongo I repair; pres. ind. 1st pers. sing. / *recomponer.*

recompuesto repaired; past part. / *recomponer.*

recompuse I repaired; past 1st pers. sing. / *recomponer.*

recompusiera 1. that I might repair; imp. subj. 1st pers. sing. / *recomponer.* 2. that he (she/it) might repair; imp. subj. 3rd pers. sing.

recompusierais that you (all) might repair; imp. subj. 2nd pers pl. / *recomponer.*

recompusiéramos that we might repair; imp. subj. 1st pers. pl. / *recomponer.*

recompusieran that they might repair; imp. subj. 3rd pers. pl. / *recomponer.*

recompusieras that you might repair; imp. subj. 2nd pers. sing. / *recomponer.*

recompusieron they repaired; past 3rd pers. pl. / *recomponer.*

recompusiese 1. that I might repair; imp. subj. 1st pers. sing. / *recomponer.* 2. that he (she/it) might repair; imp. subj. 3rd pers. sing.

recompusieseis that you (all) might repair; imp. subj. 2nd pers pl. / *recomponer.*

recompusiésemos that we might repair; imp. subj. 1st pers. pl. / *recomponer.*

recompusiesen that they might repair; imp. subj. 3rd pers. pl. / *recomponer.*

recompusieses that you might repair; imp. subj. 2nd pers. sing. / *recomponer.*

recompusimos we repaired; past 1st pers. pl. / *recomponer.*

recompusiste you repaired; past 2nd pers. sing. / *recomponer.*

recompusisteis you (all) repaired; past 2nd pers. pl. / *recomponer.*

recompuso he (she/it) repaired; past 3rd pers. sing. / *recomponer.*

reconcentrándose becoming absorbed; pres. part. / *reconcentrarse.*

reconcentraos (you all) become absorbed; impve. 2nd pers. pl. / *reconcentrarse.*

reconcentrar to concentrate. reg.

reconcentrarse to become absorbed. reg.

reconcéntrate (you) become absorbed; impve. 2nd pers. sing. / *reconcentrarse.*

reconcentrémonos let us become absorbed; impve. 1st pers. pl. / *reconcentrarse.*

reconcéntrense let them become absorbed; impve. 3rd pers. pl. / *reconcentrarse.*

reconcéntrese let him (her/it) become absorbed; impve. 3rd pers. sing. / *reconcentrarse.*

reconciliándose becoming reconciled; pres. part. / *reconciliarse.*

reconciliaos (you all) become reconciled; impve. 2nd pers. pl. / *reconciliarse.*

reconciliar to reconcile. reg.

reconciliarse to become reconciled. reg.

reconcilíate (you) become reconciled; impve. 2nd pers. sing. / *reconciliarse.*

reconciliémonos let us become reconciled; impve. 1st pers. pl. / *reconciliarse.*

reconcilíense let them become reconciled; impve. 3rd pers. pl. / *reconciliarse.*

reconcilíese let him (her/it) become reconciled; impve. 3rd pers. sing. / *reconciliarse.*

reconoceos (you all) confess; impve. 2nd pers. pl. / *reconocerse.*

reconocer to recognize. irr.

reconocerse to confess. irr.

reconócete (you) confess; impve. 2nd pers. sing. / *reconocerse.*

reconociéndose confessing; pres. part. / *reconocerse.*

reconozca 1. that I may recognize; pres. subj. 1st pers. sing. / *reconocer.* 2. that he (she/it) may recognize; pres. subj. 3rd pers. sing. 3. let him (her/it) recognize; impve. 3rd pers. sing.

reconozcáis that you (all) may recognize; pres. subj. 2nd pers. pl. / *reconocer.*

reconozcámonos let us confess; impve. 1st pers. pl. / *reconocerse.*

reconozcamos 1. that we may recognize; pres. subj. 1st pers. pl. / *reconocer.* 2. let us recognize; impve. 1st pers. pl.

reconozcan 1. that they may recognize; pres. subj. 3rd pers. pl. / *reconocer.* 2. let them recognize; impve. 3rd pers. pl.

reconózcanse let them confess; impve. 3rd pers. pl. / *reconocerse.*

reconozcas that you may recognize; pres. subj. 2nd pers. sing. / *reconocer.*

reconózcase let him (her/it) confess; impve. 3rd pers. sing. / *reconocerse.*

reconozco I recognize; pres. ind. 1st pers. sing. / *reconocer.*

reconquistar to reconquer. reg.

reconstituir to reconstitute. irr.

reconstituya 1. that I may reconstitute; pres. subj. 1st pers. sing. / *reconstituir.* 2. that he (she/it) may reconstitute; pres. subj. 3rd pers. sing. 3. let him (her/it) reconstitute; impve. 3rd pers. sing.

reconstituyáis that you (all) may reconstitute; pres. subj. 2nd pers. pl. / *reconstituir.*

reconstituyamos 1. that we may reconstitute; pres. subj. 1st pers. pl. / *reconstituir.* 2. let us reconstitute; impve. 1st pers. pl.

reconstituyan 1. that they may reconstitute; pres. subj. 3rd pers. pl. / *reconstituir.* 2. let them reconstitute; impve. 3rd pers. pl.

reconstituyas that you may reconstitute; pres. subj. 2nd pers. sing. / *reconstituir.*

reconstituye 1. he (she/it) reconstitutes; pres. ind. 3rd pers. sing. / *reconstituir.* 2. (you) reconstitute; impve. 2nd pers. sing.

reconstituyen they reconstitute; pres. ind. 3rd pers. pl. / *reconstituir.*

reconstituyendo reconstituting; pres. part. / *reconstituir.*

reconstituyera 1. that I might reconstitute; imp. subj. 1st pers. sing. / *reconstituir.* 2. that he (she/it) might reconstitute; imp. subj. 3rd pers. sing.

reconstituyerais that you (all) might reconstitute; imp. subj. 2nd pers pl. / *reconstituir.*

reconstituyéramos that we might reconstitute; imp. subj. 1st pers. pl. / *reconstituir.*

reconstituyeran that they might reconstitute; imp. subj. 3rd pers. pl. / *reconstituir.*

reconstituyeras that you might reconstitute; imp. subj. 2nd pers. sing. / *reconstituir.*

reconstituyeron they reconstituted; past 3rd pers. pl. / *reconstituir.*

reconstituyes you reconstitute; pres. ind. 2nd pers. sing. / *reconstituir.*

reconstituyese 1. that I might reconstitute; imp. subj. 1st pers. sing. / *reconstituir.* 2. that he (she/it) might reconstitute; imp. subj. 3rd pers. sing.

reconstituyeseis that you (all) might reconstitute; imp. subj. 2nd pers pl. / *reconstituir.*

reconstituyésemos that we might reconstitute; imp. subj. 1st pers. pl. / *reconstituir.*

reconstituyesen that they might reconstitute; imp. subj. 3rd pers. pl. / *reconstituir.*

reconstituyeses that you might reconstitute; imp. subj. 2nd pers. sing. / *reconstituir.*

reconstituyo I reconstitute; pres. ind. 1st pers. sing. / *reconstituir.*

reconstituyó he (she/it) reconstituted; past 3rd pers. sing. / *reconstituir.*

reconstruir to reconstruct. irr.

reconstruya 1. that I may reconstruct; pres. subj. 1st pers. sing. / *reconstruir.* 2. that he (she/it) may reconstruct; pres. subj. 3rd pers. sing. 3. let him (her/it) reconstruct; impve. 3rd pers. sing.

reconstruyáis that you (all) may reconstruct; pres. subj. 2nd pers. pl. / *reconstruir.*

reconstruyamos 1. that we may reconstruct; pres. subj. 1st pers. pl. / *reconstruir.* 2. let us reconstruct; impve. 1st pers. pl.

reconstruyan 1. that they may reconstruct; pres. subj. 3rd pers. pl. / *reconstruir.* 2. let them reconstruct; impve. 3rd pers. pl.

reconstruyas that you may reconstruct; pres. subj. 2nd pers. sing. / *reconstruir.*

reconstruye 1. he (she/it) reconstructs; pres. ind. 3rd pers. sing. / *reconstruir.* 2. (you) reconstruct; impve. 2nd pers. sing.

reconstruyen they reconstruct; pres. ind. 3rd pers. pl. / *reconstruir.*

reconstruyendo reconstructing; pres. part. / *reconstruir.*

reconstruyera 1. that I might reconstruct; imp. subj. 1st pers. sing. / *reconstruir.* 2. that he (she/it) might reconstruct; imp. subj. 3rd pers. sing.

reconstruyerais that you (all) might reconstruct; imp. subj. 2nd pers pl. / *reconstruir.*

reconstruyéramos that we might reconstruct; imp. subj. 1st pers. pl. / *reconstruir.*

reconstruyeran that they might reconstruct; imp. subj. 3rd pers. pl. / *reconstruir.*

reconstruyeras that you might reconstruct; imp. subj. 2nd pers. sing. / *reconstruir.*

reconstruyeron they reconstructed; past 3rd pers. pl. / *reconstruir.*

reconstruyes you reconstruct; pres. ind. 2nd pers. sing. / *reconstruir.*

reconstruyese 1. that I might reconstruct; imp. subj. 1st pers. sing. / *reconstruir.* 2. that he (she/it) might reconstruct; imp. subj. 3rd pers. sing.

reconstruyeseis that you (all) might reconstruct; imp. subj. 2nd pers pl. / *reconstruir.*

reconstruyésemos that we might reconstruct; imp. subj. 1st pers. pl. / *reconstruir.*

reconstruyesen that they might reconstruct; imp. subj. 3rd pers. pl. / *reconstruir.*

reconstruyeses that you might reconstruct; imp. subj. 2nd pers. sing. / *reconstruir.*

reconstruyo I reconstruct; pres. ind. 1st pers. sing. / *reconstruir.*

reconstruyó he (she/it) reconstructed; past 3rd pers. sing. / *reconstruir.*

recontar to recount. irr.

reconven (you) reproach; impve. 2nd pers. sing. / *reconvenir.*

reconvendrá he (she/it) will reproach; fut. 3rd pers. sing. / *reconvenir.*

reconvendrán they will reproach; fut. 3rd pers. pl. / *reconvenir.*

reconvendrás you will reproach; fut. 2nd pers. sing. / *reconvenir.*

reconvendré I shall reproach; fut. 1st pers. sing. / *reconvenir.*

reconvendréis you (all) will reproach; fut. 2nd pers. pl. / *reconvenir.*

reconvendremos we shall reproach; fut. 1st pers. pl. / *reconvenir.*

reconvendría 1. I should reproach; cond. 1st pers. sing. / *reconvenir.* 2. he (she/it) would reproach; cond. 3rd pers. sing.

reconvendríais you (all) would reproach; cond. 2nd pers. pl. / *reconvenir.*

reconvendríamos we should reproach; cond. 1st pers. pl. / *reconvenir.*

reconvendrían they would reproach; cond. 3rd pers. pl. / *reconvenir.*

reconvendrías you would reproach; cond. 2nd pers. sing. / *reconvenir.*

reconvenga 1. that I may reproach; pres. subj. 1st pers. sing. / *reconvenir.* 2. that he (she/it) may reproach; pres. subj. 3rd pers. sing. 3. let him (her/it) reproach; impve. 3rd pers. sing.

reconvengáis that you (all) may reproach; pres. subj. 2nd pers. pl. / *reconvenir.*

reconvengamos 1. that we may reproach; pres. subj. 1st pers. pl. / *reconvenir.* 2. let us reproach; impve. 1st pers. pl.

reconvengan 1. that they may reproach; pres. subj. 3rd pers. pl. / *reconvenir.* 2. let them reproach; impve. 3rd pers. pl.

reconvengas that you may reproach; pres. subj. 2nd pers. sing. / *reconvenir.*

reconvengo I reproach; pres. ind. 1st pers. sing. / *reconvenir.*

reconvenir to reproach. irr.

reconviene 1. he (she/it) reproaches; pres. ind. 3rd pers. sing. / *reconvenir.* 2. (you) reproach; impve. 2nd pers. sing.

reconvienen they reproach; pres. ind. 3rd pers. pl. / *reconvenir.*

reconvienes you reproach; pres. ind. 2nd pers. sing. / *reconvenir.*

reconvine I reproached; past 1st pers. sing. / *reconvenir.*

reconviniendo reproaching; pres. part. / *reconvenir.*

reconviniera 1. that I might reproach; imp. subj. 1st pers. sing. / *reconvenir.* 2. that he (she/it) might reproach; imp. subj. 3rd pers. sing.

reconvinierais that you (all) might reproach; imp. subj. 2nd pers pl. / *reconvenir.*

reconviniéramos that we might reproach; imp. subj. 1st pers. pl. / *reconvenir.*

reconvinieran that they might reproach; imp. subj. 3rd pers. pl. / *reconvenir.*

reconvinieras that you might reproach; imp. subj. 2nd pers. sing. / *reconvenir.*

reconvinieron they reproached; past 3rd pers. pl. / *reconvenir.*

reconviniese 1. that I might reproach; imp. subj. 1st pers. sing. / *reconvenir.* 2. that he (she/it) might reproach; imp. subj. 3rd pers. sing.

reconvinieseis that you (all) might reproach; imp. subj. 2nd pers pl. / *reconvenir.*

reconviniésemos that we might reproach; imp. subj. 1st pers. pl. / *reconvenir.*

reconviniesen that they might reproach; imp. subj. 3rd pers. pl. / *reconvenir.*

reconvinieses that you might reproach; imp. subj. 2nd pers. sing. / *reconvenir.*

reconvinimos we reproached; past 1st pers. pl. / *reconvenir.*

reconviniste you reproached; past 2nd pers. sing. / *reconvenir.*

reconvinisteis you (all) reproached; past 2nd pers. pl. / *reconvenir.*

reconvino he (she/it) reproached; past 3rd pers. sing. / *reconvenir.*

recopilar to compile. reg.

recordándose recalling; pres. part. / *recordarse.*

recordaos (you all) recall; impve. 2nd pers. pl. / *recordarse.*

recordar to remember. irr.

recordarse to recall. irr.

recordémonos let us recall; impve. 1st pers. pl. / *recordarse.*

recorrer to travel over. reg.

recortándose standing out; pres. part. / *recortarse.*

recortaos (you all) stand out; impve. 2nd pers. pl. / *recortarse.*

recortar to trim. reg.

recortarse to stand out. reg.

recórtate (you) stand out; impve. 2nd pers. sing. / *recortarse.*

recortémonos let us stand out; impve. 1st pers. pl. / *recortarse.*

recórtense let them stand out; impve. 3rd pers. pl. / *recortarse.*

recórtese let him (her/it) stand out; impve. 3rd pers. sing. / *recortarse.*

recoser to resew or to mend. reg.

recostándose lying down; pres. part. / *recostarse.*

recostaos (you all) lie down; impve. 2nd pers. pl. / *recostarse.*

recostar to recline. irr.

recostarse to lie down. irr.

recostémonos let us lie down; impve. 1st pers. pl. / *recostarse.*

recozáis that you (all) may recook; pres. subj. 2nd pers. pl. / *recocer.*

recozámonos let us be eaten up with passion; impve. 1st pers. pl. / *recocerse.*

recozamos 1. that we may recook; pres. subj. 1st pers. pl. / *recocer.* 2. let us recook; impve. 1st pers. pl.

recreándose relaxing; pres. part. / *recrearse.*

recreaos (you all) relax; impve. 2nd pers. pl. / *recrearse.*

recrear to amuse. reg.

recrearse to relax. reg.

recréate (you) relax; impve. 2nd pers. sing. / *recrearse.*

recreceos (you all) recover your spirits; impve. 2nd pers. pl. / *recrecerse.*

recrecer to increase. irr.

recrecerse to recover one's spirits. irr.

recrécete (you) recover your spirit; impve. 2nd pers. sing. / *recrecerse.*

recreciéndose recovering one's spirit; pres. part. / *recrecerse.*

recreémonos let us relax; impve. 1st pers. pl. / *recrearse.*

recréense let them relax; impve. 3rd pers. pl. / *recrearse.*

recréese let him (her/it) relax; impve. 3rd pers. sing. / *recrearse.*

recrezca 1. that I may increase; pres. subj. 1st pers. sing. / *recrecer.* 2. that he (she/it) may increase; pres. subj. 3rd pers. sing. 3. let him (her/it) increase; impve. 3rd pers. sing.

recrezcáis that you (all) may increase; pres. subj. 2nd pers. pl. / *recrecer.*

recrezcámonos let us recover our spirits; impve. 1st pers. pl. / *recrecerse.*

recrezcamos 1. that we may increase; pres. subj. 1st pers. pl. / *recrecer.* 2. let us increase; impve. 1st pers. pl.

recrezcan 1. that they may increase; pres. subj. 3rd pers. pl. / *recrecer.* 2. let them increase; impve. 3rd pers. pl.

recrézcanse let them recover their spirits; impve. 3rd pers. pl. / *recrecerse.*

recrezcas that you may increase; pres. subj. 2nd pers. sing. / *recrecer.*

recrézcase let him (her/it) recover his (her/its) spirit; impve. 3rd pers. sing. / *recrecerse.*

recrezco I increase; pres. ind. 1st pers. sing. / *recrecer.*

recriminar to recriminate. reg.

recrudeceos (you all) get worse; impve. 2nd pers. pl. / *recrudecerse.*

recrudecer to recur. irr.

recrudecerse to get worse. irr.

recrudécete (you) get worse; impve. 2nd pers. sing. / *recrudecerse.*

recrudeciéndose getting worse; pres. part. / *recrudecerse.*

recrudezca 1. that I may recur; pres. subj. 1st pers. sing. / *recrudecer.* 2. that he (she/it) may recur; pres. subj. 3rd pers. sing. 3. let him (her/it) recur; impve. 3rd pers. sing.

recrudezcáis that you (all) may recur; pres. subj. 2nd pers. pl. / *recrudecer.*

recrudezcámonos let us get worse; impve. 1st pers. pl. / *recrudecerse.*

recrudezcamos 1. that we may recur; pres. subj. 1st pers. pl. / *recrudecer.* 2. let us recur; impve. 1st pers. pl.

recrudezcan 1. that they may recur; pres. subj. 3rd pers. pl. / *recrudecer.* 2. let them recur; impve. 3rd pers. pl.

recrudézcanse let them get worse; impve. 3rd pers. pl. / *recrudecerse.*

recrudezcas that you may recur; pres. subj. 2nd pers. sing. / *recrudecer.*

recrudézcase let him (her/it) get worse; impve. 3rd pers. sing. / *recrudecerse.*

recrudezco I recur; pres. ind. 1st pers. sing. / *recrudecer*.

recrujir to creak loudly. reg.

rectificar to rectify. irr.

rectifique 1. that I may rectify; pres. subj. 1st pers. sing. / *rectificar*. 2. that he (she/it) may rectify; pres. subj. 3rd pers. sing. 3. let him (her/it) rectify; impve. 3rd pers. sing.

rectifiqué I rectified; past 1st pers. sing. / *rectificar*.

rectifiquéis that you (all) may rectify; pres. subj. 2nd pers. pl. / *rectificar*.

rectifiquemos 1. that we may rectify; pres. subj. 1st pers. pl. / *rectificar*. 2. let us rectify; impve. 1st pers. pl.

rectifiquen 1. that they may rectify; pres. subj. 3rd pers. pl. / *rectificar*. 2. let them rectify; impve. 3rd pers. pl.

rectifiques that you may rectify; pres. subj. 2nd pers. sing. / *rectificar*.

recubierto covered; past. part. / *recubrir*.

recubrir to cover. reg. for pp.

recudir to pay or to revert. reg.

recuece 1. he (she/it) recooks; pres. ind. 3rd pers. sing. / *recocer*. 2. (you) recook; impve. 2nd pers. sing.

recuecen they recook; pres. ind. 3rd pers. pl. / *recocer*.

recueces you recook; pres. ind. 2nd pers. sing. / *recocer*.

recuécete (you) be eaten up with passion; impve. 2nd pers. sing. / *recocerse*.

recuenta 1. he (she/it) recounts; pres. ind. 3rd pers. sing. / *recontar*. 2. (you) recount; impve. 2nd pers. sing.

recuentan they recount; pres. ind. 3rd pers. pl. / *recontar*.

recuentas you recount; pres. ind. 2nd pers. sing. / *recontar*.

recuente 1. that I may recount; pres. subj. 1st pers. sing. / *recontar*. 2. that he (she/it) may recount; pres. subj. 3rd pers. sing. 3. let him (her/it) recount; impve. 3rd pers. sing.

recuenten 1. that they may recount; pres. subj. 3rd pers. pl. / *recontar*. 2. let them recount; impve. 3rd pers. pl.

recuentes that you may recount; pres. subj. 2nd pers. sing. / *recontar*.

recuento I recount; pres. ind. 1st pers. sing. / *recontar*.

recuerda 1. he (she/it) remembers; pres. ind. 3rd pers. sing. / *recordar*. 2. (you) remember; impve. 2nd pers. sing.

recuerdan they remember; pres. ind. 3rd pers. pl. / *recordar*.

recuerdas you remember; pres. ind. 2nd pers. sing. / *recordar*.

recuérdate (you) recall; impve. 2nd pers. sing. / *recordarse*.

recuerde 1. that I may remember; pres. subj. 1st pers. sing. / *recordar*. 2. that he (she/it) may remember; pres. subj. 3rd pers. sing. 3. let him (her/it) remember; impve. 3rd pers. sing.

recuerden 1. that they may remember; pres. subj. 3rd pers. pl. / *recordar*. 2. let them remember; impve. 3rd pers. pl.

recuérdense let them recall; impve. 3rd pers. pl. / *recordarse*.

recuerdes that you may remember; pres. subj. 2nd pers. sing. / *recordar*.

recuérdese let him (her/it) recall; impve. 3rd pers. sing. / *recordarse*.

recuerdo I remember; pres. ind. 1st pers. sing. / *recordar*.

recuesta 1. he (she/it) reclines; pres. ind. 3rd pers. sing. / *recostar*. 2. (you) recline; impve. 2nd pers. sing.

recuestan they recline; pres. ind. 3rd pers. pl. / *recostar*.

recuestar to request. reg.

recuestas you recline; pres. ind. 2nd pers. sing. / *recostar*.

recuéstate (you) lie down; impve. 2nd pers. sing. / *recostarse*.

recueste 1. that I may recline; pres. subj. 1st pers. sing. / *recostar*. 2. that he (she/it) may recline; pres. subj. 3rd pers. sing. 3. let him (her/it) recline; impve. 3rd pers. sing.

recuesten 1. that they may recline; pres. subj. 3rd pers. pl. / *recostar*. 2. let them recline; impve. 3rd pers. pl.

recuéstense let them lie down; impve. 3rd pers. pl. / *recostarse*.

recuestes that you may recline; pres. subj. 2nd pers. sing. / *recostar*.

recuéstese let him (her/it) lie down; impve. 3rd pers. sing. / *recostarse*.

recuesto I recline; pres. ind. 1st pers. sing. / *recostar*.

recueza 1. that I may recook; pres. subj. 1st pers. sing. / *recocer*. 2. that he (she/it) may recook; pres. subj. 3rd pers. sing. 3. let him (her/it) recook; impve. 3rd pers. sing.

recuezan 1. that they may recook; pres. subj. 3rd pers. pl. / *recocer*. 2. let them recook; impve. 3rd pers. pl.

recuézanse let them be eaten up with passion; impve. 3rd pers. pl. / *recocerse*.

recuezas that you may recook; pres. subj. 2nd pers. sing. / *recocer*.

recuézase let him (her/it) be eaten up with passion; impve. 3rd pers. sing. / *recocerse*.

recuezo I recook; pres. ind. 1st pers. sing. / *recocer*.

recular to fall back. reg.

recuperándose recovering; pres. part. / *recuperarse*.

recuperaos (you all) recover; impve. 2nd pers. pl. / *recuperarse*.

recuperar to recuperate. reg.

recuperarse to recover. reg.

recupérate (you) recover; impve. 2nd pers. sing. / *recuperarse*.

recuperémonos let us recover; impve. 1st pers. pl. / *recuperarse*.

recupérense let them recover; impve. 3rd pers. pl. / *recuperarse*.

recupérese let him (her/it) recover; impve. 3rd pers. sing. / *recuperarse*.

recurrir to resort. reg.

recusar to decline. reg.

rechace 1. that I may reject; pres. subj. 1st pers. sing. / *rechazar*. 2. that he (she/it) may reject; pres. subj. 3rd pers. sing. 3. let him (her/it) reject; impve. 3rd pers. sing.

rechacé I rejected; past 1st pers. sing. / *rechazar*.

rechacéis that you (all) may reject; pres. subj. 2nd pers. pl. / *rechazar*.

rechacemos 1. that we may reject; pres. subj. 1st pers. pl. / *rechazar*. 2. let us reject; impve. 1st pers. pl.

rechacen 1. that they may reject; pres. subj. 3rd pers. pl. / *rechazar*. 2. let them reject; impve. 3rd pers. pl.

rechaces that you may reject; pres. subj. 2nd pers. sing. / *rechazar*.

rechazar to reject. irr.

rechiflar to hoot or to catcall. reg.

rechinar to creak or gnash. reg.

rechistar to protest. reg.

rechupándose smacking one's lips; pres. part. / *rechuparse*.

rechupaos (you all) smack your lips; impve. 2nd pers. pl. / *rechuparse*.

rechuparse to smack one's lips. reg.

rechúpate (you) smack your lips; impve. 2nd pers. sing. / *rechuparse*.

rechupémonos let us smack our lips; impve. 1st pers. pl. / *rechuparse*.

rechúpense let them smack their lips; impve. 3rd pers. pl. / *rechuparse*.

rechúpese let him (her/it) smack his (her/its) lips; impve. 3rd pers. sing. / *rechuparse*.

redactar to edit. reg.

redar to net. reg.

redargüir to answer back. irr.

redarguya 1. that I may answer back; pres. subj. 1st pers. sing. / *redargüir*. 2. that he (she/it) may answer back; pres. subj. 3rd pers. sing. 3. let him (her/it) answer back; impve. 3rd pers. sing.

redarguyáis that you (all) may answer back; pres. subj. 2nd pers. pl. / *redargüir*.

redarguyamos 1. that we may answer back; pres. subj. 1st pers. pl. / *redargüir*. 2. let us answer back; impve. 1st pers. pl.

redarguyan 1. that they may answer back; pres. subj. 3rd pers. pl. / *redargüir*. 2. let them answer back; impve. 3rd pers. pl.

redarguyas that you may answer back; pres. subj. 2nd pers. sing. / *redargüir*.

redarguye 1. he (she/it) answers back; pres. ind. 3rd pers. sing. / *redargüir*. 2. (you) answer back; impve. 2nd pers. sing.

redarguyen they answer back; pres. ind. 3rd pers. pl. / *redargüir*.

redarguyendo answering back; pres. part. / *redargüir*.

redarguyera 1. that I might answer back; imp. subj. 1st pers. sing. / *redargüir*. 2. that he (she/it) might answer back; imp. subj. 3rd pers. sing.

redarguyerais that you (all) might answer back; imp. subj. 2nd pers pl. / *redargüir*.

redarguyéramos that we might answer back; imp. subj. 1st pers. pl. / *redargüir*.

redarguyeran that they might answer back; imp. subj. 3rd pers. pl. / *redargüir*.

redarguyeras that you might answer back; imp. subj. 2nd pers. sing. / *redargüir*.

redarguyeron they answered back; past 3rd pers. pl. / *redargüir*.

redarguyes you answer back; pres. ind. 2nd pers. sing. / *redargüir*.

redarguyese 1. that I might answer back; imp. subj. 1st pers. sing. / *redargüir*. 2. that he (she/it) might answer back; imp. subj. 3rd pers. sing.

redarguyeseis that you (all) might answer back; imp. subj. 2nd pers pl. / *redargüir*.

redarguyésemos that we might answer back; imp. subj. 1st pers. pl. / *redargüir*.

redarguyesen that they might answer back; imp. subj. 3rd pers. pl. / *redargüir*.

redarguyeses that you might answer back; imp. subj. 2nd pers. sing. / *redargüir*.

redarguyo I answer back; pres. ind. 1st pers. sing. / *redargüir*.

redarguyó he (she/it) answered back; past 3rd pers. sing. / *redargüir*.

redimir to redeem. reg.

reditúa 1. he (she/it) yields interest; pres. ind. 3rd pers. sing. / *redituar*. 2. (you) yield interest; impve. 2nd pers. sing.

reditúan they yield interest; pres. ind. 3rd pers. pl. / *redituar*.

redituar to yield interest. irr.

reditúas you yield interest; pres. ind. 2nd pers. sing. / *redituar*.

reditúe 1. that I may yield interest; pres. subj. 1st pers. sing. / *redituar*. 2. that he (she/it) may yield interest; pres. subj. 3rd pers. sing. 3. let him (her/it) yield interest; impve. 3rd pers. sing.

reditúen 1. that they may yield interest; pres. subj. 3rd pers. pl. / *redituar*. 2. let them yield interest; impve. 3rd pers. pl.

reditúes that you may yield interest; pres. subj. 2nd pers. sing. / *redituar*.

reditúo I yield interest; pres. ind. 1st pers. sing. / *redituar*.

redoblar to double. reg.

redondeándose being well off; pres. part. / *redondearse*.

redondeaos (you all) be well off; impve. 2nd pers. pl. / *redondearse*.

redondear to round off. reg.

redondearse to be well off. reg.

redondéate (you) be well off; impve. 2nd pers. sing. / *redondearse*.

redondeémonos let us be well off; impve. 1st pers. pl. / *redondearse*.

redondéense let them be well off; impve. 3rd pers. pl. / *redondearse*.

redondéese let him (her/it) be well off; impve. 3rd pers. sing. / *redondearse*.

redúcete (you) adjust yourself; impve. 2nd pers. sing. / *reducirse*.

reduciéndose adjusting oneself; pres. part. / *reducirse*.

reducíos (you all) adjust yourselves; impve. 2nd pers. pl. / *reducirse*.

reducir to reduce. irr.

reducirse to adjust oneself. irr.

reduje I reduced; past 1st pers. sing. / *reducir*.

redujera 1. that I might reduce; imp. subj. 1st pers. sing. / *reducir*. 2. that he (she/it) might reduce; imp. subj. 3rd pers. sing.

redujerais that you (all) might reduce; imp. subj. 2nd pers pl. / *reducir*.

redujéramos that we might reduce; imp. subj. 1st pers. pl. / *reducir*.

redujeran that they might reduce; imp. subj. 3rd pers. pl. / *reducir*.

redujeras that you might reduce; imp. subj. 2nd pers. sing. / *reducir*.

redujeron they reduced; past 3rd pers. pl. / *reducir*.

redujese 1. that I might reduce; imp. subj. 1st pers. sing. / *reducir*. 2. that he (she/it) might reduce; imp. subj. 3rd pers. sing.

redujeseis that you (all) might reduce; imp. subj. 2nd pers pl. / *reducir*.

redujésemos that we might reduce; imp. subj. 1st pers. pl. / *reducir*.

redujesen that they might reduce; imp. subj. 3rd pers. pl. / *reducir*.

redujeses that you might reduce; imp. subj. 2nd pers. sing. / *reducir*.

redujimos we reduced; past 1st pers. pl. / *reducir*.

redujiste you reduced; past 2nd pers. sing. / *reducir*.

redujisteis you (all) reduced; past 2nd pers. pl. / *reducir*.

redujo he (she/it) reduced; past 3rd pers. sing. / *reducir*.

redundar to overflow. reg.

reduplicar to reduplicate. irr.

reduplique 1. that I may reduplicate; pres. subj. 1st pers. sing. / *reduplicar*. 2. that he (she/it) may reduplicate; pres. subj. 3rd pers. sing. 3. let him (her/it) reduplicate; impve. 3rd pers. sing.

redupliqué I reduplicated; past 1st pers. sing. / *reduplicar*.

redupliquéis that you (all) may reduplicate; pres. subj. 2nd pers. pl. / *reduplicar*.

redupliquemos 1. that we may reduplicate; pres. subj. 1st pers. pl. / *reduplicar*. 2. let us reduplicate; impve. 1st pers. pl.

redupliquen 1. that they may reduplicate; pres. subj. 3rd pers. pl. / *reduplicar*. 2. let them reduplicate; impve. 3rd pers. pl.

redupliques that you may reduplicate; pres. subj. 2nd pers. sing. / *reduplicar*.

reduzca 1. that I may reduce; pres. subj. 1st pers. sing. / *reducir*. 2. that he (she/it) may reduce; pres. subj. 3rd pers. sing. 3. let him (her/it) reduce; impve. 3rd pers. sing.

reduzcáis that you (all) may reduce; pres. subj. 2nd pers. pl. / *reducir*.

reduzcámonos let us adjust ourselves; impve. 1st pers. pl. / *reducirse*.

reduzcamos 1. that we may reduce; pres. subj. 1st pers. pl. / *reducir*. 2. let us reduce; impve. 1st pers. pl.

reduzcan 1. that they may reduce; pres. subj. 3rd pers. pl. / *reducir*. 2. let them reduce; impve. 3rd pers. pl.

redúzcanse let them adjust themselves; impve. 3rd pers. pl. / *reducirse*.

reduzcas that you may reduce; pres. subj. 2nd pers. sing. / *reducir*.

redúzcase let him (her/it) adjust himself (herself/itself); impve. 3rd pers. sing. / *reducirse*.

reduzco I reduce; pres. ind. 1st pers. sing. / *reducir*.

reedificar to rebuild. irr.

reedifique 1. that I may rebuild; pres. subj. 1st pers. sing. / *reedificar*. 2. that he (she/it) may rebuild; pres. subj. 3rd pers. sing. 3. let him (her/it) rebuild; impve. 3rd pers. sing.

reedifiqué I rebuilt; past 1st pers. sing. / *reedificar*.

reedifiquéis that you (all) may rebuild; pres. subj. 2nd pers. pl. / *reedificar*.

reedifiquemos 1. that we may rebuild; pres. subj. 1st pers. pl. / *reedificar*. 2. let us rebuild; impve. 1st pers. pl.

reedifiquen 1. that they may rebuild; pres. subj. 3rd pers. pl. / *reedificar*. 2. let them rebuild; impve. 3rd pers. pl.

reedifiques that you may rebuild; pres. subj. 2nd pers. sing. / *reedificar*.

reeditar to reprint. reg.

reelegir reelect. irr.

reeleja 1. that I may reelect; pres. subj. 1st pers. sing. / *reelegir*. 2. that he (she/it) may reelect; pres. subj. 3rd pers. sing. 3. let him (her/it) reelect; impve. 3rd pers. sing.

reelejáis that you (all) may reelect; pres. subj. 2nd pers. pl. / *reelegir*.

reelejamos 1. that we may reelect; pres. subj. 1st pers. pl. / *reelegir*. 2. let us reelect; impve. 1st pers. pl.

reelejan 1. that they may reelect; pres. subj. 3rd pers. pl. / *reelegir*. 2. let them reelect; impve. 3rd pers. pl.

reelejas that you may reelect; pres. subj. 2nd pers. sing. / *reelegir*.

reelejo I reelect; pres. ind. 1st pers. sing. / *reelegir*.

reembarcándose reembarking; pres. part. / *reembarcarse*.

reembarcaos (you all) reembark; impve. 2nd pers. pl. / *reembarcarse*.

reembarcar to reship. irr.

reembarcarse to reembark. irr.

reembárcate (you) reembark; impve. 2nd pers. sing. / *reembarcarse*.

reembarque 1. that I may reship; pres. subj. 1st pers. sing. / *reembarcar*. 2. that he (she/it) may reship; pres. subj. 3rd pers. sing. 3. let him (her/it) reship; impve. 3rd pers. sing.

reembarqué I reshiped; past 1st pers. sing. / *reembarcar*.

reembarquéis that you (all) may reship; pres. subj. 2nd pers. pl. / *reembarcar*.

reembarquémonos let us reembark; impve. 1st pers. pl. / *reembarcarse*.

reembarquemos 1. that we may reship; pres. subj. 1st pers. pl. / *reembarcar*. 2. let us reship; impve. 1st pers. pl.

reembarquen 1. that they may reship; pres. subj. 3rd pers. pl. / *reembarcar*. 2. let them reship; impve. 3rd pers. pl.

reembárquense let them reembark; impve. 3rd pers. pl. / *reembarcarse*.

reembarques that you may reship; pres. subj. 2nd pers. sing. / *reembarcar*.

reembárquese let him (her/it) reembark; impve. 3rd pers. sing. / *reembarcarse*.

reembolsar to reimburse. reg.

reemitir to emit again. reg.

reemplace 1. that I may replace; pres. subj. 1st pers. sing. / *reemplazar*. 2. that he (she/it) may replace; pres. subj. 3rd pers. sing. 3. let him (her/it) replace; impve. 3rd pers. sing.

reemplacé I replaced; past 1st pers. sing. / *reemplazar*.

reemplacéis that you (all) may replace; pres. subj. 2nd pers. pl. / *reemplazar*.

reemplacemos 1. that we may replace; pres. subj. 1st pers. pl. / *reemplazar*. 2. let us replace; impve. 1st pers. pl.

reemplacen 1. that they may replace; pres. subj. 3rd pers. pl. / *reemplazar*. 2. let them replace; impve. 3rd pers. pl.

reemplaces that you may replace; pres. subj. 2nd pers. sing. / *reemplazar*.

reemplazar to replace. irr.

reencarnar to be reincarnated. reg.

reenganchar to reenlist. reg.

reentrar to reenter. reg.

reenvía 1. he (she/it) forwards; pres. ind. 3rd pers. sing. / *reenviar*. 2. (you) forward; impve. 2nd pers. sing.

reenvían they forward; pres. ind. 3rd pers. pl. / *reenviar*.

reenviar to forward. irr.

reenvías you forward; pres. ind. 2nd pers. sing. / *reenviar*.

reenvíe 1. that I may forward; pres. subj. 1st pers. sing. / *reenviar*. 2. that he (she/it) may forward; pres. subj. 3rd pers. sing. 3. let him (her/it) forward; impve. 3rd pers. sing.

reenvíen 1. that they may forward; pres. subj. 3rd pers. pl. / *reenviar*. 2. let them forward; impve. 3rd pers. pl.

reenvíes that you may forward; pres. subj. 2nd pers. sing. / *reenviar*.

reenvío I forward; pres. ind. 1st pers. sing. / *reenviar*.

reexpedir to forward. irr.

reexpida 1. that I may forward; pres. subj. 1st pers. sing. / *reexpedir*. 2. that he (she/it) may forward; pres. subj. 3rd pers. sing. 3. let him (her/it) forward; impve. 3rd pers. sing.

reexpidáis that you (all) may forward; pres. subj. 2nd pers. pl. / *reexpedir*.

reexpidamos 1. that we may forward; pres. subj. 1st pers. pl. / *reexpedir*. 2. let us forward; impve. 1st pers. pl.

reexpidan 1. that they may forward; pres. subj. 3rd pers. pl. / *reexpedir*. 2. let them forward; impve. 3rd pers. pl.

reexpidas that you may forward; pres. subj. 2nd pers. sing. / *reexpedir*.

reexpide 1. he (she/it) forwards; pres. ind. 3rd pers. sing. / *reexpedir*. 2. (you) forward; impve. 2nd pers. sing.

reexpiden they forward; pres. ind. 3rd pers. pl. / *reexpedir*.

reexpides you forward; pres. ind. 2nd pers. sing. / *reexpedir*.

reexpidiendo forwarding; pres. part. / *reexpedir*.

reexpidiera 1. that I might forward; imp. subj. 1st pers. sing. / *reexpedir*. 2. that he (she/it) might forward; imp. subj. 3rd pers. sing.

reexpidierais that you (all) might forward; imp. subj. 2nd pers pl. / *reexpedir*.

reexpidiéramos that we might forward; imp. subj. 1st pers. pl. / *reexpedir*.

reexpidieran that they might forward; imp. subj. 3rd pers. pl. / *reexpedir*.

reexpidieras that you might forward; imp. subj. 2nd pers. sing. / *reexpedir*.

reexpidieron they forwarded; past 3rd pers. pl. / *reexpedir*.

reexpidiese 1. that I might forward; imp. subj. 1st pers. sing. / *reexpedir*. 2. that he (she/it) might forward; imp. subj. 3rd pers. sing.

reexpidieseis that you (all) might forward; imp. subj. 2nd pers pl. / *reexpedir*.

reexpidiésemos that we might forward; imp. subj. 1st pers. pl. / *reexpedir*.

reexpidiesen that they might forward; imp. subj. 3rd pers. pl. / *reexpedir*.

reexpidieses that you might forward; imp. subj. 2nd pers. sing. / *reexpedir*.

reexpidió he (she/it) forwarded; past 3rd pers. sing. / *reexpedir*.

reexpido I forward; pres. ind. 1st pers. sing. / *reexpedir*.

refaccionar to repair. reg.

referíos (you all) relate; impve. 2nd pers. pl. / *referirse*.

referir to refer. irr.

referirse to relate. irr.

refiera 1. that I may refer; pres. subj. 1st pers. sing. / *referir*. 2. that he (she/it) may refer; pres. subj. 3rd pers. sing. 3. let him (her/it) refer; impve. 3rd pers. sing.

refieran 1. that they may refer; pres. subj. 3rd pers. pl. / *referir*. 2. let them refer; impve. 3rd pers. pl.

refiéranse let them relate; impve. 3rd pers. pl. / *referirse*.

refieras that you may refer; pres. subj. 2nd pers. sing. / *referir*.

refiérase let him (her/it) relate; impve. 3rd pers. sing. / *referirse*.

refiere 1. he (she/it) refers; pres. ind. 3rd pers. sing. / *referir*. 2. (you) refer; impve. 2nd pers. sing.

refieren they refer; pres. ind. 3rd pers. pl. / *referir*.

refieres you refer; pres. ind. 2nd pers. sing. / *referir*.

refiérete (you) relate; impve. 2nd pers. sing. / *referirse*.

refiero I refer; pres. ind. 1st pers. sing. / *referir*.

refinar to refine. reg.

refiráis that you (all) may refer; pres. subj. 2nd pers. pl. / *referir*.

refirámonos let us relate; impve. 1st pers. pl. / *referirse*.

refiramos 1. that we may refer; pres. subj. 1st pers. pl. / *referir*. 2. let us refer; impve. 1st pers. pl.

refiriendo referring; pres. part. / *referir*.

refiriéndose relating; pres. part. / *referirse*.

refiriera 1. that I might refer; imp. subj. 1st pers. sing. / *referir*. 2. that he (she/it) might refer; imp. subj. 3rd pers. sing.

refirierais that you (all) might refer; imp. subj. 2nd pers pl. / *referir*.

refiriéramos that we might refer; imp. subj. 1st pers. pl. / *referir*.

refirieran that they might refer; imp. subj. 3rd pers. pl. / *referir*.

refirieras that you might refer; imp. subj. 2nd pers. sing. / *referir*.

refirieron they referred; past 3rd pers. pl. / *referir*.

refiriese 1. that I might refer; imp. subj. 1st pers. sing. / *referir*. 2. that he (she/it) might refer; imp. subj. 3rd pers. sing.

refirieseis that you (all) might refer; imp. subj. 2nd pers pl. / *referir*.

refiriésemos that we might refer; imp. subj. 1st pers. pl. / *referir*.

refiriesen that they might refer; imp. subj. 3rd pers. pl. / *referir*.

refirieses that you might refer; imp. subj. 2nd pers. sing. / *referir*.

refirió he (she/it) referred; past 3rd pers. sing. / *referir*.

refirmar to ratify. reg.

reflectar to reflect. reg.

reflejándose being reflected; pres. part. / *reflejarse*.

reflejaos (you all) be reflected; impve. 2nd pers. pl. / *reflejarse*.

reflejar to reflect. reg.

reflejarse to be reflected. reg.

refléjate (you) be reflected; impve. 2nd pers. sing. / *reflejarse*.

reflejémonos let us be reflected; impve. 1st pers. pl. / *reflejarse*.

refléjense let them be reflected; impve. 3rd pers. pl. / *reflejarse*.

refléjese let him (her/it) be reflected; impve. 3rd pers. sing. / *reflejarse*.

reflexionar to think over. reg.

refluir to flow back. irr.

refluya 1. that it may flow back; pres. subj. 3rd pers. sing. / *refluir*. 2. let it flow back; impve. 3rd pers. sing.

refluyan 1. that they may flow back; pres. subj. 3rd pers. pl. / *refluir*. 2. let them flow back; impve. 3rd pers. pl.

refluye it flows back; pres. ind. 3rd pers. sing. / *refluir*.

refluyen they flow back; pres. ind. 3rd pers. pl. / *refluir*.

refluyendo flowing back; pres. part. / *refluir*.

refluyera that it might flow back; imp. subj. 3rd pers. sing. / *refluir*.

refluyeran that they might flow back; imp. subj. 3rd pers. pl. / *refluir*.

refluyeron they flowed back; past 3rd pers. pl. / *refluir*.

refluyese that it might flow back; imp. subj. 3rd pers. sing. / *refluir*.

refluyesen that they might flow back; imp. subj. 3rd pers. pl. / *refluir*.

refluyó it flowed back; past 3rd pers. sing. / *refluir*.

refocilándose frolicing; pres. part. / *refocilarse*.

refocilaos (you all) frolic; impve. 2nd pers. pl. / *refocilarse*.

refocilar to please. reg.

refocilarse to frolic. reg.

refocílate (you) frolic; impve. 2nd pers. sing. / *refocilarse*.

refocilémonos let us frolic; impve. 1st pers. pl. / *refocilarse*.

refocílense let them frolic; impve. 3rd pers. pl. / *refocilarse*.

refocílese let him (her/it) frolic; impve. 3rd pers. sing. / *refocilarse*.

reforcé I reinforced; past 1st pers. sing. / *reforzar*.

reforcéis that you (all) may reinforce; pres. subj. 2nd pers. pl. / *reforzar*.

reforcemos 1. that we may reinforce; pres. subj. 1st pers. pl. / *reforzar*. 2. let us reinforce; impve. 1st pers. pl.

reformándose reforming; pres. part. / *reformarse*.

reformaos (you all) reform; impve. 2nd pers. pl. / *reformarse*.

reformar to reform. reg.

reformarse to reform. reg.

refórmate (you) reform; impve. 2nd pers. sing. / *reformarse*.

reformémonos let us reform; impve. 1st pers. pl. / *reformarse*.

refórmense let them reform; impve. 3rd pers. pl. / *reformarse*.

refórmese let him (her/it) reform; impve. 3rd pers. sing. / *reformarse*.

reforzar to reinforce. irr.

refractar to refract. reg.
refregar to rub. irr.
refregué I rubbed; past 1st pers. sing. / *refregar.*
refreguéis that you (all) may rub; pres. subj. 2nd pers. pl. / *refregar.*
refreguemos 1. that we may rub; pres. subj. 1st pers. pl. / *refregar.* 2. let us rub; impve. 1st pers. pl.
refreír to refry. irr.
refrenar to restrain. reg.
refrendar to countersign. reg.
refrescándose cooling off; pres. part. / *refrescarse.*
refrescaos (you all) cool off; impve. 2nd pers. pl. / *refrescarse.*
refrescar to refresh. irr.
refrescarse to cool off. irr.
refréscate (you) cool off; impve. 2nd pers. sing. / *refrescarse.*
refresque 1. that I may refresh; pres. subj. 1st pers. sing. / *refrescar.* 2. that he (she/it) may refresh; pres. subj. 3rd pers. sing. 3. let him (her/it) refresh; impve. 3rd pers. sing.
refresqué I refreshed; past 1st pers. sing. / *refrescar.*
refresquéis that you (all) may refresh; pres. subj. 2nd pers. pl. / *refrescar.*
refresquémonos let us cool off; impve. 1st pers. pl. / *refrescarse.*
refresquemos 1. that we may refresh; pres. subj. 1st pers. pl. / *refrescar.* 2. let us refresh; impve. 1st pers. pl.
refresquen 1. that they may refresh; pres. subj. 3rd pers. pl. / *refrescar.* 2. let them refresh; impve. 3rd pers. pl.
refrésquense let them cool off; impve. 3rd pers. pl. / *refrescarse.*
refresques that you may refresh; pres. subj. 2nd pers. sing. / *refrescar.*
refrésquese let him (her/it) cool off; impve. 3rd pers. sing. / *refrescarse.*
refría 1. that I may refry; pres. subj. 1st pers. sing. / *refreír.* 2. that he (she/it) may refry; pres. subj. 3rd pers. sing. 3. let him (her/it) refry; impve. 3rd pers. sing.
refriáis that you (all) may refry; pres. subj. 2nd pers. pl. / *refreír.*
refriamos that we may refry; pres. subj. 1st pers. pl. / *refreír.*
refrían 1. that they may refry; pres. subj. 3rd pers. pl. / *refreír.* 2. let them refry; impve. 3rd pers. pl.
refrías that you may refry; pres. subj. 2nd pers. sing. / *refreír.*
refríe 1. he (she/it) refries; pres. ind. 3rd pers. sing. / *refreír.* 2. (you) refry; impve. 2nd pers. sing.
refriega 1. he (she/it) rubs; pres. ind. 3rd pers. sing. / *refregar.* 2. (you) rub; impve. 2nd pers. sing.
refriegan they rub; pres. ind. 3rd pers. pl. / *refregar.*
refriegas you rub; pres. ind. 2nd pers. sing. / *refregar.*
refriego I rub; pres. ind. 1st pers. sing. / *refregar.*

refriegue 1. that I may rub; pres. subj. 1st pers. sing. / *refregar.* 2. that he (she/it) may rub; pres. subj. 3rd pers. sing. 3. let him (her/it) rub; impve. 3rd pers. sing.
refrieguen 1. that they may rub; pres. subj. 3rd pers. pl. / *refregar.* 2. let them rub; impve. 3rd pers. pl.
refriegues that you may rub; pres. subj. 2nd pers. sing. / *refregar.*
refríen they refry; pres. ind. 3rd pers. pl. / *refreír.*
refriendo refrying; pres. part. / *refreír.*
refriera 1. that I might refry; imp. subj. 1st pers. sing. / *refreír.* 2. that he (she/it) might refry; imp. subj. 3rd pers. sing.
refrierais that you (all) might refry; imp. subj. 2nd pers pl. / *refreír.*
refriéramos that we might refry; imp. subj. 1st pers. pl. / *refreír.*
refrieran that they might refry; imp. subj. 3rd pers. pl. / *refreír.*
refrieras that you might refry; imp. subj. 2nd pers. sing. / *refreír.*
refrieron they refried; past 3rd pers. pl. / *refreír.*
refríes you refry; pres. ind. 2nd pers. sing. / *refreír.*
refriese 1. that I might refry; imp. subj. 1st pers. sing. / *refreír.* 2. that he (she/it) might refry; imp. subj. 3rd pers. sing.
refrieseis that you (all) might refry; imp. subj. 2nd pers pl. / *refreír.*
refriésemos that we might refry; imp. subj. 1st pers. pl. / *refreír.*
refriesen that they might refry; imp. subj. 3rd pers. pl. / *refreír.*
refrieses that you might refry; imp. subj. 2nd pers. sing. / *refreír.*
refrigerar to refrigerate. reg.
refringir to refract. irr.
refrinja 1. that it may refract; pres. subj. 3rd pers. sing. / *refringir.* 2.let it refract; impve. 3rd pers. sing.
refrinjan 1. that they may refract; pres. subj. 3rd pers. pl. / *refringir.* 2. let them refract; impve. 3rd pers. pl.
refrió he (she/it) refried; past 3rd pers. sing. / *refreír.*
refrío I refry; pres. ind. 1st pers. sing. / *refreír.*
refrito refried; past part. / *refreír.*
refuerce 1. that I may reinforce; pres. subj. 1st pers. sing. / *reforzar.* 2. that he (she/it) may reinforce; pres. subj. 3rd pers. sing. 3. let him (her/it) reinforce; impve. 3rd pers. sing.
refuercen 1. that they may reinforce; pres. subj. 3rd pers. pl. / *reforzar.* 2. let them reinforce; impve. 3rd pers. pl.
refuerces that you may reinforce; pres. subj. 2nd pers. sing. / *reforzar.*
refuerza 1. he (she/it) reinforces; pres. ind. 3rd pers. sing. / *reforzar.* 2. (you) reinforce; impve. 2nd pers. sing.
refuerzan they reinforce; pres. ind. 3rd pers. pl. / *reforzar.*
refuerzas you reinforce; pres. ind. 2nd pers. sing. / *reforzar.*

refuerzo I reinforce; pres. ind. 1st pers. sing. / *reforzar.*

refugiándose taking refuge; pres. part. / *refugiarse.*

refugiaos (you all) take refuge; impve. 2nd pers. pl. / *refugiarse.*

refugiar to shelter. reg.

refugiarse to take refuge. reg.

refugíate (you) take refuge; impve. 2nd pers. sing. / *refugiarse.*

refugiémonos let us take refuge; impve. 1st pers. pl. / *refugiarse.*

refugíense let them take refuge; impve. 3rd pers. pl. / *refugiarse.*

refugíese let him (her/it) take refuge; impve. 3rd pers. sing. / *refugiarse.*

refulgir to shine. irr.

refulja 1. that I may shine; pres. subj. 1st pers. sing. / *refulgir.* 2. that he (she/it) may shine; pres. subj. 3rd pers. sing. 3. let him (her/it) shine; impve. 3rd pers. sing.

refuljáis that you (all) may shine; pres. subj. 2nd pers. pl. / *refulgir.*

refuljamos 1. that we may shine; pres. subj. 1st pers. pl. / *refulgir.* 2. let us shine; impve. 1st pers. pl.

refuljan 1. that they may shine; pres. subj. 3rd pers. pl. / *refulgir.* 2. let them shine; impve. 3rd pers. pl.

refuljas that you may shine; pres. subj. 2nd pers. sing. / *refulgir.*

refuljo I shine; pres. ind. 1st pers. sing. / *refulgir.*

refundir to remelt. reg.

refunfuñar to grumble. reg.

refutar to refute. reg.

regace 1. that I may tuck up; pres. subj. 1st pers. sing. / *regazar.* 2. that he (she/it) may tuck up; pres. subj. 3rd pers. sing. 3. let him (her/it) tuck up; impve. 3rd pers. sing.

regacé I tucked up; past 1st pers. sing. / *regazar.*

regacéis that you (all) may tuck up; pres. subj. 2nd pers. pl. / *regazar.*

regacemos 1. that we may tuck up; pres. subj. 1st pers. pl. / *regazar.* 2. let us tuck up; impve. 1st pers. pl.

regacen 1. that they may tuck up; pres. subj. 3rd pers. pl. / *regazar.* 2. let them tuck up; impve. 3rd pers. pl.

regaces that you may tuck up; pres. subj. 2nd pers. sing. / *regazar.*

regalándose living very well; pres. part. / *regalarse.*

regalaos (you all) live very well; impve. 2nd pers. pl. / *regalarse.*

regalar to give. reg.

regalarse to live very well. reg.

regálate (you) live very well; impve. 2nd pers. sing. / *regalarse.*

regalémonos let us live very well; impve. 1st pers. pl. / *regalarse.*

regálense let them live very well; impve. 3rd pers. pl. / *regalarse.*

regálese let him (her/it) live very well; impve. 3rd pers. sing. / *regalarse.*

regándose scattering; pres. part. / *regarse.*

regañar to scold or to growl. reg.

regaos (you all) scatter; impve. 2nd pers. pl. / *regarse.*

regar to water. irr.

regarse to scatter. irr.

regatear to haggle. reg.

regatonear to trade retail. reg.

regazar to tuck up. irr.

regenerar to regenerate. reg.

regentar to govern. reg.

regentear to boss. reg.

regimentar to regiment. irr.

regimienta 1. he (she/it) regiments; pres. ind. 3rd pers. sing. / *regimentar.* 2. (you) regiment; impve. 2nd pers. sing.

regimientan they regiment; pres. ind. 3rd pers. pl. / *regimentar.*

regimientas you regiment; pres. ind. 2nd pers. sing. / *regimentar.*

regimiente 1. that I may regiment; pres. subj. 1st pers. sing. / *regimentar.* 2. that he (she/it) may regiment; pres. subj. 3rd pers. sing. 3. let him (her/it) regiment; impve. 3rd pers. sing.

regimienten 1. that they may regiment; pres. subj. 3rd pers. pl. / *regimentar.* 2. let them regiment; impve. 3rd pers. pl.

regimientes that you may regiment; pres. subj. 2nd pers. sing. / *regimentar.*

regimiento I regiment; pres. ind. 1st pers. sing. / *regimentar.*

regir to rule or to govern. irr.

registrándose registering; pres. part. / *registrarse.*

registraos (you all) register; impve. 2nd pers. pl. / *registrarse.*

registrar to register or to inspect. reg.

registrarse to register. reg.

regístrate (you) register; impve. 2nd pers. sing. / *registrarse.*

registrémonos let us register; impve. 1st pers. pl. / *registrarse.*

regístrense let them register; impve. 3rd pers. pl. / *registrarse.*

regístrese let him (her/it) register; impve. 3rd pers. sing. / *registrarse.*

reglamentar to regulate. reg.

reglándose restricting oneself; pres. part. / *reglarse.*

reglaos (you all) restrict yourselves; impve. 2nd pers. pl. / *reglarse.*

reglar to line or to regulate. reg.

reglarse to restrict oneself. reg.

réglate (you) restrict yourself; impve. 2nd pers. sing. / *reglarse.*

reglémonos let us restrict ourselves; impve. 1st pers. pl. / *reglarse.*

réglense let them restrict themselves; impve. 3rd pers. pl. / *reglarse.*

réglese let him (her/it) restrict himself (herself/itself); impve. 3rd pers. sing. / *reglarse.*

regletear to lead. reg.

regocijándose rejoicing; pres. part. / *regocijarse.*

regocijaos (you all) rejoice; impve. 2nd pers. pl. / *regocijarse.*

regocijar to gladden. reg.

regocijarse to rejoice. reg.

regocíjate (you) rejoice; impve. 2nd pers. sing. / *regocijarse.*

regocijémonos let us rejoice; impve. 1st pers. pl. / *regocijarse.*

regocíjense let them rejoice; impve. 3rd pers. pl. / *regocijarse.*

regocíjese let him (her/it) rejoice; impve. 3rd pers. sing. / *regocijarse.*

regodeándose having fun; pres. part. / *regodearse.*

regodeaos (you all) have fun; impve. 2nd pers. pl. / *regodearse.*

regodearse to have fun. reg.

regodéate (you) have fun; impve. 2nd pers. sing. / *regodearse.*

regodeémonos let us have fun; impve. 1st pers. pl. / *regodearse.*

regodéense let them have fun; impve. 3rd pers. pl. / *regodearse.*

regodéese let him (her/it) have fun; impve. 3rd pers. sing. / *regodearse.*

regoldar to belch. irr.

regraciar to be grateful for. reg.

regresar to return. reg.

regué I watered; past 1st pers. sing. / *regar.*

reguéis that you (all) may water; pres. subj. 2nd pers. pl. / *regar.*

regüelda 1. he (she/it) belches; pres. ind. 3rd pers. sing. / *regoldar.* 2. (you) belch; impve. 2nd pers. sing.

regüeldan they belch; pres. ind. 3rd pers. pl. / *regoldar.*

regüeldas you belch; pres. ind. 2nd pers. sing. / *regoldar.*

regüelde 1. that I may belch; pres. subj. 1st pers. sing. / *regoldar.* 2. that he (she/it) may belch; pres. subj. 3rd pers. sing. 3. let him (her/it) belch; impve. 3rd pers. sing.

regüelden 1. that they may belch; pres. subj. 3rd pers. pl. / *regoldar.* 2. let them belch; impve. 3rd pers. pl.

regüeldes that you may belch; pres. subj. 2nd pers. sing. / *regoldar.*

regüeldo I belch; pres. ind. 1st pers. sing. / *regoldar.*

reguémonos let us scatter; impve. 1st pers. pl. / *regarse.*

reguemos 1. that we may water; pres. subj. 1st pers. pl. / *regar.* 2. let us water; impve. 1st pers. pl.

regular to regulate. reg.

regularice 1. that I may regularize; pres. subj. 1st pers. sing. / *regularizar.* 2. that he (she/it) may regularize; pres. subj. 3rd pers. sing. 3. let him (her/it) regularize; impve. 3rd pers. sing.

regularicé I regularized; past 1st pers. sing. / *regularizar.*

regularicéis that you (all) may regularize; pres. subj. 2nd pers. pl. / *regularizar.*

regularicemos 1. that we may regularize; pres. subj. 1st pers. pl. / *regularizar.* 2. let us regularize; impve. 1st pers. pl.

regularicen 1. that they may regularize; pres. subj. 3rd pers. pl. / *regularizar.* 2. let them regularize; impve. 3rd pers. pl.

regularices that you may regularize; pres. subj. 2nd pers. sing. / *regularizar.*

regularizar to regularize. irr.

regurgitar to regurgitate. reg.

rehabilitar to rehabilitate. reg.

rehaceos (you all) recover; impve. 2nd pers. pl. / *rehacerse.*

rehacer to remake. irr.

rehacerse to recover. irr.

rehaciéndose recovering; pres. part. / *rehacerse.*

rehaga 1. that I may remake; pres. subj. 1st pers. sing. / *rehacer.* 2. that he (she/it) may remake; pres. subj. 3rd pers. sing. 3. let him (her/it) remake; impve. 3rd pers. sing.

rehagáis that you (all) may remake; pres. subj. 2nd pers. pl. / *rehacer.*

rehagámonos let us recover; impve. 1st pers. pl. / *rehacerse.*

rehagamos 1. that we may remake; pres. subj. 1st pers. pl. / *rehacer.* 2. let us remake; impve. 1st pers. pl.

rehagan 1. that they may remake; pres. subj. 3rd pers. pl. / *rehacer.* 2. let them remake; impve. 3rd pers. pl.

reháganse let them recover; impve. 3rd pers. pl. / *rehacerse.*

rehagas that you may remake; pres. subj. 2nd pers. sing. / *rehacer.*

rehágase let him (her/it) recover; impve. 3rd pers. sing. / *rehacerse.*

rehago I remake; pres. ind. 1st pers. sing. / *rehacer.*

rehará he (she/it) will remake; fut. 3rd pers. sing. / *reharán.*

reharán they will remake; fut. 3rd pers. pl. / *rehacer.*

reharás you will remake; fut. 2nd pers. sing. / *rehacer.*

reharé I shall remake; fut. 1st pers. sing. / *rehacer.*

reharéis you (all) will remake; fut. 2nd pers. pl. / *rehacer.*

reharemos we shall remake; fut. 1st pers. pl. / *rehacer.*

reharía 1. I should remake; cond. 1st pers. sing. / *rehacer.* 2. he (she/it) would remake; cond. 3rd pers. sing.

reharíais you (all) would remake; cond. 2nd pers. pl. / *rehacer.*

reharíamos we should remake; cond. 1st pers. pl. / *rehacer.*

reharían they would remake; cond. 3rd pers. pl. / *rehacer.*

reharías you would remake; cond. 2nd pers. sing. / *rehacer.*

rehaz (you) remake; impve. 2nd pers. sing. / *rehacer.*

reházete (you) recover; impve. 2nd pers. sing. / *rehacerse.*

rehecho remade; past part. / *rehacer.*

reherir to repel. irr.

rehervir to reboil. irr.

rehervirse to ferment. irr.

rehice I remade; past 1st pers. sing. / *rehacer.*

rehiciera 1. that I might remake; imp. subj. 1st pers. sing. / *rehacer.* 2. that he (she/it) might remake; imp. subj. 3rd pers. sing.

rehicierais that you (all) might remake; imp. subj. 2nd pers pl. / *rehacer.*

rehiciéramos that we might remake; imp. subj. 1st pers. pl. / *rehacer.*

rehicieran that they might remake; imp. subj. 3rd pers. pl. / *rehacer.*

rehicieras that you might remake; imp. subj. 2nd pers. sing. / *rehacer.*

rehicieron they remade; past 3rd pers. pl. / *rehacer.*

rehiciese 1. that I might remake; imp. subj. 1st pers. sing. / *rehacer.* 2. that he (she/it) might remake; imp. subj. 3rd pers. sing.

rehicieseis that you (all) might remake; imp. subj. 2nd pers pl. / *rehacer.*

rehiciésemos that we might remake; imp. subj. 1st pers. pl. / *rehacer.*

rehiciesen that they might remake; imp. subj. 3rd pers. pl. / *rehacer.*

rehicieses that you might remake; imp. subj. 2nd pers. sing. / *rehacer.*

rehicimos we remade; past 1st pers. pl. / *rehacer.*

rehiciste you remade; past 2nd pers. sing. / *rehacer.*

rehicisteis you (all) remade; past 2nd pers. pl. / *rehacer.*

rehiera 1. that I may repel; pres. subj. 1st pers. sing. / *reherir.* 2. that he (she/it) may repel; pres. subj. 3rd pers. sing. 3. let him (her/it) repel; impve. 3rd pers. sing.

rehieran 1. that they may repel; pres. subj. 3rd pers. pl. / *reherir.* 2. let them repel; impve. 3rd pers. pl.

rehieras that you may repel; pres. subj. 2nd pers. sing. / *reherir.*

rehiere 1. he (she/it) repels; pres. ind. 3rd pers. sing. / *reherir.* 2. (you) repel; impve. 2nd pers. sing.

rehieren they repel; pres. ind. 3rd pers. pl. / *reherir.*

rehieres you repel; pres. ind. 2nd pers. sing. / *reherir.*

rehiero I repel; pres. ind. 1st pers. sing. / *reherir.*

rehierva 1. that I may reboil; pres. subj. 1st pers. sing. / *rehervir.* 2. that he (she/it) may reboil; pres. subj. 3rd pers. sing. 3. let him (her/it) reboil; impve. 3rd pers. sing.

rehiervan 1. that they may reboil; pres. subj. 3rd pers. pl. / *rehervir.* 2. let them reboil; impve. 3rd pers. pl.

rehiérvanse let them ferment; impve. 3rd pers. pl. / *rehervirse.*

rehiervas that you may reboil; pres. subj. 2nd pers. sing. / *rehervir.*

rehiérvase let it ferment; impve. 3rd pers. sing. / *rehervirse.*

rehierve 1. he (she/it) reboils; pres. ind. 3rd pers. sing. / *rehervir.* 2. (you) reboil; impve. 2nd pers. sing.

rehierven they reboil; pres. ind. 3rd pers. pl. / *rehervir.*

rehierves you reboil; pres. ind. 2nd pers. sing. / *rehervir.*

rehiervo I reboil; pres. ind. 1st pers. sing. / *rehervir.*

rehilar to quiver. reg.

rehiráis that you (all) may repel; pres. subj. 2nd pers. pl. / *reherir.*

rehiramos 1. that we may repel; pres. subj. 1st pers. pl. / *reherir.* 2. let us repel; impve. 1st pers. pl.

rehiriendo repelling; pres. part. / *reherir.*

rehiriera 1. that I might repel; imp. subj. 1st pers. sing. / *reherir.* 2. that he (she/it) might repel; imp. subj. 3rd pers. sing.

rehirierais that you (all) might repel; imp. subj. 2nd pers pl. / *reherir.*

rehiriéramos that we might repel; imp. subj. 1st pers. pl. / *reherir.*

rehirieran that they might repel; imp. subj. 3rd pers. pl. / *reherir.*

rehirieras that you might repel; imp. subj. 2nd pers. sing. / *reherir.*

rehirieron they repelled; past 3rd pers. pl. / *reherir.*

rehiriese 1. that I might repel; imp. subj. 1st pers. sing. / *reherir.* 2. that he (she/it) might repel; imp. subj. 3rd pers. sing.

rehirieseis that you (all) might repel; imp. subj. 2nd pers pl. / *reherir.*

rehiriésemos that we might repel; imp. subj. 1st pers. pl. / *reherir.*

rehiriesen that they might repel; imp. subj. 3rd pers. pl. / *reherir.*

rehirieses that you might repel; imp. subj. 2nd pers. sing. / *reherir.*

rehirió he (she/it) repelled; past 3rd pers. sing. / *reherir.*

rehirváis that you (all) may reboil; pres. subj. 2nd pers. pl. / *rehervir.*

rehirvamos 1. that we may reboil; pres. subj. 1st pers. pl. / *rehervir.* 2. let us reboil; impve. 1st pers. pl.

rehirviendo reboiling; pres. part. / *rehervir.*

rehirviéndose fermenting; pres. part. / *rehervirse.*

rehirviera 1. that I might reboil; imp. subj. 1st pers. sing. / *rehervir.* 2. that he (she/it) might reboil; imp. subj. 3rd pers. sing.

rehirvierais that you (all) might reboil; imp. subj. 2nd pers pl. / *rehervir.*

rehirviéramos that we might reboil; imp. subj. 1st pers. pl. / *rehervir.*

rehirvieran that they might reboil; imp. subj. 3rd pers. pl. / *rehervir.*

rehirvieras that you might reboil; imp. subj. 2nd pers. sing. / *rehervir.*

rehirvieron they reboiled; past 3rd pers. pl. / *rehervir.*

rehirviese 1. that I might reboil; imp. subj. 1st pers. sing. / *rehervir.* 2. that he (she/it) might reboil; imp. subj. 3rd pers. sing.

rehirvieseis that you (all) might reboil; imp. subj. 2nd pers pl. / *rehervir.*

rehirviésemos that we might reboil; imp. subj. 1st pers. pl. / *rehervir.*

rehirviesen that they might reboil; imp. subj. 3rd pers. pl. / *rehervir.*

rehirvieses that you might reboil; imp. subj. 2nd pers. sing. / *rehervir.*

rehirvió he (she/it) reboiled; past 3rd pers. sing. / *rehervir.`*

rehizo he (she/it) remade; past 3rd pers. sing. / *rehacer.*

rehogar to simmer in a covered pan. irr.

rehogue 1. that I may simmer in a covered pan; pres. subj. 1st pers. sing. / *rehogar.* 2. that he (she/it) may simmer in a covered pan; pres. subj. 3rd pers. sing. 3. let him (her/it) simmer in a covered pan; impve. 3rd pers. sing.

rehogué I simmered in a covered pan; past 1st pers. sing. / *rehogar.*

rehoguéis that you (all) may simmer in a covered pan; pres. subj. 2nd pers. pl. / *rehogar.*

rehoguemos 1. that we may simmer in a covered pan; pres. subj. 1st pers. pl. / *rehogar.* 2. let us simmer in a covered pan; impve. 1st pers. pl.

rehoguen 1. that they may simmer in a covered pan; pres. subj. 3rd pers. pl. / *rehogar.* 2. let them simmer in a covered pan; impve. 3rd pers. pl.

rehogues that you may simmer in a covered pan; pres. subj. 2nd pers. sing. / *rehogar.*

rehuíos (you all) flee; impve. 2nd pers. pl. / *rehuirse.*

rehuir to shun. irr.

rehuirse to flee. irr.

rehusándose refusing; pres. part. / *rehusarse.*

rehusaos (you all) refuse; impve. 2nd pers. pl. / *rehusarse.*

rehusar to refuse. reg.

rehusarse to refuse. reg.

rehúsate (you) refuse; impve. 2nd pers. sing. / *rehusarse.*

rehusémonos let us refuse; impve. 1st pers. pl. / *rehusarse.*

rehúsense let them refuse; impve. 3rd pers. pl. / *rehusarse.*

rehúsese let him (her/it) refuse; impve. 3rd pers. sing. / *rehusarse.*

rehuya 1. that I may shun; pres. subj. 1st pers. sing. / *rehuir.* 2. that he (she/it) may shun; pres. subj. 3rd pers. sing. 3. let him (her/it) shun; impve. 3rd pers. sing.

rehuyáis that you (all) may shun; pres. subj. 2nd pers. pl. / *rehuir.*

rehuyámonos let us flee; impve. 1st pers. pl. / *rehuirse.*

rehuyamos 1. that we may shun; pres. subj. 1st pers. pl. / *rehuir.* 2. let us shun; impve. 1st pers. pl.

rehuyan 1. that they may shun; pres. subj. 3rd pers. pl. / *rehuir.* 2. let them shun; impve. 3rd pers. pl.

rehúyanse let them flee; impve. 3rd pers. pl. / *rehuirse.*

rehuyas that you may shun; pres. subj. 2nd pers. sing. / *rehuir.*

rehúyase let him (her/it) flee; impve. 3rd pers. sing. / *rehuirse.*

rehuye 1. he (she/it) shuns; pres. ind. 3rd pers. sing. / *rehuir.* 2. (you) shun; impve. 2nd pers. sing.

rehuyen they shun; pres. ind. 3rd pers. pl. / *rehuir.*

rehuyendo shunning; pres. part. / *rehuir.*

rehuyéndose fleeing; pres. part. / *rehuirse.*

rehuyera 1. that I might shun; imp. subj. 1st pers. sing. / *rehuir.* 2. that he (she/it) might shun; imp. subj. 3rd pers. sing.

rehuyerais that you (all) might shun; imp. subj. 2nd pers pl. / *rehuir.*

rehuyéramos that we might shun; imp. subj. 1st pers. pl. / *rehuir.*

rehuyeran that they might shun; imp. subj. 3rd pers. pl. / *rehuir.*

rehuyeras that you might shun; imp. subj. 2nd pers. sing. / *rehuir.*

rehuyeron they shunned; past 3rd pers. pl. / *rehuir.*

rehuyes you shun; pres. ind. 2nd pers. sing. / *rehuir.*

rehuyese 1. that I might shun; imp. subj. 1st pers. sing. / *rehuir.* 2. that he (she/it) might shun; imp. subj. 3rd pers. sing.

rehuyeseis that you (all) might shun; imp. subj. 2nd pers pl. / *rehuir.*

rehuyésemos that we might shun; imp. subj. 1st pers. pl. / *rehuir.*

rehuyesen that they might shun; imp. subj. 3rd pers. pl. / *rehuir.*

rehuyeses that you might shun; imp. subj. 2nd pers. sing. / *rehuir.*

rehúyete (you) flee; impve. 2nd pers. sing. / *rehuirse.*

rehuyo I shun; pres. ind. 1st pers. sing. / *rehuir.*

rehuyó he (she/it) shunned; past 3rd pers. sing. / *rehuir.*

reimpreso reprinted; past part. / *reimprimir.*

reimprimir to reprint. reg. except for pp.

reinar to reign. reg.

reincidir to relapse. reg.

reingresar to reenter. reg.

reinstalar to reinstate. reg.

reintegrándose recovering; pres. part. / *reintegrarse.*

reintegraos (you all) recover; impve. 2nd pers. pl. / *reintegrarse.*

reintegrar to reintegrate or to restore. reg.

reintegrarse to recover. reg.

reintégrate (you) recover; impve. 2nd pers. sing. / *reintegrarse.*

reintegrémonos let us recover; impve. 1st pers. pl. / *reintegrarse.*

reintégrense let them recover; impve. 3rd pers. pl. / *reintegrarse.*

reintégrese let him (her/it) recover; impve. 3rd pers. sing. / *reintegrarse.*

reíos (you all) laugh at; impve. 2nd pers. pl. / *reírse.*

reír to laugh. irr.

reírse to laugh at. irr.

reiterar to reiterate. reg.

reivindicar to vindicate. irr.

reivindique 1. that I may vindicate; pres. subj. 1st pers. sing. / *reivindicar.* 2. that he (she/it) may vindicate; pres. subj. 3rd pers. sing. 3. let him (her/it) vindicate; impve. 3rd pers. sing.

reivindiqué I vindicated; past 1st pers. sing. / *reivindicar.*

reivindiquéis that you (all) may vindicate; pres. subj. 2nd pers. pl. / *reivindicar.*

reivindiquemos 1. that we may vindicate; pres. subj. 1st pers. pl. / *reivindicar.* 2. let us vindicate; impve. 1st pers. pl.

reivindiquen 1. that they may vindicate; pres. subj. 3rd pers. pl. / *reivindicar.* 2. let them vindicate; impve. 3rd pers. pl.

reivindiques that you may vindicate; pres. subj. 2nd pers. sing. / *reivindicar.*

rejonear to spear or lance a bull. reg.

rejuveneceos (you all) become rejuvenated; impve. 2nd pers. pl. / *rejuvenecerse.*

rejuvenecer to rejuvenate. irr.

rejuvenecerse to become rejuvenated. irr.

rejuvenécete (you) become rejuvenated; impve. 2nd pers. sing. / *rejuvenecerse.*

rejuveneciéndose becoming rejuvenated; pres. part. / *rejuvenecerse.*

rejuvenezca 1. that I may rejuvenate; pres. subj. 1st pers. sing. / *rejuvenecer.* 2. that he (she/it) may rejuvenate; pres. subj. 3rd pers. sing. 3. let him (her/it) rejuvenate; impve. 3rd pers. sing.

rejuvenezcáis that you (all) may rejuvenate; pres. subj. 2nd pers. pl. / *rejuvenecer.*

rejuvenezcámonos let us become rejuvenated; impve. 1st pers. pl. / *rejuvenecerse.*

rejuvenezcamos 1. that we may rejuvenate; pres. subj. 1st pers. pl. / *rejuvenecer.* 2. let us rejuvenate; impve. 1st pers. pl.

rejuvenezcan 1. that they may rejuvenate; pres. subj. 3rd pers. pl. / *rejuvenecer.* 2. let them rejuvenate; impve. 3rd pers. pl.

rejuvenézcanse let them become rejuvenated; impve. 3rd pers. pl. / *rejuvenecerse.*

rejuvenezcas that you may rejuvenate; pres. subj. 2nd pers. sing. / *rejuvenecer.*

rejuvenézcase let him (her/it) become rejuvenated; impve. 3rd pers. sing. / *rejuvenecerse.*

rejuvenezco I rejuvenate; pres. ind. 1st pers. sing. / *rejuvenecer.*

relacionándose becoming related; pres. part. / *relacionarse.*

relacionaos (you all) become related; impve. 2nd pers. pl. / *relacionarse.*

relacionar to relate. reg.

relacionarse to become related. reg.

relaciónate (you) become related; impve. 2nd pers. sing. / *relacionarse.*

relacionémonos let us become related; impve. 1st pers. pl. / *relacionarse.*

relaciónense let them become related; impve. 3rd pers. pl. / *relacionarse.*

relaciónese let him (her/it) become related; impve. 3rd pers. sing. / *relacionarse.*

relajándose getting a hernia; pres. part. / *relajarse.*

relajaos (you all) get a hernia; impve. 2nd pers. pl. / *relajarse.*

relajar to relax. reg.

relajarse to get a hernia. reg.

relájate (you) get a hernia; impve. 2nd pers. sing. / *relajarse.*

relajémonos let us get a hernia; impve. 1st pers. pl. / *relajarse.*

relájense let them get a hernia; impve. 3rd pers. pl. / *relajarse.*

relájese let him (her/it) get a hernia; impve. 3rd pers. sing. / *relajarse.*

relamámonos let us smack the lips; impve. 1st pers. pl. / *relamerse.*

relámanse let them smack the lips; impve. 3rd pers. pl. / *relamerse.*

relámase let him (her/it) smack the lips; impve. 3rd pers. sing. / *relamerse.*

relameos (you all) smack the lips; impve. 2nd pers. pl. / *relamerse.*

relamer to lick again. reg.

relamerse to smack the lips. reg.

relámete (you) smack the lips; impve. 2nd pers. sing. / *relamerse.*

relamiéndose smacking the lips; pres. part. / *relamerse.*

relampaguear to flash or to lighten. reg.

relatar to relate. reg.

releer to reread. irr.

relegar to relegate or to banish. irr.

relegue 1. that I may relegate; pres. subj. 1st pers. sing. / *relegar.* 2. that he (she/it) may relegate; pres. subj. 3rd pers. sing. 3. let him (her/it) relegate; impve. 3rd pers. sing.

relegué I relegated; past 1st pers. sing. / *relegar.*

releguéis that you (all) may relegate; pres. subj. 2nd pers. pl. / *relegar.*

releguemos 1. that we may relegate; pres. subj. 1st pers. pl. / *relegar.* 2. let us relegate; impve. 1st pers. pl.

releguen 1. that they may relegate; pres. subj. 3rd pers. pl. / *relegar.* 2. let them relegate; impve. 3rd pers. pl.

relegues that you may relegate; pres. subj. 2nd pers. sing. / *relegar.*

releí I reread; past 1st pers. sing. / *releer.*

releído reread; past part. / *releer.*

releímos we reread; past 1st pers. pl. / *releer.*

releíste you reread; past 2nd pers. sing. / *releer.*

releísteis you (all) reread; past 2nd pers. pl. / *releer.*

relevándose taking turns; pres. part. / *relevarse.*

relevaos (you all) take turns; impve. 2nd pers. pl. / *relevarse.*

relevar to relieve. reg.

relevarse to take turns. reg.

relévate (you) take turns; impve. 2nd pers. sing. / *relevarse.*

relevémonos let us take turns; impve. 1st pers. pl. / *relevarse.*

relévense let them take turns; impve. 3rd pers. pl. / *relevarse.*

relévese let him (her/it) take turns; impve. 3rd pers. sing. / *relevarse.*

releyendo rereading; pres. part. / *releer.*

releyera 1. that I might reread; imp. subj. 1st pers. sing. / *releer.* 2. that he (she/it) might reread; imp. subj. 3rd pers. sing.

releyeran that you (all) might reread; imp. subj. 2nd pers pl. / *releer.*

releyéramos that we might reread; imp. subj. 1st pers. pl. / *releer.*

releyeran that they might reread; imp. subj. 3rd pers. pl. / *releer.*

releyeras that you might reread; imp. subj. 2nd pers. sing. / *releer.*

releyeron they reread; past 3rd pers. pl. / *releer.*

releyese 1. that I might reread; imp. subj. 1st pers. sing. / *releer.* 2. that he (she/it) might reread; imp. subj. 3rd pers. sing.

releyeseis that you (all) might reread; imp. subj. 2nd pers pl. / *releer.*

releyésemos that we might reread; imp. subj. 1st pers. pl. / *releer.*

releyesen that they might reread; imp. subj. 3rd pers. pl. / *releer.*

releyeses that you might reread; imp. subj. 2nd pers. sing. / *releer.*

releyó he (she/it) reread; past 3rd pers. sing. / *releer.*

relinchar to neigh. reg.

relucir to shine. irr.

relumbrar to sparkle. reg.

reluzca 1. that I may shine; pres. subj. 1st pers. sing. / *relucir.* 2. that he (she/it) may shine; pres. subj. 3rd pers. sing. 3. let him (her/it) shine; impve. 3rd pers. sing.

reluzcáis that you (all) may shine; pres. subj. 2nd pers. pl. / *relucir.*

reluzcamos 1. that we may shine; pres. subj. 1st pers. pl. / *relucir.* 2. let us shine; impve. 1st pers. pl.

reluzcan 1. that they may shine; pres. subj. 3rd pers. pl. / *relucir.* 2. let them shine; impve. 3rd pers. pl.

reluzcas that you may shine; pres. subj. 2nd pers. sing. / *relucir.*

reluzco I shine; pres. ind. 1st pers. sing. / *relucir.*

rellanándose falling flat; pres. part. / *rellanarse.*

rellanaos (you all) fall flat; impve. 2nd pers. pl. / *rellanarse.*

rellanar to level out. reg.

rellanarse to fall flat. reg.

rellánate (you) fall flat; impve. 2nd pers. sing. / *rellanarse.*

rellanémonos let us fall flat; impve. 1st pers. pl. / *rellanarse.*

rellánense let them fall flat; impve. 3rd pers. pl. / *rellanarse.*

rellánese let him (her/it) fall flat; impve. 3rd pers. sing. / *rellanarse.*

rellenándose being stuffed; pres. part. / *rellenarse.*

rellenaos (you all) be stuffed; impve. 2nd pers. pl. / *rellenarse.*

rellenar to refill. reg.

rellenarse to be stuffed. reg.

rellénate (you) be stuffed; impve. 2nd pers. sing. / *rellenarse.*

rellenémonos let us be stuffed; impve. 1st pers. pl. / *rellenarse.*

rellénense let them be stuffed; impve. 3rd pers. pl. / *rellenarse.*

rellénese let him (her/it) be stuffed; impve. 3rd pers. sing. / *rellenarse.*

remachándose being tight-lipped; pres. part. / *remacharse.*

remachaos (you all) be tight-lipped; impve. 2nd pers. pl. / *remacharse.*

remachar to rivet. reg.

remacharse to be tight-lipped. reg.

remáchate (you) be tight-lipped; impve. 2nd pers. sing. / *remacharse.*

remachémonos let us be tight-lipped; impve. 1st pers. pl. / *remacharse.*

remáchense let them be tight-lipped; impve. 3rd pers. pl. / *remacharse.*

remáchese let him (her/it) be tight-lipped; impve. 3rd pers. sing. / *remacharse.*

remanecer to appear suddenly. irr.

remanezca 1. that I may appear suddenly; pres. subj. 1st pers. sing. / *remanecer.* 2. that he (she/it) may appear suddenly; pres. subj. 3rd pers. sing. 3. let him (her/it) appear suddenly; impve. 3rd pers. sing.

remanezcáis that you (all) may appear suddenly; pres. subj. 2nd pers. pl. / *remanecer.*

remanezcamos 1. that we may appear suddenly; pres. subj. 1st pers. pl. / *remanecer.* 2. let us appear suddenly; impve. 1st pers. pl.

remanezcan 1. that they may appear suddenly; pres. subj. 3rd pers. pl. / *remanecer.* 2. let them appear suddenly; impve. 3rd pers. pl.

remanezcas that you may appear suddenly; pres. subj. 2nd pers. sing. / *remanecer.*

remanezco I appear suddenly; pres. ind. 1st pers. sing. / *remanecer.*

remangar to roll up. irr.

remangue 1. that I may roll up; pres. subj. 1st pers. sing. / *remangar.* 2. that he (she/it) may roll up; pres. subj. 3rd pers. sing. 3. let him (her/it) roll up; impve. 3rd pers. sing.

remangué I rolled up; past 1st pers. sing. / *remangar.*

remanguéis that you (all) may roll up; pres. subj. 2nd pers. pl. / *remangar.*

remanguemos 1. that we may roll up; pres. subj. 1st pers. pl. / *remangar.* 2. let us roll up; impve. 1st pers. pl.

remanguen 1. that they may roll up; pres. subj. 3rd pers. pl. / *remangar.* 2. let them roll up; impve. 3rd pers. pl.

remangues that you may roll up; pres. subj. 2nd pers. sing. / *remangar.*

remansándose slowing; pres. part. / *remansarse.*

remansaos (you all) slow; impve. 2nd pers. pl. / *remansarse.*

remansarse to slow or to eddy. reg.

remánsate (you) slow; impve. 2nd pers. sing. / *remansarse.*

remansémonos let us slow; impve. 1st pers. pl. / *remansarse.*

remánsense let them slow; impve. 3rd pers. pl. / *remansarse.*

remánsese let him (her/it) slow; impve. 3rd pers. sing. / *remansarse.*

remar to row or to toil. reg.

rematándose being finished; pres. part. / *rematarse.*

remataos (you all) be finished; impve. 2nd pers. pl. / *rematarse.*

rematar to end. reg.

rematarse to be finished. reg.

remátate (you) be finished; impve. 2nd pers. sing. / *rematarse.*

rematémonos let us be finished; impve. 1st pers. pl. / *rematarse.*

remátense let them be finished; impve. 3rd pers. pl. / *rematarse.*

remátese let him (her/it) be finished; impve. 3rd pers. sing. / *rematarse.*

rembolsar to reimburse. reg.

remecer to rock or swing. irr.

remedar to imitate. reg.

remediar to remedy. reg.

rememorar to remember. reg.

remendar to mend. irr.

rementir to tell many lies. irr.

rementirse to tell many lies. irr.

remesar to remit or to pull hair. reg.

remeter to take in a garment. reg.

remeza 1. that I may rock; pres. subj. 1st pers. sing. / *remecer.* 2. that he (she/it) may rock; pres. subj. 3rd pers. sing. 3. let him (her/it) rock; impve. 3rd pers. sing.

remezáis that you (all) may rock; pres. subj. 2nd pers. pl. / *remecer.*

remezamos 1. that we may rock; pres. subj. 1st pers. pl. / *remecer.* 2. let us rock; impve. 1st pers. pl.

remezan 1. that they may rock; pres. subj. 3rd pers. pl. / *remecer.* 2. let them rock; impve. 3rd pers. pl.

remezas that you may rock; pres. subj. 2nd pers. sing. / *remecer.*

remezo I rock; pres. ind. 1st pers. sing. / *remecer.*

remienda 1. he (she/it) mends; pres. ind. 3rd pers. sing. / *remendar.* 2. (you) mend; impve. 2nd pers. sing.

remiendan they mend; pres. ind. 3rd pers. pl. / *remendar.*

remiendas you mend; pres. ind. 2nd pers. sing. / *remendar.*

remiende 1. that I may mend; pres. subj. 1st pers. sing. / *remendar.* 2. that he (she/it) may mend; pres. subj. 3rd pers. sing. 3. let him (her/it) mend; impve. 3rd pers. sing.

remienden 1. that they may mend; pres. subj. 3rd pers. pl. / *remendar.* 2. let them mend; impve. 3rd pers. pl.

remiendes that you may mend; pres. subj. 2nd pers. sing. / *remendar.*

remiendo I mend; pres. ind. 1st pers. sing. / *remendar.*

remienta 1. that I may tell many lies; pres. subj. 1st pers. sing. / *rementir.* 2. that he (she/it) may tell many lies; pres. subj. 3rd pers. sing. 3. let him (her/it) tell many lies; impve. 3rd pers. sing.

remientan 1. that they may tell many lies; pres. subj. 3rd pers. pl. / *rementir.* 2. let them tell many lies; impve. 3rd pers. pl.

remiéntanse let them tell many lies; impve. 3rd pers. pl. / *rementirse.*

remientas that you may tell many lies; pres. subj. 2nd pers. sing. / *rementir.*

remiéntase let him (her/it) tell many lies; impve. 3rd pers. sing. / *rementirse.*

remiente 1. he (she/it) tells many lies; pres. ind. 3rd pers. sing. / *rementir.* 2. (you) tell many lies; impve. 2nd pers. sing.

remienten they tell many lies; pres. ind. 3rd pers. pl. / *rementir.*

remientes you tell many lies; pres. ind. 2nd pers. sing. / *rementir.*

remiéntete (you) tell many lies; impve. 2nd pers. sing. / *rementirse.*

remiento I tell many lies; pres. ind. 1st pers. sing. / *rementir.*

remilgándose being fussy; pres. part. / *remilgarse.*

remilgaos (you all) be fussy; impve. 2nd pers. pl. / *remilgarse.*

remilgarse to be fussy. irr.

remílgate (you) be fussy; impve. 2nd pers. sing. / *remilgarse.*

remilgue 1. that I may be fussy; pres. subj. 1st pers. sing. / *remilgarse.* 2. that he (she/it) may be fussy; pres. subj. 3rd pers. sing.

remilgué I was fussy; past 1st pers. sing. / *remilgarse.*

remilguéis that you (all) may be fussy; pres. subj. 2nd pers. pl. / *remilgarse.*

remilguémonos let us be fussy; impve. 1st pers. pl. / *remilgarse.*

remilguemos that we may be fussy; pres. subj. 1st pers. pl. / *remilgarse.*

remilguen that they may be fussy; pres. subj. 3rd pers. pl. / *remilgarse.*

remílguense let them be fussy; impve. 3rd pers. pl. / *remilgarse.*

remilgues that you may be fussy; pres. subj. 2nd pers. sing. / *remilgarse.*

remílguese let him (her/it) be fussy; impve. 3rd pers. sing. / *remilgarse.*

remintáis that you (all) may tell many lies; pres. subj. 2nd pers. pl. / *rementir.*

remintámonos let us tell many lies; impve. 1st pers. pl. / *rementirse.*

remintamos 1. that we may tell many lies; pres. subj. 1st pers. pl. / *rementir*. 2. let us tell many lies; impve. 1st pers. pl.

remintiendo telling many lies; pres. part. / *rementir*.

remintiéndose telling many lies; pres. part. / *rementirse*.

remintiera 1. that I might tell many lies; imp. subj. 1st pers. sing. / *rementir*. 2. that he (she/it) might tell many lies; imp. subj. 3rd pers. sing.

remintierais that you (all) might tell many lies; imp. subj. 2nd pers pl. / *rementir*.

remintiéramos that we might tell many lies; imp. subj. 1st pers. pl. / *rementir*.

remintieran that they might tell many lies; imp. subj. 3rd pers. pl. / *rementir*.

remintieras that you might tell many lies; imp. subj. 2nd pers. sing. / *rementir*.

remintieron they told many lies; past 3rd pers. pl. / *rementir*.

remintiese 1. that I might tell many lies; imp. subj. 1st pers. sing. / *rementir*. 2. that he (she/it) might tell many lies; imp. subj. 3rd pers. sing.

remintieseis that you (all) might tell many lies; imp. subj. 2nd pers pl. / *rementir*.

remintiésemos that we might tell many lies; imp. subj. 1st pers. pl. / *rementir*.

remintiesen that they might tell many lies; imp. subj. 3rd pers. pl. / *rementir*.

remintieses that you might tell many lies; imp. subj. 2nd pers. sing. / *rementir*.

remintió he (she/it) told many lies; past 3rd pers. sing. / *rementir*.

remirándose taking great pains; pres. part. / *remirarse*.

remiraos (you all) take great pains; impve. 2nd pers. pl. / *remirarse*.

remirar to look at again. reg.

remirarse to take great pains. reg.

remírate (you) take great pains; impve. 2nd pers. sing. / *remirarse*.

remirémonos let us take great pains; impve. 1st pers. pl. / *remirarse*.

remírense let them take great pains; impve. 3rd pers. pl. / *remirarse*.

remírese let him (her/it) take great pains; impve. 3rd pers. sing. / *remirarse*.

remitámonos let us submit; impve. 1st pers. pl. / *remitirse*.

remítanse let them submit; impve. 3rd pers. pl. / *remitirse*.

remítase let him (her/it) submit; impve. 3rd pers. sing. / *remitirse*.

remítete (you) submit; impve. 2nd pers. sing. / *remitirse*.

remitiéndose submitting; pres. part. / *remitirse*.

remitíos (you all) submit; impve. 2nd pers. pl. / *remitirse*.

remitir to remit. reg.

remitirse to submit. reg.

remoce 1. that I may rejuvenate; pres. subj. 1st pers. sing. / *remozar*. 2. that he (she/it) may rejuvenate; pres. subj. 3rd pers. sing. 3. let him (her/it) rejuvenate; impve. 3rd pers. sing.

remocé I rejuvenated; past 1st pers. sing. / *remozar*.

remocéis that you (all) may rejuvenate; pres. subj. 2nd pers. pl. / *remozar*.

remocémonos let us look new; impve. 1st pers. pl. / *remozarse*.

remocemos 1. that we may rejuvenate; pres. subj. 1st pers. pl. / *remozar*. 2. let us rejuvenate; impve. 1st pers. pl.

remocen 1. that they may rejuvenate; pres. subj. 3rd pers. pl. / *remozar*. 2. let them rejuvenate; impve. 3rd pers. pl.

remócense let them look new; impve. 3rd pers. pl. / *remozarse*.

remoces that you may rejuvenate; pres. subj. 2nd pers. sing. / *remozar*.

remócese let him (her/it) look new; impve. 3rd pers. sing. / *remozarse*.

remojar to soak. reg.

remolcar to tow. irr.

remoler to grind up. irr.

remolinándose whirling about; pres. part. / *remolinarse*.

remolinaos (you all) whirl about; impve. 2nd pers. pl. / *remolinarse*.

remolinar to whirl about. reg.

remolinarse to whirl about. reg.

remolínate (you) whirl about; impve. 2nd pers. sing. / *remolinarse*.

remolineándose whirling about; pres. part. / *remolinearse*.

remolineaos (you all) whirl about; impve. 2nd pers. pl. / *remolinearse*.

remolinear to whirl about. reg.

remolinearse to whirl about. reg.

remolinéate (you) whirl about; impve. 2nd pers. sing. / *remolinearse*.

remolineémonos let us whirl about; impve. 1st pers. pl. / *remolinearse*.

remolinéense let them whirl about; impve. 3rd pers. pl. / *remolinearse*.

remolinéese let him (her/it) whirl about; impve. 3rd pers. sing. / *remolinearse*.

remolinémonos let us whirl about; impve. 1st pers. pl. / *remolinarse*.

remolínense let them whirl about; impve. 3rd pers. pl. / *remolinarse*.

remolínese let him (her/it) whirl about; impve. 3rd pers. sing. / *remolinarse*.

remolonear to lag or to loiter. reg.

remolque 1. that I may tow; pres. subj. 1st pers. sing. / *remolcar*. 2. that he (she/it) may tow; pres. subj. 3rd pers. sing. 3. let him (her/it) tow; impve. 3rd pers. sing.

remolqué I towed; past 1st pers. sing. / *remolcar*.

remolquéis that you (all) may tow; pres. subj. 2nd pers. pl. / *remolcar*.

remolquemos 1. that we may tow; pres. subj. 1st pers. pl. / *remolcar.* 2. let us tow; impve. 1st pers. pl.

remolquen 1. that they may tow; pres. subj. 3rd pers. pl. / *remolcar.* 2. let them tow; impve. 3rd pers. pl.

remolques that you may tow; pres. subj. 2nd pers. sing. / *remolcar.*

remontándose soaring; pres. part. / *remontarse.*

remontaos (you all) soar; impve. 2nd pers. pl. / *remontarse.*

remontar to raise or to frighten. reg.

remontarse to soar. reg.

remóntate (you) soar; impve. 2nd pers. sing. / *remontarse.*

remontémonos let us soar; impve. 1st pers. pl. / *remontarse.*

remóntense let them soar; impve. 3rd pers. pl. / *remontarse.*

remóntese let him (her/it) soar; impve. 3rd pers. sing. / *remontarse.*

remordámonos let us show worry; impve. 1st pers. pl. / *remorderse.*

remordeos (you all) show worry; impve. 2nd pers. pl. / *remorderse.*

remorder to bite again. irr.

remorderse to show worry. irr.

remordiéndose showing worry; pres. part. / *remorderse.*

removámonos let us get upset; impve. 1st pers. pl. / *removerse.*

removeos (you all) get upset; impve. 2nd pers. pl. / *removerse.*

remover to remove. irr.

removerse to get upset. irr.

removiéndose getting upset; pres. part. / *removerse.*

remozándose looking new; pres. part. / *remozarse.*

remozaos (you all) look new; impve. 2nd pers. pl. / *remozarse.*

remozar to rejuvenate. irr.

remozarse to look new. irr.

remózate (you) look new; impve. 2nd pers. sing. / *remozarse.*

remplazar to replace. reg.

rempujar to jostle. reg.

remudar to change. reg.

remuela 1. that I may grind up; pres. subj. 1st pers. sing. / *remoler.* 2. that he (she/it) may grind up; pres. subj. 3rd pers. sing. 3. let him (her/it) grind up; impve. 3rd pers. sing.

remuelan 1. that they may grind up; pres. subj. 3rd pers. pl. / *remoler.* 2. let them grind up; impve. 3rd pers. pl.

remuelas that you may grind up; pres. subj. 2nd pers. sing. / *remoler.*

remuele 1. he (she/it) grinds up; pres. ind. 3rd pers. sing. / *remoler.* 2. (you) grind up; impve. 2nd pers. sing.

remuelen they grind up; pres. ind. 3rd pers. pl. / *remoler.*

remueles you grind up; pres. ind. 2nd pers. sing. / *remoler.*

remuelo I grind up; pres. ind. 1st pers. sing. / *remoler.*

remuerda 1. that I may bite again; pres. subj. 1st pers. sing. / *remorder.* 2. that he (she/it) may bite again; pres. subj. 3rd pers. sing. 3. let him (her/it) bite again; impve. 3rd pers. sing.

remuerdan 1. that they may bite again; pres. subj. 3rd pers. pl. / *remorder.* 2. let them bite again; impve. 3rd pers. pl.

remuérdanse let them show worry; impve. 3rd pers. pl. / *remorderse.*

remuerdas that you may bite again; pres. subj. 2nd pers. sing. / *remorder.*

remuérdase let him (her/it) show worry; impve. 3rd pers. sing. / *remorderse.*

remuerde 1. he (she/it) bites again; pres. ind. 3rd pers. sing. / *remorder.* 2. (you) bite again; impve. 2nd pers. sing.

remuerden they bite again; pres. ind. 3rd pers. pl. / *remorder.*

remuerdes you bite again; pres. ind. 2nd pers. sing. / *remorder.*

remuérdete (you) show worry; impve. 2nd pers. sing. / *remorderse.*

remuerdo I bite again; pres. ind. 1st pers. sing. / *remorder.*

remueva 1. that I may remove; pres. subj. 1st pers. sing. / *remover.* 2. that he (she/it) may remove; pres. subj. 3rd pers. sing. 3. let him (her/it) remove; impve. 3rd pers. sing.

remuevan 1. that they may remove; pres. subj. 3rd pers. pl. / *remover.* 2. let them remove; impve. 3rd pers. pl.

remuévanse let them get upset; impve. 3rd pers. pl. / *removerse.*

remuevas that you may remove; pres. subj. 2nd pers. sing. / *remover.*

remuévase let him (her/it) get upset; impve. 3rd pers. sing. / *removerse.*

remueve 1. he (she/it) removes; pres. ind. 3rd pers. sing. / *remover.* 2. (you) remove; impve. 2nd pers. sing.

remueven they remove; pres. ind. 3rd pers. pl. / *remover.*

remueves you remove; pres. ind. 2nd pers. sing. / *remover.*

remuévete (you) get upset; impve. 2nd pers. sing. / *removerse.*

remuevo I remove; pres. ind. 1st pers. sing. / *remover.*

remunerar to remunerate. reg.

remusgar to suspect. irr.

remusgue 1. that I may suspect; pres. subj. 1st pers. sing. / *remusgar.* 2. that he (she/it) may suspect; pres. subj. 3rd pers. sing. 3. let him (her/it) suspect; impve. 3rd pers. sing.

remusgué I suspected; past 1st pers. sing. / *remusgar.*

remusguéis that you (all) may suspect; pres. subj. 2nd pers. pl. / *remusgar.*

remusguemos 1. that we may suspect; pres. subj. 1st pers. pl. / *remusgar.* 2. let us suspect; impve. 1st pers. pl.

remusguen 1. that they may suspect; pres. subj. 3rd pers. pl. / *remusgar*. 2. let them suspect; impve. 3rd pers. pl.

remusgues that you may suspect; pres. subj. 2nd pers. sing. / *remusgar*.

renacer to be born again. irr.

renazca 1. that I may be born again; pres. subj. 1st pers. sing. / *renacer*. 2. that he (she/it) may be born again; pres. subj. 3rd pers. sing. 3. let him (her/it) be born again; impve. 3rd pers. sing.

renazcáis that you (all) may be born again; pres. subj. 2nd pers. pl. / *renacer*.

renazcamos 1. that we may be born again; pres. subj. 1st pers. pl. / *renacer*. 2. let us be born again; impve. 1st pers. pl.

renazcan 1. that they may be born again; pres. subj. 3rd pers. pl. / *renacer*. 2. let them be born again; impve. 3rd pers. pl.

renazcas that you may be born again; pres. subj. 2nd pers. sing. / *renacer*.

renazco I am born again; pres. ind. 1st pers. sing. / *renacer*.

rendíos (you all) surrender; impve. 2nd pers. pl. / *rendirse*.

rendir to overcome. irr.

rendirse to surrender. irr.

renegar to deny strongly. irr.

renegué I denied strongly; past 1st pers. sing. / *renegar*.

reneguéis that you (all) may deny strongly; pres. subj. 2nd pers. pl. / *renegar*.

reneguemos 1. that we may deny strongly; pres. subj. 1st pers. pl. / *renegar*. 2. let us deny strongly; impve. 1st pers. pl.

renguear to limp. reg.

reniega 1. he (she/it) denies strongly; pres. ind. 3rd pers. sing. / *renegar*. 2. (you) deny strongly; impve. 2nd pers. sing.

reniegan they deny strongly; pres. ind. 3rd pers. pl. / *renegar*.

reniegas you deny strongly; pres. ind. 2nd pers. sing. / *renegar*.

reniego I deny strongly; pres. ind. 1st pers. sing. / *renegar*.

reniegue 1. that I may deny strongly; pres. subj. 1st pers. sing. / *renegar*. 2. that he (she/it) may deny strongly; pres. subj. 3rd pers. sing. 3. let him (her/it) deny strongly; impve. 3rd pers. sing.

renieguen 1. that they may deny strongly; pres. subj. 3rd pers. pl. / *renegar*. 2. let them deny strongly; impve. 3rd pers. pl.

reniegues that you may deny strongly; pres. subj. 2nd pers. sing. / *renegar*.

renovar to renovate. irr.

renquear to limp. reg.

rentar to yield or produce. reg.

renueva 1. he (she/it) renovates; pres. ind. 3rd pers. sing. / *renovar*. 2. (you) renovate; impve. 2nd pers. sing.

renuevan they renovate; pres. ind. 3rd pers. pl. / *renovar*.

renuevas you renovate; pres. ind. 2nd pers. sing. / *renovar*.

renueve 1. that I may renovate; pres. subj. 1st pers. sing. / *renovar*. 2. that he (she/it) may renovate; pres. subj. 3rd pers. sing. 3. let him (her/it) renovate; impve. 3rd pers. sing.

renueven 1. that they may renovate; pres. subj. 3rd pers. pl. / *renovar*. 2. let them renovate; impve. 3rd pers. pl.

renueves that you may renovate; pres. subj. 2nd pers. sing. / *renovar*.

renuevo I renovate; pres. ind. 1st pers. sing. / *renovar*.

renunciar to renounce. reg.

reñíos (you all) scold; impve. 2nd pers. pl. / *reñirse*.

reñir to quarrel. irr.

reñirse to scold. irr.

reorganice 1. that I may reorganize; pres. subj. 1st pers. sing. / *reorganizar*. 2. that he (she/it) may reorganize; pres. subj. 3rd pers. sing. 3. let him (her/it) reorganize; impve. 3rd pers. sing.

reorganicé I reorganized; past 1st pers. sing. / *reorganizar*.

reorganicéis that you (all) may reorganize; pres. subj. 2nd pers. pl. / *reorganizar*.

reorganicémonos let us reorganize; impve. 1st pers. pl. / *reorganizarse*.

reorganicemos 1. that we may reorganize; pres. subj. 1st pers. pl. / *reorganizar*. 2. let us reorganize; impve. 1st pers. pl.

reorganicen 1. that they may reorganize; pres. subj. 3rd pers. pl. / *reorganizar*. 2. let them reorganize; impve. 3rd pers. pl.

reorganícense let them reorganize; impve. 3rd pers. pl. / *reorganizarse*.

reorganices that you may reorganize; pres. subj. 2nd pers. sing. / *reorganizar*.

reorganícese let him (her/it) reorganize; impve. 3rd pers. sing. / *reorganizarse*.

reorganizándose reorganizing; pres. part. / *reorganizarse*.

reorganizaos (you all) reorganize; impve. 2nd pers. pl. / *reorganizarse*.

reorganizar to reorganize. irr.

reorganizarse to reorganize. irr.

reorganízate (you) reorganize; impve. 2nd pers. sing. / *reorganizarse*.

repagar to repay. irr.

repague 1. that I may repay; pres. subj. 1st pers. sing. / *repagar*. 2. that he (she/it) may repay; pres. subj. 3rd pers. sing. 3. let him (her/it) repay; impve. 3rd pers. sing.

repagué I repaid; past 1st pers. sing. / *repagar*.

repaguéis that you (all) may repay; pres. subj. 2nd pers. pl. / *repagar*.

repaguemos 1. that we may repay; pres. subj. 1st pers. pl. / *repagar*. 2. let us repay; impve. 1st pers. pl.

repaguen 1. that they may repay; pres. subj. 3rd pers. pl. / *repagar*. 2. let them repay; impve. 3rd pers. pl.

repagues that you may repay; pres. subj. 2nd pers. sing. / *repagar*.

repantigándose stretching out; pres. part. / *repantigarse.*

repantigaos (you all) stretch out; impve. 2nd pers. pl. / *repantigarse.*

repantigarse to stretch out. irr.

repantígate (you) stretch out; impve. 2nd pers. sing. / *repantigarse.*

repantigue 1. that I may stretch out; pres. subj. 1st pers. sing. / *repantigarse.* 2. that he (she/it) may stretch out; pres. subj. 3rd pers. sing.

repantigué I stretched out; past 1st pers. sing. / *repantigarse.*

repantiguéis that you (all) may stretch out; pres. subj. 2nd pers. pl. / *repantigarse.*

repantiguémonos let us stretch out; impve. 1st pers. pl. / *repantigarse.*

repantiguemos that we may stretch out; pres. subj. 1st pers. pl. / *repantigarse.*

repantiguen that they may stretch out; pres. subj. 3rd pers. pl. / *repantigarse.*

repantíguense let them stretch out; impve. 3rd pers. pl. / *repantigarse.*

repantigues that you may stretch out; pres. subj. 2nd pers. sing. / *repantigarse.*

repantíguese let him (her/it) stretch out; impve. 3rd pers. sing. / *repantigarse.*

reparándose refraining; pres. part. / *repararse.*

reparaos (you all) refrain; impve. 2nd pers. pl. / *repararse.*

reparar to repair or to stop. reg.

repararse to refrain. reg.

repárate (you) refrain; impve. 2nd pers. sing. / *repararse.*

reparémonos let us refrain; impve. 1st pers. pl. / *repararse.*

repárense let them refrain; impve. 3rd pers. pl. / *repararse.*

repárese let him (her/it) refrain; impve. 3rd pers. sing. / *repararse.*

repartir to distribute. reg.

repasar to review. reg.

repatría 1. he (she/it) repatriates; pres. ind. 3rd pers. sing. / *repatriar.* 2. (you) repatriate; impve. 2nd pers. sing.

repatrían they repatriate; pres. ind. 3rd pers. pl. / *repatriar.*

repatriándose returning to one's own country; pres. part. / *repatriarse.*

repatriaos (you all) return to your own country; impve. 2nd pers. pl. / *repatriarse.*

repatriar to repatriate. irr.

repatriarse to return to one's own country. irr.

repatrías you repatriate; pres. ind. 2nd pers. sing. / *repatriar.*

repatríate (you) return to your own country; impve. 2nd pers. sing. / *repatriarse.*

repatríe 1. that I may repatriate; pres. subj. 1st pers. sing. / *repatriar.* 2. that he (she/it) may repatriate; pres. subj. 3rd pers. sing. 3. let him (her/it) repatriate; impve. 3rd pers. sing.

repatriémonos let us return to our own country; impve. 1st pers. pl. / *repatriarse.*

repatríen 1. that they may repatriate; pres. subj. 3rd pers. pl. / *repatriar.* 2. let them repatriate; impve. 3rd pers. pl.

repatríense let them return to their own country; impve. 3rd pers. pl. / *repatriarse.*

repatríes that you may repatriate; pres. subj. 2nd pers. sing. / *repatriar.*

repatríese let him (her/it) return to his (her/its) own country; impve. 3rd pers. sing. / *repatriarse.*

repatrío I repatriate; pres. ind. 1st pers. sing. / *repatriar.*

repechar to go uphill. reg.

repelar to pull the hair of. reg.

repeler to repel. reg.

repensar to reconsider. irr.

repercutir to rebound. reg.

repetir to repeat. irr.

repicándose boasting; pres. part. / *repicarse.*

repicaos (you all) boast; impve. 2nd pers. pl. / *repicarse.*

repicar to chime or to mince. irr.

repicarse to boast. irr.

repícate (you) boast; impve. 2nd pers. sing. / *repicarse.*

repiensa 1. he (she/it) reconsiders; pres. ind. 3rd pers. sing. / *repensar.* 2. (you) reconsider; impve. 2nd pers. sing.

repiensan they reconsider; pres. ind. 3rd pers. pl. / *repensar.*

repiensas you reconsider; pres. ind. 2nd pers. sing. / *repensar.*

repiense 1. that I may reconsider; pres. subj. 1st pers. sing. / *repensar.* 2. that he (she/it) may reconsider; pres. subj. 3rd pers. sing. 3. let him (her/it) reconsider; impve. 3rd pers. sing.

repiensen 1. that they may reconsider; pres. subj. 3rd pers. pl. / *repensar.* 2. let them reconsider; impve. 3rd pers. pl.

repienses that you may reconsider; pres. subj. 2nd pers. sing. / *repensar.*

repienso I reconsider; pres. ind. 1st pers. sing. / *repensar.*

repinándose rising; pres. part. / *repinarse.*

repinaos (you all) rise; impve. 2nd pers. pl. / *repinarse.*

repinarse to rise. reg.

repínate (you) rise; impve. 2nd pers. sing. / *repinarse.*

repinémonos let us rise; impve. 1st pers. pl. / *repinarse.*

repínense let them rise; impve. 3rd pers. pl. / *repinarse.*

repínese let him (her/it) rise; impve. 3rd pers. sing. / *repinarse.*

repique 1. that I may mince; pres. subj. 1st pers. sing. / *repicar.* 2. that he (she/it) may mince; pres. subj. 3rd pers. sing. 3. let him (her/it) mince; impve. 3rd pers. sing.

repiqué I minced; past 1st pers. sing. / *repicar.*

repiquéis that you (all) may mince; pres. subj. 2nd pers. pl. / *repicar.*

repiquémonos let us boast; impve. 1st pers. pl. / *repicarse.*

repiquemos 1. that we may mince; pres. subj. 1st pers. pl. / *repicar.* 2. let us mince; impve. 1st pers. pl.

repiquen 1. that they may mince; pres. subj. 3rd pers. pl. / *repicar.* 2. let them mince; impve. 3rd pers. pl.

repíquense let them boast; impve. 3rd pers. pl. / *repicarse.*

repiques that you may mince; pres. subj. 2nd pers. sing. / *repicar.*

repíquese let him (her/it) boast; impve. 3rd pers. sing. / *repicarse.*

repiqueteándose quarreling; pres. part. / *repiquetearse.*

repiqueteaos (you all) quarrel; impve. 2nd pers. pl. / *repiquetearse.*

repiquetear to ring or clatter. reg.

repiquetearse to quarrel. reg.

repiquetéate (you) quarrel; impve. 2nd pers. sing. / *repiquetearse.*

repiqueteémonos let us quarrel; impve. 1st pers. pl. / *repiquetearse.*

repiquetéense let them quarrel; impve. 3rd pers. pl. / *repiquetearse.*

repiquetéese let him (her/it) quarrel; impve. 3rd pers. sing. / *repiquetearse.*

repisar to trample on. reg.

repita 1. that I may repeat; pres. subj. 1st pers. sing. / *repetir.* 2. that he (she/it) may repeat; pres. subj. 3rd pers. sing. 3. let him (her/it) repeat; impve. 3rd pers. sing.

repitáis that you (all) may repeat; pres. subj. 2nd pers. pl. / *repetir.*

repitamos 1. that we may repeat; pres. subj. 1st pers. pl. / *repetir.* 2. let us repeat; impve. 1st pers. pl.

repitan 1. that they may repeat; pres. subj. 3rd pers. pl. / *repetir.* 2. let them repeat; impve. 3rd pers. pl.

repitas that you may repeat; pres. subj. 2nd pers. sing. / *repetir.*

repite 1. he (she/it) repeats; pres. ind. 3rd pers. sing. / *repetir.* 2. (you) repeat; impve. 2nd pers. sing.

repiten they repeat; pres. ind. 3rd pers. pl. / *repetir.*

repites you repeat; pres. ind. 2nd pers. sing. / *repetir.*

repitiendo repeating; pres. part. / *repetir.*

repitiera 1. that I might repeat; imp. subj. 1st pers. sing. / *repetir.* 2. that he (she/it) might repeat; imp. subj. 3rd pers. sing.

repitierais that you (all) might repeat; imp. subj. 2nd pers pl. / *repetir.*

repitiéramos that we might repeat; imp. subj. 1st pers. pl. / *repetir.*

repitieran that they might repeat; imp. subj. 3rd pers. pl. / *repetir.*

repitieras that you might repeat; imp. subj. 2nd pers. sing. / *repetir.*

repitieron they repeated; past 3rd pers. pl. / *repetir.*

repitiese 1. that I might repeat; imp. subj. 1st pers. sing. / *repetir.* 2. that he (she/it) might repeat; imp. subj. 3rd pers. sing.

repitieseis that you (all) might repeat; imp. subj. 2nd pers pl. / *repetir.*

repitiésemos that we might repeat; imp. subj. 1st pers. pl. / *repetir.*

repitiesen that they might repeat; imp. subj. 3rd pers. pl. / *repetir.*

repitieses that you might repeat; imp. subj. 2nd pers. sing. / *repetir.*

repitió he (she/it) repeated; past 3rd pers. sing. / *repetir.*

repito I repeat; pres. ind. 1st pers. sing. / *repetir.*

repizcar to pinch. irr.

repizque 1. that I may pinch; pres. subj. 1st pers. sing. / *repizcar.* 2. that he (she/it) may pinch; pres. subj. 3rd pers. sing. 3. let him (her/it) pinch; impve. 3rd pers. sing.

repizqué I pinched; past 1st pers. sing. / *repizcar.*

repizquéis that you (all) may pinch; pres. subj. 2nd pers. pl. / *repizcar.*

repizquemos 1. that we may pinch; pres. subj. 1st pers. pl. / *repizcar.* 2. let us pinch; impve. 1st pers. pl.

repizquen 1. that they may pinch; pres. subj. 3rd pers. pl. / *repizcar.* 2. let them pinch; impve. 3rd pers. pl.

repizques that you may pinch; pres. subj. 2nd pers. sing. / *repizcar.*

replegándose retreating; pres. part. / *replegarse.*

replegaos (you all) retreat; impve. 2nd pers. pl. / *replegarse.*

replegar to refold. irr.

replegarse to retreat. irr.

replegué I refolded; past 1st pers. sing. / *replegar.*

repleguéis that you (all) may refold; pres. subj. 2nd pers. pl. / *replegar.*

repleguémonos let us retreat; impve. 1st pers. pl. / *replegarse.*

repleguemos 1. that we may refold; pres. subj. 1st pers. pl. / *replegar.* 2. let us refold; impve. 1st pers. pl.

replicar to reply. irr.

repliega 1. he (she/it) refolds; pres. ind. 3rd pers. sing. / *replegar.* 2. (you) refold; impve. 2nd pers. sing.

repliegan they refold; pres. ind. 3rd pers. pl. / *replegar.*

repliegas you refold; pres. ind. 2nd pers. sing. / *replegar.*

repliégate (you) retreat; impve. 2nd pers. sing. / *replegarse.*

repliego I refold; pres. ind. 1st pers. sing. / *replegar.*

repliegue 1. that I may refold; pres. subj. 1st pers. sing. / *replear.* 2. that he (she/it) may refold; pres. subj. 3rd pers. sing. 3. let him (her/it) refold; impve. 3rd pers. sing.

replieguen 1. that they may refold; pres. subj. 3rd pers. pl. / *replegar.* 2. let them refold; impve. 3rd pers. pl.

repliéguense let them retreat; impve. 3rd pers. pl. / *replegarse.*

repliegues that you may refold; pres. subj. 2nd pers. sing. / *replegar.*

repliéguese let him (her/it) retreat; impve. 3rd pers. sing. / *replegarse.*

replique 1. that I may reply; pres. subj. 1st pers. sing. / *replicar.* 2. that he (she/it) may reply; pres. subj. 3rd pers. sing. 3. let him (her/it) reply; impve. 3rd pers. sing.

repliqué I replied; past 1st pers. sing. / *replicar.*

repliquéis that you (all) may reply; pres. subj. 2nd pers. pl. / *replicar.*

repliquemos 1. that we may reply; pres. subj. 1st pers. pl. / *replicar.* 2. let us reply; impve. 1st pers. pl.

repliquen 1. that they may reply; pres. subj. 3rd pers. pl. / *replicar.* 2. let them reply; impve. 3rd pers. pl.

repliques that you may reply; pres. subj. 2nd pers. sing. / *replicar.*

repoblar repopulate. irr.

repon (you) replace; impve. 2nd pers. sing. / *reponer.*

repondrá he (she/it) will replace; fut. 3rd pers. sing. / *reponer.*

repondrán they will replace; fut. 3rd pers. pl. / *reponer.*

repondrás you will replace; fut. 2nd pers. sing. / *reponer.*

repondré I shall replace; fut. 1st pers. sing. / *reponer.*

repondréis you (all) will replace; fut. 2nd pers. pl. / *reponer.*

repondremos we shall replace; fut. 1st pers. pl. / *reponer.*

repondría 1. I should replace; cond. 1st pers. sing. / *reponer.* 2. he (she/it) would replace; cond. 3rd pers. sing.

repondríais you (all) would replace; cond. 2nd pers. pl. / *reponer.*

repondríamos we should replace; cond. 1st pers. pl. / *reponer.*

repondrían they would replace; cond. 3rd pers. pl. / *reponer.*

repondrías you would replace; cond. 2nd pers. sing. / *reponer.*

reponeos (you all) recover; impve. 2nd pers. pl. / *reponerse.*

reponer to replace. irr.

reponerse to recover. irr.

reponga 1. that I may replace; pres. subj. 1st pers. sing. / *reponer.* 2. that he (she/it) may replace; pres. subj. 3rd pers. sing. 3. let him (her/it) replace; impve. 3rd pers. sing.

repongáis that you (all) may replace; pres. subj. 2nd pers. pl. / *reponer.*

repongámonos let us recover; impve. 1st pers. pl. / *reponerse.*

repongamos 1. that we may replace; pres. subj. 1st pers. pl. / *reponer.* 2. let us replace; impve. 1st pers. pl.

repongan 1. that they may replace; pres. subj. 3rd pers. pl. / *reponer.* 2. let them replace; impve. 3rd pers. pl.

repónganse let them recover; impve. 3rd pers. pl. / *reponerse.*

repongas that you may replace; pres. subj. 2nd pers. sing. / *reponer.*

repóngase let him (her/it) recover; impve. 3rd pers. sing. / *reponerse.*

repongo I replace; pres. ind. 1st pers. sing. / *reponer.*

reponiéndose recovering; pres. part. / *reponerse.*

reponte (you) recover; impve. 2nd pers. sing. / *reponerse.*

reportándose controlling oneself; pres. part. / *reportarse.*

reportaos (you all) control yourselves; impve. 2nd pers. pl. / *reportarse.*

reportar to restrain. reg.

reportarse to control oneself. reg.

repórtate (you) control yourself; impve. 2nd pers. sing. / *reportarse.*

reportémonos let us control ourselves; impve. 1st pers. pl. / *reportarse.*

repórtense let them control themselves; impve. 3rd pers. pl. / *reportarse.*

repórtese let him (her/it) control himself (herself/itself); impve. 3rd pers. sing. / *reportarse.*

reposándose settling (liquids); pres. part. / *reposarse.*

reposar to rest. reg.

reposarse to settle (liquids). reg.

repósense let them settle (liquids); impve. 3rd pers. pl. / *reposarse.*

repósese let it settle (liquids); impve. 3rd pers. sing. / *reposarse.*

repostar to refuel. reg.

repreguntar to cross-examine. reg.

reprender to reprimand. reg.

represaliar to retaliate against. reg.

represar to dam. reg.

representándose imagining; pres. part. / *representarse.*

representaos (you all) imagine; impve. 2nd pers. pl. / *representarse.*

representar to represent. reg.

representarse to imagine. reg.

represéntate (you) imagine; impve. 2nd pers. sing. / *representarse.*

representémonos let us imagine; impve. 1st pers. pl. / *representarse.*

represéntense let them imagine; impve. 3rd pers. pl. / *representarse.*

represéntese let him (her/it) imagine; impve. 3rd pers. sing. / *representarse.*

reprimámonos let us refrain; impve. 1st pers. pl. / *reprimirse.*

reprímanse let them refrain; impve. 3rd pers. pl. / *reprimirse.*

reprímase let him (her/it) refrain; impve. 3rd pers. sing. / *reprimirse.*

reprímete (you) refrain; impve. 2nd pers. sing. / *reprimirse.*

reprimiéndose refraining; pres. part. / *reprimirse.*

reprimíos (you all) refrain; impve. 2nd pers. pl. / *reprimirse.*

reprimir to repress. reg.

reprimirse to refrain. reg.
reprobar to reprove. irr.
reprochar to reproach. reg.
reprodúcete (you) reproduce; impve. 2nd pers. sing. / *reproducirse*.
reproduciéndose reproducing; pres. part. / *reproducirse*.
reproducíos (you all) reproduce; impve. 2nd pers. pl. / *reproducirse*.
reproducir to reproduce. irr.
reproducirse to reproduce. irr.
reproduje I reproduced; past 1st pers. sing. / *reproducir*.
reprodujera 1. that I might reproduce; imp. subj. 1st pers. sing. / *reproducir*. 2. that he (she/it) might reproduce; imp. subj. 3rd pers. sing.
reprodujerais that you (all) might reproduce; imp. subj. 2nd pers pl. / *reproducir*.
reprodujéramos that we might reproduce; imp. subj. 1st pers. pl. / *reproducir*.
reprodujeran that they might reproduce; imp. subj. 3rd pers. pl. / *reproducir*.
reprodujeras that you might reproduce; imp. subj. 2nd pers. sing. / *reproducir*.
reprodujeron they reproduced; past 3rd pers. pl. / *reproducir*.
reprodujese 1. that I might reproduce; imp. subj. 1st pers. sing. / *reproducir*. 2. that he (she/it) might reproduce; imp. subj. 3rd pers. sing.
reprodujeseis that you (all) might reproduce; imp. subj. 2nd pers pl. / *reproducir*.
reprodujésemos that we might reproduce; imp. subj. 1st pers. pl. / *reproducir*.
reprodujesen that they might reproduce; imp. subj. 3rd pers. pl. / *reproducir*.
reprodujeses that you might reproduce; imp. subj. 2nd pers. sing. / *reproducir*.
reprodujimos we reproduced; past 1st pers. pl. / *reproducir*.
reprodujiste you reproduced; past 2nd pers. sing. / *reproducir*.
reprodujisteis you (all) reproduced; past 2nd pers. pl. / *reproducir*.
reprodujo he (she/it) reproduced; past 3rd pers. sing. / *reproducir*.
reproduzca 1. that I may reproduce; pres. subj. 1st pers. sing. / *reproducir*. 2. that he (she/it) may reproduce; pres. subj. 3rd pers. sing. 3. let him (her/it) reproduce; impve. 3rd pers. sing.
reproduzcáis that you (all) may reproduce; pres. subj. 2nd pers. pl. / *reproducir*.
reproduzcámonos let us reproduce; impve. 1st pers. pl. / *reproducirse*.
reproduzcamos 1. that we may reproduce; pres. subj. 1st pers. pl. / *reproducir*. 2. let us reproduce; impve. 1st pers. pl.
reproduzcan 1. that they may reproduce; pres. subj. 3rd pers. pl. / *reproducir*. 2. let them reproduce; impve. 3rd pers. pl.
reprodúzcanse let them reproduce; impve. 3rd pers. pl. / *reproducirse*.

reproduzcas that you may reproduce; pres. subj. 2nd pers. sing. / *reproducir*.
reprodúzcase let him (her/it) reproduce; impve. 3rd pers. sing. / *reproducirse*.
reproduzco I reproduce; pres. ind. 1st pers. sing. / *reproducir*.
repropiándose balking; pres. part. / *repropiarse*.
repropiaos (you all) balk; impve. 2nd pers. pl. / *repropiarse*.
repropiarse to balk. reg.
repropíate (you) balk; impve. 2nd pers. sing. / *repropiarse*.
repropiémonos let us balk; impve. 1st pers. pl. / *repropiarse*.
repropíense let them balk; impve. 3rd pers. pl. / *repropiarse*.
repropíese let him (her/it) balk; impve. 3rd pers. sing. / *repropiarse*.
reprueba 1. he (she/it) reproves; pres. ind. 3rd pers. sing. / *reprobar*. 2. (you) reprove; impve. 2nd pers. sing.
reprueban they reprove; pres. ind. 3rd pers. pl. / *reprobar*.
repruebas you reprove; pres. ind. 2nd pers. sing. / *reprobar*.
repruebe 1. that I may reprove; pres. subj. 1st pers. sing. / *reprobar*. 2. that he (she/it) may reprove; pres. subj. 3rd pers. sing. 3. let him (her/it) reprove; impve. 3rd pers. sing.
reprueben 1. that they may reprove; pres. subj. 3rd pers. pl. / *reprobar*. 2. let them reprove; impve. 3rd pers. pl.
repruebes that you may reprove; pres. subj. 2nd pers. sing. / *reprobar*.
repruebo I reprove; pres. ind. 1st pers. sing. / *reprobar*.
reptar to crawl. reg.
repudiar to repudiate. reg.
repudrámonos let us pine away; impve. 1st pers. pl. / *repudrirse*.
repúdranse let them pine away; impve. 3rd pers. pl. / *repudrirse*.
repúdrase let him (her/it) pine away; impve. 3rd pers. sing. / *repudrirse*.
repúdrete (you) pine away; impve. 2nd pers. sing. / *repudrirse*.
repudriéndose pining away; pres. part. / *repudrirse*.
repudríos (you all) pine away; impve. 2nd pers. pl. / *repudrirse*.
repudrirse to pine away. reg.
repuebla 1. he (she/it) repopulates; pres. ind. 3rd pers. sing. / *repoblar*. 2. (you) repopulate; impve. 2nd pers. sing.
repueblan they repopulate; pres. ind. 3rd pers. pl. / *repoblar*.
repueblas you repopulate; pres. ind. 2nd pers. sing. / *repoblar*.
repueble 1. that I may repopulate; pres. subj. 1st pers. sing. / *repoblar*. 2. that he (she/it) may repopulate; pres. subj. 3rd pers. sing. 3. let him (her/it) repopulate; impve. 3rd pers. sing.

repueblen 1. that they may repopulate; pres. subj. 3rd pers. pl. / *repoblar*. 2. let them repopulate; impve. 3rd pers. pl.

repuebles that you may repopulate; pres. subj. 2nd pers. sing. / *repoblar*.

repueblo I repopulate; pres. ind. 1st pers. sing. / *repoblar*.

repuesto replaced; past part. / *reponer*.

repugnar to be repugnant. reg.

repujar to emboss. reg.

repulámonos let us doll up; impve. 1st pers. pl. / *repulirse*.

repúlanse let them doll up; impve. 3rd pers. pl. / *repulirse*.

repúlase let him (her/it) doll up; impve. 3rd pers. sing. / *repulirse*.

repúlete (you) doll up; impve. 2nd pers. sing. / *repulirse*.

repulgar to hem. irr.

repulgue 1. that I may hem; pres. subj. 1st pers. sing. / *repulgar*. 2. that he (she/it) may hem; pres. subj. 3rd pers. sing. 3. let him (her/it) hem; impve. 3rd pers. sing.

repulgué I hemmed; past 1st pers. sing. / *repulgar*.

repulguéis that you (all) may hem; pres. subj. 2nd pers. pl. / *repulgar*.

repulguemos 1. that we may hem; pres. subj. 1st pers. pl. / *repulgar*. 2. let us hem; impve. 1st pers. pl.

repulguen 1. that they may hem; pres. subj. 3rd pers. pl. / *repulgar*. 2. let them hem; impve. 3rd pers. pl.

repulgues that you may hem; pres. subj. 2nd pers. sing. / *repulgar*.

repuliéndose dolling up; pres. part. / *repulirse*.

repulíos (you all) doll up; impve. 2nd pers. pl. / *repulirse*.

repulir to repolish. reg.

repulirse to doll up. reg.

repulsar to repulse. reg.

repuntándose going sour; pres. part. / *repuntarse*.

repuntaos (you all) go sour; impve. 2nd pers. pl. / *repuntarse*.

repuntar to move (tide). reg.

repuntarse to go sour. reg.

repúntate (you) go sour; impve. 2nd pers. sing. / *repuntarse*.

repuntémonos let us go sour; impve. 1st pers. pl. / *repuntarse*.

repúntense let them go sour; impve. 3rd pers. pl. / *repuntarse*.

repúntese let him (her/it) go sour; impve. 3rd pers. sing. / *repuntarse*.

repuse I replaced; past 1st pers. sing. / *reponer*.

repusiera 1. that I might replace; imp. subj. 1st pers. sing. / *reponer*. 2. that he (she/it) might replace; imp. subj. 3rd pers. sing.

repusierais that you (all) might replace; imp. subj. 2nd pers pl. / *reponer*.

repusiéramos that we might replace; imp. subj. 1st pers. pl. / *reponer*.

repusieran that they might replace; imp. subj. 3rd pers. pl. / *reponer*.

repusieras that you might replace; imp. subj. 2nd pers. sing. / *reponer*.

repusieron they replaced; past 3rd pers. pl. / *reponer*.

repusiese 1. that I might replace; imp. subj. 1st pers. sing. / *reponer*. 2. that he (she/it) might replace; imp. subj. 3rd pers. sing.

repusieseis that you (all) might replace; imp. subj. 2nd pers pl. / *reponer*.

repusiésemos that we might replace; imp. subj. 1st pers. pl. / *reponer*.

repusiesen that they might replace; imp. subj. 3rd pers. pl. / *reponer*.

repusieses that you might replace; imp. subj. 2nd pers. sing. / *reponer*.

repusimos we replaced; past 1st pers. pl. / *reponer*.

repusiste you replaced; past 2nd pers. sing. / *reponer*.

repusisteis you (all) replaced; past 2nd pers. pl. / *reponer*.

repuso he (she/it) replaced; past 3rd pers. sing. / *reponer*.

reputar to repute. reg.

requebrar to flatter. irr.

requemándose smoldering; pres. part. / *requemarse*.

requemaos (you all) smolder; impve. 2nd pers. pl. / *requemarse*.

requemar to burn again. reg.

requemarse to smolder. reg.

requémate (you) smolder; impve. 2nd pers. sing. / *requemarse*.

requemémonos let us smolder; impve. 1st pers. pl. / *requemarse*.

requémense let them smolder; impve. 3rd pers. pl. / *requemarse*.

requémese let him (her/it) smolder; impve. 3rd pers. sing. / *requemarse*.

requerir to require. irr.

requiebra 1. he (she/it) flatters; pres. ind. 3rd pers. sing. / *requebrar*. 2. (you) flatter; impve. 2nd pers. sing.

requiebran they flatter; pres. ind. 3rd pers. pl. / *requebrar*.

requiebras you flatter; pres. ind. 2nd pers. sing. / *requebrar*.

requiebre 1. that I may flatter; pres. subj. 1st pers. sing. / *requebrar*. 2. that he (she/it) may flatter; pres. subj. 3rd pers. sing. 3. let him (her/it) flatter; impve. 3rd pers. sing.

requiebren 1. that they may flatter; pres. subj. 3rd pers. pl. / *requebrar*. 2. let them flatter; impve. 3rd pers. pl.

requiebres that you may flatter; pres. subj. 2nd pers. sing. / *requebrar*.

requiebro I flatter; pres. ind. 1st pers. sing. / *requebrar*.

requiera 1. that I may require; pres. subj. 1st pers. sing. / *requerir*. 2. that he (she/it) may require; pres. subj. 3rd pers. sing. 3. let him (her/it) require; impve. 3rd pers. sing.

requieran 1. that they may require; pres. subj. 3rd pers. pl. / *requerir.* 2. let them require; impve. 3rd pers. pl.

requieras that you may require; pres. subj. 2nd pers. sing. / *requerir.*

requiere 1. he (she/it) requires; pres. ind. 3rd pers. sing. / *requerir.* 2. (you) require; impve. 2nd pers. sing.

requieren they require; pres. ind. 3rd pers. pl. / *requerir.*

requieres you require; pres. ind. 2nd pers. sing. / *requerir.*

requiero I require; pres. ind. 1st pers. sing. / *requerir.*

requiráis that you (all) may require; pres. subj. 2nd pers. pl. / *requerir.*

requiramos 1. that we may require; pres. subj. 1st pers. pl. / *requerir.* 2. let us require; impve. 1st pers. pl.

requiriendo requiring; pres. part. / *requerir.*

requiriera 1. that I might require; imp. subj. 1st pers. sing. / *requerir.* 2. that he (she/it) might require; imp. subj. 3rd pers. sing.

requirierais that you (all) might require; imp. subj. 2nd pers pl. / *requerir.*

requiriéramos that we might require; imp. subj. 1st pers. pl. / *requerir.*

requirieran that they might require; imp. subj. 3rd pers. pl. / *requerir.*

requirieras that you might require; imp. subj. 2nd pers. sing. / *requerir.*

requirieron they required; past 3rd pers. pl. / *requerir.*

requiriese 1. that I might require; imp. subj. 1st pers. sing. / *requerir.* 2. that he (she/it) might require; imp. subj. 3rd pers. sing.

requirieseis that you (all) might require; imp. subj. 2nd pers pl. / *requerir.*

requiriésemos that we might require; imp. subj. 1st pers. pl. / *requerir.*

requiriesen that they might require; imp. subj. 3rd pers. pl. / *requerir.*

requirieses that you might require; imp. subj. 2nd pers. sing. / *requerir.*

requirió he (she/it) required; past 3rd pers. sing. / *requerir.*

requisar to requisition. reg.

resaber to know completely. irr.

resabiándose spoiling; pres. part. / *resabiarse.*

resabiaos (you all) spoil; impve. 2nd pers. pl. / *resabiarse.*

resabiar to lead into bad habits. reg.

resabiarse to spoil. reg.

resabíate (you) spoil; impve. 2nd pers. sing. / *resabiarse.*

resabiémonos let us spoil; impve. 1st pers. pl. / *resabiarse.*

resabíense let them spoil; impve. 3rd pers. pl. / *resabiarse.*

resabíese let him (her/it) spoil; impve. 3rd pers. sing. / *resabiarse.*

resabrá he (she/it) will know completely; fut. 3rd pers. sing. / *resaber.*

resabrán they will know completely; fut. 3rd pers. pl. / *resaber.*

resabrás you will know completely; fut. 2nd pers. sing. / *resaber.*

resabré I shall know completely; fut. 1st pers. sing. / *resaber.*

resabréis you (all) will know completely; fut. 2nd pers. pl. / *resaber.*

resabremos we shall know completely; fut. 1st pers. pl. / *resaber.*

resabría 1. I should know completely; cond. 1st pers. sing. / *resaber.* 2. he (she/it) would know completely; cond. 3rd pers. sing.

resabríais you (all) would know completely; cond. 2nd pers. pl. / *resaber.*

resabríamos we should know completely; cond. 1st pers. pl. / *resaber.*

resabrían they would know completely; cond. 3rd pers. pl. / *resaber.*

resabrías you would know completely; cond. 2nd pers. sing. / *resaber.*

resaldrá it will jut out; fut. 3rd pers. sing. / *resalir.*

resaldrán they will jut out; fut. 3rd pers. pl. / *resalir.*

resaldría it would jut out; cond. 3rd pers. sing. / *resalir.*

resaldrían they would jut out; cond. 3rd pers. pl. / *resalir.*

resalga 1. that it may jut out; pres. subj. 3rd pers. sing. / *resalir.* 2. let it jut out; impve. 3rd pers. sing.

resalgan 1. that they may jut out; pres. subj. 3rd pers. pl. / *resalir.* 2. let them jut out; impve. 3rd pers. pl.

resalir to jut out. irr.

resaltar to stand out or to rebound. reg.

resaludar to return the greeting of. reg.

resárcete (you) recover; impve. 2nd pers. sing. / *resarcirse.*

resarciéndose recovering; pres. part. / *resarcirse.*

resarcíos (you all) recover; impve. 2nd pers. pl. / *resarcirse.*

resarcir to compensate. irr.

resarcirse to recover. irr.

resarza 1. that I may compensate; pres. subj. 1st pers. sing. / *resarcir.* 2. that he (she/it) may compensate; pres. subj. 3rd pers. sing. 3. let him (her/it) compensate; impve. 3rd pers. sing.

resarzáis that you (all) may compensate; pres. subj. 2nd pers. pl. / *resarcir.*

resarzámonos let us recover; impve. 1st pers. pl. / *resarcirse.*

resarzamos 1. that we may compensate; pres. subj. 1st pers. pl. / *resarcir.* 2. let us compensate; impve. 1st pers. pl.

resarzan 1. that they may compensate; pres. subj. 3rd pers. pl. / *resarcir.* 2. let them compensate; impve. 3rd pers. pl.

resárzanse let them recover; impve. 3rd pers. pl. / *resarcirse.*

resarzas that you may compensate; pres. subj. 2nd pers. sing. / *resarcir.*

resárzase let him (her/it) recover; impve. 3rd pers. sing. / *resarcirse.*

resarzo I compensate; pres. ind. 1st pers. sing. / *resarcir.*

resbalándose slipping; pres. part. / *resbalarse.*

resbalaos (you all) slip; impve. 2nd pers. pl. / *resbalarse.*

resbalar to slide. reg.

resbalarse to slip. reg.

resbálate (you) slip; impve. 2nd pers. sing. / *resbalarse.*

resbalémonos let us slip; impve. 1st pers. pl. / *resbalarse.*

resbálense let them slip; impve. 3rd pers. pl. / *resbalarse.*

resbálese let him (her/it) slip; impve. 3rd pers. sing. / *resbalarse.*

rescatar to ransom. reg.

rescindir to rescind. reg.

rescontrar to offset. irr.

rescuentra 1. he (she/it) offsets; pres. ind. 3rd pers. sing. / *rescontrar.* 2. (you) offset; impve. 2nd pers. sing.

rescuentran they offset; pres. ind. 3rd pers. pl. / *rescontrar.*

rescuentras you offset; pres. ind. 2nd pers. sing. / *rescontrar.*

rescuentre 1. that I may offset; pres. subj. 1st pers. sing. / *rescontrar.* 2. that he (she/it) may offset; pres. subj. 3rd pers. sing. 3. let him (her/it) offset; impve. 3rd pers. sing.

rescuentren 1. that they may offset; pres. subj. 3rd pers. pl. / *rescontrar.* 2. let them offset; impve. 3rd pers. pl.

rescuentres that you may offset; pres. subj. 2nd pers. sing. / *rescontrar.*

rescuentro I offset; pres. ind. 1st pers. sing. / *rescontrar.*

resé I know completely; pres. ind. 1st pers. sing. / *resaber.*

resecándose drying thoroughly; pres. part. / *resecarse.*

resecaos (you all) dry thoroughly; impve. 2nd pers. pl. / *resecarse.*

resecar to dry up. irr.

resecarse to dry thoroughly. irr.

resécate (you) dry thoroughly; impve. 2nd pers. sing. / *resecarse.*

resellándose becoming a turncoat; pres. part. / *resellarse.*

resellaos (you all) become a turncoat; impve. 2nd pers. pl. / *resellarse.*

resellar to restamp. reg.

resellarse to become a turncoat. reg.

reséllate (you) become a turncoat; impve. 2nd pers. sing. / *resellarse.*

resellémonos let us become a turncoat; impve. 1st pers. pl. / *resellarse.*

reséllense let them become a turncoat; impve. 3rd pers. pl. / *resellarse.*

reséllese let him (her/it) become a turncoat; impve. 3rd pers. sing. / *resellarse.*

resentíos (you all) show resentment; impve. 2nd pers. pl. / *resentirse.*

resentir to resent. irr.

resentirse to show resentment. irr.

reseñar to review. reg.

resepa 1. that I may know completely; pres. subj. 1st pers. sing. / *resaber.* 2. that he (she/it) may know completely; pres. subj. 3rd pers. sing. 3. let him (her/it) know completely; impve. 3rd pers. sing.

resepáis that you (all) may know completely; pres. subj. 2nd pers. pl. / *resaber.*

resepamos 1. that we may know completely; pres. subj. 1st pers. pl. / *resaber.* 2. let us know completely; impve. 1st pers. pl.

resepan 1. that they may know completely; pres. subj. 3rd pers. pl. / *resaber.* 2. let them know completely; impve. 3rd pers. pl.

resepas that you may know completely; pres. subj. 2nd pers. sing. / *resaber.*

reseque 1. that I may dry up; pres. subj. 1st pers. sing. / *resecar.* 2. that he (she/it) may dry up; pres. subj. 3rd pers. sing. 3. let him (her/it) dry up; impve. 3rd pers. sing.

resequé I dried up ; past 1st pers. sing. / *resecar.*

resequéis that you (all) may dry up; pres. subj. 2nd pers. pl. / *resecar.*

resequémonos let us dry thoroughly; impve. 1st pers. pl. / *resecarse.*

resequemos 1. that we may dry up; pres. subj. 1st pers. pl. / *resecar.* 2. let us dry up; impve. 1st pers. pl.

resequen 1. that they may dry up; pres. subj. 3rd pers. pl. / *resecar.* 2. let them dry up; impve. 3rd pers. pl.

reséquense let them dry thoroughly; impve. 3rd pers. pl. / *resecarse.*

reseques that you may dry up; pres. subj. 2nd pers. sing. / *resecar.*

reséquese let him (her/it) dry thoroughly; impve. 3rd pers. sing. / *resecarse.*

reservándose being wary; pres. part. / *reservarse.*

reservaos (you all) be wary; impve. 2nd pers. pl. / *reservarse.*

reservar to reserve. reg.

reservarse to be wary. reg.

resérvate (you) be wary; impve. 2nd pers. sing. / *reservarse.*

reservémonos let us be wary; impve. 1st pers. pl. / *reservarse.*

resérvense let them be wary; impve. 3rd pers. pl. / *reservarse.*

resérvese let him (her/it) be wary; impve. 3rd pers. sing. / *reservarse.*

resfría 1. he (she/it) cools; pres. ind. 3rd pers. sing. / *resfriar.* 2. (you) cool; impve. 2nd pers. sing.

resfrían they cool; pres. ind. 3rd pers. pl. / *resfriar.*

resfriándose catching cold; pres. part. / *resfriarse.*

resfriaos (you all) catch cold; impve. 2nd pers. pl. / *resfriarse.*

resfriar to cool. irr.

resfriarse to catch cold. irr.

resfrías you cool; pres. ind. 2nd pers. sing. / *resfriar.*

resfríate (you) catch cold; impve. 2nd pers. sing. / *resfriarse.*

resfríe 1. that I may cool; pres. subj. 1st pers. sing. / *resfriar.* 2. that he (she/it) may cool; pres. subj. 3rd pers. sing. 3. let him (her/it) cool; impve. 3rd pers. sing.

resfriémonos let us catch cold; impve. 1st pers. pl. / *resfriarse.*

resfríen 1. that they may cool; pres. subj. 3rd pers. pl. / *resfriar.* 2. let them cool; impve. 3rd pers. pl.

resfríense let them catch cold; impve. 3rd pers. pl. / *resfriarse.*

resfríes that you may cool; pres. subj. 2nd pers. sing. / *resfriar.*

resfríese let him (her/it) catch cold; impve. 3rd pers. sing. / *resfriarse.*

resfrío I cool; pres. ind. 1st pers. sing. / *resfriar.*

resguardándose taking shelter; pres. part. / *resguardarse.*

resguardaos (you all) take shelter; impve. 2nd pers. pl. / *resguardarse.*

resguardar to guard. reg.

resguardarse to take shelter. reg.

resguárdate (you) take shelter; impve. 2nd pers. sing. / *resguardarse.*

resguardémonos let us take shelter; impve. 1st pers. pl. / *resguardarse.*

resguárdense let them take shelter; impve. 3rd pers. pl. / *resguardarse.*

resguárdese let him (her/it) take shelter; impve. 3rd pers. sing. / *resguardarse.*

residenciar to impeach. reg.

residir to reside. reg.

resienta 1. that I may resent; pres. subj. 1st pers. sing. / *resentir.* 2. that he (she/it) may resent; pres. subj. 3rd pers. sing. 3. let him (her/it) resent; impve. 3rd pers. sing.

resientan 1. that they may resent; pres. subj. 3rd pers. pl. / *resentir.* 2. let them resent; impve. 3rd pers. pl.

resiéntanse let them show resentment; impve. 3rd pers. pl. / *resentirse.*

resientas that you may resent; pres. subj. 2nd pers. sing. / *resentir.*

resiéntase let him (her/it) show resentment; impve. 3rd pers. sing. / *resentirse.*

resiente 1. he (she/it) resents; pres. ind. 3rd pers. sing. / *resentir.* 2. (you) resent; impve. 2nd pers. sing.

resienten they resent; pres. ind. 3rd pers. pl. / *resentir.*

resientes you resent; pres. ind. 2nd pers. sing. / *resentir.*

resiéntete (you) show resentment; impve. 2nd pers. sing. / *resentirse.*

resiento I resent; pres. ind. 1st pers. sing. / *resentir.*

resignándose being resigned; pres. part. / *resignarse.*

resignaos (you all) be resigned; impve. 2nd pers. pl. / *resignarse.*

resignar to resign. reg.

resignarse to be resigned. reg.

resígnate (you) be resigned; impve. 2nd pers. sing. / *resignarse.*

resignémonos let us be resigned; impve. 1st pers. pl. / *resignarse.*

resígnense let them be resigned; impve. 3rd pers. pl. / *resignarse.*

resígnese let him (her/it) be resigned; impve. 3rd pers. sing. / *resignarse.*

resintáis that you (all) may resent; pres. subj. 2nd pers. pl. / *resentir.*

resintámonos let us show resentment; impve. 1st pers. pl. / *resentirse.*

resintamos 1. that we may resent; pres. subj. 1st pers. pl. / *resentir.* 2. let us resent; impve. 1st pers. pl.

resintiendo resenting; pres. part. / *resentir.*

resintiéndose showing resentment; pres. part. / *resentirse.*

resintiera 1. that I might resent; imp. subj. 1st pers. sing. / *resentir.* 2. that he (she/it) might resent; imp. subj. 3rd pers. sing.

resintierais that you (all) might resent; imp. subj. 2nd pers pl. / *resentir.*

resintiéramos that we might resent; imp. subj. 1st pers. pl. / *resentir.*

resintieran that they might resent; imp. subj. 3rd pers. pl. / *resentir.*

resintieras that you might resent; imp. subj. 2nd pers. sing. / *resentir.*

resintieron they resented; past 3rd pers. pl. / *resentir.*

resintiese 1. that I might resent; imp. subj. 1st pers. sing. / *resentir.* 2. that he (she/it) might resent; imp. subj. 3rd pers. sing.

resintieseis that you (all) might resent; imp. subj. 2nd pers pl. / *resentir.*

resintiésemos that we might resent; imp. subj. 1st pers. pl. / *resentir.*

resintiesen that they might resent; imp. subj. 3rd pers. pl. / *resentir.*

resintieses that you might resent; imp. subj. 2nd pers. sing. / *resentir.*

resintió he (she/it) resented; past 3rd pers. sing. / *resentir.*

resistámonos let us struggle; impve. 1st pers. pl. / *resistirse.*

resístanse let them struggle; impve. 3rd pers. pl. / *resistirse.*

resístase let him (her/it) struggle; impve. 3rd pers. sing. / *resistirse.*

resístete (you) struggle; impve. 2nd pers. sing. / *resistirse.*

resistiéndose struggling; pres. part. / *resistirse.*

resistíos (you all) struggle; impve. 2nd pers. pl. / *resistirse.*

resistir to resist. reg.

resistirse to struggle. reg.

resolvámonos let us decide; impve. 1st pers. pl. / *resolverse*.

resolveos (you all) decide; impve. 2nd pers. pl. / *resolverse*.

resolver to resolve. irr.

resolverse to decide. irr.

resolviéndose deciding; pres. part. / *resolverse*.

resollar to breathe hard. irr.

resonar to resound. irr.

resoplar to snort or to puff. reg.

respaldándose leaning back; pres. part. / *respaldarse*.

respaldaos (you all) lean back; impve. 2nd pers. pl. / *respaldarse*.

respaldar to endorse. reg.

respaldarse to lean back. reg.

respáldate (you) lean back; impve. 2nd pers. sing. / *respaldarse*.

respaldémonos let us lean back; impve. 1st pers. pl. / *respaldarse*.

respáldense let them lean back; impve. 3rd pers. pl. / *respaldarse*.

respáldese let him (her/it) lean back; impve. 3rd pers. sing. / *respaldarse*.

respectar to concern. reg.

respetar to respect. reg.

respigar to glean. irr.

respigue 1. that I may glean; pres. subj. 1st pers. sing. / *respigar*. 2. that he (she/it) may glean; pres. subj. 3rd pers. sing. 3. let him (her/it) glean; impve. 3rd pers. sing.

respigué I gleaned; past 1st pers. sing. / *respigar*.

respiguéis that you (all) may glean; pres. subj. 2nd pers. pl. / *respigar*.

respiguemos 1. that we may glean; pres. subj. 1st pers. pl. / *respigar*. 2. let us glean; impve. 1st pers. pl.

respiguen 1. that they may glean; pres. subj. 3rd pers. pl. / *respigar*. 2. let them glean; impve. 3rd pers. pl.

respigues that you may glean; pres. subj. 2nd pers. sing. / *respigar*.

respingar to balk or to buck. irr.

respingue 1. that I may balk; pres. subj. 1st pers. sing. / *respingar*. 2. that he (she/it) may balk; pres. subj. 3rd pers. sing. 3. let him (her/it) balk; impve. 3rd pers. sing.

respingué I balked; past 1st pers. sing. / *respingar*.

respinguéis that you (all) may balk; pres. subj. 2nd pers. pl. / *respingar*.

respinguemos 1. that we may balk; pres. subj. 1st pers. pl. / *respingar*. 2. let us balk; impve. 1st pers. pl.

respinguen 1. that they may balk; pres. subj. 3rd pers. pl. / *respingar*. 2. let them balk; impve. 3rd pers. pl.

respingues that you may balk; pres. subj. 2nd pers. sing. / *respingar*.

respirar to breathe. reg.

resplandecer to shine. irr.

resplandezca 1. that I may shine; pres. subj. 1st pers. sing. / *resplandecer*. 2. that he (she/it) may shine; pres. subj. 3rd pers. sing. 3. let him (her/it) shine; impve. 3rd pers. sing.

resplandezcáis that you (all) may shine; pres. subj. 2nd pers. pl. / *resplandecer*.

resplandezcamos 1. that we may shine; pres. subj. 1st pers. pl. / *resplandecer*. 2. let us shine; impve. 1st pers. pl.

resplandezcan 1. that they may shine; pres. subj. 3rd pers. pl. / *resplandecer*. 2. let them shine; impve. 3rd pers. pl.

resplandezcas that you may shine; pres. subj. 2nd pers. sing. / *resplandecer*.

resplandezco I shine; pres. ind. 1st pers. sing. / *resplandecer*.

responder to respond. reg.

responsabilice 1. that I may make responsible; pres. subj. 1st pers. sing. / *responsabilizar*. 2. that he (she/it) may make responsible; pres. subj. 3rd pers. sing. 3. let him (her/it) make responsible; impve. 3rd pers. sing.

responsabilicé I made responsible; past 1st pers. sing. / *responsabilizar*.

responsabilicéis that you (all) may make responsible; pres. subj. 2nd pers. pl. / *responsabilizar*.

responsabilicémonos let us take responsibility; impve. 1st pers. pl. / *responsabilizarse*.

responsabilicemos 1. that we may make responsible; pres. subj. 1st pers. pl. / *responsabilizar*. 2. let us make responsible; impve. 1st pers. pl.

responsabilicen 1. that they may make responsible; pres. subj. 3rd pers. pl. / *responsabilizar*. 2. let them make responsible; impve. 3rd pers. pl.

responsabilícense let them take responsibility; impve. 3rd pers. pl. / *responsabilizarse*.

responsabilices that you may make responsible; pres. subj. 2nd pers. sing. / *responsabilizar*.

responsabilícese let him (her/it) take responsibility; impve. 3rd pers. sing. / *responsabilizarse*.

responsabilizándose taking responsibility; pres. part. / *responsabilizarse*.

responsabilizaos (you all) take responsibility; impve. 2nd pers. pl. / *responsabilizarse*.

responsabilizar to make responsible. irr.

responsabilizarse to take responsibility. irr.

responsabilízate (you) take responsibility; impve. 2nd pers. sing. / *responsabilizarse*.

responsar to say prayers for the dead. reg.

responsear to recite prayers for the dead. reg.

resquebrajándose splitting; pres. part. / *resquebrajarse*.

resquebrajaos (you all) split; impve. 2nd pers. pl. / *resquebrajarse*.

resquebrajar to crack. reg.

resquebrajarse to split. reg.

resquebrájate (you) split; impve. 2nd pers. sing. / *resquebrajarse*.

resquebrajémonos let us split; impve. 1st pers. pl. / *resquebrajarse*.

resquebrajense let them split; impve. 3rd pers. pl. / *resquebrajarse*.

resquebrájese let him (her/it) split; impve. 3rd pers. sing. / *resquebrajarse*.

resquebrándose splitting; pres. part. / *resquebrarse*.

resquebraos (you all) split; impve. 2nd pers. pl. / *resquebrarse*.

resquebrar to crack. irr.

resquebrarse to split. irr.

resquebrémonos let us split; impve. 1st pers. pl. / *resquebrarse*.

resquemar to sting. reg.

resquiebra 1. he (she/it) cracks; pres. ind. 3rd pers. sing. / *resquebrar*. 2. (you) crack; impve. 2nd pers. sing.

resquiebran they crack; pres. ind. 3rd pers. pl. / *resquebrar*.

resquiebras you crack; pres. ind. 2nd pers. sing. / *resquebrar*.

resquiébrate (you) split; impve. 2nd pers. sing. / *resquebrarse*.

resquiebre 1. that I may crack; pres. subj. 1st pers. sing. / *resquebrar*. 2. that he (she/it) may crack; pres. subj. 3rd pers. sing. 3. let him (her/it) crack; impve. 3rd pers. sing.

resquiebren 1. that they may crack; pres. subj. 3rd pers. pl. / *resquebrar*. 2. let them crack; impve. 3rd pers. pl.

resquiébrense let them split; impve. 3rd pers. pl. / *resquebrarse*.

resquiebres that you may crack; pres. subj. 2nd pers. sing. / *resquebrar*.

resquiébrese let him (her/it) split; impve. 3rd pers. sing. / *resquebrarse*.

resquiebro I crack; pres. ind. 1st pers. sing. / *resquebrar*.

restableceos (you all) recover; impve. 2nd pers. pl. / *restablecerse*.

restablecer to reestablish. irr.

restablecerse to recover. irr.

restablécete (you) recover; impve. 2nd pers. sing. / *restablecerse*.

restableciéndose recovering; pres. part. / *restablecerse*.

restablezca 1. that I may reestablish; pres. subj. 1st pers. sing. / *restablecer*. 2. that he (she/it) may reestablish; pres. subj. 3rd pers. sing. 3. let him (her/it) reestablish; impve. 3rd pers. sing.

restablezcáis that you (all) may reestablish; pres. subj. 2nd pers. pl. / *restablecer*.

restablezcámonos let us recover; impve. 1st pers. pl. / *restablecerse*.

restablezcamos 1. that we may reestablish; pres. subj. 1st pers. pl. / *restablecer*. 2. let us reestablish; impve. 1st pers. pl.

restablezcan 1. that they may reestablish; pres. subj. 3rd pers. pl. / *restablecer*. 2. let them reestablish; impve. 3rd pers. pl.

restablézcanse let them recover; impve. 3rd pers. pl. / *restablecerse*.

restablezcas that you may reestablish; pres. subj. 2nd pers. sing. / *restablecer*.

restablézcase let him (her/it) recover; impve. 3rd pers. sing. / *restablecerse*.

restablezco I reestablish; pres. ind. 1st pers. sing. / *restablecer*.

restallar to crack a whip. reg.

restañar to stanch a wound. reg.

restar to subtract. reg.

restaurar to restore. reg.

restituíos (you all) go back; impve. 2nd pers. pl. / *restituirse*.

restituir to return. irr.

restituirse to go back. irr.

restituya 1. that I may return; pres. subj. 1st pers. sing. / *restituir*. 2. that he (she/it) may return; pres. subj. 3rd pers. sing. 3. let him (her/it) return; impve. 3rd pers. sing.

restituyáis that you (all) may return; pres. subj. 2nd pers. pl. / *restituir*.

restituyámonos let us go back; impve. 1st pers. pl. / *restituirse*.

restituyamos 1. that we may return; pres. subj. 1st pers. pl. / *restituir*. 2. let us return; impve. 1st pers. pl.

restituyan 1. that they may return; pres. subj. 3rd pers. pl. / *restituir*. 2. let them return; impve. 3rd pers. pl.

restitúyanse let them go back; impve. 3rd pers. pl. / *restituirse*.

restituyas that you may return; pres. subj. 2nd pers. sing. / *restituir*.

restitúyase let him (her/it) go back; impve. 3rd pers. sing. / *restituirse*.

restituye 1. he (she/it) returns; pres. ind. 3rd pers. sing. / *restituir*. 2. (you) return; impve. 2nd pers. sing.

restituyen they return; pres. ind. 3rd pers. pl. / *restituir*.

restituyendo returning; pres. part. / *restituir*.

restituyéndose going back; pres. part. / *restituirse*.

restituyera 1. that I might return; imp. subj. 1st pers. sing. / *restituir*. 2. that he (she/it) might return; imp. subj. 3rd pers. sing.

restituyerais that you (all) might return; imp. subj. 2nd pers pl. / *restituir*.

restituyéramos that we might return; imp. subj. 1st pers. pl. / *restituir*.

restituyeran that they might return; imp. subj. 3rd pers. pl. / *restituir*.

restituyeras that you might return; imp. subj. 2nd pers. sing. / *restituir*.

restituyeron they returned; past 3rd pers. pl. / *restituir*.

restituyes you return; pres. ind. 2nd pers. sing. / *restituir*.

restituyese 1. that I might return; imp. subj. 1st pers. sing. / *restituir*. 2. that he (she/it) might return; imp. subj. 3rd pers. sing.

restituyeseis that you (all) might return; imp. subj. 2nd pers pl. / *restituir*.

restituyésemos that we might return; imp. subj. 1st pers. pl. / *restituir*.

restituyesen that they might return; imp. subj. 3rd pers. pl. / *restituir*.

restituyeses that you might return; imp. subj. 2nd pers. sing. / *restituir*.

restitúyete (you) go back; impve. 2nd pers. sing. / *restituirse*.

restituyo I return; pres. ind. 1st pers. sing. / *restituir*.

restituyó he (she/it) returned; past 3rd pers. sing. / *restituir*.

restregar to scrub hard. irr.

restregué I scrubbed hard; past 1st pers. sing. / *restregar*.

restreguéis that you (all) may scrub hard; pres. subj. 2nd pers. pl. / *restregar*.

restreguemos 1. that we may scrub hard; pres. subj. 1st pers. pl. / *restregar*. 2. let us scrub hard; impve. 1st pers. pl.

restriega 1. he (she/it) scrubs hard; pres. ind. 3rd pers. sing. / *restregar*. 2. (you) scrub hard; impve. 2nd pers. sing.

restriegan they scrub hard; pres. ind. 3rd pers. pl. / *restregar*.

restriegas you scrub hard; pres. ind. 2nd pers. sing. / *restregar*.

restriego I scrub hard; pres. ind. 1st pers. sing. / *restregar*.

restriegue 1. that I may scrub hard; pres. subj. 1st pers. sing. / *restregar*. 2. that he (she/it) may scrub hard; pres. subj. 3rd pers. sing. 3. let him (her/it) scrub hard; impve. 3rd pers. sing.

restrieguen 1. that they may scrub hard; pres. subj. 3rd pers. pl. / *restregar*. 2. let them scrub hard; impve. 3rd pers. pl.

restriegues that you may scrub hard; pres. subj. 2nd pers. sing. / *restregar*.

restringir to restrict. irr.

restrinja 1. that I may restrict; pres. subj. 1st pers. sing. / *restringir*. 2. that he (she/it) may restrict; pres. subj. 3rd pers. sing. 3. let him (her/it) restrict; impve. 3rd pers. sing.

restrinjáis that you (all) may restrict; pres. subj. 2nd pers. pl. / *restringir*.

restrinjamos 1. that we may restrict; pres. subj. 1st pers. pl. / *restringir*. 2. let us restrict; impve. 1st pers. pl.

restrinjan 1. that they may restrict; pres. subj. 3rd pers. pl. / *restringir*. 2. let them restrict; impve. 3rd pers. pl.

restrinjas that you may restrict; pres. subj. 2nd pers. sing. / *restringir*.

restrinjo I restrict; pres. ind. 1st pers. sing. / *restringir*.

restriñendo restricting; pres. part. / *restriñir*.

restriñeron they restricted; past 3rd pers. pl. / *restriñir*.

restriñir to restrict. irr.

restriñó he (she/it) restricted; past 3rd pers. sing. / *restriñir*.

resucitar to resuscitate. reg.

resudar to sweat. reg.

resuelto resolved; past part. / *resolver*.

resuelva 1. that I may resolve; pres. subj. 1st pers. sing. / *resolver*. 2. that he (she/it) may resolve; pres. subj. 3rd pers. sing. 3. let him (her/it) resolve; impve. 3rd pers. sing.

resuelvan 1. that they may resolve; pres. subj. 3rd pers. pl. / *resolver*. 2. let them resolve; impve. 3rd pers. pl.

resuélvanse let them decide; impve. 3rd pers. pl. / *resolverse*.

resuelvas that you may resolve; pres. subj. 2nd pers. sing. / *resolver*.

resuélvase let him (her/it) decide; impve. 3rd pers. sing. / *resolverse*.

resuelve 1. he (she/it) resolves; pres. ind. 3rd pers. sing. / *resolver*. 2. (you) resolve; impve. 2nd pers. sing.

resuelven they resolve; pres. ind. 3rd pers. pl. / *resolver*.

resuelves you resolve; pres. ind. 2nd pers. sing. / *resolver*.

resuélvete (you) decide; impve. 2nd pers. sing. / *resolverse*.

resuelvo I resolve; pres. ind. 1st pers. sing. / *resolver*.

resuella 1. he (she/it) breathes hard; pres. ind. 3rd pers. sing. / *resollar*. 2. (you) breathe hard; impve. 2nd pers. sing.

resuellan they breathe hard; pres. ind. 3rd pers. pl. / *resollar*.

resuellas you breathe hard; pres. ind. 2nd pers. sing. / *resollar*.

resuelle 1. that I may breathe hard; pres. subj. 1st pers. sing. / *resollar*. 2. that he (she/it) may breathe hard; pres. subj. 3rd pers. sing. 3. let him (her/it) breathe hard; impve. 3rd pers. sing.

resuellen 1. that they may breathe hard; pres. subj. 3rd pers. pl. / *resollar*. 2. let them breathe hard; impve. 3rd pers. pl.

resuelles that you may breathe hard; pres. subj. 2nd pers. sing. / *resollar*.

resuello I breathe hard; pres. ind. 1st pers. sing. / *resollar*.

resuena 1. he (she/it) resounds; pres. ind. 3rd pers. sing. / *resonar*. 2. (you) resound; impve. 2nd pers. sing.

resuenan they resound; pres. ind. 3rd pers. pl. / *resonar*.

resuenas you resound; pres. ind. 2nd pers. sing. / *resonar*.

resuene 1. that I may resound; pres. subj. 1st pers. sing. / *resonar*. 2. that he (she/it) may resound; pres. subj. 3rd pers. sing. 3. let him (her/it) resound; impve. 3rd pers. sing.

resuenen 1. that they may resound; pres. subj. 3rd pers. pl. / *resonar*. 2. let them resound; impve. 3rd pers. pl.

resuenes that you may resound; pres. subj. 2nd pers. sing. / *resonar*.

resueno I resound; pres. ind. 1st pers. sing. / *resonar*.

resultar to result. reg.

resumámonos let us be reduced; impve. 1st pers. pl. / *resumirse*.

resúmanse let them be reduced; impve. 3rd pers. pl. / *resumirse*.

resúmase let him (her/it) be reduced; impve. 3rd pers. sing. / *resumirse*.

resúmete (you) be reduced; impve. 2nd pers. sing. / *resumirse*.

resumiéndose being reduced; pres. part. / *resumirse*.

resumíos (you all) be reduced; impve. 2nd pers. pl. / *resumirse*.

resumir to summarize. reg.

resumirse to be reduced. reg.

resupe I knew completely; past 1st pers. sing. / *resaber*.

resupiera 1. that I might know completely; imp. subj. 1st pers. sing. / *resaber*. 2. that he (she/it) might know completely; imp. subj. 3rd pers. sing.

resupierais that you (all) might know completely; imp. subj. 2nd pers pl. / *resaber*.

resupiéramos that we might know completely; imp. subj. 1st pers. pl. / *resaber*.

resupieran that they might know completely; imp. subj. 3rd pers. pl. / *resaber*.

resupieras that you might know completely; imp. subj. 2nd pers. sing. / *resaber*.

resupieron they knew completely; past 3rd pers. pl. / *resaber*.

resupiese 1. that I might know completely; imp. subj. 1st pers. sing. / *resaber*. 2. that he (she/it) might know completely; imp. subj. 3rd pers. sing.

resupieseis that you (all) might know completely; imp. subj. 2nd pers pl. / *resaber*.

resupiésemos that we might know completely; imp. subj. 1st pers. pl. / *resaber*.

resupiesen that they might know completely; imp. subj. 3rd pers. pl. / *resaber*.

resupieses that you might know completely; imp. subj. 2nd pers. sing. / *resaber*.

resupimos we knew completely; past 1st pers. pl. / *resaber*.

resupiste you knew completely; past 2nd pers. sing. / *resaber*.

resupisteis you (all) knew completely; past 2nd pers. pl. / *resaber*.

resupo he (she/it) knew completely; past 3rd pers. sing. / *resaber*.

resurgir to reappear. irr.

resurja 1. that I may reappear; pres. subj. 1st pers. sing. / *resurgir*. 2. that he (she/it) may reappear; pres. subj. 3rd pers. sing. 3. let him (her/it) reappear; impve. 3rd pers. sing.

resurjáis that you (all) may reappear; pres. subj. 2nd pers. pl. / *resurgir*.

resurjamos 1. that we may reappear; pres. subj. 1st pers. pl. / *resurgir*. 2. let us reappear; impve. 1st pers. pl.

resurjan 1. that they may reappear; pres. subj. 3rd pers. pl. / *resurgir*. 2. let them reappear; impve. 3rd pers. pl.

resurjas that you may reappear; pres. subj. 2nd pers. sing. / *resurgir*.

resurjo I reappear; pres. ind. 1st pers. sing. / *resurgir*.

resurtir to rebound. reg.

retar to challenge. reg.

retardándose being delayed; pres. part. / *retardarse*.

retardaos (you all) be delayed; impve. 2nd pers. pl. / *retardarse*.

retardar to retard. reg.

retardarse to be delayed. reg.

retárdate (you) be delayed; impve. 2nd pers. sing. / *retardarse*.

retardémonos let us be delayed; impve. 1st pers. pl. / *retardarse*.

retárdense let them be delayed; impve. 3rd pers. pl. / *retardarse*.

retárdese let him (her/it) be delayed; impve. 3rd pers. sing. / *retardarse*.

retemblar to tremble. irr.

reten (you) retain; impve. 2nd pers. sing. / *retener*.

retendrá he (she/it) will retain; fut. 3rd pers. sing. / *retener*.

retendrán they will retain; fut. 3rd pers. pl. / *retener*.

retendrás you will retain; fut. 2nd pers. sing. / *retener*.

retendré I shall retain; fut. 1st pers. sing. / *retener*.

retendréis you (all) will retain; fut. 2nd pers. pl. / *retener*.

retendremos we shall retain; fut. 1st pers. pl. / *retener*.

retendría 1. I should retain; cond. 1st pers. sing. / *retener*. 2. he (she/it) would retain; cond. 3rd pers. sing.

retendríais you (all) would retain; cond. 2nd pers. pl. / *retener*.

retendríamos we should retain; cond. 1st pers. pl. / *retener*.

retendrían they would retain; cond. 3rd pers. pl. / *retener*.

retendrías you would retain; cond. 2nd pers. sing. / *retener*.

retener to retain. irr.

retenga 1. that I may retain; pres. subj. 1st pers. sing. / *retener*. 2. that he (she/it) may retain; pres. subj. 3rd pers. sing. 3. let him (her/it) retain; impve. 3rd pers. sing.

retengáis that you (all) may retain; pres. subj. 2nd pers. pl. / *retener*.

retengamos 1. that we may retain; pres. subj. 1st pers. pl. / *retener*. 2. let us retain; impve. 1st pers. pl.

retengan 1. that they may retain; pres. subj. 3rd pers. pl. / *retener*. 2. let them retain; impve. 3rd pers. pl.

retengas that you may retain; pres. subj. 2nd pers. sing. / *retener*.

retengo I retain; pres. ind. 1st pers. sing. / *retener*.

retiembla 1. he (she/it) trembles; pres. ind. 3rd pers. sing. / *retemblar*. 2. (you) tremble; impve. 2nd pers. sing.

retiemblan they tremble; pres. ind. 3rd pers. pl. / *retemblar*.

retiemblas you tremble; pres. ind. 2nd pers. sing. / *retemblar*.

retiemble 1. that I may tremble; pres. subj. 1st pers. sing. / *retemblar*. 2. that he (she/it) may tremble; pres. subj. 3rd pers. sing. 3. let him (her/it) tremble; impve. 3rd pers. sing.

retiemblen 1. that they may tremble; pres. subj. 3rd pers. pl. / *retemblar.* 2. let them tremble; impve. 3rd pers. pl.

retiembles that you may tremble; pres. subj. 2nd pers. sing. / *retemblar.*

retiemblo I tremble; pres. ind. 1st pers. sing. / *retemblar.*

retiene 1. he (she/it) retains; pres. ind. 3rd pers. sing. / *retener.* 2. (you) retain; impve. 2nd pers. sing.

retienen they retain; pres. ind. 3rd pers. pl. / *retener.*

retienes you retain; pres. ind. 2nd pers. sing. / *retener.*

retiña 1. that I may jingle; pres. subj. 1st pers. sing. / *retiñir.* 2. that he (she/it) may jingle; pres. subj. 3rd pers. sing. 3. let him (her/it) jingle; impve. 3rd pers. sing.

retiñáis that you (all) may jingle; pres. subj. 2nd pers. pl. / *retiñir.*

retiñamos 1. that we may jingle; pres. subj. 1st pers. pl. / *retiñir.* 2. let us jingle; impve. 1st pers. pl.

retiñan 1. that they may jingle; pres. subj. 3rd pers. pl. / *retiñir.* 2. let them jingle; impve. 3rd pers. pl.

retiñas that you may jingle; pres. subj. 2nd pers. sing. / *retiñir.*

retiñe 1. he (she/it) jingles; pres. ind. 3rd pers. sing. / *retiñir.* 2. (you) jingle; impve. 2nd pers. sing.

retiñen they jingle; pres. ind. 3rd pers. pl. / *retiñir.*

retiñendo jingling; pres. part. / *retiñir.*

retiñera 1. that I might jingle; imp. subj. 1st pers. sing. / *retiñir.* 2. that he (she/it) might jingle; imp. subj. 3rd pers. sing.

retiñerais that you (all) might jingle; imp. subj. 2nd pers pl. / *retiñir.*

retiñéramos that we might jingle; imp. subj. 1st pers. pl. / *retiñir.*

retiñeran that they might jingle; imp. subj. 3rd pers. pl. / *retiñir.*

retiñeras that you might jingle; imp. subj. 2nd pers. sing. / *retiñir.*

retiñeron they jingled; past 3rd pers. pl. / *retiñir.*

retiñes you jingle; pres. ind. 2nd pers. sing. / *retiñir.*

retiñese 1. that I might jingle; imp. subj. 1st pers. sing. / *retiñir.* 2. that he (she/it) might jingle; imp. subj. 3rd pers. sing.

retiñeseis that you (all) might jingle; imp. subj. 2nd pers pl. / *retiñir.*

retiñésemos that we might jingle; imp. subj. 1st pers. pl. / *retiñir.*

retiñesen that they might jingle; imp. subj. 3rd pers. pl. / *retiñir.*

retiñeses that you might jingle; imp. subj. 2nd pers. sing. / *retiñir.*

retiñir to jingle. irr.

retiño I jingle; pres. ind. 1st pers. sing. / *retiñir.*

retiñó he (she/it) jingled; past 3rd pers. sing. / *retiñir.*

retirándose withdrawing; pres. part. / *retirarse.*

retiraos (you all) withdraw; impve. 2nd pers. pl. / *retirarse.*

retirar to retire. reg.

retirarse to withdraw. reg.

retírate (you) withdraw; impve. 2nd pers. sing. / *retirarse.*

retirémonos let us withdraw; impve. 1st pers. pl. / *retirarse.*

retírense let them withdraw; impve. 3rd pers. pl. / *retirarse.*

retírese let him (her/it) withdraw; impve. 3rd pers. sing. / *retirarse.*

retobándose talking back; pres. part. / *retobarse.*

retobaos (you all) talk back; impve. 2nd pers. pl. / *retobarse.*

retobar to cover with leather. reg.

retobarse to talk back. reg.

retóbate (you) talk back; impve. 2nd pers. sing. / *retobarse.*

retobémonos let us talk back; impve. 1st pers. pl. / *retobarse.*

retóbense let them talk back; impve. 3rd pers. pl. / *retobarse.*

retóbese let him (her/it) talk back; impve. 3rd pers. sing. / *retobarse.*

retocar to retouch. irr.

retoce 1. that I may frolic; pres. subj. 1st pers. sing. / *retozar.* 2. that he (she/it) may frolic; pres. subj. 3rd pers. sing. 3. let him (her/it) frolic; impve. 3rd pers. sing.

retocé I froliced; past 1st pers. sing. / *retozar.*

retocéis that you (all) may frolic; pres. subj. 2nd pers. pl. / *retozar.*

retocemos 1. that we may frolic; pres. subj. 1st pers. pl. / *retozar.* 2. let us frolic; impve. 1st pers. pl.

retocen 1. that they may frolic; pres. subj. 3rd pers. pl. / *retozar.* 2. let them frolic; impve. 3rd pers. pl.

retoces that you may frolic; pres. subj. 2nd pers. sing. / *retozar.*

retoñar to sprout. reg.

retoque 1. that I may retouch; pres. subj. 1st pers. sing. / *retocar.* 2. that he (she/it) may retouch; pres. subj. 3rd pers. sing. 3. let him (her/it) retouch; impve. 3rd pers. sing.

retoqué I retouched; past 1st pers. sing. / *retocar.*

retoquéis that you (all) may retouch; pres. subj. 2nd pers. pl. / *retocar.*

retoquemos 1. that we may retouch; pres. subj. 1st pers. pl. / *retocar.* 2. let us retouch; impve. 1st pers. pl.

retoquen 1. that they may retouch; pres. subj. 3rd pers. pl. / *retocar.* 2. let them retouch; impve. 3rd pers. pl.

retoques that you may retouch; pres. subj. 2nd pers. sing. / *retocar.*

retorceos (you all) squirm; impve. 2nd pers. pl. / *retorcerse.*

retorcer to twist. irr.

retorcerse to squirm. irr.

retorciéndose squirming; pres. part. / *retorcerse.*

retornándose returning; pres. part. / *retornarse.*

retornaos (you all) return; impve. 2nd pers. pl. / *retornarse.*

retornar to return. reg.

retornarse to return. reg.
retórnate (you) return; impve. 2nd pers. sing. / *retornarse.*
retornémonos let us return; impve. 1st pers. pl. / *retornarse.*
retórnense let them return; impve. 3rd pers. pl. / *retornarse.*
retórnese let him (her/it) return; impve. 3rd pers. sing. / *retornarse.*
retortijar to twist. reg.
retorzáis that you (all) may twist; pres. subj. 2nd pers. pl. / *retorcer.*
retorzámonos let us squirm; impve. 1st pers. pl. / *retorcerse.*
retorzamos 1. that we may twist; pres. subj. 1st pers. pl. / *retorcer.* 2. let us twist; impve. 1st pers. pl.
retozar to frolic. irr.
retractándose retracting; pres. part. / *retractarse.*
retractaos (you all) retract; impve. 2nd pers. pl. / *retractarse.*
retractar to retract. reg.
retractarse to retract. reg.
retráctate (you) retract; impve. 2nd pers. sing. / *retractarse.*
retractémonos let us retract; impve. 1st pers. pl. / *retractarse.*
retráctense let them retract; impve. 3rd pers. pl. / *retractarse.*
retráctese let him (her/it) retract; impve. 3rd pers. sing. / *retractarse.*
retraeos (you all) withdraw; impve. 2nd pers. pl. / *retraerse.*
retraer to bring back. irr.
retraerse to withdraw. irr.
retráete (you) withdraw; impve. 2nd pers. sing. / *retraerse.*
retraiga 1. that I may bring back; pres. subj. 1st pers. sing. / *retraer.* 2. that he (she/it) may bring back; pres. subj. 3rd pers. sing. 3. let him (her/it) bring back; impve. 3rd pers. sing.
retraigáis that you (all) may bring back; pres. subj. 2nd pers. pl. / *retraer.*
retraigámonos let us withdraw; impve. 1st pers. pl. / *retraerse.*
retraigamos 1. that we may bring back; pres. subj. 1st pers. pl. / *retraer.* 2. let us bring back; impve. 1st pers. pl.
retraigan 1. that they may bring back; pres. subj. 3rd pers. pl. / *retraer.* 2. let them bring back; impve. 3rd pers. pl.
retraíganse let them withdraw; impve. 3rd pers. pl. / *retraerse.*
retraigas that you may bring back; pres. subj. 2nd pers. sing. / *retraer.*
retraígase let him (her/it) withdraw; impve. 3rd pers. sing. / *retraerse.*
retraigo I bring back; pres. ind. 1st pers. sing. / *retraer.*
retraje I brought back; past 1st pers. sing. / *retraer.*

retrajera 1. that I might bring back; imp. subj. 1st pers. sing. / *retraer.* 2. that he (she/it) might bring back; imp. subj. 3rd pers. sing.
retrajerais that you (all) might bring back; imp. subj. 2nd pers pl. / *retraer.*
retrajéramos that we might bring back; imp. subj. 1st pers. pl. / *retraer.*
retrajeran that they might bring back; imp. subj. 3rd pers. pl. / *retraer.*
retrajeras that you might bring back; imp. subj. 2nd pers. sing. / *retraer.*
retrajeron they brought back; past 3rd pers. pl. / *retraer.*
retrajese 1. that I might bring back; imp. subj. 1st pers. sing. / *retraer.* 2. that he (she/it) might bring back; imp. subj. 3rd pers. sing.
retrajeseis that you (all) might bring back; imp. subj. 2nd pers pl. / *retraer.*
retrajésemos that we might bring back; imp. subj. 1st pers. pl. / *retraer.*
retrajesen that they might bring back; imp. subj. 3rd pers. pl. / *retraer.*
retrajeses that you might bring back; imp. subj. 2nd pers. sing. / *retraer.*
retrajimos we brought back; past 1st pers. pl. / *retraer.*
retrajiste you brought back; past 2nd pers. sing. / *retraer.*
retrajisteis you (all) brought back; past 2nd pers. pl. / *retraer.*
retrajo he (she/it) brought back; past 3rd pers. sing. / *retraer.*
retrancar to brake. irr.
retranque 1. that I may brake; pres. subj. 1st pers. sing. / *retrancar.* 2. that he (she/it) may brake; pres. subj. 3rd pers. sing. 3. let him (her/it) brake; impve. 3rd pers. sing.
retranqué I braked; past 1st pers. sing. / *retrancar.*
retranquéis that you (all) may brake; pres. subj. 2nd pers. pl. / *retrancar.*
retranquemos 1. that we may brake; pres. subj. 1st pers. pl. / *retrancar.* 2. let us brake; impve. 1st pers. pl.
retranquen 1. that they may brake; pres. subj. 3rd pers. pl. / *retrancar.* 2. let them brake; impve. 3rd pers. pl.
retranques that you may brake; pres. subj. 2nd pers. sing. / *retrancar.*
retrasándose falling behind; pres. part. / *retrasarse.*
retrasaos (you all) fall behind; impve. 2nd pers. pl. / *retrasarse.*
retrasar to delay. reg.
retrasarse to fall behind. reg.
retrásate (you) fall behind; impve. 2nd pers. sing. / *retrasarse.*
retrasémonos let us fall behind; impve. 1st pers. pl. / *retrasarse.*
retrásense let them fall behind; impve. 3rd pers. pl. / *retrasarse.*
retrásese let him (her/it) fall behind; impve. 3rd pers. sing. / *retrasarse.*

retratándose being photographed; pres. part. / *retratarse*.

retrataos (you all) be photographed; impve. 2nd pers. pl. / *retratarse*.

retratar to portray. reg.

retratarse to be photographed. reg.

retrátate (you) be photographed; impve. 2nd pers. sing. / *retratarse*.

retratémonos let us be photographed; impve. 1st pers. pl. / *retratarse*.

retrátense let them be photographed; impve. 3rd pers. pl. / *retratarse*.

retrátese let him (her/it) be photographed; impve. 3rd pers. sing. / *retratarse*.

retrayendo bringing back; pres. part. / *retraer*.

retrayéndose withdrawing; pres. part. / *retraerse*.

retrechar to move backward. reg.

retribuir to pay for. irr.

retribuya 1. that I may pay for; pres. subj. 1st pers. sing. / *retribuir*. 2. that he (she/it) may pay for; pres. subj. 3rd pers. sing. 3. let him (her/it) pay for; impve. 3rd pers. sing.

retribuyáis that you (all) may pay for; pres. subj. 2nd pers. pl. / *retribuir*.

retribuyamos 1. that we may pay for; pres. subj. 1st pers. pl. / *retribuir*. 2. let us pay for; impve. 1st pers. pl.

retribuyan 1. that they may pay for; pres. subj. 3rd pers. pl. / *retribuir*. 2. let them pay for; impve. 3rd pers. pl.

retribuyas that you may pay for; pres. subj. 2nd pers. sing. / *retribuir*.

retribuye 1. he (she/it) pays for; pres. ind. 3rd pers. sing. / *retribuir*. 2. (you) pay for; impve. 2nd pers. sing.

retribuyen they pay for; pres. ind. 3rd pers. pl. / *retribuir*.

retribuyendo paying for; pres. part. / *retribuir*.

retribuyera 1. that I might pay for; imp. subj. 1st pers. sing. / *retribuir*. 2. that he (she/it) might pay for; imp. subj. 3rd pers. sing.

retribuyerais that you (all) might pay for; imp. subj. 2nd pers pl. / *retribuir*.

retribuyéramos that we might pay for; imp. subj. 1st pers. pl. / *retribuir*.

retribuyeran that they might pay for; imp. subj. 3rd pers. pl. / *retribuir*.

retribuyeras that you might pay for; imp. subj. 2nd pers. sing. / *retribuir*.

retribuyeron they paid for; past 3rd pers. pl. / *retribuir*.

retribuyes you pay for; pres. ind. 2nd pers. sing. / *retribuir*.

retribuyese 1. that I might pay for; imp. subj. 1st pers. sing. / *retribuir*. 2. that he (she/it) might pay for; imp. subj. 3rd pers. sing.

retribuyeseis that you (all) might pay for; imp. subj. 2nd pers pl. / *retribuir*.

retribuyésemos that we might pay for; imp. subj. 1st pers. pl. / *retribuir*.

retribuyesen that they might pay for; imp. subj. 3rd pers. pl. / *retribuir*.

retribuyeses that you might pay for; imp. subj. 2nd pers. sing. / *retribuir*.

retribuyo I pay for; pres. ind. 1st pers. sing. / *retribuir*.

retribuyó he (she/it) paid for; past 3rd pers. sing. / *retribuir*.

retroceder to turn back. reg.

retrogradar to retrogress. reg.

retronar to thunder. irr.

retrotraer to antedate. irr.

retrotraiga 1. that I may antedate; pres. subj. 1st pers. sing. / *retrotraer*. 2. that he (she/it) may antedate; pres. subj. 3rd pers. sing. 3. let him (her/it) antedate; impve. 3rd pers. sing.

retrotraigáis that you (all) may antedate; pres. subj. 2nd pers. pl. / *retrotraer*.

retrotraigamos 1. that we may antedate; pres. subj. 1st pers. pl. / *retrotraer*. 2. let us antedate; impve. 1st pers. pl.

retrotraigan 1. that they may antedate; pres. subj. 3rd pers. pl. / *retrotraer*. 2. let them antedate; impve. 3rd pers. pl.

retrotraigas that you may antedate; pres. subj. 2nd pers. sing. / *retrotraer*.

retrotraigo I antedate; pres. ind. 1st pers. sing. / *retrotraer*.

retrotraje I antedated; past 1st pers. sing. / *retrotraer*.

retrotrajera 1. that I might antedate; imp. subj. 1st pers. sing. / *retrotraer*. 2. that he (she/it) might antedate; imp. subj. 3rd pers. sing.

retrotrajerais that you (all) might antedate; imp. subj. 2nd pers pl. / *retrotraer*.

retrotrajéramos that we might antedate; imp. subj. 1st pers. pl. / *retrotraer*.

retrotrajeran that they might antedate; imp. subj. 3rd pers. pl. / *retrotraer*.

retrotrajeras that you might antedate; imp. subj. 2nd pers. sing. / *retrotraer*.

retrotrajeron they antedated; past 3rd pers. pl. / *retrotraer*.

retrotrajese 1. that I might antedate; imp. subj. 1st pers. sing. / *retrotraer*. 2. that he (she/it) might antedate; imp. subj. 3rd pers. sing.

retrotrajeseis that you (all) might antedate; imp. subj. 2nd pers pl. / *retrotraer*.

retrotrajésemos that we might antedate; imp. subj. 1st pers. pl. / *retrotraer*.

retrotrajesen that they might antedate; imp. subj. 3rd pers. pl. / *retrotraer*.

retrotrajeses that you might antedate; imp. subj. 2nd pers. sing. / *retrotraer*.

retrotrajimos we antedated; past 1st pers. pl. / *retrotraer*.

retrotrajiste you antedated; past 2nd pers. sing. / *retrotraer*.

retrotrajisteis you (all) antedated; past 2nd pers. pl. / *retrotraer*.

retrotrajo he (she/it) antedated; past 3rd pers. sing. / *retrotraer*.

retrotrayendo antedating; pres. part. / *retrotraer*.

retruena 1. he (she/it) thunders; pres. ind. 3rd pers. sing. / *retronar*. 2. (you) thunder; impve. 2nd pers. sing.

retruenan they thunder; pres. ind. 3rd pers. pl. / *retronar*.

retruenas you thunder; pres. ind. 2nd pers. sing. / *retronar*.

retruene 1. that I may thunder; pres. subj. 1st pers. sing. / *retronar*. 2. that he (she/it) may thunder; pres. subj. 3rd pers. sing. 3. let him (her/it) thunder; impve. 3rd pers. sing.

retruenen 1. that they may thunder; pres. subj. 3rd pers. pl. / *retronar*. 2. let them thunder; impve. 3rd pers. pl.

retruenes that you may thunder; pres. subj. 2nd pers. sing. / *retronar*.

retrueno I thunder; pres. ind. 1st pers. sing. / *retronar*.

retuerce 1. he (she/it) twists; pres. ind. 3rd pers. sing. / *retorcer*. 2. (you) twist; impve. 2nd pers. sing.

retuercen they twist; pres. ind. 3rd pers. pl. / *retorcer*.

retuerces you twist; pres. ind. 2nd pers. sing. / *retorcer*.

retuércete (you) squirm; impve. 2nd pers. sing. / *retorcerse*.

retuerza 1. that I may twist; pres. subj. 1st pers. sing. / *retorcer*. 2. that he (she/it) may twist; pres. subj. 3rd pers. sing. 3. let him (her/it) twist; impve. 3rd pers. sing.

retuerzan 1. that they may twist; pres. subj. 3rd pers. pl. / *retorcer*. 2. let them twist; impve. 3rd pers. pl.

retuérzanse let them squirm; impve. 3rd pers. pl. / *retorcerse*.

retuerzas that you may twist; pres. subj. 2nd pers. sing. / *retorcer*.

retuérzase let him (her/it) squirm; impve. 3rd pers. sing. / *retorcerse*.

retuerzo I twist; pres. ind. 1st pers. sing. / *retorcer*.

retumbar to resound. reg.

retuve I retained; past 1st pers. sing. / *retener*.

retuviera 1. that I might retain; imp. subj. 1st pers. sing. / *retener*. 2. that he (she/it) might retain; imp. subj. 3rd pers. sing.

retuvierais that you (all) might retain; imp. subj. 2nd pers pl. / *retener*.

retuviéramos that we might retain; imp. subj. 1st pers. pl. / *retener*.

retuvieran that they might retain; imp. subj. 3rd pers. pl. / *retener*.

retuvieras that you might retain; imp. subj. 2nd pers. sing. / *retener*.

retuvieron they retained; past 3rd pers. pl. / *retener*.

retuviese 1. that I might retain; imp. subj. 1st pers. sing. / *retener*. 2. that he (she/it) might retain; imp. subj. 3rd pers. sing.

retuvieseis that you (all) might retain; imp. subj. 2nd pers pl. / *retener*.

retuviésemos that we might retain; imp. subj. 1st pers. pl. / *retener*.

retuviesen that they might retain; imp. subj. 3rd pers. pl. / *retener*.

retuvieses that you might retain; imp. subj. 2nd pers. sing. / *retener*.

retuvimos we retained; past 1st pers. pl. / *retener*.

retuviste you retained; past 2nd pers. sing. / *retener*.

retuvisteis you (all) retained; past 2nd pers. pl. / *retener*.

retuvo he (she/it) retained; past 3rd pers. sing. / *retener*.

reúna 1. that I may reunite; pres. subj. 1st pers. sing. / *reunir*. 2. that he (she/it) may reunite; pres. subj. 3rd pers. sing. 3. let him (her/it) reunite; impve. 3rd pers. sing.

reunámonos let us assemble; impve. 1st pers. pl. / *reunirse*.

reúnan 1. that they may reunite; pres. subj. 3rd pers. pl. / *reunir*. 2. let them reunite; impve. 3rd pers. pl.

reúnanse let them assemble; impve. 3rd pers. pl. / *reunirse*.

reúnas that you may reunite; pres. subj. 2nd pers. sing. / *reunir*.

reúnase let him (her/it) assemble; impve. 3rd pers. sing. / *reunirse*.

reúne 1. he (she/it) reunites; pres. ind. 3rd pers. sing. / *reunir*. 2. (you) reunite; impve. 2nd pers. sing.

reúnen they reunite; pres. ind. 3rd pers. pl. / *reunir*.

reúnes you reunite; pres. ind. 2nd pers. sing. / *reunir*.

reúnete (you) assemble; impve. 2nd pers. sing. / *reunirse*.

reuniéndose assembling; pres. part. / *reunirse*.

reuníos (you all) assemble; impve. 2nd pers. pl. / *reunirse*.

reunir to reunite. irr.

reunirse to assemble. irr.

reúno I reunite; pres. ind. 1st pers. sing. / *reunir*.

revalidándose taking qualifying exams for a degree; pres. part. / *revalidarse*.

revalidaos (you all) take qualifying exams for a degree; impve. 2nd pers. pl. / *revalidarse*.

revalidar to revalidate or to confirm. reg.

revalidarse to take qualifying exams for a degree. reg.

revalídate (you) take qualifying exams for a degree; impve. 2nd pers. sing. / *revalidarse*.

revalidémonos let us take qualifying exams for a degree; impve. 1st pers. pl. / *revalidarse*.

revalídense let them take qualifying exams for a degree; impve. 3rd pers. pl. / *revalidarse*.

revalídese let him (her/it) take qualifying exams for a degree; impve. 3rd pers. sing. / *revalidarse*.

revalorar to revalue. reg.

revalorice 1. that I may revalue; pres. subj. 1st pers. sing. / *revalorizar*. 2. that he (she/it) may revalue; pres. subj. 3rd pers. sing. 3. let him (her/it) revalue; impve. 3rd pers. sing.

revaloricé I revalued; past 1st pers. sing. / *revalorizar*.

revaloricéis that you (all) may revalue; pres. subj. 2nd pers. pl. / *revalorizar*.

revaloricemos 1. that we may revalue; pres. subj. 1st pers. pl. / *revalorizar*. 2. let us revalue; impve. 1st pers. pl.

revaloricen 1. that they may revalue; pres. subj. 3rd pers. pl. / *revalorizar.* 2. let them revalue; impve. 3rd pers. pl.

revalorices that you may revalue; pres. subj. 2nd pers. sing. / *revalorizar.*

revalorizar to revalue. irr.

revea 1. that I may review; pres. subj. 1st pers. sing. / *rever.* 2. that he (she/it) may review; pres. subj. 3rd pers. sing. 3. let him (her/it) review; impve. 3rd pers. sing.

reveáis that you (all) may review; pres. subj. 2nd pers. pl. / *rever.*

reveamos 1. that we may review; pres. subj. 1st pers. pl. / *rever.* 2. let us review; impve. 1st pers. pl.

revean 1. that they may review; pres. subj. 3rd pers. pl. / *rever.* 2. let them review; impve. 3rd pers. pl.

reveas that you may review; pres. subj. 2nd pers. sing. / *rever.*

revece 1. that I may work in shifts; pres. subj. 1st pers. sing. / *revezar.* 2. that he (she/it) may work in shifts; pres. subj. 3rd pers. sing. 3. let him (her/it) work in shifts; impve. 3rd pers. sing.

revecé I worked in shifts; past 1st pers. sing. / *revezar.*

revecéis that you (all) may work in shifts; pres. subj. 2nd pers. pl. / *revezar.*

revecemos 1. that we may work in shifts; pres. subj. 1st pers. pl. / *revezar.* 2. let us work in shifts; impve. 1st pers. pl.

revecen 1. that they may work in shifts; pres. subj. 3rd pers. pl. / *revezar.* 2. let them work in shifts; impve. 3rd pers. pl.

reveces that you may work in shifts; pres. subj. 2nd pers. sing. / *revezar.*

reveía 1. I was reviewing; imp. ind. 1st pers. sing. / *rever.* 2. he (she/it) was reviewing; imp. ind. 3rd pers. sing.

reveíais you (all) were reviewing; imp. ind. 2nd pers. pl. / *rever.*

reveíamos we were reviewing; imp. ind. 1st pers. pl. / *rever.*

reveían they were reviewing; imp. ind. 3rd pers. pl. / *rever.*

reveías you were reviewing; imp. ind. 2nd pers. sing. / *rever.*

revejeceos (you all) age prematurely; impve. 2nd pers. pl. / *revejecerse.*

revejecer to age prematurely. irr.

revejecerse to age prematurely. irr.

revejécete (you) age prematurely; impve. 2nd pers. sing. / *revejecerse.*

revejeciéndose aging prematurely; pres. part. / *revejecerse.*

revejezca 1. that I may age prematurely; pres. subj. 1st pers. sing. / *revejecer.* 2. that he (she/it) may age prematurely; pres. subj. 3rd pers. sing. 3. let him (her/it) age prematurely; impve. 3rd pers. sing.

revejezcáis that you (all) may age prematurely; pres. subj. 2nd pers. pl. / *revejecer.*

revejezcámonos let us age prematurely; impve. 1st pers. pl. / *revejecerse.*

revejezcamos 1. that we may age prematurely; pres. subj. 1st pers. pl. / *revejecer.* 2. let us age prematurely; impve. 1st pers. pl.

revejezcan 1. that they may age prematurely; pres. subj. 3rd pers. pl. / *revejecer.* 2. let them age prematurely; impve. 3rd pers. pl.

revejézcanse let them age prematurely; impve. 3rd pers. pl. / *revejecerse.*

revejezcas that you may age prematurely; pres. subj. 2nd pers. sing. / *revejecer.*

revejézcase let him (her/it) age prematurely; impve. 3rd pers. sing. / *revejecerse.*

revejezco I age prematurely; pres. ind. 1st pers. sing. / *revejecer.*

revelar to reveal or to develope a film. reg.

reven (you) come back; impve. 2nd pers. sing. / *revenir.*

revender to resell. reg.

revendrá he (she/it) will come back; fut. 3rd pers. sing. / *revenir.*

revendrán they will come back; fut. 3rd pers. pl. / *revenir.*

revendrás you will come back; fut. 2nd pers. sing. / *revenir.*

revendré I shall come back; fut. 1st pers. sing. / *revenir.*

revendréis you (all) will come back; fut. 2nd pers. pl. / *revenir.*

revendremos we shall come back; fut. 1st pers. pl. / *revenir.*

revendría 1. I should come back; cond. 1st pers. sing. / *revenir.* 2. he (she/it) would come back; cond. 3rd pers. sing.

revendríais you (all) would come back; cond. 2nd pers. pl. / *revenir.*

revendríamos we should come back; cond. 1st pers. pl. / *revenir.*

revendrían they would come back; cond. 3rd pers. pl. / *revenir.*

revendrías you would come back; cond. 2nd pers. sing. / *revenir.*

revénete (you) turn sour; impve. 2nd pers. sing. / *revenirse.*

revenga 1. that I may come back; pres. subj. 1st pers. sing. / *revenir.* 2. that he (she/it) may come back; pres. subj. 3rd pers. sing. 3. let him (her/it) come back; impve. 3rd pers. sing.

revengáis that you (all) may come back; pres. subj. 2nd pers. pl. / *revenir.*

revengámonos let us turn sour; impve. 1st pers pl. / *revenirse.*

revengamos 1. that we may come back; pres. subj. 1st pers. pl. / *revenir.* 2. let us come back; impve. 1st pers. pl.

revengan 1. that they may come back; pres. subj. 3rd pers. pl. / *revenir.* 2. let them come back; impve. 3rd pers. pl.

revénganse let them turn sour; impve. 3rd pers. pl. / *revenirse.*

revengas that you may come back; pres. subj. 2nd pers. sing. / *revenir.*

revéngase let him (her/it) turn sour; impve. 3rd pers. sing. / *revenirse.*

revengo I come back; pres. ind. 1st pers. sing. / *revenir.*

revenios (you all) turn sour; impve. 2nd pers. pl. / *revenirse.*

revenir to come back. irr.

revenirse to turn sour. irr.

reventándose bursting; pres. part. / *reventarse.*

reventaos (you all) burst; impve. 2nd pers. pl. / *reventarse.*

reventar to burst. irr.

reventarse to burst. irr.

reventémonos let us burst; impve. 1st pers. pl. / *reventarse.*

reveo I review; pres. ind. 1st pers. sing. / *rever.*

rever to review. irr.

reverberar to reverberate. reg.

reverdecer to turn green again. irr.

reverdezca 1. that I may turn green again; pres. subj. 1st pers. sing. / *reverdecer.* 2. that he (she/it) may turn green again; pres. subj. 3rd pers. sing. 3. let him (her/it) turn green again; impve. 3rd pers. sing.

reverdezcáis that you (all) may turn green again; pres. subj. 2nd pers. pl. / *reverdecer.*

reverdezcamos 1. that we may turn green again; pres. subj. 1st pers. pl. / *reverdecer.* 2. let us turn green again; impve. 1st pers. pl.

reverdezcan 1. that they may turn green again; pres. subj. 3rd pers. pl. / *reverdecer.* 2. let them turn green again; impve. 3rd pers. pl.

reverdezcas that you may turn green again; pres. subj. 2nd pers. sing. / *reverdecer.*

reverdezco I turn green again; pres. ind. 1st pers. sing. / *reverdecer.*

reverenciar to revere. reg.

reverter to overflow. irr.

revertir to revert. irr.

revestíos (you all) dress; impve. 2nd pers. pl. / *revestirse.*

revestir to dress. irr.

revestirse to dress. irr.

revezar to work in shifts. irr.

revi I reviewed; past 1st pers. sing. / *rever.*

reviene he (she/it) comes back; pres. ind. 3rd pers. sing. / *revenir.*

revienen they come back; pres. ind. 3rd pers. pl. / *revenir.*

revienes you come back; pres. ind. 2nd pers. sing. / *revenir.*

revienta 1. he (she/it) bursts; pres. ind. 3rd pers. sing. / *reventar.* 2. (you) burst; impve. 2nd pers. sing.

revientan they burst; pres. ind. 3rd pers. pl. / *reventar.*

revientas you burst; pres. ind. 2nd pers. sing. / *reventar.*

reviéntate (you) burst; impve. 2nd pers. sing. / *reventarse.*

reviente 1. that I may burst; pres. subj. 1st pers. sing. / *reventar.* 2. that he (she/it) may burst; pres. subj. 3rd pers. sing. 3. let him (her/it) burst; impve. 3rd pers. sing.

revienten 1. that they may burst; pres. subj. 3rd pers. pl. / *reventar.* 2. let them burst; impve. 3rd pers. pl.

reviéntense let them burst; impve. 3rd pers. pl. / *reventarse.*

revientes that you may burst; pres. subj. 2nd pers. sing. / *reventar.*

reviéntese let him (her/it) burst; impve. 3rd pers. sing. / *reventarse.*

reviento I burst; pres. ind. 1st pers. sing. / *reventar.*

revierta 1. that I may overflow; pres. subj. 1st pers. sing. / *reverter.* 2. that he (she/it) may overflow; pres. subj. 3rd pers. sing. 3. let him (her/it) overflow; impve. 3rd pers. sing.

revierta 1. that I may revert; pres. subj. 1st pers. sing. / *revertir.* 2. that he (she/it) may revert; pres. subj. 3rd pers. sing. 3. let him (her/it) revert; impve. 3rd pers. sing.

reviertan 1. that they may overflow; pres. subj. 3rd pers. pl. / *reverter.* 2. let them overflow; impve. 3rd pers. pl.

reviertan 1. that they may revert; pres. subj. 3rd pers. pl. / *revertir.* 2. let them revert; impve. 3rd pers. pl.

reviertas that you may overflow; pres. subj. 2nd pers. sing. / *reverter.*

reviertas that you may revert; pres. subj. 2nd pers. sing. / *revertir.*

revierte 1. he (she/it) overflows; pres. ind. 3rd pers. sing. / *reverter.* 2. (you) overflow; impve. 2nd pers. sing.

revierte 1. he (she/it) reverts; pres. ind. 3rd pers. sing. / *revertir.* 2. (you) revert; impve. 2nd pers. sing.

revierten they overflow; pres. ind. 3rd pers. pl. / *reverter.*

revierten they revert; pres. ind. 3rd pers. pl. / *revertir.*

reviertes you overflow; pres. ind. 2nd pers. sing. / *reverter.*

reviertes you revert; pres. ind. 2nd pers. sing. / *revertir.*

revierto I overflow; pres. ind. 1st pers. sing. / *reverter.*

revierto I revert; pres. ind. 1st pers. sing. / *revertir.*

revine I came back; past 1st pers. sing. / *revenir.*

reviniendo coming back; pres. part. / *revenir.*

reviniéndose turning sour; pres. part. / *revenirse.*

reviniera 1. that I might come back; imp. subj. 1st pers. sing. / *revenir.* 2. that he (she/it) might come back; imp. subj. 3rd pers. sing.

revinierais that you (all) might come back; imp. subj. 2nd pers pl. / *revenir.*

reviniéramos that we might come back; imp. subj. 1st pers. pl. / *revenir.*

revinieran that they might come back; imp. subj. 3rd pers. pl. / *revenir.*

revinieras that you might come back; imp. subj. 2nd pers. sing. / *revenir.*

revinieron they came back; past 3rd pers. pl. / *revenir.*

reviniese 1. that I might come back; imp. subj. 1st pers. sing. / *revenir*. 2. that he (she/it) might come back; imp. subj. 3rd pers. sing.

revinieseis that you (all) might come back; imp. subj. 2nd pers pl. / *revenir*.

reviniésemos that we might come back; imp. subj. 1st pers. pl. / *revenir*.

reviniesen that they might come back; imp. subj. 3rd pers. pl. / *revenir*.

revinieses that you might come back; imp. subj. 2nd pers. sing. / *revenir*.

revinimos we came back; past 1st pers. pl. / *revenir*.

reviniste you came back; past 2nd pers. sing. / *revenir*.

revinisteis you (all) came back; past 2nd pers. pl. / *revenir*.

revino he (she/it) came back; past 3rd pers. sing. / *revenir*.

revio he (she/it) reviewed; past 3rd pers. sing. / *rever*.

revirtáis that you (all) may revert; pres. subj. 2nd pers. pl. / *revertir*.

revirtamos 1. that we may revert; pres. subj. 1st pers. pl. / *revertir*. 2. let us revert; impve. 1st pers. pl.

revirtiendo reverting; pres. part. / *revertir*.

revirtiera 1. that I might revert; imp. subj. 1st pers. sing. / *revertir*. 2. that he (she/it) might revert; imp. subj. 3rd pers. sing.

revirtierais that you (all) might revert; imp. subj. 2nd pers pl. / *revertir*.

revirtiéramos that we might revert; imp. subj. 1st pers. pl. / *revertir*.

revirtieran that they might revert; imp. subj. 3rd pers. pl. / *revertir*.

revirtieras that you might revert; imp. subj. 2nd pers. sing. / *revertir*.

revirtieron they reverted; past 3rd pers. pl. / *revertir*.

revirtiese 1. that I might revert; imp. subj. 1st pers. sing. / *revertir*. 2. that he (she/it) might revert; imp. subj. 3rd pers. sing.

revirtieseis that you (all) might revert; imp. subj. 2nd pers pl. / *revertir*.

revirtiésemos that we might revert; imp. subj. 1st pers. pl. / *revertir*.

revirtiesen that they might revert; imp. subj. 3rd pers. pl. / *revertir*.

revirtieses that you might revert; imp. subj. 2nd pers. sing. / *revertir*.

revirtió he (she/it) reverted; past 3rd pers. sing. / *revertir*.

revisar to revise. reg.

revista 1. that I may dress; pres. subj. 1st pers. sing. / *revestir*. 2. that he (she/it) may dress; pres. subj. 3rd pers. sing. 3. let him (her/it) dress; impve. 3rd pers. sing.

revistáis that you (all) may dress; pres. subj. 2nd pers. pl. / *revestir*.

revistámonos let us dress; impve. 1st pers. pl. / *revestirse*.

revistamos 1. that we may dress; pres. subj. 1st pers. pl. / *revestir*. 2. let us dress; impve. 1st pers. pl.

revistan 1. that they may dress; pres. subj. 3rd pers. pl. / *revestir*. 2. let them dress; impve. 3rd pers. pl.

revístanse let them dress; impve. 3rd pers. pl. / *revestirse*.

revistar to review. reg.

revistas that you may dress; pres. subj. 2nd pers. sing. / *revestir*.

revístase let him (her/it) dress; impve. 3rd pers. sing. / *revestirse*.

reviste 1. he (she/it) dresses; pres. ind. 3rd pers. sing. / *revestir*. 2. (you) dress; impve. 2nd pers. sing.

revisten they dress; pres. ind. 3rd pers. pl. / *revestir*.

revistes you dress; pres. ind. 2nd pers. sing. / *revestir*.

revístete (you) dress; impve. 2nd pers. sing. / *revestirse*.

revistiendo dressing; pres. part. / *revestir*.

revistiéndose dressing; pres. part. / *revestirse*.

revistiera 1. that I might dress; imp. subj. 1st pers. sing. / *revestir*. 2. that he (she/it) might dress; imp. subj. 3rd pers. sing.

revistierais that you (all) might dress; imp. subj. 2nd pers pl. / *revestir*.

revistiéramos that we might dress; imp. subj. 1st pers. pl. / *revestir*.

revistieran that they might dress; imp. subj. 3rd pers. pl. / *revestir*.

revistieras that you might dress; imp. subj. 2nd pers. sing. / *revestir*.

revistieron they dressed; past 3rd pers. pl. / *revestir*.

revistiese 1. that I might dress; imp. subj. 1st pers. sing. / *revestir*. 2. that he (she/it) might dress; imp. subj. 3rd pers. sing.

revistieseis that you (all) might dress; imp. subj. 2nd pers pl. / *revestir*.

revistiésemos that we might dress; imp. subj. 1st pers. pl. / *revestir*.

revistiesen that they might dress; imp. subj. 3rd pers. pl. / *revestir*.

revistieses that you might dress; imp. subj. 2nd pers. sing. / *revestir*.

revistió he (she/it) dressed; past 3rd pers. sing. / *revestir*.

revisto reviewed; past part. / *rever*.

revisto I dress; pres. ind. 1st pers. sing. / *revestir*.

revivificar to revive. irr.

revivifique 1. that I may revive; pres. subj. 1st pers. sing. / *revivificar*. 2. that he (she/it) may revive; pres. subj. 3rd pers. sing. 3. let him (her/it) revive; impve. 3rd pers. sing.

revivifiqué I revived; past 1st pers. sing. / *revivificar*.

revivifiquéis that you (all) may revive; pres. subj. 2nd pers. pl. / *revivificar*.

revivifiquemos 1. that we may revive; pres. subj. 1st pers. pl. / *revivificar*. 2. let us revive; impve. 1st pers. pl.

revivifiquen 1. that they may revive; pres. subj. 3rd pers. pl. / *revivificar*. 2. let them revive; impve. 3rd pers. pl.

revivifiques that you may revive; pres. subj. 2nd pers. sing. / *revivificar*.

revivir to revive. reg.
revocar to revoke. irr.
revolar to fly about. irr.
revolcándose wallowing; pres. part. / *revolcarse.*
revolcaos (you all) wallow; impve. 2nd pers. pl. /
revolcarse.
revolcar to knock down. irr.
revolcarse to wallow. irr.
revolear to fling up. reg.
revolotear to flutter. reg.
revolqué I knocked down; past 1st pers. sing. /
revolcar.
revolquéis that you (all) may knock down; pres. subj.
2nd pers. pl. / *revolcar.*
revolquémonos let us wallow; impve. 1st pers. pl. /
revolcarse.
revolquemos 1. that we may knock down; pres. subj.
1st pers. pl. / *revolcar.* 2. let us knock down; impve.
1st pers. pl.
revolucionándose rebelling; pres. part. /
revolucionarse.
revolucionaos (you all) rebel; impve. 2nd pers. pl. /
revolucionarse.
revolucionar to revolutionize. reg.
revolucionarse to rebel. reg.
revoluciónate (you) rebel; impve. 2nd pers. sing. /
revolucionarse.
revolucionémonos let us rebel; impve. 1st pers. pl. /
revolucionarse.
revoluciónense let them rebel; impve. 3rd pers. pl. /
revolucionarse.
revoluciónese let him (her/it) rebel; impve. 3rd pers.
sing. / *revolucionarse.*
revolvámonos let us turn; impve. 1st pers. pl. /
revolverse.
revolveos (you all) turn; impve. 2nd pers. pl. /
revolverse.
revolver to revolve. irr.
revolverse to turn. irr.
revolviéndose turning; pres. part. / *revolverse.*
revoque 1. that I may revoke; pres. subj. 1st pers.
sing. / *revocar.* 2. that he (she/it) may revoke; pres.
subj. 3rd pers. sing. 3. let him (her/it) revoke;
impve. 3rd pers. sing.
revoqué I revoked; past 1st pers. sing. / *revocar.*
revoquéis that you (all) may revoke; pres. subj. 2nd
pers. pl. / *revocar.*
revoquemos 1. that we may revoke; pres. subj. 1st
pers. pl. / *revocar.* 2. let us revoke; impve. 1st pers.
pl.
revoquen 1. that they may revoke; pres. subj. 3rd
pers. pl. / *revocar.* 2. let them revoke; impve. 3rd
pers. pl.
revoques that you may revoke; pres. subj. 2nd pers.
sing. / *revocar.*
revuela 1. he (she/it) flies about; pres. ind. 3rd pers.
sing. / *revolar.* 2. (you) fly about; impve. 2nd pers.
sing.
revuelan they fly about; pres. ind. 3rd pers. pl. /
revolar.

revuelas you fly about; pres. ind. 2nd pers. sing. /
revolar.
revuelca 1. he (she/it) knocks down; pres. ind. 3rd
pers. sing. / *revolcar.* 2. (you) knock down; impve.
2nd pers. sing.
revuelcan they knock down; pres. ind. 3rd pers. pl. /
revolcar.
revuelcas you knock down; pres. ind. 2nd pers. sing. /
revolcar.
revuélcate (you) wallow; impve. 2nd pers. sing. /
revolcarse.
revuelco I knock down; pres. ind. 1st pers. sing. /
revolcar.
revuele 1. that I may fly about; pres. subj. 1st pers.
sing. / *revolar.* 2. that he (she/it) may fly about; pres.
subj. 3rd pers. sing. 3. let him (her/it) fly about;
impve. 3rd pers. sing.
revuelen 1. that they may fly about; pres. subj. 3rd
pers. pl. / *revolar.* 2. let them fly about; impve. 3rd
pers. pl.
revueles that you may fly about; pres. subj. 2nd pers.
sing. / *revolar.*
revuelo I fly about; pres. ind. 1st pers. sing. / *revolar.*
revuelque 1. that I may knock down; pres. subj. 1st
pers. sing. / *revolcar.* 2. that he (she/it) may knock
down; pres. subj. 3rd pers. sing. 3. let him (her/it)
knock down; impve. 3rd pers. sing.
revuelquen 1. that they may knock down; pres. subj.
3rd pers. pl. / *revolcar.* 2. let them knock down;
impve. 3rd pers. pl.
revuélquense let them wallow; impve. 3rd pers. pl. /
revolcarse.
revuelques that you may knock down; pres. subj. 2nd
pers. sing. / *revolcar.*
revuélquese let him (her/it) wallow; impve. 3rd pers.
sing. / *revolcarse.*
revuelto revolved; past part. / *revolver.*
revuelva 1. that I may revolve; pres. subj. 1st pers.
sing. / *revolver.* 2. that he (she/it) may revolve; pres.
subj. 3rd pers. sing. 3. let him (her/it) revolve;
impve. 3rd pers. sing.
revuelvan 1. that they may revolve; pres. subj. 3rd
pers. pl. / *revolver.* 2. let them revolve; impve. 3rd
pers. pl.
revuélvanse let them turn; impve. 3rd pers. pl. /
revolverse.
revuelvas that you may revolve; pres. subj. 2nd pers.
sing. / *revolver.*
revuélvase let him (her/it) turn; impve. 3rd pers. sing.
/ *revolverse.*
revuelve 1. he (she/it) revolves; pres. ind. 3rd pers.
sing. / *revolver.* 2. (you) revolve; impve. 2nd pers.
sing.
revuelven they revolve; pres. ind. 3rd pers. pl. /
revolver.
revuelves you revolve; pres. ind. 2nd pers. sing. /
revolver.
revuélvete (you) turn; impve. 2nd pers. sing. /
revolverse.
revuelvo I revolve; pres. ind. 1st pers. sing. / *revolver.*
rexpedir to forward. irr.

rexpida 1. that I may forward; pres. subj. 1st pers. sing. / *rexpedir.* 2. that he (she/it) may forward; pres. subj. 3rd pers. sing. 3. let him (her/it) forward; impve. 3rd pers. sing.

rexpidáis that you (all) may forward; pres. subj. 2nd pers. pl. / *rexpedir.*

rexpidamos 1. that we may forward; pres. subj. 1st pers. pl. / *rexpedir.* 2. let us forward; impve. 1st pers. pl.

rexpidan 1. that they may forward; pres. subj. 3rd pers. pl. / *rexpedir.* 2. let them forward; impve. 3rd pers. pl.

rexpidas that you may forward; pres. subj. 2nd pers. sing. / *rexpedir.*

rexpide 1. he (she/it) forwards; pres. ind. 3rd pers. sing. / *rexpedir.* 2. (you) forward; impve. 2nd pers. sing.

rexpiden they forward; pres. ind. 3rd pers. pl. / *rexpedir.*

rexpides you forward; pres. ind. 2nd pers. sing. / *rexpedir.*

rexpidiendo forwarding; pres. part. / *rexpedir.*

rexpidiera 1. that I might forward; imp. subj. 1st pers. sing. / *rexpedir.* 2. that he (she/it) might forward; imp. subj. 3rd pers. sing.

rexpidierais that you (all) might forward; imp. subj. 2nd pers pl. / *rexpedir.*

rexpidiéramos that we might forward; imp. subj. 1st pers. pl. / *rexpedir.*

rexpidieran that they might forward; imp. subj. 3rd pers. pl. / *rexpedir.*

rexpidieras that you might forward; imp. subj. 2nd pers. sing. / *rexpedir.*

rexpidieron they forwarded; past 3rd pers. pl. / *rexpedir.*

rexpidiese 1. that I might forward; imp. subj. 1st pers. sing. / *rexpedir.* 2. that he (she/it) might forward; imp. subj. 3rd pers. sing.

rexpidieseis that you (all) might forward; imp. subj. 2nd pers pl. / *rexpedir.*

rexpidiésemos that we might forward; imp. subj. 1st pers. pl. / *rexpedir.*

rexpidiesen that they might forward; imp. subj. 3rd pers. pl. / *rexpedir.*

rexpidieses that you might forward; imp. subj. 2nd pers. sing. / *rexpedir.*

rexpidió he (she/it) forwarded; past 3rd pers. sing. / *rexpedir.*

rexpido I forward; pres. ind. 1st pers. sing. / *rexpedir.*

rezagándose lagging behind; pres. part. / *rezagarse.*

rezagaos (you all) lag behind; impve. 2nd pers. pl. / *rezagarse.*

rezagar to leave behind. irr.

rezagarse to lag behind. irr.

rezágate (you) lag behind; impve. 2nd pers. sing. / *rezagarse.*

rezague 1. that I may leave behind; pres. subj. 1st pers. sing. / *rezagar.* 2. that he (she/it) may leave behind; pres. subj. 3rd pers. sing. 3. let him (her/it) leave behind; impve. 3rd pers. sing.

rezagué I left behind; past 1st pers. sing. / *rezagar.*

rezaguéis that you (all) may leave behind; pres. subj. 2nd pers. pl. / *rezagar.*

rezaguémonos let us lag behind; impve. 1st pers. pl. / *rezagarse.*

rezaguemos 1. that we may leave behind; pres. subj. 1st pers. pl. / *rezagar.* 2. let us leave behind; impve. 1st pers. pl.

rezaguen 1. that they may leave behind; pres. subj. 3rd pers. pl. / *rezagar.* 2. let them leave behind; impve. 3rd pers. pl.

rezáguense let them lag behind; impve. 3rd pers. pl. / *rezagarse.*

rezagues that you may leave behind; pres. subj. 2nd pers. sing. / *rezagar.*

rezáguese let him (her/it) lag behind; impve. 3rd pers. sing. / *rezagarse.*

rezar to pray. irr.

rezongar to grumble. irr.

rezongue 1. that I may grumble; pres. subj. 1st pers. sing. / *rezongar.* 2. that he (she/it) may grumble; pres. subj. 3rd pers. sing. 3. let him (her/it) grumble; impve. 3rd pers. sing.

rezongué I grumbled; past 1st pers. sing. / *rezongar.*

rezonguéis that you (all) may grumble; pres. subj. 2nd pers. pl. / *rezongar.*

rezonguemos 1. that we may grumble; pres. subj. 1st pers. pl. / *rezongar.* 2. let us grumble; impve. 1st pers. pl.

rezonguen 1. that they may grumble; pres. subj. 3rd pers. pl. / *rezongar.* 2. let them grumble; impve. 3rd pers. pl.

rezongues that you may grumble; pres. subj. 2nd pers. sing. / *rezongar.*

rezumándose seeping; pres. part. / *rezumarse.*

rezumar to ooze. reg.

rezumarse to seep. reg.

rezúmense let them seep; impve. 3rd pers. pl. / *rezumarse.*

rezúmese let it seep; impve. 3rd pers. sing. / *rezumarse.*

ría 1. that I may laugh; pres. subj. 1st pers. sing. / *reír.* 2. that he (she/it) may laugh; pres. subj. 3rd pers. sing. 3. let him (her/it) laugh; impve. 3rd pers. sing.

riáis that you (all) may laugh; pres. subj. 2nd pers. pl. / *reír.*

riámonos let us laugh at; impve. 1st pers. pl. / *reírse.*

riamos 1. that we may laugh; pres. subj. 1st pers. pl. / *reír.* 2. let us laugh; impve. 1st pers. pl.

rían 1. that they may laugh; pres. subj. 3rd pers. pl. / *reír.* 2. let them laugh; impve. 3rd pers. pl.

ríanse let them laugh at; impve. 3rd pers. pl. / *reírse.*

rías that you may laugh; pres. subj. 2nd pers. sing. / *reír.*

ríase let him (her/it) laugh at; impve. 3rd pers. sing. / *reírse.*

ribetear to bind or to trim. reg.

rice 1. that I may curl; pres. subj. 1st pers. sing. / *rizar.* 2. that he (she/it) may curl; pres. subj. 3rd pers. sing. 3. let him (her/it) curl; impve. 3rd pers. sing.

ricé I curled; past 1st pers. sing. / *rizar.*

ricéis that you (all) may curl; pres. subj. 2nd pers. pl. / *rizar*.

ricémonos let us frizzle; impve. 1st pers. pl. / *rizarse*.

ricemos 1. that we may curl; pres. subj. 1st pers. pl. / *rizar*. 2. let us curl; impve. 1st pers. pl.

ricen 1. that they may curl; pres. subj. 3rd pers. pl. / *rizar*. 2. let them curl; impve. 3rd pers. pl.

rícense let them frizzle; impve. 3rd pers. pl. / *rizarse*.

rices that you may curl; pres. subj. 2nd pers. sing. / *rizar*.

rícese let him (her/it) frizzle; impve. 3rd pers. sing. / *rizarse*.

ridiculice 1. that I may ridicule; pres. subj. 1st pers. sing. / *ridiculizar*. 2. that he (she/it) may ridicule; pres. subj. 3rd pers. sing. 3. let him (her/it) ridicule; impve. 3rd pers. sing.

ridiculicé I ridiculed; past 1st pers. sing. / *ridiculizar*.

ridiculicéis that you (all) may ridicule; pres. subj. 2nd pers. pl. / *ridiculizar*.

ridiculicemos 1. that we may ridicule; pres. subj. 1st pers. pl. / *ridiculizar*. 2. let us ridicule; impve. 1st pers. pl.

ridiculicen 1. that they may ridicule; pres. subj. 3rd pers. pl. / *ridiculizar*. 2. let them ridicule; impve. 3rd pers. pl.

ridiculices that you may ridicule; pres. subj. 2nd pers. sing. / *ridiculizar*.

ridiculizar to ridicule. irr.

ríe 1. he (she/it) laughs; pres. ind. 3rd pers. sing. / *reír*. 2. (you) laugh; impve. 2nd pers. sing.

riega 1. he (she/it) waters; pres. ind. 3rd pers. sing. / *regar*. 2. (you) water; impve. 2nd pers. sing.

riegan they water; pres. ind. 3rd pers. pl. / *regar*.

riegas you water; pres. ind. 2nd pers. sing. / *regar*.

riégate (you) scatter; impve. 2nd pers. sing. / *regarse*.

riego I water; pres. ind. 1st pers. sing. / *regar*.

riegue 1. that I may water; pres. subj. 1st pers. sing. / *regar*. 2. that he (she/it) may water; pres. subj. 3rd pers. sing. 3. let him (her/it) water; impve. 3rd pers. sing.

rieguen 1. that they may water; pres. subj. 3rd pers. pl. / *regar*. 2. let them water; impve. 3rd pers. pl.

riéguense let them scatter; impve. 3rd pers. pl. / *regarse*.

riegues that you may water; pres. subj. 2nd pers. sing. / *regar*.

riéguese let him (her/it) scatter; impve. 3rd pers. sing. / *regarse*.

rielar to gleam. reg.

ríen they laugh; pres. ind. 3rd pers. pl. / *reír*.

riendo laughing; pres. part. / *reír*.

riéndose laughing at; pres. part. / *reírse*.

riera 1. that I might laugh; imp. subj. 1st pers. sing. / *reír*. 2. that he (she/it) might laugh; imp. subj. 3rd pers. sing.

rierais that you (all) might laugh; imp. subj. 2nd pers pl. / *reír*.

riéramos that we might laugh; imp. subj. 1st pers. pl. / *reír*.

rieran that they might laugh; imp. subj. 3rd pers. pl. / *reír*.

rieras that you might laugh; imp. subj. 2nd pers. sing. / *reír*.

rieron they laughed; past 3rd pers. pl. / *reír*.

ríes you laugh; pres. ind. 2nd pers. sing. / *reír*.

riese 1. that I might laugh; imp. subj. 1st pers. sing. / *reír*. 2. that he (she/it) might laugh; imp. subj. 3rd pers. sing.

rieseis that you (all) might laugh; imp. subj. 2nd pers pl. / *reír*.

riésemos that we might laugh; imp. subj. 1st pers. pl. / *reír*.

riesen that they might laugh; imp. subj. 3rd pers. pl. / *reír*.

rieses that you might laugh; imp. subj. 2nd pers. sing. / *reír*.

ríete (you) laugh at; impve. 2nd pers. sing. / *reírse*.

rifar to raffle. reg.

rige 1. he (she/it) rules; pres. ind. 3rd pers. sing. / *regir*. 2. (you) rule; impve. 2nd pers. sing.

rigen they rule; pres. ind. 3rd pers. pl. / *regir*.

riges you rule; pres. ind. 2nd pers. sing. / *regir*.

rigiendo ruling; pres. part. / *regir*.

rigiera 1. that I might rule; imp. subj. 1st pers. sing. / *regir*. 2. that he (she/it) might rule; imp. subj. 3rd pers. sing.

rigierais that you (all) might rule; imp. subj. 2nd pers pl. / *regir*.

rigiéramos that we might rule; imp. subj. 1st pers. pl. / *regir*.

rigieran that they might rule; imp. subj. 3rd pers. pl. / *regir*.

rigieras that you might rule; imp. subj. 2nd pers. sing. / *regir*.

rigieron they ruled; past 3rd pers. pl. / *regir*.

rigiese 1. that I might rule; imp. subj. 1st pers. sing. / *regir*. 2. that he (she/it) might rule; imp. subj. 3rd pers. sing.

rigieseis that you (all) might rule; imp. subj. 2nd pers pl. / *regir*.

rigiésemos that we might rule; imp. subj. 1st pers. pl. / *regir*.

rigiesen that they might rule; imp. subj. 3rd pers. pl. / *regir*.

rigieses that you might rule; imp. subj. 2nd pers. sing. / *regir*.

rigió he (she/it) ruled; past 3rd pers. sing. / *regir*.

rija 1. that I may rule; pres. subj. 1st pers. sing. / *regir*. 2. that he (she/it) may rule; pres. subj. 3rd pers. sing. 3. let him (her/it) rule; impve. 3rd pers. sing.

rijáis that you (all) may rule; pres. subj. 2nd pers. pl. / *regir*.

rijamos 1. that we may rule; pres. subj. 1st pers. pl. / *regir*. 2. let us rule; impve. 1st pers. pl.

rijan 1. that they may rule; pres. subj. 3rd pers. pl. / *regir*. 2. let them rule; impve. 3rd pers. pl.

rijas that you may rule; pres. subj. 2nd pers. sing. / *regir*.

rijo I rule; pres. ind. 1st pers. sing. / *regir*.

rimar to rhyme. reg.

rimbombar to resound. reg.

rinda 1. that I may overcome; pres. subj. 1st pers. sing. / *rendir*. 2. that he (she/it) may overcome; pres. subj. 3rd pers. sing. 3. let him (her/it) overcome; impve. 3rd pers. sing.

rindáis that you (all) may overcome; pres. subj. 2nd pers. pl. / *rendir*.

rindámonos let us surrender; impve. 1st pers. pl. / *rendirse*.

rindamos 1. that we may overcome; pres. subj. 1st pers. pl. / *rendir*. 2. let us overcome; impve. 1st pers. pl.

rindan 1. that they may overcome; pres. subj. 3rd pers. pl. / *rendir*. 2. let them overcome; impve. 3rd pers. pl.

ríndanse let them surrender; impve. 3rd pers. pl. / *rendirse*.

rindas that you may overcome; pres. subj. 2nd pers. sing. / *rendir*.

ríndase let him (her/it) surrender; impve. 3rd pers. sing. / *rendirse*.

rinde 1. he (she/it) overcomes; pres. ind. 3rd pers. sing. / *rendir*. 2. (you) overcome; impve. 2nd pers. sing.

rinden they overcome; pres. ind. 3rd pers. pl. / *rendir*.

rindes you overcome; pres. ind. 2nd pers. sing. / *rendir*.

ríndete (you) surrender; impve. 2nd pers. sing. / *rendirse*.

rindiendo overcoming; pres. part. / *rendir*.

rindiéndose surrendering; pres. part. / *rendirse*.

rindiera 1. that I might overcome; imp. subj. 1st pers. sing. / *rendir*. 2. that he (she/it) might overcome; imp. subj. 3rd pers. sing.

rindierais that you (all) might overcome; imp. subj. 2nd pers pl. / *rendir*.

rindiéramos that we might overcome; imp. subj. 1st pers. pl. / *rendir*.

rindieran that they might overcome; imp. subj. 3rd pers. pl. / *rendir*.

rindieras that you might overcome; imp. subj. 2nd pers. sing. / *rendir*.

rindieron they overcame; past 3rd pers. pl. / *rendir*.

rindiese 1. that I might overcome; imp. subj. 1st pers. sing. / *rendir*. 2. that he (she/it) might overcome; imp. subj. 3rd pers. sing.

rindieseis that you (all) might overcome; imp. subj. 2nd pers pl. / *rendir*.

rindiésemos that we might overcome; imp. subj. 1st pers. pl. / *rendir*.

rindiesen that they might overcome; imp. subj. 3rd pers. pl. / *rendir*.

rindieses that you might overcome; imp. subj. 2nd pers. sing. / *rendir*.

rindió he (she/it) overcame; past 3rd pers. sing. / *rendir*.

rindo I overcome; pres. ind. 1st pers. sing. / *rendir*.

riña 1. that I may quarrel; pres. subj. 1st pers. sing. / *reñir*. 2. that he (she/it) may quarrel; pres. subj. 3rd pers. sing. 3. let him (her/it) quarrel; impve. 3rd pers. sing.

riñáis that you (all) may quarrel; pres. subj. 2nd pers. pl. / *reñir*.

riñámonos let us scold; impve. 1st pers. pl. / *reñirse*.

riñamos 1. that we may quarrel; pres. subj. 1st pers. pl. / *reñir*. 2. let us quarrel; impve. 1st pers. pl.

riñan 1. that they may quarrel; pres. subj. 3rd pers. pl. / *reñir*. 2. let them quarrel; impve. 3rd pers. pl.

ríñanse let them scold; impve. 3rd pers. pl. / *reñirse*.

riñas that you may quarrel; pres. subj. 2nd pers. sing. / *reñir*.

ríñase let him (her/it) scold; impve. 3rd pers. sing. / *reñirse*.

riñe 1. he (she/it) quarrels; pres. ind. 3rd pers. sing. / *reñir*. 2. (you) quarrel; impve. 2nd pers. sing.

riñen they quarrel; pres. ind. 3rd pers. pl. / *reñir*.

riñendo quarreling; pres. part. / *reñir*.

riñéndose scolding; pres. part. / *reñirse*.

riñera 1. that I might quarrel; imp. subj. 1st pers. sing. / *reñir*. 2. that he (she/it) might quarrel; imp. subj. 3rd pers. sing.

riñerais that you (all) might quarrel; imp. subj. 2nd pers pl. / *reñir*.

riñéramos that we might quarrel; imp. subj. 1st pers. pl. / *reñir*.

riñeran that they might quarrel; imp. subj. 3rd pers. pl. / *reñir*.

riñeras that you might quarrel; imp. subj. 2nd pers. sing. / *reñir*.

riñeron they quarreled; past 3rd pers. pl. / *reñir*.

riñes you quarrel; pres. ind. 2nd pers. sing. / *reñir*.

riñese 1. that I might quarrel; imp. subj. 1st pers. sing. / *reñir*. 2. that he (she/it) might quarrel; imp. subj. 3rd pers. sing.

riñeseis that you (all) might quarrel; imp. subj. 2nd pers pl. / *reñir*.

riñésemos that we might quarrel; imp. subj. 1st pers. pl. / *reñir*.

riñesen that they might quarrel; imp. subj. 3rd pers. pl. / *reñir*.

riñeses that you might quarrel; imp. subj. 2nd pers. sing. / *reñir*.

ríñete (you) scold; impve. 2nd pers. sing. / *reñirse*.

riño I quarrel; pres. ind. 1st pers. sing. / *reñir*.

riñó he (she/it) quarreled; past 3rd pers. sing. / *reñir*.

río I laugh; pres. ind. 1st pers. sing. / *reír*.

rió he (she/it) laughed; past 3rd pers. sing. / *reír*.

risotear to guffaw. reg.

rivalice 1. that I may rival; pres. subj. 1st pers. sing. / *rivalizar*. 2. that he (she/it) may rival; pres. subj. 3rd pers. sing. 3. let him (her/it) rival; impve. 3rd pers. sing.

rivalicé I rivaled; past 1st pers. sing. / *rivalizar*.

rivalicéis that you (all) may rival; pres. subj. 2nd pers. pl. / *rivalizar*.

rivalicemos 1. that we may rival; pres. subj. 1st pers. pl. / *rivalizar*. 2. let us rival; impve. 1st pers. pl.

rivalicen 1. that they may rival; pres. subj. 3rd pers. pl. / *rivalizar*. 2. let them rival; impve. 3rd pers. pl.

rivalices that you may rival; pres. subj. 2nd pers. sing. / *rivalizar*.

rivalizar to rival or to compete. irr.

rizándose frizzling; pres. part. / *rizarse*.

rizaos (you all) frizzle; impve. 2nd pers. pl. / *rizarse*.

rizar to curl. irr.

rizarse to frizzle. irr.

rízate (you) frizzle; impve. 2nd pers. sing. / *rizarse*.

robar to rob. reg.

roborar to reinforce. reg.

robusteceos (you all) strengthen; impve. 2nd pers. pl. / *robustecerse*.

robustecer to strengthen. irr.

robustecerse to strengthen. irr.

robustécete (you) strengthen; impve. 2nd pers. sing. / *robustecerse*.

robusteciéndose strengthening; pres. part. / *robustecerse*.

robustezca 1. that I may strengthen; pres. subj. 1st pers. sing. / *robustecer*. 2. that he (she/it) may strengthen; pres. subj. 3rd pers. sing. 3. let him (her/it) strengthen; impve. 3rd pers. sing.

robustezcáis that you (all) may strengthen; pres. subj. 2nd pers. pl. / *robustecer*.

robustezcámonos let us strengthen; impve. 1st pers. pl. / *robustecerse*.

robustezcamos 1. that we may strengthen; pres. subj. 1st pers. pl. / *robustecer*. 2. let us strengthen; impve. 1st pers. pl.

robustezcan 1. that they may strengthen; pres. subj. 3rd pers. pl. / *robustecer*. 2. let them strengthen; impve. 3rd pers. pl.

robustézcanse let them strengthen; impve. 3rd pers. pl. / *robustecerse*.

robustezcas that you may strengthen; pres. subj. 2nd pers. sing. / *robustecer*.

robustézcase let him (her/it) strengthen; impve. 3rd pers. sing. / *robustecerse*.

robustezco I strengthen; pres. ind. 1st pers. sing. / *robustecer*.

roce 1. that I may clear; pres. subj. 1st pers. sing. / *rozar*. 2. that he (she/it) may clear; pres. subj. 3rd pers. sing. 3. let him (her/it) clear; impve. 3rd pers. sing.

rocé I cleared; past 1st pers. sing. / *rozar*.

rocéis that you (all) may clear; pres. subj. 2nd pers. pl. / *rozar*.

rocémonos let us become scuffed; impve. 1st pers. pl. / *rozarse*.

rocemos 1. that we may clear; pres. subj. 1st pers. pl. / *rozar*. 2. let us clear; impve. 1st pers. pl.

rocen 1. that they may clear; pres. subj. 3rd pers. pl. / *rozar*. 2. let them clear; impve. 3rd pers. pl.

rócense let them become scuffed; impve. 3rd pers. pl. / *rozarse*.

roces that you may clear; pres. subj. 2nd pers. sing. / *rozar*.

rócese let him (her/it) become scuffed; impve. 3rd pers. sing. / *rozarse*.

rocía 1. he (she/it) sprinkles; pres. ind. 3rd pers. sing. / *rociar*. 2. (you) sprinkle; impve. 2nd pers. sing.

rocían they sprinkle; pres. ind. 3rd pers. pl. / *rociar*.

rociar to sprinkle. irr.

rocías you sprinkle; pres. ind. 2nd pers. sing. / *rociar*.

rocíe 1. that I may sprinkle; pres. subj. 1st pers. sing. / *rociar*. 2. that he (she/it) may sprinkle; pres. subj. 3rd pers. sing. 3. let him (her/it) sprinkle; impve. 3rd pers. sing.

rocíen 1. that they may sprinkle; pres. subj. 3rd pers. pl. / *rociar*. 2. let them sprinkle; impve. 3rd pers. pl.

rocíes that you may sprinkle; pres. subj. 2nd pers. sing. / *rociar*.

rocío I sprinkle; pres. ind. 1st pers. sing. / *rociar*.

rodar to roll. irr.

rodeándose twisting about; pres. part. / *rodearse*.

rodeaos (you all) twist about; impve. 2nd pers. pl. / *rodearse*.

rodear to go around or to surround. reg.

rodearse to twist about. reg.

rodéate (you) twist about; impve. 2nd pers. sing. / *rodearse*.

rodeémonos let us twist about; impve. 1st pers. pl. / *rodearse*.

rodéense let them twist about; impve. 3rd pers. pl. / *rodearse*.

rodéese let him (her/it) twist about; impve. 3rd pers. sing. / *rodearse*.

rodrigar to prop up vines. irr.

rodrigue 1. that I may prop up vines; pres. subj. 1st pers. sing. / *rodrigar*. 2. that he (she/it) may prop up vines; pres. subj. 3rd pers. sing. 3. let him (her/it) prop up vines; impve. 3rd pers. sing.

rodrigué I propped up vines; past 1st pers. sing. / *rodrigar*.

rodriguéis that you (all) may prop up vines; pres. subj. 2nd pers. pl. / *rodrigar*.

rodriguemos 1. that we may prop up vines; pres. subj. 1st pers. pl. / *rodrigar*. 2. let us prop up vines; impve. 1st pers. pl.

rodriguen 1. that they may prop up vines; pres. subj. 3rd pers. pl. / *rodrigar*. 2. let them prop up vines; impve. 3rd pers. pl.

rodrigues that you may prop up vines; pres. subj. 2nd pers. sing. / *rodrigar*.

roer to gnaw. irr.

rogar to pray. irr.

rogué I prayed; past 1st pers. sing. / *rogar*.

roguéis that you (all) may pray; pres. subj. 2nd pers. pl. / *rogar*.

roguemos 1. that we may pray; pres. subj. 1st pers. pl. / *rogar*. 2. let us pray; impve. 1st pers. pl.

roído gnawed; past part. / *roer*.

roiga that I may gnaw; pres. subj. 1st pers. sing. / *roer*.

roigo I gnaw; pres. ind. 1st pers. sing. / *roer*.

roímos we gnawed; past 1st pers. pl. / *roer*.

roíste you gnawed; past 2nd pers. sing. / *roer*.

roísteis you (all) gnawed; past 2nd pers. pl. / *roer.*

rojear to redden. reg.

rollar to rollup. reg.

romancear to translate. reg.

romanice 1. that I may romanize; pres. subj. 1st pers. sing. / *romanizar.* 2. that he (she/it) may romanize; pres. subj. 3rd pers. sing. 3. let him (her/it) romanize; impve. 3rd pers. sing.

romanicé I romanized; past 1st pers. sing. / *romanizar.*

romanicéis that you (all) may romanize; pres. subj. 2nd pers. pl. / *romanizar.*

romanicémonos let us romanize; impve. 1st pers. pl. / *romanizarse.*

romanicemos 1. that we may romanize; pres. subj. 1st pers. pl. / *romanizar.* 2. let us romanize; impve. 1st pers. pl.

romanicen 1. that they may romanize; pres. subj. 3rd pers. pl. / *romanizar.* 2. let them romanize; impve. 3rd pers. pl.

romanícense let them romanize; impve. 3rd pers. pl. / *romanizarse.*

romanices that you may romanize; pres. subj. 2nd pers. sing. / *romanizar.*

romanícese let him (her/it) romanize; impve. 3rd pers. sing. / *romanizarse.*

romanizándose romanizing; pres. part. / *romanizarse.*

romanizaos (you all) romanize; impve. 2nd pers. pl. / *romanizarse.*

romanizar to romanize. irr.

romanizarse to romanize. irr.

romanízate (you) romanize; impve. 2nd pers. sing. / *romanizarse.*

rompámonos let us break; impve. 1st pers. pl. / *romperse.*

rómpanse let them break; impve. 3rd pers. pl. / *romperse.*

rómpase let him (her/it) break; impve. 3rd pers. sing. / *romperse.*

rompeos (you all) break; impve. 2nd pers. pl. / *romperse.*

romper to tear up. reg. except for pp.

romperse to break. reg. except for pp.

rómpete (you) break; impve. 2nd pers. sing. / *romperse.*

rompiéndose breaking; pres. part. / *romperse.*

roncar to snore. irr.

roncear to dawdle or to flatter. reg.

ronchar to crunch. reg.

rondar to go around. reg.

ronque 1. that I may snore; pres. subj. 1st pers. sing. / *roncar.* 2. that he (she/it) may snore; pres. subj. 3rd pers. sing. 3. let him (her/it) snore; impve. 3rd pers. sing.

ronqué I snored; past 1st pers. sing. / *roncar.*

ronquéis that you (all) may snore; pres. subj. 2nd pers. pl. / *roncar.*

ronquemos 1. that we may snore; pres. subj. 1st pers. pl. / *roncar.* 2. let us snore; impve. 1st pers. pl.

ronquen 1. that they may snore; pres. subj. 3rd pers. pl. / *roncar.* 2. let them snore; impve. 3rd pers. pl.

ronques that you may snore; pres. subj. 2nd pers. sing. / *roncar.*

ronronear to purr. reg.

roscar to thread or to spiral. irr.

rosque 1. that I may thread; pres. subj. 1st pers. sing. / *roscar.* 2. that he (she/it) may thread; pres. subj. 3rd pers. sing. 3. let him (her/it) thread; impve. 3rd pers. sing.

rosqué I threaded; past 1st pers. sing. / *roscar.*

rosquéis that you (all) may thread; pres. subj. 2nd pers. pl. / *roscar.*

rosquemos 1. that we may thread; pres. subj. 1st pers. pl. / *roscar.* 2. let us thread; impve. 1st pers. pl.

rosquen 1. that they may thread; pres. subj. 3rd pers. pl. / *roscar.* 2. let them thread; impve. 3rd pers. pl.

rosques that you may thread; pres. subj. 2nd pers. sing. / *roscar.*

roto tore up; past part. / *romper.*

rotular to label. reg.

roturar to break ground. reg.

roya that I may gnaw; pres. subj. 1st pers. sing. / *roer.*

royendo gnawing; pres. part. / *roer.*

royera 1. that I might gnaw; imp. subj. 1st pers. sing. / *roer.* 2. that he (she/it) might gnaw; imp. subj. 3rd pers. sing.

royerais that you (all) might gnaw; imp. subj. 2nd pers pl. / *roer.*

royéramos that we might gnaw; imp. subj. 1st pers. pl. / *roer.*

royeran that they might gnaw; imp. subj. 3rd pers. pl. / *roer.*

royeras that you might gnaw; imp. subj. 2nd pers. sing. / *roer.*

royeron they gnawed; past 3rd pers. pl. / *roer.*

royese 1. that I might gnaw; imp. subj. 1st pers. sing. / *roer.* 2. that he (she/it) might gnaw; imp. subj. 3rd pers. sing.

royeseis that you (all) might gnaw; imp. subj. 2nd pers pl. / *roer.*

royésemos that we might gnaw; imp. subj. 1st pers. pl. / *roer.*

royesen that they might gnaw; imp. subj. 3rd pers. pl. / *roer.*

royeses that you might gnaw; imp. subj. 2nd pers. sing. / *roer.*

royo I gnaw; pres. ind. 1st pers. sing. / *roer.*

royó he (she/it) gnawed; past 3rd pers. sing. / *roer.*

rozándose becoming scuffed; pres. part. / *rozarse.*

rozaos (you all) become scuffed; impve. 2nd pers. pl. / *rozarse.*

rozar to clear or to clean. irr.

rozarse to become scuffed. irr.

rózate (you) become scuffed; impve. 2nd pers. sing. / *rozarse.*

ruborice 1. that I may blush; pres. subj. 1st pers. sing. / *ruborizar.* 2. that he (she/it) may blush; pres. subj. 3rd pers. sing. 3. let him (her/it) blush; impve. 3rd pers. sing.

ruboricé I blushed; past 1st pers. sing. / *ruborizar*.

ruboricéis that you (all) may blush; pres. subj. 2nd pers. pl. / *ruborizar*.

ruboricémonos let us redden; impve. 1st pers. pl. / *ruborizar*.

ruboricemos 1. that we may blush; pres. subj. 1st pers. pl. / *ruborizar*. 2. let us blush; impve. 1st pers. pl.

ruboricen 1. that they may blush; pres. subj. 3rd pers. pl. / *ruborizar*. 2. let them blush; impve. 3rd pers. pl.

ruborícense let them redden; impve. 3rd pers. pl. / *ruborizar*.

ruborices that you may blush; pres. subj. 2nd pers. sing. / *ruborizar*.

ruborícese let him (her/it) redden; impve. 3rd pers. sing. / *ruborizar*.

ruborizándose reddening; pres. part. / *ruborizar*.

ruborizaos (you all) redden; impve. 2nd pers. pl. / *ruborizar*.

ruborizar to blush. irr.

ruborizarse to redden. irr.

ruborízate (you) redden; impve. 2nd pers. sing. / *ruborizar*.

rubricar to endorse. irr.

rubrique 1. that I may endorse; pres. subj. 1st pers. sing. / *rubricar*. 2. that he (she/it) may endorse; pres. subj. 3rd pers. sing. 3. let him (her/it) endorse; impve. 3rd pers. sing.

rubriqué I endorsed; past 1st pers. sing. / *rubricar*.

rubriquéis that you (all) may endorse; pres. subj. 2nd pers. pl. / *rubricar*.

rubriquemos 1. that we may endorse; pres. subj. 1st pers. pl. / *rubricar*. 2. let us endorse; impve. 1st pers. pl.

rubriquen 1. that they may endorse; pres. subj. 3rd pers. pl. / *rubricar*. 2. let them endorse; impve. 3rd pers. pl.

rubriques that you may endorse; pres. subj. 2nd pers. sing. / *rubricar*.

rueda 1. he (she/it) rolls; pres. ind. 3rd pers. sing. / *rodar*. 2. (you) roll; impve. 2nd pers. sing.

ruedan they roll; pres. ind. 3rd pers. pl. / *rodar*.

ruedas you roll; pres. ind. 2nd pers. sing. / *rodar*.

ruede 1. that I may roll; pres. subj. 1st pers. sing. / *rodar*. 2. that he (she/it) may roll; pres. subj. 3rd pers. sing. 3. let him (her/it) roll; impve. 3rd pers. sing.

rueden 1. that they may roll; pres. subj. 3rd pers. pl. / *rodar*. 2. let them roll; impve. 3rd pers. pl.

ruedes that you may roll; pres. subj. 2nd pers. sing. / *rodar*.

ruedo I roll; pres. ind. 1st pers. sing. / *rodar*.

ruega 1. he (she/it) prays; pres. ind. 3rd pers. sing. / *rogar*. 2. (you) pray; impve. 2nd pers. sing.

ruegan they pray; pres. ind. 3rd pers. pl. / *rogar*.

ruegas you pray; pres. ind. 2nd pers. sing. / *rogar*.

ruego I pray; pres. ind. 1st pers. sing. / *rogar*.

ruegue 1. that I may pray; pres. subj. 1st pers. sing. / *rogar*. 2. that he (she/it) may pray; pres. subj. 3rd pers. sing. 3. let him (her/it) pray; impve. 3rd pers. sing.

rueguen 1. that they may pray; pres. subj. 3rd pers. pl. / *rogar*. 2. let them pray; impve. 3rd pers. pl.

ruegues that you may pray; pres. subj. 2nd pers. sing. / *rogar*.

rugir to roar. irr.

ruinar to ruin. reg.

ruja 1. that I may roar; pres. subj. 1st pers. sing. / *rugir*. 2. that he (she/it) may roar; pres. subj. 3rd pers. sing. 3. let him (her/it) roar; impve. 3rd pers. sing.

rujáis that you (all) may roar; pres. subj. 2nd pers. pl. / *rugir*.

rujamos 1. that we may roar; pres. subj. 1st pers. pl. / *rugir*. 2. let us roar; impve. 1st pers. pl.

rujan 1. that they may roar; pres. subj. 3rd pers. pl. / *rugir*. 2. let them roar; impve. 3rd pers. pl.

rujas that you may roar; pres. subj. 2nd pers. sing. / *rugir*.

rujo I roar; pres. ind. 1st pers. sing. / *rugir*.

rumbear to head towards or to go on a spree. reg.

rumiar to ruminate. reg.

rumorándose being rumored; pres. part. / *rumorarse*.

rumoraos (you all) be rumored; impve. 2nd pers. pl. / *rumorarse*.

rumorar to rumor. reg.

rumorarse to be rumored. reg.

rumórate (you) be rumored; impve. 2nd pers. sing. / *rumorarse*.

rumoreándose being rumored; pres. part. / *rumorearse*.

rumoreaos (you all) be rumored; impve. 2nd pers. pl. / *rumorearse*.

rumorear to rumor. reg.

rumorearse to be rumored. reg.

rumoréate (you) be rumored; impve. 2nd pers. sing. / *rumorearse*.

rumoréemonos let us be rumored; impve. 1st pers. pl. / *rumorearse*.

rumoréense let them be rumored; impve. 3rd pers. pl. / *rumorearse*.

rumoréese let him (her/it) be rumored; impve. 3rd pers. sing. / *rumorearse*.

rumorémonos let us be rumored; impve. 1st pers. pl. / *rumorarse*.

rumórense let them be rumored; impve. 3rd pers. pl. / *rumorarse*.

rumórese let him (her/it) be rumored; impve. 3rd pers. sing. / *rumorarse*.

runruneándose being rumored; pres. part. / *runrunearse*.

runruneaos (you all) be rumored; impve. 2nd pers. pl. / *runrunearse*.

runrunearse to be rumored. reg.

runrunéate (you) be rumored; impve. 2nd pers. sing. / *runrunearse*.

runruneémonos let us be rumored; impve. 1st pers. pl. / *runrunearse*.
runrunéense let them be rumored; impve. 3rd pers. pl. / *runrunearse*.
runrunéese let him (her/it) be rumored; impve. 3rd pers. sing. / *runrunearse*.
rutilar to shine. reg.

S

saber to know. irr.
saboreándose relishing; pres. part. / *saborearse*.
saboreaos (you all) relish; impve. 2nd pers. pl. / *saborearse*.
saborear to savor. reg.
saborearse to relish. reg.
saboréate (you) relish; impve. 2nd pers. sing. / *saborearse*.
saboreémonos let us relish; impve. 1st pers. pl. / *saborearse*.
saboréense let them relish; impve. 3rd pers. pl. / *saborearse*.
saboréese let him (her/it) relish; impve. 3rd pers. sing. / *saborearse*.
sabotear to sabotage. reg.
sabrá he (she/it) will know; fut. 3rd pers. sing. / *saber*.
sabrán they will know; fut. 3rd pers. pl. / *saber*.
sabrás you will know; fut. 2nd pers. sing. / *saber*.
sabré I shall know; fut. 1st pers. sing. / *saber*.
sabréis you (all) will know; fut. 2nd pers. pl. / *saber*.
sabremos we shall know; fut. 1st pers. pl. / *saber*.
sabría 1. I should know; cond. 1st pers. sing. / *saber*. 2. he (she/it) would know; cond. 3rd pers. sing.
sabríais you (all) would know; cond. 2nd pers. pl. / *saber*.
sabríamos we should know; cond. 1st pers. pl. / *saber*.
sabrían they would know; cond. 3rd pers. pl. / *saber*.
sabrías you would know; cond. 2nd pers. sing. / *saber*.
sacar to take out. irr.
saciándose being satiated; pres. part. / *saciarse*.
saciaos (you all) be satiated; impve. 2nd pers. pl. / *saciarse*.
saciar to satiate. reg.
saciarse to be satiated. reg.
saciate (you) be satiated; impve. 2nd pers. sing. / *saciarse*.
saciémonos let us be satiated; impve. 1st pers. pl. / *saciarse*.
saciense let them be satiated; impve. 3rd pers. pl. / *saciarse*.
saciese let him (her/it) be satiated; impve. 3rd pers. sing. / *saciarse*.
sacramentar to administer the sacrament to. reg.
sacrificar to sacrifice. irr.

sacrifique 1. that I may sacrifice; pres. subj. 1st pers. sing. / *sacrificar*. 2. that he (she/it) may sacrifice; pres. subj. 3rd pers. sing. 3. let him (her/it) sacrifice; impve. 3rd pers. sing.
sacrifiqué I sacrificed; past 1st pers. sing. / *sacrificar*.
sacrifiquéis that you (all) may sacrifice; pres. subj. 2nd pers. pl. / *sacrificar*.
sacrifiquemos 1. that we may sacrifice; pres. subj. 1st pers. pl. / *sacrificar*. 2. let us sacrifice; impve. 1st pers. pl.
sacrifiquen 1. that they may sacrifice; pres. subj. 3rd pers. pl. / *sacrificar*. 2. let them sacrifice; impve. 3rd pers. pl.
sacrifiques that you may sacrifice; pres. subj. 2nd pers. sing. / *sacrificar*.
sacudámonos let us dismiss brusquely; impve. 1st pers. pl. / *sacudirse*.
sacúdanse let them dismiss brusquely; impve. 3rd pers. pl. / *sacudirse*.
sacúdase let him (her/it) dismiss brusquely; impve. 3rd pers. sing. / *sacudirse*.
sacúdete (you) dismiss brusquely; impve. 2nd pers. sing. / *sacudirse*.
sacudiéndose dismissing brusquely; pres. part. / *sacudirse*.
sacudíos (you all) dismiss brusquely; impve. 2nd pers. pl. / *sacudirse*.
sacudir to shake. reg.
sacudirse to dismiss brusquely. reg.
sachar to weed. reg.
sahumar to perfume with incense. reg.
sajar to cut. reg.
sal (you) go out; impve. 2nd pers. sing. / *salir*.
salar to salt. reg.
salariar to salary. reg.
salcochar to boil meat. reg.
saldar to settle an account. reg.
saldrá he (she/it) will go out; fut. 3rd pers. sing. / *salir*.
saldrán they will go out; fut. 3rd pers. pl. / *salir*.
saldrás you will go out; fut. 2nd pers. sing. / *salir*.
saldré I shall go out; fut. 1st pers. sing. / *salir*.
saldréis you (all) will go out; fut. 2nd pers. pl. / *salir*.
saldremos we shall go out; fut. 1st pers. pl. / *salir*.
saldría 1. I should go out; cond. 1st pers. sing. / *salir*. 2. he (she/it) would go out; cond. 3rd pers. sing.
saldríais you (all) would go out; cond. 2nd pers. pl. / *salir*.
saldríamos we should go out; cond. 1st pers. pl. / *salir*.
saldrían they would go out; cond. 3rd pers. pl. / *salir*.
saldrías you would go out; cond. 2nd pers. sing. / *salir*.
sálete (you) overflow; impve. 2nd pers. sing. / *salirse*.
salga 1. that I may go out; pres. subj. 1st pers. sing. / *salir*. 2. that he (she/it) may go out; pres. subj. 3rd pers. sing. 3. let him (her/it) go out; impve. 3rd pers. sing.
salgáis that you (all) may go out; pres. subj. 2nd pers. pl. / *salir*.

salgámonos let us overflow; impve. 1st pers. pl. / *salirse.*

salgamos 1. that we may go out; pres. subj. 1st pers. pl. / *salir.* 2. let us go out; impve. 1st pers. pl.

salgan 1. that they may go out; pres. subj. 3rd pers. pl. / *salir.* 2. let them go out; impve. 3rd pers. pl.

sálganse let them overflow; impve. 3rd pers. pl. / *salirse.*

salgas that you may go out; pres. subj. 2nd pers. sing. / *salir.*

sálgase let him (her/it) overflow; impve. 3rd pers. sing. / *salirse.*

salgo I go out; pres. ind. 1st pers. sing. / *salir.*

saliéndose overflowing; pres. part. / *salirse.*

salíos (you all) overflow; impve. 2nd pers. pl. / *salirse.*

salir to go out. irr.

salirse to overflow. irr.

salivar to salivate. reg.

salmodiar to chant. reg.

salpicar to sprinkle. irr.

salpimentar to salt and pepper. irr.

salpimienta 1. he (she/it) salts and peppers; pres. ind. 3rd pers. sing. / *salpimentar.* 2. (you) salt and pepper; impve. 2nd pers. sing.

salpimientan they salt and pepper; pres. ind. 3rd pers. pl. / *salpimentar.*

salpimientas you salt and pepper; pres. ind. 2nd pers. sing. / *salpimentar.*

salpimiente 1. that I may salt and pepper; pres. subj. 1st pers. sing. / *salpimentar.* 2. that he (she/it) may salt and pepper; pres. subj. 3rd pers. sing. 3. let him (her/it) salt and pepper; impve. 3rd pers. sing.

salpimienten 1. that they may salt and pepper; pres. subj. 3rd pers. pl. / *salpimentar.* 2. let them salt and pepper; impve. 3rd pers. pl.

salpimientes that you may salt and pepper; pres. subj. 2nd pers. sing. / *salpimentar.*

salpimiento I salt and pepper; pres. ind. 1st pers. sing. / *salpimentar.*

salpique 1. that I may sprinkle; pres. subj. 1st pers. sing. / *salpicar.* 2. that he (she/it) may sprinkle; pres. subj. 3rd pers. sing. 3. let him (her/it) sprinkle; impve. 3rd pers. sing.

salpiqué I sprinkled; past 1st pers. sing. / *salpicar.*

salpiquéis that you (all) may sprinkle; pres. subj. 2nd pers. pl. / *salpicar.*

salpiquemos 1. that we may sprinkle; pres. subj. 1st pers. pl. / *salpicar.* 2. let us sprinkle; impve. 1st pers. pl.

salpiquen 1. that they may sprinkle; pres. subj. 3rd pers. pl. / *salpicar.* 2. let them sprinkle; impve. 3rd pers. pl.

salpiques that you may sprinkle; pres. subj. 2nd pers. sing. / *salpicar.*

salpresar to salt or to cure. reg.

saltándose skipping; pres. part. / *saltarse.*

saltaos (you all) skip; impve. 2nd pers. pl. / *saltarse.*

saltar to jump. reg.

saltarse to skip. reg.

sáltate (you) skip; impve. 2nd pers. sing. / *saltarse.*

saltear to assault. reg.

saltémonos let us skip; impve. 1st pers. pl. / *saltarse.*

sáltense let them skip; impve. 3rd pers. pl. / *saltarse.*

sáltese let him (her/it) skip; impve. 3rd pers. sing. / *saltarse.*

saludar to greet or to salute. reg.

salvaguadar to safeguard. reg.

salvándose being saved; pres. part. / *salvarse.*

salvaos (you all) be saved; impve. 2nd pers. pl. / *salvarse.*

salvar to save. reg.

salvarse to be saved. reg.

sálvate (you) be saved; impve. 2nd pers. sing. / *salvarse.*

salvémonos let us be saved; impve. 1st pers. pl. / *salvarse.*

sálvense let them be saved; impve. 3rd pers. pl. / *salvarse.*

sálvese let him (her/it) be saved; impve. 3rd pers. sing. / *salvarse.*

sallar to weed. reg.

sanar to heal. reg.

sancionar to sanction. reg.

sancochar to parboil. reg.

sanear to make sanitary or to drain. reg.

sangrar to bleed. reg.

santificar to sanctify. irr.

santifique 1. that I may sanctify; pres. subj. 1st pers. sing. / *santificar.* 2. that he (she/it) may sanctify; pres. subj. 3rd pers. sing. 3. let him (her/it) sanctify; impve. 3rd pers. sing.

santifiqué I sanctified; past 1st pers. sing. / *santificar.*

santifiquéis that you (all) may sanctify; pres. subj. 2nd pers. pl. / *santificar.*

santifiquemos 1. that we may sanctify; pres. subj. 1st pers. pl. / *santificar.* 2. let us sanctify; impve. 1st pers. pl.

santifiquen 1. that they may sanctify; pres. subj. 3rd pers. pl. / *santificar.* 2. let them sanctify; impve. 3rd pers. pl.

santifiques that you may sanctify; pres. subj. 2nd pers. sing. / *santificar.*

santiguándose crossing oneself; pres. part. / *santiguarse.*

santiguaos (you all) cross yourselves; impve. 2nd pers. pl. / *santiguarse.*

santiguar to bless. irr.

santiguarse to cross oneself. irr.

santíguate (you) cross yourself; impve. 2nd pers. sing. / *santiguarse.*

santigüe 1. that I may bless; pres. subj. 1st pers. sing. / *santiguar.* 2. that he (she/it) may bless; pres. subj. 3rd pers. sing. 3. let him (her/it) bless; impve. 3rd pers. sing.

santigüé I blessed; past 1st pers. sing. / *santiguar.*

santigüéis that you (all) may bless; pres. subj. 2nd pers. pl. / *santiguar.*

santigüémonos let us cross ourselves; impve. 1st pers. pl. / *santiguarse.*

santigüemos 1. that we may bless; pres. subj. 1st pers. pl. / *santiguar.* 2. let us bless; impve. 1st pers. pl.

santigüen 1. that they may bless; pres. subj. 3rd pers. pl. / *santiguar.* 2. let them bless; impve. 3rd pers. pl.

santigüense let them cross themselves; impve. 3rd pers. pl. / *santiguarse.*

santigües that you may bless; pres. subj. 2nd pers. sing. / *santiguar.*

santigüese let him (her) cross (himself/herself); impve. 3rd pers. sing. / *santiguarse.*

saque 1. that I may take out; pres. subj. 1st pers. sing. / *sacar.* 2. that he (she/it) may take out; pres. subj. 3rd pers. sing. 3. let him (her/it) take out; impve. 3rd pers. sing.

saqué I took out; past 1st pers. sing. / *sacar.*

saquear to sack or plunder. reg.

saquéis that you (all) may take out; pres. subj. 2nd pers. pl. / *sacar.*

saquemos 1. that we may take out; pres. subj. 1st pers. pl. / *sacar.* 2. let us take out; impve. 1st pers. pl.

saquen 1. that they may take out; pres. subj. 3rd pers. pl. / *sacar.* 2. let them take out; impve. 3rd pers. pl.

saques that you may take out; pres. subj. 2nd pers. sing. / *sacar.*

satinar to glaze. reg.

satirice 1. that I may satirize; pres. subj. 1st pers. sing. / *satirizar.* 2. that he (she/it) may satirize; pres. subj. 3rd pers. sing. 3. let him (her/it) satirize; impve. 3rd pers. sing.

satiricé I satirized; past 1st pers. sing. / *satirizar.*

satiricéis that you (all) may satirize; pres. subj. 2nd pers. pl. / *satirizar.*

satiricemos 1. that we may satirize; pres. subj. 1st pers. pl. / *satirizar.* 2. let us satirize; impve. 1st pers. pl.

satiricen 1. that they may satirize; pres. subj. 3rd pers. pl. / *satirizar.* 2. let them satirize; impve. 3rd pers. pl.

satirices that you may satirize; pres. subj. 2nd pers. sing. / *satirizar.*

satirizar to satirize. irr.

satisfaceos (you all) be satisfied; impve. 2nd pers. pl. / *satisfacerse.*

satisfacer to satisfy. irr.

satisfacerse to be satisfied. irr.

satisfaciéndose being satisfied; pres. part. / *satisfacerse.*

satisfaga 1. that I may satisfy; pres. subj. 1st pers. sing. / *satisfacer.* 2. that he (she/it) may satisfy; pres. subj. 3rd pers. sing. 3. let him (her/it) satisfy; impve. 3rd pers. sing.

satisfagáis that you (all) may satisfy; pres. subj. 2nd pers. pl. / *satisfacer.*

satisfagámonos let us be satisfied; impve. 1st pers. pl. / *satisfacerse.*

satisfagamos 1. that we may satisfy; pres. subj. 1st pers. pl. / *satisfacer.* 2. let us satisfy; impve. 1st pers. pl.

satisfagan 1. that they may satisfy; pres. subj. 3rd pers. pl. / *satisfacer.* 2. let them satisfy; impve. 3rd pers. pl.

satisfáganse let them be satisfied; impve. 3rd pers. pl. / *satisfacerse.*

satisfagas that you may satisfy; pres. subj. 2nd pers. sing. / *satisfacer.*

satisfágase let him (her/it) be satisfied; impve. 3rd pers. sing. / *satisfacerse.*

satisfago I satisfy; pres. ind. 1st pers. sing. / *satisfacer.*

satisfará he (she/it) will satisfy; fut. 3rd pers. sing. / *satisfacer.*

satisfarán they will satisfy; fut. 3rd pers. pl. / *satisfacer.*

satisfarás you will satisfy; fut. 2nd pers. sing. / *satisfacer.*

satisfaré I shall satisfy; fut. 1st pers. sing. / *satisfacer.*

satisfaréis you (all) will satisfy; fut. 2nd pers. pl. / *satisfacer.*

satisfaremos we shall satisfy; fut. 1st pers. pl. / *satisfacer.*

satisfaría 1. I should satisfy; cond. 1st pers. sing. / *satisfacer.* 2. he (she/it) would satisfy; cond. 3rd pers. sing.

satisfaríais you (all) would satisfy; cond. 2nd pers. pl. / *satisfacer.*

satisfaríamos we should satisfy; cond. 1st pers. pl. / *satisfacer.*

satisfarían they would satisfy; cond. 3rd pers. pl. / *satisfacer.*

satisfarías you would satisfy; cond. 2nd pers. sing. / *satisfacer.*

satisfaz (you) satisfy; impve. 2nd pers. sing. / *satisfacer.*

satisfázete (you) be satisfied; impve. 2nd pers. sing. / *satisfacerse.*

satisfecho satisfied; past part. / *satisfacer.*

satisfice I satisfied; past 1st pers. sing. / *satisfacer.*

satisficiera 1. that I might satisfy; imp. subj. 1st pers. sing. / *satisfacer.* 2. that he (she/it) might satisfy; imp. subj. 3rd pers. sing.

satisficierais that you (all) might satisfy; imp. subj. 2nd pers pl. / *satisfacer.*

satisficiéramos that we might satisfy; imp. subj. 1st pers. pl. / *satisfacer.*

satisficieran that they might satisfy; imp. subj. 3rd pers. pl. / *satisfacer.*

satisficieras that you might satisfy; imp. subj. 2nd pers. sing. / *satisfacer.*

satisficieron they satisfied; past 3rd pers. pl. / *satisfacer.*

satisficiese 1. that I might satisfy; imp. subj. 1st pers. sing. / *satisfacer.* 2. that he (she/it) might satisfy; imp. subj. 3rd pers. sing.

satisficieseis that you (all) might satisfy; imp. subj. 2nd pers pl. / *satisfacer.*

satisficiésemos that we might satisfy; imp. subj. 1st pers. pl. / *satisfacer.*

satisficiesen that they might satisfy; imp. subj. 3rd pers. pl. / *satisfacer.*

satisficieses that you might satisfy; imp. subj. 2nd pers. sing. / *satisfacer.*

satisficimos we satisfied; past 1st pers. pl. / *satisfacer.*

satisficiste you satisfied; past 2nd pers. sing. / *satisfacer.*

satisficisteis you (all) satisfied; past 2nd pers. pl. / *satisfacer.*

satisfizo he (she/it) satisfied; past 3rd pers. sing. / *satisfacer.*

saturar to saturate. reg.

sazonándose ripening; pres. part. / *sazonarse.*

sazonaos (you all) ripen; impve. 2nd pers. pl. / *sazonarse.*

sazonar to season. reg.

sazonarse to ripen. reg.

sazónate (you) ripen; impve. 2nd pers. sing. / *sazonarse.*

sazonémonos let us ripen; impve. 1st pers. pl. / *sazonarse.*

sazónense let them ripen; impve. 3rd pers. pl. / *sazonarse.*

sazónese let him (her/it) ripen; impve. 3rd pers. sing. / *sazonarse.*

sé I know; pres. ind. 1st pers. sing. / *saber.*

sé (you) be; impve. 2nd pers. sing. / *ser.*

sea 1. that I may be; pres. subj. 1st pers. sing. / *ser.* 2. that he (she/it) may be; pres. subj. 3rd pers. sing. 3. let him (her/it) be; impve. 3rd pers. sing.

seáis that you (all) may be; pres. subj. 2nd pers. pl. / *ser.*

seamos 1. that we may be; pres. subj. 1st pers. pl. / *ser.* 2. let us be; impve. 1st pers. pl.

sean 1. that they may be; pres. subj. 3rd pers. pl. / *ser.* 2. let them be; impve. 3rd pers. pl.

seas that you may be; pres. subj. 2nd pers. sing. / *ser.*

secándose drying up; pres. part. / *secarse.*

secaos (you all) dry up; impve. 2nd pers. pl. / *secarse.*

secar to dry. irr.

secarse to dry up. irr.

sécate (you) dry up; impve. 2nd pers. sing. / *secarse.*

seccionar to section. reg.

secretar to secrete. reg.

secreteándose whispering to each other; pres. part. / *secretearse.*

secreteaos (you all) whisper to each other; impve. 2nd pers. pl. / *secretearse.*

secretear to whisper. reg.

secretearse to whisper to each other. reg.

secretéate (you) whisper to each other; impve. 2nd pers. sing. / *secretearse.*

secreteémonos let us whisper to each other; impve. 1st pers. pl. / *secretearse.*

secretéense let them whisper to each other; impve. 3rd pers. pl. / *secretearse.*

secretéese let him (her/it) whisper to each other; impve. 3rd pers. sing. / *secretearse.*

secuestrar to kidnap. reg.

secularice 1. that I may secularize; pres. subj. 1st pers. sing. / *secularizar.* 2. that he (she/it) may secularize; pres. subj. 3rd pers. sing. 3. let him (her/it) secularize; impve. 3rd pers. sing.

secularicé I secularized; past 1st pers. sing. / *secularizar.*

secularicéis that you (all) may secularize; pres. subj. 2nd pers. pl. / *secularizar.*

secularicemos 1. that we may secularize; pres. subj. 1st pers. pl. / *secularizar.* 2. let us secularize; impve. 1st pers. pl.

secularicen 1. that they may secularize; pres. subj. 3rd pers. pl. / *secularizar.* 2. let them secularize; impve. 3rd pers. pl.

secularices that you may secularize; pres. subj. 2nd pers. sing. / *secularizar.*

secularizar to secularize. irr.

secundar to second. reg.

sedar to calm. reg.

sedimentándose being deposited as sediment; pres. part. / *sedimentarse.*

sedimentar to cause sedimentation. reg.

sedimentarse to be deposited as sediment. reg.

sediméntense let them be deposited as sediment; impve. 3rd pers. pl. / *sedimentarse.*

sediméntese let it be deposited as sediment; impve. 3rd pers. sing. / *sedimentarse.*

seducir to seduce. irr.

seduje I seduced; past 1st pers. sing. / *seducir.*

sedujera 1. that I might seduce; imp. subj. 1st pers. sing. / *seducir.* 2. that he (she/it) might seduce; imp. subj. 3rd pers. sing.

sedujerais that you (all) might seduce; imp. subj. 2nd pers pl. / *seducir.*

sedujéramos that we might seduce; imp. subj. 1st pers. pl. / *seducir.*

sedujeran that they might seduce; imp. subj. 3rd pers. pl. / *seducir.*

sedujeras that you might seduce; imp. subj. 2nd pers. sing. / *seducir.*

sedujeron they seduced; past 3rd pers. pl. / *seducir.*

sedujese 1. that I might seduce; imp. subj. 1st pers. sing. / *seducir.* 2. that he (she/it) might seduce; imp. subj. 3rd pers. sing.

sedujeseis that you (all) might seduce; imp. subj. 2nd pers pl. / *seducir.*

sedujésemos that we might seduce; imp. subj. 1st pers. pl. / *seducir.*

sedujesen that they might seduce; imp. subj. 3rd pers. pl. / *seducir.*

sedujeses that you might seduce; imp. subj. 2nd pers. sing. / *seducir.*

sedujimos we seduced; past 1st pers. pl. / *seducir.*

sedujiste you seduced; past 2nd pers. sing. / *seducir.*

sedujisteis you (all) seduced; past 2nd pers. pl. / *seducir.*

sedujo he (she/it) seduced; past 3rd pers. sing. / *seducir.*

seduzca 1. that I may seduce; pres. subj. 1st pers. sing. / *seducir*. 2. that he (she/it) may seduce; pres. subj. 3rd pers. sing. 3. let him (her/it) seduce; impve. 3rd pers. sing.

seduzcáis that you (all) may seduce; pres. subj. 2nd pers. pl. / *seducir*.

seduzcamos 1. that we may seduce; pres. subj. 1st pers. pl. / *seducir*. 2. let us seduce; impve. 1st pers. pl.

seduzcan 1. that they may seduce; pres. subj. 3rd pers. pl. / *seducir*. 2. let them seduce; impve. 3rd pers. pl.

seduzcas that you may seduce; pres. subj. 2nd pers. sing. / *seducir*.

seduzco I seduce; pres. ind. 1st pers. sing. / *seducir*.

segar to mow. irr.

segregar to segregate. irr.

segregue 1. that I may segregate; pres. subj. 1st pers. sing. / *segregar*. 2. that he (she/it) may segregate; pres. subj. 3rd pers. sing. 3. let him (her/it) segregate; impve. 3rd pers. sing.

segregué I segregated; past 1st pers. sing. / *segregar*.

segreguéis that you (all) may segregate; pres. subj. 2nd pers. pl. / *segregar*.

segreguemos 1. that we may segregate; pres. subj. 1st pers. pl. / *segregar*. 2. let us segregate; impve. 1st pers. pl.

segreguen 1. that they may segregate; pres. subj. 3rd pers. pl. / *segregar*. 2. let them segregate; impve. 3rd pers. pl.

segregues that you may segregate; pres. subj. 2nd pers. sing. / *segregar*.

segué I mowed; past 1st pers. sing. / *segar*.

seguéis that you (all) may mow; pres. subj. 2nd pers. pl. / *segar*.

seguemos 1. that we may mow; pres. subj. 1st pers. pl. / *segar*. 2. let us mow; impve. 1st pers. pl.

seguir to follow. irr.

seguirse to ensue. irr.

segundar to repeat a second time. reg.

seleccionar to select. reg.

sellar to seal. reg.

sembrar to sow. irr.

semejándose being similar; pres. part. / *semejarse*.

semejaos (you all) be similar; impve. 2nd pers. pl. / *semejarse*.

semejar to resemble. reg.

semejarse to be similar. reg.

seméjate (you) be similar; impve. 2nd pers. sing. / *semejarse*.

semejémonos let us be similar; impve. 1st pers. pl. / *semejarse*.

seméjense let them be similar; impve. 3rd pers. pl. / *semejarse*.

seméjese let him (her/it) be similar; impve. 3rd pers. sing. / *semejarse*.

sementar to sow. irr.

semienta 1. he (she/it) sows; pres. ind. 3rd pers. sing. / *sementar*. 2. (you) sow; impve. 2nd pers. sing.

semientan they sow; pres. ind. 3rd pers. pl. / *sementar*.

semientas you sow; pres. ind. 2nd pers. sing. / *sementar*.

semiente 1. that I may sow; pres. subj. 1st pers. sing. / *sementar*. 2. that he (she/it) may sow; pres. subj. 3rd pers. sing. 3. let him (her/it) sow; impve. 3rd pers. sing.

semienten 1. that they may sow; pres. subj. 3rd pers. pl. / *sementar*. 2. let them sow; impve. 3rd pers. pl.

semientes that you may sow; pres. subj. 2nd pers. sing. / *sementar*.

semiento I sow; pres. ind. 1st pers. sing. / *sementar*.

sensibilice 1. that I may sensitize; pres. subj. 1st pers. sing. / *sensibilizar*. 2. that he (she/it) may sensitize; pres. subj. 3rd pers. sing. 3. let him (her/it) sensitize; impve. 3rd pers. sing.

sensibilicé I sensitized; past 1st pers. sing. / *sensibilizar*.

sensibilicéis that you (all) may sensitize; pres. subj. 2nd pers. pl. / *sensibilizar*.

sensibilicemos 1. that we may sensitize; pres. subj. 1st pers. pl. / *sensibilizar*. 2. let us sensitize; impve. 1st pers. pl.

sensibilicen 1. that they may sensitize; pres. subj. 3rd pers. pl. / *sensibilizar*. 2. let them sensitize; impve. 3rd pers. pl.

sensibilices that you may sensitize; pres. subj. 2nd pers. sing. / *sensibilizar*.

sensibilizar to sensitize. irr.

sentándose sitting down; pres. part. / *sentarse*.

sentaos (you all) sit down; impve. 2nd pers. pl. / *sentarse*.

sentar to seat. irr.

sentarse to sit down. irr.

sentémonos let us sit down; impve. 1st pers. pl. / *sentarse*.

sentenciar to sentence. reg.

sentíos (you all) feel; impve. 2nd pers. pl. / *sentirse*.

sentir to feel. irr.

sentirse to feel. irr.

señalándose excelling; pres. part. / *señalarse*.

señalaos (you all) excel; impve. 2nd pers. pl. / *señalarse*.

señalar to mark. reg.

señalarse to excel. reg.

señálate (you) excel; impve. 2nd pers. sing. / *señalarse*.

señalémonos let us excel; impve. 1st pers. pl. / *señalarse*.

señálense let them excel; impve. 3rd pers. pl. / *señalarse*.

señálese let him (her/it) excel; impve. 3rd pers. sing. / *señalarse*.

señalizar to mark with signs. reg.

señoreándose taking command; pres. part. / *señorearse*.

señoreaos (you all) take command; impve. 2nd pers. pl. / *señorearse*.

señorear to lord it over. reg.

señorearse to take command. reg.
señoréate (you) take command; impve. 2nd pers. sing. / *señorearse.*
señoreémonos let us take command; impve. 1st pers. pl. / *señorearse.*
señoréense let them take command; impve. 3rd pers. pl. / *señorearse.*
señoréese let him (her/it) take command; impve. 3rd pers. sing. / *señorearse.*
sepa 1. that I may know; pres. subj. 1st pers. sing. / *saber.* 2. that he (she/it) may know; pres. subj. 3rd pers. sing. 3. let him (her/it) know; impve. 3rd pers. sing.
sepáis that you (all) may know; pres. subj. 2nd pers. pl. / *saber.*
sepamos 1. that we may know; pres. subj. 1st pers. pl. / *saber.* 2. let us know; impve. 1st pers. pl.
sepan 1. that they may know; pres. subj. 3rd pers. pl. / *saber.* 2. let them know; impve. 3rd pers. pl.
separándose separating; pres. part. / *separarse.*
separaos (you all) separate; impve. 2nd pers. pl. / *separarse.*
separar to separate. reg.
separarse to separate. reg.
sepárate (you) separate; impve. 2nd pers. sing. / *separarse.*
separémonos let us separate; impve. 1st pers. pl. / *separarse.*
sepárense let them separate; impve. 3rd pers. pl. / *separarse.*
sepárese let him (her/it) separate; impve. 3rd pers. sing. / *separarse.*
sepas that you may know; pres. subj. 2nd pers. sing. / *saber.*
septuplicar to septuple. irr.
septuplique 1. that I may septuple; pres. subj. 1st pers. sing. / *septuplicar.* 2. that he (she/it) may septuple; pres. subj. 3rd pers. sing. 3. let him (her/it) septuple; impve. 3rd pers. sing.
septupliqué I septupled; past 1st pers. sing. / *septuplicar.*
septupliquéis that you (all) may septuple; pres. subj. 2nd pers. pl. / *septuplicar.*
septupliquemos 1. that we may septuple; pres. subj. 1st pers. pl. / *septuplicar.* 2. let us septuple; impve. 1st pers. pl.
septupliquen 1. that they may septuple; pres. subj. 3rd pers. pl. / *septuplicar.* 2. let them septuple; impve. 3rd pers. pl.
septupliques that you may septuple; pres. subj. 2nd pers. sing. / *septuplicar.*
sepultar to bury. reg.
seque 1. that I may dry; pres. subj. 1st pers. sing. / *secar.* 2. that he (she/it) may dry; pres. subj. 3rd pers. sing. 3. let him (her/it) dry; impve. 3rd pers. sing.
sequé I dried; past 1st pers. sing. / *secar.*
sequéis that you (all) may dry; pres. subj. 2nd pers. pl. / *secar.*
sequémonos let us dry up; impve. 1st pers. pl. / *secarse.*

sequemos 1. that we may dry; pres. subj. 1st pers. pl. / *secar.* 2. let us dry; impve. 1st pers. pl.
sequen 1. that they may dry; pres. subj. 3rd pers. pl. / *secar.* 2. let them dry; impve. 3rd pers. pl.
séquense let them dry up; impve. 3rd pers. pl. / *secarse.*
seques that you may dry; pres. subj. 2nd pers. sing. / *secar.*
séquese let him (her/it) dry up; impve. 3rd pers. sing. / *secarse.*
ser to be. irr.
serenándose becoming serene; pres. part. / *serenarse.*
serenaos (you all) become serene; impve. 2nd pers. pl. / *serenarse.*
serenar to calm. reg.
serenarse to become serene. reg.
serénate (you) become serene; impve. 2nd pers. sing. / *serenarse.*
serenémonos let us become serene; impve. 1st pers. pl. / *serenarse.*
serénense let them become serene; impve. 3rd pers. pl. / *serenarse.*
serénese let him (her/it) become serene; impve. 3rd pers. sing. / *serenarse.*
sermonear to sermonize. reg.
serpentear to wind or to meander. reg.
serrar to saw. irr.
servíos (you all) be willing; impve. 2nd pers. pl. / *servirse.*
servir to serve. irr.
servirse to be willing. irr.
sesear to pronounce z and c as s in spanish. reg.
sesgar to slant. irr.
sesgue 1. that I may slant; pres. subj. 1st pers. sing. / *sesgar.* 2. that he (she/it) may slant; pres. subj. 3rd pers. sing. 3. let him (her/it) slant; impve. 3rd pers. sing.
sesgué I slanted; past 1st pers. sing. / *sesgar.*
sesguéis that you (all) may slant; pres. subj. 2nd pers. pl. / *sesgar.*
sesguemos 1. that we may slant; pres. subj. 1st pers. pl. / *sesgar.* 2. let us slant; impve. 1st pers. pl.
sesguen 1. that they may slant; pres. subj. 3rd pers. pl. / *sesgar.* 2. let them slant; impve. 3rd pers. pl.
sesgues that you may slant; pres. subj. 2nd pers. sing. / *sesgar.*
sestear to take a siesta. reg.
sextuplicar to sextuple. irr.
sextuplique 1. that I may sextuple; pres. subj. 1st pers. sing. / *sextuplicar.* 2. that he (she/it) may sextuple; pres. subj. 3rd pers. sing. 3. let him (her/it) sextuple; impve. 3rd pers. sing.
sextupliqué I sextupled; past 1st pers. sing. / *sextuplicar.*
sextupliquéis that you (all) may sextuple; pres. subj. 2nd pers. pl. / *sextuplicar.*
sextupliquemos 1. that we may sextuple; pres. subj. 1st pers. pl. / *sextuplicar.* 2. let us sextuple; impve. 1st pers. pl.

sextupliquen 1. that they may sextuple; pres. subj. 3rd pers. pl. / *sextuplicar.* 2. let them sextuple; impve. 3rd pers. pl.

sextupliques that you may sextuple; pres. subj. 2nd pers. sing. / *sextuplicar.*

siconanalice 1. that I may psychoanalyze; pres. subj. 1st pers. sing. / *sicoanalizar.* 2. that he (she/it) may psychoanalyze; pres. subj. 3rd pers. sing. 3. let him (her/it) psychoanalyze; impve. 3rd pers. sing.

siconanalicé I psychoanalyzed; past 1st pers. sing. / *sicoanalizar.*

siconanalicéis that you (all) may psychoanalyze; pres. subj. 2nd pers. pl. / *sicoanalizar.*

siconanalicemos 1. that we may psychoanalyze; pres. subj. 1st pers. pl. / *sicoanalizar.* 2. let us psychoanalyze; impve. 1st pers. pl.

siconanalicen 1. that they may psychoanalyze; pres. subj. 3rd pers. pl. / *sicoanalizar.* 2. let them psychoanalyze; impve. 3rd pers. pl.

siconanalices that you may psychoanalyze; pres. subj. 2nd pers. sing. / *sicoanalizar.*

siconanalizar to psychoanalyze. irr.

sido was; past part. / *ser.*

siega 1. he (she/it) mows; pres. ind. 3rd pers. sing. / *segar.* 2. (you) mow; impve. 2nd pers. sing.

siegan they mow; pres. ind. 3rd pers. pl. / *segar.*

siegas you mow; pres. ind. 2nd pers. sing. / *segar.*

siego I mow; pres. ind. 1st pers. sing. / *segar.*

siegue 1. that I may mow; pres. subj. 1st pers. sing. / *segar.* 2. that he (she/it) may mow; pres. subj. 3rd pers. sing. 3. let him (her/it) mow; impve. 3rd pers. sing.

sieguen 1. that they may mow; pres. subj. 3rd pers. pl. / *segar.* 2. let them mow; impve. 3rd pers. pl.

siegues that you may mow; pres. subj. 2nd pers. sing. / *segar.*

siembra 1. he (she/it) sows; pres. ind. 3rd pers. sing. / *sembrar.* 2. (you) sow; impve. 2nd pers. sing.

siembran they sow; pres. ind. 3rd pers. pl. / *sembrar.*

siembras you sow; pres. ind. 2nd pers. sing. / *sembrar.*

siembre 1. that I may sow; pres. subj. 1st pers. sing. / *sembrar.* 2. that he (she/it) may sow; pres. subj. 3rd pers. sing. 3. let him (her/it) sow; impve. 3rd pers. sing.

siembren 1. that they may sow; pres. subj. 3rd pers. pl. / *sembrar.* 2. let them sow; impve. 3rd pers. pl.

siembres that you may sow; pres. subj. 2nd pers. sing. / *sembrar.*

siembro I sow; pres. ind. 1st pers. sing. / *sembrar.*

siendo being; pres. part. / *ser.*

sienta 1. he (she/it) seats; pres. ind. 3rd pers. sing. / *sentar.* 2. (you) seat; impve. 2nd pers. sing.

sienta 1. that I may feel; pres. subj. 1st pers. sing. / *sentir.* 2. that he (she/it) may feel; pres. subj. 3rd pers. sing. 3. let him (her/it) feel; impve. 3rd pers. sing.

sientan they seat; pres. ind. 3rd pers. pl. / *sentar.*

sientan 1. that they may feel; pres. subj. 3rd pers. pl. / *sentir.* 2. let them feel; impve. 3rd pers. pl.

siéntanse let them feel; impve. 3rd pers. pl. / *sentirse.*

sientas you seat; pres. ind. 2nd pers. sing. / *sentar.*

sientas that you may feel; pres. subj. 2nd pers. sing. / *sentir.*

siéntase let him (her/it) feel; impve. 3rd pers. sing. / *sentirse.*

siéntate (you) sit down; impve. 2nd pers. sing. / *sentarse.*

siente 1. that I may seat; pres. subj. 1st pers. sing. / *sentar.* 2. that he (she/it) may seat; pres. subj. 3rd pers. sing. 3. let him (her/it) seat; impve. 3rd pers. sing.

siente 1. he (she/it) feels; pres. ind. 3rd pers. sing. / *sentir.* 2. (you) feel; impve. 2nd pers. sing.

sienten 1. that they may seat; pres. subj. 3rd pers. pl. / *sentar.* 2. let them seat; impve. 3rd pers. pl.

sienten they feel; pres. ind. 3rd pers. pl. / *sentir.*

siéntense let them sit down; impve. 3rd pers. pl. / *sentarse.*

sientes that you may seat; pres. subj. 2nd pers. sing. / *sentar.*

sientes you feel; pres. ind. 2nd pers. sing. / *sentir.*

siéntese let him (her/it) sit down; impve. 3rd pers. sing. / *sentarse.*

siéntete (you) feel; impve. 2nd pers. sing. / *sentirse.*

siento I seat; pres. ind. 1st pers. sing. / *sentar.*

siento I feel; pres. ind. 1st pers. sing. / *sentir.*

sierra 1. he (she/it) saws; pres. ind. 3rd pers. sing. / *serrar.* 2. (you) saw; impve. 2nd pers. sing.

sierran they saw; pres. ind. 3rd pers. pl. / *serrar.*

sierras you saw; pres. ind. 2nd pers. sing. / *serrar.*

sierre 1. that I may saw; pres. subj. 1st pers. sing. / *serrar.* 2. that he (she/it) may saw; pres. subj. 3rd pers. sing. 3. let him (her/it) saw; impve. 3rd pers. sing.

sierren 1. that they may saw; pres. subj. 3rd pers. pl. / *serrar.* 2. let them saw; impve. 3rd pers. pl.

sierres that you may saw; pres. subj. 2nd pers. sing. / *serrar.*

sierro I saw; pres. ind. 1st pers. sing. / *serrar.*

siga 1. that I may follow; pres. subj. 1st pers. sing. / *seguir.* 2. that he (she/it) may follow; pres. subj. 3rd pers. sing. 3. let him (her/it) follow; impve. 3rd pers. sing.

sigáis that you (all) may follow; pres. subj. 2nd pers. pl. / *seguir.*

sigamos 1. that we may follow; pres. subj. 1st pers. pl. / *seguir.* 2. let us follow; impve. 1st pers. pl.

sigan 1. that they may follow; pres. subj. 3rd pers. pl. / *seguir.* 2. let them follow; impve. 3rd pers. pl.

siganse let them ensue; impve. 3rd pers. pl. / *seguirse.*

sigas that you may follow; pres. subj. 2nd pers. sing. / *seguir.*

sígase let it ensue; impve. 3rd pers. sing. / *seguirse.*

sigilar to conceal. reg.

signándose crossing oneself three times; pres. part. / *signarse.*

signaos (you all) cross yourselves three times; impve. 2nd pers. pl. / *signarse.*

signar to sign or to mark. reg.

signarse to cross oneself three times / reg.

sígnate (you) cross yourself three times; impve. 2nd pers. sing. / *signarse.*

signémonos let us cross ourselves three times; impve. 1st pers. pl. / *signarse.*

sígnense let them cross themselves three times; impve. 3rd pers. pl. / *signarse.*

sígnese let him (her) cross himself (herself) three times / *signarse.*

significar to signify. irr.

signifique 1. that I may signify; pres. subj. 1st pers. sing. / *significar.* 2. that he (she/it) may signify; pres. subj. 3rd pers. sing. 3. let him (her/it) signify; impve. 3rd pers. sing.

signifiqué I signified; past 1st pers. sing. / *significar.*

signifiquéis that you (all) may signify; pres. subj. 2nd pers. pl. / *significar.*

signifiquemos 1. that we may signify; pres. subj. 1st pers. pl. / *significar.* 2. let us signify; impve. 1st pers. pl.

signifiquen 1. that they may signify; pres. subj. 3rd pers. pl. / *significar.* 2. let them signify; impve. 3rd pers. pl.

signifiques that you may signify; pres. subj. 2nd pers. sing. / *significar.*

sigo I follow; pres. ind. 1st pers. sing. / *seguir.*

sigue 1. he (she/it) follows; pres. ind. 3rd pers. sing. / *seguir.* 2. (you) follow; impve. 2nd pers. sing.

siguen they follow; pres. ind. 3rd pers. pl. / *seguir.*

sigues you follow; pres. ind. 2nd pers. sing. / *seguir.*

siguiendo following; pres. part. / *seguir.*

siguiéndose ensuing; pres. part. / *seguirse.*

siguiera 1. that I might follow; imp. subj. 1st pers. sing. / *seguir.* 2. that he (she/it) might follow; imp. subj. 3rd pers. sing.

siguierais that you (all) might follow; imp. subj. 2nd pers pl. / *seguir.*

siguiéramos that we might follow; imp. subj. 1st pers. pl. / *seguir.*

siguieran that they might follow; imp. subj. 3rd pers. pl. / *seguir.*

siguieras that you might follow; imp. subj. 2nd pers. sing. / *seguir.*

siguieron they followed; past 3rd pers. pl. / *seguir.*

siguiese 1. that I might follow; imp. subj. 1st pers. sing. / *seguir.* 2. that he (she/it) might follow; imp. subj. 3rd pers. sing.

siguieseis that you (all) might follow; imp. subj. 2nd pers pl. / *seguir.*

siguiésemos that we might follow; imp. subj. 1st pers. pl. / *seguir.*

siguiesen that they might follow; imp. subj. 3rd pers. pl. / *seguir.*

siguieses that you might follow; imp. subj. 2nd pers. sing. / *seguir.*

siguió he (she/it) followed; past 3rd pers. sing. / *seguir.*

silabear to syllabicate. reg.

silbar to whistle. reg.

silenciar to silence. reg.

simbolice 1. that I may symbolize; pres. subj. 1st pers. sing. / *simbolizar.* 2. that he (she/it) may symbolize; pres. subj. 3rd pers. sing. 3. let him (her/it) symbolize; impve. 3rd pers. sing.

simbolicé I symbolized; past 1st pers. sing. / *simbolizar.*

simbolicéis that you (all) may symbolize; pres. subj. 2nd pers. pl. / *simbolizar.*

simbolicemos 1. that we may symbolize; pres. subj. 1st pers. pl. / *simbolizar.* 2. let us symbolize; impve. 1st pers. pl.

simbolicen 1. that they may symbolize; pres. subj. 3rd pers. pl. / *simbolizar.* 2. let them symbolize; impve. 3rd pers. pl.

simbolices that you may symbolize; pres. subj. 2nd pers. sing. / *simbolizar.*

simbolizar to symbolize. irr.

simpatice 1. that I may sympathize; pres. subj. 1st pers. sing. / *simpatizar.* 2. that he (she/it) may sympathize; pres. subj. 3rd pers. sing. 3. let him (her/it) sympathize; impve. 3rd pers. sing.

simpaticé I sympathized; past 1st pers. sing. / *simpatizar.*

simpaticéis that you (all) may sympathize; pres. subj. 2nd pers. pl. / *simpatizar.*

simpaticemos 1. that we may sympathize; pres. subj. 1st pers. pl. / *simpatizar.* 2. let us sympathize; impve. 1st pers. pl.

simpaticen 1. that they may sympathize; pres. subj. 3rd pers. pl. / *simpatizar.* 2. let them sympathize; impve. 3rd pers. pl.

simpatices that you may sympathize; pres. subj. 2nd pers. sing. / *simpatizar.*

simpatizar to sympathize. irr.

simplificar to simplify. irr.

simplifique 1. that I may simplify; pres. subj. 1st pers. sing. / *simplificar.* 2. that he (she/it) may simplify; pres. subj. 3rd pers. sing. 3. let him (her/it) simplify; impve. 3rd pers. sing.

simplifiqué I simplified; past 1st pers. sing. / *simplificar.*

simplifiquéis that you (all) may simplify; pres. subj. 2nd pers. pl. / *simplificar.*

simplifiquemos 1. that we may simplify; pres. subj. 1st pers. pl. / *simplificar.* 2. let us simplify; impve. 1st pers. pl.

simplifiquen 1. that they may simplify; pres. subj. 3rd pers. pl. / *simplificar.* 2. let them simplify; impve. 3rd pers. pl.

simplifiques that you may simplify; pres. subj. 2nd pers. sing. / *simplificar.*

simular to simulate. reg.

sincerándose speaking frankly; pres. part. / *sincerarse.*

sinceraos (you all) speak frankly; impve. 2nd pers. pl. / *sincerarse.*

sincerar to justify. reg.

sincerarse to speak frankly. reg.

sincérate (you) speak frankly; impve. 2nd pers. sing. / *sincerarse.*

sincerémonos let us speak frankly; impve. 1st pers. pl. / *sincerarse*.

sincérense let them speak frankly; impve. 3rd pers. pl. / *sincerarse*.

sincérese let him (her/it) speak frankly; impve. 3rd pers. sing. / *sincerarse*.

sincopar to syncopate. reg.

sincronice 1. that I may synchronize; pres. subj. 1st pers. sing. / *sincronizar*. 2. that he (she/it) may synchronize; pres. subj. 3rd pers. sing. 3. let him (her/it) synchronize; impve. 3rd pers. sing.

sincronicé I synchronized; past 1st pers. sing. / *sincronizar*.

sincronicéis that you (all) may synchronize; pres. subj. 2nd pers. pl. / *sincronizar*.

sincronicemos 1. that we may synchronize; pres. subj. 1st pers. pl. / *sincronizar*. 2. let us synchronize; impve. 1st pers. pl.

sincronicen 1. that they may synchronize; pres. subj. 3rd pers. pl. / *sincronizar*. 2. let them synchronize; impve. 3rd pers. pl.

sincronices that you may synchronize; pres. subj. 2nd pers. sing. / *sincronizar*.

sincronizar to synchronize. irr.

sindicándose becoming union; pres. part. / *sindicarse*.

sindicaos (you all) become union; impve. 2nd pers. pl. / *sindicarse*.

sindicar to syndicate. irr.

sindicarse to become union. irr.

sindícate (you) become union; impve. 2nd pers. sing. / *sindicarse*.

sindique 1. that I may syndicate; pres. subj. 1st pers. sing. / *sindicar*. 2. that he (she/it) may syndicate; pres. subj. 3rd pers. sing. 3. let him (her/it) syndicate; impve. 3rd pers. sing.

sindiqué I syndicated; past 1st pers. sing. / *sindicar*.

sindiquéis that you (all) may syndicate; pres. subj. 2nd pers. pl. / *sindicar*.

sindiquémonos let us become union; impve. 1st pers. pl. / *sindicarse*.

sindiquemos 1. that we may syndicate; pres. subj. 1st pers. pl. / *sindicar*. 2. let us syndicate; impve. 1st pers. pl.

sindiquen 1. that they may syndicate; pres. subj. 3rd pers. pl. / *sindicar*. 2. let them syndicate; impve. 3rd pers. pl.

sindíquense let them become union; impve. 3rd pers. pl. / *sindicarse*.

sindiques that you may syndicate; pres. subj. 2nd pers. sing. / *sindicar*.

sindíquese let him (her/it) become union; impve. 3rd pers. sing. / *sindicarse*.

singlar to follow a course (boat). reg.

singularice 1. that I may distinguish; pres. subj. 1st pers. sing. / *singularizar*. 2. that he (she/it) may distinguish; pres. subj. 3rd pers. sing. 3. let him (her/it) distinguish; impve. 3rd pers. sing.

singularicé I distinguished; past 1st pers. sing. / *singularizar*.

singularicéis that you (all) may distinguish; pres. subj. 2nd pers. pl. / *singularizar*.

singularicémonos let us be singled out; impve. 1st pers. pl. / *singularizarse*.

singularicemos 1. that we may distinguish; pres. subj. 1st pers. pl. / *singularizar*. 2. let us distinguish; impve. 1st pers. pl.

singularicen 1. that they may distinguish; pres. subj. 3rd pers. pl. / *singularizar*. 2. let them distinguish; impve. 3rd pers. pl.

singularícense let them be singled out; impve. 3rd pers. pl. / *singularizarse*.

singularices that you may distinguish; pres. subj. 2nd pers. sing. / *singularizar*.

singularícese let him (her/it) be singled out; impve. 3rd pers. sing. / *singularizarse*.

singularizándose being singled out; pres. part. / *singularizarse*.

singularizaos (you all) be singled out; impve. 2nd pers. pl. / *singularizarse*.

singularizar to distinguish. irr.

singularizarse to be singled out. irr.

singularízate (you) be singled out; impve. 2nd pers. sing. / *singularizarse*.

sintáis that you (all) may feel; pres. subj. 2nd pers. pl. / *sentir*.

sintámonos let us feel; impve. 1st pers. pl. / *sentirse*.

sintamos 1. that we may feel; pres. subj. 1st pers. pl. / *sentir*. 2. let us feel; impve. 1st pers. pl.

sintetice 1. that I may synthesize; pres. subj. 1st pers. sing. / *sintetizar*. 2. that he (she/it) may synthesize; pres. subj. 3rd pers. sing. 3. let him (her/it) synthesize; impve. 3rd pers. sing.

sinteticé I synthesized; past 1st pers. sing. / *sintetizar*.

sinteticéis that you (all) may synthesize; pres. subj. 2nd pers. pl. / *sintetizar*.

sinteticemos 1. that we may synthesize; pres. subj. 1st pers. pl. / *sintetizar*. 2. let us synthesize; impve. 1st pers. pl.

sinteticen 1. that they may synthesize; pres. subj. 3rd pers. pl. / *sintetizar*. 2. let them synthesize; impve. 3rd pers. pl.

sintetices that you may synthesize; pres. subj. 2nd pers. sing. / *sintetizar*.

sintetizar to synthesize. irr.

sintiendo feeling; pres. part. / *sentir*.

sintiéndose feeling; pres. part. / *sentirse*.

sintiera 1. that I might feel; imp. subj. 1st pers. sing. / *sentir*. 2. that he (she/it) might feel; imp. subj. 3rd pers. sing.

sintierais that you (all) might feel; imp. subj. 2nd pers pl. / *sentir*.

sintiéramos that we might feel; imp. subj. 1st pers. pl. / *sentir*.

sintieran that they might feel; imp. subj. 3rd pers. pl. / *sentir*.

sintieras that you might feel; imp. subj. 2nd pers. sing. / *sentir*.

sintieron they felt; past 3rd pers. pl. / *sentir*.

sintiese 1. that I might feel; imp. subj. 1st pers. sing. / *sentir.* 2. that he (she/it) might feel; imp. subj. 3rd pers. sing.

sintieseis that you (all) might feel; imp. subj. 2nd pers pl. / *sentir.*

sintiésemos that we might feel; imp. subj. 1st pers. pl. / *sentir.*

sintiesen that they might feel; imp. subj. 3rd pers. pl. / *sentir.*

sintieses that you might feel; imp. subj. 2nd pers. sing. / *sentir.*

sintió he (she/it) felt; past 3rd pers. sing. / *sentir.*

sintonice 1. that I may tune in; pres. subj. 1st pers. sing. / *sintonizar.* 2. that he (she/it) may tune in; pres. subj. 3rd pers. sing. 3. let him (her/it) tune in; impve. 3rd pers. sing.

sintonicé I tuned in; past 1st pers. sing. / *sintonizar.*

sintonicéis that you (all) may tune in; pres. subj. 2nd pers. pl. / *sintonizar.*

sintonicemos 1. that we may tune in; pres. subj. 1st pers. pl. / *sintonizar.* 2. let us tune in; impve. 1st pers. pl.

sintonicen 1. that they may tune in; pres. subj. 3rd pers. pl. / *sintonizar.* 2. let them tune in; impve. 3rd pers. pl.

sintonices that you may tune in; pres. subj. 2nd pers. sing. / *sintonizar.*

sintonizar to tune in. irr.

sirva 1. that I may serve; pres. subj. 1st pers. sing. / *servir.* 2. that he (she/it) may serve; pres. subj. 3rd pers. sing. 3. let him (her/it) serve; impve. 3rd pers. sing.

sirváis that you (all) may serve; pres. subj. 2nd pers. pl. / *servir.*

sirvámonos let us be willing; impve. 1st pers. pl. / *servirse.*

sirvamos 1. that we may serve; pres. subj. 1st pers. pl. / *servir.* 2. let us serve; impve. 1st pers. pl.

sirvan 1. that they may serve; pres. subj. 3rd pers. pl. / *servir.* 2. let them serve; impve. 3rd pers. pl.

sírvanse let them be willing; impve. 3rd pers. pl. / *servirse.*

sirvas that you may serve; pres. subj. 2nd pers. sing. / *servir.*

sírvase let him (her/it) be willing; impve. 3rd pers. sing. / *servirse.*

sirve 1. he (she/it) serves; pres. ind. 3rd pers. sing. / *servir.* 2. (you) serve; impve. 2nd pers. sing.

sirven they serve; pres. ind. 3rd pers. pl. / *servir.*

sirves you serve; pres. ind. 2nd pers. sing. / *servir.*

sírvete (you) be willing; impve. 2nd pers. sing. / *servirse.*

sirviendo serving; pres. part. / *servir.*

sirviéndose being willing; pres. part. / *servirse.*

sirviera 1. that I might serve; imp. subj. 1st pers. sing. / *servir.* 2. that he (she/it) might serve; imp. subj. 3rd pers. sing.

sirvierais that you (all) might serve; imp. subj. 2nd pers pl. / *servir.* ,

sirviéramos that we might serve; imp. subj. 1st pers. pl. / *servir.*

sirvieran that they might serve; imp. subj. 3rd pers. pl. / *servir.*

sirvieras that you might serve; imp. subj. 2nd pers. sing. / *servir.*

sirvieron they served; past 3rd pers. pl. / *servir.*

sirviese 1. that I might serve; imp. subj. 1st pers. sing. / *servir.* 2. that he (she/it) might serve; imp. subj. 3rd pers. sing.

sirvieseis that you (all) might serve; imp. subj. 2nd pers pl. / *servir.*

sirviésemos that we might serve; imp. subj. 1st pers. pl. / *servir.*

sirviesen that they might serve; imp. subj. 3rd pers. pl. / *servir.*

sirvieses that you might serve; imp. subj. 2nd pers. sing. / *servir.*

sirvió he (she/it) served; past 3rd pers. sing. / *servir.*

sirvo I serve; pres. ind. 1st pers. sing. / *servir.*

sisar to pilfer. reg.

sisear to hiss. reg.

sistematice 1. that I may systematize; pres. subj. 1st pers. sing. / *sistematizar.* 2. that he (she/it) may systematize; pres. subj. 3rd pers. sing. 3. let him (her/it) systematize; impve. 3rd pers. sing.

sistematicé I systematized; past 1st pers. sing. / *sistematizar.*

sistematicéis that you (all) may systematize; pres. subj. 2nd pers. pl. / *sistematizar.*

sistematicemos 1. that we may systematize; pres. subj. 1st pers. pl. / *sistematizar.* 2. let us systematize; impve. 1st pers. pl.

sistematicen 1. that they may systematize; pres. subj. 3rd pers. pl. / *sistematizar.* 2. let them systematize; impve. 3rd pers. pl.

sistematices that you may systematize; pres. subj. 2nd pers. sing. / *sistematizar.*

sistematizar to systematize. irr.

sitiar to besiege. reg.

sitúa 1. he (she/it) situates; pres. ind. 3rd pers. sing. / *situar.* 2. (you) situate; impve. 2nd pers. sing.

sitúan they situate; pres. ind. 3rd pers. pl. / *situar.*

situándose being located; pres. part. / *situarse.*

situaos (you all) be located; impve. 2nd pers. pl. / *situarse.*

situar to situate. irr.

situarse to be located. irr.

sitúas you situate; pres. ind. 2nd pers. sing. / *situar.*

sitúate (you) be located; impve. 2nd pers. sing. / *situarse.*

sitúe 1. that I may situate; pres. subj. 1st pers. sing. / *situar.* 2. that he (she/it) may situate; pres. subj. 3rd pers. sing. 3. let him (her/it) situate; impve. 3rd pers. sing.

situémonos let us be located; impve. 1st pers. pl. / *situarse.*

sitúen 1. that they may situate; pres. subj. 3rd pers. pl. / *situar.* 2. let them situate; impve. 3rd pers. pl.

sitúense let them be located; impve. 3rd pers. pl. / *situarse.*

sitúes that you may situate; pres. subj. 2nd pers. sing. / *situar*.

sitúese let him (her/it) be located; impve. 3rd pers. sing. / *situarse*.

sitúo I situate; pres. ind. 1st pers. sing. / *situar*.

sobajar to humble or to handle. reg.

sobajear to handle or to paw. reg.

sobar to knead. reg.

sobarcar to tuck under the arm. irr.

sobarque 1. that I may tuck under the arm; pres. subj. 1st pers. sing. / *sobarcar*. 2. that he (she/it) may tuck under the arm; pres. subj. 3rd pers. sing. 3. let him (her/it) tuck under the arm; impve. 3rd pers. sing.

sobarqué I tucked under the arm; past 1st pers. sing. / *sobarcar*.

sobarquéis that you (all) may tuck under the arm; pres. subj. 2nd pers. pl. / *sobarcar*.

sobarquemos 1. that we may tuck under the arm; pres. subj. 1st pers. pl. / *sobarcar*. 2. let us tuck under the arm; impve. 1st pers. pl.

sobarquen 1. that they may tuck under the arm; pres. subj. 3rd pers. pl. / *sobarcar*. 2. let them tuck under the arm; impve. 3rd pers. pl.

sobarques that you may tuck under the arm; pres. subj. 2nd pers. sing. / *sobarcar*.

sobornar to bribe. reg.

sobrar to exceed. reg.

sobreaguar to float on. irr.

sobreagüe 1. that I may float on; pres. subj. 1st pers. sing. / *sobreaguar*. 2. that he (she/it) may float on; pres. subj. 3rd pers. sing. 3. let him (her/it) float on; impve. 3rd pers. sing.

sobreagüé I floated on; past 1st pers. sing. / *sobreaguar*.

sobreagüéis that you (all) may float on; pres. subj. 2nd pers. pl. / *sobreaguar*.

sobreagüemos 1. that we may float on; pres. subj. 1st pers. pl. / *sobreaguar*. 2. let us float on; impve. 1st pers. pl.

sobreagüen 1. that they may float on; pres. subj. 3rd pers. pl. / *sobreaguar*. 2. let them float on; impve. 3rd pers. pl.

sobreagües that you may float on; pres. subj. 2nd pers. sing. / *sobreaguar*.

sobrealce 1. that I may extol; pres. subj. 1st pers. sing. / *sobrealzar*. 2. that he (she/it) may extol; pres. subj. 3rd pers. sing. 3. let him (her/it) extol; impve. 3rd pers. sing.

sobrealcé I extoled; past 1st pers. sing. / *sobrealzar*.

sobrealcéis that you (all) may extol; pres. subj. 2nd pers. pl. / *sobrealzar*.

sobrealcemos 1. that we may extol; pres. subj. 1st pers. pl. / *sobrealzar*. 2. let us extol; impve. 1st pers. pl.

sobrealcen 1. that they may extol; pres. subj. 3rd pers. pl. / *sobrealzar*. 2. let them extol; impve. 3rd pers. pl.

sobrealces that you may extol; pres. subj. 2nd pers. sing. / *sobrealzar*.

sobrealimentar to overfeed. reg.

sobrealzar to extol. irr.

sobrecargar to overload. irr.

sobrecargue 1. that I may overload; pres. subj. 1st pers. sing. / *sobrecargar*. 2. that he (she/it) may overload; pres. subj. 3rd pers. sing. 3. let him (her/it) overload; impve. 3rd pers. sing.

sobrecargué I overloaded; past 1st pers. sing. / *sobrecargar*.

sobrecarguéis that you (all) may overload; pres. subj. 2nd pers. pl. / *sobrecargar*.

sobrecarguemos 1. that we may overload; pres. subj. 1st pers. pl. / *sobrecargar*. 2. let us overload; impve. 1st pers. pl.

sobrecarguen 1. that they may overload; pres. subj. 3rd pers. pl. / *sobrecargar*. 2. let them overload; impve. 3rd pers. pl.

sobrecargues that you may overload; pres. subj. 2nd pers. sing. / *sobrecargar*.

sobrecogeos (you all) be overcome; impve. 2nd pers. pl. / *sobrecogerse*.

sobrecoger to surprise. irr.

sobrecogerse to be overcome. irr.

sobrecógete (you) be overcome; impve. 2nd pers. sing. / *sobrecogerse*.

sobrecogiéndose being overcome; pres. part. / *sobrecogerse*.

sobrecoja 1. that I may surprise; pres. subj. 1st pers. sing. / *sobrecoger*. 2. that he (she/it) may surprise; pres. subj. 3rd pers. sing. 3. let him (her/it) surprise; impve. 3rd pers. sing.

sobrecojáis that you (all) may surprise; pres. subj. 2nd pers. pl. / *sobrecoger*.

sobrecojámonos let us be overcome; impve. 1st pers. pl. / *sobrecogerse*.

sobrecojamos 1. that we may surprise; pres. subj. 1st pers. pl. / *sobrecoger*. 2. let us surprise; impve. 1st pers. pl.

sobrecojan 1. that they may surprise; pres. subj. 3rd pers. pl. / *sobrecoger*. 2. let them surprise; impve. 3rd pers. pl.

sobrecójanse let them be overcome; impve. 3rd pers. pl. / *sobrecogerse*.

sobrecojas that you may surprise; pres. subj. 2nd pers. sing. / *sobrecoger*.

sobrecójase let him (her/it) be overcome; impve. 3rd pers. sing. / *sobrecogerse*.

sobrecojo I surprise; pres. ind. 1st pers. sing. / *sobrecoger*.

sobrecomprimir to pressurize. reg.

sobredorar to gloss over. reg.

sobreentender to understand. irr.

sobreentienda 1. that I may understand; pres. subj. 1st pers. sing. / *sobreentender*. 2. that he (she/it) may understand; pres. subj. 3rd pers. sing. 3. let him (her/it) understand; impve. 3rd pers. sing.

sobreentiendan 1. that they may understand; pres. subj. 3rd pers. pl. / *sobreentender*. 2. let them understand; impve. 3rd pers. pl.

sobreentiendas that you may understand; pres. subj. 2nd pers. sing. / *sobreentender*.

sobreentiende 1. he (she/it) understands; pres. ind. 3rd pers. sing. / *sobreentender.* 2. (you) understand; impve. 2nd pers. sing.

sobreentienden they understand; pres. ind. 3rd pers. pl. / *sobreentender.*

sobreentiendes you understand; pres. ind. 2nd pers. sing. / *sobreentender.*

sobreentiendo I understand; pres. ind. 1st pers. sing. / *sobreentender.*

sobreestimar to overestimate. reg.

sobreexceder to exceed. reg.

sobreexcitar to overexcite. reg.

sobreexpon (you) overexpose; impve. 2nd pers. sing. / *sobreexponer.*

sobreexpondrá he (she/it) will overexpose; fut. 3rd pers. sing. / *sobreexponer.*

sobreexpondrán they will overexpose; fut. 3rd pers. pl. / *sobreexponer.*

sobreexpondrás you will overexpose; fut. 2nd pers. sing. / *sobreexponer.*

sobreexpondré I shall overexpose; fut. 1st pers. sing. / *sobreexponer.*

sobreexpondréis you (all) will overexpose; fut. 2nd pers. pl. / *sobreexponer.*

sobreexpondremos we shall overexpose; fut. 1st pers. pl. / *sobreexponer.*

sobreexpondría 1. I should overexpose; cond. 1st pers. sing. / *sobreexponer.* 2. he (she/it) would overexpose; cond. 3rd pers. sing.

sobreexpondríais you (all) would overexpose; cond. 2nd pers. pl. / *sobreexponer.*

sobreexpondríamos we should overexpose; cond. 1st pers. pl. / *sobreexponer.*

sobreexpondrían they would overexpose; cond. 3rd pers. pl. / *sobreexponer.*

sobreexpondrías you would overexpose; cond. 2nd pers. sing. / *sobreexponer.*

sobreexponer to overexpose. irr.

sobreexponga 1. that I may overexpose; pres. subj. 1st pers. sing. / *sobreexponer.* 2. that he (she/it) may overexpose; pres. subj. 3rd pers. sing. 3. let him (her/it) overexpose; impve. 3rd pers. sing.

sobreexpongáis that you (all) may overexpose; pres. subj. 2nd pers. pl. / *sobreexponer.*

sobreexpongamos 1. that we may overexpose; pres. subj. 1st pers. pl. / *sobreexponer.* 2. let us overexpose; impve. 1st pers. pl.

sobreexpongan 1. that they may overexpose; pres. subj. 3rd pers. pl. / *sobreexponer.* 2. let them overexpose; impve. 3rd pers. pl.

sobreexpongas that you may overexpose; pres. subj. 2nd pers. sing. / *sobreexponer.*

sobreexpongo I overexpose; pres. ind. 1st pers. sing. / *sobreexponer.*

sobreexpuesto overexposed; past part. / *sobreexponer.*

sobreexpuse I overexposed; past 1st pers. sing. / *sobreexponer.*

sobreexpusiera 1. that I might overexpose; imp. subj. 1st pers. sing. / *sobreexponer.* 2. that he (she/it) might overexpose; imp. subj. 3rd pers. sing.

sobreexpusierais that you (all) might overexpose; imp. subj. 2nd pers pl. / *sobreexponer.*

sobreexpusiéramos that we might overexpose; imp. subj. 1st pers. pl. / *sobreexponer.*

sobreexpusieran that they might overexpose; imp. subj. 3rd pers. pl. / *sobreexponer.*

sobreexpusieras that you might overexpose; imp. subj. 2nd pers. sing. / *sobreexponer.*

sobreexpusieron they overexposed; past 3rd pers. pl. / *sobreexponer.*

sobreexpusiese 1. that I might overexpose; imp. subj. 1st pers. sing. / *sobreexponer.* 2. that he (she/it) might overexpose; imp. subj. 3rd pers. sing.

sobreexpusieseis that you (all) might overexpose; imp. subj. 2nd pers pl. / *sobreexponer.*

sobreexpusiésemos that we might overexpose; imp. subj. 1st pers. pl. / *sobreexponer.*

sobreexpusiesen that they might overexpose; imp. subj. 3rd pers. pl. / *sobreexponer.*

sobreexpusieses that you might overexpose; imp. subj. 2nd pers. sing. / *sobreexponer.*

sobreexpusimos we overexposed; past 1st pers. pl. / *sobreexponer.*

sobreexpusiste you overexposed; past 2nd pers. sing. / *sobreexponer.*

sobreexpusisteis you (all) overexposed; past 2nd pers. pl. / *sobreexponer.*

sobreexpuso he (she/it) overexposed; past 3rd pers. sing. / *sobreexponer.*

sobregirar to overdraw. reg.

sobrehilar to overcast (sewing). reg.

sobrellenar to overfill. reg.

sobrellevar to endure. reg.

sobrenadar to float. reg.

sobrentendámonos let us be obvious; impve. 1st pers. pl. / *sobrentenderse.*

sobrentendeos (you all) be obvious; impve. 2nd pers. pl. / *sobrentenderse.*

sobrentender to assume. irr.

sobrentenderse to be obvious. irr.

sobrentendiendo assuming; pres. part. / *sobrentender.*

sobrentendiéndose being obvious; pres. part. / *sobrentenderse.*

sobrentienda 1. that I may assume; pres. subj. 1st pers. sing. / *sobrentender.* 2. that he (she/it) may assume; pres. subj. 3rd pers. sing. 3. let him (her/it) assume; impve. 3rd pers. sing.

sobrentiendan 1. that they may assume; pres. subj. 3rd pers. pl. / *sobrentender.* 2. let them assume; impve. 3rd pers. pl.

sobrentiéndanse let them be obvious; impve. 3rd pers. pl. / *sobrentenderse.*

sobrentiendas that you may assume; pres. subj. 2nd pers. sing. / *sobrentender.*

sobrentiéndase let him (her/it) be obvious; impve. 3rd pers. sing. / *sobrentenderse.*

sobrentiende 1. he (she/it) assumes; pres. ind. 3rd pers. sing. / *sobrentender.* 2. (you) assume; impve. 2nd pers. sing.

sobrentienden they assume; pres. ind. 3rd pers. pl. / *sobrentender.*

sobrentiendes you assume; pres. ind. 2nd pers. sing. / *sobrentender.*

sobrentiéndete (you) be obvious; impve. 2nd pers. sing. / *sobrentenderse.*

sobrentiendo I assume; pres. ind. 1st pers. sing. / *sobrentender.*

sobrepasándose overstepping; pres. part. / *sobrepasarse.*

sobrepasaos (you all) overstep; impve. 2nd pers. pl. / *sobrepasarse.*

sobrepasar to surpass. reg.

sobrepasarse to overstep. reg.

sobrepásate (you) overstep; impve. 2nd pers. sing. / *sobrepasarse.*

sobrepasémonos let us overstep; impve. 1st pers. pl. / *sobrepasarse.*

sobrepásense let them overstep; impve. 3rd pers. pl. / *sobrepasarse.*

sobrepásese let him (her/it) overstep; impve. 3rd pers. sing. / *sobrepasarse.*

sobrepon (you) superimpose; impve. 2nd pers. sing. / *sobreponer.*

sobrepondrá he (she/it) will superimpose; fut. 3rd pers. sing. / *sobreponer.*

sobrepondrán they will superimpose; fut. 3rd pers. pl. / *sobreponer.*

sobrepondrás you will superimpose; fut. 2nd pers. sing. / *sobreponer.*

sobrepondré I shall superimpose; fut. 1st pers. sing. / *sobreponer.*

sobrepondréis you (all) will superimpose; fut. 2nd pers. pl. / *sobreponer.*

sobrepondremos we shall superimpose; fut. 1st pers. pl. / *sobreponer.*

sobrepondría 1. I should superimpose; cond. 1st pers. sing. / *sobreponer.* 2. he (she/it) would superimpose; cond. 3rd pers. sing.

sobrepondríais you (all) would superimpose; cond. 2nd pers. pl. / *sobreponer.*

sobrepondríamos we should superimpose; cond. 1st pers. pl. / *sobreponer.*

sobrepondrían they would superimpose; cond. 3rd pers. pl. / *sobreponer.*

sobrepondrías you would superimpose; cond. 2nd pers. sing. / *sobreponer.*

sobreponeos (you all) overcome; impve. 2nd pers. pl. / *sobreponerse.*

sobreponer to superimpose. irr.

sobreponerse to overcome. irr.

sobreponga 1. that I may superimpose; pres. subj. 1st pers. sing. / *sobreponer.* 2. that he (she/it) may superimpose; pres. subj. 3rd pers. sing. 3. let him (her/it) superimpose; impve. 3rd pers. sing.

sobrepongáis that you (all) may superimpose; pres. subj. 2nd pers. pl. / *sobreponer.*

sobrepongámonos let us overcome; impve. 1st pers. pl. / *sobreponerse.*

sobrepongamos 1. that we may superimpose; pres. subj. 1st pers. pl. / *sobreponer.* 2. let us superimpose; impve. 1st pers. pl.

sobrepongan 1. that they may superimpose; pres. subj. 3rd pers. pl. / *sobreponer.* 2. let them superimpose; impve. 3rd pers. pl.

sobrepónganse let them overcome; impve. 3rd pers. pl. / *sobreponerse.*

sobrepongas that you may superimpose; pres. subj. 2nd pers. sing. / *sobreponer.*

sobrepóngase let him (her/it) overcome; impve. 3rd pers. sing. / *sobreponerse.*

sobrepongo I superimpose; pres. ind. 1st pers. sing. / *sobreponer.*

sobreponiendo superimposing; pres. part. / *sobreponer.*

sobreponiéndose overcoming; pres. part. / *sobreponerse.*

sobreponte (you) overcome; impve. 2nd pers. sing. / *sobreponerse.*

sobrepuesto superimposed; past part. / *sobreponer.*

sobrepujar to surpass. reg.

sobrepuse I superimposed; past 1st pers. sing. / *sobreponer.*

sobrepusiera 1. that I might superimpose; imp. subj. 1st pers. sing. / *sobreponer.* 2. that he (she/it) might superimpose; imp. subj. 3rd pers. sing.

sobrepusierais that you (all) might superimpose; imp. subj. 2nd pers pl. / *sobreponer.*

sobrepusiéramos that we might superimpose; imp. subj. 1st pers. pl. / *sobreponer.*

sobrepusieran that they might superimpose; imp. subj. 3rd pers. pl. / *sobreponer.*

sobrepusieras that you might superimpose; imp. subj. 2nd pers. sing. / *sobreponer.*

sobrepusieron they superimposed; past 3rd pers. pl. / *sobreponer.*

sobrepusiese 1. that I might superimpose; imp. subj. 1st pers. sing. / *sobreponer.* 2. that he (she/it) might superimpose; imp. subj. 3rd pers. sing.

sobrepusieseis that you (all) might superimpose; imp. subj. 2nd pers pl. / *sobreponer.*

sobrepusiésemos that we might superimpose; imp. subj. 1st pers. pl. / *sobreponer.*

sobrepusiesen that they might superimpose; imp. subj. 3rd pers. pl. / *sobreponer.*

sobrepusieses that you might superimpose; imp. subj. 2nd pers. sing. / *sobreponer.*

sobrepusimos we superimposed; past 1st pers. pl. / *sobreponer.*

sobrepusiste you superimposed; past 2nd pers. sing. / *sobreponer.*

sobrepusisteis you (all) superimposed; past 2nd pers. pl. / *sobreponer.*

sobrepuso he (she/it) superimposed; past 3rd pers. sing. / *sobreponer.*

sobresal (you) stand out; impve. 2nd pers. sing. / *sobresalir.*

sobresaldrá he (she/it) will stand out; fut. 3rd pers. sing. / *sobresalir.*

sobresaldrán they will stand out; fut. 3rd pers. pl. / *sobresalir.*

sobresaldrás you will stand out; fut. 2nd pers. sing. / *sobresalir.*

sobresaldré I shall stand out; fut. 1st pers. sing. / *sobresalir.*

sobresaldréis you (all) will stand out; fut. 2nd pers. pl. / *sobresalir.*

sobresaldremos we shall stand out; fut. 1st pers. pl. / *sobresalir.*

sobresaldría 1. I should stand out; cond. 1st pers. sing. / *sobresalir.* 2. he (she/it) would stand out; cond. 3rd pers. sing.

sobresaldríais you (all) would stand out; cond. 2nd pers. pl. / *sobresalir.*

sobresaldríamos we should stand out; cond. 1st pers. pl. / *sobresalir.*

sobresaldrían they would stand out; cond. 3rd pers. pl. / *sobresalir.*

sobresaldrías you would stand out; cond. 2nd pers. sing. / *sobresalir.*

sobresalga 1. that I may stand out ; pres. subj. 1st pers. sing. / *sobresalir.* 2. that he (she/it) may stand out ; pres. subj. 3rd pers. sing. 3. let him (her/it) stand out ; impve. 3rd pers. sing.

sobresalgáis that you (all) may stand out ; pres. subj. 2nd pers. pl. / *sobresalir.*

sobresalgamos 1. that we may stand out ; pres. subj. 1st pers. pl. / *sobresalir.* 2. let us stand out ; impve. 1st pers. pl.

sobresalgan 1. that they may stand out ; pres. subj. 3rd pers. pl. / *sobresalir.* 2. let them stand out ; impve. 3rd pers. pl.

sobresalgas that you may stand out ; pres. subj. 2nd pers. sing. / *sobresalir.*

sobresalgo I stand out ; pres. ind. 1st pers. sing. / *sobresalir.*

sobresalir to stand out. irr.

sobresaltándose being frightened; pres. part. / *sobresaltarse.*

sobresaltaos (you all) be frightened; impve. 2nd pers. pl. / *sobresaltarse.*

sobresaltar to startle. reg.

sobresaltarse to be frightened. reg.

sobresáltate (you) be frightened; impve. 2nd pers. sing. / *sobresaltarse.*

sobresaltémonos let us be frightened; impve. 1st pers. pl. / *sobresaltarse.*

sobresáltense let them be frightened; impve. 3rd pers. pl. / *sobresaltarse.*

sobresáltese let him (her/it) be frightened; impve. 3rd pers. sing. / *sobresaltarse.*

sobresanar to heal superficially. reg.

sobrescribir to superscribe. reg. except for pp.

sobrescrito superscribed; past part. / *sobrescribir.*

sobreseí I stayed; past 1st pers. sing. / *sobreseer.*

sobreseído stayed; past part. / *sobreseer.*

sobreseímos we stayed; past 1st pers. pl. / *sobreseer.*

sobreseíste you stayed; past 2nd pers. sing. / *sobreseer.*

sobreseísteis you (all) stayed; past 2nd pers. pl. / *sobreseer.*

sobreseyendo staying; pres. part. / *sobreseer.*

sobreseyera 1. that I might stay; imp. subj. 1st pers. sing. / *sobreseer.* 2. that he (she/it) might stay; imp. subj. 3rd pers. sing.

sobreseyerais that you (all) might stay; imp. subj. 2nd pers pl. / *sobreseer.*

sobreseyeran that they might stay; imp. subj. 3rd pers. pl. / *sobreseer.*

sobreseyeras that you might stay; imp. subj. 2nd pers. sing. / *sobreseer.*

sobreseyeron they stayed; past 3rd pers. pl. / *sobreseer.*

sobreseyese 1. that I might stay; imp. subj. 1st pers. sing. / *sobreseer.* 2. that he (she/it) might stay; imp. subj. 3rd pers. sing.

sobreseyeseis that you (all) might stay; imp. subj. 2nd pers pl. / *sobreseer.*

sobreseyésemos that we might stay; imp. subj. 1st pers. pl. / *sobreseer.*

sobreseyesen that they might stay; imp. subj. 3rd pers. pl. / *sobreseer.*

sobreseyeses that you might stay; imp. subj. 2nd pers. sing. / *sobreseer.*

sobreseyó he (she/it) stayed; past 3rd pers. sing. / *sobreseer.*

sobreven (you) happen; impve. 2nd pers. sing. / *sobrevenir.*

sobrevendrá he (she/it) will happen; fut. 3rd pers. sing. / *sobrevenir.*

sobrevendrán they will happen; fut. 3rd pers. pl. / *sobrevenir.*

sobrevendrás you will happen; fut. 2nd pers. sing. / *sobrevenir.*

sobrevendré I shall happen; fut. 1st pers. sing. / *sobrevenir.*

sobrevendréis you (all) will happen; fut. 2nd pers. pl. / *sobrevenir.*

sobrevendremos we shall happen; fut. 1st pers. pl. / *sobrevenir.*

sobrevendría 1. I should happen; cond. 1st pers. sing. / *sobrevenir.* 2. he (she/it) would happen; cond. 3rd pers. sing.

sobrevendríais you (all) would happen; cond. 2nd pers. pl. / *sobrevenir.*

sobrevendríamos we should happen; cond. 1st pers. pl. / *sobrevenir.*

sobrevendrían they would happen; cond. 3rd pers. pl. / *sobrevenir.*

sobrevendrías you would happen; cond. 2nd pers. sing. / *sobrevenir.*

sobrevenga 1. that I may happen; pres. subj. 1st pers. sing. / *sobrevenir.* 2. that he (she/it) may happen; pres. subj. 3rd pers. sing. 3. let him (her/it) happen; impve. 3rd pers. sing.

sobrevengáis that you (all) may happen; pres. subj. 2nd pers. pl. / *sobrevenir.*

sobrevengamos 1. that we may happen; pres. subj. 1st pers. pl. / *sobrevenir*. 2. let us happen; impve. 1st pers. pl.

sobrevengan 1. that they may happen; pres. subj. 3rd pers. pl. / *sobrevenir*. 2. let them happen; impve. 3rd pers. pl.

sobrevengas that you may happen; pres. subj. 2nd pers. sing. / *sobrevenir*.

sobrevengo I happen; pres. ind. 1st pers. sing. / *sobrevenir*.

sobrevenir to happen. irr.

sobreviene he (she/it) happens; pres. ind. 3rd pers. sing. / *sobrevenir*.

sobrevienen they happen; pres. ind. 3rd pers. pl. / *sobrevenir*.

sobrevienes you happen; pres. ind. 2nd pers. sing. / *sobrevenir*.

sobrevine I happened; past 1st pers. sing. / *sobrevenir*.

sobreviniendo happening; pres. part. / *sobrevenir*.

sobreviniera 1. that I might happen; imp. subj. 1st pers. sing. / *sobrevenir*. 2. that he (she/it) might happen; imp. subj. 3rd pers. sing.

sobrevinierais that you (all) might happen; imp. subj. 2nd pers pl. / *sobrevenir*.

sobreviniéramos that we might happen; imp. subj. 1st pers. pl. / *sobrevenir*.

sobrevinieran that they might happen; imp. subj. 3rd pers. pl. / *sobrevenir*.

sobrevinieras that you might happen; imp. subj. 2nd pers. sing. / *sobrevenir*.

sobrevinieron they happened; past 3rd pers. pl. / *sobrevenir*.

sobreviniese 1. that I might happen; imp. subj. 1st pers. sing. / *sobrevenir*. 2. that he (she/it) might happen; imp. subj. 3rd pers. sing.

sobrevinieseis that you (all) might happen; imp. subj. 2nd pers pl. / *sobrevenir*.

sobreviniésemos that we might happen; imp. subj. 1st pers. pl. / *sobrevenir*.

sobreviniesen that they might happen; imp. subj. 3rd pers. pl. / *sobrevenir*.

sobrevinieses that you might happen; imp. subj. 2nd pers. sing. / *sobrevenir*.

sobrevinimos we happened; past 1st pers. pl. / *sobrevenir*.

sobreviniste you happened; past 2nd pers. sing. / *sobrevenir*.

sobrevinisteis you (all) happened; past 2nd pers. pl. / *sobrevenir*.

sobrevino he (she/it) happened; past 3rd pers. sing. / *sobrevenir*.

sobrevivir to survive. reg.

sobrexceder to exceed. reg.

sobrexcitar to overexcite. reg.

socaliñar to wheedle. reg.

socarrar to singe. reg.

socavar to undermine. reg.

socialice 1. that I may socialize; pres. subj. 1st pers. sing. / *socializar*. 2. that he (she/it) may socialize; pres. subj. 3rd pers. sing. 3. let him (her/it) socialize; impve. 3rd pers. sing.

socialicé I socialized; past 1st pers. sing. / *socializar*.

socialicéis that you (all) may socialize; pres. subj. 2nd pers. pl. / *socializar*.

socialicemos 1. that we may socialize; pres. subj. 1st pers. pl. / *socializar*. 2. let us socialize; impve. 1st pers. pl.

socialicen 1. that they may socialize; pres. subj. 3rd pers. pl. / *socializar*. 2. let them socialize; impve. 3rd pers. pl.

socialices that you may socialize; pres. subj. 2nd pers. sing. / *socializar*.

socializar to socialize. irr.

socorrer to succor. reg.

sofisticar to sophisticate or to falsify. irr.

sofistique 1. that I may sophisticate; pres. subj. 1st pers. sing. / *sofisticar*. 2. that he (she/it) may sophisticate; pres. subj. 3rd pers. sing. 3. let him (her/it) sophisticate; impve. 3rd pers. sing.

sofistiqué I sophisticated; past 1st pers. sing. / *sofisticar*.

sofistiquéis that you (all) may sophisticate; pres. subj. 2nd pers. pl. / *sofisticar*.

sofistiquemos 1. that we may sophisticate; pres. subj. 1st pers. pl. / *sofisticar*. 2. let us sophisticate; impve. 1st pers. pl.

sofistiquen 1. that they may sophisticate; pres. subj. 3rd pers. pl. / *sofisticar*. 2. let them sophisticate; impve. 3rd pers. pl.

sofistiques that you may sophisticate; pres. subj. 2nd pers. sing. / *sofisticar*.

soflamándose getting scorched; pres. part. / *soflamarse*.

soflamaos (you all) get scorched; impve. 2nd pers. pl. / *soflamarse*.

soflamar to embarrass. reg.

soflamarse to get scorched. reg.

soflámate (you) get scorched; impve. 2nd pers. sing. / *soflamarse*.

soflamémonos let us get scorched; impve. 1st pers. pl. / *soflamarse*.

soflámense let them get scorched; impve. 3rd pers. pl. / *soflamarse*.

soflámese let him (her/it) get scorched; impve. 3rd pers. sing. / *soflamarse*.

sofocándose suffocating; pres. part. / *sofocarse*.

sofocaos (you all) suffocate; impve. 2nd pers. pl. / *sofocarse*.

sofocar to suffocate. irr.

sofocarse to suffocate. irr.

sofócate (you) suffocate; impve. 2nd pers. sing. / *sofocarse*.

sofoque 1. that I may suffocate; pres. subj. 1st pers. sing. / *sofocar*. 2. that he (she/it) may suffocate; pres. subj. 3rd pers. sing. 3. let him (her/it) suffocate; impve. 3rd pers. sing.

sofoqué I suffocated; past 1st pers. sing. / *sofocar*.

sofoquéis that you (all) may suffocate; pres. subj. 2nd pers. pl. / *sofocar.*

sofoquémonos let us suffocate; impve. 1st pers. pl. / *sofocarse.*

sofoquemos 1. that we may suffocate; pres. subj. 1st pers. pl. / *sofocar.* 2. let us suffocate; impve. 1st pers. pl.

sofoquen 1. that they may suffocate; pres. subj. 3rd pers. pl. / *sofocar.* 2. let them suffocate; impve. 3rd pers. pl.

sofóquense let them suffocate; impve. 3rd pers. pl. / *sofocarse.*

sofoques that you may suffocate; pres. subj. 2nd pers. sing. / *sofocar.*

sofóquese let him (her/it) suffocate; impve. 3rd pers. sing. / *sofocarse.*

sofreír to fry lightly. irr.

sofrenar to check or to curb. reg.

sofría 1. that I may fry lightly; pres. subj. 1st pers. sing. / *sofreír.* 2. that he (she/it) may fry lightly; pres. subj. 3rd pers. sing. 3. let him (her/it) fry lightly; impve. 3rd pers. sing.

sofriáis that you (all) may fry lightly; pres. subj. 2nd pers. pl. / *sofreír.*

sofriamos 1. that we may fry lightly; pres. subj. 1st pers. pl. / *sofreír.* 2. let us fry lightly; impve. 1st pers. pl.

sofrían 1. that they may fry lightly; pres. subj. 3rd pers. pl. / *sofreír.* 2. let them fry lightly; impve. 3rd pers. pl.

sofrías that you may fry lightly; pres. subj. 2nd pers. sing. / *sofreír.*

sofríe 1. he (she/it) fries lightly; pres. ind. 3rd pers. sing. / *sofreír.* 2. (you) fry lightly; impve. 2nd pers. sing.

sofríen they fry lightly; pres. ind. 3rd pers. pl. / *sofreír.*

sofriendo frying lightly; pres. part. / *sofreír.*

sofriera 1. that I might fry lightly; imp. subj. 1st pers. sing. / *sofreír.* 2. that he (she/it) might fry lightly; imp. subj. 3rd pers. sing.

sofrierais that you (all) might fry lightly; imp. subj. 2nd pers pl. / *sofreír.*

sofriéramos that we might fry lightly; imp. subj. 1st pers. pl. / *sofreír.*

sofrieran that they might fry lightly; imp. subj. 3rd pers. pl. / *sofreír.*

sofrieras that you might fry lightly; imp. subj. 2nd pers. sing. / *sofreír.*

sofrieron they fried lightly; past 3rd pers. pl. / *sofreír.*

sofríes you fry lightly; pres. ind. 2nd pers. sing. / *sofreír.*

sofriese 1. that I might fry lightly; imp. subj. 1st pers. sing. / *sofreír.* 2. that he (she/it) might fry lightly; imp. subj. 3rd pers. sing.

sofrieseis that you (all) might fry lightly; imp. subj. 2nd pers pl. / *sofreír.*

sofriésemos that we might fry lightly; imp. subj. 1st pers. pl. / *sofreír.*

sofriesen that they might fry lightly; imp. subj. 3rd pers. pl. / *sofreír.*

sofrieses that you might fry lightly; imp. subj. 2nd pers. sing. / *sofreír.*

sofrío I fry lightly; pres. ind. 1st pers. sing. / *sofreír.*

sofrió he (she/it) fried lightly; past 3rd pers. sing. / *sofreír.*

sofrito fried lightly; past part. / *sofreír.*

sois you (all) are; pres. ind. 2nd pers. pl. / *ser.*

sojuzgar to subjugate. irr.

sojuzgue 1. that I may subjugate; pres. subj. 1st pers. sing. / *sojuzgar.* 2. that he (she/it) may subjugate; pres. subj. 3rd pers. sing. 3. let him (her/it) subjugate; impve. 3rd pers. sing.

sojuzgué I subjugated; past 1st pers. sing. / *sojuzgar.*

sojuzguéis that you (all) may subjugate; pres. subj. 2nd pers. pl. / *sojuzgar.*

sojuzguemos 1. that we may subjugate; pres. subj. 1st pers. pl. / *sojuzgar.* 2. let us subjugate; impve. 1st pers. pl.

sojuzguen 1. that they may subjugate; pres. subj. 3rd pers. pl. / *sojuzgar.* 2. let them subjugate; impve. 3rd pers. pl.

sojuzgues that you may subjugate; pres. subj. 2nd pers. sing. / *sojuzgar.*

solace 1. that I may solace; pres. subj. 1st pers. sing. / *solazar.* 2. that he (she/it) may solace; pres. subj. 3rd pers. sing. 3. let him (her/it) solace; impve. 3rd pers. sing.

solacé I solaced; past 1st pers. sing. / *solazar.*

solacear to solace. reg.

solacéis that you (all) may solace; pres. subj. 2nd pers. pl. / *solazar.*

solacémonos let us seek relaxation; impve. 1st pers. pl. / *solazarse.*

solacemos 1. that we may solace; pres. subj. 1st pers. pl. / *solazar.* 2. let us solace; impve. 1st pers. pl.

solacen 1. that they may solace; pres. subj. 3rd pers. pl. / *solazar.* 2. let them solace; impve. 3rd pers. pl.

solácense let them seek relaxation; impve. 3rd pers. pl. / *solazarse.*

solaces that you may solace; pres. subj. 2nd pers. sing. / *solazar.*

solácese let him (her/it) seek relaxation; impve. 3rd pers. sing. / *solazarse.*

solapar to overlap or to conceal. reg.

solar to sole shoes or to pave. irr.

solazándose seeking relaxation; pres. part. / *solazarse.*

solazaos (you all) seek relaxation; impve. 2nd pers. pl. / *solazarse.*

solazar to solace. irr.

solazarse to seek relaxation. irr.

solázate (you) seek relaxation; impve. 2nd pers. sing. / *solazarse.*

soldar to solder. irr.

solear to sun. reg.

solemnice 1. that I may solemnize; pres. subj. 1st pers. sing. / *solemnizar.* 2. that he (she/it) may solemnize; pres. subj. 3rd pers. sing. 3. let him (her/it) solemnize; impve. 3rd pers. sing.

solemnicé I solemnized; past 1st pers. sing. / *solemnizar.*

solemnicéis that you (all) may solemnize; pres. subj. 2nd pers. pl. / *solemnizar.*

solemnicemos 1. that we may solemnize; pres. subj. 1st pers. pl. / *solemnizar.* 2. let us solemnize; impve. 1st pers. pl.

solemnicen 1. that they may solemnize; pres. subj. 3rd pers. pl. / *solemnizar.* 2. let them solemnize; impve. 3rd pers. pl.

solemnices that you may solemnize; pres. subj. 2nd pers. sing. / *solemnizar.*

solemnizar to solemnize. irr.

soler to be used to. irr.

solevándose rebelling; pres. part. / *solevarse.*

solevantándose rebelling; pres. part. / *solevantarse.*

solevantaos (you all) rebel; impve. 2nd pers. pl. / *solevantarse.*

solevantar to agitate. reg.

solevantarse to rebel. reg.

solevántate (you) rebel; impve. 2nd pers. sing. / *solevantarse.*

solevantémonos let us rebel; impve. 1st pers. pl. / *solevantarse.*

solevántense let them rebel; impve. 3rd pers. pl. / *solevantarse.*

solevántese let him (her/it) rebel; impve. 3rd pers. sing. / *solevantarse.*

solevaos (you all) rebel; impve. 2nd pers. pl. / *solevarse.*

solevar to agitate. reg.

solevarse to rebel. reg.

solévate (you) rebel; impve. 2nd pers. sing. / *solevarse.*

solevémonos let us rebel; impve. 1st pers. pl. / *solevarse.*

solévense let them rebel; impve. 3rd pers. pl. / *solevarse.*

solévese let him (her/it) rebel; impve. 3rd pers. sing. / *solevarse.*

solfear to sing. reg.

solicitar to solicit. reg.

solidar to affirm. reg.

solidarice 1. that I may unite; pres. subj. 1st pers. sing. / *solidarizar.* 2. that he (she/it) may unite; pres. subj. 3rd pers. sing. 3. let him (her/it) unite; impve. 3rd pers. sing.

solidaricé I united; past 1st pers. sing. / *solidarizar.*

solidaricéis that you (all) may unite; pres. subj. 2nd pers. pl. / *solidarizar.*

solidaricémonos let us stand together with; impve. 1st pers. pl. / *solidarizarse.*

solidaricemos 1. that we may unite; pres. subj. 1st pers. pl. / *solidarizar.* 2. let us unite; impve. 1st pers. pl.

solidaricen 1. that they may unite; pres. subj. 3rd pers. pl. / *solidarizar.* 2. let them unite; impve. 3rd pers. pl.

solidarícense let them stand together with; impve. 3rd pers. pl. / *solidarizarse.*

solidarices that you may unite; pres. subj. 2nd pers. sing. / *solidarizar.*

solidarícese let him (her/it) stand together with; impve. 3rd pers. sing. / *solidarizarse.*

solidarizándose standing together with; pres. part. / *solidarizarse.*

solidarizaos (you all) stand together with; impve. 2nd pers. pl. / *solidarizarse.*

solidarizar to unite. irr.

solidarizarse to stand together with. irr.

solidarízate (you) stand together with; impve. 2nd pers. sing. / *solidarizarse.*

solidificándose solidifying; pres. part. / *solidificarse.*

solidificaos (you all) solidify; impve. 2nd pers. pl. / *solidificarse.*

solidificar to solidify. irr.

solidificarse to solidify. irr.

solidifícate (you) solidify; impve. 2nd pers. sing. / *solidificarse.*

solidifique 1. that I may solidify; pres. subj. 1st pers. sing. / *solidificar.* 2. that he (she/it) may solidify; pres. subj. 3rd pers. sing. 3. let him (her/it) solidify; impve. 3rd pers. sing.

solidifiqué I solidified; past 1st pers. sing. / *solidificar.*

solidifiquéis that you (all) may solidify; pres. subj. 2nd pers. pl. / *solidificar.*

solidifiquémonos let us solidify; impve. 1st pers. pl. / *solidificarse.*

solidifiquemos 1. that we may solidify; pres. subj. 1st pers. pl. / *solidificar.* 2. let us solidify; impve. 1st pers. pl.

solidifiquen 1. that they may solidify; pres. subj. 3rd pers. pl. / *solidificar.* 2. let them solidify; impve. 3rd pers. pl.

solidifíquense let them solidify; impve. 3rd pers. pl. / *solidificarse.*

solidifiques that you may solidify; pres. subj. 2nd pers. sing. / *solidificar.*

solidifíquese let him (her/it) solidify; impve. 3rd pers. sing. / *solidificarse.*

soliloquiar to soliloquize. reg.

soliviantar to incite. reg.

soliviar to raise. reg.

soltándose loosening; pres. part. / *soltarse.*

soltaos (you all) loosen; impve. 2nd pers. pl. / *soltarse.*

soltar to untie. irr.

soltarse to loosen. irr.

soltémonos let us loosen; impve. 1st pers. pl. / *soltarse.*

solucionar to solve. reg.

solventar to settle a debt. reg.

sollamar to singe. reg.

solloce 1. that I may sob; pres. subj. 1st pers. sing. / *sollozar.* 2. that he (she/it) may sob; pres. subj. 3rd pers. sing. 3. let him (her/it) sob; impve. 3rd pers. sing.

sollocé I sobbed; past 1st pers. sing. / *sollozar.*

sollocéis that you (all) may sob; pres. subj. 2nd pers. pl. / *sollozar*.

sollocemos 1. that we may sob; pres. subj. 1st pers. pl. / *sollozar*. 2. let us sob; impve. 1st pers. pl.

sollocen 1. that they may sob; pres. subj. 3rd pers. pl. / *sollozar*. 2. let them sob; impve. 3rd pers. pl.

solloces that you may sob; pres. subj. 2nd pers. sing. / *sollozar*.

sollozar to sob. irr.

sombrar to shade. reg.

sombreándose seeking shade; pres. part. / *sombrearse*.

sombreaos (you all) seek shade; impve. 2nd pers. pl. / *sombrearse*.

sombrear to shade. reg.

sombrearse to seek shade. reg.

sombréate (you) seek shade; impve. 2nd pers. sing. / *sombrearse*.

sombreémonos let us seek shade; impve. 1st pers. pl. / *sombrearse*.

sombréense let them seek shade; impve. 3rd pers. pl. / *sombrearse*.

sombréese let him (her/it) seek shade; impve. 3rd pers. sing. / *sombrearse*.

sometámonos let us submit; impve. 1st pers. pl. / *someterse*.

sométanse let them submit; impve. 3rd pers. pl. / *someterse*.

sométase let him (her/it) submit; impve. 3rd pers. sing. / *someterse*.

someteos (you all) submit; impve. 2nd pers. pl. / *someterse*.

someter to subdue. reg.

someterse to submit. reg.

sométete (you) submit; impve. 2nd pers. sing. / *someterse*.

sometiéndose submitting; pres. part. / *someterse*.

somorgujándose ducking; pres. part. / *somorgujarse*.

somorgujaos (you all) duck; impve. 2nd pers. pl. / *somorgujarse*.

somorgujar to dive or to dip. reg.

somorgujarse to duck. reg.

somorgújate (you) duck; impve. 2nd pers. sing. / *somorgujarse*.

somorgujémonos let us duck; impve. 1st pers. pl. / *somorgujarse*.

somorgújense let them duck; impve. 3rd pers. pl. / *somorgujarse*.

somorgújese let him (her/it) duck; impve. 3rd pers. sing. / *somorgujarse*.

somos we are; pres. ind. 1st pers. pl. / *ser*.

son they are; pres. ind. 3rd pers. pl. / *ser*.

sonándose blowing one's nose; pres. part. / *sonarse*.

sonaos (you all) blow your noses; impve. 2nd pers. pl. / *sonarse*.

sonar to sound. irr.

sonarse to blow one's nose. irr.

sondar to sound or to probe. reg.

sondear to sound or to fathom. reg.

sonémonos let us blow our noses; impve. 1st pers. pl. / *sonarse*.

sonorice 1. that I may voice; pres. subj. 1st pers. sing. / *sonorizar*. 2. that he (she/it) may voice; pres. subj. 3rd pers. sing. 3. let him (her/it) voice; impve. 3rd pers. sing.

sonoricé I voiced; past 1st pers. sing. / *sonorizar*.

sonoricéis that you (all) may voice; pres. subj. 2nd pers. pl. / *sonorizar*.

sonoricemos 1. that we may voice; pres. subj. 1st pers. pl. / *sonorizar*. 2. let us voice; impve. 1st pers. pl.

sonoricen 1. that they may voice; pres. subj. 3rd pers. pl. / *sonorizar*. 2. let them voice; impve. 3rd pers. pl.

sonorices that you may voice; pres. subj. 2nd pers. sing. / *sonorizar*.

sonorizar to voice. irr.

sonreíos (you all) smile; impve. 2nd pers. pl. / *sonreírse*.

sonreír to smile. irr.

sonreírse to smile. irr.

sonría 1. that I may smile; pres. subj. 1st pers. sing. / *sonreír*. 2. that he (she/it) may smile; pres. subj. 3rd pers. sing. 3. let him (her/it) smile; impve. 3rd pers. sing.

sonriáis that you (all) may smile; pres. subj. 2nd pers. pl. / *sonreír*.

sonriámonos let us smile; impve. 1st pers. pl. / *sonreírse*.

sonriamos 1. that we may smile; pres. subj. 1st pers. pl. / *sonreír*. 2. let us smile; impve. 1st pers. pl.

sonrían 1. that they may smile; pres. subj. 3rd pers. pl. / *sonreír*. 2. let them smile; impve. 3rd pers. pl.

sonríanse let them smile; impve. 3rd pers. pl. / *sonreírse*.

sonrías that you may smile; pres. subj. 2nd pers. sing. / *sonreír*.

sonríase let him (her/it) smile; impve. 3rd pers. sing. / *sonreírse*.

sonríe 1. he (she/it) smiles; pres. ind. 3rd pers. sing. / *sonreír*. 2. (you) smile; impve. 2nd pers. sing.

sonríen they smile; pres. ind. 3rd pers. pl. / *sonreír*.

sonriendo smiling; pres. part. / *sonreír*.

sonriéndose smiling; pres. part. / *sonreírse*.

sonriera 1. that I might smile; imp. subj. 1st pers. sing. / *sonreír*. 2. that he (she/it) might smile; imp. subj. 3rd pers. sing.

sonrierais that you (all) might smile; imp. subj. 2nd pers pl. / *sonreír*.

sonriéramos that we might smile; imp. subj. 1st pers. pl. / *sonreír*.

sonrieran that they might smile; imp. subj. 3rd pers. pl. / *sonreír*.

sonrieras that you might smile; imp. subj. 2nd pers. sing. / *sonreír*.

sonrieron they smiled; past 3rd pers. pl. / *sonreír*.

sonríes you smile; pres. ind. 2nd pers. sing. / *sonreír*.

sonriese 1. that I might smile; imp. subj. 1st pers. sing. / *sonreír*. 2. that he (she/it) might smile; imp. subj. 3rd pers. sing.

sonrieseis that you (all) might smile; imp. subj. 2nd pers pl. / *sonreír.*

sonriésemos that we might smile; imp. subj. 1st pers. pl. / *sonreír.*

sonriesen that they might smile; imp. subj. 3rd pers. pl. / *sonreír.*

sonrieses that you might smile; imp. subj. 2nd pers. sing. / *sonreír.*

sonríete (you) smile; impve. 2nd pers. sing. / *sonreírse.*

sonrío I smile; pres. ind. 1st pers. sing. / *sonreír.*

sonrió he (she/it) smiled; past 3rd pers. sing. / *sonreír.*

sonrojándose blushing; pres. part. / *sonrojarse.*

sonrojaos (you all) blush; impve. 2nd pers. pl. / *sonrojarse.*

sonrojar to make blush. reg.

sonrojarse to blush. reg.

sonrójate (you) blush; impve. 2nd pers. sing. / *sonrojarse.*

sonrojeándose blushing; pres. part. / *sonrojearse.*

sonrojeaos (you all) blush; impve. 2nd pers. pl. / *sonrojearse.*

sonrojear to make blush. reg.

sonrojearse to blush. reg.

sonrojéate (you) blush; impve. 2nd pers. sing. / *sonrojearse.*

sonrojeémonos let us blush; impve. 1st pers. pl. / *sonrojearse.*

sonrojéense let them blush; impve. 3rd pers. pl. / *sonrojearse.*

sonrojéese let him (her/it) blush; impve. 3rd pers. sing. / *sonrojearse.*

sonrojémonos let us blush; impve. 1st pers. pl. / *sonrojarse.*

sonrójense let them blush; impve. 3rd pers. pl. / *sonrojarse.*

sonrójese let him (her/it) blush; impve. 3rd pers. sing. / *sonrojarse.*

sonrosar to make blush. reg.

sonrosear to make blush. reg.

sonsacar to lure away. irr.

sonsaque 1. that I may lure away; pres. subj. 1st pers. sing. / *sonsacar.* 2. that he (she/it) may lure away; pres. subj. 3rd pers. sing. 3. let him (her/it) lure away; impve. 3rd pers. sing.

sonsaqué I lured away; past 1st pers. sing. / *sonsacar.*

sonsaquéis that you (all) may lure away; pres. subj. 2nd pers. pl. / *sonsacar.*

sonsaquemos 1. that we may lure away; pres. subj. 1st pers. pl. / *sonsacar.* 2. let us lure away; impve. 1st pers. pl.

sonsaquen 1. that they may lure away; pres. subj. 3rd pers. pl. / *sonsacar.* 2. let them lure away; impve. 3rd pers. pl.

sonsaques that you may lure away; pres. subj. 2nd pers. sing. / *sonsacar.*

soñar to dream. irr.

sopar to steep or to trample on. reg.

sopear to steep or to trample on. reg.

sopesar to try the weight of. reg.

sopetear to sop or to dunk. reg.

soplándose getting puffed up; pres. part. / *soplarse.*

soplaos (you all) get puffed up; impve. 2nd pers. pl. / *soplarse.*

soplar to blow. reg.

soplarse to get puffed up. reg.

sóplate (you) get puffed up; impve. 2nd pers. sing. / *soplarse.*

soplémonos let us get puffed up; impve. 1st pers. pl. / *soplarse.*

sóplense let them get puffed up; impve. 3rd pers. pl. / *soplarse.*

sóplese let him (her/it) get puffed up; impve. 3rd pers. sing. / *soplarse.*

soportar to support. reg.

sopuntar to underscore with dots. reg.

sorbámonos let us swallow; impve. 1st pers. pl. / *sorberse.*

sórbanse let them swallow; impve. 3rd pers. pl. / *sorberse.*

sórbase let him (her/it) swallow; impve. 3rd pers. sing. / *sorberse.*

sorbeos (you all) swallow; impve. 2nd pers. pl. / *sorberse.*

sorber to sip. reg.

sorberse to swallow. reg.

sórbete (you) swallow; impve. 2nd pers. sing. / *sorberse.*

sorbiéndose swallowing; pres. part. / *sorberse.*

sorprendámonos let us be surprised; impve. 1st pers. pl. / *sorprenderse.*

sorpréndanse let them be surprised; impve. 3rd pers. pl. / *sorprenderse.*

sorpréndase let him (her/it) be surprised; impve. 3rd pers. sing. / *sorprenderse.*

sorprendeos (you all) be surprised; impve. 2nd pers. pl. / *sorprenderse.*

sorprender to surprise. reg.

sorprenderse to be surprised. reg.

sorpréndete (you) be surprised; impve. 2nd pers. sing. / *sorprenderse.*

sorprendiéndose being surprised; pres. part. / *sorprenderse.*

sortear to raffle or to draw lots. reg.

sosegándose quieting down; pres. part. / *sosegarse.*

sosegaos (you all) quiet down; impve. 2nd pers. pl. / *sosegarse.*

sosegar to calm. irr.

sosegarse to quiet down. irr.

sosegué I calmed; past 1st pers. sing. / *sosegar.*

soseguéis that you (all) may calm; pres. subj. 2nd pers. pl. / *sosegar.*

soseguémonos let us quiet down; impve. 1st pers. pl. / *sosegarse.*

soseguemos 1. that we may calm; pres. subj. 1st pers. pl. / *sosegar.* 2. let us calm; impve. 1st pers. pl.

sosiega 1. he (she/it) calms; pres. ind. 3rd pers. sing. / *sosegar.* 2. (you) calm; impve. 2nd pers. sing.

sosiegan they calm; pres. ind. 3rd pers. pl. / *sosegar.*
sosiegas you calm; pres. ind. 2nd pers. sing. / *sosegar.*
sosiégate (you) quiet down; impve. 2nd pers. sing. / *sosegarse.*
sosiego I calm; pres. ind. 1st pers. sing. / *sosegar.*
sosiegue 1. that I may calm; pres. subj. 1st pers. sing. / *sosegar.* 2. that he (she/it) may calm; pres. subj. 3rd pers. sing. 3. let him (her/it) calm; impve. 3rd pers. sing.
sosieguen 1. that they may calm; pres. subj. 3rd pers. pl. / *sosegar.* 2. let them calm; impve. 3rd pers. pl.
sosiéguense let them quiet down; impve. 3rd pers. pl. / *sosegarse.*
sosiegues that you may calm; pres. subj. 2nd pers. sing. / *sosegar.*
sosiéguese let him (her/it) quiet down; impve. 3rd pers. sing. / *sosegarse.*
soslayar to avoid. reg.
sospechar to suspect. reg.
sosten (you) support; impve. 2nd pers. sing. / *sostener.*
sostendrá he (she/it) will support; fut. 3rd pers. sing. / *sostener.*
sostendrán they will support; fut. 3rd pers. pl. / *sostener.*
sostendrás you will support; fut. 2nd pers. sing. / *sostener.*
sostendré I shall support; fut. 1st pers. sing. / *sostener.*
sostendréis you (all) will support; fut. 2nd pers. pl. / *sostener.*
sostendremos we shall support; fut. 1st pers. pl. / *sostener.*
sostendría 1. I should support; cond. 1st pers. sing. / *sostener.* 2. he (she/it) would support; cond. 3rd pers. sing.
sostendríais you (all) would support; cond. 2nd pers. pl. / *sostener.*
sostendríamos we should support; cond. 1st pers. pl. / *sostener.*
sostendrían they would support; cond. 3rd pers. pl. / *sostener.*
sostendrías you would support; cond. 2nd pers. sing. / *sostener.*
sosteneos (you all) support yourselves; impve. 2nd pers. pl. / *sostenerse.*
sostener to support. irr.
sostenerse to support oneself. irr.
sosténete (you) support yourself; impve. 2nd pers. sing. / *sostenerse.*
sostenga 1. that I may support; pres. subj. 1st pers. sing. / *sostener.* 2. that he (she/it) may support; pres. subj. 3rd pers. sing. 3. let him (her/it) support; impve. 3rd pers. sing.
sostengáis that you (all) may support; pres. subj. 2nd pers. pl. / *sostener.*
sostengámonos let us support ourselves; impve. 1st pers. pl. / *sostenerse.*
sostengamos 1. that we may support; pres. subj. 1st pers. pl. / *sostener.* 2. let us support; impve. 1st pers. pl.

sostengan 1. that they may support; pres. subj. 3rd pers. pl. / *sostener.* 2. let them support; impve. 3rd pers. pl.
sosténganse let them support themselves; impve. 3rd pers. pl. / *sostenerse.*
sostengas that you may support; pres. subj. 2nd pers. sing. / *sostener.*
sosténgase let him (her/it) support himself (herself/itself); impve. 3rd pers. sing. / *sostenerse.*
sostengo I support; pres. ind. 1st pers. sing. / *sostener.*
sosteniendo supporting; pres. part. / *sostener.*
sosteniéndose supporting oneself; pres. part. / *sostenerse.*
sostiene he (she/it) supports; pres. ind. 3rd pers. sing. / *sostener.*
sostienen they support; pres. ind. 3rd pers. pl. / *sostener.*
sostienes you support; pres. ind. 2nd pers. sing. / *sostener.*
sostuve I supported; past 1st pers. sing. / *sostener.*
sostuviera 1. that I might support; imp. subj. 1st pers. sing. / *sostener.* 2. that he (she/it) might support; imp. subj. 3rd pers. sing.
sostuvierais that you (all) might support; imp. subj. 2nd pers pl. / *sostener.*
sostuviéramos that we might support; imp. subj. 1st pers. pl. / *sostener.*
sostuvieran that they might support; imp. subj. 3rd pers. pl. / *sostener.*
sostuvieras that you might support; imp. subj. 2nd pers. sing. / *sostener.*
sostuvieron they supported; past 3rd pers. pl. / *sostener.*
sostuviese 1. that I might support; imp. subj. 1st pers. sing. / *sostener.* 2. that he (she/it) might support; imp. subj. 3rd pers. sing.
sostuvieseis that you (all) might support; imp. subj. 2nd pers pl. / *sostener.*
sostuviésemos that we might support; imp. subj. 1st pers. pl. / *sostener.*
sostuviesen that they might support; imp. subj. 3rd pers. pl. / *sostener.*
sostuvieses that you might support; imp. subj. 2nd pers. sing. / *sostener.*
sostuvimos we supported; past 1st pers. pl. / *sostener.*
sostuviste you supported; past 2nd pers. sing. / *sostener.*
sostuvisteis you (all) supported; past 2nd pers. pl. / *sostener.*
sostuvo he (she/it) supported; past 3rd pers. sing. / *sostener.*
soterrar to bury. irr.
sotierra 1. he (she/it) buries; pres. ind. 3rd pers. sing. / *soterrar.* 2. (you) bury; impve. 2nd pers. sing.
sotierran they bury; pres. ind. 3rd pers. pl. / *soterrar.*
sotierras you bury; pres. ind. 2nd pers. sing. / *soterrar.*

sotierre 1. that I may bury; pres. subj. 1st pers. sing. / *soterrar.* 2. that he (she/it) may bury; pres. subj. 3rd pers. sing. 3. let him (her/it) bury; impve. 3rd pers. sing.

sotierren 1. that they may bury; pres. subj. 3rd pers. pl. / *soterrar.* 2. let them bury; impve. 3rd pers. pl.

sotierres that you may bury; pres. subj. 2nd pers. sing. / *soterrar.*

sotierro I bury; pres. ind. 1st pers. sing. / *soterrar.*

soy I am; pres. ind. 1st pers. sing. / *ser.*

suavice 1. that I may smooth; pres. subj. 1st pers. sing. / *suavizar.* 2. that he (she/it) may smooth; pres. subj. 3rd pers. sing. 3. let him (her/it) smooth; impve. 3rd pers. sing.

suavicé I smoothed; past 1st pers. sing. / *suavizar.*

suavicéis that you (all) may smooth; pres. subj. 2nd pers. pl. / *suavizar.*

suavicémonos let us calm down; impve. 1st pers. pl. / *suavizarse.*

suavicemos 1. that we may smooth; pres. subj. 1st pers. pl. / *suavizar.* 2. let us smooth; impve. 1st pers. pl.

suavicen 1. that they may smooth; pres. subj. 3rd pers. pl. / *suavizar.* 2. let them smooth; impve. 3rd pers. pl.

suavícense let them calm down; impve. 3rd pers. pl. / *suavizarse.*

suavices that you may smooth; pres. subj. 2nd pers. sing. / *suavizar.*

suavícese let him (her/it) calm down; impve. 3rd pers. sing. / *suavizarse.*

suavizándose calming down; pres. part. / *suavizarse.*

suavizaos (you all) calm down; impve. 2nd pers. pl. / *suavizarse.*

suavizar to smooth or to soften. irr.

suavizarse to calm down. irr.

suavízate (you) calm down; impve. 2nd pers. sing. / *suavizarse.*

subámonos let us rise; impve. 1st pers. pl. / *subirse.*

súbanse let them rise; impve. 3rd pers. pl. / *subirse.*

subarrendar to sublet. irr.

subarrienda 1. he (she/it) sublets; pres. ind. 3rd pers. sing. / *subarrendar.* 2. (you) sublet; impve. 2nd pers. sing.

subarriendan they sublet; pres. ind. 3rd pers. pl. / *subarrendar.*

subarriendas you sublet; pres. ind. 2nd pers. sing. / *subarrendar.*

subarriende 1. that I may sublet; pres. subj. 1st pers. sing. / *subarrendar.* 2. that he (she/it) may sublet; pres. subj. 3rd pers. sing. 3. let him (her/it) sublet; impve. 3rd pers. sing.

subarrienden 1. that they may sublet; pres. subj. 3rd pers. pl. / *subarrendar.* 2. let them sublet; impve. 3rd pers. pl.

subarriendes that you may sublet; pres. subj. 2nd pers. sing. / *subarrendar.*

subarriendo I sublet; pres. ind. 1st pers. sing. / *subarrendar.*

súbase let him (her/it) rise; impve. 3rd pers. sing. / *subirse.*

subastar to auction. reg.

subcontrar to subcontract. reg.

subdividir to subdivide. reg.

subentender to gather. irr.

subentienda 1. that I may gather; pres. subj. 1st pers. sing. / *subentender.* 2. that he (she/it) may gather; pres. subj. 3rd pers. sing. 3. let him (her/it) gather; impve. 3rd pers. sing.

subentiendan 1. that they may gather; pres. subj. 3rd pers. pl. / *subentender.* 2. let them gather; impve. 3rd pers. pl.

subentiendas that you may gather; pres. subj. 2nd pers. sing. / *subentender.*

subentiende 1. he (she/it) gathers; pres. ind. 3rd pers. sing. / *subentender.* 2. (you) gather; impve. 2nd pers. sing.

subentienden they gather; pres. ind. 3rd pers. pl. / *subentender.*

subentiendes you gather; pres. ind. 2nd pers. sing. / *subentender.*

subentiendo I gather; pres. ind. 1st pers. sing. / *subentender.*

subestimar to underestimate. reg.

súbete (you) rise; impve. 2nd pers. sing. / *subirse.*

subiéndose rising; pres. part. / *subirse.*

subíos (you all) rise; impve. 2nd pers. pl. / *subirse.*

subir to ascend. reg.

subirse to rise. reg.

sublevándose revolting; pres. part. / *sublevarse.*

sublevaos (you all) revolt; impve. 2nd pers. pl. / *sublevarse.*

sublevar to excite to rebellion. reg.

sublevarse to revolt. reg.

sublévate (you) revolt; impve. 2nd pers. sing. / *sublevarse.*

sublevémonos let us revolt; impve. 1st pers. pl. / *sublevarse.*

sublévense let them revolt; impve. 3rd pers. pl. / *sublevarse.*

sublévese let him (her/it) revolt; impve. 3rd pers. sing. / *sublevarse.*

sublimar to sublimate. reg.

subordinar to subordinate. reg.

subrayar to underline. reg.

subrogar to subrogate or to substitute. irr.

subrogue 1. that I may subrogate; pres. subj. 1st pers. sing. / *subrogar.* 2. that he (she/it) may subrogate; pres. subj. 3rd pers. sing. 3. let him (her/it) subrogate; impve. 3rd pers. sing.

subrogué I subrogated; past 1st pers. sing. / *subrogar.*

subroguéis that you (all) may subrogate; pres. subj. 2nd pers. pl. / *subrogar.*

subroguemos 1. that we may subrogate; pres. subj. 1st pers. pl. / *subrogar.* 2. let us subrogate; impve. 1st pers. pl.

subroguen 1. that they may subrogate; pres. subj. 3rd pers. pl. / *subrogar.* 2. let them subrogate; impve. 3rd pers. pl.

subrogues that you may subrogate; pres. subj. 2nd pers. sing. / *subrogar.*

subsanar to excuse. reg.

subscribámonos let us subscribe; impve. 1st pers. pl. / *subscribirse.*

subscríbanse let them subscribe; impve. 3rd pers. pl. / *subscribirse.*

subscríbase let him (her/it) subscribe; impve. 3rd pers. sing. / *subscribirse.*

subscríbete (you) subscribe; impve. 2nd pers. sing. / *subscribirse.*

subscribiéndose subscribing; pres. part. / *subscribirse.*

subscribíos (you all) subscribe; impve. 2nd pers. pl. / *subscribirse.*

subscribir to subscribe. reg. except for pp.

subscribirse to subscribe. reg. except for pp.

subscrito subscribed; past part. / *subscribir.*

subséguete (you) follow next; impve. 2nd pers. sing. / *subseguirse.*

subseguíos (you all) follow next; impve. 2nd pers. pl. / *subseguirse.*

subseguir to follow next. irr.

subseguirse to follow next. irr.

subsidiar to subsidize. reg.

subsiga 1. that I may follow next; pres. subj. 1st pers. sing. / *subseguir.* 2. that he (she/it) may follow next; pres. subj. 3rd pers. sing. 3. let him (her/it) follow next; impve. 3rd pers. sing.

subsigáis that you (all) may follow next; pres. subj. 2nd pers. pl. / *subseguir.*

subsigámonos let us follow next; impve. 1st pers. pl. / *subseguir.*

subsigamos 1. that we may follow next; pres. subj. 1st pers. pl. / *subseguir.* 2. let us follow next; impve. 1st pers. pl.

subsigan 1. that they may follow next; pres. subj. 3rd pers. pl. / *subseguir.* 2. let them follow next; impve. 3rd pers. pl.

subsíganse let them follow next; impve. 3rd pers. pl. / *subseguirse.*

subsigas that you may follow next; pres. subj. 2nd pers. sing. / *subseguir.*

subsígase let him (her/it) follow next; impve. 3rd pers. sing. / *subseguirse.*

subsigo I follow next; pres. ind. 1st pers. sing. / *subseguir.*

subsigue 1. he (she/it) follows next; pres. ind. 3rd pers. sing. / *subseguir.* 2. (you) follow next; impve. 2nd pers. sing.

subsiguen they follow next; pres. ind. 3rd pers. pl. / *subseguir.*

subsigues you follow next; pres. ind. 2nd pers. sing. / *subseguir.*

subsiguiendo following next; pres. part. / *subseguir.*

subsiguiéndose following next; pres. part. / *subseguirse.*

subsiguiera 1. that I might follow next; imp. subj. 1st pers. sing. / *subseguir.* 2. that he (she/it) might follow next; imp. subj. 3rd pers. sing.

subsiguierais that you (all) might follow next; imp. subj. 2nd pers pl. / *subseguir.*

subsiguiéramos that we might follow next; imp. subj. 1st pers. pl. / *subseguir.*

subsiguieran that they might follow next; imp. subj. 3rd pers. pl. / *subseguir.*

subsiguieras that you might follow next; imp. subj. 2nd pers. sing. / *subseguir.*

subsiguieron they followed next; past 3rd pers. pl. / *subseguir.*

subsiguiese 1. that I might follow next; imp. subj. 1st pers. sing. / *subseguir.* 2. that he (she/it) might follow next; imp. subj. 3rd pers. sing.

subsiguieseis that you (all) might follow next; imp. subj. 2nd pers pl. / *subseguir.*

subsiguiésemos that we might follow next; imp. subj. 1st pers. pl. / *subseguir.*

subsiguiesen that they might follow next; imp. subj. 3rd pers. pl. / *subseguir.*

subsiguieses that you might follow next; imp. subj. 2nd pers. sing. / *subseguir.*

subsiguió he (she/it) followed next; past 3rd pers. sing. / *subseguir.*

subsistir to subsist. reg.

substanciar to condense. reg.

substituir to substitute. irr.

substituya 1. that I may substitute; pres. subj. 1st pers. sing. / *substituir.* 2. that he (she/it) may substitute; pres. subj. 3rd pers. sing. 3. let him (her/it) substitute; impve. 3rd pers. sing.

substituyáis that you (all) may substitute; pres. subj. 2nd pers. pl. / *substituir.*

substituyamos 1. that we may substitute; pres. subj. 1st pers. pl. / *substituir.* 2. let us substitute; impve. 1st pers. pl.

substituyan 1. that they may substitute; pres. subj. 3rd pers. pl. / *substituir.* 2. let them substitute; impve. 3rd pers. pl.

substituyas that you may substitute; pres. subj. 2nd pers. sing. / *substituir.*

substituye 1. he (she/it) substitutes; pres. ind. 3rd pers. sing. / *substituir.* 2. (you) substitute; impve. 2nd pers. sing.

substituyen they substitute; pres. ind. 3rd pers. pl. / *substituir.*

substituyendo substituting; pres. part. / *substituir.*

substituyera 1. that I might substitute; imp. subj. 1st pers. sing. / *substituir.* 2. that he (she/it) might substitute; imp. subj. 3rd pers. sing.

substituyerais that you (all) might substitute; imp. subj. 2nd pers pl. / *substituir.*

substituyéramos that we might substitute; imp. subj. 1st pers. pl. / *substituir.*

substituyeran that they might substitute; imp. subj. 3rd pers. pl. / *substituir.*

substituyeras that you might substitute; imp. subj. 2nd pers. sing. / *substituir.*

substituyeron they substituted; past 3rd pers. pl. / *substituir.*

substituyes you substitute; pres. ind. 2nd pers. sing. / *substituir.*

substituyese 1. that I might substitute; imp. subj. 1st pers. sing. / *substituir*. 2. that he (she/it) might substitute; imp. subj. 3rd pers. sing.

substituyeseis that you (all) might substitute; imp. subj. 2nd pers pl. / *substituir*.

substituyésemos that we might substitute; imp. subj. 1st pers. pl. / *substituir*.

substituyesen that they might substitute; imp. subj. 3rd pers. pl. / *substituir*.

substituyeses that you might substitute; imp. subj. 2nd pers. sing. / *substituir*.

substituyo I substitute; pres. ind. 1st pers. sing. / *substituir*.

substituyó he (she/it) substituted; past 3rd pers. sing. / *substituir*.

substraeos (you all) withdraw; impve. 2nd pers. pl. / *substraerse*.

substraer to withhold. irr.

substraerse to withdraw. irr.

substráete (you) withdraw; impve. 2nd pers. sing. / *substraerse*.

substraiga 1. that I may withhold; pres. subj. 1st pers. sing. / *substraer*. 2. that he (she/it) may withhold; pres. subj. 3rd pers. sing. 3. let him (her/it) withhold; impve. 3rd pers. sing.

substraigáis that you (all) may withhold; pres. subj. 2nd pers. pl. / *substraer*.

substraigámonos let us withdraw; impve. 1st pers. pl. / *substraerse*.

substraigamos 1. that we may withhold; pres. subj. 1st pers. pl. / *substraer*. 2. let us withhold; impve. 1st pers. pl.

substraigan 1. that they may withhold; pres. subj. 3rd pers. pl. / *substraer*. 2. let them withhold; impve. 3rd pers. pl.

substraíganse let them withdraw; impve. 3rd pers. pl. / *substraerse*.

substraigas that you may withhold; pres. subj. 2nd pers. sing. / *substraer*.

substraígase let him (her/it) withdraw; impve. 3rd pers. sing. / *substraerse*.

substraigo I withhold; pres. ind. 1st pers. sing. / *substraer*.

substraje I withheld; past 1st pers. sing. / *substraer*.

substrajera 1. that I might withhold; imp. subj. 1st pers. sing. / *substraer*. 2. that he (she/it) might withhold; imp. subj. 3rd pers. sing.

substrajerais that you (all) might withhold; imp. subj. 2nd pers pl. / *substraer*.

substrajéramos that we might withhold; imp. subj. 1st pers. pl. / *substraer*.

substrajeran that they might withhold; imp. subj. 3rd pers. pl. / *substraer*.

substrajeras that you might withhold; imp. subj. 2nd pers. sing. / *substraer*.

substrajeron they withheld; past 3rd pers. pl. / *substraer*.

substrajese 1. that I might withhold; imp. subj. 1st pers. sing. / *substraer*. 2. that he (she/it) might withhold; imp. subj. 3rd pers. sing.

substrajeseis that you (all) might withhold; imp. subj. 2nd pers pl. / *substraer*.

substrajésemos that we might withhold; imp. subj. 1st pers. pl. / *substraer*.

substrajesen that they might withhold; imp. subj. 3rd pers. pl. / *substraer*.

substrajeses that you might withhold; imp. subj. 2nd pers. sing. / *substraer*.

substrajimos we withheld; past 1st pers. pl. / *substraer*.

substrajiste you withheld; past 2nd pers. sing. / *substraer*.

substrajisteis you (all) withheld; past 2nd pers. pl. / *substraer*.

substrajo he (she/it) withheld; past 3rd pers. sing. / *substraer*.

substrayendo withholding; pres. part. / *substraer*.

substrayéndose withdrawing; pres. part. / *substraerse*.

subsumir to subsume. reg.

subven (you) provide for; impve. 2nd pers. sing. / *subvenir*.

subvencionar to subsidize. reg.

subvendrá he (she/it) will provide for; fut. 3rd pers. sing. / *subvenir*.

subvendrán they will provide for; fut. 3rd pers. pl. / *subvenir*.

subvendrás you will provide for; fut. 2nd pers. sing. / *subvenir*.

subvendré I shall provide for; fut. 1st pers. sing. / *subvenir*.

subvendréis you (all) will provide for; fut. 2nd pers. pl. / *subvenir*.

subvendremos we shall provide for; fut. 1st pers. pl. / *subvenir*.

subvendría 1. I should provide for; cond. 1st pers. sing. / *subvenir*. 2. he (she/it) would provide for; cond. 3rd pers. sing.

subvendríais you (all) would provide for; cond. 2nd pers. pl. / *subvenir*.

subvendríamos we should provide for; cond. 1st pers. pl. / *subvenir*.

subvendrían they would provide for; cond. 3rd pers. pl. / *subvenir*.

subvendrías you would provide for; cond. 2nd pers. sing. / *subvenir*.

subvenga 1. that I may provide for; pres. subj. 1st pers. sing. / *subvenir*. 2. that he (she/it) may provide for; pres. subj. 3rd pers. sing. 3. let him (her/it) provide for; impve. 3rd pers. sing.

subvengáis that you (all) may provide for; pres. subj. 2nd pers. pl. / *subvenir*.

subvengamos 1. that we may provide for; pres. subj. 1st pers. pl. / *subvenir*. 2. let us provide for; impve. 1st pers. pl.

subvengan 1. that they may provide for; pres. subj. 3rd pers. pl. / *subvenir*. 2. let them provide for; impve. 3rd pers. pl.

subvengas that you may provide for; pres. subj. 2nd pers. sing. / *subvenir*.

subvengo I provide for; pres. ind. 1st pers. sing. / *subvenir*.

subvenir to provide for. irr.

subvertir to subvert. irr.

subviene he (she/it) provides for; pres. ind. 3rd pers. sing. / *subvenir*.

subvienen they provide for; pres. ind. 3rd pers. pl. / *subvenir*.

subvienes you provide for; pres. ind. 2nd pers. sing. / *subvenir*.

subvierta 1. that I may subvert; pres. subj. 1st pers. sing. / *subvertir*. 2. that he (she/it) may subvert; pres. subj. 3rd pers. sing. 3. let him (her/it) subvert; impve. 3rd pers. sing.

subviertan 1. that they may subvert; pres. subj. 3rd pers. pl. / *subvertir*. 2. let them subvert; impve. 3rd pers. pl.

subviertas that you may subvert; pres. subj. 2nd pers. sing. / *subvertir*.

subvierte 1. he (she/it) subverts; pres. ind. 3rd pers. sing. / *subvertir*. 2. (you) subvert; impve. 2nd pers. sing.

subvierten they subvert; pres. ind. 3rd pers. pl. / *subvertir*.

subviertes you subvert; pres. ind. 2nd pers. sing. / *subvertir*.

subvierto I subvert; pres. ind. 1st pers. sing. / *subvertir*.

subvine I provided for; past 1st pers. sing. / *subvenir*.

subviniendo providing for; pres. part. / *subvenir*.

subviniera 1. that I might provide for; imp. subj. 1st pers. sing. / *subvenir*. 2. that he (she/it) might provide for; imp. subj. 3rd pers. sing.

subvinierais that you (all) might provide for; imp. subj. 2nd pers pl. / *subvenir*.

subviniéramos that we might provide for; imp. subj. 1st pers. pl. / *subvenir*.

subvinieran that they might provide for; imp. subj. 3rd pers. pl. / *subvenir*.

subvinieras that you might provide for; imp. subj. 2nd pers. sing. / *subvenir*.

subvinieron they provided for; past 3rd pers. pl. / *subvenir*.

subviniese 1. that I might provide for; imp. subj. 1st pers. sing. / *subvenir*. 2. that he (she/it) might provide for; imp. subj. 3rd pers. sing.

subvinieseis that you (all) might provide for; imp. subj. 2nd pers pl. / *subvenir*.

subviniésemos that we might provide for; imp. subj. 1st pers. pl. / *subvenir*.

subviniesen that they might provide for; imp. subj. 3rd pers. pl. / *subvenir*.

subvinieses that you might provide for; imp. subj. 2nd pers. sing. / *subvenir*.

subvinimos we provided for; past 1st pers. pl. / *subvenir*.

subviniste you provided for; past 2nd pers. sing. / *subvenir*.

subvinisteis you (all) provided for; past 2nd pers. pl. / *subvenir*.

subvino he (she/it) provided for; past 3rd pers. sing. / *subvenir*.

subvirtáis that you (all) may subvert; pres. subj. 2nd pers. pl. / *subvertir*.

subvirtamos 1. that we may subvert; pres. subj. 1st pers. pl. / *subvertir*. 2. let us subvert; impve. 1st pers. pl.

subvirtiendo subverting; pres. part. / *subvertir*.

subvirtiera 1. that I might subvert; imp. subj. 1st pers. sing. / *subvertir*. 2. that he (she/it) might subvert; imp. subj. 3rd pers. sing.

subvirtierais that you (all) might subvert; imp. subj. 2nd pers pl. / *subvertir*.

subvirtiéramos that we might subvert; imp. subj. 1st pers. pl. / *subvertir*.

subvirtieran that they might subvert; imp. subj. 3rd pers. pl. / *subvertir*.

subvirtieras that you might subvert; imp. subj. 2nd pers. sing. / *subvertir*.

subvirtieron they subverted; past 3rd pers. pl. / *subvertir*.

subvirtiese 1. that I might subvert; imp. subj. 1st pers. sing. / *subvertir*. 2. that he (she/it) might subvert; imp. subj. 3rd pers. sing.

subvirtieseis that you (all) might subvert; imp. subj. 2nd pers pl. / *subvertir*.

subvirtiésemos that we might subvert; imp. subj. 1st pers. pl. / *subvertir*.

subvirtiesen that they might subvert; imp. subj. 3rd pers. pl. / *subvertir*.

subvirtieses that you might subvert; imp. subj. 2nd pers. sing. / *subvertir*.

subvirtió he (she/it) subverted; past 3rd pers. sing. / *subvertir*.

subyugar to subjugate. irr.

subyugue 1. that I may subjugate; pres. subj. 1st pers. sing. / *subyugar*. 2. that he (she/it) may subjugate; pres. subj. 3rd pers. sing. 3. let him (her/it) subjugate; impve. 3rd pers. sing.

subyugué I subjugated; past 1st pers. sing. / *subyugar*.

subyuguéis that you (all) may subjugate; pres. subj. 2nd pers. pl. / *subyugar*.

subyuguemos 1. that we may subjugate; pres. subj. 1st pers. pl. / *subyugar*. 2. let us subjugate; impve. 1st pers. pl.

subyuguen 1. that they may subjugate; pres. subj. 3rd pers. pl. / *subyugar*. 2. let them subjugate; impve. 3rd pers. pl.

subyugues that you may subjugate; pres. subj. 2nd pers. sing. / *subyugar*.

succionar to suck. reg.

suceder to succeed or to happen. reg.

sucumbir to succumb. reg.

sudar to sweat. reg.

suela 1. he (she/it) soles shoes; pres. ind. 3rd pers. sing. / *solar*. 2. (you) sole shoes; impve. 2nd pers. sing.

suela 1. that I may be used to; pres. subj. 1st pers. sing. / *soler*. 2. that he (she/it) may be used to; pres. subj. 3rd pers. sing. 3. let him (her/it) be used to; impve. 3rd pers. sing.

suelan they sole shoes; pres. ind. 3rd pers. pl. / *solar*.

suelan 1. that they may be used to; pres. subj. 3rd pers. pl. / *soler*. 2. let them be used to; impve. 3rd pers. pl.

suelas you sole shoes; pres. ind. 2nd pers. sing. / *solar*.

suelas that you may be used to; pres. subj. 2nd pers. sing. / *soler*.

suelda 1. he (she/it) solders; pres. ind. 3rd pers. sing. / *soldar*. 2. (you) solder; impve. 2nd pers. sing.

sueldan they solder; pres. ind. 3rd pers. pl. / *soldar*.

sueldas you solder; pres. ind. 2nd pers. sing. / *soldar*.

suelde 1. that I may solder; pres. subj. 1st pers. sing. / *soldar*. 2. that he (she/it) may solder; pres. subj. 3rd pers. sing. 3. let him (her/it) solder; impve. 3rd pers. sing.

suelden 1. that they may solder; pres. subj. 3rd pers. pl. / *soldar*. 2. let them solder; impve. 3rd pers. pl.

sueldes that you may solder; pres. subj. 2nd pers. sing. / *soldar*.

sueldo I solder; pres. ind. 1st pers. sing. / *soldar*.

suele 1. that I may sole shoes; pres. subj. 1st pers. sing. / *solar*. 2. that he (she/it) may sole shoes; pres. subj. 3rd pers. sing. 3. let him (her/it) sole shoes; impve. 3rd pers. sing.

suele 1. he (she/it) is used to; pres. ind. 3rd pers. sing. / *soler*. 2. (you) be used to; impve. 2nd pers. sing.

suelen 1. that they may sole shoes; pres. subj. 3rd pers. pl. / *solar*. 2. let them sole shoes; impve. 3rd pers. pl.

suelen they are used to ; pres. ind. 3rd pers. pl. / *soler*.

sueles that you may sole shoes; pres. subj. 2nd pers. sing. / *solar*.

sueles you are used to; pres. ind. 2nd pers. sing. / *soler*.

suelo I sole shoes; pres. ind. 1st pers. sing. / *solar*.

suelo I am used to; pres. ind. 1st pers. sing. / *soler*.

suelta 1. he (she/it) unties; pres. ind. 3rd pers. sing. / *soltar*. 2. (you) untie; impve. 2nd pers. sing.

sueltan they untie; pres. ind. 3rd pers. pl. / *soltar*.

sueltas you untie; pres. ind. 2nd pers. sing. / *soltar*.

suéltate (you) loosen; impve. 2nd pers. sing. / *soltarse*.

suelte 1. that I may untie; pres. subj. 1st pers. sing. / *soltar*. 2. that he (she/it) may untie; pres. subj. 3rd pers. sing. 3. let him (her/it) untie; impve. 3rd pers. sing.

suelten 1. that they may untie; pres. subj. 3rd pers. pl. / *soltar*. 2. let them untie; impve. 3rd pers. pl.

suéltense let them loosen; impve. 3rd pers. pl. / *soltarse*.

sueltes that you may untie; pres. subj. 2nd pers. sing. / *soltar*.

suéltese let him (her/it) loosen; impve. 3rd pers. sing. / *soltarse*.

suelto I untie; pres. ind. 1st pers. sing. / *soltar*.

suena 1. he (she/it) sounds; pres. ind. 3rd pers. sing. / *sonar*. 2. (you) sound; impve. 2nd pers. sing.

suenan they sound; pres. ind. 3rd pers. pl. / *sonar*.

suenas you sound; pres. ind. 2nd pers. sing. / *sonar*.

suénate (you) blow your nose; impve. 2nd pers. sing. / *sonarse*.

suene 1. that I may sound; pres. subj. 1st pers. sing. / *sonar*. 2. that he (she/it) may sound; pres. subj. 3rd pers. sing. 3. let him (her/it) sound; impve. 3rd pers. sing.

suenen 1. that they may sound; pres. subj. 3rd pers. pl. / *sonar*. 2. let them sound; impve. 3rd pers. pl.

suénense let them blow their noses; impve. 3rd pers. pl. / *sonarse*.

suenes that you may sound; pres. subj. 2nd pers. sing. / *sonar*.

suénese let him (her/it) blow their noses; impve. 3rd pers. sing. / *sonarse*.

sueno I sound; pres. ind. 1st pers. sing. / *sonar*.

sueña 1. he (she/it) dreams; pres. ind. 3rd pers. sing. / *soñar*. 2. (you) dream; impve. 2nd pers. sing.

sueñan they dream; pres. ind. 3rd pers. pl. / *soñar*.

sueñas you dream; pres. ind. 2nd pers. sing. / *soñar*.

sueñe 1. that I may dream; pres. subj. 1st pers. sing. / *soñar*. 2. that he (she/it) may dream; pres. subj. 3rd pers. sing. 3. let him (her/it) dream; impve. 3rd pers. sing.

sueñen 1. that they may dream; pres. subj. 3rd pers. pl. / *soñar*. 2. let them dream; impve. 3rd pers. pl.

sueñes that you may dream; pres. subj. 2nd pers. sing. / *soñar*.

sueño I dream; pres. ind. 1st pers. sing. / *soñar*.

sufragar to defray. irr.

sufrague 1. that I may defray; pres. subj. 1st pers. sing. / *sufragar*. 2. that he (she/it) may defray; pres. subj. 3rd pers. sing. 3. let him (her/it) defray; impve. 3rd pers. sing.

sufragué I defrayed; past 1st pers. sing. / *sufragar*.

sufraguéis that you (all) may defray; pres. subj. 2nd pers. pl. / *sufragar*.

sufraguemos 1. that we may defray; pres. subj. 1st pers. pl. / *sufragar*. 2. let us defray; impve. 1st pers. pl.

sufraguen 1. that they may defray; pres. subj. 3rd pers. pl. / *sufragar*. 2. let them defray; impve. 3rd pers. pl.

sufragues that you may defray; pres. subj. 2nd pers. sing. / *sufragar*.

sufrir to suffer. reg.

sugerir to suggest. irr.

sugestionar to influence. reg.

sugiera 1. that I may suggest; pres. subj. 1st pers. sing. / *sugerir*. 2. that he (she/it) may suggest; pres. subj. 3rd pers. sing. 3. let him (her/it) suggest; impve. 3rd pers. sing.

sugieran 1. that they may suggest; pres. subj. 3rd pers. pl. / *sugerir*. 2. let them suggest; impve. 3rd pers. pl.

sugieras that you may suggest; pres. subj. 2nd pers. sing. / *sugerir*.

sugiere 1. he (she/it) suggests; pres. ind. 3rd pers. sing. / *sugerir*. 2. (you) suggest; impve. 2nd pers. sing.

sugieren they suggest; pres. ind. 3rd pers. pl. / *sugerir*.

sugieres you suggest; pres. ind. 2nd pers. sing. / *sugerir*.

sugiero I suggest; pres. ind. 1st pers. sing. / *sugerir*.

sugiráis that you (all) may suggest; pres. subj. 2nd pers. pl. / *sugerir*.

sugiramos 1. that we may suggest; pres. subj. 1st pers. pl. / *sugerir*. 2. let us suggest; impve. 1st pers. pl.

sugiriendo suggesting; pres. part. / *sugerir*.

sugiriera 1. that I might suggest; imp. subj. 1st pers. sing. / *sugerir*. 2. that he (she/it) might suggest; imp. subj. 3rd pers. sing.

sugirierais that you (all) might suggest; imp. subj. 2nd pers pl. / *sugerir*.

sugiriéramos that we might suggest; imp. subj. 1st pers. pl. / *sugerir*.

sugirieran that they might suggest; imp. subj. 3rd pers. pl. / *sugerir*.

sugirieras that you might suggest; imp. subj. 2nd pers. sing. / *sugerir*.

sugirieron they suggested; past 3rd pers. pl. / *sugerir*.

sugiriese 1. that I might suggest; imp. subj. 1st pers. sing. / *sugerir*. 2. that he (she/it) might suggest; imp. subj. 3rd pers. sing.

sugirieseis that you (all) might suggest; imp. subj. 2nd pers pl. / *sugerir*.

sugiriésemos that we might suggest; imp. subj. 1st pers. pl. / *sugerir*.

sugiriesen that they might suggest; imp. subj. 3rd pers. pl. / *sugerir*.

sugirieses that you might suggest; imp. subj. 2nd pers. sing. / *sugerir*.

sugirió he (she/it) suggested; past 3rd pers. sing. / *sugerir*.

suicidándose committing suicide; pres. part. / *suicidarse*.

suicidaos (you all) commit suicide; impve. 2nd pers. pl. / *suicidarse*.

suicidarse to commit suicide. reg.

suicídate (you) commit suicide; impve. 2nd pers. sing. / *suicidarse*.

suicidémonos let us commit suicide; impve. 1st pers. pl. / *suicidarse*.

suicídense let them commit suicide; impve. 3rd pers. pl. / *suicidarse*.

suicídese let him (her/it) commit suicide; impve. 3rd pers. sing. / *suicidarse*.

sujetándose submitting; pres. part. / *sujetarse*.

sujetaos (you all) submit; impve. 2nd pers. pl. / *sujetarse*.

sujetar to subject or to hold. reg.

sujetarse to submit. reg.

sujétate (you) submit; impve. 2nd pers. sing. / *sujetarse*.

sujetémonos let us submit; impve. 1st pers. pl. / *sujetarse*.

sujétense let them submit; impve. 3rd pers. pl. / *sujetarse*.

sujétese let him (her/it) submit; impve. 3rd pers. sing. / *sujetarse*.

sulfurándose getting angry; pres. part. / *sulfurarse*.

sulfuraos (you all) get angry; impve. 2nd pers. pl. / *sulfurarse*.

sulfurar to anger. reg.

sulfurarse to get angry. reg.

sulfúrate (you) get angry; impve. 2nd pers. sing. / *sulfurarse*.

sulfurémonos let us get angry; impve. 1st pers. pl. / *sulfurarse*.

sulfúrense let them get angry; impve. 3rd pers. pl. / *sulfurarse*.

sulfúrese let him (her/it) get angry; impve. 3rd pers. sing. / *sulfurarse*.

sumámonos let us shrink; impve. 1st pers. pl. / *sumirse*.

sumándose joining; pres. part. / *sumarse*.

súmanse let them shrink; impve. 3rd pers. pl. / *sumirse*.

sumaos (you all) join; impve. 2nd pers. pl. / *sumarse*.

sumar to add. reg.

sumarse to join. reg.

súmase let him (her/it) shrink; impve. 3rd pers. sing. / *sumirse*.

súmate (you) join; impve. 2nd pers. sing. / *sumarse*.

sumémonos let us join; impve. 1st pers. pl. / *sumarse*.

súmense let them join; impve. 3rd pers. pl. / *sumarse*.

sumérgete (you) sink; impve. 2nd pers. sing. / *sumergirse*.

sumergiéndose sinking; pres. part. / *sumergirse*.

sumergíos (you all) sink; impve. 2nd pers. pl. / *sumergirse*.

sumergir to submerge. irr.

sumergirse to sink. irr.

sumerja 1. that I may submerge; pres. subj. 1st pers. sing. / *sumergir*. 2. that he (she/it) may submerge; pres. subj. 3rd pers. sing. 3. let him (her/it) submerge; impve. 3rd pers. sing.

sumerjáis that you (all) may submerge; pres. subj. 2nd pers. pl. / *sumergir*.

sumerjámonos let us sink; impve. 1st pers. pl. / *sumergirse*.

sumerjamos 1. that we may submerge; pres. subj. 1st pers. pl. / *sumergir*. 2. let us submerge; impve. 1st pers. pl.

sumerjan 1. that they may submerge; pres. subj. 3rd pers. pl. / *sumergir*. 2. let them submerge; impve. 3rd pers. pl.

sumérjanse let them sink; impve. 3rd pers. pl. / *sumergirse*.

sumerjas that you may submerge; pres. subj. 2nd pers. sing. / *sumergir*.

sumérjase let him (her/it) sink; impve. 3rd pers. sing. / *sumergirse*.

sumerjo I submerge; pres. ind. 1st pers. sing. / *sumergir*.

súmese let him (her/it) join; impve. 3rd pers. sing. / *sumarse*.

súmete (you) shrink; impve. 2nd pers. sing. / *sumirse*.

sumiéndose shrinking; pres. part. / *sumirse*.

suministrar to supply. reg.

sumíos (you all) shrink; impve. 2nd pers. pl. / *sumirse.*

sumir to sink. reg.

sumirse to shrink. reg.

supe I knew; past 1st pers. sing. / *saber.*

supeditar to oppress. reg.

superar to surpass. reg.

superentender to superintend. irr.

superentienda 1. that I may superintend; pres. subj. 1st pers. sing. / *superentender.* 2. that he (she/it) may superintend; pres. subj. 3rd pers. sing. 3. let him (her/it) superintend; impve. 3rd pers. sing.

superentiendan 1. that they may superintend; pres. subj. 3rd pers. pl. / *superentender.* 2. let them superintend; impve. 3rd pers. pl.

superentiendas that you may superintend; pres. subj. 2nd pers. sing. / *superentender.*

superentiende 1. he (she/it) superintends; pres. ind. 3rd pers. sing. / *superentender.* 2. (you) superintend; impve. 2nd pers. sing.

superentienden they superintend; pres. ind. 3rd pers. pl. / *superentender.*

superentiendes you superintend; pres. ind. 2nd pers. sing. / *superentender.*

superentiendo I superintend; pres. ind. 1st pers. sing. / *superentender.*

superpon (you) superimpose; impve. 2nd pers. sing. / *superponer.*

superpondrá he (she/it) will superimpose; fut. 3rd pers. sing. / *superponer.*

superpondrán they will superimpose; fut. 3rd pers. pl. / *superponer.*

superpondrás you will superimpose; fut. 2nd pers. sing. / *superponer.*

superpondré I shall superimpose; fut. 1st pers. sing. / *superponer.*

superpondréis you (all) will superimpose; fut. 2nd pers. pl. / *superponer.*

superpondremos we shall superimpose; fut. 1st pers. pl. / *superponer.*

superpondría 1. I should superimpose; cond. 1st pers. sing. / *superponer.* 2. he (she/it) would superimpose; cond. 3rd pers. sing.

superpondríais you (all) would superimpose; cond. 2nd pers. pl. / *superponer.*

superpondríamos we should superimpose; cond. 1st pers. pl. / *superponer.*

superpondrían they would superimpose; cond. 3rd pers. pl. / *superponer.*

superpondrías you would superimpose; cond. 2nd pers. sing. / *superponer.*

superponer to superimpose. irr.

superponga 1. that I may superimpose; pres. subj. 1st pers. sing. / *superponer.* 2. that he (she/it) may superimpose; pres. subj. 3rd pers. sing. 3. let him (her/it) superimpose; impve. 3rd pers. sing.

superpongáis that you (all) may superimpose; pres. subj. 2nd pers. pl. / *superponer.*

superpongamos 1. that we may superimpose; pres. subj. 1st pers. pl. / *superponer.* 2. let us superimpose; impve. 1st pers. pl.

superpongan 1. that they may superimpose; pres. subj. 3rd pers. pl. / *superponer.* 2. let them superimpose; impve. 3rd pers. pl.

superpongas that you may superimpose; pres. subj. 2nd pers. sing. / *superponer.*

superpongo I superimpose; pres. ind. 1st pers. sing. / *superponer.*

superpuesto superimposed; past part. / *superponer.*

superpuse I superimposed; past 1st pers. sing. / *superponer.*

superpusiera 1. that I might superimpose; imp. subj. 1st pers. sing. / *superponer.* 2. that he (she/it) might superimpose; imp. subj. 3rd pers. sing.

superpusierais that you (all) might superimpose; imp. subj. 2nd pers pl. / *superponer.*

superpusiéramos that we might superimpose; imp. subj. 1st pers. pl. / *superponer.*

superpusieran that they might superimpose; imp. subj. 3rd pers. pl. / *superponer.*

superpusieras that you might superimpose; imp. subj. 2nd pers. sing. / *superponer.*

superpusieron they superimposed; past 3rd pers. pl. / *superponer.*

superpusiese 1. that I might superimpose; imp. subj. 1st pers. sing. / *superponer.* 2. that he (she/it) might superimpose; imp. subj. 3rd pers. sing.

superpusieseis that you (all) might superimpose; imp. subj. 2nd pers pl. / *superponer.*

superpusiésemos that we might superimpose; imp. subj. 1st pers. pl. / *superponer.*

superpusiesen that they might superimpose; imp. subj. 3rd pers. pl. / *superponer.*

superpusieses that you might superimpose; imp. subj. 2nd pers. sing. / *superponer.*

superpusimos we superimposed; past 1st pers. pl. / *superponer.*

superpusiste you superimposed; past 2nd pers. sing. / *superponer.*

superpusisteis you (all) superimposed; past 2nd pers. pl. / *superponer.*

superpuso he (she/it) superimposed; past 3rd pers. sing. / *superponer.*

superven (you) happen; impve. 2nd pers. sing. / *supervenir.*

supervendrá he (she/it) will happen; fut. 3rd pers. sing. / *supervenir.*

supervendrán they will happen; fut. 3rd pers. pl. / *supervenir.*

supervendrás you will happen; fut. 2nd pers. sing. / *supervenir.*

supervendré I shall happen; fut. 1st pers. sing. / *supervenir.*

supervendréis you (all) will happen; fut. 2nd pers. pl. / *supervenir.*

supervendremos we shall happen; fut. 1st pers. pl. / *supervenir.*

supervendría 1. I should happen; cond. 1st pers. sing. / *supervenir.* 2. he (she/it) would happen; cond. 3rd pers. sing.

supervendríais you (all) would happen; cond. 2nd pers. pl. / *supervenir.*

supervendríamos we should happen; cond. 1st pers. pl. / *supervenir*.

supervendrían they would happen; cond. 3rd pers. pl. / *supervenir*.

supervendrías you would happen; cond. 2nd pers. sing. / *supervenir*.

supervenga 1. that I may happen; pres. subj. 1st pers. sing. / *supervenir*. 2. that he (she/it) may happen; pres. subj. 3rd pers. sing. 3. let him (her/it) happen; impve. 3rd pers. sing.

supervengáis that you (all) may may happen; pres. subj. 2nd pers. pl. / *supervenir*.

supervengamos 1. that we may happen; pres. subj. 1st pers. pl. / *supervenir*. 2. let us may happen; impve. 1st pers. pl.

supervengan 1. that they may happen; pres. subj. 3rd pers. pl. / *supervenir*. 2. let them happen; impve. 3rd pers. pl.

supervengas that you may happen; pres. subj. 2nd pers. sing. / *supervenir*.

supervengo I happen; pres. ind. 1st pers. sing. / *supervenir*.

supervenir to happen. irr.

superviene he (she/it) happens; pres. ind. 3rd pers. sing. / *supervenir*.

supervienen they happen; pres. ind. 3rd pers. pl. / *supervenir*.

supervienes you happen; pres. ind. 2nd pers. sing. / *supervenir*.

supervine I happened; past 1st pers. sing. / *supervenir*.

superviniendo happening; pres. part. / *supervenir*.

superviniera 1. that I might happen; imp. subj. 1st pers. sing. / *supervenir*. 2. that he (she/it) might happen; imp. subj. 3rd pers. sing.

supervinierais that you (all) might happen; imp. subj. 2nd pers pl. / *supervenir*.

superviniéramos that we might happen; imp. subj. 1st pers. pl. / *supervenir*.

supervinieran that they might happen; imp. subj. 3rd pers. pl. / *supervenir*.

supervinieras that you might happen; imp. subj. 2nd pers. sing. / *supervenir*.

supervinieron they happened; past 3rd pers. pl. / *supervenir*.

superviniese 1. that I might happen; imp. subj. 1st pers. sing. / *supervenir*. 2. that he (she/it) might happen; imp. subj. 3rd pers. sing.

supervinieseis that you (all) might happen; imp. subj. 2nd pers pl. / *supervenir*.

superviniésemos that we might happen; imp. subj. 1st pers. pl. / *supervenir*.

superviniesen that they might happen; imp. subj. 3rd pers. pl. / *supervenir*.

supervinieses that you might happen; imp. subj. 2nd pers. sing. / *supervenir*.

supervinimos we happened; past 1st pers. pl. / *supervenir*.

superviniste you happened; past 2nd pers. sing. / *supervenir*.

supervinisteis you (all) happened; past 2nd pers. pl. / *supervenir*.

supervino he (she/it) happened; past 3rd pers. sing. / *supervenir*.

supervisar to supervise. reg.

supiera 1. that I might know; imp. subj. 1st pers. sing. / *saber*. 2. that he (she/it) might know; imp. subj. 3rd pers. sing.

supierais that you (all) might know; imp. subj. 2nd pers pl. / *saber*.

supiéramos that we might know; imp. subj. 1st pers. pl. / *saber*.

supieran that they might know; imp. subj. 3rd pers. pl. / *saber*.

supieras that you might know; imp. subj. 2nd pers. sing. / *saber*.

supieron they knew; past 3rd pers. pl. / *saber*.

supiese 1. that I might know; imp. subj. 1st pers. sing. / *saber*. 2. that he (she/it) might know; imp. subj. 3rd pers. sing.

supieseis that you (all) might know; imp. subj. 2nd pers pl. / *saber*.

supiésemos that we might know; imp. subj. 1st pers. pl. / *saber*.

supiesen that they might know; imp. subj. 3rd pers. pl. / *saber*.

supieses that you might know; imp. subj. 2nd pers. sing. / *saber*.

supimos we knew; past 1st pers. pl. / *saber*.

supiste you knew; past 2nd pers. sing. / *saber*.

supisteis you (all) knew; past 2nd pers. pl. / *saber*.

suplantar to supplant. reg.

suplementar to supplement. reg.

suplicar to supplicate. irr.

suplique 1. that I may supplicate; pres. subj. 1st pers. sing. / *suplicar*. 2. that he (she/it) may supplicate; pres. subj. 3rd pers. sing. 3. let him (her/it) supplicate; impve. 3rd pers. sing.

supliqué I supplicated; past 1st pers. sing. / *suplicar*.

supliquéis that you (all) may supplicate; pres. subj. 2nd pers. pl. / *suplicar*.

supliquemos 1. that we may supplicate; pres. subj. 1st pers. pl. / *suplicar*. 2. let us supplicate; impve. 1st pers. pl.

supliquen 1. that they may supplicate; pres. subj. 3rd pers. pl. / *suplicar*. 2. let them supplicate; impve. 3rd pers. pl.

supliques that you may supplicate; pres. subj. 2nd pers. sing. / *suplicar*.

suplir to supply. reg.

supo he (she/it) knew; past 3rd pers. sing. / *saber*.

supon (you) suppose; impve. 2nd pers. sing. / *suponer*.

supondrá he (she/it) will suppose; fut. 3rd pers. sing. / *suponer*.

supondrán they will suppose; fut. 3rd pers. pl. / *suponer*.

supondrás you will suppose; fut. 2nd pers. sing. / *suponer*.

supondré I shall suppose; fut. 1st pers. sing. / *suponer.*

supondréis you (all) will suppose; fut. 2nd pers. pl. / *suponer.*

supondremos we shall suppose; fut. 1st pers. pl. / *suponer.*

supondría 1. I should suppose; cond. 1st pers. sing. / *suponer.* 2. he (she/it) would suppose; cond. 3rd pers. sing.

supondríais you (all) would suppose; cond. 2nd pers. pl. / *suponer.*

supondríamos we should suppose; cond. 1st pers. pl. / *suponer.*

supondrían they would suppose; cond. 3rd pers. pl. / *suponer.*

supondrías you would suppose; cond. 2nd pers. sing. / *suponer.*

suponer to suppose. irr.

suponga 1. that I may suppose; pres. subj. 1st pers. sing. / *suponer.* 2. that he (she/it) may suppose; pres. subj. 3rd pers. sing. 3. let him (her/it) suppose; impve. 3rd pers. sing.

supongáis that you (all) may suppose; pres. subj. 2nd pers. pl. / *suponer.*

supongamos 1. that we may suppose; pres. subj. 1st pers. pl. / *suponer.* 2. let us suppose; impve. 1st pers. pl.

supongan 1. that they may suppose; pres. subj. 3rd pers. pl. / *suponer.* 2. let them suppose; impve. 3rd pers. pl.

supongas that you may suppose; pres. subj. 2nd pers. sing. / *suponer.*

supongo I suppose; pres. ind. 1st pers. sing. / *suponer.*

suprimir to suppress. reg.

supuesto supposed; past part. / *suponer.*

supurar to fester. reg.

supuse I supposed; past 1st pers. sing. / *suponer.*

supusiera 1. that I might suppose; imp. subj. 1st pers. sing. / *suponer.* 2. that he (she/it) might suppose; imp. subj. 3rd pers. sing.

supusierais that you (all) might suppose; imp. subj. 2nd pers pl. / *suponer.*

supusiéramos that we might suppose; imp. subj. 1st pers. pl. / *suponer.*

supusieran that they might suppose; imp. subj. 3rd pers. pl. / *suponer.*

supusieras that you might suppose; imp. subj. 2nd pers. sing. / *suponer.*

supusieron they supposed; past 3rd pers. pl. / *suponer.*

supusiese 1. that I might suppose; imp. subj. 1st pers. sing. / *suponer.* 2. that he (she/it) might suppose; imp. subj. 3rd pers. sing.

supusieseis that you (all) might suppose; imp. subj. 2nd pers pl. / *suponer.*

supusiésemos that we might suppose; imp. subj. 1st pers. pl. / *suponer.*

supusiesen that they might suppose; imp. subj. 3rd pers. pl. / *suponer.*

supusieses that you might suppose; imp. subj. 2nd pers. sing. / *suponer.*

supusimos we supposed; past 1st pers. pl. / *suponer.*

supusiste you supposed; past 2nd pers. sing. / *suponer.*

supusisteis you (all) supposed; past 2nd pers. pl. / *suponer.*

supuso he (she/it) supposed; past 3rd pers. sing. / *suponer.*

suputar to compute. reg.

surcar to furrow. irr.

surgir to surge. irr.

surja 1. that I may surge; pres. subj. 1st pers. sing. / *surgir.* 2. that he (she/it) may surge; pres. subj. 3rd pers. sing. 3. let him (her/it) surge; impve. 3rd pers. sing.

surjáis that you (all) may surge; pres. subj. 2nd pers. pl. / *surgir.*

surjamos 1. that we may surge; pres. subj. 1st pers. pl. / *surgir.* 2. let us surge; impve. 1st pers. pl.

surjan 1. that they may surge; pres. subj. 3rd pers. pl. / *surgir.* 2. let them surge; impve. 3rd pers. pl.

surjas that you may surge; pres. subj. 2nd pers. sing. / *surgir.*

surjo I surge; pres. ind. 1st pers. sing. / *surgir.*

surque 1. that I may furrow; pres. subj. 1st pers. sing. / *surcar.* 2. that he (she/it) may furrow; pres. subj. 3rd pers. sing. 3. let him (her/it) furrow; impve. 3rd pers. sing.

surqué I furrowed; past 1st pers. sing. / *surcar.*

surquéis that you (all) may furrow; pres. subj. 2nd pers. pl. / *surcar.*

surquemos 1. that we may furrow; pres. subj. 1st pers. pl. / *surcar.* 2. let us furrow; impve. 1st pers. pl.

surquen 1. that they may furrow; pres. subj. 3rd pers. pl. / *surcar.* 2. let them furrow; impve. 3rd pers. pl.

surques that you may furrow; pres. subj. 2nd pers. sing. / *surcar.*

surtir to supply. reg.

suscitar to provoke. reg.

suscribámonos let us subscribe; impve. 1st pers. pl. / *suscribirse.*

suscríbanse let them subscribe; impve. 3rd pers. pl. / *suscribirse.*

suscríbase let him (her/it) subscribe; impve. 3rd pers. sing. / *suscribirse.*

suscríbete (you) subscribe; impve. 2nd pers. sing. / *suscribirse.*

suscribiéndose subscribing; pres. part. / *suscribirse.*

suscribíos (you all) subscribe; impve. 2nd pers. pl. / *suscribirse.*

suscribir to suscribe. reg. except for pp.

suscribirse to subscribe. reg. except for pp.

suscrito suscribed; past part. / *suscribir.*

suspender to suspend. reg.

suspirar to sigh. reg.

sustentar to sustain. reg.

sustituir to substitute. irr.

sustituya 1. that I may substitute; pres. subj. 1st sing. / *sustituir*. 2. that he (she/it) may substitute; pres. subj. 3rd pers. sing. 3. let him (her/it) substitute; impve. 3rd pers. sing.

sustituyáis that you (all) may substitute; pres. subj. 2nd pers. pl. / *sustituir*.

sustituyamos 1. that we may substitute; pres. subj. 1st pers. pl. / *sustituir*. 2. let us substitute; impve. 1st pers. pl.

sustituyan 1. that they may substitute; pres. subj. 3rd pers. pl. / *sustituir*. 2. let them substitute; impve. 3rd pers. pl.

sustituyas that you may substitute; pres. subj. 2nd pers. sing. / *sustituir*.

sustituye 1. he (she/it) substitutes; pres. ind. 3rd pers. sing. / *sustituir*. 2. (you) substitute; impve. 2nd pers. sing.

sustituyen they substitute; pres. ind. 3rd pers. pl. / *sustituir*.

sustituyendo substituting; pres. part. / *sustituir*.

sustituyera 1. that I might substitute; imp. subj. 1st pers. sing. / *sustituir*. 2. that he (she/it) might substitute; imp. subj. 3rd pers. sing.

sustituyerais that you (all) might substitute; imp. subj. 2nd pers pl. / *sustituir*.

sustituyéramos that we might substitute; imp. subj. 1st pers. pl. / *sustituir*.

sustituyeran that they might substitute; imp. subj. 3rd pers. pl. / *sustituir*.

sustituyeras that you might substitute; imp. subj. 2nd pers. sing. / *sustituir*.

sustituyeron they substituted; past 3rd pers. pl. / *sustituir*.

sustituyes you substitute; pres. ind. 2nd pers. sing. / *sustituir*.

sustituyese 1. that I might substitute; imp. subj. 1st pers. sing. / *sustituir*. 2. that he (she/it) might substitute; imp. subj. 3rd pers. sing.

sustituyeseis that you (all) might substitute; imp. subj. 2nd pers pl. / *sustituir*.

sustituyésemos that we might substitute; imp. subj. 1st pers. pl. / *sustituir*.

sustituyesen that they might substitute; imp. subj. 3rd pers. pl. / *sustituir*.

sustituyeses that you might substitute; imp. subj. 2nd pers. sing. / *sustituir*.

sustituyo I substitute; pres. ind. 1st pers. sing. / *sustituir*.

sustituyó he (she/it) substituted; past 3rd pers. sing. / *sustituir*.

sustraeos (you all) withdraw; impve. 2nd pers. pl. / *sustraerse*.

sustraer to subtract. irr.

sustraerse to withdraw. irr.

sustráete (you) withdraw; impve. 2nd pers. sing. / *sustraerse*.

sustraiga 1. that I may subtract; pres. subj. 1st pers. sing. / *sustraer*. 2. that he (she/it) may subtract; pres. subj. 3rd pers. sing. 3. let him (her/it) subtract; impve. 3rd pers. sing.

sustraigáis that you (all) may subtract; pres. subj. 2nd pers. pl. / *sustraer*.

sustraigámonos let us withdraw; impve. 1st pers. pl. / *sustraerse*.

sustraigamos 1. that we may subtract; pres. subj. 1st pers. pl. / *sustraer*. 2. let us subtract; impve. 1st pers. pl.

sustraigan 1. that they may subtract; pres. subj. 3rd pers. pl. / *sustraer*. 2. let them subtract; impve. 3rd pers. pl.

sustraíganse let them withdraw; impve. 3rd pers. pl. / *sustraerse*.

sustraigas that you may subtract; pres. subj. 2nd pers. sing. / *sustraer*.

sustraígase let him (her/it) withdraw; impve. 3rd pers. sing. / *sustraerse*.

sustraigo I subtract; pres. ind. 1st pers. sing. / *sustraer*.

sustraje I subtracted; past 1st pers. sing. / *sustraer*.

sustrajera 1. that I might subtract; imp. subj. 1st pers. sing. / *sustraer*. 2. that he (she/it) might subtract; imp. subj. 3rd pers. sing.

sustrajerais that you (all) might subtract; imp. subj. 2nd pers pl. / *sustraer*.

sustrajéramos that we might subtract; imp. subj. 1st pers. pl. / *sustraer*.

sustrajeran that they might subtract; imp. subj. 3rd pers. pl. / *sustraer*.

sustrajeras that you might subtract; imp. subj. 2nd pers. sing. / *sustraer*.

sustrajeron they subtracted; past 3rd pers. pl. / *sustraer*.

sustrajese 1. that I might subtract; imp. subj. 1st pers. sing. / *sustraer*. 2. that he (she/it) might subtract; imp. subj. 3rd pers. sing.

sustrajeseis that you (all) might subtract; imp. subj. 2nd pers pl. / *sustraer*.

sustrajésemos that we might subtract; imp. subj. 1st pers. pl. / *sustraer*.

sustrajesen that they might subtract; imp. subj. 3rd pers. pl. / *sustraer*.

sustrajeses that you might subtract; imp. subj. 2nd pers. sing. / *sustraer*.

sustrajimos we subtracted; past 1st pers. pl. / *sustraer*.

sustrajiste you subtracted; past 2nd pers. sing. / *sustraer*.

sustrajisteis you (all) subtracted; past 2nd pers. pl. / *sustraer*.

sustrajo he (she/it) subtracted; past 3rd pers. sing. / *sustraer*.

sustrayendo subtracting; pres. part. / *sustraer*.

sustrayéndose withdrawing; pres. part. / *sustraerse*.

susurrándose being rumored; pres. part. / *susurrarse*.

susurrar to whisper. reg.

susurrarse to be rumored. reg.

susúrrense let them be rumored; impve. 3rd pers. pl. / *susurrarse*.

susúrrese let it be rumored; impve. 3rd pers. sing. / *susurrarse*.

sutilice 1. that I may make subtle; pres. subj. 1st pers. sing. / *sutilizar*. 2. that he (she/it) may make subtle; pres. subj. 3rd pers. sing. 3. let him (her/it) make subtle; impve. 3rd pers. sing.

sutilicé I made subtle; past 1st pers. sing. / *sutilizar*.

sutilicéis that you (all) may make subtle; pres. subj. 2nd pers. pl. / *sutilizar*.

sutilicemos 1. that we may make subtle; pres. subj. 1st pers. pl. / *sutilizar*. 2. let us make subtle; impve. 1st pers. pl.

sutilicen 1. that they may make subtle; pres. subj. 3rd pers. pl. / *sutilizar*. 2. let them make subtle; impve. 3rd pers. pl.

sutilices that you may make subtle; pres. subj. 2nd pers. sing. / *sutilizar*.

sutilizar to make subtle or to refne. irr.

T

tabaleándose rocking; pres. part. / *tabalearse*.

tabaleaos (you all) rock; impve. 2nd pers. pl. / *tabalearse*.

tabalear to shake or to beat. reg.

tabalearse to rock. reg.

tabaléate (you) rock; impve. 2nd pers. sing. / *tabalearse*.

tabaleémonos let us rock; impve. 1st pers. pl. / *tabalearse*.

tabaléense let them rock; impve. 3rd pers. pl. / *tabalearse*.

tabaléese let him (her/it) rock; impve. 3rd pers. sing. / *tabalearse*.

tabicar to wall up. irr.

tabique 1. that I may wall up; pres. subj. 1st pers. sing. / *tabicar*. 2. that he (she/it) may wall up; pres. subj. 3rd pers. sing. 3. let him (her/it) wall up; impve. 3rd pers. sing.

tabiqué I walled up; past 1st pers. sing. / *tabicar*.

tabiquéis that you (all) may wall up; pres. subj. 2nd pers. pl. / *tabicar*.

tabiquemos 1. that we may wall up; pres. subj. 1st pers. pl. / *tabicar*. 2. let us wall up; impve. 1st pers. pl.

tabiquen 1. that they may wall up; pres. subj. 3rd pers. pl. / *tabicar*. 2. let them wall up; impve. 3rd pers. pl.

tabiques that you may wall up; pres. subj. 2nd pers. sing. / *tabicar*.

tablear to saw up timber. reg.

tabletear to rattle. reg.

tabular to tabulate. reg.

tacar to mark. irr.

tace 1. that I may fray; pres. subj. 1st pers. sing. / *tazar*. 2. that he (she/it) may fray; pres. subj. 3rd pers. sing. 3. let him (her/it) fray; impve. 3rd pers. sing.

tacé I frayed; past 1st pers. sing. / *tazar*.

tacéis that you (all) may fray; pres. subj. 2nd pers. pl. / *tazar*.

tacemos 1. that we may fray; pres. subj. 1st pers. pl. / *tazar*. 2. let us fray; impve. 1st pers. pl.

tacen 1. that they may fray; pres. subj. 3rd pers. pl. / *tazar*. 2. let them fray; impve. 3rd pers. pl.

taces that you may fray; pres. subj. 2nd pers. sing. / *tazar*.

taconear to click the heels. reg.

tachar to cross out or to find fault. reg.

tachonar to stud. reg.

taimándose sulking; pres. part. / *taimarse*.

taimaos (you all) sulk; impve. 2nd pers. pl. / *taimarse*.

taimarse to sulk. reg.

taímate (you) sulk; impve. 2nd pers. sing. / *taimarse*.

taimémonos let us sulk; impve. 1st pers. pl. / *taimarse*.

taímense let them sulk; impve. 3rd pers. pl. / *taimarse*.

taímese let him (her/it) sulk; impve. 3rd pers. sing. / *taimarse*.

tajar to cut. reg.

taladrar to drill. reg.

talar to fell trees. reg.

talonear to walk briskly. reg.

tallar to carve. reg.

tambaleándose staggering; pres. part. / *tambalearse*.

tambaleaos (you all) stagger; impve. 2nd pers. pl. / *tambalearse*.

tambalear to totter. reg.

tambalearse to stagger. reg.

tambaléate (you) stagger; impve. 2nd pers. sing. / *tambalearse*.

tambaleémonos let us stagger; impve. 1st pers. pl. / *tambalearse*.

tambaléense let them stagger; impve. 3rd pers. pl. / *tambalearse*.

tambaléese let him (her/it) stagger; impve. 3rd pers. sing. / *tambalearse*.

tamborear to drum. reg.

tamborilear to extol or to play the tambourine. reg.

tamice 1. that I may sift; pres. subj. 1st pers. sing. / *tamizar*. 2. that he (she/it) may sift; pres. subj. 3rd pers. sing. 3. let him (her/it) sift; impve. 3rd pers. sing.

tamicé I sifted; past 1st pers. sing. / *tamizar*.

tamicéis that you (all) may sift; pres. subj. 2nd pers. pl. / *tamizar*.

tamicemos 1. that we may sift; pres. subj. 1st pers. pl. / *tamizar*. 2. let us sift; impve. 1st pers. pl.

tamicen 1. that they may sift; pres. subj. 3rd pers. pl. / *tamizar*. 2. let them sift; impve. 3rd pers. pl.

tamices that you may sift; pres. subj. 2nd pers. sing. / *tamizar*.

tamizar to sift. irr.

tantear to probe. reg.

taña 1. that I may play an instrument; pres. subj. 1st pers. sing. / *tañer*. 2. that he (she/it) may play an instrument; pres. subj. 3rd pers. sing. 3. let him (her/it) play an instrument; impve. 3rd pers. sing.

tañáis that you (all) may play an instrument; pres. subj. 2nd pers. pl. / *tañer.*

tañamos 1. that we may play an instrument; pres. subj. 1st pers. pl. / *tañer.* 2. let us play an instrument; impve. 1st pers. pl.

tañan 1. that they may play an instrument; pres. subj. 3rd pers. pl. / *tañer.* 2. let them play an instrument; impve. 3rd pers. pl.

tañas that you may play an instrument; pres. subj. 2nd pers. sing. / *tañer.*

tañe 1. he (she/it) plays an instrument; pres. ind. 3rd pers. sing. / *tañer.* 2. (you) play an instrument; impve. 2nd pers. sing.

tañen they play an instrument; pres. ind. 3rd pers. pl. / *tañer.*

tañendo playing an instrument; pres. part. / *tañer.*

tañer to play an instrument. irr.

tañera 1. that I might play an instrument; imp. subj. 1st pers. sing. / *tañer.* 2. that he (she/it) might play an instrument; imp. subj. 3rd pers. sing.

tañerais that you (all) might play an instrument; imp. subj. 2nd pers pl. / *tañer.*

tañéramos that we might play an instrument; imp. subj. 1st pers. pl. / *tañer.*

tañeran that they might play an instrument; imp. subj. 3rd pers. pl. / *tañer.*

tañeras that you might play an instrument; imp. subj. 2nd pers. sing. / *tañer.*

tañeron they played an instrument; past 3rd pers. pl. / *tañer.*

tañes you play an instrument; pres. ind. 2nd pers. sing. / *tañer.*

tañese 1. that I might play an instrument; imp. subj. 1st pers. sing. / *tañer.* 2. that he (she/it) might play an instrument; imp. subj. 3rd pers. sing.

tañeseis that you (all) might play an instrument; imp. subj. 2nd pers pl. / *tañer.*

tañésemos that we might play an instrument; imp. subj. 1st pers. pl. / *tañer.*

tañesen that they might play an instrument; imp. subj. 3rd pers. pl. / *tañer.*

tañeses that you might play an instrument; imp. subj. 2nd pers. sing. / *tañer.*

taño I play an instrument; pres. ind. 1st pers. sing. / *tañer.*

tañó he (she/it) played an instrument; past 3rd pers. sing. / *tañer.*

tapándose covering up; pres. part. / *taparse.*

tapaos (you all) cover up; impve. 2nd pers. pl. / *taparse.*

tapar to cover. reg.

taparse to cover up. reg.

tápate (you) cover up; impve. 2nd pers. sing. / *taparse.*

tapémonos let us cover up; impve. 1st pers. pl. / *taparse.*

tápense let them cover up; impve. 3rd pers. pl. / *taparse.*

tápese let him (her/it) cover up; impve. 3rd pers. sing. / *taparse.*

tapiar to wall up. reg.

tapice 1. that I may cover with tapestry; pres. subj. 1st pers. sing. / *tapizar.* 2. that he (she/it) may cover with tapestry; pres. subj. 3rd pers. sing. 3. let him (her/it) cover with tapestry; pres. subj. 3rd pers. sing.

tapicé I covered with tapestry; past 1st pers. sing. / *tapizar.*

tapicéis that you (all) may cover with tapestry; pres. subj. 2nd pers. pl. / *tapizar.*

tapicemos 1. that we may cover with tapestry; pres. subj. 1st pers. pl. / *tapizar.* 2. let us cover with tapestry; impve. 1st pers. pl.

tapicen 1. that they may cover with tapestry; pres. subj. 3rd pers. pl. / *tapizar.* 2. let them cover with tapestry; impve. 3rd pers. pl.

tapices that you may cover with tapestry; pres. subj. 2nd pers. sing. / *tapizar.*

tapizar to cover with tapestry. irr.

taponar to plug. reg.

taque 1. that I may mark; pres. subj. 1st pers. sing. / *tacar.* 2. that he (she/it) may mark; pres. subj. 3rd pers. sing. 3. let him (her/it) mark; impve. 3rd pers. sing.

taqué I marked; past 1st pers. sing. / *tacar.*

taquéis that you (all) may mark; pres. subj. 2nd pers. pl. / *tacar.*

taquemos 1. that we may mark; pres. subj. 1st pers. pl. / *tacar.* 2. let us mark; impve. 1st pers. pl.

taquen 1. that they may mark; pres. subj. 3rd pers. pl. / *tacar.* 2. let them mark; impve. 3rd pers. pl.

taques that you may mark; pres. subj. 2nd pers. sing. / *tacar.*

taquigrafía 1. he (she/it) takes down in shorthand; pres. ind. 3rd pers. sing. / *taquigrafiar.* 2. (you) take down in shorthand; impve. 2nd pers. sing.

taquigrafían they take down in shorthand; pres. ind. 3rd pers. pl. / *taquigrafiar.*

taquigrafiar to take down in shorthand. irr.

taquigrafías you take down in shorthand; pres. ind. 2nd pers. sing. / *taquigrafiar.*

taquigrafíe 1. that I may take down in shorthand; pres. subj. 1st pers. sing. / *taquigrafiar.* 2. that he (she/it) may take down in shorthand; pres. subj. 3rd pers. sing. 3. let him (her/it) take down in shorthand; impve. 3rd pers. sing.

taquigrafíen 1. that they may take down in shorthand; pres. subj. 3rd pers. pl. / *taquigrafiar.* 2. let them take down in shorthand; impve. 3rd pers. pl.

taquigrafíes that you may take down in shorthand; pres. subj. 2nd pers. sing. / *taquigrafiar.*

taquigrafío I take down in shorthand; pres. ind. 1st pers. sing. / *taquigrafiar.*

tarace 1. that I may bite; pres. subj. 1st pers. sing. / *tarazar.* 2. that he (she/it) may bite; pres. subj. 3rd pers. sing. 3. let him (her/it) bite; impve. 3rd pers. sing.

taracé I bit; past 1st pers. sing. / *tarazar.*

taracéis that you (all) may bite; pres. subj. 2nd pers. pl. / *tarazar.*

taracemos 1. that we may bite; pres. subj. 1st pers. pl. / *tarazar*. 2. let us bite; impve. 1st pers. pl.

taracen 1. that they may bite; pres. subj. 3rd pers. pl. / *tarazar*. 2. let them bite; impve. 3rd pers. pl.

taraces that you may bite; pres. subj. 2nd pers. sing. / *tarazar*.

tararear to hum. reg.

tarascar to bite or to snap. irr.

tarasque 1. that I may bite; pres. subj. 1st pers. sing. / *tarascar*. 2. that he (she/it) may bite; pres. subj. 3rd pers. sing. 3. let him (her/it) bite; impve. 3rd pers. sing.

tarasqué I bit; past 1st pers. sing. / *tarascar*.

tarasquéis that you (all) may bite; pres. subj. 2nd pers. pl. / *tarascar*.

tarasquemos 1. that we may bite; pres. subj. 1st pers. pl. / *tarascar*. 2. let us bite; impve. 1st pers. pl.

tarasquen 1. that they may bite; pres. subj. 3rd pers. pl. / *tarascar*. 2. let them bite; impve. 3rd pers. pl.

tarasques that you may bite; pres. subj. 2nd pers. sing. / *tarascar*.

tarazar to bite. irr.

tardándose being delayed; pres. part. / *tardarse*.

tardaos (you all) be delayed; impve. 2nd pers. pl. / *tardarse*.

tardar to delay. reg.

tardarse to be delayed. reg.

tárdate (you) be delayed; impve. 2nd pers. sing. / *tardarse*.

tardecer to get late. irr.

tardémonos let us be delayed; impve. 1st pers. pl. / *tardarse*.

tárdense let them be delayed; impve. 3rd pers. pl. / *tardarse*.

tárdese let him (her/it) be delayed; impve. 3rd pers. sing. / *tardarse*.

tardezca 1. that I may get late; pres. subj. 1st pers. sing. / *tardecer*. 2. that he (she/it) may get late; pres. subj. 3rd pers. sing. 3. let him (her/it) get late; impve. 3rd pers. sing.

tardezcáis that you (all) may get late; pres. subj. 2nd pers. pl. / *tardecer*.

tardezcamos 1. that we may get late; pres. subj. 1st pers. pl. / *tardecer*. 2. let us get late; impve. 1st pers. pl.

tardezcan 1. that they may get late; pres. subj. 3rd pers. pl. / *tardecer*. 2. let them get late; impve. 3rd pers. pl.

tardezcas that you may get late; pres. subj. 2nd pers. sing. / *tardecer*.

tardezco I get late; pres. ind. 1st pers. sing. / *tardecer*.

tartajear to stammer. reg.

tartalear to stagger. reg.

tartamudear to stutter. reg.

tasar to appraise. reg.

tascar to crunch. irr.

tasque 1. that I may crunch; pres. subj. 1st pers. sing. / *tascar*. 2. that he (she/it) may crunch; pres. subj. 3rd pers. sing. 3. let him (her/it) crunch; impve. 3rd pers. sing.

tasqué I crunched; past 1st pers. sing. / *tascar*.

tasquéis that you (all) may crunch; pres. subj. 2nd pers. pl. / *tascar*.

tasquemos 1. that we may crunch; pres. subj. 1st pers. pl. / *tascar*. 2. let us crunch; impve. 1st pers. pl.

tasquen 1. that they may crunch; pres. subj. 3rd pers. pl. / *tascar*. 2. let them crunch; impve. 3rd pers. pl.

tasques that you may crunch; pres. subj. 2nd pers. sing. / *tascar*.

tatúa 1. he (she/it) tatooes; pres. ind. 3rd pers. sing. / *tatuar* 2. (you) tattoo; impve. 2nd pers. sing.

tatúan they tattoo; pres. ind. 3rd pers. pl. / *tatuar*.

tatuar to tattoo. irr.

tatúas you tattoo; pres. ind. 2nd pers. sing. / *tatuar*.

tatúe 1. that I may tattoo; pres. subj. 1st pers. sing. / *tatuar*. 2. that he (she/it) may tattoo; pres. subj. 3rd pers. sing. 3. let him (her/it) tattoo; impve. 3rd pers. sing.

tatúen 1. that they may tattoo; pres. subj. 3rd pers. pl. / *tatuar*. 2. let them tattoo; impve. 3rd pers. pl.

tatúes that you may tattoo; pres. subj. 2nd pers. sing. / *tatuar*.

tatúo I tattoo; pres. ind. 1st pers. sing. / *tatuar*.

taxear to taxi an airplane. reg.

tazar to fray. irr.

teclear to strum a keyboard. reg.

techar to roof. reg.

tediar to loathe. reg.

tejar to tile. reg.

tejer to weave. reg.

teledifundir to televise. reg.

teledirigir to operate by remote control. reg.

telefonar to telephone. reg.

telefonear to telephone. reg.

telegrafía 1. he (she/it) telegraphs; pres. ind. 3rd pers. sing. / *telegrafiar*. 2. (you) telegraph; impve. 2nd pers. sing.

telegrafían they telegraph; pres. ind. 3rd pers. pl. / *telegrafiar*.

telegrafiar to telegraph. irr.

telegrafías you telegraph; pres. ind. 2nd pers. sing. / *telegrafiar*.

telegrafíe 1. that I may telegraph; pres. subj. 1st pers. sing. / *telegrafiar*. 2. that he (she/it) may telegraph; pres. subj. 3rd pers. sing. 3. let him (her/it) telegraph; impve. 3rd pers. sing.

telegrafíen 1. that they may telegraph; pres. subj. 3rd pers. pl. / *telegrafiar*. 2. let them telegraph; impve. 3rd pers. pl.

telegrafíes that you may telegraph; pres. subj. 2nd pers. sing. / *telegrafiar*.

telegrafío I telegraph; pres. ind. 1st pers. sing. / *telegrafiar*.

telescopándose telescoping; pres. part. / *telescoparse*.

telescopaos (you all) telescope; impve. 2nd pers. pl. / *telescoparse*.

telescopar to telescope. reg.

telescoparse to telescope. reg.

telescópate (you) telescope; impve. 2nd pers. sing. / *telescoparse*.

telescopémonos let us telescope; impve. 1st pers. pl. / *telescoparse.*

telescópense let them telescope; impve. 3rd pers. pl. / *telescoparse.*

telescópese let him (her/it) telescope; impve. 3rd pers. sing. / *telescoparse.*

televisar to televise. reg.

temblar to tremble. irr.

temblequear to shiver. reg.

temer to fear. reg.

temperar to temper. reg.

tempestear to storm. reg.

templándose being moderate; pres. part. / *templarse.*

templaos (you all) be moderate; impve. 2nd pers. pl. / *templarse.*

templar to temper. reg.

templarse to be moderate. reg.

témplate (you) be moderate; impve. 2nd pers. sing. / *templarse.*

templémonos let us be moderate; impve. 1st pers. pl. / *templarse.*

témplense let them be moderate; impve. 3rd pers. pl. / *templarse.*

témplese let him (her/it) be moderate; impve. 3rd pers. sing. / *templarse.*

temporice 1. that I may temporize; pres. subj. 1st pers. sing. / *temporizar.* 2. that he (she/it) may temporize; pres. subj. 3rd pers. sing. 3. let him (her/it) temporize; impve. 3rd pers. sing.

temporicé I temporized; past 1st pers. sing. / *temporizar.*

temporicéis that you (all) may temporize; pres. subj. 2nd pers. pl. / *temporizar.*

temporicemos 1. that we may temporize; pres. subj. 1st pers. pl. / *temporizar.* 2. let us temporize; impve. 1st pers. pl.

temporicen 1. that they may temporize; pres. subj. 3rd pers. pl. / *temporizar.* 2. let them temporize; impve. 3rd pers. pl.

temporices that you may temporize; pres. subj. 2nd pers. sing. / *temporizar.*

temporizar to temporize. irr.

ten (you) have; impve. 2nd pers. sing. / *tener.*

tendámonos let us stretch out; impve. 1st pers. pl. / *tenderse.*

tendeos (you all) stretch out; impve. 2nd pers. pl. / *tenderse.*

tender to spread out or to tend. irr.

tenderse to stretch out. irr.

tendiéndose stretching out; pres. part. / *tenderse.*

tendrá he (she/it) will have; fut. 3rd pers. sing. / *tener.*

tendrán they will have; fut. 3rd pers. pl. / *tener.*

tendrás you will have; fut. 2nd pers. sing. / *tener.*

tendré I shall have; fut. 1st pers. sing. / *tener.*

tendréis you (all) will have; fut. 2nd pers. pl. / *tener.*

tendremos we shall have; fut. 1st pers. pl. / *tener.*

tendría 1. I should have; cond. 1st pers. sing. / *tener.* 2. he (she/it) would have; cond. 3rd pers. sing.

tendríais you (all) would have; cond. 2nd pers. pl. / *tener.*

tendríamos we should have; cond. 1st pers. pl. / *tener.*

tendrían they would have; cond. 3rd pers. pl. / *tener.*

tendrías you would have; cond. 2nd pers. sing. / *tener.*

teneos (you all) stand firm; impve. 2nd pers. pl. / *tenerse.*

tener to have. irr.

tenerse to stand firm. irr.

ténete (you) stand firm; impve. 2nd pers. sing. / *tenerse.*

tenga 1. that I may have; pres. subj. 1st pers. sing. / *tener.* 2. that he (she/it) may have; pres. subj. 3rd pers. sing. 3. let him (her/it) have; impve. 3rd pers. sing.

tengáis that you (all) may have; pres. subj. 2nd pers. pl. / *tener.*

tengámonos let us stand firm; impve. 1st pers. pl. / *tenerse.*

tengamos 1. that we may have; pres. subj. 1st pers. pl. / *tener.* 2. let us have; impve. 1st pers. pl.

tengan 1. that they may have; pres. subj. 3rd pers. pl. / *tener.* 2. let them have; impve. 3rd pers. pl.

ténganse let them stand firm; impve. 3rd pers. pl. / *tenerse.*

tengas that you may have; pres. subj. 2nd pers. sing. / *tener.*

téngase let him (her/it) stand firm; impve. 3rd pers. sing. / *tenerse.*

tengo I have; pres. ind. 1st pers. sing. / *tener.*

teniendo having; pres. part. / *tener.*

teniéndose standing firm; pres. part. / *tenerse.*

tensar to tighten. reg.

tentalear to feel over or to grope. reg.

tentar to tempt. irr.

teñir to dye. irr.

teorice 1. that I may theorize; pres. subj. 1st pers. sing. / *teorizar.* 2. that he (she/it) may theorize; pres. subj. 3rd pers. sing. 3. let him (her/it) theorize; impve. 3rd pers. sing.

teoricé I theorized; past 1st pers. sing. / *teorizar.*

teoricéis that you (all) may theorize; pres. subj. 2nd pers. pl. / *teorizar.*

teoricemos 1. that we may theorize; pres. subj. 1st pers. pl. / *teorizar.* 2. let us theorize; impve. 1st pers. pl.

teoricen 1. that they may theorize; pres. subj. 3rd pers. pl. / *teorizar.* 2. let them theorize; impve. 3rd pers. pl.

teorices that you may theorize; pres. subj. 2nd pers. sing. / *teorizar.*

teorizar to theorize. irr.

terciándose being all right; pres. part. / *terciarse.*

terciaos (you all) be all right; impve. 2nd pers. pl. / *terciarse.*

terciar to slant or to divide into thirds. reg.

terciarse to be all right. reg.

tercíate (you) be all right; impve. 2nd pers. sing. / *terciarse.*

terciémonos let us be all right; impve. 1st pers. pl. / *terciarse*.

tercíense let them be all right; impve. 3rd pers. pl. / *terciarse*.

tercíese let him (her/it) be all right; impve. 3rd pers. sing. / *terciarse*.

tergiversar to distort. reg.

terminándose ending; pres. part. / *terminarse*.

terminaos (you all) end; impve. 2nd pers. pl. / *terminarse*.

terminar to terminate. reg.

terminarse to end. reg.

termínate (you) end; impve. 2nd pers. sing. / *terminarse*.

terminémonos let us end; impve. 1st pers. pl. / *terminarse*.

termínense let them end; impve. 3rd pers. pl. / *terminarse*.

termínese let him (her/it) end; impve. 3rd pers. sing. / *terminarse*.

terquear to be stubborn. reg.

terraplenar to level land. reg.

tesar to make tight and smooth. reg.

testar to make a will. reg.

testificar to testify. irr.

testifique 1. that I may testify; pres. subj. 1st pers. sing. / *testificar*. 2. that he (she/it) may testify; pres. subj. 3rd pers. sing. 3. let him (her/it) testify; impve. 3rd pers. sing.

testifiqué I testified; past 1st pers. sing. / *testificar*.

testifiquéis that you (all) may testify; pres. subj. 2nd pers. pl. / *testificar*.

testifiquemos 1. that we may testify; pres. subj. 1st pers. pl. / *testificar*. 2. let us testify; impve. 1st pers. pl.

testifiquen 1. that they may testify; pres. subj. 3rd pers. pl. / *testificar*. 2. let them testify; impve. 3rd pers. pl.

testifiques that you may testify; pres. subj. 2nd pers. sing. / *testificar*.

testimoniar to give testimony. reg.

tetar to suckle. reg.

tiembla 1. he (she/it) trembles; pres. ind. 3rd pers. sing. / *temblar*. 2. (you) tremble; impve. 2nd pers. sing.

tiemblan they tremble; pres. ind. 3rd pers. pl. / *temblar*.

tiemblas you tremble; pres. ind. 2nd pers. sing. / *temblar*.

tiemble 1. that I may tremble; pres. subj. 1st pers. sing. / *temblar*. 2. that he (she/it) may tremble; pres. subj. 3rd pers. sing. 3. let him (her/it) tremble; impve. 3rd pers. sing.

tiemblen 1. that they may tremble; pres. subj. 3rd pers. pl. / *temblar*. 2. let them tremble; impve. 3rd pers. pl.

tiembles that you may tremble; pres. subj. 2nd pers. sing. / *temblar*.

tiemblo I tremble; pres. ind. 1st pers. sing. / *temblar*.

tienda 1. that I may spread out; pres. subj. 1st pers. sing. / *tender*. 2. that he (she/it) may spread out; pres. subj. 3rd pers. sing. 3. let him (her/it) spread out; impve. 3rd pers. sing.

tiendan 1. that they may spread out; pres. subj. 3rd pers. pl. / *tender*. 2. let them spread out; impve. 3rd pers. pl.

tiéndanse let them stretch; impve. 3rd pers. pl. / *tenderse*.

tiendas that you may spread out; pres. subj. 2nd pers. sing. / *tender*.

tiéndase let him (her/it) stretch; impve. 3rd pers. sing. / *tenderse*.

tiende 1. he (she/it) spreads out; pres. ind. 3rd pers. sing. / *tender*. 2. (you) spread out; impve. 2nd pers. sing.

tienden they spread out; pres. ind. 3rd pers. pl. / *tender*.

tiendes you spread out; pres. ind. 2nd pers. sing. / *tender*.

tiéndete (you) stretch; impve. 2nd pers. sing. / *tenderse*.

tiendo I spread out; pres. ind. 1st pers. sing. / *tender*.

tiene he (she/it) has; pres. ind. 3rd pers. sing. / *tener*.

tienen they have; pres. ind. 3rd pers. pl. / *tener*.

tienes you have; pres. ind. 2nd pers. sing. / *tener*.

tienta 1. he (she/it) tempts; pres. ind. 3rd pers. sing. / *tentar*. 2. (you) tempt; impve. 2nd pers. sing.

tientan they tempt; pres. ind. 3rd pers. pl. / *tentar*.

tientas you tempt; pres. ind. 2nd pers. sing. / *tentar*.

tiente 1. that I may tempt; pres. subj. 1st pers. sing. / *tentar*. 2. that he (she/it) may tempt; pres. subj. 3rd pers. sing. 3. let him (her/it) tempt; impve. 3rd pers. sing.

tienten 1. that they may tempt; pres. subj. 3rd pers. pl. / *tentar*. 2. let them tempt; impve. 3rd pers. pl.

tientes that you may tempt; pres. subj. 2nd pers. sing. / *tentar*.

tiento I tempt; pres. ind. 1st pers. sing. / *tentar*.

tijeretear to snip. reg.

tildar to brand. reg.

tillar to floor. reg.

timándose making eyes; pres. part. / *timarse*.

timaos (you all) make eyes; impve. 2nd pers. pl. / *timarse*.

timar to swindle. reg.

timarse to make eyes. reg.

tímate (you) make eyes; impve. 2nd pers. sing. / *timarse*.

timbrar to stamp. reg.

timémonos let us make eyes; impve. 1st pers. pl. / *timarse*.

tímense let them make eyes; impve. 3rd pers. pl. / *timarse*.

tímese let him (her/it) make eyes; impve. 3rd pers. sing. / *timarse*.

timonear to steer a ship. reg.

tintar to tint. reg.

tintinar to tinkle. reg.

tintinear to tinkle. reg.

tinto dyed; past part. / *teñir*.

tinturar to tincture. reg.

tiña 1. that I may dye; pres. subj. 1st pers. sing. / *teñir*. 2. that he (she/it) may dye; pres. subj. 3rd pers. sing. 3. let him (her/it) dye; impve. 3rd pers. sing.

tiñáis that you (all) may dye; pres. subj. 2nd pers. pl. / *teñir*.

tiñamos 1. that we may dye; pres. subj. 1st pers. pl. / *teñir*. 2. let us dye; impve. 1st pers. pl.

tiñan 1. that they may dye; pres. subj. 3rd pers. pl. / *teñir*. 2. let them dye; impve. 3rd pers. pl.

tiñas that you may dye; pres. subj. 2nd pers. sing. / *teñir*.

tiñe 1. he (she/it) dyes; pres. ind. 3rd pers. sing. / *teñir*. 2. (you) dye; impve. 2nd pers. sing.

tiñen they dye; pres. ind. 3rd pers. pl. / *teñir*.

tiñendo dying; pres. part. / *teñir*.

tiñera 1. that I might dye; imp. subj. 1st pers. sing. / *teñir*. 2. that he (she/it) might dye; imp. subj. 3rd pers. sing.

tiñerais that you (all) might dye; imp. subj. 2nd pers pl. / *teñir*.

tiñéramos that we might dye; imp. subj. 1st pers. pl. / *teñir*.

tiñeran that they might dye; imp. subj. 3rd pers. pl. / *teñir*.

tiñeras that you might dye; imp. subj. 2nd pers. sing. / *teñir*.

tiñeron they dyed; past 3rd pers. pl. / *teñir*.

tiñes you dye; pres. ind. 2nd pers. sing. / *teñir*.

tiñese 1. that I might dye; imp. subj. 1st pers. sing. / *teñir*. 2. that he (she/it) might dye; imp. subj. 3rd pers. sing.

tiñeseis that you (all) might dye; imp. subj. 2nd pers pl. / *teñir*.

tiñésemos that we might dye; imp. subj. 1st pers. pl. / *teñir*.

tiñesen that they might dye; imp. subj. 3rd pers. pl. / *teñir*.

tiñeses that you might dye; imp. subj. 2nd pers. sing. / *teñir*.

tiño I dye; pres. ind. 1st pers. sing. / *teñir*.

tiñó he (she/it) dyed; past 3rd pers. sing. / *teñir*.

tipiar to type. reg.

tirándose rushing; pres. part. / *tirarse*.

tiranice 1. that I may tyrannize; pres. subj. 1st pers. sing. / *tiranizar*. 2. that he (she/it) may tyrannize; pres. subj. 3rd pers. sing. 3. let him (her/it) tyrannize; impve. 3rd pers. sing.

tiranicé I tyrannized; past 1st pers. sing. / *tiranizar*.

tiranicéis that you (all) may tyrannize; pres. subj. 2nd pers. pl. / *tiranizar*.

tiranicemos 1. that we may tyrannize; pres. subj. 1st pers. pl. / *tiranizar*. 2. let us tyrannize; impve. 1st pers. pl.

tiranicen 1. that they may tyrannize; pres. subj. 3rd pers. pl. / *tiranizar*. 2. let them tyrannize; impve. 3rd pers. pl.

tiranices that you may tyrannize; pres. subj. 2nd pers. sing. / *tiranizar*.

tiranizar to tyrannize. irr.

tiraos (you all) rush; impve. 2nd pers. pl. / *tirarse*.

tirar to throw. reg.

tirarse to rush. reg.

tírate (you) rush; impve. 2nd pers. sing. / *tirarse*.

tirémonos let us rush; impve. 1st pers. pl. / *tirarse*.

tírense let them rush; impve. 3rd pers. pl. / *tirarse*.

tírese let him (her/it) rush; impve. 3rd pers. sing. / *tirarse*.

tiritar to shiver. reg.

tironear to pull. reg.

tiroteándose exchanging shots; pres. part. / *tirotearse*.

tiroteaos (you all) exchange shots; impve. 2nd pers. pl. / *tirotearse*.

tirotear to shoot at random. reg.

tirotearse to exchange shots. reg.

tirotéate (you) exchange shots; impve. 2nd pers. sing. / *tirotearse*.

tiroteémonos let us exchange shots; impve. 1st pers. pl. / *tirotearse*.

tirotéense let them exchange shots; impve. 3rd pers. pl. / *tirotearse*.

tirotéese let him (her/it) exchange shots; impve. 3rd pers. sing. / *tirotearse*.

titilar to quiver or to twinkle. reg.

titiritar to shiver. reg.

titubar to vacillate. reg.

titubear to hesitate. reg.

titulándose being called; pres. part. / *titularse*.

titulaos (you all) be called; impve. 2nd pers. pl. / *titularse*.

titular to title. reg.

titularse to be called. reg.

titúlate (you) be called; impve. 2nd pers. sing. / *titularse*.

titulémonos let us be called; impve. 1st pers. pl. / *titularse*.

titúlense let them be called; impve. 3rd pers. pl. / *titularse*.

titúlese let him (her/it) be called; impve. 3rd pers. sing. / *titularse*.

tiznándose getting drunk; pres. part. / *tiznarse*.

tiznaos (you all) get drunk; impve. 2nd pers. pl. / *tiznarse*.

tiznar to smudge. reg.

tiznarse to get drunk. reg.

tíznate (you) get drunk; impve. 2nd pers. sing. / *tiznarse*.

tiznémonos let us get drunk; impve. 1st pers. pl. / *tiznarse*.

tíznense let them get drunk; impve. 3rd pers. pl. / *tiznarse*.

tíznese let him (her/it) get drunk; impve. 3rd pers. sing. / *tiznarse*.

tizonear to stir. reg.

toar to tow. reg.

tocándose putting on a hat; pres. part. / *tocarse*.

tocaos (you all) put on a hat; impve. 2nd pers. pl. / *tocarse*.

tocar to touch. irr.

tocarse to put on a hat. irr.

tócate (you) put on a hat; impve. 2nd pers. sing. / *tocarse.*

toldar to cover with awning. reg.

tolerar to tolerate. reg.

tomándose rusting; pres. part. / *tomarse.*

tomar to take. reg.

tomarse to rust. reg.

tómense let them rust; impve. 3rd pers. pl. / *tomarse.*

tómese let it rust; impve. 3rd pers. sing. / *tomarse.*

tonificar to give tone. irr.

tonifique 1. that I may give tone; pres. subj. 1st pers. sing. / *tonificar.* 2. that he (she/it) may give tone; pres. subj. 3rd pers. sing. 3. let him (her/it) give tone; impve. 3rd pers. sing.

tonifiqué I gave tone; past 1st pers. sing. / *tonificar.*

tonifiquéis that you (all) may give tone; pres. subj. 2nd pers. pl. / *tonificar.*

tonifiquemos 1. that we may give tone; pres. subj. 1st pers. pl. / *tonificar.* 2. let us give tone; impve. 1st pers. pl.

tonifiquen 1. that they may give tone; pres. subj. 3rd pers. pl. / *tonificar.* 2. let them give tone; impve. 3rd pers. pl.

tonifiques that you may give tone; pres. subj. 2nd pers. sing. / *tonificar.*

tonsurar to tonsure. reg.

tontear to fool around. reg.

topar to butt. reg.

topetar to butt. reg.

topetear to butt. reg.

toque 1. that I may touch; pres. subj. 1st pers. sing. / *tocar.* 2. that he (she/it) may touch; pres. subj. 3rd pers. sing. 3. let him (her/it) touch; impve. 3rd pers. sing.

toqué I touched; past 1st pers. sing. / *tocar.*

toquéis that you (all) may touch; pres. subj. 2nd pers. pl. / *tocar.*

toquémonos let us put on a hat; impve. 1st pers. pl. / *tocarse.*

toquemos 1. that we may touch; pres. subj. 1st pers. pl. / *tocar.* 2. let us touch; impve. 1st pers. pl.

toquen 1. that they may touch; pres. subj. 3rd pers. pl. / *tocar.* 2. let them touch; impve. 3rd pers. pl.

tóquense let them put on a hat; impve. 3rd pers. pl. / *tocarse.*

toques that you may touch; pres. subj. 2nd pers. sing. / *tocar.*

tóquese let him (her/it) put on a hat; impve. 3rd pers. sing. / *tocarse.*

torcer to twist. irr.

torcerse to go astray. irr.

torear to fight bulls or to tease. reg.

tornándose turning; pres. part. / *tornarse.*

tornaos (you all) turn; impve. 2nd pers. pl. / *tornarse.*

tornar to return. reg.

tornarse to turn. reg.

tornasolar to make iridescent. reg.

tórnate (you) turn; impve. 2nd pers. sing. / *tornarse.*

tornear to turn in a lathe. reg.

tornémonos let us turn; impve. 1st pers. pl. / *tornarse.*

tórnense let them turn; impve. 3rd pers. pl. / *tornarse.*

tórnese let him (her/it) turn; impve. 3rd pers. sing. / *tornarse.*

torpedear to torpedo. reg.

torrar to toast. reg.

torturar to torture. reg.

torzáis that you (all) may twist; pres. subj. 2nd pers. pl. / *torcer.*

torzámonos let us go astray; impve. 1st pers. pl. / *torcerse.*

torzamos 1. that we may twist; pres. subj. 1st pers. pl. / *torcer.* 2. let us twist; impve. 1st pers. pl.

toser to cough or to defy. reg.

tostándose roasting; pres. part. / *tostarse.*

tostaos (you all) roast; impve. 2nd pers. pl. / *tostarse.*

tostar to toast. irr.

tostarse to roast. irr.

tostémonos let us roast; impve. 1st pers. pl. / *tostarse.*

totalice 1. that I may total; pres. subj. 1st pers. sing. / *totalizar.* 2. that he (she/it) may total; pres. subj. 3rd pers. sing. 3. let him (her/it) total; impve. 3rd pers. sing.

totalicé I totaled; past 1st pers. sing. / *totalizar.*

totalicéis that you (all) may total; pres. subj. 2nd pers. pl. / *totalizar.*

totalicémonos let us total; impve. 1st pers. pl. / *totalizarse.*

totalicemos 1. that we may total; pres. subj. 1st pers. pl. / *totalizar.* 2. let us total; impve. 1st pers. pl.

totalicen 1. that they may total; pres. subj. 3rd pers. pl. / *totalizar.* 2. let them total; impve. 3rd pers. pl.

totalícense let them total; impve. 3rd pers. pl. / *totalizarse.*

totalices that you may total; pres. subj. 2nd pers. sing. / *totalizar.*

totalícese let him (her/it) total; impve. 3rd pers. sing. / *totalizarse.*

totalizándose totaling; pres. part. / *totalizarse.*

totalizaos (you all) total; impve. 2nd pers. pl. / *totalizarse.*

totalizar to total. irr.

totalizarse to total. irr.

totalízate (you) total; impve. 2nd pers. sing. / *totalizarse.*

toxicar to poison. irr.

toxique 1. that I may poison; pres. subj. 1st pers. sing. / *toxicar.* 2. that he (she/it) may poison; pres. subj. 3rd pers. sing. 3. let him (her/it) poison; impve. 3rd pers. sing.

toxiqué I poisoned; past 1st pers. sing. / *toxicar.*

toxiquéis that you (all) may poison; pres. subj. 2nd pers. pl. / *toxicar.*

toxiquemos 1. that we may poison; pres. subj. 1st pers. pl. / *toxicar.* 2. let us poison; impve. 1st pers. pl.

toxiquen 1. that they may poison; pres. subj. 3rd pers. pl. / *toxicar.* 2. let them poison; impve. 3rd pers. pl.

toxiques that you may poison; pres. subj. 2nd pers. sing. / *toxicar.*

trabajándose striving; pres. part. / *trabajarse.*

trabajaos (you all) strive; impve. 2nd pers. pl. / *trabajarse.*

trabajar to work. reg.

trabajarse to strive. reg.

trabájate (you) strive; impve. 2nd pers. sing. / *trabajarse.*

trabajémonos let us strive; impve. 1st pers. pl. / *trabajarse.*

trabájense let them strive; impve. 3rd pers. pl. / *trabajarse.*

trabájese let him (her/it) strive; impve. 3rd pers. sing. / *trabajarse.*

trabándose becoming tangled; pres. part. / *trabarse.*

trabaos (you all) become tangled; impve. 2nd pers. pl. / *trabarse.*

trabar to join. reg.

trabarse to become tangled or to stammer. reg.

trábate (you) become tangled; impve. 2nd pers. sing. / *trabarse.*

trabémonos let us become tangled; impve. 1st pers. pl. / *trabarse.*

trábense let them become tangled; impve. 3rd pers. pl. / *trabarse.*

trábese let him (her/it) become tangled; impve. 3rd pers. sing. / *trabarse.*

trabucar to garble. irr.

trabuque 1. that I may garble; pres. subj. 1st pers. sing. / *trabucar.* 2. that he (she/it) may garble; pres. subj. 3rd pers. sing. 3. let him (her/it) garble; impve. 3rd pers. sing.

trabuqué I garbled; past 1st pers. sing. / *trabucar.*

trabuquéis that you (all) may garble; pres. subj. 2nd pers. pl. / *trabucar.*

trabuquemos 1. that we may garble; pres. subj. 1st pers. pl. / *trabucar.* 2. let us garble; impve. 1st pers. pl.

trabuquen 1. that they may garble; pres. subj. 3rd pers. pl. / *trabucar.* 2. let them garble; impve. 3rd pers. pl.

trabuques that you may garble; pres. subj. 2nd pers. sing. / *trabucar.*

trace 1. that I may trace; pres. subj. 1st pers. sing. / *trazar.* 2. that he (she/it) may trace; pres. subj. 3rd pers. sing. 3. let him (her/it) trace; impve. 3rd pers. sing.

tracé I traced; past 1st pers. sing. / *trazar.*

tracéis that you (all) may trace; pres. subj. 2nd pers. pl. / *trazar.*

tracemos 1. that we may trace; pres. subj. 1st pers. pl. / *trazar.* 2. let us trace; impve. 1st pers. pl.

tracen 1. that they may trace; pres. subj. 3rd pers. pl. / *trazar.* 2. let them trace; impve. 3rd pers. pl.

traces that you may trace; pres. subj. 2nd pers. sing. / *trazar.*

traducir to translate. irr.

traduje I translated; past 1st pers. sing. / *traducir.*

tradujera 1. that I might translate; imp. subj. 1st pers. sing. / *traducir.* 2. that he (she/it) might translate; imp. subj. 3rd pers. sing.

tradujerais that you (all) might translate; imp. subj. 2nd pers pl. / *traducir.*

tradujéramos that we might translate; imp. subj. 1st pers. pl. / *traducir.*

tradujeran that they might translate; imp. subj. 3rd pers. pl. / *traducir.*

tradujeras that you might translate; imp. subj. 2nd pers. sing. / *traducir.*

tradujeron they translated; past 3rd pers. pl. / *traducir.*

tradujese 1. that I might translate; imp. subj. 1st pers. sing. / *traducir.* 2. that he (she/it) might translate; imp. subj. 3rd pers. sing.

tradujeseis that you (all) might translate; imp. subj. 2nd pers pl. / *traducir.*

tradujésemos that we might translate; imp. subj. 1st pers. pl. / *traducir.*

tradujesen that they might translate; imp. subj. 3rd pers. pl. / *traducir.*

tradujeses that you might translate; imp. subj. 2nd pers. sing. / *traducir.*

tradujimos we translated; past 1st pers. pl. / *traducir.*

tradujiste you translated; past 2nd pers. sing. / *traducir.*

tradujisteis you (all) translated; past 2nd pers. pl. / *traducir.*

tradujo he (she/it) translated; past 3rd pers. sing. / *traducir.*

traduzca 1. that I may translate; pres. subj. 1st pers. sing. / *traducir.* 2. that he (she/it) may translate; pres. subj. 3rd pers. sing. 3. let him (her/it) translate; impve. 3rd pers. sing.

traduzcáis that you (all) may translate; pres. subj. 2nd pers. pl. / *traducir.*

traduzcamos 1. that we may translate; pres. subj. 1st pers. pl. / *traducir.* 2. let us translate; impve. 1st pers. pl.

traduzcan 1. that they may translate; pres. subj. 3rd pers. pl. / *traducir.* 2. let them translate; impve. 3rd pers. pl.

traduzcas that you may translate; pres. subj. 2nd pers. sing. / *traducir.*

traduzco I translate; pres. ind. 1st pers. sing. / *traducir.*

traeos (you all) dress; impve. 2nd pers. pl. / *traerse.*

traer to bring. irr.

traerse to dress. irr.

traérselas to be up to something. irr.

tráete (you) dress; impve. 2nd pers. sing. / *traerse.*

trafagar to traffic. irr.

trafague 1. that I may traffic; pres. subj. 1st pers. sing. / *trafagar.* 2. that he (she/it) may traffic; pres. subj. 3rd pers. sing. 3. let him (her/it) traffic; impve. 3rd pers. sing.

trafagué I trafficed; past 1st pers. sing. / *trafagar.*

trafaguéis that you (all) may traffic; pres. subj. 2nd pers. pl. / *trafagar.*

trafaguemos 1. that we may traffic; pres. subj. 1st pers. pl. / *trafagar*. 2. let us traffic; impve. 1st pers. pl.

trafaguen 1. that they may traffic; pres. subj. 3rd pers. pl. / *trafagar*. 2. let them traffic; impve. 3rd pers. pl.

trafagues that you may traffic; pres. subj. 2nd pers. sing. / *trafagar*.

traficar to traffic. irr.

trafique 1. that I may traffic; pres. subj. 1st pers. sing. / *traficar*. 2. that he (she/it) may traffic; pres. subj. 3rd pers. sing. 3. let him (her/it) traffic; impve. 3rd pers. sing.

trafiqué I trafficced; past 1st pers. sing. / *traficar*.

trafiquéis that you (all) may traffic; pres. subj. 2nd pers. pl. / *traficar*.

trafiquemos 1. that we may traffic; pres. subj. 1st pers. pl. / *traficar*. 2. let us traffic; impve. 1st pers. pl.

trafiquen 1. that they may traffic; pres. subj. 3rd pers. pl. / *traficar*. 2. let them traffic; impve. 3rd pers. pl.

trafiques that you may traffic; pres. subj. 2nd pers. sing. / *traficar*.

tragándose playing dumb; pres. part. / *tragarse*.

tragaos (you all) play dumb; impve. 2nd pers. pl. / *tragarse*.

tragar to swallow. irr.

tragarse to play dumb. irr.

trágate (you) play dumb; impve. 2nd pers. sing. / *tragarse*.

trague 1. that I may swallow; pres. subj. 1st pers. sing. / *tragar*. 2. that he (she/it) may swallow; pres. subj. 3rd pers. sing. 3. let him (her/it) swallow; impve. 3rd pers. sing.

tragué I swallowed; past 1st pers. sing. / *tragar*.

traguéis that you (all) may swallow; pres. subj. 2nd pers. pl. / *tragar*.

traguémonos let us play dumb; impve. 1st pers. pl. / *tragarse*.

traguemos 1. that we may swallow; pres. subj. 1st pers. pl. / *tragar*. 2. let us swallow; impve. 1st pers. pl.

traguen 1. that they may swallow; pres. subj. 3rd pers. pl. / *tragar*. 2. let them swallow; impve. 3rd pers. pl.

tráguense let them play dumb; impve. 3rd pers. pl. / *tragarse*.

tragues that you may swallow; pres. subj. 2nd pers. sing. / *tragar*.

tráguese let him (her/it) play dumb; impve. 3rd pers. sing. / *tragarse*.

traicionar to betray. reg.

traído brought; past part. / *traer*.

traiga 1. that I may bring; pres. subj. 1st pers. sing. / *traer*. 2. that he (she/it) may bring; pres. subj. 3rd pers. sing. 3. let him (her/it) bring; impve. 3rd pers. sing.

traigáis that you (all) may bring; pres. subj. 2nd pers. pl. / *traer*.

traigámonos let us dress; impve. 1st pers. pl. / *traerse*.

traigamos 1. that we may bring; pres. subj. 1st pers. pl. / *traer*. 2. let us bring; impve. 1st pers. pl.

traigan 1. that they may bring; pres. subj. 3rd pers. pl. / *traer*. 2. let them bring; impve. 3rd pers. pl.

tráiganse let them dress; impve. 3rd pers. pl. / *traerse*.

traigas that you may bring; pres. subj. 2nd pers. sing. / *traer*.

tráigase let him (her/it) dress; impve. 3rd pers. sing. / *traerse*.

traigo I bring; pres. ind. 1st pers. sing. / *traer*.

traje I brought; past 1st pers. sing. / *traer*.

trajear to dress. reg.

trajera 1. that I might bring; imp. subj. 1st pers. sing. / *traer*. 2. that he (she/it) might bring; imp. subj. 3rd pers. sing.

trajerais that you (all) might bring; imp. subj. 2nd pers pl. / *traer*.

trajéramos that we might bring; imp. subj. 1st pers. pl. / *traer*.

trajeran that they might bring; imp. subj. 3rd pers. pl. / *traer*.

trajeras that you might bring; imp. subj. 2nd pers. sing. / *traer*.

trajeron they brought; past 3rd pers. pl. / *traer*.

trajese 1. that I might bring; imp. subj. 1st pers. sing. / *traer*. 2. that he (she/it) might bring; imp. subj. 3rd pers. sing.

trajeseis that you (all) might bring; imp. subj. 2nd pers pl. / *traer*.

trajésemos that we might bring; imp. subj. 1st pers. pl. / *traer*.

trajesen that they might bring; imp. subj. 3rd pers. pl. / *traer*.

trajeses that you might bring; imp. subj. 2nd pers. sing. / *traer*.

trajimos we brought; past 1st pers. pl. / *traer*.

trajinar to carry. reg.

trajiste you brought; past 2nd pers. sing. / *traer*.

trajisteis you (all) brought; past 2nd pers. pl. / *traer*.

trajo he (she/it) brought; past 3rd pers. sing. / *traer*.

tramar to weave or to plot. reg.

tramitar to transact. reg.

tramontándose fleeing; pres. part. / *tramontarse*.

tramontaos (you all) flee; impve. 2nd pers. pl. / *tramontarse*.

tramontar to sink behind mountains. reg.

tramontarse to flee. reg.

tramóntate (you) flee; impve. 2nd pers. sing. / *tramontarse*.

tramontémonos let us flee; impve. 1st pers. pl. / *tramontarse*.

tramóntense let them flee; impve. 3rd pers. pl. / *tramontarse*.

tramóntese let him (her/it) flee; impve. 3rd pers. sing. / *tramontarse*.

trampear to cheat. reg.

trancándose secluding oneself; pres. part. / *trancarse*.

trancaos (you all) seclude yourselves; impve. 2nd pers. pl. / *trancarse*.

trancar to bar or to stride along. irr.

trancarse to seclude oneself. irr.

tráncate (you) seclude yourself; impve. 2nd pers. sing. / *trancarse.*

trance 1. that I may truncate; pres. subj. 1st pers. sing. / *tranzar.* 2. that he (she/it) may truncate; pres. subj. 3rd pers. sing. 3. let him (her/it) truncate; impve. 3rd pers. sing.

trancé I truncated; past 1st pers. sing. / *tranzar.*

trancéis that you (all) may truncate; pres. subj. 2nd pers. pl. / *tranzar.*

trancemos 1. that we may truncate; pres. subj. 1st pers. pl. / *tranzar.* 2. let us truncate; impve. 1st pers. pl.

trancen 1. that they may truncate; pres. subj. 3rd pers. pl. / *tranzar.* 2. let them truncate; impve. 3rd pers. pl.

trances that you may truncate; pres. subj. 2nd pers. sing. / *tranzar.*

tranque 1. that I may bar; pres. subj. 1st pers. sing. / *trancar.* 2. that he (she/it) may bar; pres. subj. 3rd pers. sing. 3. let him (her/it) bar; impve. 3rd pers. sing.

tranqué I barred; past 1st pers. sing. / *trancar.*

tranquear to stride along. reg.

tranquéis that you (all) may bar; pres. subj. 2nd pers. pl. / *trancar.*

tranquémonos let us seclude ourselves; impve. 1st pers. pl. / *trancarse.*

tranquemos 1. that we may bar; pres. subj. 1st pers. pl. / *trancar.* 2. let us bar; impve. 1st pers. pl.

tranquen 1. that they may bar; pres. subj. 3rd pers. pl. / *trancar.* 2. let them bar; impve. 3rd pers. pl.

tránquense let them seclude themselves; impve. 3rd pers. pl. / *trancarse.*

tranques that you may bar; pres. subj. 2nd pers. sing. / *trancar.*

tránquese let him (her/it) seclude himself (herself/itself); impve. 3rd pers. sing. / *trancarse.*

tranquilice 1. that I may tranquilize; pres. subj. 1st pers. sing. / *tranquilizar.* 2. that he (she/it) may tranquilize; pres. subj. 3rd pers. sing. 3. let him (her/it) tranquilize; impve. 3rd pers. sing.

tranquilicé I tranquilized; past 1st pers. sing. / *tranquilizar.*

tranquilicéis that you (all) may tranquilize; pres. subj. 2nd pers. pl. / *tranquilizar.*

tranquilicémonos let us calm down; impve. 1st pers. pl. / *tranquilizarse.*

tranquilicemos 1. that we may tranquilize; pres. subj. 1st pers. pl. / *tranquilizar.* 2. let us tranquilize; impve. 1st pers. pl.

tranquilicen 1. that they may tranquilize; pres. subj. 3rd pers. pl. / *tranquilizar.* 2. let them tranquilize; impve. 3rd pers. pl.

tranquilícense let them calm down; impve. 3rd pers. pl. / *tranquilizarse.*

tranquilices that you may tranquilize; pres. subj. 2nd pers. sing. / *tranquilizarse.*

tranquilícese let him (her/it) calm down; impve. 3rd pers. sing. / *tranquilizarse.*

tranquilizándose calming down; pres. part. / *tranquilizarse.*

tranquilizaos (you all) calm down; impve. 2nd pers. pl. / *tranquilizarse.*

tranquilizar to tranquilize. irr.

tranquilizarse to calm down. irr.

tranquilízate (you) calm down; impve. 2nd pers. sing. / *tranquilizarse.*

transar to compromise. reg.

transbordar to transfer. reg.

transcender to analyze or to spread. irr.

transcienda 1. that I may analyze; pres. subj. 1st pers. sing. / *transcender.* 2. that he (she/it) may analyze; pres. subj. 3rd pers. sing. 3. let him (her/it) analyze; impve. 3rd pers. sing.

transciendan 1. that they may analyze; pres. subj. 3rd pers. pl. / *transcender.* 2. let them analyze; impve. 3rd pers. pl.

transciendas that you may analyze; pres. subj. 2nd pers. sing. / *transcender.*

transciende 1. he (she/it) analyzes; pres. ind. 3rd pers. sing. / *transcender.* 2. (you) analyze; impve. 2nd pers. sing.

transcienden they analyze; pres. ind. 3rd pers. pl. / *transcender.*

transciendes you analyze; pres. ind. 2nd pers. sing. / *transcender.*

transciendo I analyze; pres. ind. 1st pers. sing. / *transcender.*

transcribir to transcribe. reg. except for pp.

transcripto transcribed; past part. / *transcribir.*

transcrito transcribed; past part. / *transcribir.*

transcurrir to elapse. reg.

transferir to transfer. irr.

transfiera 1. that I may transfer; pres. subj. 1st pers. sing. / *transferir.* 2. that he (she/it) may transfer; pres. subj. 3rd pers. sing. 3. let him (her/it) transfer; impve. 3rd pers. sing.

transfieran 1. that they may transfer; pres. subj. 3rd pers. pl. / *transferir.* 2. let them transfer; impve. 3rd pers. pl.

transfieras that you may transfer; pres. subj. 2nd pers. sing. / *transferir.*

transfiere 1. he (she/it) transfers; pres. ind. 3rd pers. sing. / *transferir.* 2. (you) transfer; impve. 2nd pers. sing.

transfieren they transfer; pres. ind. 3rd pers. pl. / *transferir.*

transfieres you transfer; pres. ind. 2nd pers. sing. / *transferir.*

transfiero I transfer; pres. ind. 1st pers. sing. / *transferir.*

transfigurándose becoming transfigured; pres. part. / *transfigurarse.*

transfiguraos (you all) become transfigured; impve. 2nd pers. pl. / *transfigurarse.*

transfigurar to transfigure. reg.

transfigurarse to become transfigured. reg.

transfigúrate (you) become transfigured; impve. 2nd pers. sing. / *transfigurarse.*

transfigurémonos let us become transfigured; impve. 1st pers. pl. / *transfigurarse.*

transfigúrense let them become transfigured; impve. 3rd pers. pl. / *transfigurarse*.

transfigúrese let him (her/it) become transfigured; impve. 3rd pers. sing. / *transfigurarse*.

transfiráis that you (all) may transfer; pres. subj. 2nd pers. pl. / *transferir*.

transfiramos 1. that we may transfer; pres. subj. 1st pers. pl. / *transferir*. 2. let us transfer; impve. 1st pers. pl.

transfiriendo transferring; pres. part. / *transferir*.

transfiriera 1. that I might transfer; imp. subj. 1st pers. sing. / *transferir*. 2. that he (she/it) might transfer; imp. subj. 3rd pers. sing.

transfirierais that you (all) might transfer; imp. subj. 2nd pers pl. / *transferir*.

transfiriéramos that we might transfer; imp. subj. 1st pers. pl. / *transferir*.

transfirieran that they might transfer; imp. subj. 3rd pers. pl. / *transferir*.

transfirieras that you might transfer; imp. subj. 2nd pers. sing. / *transferir*.

transfirieron they transferred; past 3rd pers. pl. / *transferir*.

transfiriese 1. that I might transfer; imp. subj. 1st pers. sing. / *transferir*. 2. that he (she/it) might transfer; imp. subj. 3rd pers. sing.

transfirieseis that you (all) might transfer; imp. subj. 2nd pers pl. / *transferir*.

transfiriésemos that we might transfer; imp. subj. 1st pers. pl. / *transferir*.

transfiriesen that they might transfer; imp. subj. 3rd pers. pl. / *transferir*.

transfirieses that you might transfer; imp. subj. 2nd pers. sing. / *transferir*.

transfirió he (she/it) transferred; past 3rd pers. sing. / *transferir*.

transflorar to show through. reg.

transformar to transform. reg.

transfretar to cross the sea or to spread. reg.

transfundir to transfuse or to transmit. reg.

transgredir to transgress. irr. used only in the forms that have an i in the ending.

transigir to compromise. irr.

transija 1. that I may compromise; pres. subj. 1st pers. sing. / *transigir*. 2. that he (she/it) may compromise; pres. subj. 3rd pers. sing. 3. let him (her/it) compromise; impve. 3rd pers. sing.

transijáis that you (all) may compromise; pres. subj. 2nd pers. pl. / *transigir*.

transijamos 1. that we may compromise; pres. subj. 1st pers. pl. / *transigir*. 2. let us compromise; impve. 1st pers. pl.

transijan 1. that they may compromise; pres. subj. 3rd pers. pl. / *transigir*. 2. let them compromise; impve. 3rd pers. pl.

transijas that you may compromise; pres. subj. 2nd pers. sing. / *transigir*.

transijo I compromise; pres. ind. 1st pers. sing. / *transigir*.

transitar to pass through. reg.

translimitar to go beyond. reg.

transmigrar to transmigrate. reg.

transmitir to transmit. reg.

transmutar to transmute. reg.

transparentándose becoming transparent; pres. part. / *transparentarse*.

transparentaos (you all) become transparent; impve. 2nd pers. pl. / *transparentarse*.

transparentarse to become transparent. reg.

transparéntate (you) become transparent; impve. 2nd pers. sing. / *transparentarse*.

transparentémonos let us become transparent; impve. 1st pers. pl. / *transparentarse*.

transparéntense let them become transparent; impve. 3rd pers. pl. / *transparentarse*.

transparéntese let him (her/it) become transparent; impve. 3rd pers. sing. / *transparentarse*.

transpirar to perspire. reg.

transplantar to transplant. reg.

transpon (you) transpose; impve. 2nd pers. sing. / *transponer*.

transpondrá he (she/it) will transpose; fut. 3rd pers. sing. / *transponer*.

transpondrán they will transpose; fut. 3rd pers. pl. / *transponer*.

transpondrás you will transpose; fut. 2nd pers. sing. / *transponer*.

transpondré I shall transpose; fut. 1st pers. sing. / *transponer*.

transpondréis you (all) will transpose; fut. 2nd pers. pl. / *transponer*.

transpondremos we shall transpose; fut. 1st pers. pl. / *transponer*.

transpondría 1. I should transpose; cond. 1st pers. sing. / *transponer*. 2. he (she/it) would transpose; cond. 3rd pers. sing.

transpondríais you (all) would transpose; cond. 2nd pers. pl. / *transponer*.

transpondríamos we should transpose; cond. 1st pers. pl. / *transponer*.

transpondrían they would transpose; cond. 3rd pers. pl. / *transponer*.

transpondrías you would transpose; cond. 2nd pers. sing. / *transponer*.

transponeos (you all) hide from view; impve. 2nd pers. pl. / *transponerse*.

transponer to transpose. irr.

transponerse to hide from view. irr.

transponga 1. that I may transpose; pres. subj. 1st pers. sing. / *transponer*. 2. that he (she/it) may transpose; pres. subj. 3rd pers. sing. 3. let him (her/it) transpose; impve. 3rd pers. sing.

transpongáis that you (all) may transpose; pres. subj. 2nd pers. pl. / *transponer*.

transpongámonos let us hide from view; impve. 1st pers. pl. / *transponerse*.

transpongamos 1. that we may transpose; pres. subj. 1st pers. pl. / *transponer*. 2. let us transpose; impve. 1st pers. pl.

transpongan 1. that they may transpose; pres. subj. 3rd pers. pl. / *transponer*. 2. let them transpose; impve. 3rd pers. pl.

transpónganse let them hide from view; impve. 3rd pers. pl. / *transponerse*.

transpongas that you may transpose; pres. subj. 2nd pers. sing. / *transponer*.

transpóngase let him (her/it) hide from view; impve. 3rd pers. sing. / *transponerse*.

transpongo I transpose; pres. ind. 1st pers. sing. / *transponer*.

transponiendo transposing; pres. part. / *transponer*.

transponiéndose hiding from view; pres. part. / *transponerse*.

transponte (you) hide from view; impve. 2nd pers. sing. / *transponerse*.

transportándose going into ecstacies; pres. part. / *transportarse*.

transportaos (you all) go into ecstacies; impve. 2nd pers. pl. / *transportarse*.

transportar to transport. reg.

transportarse to go into ecstacies. reg.

transpórtate (you) go into ecstacies; impve. 2nd pers. sing. / *transportarse*.

transportémonos let us go into ecstacies; impve. 1st pers. pl. / *transportarse*.

transpórtense let them go into ecstacies; impve. 3rd pers. pl. / *transportarse*.

transpórtese let him (her/it) go into ecstacies; impve. 3rd pers. sing. / *transportarse*.

transpuesto transposed; past part. / *transponer*.

transpuse I transposed; past 1st pers. sing. / *transponer*.

transpusiera 1. that I might transpose; imp. subj. 1st pers. sing. / *transponer*. 2. that he (she/it) might transpose; imp. subj. 3rd pers. sing.

transpusierais that you (all) might transpose; imp. subj. 2nd pers pl. / *transponer*.

transpusiéramos that we might transpose; imp. subj. 1st pers. pl. / *transponer*.

transpusieran that they might transpose; imp. subj. 3rd pers. pl. / *transponer*.

transpusieras that you might transpose; imp. subj. 2nd pers. sing. / *transponer*.

transpusieron they transposed; past 3rd pers. pl. / *transponer*.

transpusiese 1. that I might transpose; imp. subj. 1st pers. sing. / *transponer*. 2. that he (she/it) might transpose; imp. subj. 3rd pers. sing.

transpusieseis that you (all) might transpose; imp. subj. 2nd pers pl. / *transponer*.

transpusiésemos that we might transpose; imp. subj. 1st pers. pl. / *transponer*.

transpusiesen that they might transpose; imp. subj. 3rd pers. pl. / *transponer*.

transpusieses that you might transpose; imp. subj. 2nd pers. sing. / *transponer*.

transpusimos we transposed; past 1st pers. pl. / *transponer*.

transpusiste you transposed; past 2nd pers. sing. / *transponer*.

transpusisteis you (all) transposed; past 2nd pers. pl. / *transponer*.

transpuso he (she/it) transposed; past 3rd pers. sing. / *transponer*.

transvertir to change. irr.

transvierta 1. that I may change; pres. subj. 1st pers. sing. / *transvertir*. 2. that he (she/it) may change; pres. subj. 3rd pers. sing. 3. let him (her/it) change; impve. 3rd pers. sing.

transviertan 1. that they may change; pres. subj. 3rd pers. pl. / *transvertir*. 2. let them change; impve. 3rd pers. pl.

transviertas that you may change; pres. subj. 2nd pers. sing. / *transvertir*.

transvierte 1. he (she/it) changes; pres. ind. 3rd pers. sing. / *transvertir*. 2. (you) change; impve. 2nd pers. sing.

transvierten they change; pres. ind. 3rd pers. pl. / *transvertir*.

transviertes you change; pres. ind. 2nd pers. sing. / *transvertir*.

transvierto I change; pres. ind. 1st pers. sing. / *transvertir*.

transvirtáis that you (all) may change; pres. subj. 2nd pers. pl. / *transvertir*.

transvirtamos 1. that we may change; pres. subj. 1st pers. pl. / *transvertir*. 2. let us change; impve. 1st pers. pl.

transvirtiendo changing; pres. part. / *transvertir*.

transvirtiera 1. that I might change; imp. subj. 1st pers. sing. / *transvertir*. 2. that he (she/it) might change; imp. subj. 3rd pers. sing.

transvirtierais that you (all) might change; imp. subj. 2nd pers. pl. / *transvertir*.

transvirtiéramos that we might change; imp. subj. 1st pers. pl. / *transvertir*.

transvirtieran that they might change; imp. subj. 3rd pers. pl. / *transvertir*.

transvirtieras that you might change; imp. subj. 2nd pers. sing. / *transvertir*.

transvirtieron they changed; past 3rd pers. pl. / *transvertir*.

transvirtiese 1. that I might change; imp. subj. 1st pers. sing. / *transvertir*. 2. that he (she/it) might change; imp. subj. 3rd pers. sing.

transvirtieseis that you (all) might change; imp. subj. 2nd pers pl. / *transvertir*.

transvirtiésemos that we might change; imp. subj. 1st pers. pl. / *transvertir*.

transvirtiesen that they might change; imp. subj. 3rd pers. pl. / *transvertir*.

transvirtieses that you might change; imp. subj. 2nd pers. sing. / *transvertir*.

transvirtió he (she/it) changed; past 3rd pers. sing. / *transvertir*.

tranzar to truncate. irr.

trapacear to swindle. reg.

trapalear to clatter. reg.

trapear to mop. reg.

trapichear to retail. reg.

traquear to shake or to rattle. reg.

traquetear to rattle. reg.

trasbordar to transfer. reg.

trascender to transcend. irr.

trascienda 1. that I may transcend; pres. subj. 1st pers. sing. / *trascender*. 2. that he (she/it) may transcend; pres. subj. 3rd pers. sing. 3. let him (her/it) transcend; impve. 3rd pers. sing.

trasciendan 1. that they may transcend; pres. subj. 3rd pers. pl. / *trascender*. 2. let them transcend; impve. 3rd pers. pl.

trasciendas that you may transcend; pres. subj. 2nd pers. sing. / *trascender*.

trasciende 1. he (she/it) transcends; pres. ind. 3rd pers. sing. / *trascender*. 2. (you) transcend; impve. 2nd pers. sing.

trascienden they transcend; pres. ind. 3rd pers. pl. / *trascender*.

trasciendes you transcend; pres. ind. 2nd pers. sing. / *trascender*.

trasciendo I transcend; pres. ind. 1st pers. sing. / *trascender*.

trascolar to percolate. irr.

trascribir to transcribe. reg. except for pp.

trascrito transcribed; past part. / *trascribir*.

trascuela 1. he (she/it) percolates; pres. ind. 3rd pers. sing. / *trascolar*. 2. (you) percolate; impve. 2nd pers. sing.

trascuelan they percolate; pres. ind. 3rd pers. pl. / *trascolar*.

trascuelas you percolate; pres. ind. 2nd pers. sing. / *trascolar*.

trascuele 1. that I may percolate; pres. subj. 1st pers. sing. / *trascolar*. 2. that he (she/it) may percolate; pres. subj. 3rd pers. sing. 3. let him (her/it) percolate; impve. 3rd pers. sing.

trascuelen 1. that they may percolate; pres. subj. 3rd pers. pl. / *trascolar*. 2. let them percolate; impve. 3rd pers. pl.

trascueles that you may percolate; pres. subj. 2nd pers. sing. / *trascolar*.

trascuelo I percolate; pres. ind. 1st pers. sing. / *trascolar*.

trascurrir to pass. reg.

trasechar to waylay. reg.

trasegar to upset. irr.

trasegué I upset; past 1st pers. sing. / *trasegar*.

traseguéis that you (all) may upset; pres. subj. 2nd pers. pl. / *trasegar*.

traseguemos 1. that we may upset; pres. subj. 1st pers. pl. / *trasegar*. 2. let us upset; impve. 1st pers. pl.

trasferir to transfer. irr.

trasfiera 1. that I may transfer; pres. subj. 1st pers. sing. / *trasferir*. 2. that he (she/it) may transfer; pres. subj. 3rd pers. sing. 3. let him (her/it) transfer; impve. 3rd pers. sing.

trasfieran 1. that they may transfer; pres. subj. 3rd pers. pl. / *trasferir*. 2. let them transfer; impve. 3rd pers. pl.

trasfieras that you may transfer; pres. subj. 2nd pers. sing. / *trasferir*.

trasfiere 1. he (she/it) transfers; pres. ind. 3rd pers. sing. / *trasferir*. 2. (you) transfer; impve. 2nd pers. sing.

trasfieren they transfer; pres. ind. 3rd pers. pl. / *trasferir*.

trasfieres you transfer; pres. ind. 2nd pers. sing. / *trasferir*.

trasfiero I transfer; pres. ind. 1st pers. sing. / *trasferir*.

trasfiguándose being transfigured; pres. part. / *trasfiguarse*.

trasfiguaos (you all) be transfigured; impve. 2nd pers. pl. / *trasfiguarse*.

trasfiguarse to be transfigured. reg.

trasfíguate (you) be transfigured; impve. 2nd pers. sing. / *trasfiguarse*.

trasfiguémonos let us be transfigured; impve. 1st pers. pl. / *trasfiguarse*.

trasfíguense let them be transfigured; impve. 3rd pers. pl. / *trasfiguarse*.

trasfíguese let him (her/it) be transfigured; impve. 3rd pers. sing. / *trasfiguarse*.

trasfiráis that you (all) may transfer; pres. subj. 2nd pers. pl. / *trasferir*.

trasfiramos 1. that we may transfer; pres. subj. 1st pers. pl. / *trasferir*. 2. let us transfer; impve. 1st pers. pl.

trasfiriendo transferring; pres. part. / *trasferir*.

trasfiriera 1. that I might transfer; imp. subj. 1st pers. sing. / *trasferir*. 2. that he (she/it) might transfer; imp. subj. 3rd pers. sing.

trasfirierais that you (all) might transfer; imp. subj. 2nd pers pl. / *trasferir*.

trasfiriéramos that we might transfer; imp. subj. 1st pers. pl. / *trasferir*.

trasfirieran that they might transfer; imp. subj. 3rd pers. pl. / *trasferir*.

trasfirieras that you might transfer; imp. subj. 2nd pers. sing. / *trasferir*.

trasfirieron they transferred; past 3rd pers. pl. / *trasferir*.

trasfiriese 1. that I might transfer; imp. subj. 1st pers. sing. / *trasferir*. 2. that he (she/it) might transfer; imp. subj. 3rd pers. sing.

trasfirieseis that you (all) might transfer; imp. subj. 2nd pers pl. / *trasferir*.

trasfiriésemos that we might transfer; imp. subj. 1st pers. pl. / *trasferir*.

trasfiriesen that they might transfer; imp. subj. 3rd pers. pl. / *trasferir*.

trasfirieses that you might transfer; imp. subj. 2nd pers. sing. / *trasferir*.

trasfirió he (she/it) transferred; past 3rd pers. sing. / *trasferir*.

trasformándose changing; pres. part. / *trasformarse*.

trasformaos (you all) change; impve. 2nd pers. pl. / *trasformarse*.

trasformar to transform. reg.

trasformarse to change. reg.

trasfórmate (you) change; impve. 2nd pers. sing. / *trasformarse*.

trasformémonos let us change; impve. 1st pers. pl. / *trasformarse.*

trasfórmense let them change; impve. 3rd pers. pl. / *trasformarse.*

trasfórmese let him (her/it) change; impve. 3rd pers. sing. / *trasformarse.*

trasgredir to transgress. irr. used only in the forms that have an I in the ending.

trashojar to leaf through a book. reg.

trashumar to move to seasonal pastures. reg.

trasiega 1. he (she/it) upsets; pres. ind. 3rd pers. sing. / *trasegar.* 2. (you) upset; impve. 2nd pers. sing.

trasiegan they upset; pres. ind. 3rd pers. pl. / *trasegar.*

trasiegas you upset; pres. ind. 2nd pers. sing. / *trasegar.*

trasiego I upset; pres. ind. 1st pers. sing. / *trasegar.*

trasiegue 1. that I may upset; pres. subj. 1st pers. sing. / *trasegar.* 2. that he (she/it) may upset; pres. subj. 3rd pers. sing. 3. let him (her/it) upset; impve. 3rd pers. sing.

trasieguen 1. that they may upset; pres. subj. 3rd pers. pl. / *trasegar.* 2. let them upset; impve. 3rd pers. pl.

trasiegues that you may upset; pres. subj. 2nd pers. sing. / *trasegar.*

trasladándose moving; pres. part. / *trasladarse.*

trasladaos (you all) move; impve. 2nd pers. pl. / *trasladarse.*

trasladar to move. reg.

trasladarse to move. reg.

trasládate (you) move; impve. 2nd pers. sing. / *trasladarse.*

trasladémonos let us move; impve. 1st pers. pl. / *trasladarse.*

trasládense let them move; impve. 3rd pers. pl. / *trasladarse.*

trasládese let him (her/it) move; impve. 3rd pers. sing. / *trasladarse.*

traslapar to overlap. reg.

traslúcete (you) be translucent; impve. 2nd pers. sing. / *traslucirse.*

trasluciéndose being translucent; pres. part. / *traslucirse.*

traslucíos (you all) be translucent; impve. 2nd pers. pl. / *traslucirse.*

traslucir to infer. irr.

traslucirse to be translucent. irr.

traslumbrándose vanishing; pres. part. / *traslumbrarse.*

traslumbraos (you all) vanish; impve. 2nd pers. pl. / *traslumbrarse.*

traslumbrar to dazzle. reg.

traslumbrarse to vanish. reg.

traslúmbrate (you) vanish; impve. 2nd pers. sing. / *traslumbrarse.*

traslumbrémonos let us vanish; impve. 1st pers. pl. / *traslumbrarse.*

traslúmbrense let them vanish; impve. 3rd pers. pl. / *traslumbrarse.*

traslúmbrese let him (her/it) vanish; impve. 3rd pers. sing. / *traslumbrarse.*

trasluzca 1. that I may infer; pres. subj. 1st pers. sing. / *traslucir.* 2. that he (she/it) may infer; pres. subj. 3rd pers. sing. 3. let him (her/it) infer; impve. 3rd pers. sing.

trasluzcáis that you (all) may infer; pres. subj. 2nd pers. pl. / *traslucir.*

trasluzcámonos let us be translucent; impve. 1st pers. pl. / *traslucirse.*

trasluzcamos 1. that we may infer; pres. subj. 1st pers. pl. / *traslucir.* 2. let us infer; impve. 1st pers. pl.

trasluzcan 1. that they may infer; pres. subj. 3rd pers. pl. / *traslucir.* 2. let them infer; impve. 3rd pers. pl.

traslúzcanse let them be translucent; impve. 3rd pers. pl. / *traslucirse.*

trasluzcas that you may infer; pres. subj. 2nd pers. sing. / *traslucir.*

traslúzcase let him (her/it) be translucent; impve. 3rd pers. sing. / *traslucirse.*

trasluzco I infer; pres. ind. 1st pers. sing. / *traslucir.*

trasmañanar to leave for the morrow. reg.

trasmatar to bury. reg.

trasminándose seeping; pres. part. / *trasminarse.*

trasminar to undermine. reg.

trasminarse to seep. reg.

trasmínense let them seep; impve. 3rd pers. pl. / *trasminarse.*

trasmínese let it seep; impve. 3rd pers. sing. / *trasminarse.*

trasmitir to transmit. reg.

trasnochar to stay up all night. reg.

trasoñar to dream up. irr.

traspalar to shovel. reg.

traspapelándose getting mislaid; pres. part. / *traspapelarse.*

traspapelar to misplace a document. reg.

traspapelarse to get mislaid. reg.

traspapélense let them get mislaid; impve. 3rd pers. pl. / *traspapelarse.*

traspapélese let it get mislaid; impve. 3rd pers. sing. / *traspapelarse.*

traspasándose overstepping the mark; pres. part. / *traspasarse.*

traspasaos (you all) overstep the mark; impve. 2nd pers. pl. / *traspasarse.*

traspasar to cross over. reg.

traspasarse to overstep the mark. reg.

traspásate (you) overstep the mark; impve. 2nd pers. sing. / *traspasarse.*

traspasémonos let us overstep the mark; impve. 1st pers. pl. / *traspasarse.*

traspásense let them overstep the mark; impve. 3rd pers. pl. / *traspasarse.*

traspásese let him (her/it) overstep the mark; impve. 3rd pers. sing. / *traspasarse.*

traspirar to transpire. reg.

trasplantándose emigrating; pres. part. / *trasplantarse.*

trasplantaos (you all) emigrate; impve. 2nd pers. pl. / *trasplantarse.*

trasplantar to transplant. reg.

trasplantarse to emigrate. reg.

trasplántate (you) emigrate; impve. 2nd pers. sing. / *trasplantarse.*

trasplantémonos let us emigrate; impve. 1st pers. pl. / *trasplantarse.*

trasplántense let them emigrate; impve. 3rd pers. pl. / *trasplantarse.*

trasplántese let him (her/it) emigrate; impve. 3rd pers. sing. / *trasplantarse.*

traspon (you) transpose; impve. 2nd pers. sing. / *trasponer.*

traspondrá he (she/it) will transpose; fut. 3rd pers. sing. / *trasponer.*

traspondrán they will transpose; fut. 3rd pers. pl. / *trasponer.*

traspondrás you will transpose; fut. 2nd pers. sing. / *trasponer.*

traspondré I shall transpose; fut. 1st pers. sing. / *trasponer.*

traspondréis you (all) will transpose; fut. 2nd pers. pl. / *trasponer.*

traspondremos we shall transpose; fut. 1st pers. pl. / *trasponer.*

traspondría 1. I should transpose; cond. 1st pers. sing. / *trasponer.* 2. he (she/it) would transpose; cond. 3rd pers. sing.

traspondríais you (all) would transpose; cond. 2nd pers. pl. / *trasponer.*

traspondríamos we should transpose; cond. 1st pers. pl. / *trasponer.*

traspondrían they would transpose; cond. 3rd pers. pl. / *trasponer.*

traspondrías you would transpose; cond. 2nd pers. sing. / *trasponer.*

trasponeos (you all) detour; impve. 2nd pers. pl. / *trasponerse.*

trasponer to transpose. irr.

trasponerse to detour. irr.

trasponga 1. that I may transpose; pres. subj. 1st pers. sing. / *trasponer.* 2. that he (she/it) may transpose; pres. subj. 3rd pers. sing. 3. let him (her/it) transpose; impve. 3rd pers. sing.

traspongáis that you (all) may transpose; pres. subj. 2nd pers. pl. / *trasponer.*

traspongámonos let us detour; impve. 1st pers. pl. / *trasponerse.*

traspongamos 1. that we may transpose; pres. subj. 1st pers. pl. / *trasponer.* 2. let us transpose; impve. 1st pers. pl.

traspongan 1. that they may transpose; pres. subj. 3rd pers. pl. / *trasponer.* 2. let them transpose; impve. 3rd pers. pl.

traspónganse let them detour; impve. 3rd pers. pl. / *trasponerse.*

traspongas that you may transpose; pres. subj. 2nd pers. sing. / *trasponer.*

traspóngase let him (her/it) detour; impve. 3rd pers. sing. / *trasponerse.*

traspongo I transpose; pres. ind. 1st pers. sing. / *trasponer.*

trasponiendo transposing; pres. part. / *trasponer.*

trasponiéndose detouring; pres. part. / *trasponerse.*

trasponte (you) detour; impve. 2nd pers. sing. / *trasponerse.*

trasportándose getting carried away; pres. part. / *trasportarse.*

trasportaos (you all) get carried away; impve. 2nd pers. pl. / *trasportarse.*

trasportar to transport. reg.

trasportarse to get carried away. reg.

traspórtate (you) get carried away; impve. 2nd pers. sing. / *trasportarse.*

trasportémonos let us get carried away; impve. 1st pers. pl. / *trasportarse.*

traspórtense let them get carried away; impve. 3rd pers. pl. / *trasportarse.*

traspórtese let him (her/it) get carried away; impve. 3rd pers. sing. / *trasportarse.*

traspuesto transposed; past part. / *trasponer.*

traspuse I transposed; past 1st pers. sing. / *trasponer.*

traspusiera 1. that I might transpose; imp. subj. 1st pers. sing. / *trasponer.* 2. that he (she/it) might transpose; imp. subj. 3rd pers. sing.

traspusierais that you (all) might transpose; imp. subj. 2nd pers pl. / *trasponer.*

traspusiéramos that we might transpose; imp. subj. 1st pers. pl. / *trasponer.*

traspusieran that they might transpose; imp. subj. 3rd pers. pl. / *trasponer.*

traspusieras that you might transpose; imp. subj. 2nd pers. sing. / *trasponer.*

traspusieron they transposed; past 3rd pers. pl. / *trasponer.*

traspusiese 1. that I might transpose; imp. subj. 1st pers. sing. / *trasponer.* 2. that he (she/it) might transpose; imp. subj. 3rd pers. sing.

traspusieseis that you (all) might transpose; imp. subj. 2nd pers pl. / *trasponer.*

traspusiésemos that we might transpose; imp. subj. 1st pers. pl. / *trasponer.*

traspusiesen that they might transpose; imp. subj. 3rd pers. pl. / *trasponer.*

traspusieses that you might transpose; imp. subj. 2nd pers. sing. / *trasponer.*

traspusimos we transposed; past 1st pers. pl. / *trasponer.*

traspusiste you transposed; past 2nd pers. sing. / *trasponer.*

traspusisteis you (all) transposed; past 2nd pers. pl. / *trasponer.*

traspuso he (she/it) transposed; past 3rd pers. sing. / *trasponer.*

trasquilar to shear. reg.

trastabillar to stumble. reg.

trasteándose moving; pres. part. / *trastearse.*

trasteaos (you all) move; impve. 2nd pers. pl. / *trastearse.*

trastear to move things around or to fret. reg.

trastearse to move. reg.

trastéate (you) move; impve. 2nd pers. sing. / *trastearse.*

trasteémonos let us move; impve. 1st pers. pl. / *trastearse.*

trastéense let them move; impve. 3rd pers. pl. / *trastearse.*

trastéese let him (her/it) move; impve. 3rd pers. sing. / *trastearse.*

trastornar to upset. reg.

trastrabillar to stumble. reg.

trastrocar to invert. irr.

trastroqué I inverted; past 1st pers. sing. / *trastrocar.*

trastroquéis that you (all) may invert; pres. subj. 2nd pers. pl. / *trastrocar.*

trastroquemos 1. that we may invert; pres. subj. 1st pers. pl. / *trastrocar.* 2. let us invert; impve. 1st pers. pl.

trastrueca 1. he (she/it) inverts; pres. ind. 3rd pers. sing. / *trastrocar.* 2. (you) invert; impve. 2nd pers. sing.

trastruecan they invert; pres. ind. 3rd pers. pl. / *trastrocar.*

trastruecas you invert; pres. ind. 2nd pers. sing. / *trastrocar.*

trastrueco I invert; pres. ind. 1st pers. sing. / *trastrocar.*

trastrueque 1. that I may invert; pres. subj. 1st pers. sing. / *trastrocar.* 2. that he (she/it) may invert; pres. subj. 3rd pers. sing. 3. let him (her/it) invert; impve. 3rd pers. sing.

trastruequen 1. that they may invert; pres. subj. 3rd pers. pl. / *trastrocar.* 2. let them invert; impve. 3rd pers. pl.

trastrueques that you may invert; pres. subj. 2nd pers. sing. / *trastrocar.*

trasudar to perspire. reg.

trasueña 1. he (she/it) dreams up; pres. ind. 3rd pers. sing. / *trasoñar.* 2. (you) dream up; impve. 2nd pers. sing.

trasueñan they dream up; pres. ind. 3rd pers. pl. / *trasoñar.*

trasueñas you dream up; pres. ind. 2nd pers. sing. / *trasoñar.*

trasueñe 1. that I may dream up; pres. subj. 1st pers. sing. / *trasoñar.* 2. that he (she/it) may dream up; pres. subj. 3rd pers. sing. 3. let him (her/it) dream up; impve. 3rd pers. sing.

trasueñen 1. that they may dream up; pres. subj. 3rd pers. pl. / *trasoñar.* 2. let them dream up; impve. 3rd pers. pl.

trasueñes that you may dream up; pres. subj. 2nd pers. sing. / *trasoñar.*

trasueño I dream up; pres. ind. 1st pers. sing. / *trasoñar.*

trasverter to overflow. irr.

trasvierta 1. that I may overflow; pres. subj. 1st pers. sing. / *trasverter.* 2. that he (she/it) may overflow; pres. subj. 3rd pers. sing. 3. let him (her/it) overflow; impve. 3rd pers. sing.

trasviertan 1. that they may overflow; pres. subj. 3rd pers. pl. / *trasverter.* 2. let them overflow; impve. 3rd pers. pl.

trasviertas that you may overflow; pres. subj. 2nd pers. sing. / *trasverter.*

trasvierte 1. he (she/it) overflows; pres. ind. 3rd pers. sing. / *trasverter.* 2. (you) overflow; impve. 2nd pers. sing.

trasvierten they overflow; pres. ind. 3rd pers. pl. / *trasverter.*

trasviertes you overflow; pres. ind. 2nd pers. sing. / *trasverter.*

trasvierto I overflow; pres. ind. 1st pers. sing. / *trasverter.*

tratándose dealing; pres. part. / *tratarse.*

trataos (you all) deal; impve. 2nd pers. pl. / *tratarse.*

tratar to treat. reg.

tratarse to deal. reg.

trátate (you) deal; impve. 2nd pers. sing. / *tratarse.*

tratémonos let us deal; impve. 1st pers. pl. / *tratarse.*

trátense let them deal; impve. 3rd pers. pl. / *tratarse.*

trátese let him (her/it) deal; impve. 3rd pers. sing. / *tratarse.*

travesar to cross. irr.

travesear to romp or to misbehave. reg.

traviesa 1. he (she/it) crosses; pres. ind. 3rd pers. sing. / *travesar.* 2. (you) cross; impve. 2nd pers. sing.

traviesan they cross; pres. ind. 3rd pers. pl. / *travesar.*

traviesas you cross; pres. ind. 2nd pers. sing. / *travesar.*

traviese 1. that I may cross; pres. subj. 1st pers. sing. / *travesar.* 2. that he (she/it) may cross; pres. subj. 3rd pers. sing. 3. let him (her/it) cross; impve. 3rd pers. sing.

traviesen 1. that they may cross; pres. subj. 3rd pers. pl. / *travesar.* 2. let them cross; impve. 3rd pers. pl.

travieses that you may cross; pres. subj. 2nd pers. sing. / *travesar.*

travieso I cross; pres. ind. 1st pers. sing. / *travesar.*

trayendo bringing; pres. part. / *traer.*

trayéndose dressing; pres. part. / *traerse.*

trazar to trace. irr.

trazumar to ooze. reg.

tremer to tremble. reg.

tremolar to wave. reg.

trence 1. that I may braid; pres. subj. 1st pers. sing. / *trenzar.* 2. that he (she/it) may braid; pres. subj. 3rd pers. sing. 3. let him (her/it) braid; impve. 3rd pers. sing.

trencé I braided; past 1st pers. sing. / *trenzar.*

trencéis that you (all) may braid; pres. subj. 2nd pers. pl. / *trenzar.*

trencémonos let us tangle; impve. 1st pers. pl. / *trenzarse.*

trencemos 1. that we may braid; pres. subj. 1st pers. pl. / *trenzar.* 2. let us braid; impve. 1st pers. pl.

trencen 1. that they may braid; pres. subj. 3rd pers. pl. / *trenzar.* 2. let them braid; impve. 3rd pers. pl.

tréncense let them tangle; impve. 3rd pers. pl. / *trenzarse.*

trences that you may braid; pres. subj. 2nd pers. sing. / *trenzar*.
tréncese let him (her/it) tangle; impve. 3rd pers. sing. / *trenzarse*.
trenzándose tangling; pres. part. / *trenzarse*.
trenzaos (you all) tangle; impve. 2nd pers. pl. / *trenzarse*.
trenzar to braid or to caper. irr.
trenzarse to tangle. irr.
trénzate (you) tangle; impve. 2nd pers. sing. / *trenzarse*.
trepanar to trepan. reg.
trepándose climbing; pres. part. / *treparse*.
trepaos (you all) climb; impve. 2nd pers. pl. / *treparse*.
trepar to climb. reg.
treparse to climb. reg.
trépate (you) climb; impve. 2nd pers. sing. / *treparse*.
trepémonos let us climb; impve. 1st pers. pl. / *treparse*.
trépense let them climb; impve. 3rd pers. pl. / *treparse*.
trépese let him (her/it) climb; impve. 3rd pers. sing. / *treparse*.
trepidar to tremble. reg.
tría 1. he (she/it) sorts; pres. ind. 3rd pers. sing. / *triar*. 2. (you) sort; impve. 2nd pers. sing.
trían they sort; pres. ind. 3rd pers. pl. / *triar*.
triangular to triangulate. reg.
triar to sort. irr.
trías you sort; pres. ind. 2nd pers. sing. / *triar*.
tributar to pay tribute. reg.
trice 1. that I may shatter; pres. subj. 1st pers. sing. / *trizar*. 2. that he (she/it) may shatter; pres. subj. 3rd pers. sing. 3. let him (her/it) shatter; impve. 3rd pers. sing.
tricé I shattered; past 1st pers. sing. / *trizar*.
tricéis that you (all) may shatter; pres. subj. 2nd pers. pl. / *trizar*.
tricemos 1. that we may shatter; pres. subj. 1st pers. pl. / *trizar*. 2. let us shatter; impve. 1st pers. pl.
tricen 1. that they may shatter; pres. subj. 3rd pers. pl. / *trizar*. 2. let them shatter; impve. 3rd pers. pl.
trices that you may shatter; pres. subj. 2nd pers. sing. / *trizar*.
tríe 1. that I may sort; pres. subj. 1st pers. sing. / *triar*. 2. that he (she/it) may sort; pres. subj. 3rd pers. sing. 3. let him (her/it) sort; impve. 3rd pers. sing.
tríen 1. that they may sort; pres. subj. 3rd pers. pl. / *triar*. 2. let them sort; impve. 3rd pers. pl.
tríes that you may sort; pres. subj. 2nd pers. sing. / *triar*.
trifurcar to trifurcate. irr.
trifurque 1. that I may trifurcate; pres. subj. 1st pers. sing. / *trifurcar*. 2. that he (she/it) may trifurcate; pres. subj. 3rd pers. sing. 3. let him (her/it) trifurcate; impve. 3rd pers. sing.
trifurqué I trifurcated; past 1st pers. sing. / *trifurcar*.
trifurquéis that you (all) may trifurcate; pres. subj. 2nd pers. pl. / *trifurcar*.

trifurquemos 1. that we may trifurcate; pres. subj. 1st pers. pl. / *trifurcar*. 2. let us trifurcate; impve. 1st pers. pl.
trifurquen 1. that they may trifurcate; pres. subj. 3rd pers. pl. / *trifurcar*. 2. let them trifurcate; impve. 3rd pers. pl.
trifurques that you may trifurcate; pres. subj. 2nd pers. sing. / *trifurcar*.
trillar to thresh. reg.
trinar to trill. reg.
trincar to bind. irr.
trinchar to carve. reg.
trinque 1. that I may bind; pres. subj. 1st pers. sing. / *trincar*. 2. that he (she/it) may bind; pres. subj. 3rd pers. sing. 3. let him (her/it) bind; impve. 3rd pers. sing.
trinqué I bound; past 1st pers. sing. / *trincar*.
trinquéis that you (all) may bind; pres. subj. 2nd pers. pl. / *trincar*.
trinquemos 1. that we may bind; pres. subj. 1st pers. pl. / *trincar*. 2. let us bind; impve. 1st pers. pl.
trinquen 1. that they may bind; pres. subj. 3rd pers. pl. / *trincar*. 2. let them bind; impve. 3rd pers. pl.
trinques that you may bind; pres. subj. 2nd pers. sing. / *trincar*.
trío I sort; pres. ind. 1st pers. sing. / *triar*.
tripartir to divide into three parts. reg.
triplicándose tripling; pres. part. / *triplicarse*.
triplicaos (you all) triple; impve. 2nd pers. pl. / *triplicarse*.
triplicar to triple. irr.
triplicarse to triple. irr.
triplícate (you) triple; impve. 2nd pers. sing. / *triplicarse*.
triplique 1. that I may triple; pres. subj. 1st pers. sing. / *triplicar*. 2. that he (she/it) may triple; pres. subj. 3rd pers. sing. 3. let him (her/it) triple; impve. 3rd pers. sing.
tripliqué I tripled; past 1st pers. sing. / *triplicar*.
tripliquéis that you (all) may triple; pres. subj. 2nd pers. pl. / *triplicar*.
tripliquémonos let us triple; impve. 1st pers. pl. / *triplicarse*.
tripliquemos 1. that we may triple; pres. subj. 1st pers. pl. / *triplicar*. 2. let us triple; impve. 1st pers. pl.
tripliquen 1. that they may triple; pres. subj. 3rd pers. pl. / *triplicar*. 2. let them triple; impve. 3rd pers. pl.
triplíquense let them triple; impve. 3rd pers. pl. / *triplicarse*.
tripliques that you may triple; pres. subj. 2nd pers. sing. / *triplicar*.
triplíquese let him (her/it) triple; impve. 3rd pers. sing. / *triplicarse*.
tripular to man a ship. reg.
trisar to crack. reg.
triscar to frolic. irr.
trisecar to trisect. irr.

triseque 1. that I may trisect; pres. subj. 1st pers. sing. / *trisecar*. 2. that he (she/it) may trisect; pres. subj. 3rd pers. sing. 3. let him (her/it) trisect; impve. 3rd pers. sing.

trisequé I trisected; past 1st pers. sing. / *trisecar*.

trisequéis that you (all) may trisect; pres. subj. 2nd pers. pl. / *trisecar*.

trisequemos 1. that we may trisect; pres. subj. 1st pers. pl. / *trisecar*. 2. let us trisect; impve. 1st pers. pl.

trisequen 1. that they may trisect; pres. subj. 3rd pers. pl. / *trisecar*. 2. let them trisect; impve. 3rd pers. pl.

triseques that you may trisect; pres. subj. 2nd pers. sing. / *trisecar*.

trisque 1. that I may frolic; pres. subj. 1st pers. sing. / *triscar*. 2. that he (she/it) may frolic; pres. subj. 3rd pers. sing. 3. let him (her/it) frolic; impve. 3rd pers. sing.

trisqué I froliced; past 1st pers. sing. / *triscar*.

trisquéis that you (all) may frolic; pres. subj. 2nd pers. pl. / *triscar*.

trisquemos 1. that we may frolic; pres. subj. 1st pers. pl. / *triscar*. 2. let us frolic; impve. 1st pers. pl.

trisquen 1. that they may frolic; pres. subj. 3rd pers. pl. / *triscar*. 2. let them frolic; impve. 3rd pers. pl.

trisques that you may frolic; pres. subj. 2nd pers. sing. / *triscar*.

triturar to crush. reg.

triunfar to triumph. reg.

trizar to shatter. irr.

trocándose changing; pres. part. / *trocarse*.

trocaos (you all) change; impve. 2nd pers. pl. / *trocarse*.

trocar to exchange. irr.

trocarse to change. irr.

troce 1. that I may cut off; pres. subj. 1st pers. sing. / *trozar*. 2. that he (she/it) may cut off; pres. subj. 3rd pers. sing. 3. let him (her/it) cut off; impve. 3rd pers. sing.

trocé I cut off; past 1st pers. sing. / *trozar*.

trocéis that you (all) may cut off; pres. subj. 2nd pers. pl. / *trozar*.

trocemos 1. that we may cut off; pres. subj. 1st pers. pl. / *trozar*. 2. let us cut off; impve. 1st pers. pl.

trocen 1. that they may cut off; pres. subj. 3rd pers. pl. / *trozar*. 2. let them cut off; impve. 3rd pers. pl.

troces that you may cut off; pres. subj. 2nd pers. sing. / *trozar*.

trompeándose having a fist fight; pres. part. / *trompearse*.

trompeaos (you all) have a fist fight; impve. 2nd pers. pl. / *trompearse*.

trompearse to have a fist fight. reg.

trompéate (you) have a fist fight; impve. 2nd pers. sing. / *trompearse*.

trompeémonos let us have a fist fight; impve. 1st pers. pl. / *trompearse*.

trompéense let them have a fist fight; impve. 3rd pers. pl. / *trompearse*.

trompéese let him (her/it) have a fist fight; impve. 3rd pers. sing. / *trompearse*.

trompetear to trumpet. reg.

trompicar to stumble. irr.

trompique 1. that I may stumble; pres. subj. 1st pers. sing. / *trompicar*. 2. that he (she/it) may stumble; pres. subj. 3rd pers. sing. 3. let him (her/it) stumble; impve. 3rd pers. sing.

trompiqué I stumbled; past 1st pers. sing. / *trompicar*.

trompiquéis that you (all) may stumble; pres. subj. 2nd pers. pl. / *trompicar*.

trompiquemos 1. that we may stumble; pres. subj. 1st pers. pl. / *trompicar*. 2. let us stumble; impve. 1st pers. pl.

trompiquen 1. that they may stumble; pres. subj. 3rd pers. pl. / *trompicar*. 2. let them stumble; impve. 3rd pers. pl.

trompiques that you may stumble; pres. subj. 2nd pers. sing. / *trompicar*.

tronar to thunder. irr.

troncar to truncate. irr.

tronce 1. that I may shatter; pres. subj. 1st pers. sing. / *tronzar*. 2. that he (she/it) may shatter; pres. subj. 3rd pers. sing. 3. let him (her/it) shatter; impve. 3rd pers. sing.

troncé I shattered; past 1st pers. sing. / *tronzar*.

troncéis that you (all) may shatter; pres. subj. 2nd pers. pl. / *tronzar*.

troncemos 1. that we may shatter; pres. subj. 1st pers. pl. / *tronzar*. 2. let us shatter; impve. 1st pers. pl.

troncen 1. that they may shatter; pres. subj. 3rd pers. pl. / *tronzar*. 2. let them shatter; impve. 3rd pers. pl.

tronces that you may shatter; pres. subj. 2nd pers. sing. / *tronzar*.

tronchar to break. reg.

tronque 1. that I may truncate; pres. subj. 1st pers. sing. / *troncar*. 2. that he (she/it) may truncate; pres. subj. 3rd pers. sing. 3. let him (her/it) truncate; impve. 3rd pers. sing.

tronqué I truncated; past 1st pers. sing. / *troncar*.

tronquéis that you (all) may truncate; pres. subj. 2nd pers. pl. / *troncar*.

tronquemos 1. that we may truncate; pres. subj. 1st pers. pl. / *troncar*. 2. let us truncate; impve. 1st pers. pl.

tronquen 1. that they may truncate; pres. subj. 3rd pers. pl. / *troncar*. 2. let them truncate; impve. 3rd pers. pl.

tronques that you may truncate; pres. subj. 2nd pers. sing. / *troncar*.

tronzar to shatter. irr.

tropecé I stumbled; past 1st pers. sing. / *tropezar*.

tropecéis that you (all) may stumble; pres. subj. 2nd pers. pl. / *tropezar*.

tropecemos 1. that we may stumble; pres. subj. 1st pers. pl. / *tropezar*. 2. let us stumble; impve. 1st pers. pl.

tropezar to stumble. irr.

tropiece 1. that I may stumble; pres. subj. 1st pers. sing. / *tropezar*. 2. that he (she/it) may stumble; pres. subj. 3rd pers. sing. 3. let him (her/it) stumble; impve. 3rd pers. sing.

tropiecen 1. that they may stumble; pres. subj. 3rd pers. pl. / *tropezar*. 2. let them stumble; impve. 3rd pers. pl.

tropieces that you may stumble; pres. subj. 2nd pers. sing. / *tropezar*.

tropieza 1. he (she/it) stumbles; pres. ind. 3rd pers. sing. / *tropezar*. 2. (you) stumble; impve. 2nd pers. sing.

tropiezan they stumble; pres. ind. 3rd pers. pl. / *tropezar*.

tropiezas you stumble; pres. ind. 2nd pers. sing. / *tropezar*.

tropiezo I stumble; pres. ind. 1st pers. sing. / *tropezar*.

troqué I exchanged; past 1st pers. sing. / *trocar*.

troquéis that you (all) may exchange; pres. subj. 2nd pers. pl. / *trocar*.

troquelar to die stamp. reg.

troquémonos let us change; impve. 1st pers. pl. / *trocarse*.

troquemos 1. that we may exchange; pres. subj. 1st pers. pl. / *trocar*. 2. let us exchange; impve. 1st pers. pl.

trotar to trot. reg.

trovar to write verse. reg.

trozar to cut off. irr.

trueca 1. he (she/it) exchanges; pres. ind. 3rd pers. sing. / *trocar*. 2. (you) exchange; impve. 2nd pers. sing.

truecan they exchange; pres. ind. 3rd pers. pl. / *trocar*.

truecas you exchange; pres. ind. 2nd pers. sing. / *trocar*.

truécate (you) change; impve. 2nd pers. sing. / *trocarse*.

trueco I exchange; pres. ind. 1st pers. sing. / *trocar*.

truena 1. he (she/it) thunders; pres. ind. 3rd pers. sing. / *tronar*. 2. (you) thunder; impve. 2nd pers. sing.

truenan they thunder; pres. ind. 3rd pers. pl. / *tronar*.

truenas you thunder; pres. ind. 2nd pers. sing. / *tronar*.

truene 1. that I may thunder; pres. subj. 1st pers. sing. / *tronar*. 2. that he (she/it) may thunder; pres. subj. 3rd pers. sing. 3. let him (her/it) thunder; impve. 3rd pers. sing.

truenen 1. that they may thunder; pres. subj. 3rd pers. pl. / *tronar*. 2. let them thunder; impve. 3rd pers. pl.

truenes that you may thunder; pres. subj. 2nd pers. sing. / *tronar*.

trueno I thunder; pres. ind. 1st pers. sing. / *tronar*.

trueque 1. that I may exchange; pres. subj. 1st pers. sing. / *trocar*. 2. that he (she/it) may exchange; pres. subj. 3rd pers. sing. 3. let him (her/it) exchange; impve. 3rd pers. sing.

truequen 1. that they may exchange; pres. subj. 3rd pers. pl. / *trocar*. 2. let them exchange; impve. 3rd pers. pl.

truéquense let them change; impve. 3rd pers. pl. / *trocarse*.

trueques that you may exchange; pres. subj. 2nd pers. sing. / *trocar*.

truéquese let him (her/it) change; impve. 3rd pers. sing. / *trocarse*.

trufar to stuff with truffles. reg.

truncar to truncate. irr.

trunque 1. that I may truncate; pres. subj. 1st pers. sing. / *truncar*. 2. that he (she/it) may truncate; pres. subj. 3rd pers. sing. 3. let him (her/it) truncate; impve. 3rd pers. sing.

trunqué I truncated; past 1st pers. sing. / *truncar*.

trunquéis that you (all) may truncate; pres. subj. 2nd pers. pl. / *truncar*.

trunquemos 1. that we may truncate; pres. subj. 1st pers. pl. / *truncar*. 2. let us truncate; impve. 1st pers. pl.

trunquen 1. that they may truncate; pres. subj. 3rd pers. pl. / *truncar*. 2. let them truncate; impve. 3rd pers. pl.

trunques that you may truncate; pres. subj. 2nd pers. sing. / *truncar*.

tuerce 1. he (she/it) twists; pres. ind. 3rd pers. sing. / *torcer*. 2. (you) twist; impve. 2nd pers. sing.

tuercen they twist; pres. ind. 3rd pers. pl. / *torcer*.

tuerces you twist; pres. ind. 2nd pers. sing. / *torcer*.

tuerza 1. that I may twist; pres. subj. 1st pers. sing. / *torcer*. 2. that he (she/it) may twist; pres. subj. 3rd pers. sing. 3. let him (her/it) twist; impve. 3rd pers. sing.

tuerzan 1. that they may twist; pres. subj. 3rd pers. pl. / *torcer*. 2. let them twist; impve. 3rd pers. pl.

tuerzas that you may twist; pres. subj. 2nd pers. sing. / *torcer*.

tuerzo I twist; pres. ind. 1st pers. sing. / *torcer*.

tuesta 1. he (she/it) toasts; pres. ind. 3rd pers. sing. / *tostar*. 2. (you) toast; impve. 2nd pers. sing.

tuestan they toast; pres. ind. 3rd pers. pl. / *tostar*.

tuestas you toast; pres. ind. 2nd pers. sing. / *tostar*.

tuéstate (you) roast; impve. 2nd pers. sing. / *tostarse*.

tueste 1. that I may toast; pres. subj. 1st pers. sing. / *tostar*. 2. that he (she/it) may toast; pres. subj. 3rd pers. sing. 3. let him (her/it) toast; impve. 3rd pers. sing.

tuesten 1. that they may toast; pres. subj. 3rd pers. pl. / *tostar*. 2. let them toast; impve. 3rd pers. pl.

tuéstense let them roast; impve. 3rd pers. pl. / *tostarse*.

tuestes that you may toast; pres. subj. 2nd pers. sing. / *tostar*.

tuéstese let him (her/it) roast; impve. 3rd pers. sing. / *tostarse*.

tuesto I toast; pres. ind. 1st pers. sing. / *tostar*.

tullámonos let us become crippled; impve. 1st pers. pl. / *tullirse*.

túllanse let them become crippled; impve. 3rd pers. pl. / *tullirse*.

túllase let him (her/it) become crippled; impve. 3rd pers. sing. / *tullirse*.

tullendo crippling; pres. part. / *tullir*.
tulléndose becoming crippled; pres. part. / *tullirse*.
tullera 1. that I might cripple; imp. subj. 1st pers. sing. / *tullir*. 2. that he (she/it) might cripple; imp. subj. 3rd pers. sing.
tullerais that you (all) might cripple; imp. subj. 2nd pers pl. / *tullir*.
tulléramos that we might cripple; imp. subj. 1st pers. pl. / *tullir*.
tulleran that they might cripple; imp. subj. 3rd pers. pl. / *tullir*.
tulleras that you might cripple; imp. subj. 2nd pers. sing. / *tullir*.
tulleron they crippled; past 3rd pers. pl. / *tullir*.
tullese 1. that I might cripple; imp. subj. 1st pers. sing. / *tullir*. 2. that he (she/it) might cripple; imp. subj. 3rd pers. sing.
tulleseis that you (all) might cripple; imp. subj. 2nd pers pl. / *tullir*.
tullésemos that we might cripple; imp. subj. 1st pers. pl. / *tullir*.
tullesen that they might cripple; imp. subj. 3rd pers. pl. / *tullir*.
tulleses that you might cripple; imp. subj. 2nd pers. sing. / *tullir*.
túllete (you) become crippled; impve. 2nd pers. sing. / *tullirse*.
tullir to cripple. irr.
tullirse to become crippled. irr.
tulló he (she/it) crippled; past 3rd pers. sing. / *tullir*.
tullos (you all) become crippled; impve. 2nd pers. pl. / *tullirse*.
tumbándose lying down; pres. part. / *tumbarse*.
tumbaos (you all) lie down; impve. 2nd pers. pl. / *tumbarse*.
tumbar to knock down. reg.
tumbarse to lie down. reg.
túmbate (you) lie down; impve. 2nd pers. sing. / *tumbarse*.
tumbémonos let us lie down; impve. 1st pers. pl. / *tumbarse*.
túmbense let them lie down; impve. 3rd pers. pl. / *tumbarse*.
túmbese let him (her/it) lie down; impve. 3rd pers. sing. / *tumbarse*.
tumefaceos (you all) swell; impve. 2nd pers. pl. / *tumefacerse*.
tumefacer to swell. irr.
tumefacerse to swell. irr.
tumefaciéndose swelling; pres. part. / *tumefacerse*.
tumefaga 1. that I may swell; pres. subj. 1st pers. sing. / *tumefacer*. 2. that he (she/it) may swell; pres. subj. 3rd pers. sing. 3. let him (her/it) swell; impve. 3rd pers. sing.
tumefagáis that you (all) may swell; pres. subj. 2nd pers. pl. / *tumefacer*.
tumefagámonos let us swell; impve. 1st pers. pl. / *tumefacerse*.

tumefagamos 1. that we may swell; pres. subj. 1st pers. pl. / *tumefacer*. 2. let us swell; impve. 1st pers. pl.
tumefagan 1. that they may swell; pres. subj. 3rd pers. pl. / *tumefacer*. 2. let them swell; impve. 3rd pers. pl.
tumefáganse let them swell; impve. 3rd pers. pl. / *tumefacerse*.
tumefagas that you may swell; pres. subj. 2nd pers. sing. / *tumefacer*.
tumefágase let him (her/it) swell; impve. 3rd pers. sing. / *tumefacerse*.
tumefago I swell; pres. ind. 1st pers. sing. / *tumefacer*.
tumefará he (she/it) will swell; fut. 3rd pers. sing. / *tumefacer*.
tumefarán they will swell; fut. 3rd pers. pl. / *tumefacer*.
tumefarás you will swell; fut. 2nd pers. sing. / *tumefacer*.
tumefaré I shall swell; fut. 1st pers. sing. / *tumefacer*.
tumefaréis you (all) will swell; fut. 2nd pers. pl. / *tumefacer*.
tumefaremos we shall swell; fut. 1st pers. pl. / *tumefacer*.
tumefaría 1. I should swell; cond. 1st pers. sing. / *tumefacer*. 2. he (she/it) would swell; cond. 3rd pers. sing.
tumefaríais you (all) would swell; cond. 2nd pers. pl. / *tumefacer*.
tumefaríamos we should swell; cond. 1st pers. pl. / *tumefacer*.
tumefarían they would swell; cond. 3rd pers. pl. / *tumefacer*.
tumefarías you would swell; cond. 2nd pers. sing. / *tumefacer*.
tumefaz (you) swell; impve. 2nd pers. sing. / *tumefacer*.
tumefázete (you) swell; impve. 2nd pers. sing. / *tumefacerse*.
tumefecho swelled; past part. / *tumefacer*.
tumefice I swelled; past 1st pers. sing. / *tumefacer*.
tumeficiera 1. that I might swell; imp. subj. 1st pers. sing. / *tumefacer*. 2. that he (she/it) might swell; imp. subj. 3rd pers. sing.
tumeficierais that you (all) might swell; imp. subj. 2nd pers pl. / *tumefacer*.
tumeficiéramos that we might swell; imp. subj. 1st pers. pl. / *tumefacer*.
tumeficieran that they might swell; imp. subj. 3rd pers. pl. / *tumefacer*.
tumeficieras that you might swell; imp. subj. 2nd pers. sing. / *tumefacer*.
tumeficieron they swelled; past 3rd pers. pl. / *tumefacer*.
tumeficiese 1. that I might swell; imp. subj. 1st pers. sing. / *tumefacer*. 2. that he (she/it) might swell; imp. subj. 3rd pers. sing.
tumeficieseis that you (all) might swell; imp. subj. 2nd pers pl. / *tumefacer*.
tumeficiésemos that we might swell; imp. subj. 1st pers. pl. / *tumefacer*.

tumeficiesen that they might swell; imp. subj. 3rd pers. pl. / *tumefacer.*
tumeficieses that you might swell; imp. subj. 2nd pers. sing. / *tumefacer.*
tumeficimos we swelled; past 1st pers. pl. / *tumefacer.*
tumeficiste you swelled; past 2nd pers. sing. / *tumefacer.*
tumeficisteis you (all) swelled; past 2nd pers. pl. / *tumefacer.*
tumefizo he (she/it) swelled; past 3rd pers. sing. / *tumefacer.*
tumultuándose rioting; pres. part. / *tumultuarse.*
tumultuaos (you all) riot; impve. 2nd pers. pl. / *tumultuarse.*
tumultuar to incite to riot. reg.
tumultuarse to riot. reg.
tumultúate (you) riot; impve. 2nd pers. sing. / *tumultuarse.*
tumultuémonos let us riot; impve. 1st pers. pl. / *tumultuarse.*
tumultúense let them riot; impve. 3rd pers. pl. / *tumultuarse.*
tumultúese let him (her/it) riot; impve. 3rd pers. sing. / *tumultuarse.*
tunar to bum around. reg.
tundir to beat. reg.
tunear to behave as a scoundrel. reg.
tupámonos let us overeat; impve. 1st pers. pl. / *tupirse.*
túpanse let them overeat; impve. 3rd pers. pl. / *tupirse.*
túpase let him (her/it) overeat; impve. 3rd pers. sing. / *tupirse.*
túpete (you) overeat; impve. 2nd pers. sing. / *tupirse.*
tupiéndose overeating; pres. part. / *tupirse.*
tupíos (you all) overeat; impve. 2nd pers. pl. / *tupirse.*
tupir to pack tight. reg.
tupirse to overeat. reg.
turbándose getting disturbed; pres. part. / *turbarse.*
turbaos (you all) get disturbed; impve. 2nd pers. pl. / *turbarse.*
turbar to disturb. reg.
turbarse to get disturbed. reg.
túrbate (you) get disturbed; impve. 2nd pers. sing. / *turbarse.*
turbémonos let us get disturbed; impve. 1st pers. pl. / *turbarse.*

túrbense let them get disturbed; impve. 3rd pers. pl. / *turbarse.*
túrbese let him (her/it) get disturbed; impve. 3rd pers. sing. / *turbarse.*
turnándose taking turns; pres. part. / *turnarse.*
turnaos (you all) take turns; impve. 2nd pers. pl. / *turnarse.*
turnar to alternate. reg.
turnarse to take turns. reg.
túrnate (you) take turns; impve. 2nd pers. sing. / *turnarse.*
turnémonos let us take turns; impve. 1st pers. pl. / *turnarse.*
túrnense let them take turns; impve. 3rd pers. pl. / *turnarse.*
túrnese let him (her/it) take turns; impve. 3rd pers. sing. / *turnarse.*
turrar to toast. reg.
tusar to shear. reg.
tutear to speak familiarly. reg.
tutelar to guide. reg.
tuve I had; past 1st pers. sing. / *tener.*
tuviera 1. that I might have; imp. subj. 1st pers. sing. / *tener.* 2. that he (she/it) might have; imp. subj. 3rd pers. sing.
tuvierais that you (all) might have; imp. subj. 2nd pers pl. / *tener.*
tuviéramos that we might have; imp. subj. 1st pers. pl. / *tener.*
tuvieran that they might have; imp. subj. 3rd pers. pl. / *tener.*
tuvieras that you might have; imp. subj. 2nd pers. sing. / *tener.*
tuvieron they had; past 3rd pers. pl. / *tener.*
tuviese 1. that I might have; imp. subj. 1st pers. sing. / *tener.* 2. that he (she/it) might have; imp. subj. 3rd pers. sing.
tuvieseis that you (all) might have; imp. subj. 2nd pers pl. / *tener.*
tuviésemos that we might have; imp. subj. 1st pers. pl. / *tener.*
tuviesen that they might have; imp. subj. 3rd pers. pl. / *tener.*
tuvieses that you might have; imp. subj. 2nd pers. sing. / *tener.*
tuvimos we had; past 1st pers. pl. / *tener.*
tuviste you had; past 2nd pers. sing. / *tener.*
tuvisteis you (all) had; past 2nd pers. pl. / *tener.*
tuvo he (she/it) had; past 3rd pers. sing. / *tener.*

U

ubicándose being located; pres. part. / *ubicarse.*
ubicaos (you all) be located; impve. 2nd pers. pl. / *ubicarse.*
ubicar to locate. irr.
ubicarse to be located. irr.
ubícate (you) be located; impve. 2nd pers. sing. / *ubicarse.*
ubique 1. that I may locate; pres. subj. 1st pers. sing. / *ubicar.* 2. that he (she/it) may locate; pres. subj. 3rd pers. sing. 3. let him (her/it) locate; impve. 3rd pers. sing.
ubiqué I located; past 1st pers. sing. / *ubicar.*
ubiquéis that you (all) may locate; pres. subj. 2nd pers. pl. / *ubicar.*
ubiquémonos let us be located; impve. 1st pers. pl. / *ubicarse.*
ubiquemos 1. that we may locate; pres. subj. 1st pers. pl. / *ubicar.* 2. let us locate; impve. 1st pers. pl.
ubiquen 1. that they may locate; pres. subj. 3rd pers. pl. / *ubicar.* 2. let them locate; impve. 3rd pers. pl.
ubíquense let them be located; impve. 3rd pers. pl. / *ubicarse.*
ubiques that you may locate; pres. subj. 2nd pers. sing. / *ubicar.*
ubíquese let him (her/it) be located; impve. 3rd pers. sing. / *ubicarse.*
ufanándose boasting; pres. part. / *ufanarse.*
ufanaos (you all) boast; impve. 2nd pers. pl. / *ufanarse.*
ufanarse to boast. reg.
ufánate (you) boast; impve. 2nd pers. sing. / *ufanarse.*
ufanémonos let us boast; impve. 1st pers. pl. / *ufanarse.*
ufánense let them boast; impve. 3rd pers. pl. / *ufanarse.*
ufánese let him (her/it) boast; impve. 3rd pers. sing. / *ufanarse.*
ulcerándose becoming ulcerated; pres. part. / *ulcerarse.*
ulceraos (you all) become ulcerated; impve. 2nd pers. pl. / *ulcerarse.*
ulcerar to ulcerate. reg.
ulcerarse to become ulcerated. reg.
ulcérate (you) become ulcerated; impve. 2nd pers. sing. / *ulcerarse.*
ulcerémonos let us become ulcerated; impve. 1st pers. pl. / *ulcerarse.*
ulcérense let them become ulcerated; impve. 3rd pers. pl. / *ulcerarse.*
ulcérese let him (her/it) become ulcerated; impve. 3rd pers. sing. / *ulcerarse.*
ultimar to finish. reg.
ultrajar to outrage. reg.
ulular to howl. reg.
unámonos let us join; impve. 1st pers. pl. / *unirse.*
únanse let them join; impve. 3rd pers. pl. / *unirse.*

únase let him (her/it) join; impve. 3rd pers. sing. / *unirse.*
uncir to yoke. irr.
undular to undulate. reg.
únete (you) join; impve. 2nd pers. sing. / *unirse.*
ungir to anoint. irr.
uniéndose joining; pres. part. / *unirse.*
unificándose uniting; pres. part. / *unificarse.*
unificaos (you all) unite; impve. 2nd pers. pl. / *unificarse.*
unificar to unify. irr.
unificarse to unite. irr.
unifícate (you) unite; impve. 2nd pers. sing. / *unificarse.*
unifique 1. that I may unify; pres. subj. 1st pers. sing. / *unificar.* 2. that he (she/it) may unify; pres. subj. 3rd pers. sing. 3. let him (her/it) unify; impve. 3rd pers. sing.
unifiqué I unified; past 1st pers. sing. / *unificar.*
unifiquéis that you (all) may unify; pres. subj. 2nd pers. pl. / *unificar.*
unifiquémonos let us unite; impve. 1st pers. pl. / *unificarse.*
unifiquemos 1. that we may unify; pres. subj. 1st pers. pl. / *unificar.* 2. let us unify; impve. 1st pers. pl.
unifiquen 1. that they may unify; pres. subj. 3rd pers. pl. / *unificar.* 2. let them unify; impve. 3rd pers. pl.
unifíquense let them unite; impve. 3rd pers. pl. / *unificarse.*
unifiques that you may unify; pres. subj. 2nd pers. sing. / *unificar.*
unifíquese let him (her/it) unite; impve. 3rd pers. sing. / *unificarse.*
uniformar to make uniform. reg.
uníos (you all) join; impve. 2nd pers. pl. / *unirse.*
unir to unite. reg.
unirse to join. reg.
universalice 1. that I may universalize; pres. subj. 1st pers. sing. / *universalizar.* 2. that he (she/it) may universalize; pres. subj. 3rd pers. sing. 3. let him (her/it) universalize; impve. 3rd pers. sing.
universalicé I universalized; past 1st pers. sing. / *universalizar.*
universalicéis that you (all) may universalize; pres. subj. 2nd pers. pl. / *universalizar.*
universalicemos 1. that we may universalize; pres. subj. 1st pers. pl. / *universalizar.* 2. let us universalize; impve. 1st pers. pl.
universalicen 1. that they may universalize; pres. subj. 3rd pers. pl. / *universalizar.* 2. let them universalize; impve. 3rd pers. pl.
universalices that you may universalize; pres. subj. 2nd pers. sing. / *universalizar.*
universalizar to universalize. irr.
unja 1. that I may anoint; pres. subj. 1st pers. sing. / *ungir.* 2. that he (she/it) may anoint; pres. subj. 3rd pers. sing. 3. let him (her/it) anoint; impve. 3rd pers. sing.
unjáis that you (all) may anoint; pres. subj. 2nd pers. pl. / *ungir.*

unjamos 1. that we may anoint; pres. subj. 1st pers. pl. / *ungir*. 2. let us anoint; impve. 1st pers. pl.

unjan 1. that they may anoint; pres. subj. 3rd pers. pl. / *ungir*. 2. let them anoint; impve. 3rd pers. pl.

unjas that you may anoint; pres. subj. 2nd pers. sing. / *ungir*.

unjo I anoint; pres. ind. 1st pers. sing. / *ungir*.

untándose getting smeared; pres. part. / *untarse*.

untaos (you all) get smeared; impve. 2nd pers. pl. / *untarse*.

untar to anoint. reg.

untarse to get smeared. reg.

úntate (you) get smeared; impve. 2nd pers. sing. / *untarse*.

untémonos let us get smeared; impve. 1st pers. pl. / *untarse*.

úntense let them get smeared; impve. 3rd pers. pl. / *untarse*.

úntese let him (her/it) get smeared; impve. 3rd pers. sing. / *untarse*.

unza 1. that I may yoke; pres. subj. 1st pers. sing. / *uncir*. 2. that he (she/it) may yoke; pres. subj. 3rd pers. sing. 3. let him (her/it) yoke; impve. 3rd pers. sing.

unzáis that you (all) may yoke; pres. subj. 2nd pers. pl. / *uncir*.

unzamos 1. that we may yoke; pres. subj. 1st pers. pl. / *uncir*. 2. let us yoke; impve. 1st pers. pl.

unzan 1. that they may yoke; pres. subj. 3rd pers. pl. / *uncir*. 2. let them yoke; impve. 3rd pers. pl.

unzas that you may yoke; pres. subj. 2nd pers. sing. / *uncir*.

unzo I yoke; pres. ind. 1st pers. sing. / *uncir*.

uñendo yoking; pres. part. / *uñir*.

uñera 1. that I might yoke; imp. subj. 1st pers. sing. / *uñir*. 2. that he (she/it) might yoke; imp. subj. 3rd pers. sing.

uñerais that you (all) might yoke; imp. subj. 2nd pers pl. / *uñir*.

uñéramos that we might yoke; imp. subj. 1st pers. pl. / *uñir*.

uñeran that they might yoke; imp. subj. 3rd pers. pl. / *uñir*.

uñeras that you might yoke; imp. subj. 2nd pers. sing. / *uñir*.

uñeron they yoked; past 3rd pers. pl. / *uñir*.

uñese 1. that I might yoke; imp. subj. 1st pers. sing. / *uñir*. 2. that he (she/it) might yoke; imp. subj. 3rd pers. sing.

uñeseis that you (all) might yoke; imp. subj. 2nd pers pl. / *uñir*.

uñésemos that we might yoke; imp. subj. 1st pers. pl. / *uñir*.

uñesen that they might yoke; imp. subj. 3rd pers. pl. / *uñir*.

uñeses that you might yoke; imp. subj. 2nd pers. sing. / *uñir*.

uñir to yoke. irr.

uñó he (she/it) yoked; past 3rd pers. sing. / *uñir*.

urbanice 1. that I may urbanize; pres. subj. 1st pers. sing. / *urbanizar*. 2. that he (she/it) may urbanize; pres. subj. 3rd pers. sing. 3. let him (her/it) urbanize; impve. 3rd pers. sing.

urbanicé I urbanized; past 1st pers. sing. / *urbanizar*.

urbanicéis that you (all) may urbanize; pres. subj. 2nd pers. pl. / *urbanizar*.

urbanicemos 1. that we may urbanize; pres. subj. 1st pers. pl. / *urbanizar*. 2. let us urbanize; impve. 1st pers. pl.

urbanicen 1. that they may urbanize; pres. subj. 3rd pers. pl. / *urbanizar*. 2. let them urbanize; impve. 3rd pers. pl.

urbanices that you may urbanize; pres. subj. 2nd pers. sing. / *urbanizar*.

urbanizar to urbanize. irr.

urdir to warp. reg.

urgir to be urgent. irr.

urja 1. that I may be urgent; pres. subj. 1st pers. sing. / *urgir*. 2. that he (she/it) may be urgent; pres. subj. 3rd pers. sing. 3. let him (her/it) be urgent; impve. 3rd pers. sing.

urjáis that you (all) may be urgent; pres. subj. 2nd pers. pl. / *urgir*.

urjamos 1. that we may be urgent; pres. subj. 1st pers. pl. / *urgir*. 2. let us be urgent; impve. 1st pers. pl.

urjan 1. that they may be urgent; pres. subj. 3rd pers. pl. / *urgir*. 2. let them be urgent; impve. 3rd pers. pl.

urjas that you may be urgent; pres. subj. 2nd pers. sing. / *urgir*.

urjo I am urgent; pres. ind. 1st pers. sing. / *urgir*.

usándose being in use; pres. part. / *usarse*.

usaos (you all) be in use; impve. 2nd pers. pl. / *usarse*.

usar to use. reg.

usarse to be in use. reg.

úsate (you) be in use; impve. 2nd pers. sing. / *usarse*.

usémonos let us be in use; impve. 1st pers. pl. / *usarse*.

úsense let them be in use; impve. 3rd pers. pl. / *usarse*.

úsese let him (her/it) be in use; impve. 3rd pers. sing. / *usarse*.

usufructúa 1. he (she/it) makes use of; pres. ind. 3rd pers. sing. / *usufructuar*. 2. (you) make use of; impve. 2nd pers. sing.

usufructúan they make use of; pres. ind. 3rd pers. pl. / *usufructuar*.

usufructuar to make use of. irr.

usufructúas you make use of; pres. ind. 2nd pers. sing. / *usufructuar*.

usufructúe 1. that I may make use of; pres. subj. 1st pers. sing. / *usufructuar*. 2. that he (she/it) may make use of; pres. subj. 3rd pers. sing. 3. let him (her/it) make use of; impve. 3rd pers. sing.

usufructúen 1. that they may make use of; pres. subj. 3rd pers. pl. / *usufructuar*. 2. let them make use of; impve. 3rd pers. pl.

usufructúes that you may make use of; pres. subj. 2nd pers. sing. / *usufructuar*.

usufructúo I make use of; pres. ind. 1st pers. sing. / *usufructuar.*

usurear to profiteer. reg.

usurpar to usurp. reg.

utilice 1. that I may utilize; pres. subj. 1st pers. sing. / *utilizar.* 2. that he (she/it) may utilize; pres. subj. 3rd pers. sing. 3. let him (her/it) utilize; impve. 3rd pers. sing.

utilicé I utilized; past 1st pers. sing. / *utilizar.*

utilicéis that you (all) may utilize; pres. subj. 2nd pers. pl. / *utilizar.*

utilicemos 1. that we may utilize; pres. subj. 1st pers. pl. / *utilizar.* 2. let us utilize; impve. 1st pers. pl.

utilicen 1. that they may utilize; pres. subj. 3rd pers. pl. / *utilizar.* 2. let them utilize; impve. 3rd pers. pl.

utilices that you may utilize; pres. subj. 2nd pers. sing. / *utilizar.*

utilizar to utilize. irr.

V

va he (she/it) goes; pres. ind. 3rd pers. sing. / *ir.*

vacar to be vacant or to be idle. irr.

vacía 1. he (she/it) empties; pres. ind. 3rd pers. sing. / *vaciar.* 2. (you) empty; impve. 2nd pers. sing.

vacían they empty; pres. ind. 3rd pers. pl. / *vaciar.*

vaciándose spilling; pres. part. / *vaciarse.*

vaciaos (you all) spill; impve. 2nd pers. pl. / *vaciarse.*

vaciar to empty. irr.

vaciarse to spill. irr.

vacías you empty; pres. ind. 2nd pers. sing. / *vaciar.*

vacíate (you) spill; impve. 2nd pers. sing. / *vaciarse.*

vacíe 1. that I may empty; pres. subj. 1st pers. sing. / *vaciar.* 2. that he (she/it) may empty; pres. subj. 3rd pers. sing. 3. let him (her/it) empty; impve. 3rd pers. sing.

vaciémonos let us spill; impve. 1st pers. pl. / *vaciarse.*

vacíen 1. that they may empty; pres. subj. 3rd pers. pl. / *vaciar.* 2. let them empty; impve. 3rd pers. pl.

vaciense let them spill; impve. 3rd pers. pl. / *vaciarse.*

vacíes that you may empty; pres. subj. 2nd pers. sing. / *vaciar.*

vacíese let him (her/it) spill; impve. 3rd pers. sing. / *vaciarse.*

vacilar to vacillate. reg.

vacío I empty; pres. ind. 1st pers. sing. / *vaciar.*

vacunar to vaccinate. reg.

vadeándose behaving; pres. part. / *vadearse.*

vadeaos (you all) behave; impve. 2nd pers. pl. / *vadearse.*

vadear to ford or to wade. reg.

vadearse to behave. reg.

vadéate (you) behave; impve. 2nd pers. sing. / *vadearse.*

vadeémonos let us behave; impve. 1st pers. pl. / *vadearse.*

vadéense let them behave; impve. 3rd pers. pl. / *vadearse.*

vadéese let him (her/it) behave; impve. 3rd pers. sing. / *vadearse.*

vagabundear to wander. reg.

vagamundear to roam. reg.

vagar to wander. irr.

vague 1. that I may wander; pres. subj. 1st pers. sing. / *vagar.* 2. that he (she/it) may wander; pres. subj. 3rd pers. sing. 3. let him (her/it) wander; impve. 3rd pers. sing.

vagué I wandered; past 1st pers. sing. / *vagar.*

vaguear to roam. reg.

vaguéis that you (all) may wander; pres. subj. 2nd pers. pl. / *vagar.*

vaguemos 1. that we may wander; pres. subj. 1st pers. pl. / *vagar.* 2. let us wander; impve. 1st pers. pl.

vaguen 1. that they may wander; pres. subj. 3rd pers. pl. / *vagar.* 2. let them wander; impve. 3rd pers. pl.

vagues that you may wander; pres. subj. 2nd pers. sing. / *vagar.*

vahar to emit vapor. reg.

vahear to exhale. reg.

vais you (all) go; past 2nd pers. pl. / *ir.*

val (you) be worth; impve. 2nd pers. sing. / *valer.*

valdrá he (she/it) will be worth; fut. 3rd pers. sing. / *valer.*

valdrán they will be worth; fut. 3rd pers. pl. / *valer.*

valdrás you will be worth; fut. 2nd pers. sing. / *valer.*

valdré I shall be worth; fut. 1st pers. sing. / *valer.*

valdréis you (all) will be worth; fut. 2nd pers. pl. / *valer.*

valdremos we shall be worth; fut. 1st pers. pl. / *valer.*

valdría 1. I should be worth; cond. 1st pers. sing. / *valer.* 2. he (she/it) would be worth; cond. 3rd pers. sing.

valdríais you (all) would be worth; cond. 2nd pers. pl. / *valer.*

valdríamos we should be worth; cond. 1st pers. pl. / *valer.*

valdrían they would be worth; cond. 3rd pers. pl. / *valer.*

valdrías you would be worth; cond. 2nd pers. sing. / *valer.*

vale 1. he (she/it) is worth; pres. ind. 3rd pers. sing. / *valer.* 2. (you) be worth; impve. 2nd pers. sing.

valeos (you all) make use of; impve. 2nd pers. pl. / *valerse.*

valer to be worth. irr.

valerse to make use of. irr.

válete (you) make use of; impve. 2nd pers. sing. / *valerse.*

valga 1. that I may be worth; pres. subj. 1st pers. sing. / *valer.* 2. that he (she/it) may be worth; pres. subj. 3rd pers. sing. 3. let him (her/it) be worth; impve. 3rd pers. sing.

valgáis that you (all) may be worth; pres. subj. 2nd pers. pl. / *valer.*

valgámonos let us make use of; impve. 1st pers. pl. / *valerse.*

valgamos 1. that we may be worth; pres. subj. 1st pers. pl. / *valer*. 2. let us be worth; impve. 1st pers. pl.

valgan 1. that they may be worth; pres. subj. 3rd pers. pl. / *valer*. 2. let them be worth; impve. 3rd pers. pl.

válganse let them make use of; impve. 3rd pers. pl. / *valerse*.

valgas that you may be worth; pres. subj. 2nd pers. sing. / *valer*.

válgase let him (her/it) make use of; impve. 3rd pers. sing. / *valerse*.

valgo I am worth; pres. ind. 1st pers. sing. / *valer*.

validar to validate. reg.

valiéndose making use of; pres. part. / *valerse*.

valorar to value. reg.

valorear to evaluate. reg.

valorice 1. that I may appraise; pres. subj. 1st pers. sing. / *valorizar*. 2. that he (she/it) may appraise; pres. subj. 3rd pers. sing. 3. let him (her/it) appraise; impve. 3rd pers. sing.

valoricé I appraised; past 1st pers. sing. / *valorizar*.

valoricéis that you (all) may appraise; pres. subj. 2nd pers. pl. / *valorizar*.

valoricémonos let us increase in value; impve. 1st pers. pl. / *valorizarse*.

valoricemos 1. that we may appraise; pres. subj. 1st pers. pl. / *valorizar*. 2. let us appraise; impve. 1st pers. pl.

valoricen 1. that they may appraise; pres. subj. 3rd pers. pl. / *valorizar*. 2. let them appraise; impve. 3rd pers. pl.

valorícense let them increase in value; impve. 3rd pers. pl. / *valorizarse*.

valorices that you may appraise; pres. subj. 2nd pers. sing. / *valorizar*.

valorícese let him (her/it) increase in value; impve. 3rd pers. sing. / *valorizarse*.

valorizándose increasing in value; pres. part. / *valorizarse*.

valorizaos (you all) increase in value; impve. 2nd pers. pl. / *valorizarse*.

valorizar to appraise. irr.

valorizarse to increase in value. irr.

valorízate (you) increase in value; impve. 2nd pers. sing. / *valorizarse*.

valsar to waltz. reg.

valsear to waltz. reg.

valúa 1. he (she/it) evaluates; pres. ind. 3rd pers. sing. / *valuar*. 2. (you) evaluate; impve. 2nd pers. sing.

valúan they evaluate; pres. ind. 3rd pers. pl. / *valuar*.

valuar to evaluate. irr.

valúas you evaluate; pres. ind. 2nd pers. sing. / *valuar*.

valúe 1. that I may evaluate; pres. subj. 1st pers. sing. / *valuar*. 2. that he (she/it) may evaluate; pres. subj. 3rd pers. sing. 3. let him (her/it) evaluate; impve. 3rd pers. sing.

valúen 1. that they may evaluate; pres. subj. 3rd pers. pl. / *valuar*. 2. let them evaluate; impve. 3rd pers. pl.

valúes that you may evaluate; pres. subj. 2nd pers. sing. / *valuar*.

valúo I evaluate; pres. ind. 1st pers. sing. / *valuar*.

vallar to barricade. reg.

vámonos let us go away; impve. 1st pers. pl. / *irse*.

vamos 1. we go; pres. ind. 1st pers. pl. / *ir*. 2. let us go; impve. 1st pers. pl.

van they go; pres. ind. 3rd pers. pl. / *ir*.

vanagloria 1. he (she/it) boasts; pres. ind. 3rd pers. sing. / *vanagloriarse*. 2. (you) boast; impve. 2nd pers. sing.

vanaglorían they boast; pres. ind. 3rd pers. pl. / *vanagloriarse*.

vanagloriándose boasting; pres. part. / *vanagloriarse*.

vanagloriaos (you all) boast; impve. 2nd pers. pl. / *vanagloriarse*.

vanagloriarse to boast. irr.

vanaglorías you boast; pres. ind. 2nd pers. sing. / *vanagloriarse*.

vanagloríate (you) boast; impve. 2nd pers. sing. / *vanagloriarse*.

vanagloríe 1. that I may boast; pres. subj. 1st pers. sing. / *vanagloriarse*. 2. that he (she/it) may boast; pres. subj. 3rd pers. sing.

vanagloriémonos let us boast; impve. 1st pers. pl. / *vanagloriarse*.

vanagloriemos that we may boast; pres. subj. 1st pers. pl. / *vanagloriarse*.

vanagloríen that they may boast; pres. subj. 3rd pers. pl. / *vanagloriarse*.

vanagloríense let them boast; impve. 3rd pers. pl. / *vanagloriarse*.

vanagloríes that you may boast; pres. subj. 2nd pers. sing. / *vanagloriarse*.

vanagloríese let him (her/it) boast; impve. 3rd pers. sing. / *vanagloriarse*.

vanaglorío I boast; pres. ind. 1st pers. sing. / *vanagloriarse*.

vanear to talk rubbish. reg.

vaporar to evaporate. reg.

vaporice 1. that I may vaporize; pres. subj. 1st pers. sing. / *vaporizar*. 2. that he (she/it) may vaporize; pres. subj. 3rd pers. sing. 3. let him (her/it) vaporize; impve. 3rd pers. sing.

vaporicé I vaporized; past 1st pers. sing. / *vaporizar*.

vaporicéis that you (all) may vaporize; pres. subj. 2nd pers. pl. / *vaporizar*.

vaporicemos 1. that we may vaporize; pres. subj. 1st pers. pl. / *vaporizar*. 2. let us vaporize; impve. 1st pers. pl.

vaporicen 1. that they may vaporize; pres. subj. 3rd pers. pl. / *vaporizar*. 2. let them vaporize; impve. 3rd pers. pl.

vaporices that you may vaporize; pres. subj. 2nd pers. sing. / *vaporizar*.

vaporizar to vaporize. irr.

vapular to flog. reg.

vapulear to thrash. reg.

vaque 1. that it may be vacant; pres. subj. 3rd pers. sing. / *vacar.* 2. let it be vacant; impve. 3rd pers. sing.

vaquen 1. that they may be vacant; pres. subj. 3rd pers. pl. / *vacar.* 2. let them be vacant; impve. 3rd pers. pl.

varándose running aground; pres. part. / *vararse.*

varaos (you all) run aground; impve. 2nd pers. pl. / *vararse.*

varar to beach a boat. reg.

vararse to run aground. reg.

várate (you) run aground; impve. 2nd pers. sing. / *vararse.*

vareándose weakening; pres. part. / *varearse.*

vareaos (you all) weaken; impve. 2nd pers. pl. / *varearse.*

varear to beat. reg.

varearse to weaken. reg.

varéate (you) weaken; impve. 2nd pers. sing. / *varearse.*

vareémonos let us weaken; impve. 1st pers. pl. / *varearse.*

varéense let them weaken; impve. 3rd pers. pl. / *varearse.*

varéese let him (her/it) weaken; impve. 3rd pers. sing. / *varearse.*

varémonos let us run aground; impve. 1st pers. pl. / *vararse.*

várense let them run aground; impve. 3rd pers. pl. / *vararse.*

várese let him (her/it) run aground; impve. 3rd pers. sing. / *vararse.*

varía 1. he (she/it) varies; pres. ind. 3rd pers. sing. / *variar.* 2. (you) vary; impve. 2nd pers. sing.

varían they vary; pres. ind. 3rd pers. pl. / *variar.*

variar to vary. irr.

varías you vary; pres. ind. 2nd pers. sing. / *variar.*

varíe 1. that I may vary; pres. subj. 1st pers. sing. / *variar.* 2. that he (she/it) may vary; pres. subj. 3rd pers. sing. 3. let him (her/it) vary; impve. 3rd pers. sing.

varíen 1. that they may vary; pres. subj. 3rd pers. pl. / *variar.* 2. let them vary; impve. 3rd pers. pl.

varíes that you may vary; pres. subj. 2nd pers. sing. / *variar.*

varío I vary; pres. ind. 1st pers. sing. / *variar.*

vas you go; pres. ind. 2nd pers. sing. / *ir.*

vaticinar to prophesy. reg.

vaya 1. that I may go; pres. subj. 1st pers. sing. / *ir.* 2. that he (she/it) may go; pres. subj. 3rd pers. sing. 3. let him (her/it) go; impve. 3rd pers. sing.

vayáis that you (all) may go; pres. subj. 2nd pers. pl. / *ir.*

vayamos 1. that we may go; pres. subj. 1st pers. pl. / *ir.* 2. let us go; impve. 1st pers. pl.

vayan 1. that they may go; pres. subj. 3rd pers. pl. / *ir.* 2. let them go; impve. 3rd pers. pl.

váyanse let them go away; impve. 3rd pers. pl. / *irse.*

vayas that you may go; pres. subj. 2nd pers. sing. / *ir.*

váyase let him (her/it) go away; impve. 3rd pers. sing. / *irse.*

ve (you) go; impve. 2nd pers. sing. / *ir.*

vea 1. that I may see; pres. subj. 1st pers. sing. / *ver.* 2. that he (she/it) may see; pres. subj. 3rd pers. sing. 3. let him (her/it) see; impve. 3rd pers. sing.

veáis that you (all) may see; pres. subj. 2nd pers. pl. / *ver.*

veámonos let us appear; impve. 1st pers. pl. / *verse.*

veamos 1. that we may see; pres. subj. 1st pers. pl. / *ver.* 2. let us see; impve. 1st pers. pl.

vean 1. that they may see; pres. subj. 3rd pers. pl. / *ver.* 2. let them see; impve. 3rd pers. pl.

véanse let them appear; impve. 3rd pers. pl. / *verse.*

veas that you may see; pres. subj. 2nd pers. sing. / *ver.*

véase let him (her/it) appear; impve. 3rd pers. sing. / *verse.*

vece 1. that I may accustom; pres. subj. 1st pers. sing. / *vezar.* 2. that he (she/it) may accustom; pres. subj. 3rd pers. sing. 3. let him (her/it) accustom; impve. 3rd pers. sing.

vecé I accustomed; past 1st pers. sing. / *vezar.*

vecéis that you (all) may accustom; pres. subj. 2nd pers. pl. / *vezar.*

vecemos 1. that we may accustom; pres. subj. 1st pers. pl. / *vezar.* 2. let us accustom; impve. 1st pers. pl.

vecen 1. that they may accustom; pres. subj. 3rd pers. pl. / *vezar.* 2. let them accustom; impve. 3rd pers. pl.

veces that you may accustom; pres. subj. 2nd pers. sing. / *vezar.*

vedar to prohibit. reg.

vegetar to vegetate. reg.

veía 1. I was seeing; imp. ind. 1st pers. sing. / *ver.* 2. he (she/it) was seeing; imp. ind. 3rd pers. sing.

veíais you (all) were seeing; imp. ind. 2nd pers. pl. / *ver.*

veíamos we were seeing; imp. ind. 1st pers. pl. / *ver.*

veían they were seeing; imp. ind. 3rd pers. pl. / *ver.*

veías you were seeing; imp. ind. 2nd pers. sing. / *ver.*

vejar to vex. reg.

velándose fogging (photo); pres. part. / *velarse.*

velar to veil. reg.

velarse to fog (photo). reg.

vélense let them fog (photo); impve. 3rd pers. pl. / *velarse.*

vélese let it fog (photo); impve. 3rd pers. sing. / *velarse.*

ven (you) come; impve. 2nd pers. sing. / *venir.*

venceos (you all) control yourselves; impve. 2nd pers. pl. / *vencerse.*

vencer to conquer. irr.

vencerse to control oneself. irr.

véncete (you) control yourself; impve. 2nd pers. sing. / *vencerse.*

venciéndose controlling oneself; pres. part. / *vencerse.*

vendámonos let us be sold; impve. 1st pers. pl. / *venderse.*

véndanse let them be sold; impve. 3rd pers. pl. / *venderse.*

vendar to bandage or to blindfold. reg.

véndase let him (her/it) be sold; impve. 3rd pers. sing. / *venderse.*

vendeos (you all) be sold; impve. 2nd pers. pl. / *venderse.*

vender to sell. reg.

venderse to be sold. reg.

véndete (you) be sold; impve. 2nd pers. sing. / *venderse.*

vendiéndose being sold; pres. part. / *venderse.*

vendimiar to gather grapes. reg.

vendrá he (she/it) will come; fut. 3rd pers. sing. / *venir.*

vendrán they will come; fut. 3rd pers. pl. / *venir.*

vendrás you will come; fut. 2nd pers. sing. / *venir.*

vendré I shall come; fut. 1st pers. sing. / *venir.*

vendréis you (all) will come; fut. 2nd pers. pl. / *venir.*

vendremos we shall come; fut. 1st pers. pl. / *venir.*

vendría 1. I should come; cond. 1st pers. sing. / *venir.* 2. he (she/it) would come; cond. 3rd pers. sing.

vendríais you (all) would come; cond. 2nd pers. pl. / *venir.*

vendríamos we should come; cond. 1st pers. pl. / *venir.*

vendrían they would come; cond. 3rd pers. pl. / *venir.*

vendrías you would come; cond. 2nd pers. sing. / *venir.*

venerar to venerate. reg.

venga 1. that I may come; pres. subj. 1st pers. sing. / *venir.* 2. that he (she/it) may come; pres. subj. 3rd pers. sing. 3. let him (her/it) come; impve. 3rd pers. sing.

vengáis that you (all) may come; pres. subj. 2nd pers. pl. / *venir.*

vengamos 1. that we may come; pres. subj. 1st pers. pl. / *venir.* 2. let us come; impve. 1st pers. pl.

vengan 1. that they may come; pres. subj. 3rd pers. pl. / *venir.* 2. let them come; impve. 3rd pers. pl.

vengándose taking vengeance; pres. part. / *vengarse.*

vengaos (you all) take vengeance; impve. 2nd pers. pl. / *vengarse.*

vengar to avenge or to revenge. irr.

vengarse to take vengeance. irr.

vengas that you may come; pres. subj. 2nd pers. sing. / *venir.*

véngate (you) take vengeance; impve. 2nd pers. sing. / *vengarse.*

vengo I come; pres. ind. 1st pers. sing. / *venir.*

vengue 1. that I may avenge; pres. subj. 1st pers. sing. / *vengar.* 2. that he (she/it) may avenge; pres. subj. 3rd pers. sing. 3. let him (her/it) avenge; impve. 3rd pers. sing.

vengué I avenged; past 1st pers. sing. / *vengar.*

venguéis that you (all) may avenge; pres. subj. 2nd pers. pl. / *vengar.*

venguémonos let us take vengeance; impve. 1st pers. pl. / *vengarse.*

venguemos 1. that we may avenge; pres. subj. 1st pers. pl. / *vengar.* 2. let us avenge; impve. 1st pers. pl.

venguen 1. that they may avenge; pres. subj. 3rd pers. pl. / *vengar.* 2. let them avenge; impve. 3rd pers. pl.

vénguense let them take vengeance; impve. 3rd pers. pl. / *vengarse.*

vengues that you may avenge; pres. subj. 2nd pers. sing. / *vengar.*

vénguese let him (her/it) take vengeance; impve. 3rd pers. sing. / *vengarse.*

venir to come. irr.

ventándose splitting; pres. part. / *ventarse.*

ventaos (you all) split; impve. 2nd pers. pl. / *ventarse.*

ventar to sniff. reg.

ventarse to split. reg.

véntate (you) split; impve. 2nd pers. sing. / *ventarse.*

venteándose expelling air; pres. part. / *ventearse.*

venteaos (you all) expel air; impve. 2nd pers. pl. / *ventearse.*

ventear to sniff. reg.

ventearse to expel air. reg.

ventéate (you) expel air; impve. 2nd pers. sing. / *ventearse.*

venteémonos let us expel air; impve. 1st pers. pl. / *ventearse.*

ventéense let them expel air; impve. 3rd pers. pl. / *ventearse.*

ventéese let him (her/it) expel air; impve. 3rd pers. sing. / *ventearse.*

ventémonos let us split; impve. 1st pers. pl. / *ventarse.*

véntense let them split; impve. 3rd pers. pl. / *ventarse.*

véntese let him (her/it) split; impve. 3rd pers. sing. / *ventarse.*

ventilar to ventilate. reg.

ventiscar to blow or to snow hard. irr.

ventisque that it may blow; pres. subj. 3rd pers. sing. / *ventiscar.*

ventisquear to blow as a blizzard. reg.

ventisquen 1. that they may blow; pres. subj. 3rd pers. pl. / *ventiscar.* 2. let them blow; impve. 3rd pers. pl.

ventosear to break wind. reg.

venza 1. that I may conquer; pres. subj. 1st pers. sing. / *vencer.* 2. that he (she/it) may conquer; pres. subj. 3rd pers. sing. 3. let him (her/it) conquer; impve. 3rd pers. sing.

venzáis that you (all) may conquer; pres. subj. 2nd pers. pl. / *vencer.*

venzámonos let us control ourselves; impve. 1st pers. pl. / *vencerse.*

venzamos 1. that we may conquer; pres. subj. 1st pers. pl. / *vencer.* 2. let us conquer; impve. 1st pers. pl.

venzan 1. that they may conquer; pres. subj. 3rd pers. pl. / *vencer.* 2. let them conquer; impve. 3rd pers. pl.

vénzanse let them control themselves; impve. 3rd pers. pl. / *vencerse.*

venzas that you may conquer; pres. subj. 2nd pers. sing. / *vencer.*

vénzase let him (her/it) control himself (herself/itself); impve. 3rd pers. sing. / *vencerse.*

venzo I conquer; pres. ind. 1st pers. sing. / *vencer.*

veos (you all) appear; impve. 2nd pers. pl. / *verse.*

ver to see or to look. irr.

veranear to spend the summer. reg.

verberar to beat against. reg.

verdear to look green. reg.

verdecer to turn green. irr.

verdezca 1. that I may turn green; pres. subj. 1st pers. sing. / *verdecer.* 2. that he (she/it) may turn green; pres. subj. 3rd pers. sing. 3. let him (her/it) turn green; impve. 3rd pers. sing.

verdezcáis that you (all) may turn green; pres. subj. 2nd pers. pl. / *verdecer.*

verdezcamos 1. that we may turn green; pres. subj. 1st pers. pl. / *verdecer.* 2. let us turn green; impve. 1st pers. pl.

verdezcan 1. that they may turn green; pres. subj. 3rd pers. pl. / *verdecer.* 2. let them turn green; impve. 3rd pers. pl.

verdezcas that you may turn green; pres. subj. 2nd pers. sing. / *verdecer.*

verdezco I turn green; pres. ind. 1st pers. sing. / *verdecer.*

verguear to flog. reg.

verificándose being verified; pres. part. / *verificarse.*

verificaos (you all) be verified; impve. 2nd pers. pl. / *verificarse.*

verificar to verify. irr.

verificarse to be verified. irr.

verifícate (you) be verified; impve. 2nd pers. sing. / *verificarse.*

verifique 1. that I may verify; pres. subj. 1st pers. sing. / *verificar.* 2. that he (she/it) may verify; pres. subj. 3rd pers. sing. 3. let him (her/it) verify; impve. 3rd pers. sing.

verifiqué I verified; past 1st pers. sing. / *verificar.*

verifiquéis that you (all) may verify; pres. subj. 2nd pers. pl. / *verificar.*

verifiquémonos let us be verified; impve. 1st pers. pl. / *verificarse.*

verifiquemos 1. that we may verify; pres. subj. 1st pers. pl. / *verificar.* 2. let us verify; impve. 1st pers. pl.

verifiquen 1. that they may verify; pres. subj. 3rd pers. pl. / *verificar.* 2. let them verify; impve. 3rd pers. pl.

verifiquense let them be verified; impve. 3rd pers. pl. / *verificarse.*

verifiques that you may verify; pres. subj. 2nd pers. sing. / *verificar.*

verifíquese let him (her/it) be verified; impve. 3rd pers. sing. / *verificarse.*

versándose becoming skilled; pres. part. / *versarse.*

versaos (you all) become skilled; impve. 2nd pers. pl. / *versarse.*

versar to deal with. reg.

versarse to become skilled. reg.

vérsate (you) become skilled; impve. 2nd pers. sing. / *versarse.*

verse to appear or to seem. irr.

versémonos let us become skilled; impve. 1st pers. pl. / *versarse.*

vérsense let them become skilled; impve. 3rd pers. pl. / *versarse.*

vérsese let him (her/it) become skilled; impve. 3rd pers. sing. / *versarse.*

versificar to versify. irr.

versifique 1. that I may versify; pres. subj. 1st pers. sing. / *versificar.* 2. that he (she/it) may versify; pres. subj. 3rd pers. sing. 3. let him (her/it) versify; impve. 3rd pers. sing.

versifiqué I versified; past 1st pers. sing. / *versificar.*

versifiquéis that you (all) may versify; pres. subj. 2nd pers. pl. / *versificar.*

versifiquemos 1. that we may versify; pres. subj. 1st pers. pl. / *versificar.* 2. let us versify; impve. 1st pers. pl.

versifiquen 1. that they may versify; pres. subj. 3rd pers. pl. / *versificar.* 2. let them versify; impve. 3rd pers. pl.

versifiques that you may versify; pres. subj. 2nd pers. sing. / *versificar.*

verter to pour. irr.

vestíos (you all) dress; impve. 2nd pers. pl. / *vestirse.*

vestir to clothe. irr.

vestirse to dress. irr.

vetar to veto. reg.

vete (you) go away; impve. 2nd pers. sing. / *irse.*

vetear to grain or to streak. reg.

vezar to accustom. irr.

vi I saw; past 1st pers. sing. / *ver.*

viajar to travel. reg.

vibrar to vibrate. reg.

viciándose becoming corrupt; pres. part. / *viciarse.*

viciaos (you all) become corrupt; impve. 2nd pers. pl. / *viciarse.*

viciar to vitiate or to corrupt. reg.

viciarse to become corrupt. reg.

vicíate (you) become corrupt; impve. 2nd pers. sing. / *viciarse.*

viciémonos let us become corrupt; impve. 1st pers. pl. / *viciarse.*

vicíense let them become corrupt; impve. 3rd pers. pl. / *viciarse.*

vicíese let him (her/it) become corrupt; impve. 3rd pers. sing. / *viciarse.*

victimar to murder. reg.

victorear to cheer. reg.

vidría 1. he (she/it) glazes; pres. ind. 3rd pers. sing. / *vidriar.* 2. (you) glaze; impve. 2nd pers. sing.

vidrían they glaze; pres. ind. 3rd pers. pl. / *vidriar.*

vidriar to glaze. irr.

vidrías you glaze; pres. ind. 2nd pers. sing. / *vidriar.*

vidríe 1. that I may glaze; pres. subj. 1st pers. sing. / *vidriar.* 2. that he (she/it) may glaze; pres. subj. 3rd pers. sing. 3. let him (her/it) glaze; impve. 3rd pers. sing.

vidríen 1. that they may glaze; pres. subj. 3rd pers. pl. / *vidriar.* 2. let them glaze; impve. 3rd pers. pl.

vidríes that you may glaze; pres. subj. 2nd pers. sing. / *vidriar*.

vidrío I glaze; pres. ind. 1st pers. sing. / *vidriar*.

viendo seeing; pres. part. / *ver*.

viéndose appearing; pres. part. / *verse*.

viene he (she/it) comes; pres. ind. 3rd pers. sing. / *venir*.

vienen they come; pres. ind. 3rd pers. pl. / *venir*.

vienes you come; pres. ind. 2nd pers. sing. / *venir*.

viera 1. that I might see; imp. subj. 1st pers. sing. / *ver*. 2. that he (she/it) might see; imp. subj. 3rd pers. sing.

vierais that you (all) might see; imp. subj. 2nd pers pl. / *ver*.

viéramos that we might see; imp. subj. 1st pers. pl. / *ver*.

vieran that they might see; imp. subj. 3rd pers. pl. / *ver*.

vieras that you might see; imp. subj. 2nd pers. sing. / *ver*.

vieron they saw; past 3rd pers. pl. / *ver*.

vierta 1. that I may pour; pres. subj. 1st pers. sing. / *verter*. 2. that he (she/it) may pour; pres. subj. 3rd pers. sing. 3. let him (her/it) pour; impve. 3rd pers. sing.

viertan 1. that they may pour; pres. subj. 3rd pers. pl. / *verter*. 2. let them pour; impve. 3rd pers. pl.

viertas that you may pour; pres. subj. 2nd pers. sing. / *verter*.

vierte 1. he (she/it) pours; pres. ind. 3rd pers. sing. / *verter*. 2. (you) pour; impve. 2nd pers. sing.

vierten they pour; pres. ind. 3rd pers. pl. / *verter*.

viertes you pour; pres. ind. 2nd pers. sing. / *verter*.

vierto I pour; pres. ind. 1st pers. sing. / *verter*.

viese 1. that I might see; imp. subj. 1st pers. sing. / *ver*. 2. that he (she/it) might see; imp. subj. 3rd pers. sing.

vieseis that you (all) might see; imp. subj. 2nd pers pl. / *ver*.

viésemos that we might see; imp. subj. 1st pers. pl. / *ver*.

viesen that they might see; imp. subj. 3rd pers. pl. / *ver*.

vieses that you might see; imp. subj. 2nd pers. sing. / *ver*.

vigilar to watch over. reg.

vigorice 1. that I may invigorate; pres. subj. 1st pers. sing. / *vigorizar*. 2. that he (she/it) may invigorate; pres. subj. 3rd pers. sing. 3. let him (her/it) invigorate; impve. 3rd pers. sing.

vigoricé I invigorated; past 1st pers. sing. / *vigorizar*.

vigoricéis that you (all) may invigorate; pres. subj. 2nd pers. pl. / *vigorizar*.

vigoricemos 1. that we may invigorate; pres. subj. 1st pers. pl. / *vigorizar*. 2. let us invigorate; impve. 1st pers. pl.

vigoricen 1. that they may invigorate; pres. subj. 3rd pers. pl. / *vigorizar*. 2. let them invigorate; impve. 3rd pers. pl.

vigorices that you may invigorate; pres. subj. 2nd pers. sing. / *vigorizar*.

vigorizar to invigorate. irr.

vilipendiar to vilify or to revile. reg.

vimos we saw; past 1st pers. pl. / *ver*.

vincular to bind. reg.

vindicándose defending oneself; pres. part. / *vindicarse*.

vindicaos (you all) defend yourselves; impve. 2nd pers. pl. / *vindicarse*.

vindicar to vindicate. irr.

vindicarse to defend oneself. irr.

vindícate (you) defend yourself; impve. 2nd pers. sing. / *vindicarse*.

vindique 1. that I may vindicate; pres. subj. 1st pers. sing. / *vindicar*. 2. that he (she/it) may vindicate; pres. subj. 3rd pers. sing. 3. let him (her/it) vindicate; impve. 3rd pers. sing.

vindiqué I vindicated; past 1st pers. sing. / *vindicar*.

vindiquéis that you (all) may vindicate; pres. subj. 2nd pers. pl. / *vindicar*.

vindiquémonos let us defend ourselves; impve. 1st pers. pl. / *vindicarse*.

vindiquemos 1. that we may vindicate; pres. subj. 1st pers. pl. / *vindicar*. 2. let us vindicate; impve. 1st pers. pl.

vindiquen 1. that they may vindicate; pres. subj. 3rd pers. pl. / *vindicar*. 2. let them vindicate; impve. 3rd pers. pl.

vindíquense let them defend themselves; impve. 3rd pers. pl. / *vindicarse*.

vindiques that you may vindicate; pres. subj. 2nd pers. sing. / *vindicar*.

vindíquese let him (her/it) defend himself (herself/itself); impve. 3rd pers. sing. / *vindicarse*.

vine I came; past 1st pers. sing. / *venir*.

viniendo coming; pres. part. / *venir*.

viniera 1. that I might come; imp. subj. 1st pers. sing. / *venir*. 2. that he (she/it) might come; imp. subj. 3rd pers. sing.

vinierais that you (all) might come; imp. subj. 2nd pers pl. / *venir*.

viniéramos that we might come; imp. subj. 1st pers. pl. / *venir*.

vinieran that they might come; imp. subj. 3rd pers. pl. / *venir*.

vinieras that you might come; imp. subj. 2nd pers. sing. / *venir*.

vinieron they came; past 3rd pers. pl. / *venir*.

viniese 1. that I might come; imp. subj. 1st pers. sing. / *venir*. 2. that he (she/it) might come; imp. subj. 3rd pers. sing.

vinieseis that you (all) might come; imp. subj. 2nd pers pl. / *venir*.

viniésemos that we might come; imp. subj. 1st pers. pl. / *venir*.

viniesen that they might come; imp. subj. 3rd pers. pl. / *venir*.

vinieses that you might come; imp. subj. 2nd pers. sing. / *venir*.

vinimos we came; past 1st pers. pl. / *venir*.
viniste you came; past 2nd pers. sing. / *venir*.
vinisteis you (all) came; past 2nd pers. pl. / *venir*.
vino he (she/it) came; past 3rd pers. sing. / *venir*.
vio he (she/it) saw; past 3rd pers. sing. / *ver*.
violar to violate. reg.
violentándose getting angry; pres. part. / *violentarse*.
violentaos (you all) get angry; impve. 2nd pers. pl. / *violentarse*.
violentar to do violence. reg.
violentarse to get angry. reg.
violéntate (you) get angry; impve. 2nd pers. sing. / *violentarse*.
violentémonos let us get angry; impve. 1st pers. pl. / *violentarse*.
violéntense let them get angry; impve. 3rd pers. pl. / *violentarse*.
violéntese let him (her/it) get angry; impve. 3rd pers. sing. / *violentarse*.
virándose turning; pres. part. / *virarse*.
viraos (you all) turn; impve. 2nd pers. pl. / *virarse*.
virar to veer. reg.
virarse to turn. reg.
vírate (you) turn; impve. 2nd pers. sing. / *virarse*.
virémonos let us turn; impve. 1st pers. pl. / *virarse*.
vírense let them turn; impve. 3rd pers. pl. / *virarse*.
vírese let him (her/it) turn; impve. 3rd pers. sing. / *virarse*.
visar to visa or to countersign. reg.
visitándose being on visiting terms; pres. part. / *visitarse*.
visitaos (you all) be on visiting terms; impve. 2nd pers. pl. / *visitarse*.
visitar to visit. reg.
visitarse to be on visiting terms. reg.
visítate (you) be on visiting terms; impve. 2nd pers. sing. / *visitarse*.
visitémonos let us be on visiting terms; impve. 1st pers. pl. / *visitarse*.
visítense let them be on visiting terms; impve. 3rd pers. pl. / *visitarse*.
visítese let him (her/it) be on visiting terms; impve. 3rd pers. sing. / *visitarse*.
vislumbrándose glimmering; pres. part. / *vislumbrarse*.
vislumbrar to glimpse. reg.
vislumbrarse to glimmer. reg.
vislúmbrense let them glimmer; impve. 3rd pers. pl. / *vislumbrarse*.
vislúmbrese let it glimmer; impve. 3rd pers. sing. / *vislumbrarse*.
vista 1. that I may clothe; pres. subj. 1st pers. sing. / *vestir*. 2. that he (she/it) may clothe; pres. subj. 3rd pers. sing. 3. let him (her/it) clothe; impve. 3rd pers. sing.
vistáis that you (all) may clothe; pres. subj. 2nd pers. pl. / *vestir*.
vistámonos let us dress; impve. 1st pers. pl. / *vestirse*.

vistamos 1. that we may clothe; pres. subj. 1st pers. pl. / *vestir*. 2. let us clothe; impve. 1st pers. pl.
vistan 1. that they may clothe; pres. subj. 3rd pers. pl. / *vestir*. 2. let them clothe; impve. 3rd pers. pl.
vístanse let them dress; impve. 3rd pers. pl. / *vestirse*.
vistas that you may clothe; pres. subj. 2nd pers. sing. / *vestir*.
vístase let him (her/it) dress; impve. 3rd pers. sing. / *vestirse*.
viste you saw; past 2nd pers. sing. / *ver*.
viste 1. he (she/it) clothes; pres. ind. 3rd pers. sing. / *vestir*. 2. (you) clothe; impve. 2nd pers. sing.
visteis (you all) saw; impve. 2nd pers. pl. / *ver*.
visten they clothe; pres. ind. 3rd pers. pl. / *vestir*.
vistes you clothe; pres. ind. 2nd pers. sing. / *vestir*.
vístete (you) dress; impve. 2nd pers. sing. / *vestirse*.
vistiendo clothing; pres. part. / *vestir*.
vistiéndose dressing; pres. part. / *vestirse*.
vistiera 1. that I might clothe; imp. subj. 1st pers. sing. / *vestir*. 2. that he (she/it) might clothe; imp. subj. 3rd pers. sing.
vistierais that you (all) might clothe; imp. subj. 2nd pers pl. / *vestir*.
vistiéramos that we might clothe; imp. subj. 1st pers. pl. / *vestir*.
vistieran that they might clothe; imp. subj. 3rd pers. pl. / *vestir*.
vistieras that you might clothe; imp. subj. 2nd pers. sing. / *vestir*.
vistieron they clothed; past 3rd pers. pl. / *vestir*.
vistiese 1. that I might clothe; imp. subj. 1st pers. sing. / *vestir*. 2. that he (she/it) might clothe; imp. subj. 3rd pers. sing.
vistieseis that you (all) might clothe; imp. subj. 2nd pers pl. / *vestir*.
vistiésemos that we might clothe; imp. subj. 1st pers. pl. / *vestir*.
vistiesen that they might clothe; imp. subj. 3rd pers. pl. / *vestir*.
vistieses that you might clothe; imp. subj. 2nd pers. sing. / *vestir*.
vistió he (she/it) clothed; past 3rd pers. sing. / *vestir*.
visto saw; past part. / *ver*.
visto I clothe; pres. ind. 1st pers. sing. / *vestir*.
visualice 1. that I may visualize; pres. subj. 1st pers. sing. / *visualizar*. 2. that he (she/it) may visualize; pres. subj. 3rd pers. sing. 3. let him (her/it) visualize; impve. 3rd pers. sing.
visualicé I visualized; past 1st pers. sing. / *visualizar*.
visualicéis that you (all) may visualize; pres. subj. 2nd pers. pl. / *visualizar*.
visualicemos 1. that we may visualize; pres. subj. 1st pers. pl. / *visualizar*. 2. let us visualize; impve. 1st pers. pl.
visualicen 1. that they may visualize; pres. subj. 3rd pers. pl. / *visualizar*. 2. let them visualize; impve. 3rd pers. pl.
visualices that you may visualize; pres. subj. 2nd pers. sing. / *visualizar*.
visualizar to visualize. irr.

vitalice 1. that I may vitalize; pres. subj. 1st pers. sing. / *vitalizar.* 2. that he (she/it) may vitalize; pres. subj. 3rd pers. sing. 3. let him (her/it) vitalize; impve. 3rd pers. sing.

vitalicé I vitalized; past 1st pers. sing. / *vitalizar.*

vitalicéis that you (all) may vitalize; pres. subj. 2nd pers. pl. / *vitalizar.*

vitalicemos 1. that we may vitalize; pres. subj. 1st pers. pl. / *vitalizar.* 2. let us vitalize; impve. 1st pers. pl.

vitalicen 1. that they may vitalize; pres. subj. 3rd pers. pl. / *vitalizar.* 2. let them vitalize; impve. 3rd pers. pl.

vitalices that you may vitalize; pres. subj. 2nd pers. sing. / *vitalizar.*

vitalizar to vitalize. irr.

vitorear to cheer. reg.

vitrificándose vitrifying; pres. part. / *vitrificarse.*

vitrificaos (you all) vitrify; impve. 2nd pers. pl. / *vitrificarse.*

vitrificar to vitrify. irr.

vitrificarse to vitrify. irr.

vitrifícate (you) vitrify; impve. 2nd pers. sing. / *vitrificarse.*

vitrifique 1. that I may vitrify; pres. subj. 1st pers. sing. / *vitrificar.* 2. that he (she/it) may vitrify; pres. subj. 3rd pers. sing. 3. let him (her/it) vitrify; impve. 3rd pers. sing.

vitrifiqué I vitrified; past 1st pers. sing. / *vitrificar.*

vitrifiquéis that you (all) may vitrify; pres. subj. 2nd pers. pl. / *vitrificarse.*

vitrifiquémonos let us vitrify; impve. 1st pers. pl. / *vitrificarse.*

vitrifiquemos 1. that we may vitrify; pres. subj. 1st pers. pl. / *vitrificar.* 2. let us vitrify; impve. 1st pers. pl.

vitrifiquen 1. that they may vitrify; pres. subj. 3rd pers. pl. / *vitrificar.* 2. let them vitrify; impve. 3rd pers. pl. / *vitrificarse.*

vitrifiquense let them vitrify; impve. 3rd pers. pl. / *vitrificarse.*

vitrifiques that you may vitrify; pres. subj. 2nd pers. sing. / *vitrificar.*

vitrifíquese let him (her/it) vitrify; impve. 3rd pers. sing. / *vitrificarse.*

vituperar to vituperate. reg.

vivaquear to bivouac. reg.

vivar to cheer. reg.

vivificar to vivify. irr.

vivifique 1. that I may vivify; pres. subj. 1st pers. sing. / *vivificar.* 2. that he (she/it) may vivify; pres. subj. 3rd pers. sing. 3. let him (her/it) vivify; impve. 3rd pers. sing.

vivifiqué I vivified; past 1st pers. sing. / *vivificar.*

vivifiquéis that you (all) may vivify; pres. subj. 2nd pers. pl. / *vivificar.*

vivifiquemos 1. that we may vivify; pres. subj. 1st pers. pl. / *vivificar.* 2. let us vivify; impve. 1st pers. pl.

vivifiquen 1. that they may vivify; pres. subj. 3rd pers. pl. / *vivificar.* 2. let them vivify; impve. 3rd pers. pl.

vivifiques that you may vivify; pres. subj. 2nd pers. sing. / *vivificar.*

vivir to live. reg.

vocalice 1. that I may vocalize; pres. subj. 1st pers. sing. / *vocalizar.* 2. that he (she/it) may vocalize; pres. subj. 3rd pers. sing. 3. let him (her/it) vocalize; impve. 3rd pers. sing.

vocalicé I vocalized; past 1st pers. sing. / *vocalizar.*

vocalicéis that you (all) may vocalize; pres. subj. 2nd pers. pl. / *vocalizar.*

vocalicemos 1. that we may vocalize; pres. subj. 1st pers. pl. / *vocalizar.* 2. let us vocalize; impve. 1st pers. pl.

vocalicen 1. that they may vocalize; pres. subj. 3rd pers. pl. / *vocalizar.* 2. let them vocalize; impve. 3rd pers. pl.

vocalices that you may vocalize; pres. subj. 2nd pers. sing. / *vocalizar.*

vocalizar to vocalize. irr.

vocear to shout. reg.

vociferar to vociferate or to boast loudly. reg.

volándose getting angry; pres. part. / *volarse.*

volaos (you all) get angry; impve. 2nd pers. pl. / *volarse.*

volar to fly. irr.

volarse to get angry. irr.

volatice 1. that I may evaporate; pres. subj. 1st pers. sing. / *volatizar.* 2. that he (she/it) may evaporate; pres. subj. 3rd pers. sing. 3. let him (her/it) evaporate; impve. 3rd pers. sing.

volaticé I evaporated; past 1st pers. sing. / *volatizar.*

volaticéis that you (all) may evaporate; pres. subj. 2nd pers. pl. / *volatizar.*

volaticémonos let us evaporate; impve. 1st pers. pl. / *volatizarse.*

volaticemos 1. that we may evaporate; pres. subj. 1st pers. pl. / *volatizar.* 2. let us evaporate; impve. 1st pers. pl.

volaticen 1. that they may evaporate; pres. subj. 3rd pers. pl. / *volatizar.* 2. let them evaporate; impve. 3rd pers. pl.

volatícense let them evaporate; impve. 3rd pers. pl. / *volatizarse.*

volatices that you may evaporate; pres. subj. 2nd pers. sing. / *volatizar.*

volatícese let him (her/it) evaporate; impve. 3rd pers. sing. / *volatizar.*

volatilice 1. that it may volatilize; pres. subj. 3rd pers. sing. / *volatilizar.* 2. let it volatilize; impve. 3rd pers. sing.

volatilicen 1. that they may volatilize; pres. subj. 3rd pers. pl. / *volatilizar.* 2. let them volatilize; impve. 3rd pers. pl.

volatilícense let them volatilize; impve. 3rd pers. pl. / *volatilizarse.*

volatilícese let it volatilize; impve. 3rd pers. sing. / *volatilizarse.*

volatilizándose volatilizing; pres. part. / *volatilizarse.*

volatilizar to volatilize. irr.

volatilizarse to volatilize. irr.

volatizándose evaporating; pres. part. / *volatizarse.*
volatizaos (you all) evaporate; impve. 2nd pers. pl. / *volatizarse.*
volatizar to evaporate. irr.
volatizarse to evaporate. irr.
volatízate (you) evaporate; impve. 2nd pers. sing. / *volatizarse.*
volcándose getting upset; pres. part. / *volcarse.*
volcaos (you all) get upset; impve. 2nd pers. pl. / *volcarse.*
volcar to overturn. irr.
volcarse to get upset. irr.
volear to volley. reg.
volémonos let us get angry; impve. 1st pers. pl. / *volarse.*
volitar to flutter. reg.
volqué I overturned; past 1st pers. sing. / *volcar.*
volqueándose rolling over; pres. part. / *volquearse.*
volqueaos (you all) roll over; impve. 2nd pers. pl. / *volquearse.*
volquearse to roll over. reg.
volquéate (you) roll over; impve. 2nd pers. sing. / *volquearse.*
volqueémonos let us roll over; impve. 1st pers. pl. / *volquearse.*
volquéense let them roll over; impve. 3rd pers. pl. / *volquearse.*
volquéese let him (her/it) roll over; impve. 3rd pers. sing. / *volquearse.*
volquéis that you (all) may overturn; pres. subj. 2nd pers. pl. / *volcar.*
volquémonos let us get upset; impve. 1st pers. pl. / *volcarse.*
volquemos 1. that we may overturn; pres. subj. 1st pers. pl. / *volcar.* 2. let us overturn; impve. 1st pers. pl.
volteándose changing sides; pres. part. / *voltearse.*
volteaos (you all) change sides; impve. 2nd pers. pl. / *voltearse.*
voltear to turn. reg.
voltearse to change sides. reg.
voltéate (you) change sides; impve. 2nd pers. sing. / *voltearse.*
volteémonos let us change sides; impve. 1st pers. pl. / *voltearse.*
voltéense let them change sides; impve. 3rd pers. pl. / *voltearse.*
voltéese let him (her/it) change sides; impve. 3rd pers. sing. / *voltearse.*
volvámonos let us become; impve. 1st pers. pl. / *volverse.*
volveos (you all) become; impve. 2nd pers. pl. / *volverse.*
volver to turn. irr.
volverse to become. irr.
volviéndose becoming; pres. part. / *volverse.*
vomitar to vomit. reg.
vosear to address as vos. reg.
votar to vote. reg.

voy I go; pres. ind. 1st pers. sing. / *ir.*
vuela 1. he (she/it) flies; pres. ind. 3rd pers. sing. / *volar.* 2. (you) fly; impve. 2nd pers. sing.
vuelan they fly; pres. ind. 3rd pers. pl. / *volar.*
vuelas you fly; pres. ind. 2nd pers. sing. / *volar.*
vuélate (you) get angry; impve. 2nd pers. sing. / *volarse.*
vuelca 1. he (she/it) overturns; pres. ind. 3rd pers. sing. / *volcar.* 2. (you) overturn; impve. 2nd pers. sing.
vuelcan they overturn; pres. ind. 3rd pers. pl. / *volcar.*
vuelcas you overturn; pres. ind. 2nd pers. sing. / *volcar.*
vuélcate (you) get upset; impve. 2nd pers. sing. / *volcarse.*
vuelco I overturn; pres. ind. 1st pers. sing. / *volcar.*
vuele 1. that I may fly; pres. subj. 1st pers. sing. / *volar.* 2. that he (she/it) may fly; pres. subj. 3rd pers. sing. 3. let him (her/it) fly; impve. 3rd pers. sing.
vuelen 1. that they may fly; pres. subj. 3rd pers. pl. / *volar.* 2. let them fly; impve. 3rd pers. pl.
vuélense let them get angry; impve. 3rd pers. pl. / *volarse.*
vueles that you may fly; pres. subj. 2nd pers. sing. / *volar.*
vuélese let him (her/it) get angry; impve. 3rd pers. sing. / *volarse.*
vuelo I fly; pres. ind. 1st pers. sing. / *volar.*
vuelque 1. that I may overturn; pres. subj. 1st pers. sing. / *volcar.* 2. that he (she/it) may overturn; pres. subj. 3rd pers. sing. 3. let him (her/it) overturn; impve. 3rd pers. sing.
vuelquen 1. that they may overturn; pres. subj. 3rd pers. pl. / *volcar.* 2. let them overturn; impve. 3rd pers. pl.
vuélquense let them get upset; impve. 3rd pers. pl. / *volcarse.*
vuelques that you may overturn; pres. subj. 2nd pers. sing. / *volcar.*
vuélquese let him (her/it) get upset; impve. 3rd pers. sing. / *volcarse.*
vuelto turned; past part. / *volver.*
vuelva 1. that I may turn; pres. subj. 1st pers. sing. / *volver.* 2. that he (she/it) may turn; pres. subj. 3rd pers. sing. 3. let him (her/it) turn; impve. 3rd pers. sing.
vuelvan 1. that they may turn; pres. subj. 3rd pers. pl. / *volver.* 2. let them turn; impve. 3rd pers. pl.
vuélvanse let them become; impve. 3rd pers. pl. / *volverse.*
vuelvas that you may turn; pres. subj. 2nd pers. sing. / *volver.*
vuélvase let him (her/it) become; impve. 3rd pers. sing. / *volverse.*
vuelve 1. he (she/it) turns; pres. ind. 3rd pers. sing. / *volver.* 2. (you) turn; impve. 2nd pers. sing.
vuelven they turn; pres. ind. 3rd pers. pl. / *volver.*
vuelves you turn; pres. ind. 2nd pers. sing. / *volver.*
vuélvete (you) become; impve. 2nd pers. sing. / *volverse.*

vuelvo I turn; pres. ind. 1st pers. sing. / *volver.*
vulcanice 1. that I may vulcanize; pres. subj. 1st pers.
sing. / *vulcanizar.* 2. that he (she/it) may vulcanize;
pres. subj. 3rd pers. sing. 3. let him (her/it)
vulcanize; impve. 3rd pers. sing.
vulcanicé I vulcanized; past 1st pers. sing. /
vulcanizar.
vulcanicéis that you (all) may vulcanize; pres. subj.
2nd pers. pl. / *vulcanizar.*
vulcanicemos 1. that we may vulcanize; pres. subj. 1st
pers. pl. / *vulcanizar.* 2. let us vulcanize; impve. 1st
pers. pl.
vulcanicen 1. that they may vulcanize; pres. subj. 3rd
pers. pl. / *vulcanizar.* 2. let them vulcanize; impve.
3rd pers. pl.
vulcanices that you may vulcanize; pres. subj. 2nd
pers. sing. / *vulcanizar.*
vulcanizar to vulcanize. irr.
vulgarice 1. that I may vulgarize; pres. subj. 1st pers.
sing. / *vulgarizar.* 2. that he (she/it) may vulgarize;
pres. subj. 3rd pers. sing. 3. let him (her/it)
vulgarize; impve. 3rd pers. sing.
vulgaricé I vulgarized; past 1st pers. sing. / *vulgarizar.*
vulgaricéis that you (all) may vulgarize; pres. subj.
2nd pers. pl. / *vulgarizar.*
vulgaricémonos let us become popular; impve. 1st
pers. pl. / *vulgarizarse.*
vulgaricemos 1. that we may vulgarize; pres. subj. 1st
pers. pl. / *vulgarizar.* 2. let us vulgarize; impve. 1st
pers. pl.
vulgaricen 1. that they may vulgarize; pres. subj. 3rd
pers. pl. / *vulgarizar.* 2. let them vulgarize; impve.
3rd pers. pl.
vulgarícense let them become popular; impve. 3rd
pers. pl. / *vulgarizarse.*
vulgarices that you may vulgarize; pres. subj. 2nd
pers. sing. / *vulgarizar.*
vulgarícese let him (her/it) become popular; impve.
3rd pers. sing. / *vulgarizarse.*
vulgarizándose becoming popular; pres. part. /
vulgarizarse.
vulgarizaos (you all) become popular; impve. 2nd
pers. pl. / *vulgarizarse.*
vulgarizar to vulgarize. irr.
vulgarizarse to become popular. irr
vulgarízate (you) become popular; impve. 2nd pers.
sing. / *vulgarizarse.*
vulnerar to damage. reg.

Y

yacer to lie. irr.
yaga 1. that I may lie; pres. subj. 1st pers. sing. /
yacer. 2. that he (she/it) may lie; pres. subj. 3rd pers.
sing. 3. let him (her/it) lie; impve. 3rd pers. sing.
yago I lie; pres. ind. 1st pers. sing. / *yacer.*
yantar to eat. reg.
yaz (you) lie; impve. 2nd pers. sing. / *yacer.*

yazca 1. that I may lie; pres. subj. 1st pers. sing. /
yacer. 2. that he (she/it) may lie; pres. subj. 3rd pers.
sing. 3. let him (her/it) lie; impve. 3rd pers. sing.
yazcáis that you (all) may lie; pres. subj. 2nd pers. pl.
/ *yacer.*
yazcamos 1. that we may lie; pres. subj. 1st pers. pl. /
yacer. 2. let us lie; impve. 1st pers. pl.
yazcan 1. that they may lie; pres. subj. 3rd pers. pl. /
yacer. 2. let them lie; impve. 3rd pers. pl.
yazcas that you may lie; pres. subj. 2nd pers. sing. /
yacer.
yazco I lie; pres. ind. 1st pers. sing. / *yacer.*
yazga 1. that I may lie; pres. subj. 1st pers. sing. /
yacer. 2. that he (she/it) may lie; pres. subj. 3rd pers.
sing. 3. let him (her/it) lie; impve. 3rd pers. sing.
yazgáis that you (all) may lie; pres. subj. 2nd pers. pl.
/ *yacer.*
yazgamos 1. that we may lie; pres. subj. 1st pers. pl. /
yacer. 2. let us lie; impve. 1st pers. pl.
yazgan 1. that they may lie; pres. subj. 3rd pers. pl. /
yacer. 2. let them lie; impve. 3rd pers. pl.
yazgas that you may lie; pres. subj. 2nd pers. sing. /
yacer.
yazgo I lie; pres. ind. 1st pers. sing. / *yacer.*
yendo going; pres. part. / *ir.*
yéndose going away; pres. part. / *irse.*
yerga 1. that I may erect; pres. subj. 1st pers. sing. /
erguir. 2. that he (she/it) may erect; pres. subj. 3rd
pers. sing. 3. let him (her/it) erect; impve. 3rd pers.
sing.
yergáis that you (all) may erect; pres. subj. 2nd pers.
pl. / *erguir.*
yergámonos let us straighten; impve. 1st pers. pl. /
erguirse.
yergamos 1. that we may erect; pres. subj. 1st pers.
pl. / *erguir.* 2. let us erect; impve. 1st pers. pl.
yergan 1. that they may erect; pres. subj. 3rd pers. pl.
/ *erguir.* 2. let them erect; impve. 3rd pers. pl.
yérganse let them straighten; impve. 3rd pers. pl. /
erguirse.
yergas that you may erect; pres. subj. 2nd pers. sing. /
erguir.
yérgase let him (her/it) straighten; impve. 3rd pers.
sing. / *erguirse.*
yergo I erect; pres. ind. 1st pers. sing. / *erguir.*
yergue 1. he (she/it) erects; pres. ind. 3rd pers. sing. /
erguir. 2. (you) erect; impve. 2nd pers. sing.
yerguen they erect; pres. ind. 3rd pers. pl. / *erguir.*
yergues you erect; pres. ind. 2nd pers. sing. / *erguir.*
yérguete (you) straighten; impve. 2nd pers. sing. /
erguirse.
yermar to lay waste. reg.
yerra 1. he (she/it) errs; pres. ind. 3rd pers. sing. /
errar. 2. (you) err; impve. 2nd pers. sing.
yerran they err; pres. ind. 3rd pers. pl. / *errar.*
yerras you err; pres. ind. 2nd pers. sing. / *errar.*
yérrate (you) wander; impve. 2nd pers. sing. / *errarse.*
yerre 1. that I may err; pres. subj. 1st pers. sing. /
errar. 2. that he (she/it) may err; pres. subj. 3rd pers.
sing. 3. let him (her/it) err; impve. 3rd pers. sing.

yerren 1. that they may err; pres. subj. 3rd pers. pl. / *errar.* 2. let them err; impve. 3rd pers. pl.

yérrense let them wander; impve. 3rd pers. pl. / *errarse.*

yerres that you may err; pres. subj. 2nd pers. sing. / *errar.*

yérrese let him (her/it) wander; impve. 3rd pers. sing. / *errarse.*

yerro I err; pres. ind. 1st pers. sing. / *errar.*

yetar to hex. reg.

yuxtapon (you) juxtapose; impve. 2nd pers. sing. / *yuxtaponer.*

yuxtapondrá he (she/it) will juxtapose; fut. 3rd pers. sing. / *yuxtaponer.*

yuxtapondrán they will juxtapose; fut. 3rd pers. pl. / *yuxtaponer.*

yuxtapondrás you will juxtapose; fut. 2nd pers. sing. / *yuxtaponer.*

yuxtapondré I shall juxtapose; fut. 1st pers. sing. / *yuxtaponer.*

yuxtapondréis you (all) will juxtapose; fut. 2nd pers. pl. / *yuxtaponer.*

yuxtapondremos we shall juxtapose; fut. 1st pers. pl. / *yuxtaponer.*

yuxtapondría 1. I should juxtapose; cond. 1st pers. sing. / *yuxtaponer.* 2. he (she/it) would juxtapose; cond. 3rd pers. sing.

yuxtapondríais you (all) would juxtapose; cond. 2nd pers. pl. / *yuxtaponer.*

yuxtapondríamos we should juxtapose; cond. 1st pers. pl. / *yuxtaponer.*

yuxtapondrían they would juxtapose; cond. 3rd pers. pl. / *yuxtaponer.*

yuxtapondrías you would juxtapose; cond. 2nd pers. sing. / *yuxtaponer.*

yuxtaponer to juxtapose. irr.

yuxtaponga 1. that I may juxtapose; pres. subj. 1st pers. sing. / *yuxtaponer.* 2. that he (she/it) may juxtapose; pres. subj. 3rd pers. sing. 3. let him (her/it) juxtapose; impve. 3rd pers. sing.

yuxtapongáis that you (all) may juxtapose; pres. subj. 2nd pers. pl. / *yuxtaponer.*

yuxtapongamos 1. that we may juxtapose; pres. subj. 1st pers. pl. / *yuxtaponer.* 2. let us juxtapose; impve. 1st pers. pl.

yuxtapongan 1. that they may juxtapose; pres. subj. 3rd pers. pl. / *yuxtaponer.* 2. let them juxtapose; impve. 3rd pers. pl.

yuxtapongas that you may juxtapose; pres. subj. 2nd pers. sing. / *yuxtaponer.*

yuxtapongo I juxtapose; pres. ind. 1st pers. sing. / *yuxtaponer.*

yuxtapuesto juxtaposed; past part. / *yuxtaponer.*

yuxtapuse I juxtaposed; past 1st pers. sing. / *yuxtaponer.*

yuxtapusiera 1. that I might juxtapose; imp. subj. 1st pers. sing. / *yuxtaponer.* 2. that he (she/it) might juxtapose; imp. subj. 3rd pers. sing.

yuxtapusierais that you (all) might juxtapose; imp. subj. 2nd pers pl. / *yuxtaponer.*

yuxtapusiéramos that we might juxtapose; imp. subj. 1st pers. pl. / *yuxtaponer.*

yuxtapusieran that they might juxtapose; imp. subj. 3rd pers. pl. / *yuxtaponer.*

yuxtapusieras that you might juxtapose; imp. subj. 2nd pers. sing. / *yuxtaponer.*

yuxtapusieron they juxtaposed; past 3rd pers. pl. / *yuxtaponer.*

yuxtapusiese 1. that I might juxtapose; imp. subj. 1st pers. sing. / *yuxtaponer.* 2. that he (she/it) might juxtapose; imp. subj. 3rd pers. sing.

yuxtapusieseis that you (all) might juxtapose; imp. subj. 2nd pers pl. / *yuxtaponer.*

yuxtapusiésemos that we might juxtapose; imp. subj. 1st pers. pl. / *yuxtaponer.*

yuxtapusiesen that they might juxtapose; imp. subj. 3rd pers. pl. / *yuxtaponer.*

yuxtapusieses that you might juxtapose; imp. subj. 2nd pers. sing. / *yuxtaponer.*

yuxtapusimos we juxtaposed; past 1st pers. pl. / *yuxtaponer.*

yuxtapusiste you juxtaposed; past 2nd pers. sing. / *yuxtaponer.*

yuxtapusisteis you (all) juxtaposed; past 2nd pers. pl. / *yuxtaponer.*

yuxtapuso he (she/it) juxtaposed; past 3rd pers. sing. / *yuxtaponer.*

Z

zabordar to runaground. reg.

zabucar to shake up. irr.

zabuque 1. that I may shake up; pres. subj. 1st pers. sing. / *zabucar.* 2. that he (she/it) may shake up; pres. subj. 3rd pers. sing. 3. let him (her/it) shake up; impve. 3rd pers. sing.

zabuqué I shook up; past 1st pers. sing. / *zabucar.*

zabuquéis that you (all) may shake up; pres. subj. 2nd pers. pl. / *zabucar.*

zabuquemos 1. that we may shake up; pres. subj. 1st pers. pl. / *zabucar.* 2. let us shake up; impve. 1st pers. pl.

zabuquen 1. that they may shake up; pres. subj. 3rd pers. pl. / *zabucar.* 2. let them shake up; impve. 3rd pers. pl.

zabuques that you may shake up; pres. subj. 2nd pers. sing. / *zabucar.*

zacear to shoo or to lisp. reg.

zafándose running away; pres. part. / *zafarse.*

zafaos (you all) run away; impve. 2nd pers. pl. / *zafarse.*

zafar to adorn. reg.

zafar to loosen or to free. reg.

zafarse to run away. reg.

záfate (you) run away; impve. 2nd pers. sing. / *zafarse.*

zafémonos let us run away; impve. 1st pers. pl. / *zafarse.*

záfense let them run away; impve. 3rd pers. pl. / *zafarse.*

záfese let him (her/it) run away; impve. 3rd pers. sing. / *zafarse.*

zaherir to censure. irr.

zahiera 1. that I may censure; pres. subj. 1st pers. sing. / *zaherir.* 2. that he (she/it) may censure; pres. subj. 3rd pers. sing. 3. let him (her/it) censure; impve. 3rd pers. sing.

zahieran 1. that they may censure; pres. subj. 3rd pers. pl. / *zaherir.* 2. let them censure; impve. 3rd pers. pl.

zahieras that you may censure; pres. subj. 2nd pers. sing. / *zaherir.*

zahiere 1. he (she/it) censures; pres. ind. 3rd pers. sing. / *zaherir.* 2. (you) censure; impve. 2nd pers. sing.

zahieren they censure; pres. ind. 3rd pers. pl. / *zaherir.*

zahieres you censure; pres. ind. 2nd pers. sing. / *zaherir.*

zahiero I censure; pres. ind. 1st pers. sing. / *zaherir.*

zahiráis that you (all) may censure; pres. subj. 2nd pers. pl. / *zaherir.*

zahiramos 1. that we may censure; pres. subj. 1st pers. pl. / *zaherir.* 2. let us censure; impve. 1st pers. pl.

zahiriendo censuring; pres. part. / *zaherir.*

zahiriera 1. that I might censure; imp. subj. 1st pers. sing. / *zaherir.* 2. that he (she/it) might censure; imp. subj. 3rd pers. sing.

zahirierais that you (all) might censure; imp. subj. 2nd pers pl. / *zaherir.*

zahiriéramos that we might censure; imp. subj. 1st pers. pl. / *zaherir.*

zahirieran that they might censure; imp. subj. 3rd pers. pl. / *zaherir.*

zahirieras that you might censure; imp. subj. 2nd pers. sing. / *zaherir.*

zahirieron they censured; past 3rd pers. pl. / *zaherir.*

zahiriese 1. that I might censure; imp. subj. 1st pers. sing. / *zaherir.* 2. that he (she/it) might censure; imp. subj. 3rd pers. sing.

zahirieseis that you (all) might censure; imp. subj. 2nd pers pl. / *zaherir.*

zahiriésemos that we might censure; imp. subj. 1st pers. pl. / *zaherir.*

zahiriesen that they might censure; imp. subj. 3rd pers. pl. / *zaherir.*

zahirieses that you might censure; imp. subj. 2nd pers. sing. / *zaherir.*

zahirió he (she/it) censured; past 3rd pers. sing. / *zaherir.*

zamarrear to shake violently. reg.

zamarronear to jolt. reg.

zambucar to hide away. irr.

zambullámonos let us dive; impve. 1st pers. pl. / *zambullirse.*

zambúllanse let them dive; impve. 3rd pers. pl. / *zambullirse.*

zambúllase let him (her/it) dive; impve. 3rd pers. sing. / *zambullirse.*

zambullendo plunging; pres. part. / *zambullir.*

zambulléndose diving; pres. part. / *zambullirse.*

zambullera 1. that I might plunge; imp. subj. 1st pers. sing. / *zambullir.* 2. that he (she/it) might plunge; imp. subj. 3rd pers. sing.

zambullerais that you (all) might plunge; imp. subj. 2nd pers pl. / *zambullir.*

zambulléramos that we might plunge; imp. subj. 1st pers. pl. / *zambullir.*

zambulleran that they might plunge; imp. subj. 3rd pers. pl. / *zambullir.*

zambulleras that you might plunge; imp. subj. 2nd pers. sing. / *zambullir.*

zambulleron they plunged; past 3rd pers. pl. / *zambullir.*

zambullese 1. that I might plunge; imp. subj. 1st pers. sing. / *zambullir.* 2. that he (she/it) might plunge; imp. subj. 3rd pers. sing.

zambulleseis that you (all) might plunge; imp. subj. 2nd pers pl. / *zambullir.*

zambullésemos that we might plunge; imp. subj. 1st pers. pl. / *zambullir.*

zambullesen that they might plunge; imp. subj. 3rd pers. pl. / *zambullir.*

zambulleses that you might plunge; imp. subj. 2nd pers. sing. / *zambullir.*

zambúllete (you) dive; impve. 2nd pers. sing. / *zambullirse.*

zambullir to plunge. irr.

zambullirse to dive. irr.

zambulló he (she/it) plunged; past 3rd pers. sing. / *zambullir.*

zambullos (you all) dive; impve. 2nd pers. pl. / *zambullirse.*

zambuque 1. that I may hide away; pres. subj. 1st pers. sing. / *zambucar.* 2. that he (she/it) may hide away; pres. subj. 3rd pers. sing. 3. let him (her/it) hide away; impve. 3rd pers. sing.

zambuqué I hid away; past 1st pers. sing. / *zambucar.*

zambuquéis that you (all) may hide away; pres. subj. 2nd pers. pl. / *zambucar.*

zambuquemos 1. that we may hide away; pres. subj. 1st pers. pl. / *zambucar.* 2. let us hide away; impve. 1st pers. pl.

zambuquen 1. that they may hide away; pres. subj. 3rd pers. pl. / *zambucar.* 2. let them hide away; impve. 3rd pers. pl.

zambuques that you may hide away; pres. subj. 2nd pers. sing. / *zambucar.*

zampándose rushing in; pres. part. / *zamparse.*

zampaos (you all) rush in; impve. 2nd pers. pl. / *zamparse.*

zampar to gobble up. reg.

zamparse to rush in. reg.

zámpate (you) rush in; impve. 2nd pers. sing. / *zamparse.*

zampémonos let us rush in; impve. 1st pers. pl. / *zamparse.*

zámpense let them rush in; impve. 3rd pers. pl. / *zamparse.*

zámpese let him (her/it) rush in; impve. 3rd pers. sing. / *zamparse.*

zanganear to loaf. reg.

zangoloteándose being loose; pres. part. / *zangolotearse.*

zangoloteaos (you all) be loose; impve. 2nd pers. pl. / *zangolotearse.*

zangolotear to shake. reg.

zangolotearse to be loose. reg.

zangolotéate (you) be loose; impve. 2nd pers. sing. / *zangolotearse.*

zangoloteémonos let us be loose; impve. 1st pers. pl. / *zangolotearse.*

zangolotéense let them be loose; impve. 3rd pers. pl. / *zangolotearse.*

zangolotéese let him (her/it) be loose; impve. 3rd pers. sing. / *zangolotearse.*

zanjar to trench or to settle. reg.

zanquear to waddle. reg.

zapar to mine or to sap. reg.

zapateándose holding one's own; pres. part. / *zapatearse.*

zapateaos (you all) hold you own; impve. 2nd pers. pl. / *zapatearse.*

zapatear to tap with the feet. reg.

zapatearse to hold one's own. reg.

zapatéate (you) hold your own; impve. 2nd pers. sing. / *zapatearse.*

zapateémonos let us hold our own; impve. 1st pers. pl. / *zapatearse.*

zapatéense let them hold their own; impve. 3rd pers. pl. / *zapatearse.*

zapatéese let him (her/it) hold his (her/its) own; impve. 3rd pers. sing. / *zapatearse.*

zapear to shoo or to scare. reg.

zarandar to sieve. reg.

zarandeándose strutting; pres. part. / *zarandearse.*

zarandeaos (you all) strut; impve. 2nd pers. pl. / *zarandearse.*

zarandear to sift. reg.

zarandearse to strut. reg.

zarandéate (you) strut; impve. 2nd pers. sing. / *zarandearse.*

zarandeémonos let us strut; impve. 1st pers. pl. / *zarandearse.*

zarandéense let them strut; impve. 3rd pers. pl. / *zarandearse.*

zarandéese let him (her/it) strut; impve. 3rd pers. sing. / *zarandearse.*

zarpar to weigh anchor or to sail. reg.

zigzaguear to zigzag. reg.

zozobrándose capsizing; pres. part. / *zozobrarse.*

zozobraos (you all) capsize; impve. 2nd pers. pl. / *zozobrarse.*

zozobrar to founder. reg.

zozobrarse to capsize. reg.

zozóbrate (you) capsize; impve. 2nd pers. sing. / *zozobrarse.*

zozobrémonos let us capsize; impve. 1st pers. pl. / *zozobrarse.*

zozóbrense let them capsize; impve. 3rd pers. pl. / *zozobrarse.*

zozóbrese let him (her/it) capsize; impve. 3rd pers. sing. / *zozobrarse.*

zumbándose becoming sassy; pres. part. / *zumbarse.*

zumbaos (you all) become sassy; impve. 2nd pers. pl. / *zumbarse.*

zumbar to buzz. reg.

zumbarse to become sassy. reg.

zúmbate (you) become sassy; impve. 2nd pers. sing. / *zumbarse.*

zumbémonos let us become sassy; impve. 1st pers. pl. / *zumbarse.*

zúmbense let them become sassy; impve. 3rd pers. pl. / *zumbarse.*

zúmbese let him (her/it) become sassy; impve. 3rd pers. sing. / *zumbarse.*

zurcir to darn. irr.

zurear to coo. reg.

zurrándose being scared; pres. part. / *zurrarse.*

zurraos (you all) be scared; impve. 2nd pers. pl. / *zurrarse.*

zurrar to flog. reg.

zurrarse to be scared. reg.

zúrrate (you) be scared; impve. 2nd pers. sing. / *zurrarse.*

zurrémonos let us be scared; impve. 1st pers. pl. / *zurrarse.*

zúrrense let them be scared; impve. 3rd pers. pl. / *zurrarse.*

zúrrese let him (her/it) be scared; impve. 3rd pers. sing. / *zurrarse.*

zurza 1. that I may darn; pres. subj. 1st pers. sing. / *zurcir.* 2. that he (she/it) may darn; pres. subj. 3rd pers. sing. 3. let him (her/it) darn; impve. 3rd pers. sing.

zurzáis that you (all) may darn; pres. subj. 2nd pers. pl. / *zurcir.*

zurzamos 1. that we may darn; pres. subj. 1st pers. pl. / *zurcir.* 2. let us darn; impve. 1st pers. pl.

zurzan 1. that they may darn; pres. subj. 3rd pers. pl. / *zurcir.* 2. let them darn; impve. 3rd pers. pl.

zurzas that you may darn; pres. subj. 2nd pers. sing. / *zurcir.*

zurzo I darn; pres. ind. 1st pers. sing. / *zurcir.*